...pe

Child care policy (Western Europe/USA) pp. 91–93

Environmental refugees (Europe) p. 439

Cutbacks in social services (Eastern Europe/Central Europe/Sweden) pp. 212–214

Cohabitation (Europe) pp. 327–328

Population pyramid (Afghanistan, Italy) pp. 454

Prisons (Finland) p. 165

Pluralism (United Kingdom) p. 256

Human trafficking (Ukraine) p. 238

Middle East

36 Norms regarding touching (Iraq) p. 63

37 Terrorist attacks (Israel and Palestine) pp. 60, 391

38 Israeli-Palestinian nursery (Israel) p. 91

39 Internet filtering (Saudi Arabia) pp. 146, 380

40 Muslim hajj (Saudi Arabia) p. 346

41 Al Jazeera/U.S. news coverage (Qatar) p. 156

42 Women's dress and behavior (Iran) pp. 272–273

43 Palestinian world view (Palestine) p. 54

North America

44 Transnational crime (USA) pp. 182–183

45 Multinational corporations (USA) pp. 224–225

46 Social stratification (Mexico) p. 233–237

47 Marriage (Canada) pp. 318, 320, 330

48 Immigration (USA/Europe) pp. 265–267

49 Crime and inequality (Mexico) p. 179

50 Transnationals (USA/Mexico/Europe/Japan/Caribbean) pp. 504–506

51 Bilingual education (Quebec) p. 70

South and Central America

52 Indigenous tribes (Brazil) p. 59

53 Environmental destruction (Brazil) p. 434

54 Apparel factories that make clothes for USA (Honduras) p. 400

THE WORLD AS A VILLAGE

Imagine that the Earth is a village of only 1,000 people rather than a world with over 6.7 billion inhabitant
Though it would not be easy to walk the Earth and get a sense of its many cultures and societie
you could walk through a village of 1,000 people and get a feeling for the diversity ther

Here Is What You Would See:

280 people under the age of 15,
70 people over the age of 65

140 with no access to improved water supplies

470 people living on less than $2 a da
140 of whom live on less than a $1 a d

496 people who are female,
504 people who are male

333 Christians (**170** of them Roman Catholic),
210 Muslims, **132** Hindus, **63** Buddhists,
112 followers of other faiths, **117** nonreligious, **23** atheists

134 people speaking Mandarin, **62** people speaking Hindi,
50 people speaking Spanish, **48** people speaking English,
29 people speaking Arabic, **27** people speaking Portuguese,
26 people speaking Russian, **26** people speaking Bengali,
598 people speaking other languages as their first language

122 illiterate adults
(out of a total of **720** adults)

1 physician and **3** hospital be

540 with no access to improved sanitation facilities

118 automobiles, **890** televisions, **200** telephones,
510 cellular phones, **150** personal computers,
105 different newspapers, **23** iPods

And if you came back in a year there would
be **1,012** people in the village.

See Acknowledgments for source information.

Select Material from

Sociology

Twelfth Edition

Richard T. Schaefer
DePaul University

 Learning Solutions

Boston Burr Ridge, IL Dubuque, IA New York San Francisco St. Louis
Bangkok Bogotá Caracas Lisbon London Madrid
Mexico City Milan New Delhi Seoul Singapore Sydney Taipei Toronto

Select Material from
Sociology, Twelfth Edition

1 2 3 4 5 6 7 8 9 0 KNG KNG 12 11 10

ISBN-13: 978-0-07-746163-8
ISBN-10: 0-07-746163-0

Learning Solutions Manager: Dave Fleming
Production Editor: Jennifer Beecher
Printer/Binder: King Printing

about the author

Richard T. Schaefer: Professor, DePaul University
B.A. Northwestern University
M.A., Ph.D. University of Chicago

Growing up in Chicago at a time when neighborhoods were going through transitions in ethnic and racial composition, Richard T. Schaefer found himself increasingly intrigued by what was happening, how people were reacting, and how these changes were affecting neighborhoods and people's jobs. His interest in social issues caused him to gravitate to sociology courses at Northwestern University, where he eventually received a BA in sociology.

"Originally as an undergraduate I thought I would go on to law school and become a lawyer. But after taking a few sociology courses, I found myself wanting to learn more about what sociologists studied, and fascinated by the kinds of questions they raised." This fascination led him to obtain his MA and PhD in sociology from the University of Chicago. Dr. Schaefer's continuing interest in race relations led him to write his master's thesis on the membership of the Ku Klux Klan and his doctoral thesis on racial prejudice and race relations in Great Britain.

Dr. Schaefer went on to become a professor of sociology, and now teaches at DePaul University in Chicago. In 2004 he was named to the Vincent DePaul professorship in recognition of his undergraduate teaching and scholarship. He has taught introductory sociology for over 35 years to students in colleges, adult education programs, nursing programs, and even a maximum-security prison. Dr. Schaefer's love of teaching is apparent in his interaction with his students. "I find myself constantly learning from the students who are in my classes and from reading what they write. Their insights into the material we read or current events that we discuss often become part of future course material and sometimes even find their way into my writing."

Dr. Schaefer is the author of the eighth edition of *Sociology: A Brief Introduction* (McGraw-Hill, 2009) and of the fourth edition of *Sociology Matters* (McGraw-Hill, 2009). He is also the author of *Racial and Ethnic Groups,* now in its twelfth edition, and *Race and Ethnicity in the United States,* fifth edition, both published by Pearson. Together with William Zellner, he coauthored the eighth edition of *Extraordinary Groups,* published by Worth in 2007. Dr. Schaefer served as the general editor of the three-volume *Encyclopedia of Race, Ethnicity, and Society,* published by Sage in 2008. His articles and book reviews have appeared in many journals, including *American Journal of Sociology; Phylon: A Review of Race and Culture; Contemporary Sociology; Sociology and Social Research; Sociological Quarterly;* and *Teaching Sociology.* He served as president of the Midwest Sociological Society in 1994–1995.

Dr. Schaefer's advice to students is to "look at the material and make connections to your own life and experiences. Sociology will make you a more attentive observer of how people in groups interact and function. It will also make you more aware of people's different needs and interests—and perhaps more ready to work for the common good, while still recognizing the individuality of each person."

brief contents

Chapter-Opening Excerpts xiv
Boxed Features xv
Social Policy Sections xvii
Maps xviii
Summing Up Tables xviii
Preface xix

PART *1*   *The Sociological Perspective*
1   Understanding Sociology . . . 2
2   Sociological Research . . . 26

PART *2*   *Organizing Social Life*
3   Culture . . . 50
4   Socialization . . . 74
5   Social Interaction and Social Structure . . . 96
6   Groups and Organizations . . . 118
7   The Mass Media . . . 138
8   Deviance and Social Control . . . 162

PART *3*   *Social Inequality*
9   Stratification and Social Mobility in the United States . . . 190
10   Global Inequality . . . 218
11   Racial and Ethnic Inequality . . . 242
12   Stratification by Gender . . . 270
13   Stratification by Age . . . 292

PART *4*   *Social Institutions*
14   The Family and Intimate Relationships . . . 310
15   Religion . . . 334
16   Education . . . 358
17   Government and Politics . . . 376
18   The Economy and Work . . . 398
19   Health, Medicine, and the Environment . . . 416

Glossary 509
References 517
Acknowledgments 546
Photo Credits 549
Name Index 551
Subject Index 558

contents

Chapter-Opening Excerpts   xiv
Boxed Features   xv
Social Policy Sections   xvii
Maps   xviii
Summing Up Tables   xviii
Preface   xix

PART 1
The Sociological Perspective

1 Understanding Sociology   2

What Is Sociology?   5
The Sociological Imagination   5
Sociology and the Social Sciences   5
Sociology and Common Sense   7

What Is Sociological Theory?   8

The Development of Sociology   9
Early Thinkers   9
Émile Durkheim   10
Max Weber   10
Karl Marx   10
W. E. B. DuBois   11
Twentieth-Century Developments   12

Major Theoretical Perspectives   13
Functionalist Perspective   13
Conflict Perspective   14
Interactionist Perspective   15
The Sociological Approach   16

Applied and Clinical Sociology   16
Research Today: Looking at Sports from Four Theoretical Perspectives   17

Developing a Sociological Imagination   18
Theory in Practice   19
Research Today   19
Thinking Globally   19
The Significance of Social Inequality   19
Speaking across Race, Gender, and Religious Boundaries   19
Sociology in the Global Community: Your Morning Cup of Coffee   20
Social Policy throughout the World   20
Appendix: Careers in Sociology   21

2 Sociological Research   26

What Is the Scientific Method?   29
Defining the Problem   29
Reviewing the Literature   30
Formulating the Hypothesis   30
Collecting and Analyzing Data   30
Developing the Conclusion   33
In Summary: The Scientific Method   33

Major Research Designs   33
Surveys   33
Research Today: Surveying Cell Phone Users   35
Observation   35
Experiments   36
Use of Existing Sources   37

Ethics of Research   37
Research Today: What's in a Name?   38
Confidentiality   39
Research Funding   40
Value Neutrality   40

Feminist Methodology   41
Taking Sociology to Work: Dave Eberbach, Research Coordinator, United Way of Central Iowa   41

Technology and Sociological Research   42

SOCIAL POLICY AND SOCIOLOGICAL RESEARCH: STUDYING HUMAN SEXUALITY   43

Appendix I: Using Statistics and Graphs   44

Appendix II: Writing a Research Report   46

PART 2
Organizing Social Life

3 Culture   50

What Is Culture?   53
Cultural Universals   54
Ethnocentrism   54
Cultural Relativism   55
Sociobiology and Culture   55

Development of Culture around the World   56
Innovation   56
Globalization, Diffusion, and Technology   56
Sociology in the Global Community: Life in the Global Village   57

Cultural Variation   58
Subcultures   58
Sociology in the Global Community: Cultural Survival in Brazil   59
Countercultures   60
Culture Shock   60

Role of Language   60
Language: Written and Spoken   61
Nonverbal Communication   62

Norms and Values   62
Norms   63
Sanctions   64
Values   65

Global Culture War   66

Culture and the Dominant Ideology   66
Sociology on Campus: A Culture of Cheating?   67

Case Study: Culture at
    Wal-Mart 68

SOCIAL POLICY AND CULTURE:
    BILINGUALISM 69

4 Socialization and the Life Course 74

The Role of Socialization 77

Social Environment: The Impact of
    Isolation 77

The Influence of Heredity 78

The Self and Socialization 79

Sociological Approaches
    to the Self 79

Sociology on Campus: Impression
    Management by Students 82

Psychological Approaches to
    the Self 82

Agents of Socialization 83

Family 83

Taking Sociology to Work: Rakefet
    Avramovitz, Program Administrator,
    Child Care Law Center 85

School 85

Peer Group 86

Mass Media and Technology 86

Workplace 87

Religion and the State 87

Research Today: Online Socializing: A
    New Agent of Socialization 88

Socialization throughout the Life Course 89

The Life Course 89

Anticipatory Socialization and
    Resocialization 90

**SOCIAL POLICY AND
    SOCIALIZATION: CHILD CARE
    AROUND THE WORLD 91**

5 Social Interaction and Social Structure 96

Social Interaction and Reality 99

Elements of Social Structure 100

Statuses 100

Social Roles 101

Research Today: Disability as a Master
    Status 102

Groups 103

Social Institutions 103

Social Networks 106

Virtual Worlds 106

Research Today: Social Networks and
    Smoking 107

Sociology in the Global Community:
    The Second Life® Virtual World 108

Social Structure in Global Perspective 107

Durkheim's Mechanical and Organic
    Solidarity 107

Tönnies's *Gemeinschaft* and *Gesellschaft* 109

Lenski's Sociocultural Evolution
    Approach 109

**SOCIAL POLICY AND SOCIAL
    INTERACTION: REGULATING
    THE NET 112**

6 Groups and Organizations 118

Understanding Groups 121

Types of Groups 121

Studying Small Groups 123

Research Today: The Drinking Rape
    Victim: Jury Decision Making 124

Understanding Organizations 125

Formal Organizations and Bureaucracies 125

Characteristics of a Bureaucracy 125

Bureaucracy and Organizational Culture 127

Sociology in the Global Community:
    McDonald's and the Worldwide
    Bureaucratization of Society 128

**Case Study: Bureaucracy and the
    Space Shuttle *Columbia* 129**

Voluntary Associations 129

The Changing Workplace 131

Organizational Restructuring 131

Telecommuting 131

Sociology in the Global Community:
    Entrepreneurship, Japanese Style 132

Electronic Communication 132

**SOCIAL POLICY AND
    ORGANIZATIONS: THE STATE OF
    THE UNIONS WORLDWIDE 133**

7 The Mass Media 138

Sociological Perspectives on the Media 141

Functionalist View 141

Conflict View 144

Taking Sociology to Work: Nicole
    Martorano Van Cleve, Former Brand
    Planner, Leo Burnett USA 146

Research Today: The Color of Network
    TV 149

Feminist View 150

Interactionist View 151

The Audience 152

Who Is in the Audience? 153

The Segmented Audience 153

Audience Behavior 154

The Media's Global Reach 154

Sociology in the Global Community:
    Al Jazeera Is on the Air 156

**SOCIAL POLICY AND THE
    MASS MEDIA: MEDIA
    CONCENTRATION 157**

8 Deviance and Social Control 162

Social Control 165

Conformity and Obedience 166

Informal and Formal Social Control 168

Sociology on Campus: Binge Drinking 169

Law and Society 170

What Is Deviance? 170

Deviance and Social Stigma 172

Deviance and Technology 172

Sociological Perspectives on Deviance 173

Functionalist Perspective 173

Research Today: Does Crime Pay? 175

Interactionist Perspective 175

Labeling Theory 177

Conflict Theory 178

Feminist Perspective 179

Crime 179

Types of Crime 180

Sociology on Campus: Campus Crime 181

Crime Statistics 183

Taking Sociology to Work: Stephanie Vezzani, Special Agent, U.S. Secret Service 184

SOCIAL POLICY AND SOCIAL CONTROL: GUN CONTROL 185

PART 3
Social Inequality

9 Stratification and Social Mobility in the United States 190

Systems of Stratification 193

Slavery 193

Castes 193

Taking Sociology to Work: Jessica Houston Su, Research Assistant, Joblessness and Urban Poverty Research Program 195

Estates 195

Social Classes 195

Sociological Perspectives on Stratification 197

Karl Marx's View of Class Differentiation 197

Max Weber's View of Stratification 198

Interactionist View 198

Is Stratification Universal? 199

Functionalist View 199

Conflict View 200

Lenski's Viewpoint 200

Stratification by Social Class 201

Objective Method of Measuring Social Class 201

Gender and Occupational Prestige 201

Multiple Measures 202

Income and Wealth 202

Poverty 204

Research Today: Precarious Work 205

Studying Poverty 205

Who Are the Poor? 206

Feminization of Poverty 206

Sociology in the Global Community: It's All Relative: Appalachian Poverty and Congolese Affluence 207

The Underclass 207

Explaining Poverty 208

Life Chances 208

Social Mobility 209

Open versus Closed Stratification Systems 209

Types of Social Mobility 209

Sociology on Campus: Social Class and Financial Aid 210

Social Mobility in the United States 210

SOCIAL POLICY AND GENDER STRATIFICATION: RETHINKING WELFARE IN NORTH AMERICA AND EUROPE 212

10 Global Inequality 218

The Global Divide 221

Stratification in the World System 223

The Legacy of Colonialism 223

Multinational Corporations 224

Worldwide Poverty 227

Sociology in the Global Community: Cutting Poverty Worldwide 228

Sociology in the Global Community: The Global Disconnect 229

Modernization 229

Stratification within Nations: A Comparative Perspective 230

Distribution of Wealth and Income 230

Social Mobility 230

Sociology in the Global Community: Stratification in Japan 231

Taking Sociology to Work: Bari Katz, Program Director, National Conference for Community and Justice 233

Case Study: Stratification in Mexico 233

Mexico's Economy 234

Race Relations in Mexico: The Color Hierarchy 234

The Status of Women in Mexico 234

The Borderlands 235

SOCIAL POLICY AND GLOBAL INEQUALITY: UNIVERSAL HUMAN RIGHTS 237

Research Today: Social Mobility among
Latino Immigrants 263

Jewish Americans 263

White Ethnics 264

**SOCIAL POLICY AND RACIAL AND
ETHNIC INEQUALITY: GLOBAL
IMMIGRATION 265**

Volunteer Coordinator, Y-ME
Illinois 285

**SOCIAL POLICY AND GENDER
STRATIFICATION: THE BATTLE
OVER ABORTION FROM A GLOBAL
PERSPECTIVE 286**

11 Racial and Ethnic Inequality 242

Minority, Racial, and Ethnic Groups 245

Minority Groups 245

Race 245

Ethnicity 248

Prejudice and Discrimination 248

Prejudice 248

Color-Blind Racism 248

Discriminatory Behavior 249

The Privileges of the Dominant 250

Taking Sociology to Work: Prudence
Hannis, Liaison Officer, National
Institute of Science Research,
University of Québec 251

Institutional Discrimination 252

Sociological Perspectives on Race and Ethnicity 253

Functionalist Perspective 253

Conflict Perspective 253

Labeling Perspective 253

Interactionist Perspective 254

Patterns of Intergroup Relations 254

Amalgamation 255

Assimilation 255

Segregation 255

Pluralism 256

Race and Ethnicity in the United States 256

African Americans 256

Native Americans 258

Asian Americans 258

Sociology in the Global Community:
The Aboriginal People of
Australia 259

Arab Americans 261

Latinos 261

12 Stratification by Gender 270

Social Construction of Gender 273

Gender Roles in the United States 273

Sociology on Campus: The Debate over
Title IX 275

Cross-Cultural Perspective 276

Sociological Perspectives on Gender 277

Functionalist View 277

Conflict Response 278

Feminist Perspective 278

Interactionist Approach 279

Women: The Oppressed Majority 279

Sexism and Sex Discrimination 280

The Status of Women Worldwide 280

Sociology in the Global Community:
The Head Scarf and the Veil:
Complex Symbols 281

Women in the Workforce of the United States 281

Labor Force Participation 281

Compensation 283

Social Consequences of Women's
Employment 283

Emergence of a Collective Consciousness 284

Taking Sociology to Work: Abigail
E. Drevs, Former Program and

13 Stratification by Age 292

Aging and Society 295

Sociological Perspectives on Aging 295

Taking Sociology to Work: A. David
Roberts, Social Worker 296

Functionalist Approach: Disengagement
Theory 296

Interactionist Approach: Activity
Theory 296

Labeling Theory 297

Conflict Approach 297

Aging Worldwide 298

Role Transitions throughout the Life Course 298

Sociology in the Global Community:
Aging, Japanese Style 299

The Sandwich Generation 299

Adjusting to Retirement 299

Death and Dying 301

Age Stratification in the United States 302

The "Graying of America" 302

Wealth and Income 303

Ageism 303

Competition in the Labor Force 304

The Elderly: Emergence of a Collective
Consciousness 304

Research Today: Elderspeak and Other
Signs of Ageism 305

**SOCIAL POLICY AND AGE
STRATIFICATION: THE RIGHT TO
DIE WORLDWIDE 306**

PART 4
Social Institutions

14 The Family and Intimate Relationships 310

Global View of the Family 313

Composition: What Is the Family? 313

Sociology in the Global Community: One Wife, Many Husbands: The Nyinba 314

Kinship Patterns: To Whom Are We Related? 315

Authority Patterns: Who Rules? 315

Sociological Perspectives on the Family 316

Functionalist View 316

Conflict View 316

Interactionist View 317

Feminist View 317

Marriage and Family 317

Courtship and Mate Selection 318

Variations in Family Life and Intimate Relationships 319

Research Today: Arranged Marriage, American-Style 320

Child-Rearing Patterns 322

Divorce 325

Statistical Trends in Divorce 325

Factors Associated with Divorce 325

Research Today: Divorce and Military Deployment 326

Impact of Divorce on Children 327

Diverse Lifestyles 327

Cohabitation 327

Remaining Single 328

Marriage without Children 328

Lesbian and Gay Relationships 329

SOCIAL POLICY AND THE FAMILY: GAY MARRIAGE 329

15 Religion 334

Durkheim and the Sociological Approach to Religion 338

World Religions 338

Sociological Perspectives on Religion 341

The Integrative Function of Religion 341

Religion and Social Support 341

Research Today: Income and Education, Religiously Speaking 342

Religion and Social Change 343

Religion and Social Control: A Conflict View 344

Feminist Perspective 344

Components of Religion 345

Belief 345

Ritual 346

Experience 347

Religious Organization 347

Ecclesiae 348

Denominations 348

Sects 348

New Religious Movements or Cults 348

Research Today: Islam in the United States 349

Research Today: The Church of Scientology: Religion or Quasi-Religion? 350

Comparing Forms of Religious Organization 350

Case Study: Religion in India 352

The Religious Tapestry in India 352

Religion and the State in India 353

SOCIAL POLICY AND RELIGION: RELIGION IN THE SCHOOLS 353

16 Education 358

Sociological Perspectives on Education 361

Functionalist View 361

Sociology on Campus: Google University 362

Conflict View 363

Taking Sociology to Work: Ray Zapata, Business Owner and Former Regent, Texas State University 366

Feminist View 366

Interactionist View 367

Schools as Formal Organizations 367

Bureaucratization of Schools 368

Research Today: Violence in the Schools 369

Teachers: Employees and Instructors 369

Student Subcultures 370

Homeschooling 371

SOCIAL POLICY AND EDUCATION: NO CHILD LEFT BEHIND ACT 372

17 Government and Politics 377

Power and Authority 379

Power 379

Types of Authority 379

Sociology in the Global Community: Charisma: The Beatles and Maharishi Mahesh Yogi 381

xii

Contents

Types of Government 381
Monarchy 381
Oligarchy 382
Dictatorship and Totalitarianism 382
Democracy 382

Political Behavior in the United
States 382
Participation and Apathy 382

Taking Sociology to Work: Joshua
Johnston, Congressional Aide, Office
of Congressman Norm Dicks 383

Race and Gender in Politics 384

Research Today: Why Don't More Young
People Vote? 385

Models of Power Structure in the
United States 386
Power Elite Models 386
Pluralist Model 388

War and Peace 388
War 389
Peace 389
Terrorism 391

Political Activism on the
Internet 392

SOCIAL POLICY AND POLITICS:
CAMPAIGN FINANCING 393

18 The Economy
and Work 398
Economic Systems 401
Capitalism 401
Socialism 402
The Informal Economy 403

Sociology in the Global Community:
Working Women in Nepal 404

Case Study: Capitalism in
China 404
The Road to Capitalism 404
The Chinese Economy Today 405
Chinese Workers in the New Economy 406

Work and Alienation 406

Taking Sociology to Work: Amy
Wang, Product Manager, Norman
International Company 407

Marx's View 407
Worker Satisfaction 408

Changing Economies 409
Microfinancing 409
The Changing Face of the Workforce 409

Research Today: Affirmative
Action 410

Deindustrialization 410

SOCIAL POLICY AND THE ECONOMY:
GLOBAL OFFSHORING 412

19 Health,
Medicine, and the
Environment 416
Culture and Health 419

Sociological Perspectives on Health
and Illness 419
Functionalist Approach 419
Conflict Approach 420

Taking Sociology to Work: Lola
Adedokun, Independent Consultant,
Health Care Research 422

Interactionist Approach 422
Labeling Approach 422

Social Epidemiology and
Health 423
Social Class 424

Research Today: The AIDS
Epidemic 425

Race and Ethnicity 426

Research Today: Medical
Apartheid 427

Gender 426
Age 427

Health Care in the United
States 428
A Historical View 428
Physicians, Nurses, and Patients 429
Alternatives to Traditional Health
Care 430
The Role of Government 431

Mental Illness in the United
States 431
Theoretical Models of Mental
Disorders 432
Patterns of Care 432

Sociological Perspectives on the
Environment 433
Human Ecology 433
Conflict View of the Environment 434
Environmental Justice 435

Environmental Problems 435

Sociology in the Global Community:
The Mysterious Fall of the
Nacirema 436

Air Pollution 436
Water Pollution 436
Global Warming 436
The Impact of Globalization 439

SOCIAL POLICY AND
THE ENVIRONMENT:
ENVIRONMENTALISM 440

Glossary 509
References 517
Acknowledgments 546
Photo Credits 549
Name Index 551
Subject Index 558

chapter opening excerpts

Every chapter in this textbook begins with an excerpt from one of the works listed here. These excerpts convey the excitement and relevance of sociological inquiry and draw readers into the subject matter from each chapter.

Chapter 1
Nickel and Dimed: On (Not) Getting By in America by Barbara Ehrenreich   4

Chapter 2
"The Demedicalization of Self-Injury" by Patricia A. Adler and Peter Adler   28

Chapter 3
"Body Ritual among the Nacirema" by Horace Miner   52

Chapter 4
Black Picket Fences: Privilege and Peril among the Black Middle Class by Mary Pattillo-McCoy   76

Chapter 5
The Lucifer Effect: Understanding How Good People Turn Evil by Philip Zimbardo   98

Chapter 6
The McDonaldization of Society by George Ritzer   120

Chapter 7
iSpy: Surveillance and Power in the Interactive Era by Mark Andrejevic   140

Chapter 8
Gang Leader for a Day: A Rogue Sociologist Takes to the Streets by Sudhir Venkatesh   164

Chapter 9
Richistan: A Journey through the American Wealth Boom and the Lives of the New Rich by Robert Frank   192

Chapter 10
The Bottom Billion: Why the Poorest Countries Are Failing and What Can Be Done About It by Paul Collier   220

Chapter 11
Asian American Dreams: The Emergence of an American People by Helen Zia   244

Chapter 12
Lipstick Jihad: A Memoir of Growing Up Iranian in America and American in Iran by Azadeh Moaveni   272

Chapter 13
Tuesdays with Morrie: An Old Man, a Young Man, and Life's Greatest Lesson by Mitch Albom   294

Chapter 14
Unequal Childhoods: Class, Race, and Family Life by Annette Lareau   312

Chapter 15
For This Land: Writings on Religion in America by Vine Deloria Jr.   336

Chapter 16
The Shame of the Nation by Jonathan Kozol   360

Chapter 17
Is Voting for Young People? by Martin P. Wattenberg   378

Chapter 18
Where Am I Wearing? A Global Tour to the Countries, Factories, and People that Make Our Clothes by Kelsey Timmerman   400

Chapter 19
The Scalpel and the Silver Bear: The First Navajo Woman Surgeon Combines Western Medicine and Traditional Healing by Lori Arviso Alvord, M.D., and Elizabeth Cohen Van Pelt   418

boxed features

RESEARCH TODAY

1-1   Looking at Sports from Four Theoretical Perspectives   17
2-1   Surveying Cell Phone Users   35
2-2   What's in a Name?   38
4-2   Online Socializing: A New Agent of Socialization   88
5-1   Disability as a Master Status   102
5-2   Social Networks and Smoking   107
6-1   The Drinking Rape Victim: Jury Decision Making   124
7-1   The Color of Network TV   149
8-2   Does Crime Pay?   175
9-1   Precarious Work   205
11-2   Social Mobility among Latino Immigrants   263
13-2   Elderspeak and Other Signs of Ageism   305
14-2   Arranged Marriage, American-Style   320
14-3   Divorce and Military Deployment   326
15-1   Income and Education, Religiously Speaking   342
15-2   Islam in the United States   349
15-3   The Church of Scientology: Religion or Quasi-Religion?   350
16-2   Violence in the Schools   369
17-2   Why Don't More Young People Vote?   385
18-2   Affirmative Action   410
19-1   The AIDS Epidemic   425
19-2   Medical Apartheid   427

SOCIOLOGY IN THE GLOBAL COMMUNITY

1-2   Your Morning Cup of Coffee   20
3-1   Life in the Global Village   57
3-2   Cultural Survival in Brazil   59
5-3   The Second Life® Virtual World   108
6-2   McDonald's and the Worldwide Bureaucratization of Society   128
6-3   Entrepreneurship, Japanese Style   132
7-2   Al Jazeera Is on the Air   156
9-2   It's All Relative: Appalachian Poverty and Congolese Affluence   207
10-1   Cutting Poverty Worldwide   228
10-2   The Global Disconnect   229
10-3   Stratification in Japan   231
11-1   The Aboriginal People of Australia   259
12-2   The Head Scarf and the Veil: Complex Symbols   281
13-1   Aging, Japanese Style   299
14-1   One Wife, Many Husbands: The Nyinba   314
17-1   Charisma: The Beatles and the Maharishi Mahesh Yogi   381
18-1   Working Women in Nepal   404
19-3   The Mysterious Fall of the Nacirema   436

SOCIOLOGY ON CAMPUS

3-3   A Culture of Cheating?   67

4-1   Impression Management by Students   82

8-1   Binge Drinking   169

8-3   Campus Crime   181

9-3   Social Class and Financial Aid   210

12-1   The Debate over Title IX   275

16-1   Google University   362

TAKING SOCIOLOGY TO WORK

Dave Eberbach, Research Coordinator, United Way of Central Iowa   41

Rakefet Avramovitz, Program Administrator, Child Care Law Center   85

Nicole Martorano Van Cleve, Former Brand Planner, Leo Burnett USA   146

Stephanie Vezzani, Special Agent, U.S. Secret Service   184

Jessica Houston Su, Research Assistant, Joblessness and Urban Poverty Research Program   195

Bari Katz, Program Director, National Conference for Community and Justice   233

Prudence Hannis, Liaison Officer, National Institute of Science Research, University of Québec   251

Abigail E. Drevs, Former Program and Volunteer Coordinator, Y-ME Illinois   285

A. David Roberts, Social Worker   296

Ray Zapata, Business Owner and Former Regent, Texas State University   366

Joshua Johnston, Congressional Aide, Office of Congressman Norm Dicks   383

Amy Wang, Product Manager, Norman International Company   407

Lola Adedokun, Independent Consultant, Health Care Research   422

Kelsie Lenor Wilson-Dorsett, Deputy Director, Department of Statistics, Government of Bahamas   451

social policy sections

Chapter 2
Social Policy and Sociological Research: *Studying Human Sexuality* 43

Chapter 3
Social Policy and Culture: *Bilingualism* 69

Chapter 4
Social Policy and Socialization: *Child Care around the World* 91

Chapter 5
Social Policy and Social Interaction: *Regulating the Net* 112

Chapter 6
Social Policy and Organizations: *The State of the Unions Worldwide* 133

Chapter 7
Social Policy and the Mass Media: *Media Concentration* 157

Chapter 8
Social Policy and Social Control: *Gun Control* 185

Chapter 10
Social Policy and Global Inequality: *Universal Human Rights* 237

Chapter 9
Social Policy and Stratification: *Rethinking Welfare in North America and Europe* 212

Chapter 11
Social Policy and Racial and Ethnic Inequality: *Global Immigration* 265

Chapter 12
Social Policy and Gender Stratification: *The Battle over Abortion from a Global Perspective* 286

Chapter 13
Social Policy and Age Stratification: *The Right to Die Worldwide* 306

Chapter 14
Social Policy and the Family: *Gay Marriage* 329

Chapter 15
Social Policy and Religion: *Religion in the Schools* 353

Chapter 16
Social Policy and Education: *No Child Left Behind Act* 372

Chapter 17
Social Policy and Politics: *Campaign Financing* 393

Chapter 18
Social Policy and the Economy: *Global Offshoring* 412

Chapter 19
Social Policy and the Environment: *Environmentalism* 440

maps

Mapping Life Nationwide

Educational Level and Household Income in the United States   31

Percentage of People Who Speak a Language Other than English at Home, by State   69

Union Membership in the United States   134

Executions by State since 1976   166

The Status of Medical Marijuana   171

The 50 States: Contrasts in Income and Poverty Levels   194

Census 2000: The Image of Diversity   257

Distribution of the Arab American Population by State   261

Restrictions on Public Funding for Abortion   286

Twenty-Eight Floridas by 2030   303

Unmarried-Couple Households by State   327

Average Salary for Teachers   370

Availability of Physicians by State   428

Homeless Estimates by State   466

Mapping Life Worldwide

A Palestinian World View   54

Countries with High Child Marriage Rates   56

Branding the Globe   145

Filtering Information: Social Content   146

Gross National Income per Capita   222

Poverty Worldwide   226

The Borderlands   236

The Global Divide on Abortion   287

Religions of the World   339

Filtering Information: Political Content   380

Global Peace Index   390

The Global Reach of Terrorism   391

People Living with HIV   424

Increase in Carbon Dioxide Emissions   438

Global Urbanization 2015 (projected)   459

Labor Migration   505

summing UP tables

Major Sociological Perspectives   16

Existing Sources Used in Sociological Research   39

Major Research Designs   39

Norms and Sanctions   65

Sociological Perspectives on Culture   68

Mead's Stages of the Self   81

Theoretical Approaches to Development of the Self   83

Sociological Perspectives on Social Institutions   106

Comparison of the Gemeinschaft and Gesellschaft   110

Stages of Sociocultural Evolution   111

Comparison of Primary and Secondary Groups   121

Characteristics of a Bureaucracy   127

Sociological Perspectives on the Mass Media   153

Modes of Individual Adaptation   174

Sociological Perspectives on Deviance   180

Sociological Perspectives on Social Stratification   201

Sociological Perspectives on Global Inequality   230

Sociological Perspectives on Race and Ethnicity   254

Sociological Perspectives on Gender   280

Sociological Perspectives on Aging   298

Sociological Perspectives on the Family   317

Major World Religions   340

Sociological Perspectives on Religion   345

Components of Religion   347

Characteristics of Ecclesiae, Denominations, Sects, and New Religious Movements   351

Sociological Perspectives on Education   368

Characteristics of the Three Major Economic Systems   403

Sociological Perspectives on Health and Illness   423

Comparing Types of Cities   458

Sociological Perspectives on Urbanization   462

Forms of Collective Behavior   482

Contributions to Social Movement Theory   485

Sociological Perspectives on Social Change   497

preface

After more than 30 years of teaching sociology to students in colleges, adult education programs, nursing programs, an overseas program based in London, and even a maximum-security prison, I am convinced that the discipline can play a valuable role in building students' critical thinking skills. The distinctive emphasis on social policy found in this text shows students how to use a sociological imagination in examining public policy issues such as welfare reform, economic development, global immigration, gay marriage, and environmentalism.

My hope is that through their reading of this book, students will begin to think like sociologists and will be able to use sociological theories and concepts in evaluating human interactions and institutions. In other words, students will be able to take sociology with them when they graduate from college, pursue careers, and get involved in their own communities and the world at large. Beginning with the introduction of the concept of sociological imagination in Chapter 1, this text highlights the distinctive way in which sociologists examine human social behavior, and how their research findings can be used to understand the broader principles that guide our lives.

"Students can take sociology with them on campus, in their careers and into the community."

The first 11 editions of *Sociology* have been used in more than 800 colleges and universities. This book is often part of a student's first encounter with the engaging ideas of sociology. Many who have read it have gone on to make sociology their life's work. Equally gratifying for me is hearing that *Sociology* has also made a difference in the lives of other students, who have applied the knowledge they gained in the course to guide their life choices.

The 12th edition of *Sociology* builds on the success of earlier editions through an emphasis on the following:

- Comprehensive and balanced coverage of **theoretical perspectives** throughout the text

- Strong coverage of issues pertaining to **gender, age, race, ethnicity, and class** in all chapters
- **Cross-cultural and global content** throughout the book

As with previous editions, the 12th edition explores contemporary issues that students hear about in the media through a sociological lens. From social mobility among Latino immigrants to online social networks to environmental policy issues and health care around the world, this book helps students to develop a sociological perspective as they consider relevant topics and issues. With this objective in mind, coverage of the global economic downturn that began in 2008 and became global in its impact by 2009 is discussed in relevant chapters. Here are some examples of this coverage:

- The impact on labor unions (Chapter 6)
- Increasing numbers of people in the United States living on government support (Chapter 9)
- Scapegoating of Jewish Americans (Chapter 11)
- The social impact on older workers (Chapter 13)
- The social costs of deindustrialization and downsizing (Chapter 18)
- The impact on people's ability to buy prescription drugs (Chapter 19)
- Rising numbers of people becoming homeless for the first time (Chapter 20)

Taking Sociology with You
in College

Chapter-Opening Excerpts:
Each chapter opens with a lively excerpt from the writings of sociologists and others, clearly conveying the excitement and relevance of sociological inquiry.

Where Am I Wearing? A Global Tour to the Countries, Factories, and People that Make Our Clothes

I was made in America. My *Jingle These* Christmas boxers were made in Bangladesh.

I had an all-American childhood in rural Ohio. My all-American blue jeans were made in Cambodia.

I wore flip-flops every day for a year when I worked as a SCUBA diving instructor in Key West. They were made in China.

One day while staring at a pile of clothes on the floor, I noticed the tag of my favorite T-shirt: "Made in Honduras."

I read the tag. My mind wandered. A quest was born.

Where am I wearing? It seems like a simple question with a simple answer. It's not.

The question inspired the quest that took me around the globe. It cost me a lot of things, not the least of which was my consumer innocence. Before the quest, I could put on a piece of clothing without reading its tag and thinking about Arifa in Bangladesh or Dewan in China, about their children, their hopes and dreams, and the challenges they face.

Where am I wearing? This isn't so much a question related to geography and clothes, but about the people who make our clothes and the texture of their lives. This quest is about the way we live and the way *they* live; because when it comes to clothing, others make it, and we have it made. And there's a big, big difference. . . .

Workers flood the narrow alley beside the Delta Apparel Factory in San Pedro Sula, Honduras. They rush to catch one of the many waiting buses at the highway. Merchants hoping to part them from a portion of their daily earnings—$4 to $5—fight for their attention. Vehicles push through the crowd. A minivan knocks over a girl in her midtwenties and then runs over her foot. She curses, is helped to her feet, and limps onto a waiting bus.

The buildings behind the fence are shaded in Bahamian pastels and very well kept. The shrubs have been recently shaped, and the grass trimmed. In the bright Honduran sun, they seem as pleasant as a factory can get.

The lady at Delta Apparel, based in Georgia, giggled at me on the phone when I told her my plans. She was happy to tell me that their Honduran factory was located in the city of Villanueva just south of San Pedro Sula. She even wished me good luck.

Now that I'm in Honduras, the company doesn't think it's very funny.

I stand among the chaos overwhelmed. A thousand sets of eyes stare at me; perhaps they recognize my T-shirt. The irony that this is Tattoo's tropical paradise wore off long ago—somewhere between the confrontation with the big-bellied guards at the factory gate who had guns shoved down their pants like little boys playing cowboy and the conversation with the tight-lipped company representative who failed to reveal much of anything about my T-shirt or the people who assembled it. There was no way I was getting onto the factory floor. All I learned was that eight humans of indiscriminate age and sex stitched my shirt together in less than five minutes—not exactly information that required traveling all the way to Honduras to obtain.

Where am I wearing? This isn't so much a question related to geography and clothes, but about the people who make our clothes and the texture of their lives.

(Timmerman 2009:xiii–xiv, 14) Additional information about this excerpt can be found on the Online Learning Center at www.mhhe.com/schaefer12e.

In his book *Where Am I Wearing? A Global Tour to the Countries, Factories, and People that Make Our Clothes*, journalist where people in industrial countries would want to work, but from the foreign worker's perspective, they may be preferable to

---

SOCIOLOGY ON CAMPUS

3-3   A Culture of Cheating?

On November 21, 2002, after issuing several warnings, officials at the U.S. Naval Academy seized the computers of almost 100 midshipmen suspected of downloading movies and music illegally from the Internet. Officers at the school may have taken the unusually strong action to avoid liability on the part of the U.S. government, which owns the computers students were using. But across the nation, college administrators have been trying to restrain students from downloading pirated entertainment for free. The practice is so widespread, it has been slowing down the high-powered computer networks colleges and universities depend on for research and admissions.

Illegal downloading is just one aspect of the growing problem of copyright violation, both on campus and off. Now that college students can use personal computers to surf the Internet, most do their research online. Apparently, the temptation to cut and paste passages from Web site postings and pass them off as one's own is irresistible to many. Surveys done by the Center for Academic Integrity show that from 1999 to 2005, the percentage of students who approved of this type of plagiarism rose from 10 percent to 41 percent. At the same time, the percentage who considered cutting and pasting from the Internet to be a serious form of cheating fell from 68 percent to 23 percent. Perhaps the worst form of Internet plagiarism is the purchase of entire papers from other writers. Increasingly, the Web sites that sell essays to students are based in other countries, including India, Ukraine, Nigeria, and the Philippines.

A recent cross-cultural study compared cheating by students in Lebanon and the United States. Researchers found a high willingness to cheat among students in both countries: 54 percent of the U.S. students and 80 percent of the Lebanese

students reported having cheated in some way during the past year. In both cultures, students were more willing to cheat if they perceived their peers to be dishonest and if they thought their cheating was unlikely to be reported.

More than proctoring of exams or reliance on search engines to identify plagiarism, educating students about the need for academic honesty seems to reduce the incidence of cheating.

The Center for Academic Integrity estimates that at most schools, more than 75 percent of the students engage in some form of cheating. Students not only cut passages from the Internet and paste them into their papers without citing the source; they share questions and answers on exams, collaborate on assignments they are supposed to do independently, and even falsify the results of their laboratory experiments. Worse, many professors have become inured to the problem and have ceased to report it.

To address what they consider an alarming trend, many schools are rewriting or adopting new academic honor codes. This renewed emphasis on honor and integrity underscores the influence of cultural values on social behavior. Observers contend that the increase in student cheating reflects widely publicized instances of cheating in public life, which have served to create an alternative set of values in which the end justifies the means. When young people see sports heroes, authors, entertainers, and corporate executives exposed for cheating in one form or another, the message seems to be "Cheating is OK, as long as you don't get caught." More than proctoring of exams or reliance on search engines to identify plagiarism, then, educating students about the need for academic honesty seems to reduce the incidence of cheating. "The feeling of being treated as an adult and responding in kind," says Professor Donald McCabe of Rutgers University, "it's clearly there for many students. They don't want to violate that trust."

LET'S DISCUSS

1. Do you know anyone who has engaged in Internet plagiarism? What about cheating on tests or falsifying laboratory results? If so, how did the person justify these forms of dishonesty?
2. Even if cheaters aren't caught, what negative effects does their academic dishonesty have on them? What effects does it have on students who are honest? Could an entire college or university suffer from students' dishonesty?

Sources: Argetsinger and Krim 2002; Bartlett 2009; Center for Academic Integrity 2006; McCabe et al. 2008; R. Thomas 2003; Zernike 2002.

Sociology on Campus: These boxes apply a sociological perspective to issues of immediate interest to students.

NEW!

Thinking about Movies: Two films that underscore chapter themes are featured at the end of each chapter, along with a set of exercises that encourage students to use their sociological imagination when viewing movies.

THINKING ABOUT MOVIES

Talk to Me (Kasi Lemmons, 2007)

In Washington, D.C., in the late 1960s, R&B radio station WOL-AM struggles to hold its audience amidst the massive social change that followed the civil rights movement. Based on the real-life story of disc jockey and entertainer Petey Greene (Don Cheadle), the movie shows how Petey, hired to increase the station's listenership, used his self-professed knowledge of inner-city culture and penchant for "telling it like it is" to make his morning show a huge success. When violence breaks out after the assassination of Martin Luther King Jr., Petey helps to end the riots by giving voice to a grieving community and reminding listeners of King's message of nonviolence.

Talk to Me shows how a mass medium can support social cohesion, especially during times of crisis. Because the story is set in an era before the large-scale consolidation of media ownership, it illustrates the close connection between a community and its local broadcasting outlet that characterized the period.

For Your Consideration

1. How might Petey Greene's radio show be seen as an agent of socialization?
2. How does Talk to Me represent the media industry? How might that representation differ from what you know about today's media?

Thank You for Smoking
(Jason Reitman, 2005)

A group of tobacco lobbyists attempts to stem the tide of antismoking sentiment and block legislation designed to curtail cigarette sales. Nick Naylor (Aaron Eckhart) is a star lobbyist for the tobacco industry. Dubbed the "Sultan of Spin," he uses his rhetorical prowess to score points for big tobacco, despite overwhelming evidence of the adverse health consequences of smoking. To increase cigarette sales, Nick devises a plan to bribe decision makers in the media industry to show actors smoking on screen. Watch for the scene in which Nick meets with "superagent" Jeff Megall (Rob Lowe) to discuss how to frame such scenes for the greatest effect.

This movie shows how the media industry promotes consumption by carefully placing products in movie scenes. It also shows the inordinate amount of control that media gatekeepers like Jeff Megall exert over what is shown in a mass medium such as film.

For Your Consideration

1. How does Thank You for Smoking show the importance of product placement ("brandcasting"), and how might that reflect the way in which the mass media promote consumption?
2. Besides agents like Jeff Megall, who else might serve as media gatekeepers, and how might they influence what you see on film and television?

Getting Involved: For students who want to become involved in social policy debates, this feature refers students to relevant material on the book's Online Learning Center.

States or Australia, is not only about learning a new language. It   If so, analyze the issue from a sociological point of view.

getting**involved**

To get involved in the debate over bilingualism, visit this book's Online Learning Center, which offers links to relevant Web sites.

www.mhhe.com/schaefer12e

MASTERING THIS CHAPTER

Self-Quiz

Read each question carefully and then select the best answer.

1. Which sociologist developed the concept of the sick role?
   a. Emile Durkheim
   b. Talcott Parsons
   c. C. Wright Mills
   d. Erving Goffman

2. Regarding health care inequities, the conflict perspective would note that
   a. physicians serve as "gatekeepers" for the sick role, either verifying a patient's condition as "illness" or designating the patient as "recovered."
   b. patients play an active role in health care by failing to follow a physician's advice.
   c. emigration out of the Third World by physicians is yet another way that the world's core industrialized nations enhance their quality of life at the expense of developing countries.
   d. the designation "healthy" or "ill" generally involves social definition by others.

3. Which one of the following nations has the lowest infant mortality rate?
   a. the United States
   b. Mozambique
   c. Canada
   d. Sweden

4. Compared with Whites, Blacks have higher death rates from
   a. heart disease.
   b. diabetes.
   c. cancer.
   d. all of the above

6. Which program is essentially a compulsory health insurance plan for the elderly?
   a. Medicare
   b. Medicaid
   c. Blue Cross
   d. Healthpac

7. Which of the following is a criticism of the sick role?
   a. Patients' judgments regarding their own state of health may be related to their gender, age, social class, and ethnic group.
   b. The sick role may be more applicable to people experiencing short-term illnesses than to those with recurring long-term illnesses.
   c. Even such simple factors as whether a person is employed or not seem to affect the person's willingness to assume the sick role.
   d. all of the above

8. Which of the following terms do conflict theorists use in referring to the growing role of medicine as a major institution of social control?
   a. the sick role
   b. the medicalization of society
   c. medical labeling
   d. epidemiology

9. According to sociologists and environmentalists, which one of the following is not a basic function that the natural environment serves for humans?
   a. It provides the resources essential for life.
   b. It serves as a waste depository.
   c. It provides a natural setting for social inequalities.

Self-Quizzes: At the end of every chapter, a 20-question self-quiz allows students to test their comprehension and retention of core information presented in the chapter.

Taking Sociology with You
in Your Career

Taking Sociology to Work: These boxes underscore the value of an undergraduate degree in sociology by profiling individuals who majored in sociology and use its principles in their work.

TAKING SOCIOLOGY TO WORK

Jessica Houston Su, Research Assistant, Joblessness and Urban Poverty Research Program

Jessica Houston Su chose sociology as her major "because it was the first class that appealed to my desire to understand the roots of inequality." It also helped her to make sense of what was going on around her at Dartmouth College. "I grew up in a rural, working-class community," she explains; "it was quite a culture shock to attend an affluent, Ivy League college." Learning about social structures and institutions helped Su to navigate through a new environment filled with people from many different backgrounds.

Su went through several potential majors before taking a sociology course and realizing that she was interested in almost every course the department offered. When she was hired for a work-study job in the department, she "soon realized that I was spending a lot of time reading all of the articles I was supposed to be photocopying," she jokes. "It became very obvious to me that I had found my major."

Su works at Harvard University's John F. Kennedy School of Government on a research program directed by the well-known sociologist William Julius Wilson. She is currently assigned to a large-scale longitudinal study of welfare reform in Boston, Chicago, and San Antonio. Her primary responsibility is to analyze the qualitative data from the study, gathered through ethnographic interviews with families who are affected by welfare reform, by searching for themes that might help to explain the study's quantitative data. She finds it exciting to be able to follow the same families over a long period. "I feel like I almost know some of the people," she explains.

Of all the things she learned as a sociology major, Su thinks one of the most important was the concept of social construction. "We consider many things to simply be facts of life," she explains, "but upon further investigation it is clear that most things have been socially constructed in some way." The concept of social construction has helped her to look more carefully at the world around her: "My worldview is much more nuanced and I've gained a much better understanding of how society works, both the good and the bad."

Su uses the research methods she learned in her sociology courses all the time. "I love going to work each day," she says. "I am challenged academically and I feel fulfilled knowing that I am working on something that will benefit society and perhaps influence future policy."

LET'S DISCUSS

1. Did you experience a sense of culture shock when you entered college and were exposed to students from different social classes? If so, has studying sociology helped you to adjust to the diversity in students' backgrounds?
2. Have you begun to see the world differently since you learned about the social construction of reality? If so, what in particular do you see in a different light?

high technology has opened up India's social order, bringing new opportunities to those who possess the skills and ability to

social consequences as the estate system ended and a class system of stratification

RESEARCH TODAY

Research Today: These boxes present new sociological findings on topics such as precarious work (how secure is *your* job?) and affirmative action.

4-2 Online Socializing: A New Agent of Socialization

older. As a result, online socializing is becoming much less age-specific—more like socializing in the real world. Moreover, this new agent of socialization can continue to influence people throughout the life course.

Though these networks offer attractive opportunities for people to socialize with others, they also raise concerns about privacy and security. Unlike face-to-face socialization, in which people hesitate to disclose personal information to strangers, online interaction tends to be more open. Looking at people's online profiles, we can see an amazing amount of personal information—much more than the typical organization will disclose about members. For example, academic institutions, which are governed by the Family Education Rights and Privacy Act (FERPA) of 1974, will disclose only the barest of details about students. In contrast, millions of high school and college students reveal significant amounts of personal

Online networks—especially those that indicate how many "friends" an individual has—can also be seen in terms of social capital.

Membership in the online social networks Facebook, Friendster, and MySpace has grown exponentially in recent years. At first, young adults monopolized these social networks. Indeed, Facebook was created in 2004 as a way for students on a single campus to become acquainted with one another before actually meeting. Now there are well over 150 million

information online. As Figure B shows, many if not most students state their relationship status, occupation, interests

self-injury (see the opening of Chapter 2), eating disorders, and other socially disapproved behaviors.

Online networks—especially those that indicate how many "friends" an individual has—can also be seen in terms of social capital. In fact, "friending" is one, if not *the*, main activity on some online sites. Often the number of friends a person socializes with becomes the subject of boasting. By extension, individuals may use these sites to search for "friends" who may prove helpful to them in future endeavors. Becoming aware of new opportunities, either social or economic, through friends is a significant benefit of social capital.

Researchers have looked at the relationship between the display of friends online and the number of real-world friends people socialize with, and have proposed two competing hypotheses. According to the social enhancement hypothesis ("the rich get richer"), those who are popular offline further increase their popularity through online networking sites. According to the social compensation hypothesis ("the poor get richer"), however, social network users try to increase their popularity online to compensate for inadequate popularity offline. The social compensation hypothesis, if correct, would be an example of impression management. Research to date supports elements of both hypotheses; neither hypothesis fully defines the participants in online networking sites.

A new means of social networking

Careers in Sociology:
This appendix to Chapter 1 presents career options for students who have their undergraduate degree in sociology, and explains how this degree can be an asset in a wide variety of occupations.

APPENDIX Careers in Sociology

For the past two decades the number of U.S. college students who have graduated with a degree in sociology has risen steadily (Figure 1-2). In this appendix we'll consider some of the options these students have after completing their undergraduate education.

An undergraduate degree in sociology doesn't just serve as excellent preparation for future graduate work in sociology. It also provides a strong liberal arts background for entry-level positions in business, social services, foundations, community organizations, not-for-profit groups, law enforcement, and many government jobs. A number of fields—among them marketing, public relations, and broadcasting—now require investigative skills and an understanding of the diverse groups found in today's multiethnic and multinational environment. Moreover, a sociology degree requires accomplishment in oral and written communication, interpersonal skills, problem solving, and critical thinking—all job-related skills that may give sociology graduates an advantage

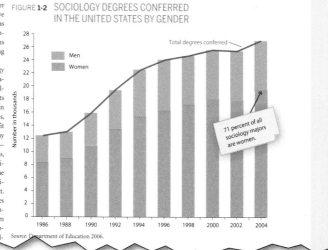

FIGURE **1-2** SOCIOLOGY DEGREES CONFERRED IN THE UNITED STATES BY GENDER

Source: Department of Education 2006.

6. Functionalists point out that discrimination is both functional and dysfunctional for a society. Conflict theorists explain racial subordination through **exploitation theory.** Interactionists pose

12. Worldwide, immigration is at an all-time high, fueling controversy not only in the United States but in the European Union. A new kind of immigrant, the **transnational,** moves back and forth across international borders in search of a better job or an education.

Critical Thinking Questions

1. Why is institutional discrimination even more powerful than individual discrimination? How would functionalists, conflict theorists, and interactionists study institutional discrimination?
2. How is color-blind racism expressed in everyday conversation? In news coverage?

3. Examine the relations between dominant and subordinate racial and ethnic groups in your hometown or your college. Can the community in which you grew up or the college you attend be viewed as a genuine example of pluralism?

267

Critical Thinking Questions:
Critical thinking questions at the end of each chapter help students to analyze the social world in which they participate.

Use Your Sociological Imagination:
These short, thought-provoking sections encourage students to apply the sociological concepts they have learned to the world around them.

www.mhhe.com/schaefer12e

use your sociological *imagination*

You are a news junkie. Where do you gather your facts or information—from newspapers, tabloids, magazines, TV newscasts, blogs, or the Internet? Why did you choose that medium?

Taking Sociology with You into the Community

casestudy Religion in India

From a sociological point of view, the nation of India is large and complex enough that it might be considered a world of its own. Four hundred languages are spoken in India, 16 of which are officially recognized by the government. Besides the two major religions that originated there—Hinduism and Buddhism—several other faiths animate this society. Demographically the nation is huge, with over a billion residents. This teeming country is expected to overtake China as the most populous nation in the world in about three decades (Third World Institute 2007).

The Religious Tapestry in India

Hinduism and Islam, the two most important religions in India, were described on pages 338 and 340. Islam arrived in India in A.D. 1000, with the first of many Muslim invasions. It flowered there during the Mogul empire (1526–1857), the period when the Taj Mahal was built. Today, Muslims account for 13 percent of India's population; Hindus make up 83 percent.

The presence of one dominant faith influences how a society views a variety of issues, even secular ones. For example, India has emerged as a leader in biotechnology, due at least partly to the Hindu faith's tolerance of stem cell research and cloning—techniques that have been questioned in nations where Christianity dominates. Hinduism is open to the latest biomedical techniques, as long as no evil is intended. The only legal prohibition is that fetuses cannot be terminated for the purpose of providing stem cells. Because of its respect for life in all its forms, Hinduism has no major conflict with engineered life-forms of any kind, such as clones (Religion Watch 2006; Sengupta 2006).

Another religion, the Sikh faith, originated in the 15th century with a Hindu named Nanak, the first of a series of gurus (prophets). Sikhism shows the influence of Islam in India, in that it is monotheistic (based on a belief in one god rather than many). It resembles Buddhism in its emphasis on meditation and spiritual transcendence of the everyday world. *Sikhs* (learners) pursue their goal of spiritual enlightenment through meditation with the help of a guru.

Sikh men have a characteristic mode of dress that makes them easy to identify. They do not cut their beards or hair, and they wrap their heads in turbans. (Because of their distinctive dress, the 400,000 Sikhs who live in the United States are often mistaken—and discriminated against—as Muslims.) Sikhs are highly patriotic. Though their 20 million members make up just 2 percent of India's population, they account for 25 percent of India's army. Their presence in the military gives them a much larger voice in the governance of the country than might be expected, given their numbers (Fausset 2003; Watson 2005).

Another faith that has been influential beyond its numbers in India is Jainism (pronounced *Jinism*). This religion was founded six centuries before the birth of Christ—about the same time as Buddhism—by a young Hindu named Mahavira. Offended by the Hindu caste system—the rigid social hierarchy that reduces some people to the status of outcastes based solely on their birth—and by the numerous Hindu deities, Mahavira left his family and his wealth behind to become a beggar monk. His teachings attracted many followers, and the faith grew and flourished until the Muslim invasions of the 12th century.

According to the Jain faith, there is no god; each person is responsible for his or her own spiritual well-being. By following a strict code of conduct, Jains believe they can ultimately free their souls from the endless cycle of death and rebirth and attain *nirvana* (spiritual enlightenment). Jains are required to meditate; forswear lying and stealing; limit their personal wealth; and practice self-denial, chastity, and nonviolence. Because they will not knowingly harm other living beings, including plants and animals, Jains shun meat, fish, or even vegetables whose harvest kills the entire plant, such as carrots and potatoes. They will not work in the military, in farming or fishing, or in the manufacture or sale of alcohol and drugs. Though the Jains are a relatively small group (about 4 million), they exercise considerable influence in India through their business dealings and charitable contributions.

Another group that forms a small segment of the faithful, Christians, also plays a disproportionate role in the country's social safety net. Christian schools, hospitals, and other social service organizations serve non-Christians as well as Christians. Interestingly, hundreds of priests who were trained at churches in India have since immigrated to the United States to ease the shortage of priests there. Together with Jains and Buddhists, Christians make up 4 percent of India's population (Embree 2003; Goodstein 2008).

Adherents of the Hindu religion participate in fire worship at a celebration in Kerala, India. The Hindu faith is enormously influential in India, the country where most Hindus live.

352

Religion and the State in India

Religion was influential in India's drive to overturn British colonialism. The great Mohandas K. Gandhi (1869–1948) led the long struggle to regain India's sovereignty, which culminated in its independence in 1947. A proponent of nonviolent resistance, Gandhi persuaded Hindus and Muslims, ancient enemies, to join in defying British domination. But his influence as a peacemaker could not override the Muslims' demand for a separate state of their own. Immediately after independence was granted, India was partitioned into two states, Pakistan for the Muslims and India for the Hindus. The new arrangement caused large-scale migrations of Indians, especially Muslims, from one nation to the other, and sparked boundary disputes that continue to this day. In many areas Muslims were forced to abandon places they considered sacred. In the chaotic months that followed, centuries of animosity between the two groups boiled over into riots, ending in Gandhi's assassination in January 1948.

Today, India is a secular state that is dominated by Hindus (see Figure 15-2 on page 339). Though the government is officially tolerant of the Muslim minority, tensions between Hindus and Muslims remain high in some states. Conflict also exists among various Hindu groups, from fundamentalists to more secular and ecumenical adherents (Embree 2003).

Many observers see religion as the moving force in Indian society. As in so many other parts of the world, religion is being redefined in India. To the dismay of Sikh spiritual leaders, increasing numbers of young Sikh men are trimming their long hair and abandoning the traditional turban. To show that the 300-year-old tradition is still cool in the 21st century, Sikh leaders now offer a CD-ROM called "Smart Turban 1.0" (Gentleman 2007b).

socialpolicy and Religion

Religion in the Schools

The Issue

Should public schools be allowed to sponsor organized prayer in the classroom? How about Bible reading, or just a collective moment of silence? Can athletes at public schools offer up a group prayer in a team huddle? Should students be able to initiate voluntary prayers at school events? Each of these situations has been an object of great dissension among those who see a role for prayer in the schools and those who want to maintain strict separation of church and state.

Another controversy concerns the teaching of theories about the origin of humans and the universe. Mainstream scientific thinking holds that humans evolved over billions of years from one-celled organisms, and that the universe came into being 15 billion years ago as a result of a "big bang." These theories are challenged by people who hold to the biblical account of the creation of humans and the universe some 10,000 years ago—a viewpoint known as **creationism.** Creationists, many of whom are Christian fundamentalists, want their belief taught in the schools as the only one—or at the very least, as an alternative to the theory of evolution.

Who has the right to decide these issues, and what is the "right" decision? Religion in the schools is one of the thorniest issues in U.S. public policy today.

The Setting

The issues just described go to the heart of the First Amendment's provisions regarding religious freedom. On the one hand, the government must protect the right to practice one's religion; on the other, it cannot take any measures that would seem to establish one religion over another (separation of church and state).

In the key case of *Engle v. Vitale,* the Supreme Court ruled in 1962 that the use of nondenominational prayer in New York schools was "wholly inconsistent" with the First Amendment's prohibition against government establishment of religion. In finding that organized school prayer violated the Constitution—even when no student was required to participate—the Court argued, in effect, that promoting religious observance was not a legitimate function of government or education. Subsequent Court decisions have allowed *voluntary* school prayer by students, but forbid school officials to *sponsor* any prayer or religious observance at school events. Despite these rulings, many public schools still regularly lead their students in prayer recitations or Bible readings. Other states have enacted "moments of silence" during the public school day, which many see as prayer in disguise (Robelon 2007).

School prayer is not the only issue that pits religion against public schools. Unlike Europeans, many people in the United States seem highly skeptical of evolutionary theory, which is taught as a matter of course in science classes. In 2007 a national survey showed that 43 percent of adults believe that God created humans in their present form. Another 38 percent believe that humans developed their present form with divine guidance. Only 14 percent believe that humans developed without divine guidance. And only 18 percent of respondents believe the central tenet of evolutionary theory, that human beings developed over millions of years from less advanced forms of life (Gallup 2009c).

The controversy over whether the biblical account of creation should be presented in school curricula recalls the famous "monkey trial" of 1925. In that trial, high school biology teacher John T. Scopes was convicted of violating a Tennessee law making it a crime to teach the scientific theory of evolution in public

353

Case Studies: Applying a sociological lens, our case studies evaluate both the local and the global community—from culture at Wal-Mart and NASA to stratification in Mexico and capitalism in China.

SOCIOLOGY IN THE GLOBAL COMMUNITY

5-3 The Second Life® Virtual World

Virtual networking is a phenomenon that is evolving so fast, its future is difficult to imagine. Consider the Second Life® world, a Web-based three-dimensional virtual world that included about 16.8 million networked "players" as of January 2009. Nearly 523,000 of those players were active over a seven-day period. Participants in such a virtual world typically assume an **avatar**—that is, a three-dimensional model, two-dimensional icon, or constructed personality provided by the Internet site. (This use of the term *avatar* originated in the 1980s, in early computer games that featured role-playing.) The avatar that a person assumes may represent a looking-glass self very different from his or her actual identity. Once equipped with an avatar, a player goes about his or her life in the virtual world, establishing a business, even buying and decorating a home.

Sociologist Manuel Castells views these emerging electronic social networks as fundamental to new organizations and the growth of existing businesses and associations. With other scholars, sociologists are now scrambling to understand these environments and their social processes. The Second Life world went public in 2003—a millennium ago in the world of cyberspace. Scholars worry that after the current period of transition, given the absence of a historical record, reconstructing these worlds as they existed when they were populated by only a hundred avatars, much less tens of thousands, will be impossible.

> *The commercialization of these spaces has been met with a good deal of antagonism: Reebok has weathered a virtual nuclear bomb attack, and "customers" have been "shot" outside the American Apparel store.*

Just like real worlds, virtual worlds have become politicized and commercialized. In 2007, Sweden became the first real-world country to place an "embassy" in the Second Life world. Elsewhere in this virtual world, virtual protesters have paraded on behalf of a far-right French group in a confrontation with anti-Nazi protesters. MySpace was commercialized when it was purchased by the global media giant News Corp, which added targeted advertising to the site. If a MySpace user con-

"islands" to use for training sessions or employee conferences—islands that are closed to the "general public." (In keeping with the spirit of the Second Life virtual world, however, employees are allowed to attend company functions in their finest avatar attire.) The commercialization of these spaces has been met with a good deal of antagonism: Reebok has weathered a virtual nuclear bomb attack, and "customers" have been "shot" outside the American Apparel store.

As in the real world, untrustworthy businesses can be found in the Second Life world. "Zania Turner," the avatar of a 33-year-old woman, could not resist the interest that her virtual money—bought with real money—could gather at the Second Life world's Ginko Financial. One day her money, along with tens of thousands of dollars that others had deposited in Ginko, vanished. Second Life operators responded by shutting down the site's virtual banks. Chaos followed as avatars flocked to the shuttered ATMs in a frenzied effort to exchange their virtual dollars for real currency.

LET'S DISCUSS

1. If you were a player in the Second Life world, what kind of avatar would you choose? What would be your reason f

Sociology in the Global Community: These boxes provide a global perspective on topics such as aging, poverty, and the women's movement.

Social Policy Sections: The end-of-chapter social policy sections play a critical role in helping students to think like sociologists. These sections apply sociological principles and theories to important social and political issues currently being debated by policymakers and the general public.

social**policy** and the Environment

Environmentalism

The Issue

On April 22, 1970, in a dramatic manifestation of growing grassroots concern over preservation of the environment, an estimated 25 million people turned out to observe the nation's first Earth Day. Two thousand communities held planned celebrations, and more than 2,000 colleges and 10,000 schools hosted environmental teach-ins. In many parts of the United States, citizens marched on behalf of specific environmental causes. That same year, the activism of these early environmentalists convinced Congress to establish the Environmental Protection Agency. The Clean Air, Clean Water, and Endangered Species acts soon followed (Brulle and Jenkins 2008).

The Setting

Several social trends helped to mobilize the environmental movement. First, the activist subculture of the 1960s and early 1970s encouraged people, especially young people, to engage in direct action regarding social issues. Second, the

Americans from around the country joined residents of the nation's capital on the Mall in Washington, D.C., on Earth Day 2009. Since its beginning in 1970, Earth Day has grown into a global celebration, a reminder of the need to preserve our fragile environment.

FIGURE **7-1** BRANDING THE GLOBE

145

The Mass Media

MAPPING LIFE WORLDWIDE

Canada
44 Thomson Reuters
73 Blackberry

Great Britain
23 HSBC
84 BP
89 Smirnoff

Netherlands
43 Philips
86 ING
97 Shell

Switzerland
24 Nescafé
41 UBS
63 Nestlé
79 Rolex

Finland
5 Nokia

Sweden
22 H&M
35 Ikea

South Korea
21 Samsung
72 Hyundai

United States
1 Coca-Cola
2 IBM
3 Microsoft
4 GE
7 Intel
8 McDonald's
9 Disney
10 Google
12 Hewlett-Packard
14 Gillette
15 American Express
17 Cisco
18 Marlboro
19 Citi

Spain
62 Zara

France
16 Louis Vuitton
51 L'Oréal
55 AXA
60 Chanel
66 Danone
76 Hermes
83 Moët & Chandon
86 Cartier
95 Hennessy

Germany
11 Mercedes-Benz
13 BMW
31 SAP
48 Siemens
53 Volkswagen
67 Audi
70 Adidas
75 Porsche
82 Allianz
98 Nivea

Italy
46 Gucci
91 Prada
93 Ferrari
94 Georgio Armani

Note: Map shows the top 100 brands in the world by country of ownership, except for the United States, for which only brands in the top
Source: Based on Interbrand 2008.
Based on revenue and name recognition, these are the brands that dominate the global marketplace.

Maps: The maps titled "Mapping Life Nationwide" and "Mapping Life Worldwide" show the prevalence of social trends in the United States as well as in the global community.

THE WORLD AS A VILLAGE

Imagine that the Earth is a village of only 1,000 people rather than a world with over 6.7 billion inhabitants. Though it would not be easy to walk the Earth and get a sense of its many cultures and societies, you could walk through a village of 1,000 people and get a feeling for the diversity there.

Here Is What You Would See:

280 people under the age of 15,
70 people over the age of 65

140 with no access to improved water supplies

470 people living on less than $2 a day,
140 of whom live on less than a $1 a day

496 people who are female,
504 people who are male

333 Christians (**170** of them Roman Catholic),
210 Muslims, **132** Hindus, **63** Buddhists,
112 followers of other faiths, **117** nonreligious, **23** atheists

134 people speaking Mandarin, **62** people speaking Hindi,
50 people speaking Spanish, **48** people speaking English,
29 people speaking Arabic, **27** people speaking Portuguese,
26 people speaking Russian, **26** people speaking Bengali,
598 people speaking other languages as their first language

122 illiterate adults
(out of a total of **720** adults)

1 physician and **3** hospital beds

540 with no access to improved sanitation facilities

118 automobiles, **890** televisions, **200** telephones,
510 cellular phones, **150** personal computers,
105 different newspapers, **23** iPods

And if you came back in a year there would
be **1,012** people in the village.

See Acknowledgments for source information.

The World as a Village: This new feature, positioned at the beginning of the book, invites students to think about the social world in which they live by figuratively shrinking the world to the size of a small village.

What's New in Each Chapter?

Chapter 1: Understanding Sociology

- Updated discussion of sociology and common sense, with new examples.
- Discussion of the high suicide rate in Las Vegas as an illustration of Durkheim's theory of suicide.
- Inclusion of W. E. B. DuBois in the same section and figure as Durkheim, Weber, and Marx, with key term coverage of *double consciousness.*
- Subsection on Pierre Bourdieu, with key term coverage of *cultural capital* and *social capital.*
- Discussion of research on "slugging," a new form of commuter behavior, as an illustration of the interactionist perspective.
- Expanded coverage of the conflict view of sports in Research Today box, "Looking at Sports from Four Theoretical Perspectives."
- Inclusion of Burawoy's concept of *public sociology.*
- Discussion of asset-based community development in Arkansas, with photo, as an example of applied sociology.
- Sociology in the Global Community box, "Your Morning Cup of Coffee."
- Figure, "Occupations of Graduating Sociology Majors."

Chapter 2: Sociological Research

- Chapter-opening excerpt from Patricia A. Adler and Peter Adler, "The Demedicalization of Self-Injury."
- Coverage of *snowball* or *convenience samples* and their uses.
- Research Today box, "Surveying Cell Phone Users."
- Discussion of undergraduate survey with table, "Top Reasons Why Men and Women Had Sex."
- Discussion of the controversial embedding of social scientists in the U.S. Army's Human Terrain System in Iraq, with photo.
- Updated Research Today box, "What's in a Name?" including coverage of most common surnames and geographical variations in most popular names.
- Updated discussion of the Exxon Corporation's use of research funding to reduce the $5.3 billion penalty for negligence in the *Exxon Valdez* disaster to $500 million.
- Section on feminist methodology, with photo of immigrant sex workers.
- Figure showing median age of first sex in eight countries.

Chapter 3: Culture

- Streamlined organization for increased readability.
- Discussion of Theodor Adorno's concept of the *culture industry,* with key term treatment.
- Discussion of child marriage as an illustration of cultural relativism, with Mapping Life Worldwide map, "Countries with High Child Marriage Rates."

- Discussion of McDonald's move toward local development of menus and marketing strategies at overseas restaurants.
- Discussion of the Navajo word for cancer as an illustration of the Sapir-Whorf hypothesis.
- Expanded discussion of cultural differences in nonverbal communication.
- Key term treatment of *symbol* in the section on nonverbal communication.
- Discussion of trends in U.S. college students' environmental values.
- Discussion of cross-cultural research on student cheating.
- Section on global *culture war,* with key term treatment.
- Mapping Life Nationwide map, "Percentage of People Who Speak a Language Other than English at Home, by State."
- Discussion of the rapidity with which immigrants to the United States learn English, with figure, "Proportion of Immigrant Group Members in Southern California Who Speak the Mother Tongue, by Generation."

Chapter 4: Socialization and the Life Course

- Summing Up table, "Mead's Stages of the Self."
- Discussion of exercise-related impression management among students.
- Research Today box, "Online Socializing: A New Agent of Socialization," with figures.
- Thinking about Movies exercise on *The Departed* (Martin Scorsese, 2006).

Chapter 5: Social Interaction and Social Structure

- Chapter-opening excerpt from Philip Zimbardo, *The Lucifer Effect: Understanding How Good People Turn Evil.*
- Discussion of cross-cultural differences in social interaction and social reality.
- Discussion of the inauguration of President Barack Obama as an example of the institutional function of providing and maintaining a sense of purpose.

- Summing Up table, "Sociological Perspectives on Social Institutions."

- Research Today box, "Social Networks and Smoking," with figure.

- Section on virtual worlds, including Sociology in the Global Community box, "The Second Life® Virtual World."

Chapter 6: Groups and Organizations

- Research Today box, "The Drinking Rape Victim: Jury Decision Making."

- Discussion of new directions in research on organizations.

- Discussion of societal changes that have weakened the bureaucratization of the workplace.

- Sociology in the Global Community box, "Entrepreneurship, Japanese Style."

- Revised Social Policy section, "The State of the Unions Worldwide," including (a) discussion of the effects of the economic downturn of 2008; (b) discussion of the activities of international trade unions; and (c) figure, "Labor Union Membership Worldwide."

Chapter 7: The Mass Media

- Chapter-opening excerpt from Mark Andrejevic, *iSpy: Surveillance and Power in the Interactive Era.*

- Coverage of prominent media events of 2009, including the transition to the Obama administration, street protests in Iran, and Michael Jackson's death.

- Discussion of *cultural convergence,* with key term treatment.

- Discussion of the degree and type of contact U.S. residents have with information and communications technologies, with table.

- Discussion of the media's role in promoting social norms regarding human sexuality.

- Mapping Life Worldwide map, "Filtering Social Content."

- Section on the "digital divide" that separates low-income groups, racial and ethnic minorities, rural residents, and citizens of developing countries from access to the latest technologies, with cartoon.

- Discussion of the use of online social networks to promote consumption, with figure.

Chapter 8: Deviance and Social Control

- Chapter-opening excerpt from *Gang Leader for a Day: A Rogue Sociologist Takes to the Streets* by Sudhir Venkatesh.

- Discussion of a recent replication of Milgram's obedience experiment.

- Research Today box, "Does Crime Pay?"

- Section on *social disorganization theory,* with key term treatment.

- Section on labeling theory and sexual deviance, with photo.

- Sociology on Campus box, "Campus Crime."

- Taking Sociology to Work box, "Stephanie Vezzani, Special Agent, U.S. Secret Service."

- Social Policy section on gun control, with cartoon.

Chapter 9: Stratification and Social Mobility in the United States

- Chapter-opening excerpt from *Richistan: A Journey through the American Wealth Boom and the Lives of the New Rich* by Robert Frank.

- Expansion of the discussion of castes to include historical contexts outside India.

- Key term treatment of *socioeconomic status (SES)* and the *feminization of poverty.*

- Expanded discussion of the growing gap in household income between the rich and the poor.

- Research Today box, "Precarious Work," including coverage of the economic downturn of 2008–2009.

- Expanded discussion of intergenerational mobility, with figure, "Intergenerational Income Mobility."

- Discussion of the generational change in women's earnings relative to men's.

- In the Social Policy section, discussion of the rise in dependence on social security, food stamps, and unemployment insurance during the economic downturn of 2008–2009.

Chapter 10: Global Inequality

- Chapter-opening excerpt from *The Bottom Billion: Why the Poorest Countries Are Failing and What Can Be Done About It* by Paul Collier.

- Explanation of how social scientists in developing nations measure poverty.

- Description of a microlending program run by the Widows Organization in the Democratic Republic of the Congo.

- Updated Sociology in the Global Community box, "Stratification in Japan," with expanded discussion of gender stratification.

- Discussion of cross-cultural studies of intergenerational mobility over the last half century.

- Discussion of growth of the middle class in some developing nations.

- Description of the effect of the recent economic downturn in the United States on Mexican immigrants and the Mexican economy.

- Discussion of the feminist perspective on human rights.

Chapter 11: Racial and Ethnic Inequality

- Discussion of the process of *racial formation,* with key term treatment.

- Expanded section on the recognition of multiple identities.

- Explanation of why race and ethnicity are still relevant despite the election or appointment of African Americans to high office in the United States.

- Section on *color-blind racism,* with key term treatment.
- Key term treatment of *White privilege.*
- Discussion of public support for the profiling of Arab Americans by airport security personnel.
- Sociology in the Global Community box, "The Aboriginal People of Australia."
- Comparison of Asian American incomes inside and outside Chinatown in New York City.
- Research Today box, "Social Mobility among Latino Immigrants."
- Key term treatment of *transnationals* in Social Policy section on global immigration.

Chapter 12: Stratification by Gender

- Key term coverage of *multiple masculinities.*
- Discussion of the social construction of gender in West Sumatra, Indonesia, with photo.
- Updated section on the interactionist approach to gender, including new examples of "doing gender" and new research on cross-sex conversations.
- Discussion of the Norwegian law requiring corporations to set aside 40 percent of managerial positions for women.
- Discussion of reasons for the pay gap between men and women in the same occupation.
- Discussion of the legal barrier to proving sex discrimination in wage payments.
- Discussion of the debate over abortion in Latin American countries.

Chapter 13: Stratification by Age

- Discussion of the trend toward the adoption of new technologies by the elderly.
- Section on labeling theory.
- Discussion of the impact of Japan's aging labor force on Japan's immigration policy.
- Key term treatment of *naturally occurring retirement communities (NORCs).*
- Expanded discussion of gender, racial, and ethnic stratification among the elderly, with figure, "Minority Population Aged 65 and Older, Projected."
- Discussion of the Age Discrimination in Employment Act (ADEA) and Supreme Court decisions favoring elderly workers.
- Research Today box, "Elderspeak and Other Signs of Ageism."
- Discussion of research on physician-assisted suicide in Oregon and the Netherlands.

Chapter 14: The Family and Intimate Relationships

- Figure, "Median Age at First Marriage in Eight Countries."
- Discussion of the impact of new media technologies on dating and mating.

- Discussion of the rise in the number of couples who live apart for reasons other than marital discord, with photo.
- Table, "Foreign-Born Adoptees by Top Ten Countries of Origin, 1989 and 2008."
- Comparison of cultural attitudes toward marriage, divorce, and cohabitation in the United States and Europe.
- Updated discussion of the impact of divorce on children.
- Updated coverage of the federal Healthy Marriage Initiative.
- Research Today box, "Divorce and Military Deployment," with photo.
- Discussion of state legislation and supreme court rulings on gay marriage.

Chapter 15: Religion

- Figure, "Major Religious Traditions in the United States."
- Discussion of the goals of the Office of Faith-Based and Neighborhood Partnerships under the Obama administration.
  - Discussion of public opinion polls in 143 countries regarding perceptions of religion as a source of oppression or social support.
  - Summing Up table, "Components of Religion."
  - Discussion of the fluidity of individual religious adherence.
  - Updated discussion of religion on the Internet, including GodTube.com and Second Life®.
- Discussion of changing dress and hairstyle among Sikh men.
- Discussion of the Christian contribution to India's social safety net.
- Discussion of a recent survey of Americans' beliefs regarding creationism and evolutionary theory.

Chapter 16: Education

- Sociology on Campus box, "Google University."
- Table, "Foreign Students by Major Countries of Origin and Destination."
- Discussion of recent research on tracking of low-income students and their performance on advanced placement exams.
- Figure, "College Campuses by Race and Ethnicity: Then, Now, and in the Future."

Chapter 17: Government and Politics

- Mapping Life Worldwide map, "Filtering Information: Political Content."

- Sociology in the Global Community box, "Charisma: The Beatles and Maharishi Mahesh Yogi," with photo.

- Discussion of the increase in online political activity during the 2008 presidential campaign.

- Figure, "Reasons for Not Voting, 18- to 24-Year-Olds."

- Coverage of the global power elite.

- Mapping Life Worldwide map, "Global Peace Index."

- Discussion of the feminist perspective on terrorism.

- Discussion of *e-government,* or the online presence of governmental authority.

- Updated Social Policy section on campaign financing, including (a) spending during the 2008 presidential campaign, (b) candidates' decisions to forgo public funding, and (c) the recent increase in online donations.

Chapter 18: The Economy and Work

- Chapter-opening excerpt from Kelsey Timmerman, *Where Am I Wearing? A Global Tour to the Countries, Factories, and People that Make Our Clothes.*

- Discussion of the federal government's bailout of banking, investment, and insurance companies during the financial crisis of 2008 and its acquisition in 2009 of majority ownership in General Motors.

- Discussion of *Karoshi* ("death from overwork") in the section on job satisfaction in Japan.

- Discussion of "color-blind policies" and preferential treatment of children of alumni in Research Today box on affirmative action.

- Discussion of the accelerating effects of the economic downturn of 2008–2009 on the processes of deindustrialization and downsizing.

- Table, "Occupations Most Vulnerable to Offshoring."

Chapter 19: Health, Medicine, and the Environment

- Combines coverage of health and medicine (Chapter 19 in the 11th edition) with coverage of the environment (Chapter 21 in the 11th edition).

- Mapping Life Worldwide map, "People Living with HIV."

- Research Today box, "The AIDS Epidemic."

- Discussion of the effect of the economic downturn of 2008–2009 on the number of people with health insurance and public opinion toward health care reform.

- Discussion of the increased death rate among people without health insurance.

- Discussion of the link between health and economic mobility.

- Figure, "Use of Complementary and Alternative Medicine."

- Discussion of the increasing use of mental health services and the growing public awareness of their necessity.

- Discussion of the higher incidence of mental illness and differential access to treatment among minority groups.

- Discussion of a recent study by the American Lung Association of air quality in U.S. communities.

- Discussion of the Obama administration's initiative to slow global warming.

- Social Policy section on environmentalism, with figure, "The Environment versus the Economy."

Chapter 20: Population, Communities, and Urbanization

- Combines coverage of population (Chapter 21 in the 11th edition) with coverage of communities and urbanization (Chapter 20 in the 11th edition).

- Figure, "Population Structure of Afghanistan, Italy, and the United States, 2012."

- Updated Social Policy section, "Seeking Shelter Worldwide," with discussions of the impact of the economic downturn of 2008–2009 on homelessness and on public opinion regarding homelessness.

Chapter 21: Collective Behavior and Social Movements

- Discussion of *crowdsourcing,* the online practice of asking Internet surfers for ideas or participation in an activity or movement.

- Discussion of the false rumor that Oscar Mayer does not support U.S. troops.

- Summing Up table, "Forms of Collective Behavior."

Chapter 22: Social Change in the Global Community

- Chapter-opening excerpt from *The Pirate's Dilemma: How Youth Culture Is Reinventing Capitalism* by Matt Mason.

- Discussion of the "not on planet Earth" campaign, an antiglobalization movement.

- Discussion of the medical advances made as a result of modern warfare, such as electronically controlled prosthetic devices.

Support for Instructors and Students

Print Resources

Student Study Guide   The Study Guide includes a detailed list of key points, key terms and their definitions, true or false self-quizzes, multiple-choice quizzes, fill-in-the-blank questions, and social policy questions.

Primis Customized Readers   An array of first-rate readings are available to adopters in a customized electronic database. Some are classic articles from the sociological literature; others are provocative pieces written especially for McGraw-Hill by leading sociologists.

Digital Resources

Online Learning Center   The Online Learning Center that accompanies this text (**www.mhhe.com/ schaefer12e**) provides robust resources for both students and instructors.

Students will find video clips, interactive quizzes, diagnostic midterm and final exams, census updates, social policy exercises, chapter glossaries, vocabulary flash cards, and more.

Schaefer's highly valued instructor resources are available on the password-protected instructor portion of the Online Learning Center. Teaching aids available include the Instructor's Resource Manual, Test Banks in computerized and Word formats, and PowerPoint slides for the convenience of instructors who choose to give multimedia lectures. The Instructor's Resource Manual provides sociology instructors with detailed chapter outlines and summaries, learning objectives, additional lecture ideas, class discussion topics, essay questions, topics for student research, critical thinking questions, video resources, and additional readings. The Test Banks include multiple-choice, true or false, and essay questions for every chapter; they will be useful in testing students on basic sociological concepts, application of

theoretical perspectives, and recall of important factual information. Correct answers are provided for all questions. The PowerPoint slides include bulleted lecture points, figures, and maps, and instructors are welcome to create overhead transparencies from the slides if they wish to do so.

McGraw-Hill's EZ Test is a flexible and easy-to-use electronic testing program. The program allows instructors to create tests from book-specific items. It accommodates a wide range of question types, and instructors may add their own questions. Multiple versions of the test can be created, and any test can be exported for use with course management systems such as WebCT, BlackBoard, and PageOut. EZ Test Online is a new service that gives you a place to easily administer your EZ Test–created exams and quizzes online. The program is available for Windows and Macintosh environments.

Also available on the instructor's portion of the Online Learning Center are book-specific questions created for use with the Classroom Performance System (CPS) by eInstruction, a wireless response system that allows instructors to receive immediate feedback from students. CPS units include easy-to-use software for instructors' use in creating their own questions and assessments, and delivering them to their students. The units also include individual wireless response pads for students' use in responding. For further details, go to **www.mhhe.com/einstruction.**

With the CourseSmart eTextbook version of this title, students can save up to 50 percent off the cost of a print book, reduce their impact on the environment, and access powerful Web tools for learning. Faculty can also review and compare the full text online without having to wait for a print desk copy. CourseSmart is an online eTextbook, which means users need to be connected to the Internet in order to access it. Students can also print sections of the book for maximum portability.

Help Feedback

sociology *12th edition*
RICHARD T. SCHAEFER

Information Center

Feature Summary
New to this Edition

Sociology, 12/e

Richard T. Schaefer, DePaul University

ISBN: 0073404330
Copyright year: 2011

Sociology provides an up-to-date and comprehensive introduction to sociology for today's student. Known for its balanced coverage of the 3 perspectives, this text continues to encourage students to think more with a sociological imagination. Through its strong coverage of globalization, race and ethnicity, careers in sociology, and current topics like mass media and social policy, *Sociology* provides students with knowledge they can use on campus, at work, in their neighborhoods, and in the global community. The new 12th edition features updated sections in various chapters reflecting recent sociological changes like the impact of the current economic downturn on social class and the global culture war. New *Research Today* boxes provide students with relevant examples of sociological research.

To obtain an instructor login for this Online Learning Center, ask your local sales representative. If you're an instructor thinking about adopting this textbook, request a free copy for review.

For further details, contact your sales representative or go to www.coursesmart.com.

Primis Online   Professors can customize this edition of *Sociology* by selecting from it only those chapters they want to use in their courses. Primis Online allows users to choose and change the order of chapters, as well as add readings from McGraw-Hill's vast database of content. Both custom-printed textbooks and electronic eBooks are available. To learn more, contact your McGraw-Hill sales representative or visit **www.primisonline.com**.

Acknowledgments

Since 1999, Elizabeth Morgan has played a most significant role in the development of my introductory sociology books. Fortunately for me, in the 12th edition, Betty has once again been responsible for the smooth integration of all changes and updates.

I deeply appreciate the contributions to this book made by my editors. Developmental editor Kate Scheinman challenged me to make this edition better than its predecessors. Rhona Robbin, director of development, at McGraw-Hill, oversaw the project.

I have received strong support and encouragement from Frank Mortimer, publisher; Gina Boedeker, senior sponsoring editor; and Caroline McGillen, marketing manager. Additional guidance and support were provided by Daniel Gonzalez, editorial coordinator; Holly Paulsen, production editor; Andrei Pasternak, design manager; Nora Agbayani, photo research coordinator; Toni Michaels, photo researcher, Rennie Evans, art editor; Judy Brody, text permissions; and Jan McDearmon, copyeditor.

Academic Reviewers

This edition continues to reflect many insightful suggestions made by reviewers of the eleven hardcover editions and the eight paperback brief editions. The current edition has benefitted from constructive and thorough evaluations provided by sociologists from both two-year and four-year institutions. These include John P. Bartkowski, Mississippi State University; Douglas Forbes, University of Wisconsin–Stevens Point; H. David Hunt, University of Southern Mississippi; Kevin Keating, Broward College; Nelson Kofie, Prince George's Community College; Richard Leveroni, Schenectady County Community College; Tina Mougouris, San Jacinto College; Gloria Nikolai, Pikes Peak Community College; Sally Raskoff, Los Angeles Valley College; Luis Salinas, University of Houston; and Rebecca Stevens, Mount Union College.

I would also like to acknowledge the contributions of the following individuals: Lynn Newhart, Rockford College, for her work on the Online Learning Center; Martha Warburton, University of Texas at Brownsville and Texas South West College, and Rebecca Matthews, PhD sociology, Cornell University, for their work on the Instructor's Resource Manual and Study Guide; Gerry Williams, for his work on the PowerPoint presentations; and Jon Bullinger, for his work on the Test Banks and CPS questions. Finally, I would like to thank Peter D. Schaefer, Marymount Manhattan College, for developing the new end-of-chapter sections, "Thinking about Movies."

As is evident from these acknowledgments, the preparation of a textbook is truly a team effort. The most valuable member of this effort continues to be my wife, Sandy. She provides the support so necessary in my creative and scholarly activities.

I have had the good fortune to introduce students to sociology for many years. These students have been enormously helpful in spurring on my own sociological imagination. In ways I can fully appreciate but cannot fully acknowledge, their questions in class and queries in the hallway have found their way into this textbook.

Richard T. Schaefer
www.schaefersociology.net
schaeferrt@aol.com

sociology

12th edition

inside

What Is Sociology?

What Is Sociological Theory?

The Development
of Sociology

Major Theoretical
Perspectives

Applied and Clinical
Sociology

Developing a Sociological
Imagination

Appendix: Careers
in Sociology

BOXES

Research Today: *Looking
at Sports from Four
Theoretical Perspectives*

Sociology in the Global
Community: *Your
Morning Cup of Coffee*

Every day we are influenced
by the people with whom we interact.

Understanding Sociology 1

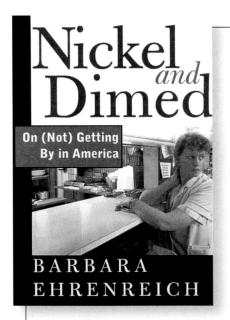

Nickel *and* Dimed

On (Not) Getting By in America

BARBARA EHRENREICH

" I am, of course, very different from the people who normally fill America's least attractive jobs, and in ways that both helped and limited me. Most obviously, I was only visiting a world that others inhabit full-time, often for most of their lives. With all the real-life assets I've built up in middle age—bank account, IRA, health insurance, multiroom home—waiting indulgently in the background, there was no way I was going to "experience poverty" or find out how it "really feels" to be a long-term low-wage worker. My aim here was much more straightforward and objective—just to see whether I could match income to expenses, as the truly poor attempt to do every day. . . .

In Portland, Maine, I came closest to achieving a decent fit between income and expenses, but only because I worked seven days a week. Between my two jobs, I was earning approximately $300 a week after taxes and paying $480 a month in rent, or a manageable 40 percent of my earnings. It helped, too, that gas and electricity were included in my rent and that I got two or three free meals each weekend at the nursing home. But I was there at the beginning of the off-season.

If I had stayed until June 2000 I would have faced the Blue Haven's summer rent of $390 a week, which would of course have been out of the question. So to survive year-round, I would have had to save enough, in the months between August 1999 and May 2000, to accumulate the first month's rent and deposit on an actual apartment. I think I could have done this—saved $800 to $1,000—at least if no car trouble or illness interfered with my budget. I am not sure, however, that I could have maintained the seven-day-a-week regimen month after month or eluded the kinds of injuries that afflicted my fellow workers in the housecleaning business.

In Minneapolis—well, here we are left with a lot of speculation. If I had been able to find an apartment for $400 a month or less, my pay at Wal-Mart—$1,120 a month before taxes—might have been sufficient, although the cost of living in a motel while I searched for such an apartment might have made it impossible for me to save enough for the first month's rent and deposit. A weekend job, such as the one I almost landed at a supermarket for about $7.75 an hour, would have helped, but I had no guarantee that I could arrange my schedule at Wal-Mart to reliably exclude weekends. If I had taken the job at Menards and the pay was in fact $10 an hour for eleven hours a day, I would have made about $440 a week after taxes—enough to pay for a motel room and still have something left over to save up for the initial costs of an apartment. But were they really offering $10 an hour? And could I have stayed on my feet eleven hours a day, five days a week? So yes, with some different choices, I probably could have survived in Minneapolis. But I'm not going back for a rematch. "

> *With all the real-life assets I've built up in middle age—bank account, IRA, health insurance, multiroom home—waiting indulgently in the background, there was no way I was going to "experience poverty" or find out how it "really feels" to be a long-term low-wage worker.*

(Ehrenreich 2001:6, 197–198) Additional information about this excerpt can be found on the Online Learning Center at www.mhhe.com/schaefer12e.

In her undercover attempts to survive as a low-wage worker in different cities in the United States, journalist Barbara Ehrenreich revealed patterns of human interaction and used methods of study that foster sociological investigation. This excerpt from her book *Nickel and Dimed: On (Not) Getting By in America* describes how she left a comfortable home and assumed the identity of a divorced, middle-aged housewife with no college degree and little working experience. She set out to get the best-paying job and the cheapest living quarters she could find, to see whether she could make ends meet. Months later, physically exhausted and demoralized by demeaning work rules, Ehrenreich confirmed what she had suspected before she began: getting by in this country as a low-wage worker is a losing proposition.

Ehrenreich's study focused on an unequal society, which is a central topic in sociology. Her investigative work, like the work of many other journalists, is informed by sociological research that documents the existence and extent of inequality in our society. Social inequality has a pervasive influence on human interactions and institutions. Certain groups of people control scarce resources, wield power, and receive special treatment.

While it might be interesting to know how one individual is affected by the need to make ends meet, sociologists consider how entire groups of people are affected by these kinds of factors, and how society itself might be altered by them. Sociologists, then, are not concerned with what one individual does or does not do, but with what people do as members of a group or in interaction with one another, and what that means for individuals and for society as a whole.

As a field of study, sociology is extremely broad in scope. You will see throughout this book the range of topics sociologists investigate—from suicide to TV viewing habits, from Amish society to global economic patterns, from peer pressure to genetic engineering. Sociology looks at how others influence our behavior; how major social institutions like the government, religion, and the economy affect us; and how we ourselves affect other individuals, groups, and even organizations.

How did sociology develop? In what ways does it differ from other social sciences? This chapter will explore the nature of sociology as both a field of inquiry and an exercise of the "sociological imagination." We'll look at the discipline as a science and consider its relationship to other social sciences. We'll meet four pioneering thinkers—Émile Durkheim, Max Weber, Karl Marx, and W. E. B. DuBois—and examine the theoretical perspectives that grew out of their work. We'll note some of the practical applications for sociological theory and research. Finally, we'll see how sociology helps us to develop a sociological imagination. For those students interested in exploring career opportunities in sociology, the chapter closes with a special appendix.

What Is Sociology?

What has sociology got to do with me or with my life?" As a student, you might well have asked this question when you signed up for your introductory sociology course. To answer it, consider these points: Are you influenced by what you see on television? Do you use the Internet? Did you vote in the last election? Are you familiar with binge drinking on campus? Do you use alternative medicine? These are just a few of the everyday life situations described in this book that sociology can shed light on. But as the opening excerpt indicates, sociology also looks at large social issues. We use sociology to investigate why thousands of jobs have moved from the United States to developing nations, what social forces promote prejudice, what leads someone to join a social movement and work for social change, how access to computer technology can reduce social inequality, and why relationships between men and women in Seattle differ from those in Singapore.

Sociology is, very simply, the scientific study of social behavior and human groups. It focuses on social relationships; how those relationships influence people's behavior; and how societies, the sum total of those relationships, develop and change.

The Sociological Imagination

In attempting to understand social behavior, sociologists rely on a unique type of critical thinking. A leading sociologist, C. Wright Mills, described such thinking as the **sociological imagination**—an awareness of the relationship between an individual and the wider society, both today and in the past. This awareness allows all of us (not just sociologists) to comprehend the links between our immediate, personal social settings and the remote, impersonal social world that surrounds and helps to shape us. Barbara Ehrenreich certainly used a sociological imagination when she studied low-wage workers (Mills [1959] 2000a).

A key element in the sociological imagination is the ability to view one's own society as an outsider would, rather than only from the perspective of personal experiences and cultural biases. Consider something as simple as sporting events. On college campuses in the United States, thousands of students cheer well-trained football players. In Bali, Indonesia, dozens of spectators gather around a ring to cheer on well-trained roosters engaged in cockfights. In both instances, the spectators debate the merits of their favorites and bet on the outcome of the events. Yet what is considered a normal sporting event in one part of the world is considered unusual in another part.

The sociological imagination allows us to go beyond personal experiences and observations to understand broader public issues. Divorce, for example, is unquestionably a personal hardship for a husband and wife who split apart. However, C. Wright Mills advocated using the sociological imagination to view divorce not simply as an individual's personal problem but rather as a societal concern. Using this perspective, we can see that an increase in the divorce rate actually redefines a major social institution—the family. Today's households frequently include stepparents and half-siblings whose parents have divorced and remarried. Through the complexities of the blended family, this private concern becomes a public issue that affects schools, government agencies, businesses, and religious institutions.

The sociological imagination is an empowering tool. It allows us to look beyond a limited understanding of human behavior to see the world and its people in a new way and through a broader lens than we might otherwise use. It may be as simple as understanding why a roommate prefers country music to hip-hop, or it may open up a whole different way of understanding other populations in the world. For example, in the aftermath of the terrorist attacks on the United States on September 11, 2001, many citizens wanted to understand how Muslims throughout the world perceived their country, and why. From time to time this textbook will offer you the chance to exercise your own sociological imagination in a variety of situations.

use your sociological *imagination*

You are walking down the street in your city or hometown. In looking around you, you can't help noticing that half or more of the people you see are overweight. How do you explain your observation? If you were C. Wright Mills, how do you think you would explain it?

www.mhhe.com/schaefer12e

Sociology and the Social Sciences

Is sociology a science? The term **science** refers to the body of knowledge obtained by methods based on systematic observation. Just like other scientific disciplines, sociology involves the organized, systematic study of phenomena (in this case, human behavior) in order to enhance understanding. All scientists, whether studying mushrooms or murderers, attempt to collect precise information through methods of study that are as objective as possible. They rely on careful recording of observations and accumulation of data.

Of course, there is a great difference between sociology and physics, between psychology and astronomy. For this reason, the sciences are commonly divided into natural and social sciences. **Natural science** is the study of the physical features of nature and the ways in which they interact and change. Astronomy, biology, chemistry, geology, and physics are all natural sciences.

Sociology is the scientific study of social behavior and human groups.

Social science is the study of the social features of humans and the ways in which they interact and change. The social sciences include sociology, anthropology, economics, history, psychology, and political science.

These social science disciplines have a common focus on the social behavior of people, yet each has a particular orientation. Anthropologists usually study past cultures and preindustrial societies that continue today, as well as the origins of humans. Economists explore the ways in which people produce and exchange goods and services, along with money and other resources. Historians are concerned with the peoples and events of the past and their significance for us today. Political scientists study international relations, the workings of government, and the exercise of power and authority. Psychologists investigate personality and individual behavior. So what do *sociologists* focus on? They study the influence that society has on people's attitudes and behavior and the ways in which people interact and shape society. Because humans are social animals, sociologists examine our social relationships with others scientifically. The range of the relationships they investigate is vast, as the current list of sections in the American Sociological Association suggests (Table 1-1).

Let's consider how different social sciences would study the impact of Hurricane Katrina, which ravaged the Gulf Coast of

TABLE **1-1** SECTIONS OF THE AMERICAN SOCIOLOGICAL ASSOCIATION

Aging and the Life Course	Ethnomethodology and Conversation Analysis	Peace, War, and Social Conflict
Alcohol, Drugs, and Tobacco	Evolution, Biology and Society	Political Economy of the World-System
Animals and Society	Family	Political Sociology
Asia and Asian America	History of Sociology	Population
Children and Youth	Human Rights	Race, Gender, and Class
Collective Behavior and Social Movements	International Migration	Racial and Ethnic Minorities
Communication and Information Technologies	Labor and Labor Movements	Rationality and Society
Community and Urban Sociology	Latino/a Sociology	Religion
Comparative and Historical Sociology	Law	Science, Knowledge, and Technology
Crime, Law, and Deviance	Marxist Sociology	Sex and Gender
Culture	Mathematical Sociology	Sexualities
Economic Sociology	Medical Sociology	Social Psychology
Education	Mental Health	Sociological Practice and Public Sociology
Emotions	Methodology	Teaching and Learning
Environment and Technology	Organizations, Occupations, and Work	Theory

The range of sociological issues is very broad. For example, sociologists who belong to the Animals and Society section of the ASA may study the animal rights movement; those who belong to the Sexualities section may study global sex workers or the gay, bisexual, and transgendered movements. Economic sociologists may investigate globalization or consumerism, among many other topics.
Source: American Sociological Association 2009b.

Think about It
Which of these topics do you think would interest you the most? Why?

the United States in 2005. Historians would compare the damage done by natural disasters in the 20th century to that caused by Katrina. Economists would conduct research on the economic impact of the damage, not just in the Southeast but throughout the nation and the world. Psychologists would study individual cases to assess the emotional stress of the traumatic event. And political scientists would study the stances taken by different elected officials, along with their implications for the government's response to the disaster.

What approach would sociologists take? They might look at Katrina's impact on different communities, as well as on different social classes. Some sociologists have undertaken neighborhood and community studies, to determine how to maintain the integrity of storm-struck neighborhoods during the rebuilding phase. Researchers have focused in particular on Katrina's impact on marginalized groups, from the inner-city poor in New Orleans to residents of rural American Indian reservations. The devastating social impact of the storm did not surprise sociologists, for the disaster area was among the poorest in the United States. In terms of family income, for example, New Orleans ranked 63rd (7th lowest) among the nation's 70 largest cities. When the storm left tens of thousands of Gulf Coast families homeless and unemployed, most had no savings to fall back on—no way to pay for a hotel room or tide themselves over until the next paycheck (Laska 2005).

Sociologists would take a similar approach to studying episodes of extreme violence. In April 2007, just as college students were beginning to focus on the impending end of the semester, tragedy struck on the campus of Virginia Tech. In a two-hour shooting spree, a mentally disturbed senior armed with semi-automatic weapons killed a total of 32 students and faculty at Virginia's largest university. Observers struggled to describe the events and place them in some social context. For sociologists in particular, the event raised numerous issues and topics for study, including the media's role in describing the attacks, the presence of violence in our educational institutions, the gun control debate, the inadequacy of the nation's mental health care system, and the stereotyping and stigmatization of people who suffer from mental illness.

Besides doing research, sociologists have a long history of advising government agencies on how to respond to disasters. Certainly the poverty of the Gulf Coast region complicated the huge challenge of evacuation in 2005. With Katrina bearing down on the Gulf Coast, thousands of poor inner-city residents had no automobiles or other available means of escaping the storm. Added to that difficulty was the high incidence of disability in the area. New Orleans ranked 2nd among the nation's 70 largest cities in the proportion of people over age 65 who are disabled—56 percent. Moving wheelchair-bound residents to safety requires specially equipped vehicles, to say nothing of handicap-accessible accommodations in public shelters. Clearly, officials must consider these factors in developing evacuation plans (Bureau of the Census 2005f).

Sociological analysis of the disaster did not end when the floodwaters receded. Long before residents of New Orleans staged a massive anticrime rally at City Hall in 2007, researchers were analyzing resettlement patterns in the city. They noted that returning residents often faced bleak job prospects. Yet families who had stayed away for that reason often had trouble enrolling

On August 29, 2005, shortly after Hurricane Katrina swept through the Gulf of Mexico, the U.S. Coast Guard took this aerial photograph of New Orleans. The widespread flooding shown in the photo grew worse as the week wore on, hampering the efforts of rescue teams. Sociologists want to know how the storm affected people from different communities and social classes, as well as how its impact varied with residents' income, race, and gender.

their children in schools unprepared for an influx of evacuees. Faced with a choice between the need to work and the need to return their children to school, some displaced families risked sending their older children home alone. Meanwhile, opportunists had arrived to victimize unsuspecting homeowners. And the city's overtaxed judicial and criminal justice systems, which had been understaffed before Katrina struck, had been only partially restored. All these social factors led sociologists and others to anticipate the unparalleled rise in reported crime the city experienced in 2006 and 2007 (Jervis 2008; Kaufman 2006).

Throughout this textbook, you will see how sociologists develop theories and conduct research to study and better understand societies. And you will be encouraged to use your own sociological imagination to examine the United States (and other societies) from the viewpoint of a respectful but questioning outsider.

Sociology and Common Sense

Sociology focuses on the study of human behavior. Yet we all have experience with human behavior and at least some knowledge of it. All of us might well have theories about why people become homeless, for example. Our theories and opinions typically come from common sense—that is, from our experiences and conversations, from what we read, from what we see on television, and so forth.

In our daily lives, we rely on common sense to get us through many unfamiliar situations. However, this commonsense knowledge, while sometimes accurate, is not always reliable, because it rests on commonly held beliefs rather than on systematic analysis of facts. It was once considered common sense to accept that the earth was flat—a view rightly questioned by Pythagoras and Aristotle. Incorrect commonsense notions are not just a part of the distant past; they remain with us today.

Contrary to the common notion that women tend to be chatty compared to men, for instance, researchers have found little difference between the sexes in terms of their talkativeness. Over a five-year period they placed unobtrusive microphones on 396 college students in various fields, at campuses in Mexico as well as the United States. They found that both men and women spoke about 16,000 words per day (Mehl et al. 2007).

Similarly, common sense tells us that in the United States today, military marriages are more likely to end in separation or divorce than in the past due to the strain of long deployments in Iraq and Afghanistan. Yet a study released in 2007 shows no significant increase in the divorce rate among U.S. soldiers over the past decade. In fact, the rate of marital dissolution among members of the military is comparable to that of nonmilitary families. Interestingly, this is not the first study to disprove the widely held notion that military service strains the marital bond. Two generations earlier, during the Vietnam era, researchers came to the same conclusion (Call and Teachman 1991; Karney and Crown 2007).

Like other social scientists, sociologists do not accept something as a fact because "everyone knows it." Instead, each piece of information must be tested and recorded, then analyzed in relation to other data. Sociologists rely on scientific studies in order to describe and understand a social environment. At times, the findings of sociologists may seem like common sense, because they deal with familiar facets of everyday life. The difference is that such findings have been *tested* by researchers. Common sense now tells us that the earth is round, but this particular commonsense notion is based on centuries of scientific work that began with the breakthroughs made by Pythagoras and Aristotle.

What Is Sociological Theory?

Why do people commit suicide? One traditional commonsense answer is that people inherit the desire to kill themselves. Another view is that sunspots drive people to take their own lives. These explanations may not seem especially convincing to contemporary researchers, but they represent beliefs widely held as recently as 1900.

Sociologists are not particularly interested in why any one individual commits suicide; they are more concerned with identifying the social forces that systematically cause some people to take their own lives. In order to undertake this research, sociologists develop a theory that offers a general explanation of suicidal behavior.

We can think of theories as attempts to explain events, forces, materials, ideas, or behavior in a comprehensive manner. In sociology, a **theory** is a set of statements that seeks to explain problems, actions, or behavior. An effective theory may have both explanatory and predictive power. That is, it can help us to see the relationships among seemingly isolated phenomena, as well as to understand how one type of change in an environment leads to other changes.

The World Health Organization (2006) estimates that some 900,000 people commit suicide every year. More than a hundred years ago, a sociologist tried to look at suicide data scientifically. Émile Durkheim ([1897] 1951) developed a highly original theory about the relationship between suicide and social factors. Durkheim was primarily concerned, not with the personalities of individual suicide victims, but rather with suicide rates and how they varied from country to country. As a result, when he looked at the number of reported suicides in France, England, and Denmark in 1869, he also noted the total population of each country in order to determine the rate of suicide in each nation. He found that whereas England had only 67 reported suicides per million inhabitants, France had 135 per million and Denmark had 277 per million. The question then became "Why did Denmark have a comparatively high rate of reported suicide?"

Durkheim went much deeper into his investigation of suicide rates. The result was his landmark work *Suicide,* published in 1897. Durkheim refused to accept unproved explanations regarding suicide, including the beliefs that cosmic forces or inherited tendencies caused such deaths. Instead, he focused on social factors, such as the cohesiveness or lack of cohesiveness of religious, social, and occupational groups.

Durkheim's research suggested that suicide, although it is a solitary act, is related to group life. He found that people with religious affiliations had a lower suicide rate than those who were unaffiliated; the unmarried had much higher rates than married people; and soldiers were more likely to take their lives than civilians. In addition, there seemed to be higher rates of suicide in times of peace than in times of war and revolution, and in times of economic instability and recession rather than in times of prosperity. Durkheim concluded that the suicide rates of a society reflected the extent to which people were or were not integrated into the group life of the society.

Émile Durkheim, like many other social scientists, developed a theory to explain how individual behavior can be understood within a social context. He pointed out the influence of groups and societal forces on what had always been viewed as a highly personal act. Clearly, Durkheim offered a more *scientific* explanation for the causes of suicide than that of sunspots or inherited tendencies. His theory has predictive power, since it suggests that suicide rates will rise or fall in conjunction with certain social and economic changes.

Las Vegas has a suicide rate that is twice the national average. Sociologists suspect that the rapidly expanding city lacks a sense of community cohesiveness.

Of course, a theory—even the best of theories—is not a final statement about human behavior. Durkheim's theory of suicide is no exception. Sociologists continue to examine factors that contribute to differences in suicide rates around the world and to a particular society's rate of suicide. They have observed that in Las Vegas, for example, the chances of dying by suicide are strikingly high—twice as high as in the United States as a whole. Noting Durkheim's emphasis on the relationship between suicide and social isolation, researchers have suggested that Las Vegas's rapid growth and constant influx of tourists have undermined the community's sense of permanence, even among longtime residents. Although gambling—or more accurately, losing while gambling—may seem a likely precipitating factor in suicides there, careful study of the data has allowed researchers to dismiss that explanation. What happens in Vegas may stay in Vegas, but the sense of community cohesiveness that the rest of the country enjoys may be lacking (Wray et al. 2008).

Harriet Martineau, an early pioneer of sociology who studied social behavior both in her native England and in the United States, proposed some of the methods still used by sociologists.

---

use your sociological *imagination*

If you were Durkheim's successor in his research on suicide, how would you investigate the factors that may explain the increase in suicide rates among young people in the United States today?

The Development of Sociology

People have always been curious about sociological matters—how we get along with others, what we do for a living, whom we select as our leaders. Philosophers and religious authorities of ancient and medieval societies made countless observations about human behavior. They did not test or verify those observations scientifically; nevertheless, their observations often became the foundation for moral codes. Several of these early social philosophers correctly predicted that a systematic study of human behavior would emerge one day. Beginning in the 19th century, European theorists made pioneering contributions to the development of a science of human behavior.

Early Thinkers

Auguste Comte The 19th century was an unsettling time in France. The French monarchy had been deposed in the revolution of 1789, and Napoleon had suffered defeat in his effort to conquer Europe. Amid this chaos, philosophers considered how society might be improved. Auguste Comte (1798–1857), credited with being the most influential of the philosophers of the early 1800s, believed that a theoretical science of society and a systematic investigation of behavior were needed to improve society. He coined the term *sociology* to apply to the science of human behavior.

Writing in the 1800s, Comte feared that the excesses of the French Revolution had permanently impaired France's stability. Yet he hoped that the systematic study of social behavior would eventually lead to more rational human interactions. In Comte's hierarchy of the sciences, sociology was at the top. He called it the "queen," and its practitioners "scientist-priests." This French theorist did not simply give sociology its name; he presented a rather ambitious challenge to the fledgling discipline.

Harriet Martineau Scholars learned of Comte's works largely through translations by the English sociologist Harriet Martineau (1802–1876). But Martineau was a pathbreaker in her own right: she offered insightful observations of the customs and social practices of both her native Britain and the United States. Martineau's book *Society in America* ([1837] 1962) examined religion, politics, child rearing, and immigration in the young nation. It gave special attention to social class distinctions and to such factors as gender and race. Martineau ([1838] 1989) also wrote the first book on sociological methods.

Martineau's writings emphasized the impact that the economy, law, trade, health, and population could have on social problems. She spoke out in favor of the rights of women, the emancipation of slaves, and religious tolerance. Later in life, deafness did not keep her from being an activist. In Martineau's ([1837] 1962) view, intellectuals and scholars should not simply offer observations of social conditions; they should *act* on their convictions in a manner that will benefit society. That is why Martineau conducted research on the nature of female employment and pointed to the need for further investigation of the issue (Deegan 2003; Hill and Hoecker-Drysdale 2001).

Herbert Spencer Another important early contributor to the discipline of sociology was Herbert Spencer (1820–1903). A relatively prosperous Victorian Englishman, Spencer (unlike Martineau) did not feel compelled to correct or improve society; instead, he merely hoped to understand it better. Drawing on Charles Darwin's study *On the Origin of Species,* Spencer applied the concept of evolution of the species to societies in order to explain how they change, or evolve, over time. Similarly, he adapted Darwin's evolutionary view of the "survival of the fittest" by arguing that it is "natural" that some people are rich while others are poor.

Spencer's approach to societal change was extremely popular in his own lifetime. Unlike Comte, Spencer suggested that since societies are bound to change eventually, one need not be highly critical of present social arrangements or work actively for social change. This viewpoint appealed to many influential people in England and the United States who had a vested interest in the status quo and were suspicious of social thinkers who endorsed change.

Émile Durkheim

Émile Durkheim made many pioneering contributions to sociology, including his important theoretical work on suicide. The son of a rabbi, Durkheim (1858–1917) was educated in both France and Germany. He established an impressive academic reputation and was appointed one of the first professors of sociology in France. Above all, Durkheim will be remembered for his insistence that behavior must be understood within a larger social context, not just in individualistic terms.

To give one example of this emphasis, Durkheim ([1912] 2001) developed a fundamental thesis to help explain all forms of society. Through intensive study of the Arunta, an Australian tribe, he focused on the functions that religion performed and underscored the role of group life in defining what we consider to be religion. Durkheim concluded that like other forms of group behavior, religion reinforces a group's solidarity.

Another of Durkheim's main interests was the consequences of work in modern societies. In his view, the growing division of labor in industrial societies, as workers became much more specialized in their tasks, led to what he called "anomie." **Anomie** refers to the loss of direction felt in a society when social control of individual behavior has become ineffective. Often, the state of anomie occurs during a time of profound social change, when people have lost their sense of purpose or direction. In a period of anomie, people are so confused and unable to cope with the new social environment that they may resort to taking their own lives.

Durkheim was concerned about the dangers that alienation, loneliness, and isolation might pose for modern industrial societies. He shared Comte's belief that sociology should provide direction for social change. As a result, he advocated the creation of new social groups—mediators between the individual's family and the state—that would provide a sense of belonging for members of huge, impersonal societies. Unions would be an example of such groups.

Like many other sociologists, Durkheim did not limit his interests to one aspect of social behavior. Later in this book we will consider his thinking on crime and punishment, religion, and the workplace. Few sociologists have had such a dramatic impact on so many different areas within the discipline.

Max Weber

Another important early theorist was Max Weber (pronounced VAY-ber). Born in Germany, Weber (1864–1920) studied legal and economic history, but gradually developed an interest in sociology. Eventually, he became a professor at various German universities. Weber taught his students that they should employ **verstehen** (pronounced fair-SHTAY-en), the German word for "understanding" or "insight," in their intellectual work. He pointed out that we cannot analyze our social behavior by the same type of objective criteria we use to measure weight or temperature. To fully comprehend behavior, we must learn the subjective meanings people attach to their actions—how they themselves view and explain their behavior.

For example, suppose that a sociologist was studying the social ranking of individuals in a fraternity. Weber would expect the researcher to employ *verstehen* to determine the significance of the fraternity's social hierarchy for its members. The researcher might examine the effects of athleticism or grades or social skills or seniority on standing within the fraternity. He or she would seek to learn how the fraternity members relate to other members of higher or lower status. While investigating these questions, the researcher would take into account people's emotions, thoughts, beliefs, and attitudes (L. Coser 1977).

We also owe credit to Weber for a key conceptual tool: the ideal type. An **ideal type** is a construct or model for evaluating specific cases. In his own works, Weber identified various characteristics of bureaucracy as an ideal type (discussed in detail in Chapter 6). In presenting this model of bureaucracy, Weber was not describing any particular business, nor was he using the term *ideal* in a way that suggested a positive evaluation. Instead, his purpose was to provide a useful standard for measuring how bureaucratic an actual organization is (Gerth and Mills 1958). Later in this book, we will use the concept of *ideal type* to study the family, religion, authority, and economic systems, as well as to analyze bureaucracy.

Although their professional careers coincided, Émile Durkheim and Max Weber never met and probably were unaware of each other's existence, let alone ideas. Such was not true of the work of Karl Marx. Durkheim's thinking about the impact of the division of labor in industrial societies was related to Marx's writings, while Weber's concern for a value-free, objective sociology was a direct response to Marx's deeply held convictions. Thus, it is not surprising that Karl Marx is viewed as a major figure in the development of sociology, as well as several other social sciences (Figure 1-1).

Karl Marx

Karl Marx (1818–1883) shared with Durkheim and Weber a dual interest in abstract philosophical issues and the concrete reality of everyday life. Unlike them, however, Marx was so critical of existing institutions that a conventional academic career was impossible. He spent most of his life in exile from his native Germany.

Marx's personal life was a difficult struggle. When a paper he had written was suppressed, he fled to France. In Paris, he met Friedrich Engels (1820–1895), with whom he formed a lifelong friendship. The two lived at a time when European and North American economic life was increasingly dominated by the factory rather than the farm.

FIGURE **1-1** CONTRIBUTORS TO SOCIOLOGY

11

Understanding Sociology

	Émile Durkheim 1858–1917	**Max Weber 1864–1920**	**Karl Marx 1818–1883**	**W. E. B. DuBois 1868–1963**
Academic training	Philosophy	Law, economics, history, philosophy	Philosophy, law	Sociology
Key works	1893—*The Division of Labor in Society* 1897—*Suicide: A Study in Sociology* 1912—*Elementary Forms of Religious Life*	1904-1905—*The Protestant Ethic and the Spirit of Capitalism* 1921—*Economy and Society*	1848—*The Communist Manifesto* 1867—*Das Kapital*	1899—*The Philadelphia Negro* 1903—*The Negro Church* 1903—*Souls of Black Folk*

While in London in 1847, Marx and Engels attended secret meetings of an illegal coalition of labor unions known as the Communist League. The following year they prepared a platform called *The Communist Manifesto,* in which they argued that the masses of people with no resources other than their labor (whom they referred to as the *proletariat*) should unite to fight for the overthrow of capitalist societies. In the words of Marx and Engels:

> The history of all hitherto existing society is the history of class struggles. . . . The proletarians have nothing to lose but their chains. They have a world to win. WORKING MEN OF ALL COUNTRIES UNITE! (L. Feuer 1989:7, 41)

After completing *The Communist Manifesto,* Marx returned to Germany, only to be expelled. He then moved to England, where he continued to write books and essays. Marx lived there in extreme poverty; he pawned most of his possessions, and several of his children died of malnutrition and disease. Marx clearly was an outsider in British society, a fact that may well have influenced his view of Western cultures.

In Marx's analysis, society was fundamentally divided between two classes that clashed in pursuit of their own interests. When he examined the industrial societies of his time, such as Germany, England, and the United States, he saw the factory as the center of conflict between the exploiters (the owners of the means of production) and the exploited (the workers). Marx viewed these relationships in systematic terms; that is, he believed that a system of economic, social, and political relationships maintained the power and dominance of the owners over the workers. Consequently, Marx and Engels argued that the working class should overthrow the existing class system. Marx's influence on contemporary thinking has been dramatic. His writings inspired those who would later lead communist revolutions in Russia, China, Cuba, Vietnam, and elsewhere.

Even apart from the political revolutions that his work fostered, Marx's significance is profound. Marx emphasized the *group* identifications and associations that influence an *individual's* place in society. This area of study is the major focus of contemporary sociology. Throughout this textbook, we will consider how membership in a particular gender classification, age group, racial group, or economic class affects a person's attitudes and behavior. In an important sense, we can trace this way of understanding society back to the pioneering work of Karl Marx.

W. E. B. DuBois

Marx's work encouraged sociologists to view society through the eyes of those segments of the population that rarely influence decision making. In the United States, some early Black sociologists, including W. E. B. DuBois (1868–1963), conducted research that they hoped would assist in the struggle for a racially egalitarian society. DuBois (pronounced doo-BOYSS) believed that knowledge was essential in combating prejudice and achieving tolerance and justice. Sociologists, he contended, needed to draw on scientific principles to study social problems such as those experienced by Blacks in the United States. To separate opinion from fact, he advocated basic research on the lives of Blacks. Through his in-depth studies of urban life, both White and Black, in cities such as Philadelphia and Atlanta, DuBois ([1899] 1996) made a major contribution to sociology.

Like Durkheim and Weber, DuBois saw the importance of religion to society. However, he tended to focus on religion at the community level and the role of the church in the lives of its members ([1903] 2003). DuBois had little patience with theorists such as Herbert Spencer, who seemed content with the status quo. He believed that the granting of full political rights to Blacks was essential to their social and economic progress.

Because many of his ideas challenged the status quo, DuBois did not find a receptive audience within either the government or the academic world. As a result, he became increasingly involved with organizations whose members questioned the established social order. In 1909 he helped to found the National Association for the Advancement of Colored People, better known today as the NAACP (Wortham 2008).

DuBois's insights have been lasting. In 1897 he coined the term **double consciousness** to refer to the division of an individual's identity into two or more social realities. He used the term to describe the experience of being Black in White America. Today, an African American holds the most powerful office in the nation, President of the United States. Yet for millions of African Americans, the reality of being Black in the United States typically is not one of power ([1903] 1961).

Twentieth-Century Developments

Sociology today builds on the firm foundation developed by Émile Durkheim, Max Weber, Karl Marx, and W. E. B. DuBois. However, the field certainly has not remained stagnant over the past hundred years. While Europeans have continued to make contributions to the discipline, sociologists from throughout the world and especially the United States have advanced sociological theory and research. Their new insights have helped us to better understand the workings of society.

In a photograph taken around 1930, social reformer Jane Addams reads to children at the Mary Crane Nursery. Addams was an early pioneer both in sociology and in the settlement house movement.

Charles Horton Cooley Charles Horton Cooley (1864–1929) was typical of the sociologists who came to prominence in the early 1900s. Born in Ann Arbor, Michigan, Cooley received his graduate training in economics but later became a sociology professor at the University of Michigan. Like other early sociologists, he had become interested in this new discipline while pursuing a related area of study.

Cooley shared the desire of Durkheim, Weber, and Marx to learn more about society. But to do so effectively, he preferred to use the sociological perspective to look first at smaller units—intimate, face-to-face groups such as families, gangs, and friendship networks. He saw these groups as the seedbeds of society, in the sense that they shape people's ideals, beliefs, values, and social nature. Cooley's work increased our understanding of groups of relatively small size.

Jane Addams In the early 1900s, many leading sociologists in the United States saw themselves as social reformers dedicated to systematically studying and then improving a corrupt society. They were genuinely concerned about the lives of immigrants in the nation's growing cities, whether those immigrants came from Europe or from the rural American South. Early female sociologists, in particular, often took active roles in poor urban areas as leaders of community centers known as *settlement houses*. For example, Jane Addams (1860–1935), a member of the American Sociological Society, cofounded the famous Chicago settlement, Hull House.

Addams and other pioneering female sociologists commonly combined intellectual inquiry, social service work, and political activism—all with the goal of assisting the underprivileged and creating a more egalitarian society. For example, working with the Black journalist and educator Ida Wells-Barnett, Addams successfully prevented racial segregation in the Chicago public schools. Addams's efforts to establish a juvenile court system and a women's trade union reveal the practical focus of her work (Addams 1910, 1930; Deegan 1991; Lengermann and Niebrugge-Brantley 1998).

By the middle of the 20th century, however, the focus of the discipline had shifted. Sociologists for the most part restricted themselves to theorizing and gathering information; the aim of transforming society was left to social workers and activists. This shift away from social reform was accompanied by a growing commitment to scientific methods of research and to value-free interpretation of data. Not all sociologists were happy with this emphasis. A new organization, the Society for the Study of Social Problems, was created in 1950 to deal more directly with social inequality and other social problems.

Robert Merton Sociologist Robert Merton (1910–2003) made an important contribution to the discipline by successfully combining theory and research. Born to Slavic immigrant parents in Philadelphia, Merton won a scholarship to Temple University. He continued his studies at Harvard, where he acquired his lifelong interest in sociology. Merton's teaching career was based at Columbia University.

Merton (1968) produced a theory that is one of the most frequently cited explanations of deviant behavior. He noted different ways in which people attempt to achieve success in life. In his view, some may deviate from the socially approved goal of accumulating material goods or the socially accepted means of achieving that goal. For example, in Merton's classification scheme, "innovators" are people who accept the goal of pursuing material wealth but use illegal means to do so, including robbery, burglary, and extortion. Although Merton based his explanation of crime on individual behavior that has been influenced by society's approved goals and means, it has wider applications. His theory helps to account for the high crime rates among the nation's poor, who may see no hope of advancing themselves through traditional roads to success. Chapter 8 discusses Merton's theory in greater detail.

Merton also emphasized that sociology should strive to bring together the "macro-level" and "micro-level" approaches to the study of society. **Macrosociology** concentrates on large-scale phenomena or entire civilizations. Émile Durkheim's cross-cultural study of suicide is an example of macro-level research. More recently, macrosociologists have examined international crime rates (see Chapter 8), the stereotype of Asian Americans as a "model minority" (see Chapter 11), and the population patterns of developing countries (see Chapter 20). In contrast, **microsociology** stresses the study of small groups, often through experimental means. Sociological research on the micro level has included studies of how divorced men and women disengage from significant social roles (see Chapter 5); of how conformity can influence the expression of prejudiced attitudes (see Chapter 8); and of how a teacher's expectations can affect a student's academic performance (see Chapter 16).

Pierre Bourdieu Increasingly, scholars in the United States have been drawing on the insights of sociologists in other countries. The ideas of the late French sociologist Pierre Bourdieu (1930–2002) have found a broad following both in North America and elsewhere. As a young man, Bourdieu did fieldwork in Algeria during its struggle for independence from France. Today, scholars study Bourdieu's research techniques as well as his conclusions.

Bourdieu wrote about how capital in its many forms sustains individuals and families from one generation to the next. To Bourdieu, *capital* included not just material goods, but cultural and social assets. **Cultural capital** refers to noneconomic goods, such as family background and education, which are reflected in a knowledge of language and the arts. Not necessarily book knowledge, cultural capital refers to the kind of education that is valued by the socially elite. Though a knowledge of Chinese cuisine is culture, for example, it is not the prestigious kind of culture that is valued by the elite. In the United States, immigrants—especially those who arrived in large numbers and settled in ethnic enclaves—have generally taken two or three generations to develop the same level of cultural capital enjoyed by more established groups. In comparison, **social capital** refers to the collective benefit of social networks, which are built on reciprocal trust. Much has been written about the importance of family and friendship networks in providing people with an opportunity to advance. In his emphasis on cultural and social capital, Bourdieu's work extends the insights of early social thinkers such as Marx and Weber (Bourdieu and Passerson 1990; Field 2008).

Today sociology reflects the diverse contributions of earlier theorists. As sociologists approach such topics as divorce, drug addiction, and religious cults, they can draw on the theoretical insights of the discipline's pioneers. A careful reader can hear Comte, Durkheim, Weber, Marx, DuBois, Cooley, Addams, and many others speaking through the pages of current research. Sociology has also broadened beyond the intellectual confines of North America and Europe. Contributions to the discipline now come from sociologists studying and researching human behavior in other parts of the world. In describing the work of these sociologists, it is helpful to examine a number of influential theoretical approaches (also known as *perspectives*).

Major Theoretical Perspectives

Sociologists view society in different ways. Some see the world basically as a stable and ongoing entity. They are impressed with the endurance of the family, organized religion, and other social institutions. Other sociologists see society as composed of many groups in conflict, competing for scarce resources. To still other

sociologists, the most fascinating aspects of the social world are the everyday, routine interactions among individuals that we sometimes take for granted. These three views, the ones most widely used by sociologists, are the functionalist, conflict, and interactionist perspectives. Together, these approaches will provide an introductory look at the discipline.

Functionalist Perspective

Think of society as a living organism in which each part of the organism contributes to its survival. This view is the **functionalist perspective,** which emphasizes the way in which the parts of a society are structured to maintain its stability.

Talcott Parsons (1902–1979), a Harvard University sociologist, was a key figure in the development of functionalist theory. Parsons was greatly influenced by the work of Émile Durkheim, Max Weber, and other European sociologists. For over four decades, he dominated sociology in the United States with his advocacy of functionalism. Parsons saw any society as a vast network of connected parts, each of which helps to maintain the system as a whole. His functionalist approach holds that if an aspect of social life does not contribute to a society's stability or survival—if it does not serve some identifiably useful function or promote value consensus among members of a society—it will not be passed on from one generation to the next.

Let's examine an example of the functionalist perspective. Many Americans have difficulty understanding the Hindu prohibition against slaughtering cows (specifically, zebu). Cattle browse unhindered through Indian street markets, helping themselves to oranges and mangoes while people bargain for the little food they can afford. What explains this devotion to the cow in the face of human deprivation—a devotion that appears to be dysfunctional?

The simple explanation is that cow worship is highly functional in Indian society, according to economists, agronomists,

Cows (zebu), considered sacred in India, wander freely through this city, respected by all who encounter them. The sanctity of the cow is functional in India, where plowing, milking, and fertilizing are far more important to subsistence farmers than a diet that includes beef.

and social scientists who have studied the matter. Cows perform two essential tasks: plowing the fields and producing milk. If eating their meat were permitted, hungry families might be tempted to slaughter their cows for immediate consumption, leaving themselves without a means of cultivation. Cows also produce dung, which doubles as a fertilizer and a fuel for cooking. Finally, cow meat sustains the neediest group in society, the *dalit,* or untouchables, who sometimes resort to eating beef in secrecy. If eating beef were socially acceptable, higher-status Indians would no doubt bid up its price, placing it beyond the reach of the hungriest.

Manifest and Latent Functions   A college catalog typically states various functions of the institution. It may inform you, for example, that the university intends to "offer each student a broad education in classical and contemporary thought, in the humanities, in the sciences, and in the arts." However, it would be quite a surprise to find a catalog that declared, "This university was founded in 1895 to assist people in finding a marriage partner." No college catalog will declare this as the purpose of the university. Yet societal institutions serve many functions, some of them quite subtle. The university, in fact, *does* facilitate mate selection.

Robert Merton (1968) made an important distinction between manifest and latent functions. **Manifest functions** of institutions are open, stated, and conscious functions. They involve the intended, recognized consequences of an aspect of society, such as the university's role in certifying academic competence and excellence. In contrast, **latent functions** are unconscious or unintended functions that may reflect hidden purposes of an institution. One latent function of universities is to hold down unemployment. Another is to serve as a meeting ground for people seeking marital partners.

Dysfunctions   Functionalists acknowledge that not all parts of a society contribute to its stability all the time. A **dysfunction** refers to an element or process of a society that may actually disrupt the social system or reduce its stability.

We view many dysfunctional behavior patterns, such as homicide, as undesirable. Yet we should not automatically interpret them in this way. The evaluation of a dysfunction depends on one's own values, or as the saying goes, on "where you sit." For example, the official view in prisons in the United States is that inmate gangs should be eradicated because they are dysfunctional to smooth operations. Yet some guards have come to view prison gangs as a functional part of their jobs. The danger posed by gangs creates a "threat to security," requiring increased surveillance and more overtime work for guards, as well as requests for special staffing to address gang problems (G. Scott 2001).

Conflict Perspective

Where functionalists see stability and consensus, conflict sociologists see a social world in continual struggle. The **conflict perspective** assumes that social behavior is best understood in terms of tension between groups over power or the allocation of resources, including housing, money, access to services, and political representation. The tension between competing groups need not be violent; it can take the form of labor negotiations, party politics, competition between religious groups for new members, or disputes over the federal budget.

Throughout most of the 1900s, the functionalist perspective had the upper hand in sociology in the United States. However, the conflict approach has become increasingly persuasive since the late 1960s. The widespread social unrest resulting from battles over civil rights, bitter divisions over the war in Vietnam, the rise of the feminist and gay liberation movements, the Watergate political scandal, urban riots, and confrontations at abortion clinics have offered support for the conflict approach—the view that our social world is characterized by continual struggle between competing groups. Currently, the discipline of sociology accepts conflict theory as one valid way to gain insight into a society.

The Marxist View   As we saw earlier, Karl Marx viewed struggle between social classes as inevitable, given the exploitation of workers that he perceived under capitalism. Expanding on Marx's work, sociologists and other social scientists have come to see conflict not merely as a class phenomenon but as a part of everyday life in all societies. In studying any culture, organization, or social group, sociologists want to know who benefits, who suffers, and who dominates at the expense of others. They are concerned with the conflicts between women and men, parents and children, cities and suburbs, Whites and Blacks, to name only a few. Conflict theorists are interested in how society's institutions—including the family, government, religion, education, and the media—may help to maintain the privileges of some groups and keep others in a subservient position. Their emphasis on social change and the redistribution of resources makes conflict theorists more radical and activist than functionalists (Dahrendorf 1959).

The Feminist View   Sociologists began embracing the feminist perspective only in the 1970s, although it has a long tradition in many other disciplines. The **feminist view** sees inequity in gender as central to all behavior and organization. Because it focuses clearly on one aspect of inequality, it is often allied with the conflict perspective. Proponents of the feminist view tend to focus on the macro level, just as conflict theorists do. Drawing on the work of Marx and Engels, contemporary feminist theorists often view women's subordination as inherent to capitalist societies. Some radical feminist theorists, however, view the oppression of women as inevitable in *all* male-dominated societies, whether capitalist, socialist, or communist.

An early example of this perspective (long before the label came into use by sociologists) can be seen in the life and writings of Ida Wells-Barnett (1862–1931). Following her groundbreaking publications in the 1890s on the practice of lynching Black Americans, she became an advocate in the women's rights campaign, especially the struggle to win the vote for women. Like feminist theorists who succeeded her, Wells-Barnett used her analysis of society as a means of resisting oppression. In her case, she researched what it meant to be Black, a woman in the United States, and a Black woman in the United States (Giddings 2008; Wells-Barnett 1970).

Feminist scholarship has broadened our understanding of social behavior by extending the analysis beyond the male point of view. In the past, studies of physical violence typically failed to include domestic violence, in which women are the chief victims. Not only was there a void in the research; in the field, law enforcement agencies were ill-prepared to deal with such

Ida Wells-Barnett explored what it meant to be female and Black in the United States. Her work established her as one of the earliest feminist theorists.

violence. Similarly, feminists have complained that studies of "children having children" focus almost entirely on the characteristics and behavior of unwed teenage mothers, ignoring the unwed father's role. They have called for more scrutiny of boys and their behavior, as well as their parents and their role models. In sum, the feminist approach moves women from the margins of scientific inquiry to the center (Ferree 2005; J. Fields 2005; hooks 1994).

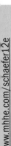

use your sociological *imagination*

You are a sociologist who uses the conflict perspective to study various aspects of our society. How do you think you would interpret the practice of prostitution? Contrast this view with the functionalist perspective. Do you think your comments would differ if you took the feminist view, and if so, how?

Interactionist Perspective

Workers interacting on the job, encounters in public places like bus stops and parks, behavior in small groups—all these aspects of microsociology catch the attention of interactionists. Whereas functionalist and conflict theorists both analyze large-scale, societywide patterns of behavior, theorists who take the **interactionist perspective** generalize about everyday forms of social interaction in order to explain society as a whole. Today, given rising concern over the cost and availability of gas, interactionists have begun to study a form of commuter behavior called "slugging." To avoid driving to work, commuters gather at certain preappointed places to seek rides from complete strangers.

When a driver pulls into the parking area or vacant lot and announces his destination, the first slug in line who is headed for that destination jumps in. Rules of etiquette have emerged to smooth the social interaction between driver and passenger. Neither the driver nor the passenger may eat or smoke; the slug may not adjust the windows or radio or talk on a cell phone. The presence of the slugs, who get a free ride, may allow the driver to use special lanes reserved for high-occupancy vehicles (Slug-Lines.com 2009).

Interactionism (also referred to as *symbolic interactionism*) is a sociological framework in which human beings are viewed as living in a world of meaningful objects. Those "objects" may include material things, actions, other people, relationships, and even symbols. Interactionists see symbols as an especially important part of human communication (thus the term *symbolic interactionism*). Symbols have a shared social meaning that is understood by all members of a society. In the United States, for example, a salute symbolizes respect, while a clenched fist signifies defiance. Another culture might use different gestures to convey a feeling of respect or defiance. These types of symbolic interaction are classified as forms of **nonverbal communication,** which can include many other gestures, facial expressions, and postures (Masuda et al. 2008).

Symbols in the form of tattoos took on special importance in the aftermath of September 11, 2001. Tattoo parlors in lower Manhattan were overwhelmed with requests from various groups for designs that carried symbolic significance for them. New York City firefighters asked for tattoos with the names of their fallen comrades; police officers requested designs incorporating their distinctive NYPD shield; recovery workers at Ground Zero sought tattoos that incorporated the image of the giant steel cross, the remnant of a massive cross-beam in a World Trade Center building. Through symbols such as these tattoos, people communicate their values and beliefs to those around them (Scharnberg 2002).

Another manipulation of symbols can be seen in dress codes. Schools frown on students who wear clothes displaying messages that appear to endorse violence or drug and alcohol consumption. Businesses stipulate the attire employees are allowed to wear on the job in order to impress their customers or clients. In 2005, the National Basketball Association (NBA) adopted a new dress code for the athletes who play professional basketball—one that involved, not the uniforms they wear on court, but the clothes they wear off court on league business. The code requires "business casual attire" when players are representing the league. Indoor sunglasses, chains, and sleeveless shirts are specifically banned (Crowe and Herman 2005:A23).

While the functionalist and conflict approaches were initiated in Europe, interactionism developed first in the United States. George Herbert Mead (1863–1931) is widely regarded as the founder of the interactionist perspective. Mead taught at the University of Chicago from 1893 until his death. As his teachings have become better known, sociologists have expressed greater interest in the interactionist perspective. Many have moved away from what may have been an excessive preoccupation with the large-scale (macro) level of social behavior and have redirected their attention toward behavior that occurs in small groups (micro level).

Erving Goffman (1922–1982) popularized a particular type of interactionist method known as the **dramaturgical approach,**

	Functionalist	Conflict	Interactionist
View of Society	Stable, well integrated	Characterized by tension and struggle between groups	Active in influencing and affecting everyday social interaction
Level of Analysis Emphasized	Macro	Macro	Micro, as a way of understanding the larger macro phenomena
Key Concepts	Manifest functions Latent functions Dysfunctions	Inequality Capitalism Stratification	Symbols Nonverbal communication Face-to-face interaction
View of the Individual	People are socialized to perform societal functions	People are shaped by power, coercion, and authority	People manipulate symbols and create their social worlds through interaction
View of the Social Order	Maintained through cooperation and consensus	Maintained through force and coercion	Maintained by shared understanding of everyday behavior
View of Social Change	Predictable, reinforcing	Change takes place all the time and may have positive consequences	Reflected in people's social positions and their communications with others
Example	Public punishments reinforce the social order	Laws reinforce the positions of those in power	People respect laws or disobey them based on their own past experience
Proponents	Émile Durkheim Talcott Parsons Robert Merton	Karl Marx W. E. B. DuBois Ida Wells-Barnett	George Herbert Mead Charles Horton Cooley Erving Goffman

in which people are seen as theatrical performers. The dramaturgist compares everyday life to the setting of the theater and stage. Just as actors project certain images, all of us seek to present particular features of our personalities while we hide other features. Thus, in a class, we may feel the need to project a serious image; at a party, we may want to look relaxed and friendly.

The Sociological Approach

Which perspective should a sociologist use in studying human behavior? Functionalist? Conflict? Interactionist? Feminist? In fact, sociologists make use of all the perspectives summarized in Table 1-2, since each offers unique insights into the same issue. We gain the broadest understanding of our society, then, by drawing on all the major perspectives, noting where they overlap and where they diverge.

Although no one approach is correct by itself, and sociologists draw on all of them for various purposes, many sociologists tend to favor one particular perspective over others. A sociologist's theoretical orientation influences his or her approach to a research problem in important ways—including the choice of what to study, how to study it, and what questions to pose (or not to pose). See Box 1-1 for an example of how a researcher would study sports from different perspectives.

Whatever the purpose of sociologists' work, their research will always be guided by their theoretical viewpoints. For example, sociologist Elijah Anderson (1990) embraces both the interactionist perspective and the groundbreaking work of W. E. B. DuBois. For 14 years Anderson conducted fieldwork in Philadelphia, where he studied the interactions of Black and White residents who lived in adjoining neighborhoods. In particular,

he was interested in their public behavior, including their eye contact—or lack of it—as they passed one another on the street. Anderson's research tells us much about the everyday social interactions of Blacks and Whites in the United States, but it does not explain the larger issues behind those interactions. Like theories, research results illuminate one part of the stage, leaving other parts in relative darkness.

Applied and Clinical Sociology

Many early sociologists—notably, Jane Addams, W. E. B. DuBois, and George Herbert Mead—were strong advocates for social reform. They wanted their theories and findings to be relevant to policymakers and to people's lives in general. For instance, Mead was the treasurer of Hull House for many years, where he applied his theory to improving the lives of those who were powerless (especially immigrants). He also served on committees dealing with Chicago's labor problems and public education. Today, **applied sociology** is the use of the discipline of sociology with the specific intent of yielding practical applications for human behavior and organizations. By extension, Michael Burawoy (2005), in his presidential address to the American Sociological Association, endorsed what he called *public sociology,* encouraging scholars to engage a broader audience in bringing about positive outcomes. In effect, the applied sociologist reaches out to others and joins them in their efforts to better society.

Often, the goal of such work is to assist in resolving a social problem. For example, in the past 50 years, eight presidents of the United States have established commissions to delve into major

RESEARCH TODAY

1-1 Looking at Sports from Four Theoretical Perspectives

We watch sports. Talk sports. Spend money on sports. Some of us live and breathe sports. Because sports occupy much of our time and directly or indirectly consume and generate a great deal of money, it should not be surprising that sports have sociological components that can be analyzed from the various theoretical perspectives.

Functionalist View

In examining any aspect of society, functionalists emphasize the contribution it makes to overall social stability. Functionalists regard sports as an almost religious institution that uses ritual and ceremony to reinforce the common values of a society:

- Sports socialize young people into such values as competition and patriotism.
- Sports help to maintain people's physical well-being.
- Sports serve as a safety valve for both participants and spectators, who are allowed to shed tension and aggressive energy in a socially acceptable way.
- Sports bring together members of a community (who support local athletes and teams) or even a nation (during World Cup matches and the Olympics) and promote an overall feeling of unity and social solidarity.

Conflict View

Conflict theorists argue that the social order is based on coercion and exploitation. They emphasize that sports reflect and even exacerbate many of the divisions of society:

- Sports are a form of big business in which profits are more important than the health and safety of the workers (athletes).
- Sports perpetuate the false idea that success can be achieved simply through hard work, while failure should be blamed on the individual alone (rather than on injustices in the larger social system). Sports also serve as an "opiate" that encourages people to seek a "fix" or temporary "high" rather than focus on personal problems and social issues.

Professional golfer Paula Creamer won more than $1.8 million in 2008, making her the 2nd most successful woman on the golf course that year. Among men, her winnings would have have put her in 42nd place.

- Communities divert scarce resources to subsidize the construction of professional sports facilities.
- Sports maintain the subordinate role of Blacks and Latinos, who toil as athletes but are less visible in supervisory positions as coaches, managers, and owners.
- Team logos and mascots (like the Washington Redskins) disparage American Indians.

Despite their differences, functionalists, conflict theorists, feminists, and interactionists would all agree that there is much more to sports than exercise or recreation.

Feminist View

Feminist theorists consider how watching or participating in sports reinforces the roles that men and women play in the larger society:

- Although sports generally promote fitness and health, they may also have an adverse effect on participants' health. Men are more likely to resort to illegal steroid use (among bodybuilders and baseball players, for example); women, to excessive dieting (among gymnasts and figure skaters, for example).
- Gender expectations encourage female athletes to be passive and gentle, qualities that do not support the emphasis

on competitiveness in sports. As a result, women find it difficult to enter sports traditionally dominated by men, such as Indy or NASCAR.

- Although professional women athletes' earnings are increasing, they typically trail those of male athletes.

Interactionist View

In studying the social order, interactionists are especially interested in shared understandings of everyday behavior. Interactionists examine sports on the micro level by focusing on how day-to-day social behavior is shaped by the distinctive norms, values, and demands of the world of sports:

- Sports often heighten parent–child involvement; they may lead to parental expectations for participation and for (sometimes unrealistically) success.
- Participation in sports provides friendship networks that can permeate everyday life.
- Despite class, racial, and religious differences, teammates may work together harmoniously and may even abandon previous stereotypes and prejudices.
- Relationships in the sports world are defined by people's social positions as players, coaches, and referees—as well as by the high or low status that individuals hold as a result of their performances and reputations.

Despite their differences, functionalists, conflict theorists, feminists, and interactionists would all agree that there is much more to sports than exercise or recreation. They would also agree that sports and other popular forms of culture are worthy subjects of serious study by sociologists.

LET'S DISCUSS

1. Have you experienced or witnessed discrimination in sports based on gender or race? If so, how did you react? Has the representation of Blacks or women on teams been controversial on your campus? In what ways?
2. Which perspective do you think is most useful in looking at the sociology of sports? Why?

Sources: Acosta and Carpenter 2001; Eitzen 2009; ESPN 2009; Fine 1987; Sharp et al. 2008; K. Young 2004; Zirin 2008.

societal concerns facing our nation. Sociologists are often asked to apply their expertise to studying such issues as violence, pornography, crime, immigration, and population. In Europe, both academic and governmental research departments are offering increasing financial support for applied studies.

One example of applied sociology is the growing interest in facilitating neighborhood economic development. Rather than focusing on social problems, sociologists and others have begun to emphasize the assets a community can offer to its residents. For example, sociologist Richard Taub (1988, 2004) took an approach that had proved successful in a working-class, mostly Black area of Chicago and applied it to a small, economically disadvantaged community in Arkansas. In both areas, efforts to attract employers and big businesses had failed. Rather than continue that failed approach, Taub conducted surveys to identify the community's strengths, as well as potential sources of credit and technical assistance. The data he collected encouraged local banks to invest locally, which would bring in more local revenue. With some outside help, the banks found ways to guarantee those investments, which did not necessarily offer quick returns. Finally, Taub identified the human capital in the community. Today, a place once thought to be beyond hope is bustling with day care centers, beauty shops, catering services, and a Mary Kay Cosmetics franchise. Although, individually, none of these businesses has the makings of a *Fortune* 500 corporation, collectively they have turned the community around.

Growing interest in applied sociology has led to such specializations as medical sociology and environmental sociology. The former includes research on how health care professionals and patients deal with disease. To give one example, medical sociologists have studied the social impact of the AIDS crisis on families, friends, and communities (see Chapter 19). Environmental sociologists examine the relationship between human societies and the physical environment. One focus of their work is the issue of "environmental justice" (see Chapter 19), raised when researchers and community activists found that hazardous waste dumps are especially likely to be situated in poor and minority neighborhoods (M. Martin 1996).

The growing popularity of applied sociology has led to the rise of the specialty of clinical sociology. Louis Wirth (1931) wrote about clinical sociology more than 75 years ago, but the term itself has become popular only in recent years. While applied sociology may simply evaluate social issues, **clinical sociology** is dedicated to facilitating change by altering social relationships (as in family therapy) or restructuring social institutions (as in the reorganization of a medical center).

The Association for Applied Clinical Sociology was founded in 1978 to promote the application of sociological knowledge to intervention for individual and social change. This professional group has developed a procedure for certifying clinical

In economically disadvantaged areas like this one in Arkansas, communities suffer from a host of social problems, including poverty, violence, and drug abuse. Applied sociologists are dedicated to finding practical applications that will improve the lives of those who are caught in cycles of poverty.

sociologists—much as physical therapists or psychologists are certified.

Applied sociologists generally leave it to others to act on their evaluations. In contrast, clinical sociologists take direct responsibility for implementation and view those with whom they work as their clients. This specialty has become increasingly attractive to graduate students in sociology because it offers an opportunity to apply intellectual learning in a practical way. A shrinking job market in the academic world has made such alternative career routes appealing.

Applied and clinical sociology can be contrasted with **basic, or pure, sociology,** which seeks a more profound knowledge of the fundamental aspects of social phenomena. This type of research is not necessarily meant to generate specific applications, although such ideas may result once findings are analyzed. When Durkheim studied suicide rates, he was not primarily interested in discovering a way to eliminate suicide. In this sense, his research was an example of basic rather than applied sociology.

---

use your sociological *imagination*

What issues facing your local community would you like to address with applied sociological research? Do you see any global connections to these local issues?

Developing a Sociological Imagination

In this book, we will be illustrating the sociological imagination in several different ways—by showing theory in practice and in current research; by thinking globally; by exploring the

Today, both the positive and negative aspects of globalization are receiving increased scrutiny from sociologists.

attacks on New York and Washington, D.C., caused an immediate economic decline not just in the United States, but throughout the world. One example of the massive global impact was the downturn in international tourism, which lasted for at least two years. The effects have been felt by people far removed from the United States, including African game wardens and Asian taxi drivers. Some observers see globalization and its effects as the natural result of advances in communications technology, particularly the Internet and satellite transmission of the mass media. Others view it more critically, as a process that allows multinational corporations to expand unchecked. We examine the impact of globalization on our daily lives and on societies throughout the world, including our own, in Box 1-2 on page 20 (on the global coffee trade) and throughout this book (Fiss and Hirsch 2005).

significance of social inequality; by speaking across race, gender, and religious boundaries; and by highlighting social policy throughout the world.

Theory in Practice

We will illustrate how the major sociological perspectives can be helpful in understanding today's issues, from capital punishment to the AIDS crisis. Sociologists do not necessarily declare "Here I am using functionalism," but their research and approaches do tend to draw on one or more theoretical frameworks, as will become clear in the pages to follow.

Research Today

Sociologists actively investigate a variety of issues and social behavior. We have already seen that research can shed light on the social factors that affect suicide rates. Sociological research often plays a direct role in improving people's lives, as in the case of increasing the participation of African Americans in diabetes testing. Throughout the rest of the book, the research performed by sociologists and other social scientists will shed light on group behavior of all types.

Thinking Globally

Whatever their theoretical perspective or research techniques, sociologists recognize that social behavior must be viewed in a global context. **Globalization** is the worldwide integration of government policies, cultures, social movements, and financial markets through trade and the exchange of ideas. Although public discussion of globalization is relatively recent, intellectuals have been pondering both its negative and positive social consequences for a long time. Karl Marx and Friedrich Engels warned in *The Communist Manifesto* (written in 1848) of a world market that would lead to production in distant lands, sweeping away existing working relationships.

Today, developments outside a country are as likely to influence people's lives as changes at home. For example, though much of the world was already in recession by September 2001, the terrorist

The Significance of Social Inequality

Who holds power? Who doesn't? Who has prestige? Who lacks it? Perhaps the major theme of analysis in sociology today is **social inequality,** a condition in which members of society have differing amounts of wealth, prestige, or power. For example, the disparity between what coffee bean pickers in developing nations are paid and the price you pay for a cup of coffee underscores global inequality (see Box 1-2). And the impact of Hurricane Katrina on residents of the Gulf Coast drew attention to social inequality in the United States. Predictably, the people who were hit the hardest by the massive storm were the poor, who had the greatest difficulty evacuating before the storm and have had the most difficulty recovering from it. Barbara Ehrenreich's research among low-wage workers uncovered some other aspects of social inequality in the United States.

Some sociologists, in seeking to understand the effects of inequality, have made the case for social justice. W. E. B. DuBois ([1940] 1968:418) noted that the greatest power in the land is not "thought or ethics, but wealth." As we have seen, the contributions of Karl Marx, Jane Addams, and Ida Wells-Barnett also stressed this sentiment for the overarching importance of social inequality and social justice. Joe Feagin (2001) echoed it in a presidential address to the American Sociological Association. Throughout, this book will highlight the work of sociologists on social inequality.

Speaking across Race, Gender, and Religious Boundaries

Sociologists include both men and women, as well as people from a variety of ethnic, national, and religious origins. In their work, sociologists seek to draw conclusions that speak to all people—not just the affluent or powerful. Doing so is not always easy. Insights into how a corporation can increase its profits tend to attract more attention and financial support than do, say, the merits of a needle exchange program for low-income inner-city

SOCIOLOGY IN THE GLOBAL COMMUNITY

1-2 Your Morning Cup of Coffee

When you drink a cup of coffee, do you give much thought to where the coffee beans came from, or do you think more about the pleasure you get from the popular beverage? Coffee certainly is popular—as an import, it is second only to petroleum, the most traded commodity in the world.

Although the coffee trade has been globalized, the customs of coffee drinking still vary from place to place. Starbucks, which now has 4,500 locations outside the United States, has over 1,000 locations in Europe. Managers find that in European countries, where the coffeehouse culture originated, 80 percent of their customers sit down to drink their coffee. In the United States, 80 percent of Starbucks' customers leave the store immediately, taking their coffee with them.

Coffee, which is thought to have originated in Ethiopia, has a long history. It first came to the attention of Europeans in the 16th century, via the Turkish Empire. A century later, the coffeehouse culture was firmly rooted in Europe. In fact, European demand for coffee helped to foster the slave trade in the Caribbean and Latin America. So today's coffeehouse, whether it is Starbucks, Dunkin' Donuts, or a local shop, is rooted in both Africa and Europe.

Today, the coffee trade continues to rely on the exploitation of cheap labor. Coffee is a labor-intensive crop: there is little that technology can do to ease the coffee picker's burden.

The typical coffee picker works in a developing nation near the equator, receiving for a day's wages an amount that matches the price of a single cup of coffee in North America. In the 1940s, advocacy groups began to promote the sale of certified *fair trade coffee,* which gives a living wage to those who harvest the crop, allowing them to become economically self-sufficient. But even now, fair trade coffee accounts for only a small fraction of the coffee that is bought and sold in the United States.

> *The typical coffee picker works in a developing nation near the equator, receiving for a day's wages an amount that matches the price of a single cup of coffee in North America.*

Political activists have sought to bring attention to the injustices brought about by the international coffee trade. Some of their messages have been very strong. For example, a television campaign that aired in the 1990s showed a mug of coffee brimming over with red blood, along with a voice-over that suggested that what was being brewed was death. The campaign, which accused a major food processor of prolonging the war in El Salvador by purchasing Salvadoran coffee, was pulled from the air in response to pressure from a distributor.

Ecological activists have drawn attention to what they see as the coffee industry's contribution to the trend toward global warming. The need to make room for more coffee fields, they charge, has encouraged the destruction of rain forests. The same criticism can be aimed at much of the consumption in industrial nations. Of all the products that emerge from developing nations, however, few have as singular a place in many people's daily ritual as that morning cup of joe. The drink in your hand is your tangible link to rural workers in some of the poorest areas of the world.

LET'S DISCUSS

1. Do you enjoy coffee? Would you willingly pay more for a cup of coffee if you knew that the worker who picked the beans would benefit from the higher price?
2. The coffee trade has been blamed for perpetuating social inequality, warfare, and global warming. Can you think of any positive effects of the coffee trade? Who benefits most from this economic activity?

Sources: Adamy 2008; Greenwald 1990; Luttinger and Dicum 2006; Pendergrast 1999; Ritzer 2008.

---

residents. Yet today more than ever, sociology seeks to better understand the experiences of all people.

Sociologists have noted, for example, that the huge tsunami that hit South Asia in 2004 affected men and women differently. When the waves hit, mothers and grandmothers were at home with the children; men were outside working, where they were more likely to become aware of the impending disaster. Moreover, most of the men knew how to swim, a survival skill that women in these traditional societies usually do not learn. As a result, many more men than women survived the catastrophe— about 10 men for every 1 woman. In one Indonesian village typical of the disaster area, 97 of 1,300 people survived; only 4 were women. The impact of this gender imbalance will be felt for some time, given women's primary role as caregivers for children and the elderly (BBC News 2005).

Social Policy throughout the World

One important way we can use a sociological imagination is to enhance our understanding of current social issues throughout the world. Beginning with Chapter 2, each chapter will conclude with a discussion of a contemporary social policy issue. In some cases, we will examine a specific issue facing national governments. For example, government funding of child care centers will be discussed in Chapter 4, Socialization; global immigration in Chapter 11, Racial and Ethnic Inequality; and religion in the schools in Chapter 15, Religion. These Social Policy sections will demonstrate how fundamental sociological concepts can enhance our critical thinking skills and help us to better understand current public policy debates taking place around the world.

In addition, sociology has been used to evaluate the success of programs or the impact of changes brought about by policymakers and political activists. For example, Chapter 9, Stratification and Social Mobility in the United States, includes a discussion of research on the effectiveness of welfare reform experiments. Such discussions underscore the many practical applications of sociological theory and research

Sociologists expect the next quarter of a century to be perhaps the most exciting and critical period in the history of the discipline. That is because of a growing recognition—both in the United States and around the world—that current social problems must be addressed before their magnitude overwhelms human societies. We can expect sociologists to play an increasing role in government by researching and developing public policy alternatives. It seems only natural for this textbook to focus on the connection between the work of sociologists and the difficult questions confronting policymakers and people in the United States and around the world.

APPENDIX Careers in Sociology

For the past two decades the number of U.S. college students who have graduated with a degree in sociology has risen steadily (Figure 1-2). In this appendix we'll consider some of the options these students have after completing their undergraduate education.

An undergraduate degree in sociology doesn't just serve as excellent preparation for future graduate work in sociology. It also provides a strong liberal arts background for entry-level positions in business, social services, foundations, community organizations, not-for-profit groups, law enforcement, and many government jobs. A number of fields—among them marketing, public relations, and broadcasting—now require investigative skills and an understanding of the diverse groups found in today's multiethnic and multinational environment. Moreover, a sociology degree requires accomplishment in oral and written communication, interpersonal skills, problem solving, and critical thinking—all job-related skills that may give sociology graduates an advantage over those who pursue more technical degrees.

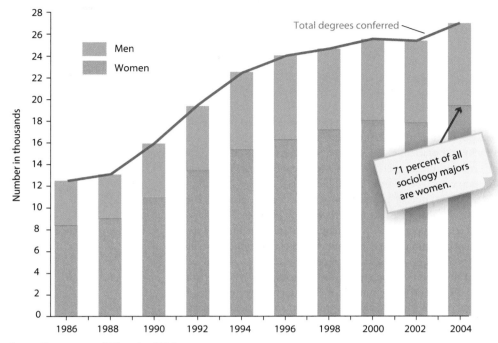

FIGURE **1-2** SOCIOLOGY DEGREES CONFERRED IN THE UNITED STATES BY GENDER

71 percent of all sociology majors are women.

Source: Department of Education 2006.

Consequently, while few occupations specifically require an undergraduate degree in sociology, such academic training can be an important asset in entering a wide range of occupations. To emphasize this point, a number of chapters in this book highlight a real-life professional who describes how the study of sociology has helped in his or her career. Look for the "Taking Sociology to Work" boxes.

Figure 1-3 on page 22 summarizes the sources of employment for those with BA or BS degrees in sociology. It shows that the areas of nonprofit organizations, education, business, and government offer major career opportunities for sociology graduates. Undergraduates who know where their career interests lie are well advised to enroll in sociology courses and specialties best suited to those interests. For example, students hoping to become health planners would take a class in medical sociology; students seeking employment as social science research assistants would focus on courses in statistics and methods. Internships, such as placements at city planning agencies and survey research organizations, afford another way for sociology students to prepare for careers. Studies show that students who choose an internship placement have less trouble finding jobs, obtain better jobs, and enjoy greater job satisfaction than students without internship placements (American Sociological Association 2006; Salem and Grabarek 1986).

Many college students view social work as the field most closely associated with sociology. Traditionally, social workers received their undergraduate training in sociology and allied fields such as psychology and counseling. After some practical experience, social workers would generally seek a master's degree in social work (MSW) to be

considered for supervisory or administrative positions. Today, however, some students choose (where it is available) to pursue a bachelor's degree in social work (BSW). This degree prepares graduates for direct service positions, such as caseworker or group worker.

Many students continue their sociological training beyond the bachelor's degree. More than 250 universities in the United States have graduate programs in sociology that offer PhD and/or master's degrees. These programs differ greatly in their areas of specialization, course requirements, costs, and the research and teaching opportunities available to graduate students. About 71 percent of the graduates are women (American Sociological Association 2005, 2009a).

Higher education is an important source of employment for sociologists with graduate degrees. About 83 percent of recent PhD recipients in sociology seek employment in colleges and universities. These sociologists teach not only majors who are committed to the discipline but also students hoping to become doctors, nurses, lawyers, police officers, and so forth (American Sociological Association 2005).

Sociologists who teach in colleges and universities may use their knowledge and training to influence public policy. For example, sociologist Andrew Cherlin (2003) recently commented on the debate over proposed federal funding to promote marriage among welfare recipients. Citing the results of two of his studies, Cherlin questioned the potential effectiveness of such a policy in strengthening low-income families. Because many single mothers choose to marry someone other than the father of their children—sometimes for good reason—their children often grow up in stepfamilies. Cherlin's research shows that children who are raised in stepfamilies are no better off than those in single-parent families. He sees government efforts to promote marriage as a politically motivated attempt to foster traditional social values in a society that has become increasingly diverse.

For sociology graduates who are interested in academic careers, the road to a PhD (or doctorate) can be long and difficult. This degree symbolizes competence in original research; each candidate must prepare a book-length study known as a dissertation. Typically, a doctoral student in sociology will engage in four to seven years of intensive work, including the time required to complete the dissertation. Yet even this effort is no guarantee of a job as a sociology professor.

The good news is that over the next 10 years, the demand for instructors is expected to increase because of high rates of retirement among faculty from the baby boom generation, as well as the anticipated slow but steady growth in the college student population in the United States. Nonetheless, anyone who launches an academic career must be prepared for considerable uncertainty and competition in the college job market (American Sociological Association 2006; Huber 1985).

Of course, not all people who work as sociologists teach or hold doctoral degrees. Take government, for example. The Census Bureau relies on people with sociological training to interpret data for other government agencies and the general public. Virtually every agency depends on survey research—a field in which sociology students can specialize—in order to assess everything from community needs to the morale of the agency's own workers. In addition, people with sociological training can put their academic knowledge to effective use in probation and parole, health sciences, community development, and recreational services. Some people working in government or private industry have a master's degree (MA or MS) in sociology; others have a bachelor's degree (BA or BS).

Currently, about 15 percent of the members of the American Sociological Association use their sociological skills outside the academic world, whether in social service agencies or in marketing positions for business firms. Increasing numbers of sociologists with graduate degrees are employed by businesses, industry, hospitals, and nonprofit organizations. Studies show that many sociology graduates are making career changes from social service areas to business and commerce. For an undergraduate major, sociology is excellent preparation for employment in many parts of the business world (Spalter-Roth and Van Vooren 2008b).

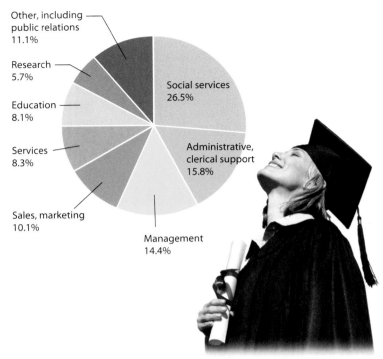

FIGURE **1-3** OCCUPATIONS OF GRADUATING SOCIOLOGY MAJORS

Other, including public relations 11.1%

Research 5.7%

Education 8.1%

Services 8.3%

Sales, marketing 10.1%

Social services 26.5%

Administrative, clerical support 15.8%

Management 14.4%

Note: Based on a national survey conducted in early 2007 of 1,800 sociology majors who graduated in 2005.
Source: Table 1 in Spalter-Roth and Van Vooren 2008a.

Whether you take a few courses in sociology or complete a degree, you will benefit from the critical thinking skills developed in this discipline. Sociologists emphasize the value of being able to analyze, interpret, and function within a variety of working situations—an asset in virtually any career. Moreover, given rapid technological change and the expanding global economy, all of us will need to adapt to substantial social change, even in our own careers. Sociology provides a rich conceptual framework that can serve as a foundation for flexible career development and assist you in taking advantage of new employment opportunities.

Connect Learn Succeed

For more information on career opportunities for individuals with a background in sociology, visit the Online Learning Center at www.mhhe.com/schaefer12e. Go to "Student Edition," and in the section titled "Course-wide Content," click on "Web Resources." Then click on "Career Opportunities," which will provide you with numerous links to sites offering career advice and information.

MASTERING THIS CHAPTER

Summary

Sociology is the scientific study of social behavior and human groups. In this chapter, we examine the nature of sociological theory, the founders of the discipline, theoretical perspectives in contemporary sociology, practical applications for sociological theory and research, and ways to exercise the "sociological imagination."

1. The **sociological imagination** is an awareness of the relationship between an individual and the wider society. It is based on the ability to view our own society as an outsider might, rather than from the perspective of our limited experiences and cultural biases.

2. In contrast to other **social sciences,** sociology emphasizes the influence that groups can have on people's behavior and attitudes and the ways in which people shape society.

3. Knowledge that relies on common sense is not always reliable. Sociologists must test and analyze each piece of information they use.

4. Sociologists employ **theories** to examine relationships between observations or data that may seem completely unrelated.

5. Nineteenth-century thinkers who contributed sociological insights included Auguste Comte, a French philosopher; Harriet Martineau, an English sociologist; and Herbert Spencer, an English scholar.

6. Other important figures in the development of sociology were Émile Durkheim, who pioneered work on suicide; Max Weber, who taught the need for insight in intellectual work; Karl Marx, who emphasized the importance of the economy and social conflict; and W. E. B. DuBois, who advocated for the usefulness of basic research in combating prejudice and fostering racial tolerance and justice.

7. In the 20th century, the discipline of sociology was indebted to the U.S. sociologists Charles Horton Cooley and Robert Merton, as well as to the French sociologist Pierre Bourdieu.

8. **Macrosociology** concentrates on large-scale phenomena or entire civilizations; **microsociology** stresses the study of small groups.

9. The **functionalist perspective** emphasizes the way in which the parts of a society are structured to maintain its stability.

10. The **conflict perspective** assumes that social behavior is best understood in terms of conflict or tension between competing groups.

11. The **interactionist perspective** is concerned primarily with fundamental or everyday forms of interaction, including symbols and other types of **nonverbal communication.**

12. The **feminist view,** which is often allied with the conflict perspective, sees inequity in gender as central to all behavior and organization.

13. Sociologists make use of all four perspectives, since each offers unique insights into the same issue.

14. **Applied** and **clinical sociology** apply the discipline of sociology to the solution of practical problems in human behavior and organizations. In contrast, **basic sociology** is sociological inquiry that seeks only a deeper knowledge of the fundamental aspects of social phenomena.

15. This textbook makes use of the sociological imagination by showing theory in practice and in current research; by thinking globally; by focusing on the significance of social inequality; by speaking across race, gender, and religious boundaries; and by highlighting social policy around the world.

Critical Thinking Questions ✗

1. What aspects of the social and work environment in a fast-food restaurant would be of particular interest to a sociologist because of his or her sociological imagination?

2. What are the manifest and latent functions of a health club?

3. How does the merchandise that is displayed in a toy store relate to issues of race, class, and gender?

Key Terms

Anomie The loss of direction felt in a society when social control of individual behavior has become ineffective. (page 10)

Applied sociology The use of the discipline of sociology with the specific intent of yielding practical applications for human behavior and organizations. (16)

Basic sociology Sociological inquiry conducted with the objective of gaining a more profound knowledge of the fundamental aspects of social phenomena. Also known as *pure sociology*. (18)

Clinical sociology The use of the discipline of sociology with the specific intent of altering social relationships or restructuring social institutions. (18)

Conflict perspective A sociological approach that assumes that social behavior is best understood in terms of tension between groups over power or the allocation of resources, including housing, money, access to services, and political representation. (14)

Cultural capital Noneconomic goods, such as family background and education, which are reflected in a knowledge of language and the arts. (13)

Double consciousness The division of an individual's identity into two or more social realities. (12)

Dramaturgical approach A view of social interaction in which people are seen as theatrical performers. (15)

Dysfunction An element or process of a society that may disrupt the social system or reduce its stability. (14)

Feminist view A sociological approach that views inequity in gender as central to all behavior and organization. (14)

Functionalist perspective A sociological approach that emphasizes the way in which the parts of a society are structured to maintain its stability. (13)

Globalization The worldwide integration of government policies, cultures, social movements, and financial markets through trade and the exchange of ideas. (19)

Ideal type A construct or model for evaluating specific cases. (10)

Interactionist perspective A sociological approach that generalizes about everyday forms of social interaction in order to explain society as a whole. (15)

Latent function An unconscious or unintended function that may reflect hidden purposes. (14)

Macrosociology Sociological investigation that concentrates on large-scale phenomena or entire civilizations. (12)

Manifest function An open, stated, and conscious function. (14)

Microsociology Sociological investigation that stresses the study of small groups, often through experimental means. (13)

Natural science The study of the physical features of nature and the ways in which they interact and change. (5)

Nonverbal communication The sending of messages through the use of gestures, facial expressions, and postures. (15)

Science The body of knowledge obtained by methods based on systematic observation. (5)

Social capital The collective benefit of social networks, which are built on reciprocal trust. (13)

Social inequality A condition in which members of society have differing amounts of wealth, prestige, or power. (19)

Social science The study of the social features of humans and the ways in which they interact and change. (6)

Sociological imagination An awareness of the relationship between an individual and the wider society, both today and in the past. (5)

Sociology The scientific study of social behavior and human groups. (5)

Theory In sociology, a set of statements that seeks to explain problems, actions, or behavior. (8)

Verstehen The German word for "understanding" or "insight"; used to stress the need for sociologists to take into account the subjective meanings people attach to their actions. (10)

Self-Quiz

Read each question carefully and then select the best answer.

1. Sociology is
   a. very narrow in scope.
   b. concerned with what one individual does or does not do.
   c. the systematic study of social behavior and human groups.
   d. an awareness of the relationship between an individual and the wider society.

2. Which of the following thinkers introduced the concept of the sociological imagination?
   a. Émile Durkheim
   b. Max Weber
   c. Karl Marx
   d. C. Wright Mills

3. Émile Durkheim's research on suicide suggested that
   a. people with religious affiliations had a higher suicide rate than those who were unaffiliated.
   b. suicide rates seemed to be higher in times of peace than in times of war and revolution.
   c. civilians were more likely to take their lives than soldiers.
   d. suicide is a solitary act, unrelated to group life.

4. Max Weber taught his students that they should employ which of the following in their intellectual work?
   a. anomie
   b. *verstehen*
   c. the sociological imagination
   d. microsociology

5. Robert Merton's contributions to sociology include
   a. successfully combining theory and research.
   b. producing a theory that is one of the most frequently cited explanations of deviant behavior.
   c. an attempt to bring macro-level and micro-level analyses together.
   d. all of the above

6. Which sociologist made a major contribution to society through his in-depth studies of urban life, including both Blacks and Whites?
   a. W. E. B. DuBois
   b. Robert Merton
   c. Auguste Comte
   d. Charles Horton Cooley

7. In the late 19th century, before the term *feminist view* could even be coined, the ideas behind this major theoretical approach appeared in the writings of
   a. Karl Marx.
   b. Ida Wells-Barnett.
   c. Charles Horton Cooley.
   d. Pierre Bourdieu.

8. Thinking of society as a living organism in which each part of the organism contributes to its survival is a reflection of which theoretical perspective?
   a. the functionalist perspective
   b. the conflict perspective
   c. the feminist perspective
   d. the interactionist perspective

9. Karl Marx's view of the struggle between social classes inspired the contemporary
   a. functionalist perspective.
   b. conflict perspective.
   c. interactionist perspective.
   d. dramaturgical approach.

10. Erving Goffman's dramaturgical approach, which postulates that people present certain aspects of their personalities while obscuring other aspects, is a derivative of what major theoretical perspective?
    a. the functionalist perspective
    b. the conflict perspective
    c. the feminist perspective
    d. the interactionist perspective

11. While the findings of sociologists may at times seem like common sense, they differ because they rest on _____ analysis of facts.

12. Within sociology, a(n) _____ is a set of statements that seeks to explain problems, actions, or behavior.

13. In _____'s hierarchy of the sciences, sociology was the "queen," and its practitioners were "scientist-priests."

14. In *Society in America,* originally published in 1837, English scholar _____ _____ examined religion, politics, child rearing, and immigration in the young nation.

15. _____ _____ adapted Charles Darwin's evolutionary view of the "survival of the fittest" by arguing that it is "natural" that some people are rich while others are poor.

16. Sociologist Max Weber coined the term _____ _____ in referring to a construct or model that serves as a measuring rod against which actual cases can be evaluated.

17. In *The Communist Manifesto,* _____ _____ and _____ _____ argued that the masses of people who have no resources other than their labor (the proletariat) should unite to fight for the overthrow of capitalist societies.

18. _____ _____, an early female sociologist, cofounded the famous Chicago settlement house called Hull House and also tried to establish a juvenile court system.

19. The university's role in certifying academic competence and excellence is an example of a(n) _____ function.

20. The _____ _____ draws on the work of Karl Marx and Friedrich Engels in that it often views women's subordination as inherent in capitalist societies.

THINKING ABOUT MOVIES

Do the Right Thing (Spike Lee, 1989)

On a hot summer day in Brooklyn, racial and social tensions between local ethnic groups boil over. Mookie (Spike Lee) is the only Black employee at a pizzeria owned and operated by Sal (Danny Aiello), where the decor features photos of notable Italian Americans. When Mookie's friends ask why there are no photos of African Americans, Sal's defensive answer leads to a neighborhood boycott. The conflict culminates in a violent attack on the pizzeria, which results in Mookie's death.

This movie lends itself to interpretation by the sociological imagination: though the characters are well drawn as individuals, their behavior can best be understood within the social context. The tension between the two competing groups exemplifies the conflict perspective.

For Your Consideration

1. How does the film suggest conflict between the two groups?
2. Name three ways that symbols are used in the film to establish group membership or identity.

Under the Same Moon (Patricia Riggen, 2008)

Rosario Reyes (Kate del Castillo) works in the United States illegally to earn money for her family in Mexico. She has left her nine-year-old son, Carlos (Adrian Alonso), in the care of his grandmother. When the grandmother dies, Carlos sets out to find his mother, confronting numerous obstacles as he attempts to evade immigration officials and cross the Mexican-American border.

This film offers a blend of macro- and micro-level approaches to the contentious issue of illegal immigration. We see individuals in the Reyes family struggle to maintain their ties in a world divided by economic, social, and geographic barriers. The story also sheds light on macrosociological concepts such as social inequality and globalization.

For Your Consideration

1. What are the differences in wealth, prestige, and power between Rosario and other characters in the film?
2. How does the movie exemplify both the macro and micro approaches to the study of society?

inside

What Is the Scientific Method?

Major Research Designs

Ethics of Research

Feminist Methodology

Technology and Sociological Research

Social Policy and Sociological Research: Studying Human Sexuality

Appendix I: Using Statistics and Graphs

Appendix II: Writing a Research Report

BOXES

Research Today: *Surveying Cell Phone Users*

Research Today: *What's in a Name?*

Taking Sociology to Work: *Dave Eberbach, Research Coordinator, United Way of Central Iowa*

On a busy street in Britain, a researcher interviews a young man about his views on contemporary social issues. Surveys are just one of the methods sociologists use to collect data.

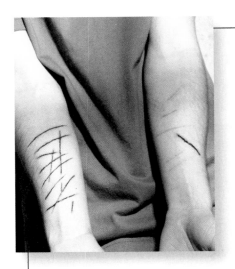

Long a subterranean topic, the deliberate, non-suicidal destruction of one's own body tissue emerged from obscurity in the 1990s and began to spread dramatically. . . . Although a range of behaviors may be considered self-injurious, . . . we focus here on . . . self-cutting, burning, branding, scratching, picking at skin or reopening wounds, biting, head banging, hair pulling (trichotillomania), hitting (with a hammer or other object), and bone breaking.

. . .

This analysis draws on eighty in-depth interviews conducted in person and on the telephone. Participants ranged in age from sixteen to their mid-fifties, with more women (sixty-five) than men (fifteen), nearly all Caucasian.

In addition, beginning in 2001–2002, we began to explore the Web sites and public postings of self-injurers. We joined several Internet self-injury groups as overt researchers and became active participants in group discussions. Because of the intimate nature of virtual communication . . . , we formed several deep and enduring relationships with people in different friendship circles that lasted for years, and we discussed with people the features of their ordinary lives and rallied around them during their many crises. We worked, with others, on the difficulties of supporting people who were disembodied and distant. Together with them, we learned to discern the seriousness of people's suicidal threats, their claims of abstinence, their presentation of different personas under different pseudonyms in different groups,

Some reported that they hung out with "the wrong crowd" and acted out or were drawn into countercultural groups such as Goths. They were nihilists who delighted in showing off by burning or cutting themselves.

and the consequences of flame wars. We networked through bulletin boards, MySpace, and the hundreds of self-injury–related Web Usenet support groups.

. . .

We . . . found a growing number of self-injurers who belonged to alternative youth subcultures. Some reported that they hung out with "the wrong crowd" and acted out or were drawn into countercultural groups such as Goths. They were nihilists who delighted in showing off by burning or cutting themselves. Natalie, a twenty-two-year-old college student, reflected back on her junior high school friends:

Eighth grade was the point at which I really started getting sociable, identifying with this alternative subculture. It wasn't like I hung out with the freaks and the rejects and, like, the outcasts. I definitely was in the subculture of the stoners and the punks, and we hung out on the bridge and I started smoking and doing drugs and, um, at that point I associated with more people who also hurt themselves.

. . .

Some self-injurers rooted their unhappiness in peer social situations. Rachel, a twenty-three-year-old college student with an intact, happy family, blamed her friends for driving her to self-injure:

It happened the first time when my group turned against me for some reason. They alienated me for a week straight, they started rumors about me. I didn't go to any activities that week and I didn't even go to school. I was so sad, I just started. I was crying and so upset and couldn't stop crying, and I just took a coat hanger, and that's how it started.

. . .

Many people continued self-injuring, either continuously or intermittently, into adulthood. Contrary to extant knowledge, roughly two-thirds of the "regulars" we encountered on the Internet were older than twenty-five, and half were older than thirty-five. . . . ❞

(P. Adler and P. Adler 2007:537–538, 540, 541, 544, 545, 547) Additional information about this excerpt can be found on the Online Learning Center at www.mhhe.com/schaefer12e.

This description of the covert practice of self-injury is taken from Patricia Adler and Peter Adler's extensive research on the little-known behavior and its social underpinnings. Over a six-year period, the Adlers conducted lengthy, emotionally intense interviews with self-injurers, becoming friends with many. They met others in virtual space, through Internet-based support groups and Web postings. "Rather than remaining strictly detached from our subjects, we became involved in their lives, helping them and giving voice to their experiences and beliefs," the Adlers admit (2007:542).

The Adlers' work on self-injury reflects all three major sociological approaches. For self-injurers, who rarely come into contact with others like themselves, the Internet functions as a meeting place, a refuge from their self-imposed social isolation.

As conflict theorists would point out, their unconventional behavior marginalizes them, preventing them from receiving assistance even when they would welcome it. Interactionists would recognize the critical nature of self-injurers' interpersonal contacts, in person and often online.

Though many people would like to ignore the phenomenon of self-injury, believing that those who practice it will eventually "grow out of it," the Adlers' research allows us to consider it intelligently and scientifically, within the social context. Self-injurers, the Adlers found, are a diverse group, whose behavior is carefully planned and considered. Surprisingly, members often begin to injure themselves in the company of others rather than in secret. They have recently begun to coalesce as a subculture (2007:559–560).

Taken as a whole, the Adlers' work illustrates the enormous breadth of the field of sociology. Over the course of their careers, Patricia Adler and Peter Adler (1991, 1993, 1998, 2004, 2008b) have published studies of college athletes, illicit drug traffickers, preadolescent peer groups, and resort workers in Hawaii. Their choice of self-injurers as their latest subject indicates the tremendous freedom sociologists have to explore and open up new topics of inquiry.

Effective sociological research can be quite thought-provoking. It may suggest many new questions that require further study, such as why we make assumptions about people who engage in atypical behaviors like self-injury. In some cases, rather than raising additional questions, a study will simply confirm previous beliefs and findings. Sociological research can also have practical applications. For instance, research results that disconfirm accepted beliefs about marriage and the family may lead to changes in public policy.

This chapter will examine the research process used in conducting sociological studies. How do sociologists go about setting up a research project? And how do they ensure that the results of the research are reliable and accurate? Can they carry out their research without violating the rights of those they study?

We will first look at the steps that make up the scientific method used in research. Then we will take a look at various techniques commonly used in sociological research, such as experiments, observations, and surveys. We will pay particular attention to the ethical challenges sociologists face in studying human behavior, and to the debate raised by Max Weber's call for "value neutrality" in social science research. We will also examine feminist methodology and the role technology plays in research today. Though sociological researchers can focus on any number of subjects, in this chapter we will concentrate on two in particular: the relationship of education to income and the controversial subject of human sexuality. The Social Policy section that closes the chapter considers the difficulties and the challenges in researching human sexuality.

Whatever the area of sociological inquiry and whatever the perspective of the sociologist—whether functionalist, conflict, feminist, interactionist, or any other—there is one crucial requirement: imaginative, responsible research that meets the highest scientific and ethical standards.

What Is the Scientific Method?

Like all of us, sociologists are interested in the central questions of our time. Is the family falling apart? Why is there so much crime in the United States? Is the world falling behind in its ability to feed a growing population? Such issues concern most people, whether or not they have academic training. However, unlike the typical citizen, the sociologist has a commitment to use the **scientific method** in studying society. The scientific method is a systematic, organized series of steps that ensures maximum objectivity and consistency in researching a problem.

Many of us will never actually conduct scientific research. Why, then, is it important that we understand the scientific method? The answer is that it plays a major role in the workings of our society. Residents of the United States are constantly bombarded with "facts" or "data." A television news report informs us that "one in every two marriages in this country now ends in divorce," yet Chapter 14 will show that this assertion is based on misleading statistics. Almost daily, advertisers cite supposedly scientific studies to prove that their products are superior. Such claims may be accurate or exaggerated. We can better evaluate such information—and will not be fooled so easily—if we are familiar with the standards of scientific research. These standards are quite stringent, and they demand as strict adherence as possible.

The scientific method requires precise preparation in developing useful research. Otherwise, the research data collected may not prove accurate. Sociologists and other researchers follow five basic steps in the scientific method: (1) defining the problem, (2) reviewing the literature, (3) formulating the hypothesis, (4) selecting the research design and then collecting and analyzing data, and (5) developing the conclusion (Figure 2-1). We'll use an actual example to illustrate the workings of the scientific method.

FIGURE **2-1** THE SCIENTIFIC METHOD

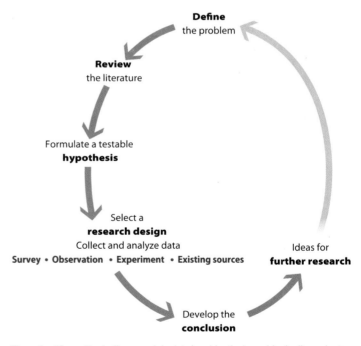

The scientific method allows sociologists to objectively and logically evaluate the data they collect. Their findings can suggest ideas for further sociological research.

Defining the Problem

Does it "pay" to go to college? Some people make great sacrifices and work hard to get a college education. Parents borrow money for their children's tuition. Students work part-time jobs or even take full-time positions while attending evening or weekend classes. Does it pay off? Are there monetary returns for getting that degree?

The first step in any research project is to state as clearly as possible what you hope to investigate—that is, *define the problem*. In this instance, we are interested in knowing how schooling relates to income. We want to find out the earnings of people with different levels of formal schooling.

Early on, any social science researcher must develop an operational definition of each concept being studied. An **operational definition** is an explanation of an abstract concept that is specific enough to allow a researcher to assess the concept. For example, a sociologist interested in status might use membership in exclusive social clubs as an operational definition of status. Someone studying prejudice might consider a person's unwillingness to hire or work with members of minority groups as an operational definition of prejudice. In our example, we need to develop two operational definitions—education and earnings—in order to study whether it pays to get an advanced educational degree. We'll define *education* as the number of years of schooling a person has achieved, and *earnings* as the income a person reports having received in the past year.

Initially, we will take a functionalist perspective (although we may end up incorporating other approaches). We will argue that opportunities for more earning power are related to level of schooling and that schools prepare students for employment.

Reviewing the Literature

By conducting a *review of the literature*—relevant scholarly studies and information—researchers refine the problem under study, clarify possible techniques to be used in collecting data, and eliminate or reduce avoidable mistakes. In our example, we would examine information about the salaries for different occupations. We would see if jobs that require more academic training are better rewarded. It would also be appropriate to review other studies on the relationship between education and income.

The review of the literature would soon tell us that many other factors besides years of schooling influence earning potential. For example, we would learn that the children of rich parents are more likely to go to college than those from modest backgrounds, so we might consider the possibility that the same parents may later help their children to secure better-paying jobs.

We might also look at macro-level data, such as state-by-state comparisons of income and educational levels. In one macro-level study based on census data, researchers found that in states whose residents have a relatively high level of education, household income levels are high as well (Figure 2-2). This finding suggests that schooling may well be related to income, though it does not speak to the micro-level relationship we are interested in. That is, we want to know whether *individuals* who are well educated are also well paid.

Formulating the Hypothesis

After reviewing earlier research and drawing on the contributions of sociological theorists, the researchers may then *formulate the hypothesis*. A **hypothesis** is a speculative statement about the relationship between two or more factors known as variables. Income, religion, occupation, and gender can all serve as variables in a study. We can define a **variable** as a measurable trait or characteristic that is subject to change under different conditions.

Researchers who formulate a hypothesis generally must suggest how one aspect of human behavior influences or affects another. The variable hypothesized to cause or influence another is called the **independent variable.** The second variable is termed the **dependent variable** because its action *depends* on the influence of the independent variable. In other words, the researcher believes that the independent variable predicts or causes change in the dependent variable. For example, a researcher in sociology might anticipate that the availability of affordable housing (the independent variable, x) affects the level of homelessness in a community (the dependent variable, y).

Our hypothesis is that the higher one's educational degree, the more money one will earn. The independent variable that is to be measured is the level of education. The variable that is thought to depend on it—income—must also be measured.

Identifying independent and dependent variables is a critical step in clarifying cause-and-effect relationships. As shown in Figure 2-3 on page 32, **causal logic** involves the relationship between a condition or variable and a particular consequence, with one event leading to the other. For instance, being less integrated into society may be directly related to, or produce a greater likelihood of, suicide. Similarly, the time students spend reviewing material for a quiz may be directly related to, or produce a greater likelihood of, getting a high score on the quiz.

A **correlation** exists when a change in one variable coincides with a change in the other. Correlations are an indication that causality *may* be present; they do not necessarily indicate causation. For example, data indicate that people who prefer to watch televised news programs are less knowledgeable than those who read newspapers and newsmagazines. This correlation between people's relative knowledge and their choice of news media seems to make sense, because it agrees with the common belief that television dumbs down information. But the correlation between the two variables is actually caused by a third variable, people's relative ability to comprehend large amounts of information. People with poor reading skills are much more likely than others to get their news from television, while those who are more educated or skilled turn more often to the print media. Though television viewing is correlated with lower news comprehension, then, it does not *cause* it. Sociologists seek to identify the *causal* link between variables; the suspected causal link is generally described in the hypothesis (Neuman 2009).

Collecting and Analyzing Data

How do you test a hypothesis to determine if it is supported or refuted? You need to collect information, using one of the research designs described later in the chapter. The research design guides the researcher in collecting and analyzing data.

Selecting the Sample In most studies, social scientists must carefully select what is known as a sample. A **sample** is a selection from a larger population that is statistically representative of that population. There are many kinds of samples, but the one social scientists use most frequently is the random sample. In a **random sample,** every member of an entire population being studied has the same chance of being selected. Thus, if

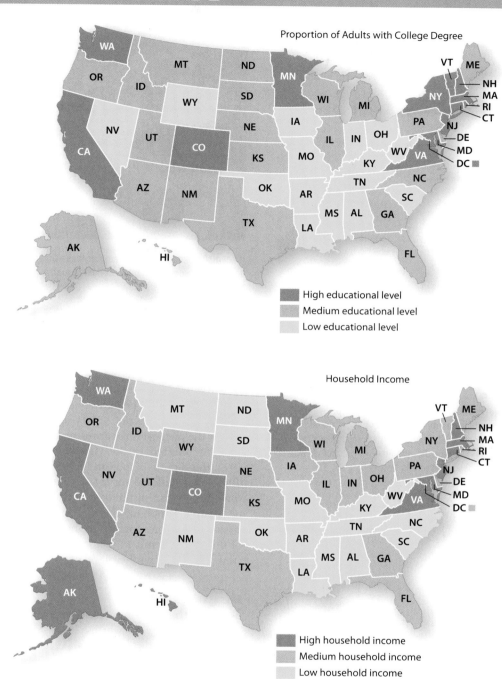

MAPPING LIFE NATIONWIDE

Proportion of Adults with College Degree

- High educational level
- Medium educational level
- Low educational level

Household Income

- High household income
- Medium household income
- Low household income

Notes: Data are for 2007. Cutoffs for high/medium and medium/low educational levels were 29.7 percent and 24.6 percent of the population with a college degree, respectively; median for the entire nation was 27.5 percent. Income data are 2004–2006, three-year average medians. Cutoffs for high/medium and medium/low household income levels were $55,200 and $45,500, respectively; national median household income was $50,740 in 2007.
Sources: American Community Survey 2008: Tables R1502 and R1901.

In general, states with high educational levels (top) also have high household incomes (bottom).

researchers want to examine the opinions of people listed in a city directory (a book that, unlike the telephone directory, lists all households), they might use a computer to randomly select names from the directory. The results would constitute a random sample. The advantage of using specialized sampling techniques

is that sociologists do not need to question everyone in a population (Igo 2007).

In some cases, the subjects researchers want to study are hard to identify, either because their activities are clandestine or because lists of such people are not readily available. How do

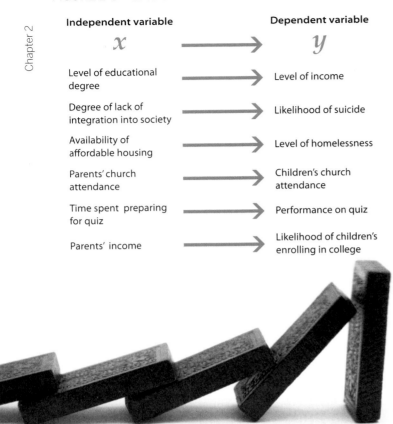

Independent variable	Dependent variable
x	y
Level of educational degree	Level of income
Degree of lack of integration into society	Likelihood of suicide
Availability of affordable housing	Level of homelessness
Parents' church attendance	Children's church attendance
Time spent preparing for quiz	Performance on quiz
Parents' income	Likelihood of children's enrolling in college

In *causal logic* an independent variable (often designated by the symbol *x*) influences a dependent variable (often designated as *y*); thus, *x* leads to *y*. For example, parents who attend church regularly (*x*) are more likely to have children who are churchgoers (*y*). Notice that the first two pairs of variables are taken from studies already described in this textbook.

Think about It
Identify two or three dependent variables that might be influenced by this independent variable: number of alcoholic drinks ingested.

researchers create a sample of illegal drug users, for instance, or of women whose husbands are at least 10 years younger than they are? In such cases, researchers employ what are called *snowball* or *convenience samples*—that is, they recruit participants through word of mouth or by posting notices on the Internet. With the help of special statistical techniques, researchers can draw conclusions from such nonrandom samples.

It is all too easy to confuse the careful scientific techniques used in representative sampling with the many *nonscientific* polls that receive much more media attention. For example, television viewers and radio listeners are often encouraged to e-mail their views on headline news or political contests. Such polls reflect nothing more than the views of those who happened to see the television program (or hear the radio broadcast) and took the time, perhaps at some cost, to register their opinions. These data do not necessarily reflect (and indeed may distort) the views of the broader population. Not everyone has access to a television

It seems reasonable to assume that these Columbia University graduates will earn more income than high school graduates. But how would you go about testing that hypothesis?

or radio, time to watch or listen to a program, or the means and/or inclination to send e-mail. Similar problems are raised by the *mail-back* questionnaires found in many magazines and by *mall intercepts,* in which shoppers are asked about some issue. Even when these techniques include answers from tens of thousands of people, they will be far less accurate than a carefully selected representative sample of 1,500 respondents.

For the purposes of our research example, we will use information collected in the General Social Survey (GSS). Since 1972, the National Opinion Research Center (NORC) has conducted this national survey 26 times, most recently in 2008. In this survey, administered in both English and Spanish, a representative sample of the adult population is interviewed on a variety of topics for about one and a half hours. The author of this book examined the responses of the 4,510 people interviewed concerning their level of education and income.

Ensuring Validity and Reliability The scientific method requires that research results be both valid and reliable. **Validity** refers to the degree to which a measure or scale truly reflects the phenomenon under study. A valid measure of income depends on the gathering of accurate data. Various studies show that people are reasonably accurate in reporting how much money they earned in the most recent year. If a question is written unclearly, however, the resulting data might not be accurate. For example, respondents to an unclear question about income might report their parents' or spouse's income instead of their own. **Reliability** refers to the extent to which a measure produces consistent results. Some people may not disclose accurate information, but most do. In the General Social Survey, only 9 percent of the respondents refused to give their income or indicated they did not know what their income was. That means 91 percent of the respondents gave their income, which we can assume is reasonably accurate (given their other responses about occupation and years in the labor force).

Developing the Conclusion

Scientific studies, including those conducted by sociologists, do not aim to answer all the questions that can be raised about a particular subject. Therefore, the conclusion of a research study represents both an end and a beginning. It terminates a specific phase of the investigation but should also generate ideas for future study.

Supporting Hypotheses   In our example, we find that the data support our hypothesis: People with more formal schooling *do* earn more money than others. Those with a high school diploma earn more than those who failed to complete high school, but those with an associate's degree earn more than high school graduates. The relationship continues through more advanced levels of schooling, so that those with graduate degrees earn the most.

The relationship is not perfect, however. Some people who drop out of high school end up with high incomes, whereas some with advanced degrees earn modest incomes, as shown in Figure 2-4. A successful entrepreneur, for example, might not have much formal schooling, while a holder of a doctorate may choose to work for a low-paying nonprofit institution. Sociologists are interested in both the general pattern that emerges from their data and exceptions to the pattern.

Sociological studies do not always generate data that support the original hypothesis. Many times, a hypothesis is refuted, and researchers must reformulate their conclusions. Unexpected results may also lead sociologists to reexamine their methodology and make changes in the research design.

Controlling for Other Factors   A **control variable** is a factor that is held constant to test the relative impact of an independent variable. For example, if researchers wanted to know how adults in the United States feel about restrictions on smoking in public places, they would probably attempt to use a respondent's smoking behavior as a control variable. That is, how do smokers versus nonsmokers feel about smoking in public places? The researchers would compile separate statistics on how smokers and nonsmokers feel about antismoking regulations.

Our study of the influence of education on income suggests that not everyone enjoys equal educational opportunities, a disparity that is one of the causes of social inequality. Since education affects a person's income, we may wish to call on the conflict perspective to explore this topic further. What impact does a person's race or gender have? Is a woman with a college degree likely to earn as much as a man with similar schooling? Later in this textbook we will consider these other factors and variables. That is, we will examine the impact that education has on income while controlling for variables such as gender and race.

---

use your sociological *imagination*

What might be the effects of a college education on society as a whole? Think of some potential effects on the family, government, and the economy.

High school diploma or less — 9%, 15%, 24%, 21%, 31%

Associate's degree or more — 31%, 24%, 19%, 12%, 14%

$60,000 and over
$40,000–59,999
$25,000–39,999
$15,000–24,999
Under $15,000

Source: Author's analysis of General Social Survey 2006 in J. Davis et al. 2007. Fifty-two percent of people with a high school diploma or less (left) earn under $25,000 a year, while only 24 percent earn $40,000 or more. In contrast, 55 percent of those with an associate's degree or higher (right) earn $40,000 or more, while only 26 percent earn less than $25,000.

Think about It

What kinds of knowledge and skills do people with an associate's degree or higher possess, compared to those with a high school education or less? Why would employers value those kinds of knowledge and skills?

In Summary: The Scientific Method

Let us briefly summarize the process of the scientific method through a review of the example. We *defined a problem* (the question of whether it pays to get a higher educational degree). We *reviewed the literature* (other studies of the relationship between education and income) and *formulated a hypothesis* (the higher one's educational degree, the more money one will earn). We *collected and analyzed the data,* making sure the sample was representative and the data were valid and reliable. Finally, we *developed the conclusion:* The data do support our hypothesis about the influence of education on income.

Major Research Designs

An important aspect of sociological research is deciding *how* to collect the data. A **research design** is a detailed plan or method for obtaining data scientifically. Selection of a research design is often based on the theories and hypotheses the researcher starts with (Merton 1948). The choice requires creativity and ingenuity, because it directly influences both the cost of the project and the amount of time needed to collect the data. Research designs that sociologists regularly use to generate data include surveys, observation, experiments, and existing sources.

Surveys

Almost all of us have responded to surveys of one kind or another. We may have been asked what kind of detergent we use, which presidential candidate we intend to vote for, or what our favorite television program is. A **survey** is a study, generally in the form of an interview or questionnaire, that provides

Doonesbury

Think about It
What would constitute a less biased question for a survey on smoking?

researchers with information about how people think and act. Among the United States' best-known surveys of opinion are the Gallup poll and the Harris poll. As anyone who watches the news during presidential campaigns knows, these polls have become a staple of political life.

When you think of surveys, you may recall seeing many person-on-the-street interviews on local television news shows. Although such interviews can be highly entertaining, they are not necessarily an accurate indication of public opinion. First, they reflect the opinions of only those people who happen to be at a certain location. Such a sample can be biased in favor of commuters, middle-class shoppers, or factory workers, depending on which street or area the newspeople select. Second, television interviews tend to attract outgoing people who are willing to appear on the air, while they frighten away others who may feel intimidated by a camera. As we've seen, a survey must be based on precise, representative sampling if it is to genuinely reflect a broad range of the population. Box 2-1 describes the challenges of conducting a public opinion survey over the telephone.

In preparing to conduct a survey, sociologists must not only develop representative samples; they must exercise great care in the wording of questions. An effective survey question must be simple and clear enough for people to understand. It must also be specific enough so that there are no problems in interpreting the results. Open-ended questions ("What do you think of the programming on educational television?") must be carefully phrased to solicit the type of information desired. Surveys can be indispensable sources of information, but only if the sampling is done properly and the questions are worded accurately and without bias.

There are two main forms of the survey: the **interview,** in which a researcher obtains information through face-to-face or telephone questioning, and the **questionnaire,** in which the researcher uses a printed or written form to obtain information from a respondent. Each of these has its own advantages. An interviewer can obtain a higher response rate because people find it more difficult to turn down a personal request for an interview than to throw away a written questionnaire. In addition, a skillful interviewer can go beyond written questions and probe for a subject's underlying feelings and reasons. On the other hand, questionnaires have the advantage of being cheaper, especially in large samples.

Why do people have sex? A straightforward question, but until recently rarely investigated scientifically, despite its significance to public health, marital counseling, and criminology. In a study published in 2007, researchers interviewed nearly 2,000 undergraduates at the University of Texas at Austin. To develop the question for the interview, they first asked a random sample of 400 students to list all the reasons why they had ever had sex. The explanations were highly diverse, ranging from "I was drunk" to "I wanted to feel closer to God." The team then asked another sample of 1,500 students to rate the importance of each of the 287 reasons given by the first group. Table 2-1 on page 36 ranks the results. Nearly every one of the reasons was rated most important by at least some respondents. Though there were some gender differences in the replies, there was significant consensus between men and women on the top 10 reasons (Meston and Buss 2007).

Studies have shown that the characteristics of the interviewer have an impact on survey data. For example, female interviewers tend to receive more feminist responses from female subjects than do male interviewers, and African American interviewers tend to receive more detailed responses about race-related issues from African American subjects than do White interviewers. The possible impact of gender and race indicates again how much care social research requires (D. W. Davis and Silver 2003).

The survey is an example of **quantitative research,** which collects and reports data primarily in numerical form. Most of the survey research discussed so far in this book has been quantitative. While this type of research can make use of large samples, it can't offer great depth and detail on a topic. That is why researchers also make use of **qualitative research,** which

RESEARCH TODAY

2-1 Surveying Cell Phone Users

"Can you hear me now?" This question, familiar to cell phone callers everywhere, could be used to characterize a debate among researchers in sociology. Until recently, calling people on the telephone was a common way for survey takers to reach a broad range of people. Though not everyone owns a telephone—particularly not low-income people—researchers managed to account for that relatively small portion of the population in other ways.

However, the recent spread of cell phones, to the point that many people now have a cell phone but no landline, presents a serious methodological problem to scholars who depend on surveys and public opinion polling. As of 2008, one in seven adults in the United States could be reached only by cell phone, and the proportion was rising. Among those under 30, the abandonment of landlines was nearly three times as common. These cell phone subscribers are more likely than others to be male and to earn a modest income.

Because the young and the poor are more likely than others to be reachable only by cell phone, scholars are reluctant to rely only on landline-based surveys. They are concerned about the potential for misleading results, such as underestimating the prevalence of health problems like binge drinking, smoking, obesity, and HIV infection. Sometimes the differences between the two sampling methods are negligible and can be ignored. In election polling done in 2008, however, some careful researchers noticed that Barack Obama had 10 percent more support among cell phone–only voters than among those with standard landlines.

Unfortunately, surveying cell phone users has its own problems. In general, cell phone users are more likely than landline users to screen incoming calls or ignore them, especially if they pay an extra charge for incoming calls.

As of 2008, one in seven adults in the United States could be reached only by cell phone, and the proportion was rising.

Studies show that because cell phone users often take calls while they are involved in other activities, they are much more likely to break off a call midsurvey than someone who is speaking on a landline. Survey takers have also found that calling cell phone numbers means they will reach a higher proportion of nonadults than when calling landline numbers. Finally, there are some ethical issues involved in randomly dialing cell phone users, who may be driving a motor vehicle or operating dangerous machinery when they answer.

In 2003, researchers who study business and the social sciences began gathering at "cell phone summits" to discuss their concerns and devise a solution. One approach to the potential for bias in surveys that exclude cell phones is to use a statistical procedure called *weighting*. That is, survey takers overcount the responses they receive from young adults and people with lower incomes, to correct for the bias in their sampling. To refine their weighting measures, they then conduct nontelephone surveys in which they ask the same questions.

Researchers are also taking steps to stay abreast of technological change. For example, they are making allowances for people who communicate without any kind of telephone, using their personal computers and the Internet. And by drawing on historical data that suggests what kinds of people tend to adopt other wireless technologies, researchers are projecting which people are likely to abandon their landlines in the near future.

LET'S DISCUSS

1. Are you a cell phone–only user? If so, do you generally accept calls from unknown numbers? Aside from underestimating certain health problems and distorting the degree of support for certain politicians, what other problems might result from excluding cell phone–only users from survey research?
2. Apply what you have just learned to the task of surveying Internet users. Which of the problems that arise during telephone surveys might also arise during Internet surveys? Might Internet surveys involve some unique problems?

Sources: Blumberg and Luke 2007; Harrisinteractive 2008; Keeter and Kennedy 2006; Keeter et al. 2008; Lavrakas et al. 2007.

---

relies on what is seen in field and naturalistic settings, and often focuses on small groups and communities rather than on large groups or whole nations. The most common form of qualitative research is observation, which we consider next. Throughout this book you will find examples of both quantitative and qualitative research, since both are used widely. Some sociologists prefer one type of research to the other, but we learn most when we draw on many different research designs and do not limit ourselves to a particular type of research.

Observation

Investigators who collect information by direct participation and/or by closely watching a group or community are engaged in **observation.** This method allows sociologists to examine certain behaviors and communities that could not be investigated through other research techniques. Though observation may seem a relatively informal method compared to surveys or experiments, researchers are careful to take detailed notes while observing their subjects.

An increasingly popular form of qualitative research in sociology today is ethnography. **Ethnography** refers to the study of an entire social setting through extended systematic observation. Typically, the emphasis is on how the subjects themselves view their social life in some setting. In some cases, the sociologist actually joins a group for a period to get an accurate sense of how it operates. This approach is called *participant observation.* In Barbara Ehrenreich's study of low-wage workers, described in Chapter 1, the researcher was a participant observer (see also P. Adler and Adler 2003, 2004, 2008a).

During the late 1930s, in a classic example of participant-observation research, William F. Whyte moved into a low-income Italian neighborhood in Boston. For nearly four years he was a member of the social circle of "corner boys" that he describes in *Street Corner Society*. Whyte revealed his identity to these men and joined in their conversations, bowling, and other leisure-time activities. His goal was to gain greater insight into the community that these men had established. As Whyte (1981:303) listened to Doc, the leader of the group, he "learned the answers to questions I would not even have had the sense to ask if I had been getting my information solely on an interviewing basis." Whyte's work was especially valuable, since at the time the academic world had little direct knowledge of the

TABLE 2-1 TOP REASONS WHY MEN AND WOMEN HAD SEX

Reason	Men	Women
I was attracted to the person	1	1
It feels good	2	3
I wanted to experience the physical pleasure	3	2
It's fun	4	8
I wanted to show my affection to the person	5	4
I was sexually aroused and wanted the release	6	6
I was "horny"	7	7
I wanted to express my love for the person	8	5
I wanted to achieve an orgasm	9	14
I wanted to please my partner	10	11
I realized I was in love	17	9
I was "in the heat of the moment"	13	10

Source: Meston and Buss 2007:506.

Sergeant Britt Damon, a social scientist on the U.S. Army Human Terrain Team, chats with Afghani children during a search operation. The participation of social scientists in the Army program, which some see as a violation of scholarly detachment, has proved controversial.

poor, and tended to rely for information on the records of social service agencies, hospitals, and courts (P. Adler et al. 1992).

The initial challenge that Whyte faced—and that every participant observer encounters—was to gain acceptance into an unfamiliar group. It is no simple matter for a college-trained sociologist to win the trust of a religious cult, a youth gang, a poor Appalachian community, or a circle of skid row residents. It requires a great deal of patience and an accepting, nonthreatening type of personality on the part of the observer.

Observation research poses other complex challenges for the investigator. Sociologists must be able to fully understand what they are observing. In a sense, then, researchers must learn to see the world as the group sees it in order to fully comprehend the events taking place around them.

This raises a delicate issue. If the research is to be successful, the observer cannot allow the close associations or even friendships that inevitably develop to influence the subjects' behavior or the conclusions of the study. Anson Shupe and David Bromley (1980), two sociologists who have used participant observation, have likened this challenge to that of walking a tightrope. Even while working hard to gain acceptance from the group being studied, the participant observer *must* maintain some degree of detachment. Thus the Adlers, in their work on self-injury, acknowledged their departure from strict detachment in describing their involvement with the subjects they studied.

Recently, the issue of detachment became a controversial one for social scientists embedded with the U.S. military in Afghanistan and Iraq. Among other studies, the academicians participated in the creation of the Army's Human Terrain System, a $4 million effort to identify the customs, kinship structures, and internal social conflicts in the two countries. The intention was to provide military leaders with information that would help them to make better decisions. Although the idea of scholars cooperating in any way with soldiers struck many people as inappropriate, others countered that the information they developed would help the military to avoid needless violence and might even facilitate the withdrawal of troops from the region (Glenn 2007).

Experiments

When sociologists want to study a possible cause-and-effect relationship, they may conduct experiments. An **experiment** is an artificially created situation that allows a researcher to manipulate variables.

In the classic method of conducting an experiment, two groups of people are selected and matched for similar characteristics, such as age or education. The researchers then assign the subjects to one of two groups: the experimental or the control group. The **experimental group** is exposed to an independent variable; the **control group** is not. Thus, if scientists were testing a new type of antibiotic, they would administer the drug to an experimental group but not to a control group.

In some experiments, just as in observation research, the presence of a social scientist or other observer may affect the behavior of the people being studied. Sociologists have used the term **Hawthorne effect** to refer to the unintended influence that observers of experiments can have on their subjects. The term originated as the result of an experiment conducted at the Hawthorne plant of the Western Electric Company during the 1920s and 1930s. Researchers found that *every* change they made in working conditions—even reduced lighting—seemed to have a positive effect on workers' productivity. They concluded that workers had made a special effort to impress their observers. Though the carefully constructed study did identify some causes for changes in the workers' behavior that did not have to do with their being observed, the term *Hawthorne effect* has become synonymous with a placebo or guinea pig effect (Franke and Kaul 1978).

> ## use your sociological *imagination*
>
> You are a researcher interested in the effect of TV watching on schoolchildren's grades. How would you go about setting up an experiment to measure this effect?

Use of Existing Sources

Sociologists do not necessarily need to collect new data in order to conduct research and test hypotheses. The term **secondary analysis** refers to a variety of research techniques that make use of previously collected and publicly accessible information and data. Generally, in conducting secondary analysis, researchers use data in ways that were unintended by the initial collectors of information. For example, census data are compiled for specific uses by the federal government but are also valuable to marketing specialists in locating everything from bicycle stores to nursing homes. And Social Security registrations, originally meant

Content analysis of popular song lyrics shows that over the past 50 years, top female artists such as Beyoncé Knowles have used fewer sexually explicit words, while male artists have used more.

for government use in administering the nation's retirement system, have been used to track cultural trends in the naming of newborn children (Box 2-2 on page 38).

Sociologists consider secondary analysis to be *nonreactive*— that is, it does not influence people's behavior. For example, Émile Durkheim's statistical analysis of suicide neither increased nor decreased human self-destruction. Researchers, then, can avoid the Hawthorne effect by using secondary analysis.

There is one inherent problem, however: the researcher who relies on data collected by someone else may not find exactly what is needed. Social scientists who are studying family violence can use statistics from police and social service agencies on *reported* cases of spouse abuse and child abuse, but how many cases are not reported? Government bodies have no precise data on *all* cases of abuse.

Many social scientists find it useful to study cultural, economic, and political documents, including newspapers, periodicals, radio and television tapes, the Internet, scripts, diaries, songs, folklore, and legal papers (Table 2-2 on page 39). In examining these sources, researchers employ a technique known as **content analysis,** which is the systematic coding and objective recording of data, guided by some rationale.

Using content analysis, Erving Goffman (1979) conducted a pioneering exploration of how advertisements portray women. The ads he studied typically showed women as subordinate to or dependent on others, or as taking instruction from men. They engaged in caressing and touching gestures more than men. Even when presented in leadership roles, women were likely to be shown striking seductive poses or gazing out into space.

Today, researchers who analyze film content are finding an increase in smoking in motion pictures, despite heightened public health concerns. Other researchers have found a growing difference in the way men and women use sexually explicit language. For example, an analysis of the lyrics of *Billboard* magazine's top 100 hits indicates that since 1958, male artists have increased their use of such language, while female artists have decreased theirs (American Lung Association 2003; Dukes et al. 2003).

Table 2-3 on page 39 summarizes the major research designs, along with their advantages and limitations.

> ## use your sociological *imagination*
>
> Imagine you are a legislator or government policymaker working on a complex social problem. What might happen if you were to base your decision on faulty research?

Ethics of Research

A biochemist cannot inject a drug into a human being unless it has been thoroughly tested and the subject agrees to the shot. To do otherwise would be both unethical and illegal. Sociologists, too, must abide by certain specific standards in

RESEARCH TODAY

2-2 What's in a Name?

Sociologists can learn a great deal using available information. For example, every year the Social Security Administration receives thousands of registrations for newborn babies. Using these data, we can identify some cultural trends in the popularity of children's names.

As the accompanying figure shows, for example, John has been an extremely popular boy's name for over a century. In 2007 over 4,000 babies were named John, making it the 19th most popular name that year. Though less than half as many babies were named Juan in 2007, that name has been gaining in popularity in recent generations, reflecting the growing impact of the Latino population in the United States.

We can see some other patterns in the annual data on name giving. In many ethnic and racial groups, parents choose names that display pride in their identity or the uniqueness they see in their children. Among African Americans, for example, names such as Ebony and Imani are the most popular ones for girls.

In 2007 over 4,000 babies were named John, making it the 19th most popular name that year.

The public data contained in name registries also reveal a trend toward "American-sounding" names among immigrants to the United States. In Italy, for example, Giuseppe is a very popular boy's name. Among Italian immigrants to the United States, the English form of Giuseppe, Joseph, is the 3rd most popular boy's name, though it ranks only 11th among other Americans. The pattern of selecting names that will allow children to fit in is not uniform, however. In some immigrant groups, parents tend to favor names that symbolize their ethnicity. For example, Kelly is popular among Irish Americans, even though it isn't a traditional girl's name in Ireland. Thus, the available data on newborns' names allows sociologists to detect cultural trends that reflect changing group identities.

The use of existing data also shows social change in people's last names (surnames). In 2007 an analysis by the Census Bureau reported that although Smith remained the most common surname in the United States, Garcia and Rodriguez had risen to the top 10 most common names. The announcement marked the first time in the nation's history that a non-Anglo name had been counted among the most common surnames.

Finally, records kept by the Social Security Administration reveal some regional variations in names. Given the large Hispanic population in Texas, we probably should not be surprised to find that Juan ranks 9th as a name for baby boys in that state. In states like Alabama, Delaware, and Mississippi, however, John is on the top 10 list.

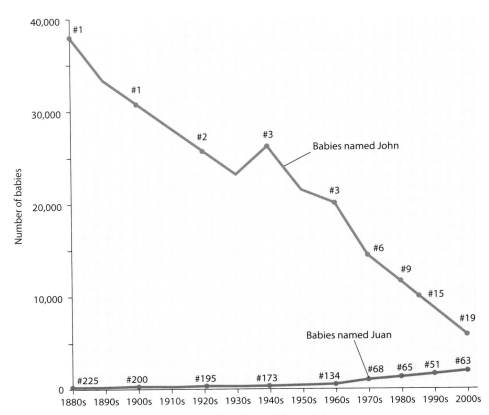

Popularity of John versus Juan

Babies named John

Babies named Juan

Note: Numbers indicate rank in popularity among all boys' names in that period.
Source: Baby Name Wizard 2009.

LET'S DISCUSS

1. Visit **www.babynamewizard.com** on the Internet, and click on "NameVoyager." According to this Web site, how popular is your first name? Is it becoming more or less fashionable over time?

2. Using the Name Mapper feature at **www .babynamewizard.com**, find out how popular your name is in the state where you were born. Is your name even more popular in some other states?

Sources: Baby Name Wizard 2009; S. Levitt and Dubner 2006; Lieberson 2000; Word et al. 2007.

---

conducting research, called a **code of ethics.** The professional society of the discipline, the American Sociological Association (ASA), first published the society's *Code of Ethics* in 1971 and revised it most recently in 1997. It puts forth the following basic principles:

1. Maintain objectivity and integrity in research.

2. Respect the subject's right to privacy and dignity.

3. Protect subjects from personal harm.

4. Preserve confidentiality.

5. Seek informed consent when data are collected from research participants or when behavior occurs in a private context.

6. Acknowledge research collaboration and assistance.

7. Disclose all sources of financial support (American Sociological Association 1997).

These basic principles probably seem clear-cut. How could they lead to any disagreement or controversy? Yet many delicate ethical questions cannot be resolved simply by reading these seven principles. For example, should a sociologist who is engaged in participant-observation research always protect the confidentiality of subjects? What if the subjects are members of a religious cult allegedly involved in unethical and possibly illegal activities? What if the sociologist is interviewing political activists and is questioned by government authorities about the research?

Because most sociological research uses *people* as sources of information—as respondents to survey questions, subjects of observation, or participants in experiments—these sorts of questions are important. In all cases, sociologists need to be certain they are not invading their subjects' privacy. Generally, they do so by assuring subjects of anonymity and by guaranteeing the confidentiality of personal information. In addition, research proposals that involve human subjects must now be overseen by a review board, whose members seek to ensure that subjects are not placed at an unreasonable level of risk. If necessary, the board may ask researchers to revise their research designs to conform to the code of ethics.

We can appreciate the seriousness of the ethical problems researchers confront by considering the experience of sociologist Rik Scarce, described in the next section. Scarce's vow to protect his subjects' confidentiality got him into considerable trouble with the law.

Confidentiality

Like journalists, sociologists occasionally find themselves subject to questions from law enforcement authorities because of knowledge they have gained in the course of their work. This uncomfortable situation raises profound ethical questions.

In May 1993, Rik Scarce, a doctoral candidate in sociology at Washington State University, was jailed for contempt of court. Scarce had declined to tell a federal grand jury what he knew—or even whether he knew anything—about a 1991 raid on a university research laboratory by animal rights activists. At the time, Scarce was conducting research for a book about environmental protestors and knew at least one suspect in the break-in. Curiously, although he was chastised by a federal judge, Scarce won respect from fellow prison inmates, who regarded him as a man who "wouldn't snitch" (Monaghan 1993:A8).

The American Sociological Association supported Scarce's position when he appealed his sentence. Scarce maintained his silence. Ultimately the judge ruled that nothing would be gained by further incarceration, and Scarce was released after serving 159 days in jail. In January 1994, the U.S. Supreme Court declined to hear Scarce's case on appeal. The Court's failure to consider his case led Scarce (1994, 1995, 2005) to argue that federal legislation is needed to clarify the right of scholars and

---

TABLE **2-2** EXISTING SOURCES USED IN SOCIOLOGICAL RESEARCH

Most Frequently Used Sources
Census data
Crime statistics
Birth, death, marriage, divorce, and health statistics

Other Sources
Newspapers and periodicals
Personal journals, diaries, e-mail, and letters
Records and archival material of religious organizations, corporations, and other organizations
Transcripts of radio programs
Videotapes of motion pictures and television programs
Web pages, Weblogs, and chatrooms
Song lyrics
Scientific records (such as patent applications)
Speeches of public figures (such as politicians)
Votes cast in elections or by elected officials on specific legislative proposals
Attendance records for public events
Videos of social protests and rallies
Literature, including folklore

TABLE **2-3** MAJOR RESEARCH DESIGNS

summing**up**

Method	Examples	Advantages	Limitations
Survey	Questionnaires Interviews	Yields information about specific issues	Can be expensive and time-consuming
Observation	Ethnography	Yields detailed information about specific groups or organizations	Involves months if not years of labor-intensive data
Experiment	Deliberate manipulation of people's social behavior	Yields direct measures of people's behavior	Ethical limitations on the degree to which subjects' behavior can be manipulated
Existing sources/ Secondary analysis	Analysis of census or health data Analysis of films or TV commercials	Cost-efficiency	Limited to data collected for some other purpose

members of the press to preserve the confidentiality of those they interview.

Research Funding

Sometimes disclosing all the sources of funding for a study, as required in principle 7 of the ASA's *Code of Ethics,* is not a sufficient guarantee of ethical conduct. Especially in the case of both corporate and government funding, money given ostensibly for the support of basic research may come with strings attached. Accepting funds from a private organization or even a government agency that stands to benefit from a study's results can call into question a researcher's objectivity and integrity (principle 1). The controversy surrounding the involvement of social scientists in the U.S. Army's Human Terrain System is one example of this conflict of interest.

Another example is the Exxon Corporation's support for research on jury verdicts. In 1989, the Exxon oil tanker *Valdez* hit a reef off the coast of Alaska, spilling over 11 million gallons of oil into Prince William Sound. Almost two decades later, the *Valdez* disaster is still regarded as the world's worst oil spill in terms of its environmental impact. In 1994 a federal court ordered Exxon to pay $5.3 billion in damages for the accident. Exxon appealed the verdict and began approaching legal scholars, sociologists, and psychologists who might be willing to study jury deliberations. The corporation's objective was to develop academic support for its lawyers' contention that the punitive judgments in such cases result from faulty deliberations and do not have a deterrent effect.

Some scholars have questioned the propriety of accepting funds under these circumstances, even if the source is disclosed. In at least one case, an Exxon employee explicitly told a sociologist that the corporation offers financial support to scholars who have shown the tendency to express views similar to its own. An argument can also be made that Exxon was attempting to set scholars' research agendas with its huge war chest. Rather than funding studies on the improvement of cleanup technologies or the assignment of long-term environmental costs, Exxon chose to shift scientists' attention to the validity of the legal awards in environmental cases.

The scholars who accepted Exxon's support deny that it influenced their work or changed their conclusions. Some received support from other sources as well, such as the National Science Foundation and Harvard University's Olin Center for Law, Economics, and Business. Many of their findings were published in respected academic journals after review by a jury of peers. Still, at least one researcher who participated in the studies refused monetary support from Exxon to avoid even the suggestion of a conflict of interest.

To date, Exxon has spent roughly $1 million on the research, and at least one compilation of studies congenial to the corporation's point of view has been published. As ethical considerations require, the academics who conducted the studies disclosed Exxon's role in funding them. Nevertheless, the investment appears to have paid off. In 2006, drawing on these studies, Exxon's lawyers succeeded in persuading an appeals court to reduce the corporation's legal punitive damages from $5.3 to $2.5 billion. In 2008 Exxon appealed that judgment to the Supreme Court, which further reduced the damages to $500 million. The final award, which is to be shared by about 32,000 plaintiffs, will result

A floating containment barrier encircles the Exxon oil tanker *Valdez* after its grounding on a reef off the coast of Alaska. Exxon executives spent $1 million to fund academic research that they hoped would support lawyers' efforts to reduce the $5.3 billion judgment against the corporation for negligence in the environmental disaster.

in payments of about $15,000 to each person (Freudenburg 2005; Liptak 2008).

Value Neutrality

The ethical considerations of sociologists lie not only in the methods they use and the funding they accept, but in the way they interpret their results. Max Weber ([1904] 1949) recognized that personal values would influence the questions that sociologists select for research. In his view, that was perfectly acceptable, but under no conditions could a researcher allow his or her personal feelings to influence the *interpretation* of data. In Weber's phrase, sociologists must practice **value neutrality** in their research.

As part of this neutrality, investigators have an ethical obligation to accept research findings even when the data run counter to their personal views, to theoretically based explanations, or to widely accepted beliefs. For example, Émile Durkheim challenged popular conceptions when he reported that social (rather than supernatural) forces were an important factor in suicide.

Some sociologists believe that neutrality is impossible. They worry that Weber's insistence on value-free sociology may lead the public to accept sociological conclusions without exploring researchers' biases. Others, drawing on the conflict perspective, as Alvin Gouldner (1970) does, have suggested that sociologists may use objectivity as a justification for remaining uncritical of existing institutions and centers of power. These arguments are attacks not so much on Weber himself as on the way his goals have been misinterpreted. As we have seen, Weber was quite clear that sociologists may bring values to their subject matter. In his view, however, they must not confuse their own values with the social reality under study (Bendix 1968).

Let's consider what might happen when researchers bring their own biases to the investigation. A person investigating the impact of intercollegiate sports on alumni contributions, for example, may focus only on the highly visible revenue-generating sports of football and basketball and neglect the so-called minor sports, such as tennis or soccer, which are more likely to involve women athletes. Despite the early work of W. E. B. DuBois and Jane Addams, sociologists still need to be reminded that the discipline often fails to adequately consider all people's social behavior.

In her book *The Death of White Sociology* (1973), Joyce Ladner called attention to the tendency of mainstream sociology to treat the lives of African Americans as a social problem. More recently, feminist sociologist Shulamit Reinharz (1992) has argued that sociological research should be not only inclusive but open to bringing about social change and to drawing on relevant research by nonsociologists. Both Reinharz and Ladner maintain that researchers should always analyze whether women's unequal social status has affected their studies in any way. For example, one might broaden the study of the impact of education on income to consider the implications of the unequal pay status of men and women. The issue of value neutrality does not mean that sociologists can't have opinions, but it does mean that they must work to overcome any biases, however unintentional, that they may bring to their analysis of research.

Peter Rossi (1987) admits to having liberal inclinations that direct him to certain fields of study. Yet in line with Weber's view of value neutrality, Rossi's commitment to rigorous research methods and objective interpretation of data has sometimes led him to controversial findings that are not necessarily supportive of his own liberal values. For example, his measure of the extent of homelessness in Chicago in the mid-1980s fell far below the estimates of the Chicago Coalition for the Homeless. Coalition members bitterly attacked Rossi for hampering their social reform efforts by minimizing the extent of homelessness.

Rossi (1987:79) concluded that "in the short term, good social research will often be greeted as a betrayal of one or another side to a particular controversy."

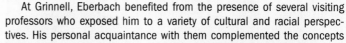

use your sociological *imagination*

You are a sociological researcher who is having difficulty maintaining a neutral attitude toward your research topic. Your topic isn't pollution, racism, or homelessness. What is it?

www.mhhe.com/schaefer12e

Feminist Methodology

Of the four theoretical approaches to sociology introduced in Chapter 1, the feminist perspective has had the greatest impact on the current generation of social researchers. How might this perspective influence research? Although researchers must be objective, their theoretical orientation may influence the questions they ask—or, just as important, the questions they fail to ask. Until recently, for example, researchers frequently studied work and the family separately. Yet feminist theorists see the two spheres of activity as being closely integrated. Similarly, work and leisure, paid and unpaid domestic work may be seen, not as two separate spheres, but as two sides of the same coin.

Feminist theorists have also drawn researchers' attention to their tendency to overlook women in their studies. For most of the history of sociology, researchers conducted studies of male subjects or male-led groups and organizations and then generalized their findings to all people. For many decades, for example, ethnographic studies of urban life focused on street corners, **41**

Feminist theorists see the global trafficking of sex workers as one sign of a close relationship between the two supposedly separate worlds of industrial nations and the developing nations that depend on them.

neighborhood taverns, and bowling alleys—places where men typically congregated. Although researchers gained some valuable insights in this way, they did not form a true impression of city life, because they overlooked the areas where women were likely to gather, such as playgrounds, grocery stores, and front stoops. These are the arenas that the feminist perspective focuses on.

These concerns can be seen in the impact of the feminist perspective on global research. To feminist theorists, the traditional distinction between industrial nations and developing nations overlooks the close relationship between these two supposedly separate worlds. Feminist theorists have called for more research on the special role that immigrant women play in maintaining their households; on the use of domestic workers from less developed nations by households in industrial nations; and on the global trafficking of sex workers (S. Cheng 2003; K. Cooper et al. 2007; Sprague 2005).

Finally, feminist researchers tend to involve and consult their subjects more than other researchers, and they are more oriented toward seeking change, raising the public consciousness, and influencing policy. They are particularly open to a multidisciplinary approach, such as making use of historical evidence or legal studies (T. Baker 1999; Lofland 1975; Reinharz 1992).

Technology and Sociological Research

Advances in technology have affected all aspects of our lives, and sociological research is no exception. The increased speed and capacity of computers are enabling sociologists to handle larger and larger sets of data. In the recent past, only people with grants or major institutional support could easily work with census data. Now anyone with a desktop computer and modem can access census information and learn more about social behavior. Moreover, data from foreign countries concerning crime statistics and health care are sometimes as available as information from the United States.

Researchers usually rely on computers to deal with quantitative data—that is, numerical measures—but electronic technology

is also assisting them with qualitative data, such as information obtained in observational research. Numerous software programs, such as Ethnograph and NVivo 7, allow the researcher not only to record observations but also to identify common behavioral patterns or concerns expressed in interviews. For example, after observing students in a college cafeteria over several weeks and putting her observations into the computer, a researcher could group all the observations according to certain variables, such as "sorority" or "study group."

The Internet affords an excellent opportunity to communicate with fellow researchers, as well as to locate useful information on social issues that has been posted on Web sites. It would be impossible to calculate all the sociological postings on Web sites or Internet mailing lists. Of course, researchers need to apply the same critical scrutiny to Internet material that they would to any printed resource.

How useful is the Internet for conducting survey research? That is still unclear. It is relatively easy to send out a questionnaire or post one on an electronic bulletin board. This technique is an inexpensive way to reach large numbers of potential respondents and get a quick response. However, there are some obvious dilemmas. How do you protect a respondent's anonymity? How do you define the potential audience? Even if you know to whom you sent the questionnaire, the respondents may forward it to others. Web-based surveys are still in their early stages. Even so, the initial results are promising. As noted in our description of the Adlers' research on self-injury, discussion groups, chat rooms, and other collectives serve as an extension of conventional face-to-face groups.

This new technology is exciting, but there is one basic limitation to the methodology. Just as telephone surveys work only with those who have access to a telephone (see Box 2-1 on page 35), Internet surveys work only with those who have access to the Internet and are online. For some market researchers, such a limitation is acceptable. For example, if you were interested in the willingness of Internet users to order books or make travel reservations online, limiting the sample population to those

Researchers use laptop computers to tabulate survey responses, access data from other studies, and record their observations.

who are already online makes sense. However, if you were surveying the general public about their plans to buy a computer in the coming year or their views on a particular candidate, your online research would need to be supplemented by more traditional sampling procedures, such as mailed questionnaires.

We have seen that researchers rely on a number of tools, from time-tested observational research and use of existing sources to the latest in computer technologies. The Social Policy section that follows will describe researchers' efforts to survey the general population about a controversial aspect of social behavior: human sexuality. This investigation was complicated by its potential social policy implications. Because in the real world, sociological research can have far-reaching consequences for public policy and public welfare, each of the following chapters in this book will close with a Social Policy section.

social policy and Sociological Research

Studying Human Sexuality

The Issue

Reality TV shows often feature an attempt to create a relationship or even a marriage between two strangers. In a picturesque setting, an eligible bachelor or bachelorette interviews potential partners—all of them good-looking—and gradually eliminates those who seem less promising. The questions that are posed on camera can be explicit. "How many sexual partners have you had?" "How often would you be willing to have sex?"

The Kaiser Family Foundation conducts regular studies of sexual content on television. The latest report, released in 2005, shows that more than two-thirds of all TV shows include some sexual content—up from about half of all shows seven years earlier (Figure 2-5). Yet the foundation's 2007 study showed that only 17 percent of parents use electronic means, such as the V-chip, to block TV content that may be inappropriate for children. Media representations of sexual behavior are important, because surveys of teens and young adults tell us that television is one of their top sources of information and ideas about sex. TV has more influence on young people's conceptions of sex than schools, parents, or peers (Kaiser Family Foundation 2007).

In this age of devastating sexually transmitted diseases, there is no time more important to increase our scientific understanding of human sexuality. As we will see, however, this is a difficult topic to research because of all the preconceptions, myths, and beliefs people bring to the subject of sexuality. How does one carry out scientific research on such a controversial and personal topic?

The Setting

Sociologists have little reliable national data on patterns of sexual behavior in the United States. Until recently, the only comprehensive study of sexual behavior was the famous two-volume *Kinsey Report,* prepared in the 1940s (Kinsey et al. 1948, 1953; see also Igo 2007). Although the *Kinsey Report* is still widely quoted, the volunteers interviewed for the report were not representative of the nation's adult population.

In part, we lack reliable data on patterns of sexual behavior because it is difficult for researchers to obtain accurate information about this sensitive subject. Moreover, until AIDS emerged in the 1980s, there was little scientific demand for data on sexual behavior, except for specific concerns such as contraception. Finally, even though the AIDS crisis has reached dramatic proportions (as will be discussed in Box 19-1 on page 425), government funding for studies of sexual behavior is controversial. Because the General Social

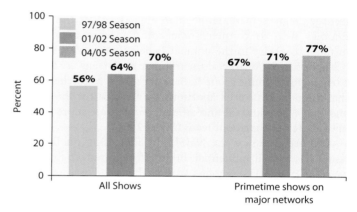

FIGURE **2-5** PERCENTAGE OF TELEVISION SHOWS THAT CONTAIN SEXUAL CONTENT

Source: Kaiser Family Foundation 2005:4.

Survey concerns sexual attitudes rather than behavior, its funding has not been jeopardized.

Sociological Insights

The controversy surrounding research on human sexual behavior raises the issue of value neutrality (page 40), which becomes especially delicate when one considers the relationship of sociology to the government. The federal government has become the major source of funding for sociological research. Yet Max Weber urged that sociology remain an autonomous discipline and not become unduly influenced by any one segment of society. According to Weber's ideal of value neutrality, sociologists must remain free to reveal information that is embarrassing to the government, or for that matter, supportive of government institutions.

Although the American Sociological Association's *Code of Ethics* requires sociologists to disclose all funding sources, it does not address the issue of whether sociologists who accept funding from a particular agency or corporation may also accept the agency's perspective on what needs to be studied. As we saw in our discussion of research funded by the Exxon Corporation (page 40), this question is a knotty one. As the next section will show, applied sociological research on human sexuality has run into political barriers.

Policy Initiatives

In 1987 the National Institute of Child Health and Human Development sought proposals for a national survey of sexual behavior. Sociologists responded with various plans that a review panel of scientists approved for funding. However, in 1991, the U.S. Senate voted to forbid funding any survey of adult sexual practices. Two years earlier, a similar debate in Great Britain had led to the denial of government funding for a national sex survey (A. Johnson et al. 1994; Laumann et al. 1994a:36).

Despite the vote by the U.S. Senate, sociologists Edward Laumann, John Gagnon, Stuart Michaels, and Robert Michael developed the National Health and Social Life Survey (NHSLS) to better understand the sexual practices of adults in the United States. The researchers raised $1.6 million of *private* funding to make their study possible (Laumann et al. 1994a, 1994b).

The authors of the NHSLS believe that their research is important. They argue that using data from their survey allows us to more easily address public policy issues such as AIDS, sexual harassment, welfare reform, sex discrimination, abortion, teenage pregnancy, and family planning. Moreover, the research findings help to counter some commonsense notions. For instance, contrary to the popular beliefs that women regularly use abortion for birth control and that poor teens are the most likely socioeconomic group to have abortions, researchers found that three-fourths of all abortions are the first for the woman, and that well-educated and affluent women are more likely to have abortions than poor teens (Sweet 2001).

The usefulness of the NHSLS in addressing public policy issues has proved influential. In an effort to reduce the occurrence of HIV/AIDS, scholars around the world are now studying human sexual behavior. Figure 2-6 shows some of their data, compiled by the United Nations.

Even in nations where government officials once shrank from collecting data on such a sensitive subject, attitudes are changing. In China, for example, scholars are aware of the NHSLS and have begun to collaborate with sociologists in the United States on a similar study in China. The data are just now being analyzed, but responses thus far indicate dramatic differences in the sexual behavior of people in their 20s, compared to behavior at the same age by people who are now in their 50s. Younger-generation Chinese are more active sexually and have more partners than their

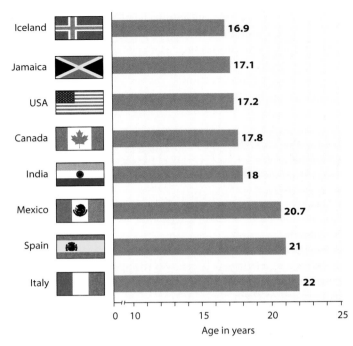

FIGURE 2-6 MEDIAN AGE OF FIRST SEX

	Age in years
Iceland	16.9
Jamaica	17.1
USA	17.2
Canada	17.8
India	18
Mexico	20.7
Spain	21
Italy	22

Source: UNICEF 2002.

parents did. Partly in response to these preliminary results, the Chinese Ministry of Health has sought U.S. assistance on HIV/AIDS prevention and research (Braverman 2002; Parish et al. 2007).

Let's Discuss

1. Do you see any merit in the position of those who oppose government funding for research on sexual behavior? Explain your reasoning.

2. Exactly how could the results of research on human sexual behavior be used to control sexually transmitted diseases?

3. Compare the issue of value neutrality in government-funded research to the same issue in corporate-funded research. Are concerns about conflict of interest more or less serious in regard to government funding?

getting**involved**

To get involved in the debate over research on human sexuality, visit this book's Online Learning Center, which offers links to relevant Web sites.

www.mhhe.com/schaefer12e

APPENDIX I Using Statistics and Graphs

In their effort to better understand social behavior, sociologists rely heavily on numbers and statistics. How have attitudes toward the legalization of marijuana changed over the past 40 years? A quick look at the results of 12 national surveys shows that while support for legalization of the drug has increased, it remains relatively weak (Figure 2-7).

Using Statistics

The most common summary measures used by sociologists are percentages, means, modes, and medians. A **percentage** shows a portion of 100. Use of percentages allows us to compare groups of different sizes. For example, if we were comparing financial contributors to a town's Baptist and Roman Catholic churches, the absolute numbers of contributors in each group could be misleading if there were many more Baptists than Catholics in the town. By using percentages, we could obtain a more meaningful comparison, showing the proportion of persons in each group who contribute to churches.

The **mean,** or *average,* is a number calculated by adding a series of values and then dividing by the number of values. For example, to find the mean of the numbers 5, 19, and 27, we add them together (for a total of 51), divide by the number of values (3), and discover that the mean is 17.

The **mode** is the single most common value in a series of scores. Suppose we were looking at the following scores on a 10-point quiz:

10	7
10	7
9	7
9	6
8	5
8	

The mode—the most frequent score on the quiz—is 7. While the mode is easier to identify than other summary measures, it tells sociologists little about all the other values. Hence, you will find much less use of the mode in this book than of the mean and the median.

The **median** is the midpoint or number that divides a series of values into two groups of equal numbers of values. For the quiz just discussed, the median, or central value, is 8. The mean, or average, would be 86 (the sum of all scores) divided by 11 (the total number of scores), or 7.8.

In the United States, the median household income for the year 2007 was $50,233; it indicates that half of all households had incomes above $50,233, while half had lower incomes (DeNavas-Walt et al. 2008:6). In many respects, the median is the most characteristic value. Although it may not reflect the full range of scores, it does approximate the typical value in a set of scores, and it is not affected by extreme scores.

Some of these statistics may seem confusing at first. But think how difficult it is to comb an endless list of numbers to identify a pattern or central tendency. Percentages, means, modes, and medians are essential time-savers in sociological research and analysis.

Reading Graphs

Tables and figures (that is, graphs) allow social scientists to display data and develop their conclusions more easily. During 2001–2005, the Gallup poll interviewed 2,034 people in the United States, ages 18 and over. Each respondent was asked, "Do you think the use of marijuana should be made legal, or not?" Without some type of summary, there is no way that analysts could examine the hundreds

FIGURE **2-7** CHANGING ATTITUDES TOWARD THE LEGALIZATION OF MARIJUANA

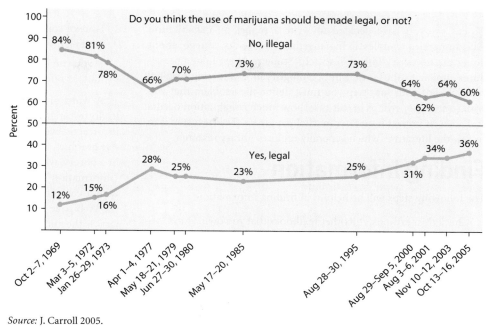

Source: J. Carroll 2005.

FIGURE **2-8** ATTITUDES TOWARD THE LEGALIZATION OF MARIJUANA BY GENDER AND AGE

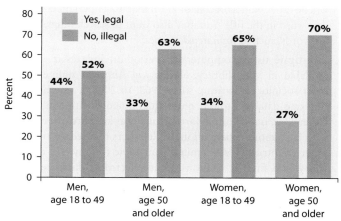

Source: J. Carroll 2005.

of individual responses to this question and reach firm conclusions. One type of summary sociologists use, a **cross-tabulation,** shows the relationship between two or more variables. Through the cross-tabulations presented graphically in Figure 2-8, we can quickly see that older people are less likely to favor the legalization of marijuana than younger people, and that women are less supportive of legalization than men.

Graphs, like tables, can be quite useful to sociologists. And illustrations are often easier for the general public to understand, whether they are in newspapers or in PowerPoint presentations. Still, as with all data, we need to be careful how they are presented.

APPENDIX II Writing a Research Report

Let's say you have decided to write a report on cohabitation (unmarried couples living together). How do you go about doing the necessary library research? Students must follow procedures similar to those used by sociologists in conducting original research. For your first step you must define the problem that you wish to study—perhaps in this case, how much cohabitation occurs and what its impact is on later marital happiness. The next step is to review the literature, which generally requires library research.

Finding Information

The following steps will be helpful in finding information:

1. Check this textbook and other textbooks that you own. Don't forget to begin with the materials closest at hand, including the Web site associated with this textbook, www.mhhe.com/schaefer12e.

2. Use the library catalog. Computerized library systems now access not only the college library's collection but also books and magazines from other libraries, available through interlibrary loans. These systems allow you to search for books by author or title. You can use title searches to locate books by subject as well. For example, if you search the title base for the keyword *cohabitation,* you will learn where books with that word somewhere in the title are located in the library's book stacks. Near these books will be other works on cohabitation that may not happen to have that word in the title. You may also want to search other, related, keywords, such as *unmarried couples.*

3. Investigate using computerized periodical indexes if they are available in your library. *Sociological Abstracts* online covers most sociological writing since 1963. In 2008, a search of just this one database found more than 1,666 documents having either *cohabitation* or *unmarried couples* as keywords. Some dealt with laws about cohabitation, while others focused on trends in other countries. If you limited your topic to same-sex couples, you would find 72 citations. Other electronic databases cover general-interest periodicals (*Time, Ms., National Review, Atlantic Monthly,* and so forth), reference materials, or newspapers. These electronic systems may be connected to a printer, allowing you to produce your own printout complete with bibliographic information, and sometimes even complete copies of articles.

4. Examine government documents. The U.S. government, states and cities, and the United Nations publish information on virtually every subject of interest to social science researchers. Publications of the Census Bureau, for example, include tables showing the number of unmarried couples living together and some social characteristics of those households. Many university libraries have access to a wide range of government reports. Consult the librarian for assistance in locating such materials.

5. Use newspapers. Major newspapers publish indexes annually or even weekly that are useful in locating information about specific events or issues. Academic Universe News is an electronic index to U.S. and international newspapers.

6. Ask people, organizations, and agencies concerned with the topic for information and assistance. Be as specific as possible in making requests. You might receive very different information on the issue of cohabitation from talking with marriage counselors and with clergy from different religions.

7. If you run into difficulties, consult the instructor, teaching assistant, or reference librarian at your college library.

A word of caution: be extremely careful in using the Internet to do research. Much of the information on the Internet is simply incorrect—even if it looks authoritative, is accompanied by impressive graphics, or has been widely circulated. Unlike the information in a library, which must be screened by a highly qualified librarian, "information" on the Internet can be created and posted by anyone with a computer. Check the sources for the information and note the Web page sponsor. Is the author qualified to write on the subject? Is the author even identified? Is the Web page sponsor likely to be biased? Whenever possible, try to confirm what you have read on the Internet through a well-known, reputable source or organization. If the accuracy of the information could be affected by how old it is, check the date on which the page or article was created or updated. Used intelligently, the Internet is a wonderful tool that offers students access to many of the reliable print sources noted earlier, including government documents and newspaper archives extending back over a century.

Writing the Report

Once you have completed all your research, you can begin writing the report. Here are a few tips:

- Be sure the topic you have chosen is not too broad. You must be able to cover it adequately in a reasonable amount of time and a reasonable number of pages.

- Develop an outline for your report. You should have an introduction and a conclusion that relate to each other—and the discussion should proceed logically throughout the paper. Use headings within the paper if they will improve clarity and organization.

- Do not leave all the writing until the last minute. It is best to write a rough draft, let it sit for a few days, and then take a fresh look before beginning revisions.

- If possible, read your paper aloud. Doing so may be helpful in locating sections or phrases that don't make sense.

Remember that you *must* cite all information you have obtained from other sources, including the Internet. Plagiarism is a serious academic offense for which the penalties are severe. If you use an author's exact words, it is essential that you place them in quotation marks. Even if you reworked someone else's ideas, you must indicate the source of those ideas.

Including Citations and References

Some professors may require that students use footnotes in research reports. Others will allow students to employ the form of referencing used in this textbook, which follows the format of the American Sociological Association (ASA). If you see "(Merton 1968:27)" listed after a statement or paragraph, it means that the material has been quoted from page 27 of a work published by Merton in 1968 and listed in the reference section at the back of this textbook. (For further guidance, visit the ASA Web site, **www.asanet.org,** and in the sidebar on the left-hand side of the home page, click on "Publications," then "Journals," and then "ASA Journals Home." You will be connected to the ASA Journals home page. In the sidebar on the right-hand side of the page, under "Author's Corner," click on "Instructions to Authors" to view the Preparation Checklist for ASA Manuscripts.)

MASTERING THIS CHAPTER

Summary

Sociologists are committed to the use of the **scientific method** in their research efforts. In this chapter we examined the basic principles of the scientific method and studied various techniques used by sociologists in conducting research.

1. There are five basic steps in the **scientific method:** defining the problem, reviewing the literature, formulating the hypothesis, collecting and analyzing the data, and developing the conclusion.

2. Whenever researchers wish to study abstract concepts, such as intelligence or prejudice, they must develop workable **operational definitions.**

3. A **hypothesis** states a possible relationship between two or more variables.

4. By using a **sample,** sociologists avoid having to test everyone in a population.

5. According to the scientific method, research results must possess both **validity** and **reliability.**

6. An important part of scientific research is devising a plan for collecting data, called a **research design.** Sociologists use four major research designs: surveys, observation, experiments, and existing sources.

7. The two principal forms of **survey** research are the **interview** and the **questionnaire.**

8. **Observation** allows sociologists to study certain behaviors and communities that cannot be investigated through other research methods.

9. When sociologists wish to study a cause-and-effect relationship, they may conduct an **experiment.**

10. Sociologists also make use of existing sources in **secondary analysis** and **content analysis.**

11. The *Code of Ethics* of the American Sociological Association calls for objectivity and integrity in research, confidentiality, and disclosure of all sources of financial support.

12. Max Weber urged sociologists to practice **value neutrality** in their research by ensuring that their personal feelings do not influence their interpretation of data.

13. Technology plays an important role in sociological research, whether it be a computer database or information obtained from the Internet.

14. Despite failure to obtain government funding, researchers developed the National Health and Social Life Survey (NHSLS) to better understand the sexual practices of adults in the United States.

Critical Thinking Questions

1. Suppose your sociology instructor has asked you to do a study of homelessness. Which research technique (survey, observation, experiment, or existing sources) would you find most useful? How would you use that technique to complete your assignment?

2. How can a sociologist genuinely maintain value neutrality while studying a group that he or she finds repugnant (for example, a White supremacist organization, a satanic cult, or a group of convicted rapists)?

3. New technologies have benefited sociological research by facilitating statistical analysis and encouraging communication among scholars. Can you think of any potential drawbacks these new technologies might have for sociological investigation?

Key Terms

Causal logic The relationship between a condition or variable and a particular consequence, with one event leading to the other. (page 30)

Code of ethics The standards of acceptable behavior developed by and for members of a profession. (38)

Content analysis The systematic coding and objective recording of data, guided by some rationale. (37)

Control group The subjects in an experiment who are not introduced to the independent variable by the researcher. (36)

Control variable A factor that is held constant to test the relative impact of an independent variable. (33)

Correlation A relationship between two variables in which a change in one coincides with a change in the other. (30)

Cross-tabulation A table or matrix that shows the relationship between two or more variables. (45)

Dependent variable The variable in a causal relationship that is subject to the influence of another variable. (30)

Ethnography The study of an entire social setting through extended systematic observation. (35)

Experiment An artificially created situation that allows a researcher to manipulate variables. (36)

Experimental group The subjects in an experiment who are exposed to an independent variable introduced by a researcher. (36)

Hawthorne effect The unintended influence that observers of experiments can have on their subjects. (37)

Hypothesis A speculative statement about the relationship between two or more variables. (30)

Independent variable The variable in a causal relationship that causes or influences a change in a second variable. (30)

Interview A face-to-face or telephone questioning of a respondent to obtain desired information. (34)

Mean A number calculated by adding a series of values and then dividing by the number of values. (45)

Median The midpoint or number that divides a series of values into two groups of equal numbers of values. (45)

Mode The single most common value in a series of scores. (45)

47

Observation A research technique in which an investigator collects information through direct participation and/or by closely watching a group or community. (35)

Operational definition An explanation of an abstract concept that is specific enough to allow a researcher to assess the concept. (30)

Percentage A portion of 100. (44)

Qualitative research Research that relies on what is seen in field or naturalistic settings more than on statistical data. (34)

Quantitative research Research that collects and reports data primarily in numerical form. (34)

Questionnaire A printed or written form used to obtain information from a respondent. (34)

Random sample A sample for which every member of an entire population has the same chance of being selected. (30)

Reliability The extent to which a measure produces consistent results. (32)

Research design A detailed plan or method for obtaining data scientifically. (33)

Sample A selection from a larger population that is statistically representative of that population. (30)

Scientific method A systematic, organized series of steps that ensures maximum objectivity and consistency in researching a problem. (29)

Secondary analysis A variety of research techniques that make use of previously collected and publicly accessible information and data. (37)

Survey A study, generally in the form of an interview or questionnaire, that provides researchers with information about how people think and act. (33)

Validity The degree to which a measure or scale truly reflects the phenomenon under study. (32)

Value neutrality Max Weber's term for objectivity of sociologists in the interpretation of data. (40)

Variable A measurable trait or characteristic that is subject to change under different conditions. (30)

Self-Quiz

Read each question carefully and then select the best answer.

1. The first step in any sociological research project is to
   a. collect data.
   b. define the problem.
   c. review previous research.
   d. formulate a hypothesis.

2. An explanation of an abstract concept that is specific enough to allow a researcher to measure the concept is a(n)
   a. hypothesis.
   b. correlation.
   c. operational definition.
   d. variable.

3. The variable hypothesized to cause or influence another is called the
   a. dependent variable.
   b. hypothetical variable.
   c. correlation variable.
   d. independent variable.

4. A correlation exists when
   a. one variable causes something to occur in another variable.
   b. two or more variables are causally related.
   c. a change in one variable coincides with a change in another variable.
   d. a negative relationship exists between two variables.

5. Through which type of research technique does a sociologist ensure that data are statistically representative of the population being studied?
   a. sampling
   b. experiments
   c. validity
   d. control variables

6. In order to obtain a random sample, a researcher might
   a. administer a questionnaire to every fifth woman who enters a business office.
   b. examine the attitudes of residents of a city by interviewing every 20th name in the city's telephone book.

   c. study the attitudes of registered Democratic voters by choosing every 10th name found on a city's list of registered Democrats.
   d. do all of the above.

7. A researcher can obtain a higher response rate by using which type of survey?
   a. an interview
   b. a questionnaire
   c. representative samples
   d. observation techniques

8. In the 1930s, William F. Whyte moved into a low-income Italian neighborhood in Boston. For nearly four years, he was a member of the social circle of "corner boys" that he describes in *Street Corner Society*. His goal was to gain greater insight into the community established by these men. What type of research technique did Whyte use?
   a. experiment
   b. survey
   c. secondary analysis
   d. participant observation

9. When sociologists want to study a possible cause-and-effect relationship, they may engage in what kind of research technique?
   a. ethnography
   b. survey research
   c. secondary analysis
   d. experiment

10. Émile Durkheim's statistical analysis of suicide was an example of what kind of research technique?
   a. ethnography
   b. observation research
   c. secondary analysis
   d. experimental research

11. Unlike the typical citizen, the sociologist has a commitment to the use of the _____ method in studying society.

12. A(n) _____ is a speculative statement about the relationship between two or more factors known as variables.

13. _____ refers to the degree to which a measure or scale truly reflects the phenomenon under study.

14. In order to obtain data scientifically, researchers need to select a research _____.

15. If scientists were testing a new type of toothpaste in an experimental setting, they would administer the toothpaste to a(n) _____ group, but not to a(n) _____ group.

16. The term _____ _____ refers to the unintended influence that observers of experiments can have on their subjects.

17. Using census data in a way unintended by its initial collectors would be an example of . _____ _____.

18. Using content analysis, _____ _____ conducted a pioneering exploration of how advertisements in 1979 portrayed women as being inferior to men.

19. The American Sociological Association's *Code of* _____ requires sociologists to maintain objectivity and integrity and to preserve the confidentiality of their subjects.

20. As part of their commitment to _____ neutrality, investigators have an ethical obligation to accept research findings even when the data run counter to their own personal views or widely accepted beliefs.

THINKING ABOUT MOVIES

Erin Brockovich (Steven Soderbergh, 2000)

In this film, based on a true story, Erin Brockovich (Julia Roberts) investigates suspicious activities by Pacific Gas & Electric. She begins as a file clerk in a law firm, but her curiosity soon takes her out of the office to do field research. By interviewing families who live near a chemical dump and combing through city documents, she builds the case for a class-action lawsuit against PG&E.

This film shows a researcher using existing sources to develop a conclusion: that Pacific Gas & Electric poisoned a community's water supply. To prove that the utility company is responsible for the diseases residents contracted, Erin needs to show a causal link, not just a correlation, between the location of residents' homes near the dump site and the prevalence of disease. Look for the scenes in which Erin conducts field interviews of community members.

For Your Consideration

1. How would you describe Erin Brockovich's research method?
2. What were the dependent and independent variables in Erin's research design?

Kinsey (Bill Condon, 2004)

In this film based on the real-life researcher, Alfred Kinsey (Liam Neeson) conducts the first wide-scale investigation of human sexuality in the United States. We see Kinsey and his team interviewing subjects about their sexual practices, work that culminates in the publication of his controversial *Kinsey Report*. We see him struggle for funding and public acceptance of his work in the prudish 1940s and 1950s, when candid talk about sex violated social norms.

One of only a few mainstream movies that show research in process, *Kinsey* illustrates the ethical challenges involved in researching human behavior. Watch for scenes in which Kinsey's team strives to be value neutral by standardizing their interviewing method. (For more about the *Kinsey Report* and its influence on contemporary research into human sexuality, see the Social Policy section on page 43.)

For Your Consideration

1. Apply the American Sociological Association's *Code of Ethics* to the Kinsey study, which was done before the code went into effect. If the study were done in the same way today, how well would it comply with the code?
2. How does *Kinsey* illustrate the attempt to establish validity and reliability in the research design?

inside

What Is Culture?

Development of Culture
around the World

Cultural Variation

Role of Language

Norms and Values

Global Culture War

Culture and the Dominant
Ideology

Case Study: Culture
at Wal-Mart

Social Policy and Culture:
Bilingualism

BOXES

Sociology in the Global
Community:
Life in the Global Village

Sociology in the Global
Community: *Cultural
Survival in Brazil*

Sociology on Campus:
A Culture of Cheating?

At a fairground in Iran, a girl
enjoys a Spiderman ride. Shared
learned behavior—what we
call culture—can move across
international borders to become
part of foreign societies

In this excerpt from his journal article "Body Ritual among the Nacirema," anthropologist Horace Miner casts his observant eye on the intriguing rituals of an exotic culture. If some aspects of this culture seem familiar to you, however, you are right, for what Miner is describing is actually the culture of the United States ("Nacirema" is "American" spelled backward). The "shrine" Miner writes of is the bathroom; he correctly informs us that in this culture, one measure of wealth is how many bathrooms one's home has. In their bathroom rituals, he goes on, the Nacirema use charms and magical potions (beauty products and prescription drugs) obtained from specialized practitioners (such as hair stylists), herbalists (pharmacists), and medicine men (physicians). Using our sociological imaginations, we could update Miner's description of the Nacirema's charms, written in 1956, by adding tooth whiteners, anti-aging creams, Waterpiks, and hair gel.

When we step back and examine a culture thoughtfully and objectively, whether it is our own culture in disguise or another less familiar to us, we learn something new about society. Take Fiji, an island in the Pacific where a robust, nicely rounded body has always been the ideal for both men and women. This is a society in which "You've gained weight" traditionally has been considered a compliment, and "Your legs are skinny," an insult. Yet a recent study shows that for the first time, eating disorders have been showing up among the young people in Fiji. What has happened to change their body image? Since the introduction of cable television in 1995, many Fiji islanders, especially young women, have begun to emulate not their mothers and aunts, but the small-waisted stars of television programs currently airing there, like *Gilmore Girls* and *Lost*. Studying culture in places like Fiji, then, sheds light on our own society (A. Becker 2007; Fiji TV 2009).

In this chapter we will study the development of culture around the world, including the cultural effects of the worldwide trend toward globalization. We will see just how basic the study of culture is to sociology. Our discussion will focus both on general cultural practices found in all societies and on the wide variations that can distinguish one society from another. We will define and explore the major aspects of culture, including language, norms, sanctions, and values. We will see how cultures develop a dominant ideology, and how functionalist and conflict theorists view culture. We'll also see what can happen when a major corporation ignores cultural variations. Finally, in the Social Policy section we will look at the conflicts in cultural values that underlie current debates over bilingualism.

What Is Culture?

Culture is the totality of learned, socially transmitted customs, knowledge, material objects, and behavior. It includes the ideas, values, and artifacts (for example, DVDs, comic books, and birth control devices) of groups of people. Patriotic attachment to the flag of the United States is an aspect of culture, as is a national passion for the tango in Argentina.

Sometimes people refer to a particular person as "very cultured" or to a city as having "lots of culture." That use of the term *culture* is different from our use in this textbook. In sociological terms, culture does not refer solely to the fine arts and refined intellectual taste. It consists of *all* objects and ideas within a society, including slang words, ice cream cones, and rock music. Sociologists consider both a portrait by Rembrandt and the work of graffiti spray painters to be aspects of culture. A tribe that cultivates soil by hand has just as much culture as a people that relies on computer-operated machinery. Each people has a distinctive culture with its own characteristic ways of gathering and preparing food, constructing homes, structuring the family, and promoting standards of right and wrong.

The fact that you share a similar culture with others helps to define the group or society to which you belong. A fairly large number of people are said to constitute a **society** when they live in the same territory, are relatively independent of people outside their area, and participate in a common culture. Metropolitan Los Angeles is more populous than at least 150 nations, yet sociologists do not consider it a society in its own right. Rather, they see it as part of—and dependent on—the larger society of the United States.

A society is the largest form of human group. It consists of people who share a common heritage and culture. Members of the society learn this culture and transmit it from one generation to the next. They even preserve their distinctive culture through literature, art, video recordings, and other means of expression.

Sociologists have long recognized the many ways in which culture influences human behavior. Through what has been termed a tool kit of habits, skills, and styles, people of a common culture construct their acquisition of knowledge, their interactions with kinfolk, their entrance into the job market—in short, the way in which they live. If it were not for the social transmission of culture, each generation would have to reinvent television, not to mention the wheel (Swidler 1986).

Having a common culture also simplifies many day-to-day interactions. For example, when you buy an airline ticket, you know you don't have to bring along hundreds of dollars in cash. You can pay with a credit card. When you are part of a society, you take for granted many small (as well as more important) cultural patterns. You assume that theaters will provide seats for the audience, that physicians will not disclose confidential

Dance, like many other aspects of culture, can be expressed in many different ways. On the left, pop star Christina Aguilera executes the latest moves on tour. On the right, traditional Irish step dancers perform in a street parade.

information, and that parents will be careful when crossing the street with young children. All these assumptions reflect basic values, beliefs, and customs of the culture of the United States.

Today, when text, sound, and video can be transmitted around the world instantaneously, some aspects of culture transcend national borders. The German philosopher Theodor Adorno and others have spoken of the worldwide **culture industry** that standardizes the goods and services demanded by consumers. Adorno contends that globally, the primary effect of popular culture is to limit people's choices. Yet others have shown that the culture industry's influence does not always permeate international borders. Sometimes the culture industry is embraced; at other times, soundly rejected (Adorno [1971] 1991:98–106; Horkheimer and Adorno [1944] 2002).

Cultural Universals

All societies have developed certain common practices and beliefs, known as **cultural universals.** Many cultural universals are, in fact, adaptations to meet essential human needs, such as the need for food, shelter, and clothing. Anthropologist George Murdock (1945:124) compiled a list of cultural universals, including athletic sports, cooking, funeral ceremonies, medicine, marriage, and sexual restrictions.

The cultural practices Murdock listed may be universal, but the manner in which they are expressed varies from culture to culture. For example, one society may let its members choose their own marriage partners; another may encourage marriages arranged by the parents.

Not only does the expression of cultural universals vary from one society to another; within a society, it may also change dramatically over time. Each generation, and each year for that matter, most human cultures change and expand through the processes of innovation and diffusion.

Ethnocentrism

Many everyday statements reflect our attitude that our own culture is best. We use terms such as *underdeveloped, backward,* and *primitive* to refer to other societies. What "we" believe is a religion; what "they" believe is superstition and mythology.

It is tempting to evaluate the practices of other cultures on the basis of our own perspectives. Sociologist William Graham Sumner (1906) coined the term **ethnocentrism** to refer to the tendency to assume that one's own culture and way of life represent the norm or are superior to all others. The ethnocentric person sees his or her own group as the center or defining point of culture and views all other cultures as deviations from what

FIGURE **3-1** A PALESTINIAN WORLD VIEW

MAPPING LIFE WORLDWIDE

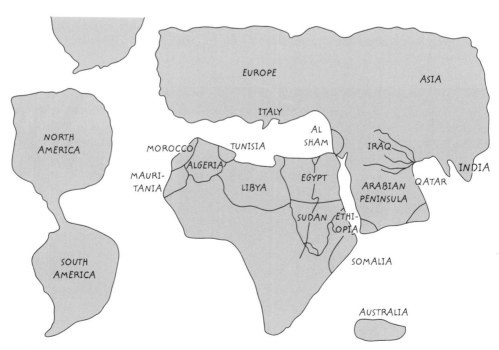

Source: Fellmann et al. 2007:76.

This map, drawn by a high school student in Gaza, reflects the emphasis on pan-Arabism in the Palestinian educational curriculum. *Al Sham* refers to "Greater Syria," a region that encompasses Syria, Jordan, Lebanon, Israel, and the Palestinian territories.

Think about It
What would be the major differences between this map and a map based on your world view? What would account for those differences?

is "normal." Westerners who think cattle are to be used for food might look down on India's Hindu religion and culture, which views the cow as sacred. Or people in one culture may dismiss as unthinkable the mate selection or child-rearing practices of another culture. As Figure 3-1 shows, our view of the world is dramatically influenced by the society in which we were raised.

Ethnocentric value judgments have complicated U.S. efforts at democratic reform of the Iraqi government. Before the 2003 war in Iraq, U.S. planners had assumed that Iraqis would adapt to a new form of government in the same way the Germans and Japanese did following World War II. But in the Iraqi culture, unlike the German and Japanese cultures, loyalty to the family and the extended clan comes before patriotism and the common good. In a country in which almost half of all people, even those in the cities, marry a first or second cousin, citizens are predisposed to favor their own kin in government and business dealings. Why trust a stranger from outside the family? What Westerners would criticize as nepotism, then, is actually an acceptable, even admirable, practice to Iraqis (J. Tierney 2003).

Conflict theorists point out that ethnocentric value judgments serve to devalue groups and to deny equal opportunities. Functionalists, on the other hand, point out that ethnocentrism serves to maintain a sense of solidarity by promoting group pride. Denigrating other nations and cultures can enhance our own patriotic feelings and belief that our way of life is superior. Yet this type of social stability is established at the expense of other peoples. Of course, ethnocentrism is hardly limited to citizens of the United States. Visitors from many African cultures are surprised at the disrespect that children in the United States show their parents. People from India may be repelled by our practice of living in the same household with dogs and cats. Many Islamic fundamentalists in the Arab world and Asia view the United States as corrupt, decadent, and doomed to destruction. All these people may feel comforted by membership in cultures that in their view are superior to ours.

Cultural Relativism

While ethnocentrism means evaluating foreign cultures using the familiar culture of the observer as a standard of correct behavior, **cultural relativism** means viewing people's behavior from the perspective of their own culture. It places a priority on understanding other cultures, rather than dismissing them as "strange" or "exotic." Unlike ethnocentrists, cultural relativists employ the kind of value neutrality in scientific study that Max Weber saw as so important.

Cultural relativism stresses that different social contexts give rise to different norms and values. Thus, we must examine practices such as polygamy, bullfighting, and monarchy within the particular contexts of the cultures in which they are found. Although cultural relativism does not suggest that we must unquestioningly accept every cultural variation, it does require a serious and unbiased effort to evaluate norms, values, and customs in light of their distinctive culture.

Consider the practice of children marrying adults. Most people in North America cannot fathom the idea of a 12-year-old girl marrying. The custom, which is illegal in the United States, is common in West Africa and South Asia. Should the United States respect such marriages? The apparent answer is no. In 2006 the U.S. government spent $623 million to discourage the

practice in 16 of the 20 countries with the highest child-marriage rates (Figure 3-2 on page 56).

From the perspective of cultural relativism, we might ask whether one society should spend its resources to dictate the norms of another. However, federal officials have defended the government's actions. They contend that child marriage deprives girls of education, threatens their health, and weakens public health efforts to combat HIV/AIDS (Jain and Kurz 2007; B. Slavin 2007).

Sociobiology and Culture

While sociology emphasizes diversity and change in the expression of culture, another school of thought, sociobiology, stresses the universal aspects of culture. **Sociobiology** is the systematic study of how biology affects human social behavior. Sociobiologists assert that many of the cultural traits humans display, such as the almost universal expectation that women will be nurturers and men will be providers, are not learned but are rooted in our genetic makeup.

Sociobiology is founded on the naturalist Charles Darwin's (1859) theory of evolution. In traveling the world, Darwin had noted small variations in species—in the shape of a bird's beak, for example—from one location to another. He theorized that over hundreds of generations, random variations in genetic makeup had helped certain members of a species to survive in a particular environment. A bird with a differently shaped beak might have been better at gathering seeds than other birds, for instance. In reproducing, these lucky individuals had passed on their advantageous genes to succeeding generations. Eventually, given their advantage in survival, individuals with the variation began to outnumber other members of the species. The species was slowly adapting to its environment. Darwin called this process of adaptation to the environment through random genetic variation *natural selection.*

Sociobiologists apply Darwin's principle of natural selection to the study of social behavior. They assume that particular forms of behavior become genetically linked to a species if they contribute to its fitness to survive (van den Berghe 1978). In its extreme form, sociobiology suggests that *all* behavior is the result of genetic or biological factors and that social interactions play no role in shaping people's conduct.

Sociobiologists do not seek to describe individual behavior on the level of "Why is Fred more aggressive than Jim?" Rather, they focus on how human nature is affected by the genetic composition of a *group* of people who share certain characteristics (such as men or women, or members of isolated tribal bands). In general, sociobiologists have stressed the basic genetic heritage that *all* humans share and have shown little interest in speculating about alleged differences between racial groups or nationalities. A few researchers have tried to trace specific behaviors, like criminal activity, to certain genetic markers, but those markers are not deterministic. Family cohesiveness, peer group behavior, and other social factors can override genetic influences on behavior (Guo et al. 2008; E. Wilson 1975, 1978).

Some researchers insist that intellectual interest in sociobiology will only deflect serious study of the more significant influence on human behavior, the social environment. Yet Lois Wladis Hoffman (1985), in her presidential address to the Society for the Psychological Study of Social Issues, argued that sociobiology poses a valuable challenge to social scientists to better document

MAPPING LIFE WORLDWIDE

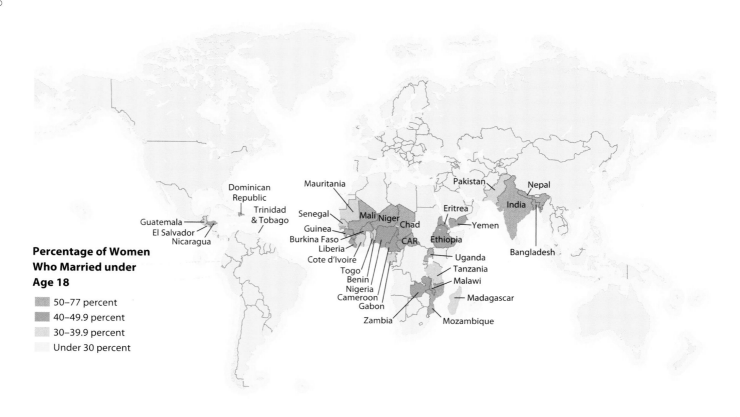

Percentage of Women Who Married under Age 18

- 50–77 percent
- 40–49.9 percent
- 30–39.9 percent
- Under 30 percent

Source: Jain and Kurz 2007:46.
In 33 countries, over 30 percent of the women under 18 are married.

their own research. Interactionists, for example, could show how social behavior is not programmed by human biology, but instead adjusts continually to the attitudes and responses of others.

Certainly most social scientists would agree that there is a biological basis for social behavior. But there is less support for the extreme positions taken by certain advocates of sociobiology. Like interactionists, conflict theorists and functionalists believe that people's behavior rather than their genetic structure defines social reality. Conflict theorists fear that the sociobiological approach could be used as an argument against efforts to assist disadvantaged people, such as schoolchildren who are not competing successfully (Guterman 2000; Segerstråle 2000; E. Wilson 2000).

Development of Culture around the World

We've come a long way from our prehistoric heritage. The human species has produced such achievements as the novels of Leo Tolstoy, the art of Pablo Picasso, and the films of Ang Lee. As we begin a new millennium, we can transmit an entire book around the world via the Internet, clone cells, and prolong lives through organ transplants. We can peer into the outermost reaches of the universe or analyze our innermost feelings. In this

section we will examine two of the social processes that make these remarkable achievements possible: innovation and the diffusion of culture through globalization and technology.

Innovation

The process of introducing a new idea or object to a culture is known as **innovation.** Innovation interests sociologists because of the social consequences of introducing something new. There are two forms of innovation: discovery and invention. **Discovery** involves making known or sharing the existence of an aspect of reality. The finding of the DNA molecule and the identification of a new moon of Saturn are both acts of discovery. A significant factor in the process of discovery is the sharing of newfound knowledge with others. In contrast, an **invention** results when existing cultural items are combined into a form that did not exist before. The bow and arrow, the automobile, and the television are all examples of inventions, as are Protestantism and democracy.

Globalization, Diffusion, and Technology

The recent emergence of Starbucks, the worldwide chain of coffeehouses, is just one illustration of the rapidly escalating trend toward globalization (see Chapter 1). While people in Asia are beginning to enjoy coffee, people in North America are discovering sushi. Some have become familiar with the *bento box,* a small

SOCIOLOGY IN THE GLOBAL COMMUNITY

3-1 Life in the Global Village

Imagine a "borderless world" in which culture, trade, commerce, money, and even people move freely from one place to another. Popular culture is widely shared, whether it be Japanese sushi or U.S. running shoes, and the English speaker who answers questions over the telephone about your credit card account is as likely to be in India or Ireland as in the United States. In this world, even the sovereignty of nations is at risk, challenged by political movements and ideologies that span nations.

There is no need to imagine this world, for we are already living in the age of globalization. African tribal youngsters wear Simpsons T-shirts; Thai teens dance to techno music; American children collect Hello Kitty items. Ethnic accessories have become a fashion statement in the United States, and Asian martial arts have swept the world.

What caused this great wave of cultural diffusion? First, sociologists take note of advances in communications technology. Satellite TV, cell phones, the Internet, and the like allow information to flow freely across the world, linking global markets. In 2008, this process reached the point where consumers could view videos on handheld devices and surf the Internet on their wireless cell phones, shopping online at Amazon.com, eBay, and other commercial Web sites from cars, airports, and cafeterias. Second, corporations in the industrial nations have become multinational, with both factories and markets in developing countries. Business leaders welcome the opportunity to sell consumer goods in populous countries such as China. Third, these multinational firms have cooperated with global financial institutions, organizations, and governments to promote free trade—unrestricted or lightly restricted commerce across national borders.

Globalization is not universally welcomed. Many critics see the dominance of "businesses without borders" as benefiting the rich, particularly the very wealthy in industrial countries,

Even James Bond movies and Britney Spears may be seen as threats to native cultures.

at the expense of the poor in less developed nations. They consider globalization to be a successor to the imperialism and colonialism that oppressed Third World nations for centuries.

Another criticism of globalization comes from people who feel overwhelmed by global culture. Embedded in the concept of globalization is the notion of the cultural domination of developing nations by more affluent nations. Simply put, people lose their traditional values and begin to identify with the culture of dominant nations. They may discard or neglect their native languages and dress as they attempt to copy the icons of mass-market entertainment and fashion. Even James Bond movies and Britney Spears may be seen as threats to native cultures, if they dominate the media at the expense of local art forms. As Sembene Ousmane, one of Africa's most prominent writers and filmmakers, noted, "[Today] we are more familiar with European fairy tales than with our own traditional stories" (World Development Forum 1990:4).

Globalization has its positive side, too. Many developing nations are taking their place in the world of commerce and bringing in much needed income. The communications revolution helps people to stay connected and gives them access to knowledge that can improve living standards and even save lives. For example, people suffering from illnesses are now accessing treatment programs that were developed outside their own nation's medical establishment. The key seems to be finding a balance between the old ways and the new—becoming modernized without leaving meaningful cultural traditions behind.

LET'S DISCUSS

1. How are you affected by globalization? Which aspects of globalization do you find advantageous and which objectionable?
2. How would you feel if the customs and traditions you grew up with were replaced by the culture or values of another country? How might you try to protect your culture?

Sources: Dodds 2000; Giddens 1991; Hirst and Thompson 1996; D. Martin et al. 2006; Ritzer 2004; Sernau 2001; Tedeschi 2006.

---

lunchbox that is often used to serve sushi. More and more cultural expressions and practices are crossing national borders and having an effect on the traditions and customs of the societies exposed to them. Sociologists use the term **diffusion** to refer to the process by which a cultural item spreads from group to group or society to society. Diffusion can occur through a variety of means, among them exploration, military conquest, missionary work, and the influence of the mass media, tourism, and the Internet (Box 3-1).

Sociologist George Ritzer coined the term *McDonaldization of society* to describe how the principles of fast-food restaurants developed in the United States have come to dominate more and more sectors of societies throughout the world (see Chapter 5). For example, hair salons and medical clinics now take walk-ins. In Hong Kong, sex selection clinics offer a menu of items, from fertility enhancement to methods of increasing the likelihood of having a child of the desired sex. Religious groups—from evangelical preachers on local stations or Web sites to priests at the Vatican Television Center—use marketing techniques similar to those that are used to sell Happy Meals.

McDonaldization is associated with the melding of cultures, through which we see more and more similarities in cultural expression. In Japan, for example, African entrepreneurs have found a thriving market for hip-hop fashions popularized by teens in the United States. And the familiar Golden Arches of McDonald's can be seen around the world. Yet corporations like McDonald's have had to make some adjustments of their own. Until 2001, McDonald's ran its overseas operations from corporate headquarters in suburban Chicago. After a few false starts, executives recognized the need to develop the restaurant's menus and marketing strategies overseas, relying on advice from local people. Now, at over 3,700 restaurants in Japan, customers can enjoy the Tamago Burger—beef, bacon, and fried egg with special sauces. In India, patrons who don't eat beef can order a double chicken-patty sandwich known as the Maharaja Mac. And in Austria, the locals' love of coffee, cake, and conversation has inspired the McCafe (Hughlett 2008; Ritzer 2002, 2008).

Technology in its many forms has increased the speed of cultural diffusion and broadened the distribution of cultural elements. Sociologist Gerhard Lenski has defined **technology** as "cultural information about how to use the material resources of the environment to satisfy human needs and desires" (Nolan and Lenski 2009:37). Today's technological developments no longer

Cultural practices may spread through diffusion, but they undergo change in the process. Because this McDonald's restaurant in Riyadh serves Saudi Arabians, McRibs are out and McArabia—grilled chicken on flatbread—is in. Note the separate lines for men and women.

await publication in journals with limited circulation. Press conferences, often carried simultaneously on the Internet, trumpet the new developments.

Technology not only accelerates the diffusion of scientific innovations but also transmits culture. The English language and North American culture dominate the Internet and World Wide Web. Such control, or at least dominance, of technology influences the direction of diffusion of culture. For example, Web sites cover even the most superficial aspects of U.S. culture but offer little information about the pressing issues faced by citizens of other nations. People all over the world find it easier to visit electronic chat rooms about the latest reality TV shows than to learn about their own governments' policies on day care or infant nutrition.

Sociologist William F. Ogburn (1922) made a useful distinction between the elements of material and nonmaterial culture. **Material culture** refers to the physical or technological aspects of our daily lives, including food, houses, factories, and raw materials. **Nonmaterial culture** refers to ways of using material objects, as well as to customs, beliefs, philosophies, governments, and patterns of communication. Generally, the nonmaterial culture is more resistant to change than the material culture. Consequently, Ogburn introduced the term **culture lag** to refer to the period of maladjustment when the nonmaterial culture is still struggling to adapt to new material conditions. For example, the ethics of using the Internet, particularly issues concerning privacy and censorship, have not yet caught up with the explosion in Internet use and technology (Griswold 2004).

Resistance to technological change can lead not only to culture lag, but to some real questions of cultural survival (Box 3-2).

use your sociological *imagination*

If you grew up in your parents' generation—without computers, e-mail, MP3 players, and cell phones—how would your daily life differ from the one you lead today?

Cultural Variation

Each culture has a unique character. Inuit tribes in northern Canada, wrapped in furs and dieting on whale blubber, have little in common with farmers in Southeast Asia, who dress for the heat and subsist mainly on the rice they grow in their paddies. Cultures adapt to meet specific sets of circumstances, such as climate, level of technology, population, and geography. Thus, despite the presence of cultural universals such as courtship and religion, great diversity exists among the world's many cultures. Moreover, even *within* a single nation, certain segments of the populace develop cultural patterns that differ from the patterns of the dominant society.

Subcultures

Rodeo riders, residents of a retirement community, workers on an offshore oil rig—all are examples of what sociologists refer to as *subcultures*. A **subculture** is a segment of society that shares a distinctive pattern of mores, folkways, and values that differs from the pattern of the larger society. In a sense, a subculture can be thought of as a culture existing within a larger, dominant culture. The existence of many subcultures is characteristic of complex societies such as the United States.

Members of a subculture participate in the dominant culture while at the same time engaging in unique and distinctive forms of behavior. Frequently, a subculture will develop an **argot,** or specialized language, that distinguishes it from the wider society. Athletes who play *parkour,* an extreme sport that combines forward running with fence leaping and the vaulting of walls, water barriers, and even moving cars, speak an argot they devised especially to describe their feats. Parkour runners talk about doing

When a society's nonmaterial culture (its values and laws) does not keep pace with rapid changes in its material culture, people experience an awkward period of maladjustment called culture lag. The transition to nuclear power generation that began in the second half of the 20th century brought widespread protests against the new technology, as well as serious accidents that government officials were poorly prepared to deal with. Tensions over the controversial technology have not run as high in some countries as in others, however. France, where this nuclear power plant is situated, generates 78 percent of all its electricity through nuclear power. The technology is not as controversial there as in the United States and Canada, which generate less than 20 percent of their electricity through nuclear reaction.

SOCIOLOGY IN THE GLOBAL COMMUNITY

3-2 Cultural Survival in Brazil

When the first Portuguese ships landed on the coast of what we now know as Brazil, more than 2 million people inhabited the vast, mineral-rich land. They lived in small, isolated settlements, spoke a variety of languages, and embraced many different cultural traditions.

Today, over five centuries later, Brazil's population has grown to more than 180 million, only about 500,000 of whom are indigenous peoples descended from the original inhabitants. Over 200 different indigenous groups have survived, living a life tied closely to the land and the rivers, just as their ancestors did. But over the past two generations, their numbers have dwindled as booms in mining, logging, oil drilling, and agriculture have encroached on their land and their settlements.

Many indigenous groups were once nomads, moving around from one hunting or fishing ground to another. Now they are hemmed in on the reservations the government confined them to, surrounded by huge farms or ranches whose owners deny their right to live off the land. State officials may insist that laws restrict the development of indigenous lands, but indigenous peoples tell a different story. In Mato Grosso, a heavily forested state near the Amazon River, loggers have been clear-cutting the land at a rate that alarms the Bororo, an indigenous group that has lived in the area for centuries. According to one elder, the Bororo are now confined to six small reservations of about 500 square miles—much less than the area officially granted them in the 19th century.

> *In Mato Grosso, a heavily forested state near the Amazon River, loggers have been clear-cutting the land at a rate that alarms the Bororo.*

Indigenous tribes are no match for powerful agribusiness interests, one of whose leaders is also governor of Mato Grosso. Blairo Maggi, head of the largest soybean producer in the world, has publicly trivialized the consequences of the massive deforestation occurring in Mato Grosso. Though Maggi said he would propose a three-year moratorium on development, opponents are skeptical that he will follow through on the promise.

Meanwhile, indigenous groups like the Bororo struggle to maintain their culture in the face of dwindling resources. Though the tribe still observes the traditional initiation rites for adolescent boys, members are finding it difficult to continue their hunting and fishing rituals, given the scarcity of game and fish in the area. Pesticides in the runoff from nearby farms have poisoned the water they fish and bathe in, threatening both their health and their culture's survival.

LET'S DISCUSS

1. How do you think the frontier in Brazil today compares to the American West in the 1800s? What similarities do you see?
2. What does society lose when indigenous cultures die?

Sources: Chu 2005; Instituto del Tercer Mundo 2005.

King Kong vaults—diving arms first over a wall or grocery cart and landing in a standing position. They may follow this maneuver with a *tic tac*—kicking off a wall to overcome some kind of obstacle (Wilkinson 2007).

Such argot allows insiders—the members of the subculture—to understand words with special meanings. It also establishes patterns of communication that outsiders can't understand. Sociologists associated with the interactionist perspective emphasize that language and symbols offer a powerful way for a subculture to feel cohesive and maintain its identity.

In India, a new subculture has developed among employees at the international call centers established by multinational corporations. To serve customers in the United States and Europe, the young men and women who work there must be fluent speakers of English. But the corporations that employ them demand more than proficiency in a foreign language; they expect their Indian employees to adopt Western values and work habits, including the grueling pace U.S. workers take for granted. In return they offer perks such as Western-style dinners, dances, and coveted consumer goods. Significantly, they allow employees to take the day off only on U.S. holidays, like Labor Day and Thanksgiving—not on Indian holidays like Diwali, the Hindu festival of lights. While most Indian families are home celebrating, call center employees see only each other; when they have the day off, no one else is free to socialize with them. As a result, these employees have formed a tight-knit subculture

Employees of an international call center in Simla, India, socialize after finishing a seven-hour shift on the telephone. Call center employees, who are isolated from other Indians by their adherence to Western holidays and odd working hours, have formed a tight-knit subculture based partly on their appreciation for Western-style consumer goods.

based on hard work and a taste for Western luxury goods and leisure-time pursuits.

Increasingly, call center workers are the object of criticism from Indians who live a more conventional lifestyle centered on family and holiday traditions. In response to such negative public opinion, the government of the Indian state where call centers are located has banned schools from teaching English rather than Kannada, the local language. Beginning in 2008, some 300,000 students were affected by the ban (Chu 2007; Kalita 2006).

Another shared characteristic among some employees at Indian call centers is their contempt for the callers they serve. In performing their monotonous, repetitive job day after day, hundreds of thousands of these workers have come to see the faceless Americans they deal with as slow, often rude customers. As described in the recent Indian bestseller *One Night @ the Call Centre,* new trainees quickly learn the "35 = 10 rule," meaning that a 35-year-old American's IQ is the same as a 10-year-old Indian's. Such shared understandings underpin this emerging subculture (Bhagat 2007; Gentleman 2006).

Functionalist and conflict theorists agree that variation exists within a culture. Functionalists view subcultures as variations of particular social environments and as evidence that differences can exist within a common culture. However, conflict theorists suggest that variations often reflect the inequality of social arrangements within a society. A conflict theorist would view the challenges to dominant social norms by African American activists, the feminist movement, and the disability rights movement as reflections of inequity based on race, gender, and disability status. Conflict theorists also argue that subcultures sometimes emerge when the dominant society unsuccessfully tries to suppress a practice, such as the use of illegal drugs.

Countercultures

By the end of the 1960s, an extensive subculture had emerged in the United States, composed of young people turned off by a society they believed was too materialistic and technological. This group included primarily political radicals and hippies who had dropped out of mainstream social institutions. These young men and women rejected the pressure to accumulate more and more cars, larger and larger homes, and an endless array of material goods. Instead, they expressed a desire to live in a culture based on more humanistic values, such as sharing, love, and coexistence with the environment. As a political force, this subculture opposed the United States' involvement in the war in Vietnam and encouraged draft resistance (Flacks 1971; Roszak 1969).

When a subculture conspicuously and deliberately opposes certain aspects of the larger culture, it is known as a **counterculture.** Countercultures typically thrive among the young, who have the least investment in the existing culture. In most cases, a 20-year-old can adjust to new cultural standards more easily than someone who has spent 60 years following the patterns of the dominant culture (Zellner 1995).

In the wake of the terrorist attacks of September 11, 2001, people around the United States learned of the existence of terrorist groups operating as a counterculture within their country. This was a situation that generations have lived with in Northern Ireland, Israel and the Palestinian territory, and many other parts of the world. But terrorist cells are not necessarily fueled only by outsiders. Frequently people become disenchanted with the policies of their own country, and a few take very violent steps.

"IT'S ENDLESS. WE JOIN A COUNTER-CULTURE; IT BECOMES THE CULTURE. WE JOIN ANOTHER COUNTER-CULTURE; IT BECOMES THE CULTURE..."

Cultures change. Fashions we once regarded as unacceptable—such as men wearing earrings and people wearing jeans in the workplace—or associated with fringe groups (such as men and women with tattoos) are now widely accepted. These countercultural practices have been absorbed by mainstream culture.

Culture Shock

Anyone who feels disoriented, uncertain, out of place, or even fearful when immersed in an unfamiliar culture may be experiencing **culture shock.** For example, a resident of the United States who visits certain areas in China and wants local meat for dinner may be stunned to learn that the specialty is dog meat. Similarly, someone from a strict Islamic culture may be shocked when first seeing the comparatively provocative dress styles and open displays of affection that are common in the United States and various European cultures.

All of us, to some extent, take for granted the cultural practices of our society. As a result, it can be surprising and even disturbing to realize that other cultures do not follow our way of life. The fact is that customs that seem strange to us may be considered normal and proper in other cultures, which may see our own mores and folkways as odd.

---

use your sociological *imagination*

You arrive in a developing African country as a Peace Corps volunteer. What aspects of a very different culture do you think would be the hardest to adjust to? What might the citizens of that country find shocking about your culture?

Role of Language

Language is one of the major elements of culture that underlie cultural variations. It is also an important component of cultural capital. Recall from Chapter 1 that Pierre Bourdieu used the term *cultural capital* to describe noneconomic assets, such as family background and past educational investments, which are reflected in a person's knowledge of language and the arts.

Members of a society generally share a common language, which facilitates day-to-day exchanges with others. When you ask a hardware store clerk for a flashlight, you don't need to draw a picture of the instrument. You share the same cultural term for a small, portable, battery-operated light. However, if you were in England and needed this item, you would have to ask for an electric torch. Of course, even within the same society, a term can have a number of different meanings. In the United States, *pot* signifies both a container that is used for cooking and an intoxicating drug. In this section we will examine the cultural influence of language, which includes both the written and spoken word and nonverbal communication.

Language: Written and Spoken

Seven thousand languages are spoken in the world today—many more than the number of countries. Within a nation's political boundaries, the number of languages spoken may range from only one (as in North Korea) to several hundred (as in Papua New Guinea, with 820). For the speakers of each one, whether they number 2,000 or 200 million, language is fundamental to their shared culture (Gordon 2005).

The English language, for example, makes extensive use of words dealing with war. We speak of "conquering" space, "fighting" the "battle" of the budget, "waging war" on drugs, making a "killing" on the stock market, and "bombing" an examination; something monumental or great is "the bomb." An observer from an entirely different and warless culture could gauge the importance that war and the military have had in our lives simply by recognizing the prominence that militaristic terms have in our language. On the other hand, in the Old West, words such as *gelding, stallion, mare, piebald,* and *sorrel* were all used to describe one animal—the horse. Even if we knew little of that period in history, we could conclude from the list of terms that horses were important to the culture. Similarly, the Sami people of northern Norway and Sweden have a rich diversity of terms for snow, ice, and reindeer (Haviland et al. 2008; Magga 2006).

Language is, in fact, the foundation of every culture. **Language** is an abstract system of word meanings and symbols for all aspects of culture. It includes speech, written characters, numerals, symbols, and nonverbal gestures and expressions. Because language is the foundation of every culture, the ability to speak other languages is crucial to intercultural relations. Throughout the Cold War era, beginning in the 1950s and continuing well into the 1970s, the U.S. government encouraged the study of Russian by developing special language schools for diplomats and military advisers who dealt with the Soviet Union. And following September 11, 2001, the nation recognized how few skilled translators it had for Arabic and other languages spoken in Muslim countries. Language quickly became a key, not only to tracking potential terrorists, but to building diplomatic bridges with Muslim countries willing to help in the war against terrorism.

Language does more than simply describe reality; it also serves to *shape* the reality of a culture. For example, most people in the United States cannot easily make the verbal distinctions concerning snow and ice that are possible in the Sami culture. As a result, they are less likely to notice such differences.

A native speaker trains instructors from the Oneida Nation of New York in the Berlitz method of language teaching. Many Native American tribes are taking steps to recover their seldom-used languages, realizing that language is the essential foundation of any culture.

The **Sapir-Whorf hypothesis,** named for two linguists, describes the role of language in shaping our interpretation of reality. According to Sapir and Whorf, because people can conceptualize the world only through language, language *precedes* thought. Thus, the word symbols and grammar of a language organize the world for us. The Sapir-Whorf hypothesis also holds that language is not a given. Rather, it is culturally determined and encourages a distinctive interpretation of reality by focusing our attention on certain phenomena (Sapir 1929).

For decades, the Navajo have referred to cancer as *lood doo na'dziihii.* Now, through a project funded by the National Cancer Institute, the tribal college is seeking to change the phrase. Why? Literally, the phrase means "the sore that does not heal," and health educators are concerned that tribal members who have been diagnosed with cancer view it as a death sentence. Their effort to change the Navajo language, not easy in itself, is complicated by the Navajo belief that to talk about the disease is to bring it on one's people (Fonseca 2008).

Similarly, feminists have noted that gender-related language can reflect—although in itself it does not determine—the traditional acceptance of men and women in certain occupations. Each time we use a term such as *mailman, policeman,* or *fireman,* we are implying (especially to young children) that these occupations can be filled only by males. Yet many women work as *letter carriers, police officers,* and *firefighters*—a fact that is being increasingly recognized and legitimized through the use of such nonsexist language.

Language can also transmit stereotypes related to race. Look up the meanings of the adjective *black* in dictionaries published in the United States. You will find *dismal, gloomy or forbidding, destitute of moral light or goodness, atrocious, evil, threatening, clouded with anger.* In contrast, dictionaries list *pure* and *innocent* among the meanings of the adjective *white.* Through such patterns of language, our culture reinforces positive associations with the term (and skin color) *white* and negative associations with *black.* Is it surprising, then, that a list meant to prevent people from working in a profession is called a *blacklist,* while a lie that we think of as somewhat acceptable is called a *white lie?*

Language can shape how we see, taste, smell, feel, and hear. It also influences the way we think about the people, ideas, and objects around us. Language communicates a culture's most important norms, values, and sanctions. That's why the decline of an old language or the introduction of a new one is such a sensitive issue in many parts of the world (see the Social Policy section at the end of this chapter).

Using American Sign Language, a form of nonverbal communication, a football coach discusses a play with his team. The Silent Warriors, four-time national champions and the pride of the Alabama School for the Deaf, have defeated both hearing and nonhearing teams.

Nonverbal Communication

If you don't like the way a meeting is going, you might suddenly sit back, fold your arms, and turn down the corners of your mouth. When you see a friend in tears, you may give a quick hug. After winning a big game, you probably high-five your teammates. These are all examples of *nonverbal communication,* the use of gestures, facial expressions, and other visual images to communicate.

We are not born with these expressions. We learn them, just as we learn other forms of language, from people who share our same culture. This statement is as true for the basic expressions of happiness and sadness as it is for more complex emotions, such as shame or distress (Fridlund et al. 1987).

Like other forms of language, nonverbal communication is not the same in all cultures. For example, sociological research done at the micro level documents that people from various cultures differ in the degree to which they touch others during the course of normal social interactions. Even experienced travelers are sometimes caught off guard by these differences. In Saudi Arabia, a middle-aged man may want to hold hands with a partner after closing a business deal. In Egypt, men walk hand in hand in the street; in cafés, they fall asleep while lounging in each other's arms. These gestures, which would shock an American businessman, are considered compliments in those cultures. The meaning of hand signals is another form of nonverbal communication that can differ from one culture to the next. In Australia, the thumbs-up sign is considered rude (Passero 2002; Vaughan 2007).

A related form of communication is the use of symbols to convey meaning to others. **Symbols** are the gestures, objects, and words that form the basis of human communication. The thumbs-up gesture, a gold star sticker, and the smiley face in an e-mail are all symbols. Often deceptively simple, many symbols are rich in meaning, and may not convey the same meaning in all social contexts. Around someone's neck, for example, a cross can symbolize religious reverence; over a grave site, a belief in everlasting life; or set in flames, racial hatred.

Some symbols or gestures, such as the basic emotional expressions—a smile, a look of horror—may be close to universal. Not long ago, a team of linguists, social scientists, and physical scientists collaborated on a system for communicating with those who live thousands of years from now, long after people have ceased to speak our languages. The challenge was to create a series of signs and explanations that would warn future generations of the dangers posed by the Waste Isolation Pilot Plant (WIPP), a nuclear waste repository in New Mexico. For the next few centuries, warning signs engraved in English, Spanish, Russian, French, Chinese, Arabic, and Navajo will alert those in the area to the presence of the underground dump, which will remain highly radioactive for at least 10,000 years. But the signs also include pictographs that researchers hope will be understandable to people who live millennia from now, no matter what their language (Figure 3-3; Department of Energy 2004; Piller 2006).

use your sociological *imagination*

Besides your language and gestures, what other aspects of your culture might seem unusual to people in India, Japan, or France?

Norms and Values

"Wash your hands before dinner." "Thou shalt not kill." "Respect your elders." All societies have ways of encouraging and enforcing what they view as appropriate behavior while discouraging and punishing what they consider to be improper behavior. They also have a collective idea of what is good and desirable in

FIGURE **3-3** A TIMELESS ALERT

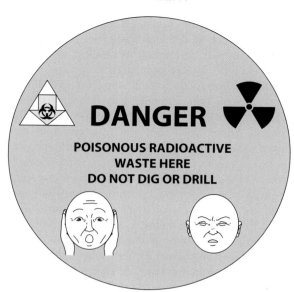

The symbols on this subsurface marker at the Waste Isolation Pilot Plant in New Mexico are an attempt to communicate the presence of hazardous waste to people who may live 10,000 years from now. Would these symbols convince you not to dig? Might future generations misinterpret them?

life—or not. In this section we will learn to distinguish between the closely related concepts of norms and values.

Norms

Norms are the established standards of behavior maintained by a society. For a norm to become significant, it must be widely shared and understood. For example, in movie theaters in the United States, we typically expect that people will be quiet while

vary, depending on the particular film and type of audience. People who are viewing a serious artistic film will be more likely to insist on the norm of silence than those who are watching a slapstick comedy or horror movie.

Types of Norms Sociologists distinguish between norms in two ways. First, norms are classified as either formal or informal. **Formal norms** generally have been written down and specify strict punishments for violators. In the United States, we often formalize norms into laws, which are very precise in defining proper and improper behavior. Sociologist Donald Black (1995) has termed **law** "governmental social control," meaning that laws are formal norms enforced by the state. Laws are just one example of formal norms. The requirements for a college major and the rules of a card game are also considered formal norms.

In contrast, **informal norms** are generally understood but not precisely recorded. Standards of proper dress are a common example of informal norms. Our society has no specific punishment or sanction for a person who comes to school, say, wearing a monkey suit. Making fun of the nonconforming student is usually the most likely response.

Norms are also classified by their relative importance to society. When classified in this way, they are known as *mores* and *folkways*. **Mores** (pronounced "MOR-ays") are norms deemed highly necessary to the welfare of a society, often because they embody the most cherished principles of a people. Each society demands obedience to its mores; violation can lead to severe penalties. Thus, the United States has strong mores against murder, treason, and child abuse, which have been institutionalized into formal norms.

Folkways are norms governing everyday behavior. Folkways play an important role in shaping the daily behavior of members

In Iraq, a female member of the U.S. Army searches a covered Muslim woman. The searches, which are necessary to prevent terrorist attacks, violate a Muslim norm that forbids touching by strangers.

When is a kiss more than a kiss? In India, public displays of affection are decidedly not the norm, even among movie stars. When Richard Gere swept actress Shilpa Shethy into his arms at an AIDS awareness event, protests erupted, and some outraged onlookers demanded that he be sanctioned.

of a culture. Society is less likely to formalize folkways than mores, and their violation raises comparatively little concern. For example, walking up a down escalator in a department store challenges our standards of appropriate behavior, but it will not result in a fine or a jail sentence.

In many societies around the world, folkways exist to reinforce patterns of male dominance. Various folkways reveal men's hierarchical position above women within the traditional Buddhist areas of Southeast Asia. In the sleeping cars of trains, women do not sleep in upper berths above men. Hospitals that house men on the first floor do not place women patients on the second floor. Even on clotheslines, folkways dictate male dominance: women's attire is hung lower than that of men (Bulle 1987).

use your sociological *imagination*

You are a high school principal. What norms would you want to govern the students' behavior? How might those norms differ from those appropriate for college students?

Acceptance of Norms People do not follow norms, whether mores or folkways, in all situations. In some cases, they can evade a norm because they know it is weakly enforced. It is illegal for U.S. teenagers to drink alcoholic beverages, yet drinking by minors is common throughout the nation. (In fact, teenage alcoholism is a serious social problem.)

In some instances, behavior that appears to violate society's norms may actually represent adherence to the norms of a particular group. Teenage drinkers are conforming to the standards of their peer group when they violate norms that condemn underage drinking. Similarly, business executives who use shady accounting techniques may be responding to a corporate culture that demands the maximization of profits at any cost, including the deception of investors and government regulatory agencies.

Norms are violated in some instances because one norm conflicts with another. For example, suppose that you live in an apartment building and one night hear the screams of the woman next door, who is being beaten by her husband. If you decide to intervene by ringing their doorbell or calling the police, you are violating the norm of minding your own business, while at the same time following the norm of assisting a victim of violence.

Even if norms do not conflict, there are always exceptions to any norm. The same action, under different circumstances, can cause one to be viewed as either a hero or a villain. Secretly taping telephone conversations is normally considered illegal and abhorrent. However, it can be done with a court order to obtain valid evidence for a criminal trial. We would heap praise on a government agent who used such methods to convict an organized crime figure. In our culture, we tolerate killing another human being in self-defense, and we actually reward killing in warfare.

Acceptance of norms is subject to change as the political, economic, and social conditions of a culture are transformed. Until the 1960s, for example, formal norms throughout much of the United States prohibited the marriage of people from different racial groups. Over the past half century, however, such legal prohibitions were cast aside. The process of change can be seen today in the increasing acceptance of single parents and growing support for the legalization of marriage between same-sex couples (see Chapter 14).

When circumstances require the sudden violation of long-standing cultural norms, the change can upset an entire population. In Iraq, where Muslim custom strictly forbids touching by strangers for men and especially for women, the war that began in 2003 has brought numerous daily violations of the norm. Outside important mosques, government offices, and other facilities likely to be targeted by terrorists, visitors must now be patted down and have their bags searched by Iraqi security guards. To reduce the discomfort caused by the procedure, women are searched by female guards and men by male guards. Despite that concession, and the fact that many Iraqis admit or even insist on the need for such measures, people still wince at the invasion of their personal privacy. In reaction to the searches, Iraqi women have begun to limit the contents of the bags they carry or simply to leave them at home (Rubin 2003).

Sanctions

Suppose a football coach sends a 12th player onto the field. Imagine a college graduate showing up in shorts for a job interview at

TABLE 3-1 NORMS AND SANCTIONS

Norms	Sanctions	
	Positive	Negative
Formal	Salary bonus	Demotion
	Testimonial dinner	Firing from a job
	Medal	Jail sentence
	Diploma	Expulsion
Informal	Smile	Frown
	Compliment	Humiliation
	Cheers	Bullying

a large bank. Or consider a driver who neglects to put any money into a parking meter. These people have violated widely shared and understood norms. So what happens? In each of these situations, the person will receive sanctions if his or her behavior is detected.

Sanctions are penalties and rewards for conduct concerning a social norm. Note that the concept of *reward* is included in this definition. Conformity to a norm can lead to positive sanctions such as a pay raise, a medal, a word of gratitude, or a pat on the back. Negative sanctions include fines, threats, imprisonment, and stares of contempt.

Table 3-1 summarizes the relationship between norms and sanctions. As you can see, the sanctions that are associated with formal norms (which are written down and codified) tend to be formal as well. If a college coach sends too many players onto the field, the team will be penalized 15 yards. The driver who fails to put money in the parking meter will receive a ticket and have to pay a fine. But sanctions for violations of informal norms can vary. The college graduate who goes to the bank interview in shorts will probably lose any chance of getting the job; on the other hand, he or she might be so brilliant that bank officials will overlook the unconventional attire.

The entire fabric of norms and sanctions in a culture reflects that culture's values and priorities. The most cherished values will be most heavily sanctioned; matters regarded as less critical will carry light and informal sanctions.

Values

Though we each have our own personal set of standards—which may include caring or fitness or success in business—we also share a general set of objectives as members of a society. Cultural **values** are these collective conceptions of what is considered good, desirable, and proper—or bad, undesirable, and improper—in a culture. They indicate what people in a given culture prefer as well as what they find important and morally right (or wrong). Values may be specific, such as honoring one's parents and owning a home, or they may be more general, such as health, love, and democracy. Of course, the members of a society do not uniformly share its values. Angry political debates and billboards promoting conflicting causes tell us that much.

Values influence people's behavior and serve as criteria for evaluating the actions of others. The values, norms, and sanctions of a culture are often directly related. For example, if a culture places a high value on the institution of marriage, it may have norms (and strict sanctions) that prohibit the act of adultery or make divorce difficult. If a culture views private property as a basic value, it will probably have stiff laws against theft and vandalism.

The values of a culture may change, but most remain relatively stable during any one person's lifetime. Socially shared, intensely felt values are a fundamental part of our lives in the United States. Sociologist Robin Williams (1970) has offered a list of basic values. It includes achievement, efficiency, material comfort, nationalism, equality, and the supremacy of science and reason over faith. Obviously, not all 307 million people in this country agree on all these values, but such a list serves as a starting point in defining the national character.

Each year more than 240,580 entering college students at 340 of the nation's four-year colleges fill out a questionnaire about their attitudes. Because this survey focuses on an array of issues, beliefs, and life goals, it is commonly cited as a barometer of the nation's values. The respondents are asked what values are personally important to them. Over the past 40 years, the value of "being very well-off financially" has shown the strongest gain in popularity; the proportion of first-year college students who endorse this value as "essential" or "very important" rose from 44 percent in 1967 to 76.8 percent in 2008 (Figure 3-4 on Page 66). In contrast, the value that has shown the most striking decline in endorsement by students is "developing a meaningful philosophy of life." While this value was the most popular in the 1967 survey, endorsed by more than 80 percent of the respondents, it had fallen to sixth place on the list by 2008, when it was endorsed by 51.4 percent of students entering college.

During the 1980s and 1990s, support for values having to do with money, power, and status grew. At the same time, support for certain values having to do with social awareness and altruism, such as "helping others," declined. According to the 2008 nationwide survey, only 44.7 percent of first-year college students stated that "influencing social values" was an "essential" or "very important" goal. The proportion of students for whom "helping to promote racial understanding" was an essential or very important goal reached a record high of 42 percent in 1992, then fell to 37.3 percent in 2008. Like other aspects of culture, such as language and norms, a nation's values are not necessarily fixed.

Whether the slogan is "Plant a Tree" or "Think Green," students have been exposed to values associated with environmentalism. How many of them accept those values? Poll results over the past 40 years show fluctuations, with a high of nearly 46 percent of students indicating a desire to become involved in cleaning up the environment. Beginning in the 1980s, student support for embracing this objective had dropped to around 20 percent or even lower (see Figure 3-4). Even with recent attention to global warming, the proportion remains level at only 29.5 percent of first-year students in 2008.

Recently, cheating has become a hot issue on college campuses. Professors who take advantage of computerized services that can identify plagiarism, such as the search engine Google, have been shocked to learn that many of the papers their students hand in

FIGURE 3-4 LIFE GOALS OF FIRST-YEAR COLLEGE STUDENTS IN THE UNITED STATES, 1966–2008

Sources: UCLA Higher Education Research Institute, as reported in Astin et al. 1994; Pryor et al. 2007, 2008.

Think about It

Why do you think values have shifted among college students in the past few decades? Which of these values is important to you?

are plagiarized in whole or in part. Box 3-3 examines the shift in values that underlies this decline in academic integrity.

Another value that has begun to change recently, not just among students but among the public in general, is the right to privacy. Americans have always valued their privacy and resented government intrusions into their personal lives. In the aftermath of the terrorist attacks of September 11, 2001, however, many citizens called for greater protection against the threat of terrorism. In response, the U.S. government broadened its surveillance powers and increased its ability to monitor people's behavior without court approval. In 2001, shortly after the attacks, Congress passed the Patriot Act, which empowers the FBI to access individuals' medical, library, student, and phone records without informing them or obtaining a search warrant.

Global Culture War

For almost a generation, public attention in the United States has focused on **culture war,** or the polarization of society over controversial cultural elements. Originally, in the 1990s, the term referred to political debates over heated issues such as abortion, religious expression, gun control, and sexual orientation. Soon, however, it took on a global meaning—especially after 9/11, as Americans wondered, "Why do they hate us?" Through 2000, global studies of public opinion had reported favorable views of the United States in countries as diverse as Morocco and Germany. But by 2003, in the wake of the U.S. invasion of Iraq,

foreign opinion of the United States had become quite negative (J. Hunter 1991; Kohut 2005, 2007).

In the past 20 years, extensive efforts have been made to compare values in different nations, recognizing the challenges in interpreting value concepts in a similar manner across cultures. Psychologist Shalom Schwartz has measured values in more than 60 countries. Around the world, certain values are widely shared, including benevolence, which is defined as "forgiveness and loyalty." In contrast, power, defined as "control or dominance over people and resources," is a value that is endorsed much less often (Hitlin and Piliavin 2004; S. Schwartz and Bardi 2001).

Despite this evidence of shared values, some scholars have interpreted the terrorism, genocide, wars, and military occupations of the early 21st century as a "clash of civilizations." According to this thesis, cultural and religious identities, rather than national or political loyalties, are becoming the prime source of international conflict. Critics of this thesis point out that conflict over values is nothing new; only our ability to create havoc and violence has grown. Furthermore, speaking of a clash of "civilizations" disguises the sharp divisions that exist within large groups. Christianity, for example, runs the gamut from Quaker-style pacifism to certain elements of the Ku Klux Klan's ideology (Berman 2003; Huntington 1993; Said 2001).

Culture and the Dominant Ideology

Functionalist and conflict theorists agree that culture and society are mutually supportive, but for different reasons. Functionalists maintain that social stability requires a consensus and the support of society's members; strong central values and common norms provide that support. This view of culture became popular in sociology beginning in the 1950s. It was borrowed from British anthropologists who saw cultural traits as a stabilizing element in a culture. From a functionalist perspective, a cultural trait or practice will persist if it performs functions that society seems to need or contributes to overall social stability and consensus.

Conflict theorists agree that a common culture may exist, but they argue that it serves to maintain the privileges of certain groups. Moreover, while protecting their own self-interest, powerful groups may keep others in a subservient position. The term **dominant ideology** describes the set of cultural beliefs and practices that helps to maintain powerful social, economic, and political interests. This concept was first used by Hungarian Marxist Georg Lukacs (1923) and Italian Marxist Antonio Gramsci (1929), but it did not gain an audience in the United States until the early 1970s. In Karl Marx's view, a capitalist society has a dominant ideology that serves the interests of the ruling class.

From a conflict perspective, the dominant ideology has major social significance. Not only do a society's most powerful groups and institutions control wealth and property; even more important, they control the means of producing beliefs about reality through religion, education, and the media. Feminists would also argue that if all a society's most important institutions tell women they should be subservient to men, that dominant

SOCIOLOGY ON CAMPUS

3-3　A Culture of Cheating?

On November 21, 2002, after issuing several warnings, officials at the U.S. Naval Academy seized the computers of almost 100 midshipmen suspected of downloading movies and music illegally from the Internet. Officers at the school may have taken the unusually strong action to avoid liability on the part of the U.S. government, which owns the computers students were using. But across the nation, college administrators have been trying to restrain students from downloading pirated entertainment for free. The practice is so widespread, it has been slowing down the high-powered computer networks colleges and universities depend on for research and admissions.

Illegal downloading is just one aspect of the growing problem of copyright violation, both on campus and off. Now that college students can use personal computers to surf the Internet, most do their research online. Apparently, the temptation to cut and paste passages from Web site postings and pass them off as one's own is irresistible to many. Surveys done by the Center for Academic Integrity show that from 1999 to 2005, the percentage of students who approved of this type of plagiarism rose from 10 percent to 41 percent. At the same time, the percentage who considered cutting and pasting from the Internet to be a serious form of cheating fell from 68 percent to 23 percent. Perhaps the worst form of Internet plagiarism is the purchase of entire papers from other writers. Increasingly, the Web sites that sell essays to students are based in other countries, including India, Ukraine, Nigeria, and the Philippines.

A recent cross-cultural study compared cheating by students in Lebanon and the United States. Researchers found a high willingness to cheat among students in both countries: 54 percent of the U.S. students and 80 percent of the Lebanese

students reported having cheated in some way during the past year. In both cultures, students were more willing to cheat if they perceived their peers to be dishonest and if they thought their cheating was unlikely to be reported.

> *More than proctoring of exams or reliance on search engines to identify plagiarism, educating students about the need for academic honesty seems to reduce the incidence of cheating.*

The Center for Academic Integrity estimates that at most schools, more than 75 percent of the students engage in some form of cheating. Students not only cut passages from the Internet and paste them into their papers without citing the source; they share questions and answers on exams, collaborate on assignments they are supposed to do independently, and even falsify the results of their laboratory experiments. Worse, many professors have become inured to the problem and have ceased to report it.

To address what they consider an alarming trend, many schools are rewriting or adopting new academic honor codes. This renewed emphasis on honor and integrity underscores the influence of cultural values on social behavior. Observers contend that the increase in student cheating reflects widely publicized instances of cheating in public life, which have served to create an alternative set of values in which the end justifies the means. When young people see sports heroes, authors, entertainers, and corporate executives exposed for cheating in one form or another, the message seems to be "Cheating is OK, as long as you don't get caught." More than proctoring of exams or reliance on search engines to identify plagiarism, then, educating students about the need for academic honesty seems to reduce the incidence of cheating. "The feeling of being treated as an adult and responding in kind," says Professor Donald McCabe of Rutgers University, "it's clearly there for many students. They don't want to violate that trust."

LET'S DISCUSS

1. Do you know anyone who has engaged in Internet plagiarism? What about cheating on tests or falsifying laboratory results? If so, how did the person justify these forms of dishonesty?
2. Even if cheaters aren't caught, what negative effects does their academic dishonesty have on them? What effects does it have on students who are honest? Could an entire college or university suffer from students' dishonesty?

Sources: Argetsinger and Krim 2002; Bartlett 2009; Center for Academic Integrity 2006; McCabe et al. 2008; R. Thomas 2003; Zernike 2002.

---

ideology will help to control women and keep them in a subordinate position.

A growing number of social scientists believe that it is not easy to identify a core culture in the United States. For support, they point to the lack of consensus on national values, the diffusion of cultural traits, the diversity within our culture, and the changing views of young people (look again at Figure 3-4). Yet there is no way of denying that certain expressions of values have greater influence than others, even in as complex a society as the United States.

If cultural values vary within the United States, they vary even more significantly from one country to the next. The

following case study illustrates what can happen when a corporation attempts to export U.S. cultural values to another country.

Table 3-2 on page 68 summarizes the major sociological perspectives on culture. How one views a culture—whether from an ethnocentric point of view or through the lens of cultural relativism—has important consequences in the area of social policy. It also has serious consequences in business, as our case study on Wal-Mart demonstrates.

A hot issue today is the extent to which a nation should accommodate non-native language speakers by sponsoring bilingual programs. We'll take a close look at this issue in the Social Policy section, on page 69.

	Functionalist Perspective	Conflict Perspective	Feminist Perspective	Interactionist Perspective
Norms	Reinforce societal standards	Reinforce patterns of dominance	Reinforce roles of men and women	Are maintained through face-to-face interaction
Values	Are collective conceptions of what is good	May perpetuate social inequality	May perpetuate men's dominance	Are defined and redefined through social interaction
Culture and Society	Culture reflects a society's strong central values	Culture reflects a society's dominant ideology	Culture reflects society's view of men and women	A society's core culture is perpetuated through daily social interactions
Cultural Variation	Subcultures serve the interests of subgroups; ethnocentrism reinforces group solidarity	Countercultures question the dominant social order; ethnocentrism devalues groups	Cultural relativism respects variations in the way men and women are viewed in different societies	Customs and traditions are transmitted through intergroup contact and through the media
Wal-Mart and Culture	Providing goods and services to customers	Treatment of unions; health benefits; women in management	Role of women in leadership	Store–customer relationships in different cultures

case**study** Culture at Wal-Mart

By some measures, Wal-Mart is the largest corporation in the world. By other measures, it is the world's 14th largest economy. Indeed, the Arkansas-based retailer's annual revenue—over one-third of a trillion dollars—surpasses the total value of goods and services produced in many countries, such as Sweden.

Wal-Mart's rise to the status of an economic superpower has not been without criticism. Opponents have criticized its policy of shutting out labor unions, its lack of commitment to elevating women to managerial positions, its slowness to provide adequate health care benefits, and its negative impact on smaller retailers in the areas where its stores are located. Nonetheless, U.S. consumers have embraced Wal-Mart's "everyday low prices." The reaction has not been as positive when the discount giant has tried to enter countries where consumers hold different cultural values (Barbaro 2008).

The company, now located in 15 countries, has not been an unqualified success abroad. In 2006 Wal-Mart pulled out of Germany, due in part to its failure to adjust to the national culture. German shoppers, accustomed to no-nonsense, impersonal service, found Wal-Mart employees' smiling, outgoing style off-putting. The company's "ten-foot attitude"—a salesperson who comes within 10 feet of a customer must look the person in the eye, greet the person, and ask if he or she needs help—simply did not play well there. Food shoppers, used to bagging their own groceries, were turned off by Wal-Mart's practice of allowing clerks to handle their purchases. Furthermore, German employees, who had grown up in a culture that accepts workplace romances, found the company's prohibition against on-the-job relationships bizarre.

Unfortunately, executives did not react quickly enough to the cultural clash. Despite their need for cultural know-how, they passed up the opportunity to install German-speaking managers in key positions. While the company struggled to adjust to unfamiliar cultural standards, fierce competition from German retailers cut into its profits. After an eight-year effort that cost the company one billion dollars, Wal-Mart's executives conceded defeat.

Wal-Mart's withdrawal from Germany was its second exit of the year. Earlier in 2006, the company sold all its facilities in South Korea, where its warehouse-style stores were not appreciated by shoppers accustomed to more elegant surroundings. Today, the successful U.S. retailer is learning not to impose its corporate culture on foreign customers and employees. No longer does the company plan to sell golf clubs in Brazil, where the game is rarely played, or ice skates in Mexico, where skating rinks are hard to find. More important, the corporate giant has begun to study the culture and social patterns of potential customers (Landler and Barbaro 2006; Saporito 2007; Wal-Mart 2007; A. Zimmerman and Nelson 2006).

Wal-Mart's mistakes in Germany and South Korea are instructive. Even without a background in sociology, most businesspeople know that culture is fundamental to society. Yet they often fail to adjust to new cultures when they enter foreign markets. Today, as Wal-Mart prepares to enter China and India, two massive consumer markets, executives are determined to repeat the company's success in Latin America, rather than its failure in Germany and South Korea (Nussbaum 2006).

socialpolicy and Culture

Bilingualism

The Issue

All over the world, nations face the challenge of how to deal with residential minorities who speak a language different from that of the mainstream culture. **Bilingualism** refers to the use of two or more languages in a particular setting, such as the workplace or schoolroom, treating each language as equally legitimate. Thus, a teacher of bilingual education may instruct children in their native language while gradually introducing them to the language of the host society. If the curriculum is also bicultural, it will teach children about the mores and folkways of both the dominant culture and the subculture.

To what degree should schools in the United States present the curriculum in a language other than English? This issue has prompted a great deal of debate among educators and policymakers.

The Setting

Because languages know no political boundaries, minority languages are common in most nations. For example, Hindi is the most widely spoken language in India, and English is used widely for official purposes, but 18 other languages are officially recognized in the nation of about 1 billion people.

According to the Bureau of the Census, 59 million residents of the United States over age five—that's about 19 percent of the population—spoke a language other than English as their primary language at home in 2007 (Figure 3-5). Indeed, 32 different languages are each spoken by at least 200,000 resi-dents of this country (Bureau of the Census 2006b; Shin and Bruno 2003).

Throughout the world, schools must deal with incoming students who speak many different languages. Do bilingual programs in the United States help these children to learn English? It is difficult to reach firm conclusions because bilingual programs in general vary so widely in their quality and approach. They differ in the length of the transition to English and in how long they allow students to remain in bilingual classrooms. Moreover, results have been mixed. In the years since California effectively dismantled its bilingual education program, reading

FIGURE **3-5** PERCENTAGE OF PEOPLE WHO SPEAK A LANGUAGE OTHER THAN ENGLISH AT HOME, BY STATE

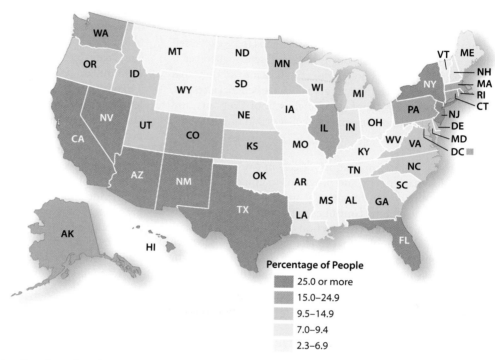

MAPPING LIFE NATIONWIDE

Percentage of People
- 25.0 or more
- 15.0–24.9
- 9.5–14.9
- 7.0–9.4
- 2.3–6.9

Note: Data drawn from the 2007 American Community Survey of people five years and over. National average was 19.7 percent.
Source: American Community Survey 2008: Table R1601.

and math scores of students with limited English proficiency rose dramatically, especially in the lower grades. Yet a major overview of 17 different studies, done at Johns Hopkins University, found that students who are offered lessons in both English and their home languages make better progress than similar students who are taught only in English (R. Slavin and Cheung 2003).

Sociological Insights

For a long time, people in the United States demanded conformity to a single language. This demand coincided with the functionalist view that language serves to unify members of a society. Immigrant children from Europe and Asia—including young Italians, Jews, Poles, Chinese, and Japanese—were expected to learn English once they entered school. In some cases, immigrant children were actually forbidden to speak their native languages on school grounds. Little respect was granted to immigrants' cultural traditions; a young person would often be teased about his or her "funny" name, accent, or style of dress.

69

Recent decades have seen challenges to this pattern of forced obedience to the dominant ideology. Beginning in the 1960s, active movements for Black pride and ethnic pride insisted that people regard the traditions of all racial and ethnic subcultures as legitimate and important. Conflict theorists explain this development as a case of subordinated language minorities seeking opportunities for self-expression. Partly as a result of these challenges, people began to view bilingualism as an asset. It seemed to provide a sensitive way of assisting millions of non-English-speaking people in the United States to *learn* English in order to function more effectively within the society.

The perspective of conflict theory also helps us to understand some of the attacks on bilingual programs. Many of them stem from an ethnocentric point of view, which holds that any deviation from the majority is bad. This attitude tends to be expressed by those who wish to stamp out foreign influence wherever it occurs, especially in our schools. It does not take into account that success in bilingual education may actually have beneficial results, such as decreasing the number of high school dropouts and increasing the number of Hispanics in colleges and universities.

Policy Initiatives

Bilingualism has policy implications largely in two areas: efforts to maintain language purity and programs to enhance bilingual education. Nations vary dramatically in their tolerance for a variety of languages. China continues to tighten its cultural control over Tibet by extending instruction of Mandarin, a Chinese dialect, from high school into the elementary schools, which will now be bilingual along with Tibetan. In contrast, nearby Singapore establishes English as the medium of instruction but allows students to take their mother tongue as a second language, be it Chinese, Malay, or Tamil.

In many nations, language dominance is a regional issue—for example, in Miami or along the Tex-Mex border, where Spanish speaking is prevalent. A particularly virulent bilingual hot spot is Quebec, the French-speaking province of Canada. The Québécois, as they are known, represent 83 percent of the province's population, but only 25 percent of Canada's total population. A law implemented in 1978 mandated education in French for all Quebec's children except those whose parents or siblings had learned English elsewhere in Canada. While special laws like this one have advanced French in the province, dissatisfied Québécois have tried to form their own separate country. In 1995, the people of Quebec indicated their preference of remaining united with Canada by only the narrowest of margins (50.5 percent). Language and language-related cultural areas both unify and divide this nation of 33 million people (*The Economist* 2005b; Schaefer 2010).

Policymakers in the United States have been somewhat ambivalent in dealing with the issue of bilingualism. In 1965, the Elementary and Secondary Education Act (ESEA) provided for bilingual, bicultural education. In the 1970s, the federal government took an active role in establishing the proper form for bilingual programs. However, more recently, federal policy has been less supportive of bilingualism, and local school districts have been forced to provide an increased share of funding for their bilingual programs. Yet bilingual programs are an expense that many communities and states are unwilling to pay for and are quick to cut back. In 1998, voters in California approved a proposition that all but eliminated bilingual education: it requires instruction in English for 1.4 million children who are not fluent in the language.

In the United States, repeated efforts have been made to introduce a constitutional amendment declaring English as the nation's official language. In 2006, the issue arose once again during debates over two extremely controversial congressional proposals—a House bill that would have criminalized the presence of illegal immigrants in the United States and expanded the penalties for aiding them, and a Senate bill that offered some illegal immigrants a path to citizenship. In an attempt to reach a compromise between the two sides, legislative leaders introduced a proposal to make English the national language. As they described it, the legislation would not completely outlaw bilingual or multilingual government services. As of 2008, 30 states had declared English their official language—an action that is now more symbolic than legislative in its significance.

Public concern over a potential decline in the use of English appears to be overblown. In reality, most immigrants and their offspring quickly become fluent in English and abandon their mother tongue. Figure 3-6 presents data from Southern California, a region with a high

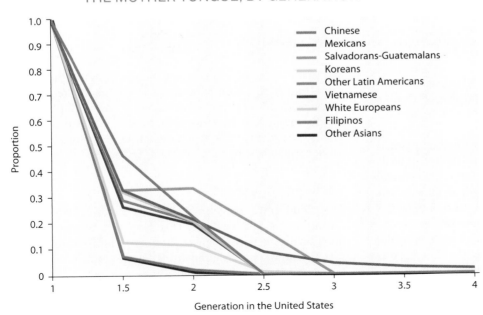

FIGURE **3-6** PROPORTION OF IMMIGRANT GROUP MEMBERS IN SOUTHERN CALIFORNIA WHO SPEAK THE MOTHER TONGUE, BY GENERATION

Chinese
Mexicans
Salvadorans-Guatemalans
Koreans
Other Latin Americans
Vietnamese
White Europeans
Filipinos
Other Asians

Proportion

Generation in the United States

Note: Based on a survey of 5,703 people in Metropolitan Los Angeles and San Diego from 2000 to 2004. Generation 1.5 includes those who came to the United States before age 15. Generation 2 includes those who were born in the United States to at least one foreign-born parent. Generation 3 includes those who were born in the United States to U.S.-born parents, but had one or more foreign-born grandparents.
Source: Rumbaut et al. 2006:456.

proportion of immigrants. It shows a steady, rapid move toward English, particularly in the first generation. Despite the presence of a large Latin enclave in the region, even Spanish-speaking immigrants quickly become speakers of English.

Nevertheless, many people are impatient with those immigrants who continue to use their mother tongue. The release in 2006 of *"Nuestro Himno,"* the Spanish-language version of the "Star-Spangled Banner," produced a strong public reaction: 69 percent of those who were surveyed on the topic said the anthem should be sung only in English. In reaction against the Spanish version, at least one congressman defiantly sang the national anthem in English—with incorrect lyrics. And the proprietor of a restaurant in Philadelphia posted signs advising patrons that he would accept orders for his famous steak sandwiches only in English. Throughout the year, passions ran high as policymakers debated how much support to afford people who speak other languages (J. Carroll 2006; U.S. English 2009).

In the end, the immigrant's experience, whether in the United States or Australia, is not only about learning a new language. It is about learning a whole new culture—a new totality of socially transmitted customs, knowledge, material objects, and behavior (Viramontes 2007).

Let's Discuss

1. Have you attended a school with a number of students for whom English is a second language? If so, did the school set up a special bilingual program? Was it effective? What is your opinion of such programs?

2. The ultimate goal of both English-only and bilingual programs is for foreign-born students to become proficient in English. Why should the type of program students attend matter so much to so many people? List all the reasons you can think of for supporting or opposing such programs. What do you see as the primary reason?

3. Besides bilingualism, can you think of another issue that has become controversial recently because of a clash of cultures? If so, analyze the issue from a sociological point of view.

getting**involved**

To get involved in the debate over bilingualism, visit this book's Online Learning Center, which offers links to relevant Web sites.

www.mhhe.com/schaefer12e

MASTERING THIS CHAPTER

Summary

Culture is the totality of learned, socially transmitted customs, knowledge, material objects, and behavior. This chapter examines the basic elements that make up a culture, social practices common to all cultures, and variations that distinguish one culture from another.

1. A shared **culture** helps to define the group or **society** to which we belong.

2. Anthropologist George Murdock compiled a list of **cultural universals,** or common practices found in every culture, including marriage, sports, cooking, medicine, and sexual restrictions.

3. People who assume that their own culture is superior to others engage in **ethnocentrism.** In contrast, **cultural relativism** is the practice of viewing other people's behavior from the perspective of their own culture.

4. Human culture is constantly expanding through the process of **innovation,** which includes both **discovery** and **invention.**

5. **Diffusion**—the spread of cultural items from one place to another—has fostered globalization. But people resist ideas that seem too foreign, as well as those they perceive as threatening to their own values and beliefs.

6. In a sense, a **subculture** can be thought of as a small culture that exists within a larger, dominant culture. **Countercultures** are subcultures that deliberately oppose aspects of the larger culture.

7. **Language,** an important element of culture, includes speech, written characters, numerals, and **symbols,** as well as gestures and other forms of nonverbal communication. Language both describes culture and shapes it.

8. Sociologists distinguish between **norms** in two ways, classifying them either as **formal** or **informal** or as **mores** or **folkways.**

9. The formal norms of a culture will carry the heaviest **sanctions;** informal norms will carry light sanctions.

10. The **dominant ideology** of a culture is the set of cultural beliefs and practices that help to maintain powerful social, economic, and political interests.

11. The social policy of **bilingualism** calls for the use of two or more languages, treating each as equally legitimate. It is supported by those who want to ease the transition of non-native-language speakers into a host society, but opposed by those who adhere to a single cultural tradition and language.

Critical Thinking Questions

1. Select three cultural universals from George Murdock's list (see page 54) and analyze them from a functionalist perspective. Why are these practices found in every culture? What functions do they serve?

2. Drawing on the theories and concepts presented in this chapter, apply sociological analysis to one subculture with which you are

familiar. Describe the norms, values, argot, and sanctions evident in that subculture.

3. In what ways is the dominant ideology of the United States evident in the nation's literature, music, movies, theater, television programs, and sporting events?

Key Terms

[handwritten: idiomatic expres. slang]

Argot Specialized language used by members of a group or subculture. (page 58)

Bilingualism The use of two or more languages in a particular setting, such as the workplace or schoolroom, treating each language as equally legitimate. (69)

Counterculture A subculture that deliberately opposes certain aspects of the larger culture. (60)

Cultural relativism The viewing of people's behavior from the perspective of their own culture. (55)

Cultural universal A common practice or belief found in every culture. (54)

Culture The totality of learned, socially transmitted customs, knowledge, material objects, and behavior. (53)

Culture industry The worldwide media industry that standardizes the goods and services demanded by consumers. (54)

Culture lag A period of maladjustment when the nonmaterial culture is still struggling to adapt to new material conditions. (58)

Culture shock The feeling of surprise and disorientation that people experience when they encounter cultural practices that are different from their own. (60)

Culture war The polarization of society over controversial cultural elements. (66)

Diffusion The process by which a cultural item spreads from group to group or society to society. (57)

Discovery The process of making known or sharing the existence of an aspect of reality. (56)

Dominant ideology A set of cultural beliefs and practices that helps to maintain powerful social, economic, and political interests. (66)

Ethnocentrism The tendency to assume that one's own culture and way of life represent the norm or are superior to all others. (54)

Folkway A norm governing everyday behavior whose violation raises comparatively little concern. (63)

Formal norm A norm that has been written down and that specifies strict punishments for violators. (63)

Informal norm A norm that is generally understood but not precisely recorded. (63)

Innovation The process of introducing a new idea or object to a culture through discovery or invention. (56)

Invention The combination of existing cultural items into a form that did not exist before. (56)

Language An abstract system of word meanings and symbols for all aspects of culture; includes gestures and other nonverbal communication. (61)

Law Governmental social control. (63)

Material culture The physical or technological aspects of our daily lives. (58)

Mores Norms deemed highly necessary to the welfare of a society. (63)

Nonmaterial culture Ways of using material objects, as well as customs, beliefs, philosophies, governments, and patterns of communication. (58)

Norm An established standard of behavior maintained by a society. (63)

Sanction A penalty or reward for conduct concerning a social norm. (65)

Sapir-Whorf hypothesis A hypothesis concerning the role of language in shaping our interpretation of reality. It holds that language is culturally determined. (61)

Society A fairly large number of people who live in the same territory, are relatively independent of people outside their area, and participate in a common culture. (53)

Sociobiology The systematic study of how biology affects human social behavior. (55)

Subculture A segment of society that shares a distinctive pattern of mores, folkways, and values that differs from the pattern of the larger society. (58)

Symbol A gesture, object, or word that forms the basis of human communication. (62)

Technology Cultural information about how to use the material resources of the environment to satisfy human needs and desires. (57)

Value A collective conception of what is considered good, desirable, and proper—or bad, undesirable, and improper—in a culture. (65)

Self-Quiz

[handwritten: Cultural genocide]

Read each question carefully and then select the best answer.

1. Which of the following is an aspect of culture?
   a. a comic book
   b. the patriotic attachment to the flag of the United States
   c. slang words
   d. all of the above

2. People's needs for food, shelter, and clothing are examples of what George Murdock referred to as
   a. norms.
   b. folkways.
   c. cultural universals.
   d. cultural practices.

3. What term do sociologists use to refer to the process by which a cultural item spreads from group to group or society to society?
   a. diffusion
   b. globalization
   c. innovation
   d. cultural relativism

4. The appearance of Starbucks coffeehouses in China is a sign of what aspect of culture?
   a. innovation
   b. globalization

   c. diffusion
   d. cultural relativism

5. Which of the following statements is true according to the Sapir-Whorf hypothesis?
   a. Language simply describes reality.
   b. Language does not transmit stereotypes related to race.
   c. Language precedes thought.
   d. Language is not an example of a cultural universal.

6. Which of the following statements about norms is correct?
   a. People do not follow norms in all situations. In some cases, they evade a norm because they know it is weakly enforced.
   b. In some instances, behavior that appears to violate society's norms may actually represent adherence to the norms of a particular group.
   c. Norms are violated in some instances because one norm conflicts with another.
   d. all of the above

7. Which of the following statements about values is correct?
   a. Values never change.
   b. The values of a culture may change, but most remain relatively stable during any one person's lifetime.
   c. Values are constantly changing; sociologists view them as being very unstable.
   d. all of the above

8. Which of the following terms describes the set of cultural beliefs and practices that help to maintain powerful social, economic, and political interests?
  a. mores
  b. dominant ideology
  c. consensus
  d. values

9. Terrorist groups are examples of
  a. cultural universals.
  b. subcultures.
  c. countercultures.
  d. dominant ideologies.

10. What is the term used when one places a priority on understanding other cultures, rather than dismissing them as "strange" or "exotic"?
  a. ethnocentrism
  b. culture shock
  c. cultural relativism
  d. cultural value

11. _____ are gestures, objects, and/or words that form the basis of human communication.

12. _____ is the process of introducing a new idea or object to a culture.

13. The bow and arrow, the automobile, and the television are all examples of _____ .

14. Sociologists associated with the _____ perspective emphasize that language and symbols offer a powerful way for a subculture to maintain its identity.

15. "Put on some clean clothes for dinner" and "Thou shalt not kill" are both examples of _____ found in U.S. culture.

16. The United States has strong _____ against murder, treason, and other forms of abuse that have been institutionalized into formal norms.

17. From a(n) _____ perspective, the dominant ideology has major social significance. Not only do a society's most powerful groups and institutions control wealth and property; more important, they control the means of production.

18. Countercultures (e.g., hippies) are typically popular among the _____, who have the least investment in the existing culture.

19. A person experiences _____ _____ when he or she feels disoriented, uncertain, out of place, even fearful, when immersed in an unfamiliar culture.

20. From the _____ perspective, enthocentrism serves to maintain a sense of solidarity by promoting group pride.

Answers
1 (d); 2 (c); 3 (a); 4 (b); 5 (c); 6 (d); 7 (b); 8 (b); 9 (c); 10 (c); 11 Symbols; 12 Innovation; 13 inventions; 14 interactionist; 15 norms; 16 mores; 17 conflict; 18 young; 19 culture shock; 20 functionalist

THINKING ABOUT MOVIES

The Namesake (Mira Nair, 2007)

An Indian couple emigrates from Calcutta to New York City to start a new life and a new family. Their firstborn son, Gogol Ganguli (Kal Penn), grows up rejecting his parents' Bengali culture, even though most of the family's social ties are to other Bengalis. He adopts colloquial American speech, chooses a wealthy Caucasian woman for his girlfriend, and rechristens himself "Nick." Then his father's sudden death makes him rethink his relationship to the Bengali culture.

This movie is rife with examples of culture seen from a sociological point of view. Look for the scenes in which Gogol's parents suffer culture shock after moving to New York City. Watch for examples of bilingualism as Gogol speaks to his family, switching back and forth from English to Bengali.

For Your Consideration

1. What are some of the differences between Gogol's parents' values and those of his Caucasian girlfriend?

2. How is language used in the film to reinforce feelings of a shared culture?

Smoke Signals (Chris Eyre, 1998)

Lanky, geeky Thomas Builds-the-Fire (Evan Adams) and athletic Victor Joseph (Adam Beach) live on a Coeur d'Alene Indian reservation in Idaho. Thomas's parents died in a fire when he was a baby; he was saved by Victor's father. After hearing that Victor's father has died in Phoenix, the two decide to take a road trip to learn more about the man who played such a pivotal role in their lives. At first Victor does not want his nerdy sidekick's company, but Thomas has saved enough money to bankroll the trip. The two grow closer as they learn more about themselves and their lost patriarch.

This movie portrays the subculture of contemporary Coeur d'Alene Indians who live in the mainstream culture but hold on to their Native American norms and values. Watch for the scene in which Victor tells Thomas how to act "properly stoic," demonstrating how members of the tribe reinforce the norms of their subculture.

For Your Consideration

1. What informal norms of the Coeur d'Alene culture does the movie show?

2. How do Thomas and Victor deal with the representations of Native American tribal people presented in mainstream films and television?

inside

The Role of Socialization

The Self and Socialization

Agents of Socialization

Socialization throughout the Life Course

Social Policy and Socialization: Child Care around the World

BOXES

Sociology on Campus: *Impression Management by Students*

Taking Sociology to Work: *Rakefet Avramovitz, Program Administrator, Child Care Law Center*

Research Today: *Online Socializing: A New Agent of Socialization*

A daughter learns; how to weave fabric from her mother in San Antonio Palopo, Guatemala. The family is the most important agent of socialization.

Socialization and the Life Course 4

BLACK PICKET FENCES

PRIVILEGE AND PERIL AMONG THE BLACK MIDDLE CLASS

MARY PATTILLO-McCOY

66 Charisse . . . is sixteen and lives with her mother and younger sister, Deanne, across the street from St. Mary's Catholic Church and School. Charisse's mother is a personnel assistant at a Chicago university, and is taking classes there to get her bachelor's degree. Mr. Baker is a Chicago firefighter. While her father and mother are separated, Charisse sees her father many times a week at the afterschool basketball hour that he supervises at St. Mary's gym. He and Charisse's mother are on very good terms, and Charisse has a loving relationship with both parents. Mr. Baker is as active as any parent could be, attending the father/daughter dances at Charisse's high school, never missing a big performance, and visiting his daughters often.

Charisse and her sister are being raised by the neighborhood family in addition to their biological parents. "We [are] real close. Like all our neighbors know us because my dad grew up over here. Since the '60s." Charisse is a third-generation Grovelandite just like Neisha Morris. Her grandparents moved into Groveland with Charisse's then-teenage father when the neighborhood first opened to African Americans. . . . Now Charisse is benefiting from the friends her family has made over their years of residence in Groveland, especially the members of St. Mary's church, who play the role of surrogate parents. When Charisse was in elementary school at St. Mary's, her late paternal grandmother was the school secretary, and so the Baker girls were always under the watchful eye of their grandmother as well as the staff, who were their grandmother's friends. And in the evenings Charisse's mother would bring her and her sister to choir practice, where they accumulated an ensemble of mothers and fathers.

After St. Mary's elementary school, Charisse went on to St. Agnes Catholic High School for girls, her father's choice. St. Agnes is located in a suburb of Chicago and is a solid, integrated Catholic school where 100 percent of the girls graduate and over 95 percent go on to college. . . .

Most of Charisse's close friends went to St. Mary's and now go to St. Agnes with her, but her choice of boyfriends shows modest signs of rebellion. . . . Many of Charisse's male interests are older than she, and irregularly employed—although some are in and out of school. She meets many of them hanging out at the mall. One evening, members of the church's youth choir sat around talking about their relationships. Charisse cooed while talking about her present boyfriend, who had just graduated from high school but did not have a job and was uncertain about his future. But in the middle of that thought, Charisse spontaneously changed her attentions to a new young man that she had just met. "Charisse changes boyfriends like she changes her clothes," her sister joked, indicating the impetuous nature of adolescent relationships.

While these young men are not in gangs or selling drugs, many of them do not seem to share Charisse's strong career goals and diligence in attaining them. Some of them would not gain the approval of her parents. However, this full list of boyfriends has not clouded Charisse's focus. 99

Charisse is a third-generation Grovelandite just like Neisha Morris. Her grandparents moved into Groveland with Charisse's then-teenage father when the neighborhood first opened to African Americans.

(Pattillo-McCoy 1999:100–102) Additional information about this excerpt can be found on the Online Learning Center at www.mhhe.com/schaefer12e.

This excerpt from *Black Picket Fences: Privilege and Peril among the Black Middle Class* describes the upbringing of a young resident of Groveland, a close-knit African American community in Chicago. The author, sociologist Mary Pattillo-McCoy, became acquainted with Charisse while living in the Groveland neighborhood, where she was doing ethnographic research. Charisse's childhood is similar to that of other youths in many respects. Regardless of race or social class, a young person's development involves a host of influences, from parents, grandparents, and siblings to friends and classmates, teachers and school administrators, neighbors and churchgoers—even youths who frequent the local mall. Yet in some ways, Charisse's development is specifically influenced by her race and social class. Contact with family and community members, for instance, has undoubtedly prepared her to deal with prejudice and the scarcity of positive images of African Americans in the media (W. Wilson et al. 2006).

Sociologists, in general, are interested in the patterns of behavior and attitudes that emerge *throughout* the life course, from infancy to old age. These patterns are part of the lifelong process of **socialization,** in which people learn the attitudes, values, and behaviors appropriate for members of a particular culture. Socialization occurs through human interactions that begin in infancy and continue through retirement. We learn a great deal from those people most important in our lives—immediate family members, best friends, and teachers. But we also learn from people we see on the street, on television, on the Internet, and in films and magazines. From a microsociological perspective, socialization helps us to discover how to behave "properly" and what to expect from others if we follow (or challenge) society's norms and values. From a macrosociological perspective, socialization provides for the transmission of a culture from one generation to the next, and thereby for the long-term continuance of a society.

Socialization also shapes our self-images. For example, in the United States, a person who is viewed as "too heavy" or "too short" does not conform to the ideal cultural standard of physical attractiveness. This kind of unfavorable evaluation can significantly influence the person's self-esteem. In this sense, socialization experiences can help to shape our personalities. In everyday speech, the term **personality** is used to refer to a person's typical patterns of attitudes, needs, characteristics, and behavior.

How much of a person's personality is shaped by culture, as opposed to inborn traits? In what ways does socialization continue into adulthood? Who are the most powerful agents of socialization? In this chapter we will examine the role of socialization in human development. We will begin by analyzing the interaction of heredity with environmental factors. We will pay particular attention to how people develop perceptions, feelings, and beliefs about themselves. The chapter will also explore the lifelong nature of the socialization process, as well as important agents of socialization, among them the family, schools, peers, the media, and technology. Finally, the Social Policy section will focus on the socialization experience of group child care for young children.

The Role of Socialization

What makes us who we are? Is it the genes we are born with, or the environment in which we grow up? Researchers have traditionally clashed over the relative importance of biological inheritance and environmental factors in human development—a conflict called the *nature versus nurture* (or *heredity versus environment*) debate. Today, most social scientists have moved beyond this debate, acknowledging instead the *interaction* of these variables in shaping human development. However, we can better appreciate how heredity and environmental factors interact and influence the socialization process if we first examine situations in which one factor operates almost entirely without the other (Homans 1979).

Social Environment: The Impact of Isolation

In the 1994 movie *Nell,* Jodie Foster played a young woman hidden from birth by her mother in a backwoods cabin. Raised without normal human contact, Nell crouches like an animal, screams wildly, and speaks or sings in a language all her own. This movie was drawn from the actual account of an emaciated 16-year-old boy who appeared mysteriously in 1828 in the town square of Nuremberg, Germany (Lipson 1994).

Isabelle and Genie: Two Cases Some viewers may have found the story of Nell difficult to believe, but the painful childhood of Isabelle was all too real. For the first six years of her life, Isabelle lived in almost total seclusion in a darkened room. She had little contact with other people, with the exception of her mother, who could neither speak nor hear. Isabelle's mother's parents had been so deeply ashamed of Isabelle's illegitimate birth that they kept her hidden away from the world. Ohio authorities finally discovered the child in 1938, when Isabelle's mother escaped from her parents' home, taking her daughter with her.

When she was discovered at age six, Isabelle could not speak; she could merely make various croaking sounds. Her only communications with her mother were simple gestures. Isabelle had been largely deprived of the typical interactions and socialization experiences of childhood. Since she had seen few people, she showed a strong fear of strangers and reacted almost like a wild animal when confronted with an unfamiliar person. As she became accustomed to seeing certain individuals, her reaction changed to one of extreme apathy. At first, observers believed that Isabelle was deaf, but she soon began to react to nearby sounds. On tests of maturity, she scored at the level of an infant rather than a six-year-old.

Specialists developed a systematic training program to help Isabelle adapt to human relationships and socialization. After a few days of training, she made her first attempt to verbalize. Although she started slowly, Isabelle quickly passed through six years of development. In a little over two months she was speaking in complete sentences. Nine months later she could identify both words and sentences. Before Isabelle reached age nine, she was ready to attend school with other children. By age 14 she was in sixth grade, doing well in school, and emotionally well adjusted.

Yet without an opportunity to experience socialization in her first six years, Isabelle had been hardly human in the social sense when she was first discovered. Her inability to communicate at the time of her discovery—despite her physical and cognitive potential to learn—and her remarkable progress over the next few years underscore the impact of socialization on human development (K. Davis 1940, 1947).

Unfortunately, other children who have been locked away or severely neglected have not fared so well as Isabelle. In many instances, the consequences of social isolation have proved much more damaging. For example, in 1970 a 14-year-old Californian named Genie was discovered in a room where she had been confined since age 20 months. During her years of isolation, no family member had spoken to her, nor could she hear anything other than swearing. Since there was no television or radio in her home, she had never heard the sounds of normal human speech. One year after beginning extensive therapy, Genie's grammar resembled that of a typical 18-month-old. Though she made further advances with continued therapy, she never achieved full language ability. Today Genie, now in her early 50s, lives in a home for developmentally disabled adults. Figure 4-1 on page 78 shows a sketch Genie made of her teacher five years after she was discovered (Curtiss 1977, 1985; Rymer 1993).

Isabelle's and Genie's experiences are important to researchers because there are only a few cases of children reared in total isolation. Unfortunately, however, there are many cases of children raised in extremely neglectful social circumstances. Recently, attention has focused on infants and young children from orphanages in the formerly communist countries of Eastern Europe. In Romanian orphanages, babies once lay in their cribs for 18 to 20 hours a day, curled against their feeding bottles and receiving little adult care. Such minimal attention continued for the first five years of their lives. Many of them were fearful of human contact and prone to unpredictable antisocial behavior.

This situation came to light as families in North America and Europe began adopting thousands of the children. The adjustment

Source: Curtiss 1977:274.
This sketch was made in 1975 by Genie—a girl who had been isolated for most of her 14 years, until she was discovered by authorities in 1970. In her drawing, her linguist friend (on the left) plays the piano while Genie listens. Genie was 18 when she drew this picture.

problems for about 20 percent of them were often so dramatic that the adopting families suffered guilty fears of being ill-fit adoptive parents. Many of them have asked for assistance in dealing with the children. Slowly, efforts are being made to introduce the deprived youngsters to feelings of attachment that they have never experienced before (Groza et al. 1999; Craig Smith 2006).

Increasingly, researchers are emphasizing the importance of the earliest socialization experiences for children who grow up in more normal environments. We now know that it is not enough to care for an infant's physical needs; parents must also concern themselves with children's social development. If, for example, children are discouraged from having friends even as toddlers,

they will miss out on social interactions with peers that are critical for emotional growth.

Primate Studies   Studies of animals raised in isolation also support the importance of socialization in development. Harry Harlow (1971), a researcher at the primate laboratory of the University of Wisconsin, conducted tests with rhesus monkeys that had been raised away from their mothers and away from contact with other monkeys. As was the case with Isabelle, the rhesus monkeys raised in isolation were fearful and easily frightened. They did not mate, and the females who were artificially inseminated became abusive mothers. Apparently, isolation had had a damaging effect on the monkeys.

A creative aspect of Harlow's experimentation was his use of "artificial mothers." In one such experiment, Harlow presented monkeys raised in isolation with two substitute mothers—one cloth-covered replica and one covered with wire that had the ability to offer milk. Monkey after monkey went to the wire mother for the life-giving milk, yet spent much more time clinging to the more motherlike cloth model. It appears that the infant monkeys developed greater social attachments from their need for warmth, comfort, and intimacy than from their need for milk.

While the isolation studies just discussed may seem to suggest that heredity can be dismissed as a factor in the social development of humans and animals, studies of twins provide insight into a fascinating interplay between hereditary and environmental factors.

use your sociological *imagination*

What events in your life have had a strong influence on who you are?

The Influence of Heredity

Identical twins Oskar Stohr and Jack Yufe were separated soon after their birth and raised on different continents, in very different cultural settings.

Despite the striking physical resemblance between these identical twins, there are undoubtedly many differences. Research points to some behavioral similarities between twins, but little beyond the likenesses found among nontwin siblings.

Oskar was reared as a strict Catholic by his maternal grandmother in the Sudetenland of Czechoslovakia. As a member of the Hitler Youth movement in Nazi Germany, he learned to hate Jews. In contrast, his brother Jack was reared in Trinidad by the twins' Jewish father. Jack joined an Israeli kibbutz (a collective settlement) at age 17 and later served in the Israeli army. When the twins were reunited in middle age, however, some startling similarities emerged: They both wore wire-rimmed glasses and mustaches. They both liked spicy foods and sweet liqueurs, were absent-minded, flushed the toilet before using it, stored rubber bands on their wrists, and dipped buttered toast in their coffee (Holden 1980).

The twins also differed in many important respects: Jack was a workaholic; Oskar enjoyed leisure-time activities. Oskar was a traditionalist who was domineering toward women; Jack was a political liberal who was much more accepting of feminism. Finally, Jack was extremely proud of being Jewish, while Oskar never mentioned his Jewish heritage (Holden 1987).

Oskar and Jack are prime examples of the interplay of heredity and environment. For a number of years, the Minnesota Twin Family Study has been following pairs of identical twins reared apart to determine what similarities, if any, they show in personality traits, behavior, and intelligence. Preliminary results from the available twin studies indicate that *both* genetic factors *and* socialization experiences are influential in human development. Certain characteristics, such as temperaments, voice patterns, and nervous habits, appear to be strikingly similar even in twins reared apart, suggesting that these qualities may be linked to hereditary causes. However, identical twins reared apart differ far more in their attitudes, values, chosen mates, and even drinking habits; these qualities, it would seem, are influenced by environmental factors. In examining clusters of personality traits among such twins, researchers have found marked similarities in their tendency toward leadership or dominance, but significant differences in their need for intimacy, comfort, and assistance.

Researchers have also been impressed with the similar scores on intelligence tests of twins reared apart in *roughly similar* social settings. Most of the identical twins register scores even closer

than those that would be expected if the same person took a test twice. At the same time, however, identical twins brought up in *dramatically different* social environments score quite differently on intelligence tests—a finding that supports the impact of socialization on human development (Joseph 2004; Kronstadt 2008a; McGue and Bouchard 1998; Minnesota Center for Twin and Family Research 2009).

We need to be cautious in reviewing studies of twin pairs and other relevant research. Widely broadcast findings have often been based on preliminary analysis of extremely small samples. For example, one study (not involving twin pairs) was frequently cited as confirming genetic links with behavior. Yet the researchers had to retract their conclusions after they increased the sample and reclassified two of the original cases. After those changes, the initial findings were no longer valid.

Critics add that studies of twin pairs have not provided satisfactory information concerning the extent to which separated identical twins may have had contact with each other, even though they were raised apart. Such interactions—especially if they were extensive—could call into question the validity of the twin studies. As this debate continues, we can certainly anticipate numerous efforts to replicate the research and clarify the interplay between heredity and environmental factors in human development (Horgan 1993; Plomin 1989).

The Self and Socialization

We all have various perceptions, feelings, and beliefs about who we are and what we are like. How do we come to develop them? Do they change as we age?

We were not born with these understandings. Building on the work of George Herbert Mead (1964b), sociologists recognize that our concept of who we are, the *self*, emerges as we interact with others. The **self** is a distinct identity that sets us apart from others. It is not a static phenomenon, but continues to develop and change throughout our lives.

Sociologists and psychologists alike have expressed interest in how the individual develops and modifies the sense of self as a result of social interaction. The work of sociologists Charles Horton Cooley and George Herbert Mead, pioneers of the interactionist approach, has been especially useful in furthering our understanding of these important issues.

Sociological Approaches to the Self

Cooley: Looking-Glass Self   In the early 1900s, Charles Horton Cooley advanced the belief that we learn who we are by interacting with others. Our view of ourselves, then, comes not only from direct contemplation of our personal qualities but also from our impressions of how others perceive us. Cooley used the phrase **looking-glass self** to emphasize that the self is the product of our social interactions.

Children imitate the people around them, especially family members they continually interact with, during the *preparatory stage* described by George Herbert Mead.

Like spoken languages, symbols vary from culture to culture, and even from one subculture to another. In North America, raising one's eyebrows may communicate astonishment or doubt. In Peru, the same gesture means "money" or "pay me," and may constitute an unspoken request for a bribe. In the Pacific island nation of Tonga, raised eyebrows mean "yes" or "I agree" (Axtell 1990).

The Play Stage   Mead was among the first to analyze the relationship of symbols to socialization. As children develop skill in communicating through symbols, they gradually become more aware of social relationships. As a result, during the *play stage,* they begin to pretend to be other people. Just as an actor "becomes" a character, a child becomes a doctor, parent, superhero, or ship captain.

Mead, in fact, noted that an important aspect of the play stage is role-playing. **Role taking** is the process of mentally assuming the perspective of another and responding from that imagined viewpoint. For example, through this process a young child will gradually learn when it is best to ask a parent for favors. If the parent usually comes home from work in a bad mood, the child will wait until after dinner, when the parent is more relaxed and approachable.

The Game Stage   In Mead's third stage, the *game stage,* the child of about age eight or nine no longer just plays roles but begins to consider several tasks and relationships simultaneously. At this point in development, children grasp not only their own social positions but also those of others around them—just as in a football game the players must understand their own and everyone else's positions. Consider a girl or boy who is part of a scout troop out on a weekend hike in the mountains. The child must understand what he or she is expected to do but must also recognize the responsibilities of other scouts as well as the leaders. This is the final stage of development under Mead's model; the child can now respond to numerous members of the social environment.

Mead uses the term **generalized other** to refer to the attitudes, viewpoints, and expectations of society as a whole that a child takes into account in his or her behavior. Simply put, this concept suggests that when an individual acts, he or she takes into account an entire group of people. For example, a child will not act courteously merely to please a particular parent. Rather, the child comes to understand that courtesy is a widespread social value endorsed by parents, teachers, and religious leaders.

At the game stage, children can take a more sophisticated view of people and the social environment. They now understand what specific occupations and social positions are and no longer equate Mr. Williams only with the role of "librarian" or Ms. Sanchez only with "principal." It has become clear to the child that Mr. Williams can be a librarian, a parent, and a marathon runner at the same time and that Ms. Sanchez is one of many principals in our society. Thus, the child has reached a new level of sophistication in observations of individuals and institutions.

Table 4-1 summarizes the three stages of self outlined by George Herbert Mead.

Mead: Theory of the Self   Mead is best known for his theory of the self. According to Mead (1964b), the self begins at a privileged, central position in a person's world. Young children picture

The process of developing a self-identity or self-concept has three phases. First, we imagine how we present ourselves to others—to relatives, friends, even strangers on the street. Then we imagine how others evaluate us (attractive, intelligent, shy, or strange). Finally, we develop some sort of feeling about ourselves, such as respect or shame, as a result of these impressions (Cooley 1902; M. Howard 1989).

A subtle but critical aspect of Cooley's looking-glass self is that the self results from an individual's "imagination" of how others view him or her. As a result, we can develop self-identities based on *incorrect* perceptions of how others see us. A student may react strongly to a teacher's criticism and decide (wrongly) that the instructor views the student as stupid. This misperception may be converted into a negative self-identity through the following process: (1) the teacher criticized me, (2) the teacher must think that I'm stupid, (3) I *am* stupid. Yet self-identities are also subject to change. If the student receives an A at the end of the course, he or she will probably no longer feel stupid.

Mead: Stages of the Self   George Herbert Mead continued Cooley's exploration of interactionist theory. Mead (1934, 1964a) developed a useful model of the process by which the self emerges, defined by three distinct stages: the preparatory stage, the play stage, and the game stage.

The Preparatory Stage   During the *preparatory stage,* children merely imitate the people around them, especially family members with whom they continually interact. Thus, a small child will bang on a piece of wood while a parent is engaged in carpentry work, or will try to throw a ball if an older sibling is doing so nearby.

As they grow older, children become more adept at using symbols, including the gestures and words that form the basis of human communication. By interacting with relatives and friends, as well as by watching cartoons on television and looking at picture books, children in the preparatory stage begin to understand symbols. They will continue to use this form of communication throughout their lives.

TABLE **4-1**   MEAD'S STAGES OF THE SELF

summing**up**   81

Stage	Self Present?	Definition	Example
Preparation	No	Child imitates the actions of others.	When adults laugh and smile, child laughs and smiles.
Play	Developing	Child takes the role of a single other, as if he or she were the other.	Child first takes the role of doctor, then the role of patient.
Game	Yes	Child considers the roles of two or more others simultaneously.	In game of hide-and-seek, child takes into account the roles of both hider and seeker.

themselves as the focus of everything around them and find it difficult to consider the perspectives of others. For example, when shown a mountain scene and asked to describe what an observer on the opposite side of the mountain might see (such as a lake or hikers), young children describe only objects visible from their own vantage point. This childhood tendency to place ourselves at the center of events never entirely disappears. Many people with a fear of flying automatically assume that if any plane goes down, it will be the one they are on. And who reads the horoscope section in the paper without looking at their own horoscope first? Why else do we buy lottery tickets, if we do not imagine ourselves winning?

Nonetheless, as people mature, the self changes and begins to reflect greater concern about the reactions of others. Parents, friends, co-workers, coaches, and teachers are often among those who play a major role in shaping a person's self. The term **significant others** is used to refer to those individuals who are most important in the development of the self. Many young people, for example, find themselves drawn to the same kind of work their parents engage in (H. Sullivan [1953] 1968).

In some instances, studies of significant others have generated controversy among researchers. For example, some researchers have contended that Black adolescents are more "peer-oriented" than their White counterparts because of presumed weaknesses in Black families. However, investigations indicate that these hasty conclusions were based on limited studies focusing on less affluent Blacks. In fact, there appears to be little difference in who Blacks and Whites from similar economic backgrounds regard as their significant others (Giordano et al. 1993; Juhasz 1989).

use your sociological *imagination*

How do you view yourself as you interact with others around you? How do you think you formed this view of yourself?

A prospective employer reviews an applicant's qualifications for the job. To present themselves in a positive manner, both interviewer and applicant may resort to *impression management* and *face-work*, two tactics described by the interactionist Erving Goffman.

Goffman: Presentation of the Self

How do we manage our "self"? How do we display to others who we are? Erving Goffman, a sociologist associated with the interactionist perspective, suggested that many of our daily activities involve attempts to convey impressions of who we are. His observations help us to understand the sometimes subtle yet critical ways in which we learn to present ourselves socially. They also offer concrete examples of this aspect of socialization.

Early in life, the individual learns to slant his or her presentation of the self in order to create distinctive appearances and satisfy particular audiences. Goffman (1959) referred to this altering of the presentation of the self as **impression management.** Box 4-1 on page 82 describes an everyday example of this concept—the way students behave after receiving their exam grades.

SOCIOLOGY ON CAMPUS

4-1 Impression Management by Students

When you and fellow classmates get an exam back, you probably react differently depending on the grades that you and they earned. This distinction is part of *impression management,* as sociologists Daniel Albas and Cheryl Albas have demonstrated. The two explored the strategies college students use to create desired appearances after receiving their grades on exams. Albas and Albas divided these encounters into three categories: those between students who have all received high grades (Ace–Ace encounters); those between students who have received high grades and those who have received low or even failing grades (Ace–Bomber encounters); and those between students who have all received low grades (Bomber–Bomber encounters).

Ace–Ace encounters occur in a rather open atmosphere, because there is comfort in sharing a high mark with another high achiever. It is even acceptable to violate the norm of modesty and brag when among other Aces, since as one student admitted, "It's much easier to admit a high mark to someone who has done better than you, or at least as well."

Ace–Bomber encounters are often sensitive. Bombers generally attempt to avoid such exchanges, because "you . . . emerge looking like the dumb one" or "feel like you are lazy or unreliable." When forced into interactions with Aces, Bombers work to appear gracious and

congratulatory. For their part, Aces offer sympathy and support to the dissatisfied Bombers and even rationalize their own "lucky" high scores. To help Bombers save face, Aces may emphasize the difficulty and unfairness of the examination.

Bomber–Bomber encounters tend to be closed, reflecting the group effort to wall off the feared disdain of others. Yet, within the safety of these encounters, Bombers openly share their disappointment and engage in expressions of

> *When forced into interactions with Aces, Bombers work to appear gracious and congratulatory.*

mutual self-pity that they themselves call "pity parties." They devise face-saving excuses for their poor performance, such as "I wasn't feeling well all week" or "I had four exams and two papers due that week." If the grade distribution in a class includes particularly low scores, Bombers may blame the professor, attacking him or her as a sadist, a slave driver, or simply an incompetent.

As is evident from these descriptions, students' impression management strategies conform to society's informal norms regarding modesty and consideration for less successful peers. In classroom settings, as in the workplace and in other

types of human interaction, efforts at impression management are most intense when status differentials are pronounced, as in encounters between the high-scoring Aces and the low-scoring Bombers.

Of course, grade comparisons are not the only occasion when students engage in impression management. Another study has shown that students' perceptions of how often fellow students work out can also influence their social encounters. In athletic terms, a bomber would be someone who doesn't work out; an ace would be someone who works hard at physical fitness. At the student lounge, then, bomber–bomber encounters might involve nonathletic students belittling those who spend a lot of time working out. At the recreation center, ace–ace encounters might involve student athletes sharing training tips.

LET'S DISCUSS

1. How do you react to those who have received higher or lower grades than you? Do you engage in impression management? How would you like others to react to your grade?

2. What social norms govern students' impression management strategies?

Sources: Albas and Albas 1988; M. Mack 2003.

In analyzing such everyday social interactions, Goffman makes so many explicit parallels to the theater that his view has been termed the **dramaturgical approach.** According to this perspective, people resemble performers in action. For example, a clerk may try to appear busier than he or she actually is if a supervisor happens to be watching. A customer in a singles' bar may try to look as if he or she is waiting for a particular person to arrive.

Goffman (1959) also drew attention to another aspect of the self—**face-work.** How often do you initiate some kind of face-saving behavior when you feel embarrassed or rejected? In response to a rejection at the singles' bar, a person may engage in face-work by saying, "There really isn't an interesting person in this entire crowd." We feel the need to maintain a proper image of the self if we are to continue social interaction.

In some cultures, people engage in elaborate deceptions to avoid losing face. In Japan, for example, where lifetime employment has until recently been the norm, "company men" thrown out of work by a deep economic recession may feign employment, rising as usual in the morning, donning suit and tie, and heading for the business district. But instead of going to the office, they congregate at places such as Tokyo's Hibiya Library, where they pass the time by reading before returning home at the usual hour. Many of these men are trying to protect family members, who would be shamed if neighbors discovered the

family breadwinner was unemployed. Others are deceiving their wives and families as well (French 2000).

Goffman's work on the self represents a logical progression of sociological studies begun by Cooley and Mead on how personality is acquired through socialization and how we manage the presentation of the self to others. Cooley stressed the process by which we create a self; Mead focused on how the self develops as we learn to interact with others; Goffman emphasized the ways in which we consciously create images of ourselves for others.

Psychological Approaches to the Self

Psychologists have shared the interest of Cooley, Mead, and other sociologists in the development of the self. Early work in psychology, such as that of Sigmund Freud (1856–1939), stressed the role of inborn drives—among them the drive for sexual gratification—in channeling human behavior. More recently, psychologists such as Jean Piaget have emphasized the stages through which human beings progress as the self develops.

Like Charles Horton Cooley and George Herbert Mead, Freud believed that the self is a social product, and that aspects of one's personality are influenced by other people (especially one's parents). However, unlike Cooley and Mead, he suggested that the self has components that work in opposition to each other. According to Freud, our natural impulsive instincts are in constant conflict

Scholar	Key Concepts and Contributions	Major Points of Theory
Charles Horton Cooley 1864–1929 sociologist (USA)	Looking-glass self	Stages of development not distinct; feelings toward ourselves developed through interaction with others
George Herbert Mead 1863–1931 sociologist (USA)	The self Generalized other	Three distinct stages of development; self develops as children grasp the roles of others in their lives
Erving Goffman 1922–1982 sociologist (USA)	Impression management Dramaturgical approach Face-work	Self developed through the impressions we convey to others and to groups
Sigmund Freud 1856–1939 psychotherapist (Austria)	Psychoanalysis	Self influenced by parents and by inborn drives, such as the drive for sexual gratification
Jean Piaget 1896–1980 child psychologist (Switzerland)	Cognitive theory of development	Four stages of cognitive development; moral development linked to socialization

with societal constraints. Part of us seeks limitless pleasure, while another part favors rational behavior. By interacting with others, we learn the expectations of society and then select behavior most appropriate to our own culture. (Of course, as Freud was well aware, we sometimes distort reality and behave irrationally.)

Research on newborn babies by the Swiss child psychologist Jean Piaget (1896–1980) has underscored the importance of social interactions in developing a sense of self. Piaget found that newborns have no self in the sense of a looking-glass image. Ironically, though, they are quite self-centered; they demand that all attention be directed toward them. Newborns have not yet separated themselves from the universe of which they are a part. For these babies, the phrase "you and me" has no meaning; they understand only "me." However, as they mature, children are gradually socialized into social relationships, even within their rather self-centered world.

In his well-known **cognitive theory of development,** Piaget (1954) identified four stages in the development of children's thought processes. In the first, or *sensorimotor,* stage, young children use their senses to make discoveries. For example, through touching they discover that their hands are actually a part of themselves. During the second, or *preoperational,* stage, children begin to use words and symbols to distinguish objects and ideas. The milestone in the third, or *concrete operational,* stage is that children engage in more logical thinking. They learn that even when a formless lump of clay is shaped into a snake, it is still the same clay. Finally, in the fourth, or *formal operational,* stage, adolescents become capable of sophisticated abstract thought and can deal with ideas and values in a logical manner.

Piaget suggested that moral development becomes an important part of socialization as children develop the ability to think more abstractly. When children learn the rules of a game such as checkers or jacks, they are learning to obey societal norms. Those under age eight display a rather basic level of morality: rules are rules, and there is no concept of "extenuating circumstances." As they mature, children become capable of greater autonomy and begin to experience moral dilemmas and doubts as to what constitutes proper behavior.

According to Jean Piaget, social interaction is the key to development. As children grow older, they pay increasing attention to how other people think and why they act in particular ways. In order to develop a distinct personality, each of us needs opportunities to interact with others. As we saw earlier, Isabelle was deprived of the chance for normal social interactions, and the consequences were severe (Kitchener 1991).

We have seen that a number of thinkers considered social interaction the key to the development of an individual's sense of self. As is generally true, we can best understand this topic by drawing on a variety of theory and research. Table 4-2 summarizes the rich literature, both sociological and psychological, on the development of the self.

Agents of Socialization

As we have seen, the culture of the United States is defined by rather gradual movements from one stage of socialization to the next. The continuing and lifelong socialization process involves many different social forces that influence our lives and alter our self-images.

The family is the most important agent of socialization in the United States, especially for children. In this chapter, we'll also discuss six other agents of socialization: the school, the peer group, the mass media and technology, the workplace, religion, and the state. We'll explore the role of religion in socializing young people into society's norms and values more fully in Chapter 15.

Family

Children in Amish communities are raised in a highly structured and disciplined manner. But they are not immune to the temptations posed by their peers in the non-Amish world—"rebellious" acts such as dancing, drinking, and riding in cars. Still, Amish families don't become too concerned; they know the strong influence they ultimately exert over their offspring. The same is true for all families. It is tempting to say that the peer group or

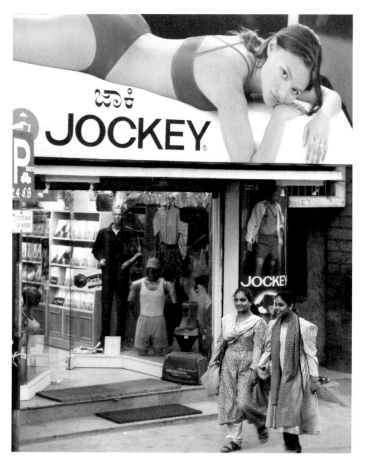

On a busy commercial street in Bangalore, India, pedestrians dressed in traditional garb stroll past a shop and billboard advertising Western fashions. Socialization comes from cultural influences as well as from family and friends. In today's globalized world, Western media expose children to cultural values that their parents and other authorities may not embrace.

even the media really raise children these days, especially when the spotlight falls on young people involved in shooting sprees and hate crimes. Almost all available research, however, shows that the role of the family in socializing a child cannot be overestimated (Matthews 2007; W. Williams 1998).

The lifelong process of learning begins shortly after birth. Since newborns can hear, see, smell, taste, and feel heat, cold, and pain, they are constantly orienting themselves to the surrounding world. Human beings, especially family members, constitute an important part of their social environment. People minister to the baby's needs by feeding, cleansing, carrying, and comforting the baby.

Cultural Influences As both Charles Horton Cooley and George Herbert Mead noted, the development of the self is a critical aspect of the early years of one's life. How children develop this sense of self can vary from one society to another, however. For example, most parents in the United States do not send six-year-olds to school unsupervised. But that is the norm in Japan, where parents push their children to commute to school on their own from an early age. In cities like Tokyo, first-graders must learn to negotiate buses, subways, and long walks. To ensure their safety, parents carefully lay out rules: never talk

to strangers; check with a station attendant if you get off at the wrong stop; if you miss your stop stay on to the end of the line, then call; take stairs, not escalators; don't fall asleep. Some parents equip the children with cell phones or pagers. One parent acknowledges that she worries, "but after they are 6, children are supposed to start being independent from the mother. If you're still taking your child to school after the first month, everyone looks at you funny" (Tolbert 2000:17).

As we consider the family's role in socialization, we need to remember that children do not play a passive role. They are active agents, influencing and altering the families, schools, and communities of which they are a part.

The Impact of Race and Gender In the United States, social development includes exposure to cultural assumptions regarding gender and race. Black parents, for example, have learned that children as young as age two can absorb negative messages about Blacks in children's books, toys, and television shows—all of which are designed primarily for White consumers. At the same time, Black children are exposed more often than others to the inner-city youth gang culture. Because most Blacks, even those who are middle class, live near very poor neighborhoods, children such as Charisse (see the chapter-opening excerpt) are susceptible to these influences, despite their parents' strong family values (Linn and Poussaint 1999; Pattillo-McCoy 1999).

The term **gender role** refers to expectations regarding the proper behavior, attitudes, and activities of males and females. For example, we traditionally think of "toughness" as masculine—and desirable only in men—while we view "tenderness" as feminine. As we will see in Chapter 12, other cultures do not necessarily assign these qualities to each gender in the way that our culture does. The existence of gender roles does not imply that inevitably, males and females will assume certain roles, nor does it imply that those roles are quite distinct from one another. Rather, gender roles emphasize the fact that males and females are not genetically predetermined to occupy certain roles.

As the primary agents of childhood socialization, parents play a critical role in guiding children into those gender roles deemed appropriate in a society. Other adults, older siblings, the mass media, and religious and educational institutions also have a noticeable impact on a child's socialization into feminine and masculine norms. A culture or subculture may require that one sex or the other take primary responsibility for the socialization of children, economic support of the family, or religious or intellectual leadership. In some societies, girls are socialized mainly by their mothers and boys by their fathers—an arrangement that may prevent girls from learning critical survival skills. In South Asia, fathers teach their sons to swim to prepare them for a life as fishermen; girls typically do not learn to swim. When a deadly tsunami hit the coast of South Asia in 2004, many more men survived than women.

Interactionists remind us that socialization concerning not only masculinity and femininity but also marriage and parenthood begins in childhood as a part of family life. Children observe their parents as they express affection, deal with finances, quarrel, complain about in-laws, and so forth. Their learning represents an informal process of anticipatory socialization in which they develop a tentative model of what being married and being a parent are like. (We will explore socialization for marriage and parenthood more fully in Chapter 14.)

School

Where did you learn the national anthem? Who taught you about the heroes of the American Revolution? Where were you first tested on your knowledge of your culture? Like the family, schools have an explicit mandate to socialize people in the United States—especially children—into the norms and values of our culture.

As conflict theorists Samuel Bowles and Herbert Gintis (1976) have observed, schools in this country foster competition through built-in systems of reward and punishment, such as grades and evaluations by teachers. Consequently, a child who is experiencing difficulty trying to learn a new skill can sometimes come to feel stupid and unsuccessful. However, as the self matures, children become capable of increasingly realistic assessments of their intellectual, physical, and social abilities.

Functionalists point out that schools, as agents of socialization, fulfill the function of teaching children the values and customs of the larger society. Conflict theorists agree, but add that schools can reinforce the divisive aspects of society, especially those of social class. For example, higher education in the United States is costly despite the existence of financial aid programs. Students from affluent backgrounds therefore have an advantage in gaining access to universities and professional training. At the same time, less affluent young people may never receive the preparation that would qualify them for the best-paying and most prestigious jobs. The contrast between the functionalist and conflict views of education will be discussed in more detail in Chapter 16.

In other cultures as well, schools serve socialization functions. Until the overthrow of Saddam Hussein in 2003, the sixth-grade textbooks used in Iraqi schools concentrated almost entirely on the military and its values of loyalty, honor, and sacrifice. Children were taught that their enemies were Iran, the

In her Michigan home, a young girl displays Razanne, a modestly dressed doll made especially for Muslim children. Because girls learn about themselves and their social roles by playing with dolls, having a doll that represents their own heritage is important to them.

TABLE **4-3**   HIGH SCHOOL POPULARITY

What makes high school girls popular?		What makes high school boys popular?	
According to college men:	According to college women:	According to college men:	According to college women:
1. Physical attractiveness	1. Grades/intelligence	1. Participation in sports	1. Participation in sports
2. Grades/intelligence	2. Participation in sports	2. Grades/intelligence	2. Grades/intelligence
3. Participation in sports	3. General sociability	3. Popularity with girls	3. General sociability
4. General sociability	4. Physical attractiveness	4. General sociability	4. Physical attractiveness
5. Popularity with boys	5. Clothes	5. Car	5. School clubs/government

Note: Students at the following universities were asked in which ways adolescents in their high schools had gained prestige with their peers: Cornell University, Louisiana State University, Southeastern Louisiana University, State University of New York at Albany, State University of New York at Stony Brook, University of Georgia, and University of New Hampshire.
Source: Suitor et al. 2001:445.

United States, Israel and its supporters, and NATO, the European military alliance. Within months of the regime's fall, the curriculum had been rewritten to remove indoctrination on behalf of Hussein, his army, and his Baath Socialist Party (Marr 2003).

Peer Group

Ask 13-year-olds who matters most in their lives and they are likely to answer "friends." As a child grows older, the family becomes somewhat less important in social development. Instead, peer groups increasingly assume the role of Mead's significant others. Within the peer group, young people associate with others who are approximately their own age, and who often enjoy a similar social status (Giordano 2003).

We can see how important peer groups are to young people when their social lives are strained by war or disaster. In Baghdad, the overthrow of Saddam Hussein has profoundly changed teenagers' world, casting doubt on their future. Some young people have lost relatives or friends; others have become involved with fundamentalist groups or fled with their families to safer countries. Those youths who are left behind can suffer intense loneliness and boredom. Confined to their homes by crime and terrorism, those fortunate enough to have computers turn to Internet chat rooms or immerse themselves in their studies. Through e-mail, they struggle to maintain old friendships interrupted by wartime dislocation (Sanders 2004).

Gender differences are noteworthy among adolescents. Boys and girls are socialized by their parents, peers, and the media to identify many of the same paths to popularity, but to different degrees. Table 4-3 compares male and female college students' reports of how girls and boys they knew became popular in high school. The two groups named many of the same paths to popularity but gave them a different order of importance. While neither men nor women named sexual activity, drug use, or alcohol use as one of the top five paths, college men were much more likely than women to mention those behaviors as a means to becoming popular, for both boys and girls.

Mass Media and Technology

In the past 80 years, media innovations—radio, motion pictures, recorded music, television, and the Internet—have become important agents of socialization. Television, and increasingly the Internet, are critical forces in the socialization of children in the United States. One national survey indicates that 68 percent of U.S. children have a television in their bedroom, and nearly half of all youths ages 8 to 18 use the Internet every day (Figure 4-2).

These media, however, are not always a negative socializing influence. Television programs and even commercials can introduce young people to unfamiliar lifestyles and cultures. Not only do children in the United States learn about life in "faraway

FIGURE **4-2**   HOW YOUNG PEOPLE USE THE MEDIA ON A TYPICAL DAY

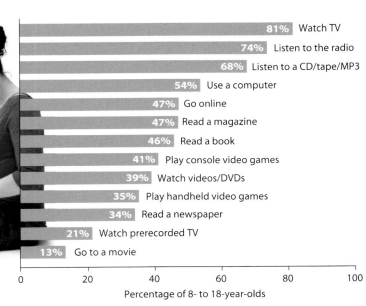

81%	Watch TV
74%	Listen to the radio
68%	Listen to a CD/tape/MP3
54%	Use a computer
47%	Go online
47%	Read a magazine
46%	Read a book
41%	Play console video games
39%	Watch videos/DVDs
35%	Play handheld video games
34%	Read a newspaper
21%	Watch prerecorded TV
13%	Go to a movie

Percentage of 8- to 18-year-olds

Note: Based on a national representative sample of 2,032 people surveyed between October 2003 and March 2004.
Source: Rideout et al. 2005:7.

lands," but inner-city children learn about the lives of farm children, and vice versa. The same thing happens in other countries.

Sociologists and other social scientists have begun to consider the impact of technology on socialization. They are particularly interested in the online friendship networks, like Facebook. Does this way of communicating resemble face-to-face interaction, or does it represent a new form of social interaction? Box 4-2 on page 88 explores the significance of this social phenomenon.

Not just in industrial nations, but in Africa and other developing areas, people have been socialized into relying on new communications technologies. Not long ago, if Zadhe Iyombe wanted to talk to his mother, he had to make an eight-day trip from the capital city of Kinshasa up the Congo River by boat to the rural town where he was born. Now both he and his mother have access to a cell phone, and they send text messages to each other daily. Iyombe and his mother are not atypical. Although cell phones aren't cheap, 1.4 billion owners in developing countries have come to consider them a necessity. Today, there are more cell phones in developing nations than in industrial nations—the first time in history that developing nations have outpaced the developed world in the adoption of a telecommunications technology (K. Sullivan 2006).

This girl's day doesn't end when school lets out. So many teenagers now work after school, the workplace has become another important agent of socialization for adolescents.

Workplace

Learning to behave appropriately in an occupation is a fundamental aspect of human socialization. In the United States, working full-time confirms adult status; it indicates that one has passed out of adolescence. In a sense, socialization into an occupation can represent both a harsh reality ("I have to work in order to buy food and pay the rent") and the realization of an ambition ("I've always wanted to be an airline pilot") (W. Moore 1968:862).

It used to be that going to work began with the end of our formal schooling, but that is no longer the case, at least not in the United States. More and more young people work today, and not just for a parent or relative. Adolescents generally seek jobs in order to make spending money; 80 percent of high school seniors say that little or none of what they earn goes to family expenses. These teens rarely look on their employment as a means of exploring vocational interests or getting on-the-job training.

Some observers feel that the increasing number of teenagers who are working earlier in life and for longer hours are finding the workplace almost as important an agent of socialization as school. In fact, a number of educators complain that student time at work is adversely affecting schoolwork. The level of teenage employment in the United States is the highest among industrial countries, which may provide one explanation for why U.S. high school students lag behind those in other countries on international achievement tests.

Socialization in the workplace changes when it involves a more permanent shift from an after-school job to full-time employment. Occupational socialization can be most intense during the transition from school to job, but it continues throughout one's work history. Technological advances may alter the requirements of the position and necessitate some degree of resocialization. Today, men and women change occupations, employers, or places of work many times during their adult years. Occupational socialization continues, then, throughout a person's years in the labor market.

College students today recognize that occupational socialization is not socialization into one lifetime occupation. They anticipate going through a number of jobs. The Bureau of Labor Statistics (2006) has found that from ages 18 to 40, the typical person holds 11 different jobs. This high rate of turnover in employment applies to both men and women, and to those with a college degree as well as those with a high school diploma.

Religion and the State

Increasingly, social scientists are recognizing the importance of both government ("the state") and religion as agents of socialization, because of their impact on the life course. Traditionally, family members have served as the primary caregivers in our culture, but in the 20th century, the family's protective function was steadily transferred to outside agencies such as hospitals, mental health clinics, and child care centers. Many of these agencies are run by the state or by groups affiliated with certain religions.

Both government and organized religion have impacted the life course by reinstituting some of the rites of passage once observed in agricultural communities and early industrial societies. For example, religious organizations stipulate certain traditional rites that may bring together all the members of an extended family, even if they never meet for any other reason. And government regulations stipulate the ages at which a person may drive a car, drink alcohol, vote in elections, marry without parental permission, work overtime, and retire. These regulations do not constitute strict rites of passage: most 18-year-olds choose not to vote, and most people choose their age of retirement without reference to government dictates.

In the Social Policy section at the end of this chapter, we will see that government is under pressure to become a provider

4-2 Online Socializing: A New Agent of Socialization

Membership in the online social networks Facebook, Friendster, and MySpace has grown exponentially in recent years. At first, young adults monopolized these social networks. Indeed, Facebook was created in 2004 as a way for students on a single campus to become acquainted with one another before actually meeting. Now there are well over 150 million profiles online, more than 70 percent of them from outside the United States. Sociologists are interested in these new social networks not because of the sophisticated technology that supports them, but because of their social significance. Much like face-to-face encounters with schoolmates or fellow workers, online social encounters serve as an agent of socialization. They affect both the development of the self and the identification of significant others, especially among youths, for whom online social networks are a particularly dominant agent of socialization.

Even in the brief history of online networking, sociologists can see social trends. For example, older people are now creating profiles on these sites. As Figure A shows, there is still a clear correlation between age and online profiles: younger people are much more likely than older people to be online. However, the fastest-growing age groups are now those over 30, including those who are much older. As a result, online socializing is becoming much less age-specific—more like socializing in the real world. Moreover, this new agent of socialization can continue to influence people throughout the life course.

Though these networks offer attractive opportunities for people to socialize with others, they also raise concerns about privacy and security. Unlike face-to-face socialization, in which people hesitate to disclose personal information to strangers, online interaction tends to be more open. Looking at people's online profiles, we can see an amazing amount of personal information—much more than the typical organization will disclose about members. For example, academic institutions, which are governed by the Family Education Rights and Privacy Act (FERPA) of 1974, will disclose only the barest of details about students. In contrast, millions of high school and college students reveal significant amounts of personal

> *Online networks—especially those that indicate how many "friends" an individual has—can also be seen in terms of social capital.*

information online. As Figure B shows, many if not most students state their relationship status, occupation, interests (often termed "passions"), and sexual orientation in their online profiles—all of which are considered privileged information under FERPA. Students may also admit to drinking, drug use, sexual promiscuity, self-injury (see the opening of Chapter 2), eating disorders, and other socially disapproved behaviors.

Online networks—especially those that indicate how many "friends" an individual has—can also be seen in terms of social capital. In fact, "friending" is one, if not *the*, main activity on some online sites. Often the number of friends a person socializes with becomes the subject of boasting. By extension, individuals may use these sites to search for "friends" who may prove helpful to them in future endeavors. Becoming aware of new opportunities, either social or economic, through friends is a significant benefit of social capital.

Researchers have looked at the relationship between the display of friends online and the number of real-world friends people socialize with, and have proposed two competing hypotheses. According to the social enhancement hypothesis ("the rich get richer"), those who are popular offline further increase their popularity through online networking sites. According to the social compensation hypothesis ("the poor get richer"), however, social network users try to increase their popularity online to compensate for inadequate popularity offline. The social compensation hypothesis, if correct, would be an example of impression management. Research to date supports elements of both hypotheses; neither hypothesis fully defines the participants in online networking sites.

A new means of social networking, Twitter, emerged recently. A way of tracking people online, Twitter allows members to receive very brief instant messages from friends and acquaintances, who may signal their whereabouts or remark on what they are doing or seeing. This form of networking is even more passive than the original social networking sites. Once a member agrees to accept a tweet from someone, the alerts keep coming.

Viewed from a societal perspective, socializing online can have both positive and negative functions. For members of some marginalized populations, it is a way to socialize with like-minded people. For example, Muslims in Great Britain connect with friends online to learn how to navigate through a society in which they form a distinct minority. For other people, such as members of the Nazis in Germany and the Mafia in Italy, online networking is a way to proclaim allegiance to socially objectionable organizations. Governments frown on such online

FIGURE A ADULTS WITH ONLINE PROFILES

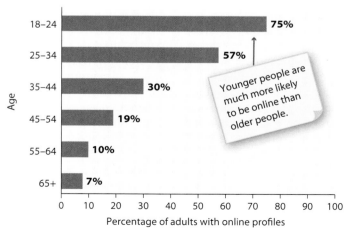

Age	Percentage of adults with online profiles
18–24	75%
25–34	57%
35–44	30%
45–54	19%
55–64	10%
65+	7%

Younger people are much more likely to be online than older people.

Note: Data collected in May 2008 and limited to adult participants because of ethical guidelines governing survey research.
Source: Lenhart 2009:1.

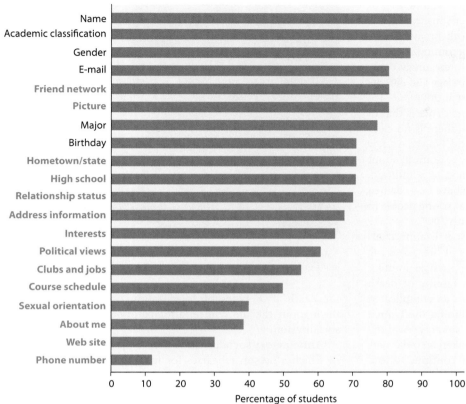

Red type indicates information not typically disclosed by colleges.

Note: Based on a review of 200 online profiles posted by college students in Facebook. Information on friend networks, majors, hometowns/states, and clubs and jobs was drawn from more than one possible field.
Source: Adapted from Stutzman 2007: Figure 1.

organizing, seeing it as dysfunctional, and periodically monitor these sites to see whether any laws have been violated.

LET'S DISCUSS

1. Do you list your "friends" on an online social networking site? If so, what is your motivation for doing so? How much social capital do you think your list represents?
2. Which of the drawbacks of online social networking—privacy lapses, extremist organizing—concerns you more? Do you think the advantages of online social networking outweigh the disadvantages?

Sources: Donadio 2009; N. Ellison et al. 2007; Facebook 2009; Gentile 2009; Hundley and Ramirez 2008; Lenhart 2009; Zywica and Danowski 2008.

---

of child care, which would give it a new and direct role in the socialization of infants and young children.

use your sociological *imagination*

You are Muslim (or another religion that is different from your own). How does your self-concept differ from the one you developed as a child?

Socialization throughout the Life Course

The Life Course

Among the Kota people of the Congo in Africa, adolescents paint themselves blue. Mexican American girls go on a daylong religious retreat before dancing the night away. Egyptian mothers step over their newborn infants seven times, and students at the Naval Academy throw their hats in the air. These are all ways

of celebrating **rites of passage,** a means of dramatizing and validating changes in a person's status. Rites of passage can mark a separation, as in a graduation ceremony, or an incorporation, as in an initiation into an organization (Gennep [1909]1960).

Rites of passage are a worldwide social phenomenon. The Kota rite marks the passage to adulthood. The color blue, viewed as the color of death, symbolizes the death of childhood. Hispanic girls celebrate reaching womanhood with a *quinceañera* ceremony at age 15. In the Cuban American community of Miami, the popularity of the *quinceañera* supports a network of party planners, caterers, dress designers, and the Miss Quinceañera Latina pageant. For thousands of years, Egyptian mothers have welcomed their newborns to the world in the Soboa ceremony by stepping over the seven-day-old infant seven times. And Naval Academy seniors celebrate their graduation from college by hurling their hats skyward.

These specific ceremonies mark stages of development in the life course. They indicate that the process of socialization continues through all stages of the life cycle. In fact, some researchers have chosen to concentrate on socialization as a lifelong process. Sociologists and other social scientists who take such a **life course approach** look closely at the social factors that influence people throughout their lives, from birth to death, including gender and income. They recognize that biological changes mold but do not dictate human behavior.

Several life events mark the passage to adulthood. Of course, these turning points vary from one society and even one generation to the next. According to a national survey done in 2002, in the United States the key event seems to be the completion of formal schooling (Table 4-4). On average, Americans expect this milestone to occur by a person's 23rd birthday. Other major events in the life course, such as getting married or becoming a parent, are expected to follow three or four years later. Interestingly, comparatively few survey respondents identified marriage and parenthood as important milestones (S. Furstenberg et al. 2004).

One result of these staggered steps to independence is that in the United States, unlike some other societies, there is no clear dividing line between adolescence and adulthood. Nowadays, few young people finish school, get married, and leave home at about the same age, clearly establishing their transition to adulthood. The terms *youthhood* and *emerging adulthood* have been coined to describe the prolonged ambiguous status that young people in their 20s experience (Côté 2000; Christian Smith 2007).

We encounter some of the most difficult socialization challenges (and rites of passage) in the later years of life. Assessing one's accomplishments, coping with declining physical abilities, experiencing retirement, and facing the inevitability of death may lead to painful adjustments. Old age is further complicated by the negative way that many societies, including the United States, view and treat the elderly. The common stereotypes of the elderly as helpless and dependent may well weaken an older person's self-image. However, many older people continue to lead active, productive, fulfilled lives, whether in the paid labor force or as retirees.

Anticipatory Socialization and Resocialization

The development of a social self is literally a lifelong transformation that begins in the crib and continues as one prepares

A young Apache woman undergoes a mudding ceremony traditionally used in rites of passage such as puberty and in some cases weddings.

for death. Two types of socialization occur at many points throughout the life course: anticipatory socialization and resocialization.

Anticipatory socialization refers to processes of socialization in which a person rehearses for future positions, occupations, and social relationships. A culture can function more efficiently and smoothly if members become acquainted with the norms, values, and behavior associated with a social position before actually assuming that status. Preparation for many aspects of adult life begins with anticipatory socialization during childhood and adolescence, and continues throughout our lives as we prepare for new responsibilities.

TABLE **4-4** MILESTONES IN THE TRANSITION TO ADULTHOOD

Life Event	Expected Age	Percentage of People Who View Event as Extremely/Quite Important
Financial independence from parents/guardians	20.9 years	80.9%
Separate residence from parents	21.1	57.2
Full-time employment	21.2	83.8
Completion of formal schooling	22.3	90.2
Capability of supporting a family	24.5	82.3
Marriage	25.7	33.2
Parenthood	26.2	29.0

Note: Based on the 2002 General Social Survey of 1,398 people.
Source: T. Smith 2003.

Think about It
Why did so few respondents consider marriage and parenthood to be important milestones? Which milestones do you think are most important?

Prisons are centers of resocialization, where people are placed under pressure to discard old behavior patterns and accept new ones. These prisoners are learning to use weights to release tension and exert their strength—a socially acceptable method of handling antisocial impulses.

Resocialization is particularly effective when it occurs within a total institution. Erving Goffman (1961) coined the term **total institution** to refer to an institution that regulates all aspects of a person's life under a single authority, such as a prison, the military, a mental hospital, or a convent. Because the total institution is generally cut off from the rest of society, it provides for all the needs of its members. Quite literally, the crew of a merchant vessel at sea becomes part of a total institution. So elaborate are its requirements, so all-encompassing its activities, a total institution often represents a miniature society.

Goffman (1961) identified four common traits of total institutions:

- All aspects of life are conducted in the same place under the control of a single authority.

- Any activities within the institution are conducted in the company of others in the same circumstances—for example, army recruits or novices in a convent.

- The authorities devise rules and schedule activities without consulting the participants.

- All aspects of life within a total institution are designed to fulfill the purpose of the organization. Thus, all activities in a monastery might be centered on prayer and communion with God. (Davies 1989; P. Rose et al. 1979)

People often lose their individuality within total institutions. For example, a person entering prison may experience the humiliation of a **degradation ceremony** as he or she is stripped of clothing, jewelry, and other personal possessions. From this point on, scheduled daily routines allow for little or no personal initiative. The individual becomes secondary and rather invisible in the overbearing social environment (Garfinkel 1956).

You can see the process of anticipatory socialization take place when high school students start to consider what colleges they may attend. Traditionally, this task meant looking at publications received in the mail or making campus visits. However, with new technology, more and more students are using the Web to begin their college experience. Colleges are investing more time and money in developing attractive Web sites through which students can take virtual campus tours and hear audio clips of everything from the college anthem to a sample zoology lecture.

Occasionally, assuming a new social or occupational position requires us to *unlearn* an established orientation. **Resocialization** refers to the process of discarding former behavior patterns and accepting new ones as part of a transition in one's life. Often resocialization occurs during an explicit effort to transform an individual, as happens in reform schools, therapy groups, prisons, religious conversion settings, and political indoctrination camps. The process of resocialization typically involves considerable stress for the individual—much more so than socialization in general, or even anticipatory socialization (Gecas 2004).

social**policy** and Socialization

Child Care around the World

In Israel, Aisheh and Eliza run a nursery for 29 Israeli and Palestinian children, ages four to six. Aisheh, who is Palestinian, speaks to the children in Arabic. Eliza, who is Jewish, speaks to them in Hebrew. The result: a bilingual, binational classroom that supports both Arab and Jewish culture—a first for Israel.

This unusual educational setting underscores the importance of early childhood socialization outside the home. Child care programs are not just babysitting services; they have an enormous influence on the development of young children—an influence that has been growing with the movement of more and more women into the paid labor force.

The Issue

The rise in single-parent families, increased job opportunities for women, and the need for additional family income have all propelled an increasing number of mothers of young children into the paid labor force of the United States. Who takes care of the children of these women during work hours?

Preschoolers typically are not cared for by their parents. Seventy-three percent of employed mothers depend on others to care for their children, and 30 percent of mothers who aren't employed have regular care arrangements. In fact, children under age five are more likely to be cared for on a daily basis by their grandparents than by their parents. Over a third of them are cared for by nonrelatives in nursery schools, Head Start programs, day care centers, family day care, and other arrangements (Bureau of the Census 2008c).

The Setting

Few people in the United States or elsewhere can afford the luxury of having a parent stay at home, or of paying for high-quality live-in child care. For millions of mothers and fathers, finding the right kind of child care is a challenge both to parenting and to the pocketbook.

Researchers have found that high-quality child care centers do not adversely affect the socialization of children; in fact, good day care benefits children. The value of preschool programs was documented in a series of studies conducted in the United States. Researchers found no significant differences in infants who had received extensive nonmaternal care compared with those who had been cared for solely by their mothers. They also reported that more and more infants in the United States are being placed in child care outside the home, and that overall, the quality of those arrangements is better than has been found in previous studies. It is difficult, however, to generalize about child care, since there is so much variability among day care providers, and even among government policies from one state to another (Loeb et al. 2004; Ludwig and Sawhill 2007; NICHD 2007).

At present, the federal government supports child care through subsidized programs, which target low-income families, and income tax credits, which benefit families with more moderate incomes. The annual expenditure to assist low-income parents is about $12 billion; the expenditure to support more affluent parents is $58 billion (Cushing-Daniels and Zedlewski 2008).

Sociological Insights

Studies that assess the quality of child care outside the home reflect the micro level of analysis and the interest of interactionists in the impact of face-to-face interaction. These studies also explore macro-level implications for the functioning of social institutions like the family. But some of the issues surrounding day care have also been of interest to those who take the conflict perspective.

In the United States, high-quality day care is not equally available to all families. Parents in wealthy communities have an easier time finding day care than those in poor or working-class communities. Finding *affordable* child care is also a problem. Viewed from a conflict perspective, child care costs are an especially serious burden for lower-class families. The poorest families spend 25 percent of their income for preschool child care, while families who are *not* poor pay only 6 percent or less of their income.

Feminist theorists echo the concern of conflict theorists that high-quality child care receives little government support because it is regarded as "merely a way to let women work." Nearly all child care workers (95 percent) are women; many find themselves in low-status, minimum-wage jobs.

Children play at the Communicare day care center in Perth, Australia. The Australian government subsidizes children's attendance at day care and after-school programs from birth to age 12.

Typically, food servers, messengers, and gas station attendants make more money than the 1.2 million child care workers in the United States, who average $9.05 per hour. Not surprisingly, turnover among employees in child care centers runs at about 30 percent per year (Bureau of the Census 2008a:Table 596; Clawson and Gerstel 2002; NACCRRA 2008).

Policy Initiatives

Policies regarding child care outside the home vary throughout the world. As Figure 4-3 shows, the cost of child care as a proportion of one's income can vary dramatically, but at least it is available in industrial nations. Most developing nations do not have the economic base to provide subsidized child care. Thus, working mothers rely largely on relatives or take their children to work. In the comparatively wealthy industrialized countries of Western Europe, government provides child care as a basic service, at little or no expense to parents. But even those countries with tax-subsidized programs occasionally fall short of the need for high-quality child care.

When policymakers decide that child care is desirable, they must determine the degree to which taxpayers should subsidize it. In Sweden and Denmark, one-half to two-thirds of preschoolers were in government-subsidized child care full-time in 2003. In the United States, where government subsidies are very limited, the total cost of child care can easily run between $9,100 and $13,200 per family per year (Immervoll and Barber 2005; NACCRRA 2007:2).

We have a long way to go in making high-quality child care more affordable and accessible, not just in the United States but throughout the world. In an attempt to reduce government

FIGURE **4-3** CHILD CARE COSTS IN INDUSTRIAL NATIONS

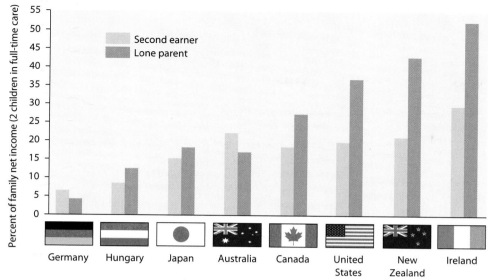

Source: Data collected by the Organisation for Economic Co-operation and Development (OECD) in 2002 and reported in Immervoll and Barber 2005.

reunification has reduced the options previously open to East German mothers, who had become accustomed to government-supported child care. Experts in child development view such reports as a vivid reminder of the need for greater government and private-sector support for child care (Hank 2001; L. King 1998).

Let's Discuss

1. Were you ever in a day care program? Do you recall the experience as good or bad? In general, do you think it is desirable to expose young children to the socializing influence of day care?

2. In the view of conflict theorists, child care receives little government support because it is "merely a way to let women work." Can you think of other explanations?

spending, France is considering cutting back the budgets of subsidized nurseries, even though waiting lists exist and the French public heartily disapproves of cutbacks. In Germany,

3. Should the costs of day care programs be paid by government, by the private sector, or entirely by parents?

getting**involved**

To get involved in the debate over day care, visit this book's Online Learning Center, which offers links to relevant Web sites.

www.mhhe.com/schaefer12e

MASTERING THIS CHAPTER

Summary

Socialization is the process through which people learn the attitudes, values, and actions appropriate for members of a particular culture. This chapter examines the role of socialization in human development; the way in which people develop perceptions, feelings, and beliefs about themselves; the lifelong nature of the socialization process; and the important agents of socialization.

1. **Socialization** affects the overall cultural practices of a society; it also shapes the images that we hold of ourselves.

2. Heredity and environmental factors interact in influencing the socialization process.

3. In the early 1900s, Charles Horton Cooley advanced the belief that we learn who we are by interacting with others, a phenomenon he called the **looking-glass self.**

4. George Herbert Mead, best known for his theory of the **self,** proposed that as people mature, their selves begin to reflect their concern about reactions from others—both **generalized others** and **significant others.**

5. Erving Goffman has shown that in many of our daily activities, we try to convey distinct impressions of who we are, a process he called **impression management.**

6. As the primary agents of socialization, parents play a critical role in guiding children into those **gender roles** deemed appropriate in a society.

7. Like the family, schools in the United States have an explicit mandate to socialize people—especially children—into the norms and values of our culture.

8. Peer groups and the mass media, especially television and the Internet, are important agents of socialization for adolescents.

9. Socialization in the workplace begins with part-time employment while we are in school and continues as we work full-time and change jobs throughout our lives.

10. Religion and the state shape the socialization process by regulating the life course and influencing our views of appropriate behavior at particular ages.

11. Socialization proceeds throughout the life course. Some societies mark stages of development with formal **rites of passage.** In the culture of the United States, significant events such as marriage and parenthood serve to change a person's status.

12. As more and more mothers of young children have entered the labor market, the demand for child care has increased dramatically, posing policy questions for many nations around the world.

Critical Thinking Questions

1. Should social research be conducted on issues such as the influence of heredity and environment, even though many investigators believe that this type of analysis is potentially detrimental to large numbers of people?

2. Drawing on Erving Goffman's dramaturgical approach, discuss how the following groups engage in impression management: athletes, college instructors, parents, physicians, and politicians.

3. How would functionalists and conflict theorists differ in their analysis of socialization by the mass media?

Key Terms

Anticipatory socialization Processes of socialization in which a person rehearses for future positions, occupations, and social relationships. (page 90)

Cognitive theory of development The theory that children's thought progresses through four stages of development. (83)

Degradation ceremony An aspect of the socialization process within some total institutions, in which people are subjected to humiliating rituals. (91)

Dramaturgical approach A view of social interaction in which people are seen as theatrical performers. (82)

Face-work The efforts people make to maintain the proper image and avoid public embarrassment. (82)

Gender role Expectations regarding the proper behavior, attitudes, and activities of males and females. (84)

Generalized other The attitudes, viewpoints, and expectations of society as a whole that a child takes into account in his or her behavior. (80)

Impression management The altering of the presentation of the self in order to create distinctive appearances and satisfy particular audiences. (81)

Life course approach A research orientation in which sociologists and other social scientists look closely at the social factors that influence people throughout their lives, from birth to death. (89)

Looking-glass self A concept that emphasizes the self as the product of our social interactions. (79)

Personality A person's typical patterns of attitudes, needs, characteristics, and behavior. (77)

Resocialization The process of discarding former behavior patterns and accepting new ones as part of a transition in one's life. (91)

Rite of passage A ritual marking the symbolic transition from one social position to another. (89)

Role taking The process of mentally assuming the perspective of another and responding from that imagined viewpoint. (80)

Self A distinct identity that sets us apart from others. (79)

Significant other An individual who is most important in the development of the self, such as a parent, friend, or teacher. (81)

Socialization The lifelong process in which people learn the attitudes, values, and behaviors appropriate for members of a particular culture. (76)

Total institution An institution that regulates all aspects of a person's life under a single authority, such as a prison, the military, a mental hospital, or a convent. (91)

Self-Quiz

Read each question carefully and then select the best answer.

1. Which of the following social scientists used the phrase *looking-glass self* to emphasize that the self is the product of our social interactions with other people?
   a. George Herbert Mead
   b. Charles Horton Cooley
   c. Erving Goffman
   d. Jean Piaget

2. In what he called the *play stage* of socialization, George Herbert Mead asserted that people mentally assume the perspectives of others, thereby enabling them to respond from that imagined viewpoint. This process is referred to as
   a. role taking.
   b. the generalized other.
   c. the significant other.
   d. impression management.

3. George Herbert Mead is best known for his theory of what?
   a. presentation of the self
   b. cognitive development
   c. the self
   d. impression management

4. Suppose a clerk tries to appear busier than he or she actually is when a supervisor happens to be watching. Erving Goffman would study this behavior from what approach?
   a. functionalist
   b. conflict
   c. psychological
   d. interactionist

5. According to child psychologist Jean Piaget's cognitive theory of development, children begin to use words and symbols to distinguish objects and ideas during which stage in the development of the thought process?
   a. the sensorimotor stage
   b. the preoperational stage
   c. the concrete operational stage
   d. the formal operational stage

6. On the first day of basic training in the army, a recruit has his civilian clothes replaced with army "greens," has his hair shaved off, loses his privacy, and finds that he must use a communal bathroom. All these humiliating activities are part of
   a. becoming a significant other.
   b. impression management.
   c. a degradation ceremony.
   d. face-work.

7. Which social institution is considered to be the most important agent of socialization in the United States, especially for children?
   a. the family
   b. the school
   c. the peer group
   d. the mass media

8. The term *gender role* refers to
   a. the biological fact that we are male or female.
   b. a role that is given to us by a teacher.
   c. a role that is given to us in a play.
   d. expectations regarding the proper behavior, attitudes, and activities of males and females.

9. Which sociological perspective emphasizes that schools in the United States foster competition through built-in systems of reward and punishment?
   a. the functionalist perspective
   b. the conflict perspective
   c. the interactionist perspective
   d. the psychological perspective

10. Which of the following statements about teenagers in Baghdad is true?
   a. They have lost much of their peer group due to death and relocation.
   b. They have lost peers who have joined fundamentalist groups.
   c. If they own a computer, they use it in an attempt to stay in contact with their pre-war peer group.
   d. all of the above

11. _____ is the term used by sociologists in referring to the lifelong process whereby people learn the attitudes, values, and behaviors appropriate for members of a particular culture.

12. In everyday speech, the term _____ is used to refer to a person's typical patterns of attitudes, needs, characteristics, and behavior.

13. Studies of twins raised apart suggest that both _____ and _____ influence human development.

14. A _____ _____ is an individual such as a parent, friend, or teacher who is most important in the development of the self.

15. Those individuals who are most important in shaping a person's identity (e.g., parents, friends, co-workers, coaches, and teachers) are referred to as

_____ _____.

16. Early work in _____ such as that by Sigmund Freud, stressed the role of inborn drives—among them the drive for sexual gratification—in channeling human behavior.

17. Preparation for many aspects of adult life begins with _____ socialization during childhood and adolescence and continues throughout our lives as we prepare for new responsibilities.

18. Resocialization is particularly effective when it occurs within a(n) _____ institution.

19. The _____ perspective emphasizes the role of schools in teaching the values and customs of the larger society.

20. As children grow older, the family becomes less important in social development, while _____ groups become more important.

Answers

1 (b); 2 (a); 3 (c); 4 (d); 5 (b); 6 (c); 7 (a); 8 (d); 9 (b); 10 (d); 11 Socialization; 12 personality; 13 heredity; environment; 14 significant other; 15 significant others; 16 psychology; 17 anticipatory; 18 total; 19 functionalist; 20 peer

THINKING ABOUT MOVIES

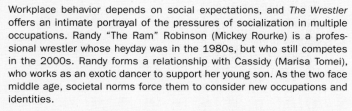

The Departed (Martin Scorsese, 2006)

Frank Costello (Jack Nicholson), an organized-crime boss in South Boston, is under investigation by the Massachusetts State Police. To infiltrate Frank's syndicate, the agency assigns a new recruit named Billy Costigan (Leonardo DiCaprio). Meanwhile, Frank sends one of his men, Collin Sullivan (Matt Damon), to covertly gather intelligence on the police. As both sides realize they have traitors in their midst, the two impostors try to avoid exposure.

This movie contains an example of the looking-glass self, or the development of self-identity in relation to social groups. Because Billy Costigan was raised by divorced parents, one working class and the other middle class, he grew up with dual identities, complete with distinctive accents. Pay particular attention to the scene in which Billy interviews for the undercover job.

For Your Consideration

1. How does Billy Costigan present his "self" in different social situations?
2. Give three examples of impression management by the two undercover agents, and explain why they used the strategy to support a particular social identity.

The Wrestler
(Darren Aronofsky, 2008)

Workplace behavior depends on social expectations, and *The Wrestler* offers an intimate portrayal of the pressures of socialization in multiple occupations. Randy "The Ram" Robinson (Mickey Rourke) is a professional wrestler whose heyday was in the 1980s, but who still competes in the 2000s. Randy forms a relationship with Cassidy (Marisa Tomei), who works as an exotic dancer to support her young son. As the two face middle age, societal norms force them to consider new occupations and identities.

The Wrestler shows how individuals undergo processes of resocialization as they pass through the life course. Watch for the scene in which Randy accepts a full-time job at a supermarket deli counter after retiring as a wrestler, and then struggles to cope with his new identity. Note how Randy and Cassidy present different "selves" on the job and off.

For Your Consideration

1. What might be some of the factors that contribute to Randy and Cassidy's socialization?
2. How could you use Mead's theory of the self to understand the actions of the main characters in this film?

inside

Social Interaction and Reality

Elements of Social Structure

Social Networks

Virtual Worlds

Social Structure in
    Global Perspective

Social Policy and
    Social Interaction:
    Regulating the Net

BOXES

Research Today: *Disability
    as a Master Status*

Research Today: *Social
    Networks and Smoking*

Sociology in the Global
    Community: *The* Second
    Life® *Virtual World*

Much of our social activity takes place in groups. These young adults are Explorers, volunteers who train with the Miami Police Department while considering a career in law enforcement.

Social Interaction and Social Structure 5

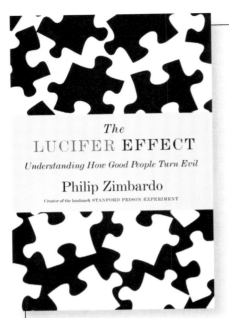

The
LUCIFER EFFECT
Understanding How Good People Turn Evil

Philip Zimbardo
Creator of the landmark STANFORD PRISON EXPERIMENT

❝ As each of the blindfolded prisoners is escorted down the flight of steps in front of Jordan Hall into our little jail, our guards order them to strip and remain standing naked with their arms outstretched against the wall and legs spread apart. They hold that uncomfortable position for a long time as the guards ignore them because they are busy with last-minute chores, like packing away the prisoners' belongings for safekeeping, fixing up their guards quarters, and arranging beds in the three cells. Before being given his uniform, each prisoner is sprayed with powder, alleged to be a delouser, to rid him of lice that might be brought in to contaminate our jail. . . . The humiliation of being a prisoner has begun, much as it does in many institutions from military boot camps to prisons, hospitals, and low-level jobs. . . .

The morning shift comes on in the middle of the night, 2 A.M. . . .

The prisoners are sound asleep. Some are snoring in their dark, cramped cells. Suddenly the silence is shattered. Loud whistles shriek, voices yell, "Up and at 'em." "Wake up and get out here for the count!" "Okay, you sleeping beauties, it's time to see if you learned how to count." Dazed prisoners line up against the wall and count off mindlessly as the three guards alternate in coming up with new variations on count themes. The count and its attendant push-ups and jumping jacks for failures continue on and on for nearly a weary hour. Finally, the prisoners are ordered back to sleep—until reveille a few hours later. . . .

[By Tuesday] our prisoners are looking raggedy and bleary-eyed, and our little prison is beginning to smell like a men's toilet in a New York subway station. Seems that some guards have made toilet visits a privilege to be awarded infrequently and never after lights out. During the night, prisoners have to urinate and defecate in buckets in their cells, and some guards refuse to allow them to be emptied till morning. Complaints are coming fast and furiously from many of the prisoners. . . .

After less than three days into this bizarre situation, some of the students role-playing prison guards have moved far beyond mere playacting. They have internalized the hostility, negative affect, and mindset characteristic of some real prison guards, as is evident from their shift reports, retrospective diaries, and personal reflections.

. . .

The depersonalization of the prisoners and the spreading extent of dehumanization are beginning to affect [one of the guards], too: "As I got angrier and angrier, I didn't question this behavior as much. I couldn't let it affect me, so I started hiding myself deeper behind my role. It was the only way of not hurting yourself. I was really lost on what was happening but didn't even think about quitting."

Blaming the victims for their sorry condition—created by our failure to provide adequate shower and sanitation facilities—became common among the staff. We see this victim blame in operation as [the guard] complains, "I got tired of seeing the prisoners in rags, smelling bad, and the prison stink." ❞

After less than three days into this bizarre situation, some of the students role-playing prison guards have moved far beyond mere playacting. They have internalized the hostility, negative affect, and mind-set characteristic of some real prison guards.

(Zimbardo 2007b:40, 41, 52, 53, 80, 86) Additional information about this excerpt can be found on the Online Learning center at www.mhhe.com/schaefer12e.

In this study, directed and described by social psychologist Philip Zimbardo, college students adopted the patterns of social interaction expected of guards and prisoners when they were placed in a mock prison. Sociologists use the term **social interaction** to refer to the ways in which people respond to one another, whether face-to-face or over the telephone or on the computer. In the mock prison, social interactions between guards and prisoners were highly impersonal. The guards addressed the prisoners by number rather than name, and they wore reflective sunglasses that made eye contact impossible.

As in many real-life prisons, the simulated prison at Stanford University had a social structure in which guards held virtually total control over prisoners. The term **social structure** refers to the way in which a society is organized into predictable relationships. The social structure of Zimbardo's mock prison influenced how the guards and prisoners interacted. Zimbardo and his colleagues (2003:546) note that it was a real prison "in the minds of the jailers and their captives." His simulated prison experiment, first conducted more than 30 years ago, has subsequently been repeated (with similar findings) both in the United States and in other countries.

Zimbardo's experiment took on new relevance in 2004, in the wake of shocking revelations of prisoner abuse at the U.S.-run Abu Ghraib military facility in Iraq. Graphic "trophy photos" showed U.S. soldiers humiliating naked Iraqi prisoners and threatening to attack them with police dogs. The structure of the wartime prison, coupled with intense pressure on military intelligence officers to secure information regarding terrorist plots, contributed to the breakdown in the guards' behavior. But Zimbardo himself noted that the guards' depraved conduct could have been predicted simply on the basis of his research. So strong was public reaction to the Abu Ghraib scandal that in

2009, during his first week in office, President Barack Obama declared that henceforth interrogators will use only noncoercive methods for questioning suspected terrorists (Zimbardo 2007a).

The two concepts of social interaction and social structure are central to sociological study. They are closely related to socialization (see Chapter 4), the process through which people learn the attitudes, values, and behaviors appropriate to their culture. When the students in Zimbardo's experiment entered the mock prison, they began a process of resocialization. In that process, they adjusted to a new social structure and learned new rules for social interaction.

In this chapter we will study social structure and its effect on our social interactions. What determines a person's status in society? How do our social roles affect

In Zimbardo's mock prison experiment, a guard orders prisoners to line up against the wall. The social interactions fostered by the prison's social structure quickly led to a breakdown in the guards' and prisoners' behavior.

our social interactions? What is the place of social institutions such as the family, religion, and government in our social structure? We'll begin by considering how social interactions shape the way we view the world around us. Next, we'll focus on the five basic elements of social structure: statuses, social roles, groups, social networks, and social institutions such as the family, religion, and government. We'll also touch on a new element of social structure, *virtual worlds*. We'll see that functionalists, conflict theorists, and interactionists approach these institutions quite differently. Finally, we'll compare our modern social structure with simpler forms, using typologies developed by Émile Durkheim, Ferdinand Tönnies, and Gerhard Lenski. The Social Policy section at the end of the chapter focuses on the debate over how best—if at all—to regulate the Internet.

Social Interaction and Reality

When someone in a crowd shoves you, do you automatically push back? Or do you consider the circumstances of the incident and the attitude of the instigator before you react? Chances are you do the latter. According to sociologist Herbert Blumer (1969:79), the distinctive characteristic of social interaction among people is that "human beings interpret or 'define' each other's actions instead of merely reacting to each other's actions." In other words, our response to someone's behavior is based on the *meaning* we attach to his or her actions. Reality is shaped by our perceptions, evaluations, and definitions.

These meanings typically reflect the norms and values of the dominant culture and our socialization experiences within that culture. As interactionists emphasize, the meanings that we attach to people's behavior are shaped by our interactions with them and with the larger society. Social reality is literally constructed from our social interactions (Berger and Luckmann 1966).

How do we define our social reality? Consider something as simple as how we regard tattoos. At one time, most of us in the United States considered tattoos weird or kooky. We associated them with fringe countercultural groups, such as punk rockers, biker gangs, and skinheads. Among many people, a tattoo elicited an automatic negative response. Now, however, so many people have tattoos—including society's trendsetters and major sports figures—and the ritual of getting a tattoo has become so legitimized, that mainstream culture regards tattoos

differently. At this point, as a result of increased social interaction with tattooed people, tattoos look perfectly at home to us in a number of settings.

The nature of social interaction and what constitutes reality varies across cultures. In Western societies, with their emphasis on romantic love, couples see marriage as a relationship as well as a social status. From Valentine's Day flowers to more informal, everyday gestures, professions of love are an expected part of marriage. In Japan, however, marriage is considered more a social status than a relationship. Although many or most Japanese couples undoubtedly do love each other, saying "I love you" does not come easily to them, especially not to husbands. Nor do most husbands call their wives by name (they prefer "Mother") or look them in the eyes. In 2006, in an effort to change these restrictive customs, some Japanese men formed the Devoted Husband Organization, which has been sponsoring a new holiday, Beloved Wives Day. Recently, the group organized an event called Shout Your Love from the Middle of a Cabbage Patch Day. Dozens of men stood in a cabbage patch north of Tokyo and shouted "I love you!" to their wives, some of whom had never heard their husbands say those words (Kambayashi 2008).

The ability to define social reality reflects a group's power within a society. In fact, one of the most crucial aspects of the relationship between dominant and subordinate groups is the ability of the dominant or majority group to define a society's values. Sociologist William I. Thomas (1923), an early critic of theories of racial and gender differences, recognized that the "definition of the situation" could mold the thinking and personality of the individual. Writing from an interactionist perspective, Thomas observed that people respond not only to the objective features of a person or situation but also to the *meaning* that person or situation has for them. For example, in Philip Zimbardo's mock prison experiment, student "guards" and "prisoners" accepted the definition of the situation (including the traditional roles and behavior associated with being a guard or prisoner) and acted accordingly.

As we have seen throughout the past 50 years—first in the civil rights movement of the 1960s and since then among such groups as women, the elderly, gays and lesbians, and people with disabilities—an important aspect of the process of social change involves redefining or reconstructing social reality. Members of subordinate groups challenge traditional definitions and begin to perceive and experience reality in a new way. An example of this challenge can be seen in the career of world champion boxer Muhammad Ali.

Ali began his career working for a White male syndicate, which sponsored his early matches when he was known as Cassius Clay. Soon, however, the young boxer rebelled against those who would keep him or his race down. He broke the old stereotypes of the self-effacing Black athlete, insisting on his own political views (including refusing to serve in the Vietnam War), his own religion (Black Muslim), and his own name (Muhammad Ali). Not only did Ali change the world of sports; he also helped to alter the world of race relations. Viewed from a sociological perspective, then, Ali was redefining social reality by rebelling against the racist thinking and terminology that restricted him and other African Americans.

Elements of Social Structure

All social interaction takes place within a social structure, including those interactions that redefine social reality. For purposes of study, we can break down any social structure into five elements: statuses, social roles, groups, social networks, and social institutions. These elements make up social structure just as a foundation, walls, and ceilings make up a building's structure. The elements of social structure are developed through the lifelong process of socialization described in Chapter 4.

Statuses

We normally think of a person's "status" as having to do with influence, wealth, and fame. However, sociologists use the term **status** to refer to any of the full range of socially defined positions within a large group or society, from the lowest to the highest. Within our society, a person can occupy the status of president of the United States, fruit picker, son or daughter, violinist, teenager, resident of Minneapolis, dental technician, or neighbor. A person can hold a number of statuses at the same time.

Ascribed and Achieved Status Sociologists view some statuses as *ascribed* and others as *achieved* (Figure 5-1). An **ascribed status** is assigned to a person by society without regard for the person's unique talents or characteristics. Generally, the assignment takes place at birth; thus, a person's racial background, gender, and age are all considered ascribed statuses. Though these characteristics are biological in origin, they are significant mainly because of the *social* meanings they have in our culture. Conflict

FIGURE **5-1** SOCIAL STATUSES

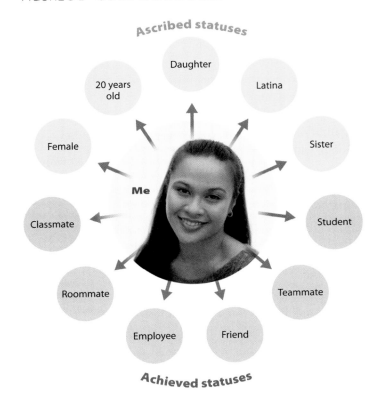

Think about It
The young woman in this figure—"me"—occupies many positions in society, each of which involves distinct statuses. How would you define your statuses? Which have the most influence in your life?

theorists are especially interested in ascribed statuses, since they often confer privileges or reflect a person's membership in a subordinate group. The social meanings of race, ethnicity, and gender will be analyzed more fully in Chapters 11 and 12.

In most cases, we can do little to change an ascribed status, but we can attempt to change the traditional constraints associated with it. For example, the Gray Panthers—an activist political group founded in 1971 to work for the rights of older people—have tried to modify society's negative and confining stereotypes of the elderly. As a result of their work and that of other groups supporting older citizens, the ascribed status of "senior citizen" is no longer as difficult for millions of older people.

An ascribed status does not necessarily have the same social meaning in every society. In a cross-cultural study, sociologist Gary Huang (1988) confirmed the long-held view that respect for the elderly is an important cultural norm in China. In many cases, the prefix "old" is used respectfully: calling someone "old teacher" or "old person" is like calling a judge in the United States "your honor." Huang points out that positive age-seniority language distinctions are uncommon in the United States; consequently, we view the term *old man* as more of an insult than a celebration of seniority and wisdom.

Unlike ascribed statuses, an **achieved status** comes to us largely through our own efforts. Both "computer programmer"

Ascribed status may intersect with a person's achieved status. As this doorman greets a resident, the worker's achieved status as a low-wage worker combines with his ethnic status as an African American, an identity that many in this society consider to be lower than that of whites.

and "prison guard" are achieved statuses, as are "lawyer," "pianist," "sorority member," "convict," and "social worker." We must do something to acquire an achieved status—go to school, learn a skill, establish a friendship, invent a new product. But as we will see in the next section, our ascribed status heavily influences our achieved status. Being male, for example, would decrease the likelihood that we would consider child care as a career.

Master Status   Each person holds many different and sometimes conflicting statuses; some may connote higher social position and some, lower position. How, then, do others view one's overall social position? According to sociologist Everett Hughes (1945), societies deal with inconsistencies by agreeing that certain statuses are more important than others. A **master status** is a status that dominates others and thereby determines a person's general position in society. For example, Arthur Ashe, who died of AIDS in 1993, had a remarkable career as a tennis star, but at the end of his life, his status as a well-known personality with AIDS may have outweighed his statuses as a retired athlete, author, and political activist. Throughout the world, many people with disabilities find that their status as disabled receives undue weight, overshadowing their actual ability to perform successfully in meaningful employment (Box 5-1 on page 102).

Our society gives such importance to race and gender that they often dominate our lives. These ascribed statuses frequently influence our achieved status. The Black activist Malcolm X (1925–1965), an eloquent and controversial advocate of Black power and Black pride during the early 1960s, recalled that his feelings and perspectives changed dramatically while in eighth grade. When his English teacher, a White man, advised him that his goal of becoming a lawyer was "no realistic goal for a nigger" and encouraged him instead to become a carpenter, Malcolm X (1964:37) found that his position as a Black man

(ascribed status) was an obstacle to his dream of becoming a lawyer (achieved status). In the United States, the ascribed statuses of race and gender can function as master statuses that have an important impact on one's potential to achieve a desired professional and social status.

Social Roles

What Are Social Roles?   Throughout our lives, we acquire what sociologists call social roles. A **social role** is a set of expectations for people who occupy a given social position or status. Thus, in the United States, we expect that cab drivers will know how to get around a city, that receptionists will be reliable in handling phone messages, and that police officers will take action if they see a citizen being threatened. With each distinctive social status—whether ascribed or achieved—come particular role expectations. However, actual performance varies from individual to individual. One secretary may assume extensive administrative responsibilities, while another may focus on clerical duties. Similarly, in Philip Zimbardo's mock prison experiment, some students were brutal and sadistic guards; others were not.

Roles are a significant component of social structure. Viewed from a functionalist perspective, roles contribute to a society's stability by enabling members to anticipate the behavior of others and to pattern their own actions accordingly. Yet social roles can also be dysfunctional if they restrict people's interactions and relationships. If we view a person *only* as a "police officer" or "supervisor," it will be difficult to relate to him or her as a friend or neighbor.

Role Conflict   Imagine the delicate situation of a woman who has worked for a decade on an assembly line in an electrical plant, and has recently been named supervisor of her unit. How is this woman expected to relate to her longtime friends and co-workers? Should she still go out to lunch with them, as she has done almost daily for years? Is it her responsibility to recommend the firing of an old friend who cannot keep up with the demands of the assembly line?

Role conflict occurs when incompatible expectations arise from two or more social positions held by the same person. Fulfillment of the roles associated with one status may directly violate the roles linked to a second status. In the example just given, the newly promoted supervisor will most likely experience a sharp conflict between her social and occupational roles. Such role conflicts call for important ethical choices. The new supervisor will have to make a difficult decision about how much allegiance she owes her friend and how much she owes her employers, who have given her supervisory responsibilities.

Another type of role conflict occurs when individuals move into occupations that are not common among people with their ascribed status. Male preschool teachers and female police

RESEARCH TODAY

5-1 Disability as a Master Status

When officials in New Hampshire required a handicap access ramp for a mountain shelter, they were ridiculed. Who could climb a mountain in a wheelchair? critics asked. In the summer of 2000 that challenge impelled several intrepid climbers, some in wheelchairs, to make a 12-hour trek over rocks and rough trail so that they could enter the shelter in triumph. As a result of such feats, stereotypes of the disabled are gradually falling away. But the status of "disabled" still carries a stigma.

Throughout history and around the world, people with disabilities have been subjected to cruel and inhuman treatment. For example, in the 20th century, the disabled were frequently viewed as subhuman creatures who were a menace to society. In Japan more than 16,000 women with disabilities were involuntarily sterilized with government approval from 1945 to 1995. Sweden apologized for the same action taken against 62,000 of its citizens in the 1970s.

Such blatantly hostile treatment of people with disabilities has given way to a *medical model*, in which the disabled are viewed as chronic patients. Increasingly, however, people concerned with the rights of the disabled have criticized this model as well. In their view, it is the unnecessary and discriminatory barriers present in the environment—both physical and attitudinal—that stand in the way of people with disabilities, more than any biological limitations. Applying a *civil rights model*, activists emphasize that those with disabilities face widespread

prejudice, discrimination, and segregation. For example, most voting places are inaccessible to wheelchair users and fail to provide ballots that can be used by those unable to read print.

Drawing on the earlier work of Erving Goffman, contemporary sociologists have suggested that society attaches a stigma to many forms of disability, a stigma that leads to prejudicial treatment. People with disabilities frequently observe that the nondisabled see them only as blind, wheelchair users, and so forth, rather than as complex human beings with individual strengths and weaknesses, whose blindness or use of a wheelchair is merely one aspect of their lives.

> *In Japan more than 16,000 women with disabilities were involuntarily sterilized with government approval from 1945 to 1995.*

Although discrimination against the disabled occurs around the world, attitudes are changing. The African nation of Botswana has plans to assist its disabled, most of whom live in rural areas and need special services for mobility and economic development. In many countries, disability rights activists are targeting issues essential to overcoming this master status and becoming a full citizen, including

Would an employee who entered this room see a member of a consulting team or a man in a wheelchair? Disability often functions as a master status.

employment, housing, education, and access to public buildings.

LET'S DISCUSS

1. Does your campus present barriers to disabled students? If so, what kinds of barriers—physical, attitudinal, or both? Describe some of them.

2. Why do you think nondisabled people see disability as the most important characteristic of a disabled person? What can be done to help people see beyond the wheelchair and the seeing-eye dog?

Sources: Albrecht 2004; Barnow 2008; Goffman 1963; D. Murphy 1997; *Newsday* 1997; Schaefer 2010: 407–412; Shapiro 1993.

---

use your sociological *imagination*

If you were a male nurse, what aspects of role conflict might you experience? Now imagine you are a professional boxer and a woman. What conflicting role expectations might that involve? In both cases, how well do you think you would handle role conflict?

officers experience this type of role conflict. In the latter case, female officers must strive to reconcile their workplace role in law enforcement with the societal view of a woman's role, which does not embrace many skills needed in police work. And while female police officers encounter sexual harassment, as women do throughout the labor force, they must also deal with the "code of silence," an informal norm that precludes their implicating fellow officers in wrongdoing (Fletcher 1995; S. Martin 1994).

Role Strain Role conflict describes the situation of a person dealing with the challenge of occupying two social positions simultaneously. However, even a single position can cause problems. Sociologists use the term **role strain** to describe the difficulty that arises when the same social position imposes conflicting demands and expectations.

People who belong to minority cultures may experience role strain while working in the mainstream culture. Criminologist Larry Gould (2002) interviewed officers of the Navajo Nation Police Department about their relations with conventional law enforcement officials, such as sheriffs and FBI agents. Besides enforcing the law, Navajo Nation officers practice an alternative form of justice known as Peacemaking, in which they seek reconciliation between the parties to a crime. The officers expressed great confidence in Peacemaking, but worried that if they did not make arrests, other law enforcement officials would think they were too soft, or "just taking care of their own." Regardless of the strength of their ties to traditional Navajo ways, all felt the strain of being considered "too Navajo" or "not Navajo enough."

Role Exit Often, when we think of assuming a social role, we focus on the preparation and anticipatory socialization a

According to sociologist Helen Rose Fuchs Ebaugh, role exit is a four-stage process. Is this transexual in the first or the fourth stage of changing genders?

person undergoes for that role. Such is true if a person is about to become an attorney, a chef, a spouse, or a parent. Yet until recently, social scientists have given little attention to the adjustments involved in *leaving* social roles.

Sociologist Helen Rose Fuchs Ebaugh (1988) developed the term **role exit** to describe the process of disengagement from a role that is central to one's self-identity in order to establish a new role and identity. Drawing on interviews with 185 people—among them ex-convicts, divorced men and women, recovering alcoholics, ex-nuns, former doctors, retirees, and transexuals—Ebaugh (herself a former nun) studied the process of voluntarily exiting from significant social roles.

Ebaugh has offered a four-stage model of role exit. The first stage begins with *doubt*. The person experiences frustration, burnout, or simply unhappiness with an accustomed status and the roles associated with the social position. The second stage involves a *search for alternatives*. A person who is unhappy with his or her career may take a leave of absence; an unhappily married couple may begin what they see as a temporary separation.

The third stage of role exit is the *action stage* or *departure*. Ebaugh found that the vast majority of her respondents could identify a clear turning point that made them feel it was essential to take final action and leave their jobs, end their marriages, or engage in another type of role exit. Twenty percent of respondents saw their role exit as a gradual, evolutionary process that had no single turning point.

The last stage of role exit involves the *creation of a new identity*. Many of you participated in a role exit when you made the transition from high school to college. You left behind the role

of offspring living at home and took on the role of a somewhat independent college student living with peers in a dorm. Sociologist Ira Silver (1996) has studied the central role that material objects play in this transition. The objects students choose to leave at home (like stuffed animals and dolls) are associated with their prior identities. They may remain deeply attached to those objects, but do not want them to be seen as part of their new identities at college. The objects they bring with them symbolize how they now see themselves and how they wish to be perceived. iPods and wall posters, for example, are calculated to say, "This is me."

Groups

In sociological terms, a **group** is any number of people with similar norms, values, and expectations who interact with one another on a regular basis. The members of a women's basketball team, a hospital's business office, a synagogue, or a symphony orchestra constitute a group. However, the residents of a suburb would not be considered a group, since they rarely interact with one another at one time.

Groups play a vital part in a society's social structure. Much of our social interaction takes place within groups and is influenced by their norms and sanctions. Being a teenager or a retired person takes on special meanings when we interact within groups designed for people with that particular status. The expectations associated with many social roles, including those accompanying the statuses of brother, sister, and student, become more clearly defined in the context of a group.

Social Institutions

The mass media, the government, the economy, the family, and the health care system are all examples of social institutions found in our society. **Social institutions** are organized patterns of beliefs and behavior centered on basic social needs, such as replacing personnel (the family) and preserving order (the government).

A close look at social institutions gives sociologists insight into the structure of a society. Consider religion, for example. The institution of religion adapts to the segment of society that it serves. Church work has very different meanings for ministers who serve a skid row area and those who serve a suburban middle-class community. Religious leaders assigned to a skid row mission will focus on tending to the ill and providing food and shelter. In contrast, clergy in affluent suburbs will be occupied with counseling those considering marriage and divorce, arranging youth activities, and overseeing cultural events (Schaefer 2008b).

Functionalist View One way to understand social institutions is to see how they fulfill essential functions. Anthropologist David F. Aberle and his colleagues (1950) and sociologists Raymond Mack and Calvin Bradford (1979) have identified five major tasks, or functional prerequisites, that a society or relatively permanent group must accomplish if it is to survive:

1. *Replacing personnel.* Any group or society must replace personnel when they die, leave, or become incapacitated. This task is accomplished through such means as immigration, annexation of neighboring groups, acquisition of slaves, or sexual reproduction. The Shakers, a religious sect that came to the United States in 1774, are a conspicuous example of a group that has *failed* to replace personnel. Their religious beliefs commit the Shakers to celibacy; to survive, the group

must recruit new members. At first, the Shakers proved quite successful in attracting members, reaching a peak of about 6,000 members in the United States during the 1840s. As of 2008, however, the only Shaker community left in this country was a farm in Maine with four members—one man and three women (Sabbathday Lake 2008).

2. *Teaching new recruits.* No group or society can survive if many of its members reject the group's established behavior and responsibilities. Thus, finding or producing new members is not sufficient; the group or society must also encourage recruits to learn and accept its values and customs. Such learning can take place formally, within schools (where learning is a manifest function), or informally, through interaction in peer groups (where instruction is a latent function).

3. *Producing and distributing goods and services.* Any relatively permanent group or society must provide and distribute desired goods and services to its members. Each society establishes a set of rules for the allocation of financial and other resources. The group must satisfy the needs of most members to some extent, or it will risk the possibility of discontent and ultimately disorder.

4. *Preserving order.* Throughout the world, indigenous and aboriginal peoples have struggled to protect themselves from outside invaders, with varying degrees of success. Failure to preserve order and defend against conquest leads to the death not only of a people, but of a culture.

5. *Providing and maintaining a sense of purpose.* People must feel motivated to continue as members of a group or society in order to fulfill the first four requirements. On January 20, 2009, in the midst of what would prove the worst economic crisis since the Great Depression, 2 million Americans crowded the National Mall to witness the inauguration of President Barack Obama, the first African American to be elected to the nation's highest office. The celebration, an expression of both patriotism and Black pride, convinced people of all races that change was possible and better times lay ahead. Faced with huge layoffs and massive home foreclosures, Americans heard the new president's call to serve their nation. Patriotism and racial pride, then, can help people to develop and maintain a sense of purpose. For others, tribal identities, religious values, or personal moral codes are especially meaningful. Whatever the motivator, in any society there remains one common and critical reality: if an individual does not have a sense of purpose, he or she has little reason to contribute to a society's survival.

This list of functional prerequisites does not specify *how* a society and its corresponding social institutions will perform each task. For example, one society may protect itself from external attack by amassing a frightening arsenal of weaponry, while another may make determined efforts to remain neutral in world politics and to promote cooperative relationships with its neighbors. No matter what its particular strategy, any society or relatively permanent group must attempt to satisfy all

What do we make of this group, photographed on the Brooklyn waterfront on September 11, 2001? The photographer who snapped the photo immediately realized that the ambiguous scene would trouble many viewers. Not until 2006 was it displayed; another year passed before it was published in a book. Public reaction was swift: some people criticized what appeared to be a group of young adults enjoying themselves as the World Trade Center burned; others speculated that the image had been manipulated. In reality, the people in the photo were not unconcerned or disaffected, nor was the image manipulated. The young woman sitting on the wall was actually deeply touched, because her mother worked for Minoru Yamasaki, the World Trade Center's architect. This group scene was caught just as the couple stopped to speak with three strangers about the tragedy that was unfolding across the river. As they talked, and from time to time stopped to help workers who were trying to get to Brooklyn, these strangers evolved into a secondary group through their shared experiences (Friend 2007; Hoepker 2006; Masur 2007; Sipser 2006).

these functional prerequisites for survival. If it fails on even one condition, the society runs the risk of extinction.

Conflict View Conflict theorists do not agree with the functionalist approach to social institutions. Although proponents of both perspectives agree that social institutions are organized to meet basic social needs, conflict theorists object to the idea that the outcome is necessarily efficient and desirable.

From a conflict perspective, the present organization of social institutions is no accident. Major institutions, such as education, help to maintain the privileges of the most powerful individuals and groups within a society, while contributing to the powerlessness of others. To give one example, public schools in the United States are financed largely through property taxes. This arrangement allows more affluent areas to provide their children with better-equipped schools and better-paid teachers than low-income areas can afford. As a result, children from prosperous communities are better prepared to compete academically than children from impoverished communities. The structure of the nation's educational system permits and even promotes such unequal treatment of schoolchildren.

Conflict theorists argue that social institutions such as education have an inherently conservative nature. Without question,

Waving flags and dressed in red, white, and blue, nearly 2 million Americans came together to celebrate the inauguration of President Barack Obama, the nation's first African American president, in January 2009. In the midst of a deepening economic and financial crisis, Obama's election brought hope to Americans of all races, helping them to maintain a sense of purpose in the face of adversity.

it has been difficult to implement educational reforms that promote equal opportunity—whether bilingual education, school desegregation, or mainstreaming of students with disabilities. From a functionalist perspective, social change can be dysfunctional, since it often leads to instability. However, from a conflict view, why should we preserve the existing social structure if it is unfair and discriminatory?

Social institutions also operate in gendered and racist environments, as conflict theorists, as well as feminists and interactionists, have pointed out. In schools, offices, and government institutions, assumptions about what people can do reflect the sexism and racism of the larger society. For instance, many people assume that women cannot make tough decisions—even those in the top echelons of corporate management. Others assume that all Black students at elite colleges represent affirmative action admissions. Inequality based on gender, economic status, race, and ethnicity thrives in such an environment—to which we might add discrimination based on age, physical disability, and sexual orientation. The truth of this assertion can be seen in routine decisions by employers on how to advertise jobs,

Social institutions affect the way we behave. How might these teens socializing at a mall in South Korea interact differently in school or at home?

as well as whether to provide fringe benefits such as child care and parental leave.

Interactionist View Social institutions affect our everyday behavior, whether we are driving down the street or waiting in a long shopping line. Sociologist Mitchell Duneier (1994a, 1994b) studied the social behavior of the word processors, all women, who work in the service center of a large Chicago law firm. Duneier was interested in the informal social norms that emerged in this work environment and the rich social network these female employees created.

The Network Center, as it is called, is a single, windowless room in a large office building where the law firm occupies seven floors. The center is staffed by two shifts of word processors, who work either from 4:00 p.m. to midnight or from midnight to 8:00 a.m. Each word processor works in a cubicle with just enough room for her keyboard, terminal, printer, and telephone. Work assignments for the word processors are placed in a central basket and then completed according to precise procedures.

At first glance, we might think that these women labor with little social contact, apart from limited breaks and occasional conversations with their supervisor. However, drawing on the interactionist perspective, Duneier learned that despite working in a large office, these women find private moments to talk (often in the halls or outside the washroom) and share a critical view of the law firm's attorneys and day-shift secretaries. Indeed, the word processors routinely suggest that their assignments represent work that the "lazy" secretaries should have completed during the normal workday. Duneier (1994b) tells of one word processor who resented the lawyers' superior attitude and pointedly refused to recognize or speak with any attorney who would not address her by name.

Interactionist theorists emphasize that our social behavior is conditioned by the roles and statuses we accept, the groups to which we belong, and the institutions within which we function. For example, the social roles associated with being a judge occur within the larger context of the criminal justice system. The status of judge stands in relation to other statuses, such as attorney, plaintiff, defendant, and witness, as well as to the social

Perspective	Role of Social Institutions	Focus
Functionalist	Meeting basic social needs	Essential functions
Conflict	Meeting basic social needs	Maintenance of privileges and inequality
Interactionist	Fostering everyday behavior	Influence of the roles and statuses we accept

institution of government. Although courts and jails have great symbolic importance, the judicial system derives its continued significance from the roles people carry out in social interactions (Berger and Luckmann 1966).

Table 5-1 summarizes the three major sociological perspectives on social institutions.

Social Networks

Groups do not merely serve to define other elements of the social structure, such as roles and statuses; they also link the individual with the larger society. We all belong to a number of different groups, and through our acquaintances make connections with people in different social circles. These connections are known as a **social network**—a series of social relationships that links a person directly to others, and through them indirectly to still more people.

Social networks can center on virtually any activity, from sharing job information to exchanging news and gossip, or even sharing sex. In the mid-1990s, sociologists Peter Bearman, James Moody, and Katherine Stovel (2004) studied romantic relationships at a high school with about 1,000 students. They found that about 61 percent of the girls had been sexually active over the past 18 months. Among the sexually active respondents, the researchers counted only 63 steady couples, or pairs with no other partners. A much larger group of 288 students—almost a third of the sample—was involved in a free-flowing network of relationships.

This research on high schoolers' sexual activity, an example of applied sociology, has clear implications for public health. Box 5-2 describes a similar but longer-term study that used network analysis to inform government efforts to discourage smoking.

Involvement in social networks—commonly known as *networking*—is especially valuable in finding employment. Albert Einstein was successful in finding a job only when a classmate's father put him in touch with his future employer. These kinds of contacts—even those that are weak and distant—can be crucial in establishing social networks and facilitating the transmission of information.

In the workplace, networking pays off more for men than for women because of the traditional presence of men in leadership positions. One survey of executives found that 63 percent of the men used networking to find new jobs, compared to 41 percent of the women. Women were more likely than men to rely on classified advertisements to find jobs. Still, women at all levels of the paid labor force are beginning to make effective use of social networks. Now that job advertisements have largely migrated to the Internet, new research is needed on whether gender differences persist in in-person and online networking (L. Flynn 2008; Henly 1999).

Virtual Worlds

Today, with recent advances in technology, people can maintain their social networks electronically; they don't need face-to-face contacts. Whether through text-messaging, handheld devices, or social networking sites like Facebook, a significant amount of networking occurs online. Adolescents can now interact freely with distant friends, even under close scrutiny by parents or teachers. Without leaving their cubicles, employees with a taste for adventure can escape their work environments. In Box 4-2 (page 88) we considered the impact of online social networks on the process of socialization. Facebook and MySpace are only the first stage in the creation of alternative forms of reality through new technology. Box 5-3 on page 108 examines the establishment of a whole new society, called the Second Life® virtual world.

Virtual life can and does migrate into real life. In 2007, college housing officials became worried when freshmen and their parents began checking out the Facebook profiles of prospective roommates. Soon, colleges were fielding requests for new roommates before students even arrived on campus. Concerns went far beyond tastes in music; the reservations expressed most often by parents included a potential roommate's race, religion, and sexual orientation (Collura 2007).

Online socialization may not necessarily reinforce people's prejudices, however. Researchers at Pennsylvania State University argue that participating in the Second Life world opens us up to people from different cultural and linguistic backgrounds. In their view, online friendships among avatars may enhance cross-cultural encounters and friendships in the first life—that is, the real world (Diehl and Prins 2008).

RESEARCH TODAY

Over the past two generations, the incidence of smoking in the United States has decreased significantly. Scholars have been trying to determine the reasons for this shift in behavior. Certainly the health benefits of quitting must have influenced many people. But smoking is an addictive behavior that is difficult to stop. Could something more than potential health benefits lie behind its steep decline?

To find out, researchers repeatedly assessed the smoking habits of 12,067 subjects of a long-term survey of heart health. From the beginning, they examined the role of social networks in respondents' smoking. Not surprisingly, they found that social networks typically linked those who either smoked or did not smoke. The two groups rarely mixed.

Over the more than three decades since this survey began, researchers saw marked changes in respondents' smoking behavior. Although the size of their family and friendship clusters remained the same, in many clusters, members totally abandoned smoking. This finding suggests that whole groups of friends and family were quitting together.

The accompanying figure shows the same social network at the beginning and end of the study's 30-year span. As might be expected, group membership and the links that connected members changed over time. More remarkable was the decline or outright disappearance of smoking in some clusters. The remaining smokers, especially heavy smokers, were marginalized—that is, their ties to other members of the network declined.

Social pressure to quit smoking seems to underlie these changes. Notably, friends but not neighbors of those who quit were influenced by a person's decision to stop smoking. Among friends, smoking cessation by one person decreased the chances that the other would continue to smoke by 36 percent. Among siblings, the risk of the other person continuing to smoke fell by

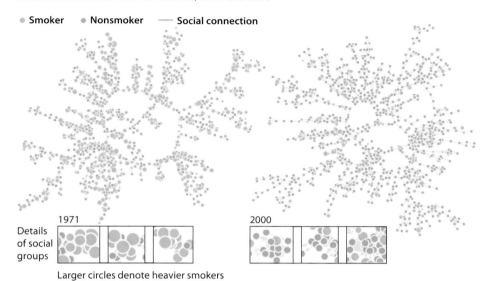

A Network of Smokers and Non-Smokers, 1971 and 2000

● Smoker   ● Nonsmoker   —— Social connection

1971

2000

Details of social groups

Larger circles denote heavier smokers

Source: Stein 2008 based on Christakis and Fowler 2008.

25 percent, and among spouses, by 67 percent. Among co-workers at small firms, the drop in the chances of one smoking after the other stopped was 34 percent.

In many clusters, members totally abandoned smoking. This finding suggests that whole groups of friends and family were quitting together.

This study shows that social networks influence the way people behave. In this case, they strengthened their members' willpower to quit smoking. The practical, or applied, implication of the research is that public health programs that promote smoking cessation should target friendship groups or couples rather than individuals. Because this insight may also prove useful in other areas of public health, researchers are now planning to investigate the relationship between social networks and obesity, drinking, and drug abuse.

LET'S DISCUSS

1. In your experience, do smokers and nonsmokers tend to cluster in separate groups? Have you ever tried to quit smoking, and if so, did your cluster of friends and family help or hinder you?
2. Besides public health campaigns, what other applications can you think of for social network research?

Sources: Christakis and Fowler 2008; Kolata 2008; K. Smith and Christakis 2008; R. Stein 2008.

Finally, virtual networks can help to preserve real-world networks interrupted by war and other dislocations. In 2003, the deployment of U.S. troops in the Middle East increased many people's reliance on e-mail. Today, digital photos and sound files accompany e-mail messages between soldiers and their families and friends. GIs can even view siblings' graduations or children's birthday parties live, via Webcams. And U.S. soldiers and Iraqi citizens have begun to post their opinions of the war in Iraq in online journals called Web logs, or blogs. Though critics are skeptical of the identity of some of the authors, these postings have become yet another source of news about the war (Faith 2005; O'Connor 2004; Sisson 2007).

Social Structure in Global Perspective

Modern societies are complex, especially compared to earlier social arrangements. Sociologists Émile Durkheim, Ferdinand Tönnies, and Gerhard Lenski developed ways to contrast modern societies with simpler forms of social structure.

Durkheim's Mechanical and Organic Solidarity

In his *Division of Labor* ([1893] 1933), Durkheim argued that social structure depends on the division of labor in a society—in other words, on the manner in which tasks are performed. Thus, a task such as providing food can be carried out almost totally

SOCIOLOGY IN THE GLOBAL COMMUNITY

5-3 The Second Life® Virtual World

Virtual networking is a phenomenon that is evolving so fast, its future is difficult to imagine. Consider the Second Life® world, a Web-based three-dimensional virtual world that included about 16.8 million networked "players" as of January 2009. Nearly 523,000 of those players were active over a seven-day period. Participants in such a virtual world typically assume an **avatar**—that is, a three-dimensional model, two-dimensional icon, or constructed personality provided by the Internet site. (This use of the term *avatar* originated in the 1980s, in early computer games that featured role-playing.) The avatar that a person assumes may represent a looking-glass self very different from his or her actual identity. Once equipped with an avatar, a player goes about his or her life in the virtual world, establishing a business, even buying and decorating a home.

Sociologist Manuel Castells views these emerging electronic social networks as fundamental to new organizations and the growth of existing businesses and associations. With other scholars, sociologists are now scrambling to understand these environments and their social processes. The Second Life world went public in 2003—a millennium ago in the world of cyberspace. Scholars worry that after the current period of transition, given the absence of a historical record, reconstructing these worlds as they existed when they were populated by only a hundred avatars, much less tens of thousands, will be impossible.

> *The commercialization of these spaces has been met with a good deal of antagonism: Reebok has weathered a virtual nuclear bomb attack, and "customers" have been "shot" outside the American Apparel store.*

Just like real worlds, virtual worlds have become politicized and commercialized. In 2007, Sweden became the first real-world country to place an "embassy" in the Second Life world. Elsewhere in this virtual world, virtual protesters have paraded on behalf of a far-right French group in a confrontation with anti-Nazi protesters. MySpace was commercialized when it was purchased by the global media giant News Corp, which added targeted advertising to the site. If a MySpace user confesses to liking tacos, a banner ad for Taco Bell may appear at the top of the page. And the Second Life world is now open to real-world corporations that want to "build" their stores in it. Some corporations have even purchased "islands" to use for training sessions or employee conferences—islands that are closed to the "general public." (In keeping with the spirit of the Second Life virtual world, however, employees are allowed to attend company functions in their finest avatar attire.) The commercialization of these spaces has been met with a good deal of antagonism: Reebok has weathered a virtual nuclear bomb attack, and "customers" have been "shot" outside the American Apparel store.

As in the real world, untrustworthy businesses can be found in the Second Life world. "Zania Turner," the avatar of a 33-year-old woman, could not resist the interest that her virtual money—bought with real money—could gather at the Second Life world's Ginko Financial. One day her money, along with tens of thousands of dollars that others had deposited in Ginko, vanished. Second Life operators responded by shutting down the site's virtual banks. Chaos followed as avatars flocked to the shuttered ATMs in a frenzied effort to exchange their virtual dollars for real currency.

A group of avatars interacting in the Second Life® virtual world.

LET'S DISCUSS

1. If you were a player in the Second Life world, what kind of avatar would you choose? What would be your reason for living a virtual second life, parallel to your life in the real world?
2. Assume you are a sociologist. What features of the Second Life world would you like to investigate, and why? How would you go about doing so?

Sources: Bainbridge 2007; Burkeman 2007; Castells 1997, 1998, 2000; Hamilton 2007; Second Life 2009; Semuels 2007, 2008; Talbot 2008.

use your sociological *imagination*

If you were deaf, what impact might instant messaging, or texting, have on you?

by one individual, or it can be divided among many people. The latter pattern is typical of modern societies, in which the cultivation, processing, distribution, and retailing of a single food item are performed by literally hundreds of people.

In societies in which there is minimal division of labor, a collective consciousness develops that emphasizes group solidarity. Durkheim termed this collective frame of mind **mechanical solidarity,** implying that all individuals perform the same tasks. In this type of society, no one needs to ask, "What do your parents do?" since all are engaged in similar work. Each person prepares food, hunts, makes clothing, builds homes, and so forth. Because people have few options regarding what to do with their lives, there is little concern for individual needs. Instead, the group is the dominating force in society. Both social interaction and negotiation are based on close, intimate, face-to-face social contacts. Since there is little specialization, there are few social roles.

As societies become more advanced technologically, they rely on greater division of labor. The person who cuts down timber is not the same person who puts up your roof. With increasing specialization, many different tasks must be performed by many different individuals—even in manufacturing a single item, such as a radio or stove. In general, social interactions become less personal than in societies characterized by mechanical solidarity. People begin relating to others on the basis of their social positions ("butcher," "nurse") rather than their distinctive human qualities. Because the overall social structure of the society continues to change, statuses and social roles are in perpetual flux.

Once society has become more complex and division of labor is greater, no individual can go it alone. Dependence on others becomes essential for group survival. In Durkheim's terms, mechanical solidarity is replaced by **organic solidarity,** a collective consciousness resting on the need a society's members have for one another. Durkheim chose the term *organic solidarity* because in his view, individuals become interdependent in much the same way as organs of the human body.

"I'd like to think of you as a person, David, but it's my job to think of you as personnel."

In a *Gesellschaft,* people are likely to relate to one another in terms of their roles rather than their relationships.

Tönnies's *Gemeinschaft* and *Gesellschaft*

Ferdinand Tönnies (1855–1936) was appalled by the rise of an industrial city in his native Germany during the late 1800s. In his view, the city marked a dramatic change from the ideal of a close-knit community, which Tönnies termed a *Gemeinschaft,* to that of an impersonal mass society, known as a *Gesellschaft* (Tönnies [1887] 1988).

The **Gemeinschaft** (pronounced guh-MINE-shoft) is typical of rural life. It is a small community in which people have similar backgrounds and life experiences. Virtually everyone knows one another, and social interactions are intimate and familiar, almost as among kinfolk. In this community there is a commitment to the larger social group and a sense of togetherness among members. People relate to others in a personal way, not just as "clerk" or "manager." With this personal interaction comes little privacy, however: we know too much about everyone.

Social control in the *Gemeinschaft* is maintained through informal means such as moral persuasion, gossip, and even gestures. These techniques work effectively because people genuinely care how others feel about them. Social change is relatively limited in the *Gemeinschaft;* the lives of members of one generation may be quite similar to those of their grandparents.

In contrast, the **Gesellschaft** (pronounced guh-ZELL-shoft) is an ideal community that is characteristic of modern urban life. In this community most people are strangers who feel little in common with other residents. Relationships are governed by social roles that grow out of immediate tasks, such as purchasing a product or arranging a business meeting. Self-interest dominates, and there is little consensus concerning values or commitment to the group. As a result, social control must rest on more formal techniques, such as laws and legally defined punishments. Social change is an important aspect of life in the *Gesellschaft;* it can be strikingly evident even within a single generation.

Table 5-2 on page 110 summarizes the differences between the *Gemeinschaft* and the *Gesellschaft.* Sociologists have used these terms to compare social structures that stress close relationships with those that emphasize less personal ties. It is easy to view the *Gemeinschaft* with nostalgia, as a far better way of life than the rat race of contemporary existence. However, the more intimate relationships of the *Gemeinschaft* come at a price. The prejudice and discrimination found there can be quite confining; ascribed statuses such as family background often outweigh a person's unique talents and achievements. In addition, the *Gemeinschaft* tends to distrust individuals who seek to be creative or just to be different.

Lenski's Sociocultural Evolution Approach

Sociologist Gerhard Lenski takes a very different view of society and social structure. Rather than distinguishing between two opposite types of society, as Tönnies did, Lenski sees human societies as undergoing a process of change characterized by a dominant pattern known as **sociocultural evolution.** This term refers to long-term trends in societies resulting from the interplay of continuity, innovation, and selection (Nolan and Lenski 2009:361).

In Lenski's view, a society's level of technology is critical to the way it is organized. Lenski defines **technology** as "information about how to use the material resources of the environment to satisfy human needs and desires" (Nolan and Lenski 2009:37). The available technology does not completely define the form that a particular society and its social structure take. Nevertheless, a low level of technology may limit the degree to which a society can depend on such things as irrigation or complex machinery. As technology advances, Lenski writes, a community evolves from a preindustrial to an industrial and finally a postindustrial society.

Preindustrial Societies How does a preindustrial society organize its economy? If we know that, we can categorize the society. The first type of preindustrial society to emerge in human history was the **hunting-and-gathering society,** in which people simply rely on whatever foods and fibers are readily available. Technology in such societies is minimal. Organized into groups, people move constantly in search of food. There is little division of labor into specialized tasks.

Hunting-and-gathering societies are composed of small, widely dispersed groups. Each group consists almost entirely of people who are related to one another. As a result, kinship

Gemeinschaft	Gesellschaft
Rural life typifies this form.	Urban life typifies this form.
People share a feeling of community that results from their similar backgrounds and life experiences.	People have little sense of commonality. Their differences appear more striking than their similarities.
Social interactions are intimate and familiar.	Social interactions are likely to be impersonal and task-specific.
People maintain a spirit of cooperation and unity of will.	Self-interest dominates.
Tasks and personal relationships cannot be separated.	The task being performed is paramount; relationships are subordinate.
People place little emphasis on individual privacy.	Privacy is valued.
Informal social control predominates.	Formal social control is evident.
People are not very tolerant of deviance.	People are more tolerant of deviance.
Emphasis is on ascribed statuses.	Emphasis is on achieved statuses.
Social change is relatively limited.	Social change is very evident, even within a generation.

Think about It
How would you classify the communities with which you are familiar? Are they more *Gemeinschaft* or *Gesellschaft*?

ties are the source of authority and influence, and the social institution of the family takes on a particularly important role. Tönnies would certainly view such societies as examples of the *Gemeinschaft*.

Preindustrial societies like this one in South America still exist in remote areas of the world. These indigenous Indians—a people who have never before had contact with the outside world—are reacting to their first sight of an airplane as it flies over their camp in Brazil, close to the Peruvian border. "We did the overflight to show their houses, to show they are there, to show they exist," explained a representative of the advocacy group Survival International.

Social differentiation within the hunting-and-gathering society is based on ascribed statuses such as gender, age, and family background. Since resources are scarce, there is relatively little inequality in terms of material goods. By the close of the 20th century, hunting-and-gathering societies had virtually disappeared (Nolan and Lenski 2009).

Horticultural societies, in which people plant seeds and crops rather than merely subsist on available foods, emerged about 12,000 years ago. Members of horticultural societies are much less nomadic than hunters and gatherers. They place greater emphasis on the production of tools and household objects. Yet technology remains rather limited in these societies, whose members cultivate crops with the aid of digging sticks or hoes (Wilford 1997).

The last stage of preindustrial development is the **agrarian society,** which emerged about 5,000 years ago. As in horticultural societies, members of agrarian societies are engaged primarily in the production of food. However, new technological innovations such as the plow allow farmers to dramatically increase their crop yields. They can cultivate the same fields over generations, allowing the emergence of larger settlements.

The agrarian society continues to rely on the physical power of humans and animals (as opposed to mechanical power). Nevertheless, its social structure has more carefully defined roles than that of horticultural societies. Individuals focus on specialized tasks, such as the repair of fishing nets or blacksmithing. As human settlements become more established and stable, social institutions become more elaborate and property rights more important. The comparative permanence and greater surpluses of an agrarian society allow members to create artifacts such as statues, public monuments, and art objects and to pass them on from one generation to the next.

TABLE **5-3** STAGES OF SOCIOCULTURAL EVOLUTION summing**up** 111

Societal Type	First Appearance	Characteristics
Hunting-and-gathering	Beginning of human life	Nomadic; reliance on readily available food and fibers
Horticultural	About 12,000 years ago	More settled; development of agriculture and limited technology
Agrarian	About 5,000 years ago	Larger, more stable settlements; improved technology and increased crop yields
Industrial	1760–1850	Reliance on mechanical power and new sources of energy; centralized workplaces; economic interdependence; formal education
Postindustrial	1960s	Reliance on services, especially the processing and control of information; expanded middle class
Postmodern	Latter 1970s	High technology; mass consumption of consumer goods and media images; cross-cultural integration

Table 5-3 summarizes Lenski's three stages of sociocultural evolution, as well as the stages that follow, described next.

Industrial Societies Although the industrial revolution did not topple monarchs, it produced changes every bit as significant as those resulting from political revolutions. The industrial revolution, which took place largely in England during the period 1760 to 1830, was a scientific revolution focused on the application of nonanimal (mechanical) sources of power to labor tasks. An **industrial society** is a society that depends on mechanization to produce its goods and services. Industrial societies rely on new inventions that facilitate agricultural and industrial production, and on new sources of energy, such as steam.

As the industrial revolution proceeded, a new form of social structure emerged. Many societies underwent an irrevocable shift from an agrarian-oriented economy to an industrial base. No longer did an individual or a family typically make an entire product. Instead, specialization of tasks and manufacturing of goods became increasingly common. Workers, generally men but also women and even children, left their family homesteads to work in central locations such as factories.

The process of industrialization had distinctive social consequences. Families and communities could not continue to function as self-sufficient units. Individuals, villages, and regions began to exchange goods and services and to become more interdependent. As people came to rely on the labor of members of other communities, the family lost its unique position as the source of power and authority. The need for specialized knowledge led to more formalized schooling, and education emerged as a social institution distinct from the family.

Postindustrial and Postmodern Societies When Lenski first proposed the sociocultural evolutionary approach in the 1960s, he paid relatively little attention to how maturing industrialized societies may change with the emergence of even more advanced forms of technology. More recently, he and other sociologists have studied the significant changes in the occupational structure of industrial societies as they shift from manufacturing to service economies. In the 1970s sociologist Daniel Bell wrote about the technologically advanced **postindustrial society,** whose economic system is engaged primarily in the processing and control of information. The main output of a postindustrial society is services rather than manufactured goods. Large numbers of people become involved in occupations devoted to the teaching, generation, or dissemination of ideas. Jobs in fields such as advertising, public relations, human resources, and computer information systems would be typical of a postindustrial society (D. Bell 1999).

Bell views the transition from industrial to postindustrial society as a positive development. He sees a general decline in organized working-class groups and a rise in interest groups concerned with national issues such as health, education, and the environment. Bell's outlook is functionalist, because he portrays the postindustrial society as basically consensual. As organizations and interest groups engage in an open and competitive process of decision making, Bell believes, the level of conflict between diverse groups will diminish, strengthening social stability.

Conflict theorists take issue with Bell's functionalist analysis of the postindustrial society. For example, Michael Harrington (1980), who alerted the nation to the problems of the poor in his book *The Other America,* questioned the significance that Bell attached to the growing class of white-collar workers. Harrington conceded that scientists, engineers, and economists are involved in important political and economic decisions, but he disagreed with Bell's claim that they have a free hand in decision making, independent of the interests of the rich. Harrington followed in the tradition of Marx by arguing that conflict between social classes will continue in the postindustrial society.

Sociologists have recently gone beyond discussion of the postindustrial society to the ideal of the postmodern society. A **postmodern society** is a technologically sophisticated society that is preoccupied with consumer goods and media images (Brannigan 1992). Such societies consume goods and information on a mass scale. Postmodern theorists take a global perspective, noting the ways that culture crosses national boundaries. For example, residents of the United States may listen to reggae music from Jamaica, eat sushi and other Japanese

Believe it or not, this photograph was taken in France, just 20 miles from the center of Paris. In a postmodern society, people consume goods, information, and media images en masse. Disneyland Paris is popularizing U.S. media images abroad, illustrating another characteristic of postmodern societies, globalization.

technologies, postindustrial and postmodern societies can be expected to display the same problems of inequality that plague industrial societies (Denzin 2004; Smart 1990; B. Turner 1990; van Vucht Tijssen 1990).

Durkheim, Tönnies, and Lenski present three visions of society's social structure. While they differ, each is useful, and this textbook will draw on all three. The sociocultural evolutionary approach emphasizes a historical perspective. It does not picture different types of social structure coexisting within the same society. Consequently, one would not expect a single society to include hunters and gatherers along with a postmodern culture. In contrast, Durkheim's and Tönnies's theories allow for the existence of different types of community—such as a *Gemeinschaft* and a *Gesellschaft*—in the same society. Thus, a rural New Hampshire community located 100 miles from Boston can be linked to the city by modern information technology. The main difference between these two theories is a matter of emphasis. While Tönnies emphasized the overriding concern in each type of community—one's own self-interest or the well-being of the larger society—Durkheim emphasized the division (or lack of division) of labor.

The work of these three thinkers reminds us that a major focus of sociology has been to identify changes in social structure and the consequences for human behavior. At the macro level, we see society shifting to more advanced forms of technology. The social structure becomes increasingly complex, and new social institutions emerge to assume some functions that once were performed by the family. On the micro level, these changes affect the nature of social interactions. Each individual takes on multiple social roles, and people come to rely more on social networks and less on kinship ties. As the social structure becomes more complex, people's relationships become more impersonal, transient, and fragmented.

foods, and wear clogs from Sweden. And the online social networks discussed in the Social Policy section know no national boundaries.

The emphasis of postmodern theorists is on observing and describing newly emerging cultural forms and patterns of social interaction. Within sociology, the postmodern view offers support for integrating the insights of various theoretical perspectives—functionalism, conflict theory, feminist theory, and interactionism—while incorporating other contemporary approaches. Feminist sociologists argue optimistically that with its indifference to hierarchies and distinctions, the postmodern society will discard traditional values of male dominance in favor of gender equality. Yet others contend that despite new

---

use your sociological *imagination*

Of all the different forms of social structure described by Durkheim, Tönnies, and Lenski, which comes closest to matching your social setting?

www.mhhe.com/schaefer12e

social**policy** and **Social Interaction**

Regulating the Net

The Issue

In 1991 the first Webcam went online. The years that followed saw the widespread adoption of the cell phone and the digital camera, not to mention the Internet. By 1998, eHarmony.com, the first online dating service, had been founded. MySpace followed in 2003, and YouTube in 2005.

All these technological innovations have affected the way we shop and share information. But just as important is their impact on our social interactions. No longer are we limited to face-to-face encounters, letters and greeting cards, and long-distance telephone calls. Not only can we communicate with others instantaneously online; we can find and scan the profiles of strangers. Unfortunately, people are using these complex communication systems without any real understanding of the technology underlying them, and thus of their potential for misuse (Shortliffe and Patel 2004).

The Setting

Though people of all ages use the Internet, it has become especially important to young people's social interactions. By 2005, 87 percent of those age 12 to 17 used the Internet; every day, 11 million teens went online. Today young people supplement conventional e-mail with texting, instant messages, and shared images and video files. Increasingly, however, they regard e-mail—in widespread use for less than 20 years—as a way of communicating with "old people" or businesses. Instead, the majority of teens text-message or make daily visits to online social networking sites, such as Facebook and MySpace—a part of the social scene that is alien to older adults (Lenhart et al. 2005, 2007).

Sociological Insights

The ease of communication that the Internet offers would seem the epitome of functionality, allowing people to access new technologies in order to conduct meetings, select colleges, find jobs, monitor their health, and even expand their religious or spiritual horizons. But through misuse or abuse, the Internet can easily become dysfunctional. About one in five (21 percent) of young people who go online report having sent an e-mail, instant message, or text message that was meant to be private but was forwarded to others by the recipient. Another dysfunction (discussed later) is the victimization of young people by online predators.

The Internet is not a level playing field. While the digital divide that separates Internet use by race and social class is narrowing, it has not disappeared. Conflict theorists have documented the gap between White and Black or Hispanic youths in the use of electronic communication. Still, the greatest divide is not that of race, ethnicity, or even social class, but of age. Low-income Blacks are more likely to send instant messages than are older White adults, even those who are affluent.

Interactionists have investigated the implications of online communication for everyday social interaction. Their research shows that young people have a fairly significant network of regular online communicators, which gives them daily contact with about 20 friends. Maintaining face-to-face or even telephone contact with that many people would be difficult on a daily basis. But that is not all the Internet offers. Instant messaging has led to buddy lists (begun by AOL in 1996), which allow users to monitor which friends are online at any given moment. Most teens who go online have a buddy list of more than 25 names; about a quarter of them have over 100 buddies that they monitor 24/7. Just as they can access friends more easily online, they can also block them much more easily online than they can in person, in the workplace, or in the school cafeteria (Lenhart et al. 2005, 2007).

In any social interaction, knowing your partner is critical. Obviously, anonymity is not an issue in face-to-face conversation or even in the typical phone call. Online messages are a different matter, however, since people can easily disguise their gender, age, and other characteristics through the use of avatars. Most online users have more than one screen name, some of them

"WHAT'S UP? ON FACEBOOK YOU'RE INTO HIP-HOP, ON MYSPACE IT'S ALL R. AND B."

By creating profiles on more than one social networking site, people can engage in online impression management, presenting one image to one group of friends and another image to others.

because they lost or forgot a password. But others use multiple screen names to present one image to one group of intimates and another image to others. This manipulative use of screen names allows people to engage in online impression management. Some of the profiles people create at MySpace, Facebook, Xanga, Friendster, Yahoo, Piczo, Gaianonline, and Tagged show enormous creativity and depth of detail.

Feminist researchers have noted that women and girls have embraced the Internet even more than men. While male dominance is well established in online game playing, women are more likely than men to engage in online chats or to access online social networks, and to do so for longer periods than men.

Policy Initiatives

Although the U.S. Constitution does not explicitly extend the right of privacy to citizens, the Fourth Amendment's protection against unreasonable searches has often been interpreted as offering that right. As a general principle, then, our social interactions should not be monitored by outsiders, including government officials.

Most parents use filtering and monitoring to oversee their children's online communications. Indeed, it is much easier for parents to monitor their children's electronic communications than their face-to-face encounters. Every time a new operating system, such as Windows Vista or Mac Leopard, is unveiled, the originator markets "parental controls" as a compelling feature.

In private companies as well, self-regulation is outstripping government regulation. For example, Google's YouTube bans nudity and takes down copyrighted material that is used without permission, but only when the rights holder files a specific complaint. One challenge to any effort to monitor such sites more closely is that thousands of videos are posted daily, and millions of people may access the sites every hour (Stone 2007).

Policy issues that have led to significant legislation include the harassment or stalking of young users and the file sharing of pornographic images. Needless to say, government administrators are also concerned about the sharing of unflattering communications that seem to show officials, police, or the military behaving unprofessionally. Despite outcries by policymakers and the general public about online abuses, however, regulation has been very limited. Except for obscenity, pornography, and government-classified information, the online social world is less regulated than everyday social life (Clemmitt 2006).

Instead of regulation, policymakers have embraced the concept of **net neutrality** (short for *Internet neutrality*), or the principle that the government should remain nonselective or neutral toward online content. The driving force behind net neutrality is not Facebook profilers, but big business. Corporate supporters of net neutrality speak of their "freedoms" and condemn any effort to limit online communication as "discrimination." Google, in fact, has an executive whose title is "Vice President and Chief Internet Evangelist," whose job is to lobby Congress to block almost all regulation of online activities.

The net neutrality campaign arose around 2003, when large telephone conglomerates, seeing a future in the transmission of telephone calls over the Internet, began to monitor pending legislation to ensure the deregulation of online content. Several years earlier, in the Internet Tax Freedom Act (1998), Congress had declared a moratorium on the taxation of online commercial transactions. In 2006, continuing its hands-off policy, the Federal Election Commission declared that campaign finance laws would not apply to most online political activity (Pace 2006; *Wall Street Journal* 2006; Weil 1998).

Despite corporate pleas for net neutrality, concern has arisen that information gathered over the Internet is being shared in ways unknown to online users. Beginning in 2006, critics charged that computer applications had been developed which would allow Internet service providers to monitor and redirect online communications for commercial or government use. Citing the Fourth Amendment, they warned against "e-mail warehouses" where data is stored with little thought to who may later access it. While online communications may be less subject to regulation than everyday interactions, they are definitely less private. We will consider the implications of monitoring these communications in Chapter 7 (Tessler 2006).

The impact of new technologies over the past decade has been amazing, but research indicates that even savvy surfers still socialize in person rather than solely online. The more serious the event, the more likely it is to occur offline (Lenhart et al. 2005, 2007). Will that change someday, so that everything from Super Bowl parties to dating and fighting will occur online? What would be the social policy implications of such a shift in social interactions?

Let's Discuss

1. Do you know people whose online profiles are more revealing than their everyday interactions? If so, why do you think people are more open about themselves online?

2. Have your face-to-face social interactions ever been affected by something you learned in an online social network, such as MySpace or Facebook? If so, in what ways?

3. What role should the government take in regulating the information people post about themselves online? Would your answer differ depending on a person's age—say, under 21? Under 18?

getting**involved**

To get involved in the debate over regulating the Internet and censorship, visit this book's Online Learning Center, which offers links to relevant Web sites.

www.mhhe.com/schaefer12e

MASTERING THIS CHAPTER

Summary

Social interaction refers to the ways in which people respond to one another. **Social structure** refers to the way in which a society is organized into predictable relationships. This chapter examines the five basic elements of social structure: **statuses, social roles, groups, social networks,** and **social institutions.**

1. People shape their social reality based on what they learn through their **social interactions.** Social change comes from redefining or reconstructing social reality.

2. An **ascribed status** is generally assigned to a person at birth, whereas an **achieved status** is largely attained through one's own effort. Some ascribed statuses, such as race and gender, can function as **master statuses** that affect one's potential to achieve a certain professional or social status.

3. With each distinctive status—whether ascribed or achieved—come particular **social roles,** the set of expectations for people who occupy that status.

4. Much of our social behavior takes place in **groups,** which are often linked to **social networks** and their vast resources.

5. **Social institutions** fulfill essential functions, such as replacing personnel, training new recruits, and preserving order. The mass media, the government, the economy, the family, and the health care system are all examples of social institutions.

6. Conflict theorists charge that social institutions help to maintain the privileges of the powerful while contributing to the powerlessness of others.

7. Interactionist theorists stress that our social behavior is conditioned by the roles and statuses we accept, the groups to which we belong, and the institutions within which we function.

8. Recent advances in technology have created virtual worlds in which people can socialize electronically, without face-to-face contacts. Sociologist Manual Castells sees these emerging social networks as

fundamental to new organizations and the growth of existing businesses and associations.

9. Émile Durkheim thought that social structure depends on the division of labor in a society. According to Durkheim, societies with minimal division of labor have a collective consciousness called **mechanical solidarity;** those with greater division of labor show an interdependence called **organic solidarity.**

10. Ferdinand Tönnies distinguished the close-knit community of *Gemeinschaft* from the impersonal mass society known as *Gesellschaft.*

11. Gerhard Lenski thinks that a society's social structure changes as its culture and technology become more sophisticated, a process he calls **sociocultural evolution.**

12. The rise of the Internet has changed the nature of our social interactions, greatly expanding our social networks but raising concerns about privacy, unequal access, and the protection of young people from sexual predators.

Critical Thinking Questions

1. People in certain professions seem particularly susceptible to role conflict. For example, journalists commonly experience role conflict during disasters, crimes, and other distressing situations. Should they offer assistance to the needy or cover breaking news? Select two other professions and discuss the role conflicts people in them might experience.

2. The functionalist, conflict, and interactionist perspectives can all be used in analyzing social institutions. What are the strengths and weaknesses in each perspective's analysis of those institutions?

3. What are the pros and cons of net neutrality? Which approach do you favor, government regulation of online content or government neutrality toward that content? Explain your position.

Key Terms

Achieved status A social position that a person attains largely through his or her own efforts. (page 100)

Agrarian society The most technologically advanced form of preindustrial society. Members are engaged primarily in the production of food, but increase their crop yields through technological innovations such as the plow. (110)

Ascribed status A social position assigned to a person by society without regard for the person's unique talents or characteristics. (100)

Avatar A three-dimensional model, two-dimensional icon, or constructed personality that is assumed by the user of an Internet site. (108)

Gemeinschaft A close-knit community, often found in rural areas, in which strong personal bonds unite members. (109)

Gesellschaft A community, often urban, that is large and impersonal, with little commitment to the group or consensus on values. (109)

Group Any number of people with similar norms, values, and expectations who interact with one another on a regular basis. (103)

Horticultural society A preindustrial society in which people plant seeds and crops rather than merely subsist on available foods. (110)

Hunting-and-gathering society A preindustrial society in which people rely on whatever foods and fibers are readily available in order to survive. (109)

Industrial society A society that depends on mechanization to produce its goods and services. (111)

Master status A status that dominates others and thereby determines a person's general position in society. (101)

Mechanical solidarity A collective consciousness that emphasizes group solidarity, characteristic of societies with minimal division of labor. (108)

Net neutrality The principle that the government should remain nonselective or neutral toward online content. (114)

Organic solidarity A collective consciousness that rests on mutual interdependence, characteristic of societies with a complex division of labor. (109)

Postindustrial society A society whose economic system is engaged primarily in the processing and control of information. (111)

Postmodern society A technologically sophisticated society that is preoccupied with consumer goods and media images. (111)

Role conflict The situation that occurs when incompatible expectations arise from two or more social positions held by the same person. (101)

Role exit The process of disengagement from a role that is central to one's self-identity in order to establish a new role and identity. (103)

Role strain The difficulty that arises when the same social position imposes conflicting demands and expectations. (102)

Social institution An organized pattern of beliefs and behavior centered on basic social needs. (103)

Social interaction The ways in which people respond to one another. (98)

Social network A series of social relationships that links a person directly to others, and through them indirectly to still more people. (106)

Social role A set of expectations for people who occupy a given social position or status. (101)

Social structure The way in which a society is organized into predictable relationships. (98)

Sociocultural evolution Long-term trends in societies resulting from the interplay of continuity, innovation, and selection. (109)

Status A term used by sociologists to refer to any of the full range of socially defined positions within a large group or society. (100)

Technology Information about how to use the material resources of the environment to satisfy human needs and desires. (109)

Self-Quiz

Read each question carefully and then select the best answer.

1. In the United States, we expect that cab drivers will know how to get around a city. This expectation is an example of which of the following?
   a. role conflict
   b. role strain
   c. social role
   d. master status

2. What occurs when incompatible expectations arise from two or more social positions held by the same person?
   a. role conflict
   b. role strain
   c. role exit
   d. both a and b

3. In sociological terms, what do we call any number of people with similar norms, values, and expectations who interact with one another on a regular basis?
- **a.** a category
- **b.** a group
- **c.** an aggregate
- **d.** a society

4. Which sociological perspective argues that the present organization of social institutions is no accident?
- **a.** the functionalist perspective
- **b.** the conflict perspective
- **c.** the interactionist perspective
- **d.** the global perspective

5. The Shakers, a religious sect that came to the United States in 1774, has seen its group membership diminish significantly due to its inability to
- **a.** teach new recruits.
- **b.** preserve order.
- **c.** replace personnel.
- **d.** provide and maintain a sense of purpose.

6. Which sociologist saw that the "definition of the situation" could mold the thinking and personality of the individual?
- **a.** Philip Zimbardo
- **b.** Herbert Blumer
- **c.** William I. Thomas
- **d.** Erving Goffman

7. In Zimbardo's mock prison experiment at Stanford University,
- **a.** the social interactions between the prisoners and the guards influenced the social structure of the prison.
- **b.** the social structure of the prison influenced the social interactions between the prisoners and the guards.
- **c.** there was no relationship between social interaction and social structure.
- **d.** Zimbardo believed that social structure and social interaction influence each other.

8. Social control in what Ferdinand Tönnies termed a *Gemeinschaft* community is maintained through all but which of the following means?
- **a.** moral persuasion
- **b.** gossip
- **c.** legally defined punishment
- **d.** gestures

9. Sociologist Daniel Bell uses which of the following terms to refer to a society whose economic system is engaged primarily in the processing and control of information?
- **a.** postmodern
- **b.** horticultural
- **c.** industrial
- **d.** postindustrial

10. A key challenge for sociologists who study virtual social networks is that
- **a.** people using online social networking often lie about themselves.
- **b.** technology changes too rapidly.
- **c.** due to their rapid growth and lack of historical record, reconstructing these virtual worlds as they existed when they were first populated will be impossible.
- **d.** it's expensive to join a virtual social network.

11. The term _____ _____ refers to the way in which a society is organized into predictable relationships.

12. The Black activist Malcolm X wrote in his autobiography that his position as a Black man, a(n) _____ status, was an obstacle to his dream of becoming a lawyer, a(n) _____ status.

13. Sociologist Helen Rose Fuchs Ebaugh developed the term _____ _____ to describe the process of disengagement from a role that is central to one's self-identity in order to establish a new role and identity.

14. The mass media, the government, the economy, the family, and the health care system are all examples of _____ _____ found in the United States.

15. According to Herbert Blumer, our response to someone's behavior is based on the _____ we attach to his or her actions.

16. In studying the social behavior of word processors in a Chicago law firm, sociologist Mitchell Duneier drew on the _____ perspective.

17. Policymakers have embraced the concept of _____ _____, or the principle that the government should remain nonselective toward online content.

18. According to Émile Durkheim, societies with a minimal division of labor are characterized by _____ solidarity, while societies with a complex division of labor are characterized by _____ solidarity.

19. In Gerhard Lenski's theory of sociocultural evolution, a society's level of _____ is critical to the way it is organized.

20. A(n) _____ society is a technologically sophisticated society that is preoccupied with consumer goods and media images.

THINKING ABOUT MOVIES

Trading Places (John Landis, 1983)

The Duke brothers (Ralph Bellamy and Don Ameche), both powerful commodities brokers, bet that they can successfully trade the social positions of two very different individuals. When the brothers attempt to swap the lives of Louis Winthrope III (Dan Aykroyd), another wealthy broker, and Billy Ray Valentine (Eddie Murphy), a homeless beggar, their unlikely plan seems to work at first. Billy Ray succeeds as a broker, while Louis sinks to the very bottom of society. But when Billy Ray finds out about the bet, he joins with Louis to plot revenge against the Duke brothers.

This movie shows how people in positions of power maintain their social positions. Louis Winthrope's privileged upbringing gives him an ascribed status that he takes for granted, but cannot retain when others who are even more powerful undermine his position.

For Your Consideration

1. How does this movie demonstrate the difference between ascribed status and achieved status?

2. What are some of the different social roles portrayed in the movie? How is role conflict shown?

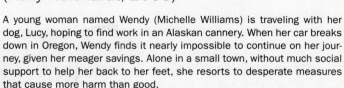

Wendy and Lucy
(Kelly Reichardt, 2008)

A young woman named Wendy (Michelle Williams) is traveling with her dog, Lucy, hoping to find work in an Alaskan cannery. When her car breaks down in Oregon, Wendy finds it nearly impossible to continue on her journey, given her meager savings. Alone in a small town, without much social support to help her back to her feet, she resorts to desperate measures that cause more harm than good.

Wendy and Lucy offers a glimpse of a life disconnected from social institutions. Wendy interacts with a few groups and individuals, and she manages to find help in unexpected places. Still, much of her contact with others is cold and impersonal—a characteristic of modern social interactions. Watch for the scene in which an authority figure at a local store upholds his managerial responsibilities, at Wendy's peril.

For Your Consideration

1. How might Wendy's struggles exemplify the *Gesellschaft*?

2. How does Wendy experience role conflict because of her relationship with Lucy? How does she attempt to alleviate the conflict?

inside

Understanding Groups

Understanding Organizations

Case Study: Bureaucracy
and the Space Shuttle
Columbia

Voluntary Associations

The Changing Workplace

Social Policy and
Organizations: The State
of the Unions Worldwide

BOXES

Research Today: *The
Drinking Rape Victim:
Jury Decision Making*

Sociology in the Global
Community: *McDonald's
and the Worldwide
Bureaucratization
of Society*

Sociology in the Global
Community:
*Entrepreneurship,
Japanese Style*

The women's rugby team of
Brown University struggles for
victory. Groups help individuals to
navigate through the larger
social world, including complex
social organizations like
educational institutions.

Groups and Organizations 6

GEORGE RITZER

The McDonaldization of Society 5

❝ Ray Kroc (1902–1984), the genius behind the franchising of McDonald's restaurants, was a man with big ideas and grand ambitions. But even Kroc could not have anticipated the astounding impact of his creation. McDonald's is the basis of one of the most influential developments in contemporary society. Its reverberations extend far beyond its point of origin in the United States and in the fast-food business. It has influenced a wide range of undertakings, indeed the way of life, of a significant portion of the world. And having rebounded from some well-publicized economic difficulties, that impact is likely to expand at an accelerating rate in the early 21st century.

However, this is not a book about McDonald's, or even about the fast-food business. . . . I devote all this attention to McDonald's . . . because it serves here as the major example of, and the paradigm for, a wide-ranging process I call McDonaldization. . . . McDonaldization has shown every sign of being an inexorable process, sweeping through seemingly impervious institutions (e.g., religion) and regions (European nations such as France) of the world.

Other types of business are increasingly adapting the principles of the fast-food industry to their needs. Said the vice chairman of Toys "R" Us, "We want to be thought of as a sort of McDonald's of toys." . . . Other chains with similar ambitions include Gap, Jiffy Lube, AAMCO Transmissions, Midas Muffler & Brake Shops, Great Clips, H&R Block, Pearle Vision, Bally's. . . .

Other nations have developed their own variants on the McDonald's chain. . . . Paris, a city whose love for fine cuisine might lead you to think it would prove immune to fast food, has a large number of fast-food croissanteries; the revered French bread has also been McDonaldized. India has a chain of fast-food restaurants, Nirula's, that sells mutton burgers (about 80% of Indians are Hindus, who eat no beef) as well as local Indian cuisine. Mos Burger is a Japanese chain with over 1,600 restaurants that, in addition to the usual fare, sell Teriyaki chicken burgers, rice burgers, and "Oshiruko with brown rice cake." . . .

McDonald's is such a powerful model that many businesses have acquired nicknames beginning with Mc. Examples include "McDentists" and "McDoctors," meaning drive-in clinics designed to deal quickly and efficiently with minor dental and medical problems; "McChild" care centers, meaning child care centers such as KinderCare; "McStables," designating the nationwide race horse–training operation of Wayne Lucas; and "McPaper," describing the newspaper *USA TODAY*. ❞

Ray Kroc (1902–1984), the genius behind the franchising of McDonald's restaurants, was a man with big ideas and grand ambitions.

(Ritzer 2008:1–2, 3, 4, 11) Additional information about this excerpt can be found on the Online Learning Center at www.mhhe.com/schaefer12e.

In this excerpt from *The McDonaldization of Society,* sociologist George Ritzer contemplates the enormous influence of a well-known fast-food organization on modern-day culture and social life. Ritzer defines **McDonaldization** as "the process by which the principles of the fast-food restaurant are coming to dominate more and more sectors of American society as well as of the rest of the world" (Ritzer 2008:1). In his book, he shows how the business principles on which the fast-food industry is founded—efficiency, calculability, predictability, and control—have changed, not only the way Americans do business and run their organizations, but the way they live their lives. Today, busy families rely on the takeout meals served up by fast-food establishments, and McDonald's has become a regular meeting place for social groups from adolescents to senior citizens.

Despite the runaway success of McDonald's and its imitators, and the advantages these enterprises bring to millions of people around the world (see Box 6-2, page 128), Ritzer is critical of their effect on society. The waste and environmental degradation created by billions of disposable containers and the dehumanized work routines of fast-food crews are two of the disadvantages he cites in his critique. Would the modern world be a better one, Ritzer asks, if it were less McDonaldized?

This chapter considers the impact of groups and organizations on social interaction. Do we behave differently in large groups than in small ones? How do we make large organizations manageable? What effect are current social changes having on the structure of groups? We'll begin by noting the distinctions between various types of groups, with particular attention to the dynamics of small groups. We'll examine how and why formal organizations came into existence and describe Max Weber's model of the modern bureaucracy. In a case study of the loss of the space shuttle *Columbia,* we'll see how NASA's bureaucratic culture contributed to the ship's disastrous accident. And we'll examine a special kind of organization, the voluntary association. Finally, we'll look at recent changes in the workplace, some of which are designed to counteract the failures of bureaucracies. The Social Policy section at the end of the chapter focuses on the status of organized labor today.

Understanding Groups

Most of us use the term *group* loosely to describe any collection of individuals, whether three strangers sharing an elevator or hundreds attending a rock concert. However, in sociological terms a **group** is any number of people with similar norms, values, and expectations who interact with one another on a regular basis. College sororities and fraternities, dance companies, tenants' associations, and chess clubs are all considered groups. The important point is that members of a group share some sense of belonging. This characteristic distinguishes groups from mere *aggregates* of people, such as passengers who happen to be together on an airplane flight, or from *categories* of people, such as those who share a common feature (such as being retired) but otherwise do not act together.

Consider the case of a college singing group. It has agreed-on values and social norms. All members want to improve their singing skills and schedule lots of performances. In addition, like many groups, the singing ensemble has both a formal and an informal structure. The members meet regularly to rehearse; they choose leaders to run the rehearsals and manage their affairs. At the same time, some group members may take on unofficial leadership roles by coaching new members in singing techniques and performing skills.

The study of groups has become an important part of sociological investigation because they play such a key role in the transmission of culture. As we interact with others, we pass on our ways of thinking and acting—from language and values to ways of dressing and leisure activities.

Types of Groups

Sociologists have made a number of useful distinctions between types of groups—primary and secondary groups, in-groups and out-groups, and reference groups.

Primary and Secondary Groups Charles Horton Cooley (1902) coined the term **primary group** to refer to a small group characterized by intimate, face-to-face association and cooperation. The members of a street gang constitute a primary group; so do members of a family living in the same household, as do a group of "sisters" in a college sorority.

Primary groups play a pivotal role both in the socialization process (see Chapter 4) and in the development of roles and statuses (see Chapter 5). Indeed, primary groups can be instrumental in a person's day-to-day existence. When we find ourselves identifying closely with a group, it is probably a primary group.

We also participate in many groups that are not characterized by close bonds of friendship, such as large college classes and business associations. The term **secondary group** refers to a formal, impersonal group in which there is little social intimacy or mutual understanding (Table 6-1). Secondary groups often emerge in the workplace among those who share special understandings about their occupation. The distinction between primary and secondary groups is not always clear-cut, however. Some social clubs may become so large and impersonal that they no longer function as primary groups.

In-Groups and Out-Groups A group can hold special meaning for members because of its relationship to other groups.

A pizza delivery crew is an example of a *secondary group*—a formal, impersonal group in which there is little social intimacy or mutual understanding. While waiting for the next delivery, members of this crew will become well enough acquainted to distinguish those who see the job as temporary from those who view it as permanent. They will learn who looks forward to deliveries in perceived high-risk areas and who does not. They may even spend time together after work, joking or boasting about their exploits on the job, but their friendship typically will not develop beyond that point.

TABLE **6-1** COMPARISON OF PRIMARY AND SECONDARY GROUPS

summing up

Primary Group	Secondary Group
Generally small	Usually large
Relatively long period of interaction	Relatively short duration, often temporary
Intimate, face-to-face association	Little social intimacy or mutual understanding
Some emotional depth to relationships	Relationships generally superficial
Cooperative, friendly	More formal and impersonal

For example, people in one group sometimes feel antagonistic toward or threatened by another group, especially if that group is perceived as being different either culturally or racially. To identify these "we" and "they" feelings, sociologists use two terms

"*So long, Bill. This is my club. You can't come in.*"

An exclusive social club is an in-group whose members consider themselves superior to others.

first employed by William Graham Sumner (1906): *in-group* and *out-group.*

An **in-group** can be defined as any group or category to which people feel they belong. Simply put, it comprises everyone who is regarded as "we" or "us." The in-group may be as narrow as a teenage clique or as broad as an entire society. The very existence of an in-group implies that there is an out-group that is viewed as "they" or "them." An **out-group** is a group or category to which people feel they do *not* belong.

In-group members typically feel distinct and superior, seeing themselves as better than people in the out-group. Proper behavior for the in-group is simultaneously viewed as unacceptable behavior for the out-group. This double standard enhances the sense of superiority. Sociologist Robert Merton (1968) described this process as the conversion of "in-group virtues" into "out-group vices." We can see this differential standard operating in worldwide discussions of terrorism. When a group or a nation takes aggressive actions, it usually justifies them as necessary, even if civilians are hurt or killed. Opponents are quick to label such actions with the emotion-laden term of *terrorist* and appeal to the world community for condemnation. Yet these same people may themselves retaliate with actions that hurt civilians, which the first group will then condemn.

Conflict between in-groups and out-groups can turn violent on a personal

as well as a political level. In 1999 two disaffected students at Columbine High School in Littleton, Colorado, launched an attack on the school that left 15 students and teachers dead, including themselves. The gunmen, members of an out-group that other students referred to as the Trenchcoat Mafia, apparently resented taunting by an in-group referred to as the Jocks. Similar episodes have occurred in schools across the nation, where rejected adolescents, overwhelmed by personal and family problems, peer group pressure, academic responsibilities, or media images of violence, have struck out against more popular classmates.

---

use your sociological *imagination*

Try putting yourself in the shoes of an out-group member. What does your in-group look like from that perspective?

Reference Groups Both primary groups and in-groups can dramatically influence the way an individual thinks and behaves. Sociologists call any group that individuals use as a standard for evaluating themselves and their own behavior a **reference group.** For example, a high school student who aspires to join a social circle of hip-hop music devotees will pattern his or her behavior after that of the group. The student will begin dressing like these peers, listening to the same downloads and DVDs, and hanging out at the same stores and clubs.

Reference groups have two basic purposes. They serve a normative function by setting and enforcing standards of conduct and belief. The high school student who wants the approval of the hip-hop crowd will have to follow the group's dictates, at least to some extent. Reference groups also perform a comparison function by serving as a standard against which people can measure themselves and others. An actor will evaluate himself

At a powwow, a drum circle breathes spirit into an ancient tribal tradition. These accomplished ceremonial musicians may serve as a reference group for onlookers who want to know more about drumming.

or herself against a reference group composed of others in the acting profession (Merton and Kitt 1950).

Reference groups may help the process of anticipatory socialization. For example, a college student majoring in finance may read the *Wall Street Journal*, study the annual reports of corporations, and listen to midday stock market news on the radio. Such a student is using financial experts as a reference group to which he or she aspires.

Often, two or more reference groups influence us at the same time. Our family members, neighbors, and co-workers all shape different aspects of our self-evaluation. In addition, reference group attachments change during the life cycle. A corporate executive who quits the rat race at age 45 to become a social worker will find new reference groups to use as standards for evaluation. We shift reference groups as we take on different statuses during our lives.

Coalitions As groups grow larger, coalitions begin to develop. A **coalition** is a temporary or permanent alliance geared toward a common goal. Coalitions can be broad-based or narrow and can take on many different objectives. Sociologist William Julius Wilson (1999) has described community-based organizations in Texas that include Whites and Latinos, working class and affluent, who have banded together to work for improved sidewalks, better drainage systems, and comprehensive street paving. Out of this type of coalition building, Wilson hopes, will emerge better interracial understanding.

Some coalitions are intentionally short-lived. Short-term coalition building is a key to success in popular TV programs like *Survivor*. In *Survivor I*, broadcast in 2000, the four members of the "Tagi alliance" banded together to vote fellow castaways off the island. The political world is also the scene of many temporary coalitions. For example, in 1997 big tobacco companies joined with antismoking groups to draw up a settlement for reimbursing states for tobacco-related medical costs. Soon after the settlement was announced the coalition members returned to their decades-long fight against each other (Pear 1997).

Can you outwit, outplay, outlast your competition? Maybe a coalition can help. In *Survivor: Tocantins,* coalition building continued to be one of the keys to success in the long-running television series, now in its 18th season.

---

use your sociological *imagination*

Do coalitions always work toward positive goals? Imagine a coalition that was formed to achieve a socially undesirable goal. Who are the members, and why did they band together?

Studying Small Groups

Sociological research done on the micro level and research done from the interactionist perspective usually focus on the study of small groups. Box 6-1 on page 124, for example, describes microsociological research on juries. The term **small group** refers to a group small enough for all members to interact simultaneously—that is, to talk with one another or at least be well acquainted. Certain primary groups, such as families, may also be classified as small groups. However, many small groups differ from primary groups in that they do not necessarily offer the intimate personal relationships characteristic of primary groups. For example, a manufacturer may bring together its seven-member regional sales staff twice a year for an intensive sales conference. The salespeople, who live in different cities and rarely see one another, constitute a small secondary group, not a primary group.

We may think of small groups as being informal and unpatterned; yet, as interactionist researchers have revealed, distinct and predictable processes are at work in the functioning of small groups. A long-term ethnographic study of street gangs in Chicago revealed an elaborate structure resembling that of a family business. A street gang there is composed of several geographically based units called sets, each of which possesses a leader, lower-ranking officers, and a rank-and-file membership. Besides staffing the economic network of the drug trade, gang members develop relationships with tenant leaders in public housing projects and participate in nondelinquent social activities important to the maintenance of their authority in the neighborhood (Venkatesh 2000, 2008).

Size of a Group At what point does a collection of people become too large to be called a small group? That is not clear. In a group with more than 20 members, it is difficult for individuals to interact regularly in a direct and intimate manner. But even within a range of 2 to 20 people, group size can substantially alter the quality of social relationships. For example, as the number of group participants increases, the most active communicators become even more active relative to others. Therefore, a person who dominates a group of 3 or 4 members will be relatively more dominant in a 15-person group.

Group size also has noticeable social implications for members who do not assume leadership roles. In a larger group, each member has less time to speak, more points of view to absorb,

RESEARCH TODAY

She was heavily intoxicated. He had drunk a few beers. They had sex. She said she was raped. He said it was consensual. The jury deliberated, and the verdict was. . . .

This is not an actual case, but an experiment in group decision making. Few small groups have received as much attention from sociologists over the past decade and a half as juries. Scholars have used several research methods to investigate juries' decision making: interviews with jury members after they have reached a verdict; observation of jurors as they sit through and react to courtroom events; observation of actual jury deliberations, which presiding judges have permitted in a few instances; and experiments involving mock juries. The findings indicate that jurors do not always make decisions the way they are supposed to.

For example, a jury's decision making may occur even before the first ballot is taken. Despite judges' instructions to the contrary, many jurors form tentative verdicts early in the trial. Studies suggest that jurors who have reached an initial judgment of "guilty" or "not guilty" give disproportionate weight to testimony that reinforces their impressions, while they tend to discount testimony that undermines them.

How do jurors form impressions in rape cases, especially those that involve intoxication?

To find out, legal scholars Emily Finch and Vanessa Munro simulated a rape trial in which intoxication was an issue. The two researchers varied the story to see what the effect might be on the verdict: in one version the alleged victim was drunk; in another she was drugged by a third person; in another she was drugged by the defendant. Finch and Munro found that although mock jurors generally disapproved of a man's taking advantage of a woman who was drunk, they did not always return a guilty verdict. In these cases, the

Finch and Munro found that although mock jurors generally disapproved of a man's taking advantage of a woman who was drunk, they did not always return a guilty verdict.

source of the intoxication often influenced the verdict. Even if the physical effect on the victim was the same, jurors were much less troubled by alcohol intoxication than by drug intoxication. Liquor and sex had come to be almost normalized in their view, to the extent that they were much less likely to convict the defendant when the victim had been drinking than when she had been using drugs.

Today, research on juries is expanding to deal with generational changes in the experience of being a juror. Some jurors arrive at court expecting to see the kind of sophisticated DNA analysis or investigative methods featured on televised crime shows, such as *CSI*. Improved methods of documenting crime scenes, including the use of computer-generated re-creations, mean that today's jurors are more likely than past jurors to be exposed to images of graphic violence and gore. Mental health professionals and social scientists have documented that the trauma jurors sometimes suffer from such exposure can trigger classic symptoms of stress, including depression, anxiety, weight loss, sleep loss, and disruptions in close social relationships. As with membership in other small groups, serving on a jury can be an intense experience—especially during a long, combative criminal trial with a focus on violence and bloodshed.

LET'S DISCUSS

1. Have you ever served on a jury? If so, were you aware of jurors who made up their minds early in the trial, despite the judge's instructions? Did you experience stress from being exposed to graphic images of violence and bloodshed?
2. Relate what you have learned about small groups to juries. Is a jury a typical small group? Why or why not? Would a large group be more effective than a small group in determining a defendant's guilt or innocence?

Sources: S. Diamond and Rose 2005; Finch and Munro 2005, 2007, 2008.

---

and a more elaborate structure to function in. At the same time, an individual has greater freedom to ignore certain members or viewpoints than he or she would in a smaller group. It is harder to disregard someone in a 4-person workforce than someone in an office with 30 employees, harder to disregard someone in a string quartet than someone in a college band with 50 members.

The German sociologist Georg Simmel (1858–1918) is credited as the first sociologist to emphasize the importance of interactive processes within groups and to note how they change as the group's size changes. The simplest of all social groups or relationships is the **dyad**, or two-member group. A wife and a husband constitute a dyad, as does a business partnership or a singing duo. The dyad offers a special level of intimacy that cannot be duplicated in larger groups. However, as Simmel ([1917] 1950) noted, a dyad, unlike any other group, can be destroyed by the loss of a single member. Therefore, the threat of termination hangs over a dyadic relationship perhaps more than over any other.

Obviously, the introduction of one additional person to a dyad dramatically transforms the character of the small group.

The dyad becomes a three-member group, or **triad**. The third member has many ways of interacting with and influencing the dynamics of the group. The new person may play a *unifying* role in the triad. When a married couple has their first child, the baby may serve to bind the group closer together. A newcomer also may play a *mediating* role in a three-person group. If two roommates are perpetually sniping at each other, the third roommate may attempt to remain on good terms with both and to arrange compromise solutions to problems. Finally, a member of a triad can choose to employ a *divide-and-rule* strategy. Such is the case, for example, with a coach who tries to gain greater control over two assistants by making them rivals (Lawler et al. 2008; Nixon 1979).

Groupthink   Can mere membership in a group cause those who belong to reach faulty decisions? William H. Whyte Jr. (1952) thought so. To describe the uncritical acceptance of or conformity to the prevailing viewpoint—a phenomenon that too often characterizes group decision making—Whyte coined the term **groupthink**. Simply put, group members experience a collective pressure to conform to the predominant line of thought. This social pressure effectively discourages the open expression of dissent.

In Whyte's opinion, high-level government leaders and their advisers are particularly prone to groupthink. These people confer regularly with one another, often in closed meetings in which they hear no one else's viewpoint. When decision makers are isolated from others in this way, they are liable to adopt unpopular or even disastrous policies. Of course, groupthink is not limited to the upper echelons of government. It occurs in jury rooms, corporate boardrooms, and even among high school students selecting a theme for their senior prom.

There are ways to avoid the illusion of unanimity created by groupthink. Small-group studies have shown the value of having outside facilitators lead groups. Dividing an established group into smaller units also encourages the expression of new perspectives (Janis 1967; Street 1997).

The effects of group size and groupthink on group dynamics are but two of the many aspects of the small group that sociologists have studied. Another aspect, conformity and deviance, is examined in Chapter 8. Although it is clear that small-group encounters have a considerable influence on our lives, we are also deeply affected by much larger groups of people, as we'll see in the next section.

Understanding Organizations

Formal Organizations and Bureaucracies

As contemporary societies have shifted to more advanced forms of technology and their social structures have become more complex, our lives have become increasingly dominated by large secondary groups referred to as *formal organizations*. A **formal organization** is a group designed for a special purpose and structured for maximum efficiency. The U.S. Postal Service, McDonald's, and the Boston Pops orchestra are examples of formal organizations. Though organizations vary in their size, specificity of goals, and degree of efficiency, they are all structured to facilitate the management of large-scale operations. They also have a bureaucratic form of organization, described in the next section.

In our society, formal organizations fulfill an enormous variety of personal and societal needs, shaping the lives of every one of us. In fact, formal organizations have become such a dominant force that we must create organizations to supervise other organizations, such as the Securities and Exchange Commission (SEC) to regulate brokerage companies. Although it sounds much more exciting to say that we live in the "computer age" than to say that we live in the "age of formal organization," the latter is probably a more accurate description (Azumi and Hage 1972; Etzioni 1964).

Ascribed statuses such as gender, race, and ethnicity can influence how we see ourselves within formal organizations. For example, a study of female lawyers in the nation's largest law firms found significant differences in the women's self-images, depending on the relative presence or absence of women in positions of power.

In firms in which less than 15 percent of partners were women, the female lawyers were likely to believe that "feminine" traits were strongly devalued and that "masculine" traits were equated with success. As one female attorney put it, "Let's face it: this is a man's environment, and it's sort of Jock City, especially at my firm." Women in firms where female lawyers were better represented in positions of power had a stronger desire for and higher expectations of promotion (Ely 1995:619).

Characteristics of a Bureaucracy

A **bureaucracy** is a component of formal organization that uses rules and hierarchical ranking to achieve efficiency. Rows of desks staffed by seemingly faceless people, endless lines and forms, impossibly complex language, and frustrating encounters with red tape—all these unpleasant images have combined to make *bureaucracy* a dirty word and an easy target in political campaigns. As a result, few people want to identify their occupation as "bureaucrat," despite the fact that all of us perform various bureaucratic tasks. In an industrial society, elements of bureaucracy enter into almost every occupation.

Max Weber ([1913–1922] 1947) first directed researchers to the significance of bureaucratic structure. In an important sociological advance, Weber emphasized the basic similarity of structure and process found in the otherwise dissimilar enterprises of religion, government, education, and business. Weber saw bureaucracy as a form of organization quite different from the family-run business. For analytical purposes, he developed an ideal type of bureaucracy that would reflect the most characteristic aspects of all human organizations. By **ideal type** Weber meant a construct or model for evaluating specific cases. In actuality, perfect bureaucracies do not exist; no real-world organization corresponds exactly to Weber's ideal type.

Weber proposed that whether the purpose is to run a church, a corporation, or an army, the ideal bureaucracy displays five basic characteristics. A discussion of those characteristics, as well as the dysfunctions of a bureaucracy, follows.

1. **Division of labor.** Specialized experts perform specific tasks. In your college bureaucracy, the admissions officer does not do the job of registrar; the guidance counselor does not see to the maintenance of buildings. By working at a specific task, people are more likely to become highly skilled and carry out a job with maximum efficiency. This emphasis on specialization is so basic a part of our lives that we may not realize it is a fairly recent development in Western culture.

The downside of division of labor is that the fragmentation of work into smaller and smaller tasks can divide workers and remove any connection they might feel to the overall objective of the bureaucracy. In *The Communist Manifesto* (written in 1848), Karl Marx and Friedrich Engels charged that the capitalist system reduces workers to a mere "appendage of the machine" (Tucker 1978). Such a work arrangement, they wrote, produces extreme **alienation**—a condition of estrangement or dissociation from the surrounding society. According to both Marx and conflict theorists, restricting workers to very small tasks also weakens their job security, since new employees can easily be trained to replace them.

Being an accountant in a large corporation may be a relatively high-paying occupation. In Marxist terms, however, accountants are vulnerable to alienation, since they are far removed from the product or service that the corporation creates.

Although division of labor has certainly enhanced the performance of many complex bureaucracies, in some cases it can lead to **trained incapacity;** that is, workers become so specialized that they develop blind spots and fail to notice obvious problems. Even worse, they may not care about what is happening in the next department. Some observers believe that such developments have caused workers in the United States to become less productive on the job.

In some cases, the bureaucratic division of labor can have tragic results. In the wake of the coordinated attacks on the World Trade Center and the Pentagon on September 11, 2001, Americans wondered aloud how the FBI and CIA could have failed to detect the terrorists' elaborately planned operation. The problem, in part, turned out to be the division of labor between the FBI, which focuses on domestic matters, and the CIA, which operates overseas. Officials at these intelligence-gathering organizations, both of which are huge bureaucracies, are well known for jealously guarding information from one another. Subsequent investigations revealed that they knew about Osama bin Laden and his Al-Qaeda terrorist network in the early 1990s. Unfortunately, five federal agencies—the CIA, FBI, National Security Agency, Defense Intelligence Agency, and National Reconnaissance Office—failed to share their leads on the network. Although the hijacking of the four commercial airliners used in the massive attacks may not have been preventable, the bureaucratic division of labor definitely hindered efforts to defend against terrorism, undermining U.S. national security.

2. **Hierarchy of authority.** Bureaucracies follow the principle of hierarchy; that is, each position is under the supervision of a higher authority. A president heads a college bureaucracy; he or she selects members of the administration, who in turn hire their own staff. In the Roman Catholic Church, the pope is the supreme authority; under him are cardinals, bishops, and so forth.

3. **Written rules and regulations.** What if your sociology professor gave your classmate an A for having such a friendly smile? You might think that wasn't fair, that it was against the rules.

Through written rules and regulations, bureaucracies generally offer employees clear standards for an adequate (or exceptional) performance. In addition, procedures provide a valuable sense of continuity in a bureaucracy. Individual workers will come and go, but the structure and past records of the organization give it a life of its own that outlives the services of any one bureaucrat.

Of course, rules and regulations can overshadow the larger goals of an organization to the point that they become dysfunctional. What if a hospital emergency room physician failed to treat a seriously injured person because he or she had no valid proof of U.S. citizenship? If blindly applied, rules no longer serve as a means to achieving an objective, but instead become important (and perhaps too important) in their own right. Robert Merton (1968) used the term **goal displacement** to refer to overzealous conformity to official regulations.

4. **Impersonality.** Max Weber wrote that in a bureaucracy, work is carried out *sine ira et studio,* "without hatred or passion." Bureaucratic norms dictate that officials perform their duties without giving personal consideration to people as individuals. Although this norm is intended to guarantee equal treatment for each person, it also contributes to the often cold and uncaring feeling associated with modern organizations. We typically think of big government and big business when we think of impersonal bureaucracies. In some cases, the impersonality that is associated with a bureaucracy can have tragic results. More frequently, bureaucratic impersonality produces frustration and disaffection. Today, even small firms filter callers with electronic menus.

5. **Employment based on technical qualifications.** Within the ideal bureaucracy, hiring is based on technical qualifications rather than on favoritism, and performance is measured against specific standards. Written personnel policies dictate who gets promoted, and people often have a right to appeal if they believe that particular rules have been violated. Such procedures protect bureaucrats against arbitrary dismissal, provide a measure of security, and encourage loyalty to the organization.

Although any bureaucracy ideally will value technical and professional competence, personnel decisions do not always follow that ideal pattern. Dysfunctions within bureaucracy have become well publicized, particularly because of the work of Laurence J. Peter. According to the **Peter principle**, every employee within a hierarchy tends to rise to his or her level of incompetence (Peter and Hull 1969). This hypothesis, which has not been directly or systematically tested, reflects a possible dysfunctional outcome of advancement on the basis of merit. Talented people receive promotion after promotion, until sadly, some of them finally achieve positions that they cannot handle with their usual competence.

Table 6-2 summarizes the five characteristics of bureaucracy. These characteristics, developed by Max Weber more than 80 years ago, describe an ideal type rather than an actual bureaucracy. Not every formal organization will possess all five of Weber's characteristics. In fact, wide variation exists among actual bureaucratic organizations.

Bureaucracy pervades modern life. Through a concept known as McDonaldization—"the process by which the principles of the fast-food restaurant are coming to dominate more and more sectors of American society as well as of the rest of the world"—bureaucratization has reached new heights (see Chapter 3). As

TABLE **6-2** CHARACTERISTICS OF A BUREAUCRACY   summing**up** 127

Characteristic	Positive Consequence	Negative Consequence	
		For the Individual	For the Organization
Division of labor	Produces efficiency in a large-scale corporation	Produces trained incapacity	Produces a narrow perspective
Hierarchy of authority	Clarifies who is in command	Deprives employees of a voice in decision making	Permits concealment of mistakes
Written rules and regulations	Let workers know what is expected of them	Stifle initiative and imagination	Lead to goal displacement
Impersonality	Reduces bias	Contributes to feelings of alienation	Discourages loyalty to company
Employment based on technical qualifications	Discourages favoritism and reduces petty rivalries	Discourages ambition to improve oneself elsewhere	Fosters Peter principle

Box 6-2 on page 128 shows, the McDonald's organization provides an excellent illustration of Weber's concept of bureaucracy (Ritzer 2008:1).

---

use your sociological *imagination*

Your school or workplace suddenly ceases to exhibit one of the five characteristics of bureaucracy. Which characteristic is it, and what are the consequences?

Bureaucratization as a Process   Have you ever had to speak to 10 or 12 individuals in a corporation or government agency just to find out which official has jurisdiction over a particular problem? Ever been transferred from one department to another until you finally hung up in disgust? Sociologists have used the term **bureaucratization** to refer to the process by which a group, organization, or social movement becomes increasingly bureaucratic.

Normally, we think of bureaucratization in terms of large organizations. But bureaucratization also takes place within small-group settings. Sociologist Jennifer Bickman Mendez (1998) studied domestic houseworkers employed in central California by a nationwide franchise. She found that housekeeping tasks were minutely defined, to the point that employees had to follow 22 written steps for cleaning a bathroom. Complaints and special requests went not to the workers, but to an office-based manager.

Oligarchy: Rule by a Few   Conflict theorists have examined the bureaucratization of social movements. The German sociologist Robert Michels (1915) studied socialist parties and labor unions in Europe before World War I and found that such organizations were becoming increasingly bureaucratic. The emerging leaders of the organizations—even some of the most radical—had a vested interest in clinging to power. If they lost their leadership posts, they would have to return to full-time work as manual laborers. (For a discussion of the status of labor unions today, see the Social Policy section at the end of this chapter.)

Through his research, Michels originated the idea of the **iron law of oligarchy,** which describes how even a democratic organization will eventually develop into a bureaucracy ruled by a few: called an oligarchy. Why do oligarchies emerge? People who achieve leadership roles usually have the skills, knowledge, or charismatic appeal (as Weber noted) to direct, if not control, others. Michels argued that the rank and file of a movement or organization look to leaders for direction and thereby reinforce the process of rule by a few. In addition, members of an oligarchy are strongly motivated to maintain their leadership roles, privileges, and power.

Bureaucracy and Organizational Culture

How does bureaucratization affect the average individual who works in an organization? The early theorists of formal organizations tended to neglect this question. Max Weber, for example, focused on the management personnel in bureaucracies, but had little to say about workers in industry or clerks in government agencies.

According to the **classical theory** of formal organizations, also known as the **scientific management approach,** workers are motivated almost entirely by economic rewards. This theory stresses that only the physical constraints on workers limit their productivity. Therefore, workers may be treated as a resource, much like the machines that began to replace them in the 20th century. Under the scientific management approach, management attempts to achieve maximum work efficiency through scientific planning, established performance standards, and careful supervision of workers and production. Planning involves efficiency studies but not studies of workers' attitudes or job satisfaction.

Not until workers organized unions—and forced management to recognize that they were not objects—did theorists of formal organizations begin to revise the classical approach.

SOCIOLOGY IN THE GLOBAL COMMUNITY

6-2 McDonald's and the Worldwide Bureaucratization of Society

In his book *The McDonaldization of Society*, sociologist George Ritzer notes the enormous influence of a well-known fast-food organization on modern-day culture and social life.

Not surprisingly, Max Weber's five characteristics of bureaucracy are apparent in McDonald's restaurants, as well as in the global corporation behind them. Food preparation and order-taking reflect a painstaking *division of labor*, implemented by a *hierarchy of authority* that stretches from the food workers up to the shift manager and store operator, and ultimately to the corporate board of directors. Store operators learn McDonald's *written rules and regulations*, which govern even the amount of ketchup or mustard placed on a hamburger, at McDonald's Hamburger University. Little bonding occurs between servers and customers, creating a pervasive sense of *impersonality*. Together with McDonald's cookie-cutter architectural designs, this lack of personal character tends to disguise a restaurant's locale—not just the town or city it serves, but often the country or continent as well. Finally, employees are expected to have specific *technical qualifications*, although most of the skills they need to perform routine tasks can be learned in a brief training period.

The real significance of McDonaldization is that it is not confined to the food-service industry or to coffee shops like Starbucks. Worldwide, McDonald's brand of predictability, efficiency, and dependence on nonhuman technology have become customary in a number of services, ranging from medical care to wedding planning to education. Even sporting events reflect the influence of bureaucratization. Around the world, stadiums are becoming increasingly similar, both physically and in the way they present the sport to spectators. Swipe cards, "sports city" garages and parking lots, and automated ticket sales maximize efficiency. All seats offer spectators an unrestricted view, and a big screen guarantees them access to instant replays. Scores, player statistics, and attendance figures are updated automatically by computer and

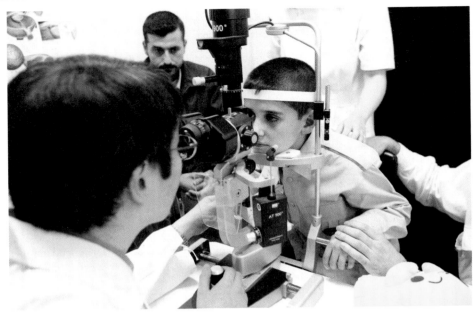

The worldwide success of highly efficient fast-food operations has led to the bureaucratization of many other services, including eye care and other forms of medical treatment.

displayed on an automated scoreboard. Spectator enthusiasm is manufactured through digital displays urging applause or rhythmic chanting. At food counters, refreshments include well-known brands whose customer loyalty has been

> *Worldwide, McDonald's brand of predictability, efficiency, and dependence on nonhuman technology have become customary in a number of services, ranging from medical care to wedding planning to education.*

nourished by advertisers for decades. And of course, the merchandising of teams' and even players' names and images is highly controlled.

McDonald's reliance on the five characteristics of bureaucracy is not revolutionary. What is new is the bureaucratization of services and life events that once were highly individualized, at times even spontaneous. More and more, society itself is becoming McDonaldized.

LET'S DISCUSS

1. Do you patronize McDonald's and other fast-food establishments? If so, what features of these restaurants do you appreciate? Do you have any complaints about them?
2. Analyze life at your college using Weber's model of bureaucracy. What elements of McDonaldization do you see? Do you wish life were less McDonaldized?

Sources: Ormond 2005; Ritzer 2008.

Social scientists became aware that, along with management and administrators, informal groups of workers have an important impact on organizations. An alternative way of considering bureaucratic dynamics, the **human relations approach**, emphasizes the role of people, communication, and participation in a bureaucracy. This type of analysis reflects the interest of interactionist theorists in small-group behavior. Unlike planning under the scientific management approach, planning based on the human relations approach focuses on workers' feelings, frustrations, and emotional need for job satisfaction.

The gradual move away from a sole focus on the physical aspects of getting the job done—and toward the concerns and needs of workers—led advocates of the human relations approach to stress the less formal aspects of bureaucratic structure. Informal groups and social networks within organizations develop partly as a result of people's ability to create more direct forms of communication than under the formal structure. Charles Page (1946) used the term *bureaucracy's other face* to refer to the unofficial activities and interactions that are such a basic part of daily organizational life.

Today, research on formal organizations is following new avenues. Among them are

- the recent arrival of a small number of women and minority group members in high-level management;

- in large corporations, the decision-making role of groups that lie outside the top ranks of leadership;

- the loss of fixed boundaries in organizations that have outsourced key functions; and

- the role of the Internet and virtual worlds in influencing business and consumer preferences.

Though research on organizations still embraces Max Weber's insights, it has gone well beyond them (Hamm 2007; Kleiner 2003; W. Scott 2004).

case study BUREAUCRACY AND THE SPACE SHUTTLE *COLUMBIA*

In February 2003, the space shuttle *Columbia* disintegrated as it reentered the earth's atmosphere. Seven astronauts died in the accident, which was blamed at first on a piece of foam weighing less than two pounds that had struck the spacecraft's wing during liftoff. But by August, the *Columbia* Accident Investigation Board (2003) had identified a second cause: NASA's bureaucratic organizational culture.

The board's blistering report cited NASA's emphasis on bureaucratic rules and regulations at the expense of astronauts' safety. Though engineers had voiced safety concerns over the years, especially after the shuttle *Challenger*'s explosion in 1986, their memos rarely reached the top of NASA's hierarchy, where costs and scheduling were considered paramount. In fact, the organization's culture discouraged the expression of safety concerns. When engineers tried to obtain special images of the *Columbia*'s wing during its last flight so that they could check for damage, managers denied their request. Aside from cost concerns, officials may have been unwilling to admit that something had gone wrong. In general, hierarchical organizations tend to encourage the concealment of mistakes (Vaughan 1996, 1999).

Another part of the problem was that over the years, foam debris had fallen during liftoff in about 10 percent of NASA's launches, without disastrous results. Officials had come to expect that a shower of debris might occur, and to speak of it as an "acceptable risk." Rather than treating it as a safety issue, they labeled it a maintenance problem. When the program resumed with *Discovery* in 2005, more foam debris broke off at launch, causing NASA to suspend further flights (J. Schwartz 2005).

Investigators had condemned the "acceptable risk" attitude following the *Challenger* explosion in 1986, but NASA's organizational culture had not changed. In a bureaucratic organization, bringing about real change can be extremely difficult. Those intrepid individuals who attempt to consider new alternatives often run into groupthink. Thus, in the wake of the second disaster, members of the *Columbia* Accident Investigation Board (2003:13) predicted, "The changes we recommend will be difficult to accomplish—and will be internally resisted."

Voluntary Associations

In the mid-19th century, the French writer Alexis de Tocqueville noted that people in the United States are "forever forming associations." By 2009, there were more than 456,000 voluntary associations in a U.S. national database. **Voluntary associations** are organizations established on the basis of common interest, whose members volunteer or even pay to participate. The Girl Scouts of America, the American Jewish Congress, the Kiwanis Club, and the League of Women Voters are all considered voluntary associations; so, too, are the American Association of Aardvark Aficionados, the Cats on

Stamps Study Group, the Mikes of America, the New York Corset Club, and the William Shatner Fellowship (Gale Cengage Learning 2009).

The categories of "formal organization" and "voluntary association" are not mutually exclusive. Large voluntary associations such as the Lions Club and the Masons have structures similar to those of profit-making corporations. At the same time, certain formal organizations, such as the Young Men's Christian Association (YMCA) and the Peace Corps, have philanthropic and educational goals usually found in voluntary associations. The Democratic Party and the United Farm Workers union are considered examples of voluntary associations. Even though membership in a political party or union can be a condition of employment and therefore not genuinely voluntary, political parties and labor unions are usually included in discussions of voluntary associations.

Participation in voluntary associations is not unique to the United States. This textbook's author attended a carnival in London featuring bungee-jumping, at which participants were expected to jump from a height of 180 feet. Skeptics were given assurances of the attraction's safety by being told that the proprietor belonged to a voluntary association: the British Elastic Rope Sports Association. An analysis of 15 industrial nations, including the United States, shows that active memberships in voluntary associations typically increased during the 1980s and 1990s. Only relatively inactive memberships in religious organizations and labor unions have showed a decline. On the whole, then, voluntary associations are fairly healthy (Curtis et al. 2001).

Voluntary associations can provide support to people in preindustrial societies. During the post–World War II period, migration from rural areas of Africa to the cities was accompanied by a growth in voluntary associations, including trade unions, occupational societies, and mutual aid organizations developed along old tribal lines. As people moved from the *Gemeinschaft* of the countryside to the *Gesellschaft* of the city, these voluntary associations provided immigrants with substitutes for the extended groups of kinfolk in their villages (Little 1988).

Voluntary associations in the United States are largely segregated by gender. Half of them are exclusively female, and one-fifth are all-male. Because the exclusively male associations tend to be larger and more heterogeneous, in terms of the background of members, all-male associations hold more promise for networking than all-female groups. Although participation varies across the population of the United States, most people belong to at least one voluntary association (Figure 6-1), while one-fourth maintain three or more memberships.

The importance of voluntary associations—and especially of their unpaid workers (or volunteers)—is increasingly being recognized. Traditionally, society has devalued unpaid work, even though the skill levels, experience, and training demands are often comparable with those of wage labor. Viewed from a conflict perspective, the critical difference has been that women perform a substantial amount of volunteer work. Feminists and conflict theorists agree that like the unpaid child care and household labor of homemakers, the effort of volunteers has too often been ignored by scholars—and awarded too little respect by the larger society—because it is viewed as "women's work." Failure to

AARP volunteers staff a phone bank in an effort to get out the vote in Des Moines, Iowa. The AARP is a voluntary association of people age 50 and older, both retired and working, that advocates for the needs of older Americans. A huge organization, it has been instrumental in maintaining Social Security benefits to retirees.

recognize women's volunteerism obscures a critical contribution women make to a society's social structure (Daniels 1987, 1988).

Besides contributing to the well-being of society, voluntary associations also serve as training grounds for civic engagement. Research shows that youthful involvement in a variety of organizations, from sports teams to debating societies and musical groups, influences a person's adult behavior. Specifically, adults who were active in voluntary associations as youths are more likely than others to participate in political activity, from voting to campaign work (McFarland and Thomas 2006).

use your sociological *imagination*

How many voluntary associations do you belong to? How do you benefit from your membership in them? How might your membership benefit others?

FIGURE **6-1** MEMBERSHIP IN VOLUNTARY ASSOCIATIONS IN THE UNITED STATES

About 4 out of 10 people belong to two or more organizations.

Source: J. Davis et al. 2007:409.

The Changing Workplace

Weber's work on bureaucracy and Michels's thinking on oligarchy are still applicable to the organizational structure and culture of the workplace. But today's factories and offices are undergoing rapid, profound changes unanticipated a century or more ago. Besides the far-reaching impact of technological advances such as computerization, workers must cope with organizational restructuring. This section will detail the dramatic changes evident in today's workplace.

Organizational Restructuring

To some extent, individual businesses, community organizations, and government agencies are always changing, if only because of personnel turnover. But since the late 20th century, formal organizations have been experimenting with new ways of getting the job done, some of which have significantly altered the workplace.

Collective decision making, or the active involvement of employee problem-solving groups in corporate management, first became popular in the United States in the 1980s. Management gurus had noted the dazzling success of Japanese automobile and consumer products manufacturers. In studying these companies, they found that problem-solving groups were one key to success. At first, such groups concentrated on small problems at specific points in the production line. But today, these groups often cross departmental and divisional boundaries to attack problems rooted in the bureaucratic division of labor. Thus, they require significant adjustment by employees long used to working in a bureaucracy (P. Hirsch and De Soucey 2006; Ouchi 1981).

Another innovation in the workplace, called *minimal hierarchy*, replaces the traditional bureaucratic hierarchy of authority with a flatter organizational structure. Minimal hierarchy offers workers greater access to those in authority, giving them an opportunity to voice concerns that might not be heard in a traditional bureaucracy. This new organizational structure is thought to minimize the potential for costly and dangerous bureaucratic oversights.

Finally, organizational *work teams* have become increasingly common, even in smaller organizations. There are two types of work team. *Project teams* address ongoing issues, such as safety or compliance with the Americans with Disabilities Act. *Task forces* pursue nonrecurring issues, such as a major building renovation. In both cases, team members are released to some degree from their regular duties in order to contribute to the organizationwide effort (W. Scott 2003; Huff 2007).

The common purpose of work teams, minimal hierarchy, and collective decision making is to empower workers. For that reason, these new organizational structures can be exciting for the employees who participate in them. But these innovations rarely touch the vast numbers of workers who perform routine jobs in factories and office buildings. The 1.7 million who are paid by the hour and who earn the minimum wage or lower know little about organizational restructuring (Bureau of Labor Statistics 2009b).

Together with organizational restructuring, societal changes well in place at the beginning of the 21st century have

Work teams are becoming an increasingly common form of organizational restructuring.

weakened the impact of bureaucratization on the workplace. As a result of globalization, today's formal organizations are less likely than those of the past to be self-contained. New information technologies have both increased employers' reliance on outside providers and facilitated direct communication between those at the very top and the very bottom of corporate hierarchies.

In Chapter 3 we discussed the role of innovation in society. Can the way that a business or any other bureaucratic organization operates influence the process of combining existing cultural items into a totally new form? See Box 6-3 on page 132.

Telecommuting

Increasingly, in many industrial countries, workers are turning into telecommuters. **Telecommuters** are employees who work full-time or part-time at home rather than in an outside office, and who are linked to their supervisors and colleagues through phone lines, Wi-Fi, the Internet, and smartphones. One national survey showed that next to on-site day care, most office workers want virtual offices that allow them to work off-site. Not surprisingly, the number of telecommuters increased from 8.5 million in 1995 to 50 million in 2005 (Donald Davis and Polonko 2001; Mokhtarian et al. 2005; Turek 2006).

What are the social implications of this shift toward the virtual office? From an interactionist perspective, the workplace is a major source of friendships; restricting face-to-face social opportunities could destroy the trust that is created by "handshake agreements." Thus, telecommuting may move society further along the continuum from *Gemeinschaft* to *Gesellschaft*. And like it or not, when employees work at home, they tend to become available 24/7. On a more positive note, telecommuting may be the first social change that pulls fathers and mothers back into the home rather than pushing them out. The trend, if it continues, should also increase autonomy and job satisfaction for many employees (Castells 2001; DiMaggio et al. 2001; P. Hirsch and De Soucey 2006).

SOCIOLOGY IN THE GLOBAL COMMUNITY

6-3 Entrepreneurship, Japanese Style

You take a group of talented employees and give them the freedom to come up with a brand-new product, like 3M's innovative Post-it® notes. It sounds like a great idea, but for many corporations, fostering a new product or business through entrepreneurship is not easy. In a profitable business, the existing organizational structure has worked well for so long, executives wonder why they should change it. Perhaps that is why the young Steve Jobs, unable to interest his employer, Hewlett-Packard, in the concept of a really small computer that could be hooked up to a home television set, quit to found Apple Computer.

The tendency of corporate culture to discourage innovation is especially strong in Japan. That may surprise North Americans, who for a generation have watched new automotive and electronic products emerge from the Asian powerhouse. Indeed, Japanese manufacturers like Toyota spearheaded the technique of continuous improvement, through which workers are encouraged to share their ideas for making the manufacturing process a little bit better (while keeping within strict limits). Yet in Japan, persuading wealthy individuals to invest in untested ideas is very difficult. Reliance on *venture capital*—private investment in the early stages of an innovation, in return for a generous payoff if the product is successful—is not well accepted in Japan. Entrepreneurs in Japan raise venture capital at less than half the rate of European entrepreneurs and a third of the rate of U.S. entrepreneurs. Among 27 of the world's industrial countries, Japan ranks 26 in venture capital investment—behind Hungary and just before the Slovak Republic.

Why this reluctance to fund innovative products and companies? Cultural factors are the primary reason. In Japan, conformity to societal norms in general, and to corporate norms in particular, is highly rewarded; individualism is frowned on. As an old Japanese saying warns, "The nail that sticks out is hammered down." Thus the Japanese people avoid displays of personal

> *Among 27 of the world's industrial countries, Japan ranks 26 in venture capital investment—behind Hungary and just before the Slovak Republic.*

wealth but celebrate corporate success. Historically, Japanese corporations have been reluctant to collaborate with other companies, much less to accept funds from venture capitalists. Collaboration between companies is four times more likely in the United States than in Japan.

Government policy is another factor that discourages innovation. The Japanese government frowns on collaboration among companies, along with partnerships between businesses and universities. Moreover, bureaucratic barriers to patent creation make it difficult for entrepreneurs, especially first-time innovators, to protect their ideas. In this inhospitable business environment, entrepreneurs typically fail.

Many are forced to declare bankruptcy, both as a business and as a person. The economist Joseph Schumpeter has referred to this high failure rate among Japanese entrepreneurs as "creative destruction."

Given the cultural barriers to innovation, it is hard to imagine a television show like *American Inventor* succeeding in Japan. In the United States, where almost everyone wants to be an inventor, audiences watch with amusement as a small business owner from Kentucky demonstrates a motion-sensitive device called the "Perfect Pet Petter," which talks to a lonely dog while stroking it. They cheer for the firefighter who invented a fire extinguisher called the "Guardian Angel," a treetop ornament connected to a small tank of water disguised as a Christmas present. Certainly, the Japanese applaud success in business, but not necessarily because they welcome innovation, either from the outside or from within.

LET'S DISCUSS

1. Have you ever thought of becoming an entrepreneur—of inventing something completely new and different, something that might make you rich? From a personal point of view, what would be the pros and cons of being an entrepreneur?
2. In Japan, do entrepreneurs constitute a counterculture? Why or why not?

Sources: *The Economist* 2006b, 2007c; Ibata-Irens 2007; Peng 2008; Sadeghi 2008; Schumpeter [1942] 1975.

---

www.mhhe.com/schaefer12e

use your sociological *imagination*

If your first full-time job after college involved telecommuting, what do you think would be the advantages and disadvantages of working out of a home office? Do you think you would be satisfied as a telecommuter? Why or why not?

Electronic Communication

Electronic communication in the workplace has generated some heat lately. On the one hand, e-mailing is a convenient way to push messages around, especially with the copy button. It's democratic, too: lower-status employees are more likely to participate in e-mail discussions than in face-to-face communications, giving organizations the benefit of their experience and views. But e-mail doesn't convey body language, which in face-to-face communication can soften insensitive phrasing and make unpleasant messages (such as a reprimand) easier to take. It also leaves a permanent record, which can be a problem if messages are written thoughtlessly (DiMaggio et al. 2001).

Electronic communication has contributed significantly to the fragmentation of work. Today, work is frequently interrupted by e-mail, pagers, and pop-up windows, as well as face-to-face interruptions. In one observation study of office workers, researchers found that employees spent an average of only 11 minutes on any given project before being interrupted. Typically, 25 minutes passed before they returned to their original tasks. While multitasking may increase a person's efficiency in some situations, it has become an integral and not necessarily helpful feature of work for many employees (Mark et al. 2005; C. Thompson 2005).

socialpolicy and Organizations

The State of the Unions Worldwide

The Issue

How many people do you know who belong to a labor union? Chances are you can name a lot fewer people than someone could 50 years ago. In 1954, unions represented 39 percent of workers in the private sector of the U.S. economy; in 2008 they represented only 12.4 percent. As Figure 6-2 shows, the decline in unionization is common to virtually all industrial nations. What has happened to diminish the importance of organized labor? Have unions outlived their usefulness in a rapidly changing global economy that is dominated by the service sector?

The Setting

Labor unions consist of organized workers who share either the same skill (as in electronics) or the same employer (as in the case of postal employees). Unions began to emerge during the Industrial Revolution in England, in the 1700s. Groups of workers banded together to extract concessions from employers (e.g., safer working conditions, a shorter workweek), as well as to protect their positions.

Historically, labor unions have engaged in restrictive practices that are regarded today as discriminatory. They frequently tried to protect their jobs by limiting entry to their occupation based on gender, race, ethnicity, citizenship, age, and sometimes rather arbitrary measures of skill levels. Today we see less of this protection of special interests, but individual labor unions are still the target of charges of discrimination, as are employers (Durrenberger 2007).

The power of labor unions varies widely from country to country. In some countries, such as Britain and Mexico, unions play a key role in the foundation of governments. In others, such as Japan and Korea, their role in politics is very limited, and even their ability to influence the private sector is relatively weak. In the United States, unions sometimes have a significant influence on employers and elected officials, but their effect varies dramatically by type of industry and even region of the country (Figure 6-3 on page 134; S. Zimmerman 2008c).

Few people today would dispute the fact that union membership is declining. Among the reasons for the decline are the following:

1. **Changes in the type of industry.** Manufacturing jobs, the traditional heart of the labor union, have declined, giving way to postindustrial service jobs.

2. **Growth in part-time jobs.** Between 1982 and 1998 the number of temporary jobs in the United States rose 577 percent, while total employment increased only 41 percent. Only in 2000 did laws governing collective bargaining allow temporary workers to join a union.

3. **The legal system.** The United States has not made it particularly easy for unions to organize and bargain, and some government measures have made it more difficult. A dramatic

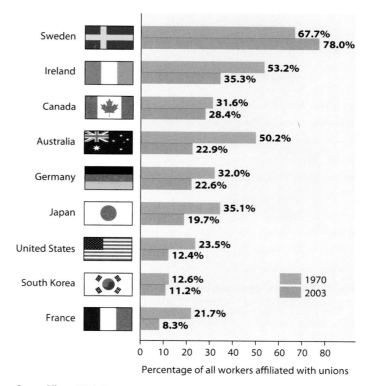

FIGURE **6-2** LABOR UNION MEMBERSHIP WORLDWIDE

Country	1970	2003
Sweden	67.7%	78.0%
Ireland	53.2%	35.3%
Canada	31.6%	28.4%
Australia	50.2%	22.9%
Germany	32.0%	22.6%
Japan	35.1%	19.7%
United States	23.5%	12.4%
South Korea	12.6%	11.2%
France	21.7%	8.3%

Percentage of all workers affiliated with unions

Source: Visser 2006:45.

example was President Ronald Reagan's firing of 11,000 air traffic controllers in 1981, when their union threatened they would walk off the job while seeking a new contract.

4. **Globalization.** The threat of jobs leaving the country has undercut the ability of union leaders to organize workers at home. Some say that labor union demands for wage increases and additional benefits have themselves spurred the exodus of jobs to developing nations, where wages are significantly lower and unions are virtually nonexistent.

5. **Employer offensives.** Increasingly hostile employers have taken court action to block unions' efforts to represent their members.

6. **Union rigidity and bureaucratization.** In the past, labor has been slow to embrace women, minorities, and immigrants. Furthermore, in some unions the election of leaders seems to dominate the organization's activity (Prah 2005).

Around the world, the economic downturn that began in 2008 has had special consequences for labor unions. Like non-union workers, many union members lost their jobs in the recession; others saw their contracts renegotiated. As part of the $17.4 billion auto bailout legislation passed by the U.S. Congress, the

FIGURE 6-3 UNION MEMBERSHIP IN THE UNITED STATES

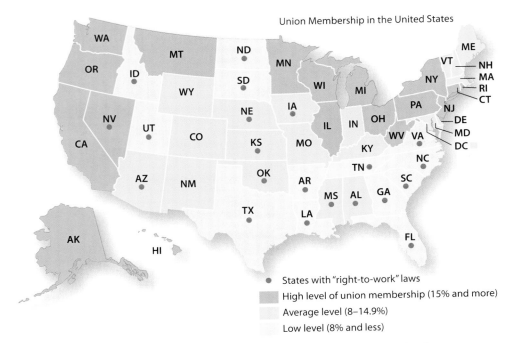

MAPPING LIFE NATIONWIDE

Union Membership in the United States

- ● States with "right-to-work" laws
- High level of union membership (15% and more)
- Average level (8–14.9%)
- Low level (8% and less)

Note: "Right to work" means that, legally, workers cannot be required to join a union or pay union dues.
Source: Developed by the author based on data for 2008 from Bureau of Labor Statistics 2009a and National Right to Work Legal Defense Foundation 2009.

---

leadership can change significantly. Smaller unions are vulnerable to changes in leadership, as are unions whose membership shifts in composition from predominantly White to African American or Latino.

Many union employees encounter role conflict (see page 101). For example, they may agree to provide a needed service and then organize a strike to withhold it. Role conflict is especially apparent in the helping occupations: teaching, social work, nursing, law enforcement, and firefighting. These workers may feel torn between carrying out their professional responsibilities and enduring working conditions they find unacceptable.

Policy Initiatives

U.S. law grants workers the right to self-organize via unions. But the United States is unique among industrial democracies in allowing employers to actively oppose their employees' decision to organize (Comstock and Fox 1994).

UAW accepted a nearly 20 percent pay cut. This and other rollbacks of benefits were largely accepted by U.S. unions, but in Europe, thousands of workers turned out in protest. In a few highly publicized cases, unions took the company bosses hostage. Although some union leaders in the United States expect the hardship caused by the economic slowdown to raise union membership, how well unions will be able to represent their members through tough times remains to be seen (S. Greenhouse 2008a, 2009b).

Sociological Insights

Both Marxists and functionalists would view unions as a logical response to the emergence of impersonal, large-scale, formal, and often alienating organizations. This view certainly characterized the growth of unions in major manufacturing industries with a sharp division of labor. However, as manufacturing has declined, unions have had to look elsewhere for growth.

Worldwide, today's labor unions bear little resemblance to those early unions organized spontaneously by exploited workers. In line with Robert Michels's iron law of oligarchy (see page 127), unions have become increasingly bureaucratized under a self-serving leadership. Conflict theorists would point out that the longer union leaders are in office, the less responsive they are to the needs and demands of the rank and file, and the more concerned with maintaining their own positions and power. Yet research shows that under certain circumstances, union

A major barrier to union growth exists in the 22 states that have right-to-work laws (see Figure 6-3). In these states, workers cannot be *required* to join or pay dues or fees to a union. The very term *right to work* reflects the anti-union view that a worker should not be forced to join a union, even if the union may negotiate on his or her behalf and achieve results that benefit the worker. This situation is unlikely to change. That is, right-to-work states will remain so; those without such laws typically have a strong union tradition or restrict union activities in other ways.

On the national level, union power is waning. In the security buildup that followed the terrorist attacks of September 11, 2001, federal officials created many new jobs and reorganized existing agencies into the Department of Homeland Security. In doing so, they specified that some 170,000 workers would not have collective bargaining rights, and that 43,000 newly federalized airport security screeners could not be unionized. These stipulations barring unions have been maintained and represent another sign of growing anti-union sentiment (Frank 2007).

In Europe, labor unions tend to play a major role in political elections. The ruling party in Great Britain, in fact, is called the Labour Party. Unions play a lesser role in U.S. politics, although they have recently been attacked for their large financial contributions to political campaigns. In addition to the role of unions in national politics, international trade unions sometimes speak out on common issues. In 2009 one of them condemned "corporate grand theft"—a reference to corporate executives who spend lavishly on themselves while laying off workers. Despite efforts dating back to Karl Marx and Friedrich Engels's call for the workers of all countries to unite (1847), no global union has emerged (International Trade Union Confederation 2009).

Though unions are a global force, their form and substance varies from country to country. In China, where there is only one political party, the government ordered Wal-Mart's 31,000 workers to unionize, over the corporation's objections. Chinese unions are controlled by the Communist Party, whose membership has declined as the party's pervasive control has weakened. Nevertheless, these unions are more likely to listen to the government than independent unions, which respond to the workers who are their members (Lague 2006).

Let's Discuss

1. What unions are represented on your college campus? Have you been aware of union activity? Has there been any opposition to the unions on the part of the administration?

2. Do you think nurses should be allowed to strike? Why or why not? What about teachers or police officers?

3. If a union is working on behalf of all the workers of a company, should all the employees be required to join the union and pay dues? Why or why not?

getting**involved**

To get involved in the debate over the labor movement, visit this book's Online Learning Center, which offers links to relevant Web sites.

www.mhhe.com/schaefer12e

MASTERING THIS CHAPTER

Summary

Social interaction among human beings is necessary to the transmission of culture and the survival of every society. This chapter examines the social behavior of *groups, formal organizations,* and *voluntary associations.*

1. When we find ourselves identifying closely with a group, it is probably a *primary group.* A *secondary group* is more formal and impersonal.

2. People tend to see the world in terms of *in-groups* and *out-groups,* a perception often fostered by the very groups to which they belong.

3. *Reference groups* set and enforce standards of conduct and serve as a source of comparison for people's evaluations of themselves and others.

4. Interactionist researchers have noted distinct and predictable processes in the functioning of *small groups.* The simplest group is a *dyad,* composed of two members. *Triads* and larger groups increase the ways of interacting and allow for *coalitions* to form.

5. As societies have become more complex, large *formal organizations* have become more powerful and pervasive.

6. Max Weber argued that in its ideal form, every *bureaucracy* has five basic characteristics: division of labor, hierarchical authority, written rules and regulations, impersonality, and employment based on technical qualifications.

7. Bureaucracy can be understood both as a process and as a matter of degree. Thus, an organization may be more or less bureaucratic than other organizations.

8. When leaders of an organization build up their power, the result can be *oligarchy* (rule by a few).

9. The informal structure of an organization can undermine and redefine official bureaucratic policies.

10. People join *voluntary associations* for a variety of purposes—for example, to share in joint activities or to get help with personal problems.

11. Organizational restructuring and new technologies have transformed the workplace through innovations such as *collective decision making* and *telecommuting.*

12. *Labor unions* are on the decline because of major shifts in the economy.

Critical Thinking Questions

1. Think about how behavior is shaped by reference groups. What different reference groups have shaped your outlook and your goals at different periods in your life? How have they done so?

2. Are primary groups, secondary groups, in-groups, out-groups, and reference groups likely to be found within a formal organization? What functions do these groups serve for a formal organization? What dysfunctions might occur as a result of their presence?

3. Max Weber identified five basic characteristics of bureaucracy. Select an actual organization familiar to you (for example, your college, a workplace, or a religious institution or civic association you belong to) and apply Weber's five characteristics to that organization. To what degree does it correspond to Weber's ideal type of bureaucracy?

Key Terms

Alienation A condition of estrangement or dissociation from the surrounding society. (page 125)

Bureaucracy A component of formal organization that uses rules and hierarchical ranking to achieve efficiency. (125)

Bureaucratization The process by which a group, organization, or social movement becomes increasingly bureaucratic. (127)

Classical theory An approach to the study of formal organizations that views workers as being motivated almost entirely by economic rewards. (127)

Coalition A temporary or permanent alliance geared toward a common goal. (123)

Dyad A two-member group. (124)

Formal organization A group designed for a special purpose and structured for maximum efficiency. (125)

Goal displacement Overzealous conformity to official regulations of a bureaucracy. (126)

Group Any number of people with similar norms, values, and expectations who interact with one another on a regular basis. (121)

Groupthink Uncritical acceptance of or conformity to the prevailing viewpoint. (124)

Human relations approach An approach to the study of formal organizations that emphasizes the role of people, communication, and participation in a bureaucracy and tends to focus on the informal structure of the organization. (128)

Ideal type A construct or model for evaluating specific cases. (125)

In-group Any group or category to which people feel they belong. (122)

Iron law of oligarchy A principle of organizational life under which even a democratic organization will eventually develop into a bureaucracy ruled by a few individuals. (127)

Labor union Organized workers who share either the same skill or the same employer. (133)

McDonaldization The process by which the principles of the fast-food restaurant are coming to dominate more and more sectors of American society as well as of the rest of the world. (120)

Out-group A group or category to which people feel they do not belong. (122)

Peter principle A principle of organizational life according to which every employee within a hierarchy tends to rise to his or her level of incompetence. (126)

Primary group A small group characterized by intimate, face-to-face association and cooperation. (121)

Reference group Any group that individuals use as a standard for evaluating themselves and their own behavior. (122)

Scientific management approach Another name for the classical theory of formal organizations. (127)

Secondary group A formal, impersonal group in which there is little social intimacy or mutual understanding. (121)

Small group A group small enough for all members to interact simultaneously—that is, to talk with one another or at least be well acquainted. (123)

Telecommuter An employee who works full-time or part-time at home rather than in an outside office, and who is linked to supervisor and colleagues through phone lines, Wi-Fi, the Internet and smartphones. (131)

Trained incapacity The tendency of workers in a bureaucracy to become so specialized that they develop blind spots and fail to notice obvious problems. (126)

Triad A three-member group. (124)

Voluntary association An organization established on the basis of common interest, whose members volunteer or even pay to participate. (129)

Self-Quiz

Read each question carefully and then select the best answer.

1. George Ritzer's belief that business principles of the fast-food industry have greatly influenced how we live and do business has been coined
   a. Fast Food Nation.
   b. Drive-Through Life.
   c. McDonaldization.
   d. Burger USA.

2. _____ groups often emerge in the workplace among those who share special understandings about their occupation.
   a. Primary
   b. Secondary
   c. Out-
   d. Formal

3. The purpose of a reference group is to serve a(n)
   a. normative function by enforcing standards of conduct and belief.
   b. comparison function by setting a standard against which people can measure themselves and others.
   c. elimination function by dissolving groups that no longer have a social purpose.
   d. both a and b

4. The president of the United States need not be a good typist, and a surgeon need not be able to fill a cavity, because of the bureaucratic characteristic of
   a. division of labor.
   b. impersonality.
   c. employment based on technical qualifications.
   d. written rules and regulations.

5. Which pioneer of sociology first directed researchers to the significance of bureaucratic structure?
   a. Émile Durkheim
   b. Max Weber
   c. Karl Marx
   d. Ferdinand Tönnies

6. Minimal hierarchy involves a(n)
   a. traditional bureaucracy.
   b. lack of rules in the workplace.
   c. flatter organizational structure.
   d. absence of traditional job titles.

7. The U.S. Postal Service, the Boston Pops orchestra, and the college or university in which you are currently enrolled as a student are all examples of
   a. primary groups.
   b. reference groups.
   c. formal organizations.
   d. triads.

8. One positive consequence of bureaucracy is that it reduces bias. Reduction of bias results from which characteristic of a bureaucracy?
   a. impersonality
   b. hierarchy of authority
   c. written rules and regulations
   d. employment based on technical qualifications

9. According to the Peter principle,
   a. all bureaucracies are notoriously inefficient.
   b. if something *can* go wrong, it *will*.
   c. every employee within a hierarchy tends to rise to his or her level of incompetence.
   d. all line workers get burned in the end.

10. What are the social implications of a shift toward the virtual office as a result of the increasing number of telecommuters?
   a. Supervisors will find that performance goals must be defined more clearly, which may lead to further bureaucratization.
   b. It should increase autonomy and job satisfaction for many employees.
   c. It will lead to greater worker privacy and job security.
   d. both a and b

11. William Graham Sumner distinguished between _____ and _____.

12. Formal organizations have a(n) _____ form of organization.

13. A third member of a group may try to gain control by having the other two members become rivals. This is known as the _____ _____ _____ strategy.

14. _____ groups often emerge in the workplace among those who share special understandings about their occupation.

15. In many cases, people model their behavior after groups to which they may not belong. These groups are called _____ groups.

16. Trained incapacity, goal displacement, and the Peter principle are all examples of bureaucratic _____.

17. The iron law of oligarchy was developed by German sociologist _____ _____.

18. People who happen to be in the same place at the same time, such as members of a Broadway theatre audience, are a(n) _____.

19. When we find ourselves identifying closely with a group, it is probably a(n) _____ group.

20. Max Weber developed a(n) _____ _____ of bureaucracy, which reflects the most characteristic aspects of all human organizations.

THINKING ABOUT MOVIES

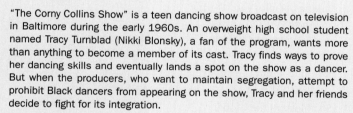

Frozen River (Courtney Hunt, 2008)

Ray Eddy (Melissa Leo) and Lila Littlewolf (Misty Upham) form an unlikely two-member group. Lila, a Native American who belongs to the Mohawk tribe, is cautious toward Ray, claiming she doesn't like to work with Whites. Ray is suspicious of Lila, whom she considers different from herself. Though the two women resent each other, they join together to achieve their economic goals by smuggling illegal immigrants across the Canadian border. Eventually, they recognize what they have in common and overcome their prejudice.

Not only does *Frozen River* illustrate the sociology of a dyad; the film shows how the rules and regulations of a formal organization can affect particular individuals. Watch for the scene in which Ray and Lila contend with the bureaucracy of the Mohawk tribal council.

For Your Consideration

1. What are the primary and secondary groups in Ray and Lila's story, and what roles do they play in the women's socialization?

2. How does Lila and Ray's group membership affect their work environment?

Hairspray

(Adam Shankman, 2007)

"The Corny Collins Show" is a teen dancing show broadcast on television in Baltimore during the early 1960s. An overweight high school student named Tracy Turnblad (Nikki Blonsky), a fan of the program, wants more than anything to become a member of its cast. Tracy finds ways to prove her dancing skills and eventually lands a spot on the show as a dancer. But when the producers, who want to maintain segregation, attempt to prohibit Black dancers from appearing on the show, Tracy and her friends decide to fight for its integration.

This movie illustrates in-groups and out-groups on two levels. Racial conflict separates Baltimore's high school students into an in-group of White cast members and an out-group of excluded Blacks. And Tracy's large body type puts her into the out-group until her dancing skill earns her a place in the in-group.

For Your Consideration

1. How does this movie represent in-group virtues and out-group vices?

2. Who joins the coalition of youths who work to integrate "The Corny Collins Show"? How does their social network help them to achieve their goal?

inside

Sociological Perspectives
    on the Media

The Audience

The Media's Global Reach

Social Policy and the
    Mass Media: Media
    Concentration

BOXES

Taking Sociology to Work:
    *Nicole Martorano Van
    Cleve, Former Brand
    Planner, Leo Burnett USA*

Research Today: *The Color
    of Network TV*

Sociology in the Global
    Community: *Al Jazeera
    Is on the Air*

The mass media are an integral part of modern culture. In Chicago, the classic black-and-white film *Casablanca* (1942), once seen only in movie theaters, received an open-air showing on a billboard-sized screen during the city's recent summer film festival.

66 In the spring of 2006, search engine giant Google announced its plans to bring the holy grail of next-generation Internet access to the United States' first city of technology: the entire city of San Francisco would be equipped with free wireless Internet access. The company wasn't doing this out of the kindness of its heart or to rid itself of an embarrassingly large budget surplus; it had a business model. In return for free wireless access, Google announced its plans to use the information it gathered about users' locations within the city to bombard them with time- and location-specific ads, or what it calls "contextual advertising." If, in other words, you happened to be working on your laptop in a city park during lunchtime, you might find an ad on your computer screen for a lunch discount at the sandwich shop across the street. Given the fact that Google can also keep track of the search requests entered into its search engines and the e-mail messages sent over its popular Gmail service, it's not hard to imagine just how "contextual" the advertising it doles out might eventually become. Say you happen to be searching for information about a particular author while working in a neighborhood café. Perhaps you might find an ad for discounts on that author's work in the bookstore around the corner. Writing a friend about a trip you're planning to take to Las Vegas the following weekend? Maybe the ad will be for poker how-to manuals instead.

When we turn on our wireless connection in the San Francisco of the future, we will find ourselves in a digital enclosure for which the terms of entry include submission to always-on, location-based monitoring.

Google's plans for San Francisco represent the physical version of . . . a *digital enclosure*—the creation of an interactive realm wherein every action and transaction generates information about itself. Although the term implies a physical space, the same characteristics can apply to virtual spaces. The Internet, for example, provides the paradigmatic example of a virtual digital enclosure—one in which every virtual "move" has the potential to leave a digital trace or record of itself. When we surf the Internet, for example, Internet browsers can gather information about the paths we take—the sites we've visited and the clickstreams that take us from one site to the next. When we purchase items online, we leave detailed records of our transactions. Even our search requests are logged and preserved in the database memories of search engines. Google's plans for downtown San Francisco are, in other words, merely the implementation of this Internet model in physical space. . . .

I use the term *enclosure* not just to invoke the notion of a space—virtual or otherwise—that is rendered interactive, but also to highlight the *process* of enclosure, whereby places and activities become encompassed by the monitoring embrace of an interactive (virtual) space. Accompanying this movement is a not-so-subtle shift in social relations: entry into the digital enclosure carries with it, in most cases, the condition of surveillance. We can go into a bookstore and make a cash purchase without generating information about the transaction. But when we go online, we generate increasingly detailed forms of transactional information that become secondary information commodities: information that may eventually be sold to third parties or used by marketers for targeted advertising campaigns. When we turn on our wireless connection in the San Francisco of the future, we will find ourselves in a digital enclosure for which the terms of entry include submission to always-on, location-based monitoring. 99

(Andrejevic 2007:1–2) Additional information about this excerpt can be found on the Online Learning Center at www.mhhe.com/schaefer12e.

Imagine relaxing under a tree at your local park. You can preview the latest episode of your favorite reality program, watch your baby sister play at her day care center, or listen to a lecture at a local college. Communications scholar Mark Andrejevic outlined a multitude of such possibilities recently as San Francisco debated whether to go wireless. So far, the City by the Bay has not adopted universal Wi-Fi, not because the technology doesn't exist or because thousands of citizens aren't ready for it. Charges of secret negotiations between the mayor and a would-be provider of wireless service scuttled the project. In 2008, however, a second wireless provider began handing out transmitters to residents, and several hundred people started using them. Today, a wireless area of about two square miles links 100,000 people. And in 2009, the local rapid transit system announced that all 104 miles of track and 43 stations would be Wi-Fi accessible by 2011 (Rachel Gordon 2009; Ha 2008).

We have come a long way from the 1950s, when rabbit-ear antennas sat atop black-and-white television sets. Both television and the Net are forms of **mass media,** a term that refers to the print and electronic means of communication that carry messages to widespread audiences. Print media include newspapers, magazines, and books; electronic media include radio, satellite radio, television, motion pictures, and the Internet. Advertising, which falls into both categories, is also a form of mass media.

The social impact of the mass media is obvious. Consider a few examples. TV dinners were invented to accommodate the millions of couch potatoes who can't bear to miss their favorite television programs. Today, *screen time* encompasses not just television viewing but playing video games and surfing the Internet. Candidates for political office rely on their media consultants to project a winning image both in print and in the electronic media. World leaders use all forms of media for political advantage, whether to gain territory or to bid on hosting the Olympics. In parts of Africa and Asia, AIDS education projects owe much of their success to media campaigns. And during the 2003 war in Iraq, both the British and U.S. governments allowed journalists to be embedded with frontline troops as a means of "telling their story."

Few aspects of society are as central as the mass media. Through the media we expand our understanding of people and events beyond what we experience in person. The media inform us about different cultures and lifestyles and about the latest forms of technology. For sociologists, the key questions are how the mass media affect our social institutions and how they influence our social behavior.

The social impact of the mass media has become so huge, in fact, that scholars have begun to speak of *cultural convergence*. The term **cultural convergence** refers to the flow of content across multiple media, and the accompanying migration of media audiences. As you watch a television program, for example, you wonder what the star of the show is doing at the moment, and turn to the Internet. Later, while texting your best friend, you tell her what you learned, accompanied by a Google Earth map showing the celebrity's location. Using Photoshop, you may even include the star's image next to your own, post the photo on your Facebook page, and then tweet your friends (send them a mini-blog) to create a caption. Media convergence is not orchestrated by the media, sophisticated though they may be. You initiate it, using techniques you likely learned by interacting with others, either face-to-face or through the media (H. Jenkins 2006).

Why are the media so influential? Who benefits from media influence and why? How do we maintain cultural and ethical standards in the face of negative media images? In this chapter we will consider the ways sociology helps us to answer these questions. First we will look at how proponents of the various sociological perspectives view the media. Then we will examine just who makes up the media's audience, not just at home but around the world. The chapter closes with a Social Policy section on the concentration of the media in the hands of a few powerful corporations.

Sociological Perspectives on the Media

Over the past decade, new technologies have made new forms of mass media available to U.S. households. These new technologies have changed people's viewing and listening habits. People spend a lot of time with the media, more and more of it on the Internet. Media consumers have moved away from television and toward digital images downloaded to their computers and portable devices. Increasingly, they learn not just about the famous but about ordinary people by viewing their personal Web sites or their pages in Facebook or MySpace. People also spend less time listening to recorded music than they did just a few years ago; they spend more time surfing the Internet. These patterns tend to vary by age group, however. Among 18- to 34-year-olds, for example, time spent watching prime-time TV—both broadcast and cable—declined by 19 percent between 1991 and 2003, as video games and the Internet took up more of their media time.

In studying the impact of the mass media on socialization, sociologists must consider the wide variety of contact people have with communication outlets, from immersion in all types of media to relative isolation, especially from recent innovations. In 2007 the Pew Research Center released a report that sorted U.S. residents into 10 categories based on their use of information and communications technologies (ICTs) (Table 7-1 on page 142). According to the report, about 31 percent of the adult population falls into the top four categories, from the "Omnivores," who use these devices as a means of self-expression, to the "Productivity Enhancers," who use them to get the job done. Middle-of-the-road users, who represent about 20 percent of the population, take advantage of new technologies but aren't as excited about them. They range from the "Mobile Centrics," who are strongly attached to their cell phones, to the "Connected but Hassled." Close to half the people in the nation have few if any technology devices, or if they do, they are not wedded to them. Typically, younger people embrace technological change more than older people, who tend either to be indifferent toward new technologies or to find them annoying.

How do people's viewing and listening habits affect their social behavior? In the following sections we'll use the three major sociological perspectives to examine the impact of the mass media and changes in their usage patterns (E. Nelson 2004).

Functionalist View

One obvious function of the mass media is to entertain. Except for clearly identified news or educational programming, we often think the explicit purpose of the mass media is to occupy our leisure time—from newspaper comics and crossword puzzles to the latest music releases on the Internet. While that is true, the media have other important functions. They also socialize us, enforce social norms, confer status, and promote consumption. An important dysfunction of the mass media is that they may act as a narcotic, desensitizing us to distressing events (Lazarsfeld and Merton 1948; C. Wright 1986).

Agent of Socialization The media increase social cohesion by presenting a common, more or less standardized view of culture through mass communication. Sociologist Robert Park (1922) studied how newspapers helped immigrants to the United States adjust to their environment by changing their customary habits and teaching them the opinions of people in their new home country. Unquestionably, the mass media play a significant role in providing a collective experience for members of society. Think about how the mass media bring together members of a community or even a nation by broadcasting important events and ceremonies (such as inaugurations, press conferences, parades, state funerals, and the Olympics) and by covering disasters.

Omnivores: 8% of American adults constitute the most active participants in the information society, consuming information goods and services at a high rate and using them as a platform for participation and self-expression.

The Connectors: 7% of the adult population surround themselves with technology and use it to connect with people and digital content. They get a lot out of their mobile devices and participate actively in online life.

Lackluster Veterans: 8% of American adults make up a group who are not at all passionate about their abundance of modern ICTs. Few like the intrusiveness their gadgets add to their lives and not many see ICTs adding to their personal productivity.

Productivity Enhancers: 9% of American adults happily get a lot of things done with information technology, both at home and at work.

Mobile Centrics: 10% of the general population are strongly attached to their cell phones and take advantage of a range of mobile applications.

Connected but Hassled: 9% of American adults fit into this group. They have invested in a lot of technology, but the connectivity is a hassle for them.

Inexperienced Experimenters: 8% of adults have less ICT on hand than others. They feel competent in dealing with technology, and might do more with it if they had more.

Light but Satisfied: 15% of adults have the basics of information technology, use it infrequently, and it does not register as an important part of their lives.

Indifferents: 11% of adults have a fair amount of technology on hand, but it does not play a central role in their daily lives.

Off the Net: 15% of the population, mainly older Americans, is off the modern information network.

Note: From a Pew Internet and American Life Project survey conducted in April 2006.
Source: Horrigan 2007:vii.

Think about It
What category would you place yourself in?

Which media outlets did people turn to in the aftermath of the September 11, 2001, tragedy? Television, radio, and the telephone were the primary means by which people in the United States bonded. But the Internet also played a prominent role. About half of all Internet users—more than 5 million people—received some kind of news about the attacks online (D. Miller and Darlington 2002).

By 2009, the media landscape moved further online. The White House routinely connected with the general public via Facebook, Twitter, Flickr, MySpace, YouTube, and iTunes. The June uprising over election results in Iran was furthered by protesters connecting through Twitter and receiving encouragement from overseas viewers of their YouTube videos. A spontaneous global sharing of Michael Jackson's sudden death in 2009 led to Web sites from Google, *Los Angeles Times*, celebrity news site TMZ, Perez Hilton's blog, to Twitter all experiencing outages (Rawlinson and Hunt 2009).

The Internet has also become a political arena. An analysis of the 2008 presidential campaign showed that 24 percent of U.S. citizens turned regularly to the Internet to research the candidates. That is a sharp increase from the 2004 campaign, when 13 percent used the Internet to gather information on politics. The online marketplace for political information is becoming broader as well, expanding from the usual candidates' Web sites to include MySpace, Facebook, and YouTube (Kohut 2008).

Some are concerned about the socialization function of the mass media, however. For instance, many people worry about the effect of using television as a babysitter and the impact of violent programming on viewer behavior. Some people adopt a blame-the-media mentality, holding the media accountable for anything that goes wrong, especially with young people. Yet the media also have positive effects on young people. For young and even not-so-young adults, for example, a new sort of tribalism is emerging online, in which communities develop around common interests or shared identities (T. Adams and Smith 2008).

Enforcer of Social Norms The media often reaffirm proper behavior by showing what happens to people who act in a way that violates societal expectations. These messages are conveyed when the bad guy gets clobbered in cartoons or is thrown in jail on *CSI*. Yet the media also sometimes glorify disapproved behavior, whether it is physical violence, disrespect to a teacher, or drug use.

The media play a critical role in human sexuality. Many people object to the widespread availability of pornography on the Web; others are concerned about the way sexual predators use chat rooms to take advantage of children. Yet innovative uses of new media may also have positive consequences. On Valentine's Day 2007, New York City introduced the official "NYC Condom" on Facebook, in an attempt to make safe sex a social norm. Not only has New York's Department of Health and Mental Hygiene given away millions of condoms, but thousands of e-condoms, as they are called, have been distributed to Facebook users.

Programs have also been created to persuade teens not to send nude images of themselves to selected friends. Such images often go viral (that is, spread across the Internet) and may be used to harass teens and their parents. To define normative behavior regarding these images, one organization has launched a "That's not cool" campaign, complete with "stalker messages" that can be e-mailed to those who misuse such images. The widespread dissemination of compromising images that were meant to be shared only among close friends is just one aspect of the new social phenomenon called cyberbullying (Chan 2009; Clifford 2009; Gentile 2009).

Conferral of Status The mass media confer status on people, organizations, and public issues. Whether it is an issue like the homeless or a celebrity like Cameron Diaz, they single out one from thousands of other similarly placed issues or people to become significant. Table 7-2 shows how often certain public figures are prominently featured on weekly magazine covers. Obviously, *People* magazine alone was not responsible for

TABLE **7-2** STATUS CONFERRED BY MAGAZINES 143

The Mass Media

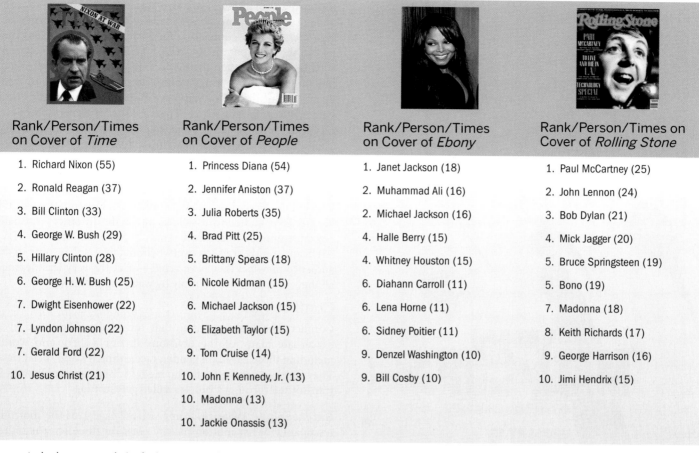

Rank/Person/Times on Cover of *Time*	Rank/Person/Times on Cover of *People*	Rank/Person/Times on Cover of *Ebony*	Rank/Person/Times on Cover of *Rolling Stone*
1. Richard Nixon (55)	1. Princess Diana (54)	1. Janet Jackson (18)	1. Paul McCartney (25)
2. Ronald Reagan (37)	2. Jennifer Aniston (37)	2. Muhammad Ali (16)	2. John Lennon (24)
3. Bill Clinton (33)	3. Julia Roberts (35)	2. Michael Jackson (16)	3. Bob Dylan (21)
4. George W. Bush (29)	4. Brad Pitt (25)	4. Halle Berry (15)	4. Mick Jagger (20)
5. Hillary Clinton (28)	5. Brittany Spears (18)	4. Whitney Houston (15)	5. Bruce Springsteen (19)
6. George H. W. Bush (25)	6. Nicole Kidman (15)	6. Diahann Carroll (11)	5. Bono (19)
7. Dwight Eisenhower (22)	6. Michael Jackson (15)	6. Lena Horne (11)	7. Madonna (18)
7. Lyndon Johnson (22)	6. Elizabeth Taylor (15)	6. Sidney Poitier (11)	8. Keith Richards (17)
7. Gerald Ford (22)	9. Tom Cruise (14)	9. Denzel Washington (10)	9. George Harrison (16)
10. Jesus Christ (21)	10. John F. Kennedy, Jr. (13)	9. Bill Cosby (10)	10. Jimi Hendrix (15)
	10. Madonna (13)		
	10. Jackie Onassis (13)		

Source: Author's content analysis of primary cover subject for full run of the periodicals beginning with *Time,* March 3, 1923; *People,* March 4, 1974; *Ebony,* November 1945; and *Rolling Stone,* September 1967 through January 1, 2009. When a periodical runs multiple covers, each version is counted. In case of ties, the more recent cover person is listed first.

Think about It

How do these magazines differ in the types of people they feature on their covers? Which type do you think enjoys the most status? Why?

making Princess Diana into a worldwide figure, but collectively, all the media outlets created a notoriety that Princess Victoria of Sweden, for one, did not enjoy.

Another way the media confer celebrity status on individuals is by publishing information about the frequency of Internet searches. Some newspapers and Web sites carry regularly updated lists of the most heavily researched individuals and topics of the week. The means may have changed since the first issue of *Time* magazine hit the stands in 1923, but the media still confer status—often electronically.

Promotion of Consumption   Twenty thousand commercials a year—that is the number the average child in the United States watches on television, according to the American Academy of Pediatrics. Young people cannot escape commercial messages. They show up on high school scoreboards, at rock concerts, and as banners on Web pages. They are even embedded in motion pictures (remember Reese's Pieces in 1982's *E.T.: The Extra Terrestrial?*). Such *product placement* is nothing new. In 1951 *The*

African Queen prominently displayed Gordon's Gin aboard the boat carrying Katharine Hepburn and Humphrey Bogart. But commercial promotion has become far more common today. Moreover, advertisers are attempting to develop brand or logo loyalty at younger and younger ages (Buckingham 2007).

Using advertising to develop a brand name with global appeal is an especially powerful way to encourage consumption. U.S. corporations have been particularly successful in creating global brands. An analysis of the 100 most successful brands worldwide, each of which derives at least a third of its earnings outside the home country, shows that 52 of them originated in the United States; 48 others come from 12 different countries (Figure 7-1 on page 145).

Media advertising has several clear functions: it supports the economy, provides information about products, and underwrites the cost of media. In some cases, advertising becomes part of the entertainment industry. A national survey showed that 44 percent of female viewers and 22 percent of male viewers watch the Super Bowl primarily for the commercials. Yet related to these functions

Product placement ("brand casting") is an increasingly important source of revenue for motion picture studios. The movie *Mall Cop* (2009), the saga of a security worker who takes on an armed gang, featured at least 50 different brands, including Bath and Body Works, Brookstone, Budweiser, Hello Kitty, Orange Julius, Perfectmatch.com, Sony, Sunglass Hut, and Verizon (Brandchannel.com 2009).

are dysfunctions. Media advertising contributes to a consumer culture that creates needs and raises unrealistic expectations of what is required to be happy or satisfied. Moreover, because the media depend heavily on advertising revenue, advertisers can influence media content (J. Jones and Carroll 2007).

---

use your sociological *imagination*

You are a news junkie. Where do you gather your facts or information—from newspapers, tabloids, magazines, TV newscasts, blogs, or the Internet? Why did you choose that medium?

Dysfunction: The Narcotizing Effect   In addition to the functions just noted, the media perform a *dysfunction*. Sociologists

Paul Lazarsfeld and Robert Merton (1948) created the term **narcotizing dysfunction** to refer to the phenomenon in which the media provide such massive amounts of coverage that the audience becomes numb and fails to act on the information, regardless of how compelling the issue. Interested citizens may take in the information but make no decision or take no action.

Consider how often the media initiate a great outpouring of philanthropic support in response to natural disasters or family crises. But then what happens? Research shows that as time passes, viewer fatigue sets in. The mass media audience becomes numb, desensitized to the suffering, and may even conclude that a solution to the crisis has been found (Moeller 1999).

The media's narcotizing dysfunction was identified 60 years ago, when just a few homes had television—well before the advent of electronic media. At that time, the dysfunction went largely unnoticed, but today commentators often point out the ill effects of addiction to television or the Internet, especially among young people. Street crime, explicit sex, war, and HIV/AIDS apparently are such overwhelming topics that some in the audience may feel they have acted—or at the very least learned all they need to know—simply by watching the news.

Conflict View

Conflict theorists emphasize that the media reflect and even exacerbate many of the divisions in our society and world, including those based on gender, race, ethnicity, and social class. They point in particular to the media's ability to decide what is transmitted through a process called gatekeeping.

Gatekeeping   What story appears on page 1 of the morning newspaper? What motion picture plays on three screens rather than one at the local cineplex? What picture isn't released at all? Behind these decisions are powerful figures—publishers, editors, and other media moguls.

The mass media constitute a form of big business in which profits are generally more important than the quality of the programming. Within the mass media, a relatively small number of people control what eventually reaches the audience through a process known as **gatekeeping.** This term describes how material must travel through a series of checkpoints (or gates) before reaching the public. Thus, a select few decide what images to bring to a broad audience. In many countries the government plays a gatekeeping role. A study done for the World Bank found that in 97 countries, 60 percent of the top five TV stations and 72 percent of the largest radio stations are government-owned (World Bank 2001:183).

Gatekeeping, which prevails in all kinds of media, is not a new concept. The term was coined by a journalism scholar in the 1940s to refer to the way that small-town newspaper editors control which events receive public attention. As sociologist C. Wright Mills ([1956] 2000b) observed, the real power of the media is that they can control what is being presented. In the recording industry, gatekeepers may reject a popular local band because it competes with a group already on their label. Even if the band is recorded, radio programmers may reject the music because it does not fit the station's sound. Television programmers may keep a pilot for a new TV series off the air because they believe it does not appeal to the target audience (which is sometimes determined by advertising sponsors). Similar decisions are made by gatekeepers in the publishing industry (Hanson 2005; White 1950).

FIGURE **7-1** BRANDING THE GLOBE
145

The Mass Media

MAPPING LIFE WORLDWIDE

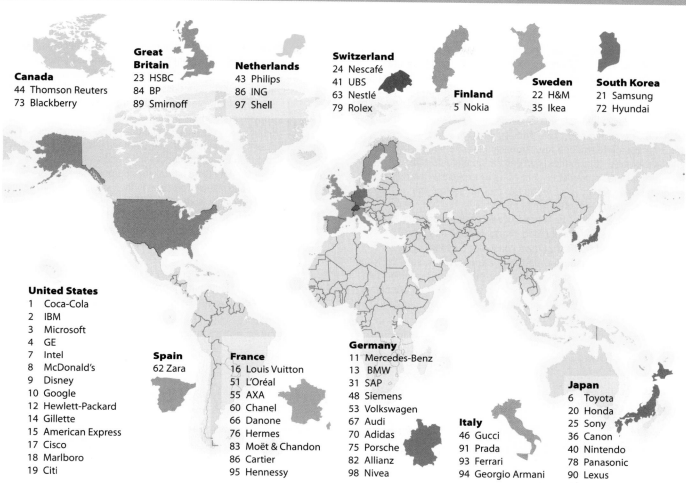

Canada
44 Thomson Reuters
73 Blackberry

Great Britain
23 HSBC
84 BP
89 Smirnoff

Netherlands
43 Philips
86 ING
97 Shell

Switzerland
24 Nescafé
41 UBS
63 Nestlé
79 Rolex

Finland
5 Nokia

Sweden
22 H&M
35 Ikea

South Korea
21 Samsung
72 Hyundai

United States
1 Coca-Cola
2 IBM
3 Microsoft
4 GE
7 Intel
8 McDonald's
9 Disney
10 Google
12 Hewlett-Packard
14 Gillette
15 American Express
17 Cisco
18 Marlboro
19 Citi

Spain
62 Zara

France
16 Louis Vuitton
51 L'Oréal
55 AXA
60 Chanel
66 Danone
76 Hermes
83 Moët & Chandon
86 Cartier
95 Hennessy

Germany
11 Mercedes-Benz
13 BMW
31 SAP
48 Siemens
53 Volkswagen
67 Audi
70 Adidas
75 Porsche
82 Allianz
98 Nivea

Italy
46 Gucci
91 Prada
93 Ferrari
94 Georgio Armani

Japan
6 Toyota
20 Honda
25 Sony
36 Canon
40 Nintendo
78 Panasonic
90 Lexus

Note: Map shows the top 100 brands in the world by country of ownership, except for the United States, for which only brands in the top 20 are shown.
Source: Based on Interbrand 2008.
Based on revenue and name recognition, these are the brands that dominate the global marketplace.

Think about It
How many of these brands do you recognize?

Gatekeeping is not as dominant in at least one form of mass media, the Internet. You can send virtually any message to an electronic bulletin board, and create a Web page or Web log (blog) to advance any argument, including one that insists the earth is flat. The Internet is a means of quickly disseminating information (or misinformation) without going through any significant gatekeeping process.

Nevertheless, the Internet is not totally without restrictions. In many nations laws regulate content on issues such as gambling, pornography, and even politics. Popular Internet service providers will terminate accounts for offensive behavior. After the terrorist attacks in 2001, eBay did not allow people to sell parts of the World Trade Center via its online auction. As of 2008, 21 countries had placed significant controls on Internet content (Figure 7-2 on page 146). China, for example, routinely blocks search engines like Google and AltaVista from accessing the names of groups or individuals critical of the government. Despite the government's gatekeeping, however, 300 million Chinese use the Internet, 70 million of whom are bloggers (A. Jacobs 2009).

Critics of the content of mass media argue that the gatekeeping process reflects a desire to maximize profits. Why else, they argue, would movie star George Clooney, rather than Afghanistan's leader Hamid Karzai, make the cover of *Time* magazine? Later in this chapter we will consider the role that corporate structure plays in the content and delivery of mass media. Another criticism of the gatekeeping process is that the content that makes it through the gates does not reflect the diversity of the audience.

Media Monitoring The term *media monitoring* is used most often to refer to interest groups' monitoring of media content.

TAKING SOCIOLOGY TO WORK

Nicole Martorano Van Cleve, Former Brand Planner, Leo Burnett USA

When Nicole Van Cleve graduated from Northwestern University in 1999 with a degree in sociology, she had no idea how useful it would be in her business career. But she soon found that her training in observing and analyzing social phenomena was in demand, especially in consumer research. "While my friends were trying to land a job in advertising using their 'business' know-how, I leveraged what I knew best—the sociological perspective," she says.

Van Cleve was hired by Leo Burnett, Chicago's largest advertising agency, to work on the campaigns for internationally known brands. "Big brands like Hallmark, Polaroid, and Disney are socially constructed entities," she explains. "The sociological imagination is an essential tool in 'seeing' the cultural phenomenon that others might miss."

In 2003 Van Cleve became a specialist in strategic brand planning, or the development of brand images to appeal to the passions and cultural truths that drive consumer purchases. As a brand planner, she conducted and analyzed interviews, surveys, focus groups, and ethnographic studies. Once, for example, she studied families on vacation in Disneyland, which involved everything from videotaping them to conducting focus groups and reading through the diaries they kept.

In the results to these studies, Van Cleve found clues to the human motivations that underlie consumers' purchasing habits and brand preferences.

Van Cleve loved the variety inherent in her work at Burnett. "In advertising, no week is ever the same," she enthuses. When she wasn't working in the field with consumers or analyzing the results of her studies, she wrote the creative briefs that inspire the agency's copywriters and art directors. Van Cleve knew that if she did her job well, the insights she developed through her consumer research would infuse the commercials and print advertisements that support her clients' brands.

Today, Van Cleve has taken her passion for sociological observation and research one step further: she is now a PhD candidate in sociology at Northwestern University. "As a student, sociology gave me an intellectual passion that I never knew I had," she muses. "As a profession, sociology gave me a job that I love."

LET'S DISCUSS

1. Can you think of some other careers in the mass media in which the sociological imagination might prove useful? If so, how?
2. What might be some ethical considerations in consumer research?

FIGURE **7-2** FILTERING INFORMATION: SOCIAL CONTENT

MAPPING LIFE WORLDWIDE

Note: "No data" sections, shown in gray, do not necessarily indicate an absence of filtering.
Source: OpenNet Initiative 2008; see also Deibert et al. 2008; Faris and Villeneuve 2008.
This map highlights nations that restrict public access to the Internet or filter its content, including material related to sexuality, gambling, illegal drugs, and alcohol, as well as other socially sensitive or offensive topics.

From television and newspapers to bloggers, media outlets were both applauded and harshly criticized for their coverage of the shootings at Virginia Tech in 2007.

efforts to obtain company records of users' Web-browsing activities. At the same time, members of the general public expressed concern both that companies like Google were maintaining such records and that government agencies were interested in them. In Chapter 10 we will see that media and computer giants don't always oppose government efforts to monitor media usage. For example, Yahoo, Google, Microsoft, and Dell have cooperated with the Chinese government's efforts to restrict and monitor Internet use, raising human rights concerns in the process.

The federal government has also come under criticism recently for authorizing wiretaps of U.S. citizens' telephone conversations without judicial approval. Government officials argue that the wiretaps were undertaken in the interest of national security, to monitor contacts between U.S. citizens and known terrorist groups following the terrorist attacks of September 11, 2001. But critics who take the conflict perspective, among others, are concerned by the apparent invasion of people's privacy (Gertner 2005).

What are the practical and ethical limits of media monitoring? In daily life, parents often oversee their children's online activities and scan the blogs they read—which are, of course, available for anyone to see. Most parents see such monitoring of children's media use and communications as an appropriate part of adult supervision. Yet their snooping sets an example for their children, who may use the technique for their own ends. Some media analysts have noted a growing trend among adolescents: the use of new media to learn not-so-public information about their parents (Delaney 2005).

The Digital Divide   As numerous studies have shown, advances in communications technology are not evenly distributed. Worldwide, low-income groups, racial and ethnic minorities, rural residents, and the citizens of developing countries have far less access than others to the latest technologies—a gap that is called the **digital divide.** People in low-income households and developing countries, for example, are less likely than others to have Internet access. When marginalized people do gain Internet access, they are still likely to trail the privileged. They may have dial-up service instead of broadband, or broadband instead of wireless Internet.

The implications of the digital divide go well beyond an inability to check sports results or celebrity comings and goings. The Internet and other new media are becoming essential to economic progress, whether it is finding a job or accessing information needed to improve one's skills.

The digital divide is most evident in developing countries. In Africa, 4 percent of the population has Internet access. These fortunate few typically pay the highest rates in the world—$250 to $300 a month—for the slowest connection speeds. In 2005 the United Nations called for digital solidarity, but thus far,

The public reaction to the shootings at Virginia Tech in April 2007 provides one example. People did not need to be constant news monitors to learn of the rampage. Ever since the mass shootings at Columbine High School near Littleton, Colorado, in 1999, news outlets of every type have descended on the sites of such school shootings, offering insight into the perpetrators and their families, covering the mass expressions of grief, and following the communities' efforts to recover. Once again, though media outlets provided valuable information and quickly reassured viewers, listeners, and readers that the shooter posed no further danger, many people criticized the reality that they constructed in their coverage.

Reactions ran the gamut. Some observers, including groups representing Asian Americans, questioned the recurring racial identifier used to describe the shooter at Virginia Tech. Indeed, when the news began to leak out that the shooter was "foreign" or "Asian," many people of color commented that they hoped he would not turn out to be one of their own, since people of color appear so rarely, if at all, in news coverage. Other observers objected to another form of stigmatization, the detailed disclosure of the shooter's history of mental illness, which seemed to some to vilify anyone who has ever suffered from a mental health problem. Still others felt that any presentation of the shooter's thinking, including the controversial release of the package of documents and videos he sent to NBC news, only served to glorify those who commit such wanton violence. Others objected to what they saw as the media's heavily antigun posture, which damned those who work to preserve the right to own firearms. In such emotional circumstances, the media's construction of reality certainly is not to everyone's liking and rarely satisfies anyone completely (Asian American Journalists Association 2007; Groening 2007; Stanley 2007).

Recently, use of the term *media monitoring* has expanded to include monitoring of individuals' media usage and choices without their knowledge. New technologies related to video on demand, downloading of audio/video clips, and satellite programming have created records of individual viewing and listening preferences. In 2006, Google opposed U.S. government

The digital divide refers not only to the gap in access to new media among different social classes, but to the gap between developing and less developed nations, including those in Africa.

results have been disappointing. Even the modest goal of getting two-thirds of Africa's government agencies, hospitals, and schools online by 2012 will not be realized (*The Economist* 2007b; Global Digital Solidarity Fund 2008; Pew Internet Project 2009; P. Schaefer 2008).

Dominant Ideology: Constructing Reality   Conflict theorists argue that the mass media maintain the privileges of certain groups. Moreover, powerful groups may limit the media's representation of others to protect their own interests. The term **dominant ideology** describes a set of cultural beliefs and practices that helps to maintain powerful social, economic, and political interests. The media transmit messages that essentially define what we regard as the real world, even though those images frequently vary from the ones that the larger society experiences.

Mass media decision makers are overwhelmingly White, male, and wealthy. It may come as no surprise, then, that the media tend to ignore the lives and ambitions of subordinate groups, among them working-class people, African Americans, Hispanics, gays and lesbians, people with disabilities, overweight people, and older people. Worse, media content may create false images or stereotypes of these groups that then become accepted as accurate portrayals of reality. **Stereotypes** are unreliable generalizations about all members of a group that do not recognize individual differences within the group. Some broadcasters use stereotypes deliberately in a desperate bid for attention, with the winking approval of media executives. Shock radio host Don Imus may have been banned from the airwaves for his stereotyped description of Black female athletes, but within 10 months he was back on the air, earning a seven-figure income.

Television content is another example of this tendency to ignore reality. How many overweight TV characters can you name? Even though in real life one out of every four women is obese (30 or more pounds over a healthy body weight), only 3

out of 100 TV characters are portrayed as obese. Heavyset television characters have fewer romances, talk less about sex, eat more often, and are more often the object of ridicule than their thin counterparts (Hellmich 2001).

Minority groups are often stereotyped in TV shows. Almost all the leading roles are cast as White, even in urban-based programs such as *Friends,* which is situated in ethnically diverse New York City. Asian Americans and Native Americans rarely appear in general roles; Blacks tend to be featured mainly in crime-based dramas; Latinos are virtually ignored. Box 7-1 discusses the distorted picture of society presented on prime-time television programs.

Another concern about the media, from the conflict perspective, is that television distorts the political process. Until the U.S. campaign finance system is truly reformed and the law enforced, the candidates with the most money (often backed by powerful lobbying groups) will be able to buy exposure to voters and saturate the air with commercials attacking their opponents.

Dominant Ideology: Whose Culture?   In the United States, on the popular television contest *The Apprentice,* the dreaded dismissal line is "You're fired." In Finland, on *Dilli (The Deal),* it's "*Olet vapautettu*" ("You're free to leave"); in Germany, on *Big Boss,* it's "*Sie haben frei*" ("You're off"). Although people throughout the world decry U.S. exports, from films to language to Bart Simpson, the U.S. media are still widely imitated. Sociologist Todd Gitlin describes American popular culture as something that "people love, and love to hate" (2002:177; Wentz and Atkinson 2005).

This love–hate relationship is so enduring that the U.S. media have come to rely on the overseas market. In fact, many motion pictures have brought in more revenue abroad than at home. Through early 2008, for example, *Titanic* had earned a record-breaking $600 million in the United States and a total of $1.8 billion worldwide. Of the top 100 top-grossing movies in 2009, in fact, 99 were U.S.-made. Some Hollywood movies, however, are so insensitive to the global audience that they fail miserably overseas. The 2005 film *Memoirs of a Geisha,* set in 20th-century Japan, greatly offended Japanese moviegoers because the title role went to the Chinese actress Ziyi Zhang. Ironically, her casting also upset the Chinese, who were outraged to see a leading Chinese actress portray a Japanese geisha. In 2006, Chinese government officials banned the film's release (Barboza 2006; Box Office Mojo 2009).

We risk being ethnocentric if we overstress U.S. dominance. For example, *Survivor, Who Wants to Be a Millionaire, Big Brother,* and *Iron Chef*—immensely popular TV programs in the United States—came from Sweden, Britain, the Netherlands, and Japan, respectively. Even *American Idol* originated in Britain as *Pop Idol,* featuring Simon Cowell. And the steamy telenovelas of Mexico and other Spanish-speaking countries owe very little of their origin to the soap operas on U.S. television. Unlike motion pictures, television is gradually moving away from U.S. domination and is more likely to be locally produced. By 2003, all the top 50 British TV shows were locally produced. *Medium* may appear on television in London, but it is shown late at night. Even U.S.-owned TV ventures such as Disney, MTV, and CNN have dramatically increased their locally produced programming overseas. Still, *CSI: NY* was on top in France, where only sports programs had a higher rating (Bielby and Harrington 2008; Colucci 2008; *The Economist* 2003b).

RESEARCH TODAY

Today, 40 percent of all youths in the United States are children of color, yet few of the faces they see on television reflect their race or cultural heritage. As of spring 2009, the only network show centered on minority performers was *Ugly Betty,* with America Ferrera. A handful of others, like *CSI* and *Grey's Anatomy,* included minority actors in an ensemble cast. In that year American Indians were completely absent from network TV, except for one actress with a recurring role in *Terminator: Sarah Connor Chronicles.* What is more, the programs shown earlier in the evening, when young people are most likely to watch television, were the *least* diverse.

There is one bright spot in prime time. Often, unscripted reality shows do reflect the audience's racial and ethnic composition, so that Latinos, African Americans, and Asian Americans appear quite regularly. Although racial balance is not an explicit consideration in casting these shows, producers admit that they edit programs so as to highlight interethnic tensions, which they see as entertaining. Casting directors for programs like *The Bachelor,* which try deliberately to match people, typically do not attempt to create interracial couples, however.

When minority groups do appear on television and in other forms of media, their roles tend to reinforce the stereotypes associated with their ethnic or racial groups. In 2004, nearly half of all Middle Eastern characters shown on television were criminals, compared to only 5 percent of White characters. Latino roles were just as stereotyped. Latinas have been featured as maids on *Will and Grace* (Rosario), *Dharma and Greg* (Celia), and even the animated *King of the Hill* (Lupino), to name just three shows.

Producers, writers, executives, and advertisers blame one another for the rampant underrepresentation of racial and ethnic minorities. More important, in recent years, the rise of more networks, cable TV, and the Internet has fragmented the broadcast entertainment market, siphoning viewers away from the general-audience sitcoms and dramas of the past. The CW cable network produces situation comedies geared toward African American audiences. With the proliferation of cable channels such as Black Entertainment Television (BET) and the Spanish-language Telemundo and Univision, as well as Web sites that cater to every imaginable taste, there no longer seems to be a need for broadly popular series such as *The Cosby Show,* the tone and content of which appealed to Whites as well as Blacks in a way the newer series do not. The result of these sweeping technological changes has been a sharp divergence in viewer preferences.

A rare sight on prime-time television: in CW's *Girlfriends,* which ran from 2000 through 2008, all the leading roles are played by African Americans.

Despite these advances in cable programming, problems persist, though they may go unnoticed by White non-Hispanics. In a 2007 episode of Showtime's *Dexter,* for example, two non-Spanish-

When minority groups do appear on television and in other forms of media, their roles tend to reinforce the stereotypes associated with their ethnic or racial groups.

speaking Hispanic actors expressed their condolences to a crime victim. Because of their incorrect Spanish pronunciation, they flubbed their lines: instead of telling the grieving mother, "I'm sorry for your loss," they said, "Sorry that you got lost."

In 2009, some observers hoped that the casting of television programs might change during the "Obama era." After all, during the 2008 election season, the cast of the popular *Saturday Night Live* depended on a White man to portray Barack Obama. The show, whose cast lacked African American women as well as men, did not even attempt to portray Michelle Obama.

From an economic perspective, it is difficult to understand why the television industry has not risen above the traditional racial and ethnic stereotypes. Between 2007 and 2008, Latino buying power exceeded $800 billion a year. Asian American and Hispanic American households with televisions grew three times faster than White households with televisions, and Black households with televisions grew twice as fast.

In the long run, media observers believe, the major networks will need to integrate the ranks of gatekeepers before they achieve true diversity

in programming. Adonis Hoffman, director of the Corporate Policy Institute, has urged network executives to throw open their studios and boardrooms to minorities. Hoffman thinks such a move would empower Black writers and producers to present a true-to-life portrait of Blacks. There are some signs of agreement from the networks. According to Doug Herzog, president of Fox Entertainment, real progress means incorporating diversity from within.

Why should it matter that minority groups aren't visible on major network television, if they are well represented on other channels such as CW, BET, and Univision? The problem is that Whites as well as minorities see a distorted picture of their society every time they turn on network TV. In Hoffman's words, "African Americans, Latinos and Asians, while portrayed as such, are not merely walk-ons in our society—they are woven into the fabric of what has made this country great" (A. Hoffman 1997:M6).

LET'S DISCUSS

1. Do you watch network TV? If so, how well do you think it represents the diversity of U.S. society?

2. Have you seen a movie or TV show recently that portrayed members of a minority group in a sensitive and realistic way—as real people rather than as stereotypes or token walk-ons? If so, describe the show.

Sources: Bielby and Bielby 2002; Braxton 2007, 2009; Carter 2008; Children Now 2004; Directors Guild of America 2002; A. Hoffman 1997; James 2007; NAACP 2008; Navarro 2002; Nielsen Media Research 2009; Poniewozik 2001; Reed 2008.

Nations that feel a loss of identity may try to defend against the cultural invasion from foreign countries, especially the economically dominant United States. Yet as sociologists know, audiences are not necessarily passive recipients of foreign cultural messages, either in developing countries or in industrial nations. Thus, research on consumers of cultural products like television, music, and film must be placed in social context. Although people may watch and even enjoy media content, that does not mean that they will accept values that are alien to their own (Bielby and Harrington 2008).

Many developing nations have long argued for a greatly improved two-way flow of news and information between industrialized nations and developing nations. They complain that news from the Third World is scant, and what news there is reflects unfavorably on the developing nations. For example, what do you know about South America? Most people in the United States will mention the two topics that dominate the news from countries south of the border: revolution and drugs. Most know little else about the continent.

Live from Dubai! MTV Arabia debuted in November 2007, with 60 percent of its programming devoted to international music and 40 percent to Arabic music. The channel also offers Arabic versions of popular MTV shows, such as *Made.* In *Al Helm* ("The Dream"), awkward teens blossom into models or rap stars. Predictably, MTV Arabia features less skin and profanity than other versions of the channel. Editors trim Western music videos according to the "4-3, 2-1 rule": close-ups of a bikini may last for 1 second but not for 2; in a moving shot, the skimpy suits may be shown for 3 seconds but not 4 (Surk 2007).

To remedy this imbalance, a resolution to monitor the news and content that cross the borders of developing nations was passed by the United Nations Educational, Scientific, and Cultural Organization (UNESCO) in the 1980s. The United States disagreed with the proposal, which became one factor in the U.S. decision to withdraw from UNESCO in the mid-1980s. In 2005, the United States opposed another UNESCO plan, meant to reduce the diminishment of cultural differences. Hailed as an important step toward protecting threatened cultures, particularly the media markets in developing nations, the measure passed the UN's General Assembly by a vote of 148–2. The United States, one of the two dissenters, objected officially to the measure's vague wording, but the real concern was clearly the measure's potential impact on a major U.S. export (Dominick 2009; Riding 2005).

Famed Chinese actress Ziyi Zhang played a Japanese geisha in the U.S.-made film *Memoirs of a Geisha* (2005). The decision to cast her in a Japanese role backfired in both Japan and China. Though U.S. films are usually well received abroad, cultural insensitivity can damage their box-office receipts.

use your sociological *imagination*

How do your favorite media reflect U.S. culture? How do they reflect the cultures of the rest of the world?

Feminist View

Feminists share the view of conflict theorists that the mass media stereotype and misrepresent social reality. According to this view, the media powerfully influence how we look at men and women, communicating unrealistic, stereotypical, and limiting images of the sexes. Here are three problems feminists believe arise from media coverage (Wood 1994):

1. Women are underrepresented, which suggests that men are the cultural standard and women are insignificant.

2. Men and women are portrayed in ways that reflect and perpetuate stereotypical views of gender. Women, for example, are often shown in peril, needing to be rescued by a male—rarely the reverse.

3. Depictions of male–female relationships emphasize traditional sex roles and normalize violence against women.

Educators and social scientists have long noted the stereotypical portrayal of women and men in the mass media. Women are often shown as being shallow and obsessed with beauty. They are more likely than men to be presented unclothed, in danger, or even physically victimized. When women achieve newsworthy feats in fields traditionally dominated by men, such as professional sports, the media are often slow to recognize their accomplishments. As Figure 7-3 shows, only about 6 percent of network sports coverage is devoted to women. The situation is even worse on ESPN Sports Center, where content analysis shows that only 2 percent of airtime is devoted to women's sports.

A continuing, troubling issue for feminists and society as a whole is pornography. Feminists tend to be very supportive of freedom of expression and self-determination, rights that are denied to women more often than to men. Yet pornography presents women as sex objects and seems to make viewing women that way acceptable. Nor are concerns about pornography limited to this type of objectification and imagery, as well as their implicit endorsement of violence against women. The industry that creates risqué adult images for videos, DVDs, and the Internet is largely unregulated, putting its own performers at

On Eighth Avenue in New York City, two sailors watch as an electronic billboard plays a trailer for an upcoming television miniseries. As they watch, a tiny camera photographs them, and a computer determines their gender, estimates their age, and measures their attention span. Interactionists study the ways in which the media reshape our social behavior, including our consumption habits (Clifford 2008).

risk. A 2002 health survey of triple-X, as the porn industry refers to itself, found that 40 percent of actors and actresses had at least one sexually transmitted disease, compared to 0.1 percent of the general population. The career span of these women and men is short, usually about 18 months, but the profits for the industry are continuous and enormous (Huffstutter 2003).

Feminist scholars are cautiously optimistic about new media. Although women are represented among bloggers, by some measures they are responsible for only about 10 percent of the most popular blogs. Still, in conservative cultures like Saudi Arabia, online media offer women the opportunity to explore lifestyles that traditional media outlets largely ignore (Jesella 2008; Worth 2008).

As in other areas of sociology, feminist researchers caution against assuming that what holds true for men's media use is true for everyone. Researchers, for example, have studied the different ways that women and men approach the Internet. Though men are only slightly more likely than women ever to have used the Internet, they are much more likely to use it daily. Yet according to a 2009 study, more women than men use the Internet. Not surprisingly, men account for 91 percent of the players in online sports fantasy leagues. Perhaps more socially significant, however, is the finding that women are more likely than men to maintain friendship networks through e-mail (Boase et al. 2006; Fallows 2006; Pew Internet Project 2009; Rainie 2005).

Interactionist View

Interactionists are especially interested in shared understandings of everyday behavior. These scholars examine the media on the micro level to see how they shape day-to-day social behavior. Increasingly, researchers point to the mass media as the source of major daily activity; some argue that television serves essentially as a primary group for many individuals who share TV viewing. Other mass-media participation is not necessarily face-to-face. For example, we usually listen to the radio or read the newspaper as a solitary activity, although it is possible to share it with others (Cerulo et al. 1992; Waite 2000).

FIGURE **7-3** NETWORK COVERAGE OF WOMEN'S VERSUS MEN'S SPORTS

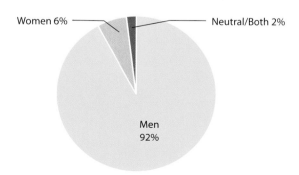

Women 6% — Neutral/Both 2%

Men 92%

Note: Based on a content analysis of 2004 televised sports news and highlights shows.
Source: Messner et al. 2006:35.

Online social networks, in fact, have become a new way of promoting consumption. As Figure 7-4 shows, advertisers have traditionally marketed products and services through spot ads, mass mailings, or billboards, whether they are promoting flat-screen televisions or public service messages like "Don't drink and drive." Now, using social networks (see Box 4-2 on page 88), they can find consumers online and attempt to develop a relationship with them there. Through Facebook, for example, Burger King awarded a free Whopper to anyone who would delete 10 friends. Facebook's staff was not happy with Burger King's promotion, which notified 239,906 Facebook users that they had been dropped for a burger—an action that violated the network's policy. Nevertheless, Burger King created a vast network of consumers who enjoy Whoppers. Similarly, Kraft Foods encouraged people to post images of the Wienermobile on the photo site Flickr (Bacon Lovers' Talk 2009; Burger King 2009; Gaudin 2009).

Interactionists note, too, that friendship networks can emerge from shared viewing habits or from recollection of a cherished television series from the past. Family members and friends often gather for parties centered on the broadcasting of popular events such as the Super Bowl or the Academy Awards. And as we've seen, television often serves as a babysitter or playmate for children and even infants.

Interactionists pay close attention to the use of symbols. The power of the mass media encourages political leaders and entertainment figures to carefully manipulate their images through public appearances called photo opportunities, or photo ops. By embracing symbols (posing with celebrities or in front of prestigious landmarks), participants in these staged events attempt to convey self-serving definitions of social reality (M. Weinstein and Weinstein 2002).

FIGURE **7-4** MARKETING ONLINE THROUGH SOCIAL NETWORKS

Traditional Marketing   **Online Marketing**

Advertiser   **Advertiser**

Traditional forms of advertising (left) allow only one-way communication, from the advertiser to the consumer. Online social networks (right) offer two-way communication, allowing advertisers to develop a relationship with consumers.

The rise of the Internet has facilitated new forms of communication and social interaction. Grandparents can now keep up with their grandchildren via e-mail, or even watch them on their laptops via Skype. Gay and lesbian teens have online resources for support and information. People can even find their lifetime partners through computer dating services.

Some troubling issues have been raised about day-to-day life on the Internet, however. What, if anything, should be done about terrorists and other extremist groups who use the Internet to exchange messages of hatred and even bomb-making recipes? What, if anything, should be done about the issue of sexual expression on the Internet? How can children be protected from it? Should "hot chat" and X-rated film clips be censored? Or should expression be completely free?

Though the Internet has created a new platform for extremists, hate groups, and pornographers, it has also given people greater control over what they see and hear. That is, the Internet allows people to manage their media exposure so as to avoid sounds, images, and ideas they do not enjoy or approve of. The legal scholar Cass Sunstein (2002) has referred to this personalized approach to news information gathering as *egocasting*. One social consequence of this trend may be a less tolerant society. If we read, see, and hear only what we know and agree with, we may be much less prepared to meet people from different backgrounds or converse with those who express new viewpoints.

Finally, while many people in the United States embrace the Internet, we should note that information is not evenly distributed throughout the population. The same people, by and large, who experience poor health and have few job opportunities have been left off the information highway. Figure 7-5 breaks down Internet usage by gender, age, race, income, and education. Note the large disparities in usage between those with high and low incomes, and between those with more and less education. The data also show a significant racial disparity. Though educators and politicians have touted the potential benefits to the disadvantaged, Internet usage may be reinforcing existing social-class barriers.

The interactionist perspective helps us to understand one important aspect of the entire mass media system—the audience. How do we actively participate in media events? How do we construct with others the meaning of media messages? We will explore these questions in the section that follows. (Table 7-3 summarizes the various sociological perspectives on the media.)

The Audience

Ever feel like text-messaging everyone you know, to encourage them to vote for your favorite performer on a certain reality program? Ever looked over someone's shoulder as he watched last week's episode of *Grey's Anatomy* on his handheld video player—and been tempted to reveal the ending to him? Ever come across an old CD and tried to remember the last time you or a friend listened to one, or heard the songs in the order in which they were recorded? In this and many other ways, we are reminded that we are all part of a larger audience.

FIGURE **7-5** WHO'S ON THE INTERNET

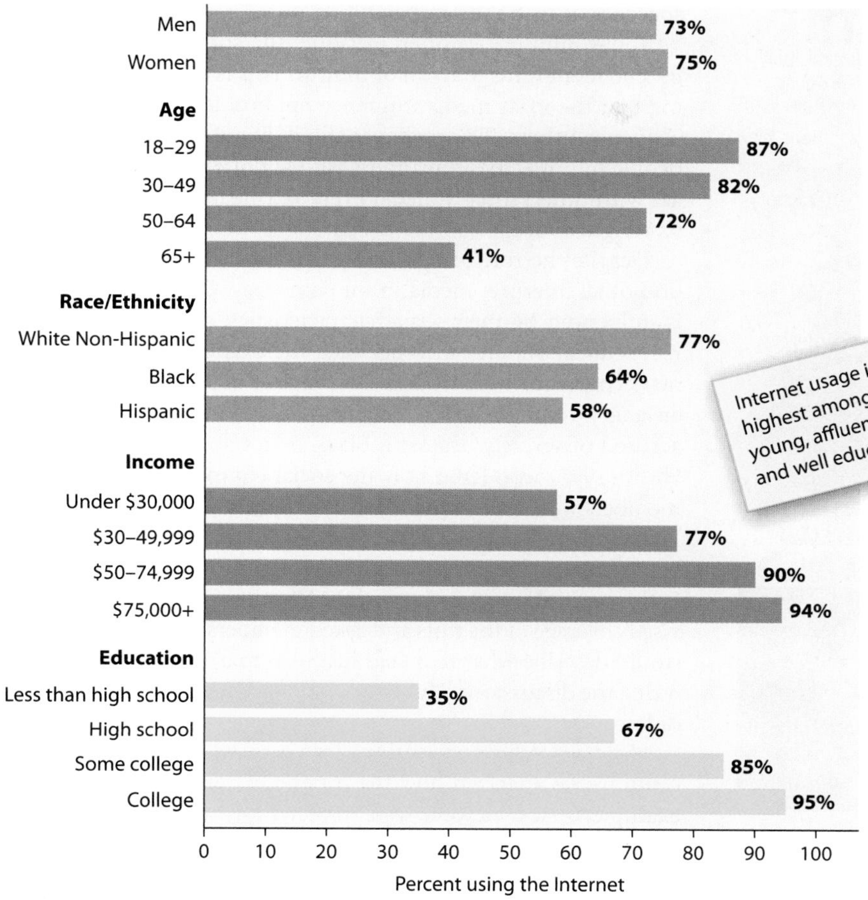

Note: Based on a November–December 2008 national survey released on January 6, 2009. Data for Blacks and Whites are for non-Hispanics. Hispanic data are for English-speaking Hispanics.
Source: Pew Internet Project 2009.

Who Is in the Audience?

The mass media are distinguished from other social institutions by the necessary presence of an audience. It can be an identifiable, finite group, such as an audience at a jazz club or a Broadway musical, or a much larger and undefined group, such as VH-1 viewers or readers of the same issue of *USA Today.* The audience may be a secondary group gathered in a large auditorium or a primary group, such as a family watching the latest Disney video at home.

We can look at the audience from the level of both *microsociology* and *macrosociology.* At the micro level, we might consider how audience members, interacting among themselves, respond to the media, or in the case of live performances, actually influence the performers. At the macro level, we might examine broader societal consequences of the media, such as the early childhood education delivered through programming like *Sesame Street.*

Even if an audience is spread out over a wide geographic area and members don't know one another, it is still distinctive in terms of age, gender, income, political party, formal schooling, race, and ethnicity. The audience for a ballet, for example, would differ substantially from the audience for alternative music.

use your sociological *imagination*

Think about the last time you were part of an audience. Describe the performance. How similar to or different from yourself were the other audience members? What might account for whatever similarities or differences you noticed?

The Segmented Audience

Increasingly, the media are marketing themselves to a *particular* audience. Once a media outlet, such as a radio station or a magazine, has identified its audience, it targets that group. To some degree, this specialization is driven by advertising. Media specialists have sharpened their ability, through survey research, to identify particular target audiences. As a result, Nike would be much more likely to promote a new line of golf clubs on the Golf Channel than on an episode of *SpongeBob.* The many more choices that the growing Internet and satellite broadcast channels offer audiences also foster specialization. Members of these audiences are more likely to *expect* content geared to their own interests.

TABLE **7-3** SOCIOLOGICAL PERSPECTIVES ON THE MASS MEDIA

summing**up**

Theoretical Perspective	Emphasis
Functionalist	Socialization
	Enforcement of social norms
	Conferral of status
	Promotion of consumption
	Narcotizing effect (dysfunction)
Conflict	Gatekeeping
	Media monitoring
	Digital divide
	Construction of reality
Feminist	Underrepresentation of women
	Misrepresentation of women
Interactionist	Impact on social behavior
	Source of friendship networks

Where's the President? The media targets audience interests, so in 2009 *Us Weekly* featured the new family in the White House on its cover, but blocked out President Barack Obama with a photo of the supposedly overweight Jessica Simpson. If you look closely, you can see the President's white-shirted arm around First Lady Michelle Obama.

The specialized targeting of audiences has led some scholars to question the "mass" in mass media. For example, the British social psychologist Sonia Livingstone (2004) has written that the media have become so segmented, they have taken on the appearance almost of individualization. Are viewing audiences so segmented that large collective audiences are a thing of the past? That is not yet clear. Even though we seem to be living in an age of *personal* computers and *personal* digital assistants (PDAs), large formal organizations still do transmit public messages that reach a sizable, heterogeneous, and scattered audience.

Audience Behavior

Sociologists have long researched how audiences interact with one another and how they share information after a media event. The role of audience members as opinion leaders particularly intrigues social researchers. An **opinion leader** is someone who influences the opinions and decisions of others through day-to-day personal contact and communication. For example, a movie or theater critic functions as an opinion leader. Sociologist Paul Lazarsfeld and his colleagues (1948) pioneered the study of opinion leaders in their research on voting behavior in

the 1940s. They found that opinion leaders encourage their relatives, friends, and co-workers to think positively about a particular candidate, perhaps pushing them to listen to the politician's speeches or read the campaign literature.

Today, film critics often attribute the success of low-budget independent films to word of mouth. This is another way of saying that the mass media influence opinion leaders, who in turn influence others. The audience, then, is not a group of passive people but of active consumers who are often impelled to interact with others after a media event (Croteau and Hoynes 2003; C. Wright 1986).

Despite the role of opinion leaders, members of an audience do not all interpret media in the same way. Often their response is influenced by their social characteristics, such as occupation, race, education, and income. Take the example of the televised news coverage of the riots in Los Angeles in 1992. The riots were an angry response to the acquittal of two White police officers accused of severely beating a Black motorist. Sociologist Darnell Hunt (1997) wondered how the social composition of audience members would affect the way they interpreted the news coverage. Hunt gathered 15 groups from the Los Angeles area, whose members were equally divided among Whites, African Americans, and Latinos. He showed each group a 17-minute clip from the televised coverage of the riots and asked members to discuss how they would describe what they had just seen to a 12-year-old. In analyzing the discussions, Hunt found that although gender and class did not cause respondents to vary their answers much, race did.

Hunt went beyond noting simple racial differences in perceptions; he analyzed how the differences were manifested. For example, Black viewers were much more likely than Latinos or Whites to refer to the events in terms of "us" versus "them." Another difference was that Black and Latino viewers were more animated and critical than White viewers as they watched the film clip. White viewers tended to sit quietly, still and unquestioning, suggesting that they were more comfortable with the news coverage than the Blacks or Hispanics.

use your sociological *imagination*

On what occasions might you be part of an audience in which you feel you are in the minority?

The Media's Global Reach

Has the rise of the electronic media created a "global village"? Canadian media theorist Marshall McLuhan predicted it would over 45 years ago. Today, physical distance is no longer a barrier, and instant messaging is possible across the world. The mass media have indeed created a global village. Not all countries are equally connected, as Figure 7-6 shows, but the progress has been staggering, considering that voice transmission was just beginning 100 years ago (McLuhan 1964; McLuhan and Fiore 1967).

FIGURE **7-6** MEDIA PENETRATION IN SELECTED COUNTRIES

155

The Mass Media

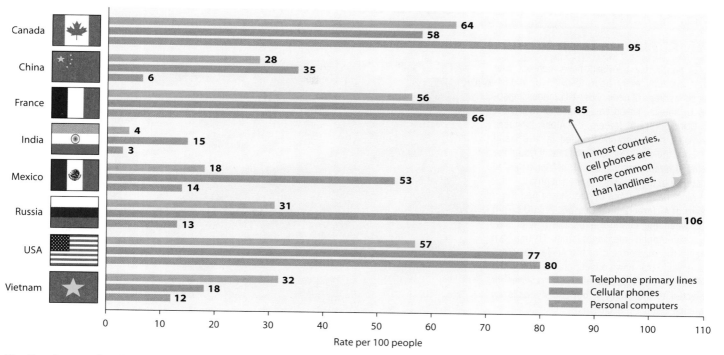

Note: Data for 2006 released in 2008.
Source: Bureau of the Census 2008a:Table 1345.

Think about It
What is the economic and political significance of media penetration?

In 2008, Lil Wayne's "Lollipop" was the most frequently downloaded cell phone ring tone. Because today's media provide multiple services, music fans can use the Internet to access recorded music and listen to it on their cell phones.

Sociologist Todd Gitlin considers "global torrent" a more apt metaphor for the media's reach than "global village." The media permeate all aspects of everyday life. Take advertising, for example. Consumer goods are marketed vigorously worldwide, from advertisements on airport baggage carriers to imprints on sandy beaches. Little wonder that people around the world develop loyalty to a brand and are as likely to sport a Nike, Coca-Cola, or Harley-Davidson logo as they are their favorite soccer or baseball insignia (Gitlin 2002; Klein 1999).

A highly visible part of the media, whether it be print or electronic, is news. In the past, most people in the United States had little familiarity with news outlets outside their own country, with the possible exception of the British-based Reuters and BBC News. Like so many other things, however, that changed after September 11, 2001, when an Arab news network took center stage (Box 7-2 on page 156).

The key to creating a truly global network that reaches directly into workplaces, schools, and homes is the Internet. Although much of the online global transmission today is limited to print and pictures, the potential to send audio and video via the Internet will increasingly

SOCIOLOGY IN THE GLOBAL COMMUNITY

7-2 Al Jazeera Is on the Air

A 24-hour-a-day televised news network with short bulletins every hour, followed by a fast-paced montage of news clips—all broadcast globally by satellite-linked cable stations. This could be CNN, but it's Al Jazeera, the Arabic-language television news network founded in 1996 and based in the small Persian Gulf state of Qatar. The name Al Jazeera means "island" or "peninsula," in reference to the network's home country.

Most people in the United States had never heard of Al Jazeera until October 7, 2001. That was when the channel aired the first of several videotaped messages from Osama bin Laden, the mastermind of the Al-Qaeda terrorist network. U.S. news outlets also televised the messages, but stopped after the government objected to the airing of bin Laden's calls for violence against U.S. citizens.

Al Jazeera refused to acquiesce to the government request, invoking its motto, "The Opinion, and the Other Opinion Too." Al Jazeera officials insist that they promote a forum for independent dialogue and debate, an unusual practice in the Arab world, where most media outlets are state controlled. In fact, several Arab states, including Saudi Arabia, Jordan, and Bahrain, have banned or restricted Al Jazeera because of the network's critical coverage of affairs in their countries. Other Arab nations criticize Al Jazeera for giving too much airplay to U.S. news.

> *"You have to be a supporter of Al Jazeera, even if you have to hold your nose sometimes."*

Though many media observers see Al Jazeera as biased, many viewers around the world might see CNN, ABC, and Fox News as biased. According to Kenton Keith, a former U.S. ambassador to Qatar, Al Jazeera has a slant, but no more than other news organizations. It just happens to be a slant that most Americans aren't comfortable with.

Al Jazeera does offer diverse views. On its popular talk show *The Opposing View*, two women hotly debated polygamy among Muslim men. On another popular program, *Shari'a [Islamic Law] and Life*, the speaker dared to reassure Muslim women that the Koran does

In 2006, Al Jazeera expanded its programming to include an all-English channel; since then its following has grown. Israel's top cable company, for example, dropped CNN and added AJE to its lineup.

not force them to marry suitors designated by their parents. Ambassador Keith believes that "for the long-range importance of press freedom in the Middle East and the advantages that will ultimately have for the West, you have to be a supporter of Al Jazeera, even if you have to hold your nose sometimes" (Barr 2002:7).

To counter Al Jazeera's influence, in 2004 the U.S. State Department established its own satellite network, Al Hurra, in the Middle East. Based in Springfield, Virginia, and staffed by veteran Arab journalists, the new network promises balanced and objective reporting on regional issues and events. Its ultimate purpose, however, is to win over the hearts and minds of a population that is deeply suspicious of U.S. motives. Al Hurra, whose name means "The Free One," is the latest in a series of U.S. attempts at improving public relations with the Islamic world. Knowledgeable observers view the effort with some skepticism, however. Al Hurra now ranks seventh out of seven among international news channels in the Middle East. Only 8 percent of the potential audience watches it even once a week.

President Barack Obama took his message directly to Arabs less than 10 days into his term by granting an interview with the Dubai-based Al-Arabiya, a more moderate alternative to Al Jazeera. Crossing the media language barrier, Obama declared that the United States has a "stake in the well-being of the Muslim world," and should speak, write, and refer to Muslims with respect.

LET'S DISCUSS

1. Do you find news outlets in the United States biased? How would you judge?
2. What do you think of the new Al Hurra network in the Middle East? Can it win over the hearts and minds of viewers there? Should the U.S. government be using taxpayers' dollars to fund the effort?

Sources: Al-Jadda 2007; Al Jazeera 2009; Barr 2002; Daniszewski 2003; Dorning 2009; MacLeod and Walt 2005; H. Rosenberg 2003; Urbina 2002; Whitlock 2008.

reach into every part of the world. Social interaction will then truly take place on a global scale.

The Internet has also facilitated other forms of communication. Reference materials and data banks can now be made accessible across national boundaries. Information related to international finance, marketing, trade, and manufacturing is literally just a keystroke away. We have seen the emergence of true world news outlets and the promotion of a world music that is not clearly identifiable with any single culture. Even the most future-oriented thinker would find the growth in the reach of the mass media in postindustrial and postmodern societies remarkable (Castells 2000, 2001; Croteau and Hoynes 2003, 2006).

These Bhutanese householders are watching the *Oprah Winfrey Show* on their brand-new television set. The Bhutanese were introduced to television in 1999. Since then, Marshall McLuhan's global village has become a reality in their remote Asian kingdom, where rulers have become concerned about the cultural impact of Western media.

The lack of one national home for the various forms of mass media raises a potential dilemma for users. People worry that unhealthy influences and even crime pervade today's electronic global village, and that few if any controls prevent them. For example, the leaders of Bhutan worry about the impact of newly introduced television programming on their culture and their people. When Bhutanese boys started to mimic professional wrestling stars, wrestling shows were taken off the air. Similarly, in industrial countries, including the United States, officials are concerned about everything from video poker to online pornography and the menace posed by hackers. And in the Social Policy section that follows, we'll see that just a few powerful corporations dominate the mass media, controlling the content that is presented to billions of people.

social**policy** and the Mass Media

Media Concentration

The Issue

Early on the morning of January 18, 2002, a train derailed four miles from the center of Minot, North Dakota. In the hours that followed, a cloud of toxic ammonia spread over the city of 36,000 people. To alert residents to the hazard, police called the town's six radio stations, but no one answered. All the stations were operating on automated programming, after having been acquired by the media conglomerate Clear Channel Communications.

Eventually, police did manage to warn citizens to close their doors and windows, boil water, and cover their faces with wet cloths. For the one person who died and the more than a thousand who were injured, however, the warning came too late. Although Clear Channel does not deserve total blame for the unfortunate blackout in communications—many communities have no overnight media outlets—the people of Minot were not well served (Klinenberg 2007; Nislow 2003).

Who owns the media production and distribution process? Increasingly, the answer is a small number of very large corporations. The social consequences of this trend toward the concentration of media ownership are a reduction in the number of information outlets and an increase in the cross-promotion of films and television shows through multiple media channels.

The Setting

The United States still has thousands of independent media outlets—small-town newspapers, radio stations, and television broadcasters—but the clear trend in the media industry is toward the consolidation of ownership. The fact is, a few multinational corporations dominate the publishing, broadcasting, and film industries, though their influence may be hard to identify, since global conglomerates manage many different product names. Walt Disney alone owns 16 television channels that reach 140 countries. But Disney is only one of several media giants. Add to the list Time Warner (HBO, CNN, AOL, *Time* and *People* magazines); Rupert Murdoch's News Corporation, founded in Australia (Fox Network Television, several book publishers, numerous newspapers and magazines, MySpace.com, and 20th Century Fox); Sony of Japan (Columbia Pictures, IMAX, CBS Records, and Columbia Records); Clear Channel Communications (over 1,200 radio and 51 television stations); and Viacom/CBS (Paramount, DreamWorks SKG, MTV, and Black Entertainment Television), and the extent of their power becomes clear. This concentration of media giants fosters considerable cross-promotion. For example, the release of Warner Brothers' film *The Matrix Reloaded* in 2003 was heavily promoted by both CNN and *Time* magazine. In fact, *Time* somehow managed to devote its cover to the film's release in the midst of the war in Iraq.

Similar concerns have been raised about the situation in countries such as China, Cuba, Iraq, and North Korea, where the ruling party owns and controls the media. The difference, which is considerable, is that in the United States the gatekeeping process lies in the hands of private individuals, whose main desire is to maximize profits. In totalitarian countries, the gatekeeping process belongs to political leaders, whose desire is to maintain control of the government (P. Thomas and Nain 2004).

We should note one significant exception to the centralization and concentration of the media: the Internet. Research shows that more and more people, especially those under age 35, are

★ Media Ownership Consolidation ★

Before

After

DARYL CAGLE SLATE.com
www.caglecartoons.com

The 2003 FCC ruling that allowed further consolidation of media outlets by already huge conglomerates may have increased the companies' profitability, but it has had little positive impact on media content.

Interactionists see a change in the way people get their news, though not in their interest in it. In the past people may have met or called one another to discuss the latest episode of *Survivor;* now they share the latest Internet news via e-mail or buddy list. Why wait for the evening news, or even for breaking news on CNN, when Yahoo and Google are at your fingertips? Because savvy media users can seek out the media they consume, interactionists suggest that warnings about media concentration may be overdone (Bielby and Harrington 2008).

Policy Initiatives

Any discussion of media regulation must begin with the Telecommunications Act of 1996, which marked the first overhaul of media policy since the early 1930s. The act, which covers everything from cable service to social issues such as obscenity and violence, made a significant distinction between information services, such as the Internet, and promoters of telecommunications service—that is, traditional telephone and wireless phone companies, as well as cable companies that offer phone service. Nevertheless, rapid technological development has rendered the act obsolete in many people's minds. With the convergence of telephone service, videocasting, and the Internet, not to mention the delivery of motion pictures online, such distinctions have become archaic only a decade after the act was passed.

Significantly, the act eliminated most restrictions on media ownership; those that remain appear to be on their way out, as well. In 2007 the Federal Communications Commission went even further by allowing the consolidation of newspaper and television ownership in cities with only one local newspaper and one local television station. Critics worried that once the transition to digital television was completed in 2009, a single local media outlet could transmit a dozen signals *and* deliver the daily newspaper (C. Baker 2007; Lear and McChesney 2006).

For generations, media conglomerates have battled efforts to regulate their industry, but in 2007 they began to pull back from their lobbying efforts. More and more, they are looking to new media like the Internet as their future source of profits. By 2010, if not sooner, Internet advertising revenue is projected to surpass total television ad revenues. People are now more likely to discuss the videos available on YouTube than the new season's lineup on prime-time television (Lieberman 2007).

receiving their media content through the Internet. Currently, the World Wide Web is accessible through independent outlets to millions of producers of media content. Obviously, the producer must be technologically proficient and must have access to a computer, but compared to other media outlets, the Internet is much more readily available. Media conglomerates, well aware of the Internet's potential, are already delivering their material via the Web. But for now, the Internet is the only medium that allows the average individual to become a media entrepreneur with a potential audience of millions (Gamson and Latteier 2004; J. Schwartz 2004; Winseck 2008).

Though concentration of ownership is not unique to the media (consider aircraft and automobile manufacturers), the media deserve special attention given the way they filter how we view reality.

Sociological Insights

Functionalists see media concentration—or the consolidation of any business—as a step toward greater economic efficiency. In their view, consolidation reduces the cost of operations, freeing capital for the development of new creative outlets. Furthermore, they believe that global trade in the media facilitates the free exchange of intellectual property, which is often hampered by arbitrary local restrictions (Croteau and Hoynes 2006).

Conflict theorists believe that media concentration stifles opportunities for minority ownership. According to the most recent FCC data, fewer than 4 percent of television stations in the United States are owned by racial and ethnic minorities; fewer than 5 percent are owned by women. Minority owners are underrepresented even in markets where minorities make up the majority of the audience. Nor is the Internet a level playing field for developing nations, as noted earlier. For example, with 10 percent of the world's population, the whole of Africa provides less than 1 percent of the Internet's online content (P. Thomas and Nain 2004; S. Turner and Cooper 2006).

Let's Discuss

1. Are you aware of who owns or manages the media you watch or listen to?

2. Do concerns about media concentration differ from concerns over the monopoly of certain products or services?

3. Does the trend toward media concentration affect traditional media outlets (print, radio, and broadcast television) differently from the Internet?

gettinginvolved

To get involved in the debate over media concentration, visit this book's Online Learning Center, which offers links to relevant Web sites.

www.mhhe.com/schaefer12e

MASTERING THIS CHAPTER

Summary

The **mass media** are print and electronic instruments of communication that carry messages to often widespread audiences. They pervade all social institutions, from entertainment to education to politics. This chapter examines how the mass media affect those institutions and influence our social behavior.

1. From the functionalist perspective, the media entertain, socialize, enforce social norms, confer status, and promote consumption. They can be dysfunctional to the extent that they desensitize us to serious events and issues (the **narcotizing dysfunction**).

2. Conflict theorists think the media reflect and even deepen the divisions in society through **gatekeeping,** or control over which material reaches the public; media monitoring, the covert observation of people's media usage and choices; and support of the **dominant ideology,** which defines reality, overwhelming local cultures.

3. Feminist theorists point out that media images of the sexes communicate unrealistic, stereotypical, limiting, and sometimes violent perceptions of women.

4. Interactionists examine the media on the micro level to see how they shape day-to-day social behavior. Interactionists have studied shared

TV viewing and staged public appearances intended to convey self-serving definitions of reality.

5. The mass media require the presence of an audience—whether it is small and well defined or large and amorphous. With increasing numbers of media outlets has come more and more targeting of segmented (or specialized) audiences.

6. Social researchers have studied the role of **opinion leaders** in influencing audiences.

7. The media have a global reach thanks to new communications technologies, especially the Internet. Some people are concerned that the media's global reach will spread unhealthy influences to other cultures.

8. The media industry is becoming more and more concentrated, creating media conglomerates. This concentration raises concerns about how innovative and independent the media can be. In some countries, governments own and control the media.

9. The Internet is the one significant exception to the trend toward media concentration, allowing millions of people to produce their own media content.

Critical Thinking Questions

1. What kind of audience is targeted by the producers of televised professional wrestling? By the creators of an animated film? By a rap group? What factors determine who makes up a particular audience?

2. Trace the production process for a new televised situation comedy (sitcom). Who do you imagine are the gatekeepers in the process?

3. Use the functionalist, conflict, and interactionist perspectives to assess the effects of global TV programming on developing countries.

Key Terms

Cultural convergence The flow of content across multiple media, and the accompanying migration of media audiences. (page 141)

Digital divide The relative lack of access to the latest technologies among low-income groups, racial and ethnic minorities, rural residents, and the citizens of developing countries. (147)

Dominant ideology A set of cultural beliefs and practices that helps to maintain powerful social, economic, and political interests. (148)

Gatekeeping The process by which a relatively small number of people in the media industry control what material eventually reaches the audience. (144)

Mass media Print and electronic means of communication that carry messages to widespread audiences. (140)

Narcotizing dysfunction The phenomenon in which the media provide such massive amounts of coverage that the audience becomes numb and fails to act on the information, regardless of how compelling the issue. (144)

Opinion leader Someone who influences the opinions and decisions of others through day-to-day personal contact and communication. (154)

Stereotype An unreliable generalization about all members of a group that does not recognize individual differences within the group. (148)

Self-Quiz

Read each question carefully and then select the best answer.

1. From the functionalist perspective, the media can be dysfunctional in what way?
   a. They enforce social norms.
   b. They confer status.
   c. They desensitize us to events.
   d. They are agents of socialization.

2. Sociologist Robert Park studied how newspapers helped immigrants to the United States adjust to their environment by changing their customary

habits and by teaching them the opinions held by people in their new home country. His study was conducted from which sociological perspective?
   a. the functionalist perspective
   b. the conflict perspective
   c. the interactionist perspective
   d. the dramaturgical perspective

3. There are problems inherent in the socialization function of the mass media. For example, many people worry about
    a. the effect of using the television as a babysitter.
    b. the impact of violent programming on viewer behavior.
    c. the unequal ability of all individuals to purchase televisions.
    d. both a and b

4. Media advertising has several clear functions, but it also has dysfunctions. Sociologists are concerned that
    a. it creates unrealistic expectations of what is required to be happy.
    b. it creates new consumer needs.
    c. advertisers are able to influence media content.
    d. all of the above

5. Gatekeeping, the process by which a relatively small number of people control what material reaches an audience, is largely dominant in all but which of the following media?
    a. television
    b. the Internet
    c. publishing
    d. music

6. Which sociological perspective is especially concerned with the media's ability to decide what gets transmitted through gatekeeping?
    a. the functionalist perspective
    b. the conflict perspective
    c. the interactionist perspective
    d. the dramaturgical perspective

7. Which of the following is *not* a problem feminist theorists see with media coverage?
    a. Women are underrepresented, suggesting that men are the cultural standard and that women are insignificant.

    b. Men and women are portrayed in ways that reflect and perpetuate stereotypical views of gender.
    c. Depictions of male–female relationships emphasize traditional sex roles and normalize violence against women.
    d. The increasing frequency of single moms in the media is providing a negative role model for women.

8. Which of the following is *not* true concerning how men and women use the Internet?
    a. Men are more likely to use the Internet daily.
    b. Women are more likely to use e-mail to maintain friendships.
    c. Men account for 100 percent of players in online sports fantasy leagues.
    d. Men are slightly more likely to have ever used the Internet than women are.

9. Sociologist Paul Lazarsfeld and his colleagues pioneered the study of
    a. the audience.
    b. opinion leaders.
    c. the media's global reach.
    d. media violence.

10. In his study of how the social composition of audience members affected how they interpreted the news coverage of riots in Los Angeles in 1992, sociologist Darnell Hunt found what kind of differences in perception?
    a. racial
    b. gender
    c. class
    d. religious

11. The mass media increase social cohesion by presenting a more or less standardized, common view of culture through mass communication. This statement reflects the _____ perspective.

12. Paul Lazarsfeld and Robert Merton created the term _____ _____ to refer to the phenomenon whereby the media provide such massive amounts of information that the audience becomes numb and generally fails to act on the information, regardless of how compelling the issue.

13. _____ _____ is the term used to describe the set of cultural beliefs and practices that helps to maintain powerful social, economic, and political interests.

14. Sociologists blame the mass media for the creation and perpetuation of _____, or generalizations about all members of a group that do not recognize individual differences within the group.

15. The _____ perspective contends that television distorts the political process.

16. We risk being _____ if we overstress U.S. dominance and assume other nations do not play a role in media cultural exports.

17. Both _____ and _____ theorists are troubled that the victims depicted in violent imagery are often those who are given less respect in real life: women, children, the poor, racial minorities, citizens of foreign countries, and even the physically disabled.

18. The _____ perspective examines the media on the micro level to see how they shape day-to-day social behavior.

19. We can point to a handful of _____ _____ that now dominate the publishing, broadcasting, and film industries, although they may be hard to identify, since global conglomerates manage many different product names.

20. Some 40 years ago, Canadian media theorist _____ _____ predicted that the rise of the electronic media would create a "global village."

THINKING ABOUT MOVIES

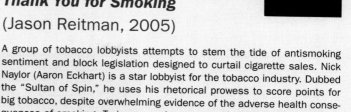

Talk to Me (Kasi Lemmons, 2007)

In Washington, D.C., in the late 1960s, R&B radio station WOL-AM struggles to hold its audience amidst the massive social change that followed the civil rights movement. Based on the real-life story of disc jockey and entertainer Petey Greene (Don Cheadle), the movie shows how Petey, hired to increase the station's listenership, used his self-professed knowledge of inner-city culture and penchant for "telling it like it is" to make his morning show a huge success. When violence breaks out after the assassination of Martin Luther King Jr., Petey helps to end the riots by giving voice to a grieving community and reminding listeners of King's message of nonviolence.

Talk to Me shows how a mass medium can support social cohesion, especially during times of crisis. Because the story is set in an era before the large-scale consolidation of media ownership, it illustrates the close connection between a community and its local broadcasting outlet that characterized the period.

For Your Consideration

1. How might Petey Greene's radio show be seen as an agent of socialization?

2. How does *Talk to Me* represent the media industry? How might that representation differ from what you know about today's media?

Thank You for Smoking
(Jason Reitman, 2005)

A group of tobacco lobbyists attempts to stem the tide of antismoking sentiment and block legislation designed to curtail cigarette sales. Nick Naylor (Aaron Eckhart) is a star lobbyist for the tobacco industry. Dubbed the "Sultan of Spin," he uses his rhetorical prowess to score points for big tobacco, despite overwhelming evidence of the adverse health consequences of smoking. To increase cigarette sales, Nick devises a plan to bribe decision makers in the media industry to show actors smoking on screen. Watch for the scene in which Nick meets with "superagent" Jeff Megall (Rob Lowe) to discuss how to frame such scenes for the greatest effect.

This movie shows how the media industry promotes consumption by carefully placing products in movie scenes. It also shows the inordinate amount of control that media gatekeepers like Jeff Megall exert over what is shown in a mass medium such as film.

For Your Consideration

1. How does *Thank You for Smoking* show the importance of product placement ("brandcasting"), and how might that reflect the way in which the mass media promote consumption?

2. Besides agents like Jeff Megall, who else might serve as media gatekeepers, and how might they influence what you see on film and television?

inside

Social Control

Law and Society

What Is Deviance?

Sociological Perspectives
    on Deviance

Crime

Social Policy and Social
    Control: Gun Control

BOXES

Sociology on Campus:
    Binge Drinking

Research Today: *Does
    Crime Pay?*

Sociology on Campus:
    Campus Crime

Taking Sociology to Work:
    *Stephanie Vezzani, Special
    Agent, U.S. Secret Service*

In Toronto, Canada, protesters confront police wearing riot gear. Law enforcement is only one of many different sources of social control.

Deviance and Social Control

8

A ROGUE SOCIOLOGIST TAKES TO THE STREETS

GANG LEADER
FOR A DAY

SUDHIR VENKATESH

Foreword by Stephen J. Dubner, coauthor of FREAKONOMICS

66 I began spending time with J.T. We'd usually hang out for a little while with some of the more senior members of his gang, and then we'd go for a ride around the South Side.

Although it would take me a few years to learn about J.T.'s life in detail, he did tell me a good bit during our first few weeks together: He had grown up in this neighborhood, then gone to college on an athletic scholarship and found that he loved reading about history and politics. After college he took a job selling office supplies and industrial textiles at a midsize corporation in downtown Chicago. But he felt that his chances of success were limited because he was black; he got angry when he saw white people with lesser skills get promoted ahead of him. Within two years he left the mainstream to return to the projects and the gang life.

. . .

One day at J.T.'s project, his cousin Clarisse talked about the prostitution that went on there. Even though J.T.'s gang didn't actually control the prostitutes in his buildings, Clarisse [a prostitute] explained that he did extract a monthly fee from both the hypes and the regulars. The regulars usually paid a flat fee (anywhere from fifteen to seventy-five dollars a month), and in return the gang would beat up any johns who abused the women. The hypes, meanwhile, turned over a cut of their income (ranging from 10 to 25 percent) to J.T.'s foot soldiers, who tried to keep track of how many tricks each woman turned. Clarisse said that J.T. was actually one of the nicer gang leaders on the South Side. He regularly lent money to women, helped them get medical care, even kept a few vacant apartments for them to use as brothels. So although J.T. didn't technically run a prostitution ring, he certainly controlled the flow of prostitution on his turf and profited from it.

The conversation with Clarisse that night made me realize that I was hardly the only person in the projects whose movements were dictated by J.T.

Whenever he took me on a survey of his buildings, I'd watch him deal with the various people who hung out in lobbies, stairwells, galleries, parking lots, and playgrounds. He warned a prostitute not to hustle out in the open. He told a man selling sneakers—they looked like counterfeit Nikes—to move away from the lobby where J.T.'s gang members were selling drugs. J.T. often forbade homeless men from hanging out in the playground, especially if they were drinking. And if he spotted a stranger on the premises, he'd have one of his senior officers interrogate that person to learn his business. J.T. hardly knew every single person out of the roughly five thousand in his domain, but he usually managed to figure out whether someone was a local, and if he couldn't figure it out, he had plenty of people to ask.

All of this was accomplished with little drama. "You folks need to move this activity somewhere else," he'd say matter-of-factly. Or, "What did I tell you about hustling in the park when kids are playing?" Or, "You can't stay in this apartment unless you deal with Creepy first." I saw a few people resist, but none for any great length of time. Most of them seemed to respect his authority, or at least fear it. 99

Clarisse said that J. T. was actually one of the nicer gang leaders on the South Side. He regularly lent money to women, helped them get medical care, even kept a few vacant apartments for them to use as brothels.

(Venkatesh 2008a:27, 58–59) Additional information about this excerpt can be found on the Online Learning Center at www.mhhe.com/schaefer12e.

Sudhir Venkatesh, now a professor of sociology at Columbia University, spent six years doing fieldwork in Chicago's public housing projects. As this excerpt from his book *Gang Leader for a Day* shows, over time Venkatesh, the son of Indian immigrants, observed and became accepted by a gang that managed one section of a low-income neighborhood. His work, as well as that of others, illustrates the thin line that often separates legal behavior from *deviant behavior*—behavior that violates social norms. Though most people would see prostitution, drug dealing, and the sale of stolen goods as unacceptable, J.T. and his gang try to create a certain level of stability for people in their neighborhood, whether they are tenants of public housing or the homeless seeking refuge in the buildings' stairwells. Are J.T. and his gang wrong, or are they survivors?

Another example of the difficulty of determining what is and is not socially acceptable is binge drinking on campus. On the one hand, we can view binge drinking as *deviant*, as violating a school's standards of conduct and endangering one's health. On the other hand, we can see it as *conforming*, or complying with peer culture. In the United States, people are socialized to have mixed feelings about both conforming and nonconforming behavior. The term *conformity* can conjure up images of mindless imitation of one's peer group—whether a circle of teenagers wearing "phat pants" or a group of business executives all dressed in gray suits. Yet the same term can also suggest that an individual is cooperative, or a "team player." What about those who do not conform? They may be respected as individualists, leaders, or creative thinkers who break new ground. Or they may be labeled as "troublemakers" and "weirdos."

This chapter examines the relationship between conformity, deviance, and social control. When does conformity verge on deviance? How does a society manage to control its members and convince them to conform to its rules and laws? What are the consequences of deviance? We will begin by distinguishing between conformity and obedience and then look at an experiment on obedience to authority. Next, we will analyze the informal and formal mechanisms societies use to encourage conformity and discourage deviance. We will pay particular attention to the legal order and how it reflects underlying social values.

The chapter then focuses on theoretical explanations for deviance, including the functionalist approach employed by Émile Durkheim and Robert Merton; interactionist-based theories; labeling theory, which draws on both the interactionist and the conflict perspectives; and conflict theory.

The next part of the chapter focuses on crime, a specific type of deviant behavior. As a form of deviance that is subject to official, written norms, crime has been a special concern of both policymakers and the public in general. We will look at various types of crime found in the United States, the ways crime is measured, and international crime rates. Finally, the Social Policy section considers the controversial topic of gun control.

Social Control

As we saw in Chapter 3, each culture, subculture, and group has distinctive norms governing appropriate behavior. Laws, dress codes, organizational bylaws, course requirements, and the rules of sports and games all express social norms.

How does a society bring about acceptance of basic norms? The term **social control** refers to the techniques and strategies for preventing deviant human behavior in any society. Social control occurs on all levels of society. In the family, we are socialized to obey our parents simply because they are our parents. Peer groups introduce us to informal norms, such as dress codes, that govern the behavior of their members. Colleges establish standards they expect of students. In bureaucratic organizations, workers encounter a formal system of rules and regulations. Finally, the government of every society legislates and enforces social norms.

Most of us respect and accept basic social norms and assume that others will do the same. Even without thinking, we obey the instructions of police officers, follow the day-to-day rules at our jobs, and move to the rear of elevators when people enter. Such behavior reflects an effective process of socialization to the dominant standards of a culture. At the same time, we are well aware that individuals, groups, and institutions *expect* us to act "properly." This expectation carries with it **sanctions,** or penalties and rewards for conduct concerning a social norm. If we fail to live up to the norm, we may face punishment through informal sanctions such as fear and ridicule or formal sanctions such as jail sentences or fines.

The ultimate formal sanction is the death penalty, which has been the subject of much controversy recently. As Figure 8-1 on page 166 shows, 1,150 people were executed in the United States from 1976 through early 2009. Much of the controversy centers on the effectiveness of this sanction as a form of social control. Other than eliminating the person who is executed, what does the death penalty accomplish? Does it actually control others' behavior by deterring them from committing a capital offense? To answer this question, researchers must consider the motivation behind capital crimes as well as the criminal's understanding of the resulting penalties. Taking these factors into consideration, researchers have found little evidence that execution is any more a deterrent to capital crimes than an extended prison term (Lanier et al. 2009).

The challenge to effective social control is that people often receive competing messages about how to behave. While the state or government may clearly define acceptable behavior, friends or fellow employees may encourage quite different behavior patterns. Historically, legal measures aimed at blocking discrimination based on race, religion, gender, age, and sexual orientation have been difficult to implement, because many people tacitly encourage the violation of such measures.

In Finland (left), a young man relaxes in his prison cell, which resembles a college dorm room. In the United States (right), prisoners at a super-maximum-security prison watch television in cages that prevent them from making physical contact with guards or other prisoners. The rate of imprisonment in Finland is less than one-half that of England and one-fourth that of the United States.

MAPPING LIFE NATIONWIDE

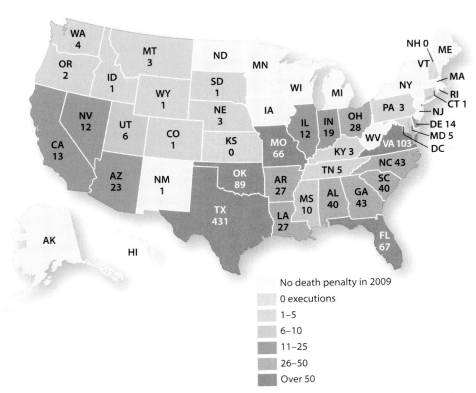

Note: Number of executions carried out from January 17, 1977, to February 20, 2009. Three federal executions not included. New Mexico abolished the death penalty in 2009, but since the appeal was not retroactive, one person remains on the state's death row.
Source: Death Penalty Information Center 2009.

Think about It
Why is there so much variation in the number of executions from one state to the next? What might cause that variation?

Functionalists maintain that people must respect social norms if any group or society is to survive. In their view, societies literally could not function if massive numbers of people defied standards of appropriate conduct. In contrast, conflict theorists contend that the "successful functioning" of a society will consistently benefit the powerful and work to the disadvantage of other groups. They point out that in the United States, widespread resistance to social norms was necessary to win our independence from England, to overturn the institution of slavery, to allow women to vote, to secure civil rights, and to force an end to the war in Vietnam.

Conformity and Obedience

Techniques for social control operate on both the group level and the societal level. People we think of as peers or equals influence us to act in particular ways; the same is true of people who hold authority over us or occupy awe-inspiring positions. Social psychologist Stanley Milgram (1975) made a useful distinction between these two levels of social control.

The Milgram Experiment Milgram used the term **conformity** to mean going along with peers—individuals of our own status

who have no special right to direct our behavior. In contrast, **obedience** is compliance with higher authorities in a hierarchical structure. Thus, a recruit entering military service will typically *conform* to the habits and language of other recruits and *obey* the orders of superior officers. Students will *conform* to the drinking behavior of their peers and *obey* the requests of campus security officers.

We often think of conformity and obedience as rather harmless behaviors. When members of an expensive health club all don the same costly sportswear, we may see their conformity as unimaginative, but we do not think of it as harmful. Nevertheless, researchers have found that under certain circumstances, both conformity and obedience can have negative consequences. Obedience, in particular, can cause immense damage—a potential that Milgram demonstrated in the laboratory.

If ordered to do so, would you comply with an experimenter's instruction to administer increasingly painful electric shocks to a subject? Most people would say no; yet Milgram's research (1963, 1975) suggests that most of us *would* obey such orders. In his words (1975:xi), "Behavior that is unthinkable in an individual . . . acting on his own may be executed without hesitation when carried out under orders."

In one of Stanley Milgram's experiments, the learner supposedly received an electric shock from a shock plate when he answered a question incorrectly. At the 150-volt level, the learner would demand to be released and would refuse to place his hand on the shock plate. The experimenter would then order the actual subject, the teacher, to force the hand onto the plate, as shown in the photo. Though 40 percent of the true subjects stopped complying with Milgram at this point, 30 percent did force the learner's hand onto the shock plate, despite his pretended agony.

Milgram placed advertisements in New Haven, Connecticut, newspapers to recruit subjects for a learning experiment at Yale University. Participants included postal clerks, engineers, high school teachers, and laborers. They were told that the purpose of the research was to investigate the effects of punishment on learning. The experimenter, dressed in a gray technician's coat, explained that in each test, one subject would be randomly selected as the "learner," while another would function as the "teacher." However, the experiment was rigged so that the real subject would always be the teacher, while an associate of Milgram's served as the learner.

At this point, the learner's hand was strapped to an electric apparatus. The teacher was taken to an electronic "shock generator" with 30 levered switches labeled from 15 to 450 volts. Before beginning the experiment, all subjects received sample shocks of 45 volts, to convince them of the authenticity of the experiment. The experimenter then instructed the teacher to apply shocks of increasing voltage each time the learner gave an incorrect answer on a memory test. Teachers were told that "although the shocks can be extremely painful, they cause no permanent tissue damage." In reality, the learner did not receive any shocks.

In a prearranged script, the learner deliberately gave incorrect answers and expressed pain when "shocked." For example, at 150 volts, the learner would cry out, "Get me out of here!" At 270 volts, the learner would scream in agony. When the shock reached 350 volts, the learner would fall silent. If the teacher wanted to stop the experiment, the experimenter would insist that the teacher continue, using such statements as "The experiment requires that you continue" and "You have no other choice; you *must* go on" (Milgram 1975:19–23).

Reflecting on the Milgram Experiment   The results of this unusual experiment stunned and dismayed Milgram and other social scientists. A sample of psychiatrists had predicted that virtually all subjects would refuse to shock innocent victims. In their view, only a "pathological fringe" of less than 2 percent would continue administering shocks up to the maximum level. Yet almost *two-thirds* of participants fell into the category of "obedient subjects."

Why did these subjects obey? Why were they willing to inflict seemingly painful shocks on innocent victims who had never done them any harm? There is no evidence that these subjects were unusually sadistic; few seemed to enjoy administering the shocks. Instead, in Milgram's view, the key to obedience was the experimenter's social role as a "scientist" and "seeker of knowledge."

Milgram pointed out that in the modern industrial world, we are accustomed to submitting to impersonal authority figures whose status is indicated by a title (professor, lieutenant, doctor) or by a uniform (the technician's coat). Because we view the authority as larger and more important than the individual, we shift responsibility for our behavior to the authority figure. Milgram's subjects frequently stated, "If it were up to me, I would not have administered shocks." They saw themselves as merely doing their duty (Milgram 1975).

From a conflict perspective, our obedience may be affected by the value we place on those whom our behavior affects. While Milgram's experiment shows that, in general, people are willing to obey authority figures, other studies show that they are even more willing to obey if they feel the "victim" is deserving of punishment. Sociologist Gary Schulman (1974) re-created Milgram's experiment and found that White students were significantly more likely to shock Black learners than White learners. By a margin of 70 percent to 48 percent, they imposed more shocks on the Black learners than on the White learners.

From an interactionist perspective, one important aspect of Milgram's findings is the fact that subjects in follow-up studies were less likely to inflict the supposed shocks as they were moved physically closer to their victims. Moreover, interactionists emphasize the effect of *incrementally* administering additional dosages of 15 volts. In effect, the experimenter negotiated with the teacher and convinced the teacher to continue inflicting higher levels of punishment. It is doubtful that anywhere near the two-thirds rate of obedience would have been reached had the experimenter told the teachers to administer 450 volts immediately (B. Allen 1978; Katovich 1987).

Milgram launched his experimental study of obedience to better understand the involvement of Germans in the annihilation of 6 million Jews and millions of other people during World War II. In an interview conducted long after the publication of his study, he suggested that "if a system of death camps were set up in the United States of the sort we had seen in Nazi Germany, one would be able to find sufficient personnel for those camps in any medium-sized American town." Though many people questioned his remark, the revealing photos taken at Iraq's Abu Ghraib prison in 2004, showing U.S. military guards humiliating if not torturing Iraqi prisoners, recalled the experiment Milgram had done two generations earlier. Under conducive circumstances, otherwise normal people can and often do treat one another inhumanely (CBS News 1979:7–8; Hayden 2004; Zimbardo 2007a).

How willing would participants in this experiment be to shock learners today? Although many people may be skeptical of the high levels of conformity Milgram found, recent replications of his experiment confirm his findings. In 2006, using additional safeguards to protect participants' welfare, psychologist Jerry Burger (2009) repeated part of Milgram's experiment with college undergraduates. To avoid biasing the participants, Burger was careful to screen out students who had heard of Milgram's study. The results of the replication were startlingly similar to Milgram's: participants showed a high level of willingness to shock the learner, just as the participants in Milgram's experiment had almost half a century earlier. At the most comparable point in the two studies, Burger measured a rate of 70 percent full obedience—lower, but not significantly so, than the rate of 82.5 percent measured two generations earlier (Twenge 2009).

use your sociological *imagination*

If you were a participant in Milgram's research on conformity, how far do you think you would go in carrying out orders? Do you see any ethical problem with the experimenter's manipulation of the control subjects?

Informal and Formal Social Control

The sanctions that are used to encourage conformity and obedience—and to discourage violation of social norms—are carried out through both informal and formal social control. As the term implies, people use **informal social control** casually to enforce norms. Examples include smiles, laughter, a raised eyebrow, and ridicule.

In the United States and many other cultures, adults often view spanking, slapping, or kicking children as a proper and necessary means of informal social control. Child development specialists counter that such corporal punishment is inappropriate because it teaches children to solve problems through violence. They warn that slapping and spanking can escalate into more serious forms of abuse. Yet, despite a 1998 policy statement by the American Academy of Pediatrics that corporal punishment is not effective and can indeed be harmful, 59 percent of pediatricians support the use of corporal punishment, at least in certain situations. Our culture widely accepts this form of informal social control (Wolraich et al. 1998).

Formal social control is carried out by authorized agents, such as police officers, judges, school administrators, employers, military officers, and managers of movie theaters. It can serve as a last resort when socialization and informal sanctions do not bring about desired behavior. Sometimes, informal social control can actually undermine formal social control, encouraging people to violate social norms. Box 8-1 examines binge drinking among college students, who receive conflicting messages about the acceptability of the behavior from sources of social control.

An increasingly significant means of formal social control in the United States is to imprison people. During the course of a year, 7 million adults undergo some form of correctional supervision—jail, prison, probation, or parole. Put another way,

almost 1 out of every 30 adult Americans is subject to this very formal type of social control every year. Little wonder that housing prisoners is a major problem. Many states must send their convicts to prisons in other states, wherever room can be found for them. To accommodate the overflow, privately run (nongovernmental) prisons have been constructed. Nearly 118,000 prisoners reside in such facilities, which serve 30 states as well as the federal government (S. Moore 2007; Sabol and Couture 2008; H. West and Sabol 2009).

In 2007, in the wake of the mass shootings at Virginia Tech, many college officials reviewed security measures on their campuses. Administrators were reluctant to end or even limit the relative freedom of movement students on their campuses enjoyed. Instead, they concentrated on improving emergency communications between campus police and students, faculty, and staff. Reflecting a reliance on technology to maintain social control, college leaders called for replacement of the "old" technology of e-mail with instant alerts that could be sent to people's cell phones via instant messaging.

Six years earlier, in the aftermath of September 11, 2001, new measures of social control became the norm in the United States. Some of them, such as stepped-up security at airports and high-rise buildings, were highly visible to the public. The federal government has also publicly urged citizens to engage

Though formal social control usually involves fines, probation, or incarceration, some judges have used public humiliation as a sanction.

SOCIOLOGY ON CAMPUS

8-1 Binge Drinking

On December 2, 2008, Carson Starkey, an 18-year-old student at California Polytechnic Institute, was looking forward to becoming a full-fledged member of Sigma Alpha Epsilon. But Starkey didn't live to celebrate the occasion. That day, during a hazing incident that was part of his initiation, the 155-pound student died of acute alcohol poisoning. An autopsy showed a blood-alcohol concentration of between .39 and .447 percent—about five times the legal driving limit in California.

Starkey's case was not unique. About 1,700 college students die each year of unintentional alcohol-related injuries. According to a study published by the Harvard School of Public Health, 44 percent of college students indulge in binge drinking (defined as at least five drinks in a row for men and four in a row for women). For those who live in a Greek fraternity or sorority, the rates are even higher—83 percent are binge drinkers (see the figure). These numbers represent an increase from 1990s data, despite efforts on many campuses across the nation to educate students about the risks of binge drinking.

The problem is not confined to the United States—Britain, Russia, and South Africa all report regular "drink till you drop" alcoholic consumption among young people. According to a 2007 study that compared data from 22 countries, however, college students in the United States have the highest rate of drinking and driving (50 percent of male drinkers and 35 percent of female drinkers). Nor does binge drinking begin in college. A national study published in 2007 by the American Academy of Pediatrics found that, over a 30-day period, 29 percent of high school students engaged in binge drinking.

Binge drinking on campus presents a difficult social problem. On the one hand, it can be regarded as *deviant,* violating the standards of conduct expected of those in an academic setting. In fact, Harvard researchers consider binge drinking the most serious public health hazard facing colleges. Not only does it cause about 50 fatalities a year and hundreds of cases of alcohol poisoning; it increases the likelihood of falling behind in schoolwork, getting injured, and damaging property.

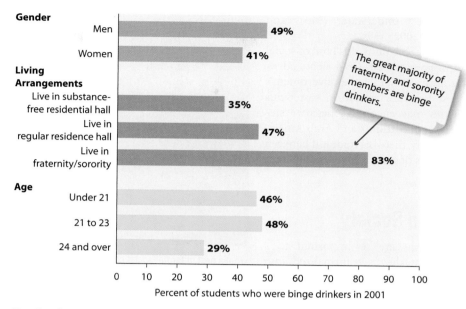

Note: Based on a 2001 national survey of more than 10,000 college students. Binge drinking was defined as one drinking session of at least five drinks for men or four drinks for women during the two weeks prior to the self-administered questionnaire.
Source: Wechsler et al. 2002:208.

The other side of this potentially self-destructive behavior is that binge drinking represents *conformity* to the peer culture, especially in fraternities and sororities, which serve as social centers on many campuses. Most students seem to take an "everybody does it—no big deal" attitude toward the behavior. Many find that taking five drinks in a row is fairly typical. As one student at Boston University noted, "Anyone that goes to a party does that or worse. If you talk to anyone college age, it's normal."

> *44 percent of college students indulge in binge drinking.*

Some colleges and universities are taking steps to make binge drinking a bit less "normal" by means of *social control*—banning kegs, closing fraternities and sororities, encouraging liquor retailers not to sell in high volume to students, and expelling students after three alcohol-related infractions. Despite privacy laws, many schools are notifying parents whenever their underage children are caught drinking. Even with these measures, however, curbing underage drinking is a challenge. The latest study, released in 2009, shows that, as in earlier studies, undergraduates who drank alcohol over a two-week period (about 70 percent of them) typically spent more hours per week drinking than studying.

LET'S DISCUSS

1. Why do you think most college students regard binge drinking as a normal rather than a deviant behavior?
2. Which do you think would be more effective in stopping binge drinking on your campus, informal or formal social control?

Sources: E. Bernstein 2007; J. Miller et al. 2007; National Center on Addiction and Substance Abuse at Columbia University 2007; National Institute on Alcohol Abuse and Alcoholism 2009; Outside the Classroom 2009; Julianne Shapiro 2009; Wechsler et al. 2002, 2004.

in informal social control by watching for and reporting people whose actions seem suspicious. But many other measures taken by the government have increased the covert surveillance of private records and communications.

Just 45 days after September 11, with virtually no debate, Congress passed the Patriot Act of 2001. Sections of this sweeping legislation revoked legal checks on the power of law enforcement agencies. Without a warrant or probable cause, the Federal Bureau of Investigation (FBI) can now secretly access most private records, including medical histories, library accounts, and student registrations. In 2002, for example, the FBI searched the records of hundreds of dive shops and scuba organizations. Agents had been directed to identify every person who had taken diving lessons in the past three years because of speculation that terrorists might try to approach their targets underwater (Moss and Fessenden 2002).

Many people think this kind of social control goes too far. Civil rights advocates also worry that the government's request for information on suspicious activities may encourage negative stereotyping of Muslims and Arab Americans. Clearly, there is a trade-off between the benefits of surveillance and the right to privacy.

Law and Society

Some norms are so important to a society that they are formalized into laws regarding people's behavior. **Law** may be defined as governmental social control (Black 1995). Some laws, such as the prohibition against murder, are

What's next in formal social control—iris checks? At Amsterdam's Schiphol airport, a security official scans a passenger's irises. Like fingerprints, iris patterns are unique, but their greater complexity makes them a more accurate form of identification. This passenger may choose to store her iris patterns on an identification card to expedite her boarding process.

directed at all members of society. Others, such as fishing and hunting regulations, primarily affect particular categories of people. Still others govern the behavior of social institutions (for instance, corporate law and laws regarding the taxing of nonprofit enterprises).

Sociologists see the creation of laws as a social process. Because laws are passed in response to a perceived need for formal social control, sociologists have sought to explain how and why such a perception arises. In their view, law is not merely a static body of rules handed down from generation to generation. Rather, it reflects continually changing standards of what is right and wrong, of how violations are to be determined, and of what sanctions are to be applied (Schur 1968).

Sociologists representing varying theoretical perspectives agree that the legal order reflects the values of those in a position to exercise authority. Therefore, the creation of civil and criminal law can be a most controversial matter. Should it be against the law to employ illegal immigrants, to have an abortion (see Chapter 12), to allow prayer in public schools (see Chapter 15), or to smoke on an airplane? Such issues have been bitterly debated, because they require a choice among competing values. Not surprisingly, laws that are unpopular—such as the one-time prohibition of alcohol under the Eighteenth Amendment and the widespread establishment of a 55-mile-per-hour speed limit on highways—become difficult to enforce when there is no consensus supporting the norms.

One current and controversial debate over laws governing behavior is whether people should be allowed to use marijuana legally, for medical purposes. Although the majority of adults polled in national surveys support such a use, the federal government continues to regard all uses of marijuana as illegal. In 2005 the Supreme Court upheld the federal government's position. Nevertheless, 12 states have granted citizens the right to use

marijuana for medical purposes—even if that privilege rests on dubious legal grounds (Figure 8-2).

Socialization is the primary source of conforming and obedient behavior, including obedience to law. Generally, it is not external pressure from a peer group or authority figure that makes us go along with social norms. Rather, we have internalized such norms as valid and desirable and are committed to observing them. In a profound sense, we want to see ourselves (and to be seen) as loyal, cooperative, responsible, and respectful of others. In the United States and other societies around the world, people are socialized both to want to belong and to fear being viewed as different or deviant.

Control theory suggests that our connection to members of society leads us to systematically conform to society's norms. According to sociologist Travis Hirschi and other control theorists, our bonds to family members, friends, and peers induce us to follow the mores and folkways of our society. We give little conscious thought to whether we will be sanctioned if we fail to conform. Socialization develops our self-control so well that we don't need further pressure to obey social norms. Although control theory does not effectively explain the rationale for every conforming act, it nevertheless reminds us that while the media may focus on crime and disorder, most members of most societies conform to and obey basic norms (Gottfredson and Hirschi 1990; Hirschi 1969).

What Is Deviance?

For sociologists, the term *deviance* does not mean perversion or depravity. **Deviance** is behavior that violates the standards of conduct or expectations of a group or society (Wickman 1991:85). In the United States, alcoholics, compulsive gamblers, and the mentally ill would all be classified as deviants. Being late for class is categorized as a deviant act; the same is true of

FIGURE **8-2** THE STATUS OF MEDICAL MARIJUANA   171

MAPPING LIFE NATIONWIDE

- 13 states have laws that allow the cultivation of medical marijuana and that protect patients who possess medical marijuana (with their doctors' recommendations or certifications) from criminal penalties.

- Maryland protects medical marijuana patients from jail, but not from the threat of arrest.

- 17 states and the District of Columbia have laws that recognize marijuana's medical value, but these laws are ineffective because they rely on federal cooperation.

- 19 states have no provisions for medical marijuana

Source: Marijuana Policy Project 2008.

The actions some states have taken to legalize marijuana are largely symbolic. Federal law still prohibits doctors from writing prescriptions for marijuana, and pharmacies from distributing the substance. Although patients can still be prosecuted by the federal government for possessing or using marijuana, however, the Obama administration has decided not to prosecute in those states where medical use of the substance is legal.

wearing jeans to a formal wedding. On the basis of the sociological definition, we are all deviant from time to time. Each of us violates common social norms in certain situations.

Is being overweight an example of deviance? In the United States and many other cultures, unrealistic standards of appearance and body image place a huge strain on people—especially adult women and girls—based on how they look. Journalist Naomi Wolf (1992) has used the term *beauty myth* to refer to an exaggerated ideal of beauty, beyond the reach of all but a few females, which has unfortunate consequences. In order to shed their "deviant" image and conform to unrealistic societal norms, many women and girls become consumed with adjusting their appearances. Yet what is deviant in one culture may be celebrated in another.

Deviance involves the violation of group norms, which may or may not be formalized into law. It is a comprehensive concept that includes not only criminal behavior but also many actions that are not subject to prosecution. The public official who takes a bribe has defied social norms, but so has the high school student who refuses to sit in an assigned seat or cuts class. Of course, deviation from norms is not always negative, let alone criminal. A member of an exclusive social club who speaks out against a

Think about It

If your friends or teammates violate a social norm, is that behavior still deviant?

In 2009 baseball fans were shocked by the revelation that, like several other baseball greats, superstar Alex Rodriguez had used banned substances and lied about it.

Increasingly, tattoos are seen as a fashion statement—in the United States, about 36 percent of people between ages 18 and 29 have at least one. Though tattoos may not seem deviant or even unusual to many people, in some circles they may create quite the opposite impression. In 2006 a U.S. appeals court ruled that police officers' tattoos are not protected under the First Amendment, and a year later, the U.S. Marine Corps banned tattoos that would be visible when Marines wear their exercise uniforms (Laumann and Derick 2006; Reed 2007).

traditional policy of not admitting women, Blacks, and Jews is deviating from the club's norms. So is a police officer who blows the whistle on corruption or brutality within the department.

From a sociological perspective, deviance is hardly objective or set in stone. Rather, it is subject to social definition within a particular society and at a particular time. For that reason, what is considered deviant can shift from one social era to another. In most instances, those individuals and groups with the greatest status and power define what is acceptable and what is deviant. For example, despite serious medical warnings against the dangers of tobacco, made since 1964, cigarette smoking continued to be accepted for decades—in good part because of the power of tobacco farmers and cigarette manufacturers. Only after a long campaign led by public health and anticancer activists did cigarette smoking become more of a deviant activity. Today, many state and local laws limit where people can smoke.

Deviance and Social Stigma

A person can acquire a deviant identity in many ways. Because of physical or behavioral characteristics, some people are unwillingly cast in negative social roles. Once assigned a deviant role, they have trouble presenting a positive image to others and may even experience lowered self-esteem. Whole groups of people—for instance, "short people" or "redheads"—may be labeled in this way. The interactionist Erving Goffman coined the term **stigma** to describe the labels society uses to devalue members of certain social groups (Goffman 1963; Heckert and Best 1997).

Prevailing expectations about beauty and body shape may prevent people who are regarded as ugly or obese from advancing as rapidly as their abilities permit. Both overweight and anorexic people are assumed to be weak in character, slaves to their appetites or to media images. Because they do not conform to the beauty myth, they may be viewed as "disfigured" or "strange" in

appearance, bearers of what Goffman calls a "spoiled identity." However, what constitutes disfigurement is a matter of interpretation. Of the 1 million cosmetic procedures done every year in the United States alone, many are performed on women who would be defined objectively as having a normal appearance. And while feminist sociologists have accurately noted that the beauty myth makes many women feel uncomfortable with themselves, men too lack confidence in their appearance. The number of males who choose to undergo cosmetic procedures has risen sharply in recent years; men now account for 20 percent of such surgeries (American Academy of Cosmetic Surgery 2008).

Often people are stigmatized for deviant behaviors they may no longer engage in. The labels "compulsive gambler," "ex-convict," "recovering alcoholic," and "ex–mental patient" can stick to a person for life. Goffman draws a useful distinction between a prestige symbol that draws attention to a positive aspect of one's identity, such as a wedding band or a badge, and a stigma symbol that discredits or debases one's identity, such as a conviction for child molestation. While stigma symbols may not always be obvious, they can become a matter of public knowledge. Starting in 1994, many states required convicted sex offenders to register with local police departments. Some communities publish the names and addresses, and in some instances even the pictures, of convicted sex offenders on the Web.

A person need not be guilty of a crime to be stigmatized. Homeless people often have trouble getting a job, because employers are wary of applicants who cannot give a home address. Moreover, hiding one's homelessness is difficult, since agencies generally use the telephone to contact applicants about job openings. If a homeless person has access to a telephone at a shelter, the staff generally answers the phone by announcing the name of the institution—a sure way to discourage prospective employers. Even if a homeless person surmounts these obstacles and manages to get a job, she or he is often fired when the employer learns of the situation. Regardless of a person's positive attributes, employers regard the spoiled identity of homelessness as sufficient reason to dismiss an employee.

While some types of deviance will stigmatize a person, other types do not carry a significant penalty. Examples of socially tolerated forms of deviance can be found in the world of high technology.

Deviance and Technology

Technological innovations such as pagers and voice mail can redefine social interactions and the standards of behavior related to them. When the Internet was first made available to the general public, no norms or regulations governed its use. Because online communication offers a high degree of anonymity, uncivil behavior—speaking harshly of others or monopolizing chat room "space"—quickly became common. Online bulletin boards designed to carry items of community interest became littered with commercial advertisements. Such deviant acts are beginning to provoke calls for the establishment of formal rules for online behavior. For example, policymakers have debated whether to regulate the content of Web sites featuring hate speech and pornography.

Some deviant uses of technology are criminal, though not all participants see it that way. The pirating of software, motion pictures, and music has become a big business. At conventions and swap meets, pirated copies of DVDs are sold openly. Some of the

Sociological Perspectives on Deviance

Why do people violate social norms? We have seen that deviant acts are subject to both informal and formal social control. The nonconforming or disobedient person may face disapproval, loss of friends, fines, or even imprisonment. Why, then, does deviance occur?

Early explanations for behavior that deviated from societal expectations blamed supernatural causes or genetic factors (such as "bad blood" or evolutionary throwbacks to primitive ancestors). By the 1800s, substantial research efforts were being made to identify biological factors that lead to deviance, and especially to criminal activity. Though such research was discredited in the 20th century, contemporary studies, primarily by biochemists, have sought to isolate genetic factors that suggest a likelihood of certain personality traits. Although criminality (much less deviance) is hardly a personality characteristic, researchers have focused on traits that might lead to crime, such as aggression. Of course, aggression can also lead to success in the corporate world, in professional sports, or in other walks of life.

The contemporary study of the possible biological roots of criminality is but one aspect of the larger debate over sociobiology. In general, sociologists reject any emphasis on the genetic roots of crime and deviance. The limitations of current knowledge, the possibility of reinforcing racist and sexist assumptions, and the disturbing implications for the rehabilitation of criminals have led sociologists to draw largely on other approaches to explain deviance (Sagarin and Sanchez 1988).

Functionalist Perspective

According to functionalists, deviance is a common part of human existence, with positive as well as negative consequences for social stability. Deviance helps to define the limits of proper behavior. Children who see one parent scold the other for belching at the dinner table learn about approved conduct. The same is true of the driver who receives a speeding ticket, the department store cashier who is fired for yelling at a customer, and the college student who is penalized for handing in papers weeks overdue.

Durkheim's Legacy Émile Durkheim ([1895] 1964) focused his sociological investigations mainly on criminal acts, yet his conclusions have implications for all types of deviant behavior. In Durkheim's view, the punishments established within a culture (including both formal and informal mechanisms of social control) help to define acceptable behavior and thus contribute to stability. If improper acts were not sanctioned, people might stretch their standards of what constitutes appropriate conduct.

Kai Erikson (1966) illustrated the boundary-maintenance function of deviance in his study of the Puritans of 17th-century New England. By today's standards, the Puritans placed tremendous emphasis on conventional morals. Their persecution and execution of women as witches represented a continuing attempt to define and redefine the boundaries of their community. In effect, their changing social norms created crime waves, as people whose behavior was previously acceptable suddenly faced punishment for being deviant (Abrahamson 1978; N. Davis 1975).

Spectators watch a cage fight in Sioux Falls, South Dakota. In the United States, cage fighting is banned in some places but permitted in others. Even within the same culture, not everyone shares the same idea of proper behavior.

products are obviously counterfeit, but many come in sophisticated packaging, complete with warranty cards. The vendors say they merely want to be compensated for their time and the cost of materials, or that the software they have copied is in the public domain.

Similarly, the downloading of music from the Internet, which is typically protected by copyright, is widely accepted. But file sharing, like the pirating of DVDs, has grown to the point that it is threatening the profits of copyright owners. Napster, the renegade Web site that allowed thousands of people to download from a wide selection of music files for free, has been shut down, the victim of a court challenge by the music industry. Nevertheless, its fleeting success has encouraged imitators, many of them college students who run file-sharing programs from their dorm rooms. The music industry is fighting back by urging law enforcement agents to track the pirates down and prosecute them.

Though most of these black market activities are clearly illegal, many consumers and small-time pirates are proud of their behavior. They may even think themselves smart for figuring out a way to avoid the "unfair" prices charged by "big corporations." Few people see the pirating of a new software program or a first-run movie as a threat to the public good, as they would see embezzling from a bank. Similarly, most businesspeople who "borrow" software from another department, even though they lack a site license, do not think they are doing anything wrong. No social stigma attaches to their illegal behavior.

Deviance, then, is a complex concept. Sometimes it is trivial, sometimes profoundly harmful. Sometimes it is accepted by society and sometimes soundly rejected. What accounts for deviant behavior and people's reaction to it? In the next section we will examine five theoretical explanations for deviance.

use your sociological *imagination*

What kinds of file sharing do you and your friends regard as acceptable? What do you regard as illegal?

By permission of John L. Hart FLP and Creators Syndicate, Inc.

Though functionalists believe that crime and deviance serve a purpose in society, they do not condone rule violations.

Durkheim ([1897] 1951) introduced the term **anomie** into sociological literature to describe the loss of direction felt in a society when social control of individual behavior has become ineffective. Anomie is a state of normlessness that typically occurs during a period of profound social change and disorder, such as a time of economic collapse. People become more aggressive or depressed, which results in higher rates of violent crime and suicide. Since there is much less agreement on what constitutes proper behavior during times of revolution, sudden prosperity, or economic depression, conformity and obedience become less significant as social forces. It also becomes much more difficult to state exactly what constitutes deviance.

Merton's Theory of Deviance   What do a mugger and a teacher have in common? Each is "working" to obtain money

that can then be exchanged for desired goods. As this example illustrates, behavior that violates accepted norms (such as mugging) may be performed with the same basic objectives in mind as those of people who pursue more conventional lifestyles.

On the basis of this kind of analysis, sociologist Robert Merton (1968) adapted Durkheim's notion of anomie to explain why people accept or reject the goals of a society, the socially ap-proved means of fulfilling their aspirations, or both. Merton maintained that one important cultural goal in the United States is success, measured largely in terms of money. In addition to providing this goal for people, our society offers specific instructions on how to pursue success—go to school, work hard, do not quit, take advantage of opportunities, and so forth.

What happens to individuals in a society with a heavy emphasis on wealth as a basic symbol of success? Merton reasoned that people adapt in certain ways, either by conforming to or by deviating from such cultural expectations. His **anomie theory of deviance** posits five basic forms of adaptation (Table 8-1).

Conformity to social norms, the most common adaptation in Merton's typology, is the opposite of deviance. It involves acceptance of both the overall societal goal ("become affluent") and the approved means ("work hard"). In Merton's view, there must be some consensus regarding accepted cultural goals and the legitimate means for attaining them. Without such a consensus, societies could exist only as collectives of people rather than as unified cultures, and might experience continual chaos.

The other four types of behavior represented in Table 8-1 all involve some departure from conformity. The "innovator" accepts the goals of society but pursues them with means that are regarded as improper. For instance, a safecracker may steal money to buy consumer goods and expensive vacations.

In Merton's typology, the "ritualist" has abandoned the goal of material success and become compulsively committed to the institutional means. Work becomes simply a way of life rather than a means to the goal of success. An example would be the bureaucratic official who blindly applies rules and regulations without remembering the larger goals of the organization. Certainly that would be true of a welfare caseworker who refuses to assist a homeless family because their last apartment was in another district.

The "retreatist," as described by Merton, has basically withdrawn (or retreated) from both the goals and the

TABLE **8-1**   MODES OF INDIVIDUAL ADAPTATION

summing up

Mode	Institutionalized Means (hard work)	Societal Goal (acquisition of wealth)
Nondeviant		
Conformity	Accept	Accept
Deviant		
Innovation	Reject	Accept
Ritualism	Accept	Reject
Retreatism	Reject	Reject
Rebellion	Replace with new means	Replace with new goals

Source: Adapted from Merton 1968:194.

RESEARCH TODAY

8-2 Does Crime Pay?

A driver violates the speed limit to get to a job interview on time. A financially strapped parent shoplifts goods that her family needs. These people may feel justified in violating the law because they do so to meet a reasonable objective. In Robert Merton's terms, they are *innovators*—people who violate social norms to achieve a commonly shared societal goal. Although their actions are criminal and potentially hurtful to others, from their own short-term perspective, their actions are functional.

Carried to its logical conclusion, innovation can and does become a career for some people. Yet from a purely economic point of view, even considering the fact that crime may pay is controversial, because doing so may seem to tolerate or encourage rule violation. Nothing is more controversial than the suggestion that gang-run drug deals are profitable and produce "good jobs." Although some people may see drug dealers as a cross between MBA-educated professionals and streetwise entrepreneurs, society in general does not admire these innovators.

Sociologist Sudhir Venkatesh collected detailed data on the illegal drug trade during his observation research on a Chicago street gang. Working with economist Steven Levitt, coauthor of the best seller *Freakonomics*, to analyze the business of selling crack cocaine, he found that less than 5 percent of even the gang leaders earned $100,000 per year. The rest of the leaders and virtually all the rank and file earned less than the minimum wage. In fact, most were unpaid workers seeking to move up in the gang hierarchy. (Thus the title of a chapter in Levitt's book, "Why Do Drug Dealers Still Live with Their Moms?") As Levitt notes, the drug gang is like most corporations: the top 2 percent of workers take home most of the money.

Why, from a sociological *and* an economic perspective, do these nonprofitable practices persist, especially considering that one in every four members of drug-oriented street

> *Less than 5 percent of even the gang leaders earned $100,000 per year. The rest of the leaders and virtually all the rank and file earned less than the minimum wage.*

gangs are eventually killed? One reason, of course, is the public's almost insatiable demand for illegal drugs. And from the drug peddler's perspective, few legitimate jobs are available to young adults in poverty-stricken areas, urban or rural. Functionally, these youths are contributing to their household incomes by dealing drugs.

In an interesting footnote to Venkatesh's observation research, the sociologist revealed that he shared in the gang's poor earnings. In fact, his cut of the meager take led members to increase the amount of money they demanded from residents for "protection." "I felt awful when I found out that my work was unwittingly hurting people," he reflected. "All of a sudden I was finding out that information was a commodity, and if I wanted something from them, they wanted something from me" (Venkatesh 2008b:45).

Scholars see a need for further research on Merton's concept of innovation. Why, for example, do some disadvantaged groups have lower rates of reported crime than others? Why do many people who are caught in adverse circumstances reject criminal activity as a viable alternative? Merton's theory of deviance does not easily answer such questions.

LET'S DISCUSS

1. Do you know anyone who has stolen out of need? If so, did the person feel justified in stealing, or did he or she feel guilty? How long did the theft continue?
2. Economically, profit is the difference between revenues and costs. What are the costs of the illegal drug trade, both economic and social? Is this economic activity profitable for society?

Sources: Clinard and Miller 1998; Kingsbury 2008; Levitt and Dubner 2006; Venkatesh 2000, 2008a, 2008b.

---

means of society. In the United States, drug addicts and vagrants are typically portrayed as retreatists. Concern has been growing that adolescents who are addicted to alcohol will become retreatists at an early age.

The final adaptation identified by Merton reflects people's attempts to create a *new* social structure. The "rebel" feels alienated from the dominant means and goals and may seek a dramatically different social order. Members of a revolutionary political organization, such as a militia group, can be categorized as rebels according to Merton's model. Although this theory of deviance is popular, it has not been applied systematically to real-world crime. Box 8-2 examines scholars' efforts to confirm the theory's validity.

Merton made a key contribution to the sociological understanding of deviance by pointing out that deviants such as innovators and ritualists share a great deal with conforming people. The convicted felon may hold many of the same aspirations as people with no criminal background. The theory helps us to understand deviance as a socially created behavior rather than as the result of momentary pathological impulses.

Interactionist Perspective

The functionalist approach to deviance explains why rule violations continue to happen despite pressure to conform and obey. However, functionalists do not indicate how a given person comes to commit a deviant act or why on some occasions crimes do or do not occur. The emphasis on everyday behavior that is the focus of the interactionist perspective offers two explanations of crime—cultural transmission and routine activities theory.

Cultural Transmission In the course of studying graffiti writing by gangs in Los Angeles, sociologist Susan A. Phillips (1999) discovered that the writers learned from one another. In fact, Phillips was surprised by how stable their focus was over time. She also noted how other ethnic groups built on the models of the African American and Chicano gangs, superimposing Cambodian, Chinese, or Vietnamese symbols.

Humans *learn* how to behave in social situations, whether properly or improperly. There is no natural, innate manner in which people interact with one another. These simple ideas are

Under cover of darkness, drag racers await the start signal on a deserted Los Angeles street. Sutherland's concepts of differential association and cultural transmission would both apply to the practice of drag racing on city streets.

not disputed today, but such was not the case when sociologist Edwin Sutherland (1883–1950) first advanced the idea that an individual undergoes the same basic socialization process in learning conforming and deviant acts.

Sutherland's ideas have been the dominating force in criminology. He drew on the **cultural transmission** school, which emphasizes that one learns criminal behavior by interacting with others. Such learning includes not only the techniques of lawbreaking (for example, how to break into a car quickly and quietly) but also the motives, drives, and rationalizations of the criminal. The cultural transmission approach can also be used to explain the behavior of those who habitually abuse alcohol or drugs.

Sutherland maintained that, through interactions with a primary group and significant others, people acquire definitions of proper and improper behavior. He used the term **differential association** to describe the process through which exposure to attitudes *favorable* to criminal acts leads to the violation of rules. Research suggests that this view of differential association also applies to noncriminal deviant acts, such as smoking, truancy, and early sexual behavior (E. Jackson et al. 1986).

To what extent will a given person engage in activity that is regarded as proper or improper? For each individual, it will depend on the frequency, duration, and importance of two types of social interaction—those experiences that endorse deviant behavior and those that promote acceptance of social norms. People are more likely to engage in norm-defying behavior if they are part of a group or subculture that stresses deviant values, such as a street gang.

Sutherland offers the example of a boy who is sociable, outgoing, and athletic and who lives in an area with a high rate of delinquency. The youth is very likely to come into contact with peers who commit acts of vandalism, fail to attend school, and so forth, and may come to adopt such behavior. However, an introverted boy who lives in the same neighborhood may stay away from his peers and avoid delinquency. In another community, an outgoing and athletic boy may join a Little League baseball team or a scout troop because of his interactions with peers. Thus, Sutherland views improper behavior as the result of the types of groups to which one belongs and the kinds of friendships one has (Sutherland et al. 1992).

According to critics, however, the cultural transmission approach may explain the deviant behavior of juvenile delinquents or graffiti artists, but it fails to explain the conduct of the first-time impulsive shoplifter or the impoverished person who steals out of necessity. While it is not a precise statement of the process through which one becomes a criminal, differential association theory does direct our attention to the paramount role of social interaction in increasing a person's motivation to engage in deviant behavior (Morselli et al. 2006; Sutherland et al. 1992).

Social Disorganization Theory   The social relationships that exist in a community or neighborhood affect people's behavior. Philip Zimbardo (2007a:24–25), author of the mock prison experiment described in Chapter 5, once did an experiment that demonstrated the power of communal relationships. He abandoned a car in each of two different neighborhoods, leaving its hood up and removing its hub caps. In one neighborhood, people started to strip the car for parts before Zimbardo had finished setting up a remote video camera to record their behavior. In the other neighborhood, weeks passed without the car being touched, except for a pedestrian who stopped to close the hood during a rainstorm.

What accounts for the strikingly different outcomes of Zimbardo's experiment in the two communities? According to **social disorganization theory,** increases in crime and deviance can be attributed to the absence or breakdown of communal relationships and social institutions, such as the family, school, church, and local government. This theory was developed at the University of Chicago in the early 1900s to describe the apparent disorganization that occurred as cities expanded with rapid immigration and migration from rural areas. Using the latest survey techniques, Clifford Shaw and Henry McKay literally mapped the distribution of social problems in Chicago. They found high rates of social problems in neighborhoods where buildings had deteriorated and the population had declined. Interestingly, the patterns persisted over time, despite changes in the neighborhoods' ethnic and racial composition.

This theory is not without its critics. To some, social disorganization theory seems to "blame the victim," leaving larger societal forces, such as the lack of jobs or high-quality schools, unaccountable. Critics also argue that even troubled neighborhoods have viable, healthy organizations, which persist despite the problems that surround them.

More recently, social disorganization theorists have taken to emphasizing the effect of social networks on communal bonds. These researchers acknowledge that communities are not isolated islands. Residents' bonds may be enhanced or weakened by their ties to groups outside the immediate community (Jensen 2005; Sampson and Graves 1989; Shaw and McKay 1942).

Labeling Theory

The Saints and Roughnecks were two groups of high school males who were continually engaged in excessive drinking, reckless driving, truancy, petty theft, and vandalism. There the similarity ended. None of the Saints was ever arrested, but every Roughneck was frequently in trouble with police and townspeople. Why the disparity in their treatment? On the basis of observation research in their high school, sociologist William Chambliss (1973) concluded that social class played an important role in the varying fortunes of the two groups.

The Saints hid behind a facade of respectability. They came from "good families," were active in school organizations, planned on attending college, and received good grades. People generally viewed their delinquent acts as a few isolated cases of sowing wild oats. The Roughnecks had no such aura of respectability. They drove around town in beat-up cars, were generally unsuccessful in school, and aroused suspicion no matter what they did.

We can understand such discrepancies by using an approach to deviance known as **labeling theory.** Unlike Sutherland's work, labeling theory does not focus on why some individuals come to commit deviant acts. Instead, it attempts to explain why certain people (such as the Roughnecks) are *viewed* as deviants, delinquents, bad kids, losers, and criminals, while others whose behavior is similar (such as the Saints) are not seen in such harsh terms. Reflecting the contribution of interactionist theorists, labeling theory emphasizes how a person comes to be labeled as deviant or to accept that label. Sociologist Howard Becker (1963:9; 1964), who popularized this approach, summed it up with this statement: "Deviant behavior is behavior that people so label."

Labeling theory is also called the **societal-reaction approach,** reminding us that it is the *response* to an act, not the behavior itself, that determines deviance. For example, studies have shown that some school personnel and therapists expand educational programs designed for learning-disabled students to include those with behavioral problems. Consequently, a "troublemaker" can be improperly labeled as learning-disabled, and vice versa.

Labeling and Agents of Social Control

Traditionally, research on deviance has focused on people who violate social norms. In contrast, labeling theory focuses on police, probation officers, psychiatrists, judges, teachers, employers, school officials, and other regulators of social control. These agents, it is argued, play a significant role in creating the deviant identity by designating certain people (and not others) as deviant. An important aspect of labeling theory is the recognition that some individuals or groups have the power to *define* labels and apply them to others. This view ties into the conflict perspective's emphasis on the social significance of power.

In recent years the practice of *racial profiling,* in which people are identified as criminal suspects purely on the basis of their race, has come under public scrutiny. Studies confirm the public's suspicions that, in some jurisdictions, police officers are much more likely to stop African American males than White males for routine traffic violations, in the expectation of finding drugs or guns in their cars. Civil rights activists refer to these cases sarcastically as DWB (Driving While Black) violations.

Beginning in 2001, profiling took a new turn as people who appeared to be Arab or Muslim came under special scrutiny. (Racial profiling will be examined in more detail in Chapter 11).

The labeling approach does not fully explain why certain people accept a label and others manage to reject it. In fact, this perspective may exaggerate the ease with which societal judgments can alter our self-images. Labeling theorists do suggest, however, that the power one has relative to others is important in determining a person's ability to resist an undesirable label. Competing approaches (including that of Sutherland) fail to explain why some deviants continue to be viewed as conformists rather than as violators of rules. According to Howard Becker (1973), labeling theory was not conceived as the *sole* explanation for deviance; its proponents merely hoped to focus more attention on the undeniably important actions of those people who are officially in charge of defining deviance (N. Davis 1975; compare with F. Cullen and Cullen 1978).

The popularity of labeling theory is reflected in the emergence of a related perspective, called social constructionism. According to the **social constructionist perspective,** deviance is the product of the culture we live in. Social constructionists focus specifically on the decision-making process that creates the deviant identity. They point out that "child abductors," "deadbeat dads," "spree killers," and "date rapists" have always been with us, but at times have become *the* major social concern of policymakers because of intensive media coverage (Liska and Messner 1999; E. R. Wright et al. 2000).

How do certain behaviors come to be viewed as a problem? Cigarette smoking, which was once regarded as a polite, gentlemanly activity, is now considered a serious health hazard, not only to the smoker but to others who don't smoke. Recently, people have become concerned about the danger, especially to children, posed by *thirdhand smoke*—smoke-related chemicals that cling to clothes and linger in rooms, cars, even elevators (Winickoff et al. 2009).

Labeling and Sexual Deviance

Labels have been applied to many types of deviance. Certainly one of the most visible examples has to do with human sexuality and gender. What is deviant sexual behavior? What is criminal sexual behavior? Labeling theory focuses on the process through which these behaviors come to be considered deviant.

The definition of deviant sexual behavior has varied significantly both over time and from culture to culture. Until 1973, the American Psychiatric Association considered homosexuality a "sociopathic personality disorder," which in effect meant that homosexuals should seek therapy. Two years later, however, the association removed homosexuality from its list of mental illnesses. Today, the organization publicly proclaims that "being gay is just as healthy as being straight." In Goffman's term (see page 172), mental health professionals have removed the stigma from this form of sexual expression. As a result, in the United States and many other countries, consensual sex between same-sex adults is no longer a crime. Nevertheless, acknowledged homosexuals are still excluded from the ranks of the U.S. military (American Psychological Association 2008; International Gay and Lesbian Human Rights Commission 2009).

The true story of Brandon Teena, presented in the 1999 motion picture *Boys Don't Cry*, illustrates the complexity of human sexuality. The transgendered teen from Nebraska, played by Hilary Swank (right), was born female but preferred life as a male.

Despite the change in health professionals' attitudes, the stigma of homosexuality lingers. As a result, many people prefer the more positive terms *gay* and *lesbian*. Others, in defiance of the stigma, have proudly adopted the pejorative term *queer* in a deliberate reaction to the ridicule they have borne because of their sexual orientation. Still others maintain that constructing one's sexual orientation as either homosexual or heterosexual is too limiting. Indeed, such either/or language ignores those who are *bisexual,* or sexually attracted to both sexes.

Another group whose sexual orientation does not fit into the usual categories is *transgendered persons,* or those people whose current gender identity does not match their physical identity at birth. Some transgendered persons see themselves as both male and female. Others, called *transsexuals,* may take hormones or undergo surgery in an effort to draw physically closer to their chosen gender identity. Transgendered persons are sometimes confused with *transvestites,* or cross-dressers who wear the clothing of the opposite sex. Transvestites are typically men, either gay or heterosexual, who choose to wear women's clothing.

The use of all these terms even in a positive or nonjudgmental way is problematic, since they imply that human sexuality can be confined in neat, mutually exclusive categories. Moreover, the destigmatization of these labels tends to reflect the influence of the socially privileged—that is, the affluent—who have the resources to overcome the stigma. In contrast, the traditional Native American concept of the *two spirit,* a personality that blends the masculine and the feminine, has been largely ridiculed or ignored (Gilley 2006; Wentling et al. 2008).

What does constitute sexual deviance, then? The answer to this question seems to change with each generation. Today, U.S. laws allow married women to accuse their husbands of rape, when a generation ago such an offense was not recognized. Similarly, *pedophilia*—an adult having sex with a minor—is generally regarded with disgust today, even when it is consensual. Yet in many countries, fringe groups now speak positively of "intergenerational sex," arguing that "childhood" is not a biological given (Hendershott 2002).

Though this and some other aspects of sexual expression are still against the law, the meaning of the labels is beginning to blur. Similarly, child pornography is both illegal and abhorrent to most people, yet many of the fashion advertisements in mainstream magazines seem to verge on it. And while sex work and sex trafficking seem wrong to most of us, society tolerates and even regulates many aspects of those activities (Barton 2006).

www.mhhe.com/schaefer12e

use your sociological *imagination*

You are a teacher. What labels, freely used in educational circles, might you attach to your students?

Conflict Theory

Conflict theorists point out that people with power protect their own interests and define deviance to suit their own needs. Sociologist Richard Quinney (1974, 1979, 1980) is a leading exponent of the view that the criminal justice system serves the interests of the powerful. Crime, according to Quinney (1970), is a definition of conduct created by authorized agents of social control—such as legislators and law enforcement officers—in a politically organized society. He and other conflict theorists argue that law-making is often an attempt by the powerful to coerce others into their own morality (see also Spitzer 1975).

This theory helps to explain why our society has laws against gambling, drug use, and prostitution, many of which are violated on a massive scale. (We will examine these "victimless crimes" later in the chapter.) According to conflict theorists, criminal law does not represent a consistent application of societal values, but instead reflects competing values and interests. Thus, the U.S. criminal code outlaws marijuana because of its alleged harm to users, yet cigarettes and alcohol—both of which can be harmful to users—are sold legally almost everywhere.

In fact, conflict theorists contend that the entire criminal justice system in the United States treats suspects differently based on their racial, ethnic, or social-class background. In many cases, officials in the system use their own discretion to make biased decisions about whether to press charges or drop them, whether to set bail and how much, whether to offer parole or deny it. Researchers have found that this kind of **differential justice**—differences in the way social control is exercised over different groups—puts African Americans and Latinos at a disadvantage in the justice system, both as juveniles and as adults. On average, White offenders receive shorter sentences than comparable Latino and African American offenders, even when prior arrest records and the relative severity of the crime are taken into consideration (R. Brewer and Heitzeg 2008; Quinney 1974; Sandefur 2008; Schlesinger 2008).

Differential justice is not limited to the United States. In 2007, the people of India were alarmed to learn that a series of killings in the slums of New Delhi had never been investigated by police. Only after 17 bodies of recently murdered children were found in a sewer drain on the edge of a slum were police moved to act. For many onlookers, it was just the

In the 1930s, the Federal Bureau of Narcotics launched a campaign to portray marijuana as a dangerous drug rather than a pleasure-inducing substance. From a conflict perspective, those in power often use such tactics to coerce others into adopting a different point of view.

Feminist Perspective

Feminist criminologists such as Freda Adler and Meda Chesney-Lind have suggested that many of the existing approaches to deviance and crime were developed with only men in mind. For example, in the United States, for many years any husband who forced his wife to have sexual intercourse—without her consent and against her will—was not legally considered to have committed rape. The law defined rape as pertaining only to sexual relations between people who were not married to each other, reflecting the overwhelmingly male composition of state legislatures at the time.

It took repeated protests by feminist organizations to get changes in the criminal law defining rape. Beginning in 1993, husbands in all 50 states could be prosecuted under most circumstances for the rape of their wives. There remain alarming exceptions in no fewer than 30 states, however. For example, the husband is exempt when he does not need to use force because his wife is asleep, unconscious, or mentally or physically impaired. These interpretations rest on the notion that the marriage contract entitles a husband to sex (Bergen 2006).

When it comes to crime and to deviance in general, society tends to treat women in a stereotypical fashion. For example, consider how women who have many and frequent sexual partners are more likely to be viewed with scorn than men who are promiscuous. Cultural views and attitudes toward women influence how they are perceived and labeled. The feminist perspective also emphasizes that deviance, including crime, tends to flow from economic relationships. Traditionally, men have had greater earning power than their wives. As a result, wives may be reluctant to report acts of abuse to the authorities, and lose what may be their primary or even sole source of income. In the workplace, men have exercised greater power than women in pricing, accounting, and product control, giving them greater opportunity to engage in such crimes as embezzlement and fraud. But as women have taken more active and powerful roles both in the household and in business, these gender differences in deviance and crime have narrowed (F. Adler 1975; F. Adler et al. 2007; Chesney-Lind 1989).

In the future, feminist scholarship can be expected to grow dramatically. Particularly on topics such as white-collar crime, drinking behavior, drug abuse, and differential sentencing rates between the genders, as well as on the fundamental question of how to define deviance, feminist scholars will have much to say.

We have seen that over the past century, sociologists have taken many different approaches in studying deviance, arousing some controversy in the process. Table 8-2 on page 180 summarizes the various theoretical approaches to this topic.

Crime

Crime is a violation of criminal law for which some governmental authority applies formal penalties. It represents a deviation from formal social norms administered by the state. Laws divide crimes into various categories, depending on the severity of the offense, the age of the offender, the potential punishment, and the court that holds jurisdiction over the case.

Crime is on everyone's mind. Until recently, college campuses were viewed as "safe havens" from crime. But as Box 8-3 on page 181

latest example of the two-tier justice system found in India and many other countries throughout the world (Gentleman 2007a).

Such dramatic differences in social treatment may lead to heightened violence and crime. People who view themselves as the victims of unfair treatment may strike out, not against the powerful so much as against fellow victims. In studying crime in rural Mexico, Andrés Villarreal (2004) found that crime rates were high in the areas where land distribution was most inequitable. In areas where land was distributed more equally, communities appeared to suffer less violence and to enjoy greater social cohesion.

The perspective advanced by conflict and labeling theorists forms quite a contrast to the functionalist approach to deviance. Functionalists see standards of deviant behavior as merely reflecting cultural norms; conflict and labeling theorists point out that the most powerful groups in a society can shape laws and standards and determine who is (or is not) prosecuted as a criminal. These groups would be unlikely to apply the label "deviant" to the corporate executive whose decisions lead to large-scale environmental pollution. In the opinion of conflict theorists, agents of social control and other powerful groups can impose their own self-serving definitions of deviance on the general public.

TABLE 8-2 SOCIOLOGICAL PERSPECTIVES ON DEVIANCE summing**up**

Approach	Theoretical Perspective	Proponents	Emphasis
Anomie	Functionalist	Émile Durkheim Robert Merton	Adaptation to societal norms
Cultural transmission/ Differential association	Interactionist	Edwin Sutherland	Patterns learned through others
Social disorganization	Interactionist	Clifford Shaw Henry McKay	Communal relationships
Labeling/Social constructionist	Interactionist	Howard Becker	Societal response to acts
Conflict	Conflict	Richard Quinney	Dominance by authorized agents Discretionary justice
Feminist	Conflict/Feminist	Freda Adler Meda Chesney-Lind	Role of gender Women as victims and perpetrators

shows, at today's colleges and universities, crime goes well beyond cheating and senior class pranks.

The term **index crimes** refers to the eight types of crime that are tabulated each year by the Federal Bureau of Investigation (FBI). This category of criminal behavior generally consists of those serious offenses that people think of when they express concern about the nation's crime problem. Index crimes include murder, rape, robbery, and assault—all of which are violent crimes committed against people—as well as the property crimes of burglary, theft, motor vehicle theft, and arson.

Types of Crime

Rather than relying solely on legal categories, sociologists classify crimes in terms of how they are committed and how society views the offenses. In this section, we will examine five types of crime differentiated by sociologists: victimless crimes, professional crime, organized crime, white-collar and technology-based crime, and transnational crime.

Victimless Crimes When we think of crime, we tend to think of acts that endanger people's economic or personal well-being against their will (or without their direct knowledge). In contrast, sociologists use the term **victimless crime** to describe the willing exchange among adults of widely desired, but illegal, goods and services, such as prostitution (Schur 1965, 1985).

Some activists are working to decriminalize many of these illegal practices. Supporters of decriminalization are troubled by the attempt to legislate a moral code for adults. In their view, prostitution, drug abuse, gambling, and other victimless crimes are impossible to prevent. The already overburdened criminal justice system should instead devote its resources to "street crimes" and other offenses with obvious victims.

Despite widespread use of the term *victimless crime,* however, many people object to the notion that there is no victim other than the offender in such crimes. Excessive drinking, compulsive gambling, and illegal drug use contribute to an enormous amount of personal and property damage. A person

with a drinking problem can become abusive to a spouse or children; a compulsive gambler or drug user may steal to pursue his or her obsession. And feminist sociologists contend that prostitution, as well as the more disturbing aspects of pornography, reinforce the misconception that women are "toys" who can be treated as objects rather than people. According to critics of decriminalization, society must not give tacit approval to conduct that has such harmful consequences (Melissa Farley and Malarek 2008).

The controversy over decriminalization reminds us of the important insights of labeling and conflict theorists presented earlier. Underlying this debate are two questions: Who has the power to define gambling, prostitution, and public drunkenness as "crimes"? and Who has the power to label such behaviors as "victimless"? The answer is generally the state legislatures and, in some cases, the police and the courts.

Again, we can see that criminal law is not simply a universal standard of behavior agreed on by all members of society. Rather, it reflects a struggle among competing individuals and groups to gain government support for their moral and social values. For example, organizations such as Mothers Against Drunk Driving (MADD) and Students Against Drunk Driving (SADD) have been successful in recent years in modifying public attitudes toward drunkenness. Rather than being viewed as a victimless crime, drunkenness is increasingly associated with the potential dangers of driving while under the influence of alcohol. As a result, the mass media are giving greater (and more critical) attention to people found guilty of drunk driving, and many states have instituted severe fines and jail terms for a wide variety of alcohol-related offenses.

Professional Crime Although the adage "Crime doesn't pay" is familiar, many people do make a career of illegal activities. A **professional criminal** (or *career criminal*) is a person who pursues crime as a day-to-day occupation, developing skilled techniques and enjoying a certain degree of status among other criminals. Some professional criminals specialize in burglary,

SOCIOLOGY ON CAMPUS

8-3 Campus Crime

According to a national survey released in 2008, 72 percent of college students consider campus safety "very important" in selecting a college. A generation earlier, would campus crime have been uppermost in the minds of prospective students?

Research on crime in college has focused on interpersonal violence ("date rape," as it is sometimes trivialized) and the way in which colleges handle such incidents. In 2007, two very different events brought campus crime to national attention. First, there was the April 16, 2007, rampage at Virginia Tech. In its aftermath, observers questioned whether campus officials should have notified students and employees of the first shootings, at a dormitory, during the two hours that passed before the gunman's second attack in a classroom building. The federal law known as the Clery Act, passed in 1990, requires timely warnings of campus crime, but how they should be delivered and how specific they should be (for example, whether the names of alleged assailants should be revealed) is unclear.

The second incident, the death of a girl in her dormitory room at Eastern Michigan University, led to the resignation of the university's president. For two months, officials had assured her parents that she died a natural death. Later, her family learned that she had been raped and murdered, and that her body had been missing for three days.

The federal law known as the Clery Act, passed in 1990, requires timely warnings of campus crime, but how they should be delivered and how specific they should be is unclear.

These and other less publicized incidents have prompted colleges to become more forthcoming about campus crime and to provide better security. However, the growing trend toward living (and partying) off campus poses a challenge to their efforts. Student safety at internship sites and study-abroad programs is even more difficult to ensure.

Making judgments about campus crime based on the reports mandated by the Clery Act is difficult. Because these documents include only reported incidents, they may or may not be accurate. The latest data from the University of California, which has over 20,000 students, for example, show that the total number of forcible sex offenses per year ranges from 2 to more than 62.

LET'S DISCUSS

1. Is crime a problem on your campus? If so, what kinds of crime? What have college officials done to discourage it?
2. Choose two theories of crime discussed in this chapter and apply them to crimes that have occurred on your campus. Which theory seems to fit better?

Sources: Department of Justice 2008a; Interface Group Report (Virginia Tech) 2007; Lipka 2009; National Institute of Justice 2005; *New York Times* 2007, 2008; Security on Campus 2008.

---

safecracking, hijacking of cargo, pickpocketing, and shoplifting. Such people have acquired skills that reduce the likelihood of arrest, conviction, and imprisonment. As a result, they may have long careers in their chosen "professions."

Edwin Sutherland (1937) offered pioneering insights into the behavior of professional criminals by publishing an annotated account written by a professional thief. Unlike the person who engages in crime only once or twice, professional thieves make a business of stealing. They devote their entire working time to planning and executing crimes, and sometimes travel across the nation to pursue their "professional duties." Like people in regular occupations, professional thieves consult with their colleagues concerning the demands of work, becoming part of a subculture of similarly occupied individuals. They exchange information on places to burglarize, on outlets for unloading stolen goods, and on ways of securing bail bonds if arrested.

Organized Crime A 1976 government report devotes three pages to defining the term *organized crime*. For our purposes, we will consider **organized crime** to be the work of a group that regulates relations among criminal enterprises involved in illegal activities, including prostitution, gambling, and the smuggling and sale of illegal drugs. Organized crime dominates the world of illegal business just as large corporations dominate the conventional business world. It allocates territory, sets prices for goods and services, and acts as an arbitrator in internal disputes. A secret, conspiratorial activity, it generally evades law enforcement. It takes over legitimate businesses, gains influence over labor unions, corrupts public officials, intimidates witnesses in criminal trials, and even "taxes" merchants in exchange for "protection" (National Advisory Commission on Criminal Justice 1976).

Organized crime serves as a means of upward mobility for groups of people struggling to escape poverty. Sociologist Daniel Bell (1953) used the term *ethnic succession* to describe the sequential passage of leadership from Irish Americans in the early part of the 20th century to Jewish Americans in the 1920s and then to Italian Americans in the early 1930s. Ethnic succession has become more complex, reflecting the diversity of the nation's latest immigrants. Colombian, Mexican, Russian, Chinese, Pakistani, and Nigerian immigrants are among those who have begun to play a significant role in organized crime activities (Chin 1996; Kleinknecht 1996).

There has always been a global element in organized crime. But law enforcement officials and policymakers now acknowledge the emergence of a new form of organized crime that takes advantage of advances in electronic communications. *Transnational* organized crime includes drug and arms smuggling, money laundering, and trafficking in illegal immigrants and stolen goods; see the discussion on pages 182–183 (Lumpe 2003; Office of Justice Programs 1999).

Our society's growing dependence on electronic transactions has greatly increased the white-collar crime of identity theft.

White-Collar and Technology-Based Crime Income tax evasion, stock manipulation, consumer fraud, bribery and extraction of kickbacks, embezzlement, and misrepresentation in advertising—these are all examples of **white-collar crime,** illegal acts committed in the course of business activities, often by affluent, "respectable" people. Edwin Sutherland (1949, 1983) likened these crimes to organized crime because they are often perpetrated through occupational roles.

A new type of white-collar crime has emerged in recent decades: computer crime. The use of high technology allows criminals to carry out embezzlement or electronic fraud, often leaving few traces, or to gain access to a company's inventory without leaving home. According to a study by the FBI and the National White Collar Crime Center, over 270,000 Internet crimes are reported every year, ranging from scams on online auction sites to identity theft (Internet Crime Complaint Center 2009).

When Charles Horton Cooley spoke of the self and Erving Goffman of impression management, surely neither scholar could have envisioned the insidious crime of identity theft. Each year 3.7 percent of all adults find that their personal information has been misused for criminal purposes. Unfortunately, with our society's growing reliance on electronic financial transactions, assuming someone else's identity has become increasingly easy (Baum 2006; Monahan 2007).

Identity theft does not necessarily require technology. A criminal can obtain someone's personal information by pickpocketing or by intercepting mail. However, the widespread exchange of information online has allowed criminals to access large amounts of personal information. Public awareness of the potential harm from identity theft took a giant leap in the

aftermath of September 11, 2001, when investigations revealed that several hijackers had used fraudulent IDs to open bank accounts, rent apartments, and board planes. A law enacted in 2004 makes identity theft punishable by a mandatory prison sentence if it is linked to other crimes. Still, unauthorized disclosures of information, even if accidental, persist (Brubaker 2008).

Sutherland (1940) coined the term *white-collar crime* in 1939 to refer to acts by individuals, but the term has been broadened more recently to include offenses by businesses and corporations as well. *Corporate crime,* or any act by a corporation that is punishable by the government, takes many forms and includes individuals, organizations, and institutions among its victims. Corporations may engage in anticompetitive behavior, environmental pollution, medical fraud, tax fraud, stock fraud and manipulation, accounting fraud, the production of unsafe goods, bribery and corruption, and health and safety violations (J. Coleman 2006).

For many years, corporate wrongdoers got off lightly in court by documenting their long history of charitable contributions and agreeing to help law enforcement officials find other white-collar criminals. Unfortunately, that is still the case. The highly visible jailing of multimedia personality Martha Stewart in 2004, as well as recent stories of "Wall Street greed," may lead the casual observer to think that government is cracking down on white-collar crime. However, an independent analysis found that the number of white-collar crimes prosecuted in 2008 was lower than the number prosecuted in 2000 (Transactional Records Access Clearinghouse 2008).

Even when a person is convicted of corporate crime, the verdict generally does not harm his or her reputation and career aspirations nearly so much as conviction for street crime would. Apparently, the label "white-collar criminal" does not carry the stigma of the label "felon convicted of a violent crime." Conflict theorists don't find such differential treatment surprising. They argue that the criminal justice system largely disregards the crimes of the affluent, focusing on crimes committed by the poor. Generally, if an offender holds a position of status and influence, his or her crime is treated as less serious than others' crimes, and the sanction is much more lenient.

Transnational Crime More and more, scholars and police officials are turning their attention to **transnational crime,** or crime that occurs across multiple national borders. In the past, international crime was often limited to the clandestine shipment of goods across the border between two countries. But increasingly, crime is no more restricted by such borders than is legal commerce. Rather than concentrating on specific countries, international crime now spans the globe.

TABLE 8-3 TYPES OF TRANSNATIONAL CRIME

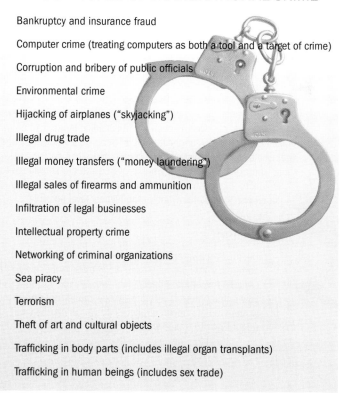

Bankruptcy and insurance fraud

Computer crime (treating computers as both a tool and a target of crime)

Corruption and bribery of public officials

Environmental crime

Hijacking of airplanes ("skyjacking")

Illegal drug trade

Illegal money transfers ("money laundering")

Illegal sales of firearms and ammunition

Infiltration of legal businesses

Intellectual property crime

Networking of criminal organizations

Sea piracy

Terrorism

Theft of art and cultural objects

Trafficking in body parts (includes illegal organ transplants)

Trafficking in human beings (includes sex trade)

Source: Compiled and updated by the author based on Mueller 2001 and United Nations Office on Drugs and Crime 2005.

Historically, probably the most dreaded example of transnational crime has been slavery. At first, governments did not regard slavery as a crime, but merely regulated it as they would the trade in goods. In the 20th century, transnational crime grew to embrace trafficking in endangered species, drugs, and stolen art and antiquities.

Transnational crime is not exclusive of some of the other types of crime we have discussed. For example, organized criminal networks are increasingly global. Technology definitely facilitates their illegal activities, such as trafficking in child pornography. Beginning in the 1990s, the United Nations began to categorize transnational crimes; Table 8-3 lists some of the more common types. In the Social Policy section of Chapter 10 we will consider the crime of trafficking in human beings in the context of universal human rights.

Bilateral cooperation in the pursuit of border criminals such as smugglers has been common for many years. The first global effort to control international crime was the International Criminal Police Organization (Interpol), a cooperative network of European police forces founded to stem the movement of political revolutionaries across borders. While such efforts to fight transnational crime may seem lofty—an activity with which any government should cooperate—they are complicated by sensitive legal and security issues. Most nations that have signed protocols issued by the United Nations, including the United States, have expressed concern over potential encroachments on their national judicial systems, as well as concern over their national security. Thus, they have been reluctant to share certain types of intelligence data. The terrorist attacks of September 11, 2001,

increased both the interest in combating transnational crime and sensitivity to the risks of sharing intelligence data (Deflem 2005; Felson and Kalaitzidis 2005).

www.mhhe.com/schaefer12e

---

use your sociological *imagination*

As a newspaper editor, how might you treat stories on corporate or white-collar crime differently from those on violent crime?

Crime Statistics

Crime statistics are not as accurate as social scientists would like, especially since they deal with an issue of grave concern to the people of the United States. Unfortunately, they are frequently cited as if they were completely reliable. Such data do serve as an indicator of police activity, as well as an approximate indication of the level of certain crimes. Yet it would be a mistake to interpret these data as an exact representation of the incidence of crime.

Understanding Crime Statistics Because reported crime is very high in the United States, the public regards crime as a major social problem. However, there has been a significant decline in violent crime nationwide following many years of increases. A number of explanations have been offered, including these:

- Community-oriented policing and crime prevention programs
- New gun control laws
- A massive increase in the prison population, which at least prevents inmates from committing crimes outside prison

It remains to be seen whether this pattern will continue, but even with current declines, reported crimes remain well above those of other nations. Yet reported rates in the United States are still the lowest in about 40 years. Feminist scholars draw our attention to one significant variation: the proportion of major crimes committed by women has increased. In a recent 10-year period (1998–2007), female arrests for major reported crimes increased 7 percent, while comparable male arrests declined 6 percent (Department of Justice 2008a:Table 33; Sutch and Carter 2006).

Typically, the crime data used in the United States are based on the index crimes described earlier. The crime index, published annually by the FBI as part of the *Uniform Crime Reports,* includes statistics on murder, rape, robbery, assault, burglary, larceny-theft, motor vehicle theft, and arson (Table 8-4 on page 184). Obviously, many serious offenses, such as white-collar crimes, are not included in this index (although they are recorded elsewhere). In addition, the crime index is disproportionately devoted to property crimes, whereas most citizens are more worried about violent crimes. Thus, a significant decrease in the number of rapes and robberies could be overshadowed by a slightly larger increase in the number of automobiles stolen, leading to the mistaken impression that *personal* safety is more at risk than before.

TAKING SOCIOLOGY TO WORK

Stephanie Vezzani, **Special Agent, U.S. Secret Service**

Stephanie Vezzani wasn't sure what she wanted to major in when she entered the University of Akron, but she did know what she wanted to do with her life: she wanted a career as a crime fighter. Vezzani began as an accounting major, but switched to sociology when she discovered the department offered a special concentration in law enforcement.

Vezzani is now an agent with the U.S. Secret Service, whose twofold mission is to protect high-ranking officials and their families and to investigate financial crimes, including counterfeiting, identity theft, and computer-based attacks on the financial, banking, and telecommunications industries. She has tackled both aspects of the job. For her, a typical week would include working on a criminal investigation in a field office or traveling around the country with a government official in need of protection.

Vezzani finds that travel is one of the most exciting aspects of her job. Over the past six years she has visited Russia, Turkey, Jordan, Vietnam, and South Korea. She also attended the 2002 Winter Olympics in Salt Lake City, where she provided protection for the athletes living in the Olympic Village. Vezzani relishes meeting people from different cultures, and, of course, she loves the sights she gets to see. "The architecture in St. Petersburg, Russia, was amazing," she says.

Vezzani uses her training in sociology on a daily basis, as she interviews suspects, witnesses, and victims of crime. "It is critical in the field of law enforcement to have an understanding of people's relationships and the beliefs and value systems that contribute to their decision making," she explains. "Sociology has provided me the knowledge to speak to and listen to people with different values and cultures in order to complete my job at the highest level possible."

LET'S DISCUSS

1. Besides an awareness of different beliefs, values, and cultures, what else might sociology offer to those who serve in law enforcement?
2. Law enforcement is a relatively new career option for women. What special strengths do you think a woman might bring to police work?

TABLE 8-4 NATIONAL CRIME RATES AND PERCENTAGE CHANGE

Crime Index Offenses in 2006	Number Reported	Rate per 100,000 Inhabitants	Percentage Change in Rate	
			Since 2003	Since 1998
Violent crime				
Murder	16,929	6	−2	−11
Forcible rape	90,427	30	−1	−13
Robbery	445,125	148	−7	−11
Aggravated assault	855,856	284	+4	−18
Total	1,408,337	367	−18	−20
Property crime				
Burglary	2,179,140	773	−16	−16
Larceny-theft	6,568,572	2,178	−20	−20
Motor vehicle theft	1,095,769	363	−21	−21
Total	9,843,481	3,264	−9	−20

Notes: Arson was designated an index offense beginning in 1979; data on arson were still incomplete as of 2007. Because of rounding, the offenses may not add to totals.
Source: Department of Justice 2008a:Tables 1, 1a.

The most serious limitation of official crime statistics is that they include only those crimes actually *reported* to law enforcement agencies. Because members of racial and ethnic minority groups often distrust law enforcement agencies, they may not contact the police. Feminist sociologists and others have noted that many women do not report rape or spousal abuse out of fear they will be blamed for the crime.

Partly because of these deficiencies in official statistics, the National Crime Victimization Survey was initiated in 1972. The Bureau of Justice Statistics, in compiling this annual report, seeks information from law enforcement agencies, but also interviews members of over 76,000 households and asks if they were victims of a specific set of crimes during the preceding year. In general, those who administer **victimization surveys** question ordinary people, not police officers, to determine whether they have been victims of crime.

Unfortunately, like other crime data, victimization surveys have particular limitations. They require that victims understand what has happened to them and are willing to disclose such information to interviewers. Fraud, income tax evasion, and blackmail are examples of crimes that are unlikely to be reported in victimization studies. Nevertheless, 91 percent of all households have been willing to cooperate with investigators for the National Crime Victimization Survey. As shown in Figure 8-3, data from these surveys reveal a fluctuating crime rate, with significant declines in both the 1980s and 1990s.

International Crime Rates If developing reliable crime data is difficult in the United States, making useful cross-national comparisons is even more difficult. Nevertheless, with some care, we can offer preliminary conclusions about how crime rates differ around the world.

During the 1980s and 1990s, violent crimes were much more common in the United States than in Western Europe. Murders, rapes, and robberies were reported to the police at much higher rates in the United States. Yet the incidence of certain other types of crime appears to be higher elsewhere. For example, England, Italy, Australia, and New Zealand all have higher rates of car theft than the United States. Developing nations have significant rates of reported homicide due to civil unrest and political conflict among civilians (International Crime Victim Survey 2004; World Bank 2003).

Why are rates of violent crime so much higher in the United States than in Western Europe? Sociologist Elliot Currie (1985, 1998) has suggested that our society places greater emphasis on individual economic achievement than other societies. At the same time, many observers have noted that the culture of the United States has long tolerated, if not condoned, many forms of violence. Coupled with sharp disparities between poor and affluent citizens, significant unemployment, and substantial alcohol and drug abuse, these factors combine to produce a climate conducive to crime.

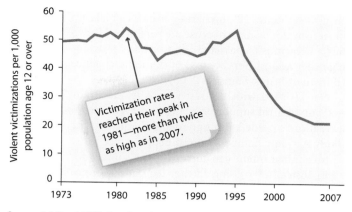

FIGURE **8-3** VICTIMIZATION RATES, 1973–2007

Victimization rates reached their peak in 1981—more than twice as high as in 2007.

Sources: M. Rand 2008; Rennison 2002.

However, disturbing increases in violent crime are evident in other Western societies. For example, certain types of crime have skyrocketed in Russia since the overthrow of Communist Party rule (with its strict controls on guns and criminals) in 1991. In 1998 there were fewer than 260 homicides in Moscow; now there are more than 1,000 homicides a year. Organized crime has filled the power vacuum in Moscow: one result is that gangland shoot-outs and premeditated "contract hits" have become more common. Some prominent reformist politicians have been targeted as well. Russia incarcerates an extremely high proportion of its citizens—almost as high as the United States. On a typical day, the United States imprisons 756 of every 100,000 adults, compared to 626 in Russia, 207 in Mexico, and 116 in Canada (International Centre for Prison Studies 2009; Winslow and Zhang 2008a, 2008b).

In the United States, high rates of violent crime, especially in the cities, have long fueled calls for stricter controls on the purchase and use of firearms. We will take a close look at the contentious issue of gun control in the Social Policy section that follows.

socialpolicy and Social Control

Gun Control

Two high school students present themselves at Kmart's national headquarters. They are not looking for jobs. Survivors of the mass murders at Columbine High School in 1999, they still have bullets lodged in their bodies—bullets their attackers bought at Kmart. In a symbolic protest, the two young people ask Kmart's representative if they may return the bullets.

This scene was shown in the 2004 Academy Award–winning documentary *Bowling for Columbine*. Producer-director Michael Moore was amazed when the day after he filmed the encounter, Kmart announced that the store would stop selling handgun ammunition.

The Issue

While reported crime has declined in recent years, the role of firearms in crime has remained fairly consistent. Over the past five years, two-thirds of all murders were committed with firearms. Although handgun owners frequently insist that they need to own firearms to protect themselves and their loved ones from violent crime, over the years, high-profile assassinations of public figures such as President John F. Kennedy, Senator Robert Kennedy, Dr. Martin Luther King Jr., and Beatle John Lennon have forced legislators to consider stricter gun control measures (Department of Justice 2008a).

Gun control legislation began with the Brady Handgun Violence Prevention Act, named after White House press secretary Jim Brady, who was seriously wounded in the 1981 assassination attempt against President Ronald Reagan. John Hinckley, the would-be assassin, had given false information about himself at the pawnshop where he bought the gun he used to shoot Reagan and Brady. The Brady Act, which took effect in 1994, mandates that firearms dealers run criminal history background checks on people who wish to purchase handguns. About 2 percent of all purchases are denied as a result of the checks—around 320 purchases per day. Denials are most commonly made because the person seeking to buy a firearm is a convicted felon or has a restraining order against him because of domestic violence (Bureau of Justice Statistics 2008).

Not satisfied with the restrictions in the Brady Act, gun control supporters claim that even stricter legislation is needed. But opponents charge that the Brady Act only hampers honest people, since those with criminal intent can turn to other sources for guns. Instead of passing further legislation, opponents suggest strengthening and enforcing existing criminal penalties for the illegal use of guns.

In 2008, in the landmark case *District of Columbia v. Heller,* the Supreme Court struck down a near-total ban on handguns in the nation's capitol by a 5–4 ruling. The verdict was lauded by those who favor gun rights but denounced by advocates of gun control. Gun rights groups are now testing the constitutionality of other restrictions on gun ownership. Gun control advocates are working to craft legislation that will be acceptable to the justices (Winkler 2009).

This dramatic pro–gun control cartoon may appear to be directed at gun rights advocates in the United States, but it was published in South Africa during a similar debate there.

The Setting

Guns and ammunition are big business in the United States, where the Second Amendment to the Constitution guarantees the "right of the people to keep and bear arms." Currently, about 42 percent of U.S. households have some type of firearm on the premises. Informal gun clubs of both a primary- and secondary-group nature flourish across the country. On a national basis, powerful formal organizations promote gun ownership. Clearly, owning a gun is not a deviant act in our society (Gallup 2009a).

Since the Brady Act went into effect, support for stricter gun control measures has declined. In 2009, 45 percent of people supported protecting gun owners' rights compared to only 34 percent in 1993. By comparison, 49 percent favored controlling gun ownership compared to 57 percent back in 1993. The National Rifle Association (NRA) has been able to use its impressive power to block or dilute gun control efforts (Pew Research Center 2009).

Sociological Insights

Conflict theorists contend that powerful groups like the NRA can dominate the legislative process because of their ability to mobilize resources in opposition to the will of the majority. Founded in 1871, the NRA has nearly 4 million members; state rifle associations, with 4 to 5 million members, support many of the NRA's goals. In contrast, Handgun Control, a key organization in the gun control battle, has only 400,000 members. Compared to the NRA's formidable war chest, Handgun Control's resources are limited.

Interactionists note that both opponents and proponents of gun control use symbols to their advantage. Opponents typically point to the Constitution and the tradition of gun ownership. Proponents point to spectacular episodes of violence, such as spree shootings on college campuses, as proof of the need to restrict firearms sales. Yet gun rights supporters see the same events as proof that students need guns to defend themselves (Lio et al. 2008).

Interactionists have also studied how gun rights organizations like the National Rifle Association present their argument to their own members. Among sympathizers, they frame the issue not so much as one of safety or crime, but of civil rights. They see the Constitution as the basis for their campaign to facilitate gun ownership (Gregory 2007).

Policy Implications

Advocates for stricter gun control laws have identified a series of measures they would like to see enacted:

- Strengthen the tools law enforcement officers need to crack down on corrupt gun dealers and curb illegal gun trafficking.
- Extend Brady background checks to all gun sales.
- Stop large-volume gun sales that supply gun traffickers.

Because towns, states, and the federal government all have the authority to regulate the possession and sale of firearms, advocates have attempted to pass these measures at all levels of government (Brady Campaign 2009).

The proposed legal restrictions on gun ownership have met strong opposition from both the NRA and firearms manufacturers. The NRA has been particularly successful in defeating political candidates who favor stricter gun control, and in backing those who seek to weaken such restrictions. Except in a handful of states, office seekers rarely risk taking an antigun position. Alarmed by the NRA's rhetoric, many voters fear that gun control will restrict their ability to protect themselves, independent of law enforcement. Indeed, in light of growing concern over terrorism, the handgun debate has turned to legislation allowing airline pilots to carry guns in the cockpit.

Recently, public health advocates have weighed in on the issue, noting the 30,000 people in the United States who die every year through gun violence, whether by suicide, homicide, or accidental discharge. This group advocates making guns safer—for example, by adding an indicator that the gun is loaded and/or a latch that prevents a magazine from being removed with a bullet still in the firing chamber. A more sophisticated approach to increasing safety would be to "personalize" firearms by requiring the owner/user to activate a code before the gun can be used (G. Brown 2008a, 2008b).

The unlawful use of guns is an issue that is not limited to the United States; it is a global issue. In the 1990s the International Committee of the Red Cross expressed concern over the global glut of firearms—one gun for every 10 people on earth. Worldwide, six nations (Britain, France, Germany, Netherlands, Russia, and the United States) account for about 85 percent of arms transfers. South Africa has moved to clamp down on guns, however. In 2005 the government launched a campaign to eliminate "surplus" weapons and toughened the procedure for acquiring new firearms (Kirsten 2008; Lumpe 2003; Springwood 2007).

Let's Discuss

1. Do you see guns more as weapons that could jeopardize your safety or as protection against those who would harm you? What formal or informal sources of social control may have influenced you to form this attitude?

2. What are the statistics on crimes committed with a firearm in your state? How many people die or are injured by guns every year? How strict are restrictions on gun ownership?

3. Should weapons manufacturers be allowed to sell guns to anyone in the world who wants them? Why or why not?

getting**involved**

To get involved in the debate over gun control, visit this book's Online Learning Center, which offers links to relevant Web sites.

www.mhhe.com/schaefer12e

MASTERING THIS CHAPTER

Summary

Conformity and **deviance** are two ways in which people respond to real or imagined pressure from others. In this chapter, we examine the relationship between conformity, deviance, and mechanisms of **social control**.

1. A society uses **social control** to encourage the acceptance of basic norms.

2. Stanley Milgram defined **conformity** as going along with one's peers; **obedience** is defined as compliance with higher authorities in a hierarchical structure.

3. Some norms are so important to a society, they are formalized into **laws**. Socialization is a primary source of conforming and obedient behavior, including obedience to law.

4. Deviant behavior violates social norms. Some forms of **deviance** carry a negative social **stigma**, while other forms are more or less accepted.

5. From a functionalist point of view, deviance and its consequences help to define the limits of proper behavior.

6. Some interactionists maintain that people learn criminal behavior by interacting with others (**cultural transmission**). To them, deviance results from exposure to attitudes that are favorable to criminal acts (**differential association**).

7. Other interactionists attribute increases in crime and deviance to the absence or breakdown of communal relationships and social institutions, such as the family, school, church, and local government (**social disorganization theory**).

8. An important aspect of **labeling theory** is the recognition that some people are viewed as deviant, while others who engage in the same behavior are not.

9. From the conflict perspective, laws and punishments are a reflection of the interests of the powerful.

10. The feminist perspective emphasizes that cultural attitudes and differential economic relationships help to explain gender differences in deviance and crime.

11. **Crime** represents a deviation from formal social norms administered by the state.

12. Sociologists differentiate among **victimless crimes** (such as drug use and prostitution), *professional crime*, **organized crime, white-collar crime,** and **transnational crime.**

13. Crime statistics are among the least reliable social data, partly because so many crimes are not reported to law enforcement agencies. Rates of violent crime are higher in the United States than in other Western societies, although they have been dropping.

14. Illegal gun trafficking has become a major problem, not just in the United States, but around the world. Yet gun control is extremely controversial, opposed by powerful interest groups whose members see it as an abridgment of their constitutional right to bear arms.

Critical Thinking Questions

1. What mechanisms of formal and informal social control are evident in your college classes and in day-to-day life and social interactions at your school?

2. What approach to deviance do you find most persuasive: that of functionalists, conflict theorists, feminists, interactionists, or labeling theorists? Why do you consider that approach more convincing than the others? What are the main weaknesses of each approach?

3. Rates of violent crime are higher in the United States than they are in Western Europe, Canada, Australia, or New Zealand. Draw on as many of the theories discussed in this chapter as possible to explain why the United States is such a comparatively violent society.

Key Terms

Anomie Durkheim's term for the loss of direction felt in a society when social control of individual behavior has become ineffective. (page 174)

Anomie theory of deviance Robert Merton's theory of deviance as an adaptation of socially prescribed goals or of the means governing their attainment, or both. (174)

Conformity Going along with peers—individuals of our own status who have no special right to direct our behavior. (166)

Control theory A view of conformity and deviance that suggests that our connection to members of society leads us to systematically conform to society's norms. (170)

Crime A violation of criminal law for which some governmental authority applies formal penalties. (179)

Cultural transmission A school of criminology that argues that criminal behavior is learned through social interactions. (176)

Deviance Behavior that violates the standards of conduct or expectations of a group or society. (170)

Differential association A theory of deviance that holds that violation of rules results from exposure to attitudes favorable to criminal acts. (176)

Differential justice Differences in the way social control is exercised over different groups. (178)

Formal social control Social control that is carried out by authorized agents, such as police officers, judges, school administrators, and employers. (168)

Index crimes The eight types of crime reported annually by the FBI in the *Uniform Crime Reports*: murder, rape, robbery, assault, burglary, theft, motor vehicle theft, and arson. (180)

Informal social control Social control that is carried out casually by ordinary people through such means as laughter, smiles, and ridicule. (168)

Labeling theory An approach to deviance that attempts to explain why certain people are viewed as deviants while others engaged in the same behavior are not. (177)

Law Governmental social control. (170)

Obedience Compliance with higher authorities in a hierarchical structure. (166)

Organized crime The work of a group that regulates relations among criminal enterprises involved in illegal activities, including prostitution, gambling, and the smuggling and sale of illegal drugs. (181)

Professional criminal A person who pursues crime as a day-to-day occupation, developing skilled techniques and enjoying a certain degree of status among other criminals. (180)

Sanction A penalty or reward for conduct concerning a social norm. (165)

Social constructionist perspective An approach to deviance that emphasizes the role of culture in the creation of the deviant identity. (177)

Social control The techniques and strategies for preventing deviant human behavior in any society. (165)

Social disorganization theory The theory that crime and deviance are caused by the absence or breakdown of communal relationships and social institutions. (176)

Societal-reaction approach Another name for *labeling theory*. (177)

Stigma A label used to devalue members of certain social groups. (172)

Transnational crime Crime that occurs across multiple national borders. (182)

Victimization survey A questionnaire or interview given to a sample of the population to determine whether people have been victims of crime. (184)

Victimless crime A term used by sociologists to describe the willing exchange among adults of widely desired, but illegal, goods and services. (180)

White-collar crime Illegal acts committed by affluent, "respectable" individuals in the course of business activities. (182)

Self-Quiz

Read each question carefully and then select the best answer.

1. Society brings about acceptance of basic norms through techniques and strategies for preventing deviant human behavior. This process is termed
   a. stigmatization.
   b. labeling.
   c. law.
   d. social control.

2. Which sociological perspective argues that people must respect social norms if any group or society is to survive?
   a. the conflict perspective
   b. the interactionist perspective
   c. the functionalist perspective
   d. the feminist perspective

3. Stanley Milgram used the word *conformity* to mean
   a. going along with peers.
   b. compliance with higher authorities in a hierarchical structure.
   c. techniques and strategies for preventing deviant human behavior in any society.
   d. penalties and rewards for conduct concerning a social norm.

4. Which sociological theory suggests that our connection to members of society leads us to conform systematically to society's norms?
   a. feminist theory
   b. control theory
   c. interactionist theory
   d. functionalist theory

5. Which of the following statements is true of deviance?
   a. Deviance is always criminal behavior.
   b. Deviance is behavior that violates the standards of conduct or expectations of a group or society.

   c. Deviance is perverse behavior.
   d. Deviance is inappropriate behavior that cuts across all cultures and social orders.

6. Which sociologist illustrated the boundary-maintenance function of deviance in his study of Puritans in 17th-century New England?
   a. Kai Erikson
   b. Émile Durkheim
   c. Robert Merton
   d. Edwin Sutherland

7. Which of the following is *not* one of the basic forms of adaptation specified in Robert Merton's anomie theory of deviance?
   a. conformity
   b. innovation
   c. ritualism
   d. hostility

8. Which sociologist first advanced the idea that an individual undergoes the same basic socialization process whether learning conforming or deviant acts?
   a. Robert Merton
   b. Edwin Sutherland
   c. Travis Hirschi
   d. William Chambliss

9. Which of the following theories contends that criminal victimization increases when communal relationships and social institutions break down?
   a. labeling theory
   b. conflict theory
   c. social disorganization theory
   d. differential association theory

10. Which of the following conducted observation research on two groups of high school males (the Saints and the Roughnecks) and concluded that social class played an important role in the varying fortunes of the two groups?

    a. Richard Quinney
    b. Edwin Sutherland
    c. Émile Durkheim
    d. William Chambliss

11. If we fail to respect and obey social norms, we may face punishment through informal or formal _____ .

12. Police officers, judges, administrators, employers, military officers, and managers of movie theaters are all instruments of _____ social control.

13. Some norms are considered so important by a society that they are formalized into _____ controlling people's behavior.

14. It is important to underscore the fact that _____ is the primary source of conformity and obedience, including obedience to law.

15. _____ is a state of normlessness that typically occurs during a period of profound social change and disorder, such as a time of economic collapse.

16. Labeling theory is also called the _____-_____ approach.

17. _____ theorists view standards of deviant behavior as merely reflecting cultural norms, whereas _____ and _____ theorists point out that the most powerful groups in a society can shape laws and standards and determine who is (or is not) prosecuted as a criminal.

18. Organizations such as Mothers Against Drunk Driving (MADD) and Students Against Drunk Driving (SADD) have had success in recent years in shifting public attitudes about drunkenness, so that it is no longer viewed as a _____ crime.

19. Daniel Bell used the term _____ _____ to describe the process during which leadership of organized crime was transferred from Irish Americans to Jewish Americans and later to Italian Americans and others.

20. Consumer fraud, bribery, and income tax evasion are considered _____-_____ crimes.

THINKING ABOUT MOVIES

American Gangster (Ridley Scott, 2007)

An organized crime leader in New York dies, leaving a vacancy that is quickly filled by ambitious, business-savvy Frank Lucas (Denzel Washington). Borrowing a strategy from the corporate world, Frank rises to power in the drug trade by importing heroin directly from Southeast Asia. Meanwhile, detective Ritchie Roberts (Russell Crowe), an honest cop in a corrupt system, searches for the source of the higher-quality product that has been hitting the streets.

This movie shows the drug business as a transnational criminal network. Watch for the scene in which Frank travels to Thailand and Vietnam to set up the distribution network he will use to import the drug into the United States. *American Gangster* also shows organized crime as a form of entrepreneurship. Finally, we see the bureaucratic nature of organized crime, as Frank takes measures to assure obedience within his organization's hierarchy.

For Your Consideration

1. From a functionalist perspective, what are some major characteristics of Frank Lucas's crime organization? From a conflict perspective?

2. What are some of the implications of transnational crime for society, both locally and globally?

Knocked Up

(Judd Apatow, 2007)

Allison Scott (Katherine Heigl) is celebrating her promotion at a club when she meets Ben Stone (Seth Rogen). The two have a one-night stand that results in Allison's pregnancy. Notwithstanding the fact that the two hardly know each other, neither of them is ready for family life. Allison has just landed a job as an anchor for the E! television network, and Ben is stalled in a perpetual state of adolescence. Nevertheless, for the sake of the baby, they try to make something of the relationship.

Allison's pregnancy can be seen as deviant in two ways. First, her unwed status is a violation of social norms. Watch for the scene in which Ben and Allison visit a doctor to verify her pregnancy. Assuming that no norms have been broken, the physician refers to them as Mr. and Mrs. Stone. Second, Allison's pregnancy stigmatizes her in the entertainment industry, which expects women to adhere to an ideal body shape.

For Your Consideration

1. Give some examples of the informal social control Allison faces once her pregnancy is out in the open.

2. In what ways is Allison's pregnancy portrayed as deviant? In what ways is it portrayed as normal?

inside

Systems of Stratification

Sociological Perspectives
    on Stratification

Is Stratification Universal?

Stratification by Social Class

Income and Wealth

Poverty

Life Chances

Social Mobility

Social Policy and
    Stratification: Rethinking
    Welfare in North America
    and Europe

BOXES

Taking Sociology to Work:
    *Jessica Houston Su,
    Research Assistant,
    Joblessness and Urban
    Poverty Research Program*

Research Today: *Precarious
    Work*

Sociology in the Global
    Community: *It's All
    Relative: Appalachian
    Poverty and Congolese
    Affluence*

Sociology on Campus: *Social
    Class and Financial Aid*

Pedestrians pass by a homeless man panhandling for change in New York City. The United States is a society of contrasts between great wealth, modest means, and deep poverty.

Stratification and Social Mobility in the United States

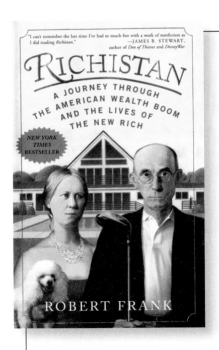

RICHISTAN

A JOURNEY THROUGH THE AMERICAN WEALTH BOOM AND THE LIVES OF THE NEW RICH

ROBERT FRANK

❝ In 2003, while writing a routine article about Wall Street bonuses, I stumbled onto a chart from the Federal Reserve Board. It showed that the number of millionaire households had more than doubled since 1995 to more than eight million.

Granted, a million dollars doesn't mean what it used to. But no matter how far up I looked on the wealth ladder—to households worth $10 million, $20 million, $50 million—all the populations were doubling.

Even more surprising was the fact that the United States was minting millionaires long after the tech bust, recession and terrorist attacks of 2001. The wealth boom, as the numbers showed, went far beyond the 20-something dotcommers in Silicon Valley and Wall Streeters in New York. It stretched across the country, to all age groups and to almost every industry. Never before had so many Americans become so rich, so quickly. The United States is now the world leader in producing millionaires. . . .

After seeing the Fed numbers, I started to wonder about all these rich people. Who were they? How did they get rich? How was money changing their lives? Most importantly, how were they changing life for the rest of us? . . .

I immersed myself in their world, hanging around yacht marinas, slipping into charity balls, loitering in Ferrari dealerships and scoping out the Sotheby's and Christie's auctions. I studied up on trust law, high-end investing and the latest trends in charitable giving. I grilled the top luxury realtors, jet brokers, party planners and resort managers. Mostly, I bothered rich people. I asked them endless questions and tried to get them to talk openly about their money and their lives. Surprisingly, many did. . . .

This book began with that reporting. But its central premise—of a parallel country of the rich—took shape later, with a chance conversation at a yacht club. In 2004, I was walking along the docks of Ft. Lauderdale's Bahia Mar Marina during an annual yacht convention when I met up with a boat owner from Texas. As we stared out over the hundreds of megayachts lined up along the docks—most 150 feet or more, flying Caribbean flags emblazoned with fruit—he turned to me and said, "You look at all these boats and you'd think everyone's making loads of money. It's like it's a different country."

The words stuck with me. Today's rich had formed their own virtual country. They were, in fact, wealthier than most nations. By 2004, the richest 1 percent of Americans were earning about $1.35 trillion a year—greater than the total national incomes of France, Italy or Canada.

And with their huge numbers, they had built a self-contained world unto themselves, complete with their own health-care system (concierge doctors), travel network (Net Jets, destination clubs), separate economy (double-digit income gains and double-digit inflation), and language ("Who's your household manager?"). They didn't just hire gardening crews; they hired "personal arborists." The rich weren't just getting richer; they were becoming financial foreigners, creating their own country within a country, their own society within a society, and their economy within an economy.

They were creating Richistan. ❞

The rich weren't just getting richer; they were becoming financial foreigners, creating their own country within a country, their own society within a society, and their economy within an economy.

(Frank 2007:1–4) Additional information about this excerpt can be found on the Online Learning Center at www.mhhe.com/schaefer12e.

In this excerpt from his book *Richistan,* senior writer Robert Frank of the *Wall Street Journal* describes a foreign country within our home country of the United States: the exclusive club of the very, very rich. To investigate this unknown territory, Frank pursued its inhabitants, hanging around the marinas where they moor their yachts, socializing with them at charity balls, and interviewing their real estate agents—the ones who specialize in huge mansions. More recently, during the severe economic downturn that began in 2008, Frank (2009a, 2009b) noted signs of a contraction in the lifestyles of the very rich. Rolls-Royce unveiled a luxury car for the cost-conscious millionaire, priced at a mere $280,000. And a Florida builder advertised a 15,000-square-foot mansion as "green" because it boasts renewable-wood floors.

The economist John Kenneth Galbraith (1977:44) observed that "of all classes the rich are the most noticed and the least studied." The poor receive a good deal of attention from reporters, social activists, and policymakers seeking to alleviate their poverty, but the very affluent, who live apart from the rest of the population, are largely a mystery. Since Galbraith's comment, moreover, the residential separation of the rich has grown. The newspaper's society page may give us a peek at members of this class, but as Frank points out, we know very little about their everyday lives. Statistically, over 2 million households in the United States are worth more than $10 million each. Less than 10 percent of these people inherited their money, and very few of them are celebrities (Massey 2007).

Ever since people first began to speculate about the nature of human society, their attention has been drawn to the differences between individuals and groups within society. The term **social inequality** describes a condition in which members of society have differing amounts of wealth, prestige, or power. Some degree of social inequality characterizes every society.

When a system of social inequality is based on a hierarchy of groups, sociologists refer to it as **stratification:** a structured ranking of entire groups of people that perpetuates unequal economic rewards and power in a society. These unequal rewards are evident not only in the distribution of wealth and income, but even in the distressing mortality rates of impoverished communities. Stratification involves the ways in which one generation passes on social inequalities to the next, producing groups of people arranged in rank order, from low to high.

Stratification is a crucial subject of sociological investigation because of its pervasive influence on human interactions and institutions. It results inevitably in social inequality, because certain groups of people stand higher in social rankings, control scarce resources, wield power, and receive special treatment. As we will see in this chapter, the consequences of stratification are evident in the unequal distribution of both income and wealth in industrial societies. The term **income** refers to salaries and wages. In contrast, **wealth** is an inclusive term encompassing all a person's material assets, including land, stocks, and other types of property.

Is social inequality an inescapable part of society? How does government policy affect the life chances of the working poor? Is this country still a place where a hardworking person can move up the social ladder? This chapter focuses on the unequal distribution of socially valued rewards and its consequences. We will begin by examining four general systems of stratification, including the one most familiar to us, the social class system. We will examine three sociological perspectives on stratification, paying particular attention to the theories of Karl Marx and Max Weber. We'll also ask whether stratification is universal, and see what sociologists, including functionalist and conflict theorists, have to say about that question. We will see how sociologists define social class and examine the consequences of stratification for people's wealth and income, safety, and educational opportunities. Then we will take a close look at poverty, particularly the question of who belongs to the underclass and why. And we will confront the question of social mobility, both upward and downward. Finally, in the Social Policy section, we will address welfare reform, an issue that is complicated by the attitudes that people, particularly those in the United States, hold toward those who do not work.

Systems of Stratification

Sociologists consider stratification on many levels, ranging from its impact on the individual to worldwide patterns of inequality. No matter where we look, however, disparities in wealth and income are substantial. Take income and poverty patterns in the United States, for example. As the top part of Figure 9-1 on page 194 shows, in many states the median household income is 25 percent higher than that in other states. And as the bottom part of the figure shows, the poverty rate in many states is double that of other states. Later in this chapter we will address the meaning of such statistics. We'll begin our discussion here with an overview of the four basic systems of stratification. Then we'll see what sociologists have had to say on the subject of social inequality.

Look at the four general systems of stratification examined here—slavery, castes, estates, and social classes—as ideal types useful for purposes of analysis. Any stratification system may include elements of more than one type. For example, prior to the Civil War, you could find in the southern states of the United States both social classes dividing Whites from Whites and the institutionalized enslavement of Blacks.

To understand these systems better, it may be helpful to review the distinction between *achieved status* and *ascribed status*, explained in Chapter 5. **Ascribed status** is a social position assigned to a person by society without regard for the person's unique talents or characteristics. In contrast, **achieved status** is a social position that a person attains largely through his or her own efforts. The two are closely linked. The nation's most affluent families generally inherit wealth and status, while many members of racial and ethnic minorities inherit disadvantaged status. Age and gender, as well, are ascribed statuses that influence a person's wealth and social position.

Slavery

The most extreme form of legalized social inequality for individuals and groups is **slavery.** What distinguishes this oppressive system of stratification is that enslaved individuals are *owned* by other people, who treat these human beings as property, just as if they were household pets or appliances.

Slavery has varied in the way it has been practiced. In ancient Greece, the main source of slaves was piracy and captives of war. Although succeeding generations could inherit slave status, it was not necessarily permanent. A person's status might change, depending on which city-state happened to triumph in a military conflict. In effect, all citizens had the potential of becoming slaves or of receiving freedom, depending on the circumstances of history. In contrast, in the United States and Latin America, where slavery was an ascribed status, racial and legal barriers prevented the freeing of slaves.

Today, the Universal Declaration of Human Rights, which is binding on all members of the United Nations, prohibits slavery in all its forms. Yet more people are enslaved today than at any point in world history. In many developing countries, bonded laborers are imprisoned in virtual lifetime employment; in some countries, human beings are owned outright. But a form of slavery also exists in Europe and the United States, where guest workers and illegal immigrants have been forced to labor for years under terrible conditions, either to pay off debts or to avoid being turned over to immigration authorities. In 2007 a wealthy couple from New York was convicted of holding two Indonesian women as slaves in their home for four years. Their shocking story gave newspaper readers an unsettling glimpse into the lives of the very rich (S. Greenhouse 2007; Skinner 2008).

Castes

Castes are hereditary ranks that are usually religiously dictated and that tend to be fixed and immobile. Caste membership is an ascribed status (at birth, children automatically assume the same position as their parents). Each caste is quite sharply defined, and members are expected to marry within that caste.

The caste system is generally associated with Hinduism in India and other countries. In India there are four major castes, called

MAPPING LIFE NATIONWIDE

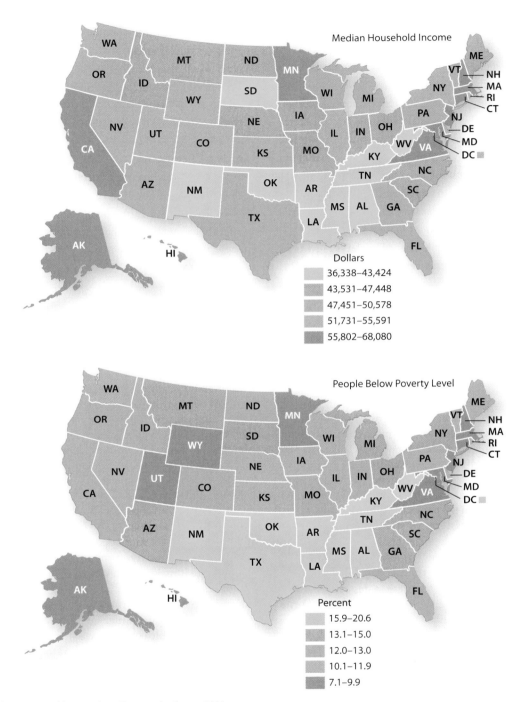

Source: 2006 census data presented in American Community Survey 2008.

varnas. A fifth category of outcastes, referred to as the *untouchables,* represents 16 percent of the population; its members are considered so lowly and unclean as to have no place within this stratification system. In an effort to avoid perpetuating the historical stigma these people bear, the government now refers to the untouchables as *scheduled castes.* The untouchables themselves prefer *Dalit* ("the repressed"), a term that communicates their desire to overcome their disadvantaged status (P. Smith 2008).

In 1950, after gaining independence from Great Britain, India adopted a new constitution that formally outlawed the caste system. Over the past decade or two, however, urbanization and technological advances have brought more change to India's caste system than the government or politics has in more than half a century. The anonymity of city life tends to blur caste boundaries, allowing the *Dalit* to pass unrecognized in temples, schools, and places of employment. And the globalization of

Jessica Houston Su, **Research Assistant, Joblessness and Urban Poverty Research Program**

Jessica Houston Su chose sociology as her major "because it was the first class that appealed to my desire to understand the roots of inequality." It also helped her to make sense of what was going on around her at Dartmouth College. "I grew up in a rural, working-class community," she explains; "it was quite a culture shock to attend an affluent, Ivy League college." Learning about social structures and institutions helped Su to navigate through a new environment filled with people from many different backgrounds.

Su went through several potential majors before taking a sociology course and realizing that she was interested in almost every course the department offered. When she was hired for a work-study job in the department, she "soon realized that I was spending a lot of time reading all of the articles I was supposed to be photocopying," she jokes. "It became very obvious to me that I had found my major."

Su works at Harvard University's John F. Kennedy School of Government on a research program directed by the well-known sociologist William Julius Wilson. She is currently assigned to a large-scale longitudinal study of welfare reform in Boston, Chicago, and San Antonio. Her primary responsibility is to analyze the qualitative data from the study, gathered through ethnographic interviews with families who are affected by welfare reform, by searching for themes that might help to explain the study's quantitative data. She finds it exciting to be able to follow the same families over a long period. "I feel like I almost know some of the people," she explains.

Of all the things she learned as a sociology major, Su thinks one of the most important was the concept of social construction. "We consider many things to simply be facts of life," she explains, "but upon further investigation it is clear that most things have been socially constructed in some way." The concept of social construction has helped her to look more carefully at the world around her: "My worldview is much more nuanced and I've gained a much better understanding of how society works, both the good and the bad."

Su uses the research methods she learned in her sociology courses all the time. "I love going to work each day," she says. "I am challenged academically and I feel fulfilled knowing that I am working on something that will benefit society and perhaps influence future policy."

LET'S DISCUSS

1. Did you experience a sense of culture shock when you entered college and were exposed to students from different social classes? If so, has studying sociology helped you to adjust to the diversity in students' backgrounds?
2. Have you begun to see the world differently since you learned about the social construction of reality? If so, what in particular do you see in a different light?

---

high technology has opened up India's social order, bringing new opportunities to those who possess the skills and ability to capitalize on them.

The term *caste* can also be applied in recent historical contexts outside India. For example, the system of stratification that characterized the southern United States from the end of the Civil War through the 1960s resembled a caste system. So did the rigid system of segregation that prevailed in the Republic of South Africa under apartheid, from 1948 through the 1990s. In both cases, race was the defining factor that placed a person in the social hierarchy.

Estates

A third type of stratification system, called *estates*, was associated with feudal societies during the Middle Ages. The **estate system,** or *feudalism*, required peasants to work land leased to them by nobles in exchange for military protection and other services. The basis for the system was the nobles' ownership of land, which was critical to their superior and privileged status. As in systems based on slavery and caste, inheritance of one's position largely defined the estate system. The nobles inherited their titles and property; the peasants were born into a subservient position within an agrarian society.

As the estate system developed, it became more differentiated. Nobles began to achieve varying degrees of authority. By the 12th century, a priesthood had emerged in most of Europe, along with classes of merchants and artisans. For the first time there were groups of people whose wealth did not depend on land ownership or agriculture. This economic change had profound

social consequences as the estate system ended and a class system of stratification came into existence.

Social Classes

A **class system** is a social ranking based primarily on economic position in which achieved characteristics can influence social mobility. In contrast to slavery and caste systems, the boundaries between classes are imprecisely defined, and one can move from one stratum, or level, of society to another. Even so, class systems maintain stable stratification hierarchies and patterns of class divisions, and they, too, are marked by unequal distribution of wealth and power. Class standing, though it is achieved, is heavily dependent on family and ascribed factors, such as race and ethnicity.

Income inequality is a basic characteristic of a class system. In 2007, the median household income in the United States was $50,233. In other words, half of all households had higher incomes in that year and half had lower incomes. But this fact does not fully convey the income disparities in our society. As Figure 9-2 on page 196 shows, there is a broad range around the median household income. Furthermore, considerable numbers of people fall at the extremes. In 2005, about 304,000 tax returns reported incomes in excess of $1 million. At the same time, over 13.3 million households reported incomes under $5,000 (Bureau of the Census 2007a:312; DeNavas-Walt et al. 2008).

Sociologist Daniel Rossides (1997) uses a five-class model to describe the class system of the United States: the upper class, the upper-middle class, the lower-middle class, the working class, and the lower class. Although the lines separating social classes **195**

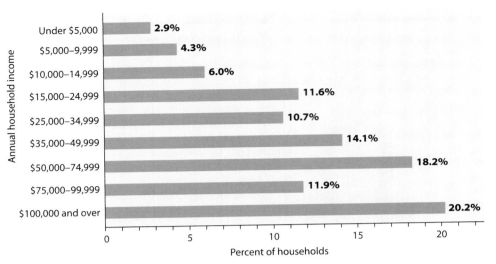

Annual household income

Under $5,000	**2.9%**
$5,000–9,999	**4.3%**
$10,000–14,999	**6.0%**
$15,000–24,999	**11.6%**
$25,000–34,999	**10.7%**
$35,000–49,999	**14.1%**
$50,000–74,999	**18.2%**
$75,000–99,999	**11.9%**
$100,000 and over	**20.2%**

Percent of households

Source: DeNavas-Walt et al. 2008:31.

in his model are not so sharp as the divisions between castes, members of the five classes differ significantly in ways other than just income level.

Upper and Lower Classes   Rossides characterizes about 1 to 2 percent of the people of the United States as *upper class.* This group is limited to the very wealthy—the people who inhabit the country within a country described by Robert Frank in *Richistan.* These people associate in exclusive clubs and social circles. In contrast, the *lower class,* consisting of approximately 20 to 25 percent of the population, disproportionately consists of Blacks, Hispanics, single mothers with dependent children, and people who cannot find regular work or must make do with low-paying work. This class lacks both wealth and income and is too weak politically to exercise significant power.

Both these classes, at opposite ends of the nation's social hierarchy, reflect the importance of ascribed status and achieved status. Ascribed statuses such as race clearly influence a person's wealth and social position. Sociologist Richard Jenkins (1991) has shown how the ascribed status of being disabled marginalizes a person in the U.S. labor market. People with disabilities are particularly vulnerable to unemployment, are often poorly paid, and tend to occupy the lower rung of the occupational ladder. Regardless of their actual performance on the job, the disabled are stigmatized as not earning their keep. Such are the effects of ascribed status. We will look again at the plight of the lower class when we consider poverty and welfare policies.

Middle Class   Sandwiched between the upper and lower classes in this model are the upper-middle class, the lower-middle class, and the working class. The *upper-middle class,* about 10 to 15 percent of the population, includes professionals such as doctors, lawyers, and architects. They participate extensively in politics and take leadership roles in voluntary associations. The *lower-middle class,* about 30 to 35 percent of the

population, includes less affluent professionals (such as elementary school teachers and nurses), owners of small businesses, and a sizable number of clerical workers. While not all members of the middle class hold degrees from a college, they share the goal of sending their children there.

The middle class is currently under a great deal of economic pressure. Close analysis indicates that of those who lost their middle-class standing during the latter 20th century, about half rose to a higher ranking in the social class system, while half dropped to a lower position. These data mean that the United States is moving toward a "bipolar income distribution." That is, a broadly based middle class is slowly being replaced by two growing groups of rich and poor.

Sociologists and other scholars have identified several factors that have contributed to the shrinking size of the middle class:

- *Disappearing opportunities for those with little education.* Today, most jobs require formal schooling, yet less than a third of adults between ages 35 and 44 have prepared themselves with a college degree.

- *Global competition and rapid advances in technology.* These two trends, which began several decades ago, mean that workers are more easily replaced now than they were in the past. Increasingly, globalization and technological advances are affecting the more complex jobs that were once the bread and butter of middle-class workers.

Supersized homes like this one typically belong to upper-middle-class families, who may also enjoy vacation retreats and luxury condos in the city. These conspicuous homes mark their owners as members of a privileged 10 to 15 percent of the population—just shy of the truly wealthy 1 or 2 percent who constitute the upper class.

- *Growing dependence on the temporary workforce.* For those workers who have no other job, temporary positions are tenuous at best, because they rarely offer health care coverage or retirement benefits.

- *The rise of new growth industries and nonunion workplaces, like fast-food restaurants.* Industries may have added employment opportunities, but they are at the lower end of the wage scale.

Middle-class families want large homes, college degrees for their children, and high-quality health care—the cost of which has been growing faster than inflation. The answer, for many people, is either to go without or to work longer hours at multiple jobs (Greenblatt 2005; Leonhardt 2007; Massey 2007; Shipler 2005; Thurow 1984; Witte 2005).

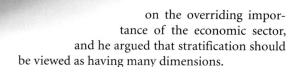

Working Class Rossides describes the *working class*—about 40 to 45 percent of the population—as people who hold regular manual or blue-collar jobs. Certain members of this class, such as electricians, may have higher incomes than people in the lower-middle class. Yet even if they have achieved some degree of economic security, they tend to identify with manual workers and their long history of involvement in the labor movement of the United States. Of the five classes, the working class is declining noticeably in size. In the economy of the United States, service and technical jobs are replacing those involved in the actual manufacturing or transportation of goods.

Social class is one of the independent or explanatory variables most frequently used by social scientists to shed light on social issues. In later chapters, we will analyze the relationships between social class and child rearing (Chapter 14), religious affiliation (Chapter 15), and formal schooling (Chapter 16), as well as other relationships in which social class is a variable.

---

use your sociological *imagination*

How can you tell someone's social class? What indicators can be misleading?

Sociological Perspectives on Stratification

Sociologists have hotly debated stratification and social inequality and have reached varying conclusions. No theorist stressed the significance of class for society—and for social change—more strongly than Karl Marx. Marx viewed class differentiation as the crucial determinant of social, economic, and political inequality. In contrast, Max Weber questioned Marx's emphasis on the overriding importance of the economic sector, and he argued that stratification should be viewed as having many dimensions.

Karl Marx's View of Class Differentiation

Karl Marx has been aptly described as both a revolutionary and a social scientist. Marx was concerned with stratification in all types of human society, beginning with primitive agricultural tribes and continuing into feudalism. But his main focus was on the effects of economic inequality on all aspects of 19th-century Europe. The plight of the working class made him feel that it was imperative to strive for changes in the class structure of society.

In Marx's view, social relations during any period of history depend on who controls the primary mode of economic production, such as land or factories. Differential access to scarce resources shapes the relationship between groups. Thus, under the feudal estate system, most production was agricultural, and the land was owned by the nobility. Peasants had little choice but to work according to terms dictated by those who owned the land.

Using this type of analysis, Marx examined social relations within **capitalism**—an economic system in which the means of production are held largely in private hands and the main incentive for economic activity is the accumulation of profits. Marx focused on the two classes that began to emerge as the feudal estate system declined, the bourgeoisie and the proletariat. The **bourgeoisie,** or capitalist class, owns the means of production, such as factories and machinery; the **proletariat** is the working class. In capitalist societies, the members of the bourgeoisie maximize profit in competition with other firms. In the process, they exploit workers, who must exchange their labor for subsistence wages. In Marx's view, members of each class share a distinctive culture. Marx was most interested in the culture of the proletariat, but he also examined the ideology of the bourgeoisie, through which that class justifies its dominance over workers.

According to Marx, exploitation of the proletariat will inevitably lead to the destruction of the capitalist system, because the workers will revolt. But first, the working class must develop **class consciousness**—a subjective awareness of common vested interests and the need for collective political action to bring

Chapter 9

about social change. Often, workers must overcome what Marx termed **false consciousness,** or an attitude held by members of a class that does not accurately reflect their objective position. A worker with false consciousness may adopt an individualistic viewpoint toward capitalist exploitation ("*I* am being exploited by *my* boss"). In contrast, the class-conscious worker realizes that all workers are being exploited by the bourgeoisie and have a common stake in revolution.

For Marx, class consciousness was part of a collective process in which the proletariat comes to identify the bourgeoisie as the source of its oppression. Revolutionary leaders will guide the working class in its struggle. Ultimately, the proletariat will overthrow the rule of both the bourgeoisie and the government (which Marx saw as representing the interests of capitalists) and will eliminate private ownership of the means of production. In Marx's rather utopian view, classes and oppression will cease to exist in the postrevolutionary workers' state.

How accurate were Marx's predictions? He failed to anticipate the emergence of labor unions, whose power in collective bargaining weakens the stranglehold that capitalists maintain over workers. Moreover, as contemporary conflict theorists note, he did not foresee the extent to which political liberties and relative prosperity could contribute to false consciousness. Many workers have come to view themselves as individuals striving for improvement within free societies that offer substantial mobility, rather than as downtrodden members of a social class who face a collective fate. Finally, Marx did not predict that Communist Party rule would be established and later overthrown in the former Soviet Union and throughout Eastern Europe. Still, the Marxist approach to the study of class is useful in stressing the importance of stratification as a determinant of social behavior and the fundamental separation in many societies between two distinct groups, the rich and the poor.

Max Weber's View of Stratification

Unlike Karl Marx, Max Weber ([1913–1922] 1947) insisted that no single characteristic (such as class) totally defines a person's position within the stratification system. Instead, writing in 1916, he identified three distinct components of stratification: class, status, and power.

Weber used the term **class** to refer to a group of people who have a similar level of wealth and income. For example, certain workers in the United States try to support their families through minimum-wage jobs. According to Weber's definition, these wage earners constitute a class because they share the same economic position and fate. Although Weber agreed with Marx on the importance of this economic dimension of stratification, he argued that the actions of individuals and groups cannot be understood *solely* in economic terms.

Weber used the term **status group** to refer to people who have the same prestige or lifestyle. An individual gains status through membership in a desirable group, such as the medical profession. But status is not the same as economic class standing. In our culture, a successful pickpocket may belong to the same income class as a college professor. Yet the thief is widely regarded as holding a low status, whereas the professor holds high status.

For Weber, the third major component of stratification has a political dimension. **Power** is the ability to exercise one's will

Karl Marx would identify these coal miners as members of the *proletariat,* or working class. Even today, miners are poorly compensated for the considerable dangers they face. The exploitation of the working class is a core principle of Marxist theory.

over others. In the United States, power stems from membership in particularly influential groups, such as corporate boards of directors, government bodies, and interest groups. Conflict theorists generally agree that two major sources of power—big business and government—are closely interrelated. For instance, many of the heads of major corporations also hold powerful positions in the government or military.

The corporate executives who head private companies in the United States earn the highest incomes in the nation. In fact, the gap between their salaries and those of the average worker has widened significantly over time. In 1980, top U.S. executives earned more than 42 times the average worker's pay, and by 2007, 344 times the average.

These highly compensated individuals represent the pinnacle not just of U.S. society, but of corporate executives around the world. Heads of U.S. corporations are paid significantly better than chief executive officers (CEOs) in other industrial countries—double the salaries of CEOs in Germany and about four times the salaries of CEOs in Japan. Even when their performance is less than stellar, many of them receive handsome raises. Departing executives at poorly performing corporations such as Morgan Stanley, Time Warner, and Hewlett-Packard received over $100 million each in their final year of leadership. During the economic downturn that began in 2008, the value of the stock top executives received in their compensation packages did decline. Yet overall, CEO salaries in the 500 largest companies still rose 3 percent that year (D. Jones and Hansen 2009; Landy 2008; Lerach 2007).

To summarize, in Weber's view, each of us has not one rank in society but three. Our position in a stratification system reflects some combination of class, status, and power. Each factor influences the other two, and in fact the rankings on these three dimensions often tend to coincide. John F. Kennedy came from an extremely wealthy family, attended exclusive preparatory schools, graduated from Harvard University, and went on to become president of the United States. Like Kennedy, many people from affluent backgrounds achieve impressive status and power.

Interactionist View

Both Karl Marx and Max Weber looked at inequality primarily from a macrosociological perspective, considering the entire

Robert Arail: © The State/Dist. by Newspaper Enterprise Association, Inc.
The economic downturn that began in 2008 with the threatened failure of several major investment banks has brought public scrutiny of the salaries and bonuses awarded to financial executives.

society or even the global economy. Marx did suggest the importance of a more microsociological analysis, however, when he stressed the ways in which individuals develop a true class consciousness.

Interactionists, as well as economists, have long been interested in the importance of social class in shaping a person's lifestyle. The theorist Thorstein Veblen (1857–1929) noted that those at the top of the social hierarchy typically convert part of their wealth into *conspicuous consumption,* purchasing more automobiles than they can reasonably use and building houses with more rooms than they can possibly occupy. Or they may engage in *conspicuous leisure,* jetting to a remote destination and staying just long enough to have dinner or view a sunset over some historic locale (Veblen [1899] 1964).

At the other end of the spectrum, behavior that is judged to be typical of the lower class is subject not only to ridicule but even to legal action. Communities have, from time to time, banned trailers from people's front yards and sofas from their front porches. In some communities, it is illegal to leave a pickup truck in front of the house overnight.

Is Stratification Universal?

Must some members of society receive greater rewards than others? Do people need to feel socially and economically superior to others? Can social life be organized without structured inequality? These questions have been debated for centuries, especially among political activists. Utopian socialists, religious minorities, and members of recent countercultures have all attempted to establish communities that to some extent or other would abolish inequality in social relationships.

Social scientists have found that inequality exists in all societies—even the simplest. For example, when anthropologist Gunnar Landtman ([1938] 1968) studied

the Kiwai Papuans of New Guinea, at first he noticed little differentiation among them. Every man in the village did the same work and lived in similar housing. However, on closer inspection, Landtman observed that certain Papuans—men who were warriors, harpooners, and sorcerers—were described as "a little more high" than others. In contrast, villagers who were female, unemployed, or unmarried were considered "down a little bit" and were barred from owning land.

Stratification is universal in that all societies maintain some form of social inequality among members. Depending on its values, a society may assign people to distinctive ranks based on their religious knowledge, skill in hunting, beauty, trading expertise, or ability to provide health care. But why has such inequality developed in human societies? And how much differentiation among people, if any, is actually essential?

Functionalist and conflict sociologists offer contrasting explanations for the existence and necessity of social stratification. Functionalists maintain that a differential system of rewards and punishments is necessary for the efficient operation of society. Conflict theorists argue that competition for scarce resources results in significant political, economic, and social inequality.

Functionalist View

Would people go to school for many years to become physicians if they could make as much money and gain as much respect working as street cleaners? Functionalists say no, which is partly why they believe that a stratified society is universal.

In the view of Kingsley Davis and Wilbert Moore (1945), society must distribute its members among a variety of social positions. It must not only make sure that these positions are filled but also see that they are filled by people with the appropriate talents

Buying an Andy Warhol painting for $21 million is an example of Thorstein Veblen's concept of conspicuous consumption, a spending pattern common to those at the very top of the social ladder.

and abilities. Rewards, including money and prestige, are based on the importance of a position and the relative scarcity of qualified personnel. Yet this assessment often devalues work performed by certain segments of society, such as women's work in the home, or in occupations traditionally filled by women, or low-status work in fast-food outlets.

Davis and Moore argue that stratification is universal and that social inequality is necessary so that people will be motivated to fill functionally important positions. But critics say that unequal rewards are not the only means of encouraging people to fill critical positions and occupations. Personal pleasure, intrinsic satisfaction, and value orientations also motivate people to enter particular careers. Functionalists agree, but they note that society must use some type of reward to motivate people to enter unpleasant or dangerous jobs and professions that require a long training period. This response does not address stratification systems in which status is largely inherited, such as slave or caste societies. Moreover, even if stratification is inevitable, the functionalist explanation for differential rewards does not explain the wide disparity between the rich and the poor (R. Collins 1975; Kerbo 2009; Tumin 1953, 1985).

As popular songs and movies suggest, long-haul truck drivers take pride in their low-prestige job. According to the conflict perspective, the cultural beliefs that form a society's dominant ideology, such as the popular image of the truck driver as hero, help the wealthy to maintain their power and control at the expense of the lower classes.

Conflict View

The writings of Karl Marx lie at the heart of conflict theory. Marx viewed history as a continuous struggle between the oppressors and the oppressed, which ultimately would culminate in an egalitarian, classless society. In terms of stratification, he argued that under capitalism, the dominant class—the bourgeoisie—manipulates the economic and political systems in order to maintain control over the exploited proletariat. Marx did not believe that stratification was inevitable, but he did see inequality and oppression as inherent in capitalism (E. O. Wright et al. 1982).

Like Marx, contemporary conflict theorists believe that human beings are prone to conflict over scarce resources such as wealth, status, and power. However, Marx focused primarily on class conflict; more recent theorists have extended the analysis to include conflicts based on gender, race, age, and other dimensions. British sociologist Ralf Dahrendorf is one of the most influential contributors to the conflict approach.

Dahrendorf (1959) has modified Marx's analysis of capitalist society to apply to *modern* capitalist societies. For Dahrendorf, social classes are groups of people who share common interests resulting from their authority relationships. In identifying the most powerful groups in society, he includes not only the bourgeoisie—the owners of the means of production—but also the managers of industry, legislators, the judiciary, heads of the government bureaucracy, and others. In that respect, Dahrendorf has merged Marx's emphasis on class conflict with Weber's recognition that power is an important element of stratification (Cuff et al. 1990).

Conflict theorists, including Dahrendorf, contend that the powerful of today, like the bourgeoisie of Marx's time, want

society to run smoothly so that they can enjoy their privileged positions. Because the status quo suits those with wealth, status, and power, they have a clear interest in preventing, minimizing, or controlling societal conflict.

One way for the powerful to maintain the status quo is to define and disseminate the society's dominant ideology. The term **dominant ideology** describes a set of cultural beliefs and practices that helps to maintain powerful social, economic, and political interests. For Marx, the dominant ideology in a capitalist society served the interests of the ruling class. From a conflict perspective, the social significance of the dominant ideology is that not only do a society's most powerful groups and institutions control wealth and property; even more important, they control the means of producing beliefs about reality through religion, education, and the media (Abercrombie et al. 1980, 1990; Robertson 1988).

The powerful, such as leaders of government, also use limited social reforms to buy off the oppressed and reduce the danger of challenges to their dominance. For example, minimum-wage laws and unemployment compensation unquestionably give some valuable assistance to needy men and women. Yet these reforms also serve to pacify those who might otherwise rebel. Of course, in the view of conflict theorists, such maneuvers can never entirely eliminate conflict, since workers will continue to demand equality, and the powerful will not give up their control of society.

Conflict theorists see stratification as a major source of societal tension and conflict. They do not agree with Davis and Moore that stratification is functional for a society or that it serves as a source of stability. Rather, conflict sociologists argue that stratification will inevitably lead to instability and social change (R. Collins 1975; L. Coser 1977).

Table 9-1 summarizes and compares the three major perspectives on social stratification.

Lenski's Viewpoint

Let's return to the question posed earlier—Is stratification universal?—and consider the sociological response. Some form of differentiation is found in every culture, from the most primitive to the most advanced industrial societies of our time. Sociologist

	Functionalist	Conflict	Interactionist
Purpose of social stratification	Facilitates filling of social positions	Facilitates exploitation	Influences people's lifestyles
Attitude toward social inequality	Necessary to some extent	Excessive and growing	Influences intergroup relations
Analysis of the wealthy	Talented and skilled, creating opportunities for others	Use the dominant ideology to further their own interests	Exhibit conspicuous consumption and conspicuous leisure

Gerhard Lenski, in his sociocultural evolution approach, described how economic systems change as their level of technology becomes more complex, beginning with hunting and gathering and culminating eventually with industrial society.

In subsistence-based hunting-and-gathering societies, people focus on survival. While some inequality and differentiation are evident, a stratification system based on social class does not emerge because there is no real wealth to be claimed. As a society advances technologically, it becomes capable of producing a considerable surplus of goods. The emergence of surplus resources greatly expands the possibilities for inequality in status, influence, and power, allowing a well-defined, rigid social class system to develop. To minimize strikes, slowdowns, and industrial sabotage, the elites may share a portion of the economic surplus with the lower classes, but not enough to reduce their own power and privilege.

As Lenski argued, the allocation of surplus goods and services controlled by those with wealth, status, and power reinforces the social inequality that accompanies stratification systems. While this reward system may once have served the overall purposes of society, as functionalists contend, the same cannot be said for the large disparities separating the haves from the have-nots in current societies. In contemporary industrial society, the degree of social and economic inequality far exceeds what is needed to provide for goods and services (Lenski 1966; Nolan and Lenski 2009).

Stratification by Social Class

We continually assess how wealthy people are by looking at the cars they drive, the houses they live in, the clothes they wear, and so on. Yet it is not so easy to locate an individual within our social hierarchies as it would be in slavery or caste systems of stratification. To determine someone's class position, sociologists generally rely on the objective method.

Objective Method of Measuring Social Class

In the **objective method** of measuring social class, class is viewed largely as a statistical category. Researchers assign individuals to social classes on the basis of criteria such as occupation, education, income, and place of residence. The key to the objective method is that the *researcher,* rather than the person being classified, identifies an individual's class position.

The first step in using this method is to decide what indicators or causal factors will be measured objectively, whether wealth, income, education, or occupation. The prestige ranking of occupations has proved to be a useful indicator of a person's class position. For one thing, it is much easier to determine accurately than income or wealth. The term **prestige** refers to the respect and admiration that an occupation holds in a society. "My daughter, the physicist" connotes something very different from "my daughter, the waitress." Prestige is independent of the particular individual who occupies a job, a characteristic that distinguishes it from esteem. **Esteem** refers to the reputation that a specific person has earned within an occupation. Therefore, one can say that the position of president of the United States has high prestige, even though it has been occupied by people with varying degrees of esteem. A hairdresser may have the esteem of his clients, but he lacks the prestige of a corporate executive.

Table 9-2 on page 202 ranks the prestige of a number of well-known occupations. In a series of national surveys, sociologists assigned prestige rankings to about 500 occupations, ranging from surgeon to panhandler. The highest possible prestige score was 100; the lowest was 0. Surgeon, physician, lawyer, dentist, and college professor were the most highly regarded occupations. Sociologists have used such data to assign prestige rankings to virtually all jobs and have found a stability in rankings from 1925 to the present. Similar studies in other countries have also developed useful prestige rankings of occupations (Nakao and Treas 1994).

Gender and Occupational Prestige

For many years, studies of social class tended to neglect the occupations and incomes of *women* as determinants of social rank. With more than half of all married women now working outside the home (see Chapter 12), this approach seems outmoded. How should we judge class or status in dual-career families—by the occupation regarded as having greater prestige, the average, or some other combination of the two? Sociologists—in particular, feminist sociologists in Great Britain—are drawing on new approaches to assess women's social class standing. One approach is to focus on the individual (rather than the family or household) as the basis for categorizing a woman's class position. Thus, a woman would be classified according to her own occupational status rather than that of her spouse (M. O'Donnell 1992).

Another feminist effort to measure the contribution of women to the economy reflects a more clearly political agenda. International Women Count Network, a global grassroots feminist organization, has sought to give a monetary value to women's unpaid work. Besides providing symbolic recognition of women's role in labor, this value would also be used to calculate pension and other benefits that are based on wages received. The United Nations has placed an $11 trillion price tag on unpaid

TABLE **9-2** PRESTIGE RANKINGS OF OCCUPATIONS

Occupation	Score	Occupation	Score
Surgeon	87	Farm manager	48
Physician	86	Mail carrier	47
Lawyer	75	Secretary	46
Dentist	74	Insurance agent	45
College professor	74	Bank teller	43
Architect	73	Nurse's aide	42
Psychiatrist	72	Farmer	40
Clergy	69	Correctional officer	40
Pharmacist	68	Receptionist	39
Registered nurse	66	Carpenter	39
High school teacher	66	Barber	36
Accountant	65	Child care worker	35
Optician	65	Hotel clerk	32
Elementary school teacher	64	Bus driver	32
Banker	63	Auto body repairer	31
Veterinarian	62	Truck driver	30
Legislator	61	Salesworker (shoes)	28
Airline pilot	60	Garbage collector	28
Police officer or detective	60	Waiter and waitress	28
Prekindergarten teacher	55	Cook in a pizza shop	27
Librarian	54	Bartender	25
Firefighter	53	Farmworker	23
Social worker	52	Janitor	22
Dental hygienist	52	Newspaper vendor	19
Electrician	51	Prostitute	14
Funeral director	49	Panhandler	11

Note: 100 is the highest and 0 the lowest possible prestige score.
Source: J. Davis et al. 2007. See also Nakao and Treas 1994.

Think about It

Can you name what you think are two more high-prestige occupations?
Two more low-prestige occupations?

labor by women, largely in child care, housework, and agriculture. Whatever the figure, the continued undercounting of many workers' contributions to a family and to an entire economy means that virtually all measures of stratification are in need of reform (United Nations Development Programme 1995; Wages for Housework Campaign 1999).

Multiple Measures

Another complication in measuring social class is that advances in statistical methods and computer technology have multiplied the factors used to define class under the objective method. No longer are sociologists limited to annual income and education in evaluating a person's class position. Today, studies use as criteria the value of homes, sources of income, assets, years in present occupations, neighborhoods, and considerations regarding dual careers. Adding these variables will not necessarily paint a different picture of class differentiation in the United States, but it does allow sociologists to measure class in a more complex and multidimensional way. When researchers use multiple measures, they typically speak of **socioeconomic status (SES),** a measure of social class that is based on income, education, and occupation. To determine the socioeconomic status of a young person, such as a college student under age 25, they use *parental* income, education, and occupation.

Whatever the technique used to measure class, the sociologist is interested in real and often dramatic differences in power, privilege, and opportunity in a society. The study of stratification is a study of inequality. Nowhere is the truth of that statement more evident than in the distribution of income and wealth.

Income and Wealth

By all measures, income in the United States is distributed unevenly. Nobel Prize–winning economist Paul Samuelson has described the situation in the following words: "If we made an income pyramid out of building blocks, with each layer portraying $500 of income, the peak would be far higher than Mount Everest, but most people would be within a few feet of the ground" (Samuelson and Nordhaus 2010:324).

Recent data support Samuelson's analogy. Figure 9-3 shows the distribution of U.S. income in the form of a section sliced from a three-dimensional pyramid—one whose needle nose is so tall that it won't fit onto the page. The box to the right of the pyramid represents the very top of the graph, collapsed to a much smaller scale. This box includes those fortunate Americans who received an income of $500,000 or more in 2005, a very select group representing

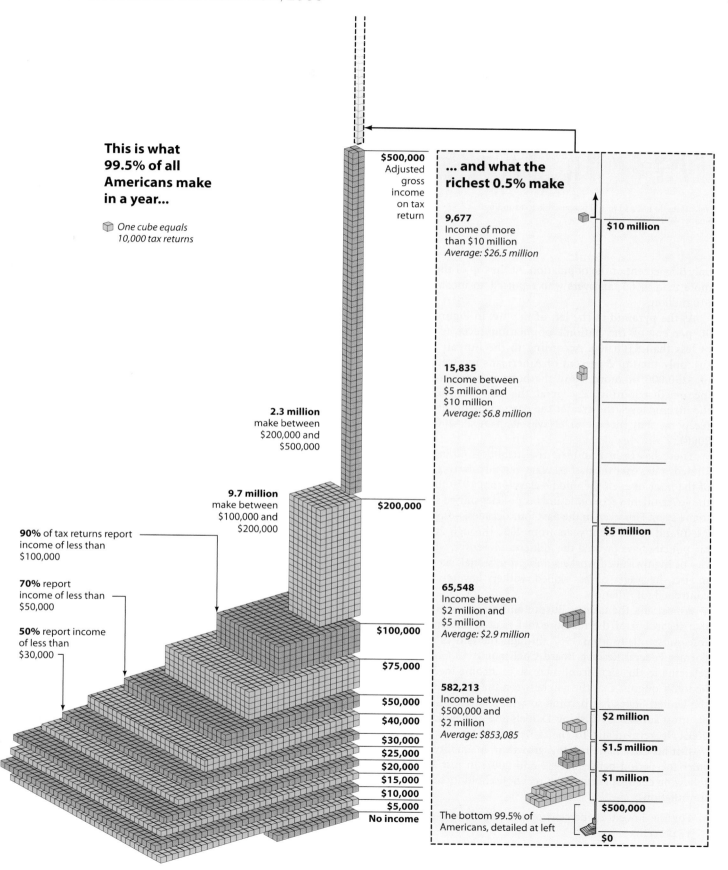

This is what 99.5% of all Americans make in a year...

One cube equals 10,000 tax returns

$500,000
Adjusted gross income on tax return

... and what the richest 0.5% make

9,677
Income of more than $10 million
Average: $26.5 million

$10 million

15,835
Income between $5 million and $10 million
Average: $6.8 million

2.3 million make between $200,000 and $500,000

9.7 million make between $100,000 and $200,000

$200,000

90% of tax returns report income of less than $100,000

$5 million

70% report income of less than $50,000

65,548
Income between $2 million and $5 million
Average: $2.9 million

50% report income of less than $30,000

$100,000

$75,000

$50,000

582,213
Income between $500,000 and $2 million
Average: $853,085

$40,000

$2 million

$30,000

$1.5 million

$25,000

$20,000

$1 million

$15,000

$10,000

$500,000

$5,000

The bottom 99.5% of Americans, detailed at left

No income

$0

Source: Dykman 2006:48–49, based on data from Bureau of Labor Statistics, Internal Revenue Service, *The State of Working America 2006/2007,* Salary.com, and Forbes.com.

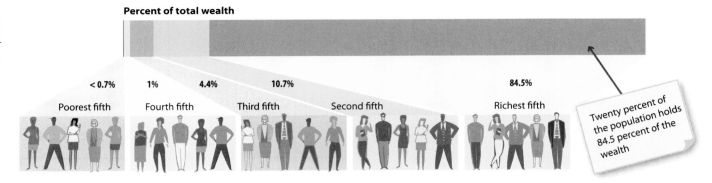

Percent of total wealth

< 0.7%   1%   4.4%   10.7%   84.5%

Poorest fifth   Fourth fifth   Third fifth   Second fifth   Richest fifth

Twenty percent of the population holds 84.5 percent of the wealth

Note: Data do not add to 100 percent due to rounding.
Source: Wolff 2002.

only 0.5 percent of the population. At the top of the box are the more than 9,600 taxpayers who reported an income exceeding $10 million.

As the pyramid to the left of the box in Figure 9-3 shows, 90 percent of the nation's population received an income of less than $100,000. According to the Bureau of the Census, only the top 2 percent of Americans received an income of $250,000 or more. Note the bottom-heavy nature of the income distribution. Except at the very bottom, the lower the income level, the greater the percentage of the population receiving that income (DeNavas-Walt et al. 2008; Dykman 2006).

There has been a modest redistribution of income in the United States over the past 80 years, but not always to the benefit of the poor or even the middle class. From 1929 through 1970, the government's economic and tax policies shifted some income to the poor. However, in the past four decades—especially in the 1980s and in the eight years from 2001 through 2008—federal tax policies have favored the affluent. Moreover, while the salaries of highly skilled workers and professionals have continued to rise, the wages of less skilled workers have *decreased* when controlled for inflation.

As a result, the Census Bureau and other researchers report that regardless of the measure that is used, income inequality rose substantially from 1967 through the end of the century. Former Federal Reserve Board Chairman Alan Greenspan was referring to this significant increase in income inequality when he told Congress that the gap between the rich and the poor in the United States has become so wide that a democratic society must address it (Cushing-Daniels and Zedlewski 2008; Grier 2005; Neckerman and Torche 2007; Saez 2008).

Just how dramatic has this growth in inequality been? Consider the period between 1982 and 2007. In just 25 years, the following changes occurred in real household income (adjusted for inflation):

- For the lowest 20 percent of the population, income rose 17 percent.
- For the next lowest 20 percent of the population, income rose 18 percent.
- For the middle 20 percent of the population, income rose 21 percent.

- For the next highest 20 percent of the population, income rose 29 percent.
- For the top 20 percent of the population, income rose a whopping 50 percent.

The pattern is clear. Though everyone has done better, by far the biggest winners have been the affluent (DeNavas-Walt et al. 2008: 40–41).

Globalization is often blamed for this growing inequality, because it has forced less skilled workers to compete with lower-paid foreign-born workers. While that is true, research suggests that the number of displaced workers who are reemployed at similarly paid or even higher-paid jobs roughly equals the number of workers whose earnings drop (S. Zimmerman 2008a).

Americans often seem not to be seriously concerned about income and wealth inquality in the United States. In a comparison of opinions about social inequality in 27 different countries, respondents in the United States were less aware than those in other countries of the extent of inequality at the top of the income distribution. Americans would prefer to "level down" the top of the nation's earning distribution, but compared to people in other countries, they are less concerned about reducing income differentials at the bottom of the distribution (Osberg and Smeeding 2006).

Wealth in the United States is much more unevenly distributed than income. As Figure 9-4 shows, in 2001, the richest fifth of the population held 84.5 percent of the nation's wealth. Government data indicate that more than 1 out of every 100 households had assets over $2.4 million, while 1 out of 5 households were so heavily in debt they had a negative net worth. Researchers have also found a dramatic disparity in wealth between African Americans and Whites. This disparity is evident even when educational backgrounds are held constant: the households of college-educated Whites have about three times as much wealth as the households of college-educated Blacks (Grawe 2008b; Oliver and Shapiro 2006, 2008; Wolff 2002).

Poverty

Approximately one out of every nine people in the United States lives below the poverty line established by the federal government. In 2007, no fewer than 37.2 million people were living in

RESEARCH TODAY

9-1 Precarious Work

In 2008 Jim Marshall, age 39, lost his job in Detroit's faltering auto industry. Figuring that job prospects had to be better elsewhere, he moved to Florida. But by May 2009 Jim was homeless, living in a tent city just north of St. Petersburg. "My parents always taught me to work hard in school, graduate high school, go to college, get a degree and you'll do fine. You'll do better than your parents' generation," Marshall says. "I did all those things. . . . For a while, I did have that good life, but nowadays that's not the reality" (Bazar 2009:A2).

Jim's story is all too common. He is one of the millions of Americans who have been reduced to doing **precarious work**—employment that is poorly paid, and from the worker's perspective, insecure and unprotected. People who engage in precarious work often cannot support a household, and they are vulnerable to falling into poverty.

Even before economists recognized the economic downturn in 2009, there was ample statistical evidence that precarious work was increasing, despite the fact that the unemployment rate remained steady. In his presidential address to the ASA, Arne L. Kalleberg offered the following five social indicators:

1. *A decline in the average length of time workers remain with an employer.* This trend has been especially noticeable among older White men, who in the past were protected by employers.
2. *An increase in long-term unemployment.* The proportion of workers who remained unemployed after six months rose in the 2000s, when the number of manufacturing jobs shrank and fewer new jobs were created.
3. *A decrease in job security.* Given the increase in long-term unemployment and the decrease in average time spent with an employer, workers became increasingly insecure about their ability to replace a lost job.
4. *An increase in outsourcing and temporary work.* To meet cyclical fluctuations in supply and demand, employers have turned more and more to nontraditional labor sources. Today, virtually any job can be outsourced, including accounting, legal, and military services.

To meet cyclical fluctuations in supply and demand, employers have turned more and more to nontraditional labor sources. Today, virtually any job can be outsourced, including accounting, legal, and military services.

5. *A shift in risk from employers to employees.* Few companies offer traditional pensions anymore. Employees are being asked to shoulder at least part of the cost and risk, not only of their retirement investments, but of their health insurance plans.

Although precarious work is becoming more common, people differ in their vulnerability to it. Members of racial and ethnic minorities are more likely than others to be engaged in precarious work. Immigrants, including those who are in the United States legally, are also more likely than others to be precariously employed. Around the world—in the United States, other industrial countries, and developing nations—women are much more likely than men to do precarious work.

What can be done to revitalize labor markets so that fewer workers end up doing substandard work—or at least, that those who do will suffer less from it? Denmark is one country that has tried to deal with the problem. Although the government there cannot make jobs more secure, it does provide significant assistance to the unemployed. Help finding a job, significant income compensation (90 percent of a worker's previous wage for one year, without conditions), and subsidized education and training are all available to Danish workers who have lost their jobs.

LET'S DISCUSS

1. Has the trend toward increasing reliance on precarious work touched your family or friends? Has anyone you know been unemployed longer than six months? If so, did that person or persons belong to one or more of the groups that are particularly vulnerable to precarious work?
2. Looking forward to your own career, can you think of a strategy for avoiding precarious work, frequent job loss, and long-term unemployment?

Sources: Bazar 2009; Fudge and Owens 2006; Kalleberg 2009; Somavia 2008; Westergaard-Nielsen 2008.

---

poverty. The economic boom of the 1990s passed these people by. A Bureau of the Census report showed that one in five households has trouble meeting basic needs, from paying the utility bills to buying dinner (Bauman 1999; DeNavas-Walt et al. 2008).

One contributor to the United States' high poverty rate has been the large number of workers employed at minimum wage. The federal government has raised the minimum wage over the past half century from 75 cents in 1950 to $6.55 in 2008 and $7.25 in 2009. But in terms of its real value adjusted for inflation, the minimum wage has frequently failed to keep pace with the cost of living. Little wonder, then, that Barbara Ehrenreich could barely scrape by when she experimented with life as a low-wage worker (see the excerpt that opened Chapter 1). Sociologists have long had an interest in the impact of substandard work on society, beginning with the writings of Karl Marx, Émile Durkheim, and

Max Weber. Their interest increased with the global economic decline that began in 2008, which trapped many people in jobs they did not want or left them unemployed. Box 9-1 considers recent sociological work on *precarious work*.

In this section, we'll consider just how social scientists define *poverty*. We'll also take a closer look at the people who fall into that category—including the working poor.

Studying Poverty

The efforts of sociologists and other social scientists to better understand poverty are complicated by the difficulty of defining it. This problem is evident even in government programs that conceive of poverty in either absolute or relative terms. **Absolute poverty** refers to a minimum level of subsistence that no family should be expected to live below.

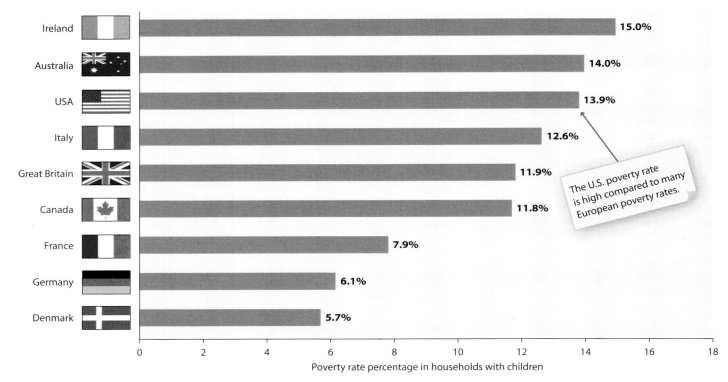

Note: Data are averages for a three-year period reported in 2007. Poverty threshold is 50 percent of a nation's median income.
Source: Organization for Economic Co-operation and Development 2007.

One commonly used measure of absolute poverty is the federal government's *poverty line,* a money income figure that is adjusted annually to reflect the consumption requirements of families based on their size and composition. The poverty line serves as an official definition of which people are poor. In 2007, for example, any family of four (two adults and two children) with a combined income of $21,000 or less fell below the poverty line. This definition determines which individuals and families will be eligible for certain government benefits (DeNavas-Walt et al. 2008).

Although by absolute standards, poverty has declined in the United States, it remains higher than in many other industrial nations. As Figure 9-5 shows, a comparatively high proportion of U.S. households are poor, meaning that they are unable to purchase basic consumer goods. If anything, this cross-national comparison understates the extent of poverty in the United States, since U.S. residents are likely to pay more for housing, health care, child care, and education than residents of other countries, where such expenses are often subsidized (Smeeding 2008).

In contrast, **relative poverty** is a floating standard of deprivation by which people at the bottom of a society, whatever their lifestyles, are judged to be disadvantaged *in comparison with the nation as a whole.* Therefore, even if the poor of 2005 are better off in absolute terms than the poor of the 1930s or 1960s, they are still seen as deserving of special assistance. Box 9-2 explores the difference between relative poverty in Appalachia and relative affluence in the Congo.

Since the 1990s, debate has grown over the accuracy of the federal government's measure of poverty. If noncash benefits such as Medicare, Medicaid, food stamps, public housing, and health care and other employer-provided fringe benefits were

included, the reported poverty rate would be lower. On the other hand, if out-of-pocket medical expenses and mandatory work expenses for transportation and child care were included, the poverty rate would be higher. The Census Bureau estimates that on balance, if both these recommendations were followed, the official poverty rate would be 2 percent higher, and 5 million more people would fall below the poverty line (Bernasek 2006).

Who Are the Poor?

Not only does the category of the poor defy any simple definition; it counters the common stereotypes about "poor people" that Barbara Ehrenreich addressed in her book *Nickel and Dimed* (see the opening excerpt in Chapter 1). For example, many people in the United States believe that the vast majority of the poor are able to work but will not. Yet many poor adults do work outside the home, although only a small portion of them work full-time throughout the year. In 2006, about 32 percent of all poor working adults worked full-time, compared to 66 percent of all adults. Of those poor adults who do not work, most are ill or disabled, or are occupied in maintaining a home (DeNavas-Walt et al. 2008).

Though many of the poor live in urban slums, a majority live outside those poverty-stricken areas. Poverty is no stranger in rural areas, from Appalachia to hard-hit farming regions to Native American reservations. Table 9-3 provides additional statistical information regarding low-income people in the United States.

Feminization of Poverty

Since World War II, an increasing proportion of the poor people of the United States have been women, many of whom are divorced or never-married mothers. In 1959, female householders

SOCIOLOGY IN THE GLOBAL COMMUNITY

9-2 It's All Relative: Appalachian Poverty and Congolese Affluence

What does it mean to be well off? To be poor? To explore this question, the editors of the London-based publication *The Economist* compared the situations of two men living very different lives: an unemployed truck driver in the Appalachian Mountains and a physician in Congo.

Enos Banks makes his home in a forgotten pocket of rural poverty, described over 40 years ago in Michael Harrington's *The Other America*. Banks once worked for a coal-mining company, but a heart attack forced him to quit his job. In his 60s, he lives in a trailer and gets by on a little more than $500 a month in supplemental security income (SSI). Because he owns a truck, he is not eligible for food stamps.

On the other side of the world, in the Democratic Republic of Congo, Mbwebwe Kabamba earns about $100 or $200 more per month than Enos Banks. Kabamba is a surgeon and head of the emergency room at a hospital in Kinshasa, the country's capital. His hospital salary is only $250 a month, but he supplements it by performing surgery on the side. In Congo, a similar income to that which impoverishes Enos

Banks places Kabamba near the middle of his society's income distribution.

Though Kabamba may seem better off than Banks, especially given the Congo's lower cost of living, such is not the case. Kabamba supports a family of 12, while Banks supports only himself. By U.S. standards, Kabamba's four-bedroom home, spacious compared to Banks's trailer, is overcrowded with 12 inhabitants. And though Kabamba's home has a kitchen, it lacks running water, dependable

> *By U.S. standards, Kabamba's four-bedroom home, spacious compared to Banks's trailer, is overcrowded with 12 inhabitants.*

electric service, and air-conditioning—services most Americans take for granted. Considered wealthy in his own country, Kabamba is worse off than a poor person in the United States.

Nevertheless, Banks's poverty is real; he occupies a position close to the bottom of the

pyramid in Figure 9-3. In absolute terms defined by his own society, Kabamba is not poor, even though he is less well off than Enos Banks. Relative to most of the world's population, however, both men are doing well.

LET'S DISCUSS

1. Have you ever lived in or traveled to a foreign country where income and living standards were very different from those in the United States? If so, did the contrast give you a new perspective on poverty? What differences between the living standards in the two societies stand out in your mind?
2. If absolute measures of poverty, such as household income, are inconsistent from one country to the next, what other measures might give a clearer picture of people's relative well-being? Should the poverty level be the same everywhere in the world? Why or why not?

Sources: *The Economist* 2005f; Harrington 1962; Haub 2008.

TABLE **9-3**   WHO ARE THE POOR IN THE UNITED STATES?

Group	Percentage of the Population of the United States	Percentage of the Poor of the United States
Under 18 years old	26%	36%
18 to 64 years old	61	54
65 years and older	13	10
Whites (non-Hispanic)	83	43
Blacks	12	27
Hispanics	11	25
Asians and Pacific Islanders	4	4
Married couples and families with male householders	82	47
Families with female householders	18	53

Note: Data are for 2007, as reported by the Bureau of the Census in 2008.
Source: DeNavas-Walt et al. 2008:13.

departure, disability, or death of a husband. The other half tend to be economically dependent either on the welfare system or on friends and relatives living nearby. A major factor in the feminization of poverty has been the increase in families with women as single heads of the household (see Chapter 14). Conflict theorists and other observers trace the higher rates of poverty among women to three distinct factors: the difficulty in finding affordable child care, sexual harassment, and sex discrimination in the labor market.

The Underclass

In 2007, 42 percent of poor people in the United States were living in central cities. These highly visible urban residents are the focus of most government efforts to alleviate poverty. Yet according to many observers, the plight of the urban poor is growing worse, owing to the devastating interplay of inadequate education and limited employment prospects. Traditional employment opportunities in the industrial sector are largely closed to the unskilled poor. Past and present discrimination heightens these problems for those low-income urban residents who are Black and Hispanic (DeNavas-Walt et al. 2008:13).

accounted for 26 percent of the nation's poor; by 2007, that figure had risen to 53 percent (see Table 9-3). This alarming trend, known as the **feminization of poverty**, is evident not just in the United States but around the world.

About half of all women living in poverty in the United States are in transition, coping with an economic crisis caused by the

Along with other social scientists, sociologist William Julius Wilson (1980, 1987, 1996) and his colleagues (2004) have used the term **underclass** to describe the long-term poor who lack training and skills. According to an analysis of Census 2000 data, 7.9 million people live in high-poverty neighborhoods. About 30 percent of the population in these neighborhoods is Black, 29 percent Hispanic, and 24 percent White. In central cities, about 49 percent of the underclass is Black, 29 percent Hispanic, 17 percent White, and 5 percent "other" (Jargowsky and Yang 2006; O'Hare and Curry-White 1992).

Conflict theorists, among others, have expressed alarm at the portion of the nation's population living on this lower rung of the stratification ladder, and at society's reluctance to address the lack of economic opportunities for these people. Often, portraits of the underclass seem to blame the victims for their plight, while ignoring the other factors that push people into poverty.

Analyses of the poor in general reveal that they are not a static social class. The overall composition of the poor changes continually, because some individuals and families near the top edge of poverty move above the poverty level after a year or two, while others slip below it. Still, hundreds of thousands of people remain in poverty for many years at a time. Blacks and Latinos are more likely than Whites to be persistently poor. Over a 21-year period, 15 percent of African Americans and 10 percent of Latinos were persistently poor, compared to 3 percent of Whites. Both Latinos and Blacks are less likely than Whites to leave the welfare rolls as a result of welfare reform, discussed in the Social Policy section of this chapter (Mangum et al. 2003).

Even if this single parent works her way up the chain of command, supporting her family will still be difficult.

Explaining Poverty

Why is it that poverty pervades a nation of such vast wealth? Sociologist Herbert Gans (1995), who has applied functionalist analysis to the existence of poverty, argues that various segments of society actually *benefit* from the existence of the poor. Gans has identified a number of social, economic, and political functions that the poor perform for society:

- The presence of poor people means that society's dirty work—physically dirty or dangerous, dead-end and underpaid, undignified and menial jobs—will be performed at low cost.

- Poverty creates jobs for occupations and professions that serve the poor. It creates both legal employment (public health experts, welfare caseworkers) and illegal jobs (drug dealers, numbers runners).

- The identification and punishment of the poor as deviants upholds the legitimacy of conventional social norms and mainstream values regarding hard work, thrift, and honesty.

- Within a relatively hierarchical society, the existence of poor people guarantees the higher status of the more affluent. As psychologist William Ryan (1976) noted, affluent people may justify inequality (and gain a measure of satisfaction) by *blaming the victims* of poverty for their disadvantaged condition.

- Because of their lack of political power, the poor often absorb the costs of social change. Under the policy of deinstitutionalization, mental patients released from long-term hospitals have been transferred primarily to low-income communities

and neighborhoods. Similarly, halfway houses for rehabilitated drug abusers, rejected by more affluent communities, often end up in poorer neighborhoods.

In Gans's view, then, poverty and the poor actually satisfy positive functions for many nonpoor groups in the United States.

Life Chances

Max Weber saw class as being closely related to people's **life chances**—that is, their opportunities to provide themselves with material goods, positive living conditions, and favorable life experiences (Gerth and Mills 1958). Life chances are reflected in measures such as housing, education, and health. Occupying a higher position in a society improves your life chances and brings greater access to social rewards. In contrast, people in the lower social classes are forced to devote a larger proportion of their limited resources to the necessities of life.

In times of danger, the affluent and powerful have a better chance of surviving than people of ordinary means. When the supposedly unsinkable British ocean liner *Titanic* hit an iceberg in 1912, it was not carrying enough lifeboats to accommodate all passengers. Plans had been made to evacuate only first- and second-class passengers. About 62 percent of the first-class passengers survived the disaster. Despite a rule that women and children would go first, about a third of those passengers were male. In contrast, only 25 percent of the passengers in third class survived. The first attempt to alert them to the need to abandon ship came well after other passengers had been notified (Butler 1998; Crouse 1999; Riding 1998).

Class position also affects people's vulnerability to natural disasters. When Hurricane Katrina hit the Gulf Coast of the United States in 2005, affluent and poor people alike became its victims. However, poor people who did not own automobiles (100,000 of them in New Orleans alone) were less able than others to evacuate in advance of the storm. The poor survived its fury had no nest egg to draw on, and thus were more likely than others to accept relocation wherever social service agencies could place them—sometimes hundreds or thousands of miles from home. Those who were able to return are still dealing with the toxic debris left behind (Bullard and Wright 2009).

Some people have hoped that the Internet revolution would help to level the playing field by making information and markets uniformly available. Unfortunately, however, not everyone can get onto the information superhighway, so yet another aspect of social inequality has emerged—the **digital divide** (see page 147). The poor, minorities, and those who live in rural communities and inner cities are not getting connected at home or at work. A recent government study found that despite falling computer prices, the Internet gap between the haves and have-nots has not narrowed: although 70 percent of all people in the United States used the Internet in 2006, that group included 94 over $75,000 but fewer than 57 less than $30,000. As wealthier people switch to high-speed Internet connections, they will be

Class position affects people's vulnerability to natural disasters. Today, years after Hurricane Katrina forced the evacuation of New Orleans, many of the city's poor still have not returned home.

able to take advantage of even more sophisticated interactive services, and the digital divide will grow even wider (Pew Internet Project 2009).

Wealth, status, and power may not ensure happiness, but they certainly provide additional ways of coping with problems and disappointments. For this reason, the opportunity for advancement—for social mobility—is of special significance to those on the bottom of society. Most people want the rewards and privileges that are granted to high-ranking members of a culture. What can society do to increase their social mobility? One strategy is to offer financial aid to college students from low-income families, on the theory that education lifts people out of poverty. Yet such programs are not having as great an effect as their authors once hoped (Box 9-3 on page 210).

www.mhhe.com/schaefer12e

use your sociological *imagination*

Imagine a society in which there are no social classes—no differences in people's wealth, income, and life chances. What would such a society be like? Would it be stable, or would its social structure change over time?

Social Mobility

In the movie *Maid in Manhattan,* Jennifer Lopez plays the lead in a modern-day Cinderella story, rising from the lowly status of chambermaid in a big-city hotel to a company supervisor and the girlfriend of a well-to-do politician. The ascent of a person from a poor background to a position of prestige, power, or financial reward is an example of social mobility. Formally defined, the term **social mobility** refers to the movement of individuals or groups from one position in a society's stratification system to another. But how significant—how frequent, how dramatic—is mobility in a class society such as the United States?

Open versus Closed Stratification Systems

Sociologists use the terms *open stratification system* and *closed stratification system* to indicate the degree of social mobility in a society. An **open system** implies that the position of each individual is influenced by his or her *achieved* status. Such a system encourages competition among members of society. The United States is moving toward this ideal type as the government attempts to reduce the barriers faced by women, racial and ethnic minorities, and people born in lower social classes. Even in the midst of the economic downturn of 2008–2009, nearly 80 percent of people in the United States felt they could get ahead (Economic Mobility Project 2009).

At the other extreme of social mobility is the **closed system,** which allows little or no possibility of individual social mobility. The slavery and caste systems of stratification are examples of closed systems. In such societies, social placement is based on *ascribed* statuses, such as race or family background, which cannot be changed.

Types of Social Mobility

An airline pilot who becomes a police officer moves from one social position to another of the same rank. Each occupation has the same prestige ranking: 60 on a scale ranging from a low of 0 to a high of 100 (see Table 9-2 on page 202). Sociologists call this kind of movement **horizontal mobility.** However, if the pilot were to become a lawyer (prestige ranking of 75), he or she would experience **vertical mobility,** the movement of an individual from one social position to another of a different rank. Vertical mobility can also involve moving *downward* in a society's stratification system, as would be the case if the airline pilot became a bank teller (ranking of 43). Pitirim Sorokin ([1927] 1959) was the first sociologist to distinguish between horizontal and vertical mobility. Most sociological analysis, however, focuses on vertical rather than horizontal mobility.

One way of examining vertical social mobility is to contrast its two types, intergenerational and intragenerational mobility. **Intergenerational mobility** involves changes in the social position of children relative to their parents. Thus, a plumber whose father was a physician provides an example of downward intergenerational mobility. A film star whose parents were both factory workers illustrates upward intergenerational mobility. Because education contributes significantly to upward mobility, any barrier to the pursuit of advanced degrees can definitely limit intergenerational mobility (see Box 9-3; Isaacs 2007a; Isaacs et al. 2008; Sawhill and Morton 2007).

Figure 9-7 on page 211 shows intergenerational mobility based on income. In 1978–1980, a national survey looked at the family income of 6,000 young people. Two decades later, in 1997–2003, researchers followed up on those young adults and their income. The results showed a strong "stickiness" in both the bottom and top quintiles, or fifths, of the income distribution. Just over 33 percent of those whose parents were in the bottom quintile and 37 percent of those who were in the top quintile remained in the same quintile as adults. Yet the study also showed mobility: almost 66 percent of those in the bottom quintile moved up, and over 60 percent of those at the top experienced downward mobility.

Intragenerational mobility involves changes in social position within a person's adult life. A woman begins work as a teacher's

SOCIOLOGY ON CAMPUS

9-3 Social Class and Financial Aid

Today's young people have been dubbed Generation Y, but a more appropriate name for them could be Generation Debt. Every year, millions of prospective college students and their parents struggle through the intricate and time-consuming process of applying for financial aid. Originally, financial aid programs were intended to level the playing field—to allow qualified students from all walks of life to attend college, regardless of the cost. But have these programs fulfilled their promise?

Statistics that show the educational level in the United States rising overall obscure the widening gap between the advantaged and the less advantaged.

In 2004, 40 percent of first-year students at major state universities came from families with incomes of more than $100,000 a year. In other words, close to half of all students came from high-income families. This statistic should not be surprising, given the high cost of tuition, room, and board at state universities. For students from families with the lowest incomes, the cost can be prohibitive. Only 11 percent of children from the poorest families in the United States have earned college degrees, compared to 53 percent of children from families in the top fifth of the population. Those moderate-income students who do graduate, and even those who fail to complete their degrees, are often saddled with heavy postgraduate debt.

Besides the spiraling cost of an education, the widespread difficulty in paying for college stems from three trends. First, over the past few decades, colleges and universities have been moving away from making outright grants, such as scholarships, to deserving students, and toward low-interest student loans. Second, much of the assistance schools offer in the form of loans is not based strictly on need. Third, interest rates on federally guaranteed loans have risen steadily, increasing the burden of repayment.

These trends in financial aid for higher education are closely tied to trends in social inequality. As noted earlier in this chapter, over the past half century, rather than declining, inequality in income and wealth has actually increased. According to one analysis of U.S. economic trends over the past 30 years, this increase in wealth and income inequality has contributed to a modest increase in educational inequality, as measured by the number of years of formal schooling students achieve. In a variation on the truism that the rich tend to get richer while the poor get poorer, the rich are getting better educations and the poor are getting poorer educations. Statistics that show the educational level in the United States rising overall obscure the widening gap between the advantaged and the less advantaged.

LET'S DISCUSS

1. How important is financial aid (grants, loans, work-study income) to you and your friends? Without these types of aid, would you be able to cover your college expenses?

2. Aside from a reduction in individual social mobility, what might be the long-term effects of the shortage of need-based financial aid? Relate your answer to the trend toward globalization.

Sources: Boushey 2005; Campbell et al. 2005; Isaacs et al. 2008; Kamenetz 2006; Leonhardt 2004; Michals 2003; Trumbull 2006.

PUMP & CIRCUMSTANCE.

---

aide and eventually becomes superintendent of the school district experiences upward intragenerational mobility. A man who becomes a taxicab driver after his accounting firm goes bankrupt undergoes downward intragenerational mobility.

Social Mobility in the United States

The belief in upward mobility is an important value in our society. Does that mean that the United States is indeed the land of opportunity? Not unless such ascriptive characteristics as race, gender, and family background have ceased to be significant in determining one's future prospects. We can see the impact of these factors in the occupational structure.

Occupational Mobility Two sociological studies conducted a decade apart offer insight into the degree of mobility in the nation's occupational structure (Blau and Duncan 1967; Featherman and Hauser 1978). Taken together, these investigations lead to several noteworthy conclusions. First, occupational mobility (both intergenerational and intragenerational) has been common among males. Approximately 60 to 70 percent of sons are employed in higher-ranked occupations than their fathers.

Second, although there is a great deal of mobility in the United States, much of it is minor. That is, people who reach an occupational level above or below that of their parents usually advance or fall back only one or two out of a possible eight occupational levels. Thus, the child of a laborer may become an artisan or a technician, but he or she is less likely to become a manager or professional. The odds against reaching the top are extremely high unless one begins from a relatively privileged position.

If this lawyer were the son of a car mechanic, his rise to the upper-middle class would illustrate intergenerational mobility. If he had begun as a paralegal and worked his way up the occupational ladder, his career would illustrate intragenerational mobility.

FIGURE **9-7**   INTERGENERATIONAL INCOME MOBILITY

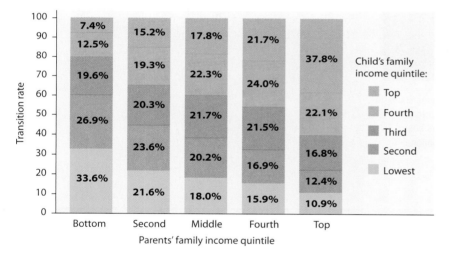

Source: Mazumder 2008:10.

Over a 25-year period, adult children often end up in the same income bracket as their parents. About 7 percent of those who begin in the bottom quintile reach the top quintile as adults; their story is one of rags to riches. About 11 percent of those who start in the top quintile fall to the bottom.

The Impact of Education   Another conclusion of both studies is that education plays a critical role in social mobility. The impact of formal schooling on adult status is even greater than that of family background (although as we have seen, family background influences the likelihood that one will receive higher education). Furthermore, education represents an important means of intergenerational mobility. A person who was born into a poor family but who graduates from college has a one in five chance of entering the top fifth of all income earners as an adult (Isaacs et al. 2008).

The impact of education on mobility has diminished somewhat in the past decade, however. An undergraduate degree—a BA or a BS—serves less as a guarantee of upward mobility now than it did in the past, simply because more and more entrants into the job market hold such a degree. Moreover, intergenerational mobility is declining, since there is no longer such a stark difference between generations. In earlier decades, many high school–educated parents successfully sent their children to college, but today's college students are increasingly likely to have college-educated parents (Sawhill and Morton 2007).

The Impact of Race and Ethnicity
Sociologists have long documented the fact that the class system is more rigid for African Americans than it is for members of other racial groups. African American men who have good jobs, for example, are less likely than White men to see their adult children attain the same status. The cumulative disadvantage of discrimination plays a significant role in the disparity between the two groups' experiences. Compared to White households, the relatively modest wealth of African American households means that adult African American children are less likely than adult White children to receive financial support from their parents. Indeed, young African American couples are much more likely than young White couples to be assisting their parents—a sacrifice that hampers their social mobility (Favreault 2008).

The African American middle class has grown over the past few decades, due to economic expansion and the benefits of the civil rights movement of the 1960s. Yet many of these middle-class households have little savings, a fact that puts them in danger during times of crisis. Studies have consistently shown that downward mobility is significantly higher for Blacks than it is for Whites (Oliver and Shapiro 2006; Sernau 2001; W. Wilson 1996).

The Latino population is not doing much better. The typical Hispanic has less than 10 percent of the wealth that a White person has. A 2008 study suggests that in recent years, Latinos have even lost ground. Their continuing immigration accounts for part of the disparity: most of the new arrivals are destitute. But even the wealthiest 5 percent of Latino households have only a third as much net worth as the top 5 percent of White households (Kochhar 2008).

The Impact of Gender   Studies of mobility, even more than those of class, have traditionally ignored the significance of gender, but some research findings are now available that explore the relationship between gender and mobility.

Andrea Jung, chairman and chief executive officer of Avon Corporation since 1999, is one of the few women in the United States who have risen to the top of the corporate hierarchy. In 2008, Jung was elected to Apple's board of directors. Despite the passage of equal opportunity laws, occupational barriers still limit most women's social mobility.

Women's employment opportunities are much more limited than men's (as Chapter 12 will show). Moreover, according to recent research, women whose skills far exceed the jobs offered them are more likely than men to withdraw entirely from the paid labor force. Their withdrawal violates an assumption common to traditional mobility studies: that most people will aspire to upward mobility and seek to make the most of their opportunities.

In contrast to men, women have a rather large range of clerical occupations open to them. But the modest salary ranges and few prospects for advancement in many of these positions limit the possibility of upward mobility. Self-employment as shopkeepers, entrepreneurs, independent professionals, and the like—an important road to upward mobility for men—is more difficult for women, who find it harder to secure the necessary financing. Although sons commonly follow in the footsteps of their fathers, women are unlikely to move into their fathers' positions. Consequently, gender remains an important factor in shaping social mobility. Women in the United States (and in other parts of the world) are especially likely to be trapped in poverty, unable to rise out of their low-income status (Heilman 2001).

On the positive side, though today's women lag behind men in employment, their earnings have increased faster than their mothers' did at a comparable age, so that their incomes are substantially higher. The one glaring exception to this trend is the daughters of low-income parents. Because these women typically care for children—many as single parents—and sometimes for other relatives as well, their mobility is severely restricted (Isaacs 2007b).

social**policy** and Gender Stratification

Rethinking Welfare in North America and Europe

The Issue

- In Milwaukee, a single mother of six has just lost her job as a security guard. Once considered a success story of the welfare reform program, she has fallen victim to the economic recession that followed the boom years of the 1990s. Because she has been on welfare before, she is ineligible to receive additional assistance from the state of Wisconsin. Yet like many other workers who made the transition from welfare to work in the late 1990s, she does not qualify for unemployment benefits; food stamps are all she can count on (Pierre 2002).

- In Paris, France, Hélène Desegrais, another single mother, waited four months to place her daughter in government-subsidized day care. Now she can seek a full-time job, but

she is concerned about government threats to curtail such services in order to keep taxes down (Simons 1997).

These are the faces of people living on the edge—often women with children seeking to make a go of it amid changing social policies. Governments in all parts of the world are searching for the right solution to welfare: How much subsidy should they provide? How much responsibility should fall on the shoulders of the poor?

The Setting

In the 1990s, an intense debate took place in the United States over the issue of welfare. Welfare programs were costly, and concern was widespread (however unfounded) that welfare payments discouraged recipients from seeking jobs. Both Democrats and Republicans vowed to "end welfare as we know it."

In late 1996, in a historic shift in federal policy, Congress passed the Personal Responsibility and Work Opportunity Reconciliation Act, ending the long-standing federal guarantee of assistance to every poor family that meets eligibility requirements. The law set a lifetime limit of five years of welfare benefits, and required all able-bodied adults to work after receiving two years of benefits (although hardship exceptions were allowed). The federal government would give block grants to the states to use as they wished in assisting poor a nd needy residents, and it would permit states to experiment with ways to move people off welfare (Cherlin 2008b; Jenness et al. 2008).

A decade later, however, the severe economic downturn of 2008–2009 forced many more people into this shrunken safety net. By 2009, over 16 percent of all personal income in the United States was coming from Social Security, food stamps, and unemployment insurance. That was the highest percentage since the government began compiling such data in 1929. In the 1960s, the proportion of income coming from these sources was less than 8 percent (Bureau of Economic Analysis 2009).

Despite this increase in dependency, reliance on the government safety net still falls far short of that in Europe, even after recent cutbacks there. Available data indicate that in Great Britain, 87 percent of health expenditures are paid for by the government; in Sweden, 82 percent; in Canada, 70 percent; but in the United States, only 46 percent. In fact, most industrialized nations devote higher proportions of their expenditures to housing, social security, welfare, health care, and unemployment compensation than the United States does. As U.S. economist Dean Baker declared recently, "The increase in social spending is still relatively modest given the severity of the downturn. We're not France" (Cauchon 2009; World Bank 2009:98–100).

For nations like Sweden, which have comparatively little income disparity, programs aimed at alleviating poverty are not as necessary as they are in the United States.

Sociological Insights

Many sociologists tend to view the debate over welfare reform in industrialized nations from a conflict perspective: the "haves" in positions of policymaking listen to the interests of other "haves," while the cries of the "have-nots" are drowned out. Critics of welfare reform believe that the nation's economic problems are unfairly blamed on welfare spending and the poor. From a conflict perspective, this backlash against welfare recipients reflects deep fears and hostility toward the nation's urban, predominantly African American and Hispanic underclass.

Those who are critical of the backlash note that "welfare scapegoating" conveniently ignores the lucrative federal handouts that go to *affluent* individuals and families. For example, while federal housing aid to the poor was cut drastically in the 1980s, tax deductions for mortgage interest and property taxes more than doubled.

Those who take a conflict perspective also urge policymakers and the general public to look closely at **corporate welfare**—the tax breaks, direct payments, and grants that the government makes to corporations—rather than looking closely at the comparatively small allowances being given to welfare mothers and their children. Yet any suggestion to curtail such corporate welfare brings a strong response from special-interest groups that are much more powerful than any coalition on behalf of the poor. One example of corporate welfare was the huge federal bailout of distressed financial institutions that occurred in fall 2008. Although the layout of hundreds of billions of dollars was vital to the nation's economic recovery, the measure received relatively little scrutiny from Congress. Just a few months later, however, when legislation was proposed to extend the safety net for laid-off workers—unemployment compensation, food stamps, subsidized child care, assistance to the homeless, disability support, and infant nutrition—it met with loud demands for the monitoring of expenditures (DeParle 2009; Piven and Cloward 1996).

Policy Initiatives

The government likes to highlight welfare reform success stories. Though many people who once depended on tax dollars are now working and paying taxes themselves, it is much too soon to see if "workfare" will be successful. The new jobs that were generated by the booming economy of the late 1990s were an unrealistic test of the system. Prospects have faded for the hard-core jobless—people who are difficult to train or are encumbered by drug or alcohol abuse, physical disabilities, or child care needs—since the boom passed and the economy moved into recession (Jencks et al. 2006; M. Turner et al. 2007).

True, fewer people remain on the rolls since welfare reform was enacted in August 1996. By April 2008 less than 1.7 million families were still on the rolls, down 65 percent from a high of 5.1 million in 1994. But while those families that have left the rolls are modestly better off now, most of their breadwinners continue to hold low-paying, unskilled jobs. For them, the economic downturn that was well in place by 2009 made finding work tougher than ever. Of those adults who remain on welfare, nearly 60 percent are not in school or in welfare-to-work programs, as the law requires them to be. This group tends to face the greatest challenges—substance abuse, mental illness, or a criminal record. Finally, while the welfare rolls have declined, the number of people who receive Medicaid and food stamps has increased by 50 percent since 2000 (Cherlin 2008b; A. Goldstein 2009; Haskins 2006; Health and Human Services 2009; R. Wolf 2006).

European governments have encountered many of the same citizen demands as in North America: keep our taxes low, even if it means reducing services to the poor. However, nations in eastern and central Europe have faced a special challenge since the end of communism. Though governments in those nations traditionally provided an impressive array of social services, they differed from capitalist systems in several important respects. First, the communist system was premised on full employment, so there was no need to provide unemployment insurance; social services focused on the old and the disabled. Second, subsidies for housing and even utilities played an important role. With new competition from the West and tight budgets, some of these countries are beginning to realize that universal coverage is no longer affordable and must be replaced with targeted programs. Even Sweden, despite its long history of social welfare programs, is feeling the pinch. Yet, by any standard, the European safety net is still significantly better than that of the United States (Petrášová 2006; M. Walker and Thurow 2009).

Both in North America and in Europe, people are beginning to turn to private means to support themselves. For instance, they are investing money for their later years rather than depending on government social security programs. But that solution works only if you have a job and can save money. Increasingly, people are seeing the gap between themselves and the affluent grow, with fewer government programs available to assist them. Solutions are frequently left to the private sector, while government policy initiatives at the national level all but disappear.

Let's Discuss

1. Do you personally know anyone who has had to depend on public assistance, such as food stamps? If so, what were the circumstances? Would you yourself need government assistance under such circumstances?

2. Do you think welfare recipients should be required to work? If so, what kind of support should they receive? Should any exceptions be granted to the work requirement?

3. Why do you think western and northern European countries have more generous welfare programs than the United States?

getting**involved**

To get involved in the debate over welfare reform, visit this book's Online Learning Center, which offers links to relevant Web sites.

www.mhhe.com/schaefer12e

MASTERING THIS CHAPTER

Summary

Stratification is the structured ranking of entire groups of people that perpetuates unequal economic rewards and **power** in a society. In this chapter we examine four general systems of stratification, the explanations offered by functionalist and conflict theorists for the existence of **social inequality,** and the relationship between stratification and **social mobility.**

1. Some degree of **social inequality** characterizes all cultures.

2. Systems of social **stratification** include **slavery, castes,** the **estate system,** and social classes.

3. Karl Marx saw that differences in access to the means of production created social, economic, and political inequality, as well as two distinct classes, owners and laborers.

4. Max Weber identified three analytically distinct components of stratification: **class, status group,** and **power.**

5. Functionalists argue that stratification is necessary to motivate people to fill society's important positions. Conflict theorists see stratification as a major source of societal tension and conflict. Interactionists stress the importance of social class in determining a person's lifestyle.

6. One consequence of social class in the United States is that both **income** and **wealth** are distributed unevenly.

7. Many of those who live in poverty are full-time workers who struggle to support their families at minimum-wage jobs. The long-term poor—those who lack the training and skills to lift themselves out of poverty—form an **underclass.**

8. Functionalists find that the poor satisfy positive functions for many of the nonpoor in the United States.

9. One's **life chances**—opportunities for obtaining material goods, positive living conditions, and favorable life experiences—are related to one's social class. Occupying a high social position improves a person's life chances.

10. **Social mobility** is more likely to be found in an **open system** that emphasizes **achieved status** than in a **closed system** that emphasizes **ascribed status.** Race, gender, and family background are important factors in social mobility.

11. Today, many governments are struggling with the question of how much tax revenue to spend on welfare programs. The trend in the United States is to put welfare recipients to work.

Critical Thinking Questions

1. Sociologist Daniel Rossides has conceptualized the class system of the United States using a five-class model. According to Rossides, the upper-middle class and the lower-middle class together account for about 40 percent of the nation's population. Yet studies suggest that a higher proportion of respondents identify themselves as middle class. Drawing on the model presented by Rossides, suggest why members of both the upper class and the working class might prefer to identify themselves as middle class.

2. Sociological study of stratification is generally conducted at the macro level and draws most heavily on the functionalist and conflict perspectives. How might sociologists use the *interactionist* perspective to examine social class inequalities in a college community?

3. Imagine you have the opportunity to do research on changing patterns of social mobility in the United States. What specific question would you want to investigate, and how would you go about it?

Key Terms

Absolute poverty A minimum level of subsistence that no family should be expected to live below. (page 205)

Achieved status A social position that a person attains largely through his or her own efforts. (193)

Ascribed status A social position assigned to a person by society without regard for the person's unique talents or characteristics. (193)

Bourgeoisie Karl Marx's term for the capitalist class, comprising the owners of the means of production. (197)

Capitalism An economic system in which the means of production are held largely in private hands and the main incentive for economic activity is the accumulation of profits. (197)

Caste A hereditary rank, usually religiously dictated, that tends to be fixed and immobile. (193)

Class A group of people who have a similar level of income and wealth. (198)

Class consciousness In Karl Marx's view, a subjective awareness held by members of a class regarding their common vested interests and need for collective political action to bring about social change. (197)

Class system A social ranking based primarily on economic position in which achieved characteristics can influence social mobility. (195)

Closed system A social system in which there is little or no possibility of individual social mobility. (209)

Corporate welfare Tax breaks, direct payments, and grants that the government makes to corporations. (213)

Digital divide The relative lack of access to the latest technologies among low-income groups, racial and ethnic minorities, rural residents, and the citizens of developing countries. (208)

Dominant ideology A set of cultural beliefs and practices that helps to maintain powerful social, economic, and political interests. (200)

Estate system A system of stratification under which peasants were required to work land leased to them by nobles in exchange for military protection and other services. Also known as *feudalism*. (195)

Esteem The reputation that a specific person has earned within an occupation. (201)

False consciousness A term used by Karl Marx to describe an attitude held by members of a class that does not accurately reflect their objective position. (198)

Feminization of poverty A trend in which women constitute an increasing proportion of the poor people of the United States. (207)

Horizontal mobility The movement of an individual from one social position to another of the same rank. (209)

Income Salaries and wages. (193)

Intergenerational mobility Changes in the social position of children relative to their parents. (209)

Intragenerational mobility Changes in social position within a person's adult life. (209)

Life chances The opportunities people have to provide themselves with material goods, positive living conditions, and favorable life experiences. (208)

Objective method A technique for measuring social class that assigns individuals to classes on the basis of criteria such as occupation, education, income, and place of residence. (201)

Open system A social system in which the position of each individual is influenced by his or her achieved status. (209)

Power The ability to exercise one's will over others. (198)

Precarious work Employment that is poorly paid, and from the worker's perspective, insecure and unprotected. (205)

Prestige The respect and admiration that an occupation holds in a society. (201)

Proletariat Karl Marx's term for the working class in a capitalist society. (197)

Relative poverty A floating standard of deprivation by which people at the bottom of a society, whatever their lifestyles, are judged to be disadvantaged *in comparison with the nation as a whole*. (206)

Slavery A system of enforced servitude in which some people are owned by other people. (193)

Social inequality A condition in which members of society have differing amounts of wealth, prestige, or power. (192)

Social mobility Movement of individuals or groups from one position in a society's stratification system to another. (209)

Socioeconomic status (SES) A measure of social class that is based on income, education, and occupation. (202)

Status group People who have the same prestige or lifestyle, independent of their class positions. (198)

Stratification A structured ranking of entire groups of people that perpetuates unequal economic rewards and power in a society. (192)

Underclass The long-term poor who lack training and skills. (208)

Vertical mobility The movement of an individual from one social position to another of a different rank. (209)

Wealth An inclusive term encompassing all of a person's material assets, including land, stocks, and other types of property. (193)

Self-Quiz

Read each question carefully and then select the best answer.

1. Which of the following describes a condition in which members of a society have different amounts of wealth, prestige, or power?
   a. stratification
   b. status inconsistency
   c. slavery
   d. social inequality

2. In Karl Marx's view, the destruction of the capitalist system will occur only if the working class first develops
   a. bourgeois consciousness.
   b. false consciousness.
   c. class consciousness.
   d. caste consciousness.

3. Which of the following were viewed by Max Weber as analytically distinct components of stratification?
   a. conformity, deviance, and social control
   b. class, status, and power
   c. class, caste, and age
   d. class, prestige, and esteem

4. Which sociological perspective argues that stratification is universal and that social inequality is necessary so that people will be motivated to fill socially important positions?
   a. the functionalist perspective
   b. the conflict perspective
   c. the interactionist perspective
   d. the labeling perspective

5. British sociologist Ralf Dahrendorf views social classes as groups of people who share common interests resulting from their authority relationships. Dahrendorf's ideology aligns best with which theoretical perspective?
   a. the functionalist perspective
   b. the conflict perspective
   c. the interactionist perspective
   d. sociocultural evolution

6. The respect or admiration that an occupation holds in a society is referred to as
   a. status.
   b. esteem.
   c. prestige.
   d. ranking.

7. Approximately how many out of every nine people in the United States live(s) below the poverty line established by the federal government?
   a. one
   b. two
   c. three
   d. four

8. Which sociologist has applied functionalist analysis to the existence of poverty and argues that various segments of society actually benefit from the existence of the poor?
   a. Émile Durkheim
   b. Max Weber
   c. Karl Marx
   d. Herbert Gans

9. The poor, minorities, and those who live in rural communities and inner cities are not as likely to have access to the Internet as other members of the United States. This situation is called
   a. the cybervoid.
   b. electronic redlining.
   c. the digital divide.
   d. none of the above

10. A plumber whose father was a physician is an example of
    a. downward intergenerational mobility.
    b. upward intergenerational mobility.
    c. downward intragenerational mobility.
    d. upward intragenerational mobility.

11. _____ is the most extreme form of legalized social inequality for individuals or groups.

12. In the _____ system of stratification, or feudalism, peasants were required to work land leased to them by nobles in exchange for military protection and other services.

13. Karl Marx viewed _____ differentiation as the crucial determinant of social, economic, and political inequality.

14. _____ _____ is the term Thorstein Veblen used to describe the extravagant spending patterns of those at the top of the class hierarchy.

15. _____ poverty is the minimum level of subsistence that no family should be expected to live below.

16. _____ poverty is a floating standard of deprivation by which people at the bottom of a society, whatever their lifestyles, are judged to be disadvantaged in comparison with the nation as a whole.

17. Sociologist William Julius Wilson and other social scientists have used the term _____ to describe the long-term poor who lack training and skills.

18. Max Weber used the term _____ _____ to refer to people's opportunities to provide themselves with material goods, positive living conditions, and favorable life experiences.

19. An open class system implies that the position of each individual is influenced by the person's _____ status.

20. _____ mobility involves changes in social position within a person's adult life.

Answers

1 (d); 2 (c); 3 (b); 4 (a); 5 (b); 6 (c); 7 (a); 8 (d); 9 (c); 10 (a); 11 Slavery; 12 estate; 13 class; 14 Conspicuous consumption; 15 Absolute; 16 Relative; 17 underclass; 18 life chances; 19 achieved; 20 Intragenerational

216

THINKING ABOUT MOVIES

Titanic (James Cameron, 1997)

This fictionalized version of the famous ocean liner offers a glimpse of British social structure in the early 20th century. The cruise ship is partitioned along class lines—divisions that become clear when Jack Dawson (Leonardo DiCaprio), a third-class steerage passenger, falls in love with the wealthy socialite Rose Bukater (Kate Winslet). Despite her family's disapproval, the two young lovers experience a few brief moments of joy before the ship's maiden voyage ends in disaster. When the ship sinks, many wealthy passengers (like Rose) are rescued as poorer travelers (like Jack) drown.

This film illustrates Weber's concept of life chances. Notice how the ship's closed stratification system inhibits Jack's upward mobility. Watch for the scenes in which Jack and Rose take turns in each other's social worlds, using their unequal social resources to pursue vertical mobility with greater or lesser success.

For Your Consideration

1. How do Jack and Rose's life chances differ? Relate their unequal social positions to social stratification in the United States today.

2. What are some of the constraints on social mobility shown in this film?

The Pursuit of Happyness (Gabriele Muccino, 2006)

Chris Gardner (Will Smith), recently separated from his wife and entrusted with his son's care, has landed an internship at a stockbrokerage firm. The only problem is that it is unpaid, and Chris is broke. Despite his limited life chances, Chris resolves to break into the relatively high-prestige stockbroker's world even as he struggles to provide for his son.

From a sociological perspective, *The Pursuit of Happyness* is both realistic and unrealistic. The movie offers a compassionate, true-to-life portrait of the underclass, showing how Chris works tirelessly to acquire the resources many of us take for granted, including food and housing. Yet there is no explicit mention of the effect of race. The relative ease with which Chris is accepted in the overwhelmingly White brokerage ignores the rigidity of the social class system toward members of minority groups.

For Your Consideration

1. What type of social mobility does this film illustrate? Describe some of the barriers to mobility that are shown in the film.

2. Would you consider the stockbrokerage firm shown in the movie to be an organization that facilitates an open or a closed social system? Explain.

inside

The Global Divide

Stratification in the World System

Stratification within Nations: A Comparative Perspective

Case Study: Stratification in Mexico

Social Policy and Global Inequality: Universal Human Rights

BOXES

Sociology in the Global Community: *Cutting Poverty Worldwide*

Sociology in the Global Community: *The Global Disconnect*

Sociology in the Global Community: *Stratification in Japan*

Taking Sociology to Work: *Bari Katz, Program Director, National Conference for Community and Justice*

In Mexico, a mother and daughter scavenge for tin at a municipal dump. Located on the border with one of the wealthiest countries in the world, Mexico is a highly stratified society in which the vast majority of the population lives in poverty.

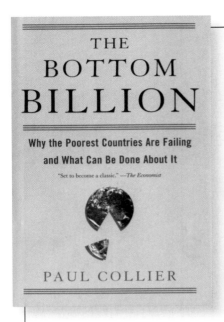

THE
BOTTOM
BILLION

Why the Poorest Countries Are Failing
and What Can Be Done About It

"Set to become a classic." —*The Economist*

PAUL COLLIER

66 The third world has shrunk. For forty years the development challenge has been a rich world of one billion people facing a poor world of five billion people.... By 2015, however, it will be apparent that this way of conceptualizing development has become outdated. Most of the five billion, about 80 percent, live in countries that are indeed developing, often at amazing speed. The real challenge of development is that there is a group of countries at the bottom that are falling behind, and often falling apart.

The countries at the bottom coexist with the twenty-first century, but their reality is the fourteenth century: civil war, plague, ignorance. They are concentrated in Africa and Central Asia, with a scattering elsewhere. Even during the 1990s, in retrospect the golden decade between the end of the Cold War and 9/11, incomes in this group declined by 5 percent. We must learn to turn the familiar numbers upside down: a total of five billion people who are already prosperous, or at least are on track to be so, and one billion who are stuck at the bottom.

This problem matters, and not just to the billion people who are living and dying in fourteenth-century conditions. It matters to us. The twenty-first-century world of material comfort, global travel, and

The real challenge of development is that there is a group of countries at the bottom that are falling behind, and often falling apart.

economic interdependence will become increasingly vulnerable to these large islands of chaos. And it matters now. As the bottom billion diverges from an increasingly sophisticated world economy, integration will become harder, not easier.

And yet it is a problem denied, both by development *biz* and by development *buzz*. Development biz is run by the aid agencies and the companies that get the contracts for their projects. They will fight this thesis with the tenacity of bureaucracies endangered, because they like things the way they are. A definition of development that encompasses five billion people gives them license to be everywhere, or more honestly, everywhere but the bottom billion. At the bottom, conditions are rather rough. Every development agency has difficulty getting its staff to serve in Chad and Laos; the glamour postings are for countries such as Brazil and China. The World Bank has large offices in every major middle-income country but not a single person resident in the Central African Republic....

. . .

What of the governments of the countries at the bottom? The prevailing conditions bring out extremes. Leaders are sometimes psychopaths who have shot their way to power, sometimes crooks who have bought it, and sometimes brave people who, against the odds, are trying to build a better future. Even the appearance of modern government in these states is sometimes a façade, . . . the government of Somalia continued to be officially "represented" in the international arena for years after Somalia ceased to have a functioning government in the country itself. So don't expect the governments of the bottom billion to unite in formulating a practical agenda. 99

(Collier 2007:3–5) Additional information about this excerpt can be found on the Online Learning Center at www.mhhe.com/schaefer12e.

How should we help the poor—not just a poor household or a poor neighborhood, but hundreds of millions of the world's poorest people? For most of his adult life, Paul Collier, an economist at Oxford University, has pondered this question. In this excerpt from his book *The Bottom Billion: Why the Poorest Countries Are Failing and What Can Be Done About It,* Collier outlines the magnitude of the challenge. He thinks that the answer lies in avoiding the traps that developing countries often fall into: wasteful depletion of their natural resources, ineffective government, prolonged internal conflict, protracted wars, and insufficient economic development.

In this chapter we will consider social inequality both *between* developing and developed nations and *within* them. Consider the contrast between "Richistan," the virtual country within a country described by Robert Frank in the opening excerpt to Chapter 9, and the world's poorest countries, described here by Collier. Inequality of the kind described by Frank exists within all countries, not just

in the United States. Even in the poorest countries, Collier writes, the very wealthy rub shoulders with the very poor.

What economic and political conditions explain the divide between rich nations and poor? Within developing nations, how are wealth and income distributed, and how much opportunity does the average worker have to move up the social ladder? How do race and gender affect social mobility in these countries? In this chapter we will focus on global inequality, beginning with the global divide. We will consider the impact of colonialism and neocolonialism, globalization, the rise of multinational corporations, grinding poverty, and the trend toward modernization. Then we will focus on stratification within nations, in terms of the distribution of wealth and income as well as social mobility. In a special case study, we will look closely at social stratification in Mexico, including the social impact of race and gender and the economic effects of industrialization. The chapter closes with a Social Policy section on universal human rights.

In some parts of the world, the people who have dedicated their lives to fighting starvation refer to what they call "coping mechanisms"—ways in which the desperately poor attempt to control their hunger. Eritrean women will strap flat stones to their stomachs to lessen their hunger pangs. In Mozambique, people eat the grasshoppers that have destroyed their crops, calling them "flying shrimp." Though dirt eating is considered a pathological condition (called *pica*) among the well-fed, the world's poor eat dirt to add minerals to their diet. And in many countries, mothers have been known to boil stones in water, to convince their hungry children that supper is almost ready. As they hover over the pot, these women hope that their malnourished children will fall asleep (McNeil 2004).

Around the world, inequality is a significant determinant of human behavior, opening doors of opportunity to some and closing them to others. Indeed, disparities in life chances are so extreme that in some places, the poorest of the poor may not be aware of them. Western media images may have circled the globe, but in extremely depressed rural areas, those at the bottom of society are not likely to see them.

A few centuries ago, such vast divides in global wealth did not exist. Except for a very few rulers and landowners, everyone in the world was poor. In much of Europe, life was as difficult as it was in Asia or South America. This was true until the Industrial Revolution and rising agricultural productivity produced explosive economic growth. The resulting rise in living standards was not evenly distributed across the world.

Figure 10-1 compares the industrial nations of the world to the developing nations. Using total population as a yardstick, we see that the developing countries have more than their fair share of rural population, as well as of total births, disease, and childhood deaths. At the same time, the industrial nations of the world, with a much smaller share of total population, have much more income and exports than the developing nations. Industrial nations also spend more on health and the military than other nations, and they emit more carbon dioxide (CO_2) (Sachs 2005; Sutcliffe 2002).

	Developing nations	Industrial nations
Deaths of children	99%	1%
Rural population	94%	6%
Total births	94%	6%
The burden of disease	93%	7%
TOTAL POPULATION	85%	15%
Cultivated land	74%	26%
Urban population	73%	27%
Income	46%	54%
CO_2 emissions	36%	64%
Health spending	24%	76%
Exports	22%	78%
Military spending	12%	88%

Note: In this comparison, industrial nations include the United States and Canada, Japan, Western Europe, and Australasia. Developing nations include Africa, Asia (except for Japan), Latin America, Eastern Europe, the Caribbean, and the Pacific.
Source: Adapted from Sutcliffe 2002:18.

Think about It

What is the relationship between health spending, disease, and deaths of children? Between CO_2 emissions, income, and exports?

What do we stand in line for? People's needs and desires differ dramatically depending on where they live. On the left, eager customers line up outside a store in New York City to purchase the newly released version of X-Box 360. On the right, residents of Ethiopia line up to receive water.

FIGURE **10-2** GROSS NATIONAL INCOME PER CAPITA

MAPPING LIFE WORLDWIDE

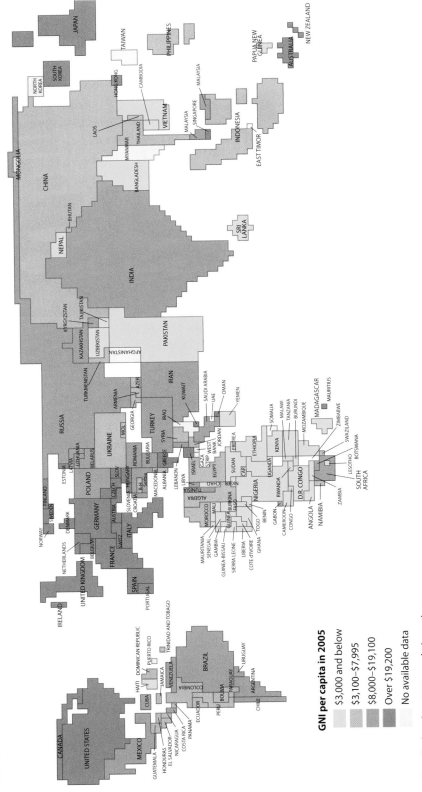

GNI per capita in 2005

- $3,000 and below
- $3,100–$7,995
- $8,000–$19,100
- Over $19,200
- No available data

Note: Size based on 2000 population estimates.
Sources: Haub 2008; Weeks 2008:30–31.

This stylized map reflects the relative population sizes of the world's nations. The color for each country shows the 2005 estimated gross national income (the total value of goods and services produced by the nation in a given year) per capita. As the map shows, some of the world's most populous countries—such as Nigeria, Bangladesh, and Pakistan—are among the nations with the lowest standard of living, as measured by per capita gross national income.

Stratification in the World System

Although the divide between industrial and developing nations is sharp, sociologists recognize a continuum of nations, from the richest of the rich to the poorest of the poor. For example, in 2006, the average value of goods and services produced per citizen (or per capita gross national income) in the industrialized countries of the United States, Japan, Switzerland, Belgium, and Norway was more than $31,000. In at least 10 poorer countries, the value was just $900 or less. However, most countries fell somewhere between those extremes, as Figure 10-2 shows.

Still, the contrasts are stark. Three forces discussed here are particularly responsible for the domination of the world marketplace by a few nations: the legacy of colonialism, the advent of multinational corporations, and modernization.

The Legacy of Colonialism

Colonialism occurs when a foreign power maintains political, social, economic, and cultural domination over a people for an extended period. In simple terms, it is rule by outsiders. The long reign of the British Empire over much of North America, parts of Africa, and India was an example of colonial domination. The same can be said of French rule over Algeria, Tunisia, and other parts of North Africa. Relations between the colonial nation and colonized people are similar to those between the dominant capitalist class and the proletariat, as described by Karl Marx.

By the 1980s, colonialism had largely disappeared. Most of the nations that were colonies before World War I had achieved political independence and established their own governments. However, for many of those countries, the transition to genuine self-rule was not yet complete. Colonial domination had established patterns of economic exploitation that continued even after nationhood was achieved—in part because former colonies were unable to develop their own industry and technology. Their dependence on more industrialized nations, including their former colonial masters, for managerial and technical expertise, investment capital, and manufactured goods kept former colonies in a subservient position. Such continuing dependence and foreign domination are referred to as **neocolonialism.**

The economic and political consequences of colonialism and neocolonialism are readily apparent. Drawing on the conflict perspective, sociologist Immanuel Wallerstein (1974, 1979a, 2000) views the global economic system as being divided between nations that control wealth and nations from which resources are taken. Through his **world systems analysis,** Wallerstein has described the unequal economic and political relationships in which certain industrialized nations (among them the United States, Japan, and Germany) and their global corporations dominate the *core* of this system (Figure 10-3). At the *semiperiphery* of the system are countries with marginal economic status, such as Israel, Ireland, and South Korea. Wallerstein suggests that the poor developing countries of Asia, Africa, and Latin America are on the *periphery* of the world economic system. The key to Wallerstein's analysis is the exploitative relationship of *core* nations toward noncore nations. Core nations and their corporations control and exploit noncore nations' economies. Unlike

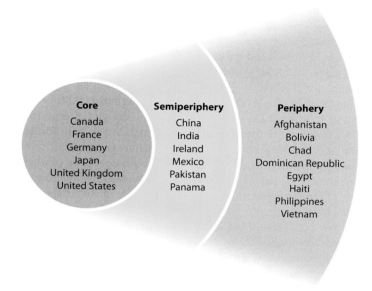

Note: Figure shows only a partial listing of countries, selected by author.

other nations, they are relatively independent of outside control (Chase-Dunn and Grimes 1995).

The division between core and periphery nations is significant and remarkably stable. A study by the International Monetary Fund (2000) found little change over the course of the *past 100 years* for the 42 economies that were studied. The only changes were Japan's movement up into the group of core nations and China's movement down toward the margins of the semiperiphery nations. Yet Immanuel Wallerstein (2000) speculates that the world system as we currently understand it may soon undergo unpredictable changes. The world is becoming increasingly urbanized, a trend that is gradually eliminating the large pools of low-cost workers in rural areas. In the future, core nations will have to find other ways to reduce their labor costs. Exhaustion of land and water resources through clear-cutting and pollution is also driving up the costs of production.

Wallerstein's world systems analysis is the most widely used version of **dependency theory.** According to this theory, even as developing countries make economic advances, they remain weak and subservient to core nations and corporations in an increasingly intertwined global economy. This interdependency allows industrialized nations to continue to exploit developing countries for their own gain. In a sense, dependency theory applies the conflict perspective on a global scale.

In the view of world systems analysts and dependency theorists, a growing share of the human and natural resources of developing countries is being redistributed to the core industrialized nations. This redistribution happens in part because developing countries owe huge sums of money to industrialized nations as a result of foreign aid, loans, and trade deficits. The global debt crisis has intensified the Third World dependency begun under colonialism, neocolonialism, and multinational investment. International financial institutions are pressuring indebted countries to take severe measures to meet their interest payments. The result is that developing nations may be forced to devalue their currencies, freeze workers' wages, increase the privatization of industry, and reduce government services and employment.

Closely related to these problems is **globalization,** the worldwide integration of government policies, cultures, social movements, and financial markets through trade and the exchange of ideas. Because world financial markets transcend governance by conventional nation-states, international organizations such as the World Bank and the International Monetary Fund have emerged as major players in the global economy. The function of these institutions, which are heavily funded and influenced by core nations, is to encourage economic trade and development and to ensure the smooth operation of international financial markets. As such, they are seen as promoters of globalization and defenders primarily of the interests of core nations.

Critics call attention to a variety of issues, including violations of workers' rights, the destruction of the environment, the loss of cultural identity, and discrimination against minority groups in periphery nations. The impact of globalization appears to be most problematic for developing countries in Latin America and Africa. In Asia, developing nations seem to do better. Foreign investment there involves the high-tech sector, which produces more sustainable economic growth (Kerbo 2006).

Some observers see globalization and its effects as the natural result of advances in communications technology, particularly the Internet and worldwide transmission of the mass media. Others view it more critically, as a process that allows multinational corporations to expand unchecked, as we will see in the next section (Chase-Dunn et al. 2000).

use your sociological *imagination*

You are traveling through a developing country. What evidence do you see of neocolonialism and globalization?

Multinational Corporations

Worldwide, corporate giants play a key role in neocolonialism. The term **multinational corporations** refers to commercial organizations that are headquartered in one country but do business throughout the world. Such private trade and lending relationships are not new; merchants have conducted business abroad for hundreds of years, trading gems, spices, garments, and other goods. However, today's multinational giants are not merely buying and selling overseas; they are also *producing* goods all over the world (Wallerstein 1974).

Moreover, today's "global factories" (factories throughout the developing world that are run by multinational corporations) may now have the "global office" alongside them.

The pitfalls of globalization were brought home—literally—to U.S. consumers in 2007, when U.S. companies were forced to recall toys manufactured in China because they were painted with lead-based paint.

Multinationals based in core countries are beginning to establish reservation services and centers for processing data and insurance claims in the periphery nations. As service industries become a more important part of the international marketplace, many companies are concluding that the low costs of overseas operations more than offset the expense of transmitting information around the world.

Do not underestimate the size of these global corporations. As Table 10-1 shows, the total revenues of multinational businesses are on a par with the total value of goods and services exchanged in *entire nations*. Foreign sales represent an important source of profit for multinational corporations, which are constantly seeking to expand into other countries (in many cases, developing nations). The economy of the United States depends heavily on foreign commerce, much of which is conducted by multinationals. Over 10 percent of all goods and services produced in the United States relates to the export of goods to foreign countries and accounts for 20 percent of the nation's annual growth (U.S. Trade Representative 2007).

Functionalist View Functionalists believe that multinational corporations can actually help the developing nations of the world. They bring jobs and industry to areas where subsistence agriculture once served as the only means of survival. Multinationals also promote

Rank	Corporation	Revenues ($ millions)	Comparison Nation(s)	Gross Domestic Product ($ millions)
1.	Wal-Mart (USA)	$378,799	Belgium	$375,300
2.	Exxon Mobil (USA)	372,824	Switzerland and Latvia	371,200
3.	Royal Dutch/Shell (Britain/Netherlands)	355,782	Malaysia	351,200
4.	BP British Petroleum (Britain)	291,438	Nigeria and Honduras	286,400
5.	Toyota Motor (Japan)	230,201	Portugal	231,100
6.	Chevron	210,783	Bangladesh	211,400
7.	ING Group	201,516	Peru	200,900
8.	Total (France)	187,280	Ireland and Morocco	185,400
9.	General Motors (USA)	182,347	Finland	183,900
10.	ConocoPhillips	178,558	Hungary	175,600

Notes: Total is an oil, petroleum, and chemical company. Where two nations are listed, the country with the larger GDP is listed first. Revenues tabulated by *Fortune* for 2008. GDP collected by the World Bank for 2006. Although the value of many corporations eroded between 2007 and 2010, so did the GDP of most countries, so these comparisons remain relevant.

Sources: For corporate data, *Fortune* 2008; for GDP data, World Bank 2009:14–16.

Think about It

What happens to society when corporations grow richer than countries and spill across international borders?

rapid development through the diffusion of inventions and innovations from industrial nations. Viewed from a functionalist perspective, the combination of skilled technology and management provided by multinationals and the relatively cheap labor available in developing nations is ideal for a global enterprise. Multinationals can take maximum advantage of technology while reducing costs and boosting profits.

Through their international ties, multinational corporations also make the nations of the world more interdependent. These ties may prevent certain disputes from reaching the point of serious conflict. A country cannot afford to sever diplomatic relations or engage in warfare with a nation that is the headquarters for its main business suppliers or a key outlet for its exports.

Conflict View Conflict theorists challenge this favorable evaluation of the impact of multinational corporations. They emphasize that multinationals exploit local workers to maximize profits. Starbucks—the international coffee retailer based in Seattle—gets some of its coffee from farms in Guatemala. But to earn enough money to buy a pound of Starbucks coffee, a Guatemalan farmworker would have to pick 500 pounds of beans, representing five days of work: see Box 1-2, page 20 (Entine and Nichols 1996).

The pool of cheap labor in the developing world prompts multinationals to move factories out of core countries. An added bonus for the multinationals is that the developing world discourages strong trade unions. In industrialized countries, organized labor insists on decent wages and humane working conditions, but governments seeking to attract or keep multinationals may develop a "climate for investment" that includes repressive anti-labor laws that restrict union activity and collective bargaining. If labor's demands become too threatening, the multinational firm will simply move its plant elsewhere, leaving a trail of unemployment behind. Nike, for example, moved its factories from the United States to Korea to Indonesia to Vietnam in search of the lowest labor costs. Conflict theorists conclude that on the whole, multinational corporations have a negative social impact on workers in *both* industrialized and developing nations.

Workers in the United States and other core countries are beginning to recognize that their own interests are served by helping to organize workers in developing nations. As long as multinationals can exploit cheap labor abroad, they will be in a strong position to reduce wages and benefits in industrialized countries. With this in mind, in the 1990s, labor unions, religious organizations, campus groups, and other activists mounted public campaigns to pressure companies such as Nike, Starbucks, Reebok, Gap, and Wal-Mart to improve wages and working conditions in their overseas operations (Global Alliance for Workers and Communities 2003; Gonzalez 2003).

Several sociologists who have surveyed the effects of foreign investment by multinationals conclude that although it may at first contribute to a host nation's wealth, it eventually increases economic inequality within developing nations. This conclusion holds true for both income and land ownership. The upper and middle classes benefit most from economic expansion; the lower classes benefit least. As conflict theorists point out, multinationals invest in limited economic sectors and restricted regions of a nation. Although certain sectors of the host nation's

226

FIGURE **10-4** POVERTY WORLDWIDE

MAPPING LIFE WORLDWIDE

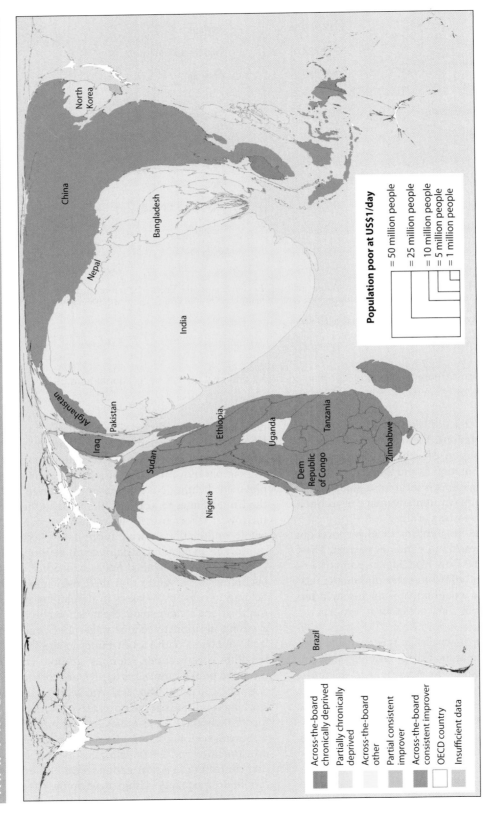

Sources: Chronic Poverty Research Centre 2009.

The scale of this map is based on the number of people in each region who are chronically poor. The colors represent the income levels of those who are poorest. In OECD countries—those that belong to the Organisation for Economic Co-Operation and Development (white)—chronic poverty is not a nationwide issue.

Think about It

To what degree does this map minimize those countries you have studied or might want to visit?
To what degree does it emphasize parts of the world about which you know very little?

economy expand, such as hotels and expensive restaurants, their very expansion appears to retard growth in agriculture and other economic sectors. Moreover, multinational corporations often buy out or force out local entrepreneurs and companies, thereby increasing economic and cultural dependence (Chase-Dunn and Grimes 1995; Kerbo 2009; Wallerstein 1979b).

Worldwide Poverty

In developing countries, any deterioration of the economic well-being of those who are least well off threatens their very survival. As we saw in Chapter 9 (see Box 9-2 on page 207), even the wealthy in the developing world are poor by U.S. standards. Those who are poor in developing countries are truly destitute.

What would a map of the world look like if we drew it to a scale that reflects the number of *poor* people in each country instead of the number of people, as in Figure 10-2 (page 222)? As Figure 10-4 shows, when we focus on the poverty level rather than the population, the world looks quite different. Note the huge areas of poverty in Africa and Asia, and the comparatively small areas of affluence in industrialized North America and Europe. Poverty is a worldwide problem that blights the lives of billions of people.

How do social scientists measure global poverty? As we saw in Chapter 9, there is significant disagreement over where to draw the poverty line in the United States. Adding the rest of the world to the equation further complicates the task. Individually, many developing nations define poverty based on the minimum income a person needs to survive—an amount that typically ranges from a low of $1 a day to a high of $2 a day. Zambia defines poverty in terms of the inability to afford specific foods in a subsistence diet (Chen and Ravallion 2008; *The Economist* 2008c).

In 2000 the United Nations launched the Millennium Project, whose objective is to eliminate extreme poverty worldwide by the year 2015 (Box 10-1 on page 228). Although 15 years may seem a long time, the challenge is great. Today, almost 3 billion people subsist on $2 a day or less. To accomplish the project's goal, planners estimate that industrial nations must set aside 0.7 percent of their **gross national product (GNP)**—the value of a nation's goods and services—to aid developing nations.

At the time the Millennium Project was launched, only five countries were giving at that target rate: Denmark, Luxembourg, the Netherlands, Norway, and Sweden. To match their contribution proportionally, the United States would need to multiply its present aid level by 45. Though in dollar terms the U.S. government delivers far more aid to foreign countries and multinational organizations than any other nation, the amount is not impressive considering the nation's tremendous wealth relative to other countries. In terms of per capita giving, the United States ranks 18th highest of the 22 most advanced industrial countries—below countries such as Great Britain, Germany, and

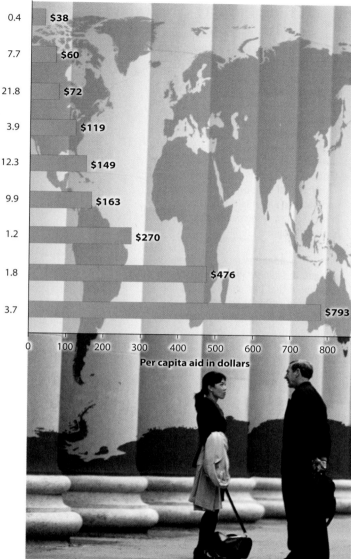

Total aid in $ millions

Country	Total aid in $ millions	Per capita aid in dollars
Portugal	0.4	$38
Japan	7.7	$60
USA	21.8	$72
Canada	3.9	$119
Germany	12.3	$149
Great Britain	9.9	$163
Ireland	1.2	$270
Sweden	1.8	$476
Norway	3.7	$793

Per capita aid in dollars (0, 100, 200, 300, 400, 500, 600, 700, 800)

Note: Data for bilateral aid in 2007 released in 2009.
Source: Organisation for Economic Co-Operation and Development 2009.

Ireland, as Figure 10-5 shows (Kerbo 2009; Sachs 2005; World Bank 2007).

Direct government-to-government foreign aid is only one way of alleviating poverty, however. Although per capita aid from the U.S. government may not be strong, private spending by U.S. residents is. Individual charitable giving is much higher in the United States than in other industrial nations. Even more significant are remittances, the money that immigrants to the United States send home to relatives. In 2006, remittances from the United States to developing countries were estimated at $199 billion—twice the total of foreign aid from all countries (*The Economist* 2007a; World Bank 2006b).

Privileged people in industrialized nations tend to assume that the world's poor lack significant assets. Yet again and again, observers from these countries have been startled to discover

SOCIOLOGY IN THE GLOBAL COMMUNITY

10-1 Cutting Poverty Worldwide

The goal of the United Nations' Millennium Project is to cut the world's poverty level in half by 2015. The project has eight objectives:

1. *Eradicate extreme poverty and hunger.* Poverty rates are falling in many parts of the globe, particularly in Asia. But in sub-Saharan Africa, where the poor are hard-pressed, millions more have sunk deeper into poverty.
2. *Achieve universal primary education.* While many parts of the developing world are approaching universal school enrollment, in sub-Saharan Africa, only 30 percent of all children are enrolled in high school.
3. *Promote gender equality and empower women.* The gender gap in primary school enrollment that has characterized the developing world for so long is slowly closing. However, women still lack equal representation at the highest levels of government.
4. *Reduce child mortality.* Death rates among children under age 5 are dropping, but not nearly fast enough. In the least developed nations, about 85 of every 1,000 children die in the first year of life, compared to 6 of every 1,000 in the more developed nations. Sadly, evidence indicates that progress toward reducing child mortality has slowed in recent decades.
5. *Improve maternal health.* Each year more than half a million women die during pregnancy or childbirth. Progress has been made in reducing maternal death rates in some developing regions, but not in countries where the risk of giving birth is highest.
6. *Combat HIV/AIDS, malaria, and other diseases.* AIDS has become the leading cause of premature death in sub-Saharan Africa, where two-thirds of the world's AIDS patients reside. Worldwide, the disease is the fourth most frequent killer. Though new drug treatments can prolong life, there is still no cure for this scourge. Moreover, each year malaria and tuberculosis kill almost as many people as AIDS, severely draining the labor pool in many countries.
7. *Ensure environmental sustainability.* Sufficient progress has not been made toward reversing the loss of the world's

environmental resources through rampant clear-cutting of forests and other forms of environmental destruction. Even so, many developing countries lack the infrastructure needed to support public health. Though access to safe drinking water has increased, half the developing world lacks toilets and other forms of basic sanitation.

Each year malaria and tuberculosis kill almost as many people as AIDS, severely draining the labor pool in many countries.

8. *Develop a global partnership for development.* The United Nations Millennium Declaration seeks a global social compact in which developing countries pledge to do more to ensure their own development, while developed countries support them through aid, debt relief, and improved trade opportunities.

What progress has been made in meeting these objectives? Despite the much-publicized Live 8 global benefit concerts, held in connection with a meeting of the world's eight major economies (Canada, France, Germany, Great Britain, Italy, Japan, Russia, and the United States), called the G8, in 2005, developed nations have fallen far short of the targets they set for themselves. By mid-2008, well before the global recession began, the G8 had contributed much less than their interim goals. The following year, at an even larger meeting, the economic superpowers pledged $1.1 trillion to help developing nations weather the worldwide economic crisis—which of course had not even been contemplated when the Millennium Project was conceived. In response, the watchdog Africa Progress Panel called on donor nations to consider establishing a tax or an international lottery to meet the Millennium Project's goals.

LET'S DISCUSS

1. Do you think the Millennium Project's objectives are realistic, given the enormity of the obstacles that must be overcome? Why do you think the project's founders gave themselves 15 years to accomplish their goal?
2. How are the project's eight objectives related to one another? Could some of the objectives be reached successfully without addressing the others? If you were a government planner with the resources to address just one objective, which would you pick, and why?

Sources: Annan 2009; Haub 2008; Katel 2005; Landler and Sanger 2009; Sachs 2005; United Nations 2005a; Weisbrot et al. 2005; World Bank 2006a, 2007:63, 80.

how far even a small amount of capital can go. Numerous microfinance programs, which involve relatively small grants or loans, have encouraged marginalized people to invest not in livestock, which may die, or jewelry, which may be stolen, but in technological improvements such as small stoves. These loans can lift a family out of poverty. In the Democratic Republic of the Congo, a local Widows Organization collects $1 from each member at every meeting and uses the proceeds to fund

SOCIOLOGY IN THE GLOBAL COMMUNITY

10-2 The Global Disconnect

Bogdan Ghirda, a Romanian, is paid 50 cents an hour to participate in multiplayer Internet games like City of Heroes and Star Wars. He is sitting in for someone in an industrialized country who does not want to spend days ascending to the highest levels of competition in order to compete with players who are already "well armed." This arrangement is not unusual. U.S.-based services can earn hundreds of dollars for recruiting someone in a less developed country, like Ghirda, to represent a single player in an affluent industrial country.

Meanwhile, villagers in Arumugam, India, are beginning to benefit from their new Knowledge Centre. The facility, funded by a nonprofit organization, contains five computers that offer Internet access—an amenity unknown until now to thousands of villagers.

These two situations illustrate the technological disconnect between the developing and industrial nations. Around the world, developing nations lag far behind industrial nations in their access to and use of new technologies. The World Economic Forum's Networked Readiness Index (NRI), a ranking of 134 nations, shows the relative preparedness of individuals, businesses, and governments to benefit from information technologies. As the accompanying table shows, the haves of the world—countries like Singapore, the United States, and Denmark—are network ready; the have-nots—countries like Ethiopia, Chad, and Bolivia—are not.

For developing nations, the consequences of the global disconnect are far more serious than an inability to surf the Net. Thanks to the Internet, multinational organizations can now function as a single global unit, responding instantly in real time, 24 hours a day. This new capability has fostered the emergence of what sociologist Manuel Castells calls a "global economy." But if large numbers of people—indeed, entire nations—are disconnected from the new global economy, their economic growth will remain slow and the well-being of their people will remain

For developing nations, the consequences of the global disconnect are far more serious than an inability to surf the Net.

retarded. Those citizens who are educated and skilled will immigrate to other labor markets, deepening the impoverishment of these nations on the periphery.

Remedying the global disconnect is not a simple matter. To gain access to new technologies, people in developing nations typically must serve the world's industrial giants, as Bogdan Ghirda does. Some may benefit from investment by nongovernmental organizations, as the villagers in India have. But progress to date has been slow. In 2005, in an effort to accelerate the diffusion of new technologies, the United Nations launched the Digital Solidarity Fund. The hope is that global information technology companies can be persuaded to set aside some of their profits to help developing nations connect to the Internet.

NETWORKED READINESS INDEX

Top 10 Countries	Bottom 10 Countries
1. Denmark	125. Nicaragua
2. Sweden	126. Cambodia
3. United States	127. Nepal
4. Singapore	128. Bolivia
5. Switzerland	129. Ethiopia
6. Finland	130. Bangladesh
7. Iceland	131. Burundi
8. Norway	132. Zimbabwe
9. Netherlands	133. Timor-Leste
10. Canada	134. Chad

LET'S DISCUSS

1. For nations on the periphery, what are some of the social and economic consequences of the global disconnect?
2. What factors might complicate efforts to remedy the global disconnect in developing nations?

Sources: Castells 2000; *The Economist* 2005c; Lim 2007; T. Thompson 2005; United Nations 2005b; World Economic Forum 2009.

$50 microloans. The widows use the loans to generate income for their families; most have already paid back about half the money (Chronic Poverty Research Centre 2008; Mumbere 2008).

Modernization

Around the world, millions of people are witnessing a revolutionary transformation of their day-to-day life. Contemporary social scientists use the term **modernization** to describe the far-reaching process by which periphery nations move from traditional or less developed institutions to those characteristic of more developed societies.

Wendell Bell (1981), whose definition of modernization we are using, notes that modern societies tend to be urban, literate, and industrial. These societies have sophisticated transportation and media systems. Their families tend to be organized within the nuclear family unit rather than the extended-family model (see Chapter 14). Thus, members of societies that undergo modernization must shift their allegiance from traditional sources of authority, such as parents and priests, to newer authorities, such as government officials.

Many sociologists are quick to note that terms such as *modernization* and even *development* contain an ethnocentric bias. The unstated assumption behind these terms is that "they" (people living in developing nations) are struggling to become more like "us" (in the core industrialized nations). Viewed from a conflict perspective, these terms perpetuate the dominant ideology of capitalist societies.

The term *modernization* also suggests positive change. Yet change, if it comes, often comes slowly, and when it does it tends to serve the affluent segments of industrial nations. This truism seems to apply to the spread of the latest electronic technologies to the developing world (Box 10-2).

A similar criticism has been made of **modernization theory,** a functionalist approach that proposes that modernization and development will gradually improve the lives of people in developing nations. According to this theory, even though nations develop at uneven rates, the development of peripheral nations will be assisted by innovations transferred from the industrialized world. Critics of modernization theory, including dependency theorists, counter that any such technology transfer only increases the dominance of core nations over developing nations and facilitates further exploitation.

When we see all the Coca-Cola and IBM signs going up in developing nations, it is easy to assume that globalization and economic change are effecting cultural change. But that is not always the case, researchers note. Distinctive cultural traditions, such as a particular religious orientation or a nationalistic identity, often persist and can soften the impact of modernization on a developing nation. Some contemporary sociologists emphasize that both industrialized and developing countries are "modern." Increasingly, researchers view modernization as movement along a series of social indicators—among them degree of urbanization, energy use, literacy, political democracy, and use of birth control. Clearly, some of these are subjective indicators; even in industrialized nations, not everyone would agree that wider use of birth control represents an example of progress (Armer and Katsillis 1992; Hedley 1992; Inglehart and Baker 2000).

Current modernization studies generally take a convergence perspective. Using the indicators just noted, researchers focus on how societies are moving closer together, despite traditional differences. From a conflict perspective, the modernization of developing nations often perpetuates their dependence on and continued exploitation by more industrialized nations. Conflict theorists view such continuing dependence on foreign powers as an example of contemporary neocolonialism.

Table 10-2 summarizes the three major approaches to global inequality.

---

use your sociological *imagination*

When you see a developing nation on television or in the movies, does the film or program emphasize the nation's progress or its problems?

TABLE **10-2** SOCIOLOGICAL PERSPECTIVES ON GLOBAL INEQUALITY

summing**UP**

Approach	Sociological Perspective	Explanation
World systems analysis	Functionalist and conflict	Unequal economic and political relationships maintain sharp divisions between nations.
Dependency theory	Conflict	Industrial nations exploit developing nations through colonialism and multinational corporations.
Modernization theory	Functionalist	Developing nations are moving away from traditional cultures and toward the cultures of industrialized nations.

This UNICEF poster reminds affluent Western consumers that the brand-name jeans they wear may be produced by exploited workers in developing countries. In sweatshops throughout the developing world, nonunion garment workers—some of them children—labor long hours for what we would consider extremely low wages—even if for the workers in those semiperiphery countries, those wages are relatively high.

Stratification within Nations: A Comparative Perspective

At the same time that the gap between rich and poor nations is widening, so too is the gap between rich and poor citizens *within* nations. As discussed earlier, stratification in developing nations is closely related to their relatively weak and dependent position in the global economy. Local elites work hand in hand with multinational corporations and prosper from such alliances. At the same time, the economic system creates and perpetuates the exploitation of industrial and agricultural workers. That is why foreign investment in developing countries tends to increase economic inequality. As Box 10-3 makes clear, inequality within a society is also evident in industrialized nations such as Japan (Bornschier et al. 1978; Kerbo 2009).

Distribution of Wealth and Income

Global inequality is staggering. Worldwide, the richest 2 percent of adults own more than 50 percent of the world's household wealth. In at least 19 nations around the world, the most affluent 10 percent of the population receives at least 40 percent of all income. The list includes the African nation of Namibia (the leader, at 65 percent of all income), as well as Colombia, Nigeria, and South Africa. Figure 10-6 on page 232 compares the distribution of income in selected industrialized and developing nations (World Bank 2009:72–74).

Social Mobility

Mobility in Industrial Nations Studies of intergenerational mobility in industrialized nations have found the following patterns:

1. Substantial similarities exist in the ways that parents' positions in stratification systems are transmitted to their children.

2. As in the United States, mobility opportunities in other nations have been influenced by structural factors, such as

SOCIOLOGY IN THE GLOBAL COMMUNITY

10-3 Stratification in Japan

Takako Ariishi is the exception that proves the rule: one of the few Japanese women who hold positions of authority in the working world. Ariishi's father, the head of a family-owned business that supplies auto parts to Nissan, raised her to succeed him. But when she gave birth to a son, he fired her and named her son his successor. Losing your job for becoming a mother is a common experience for working women in Japan. But Ariishi ultimately prevailed, taking her father's place after his death. Today, her company is the only one of Nissan's 160 suppliers that is headed by a woman.

To hold her own in a man's world, Ariishi works long hours, leaving work at 7:00 p.m. to put her son to bed and then returning to the office. Long hours are the norm in Japan, which is one reason why Japanese women have difficulty advancing in their careers. Combining work with motherhood is so difficult, most career-minded women have quit their jobs by their early 30s. Others forgo marriage and in effect become married to their companies. Even for them, achieving a managerial position is a challenge. About 10 percent of such jobs are held by women, though women make up nearly half of Japan's workforce. In the United States, about 40 percent of managerial positions are held by women.

Although Japan has an exceptionally high degree of gender stratification, research shows that its level of income inequality is among the lowest of major industrial societies (see Figure 10.6). The pay gap between Japan's top corporate executives and the nation's lowest-paid workers is about 10.8 to 1; the comparable figure for the United States would be 39 to 1.

One factor that works against inequality is

Even in developing countries, women are twice as likely to be managers as women in Japan.

that Japan is rather homogeneous—certainly when compared with the United States—in terms of race, ethnicity, nationality, and language. Japan's population is only 1.7 percent foreign-born. Still, there is discrimination against the nation's Chinese and Korean minorities, and the *Burakumin,* a low-status subculture, encounter extensive prejudice.

Gender discrimination, then, is perhaps the most pervasive form of inequality in Japan today. Overall, women earn about 65 percent of men's wages. The proportion of managerial positions that they hold (10 percent) is one of the lowest in the world. Even in developing countries, women are twice as likely to be managers as women in Japan.

In 1985, Japan's parliament—at the time, 97 percent male—passed an Equal Employment bill that encourages employers to end sex discrimination in hiring, assignment, and promotion policies. However, feminist organizations were dissatisfied because the law lacked strong sanctions. In a landmark ruling issued in late 1996, a Japanese court for the first time held an employer liable for denying promotions due to sex discrimination.

Progress has also been made in terms of public opinion. In 1987, 43 percent of Japanese adults agreed that married women should stay home, but by 2000 the proportion had dropped to 25 percent. On the political front, Japanese women have made progress but remain underrepresented. In a 2008 study of women in government around the world, Japan ranked near the bottom of the countries studied, with only 9.4 percent of its national legislators female.

LET'S DISCUSS

1. What factors might contribute to the relatively low level of income inequality in Japan?
2. Describe the types of gender discrimination found in Japan. Why do you think Japanese women occupy such a subordinate social position?

Sources: Bondy 2008; Fackler 2007; Haines et al. 2007; Harden 2009; Inter-Parliamentary Union 2009; Landy 2008; Nemoto 2008; Onishi 2009; Suzuki 2007.

---

labor market changes that lead to the rise or decline of an occupational group within the social hierarchy.

3. Immigration continues to be a significant factor in shaping a society's level of intergenerational mobility.

Cross-cultural studies suggest that intergenerational mobility has been increasing over the past 50 years in most but not all countries. In particular, researchers have noted a common pattern of movement away from agriculture-based occupations. However, they are quick to point out that growth in mobility does not necessarily bring growth in equality. Indeed, despite the evidence of steady upward mobility, their studies show that the gap between the rich and the poor has grown. Over the past 20 years, poverty levels in the 30 largest industrial economies have remained relatively constant (Organisation for Economic Co-Operation and Development 2008).

Mobility in Developing Nations Mobility patterns in industrialized countries are usually associated with intergenerational and intragenerational mobility. However, in developing nations, macro-level social and economic changes often overshadow micro-level movement from one occupation to another. For example, there is typically a substantial wage differential between rural and urban areas, which leads to high levels of migration to the cities. Yet the urban industrial sectors of developing countries generally cannot provide sufficient employment for all those seeking work.

In large developing nations, the most socially significant mobility is the movement out of poverty. This type of mobility is difficult to measure and confirm, however, because economic trends can differ from one area of a country to another. For instance, China's rapid income growth has been accompanied by a growing disparity in income between urban and rural areas and among different regions. Similarly, in India during the 1990s, poverty declined in urban areas but may have remained static at best in rural areas. Around the world, downward social mobility is also dramatically influenced by catastrophes such as crop failure and warfare.

Despite the continuing struggles of massive numbers of people, the global economic situation is not entirely bleak.

FIGURE **10-6** DISTRIBUTION OF INCOME IN NINE NATIONS

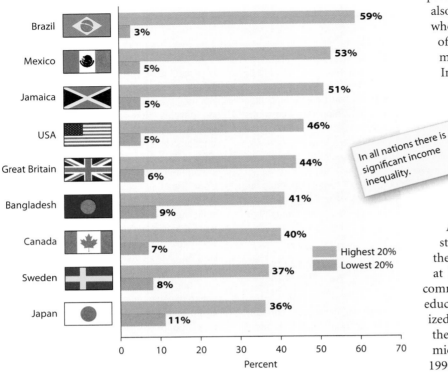

In all nations there is significant income inequality.

Highest 20%
Lowest 20%

Note: Data are considered comparable although based on statistics covering 1993 to 2001.
Source: World Bank 2007: 66–68.

In developing countries, people who hope to rise out of poverty often move from the country to the city, where employment prospects are better. The jobs available in industrialized urban areas offer perhaps the best means of upward mobility. This woman works in an electronics factory in Kuala Lumpur, Malaysia.

Although economists have documented the stubborn persistence of poverty around the world, they have also noted some growth in the number of people who enjoy a middle-class lifestyle. At the beginning of the 21st century, millions of people entered the middle class in the populous nations of China, India, Russia, Brazil, and Mexico. Entrepreneurship, microfinancing, merchandising, and in some countries, a growing, relatively well-paid government sector have fostered this increase in upward social mobility (R. Adler 2008; *The Economist* 2009).

Gender Differences and Mobility

Women in developing countries find life especially difficult. Karuna Chanana Ahmed, an anthropologist from India who has studied women in developing nations, calls women the most exploited of oppressed people. Beginning at birth women face sex discrimination. They are commonly fed less than male children, are denied educational opportunities, and are often hospitalized only when they are critically ill. Inside or outside the home, women's work is devalued. When economies fail, as they did in Asian countries in the late 1990s, women are the first to be laid off from work (J. Anderson and Moore 1993; Kristof 1998).

Surveys show a significant degree of *female infanticide* (the killing of baby girls) in China and rural areas of India. Only one-third of Pakistan's sexually segregated schools are for women, and one-third of those schools have no buildings. In Kenya and Tanzania, it is illegal for a woman to own a house. In Saudi Arabia, women are prohibited from driving, walking alone in public, and socializing with men outside their families. We will explore women's second-class status throughout the world more fully in Chapter 12.

Only recently have researchers begun to investigate the impact of gender on the mobility patterns of developing nations. Many aspects of the development process—especially modernization in rural areas and the rural-to-urban migration just described—may result in the modification or abandonment of traditional cultural practices and even marital systems. The effects on women's social standing and mobility are not necessarily positive. As a country develops and modernizes, women's vital role in food production deteriorates, jeopardizing both their autonomy and their material well-being. Moreover, the movement of families to the cities weakens women's ties to relatives who can provide food, financial assistance, and social support (Lawson 2008).

In the Philippines, however, women have moved to the forefront of the indigenous peoples' struggle to protect their ancestral land from exploitation by outsiders. Having established their right to its rich minerals and forests, members of indigenous

TAKING SOCIOLOGY TO WORK

Bari Katz, **Program Director, National Conference for Community and Justice**

"Though it may sound like a cliché, I have always known that my goal in life is to change the world," says Bari Katz. Since ninth grade this sociology major has known that her mission is to end injustice and cycles of oppression, both at home and abroad.

Katz began working for human rights while studying for her BA and MA at New York University. While there, she joined with the Human Rights Initiative at New York's Urban Justice Center to tackle issues such as immigration, hate crimes, and housing for the homeless. In her final year at NYU, eager to involve other students in the hands-on advocacy work she had been doing, she founded an internship program in human rights. Today, thanks to Katz's efforts, NYU students can work for human rights in New York City and South Africa.

Katz is currently program director at the National Conference for Community and Justice, where she develops, implements, and evaluates programs to promote respect and understanding among all races, religions, and cultures. Her long-range goal is to educate people about social justice issues, teach them to manage conflict, and inspire them to become advocates for positive social change. For Katz, every week brings new challenges and opportunities. She trains personnel at other organizations, develops youth programs, and researches and writes on issues that affect her community. "I have the amazing opportunity to be creative, independent, and influential in effecting real change," she says.

As a student, Katz found sociology to be extremely relevant to her interest in human rights. In her sophomore year she took a class on social movements, which climaxed with class attendance at an antiwar protest. "This was the first time I realized that sociology wasn't just about theories and research—it is a discipline that applies this knowledge to social problems and real-world events," she says. Katz also took a class called Public Sociology, which emphasized the importance of connecting sociology to the larger world. As part of the course, she joined the editorial board of *Contexts*, a sociological journal aimed at bridging the gap between the academic and practical sides of the discipline.

Looking back on her education, Katz says it has been invaluable to her. Sociology gave her both analytical skills and a broad understanding of systems and societies. "My training has taught me to look at the root causes of a problem, which is a principle I use every day in designing curriculum and programs," she says.

LET'S DISCUSS

1. Katz found that sociology supported her interest in human rights, allowing her to make it her life's work. How can sociology help you to develop your interests?
2. What human rights issues are you aware of in your own community? What could you do to support human rights?

---

groups had begun to feud among themselves over the way in which the land's resources should be developed. Aided by the United Nations Partners in Development Programme, women volunteers established the Pan-Cordillera Women's Network for Peace and Development, a coalition of women's groups dedicated to resolving local disputes. The women mapped boundaries, prepared development plans, and negotiated more than 2,000 peace pacts among community members. They have also run in elections, campaigned against social problems, and organized residents to work together for the common good (United Nations Development Programme 2000:87).

Studies of the distribution of wealth and income within various countries, together with cross-cultural research on mobility, consistently reveal stratification based on class, gender, and other factors within a wide range of societies. Clearly, a worldwide view of stratification must include not only the sharp contrast *between* wealthy and impoverished nations but also the layers of hierarchy *within* industrialized societies and developing countries.

---

use your sociological *imagination*

Imagine that the United States borders a country with a much higher standard of living. In this neighboring country, the salaries of workers with a college degree start at $120,000 a year. What is life in the United States like?

www.mhhe.com/schaefer12e

---

case**study** Stratification in Mexico

In May 2003, on a stretch of highway in southern Arizona, the open doors of an abandoned tractor-trailer revealed the dead bodies of 19 Mexicans. The truck had been carrying a group of illegal immigrants across the Sonoran Desert when the people hidden inside began to suffer from the intense desert heat. Their story was not unusual. Each year several hundred illegal immigrants die attempting to traverse the U.S.–Mexican border in the hot, arid corridor that connects the state of Sonora in Mexico to the state of Arizona in the United States.

Why do Mexicans risk their lives crossing the dangerous desert that lies between the two countries? The answer to this question can be found in the income disparity between the two nations—one an industrial giant and the other a partially developed country still recovering from a history of colonialism and neocolonialism. In this section we will look in some detail at the

A worker cleans the reflecting pool at the opulent Casa del Mar Hotel in San Jose del Cabo, Mexico. Though international tourism is a major industry in Mexico, most Mexicans have not benefited much from it. Mexican workers who are employed in the industry earn low wages, and their jobs are jeopardized by the travel industry's frequent boom and bust cycles.

dynamics of stratification in Mexico, a country of 108 million people. Since the early 20th century there has been a close cultural, economic, and political relationship between Mexico and the United States, one in which the United States is the dominant party. According to Immanuel Wallerstein's analysis, the United States is at the core while neighboring Mexico is still on the semiperiphery of the world economic system.

Mexico's Economy

Although the faltering U.S. economy is no longer a magnet for foreigners seeking work, Mexico's economy has faltered even more. Many out-of-work Mexicans have begun to return home from the United States, increasing the ranks of the unemployed in Mexico. Those who remain in the United States are less likely than they once were to send money back to their families in Mexico (Jordan 2009).

If we compare Mexico's economy to that of the United States, differences in the standard of living and in life chances are quite dramatic, even though Mexico is considered a semiperiphery nation. Gross national income is a commonly used measure of an average resident's well-being. In 2008 the gross national income per person in the United States came to $45,850; in Mexico, it was $12,580. About 88 percent of adults in the United States have a high school education, compared to only 21 percent of those in Mexico. And about 7 of every 1,000 infants in the United States die in the first year of life, compared to about 23 per 1,000 in Mexico (Bureau of the Census 2008a: Table 823; Haub 2008).

Although Mexico is unquestionably a poor country, the gap between its richest and poorest citizens is one of the widest in the world (refer back to Figure 10-6 on page 232). The World Bank reports that in 2006, 20 percent of Mexico's population survived on $2 per day. At the same time, the wealthiest 10 percent of Mexico's people accounted for 39 percent of the entire nation's income. According to *Forbes* magazine's 2009 portrait of the world's wealthiest individuals, that year Mexico was home to many billionaires who had gained their wealth through banking and media ventures (Kroll et al. 2009; World Bank 2007a:67).

Political scientist Jorge Castañeda (1995:71) calls Mexico a "polarized society with enormous gaps between rich and poor, town and country, north and south, white and brown (or *criollos* and *mestizos*)." He adds that the country is also divided along lines of class, race, religion, gender, and age. We will examine stratification within Mexico by focusing on race relations and the plight of Mexican Indians, the status of Mexican women, and emigration to the United States and its impact on the U.S.–Mexican borderlands.

Race Relations in Mexico: The Color Hierarchy

Mexico's indigenous Indians account for an estimated 14 percent of the nation's population. More than 90 percent of them live in houses without sewers, compared with 21 percent of the population as a whole. And whereas just 10 percent of Mexican adults are illiterate, the proportion for Mexican Indians is 44 percent (Boudreaux 2002; *The Economist* 2004; G. Thompson 2001).

The subordinate status of Mexico's Indians is but one reflection of the nation's color hierarchy, which links social class to the appearance of racial purity. At the top of this hierarchy are the *criollos*, the 10 percent of the population who are typically White, well-educated members of the business and intellectual elites, with familial roots in Spain. In the middle is the large, impoverished *mestizo* majority, most of whom have brown skin and a mixed racial lineage as a result of intermarriage. At the bottom of the color hierarchy are the destitute, full-blooded Mexican Indian minority and a small number of Blacks, some descended from 200,000 African slaves brought to Mexico. This color hierarchy is an important part of day-to-day life—enough so that some Mexicans in the cities use hair dyes, skin lighteners, and blue or green contact lenses to appear more White and European. Ironically, however, nearly all Mexicans are considered part Indian because of centuries of intermarriage (Castañeda 1995; Stahler-Sholk 2008).

Many observers take note of widespread denial of prejudice and discrimination against people of color in Mexico. Schoolchildren are taught that the election of Benito Juárez, a Zapotec Indian, as president of Mexico in the 19th century proves that all Mexicans are equal. Yet there has been a marked growth in the past decade of formal organizations and voluntary associations representing indigenous Indians (Escárcega 2008; Muñoz 2008).

The Status of Women in Mexico

In 1975, Mexico City hosted the first international conference on the status of women, convened by the United Nations. Much of the discussion concerned the situation of women in developing countries; in that regard, the situation is mixed. Women now constitute 45 percent of the labor force—an increase from 31 percent in 1980, but still less than in industrial countries. Unfortunately, Mexican women are even more mired in the lowest-paying jobs than their counterparts in industrial nations. In the political arena, although they rarely occupy top decision-making positions, women have significantly increased their representation in the national legislature, to 23 percent. Mexico now ranks

In 2000, a group of masked women demonstrated outside the Mexican Army's barracks in the state of Chiapas, demanding that the soldiers leave. The women were supporters of the Zapatista National Liberation Army, an insurgent group that protests economic injustices and discrimination against the Indian population in Chiapas.

States. The term **borderlands** refers to the area of common culture along the border between these two countries. Legal and illegal emigration from Mexico to the United States, day laborers crossing the border regularly to go to jobs in the United States, the implementation of the North American Free Trade Agreement, and the exchange of media across the border all make the notion of separate Mexican and U.S. cultures obsolete in the borderlands.

The economic position of the borderlands is rather complicated, as we can see in the emergence of *maquiladoras* on the Mexican side (Figure 10-7 on page 236). These are foreign-owned factories established just across the border in Mexico, where the companies that own them do not have to pay taxes or provide insurance and benefits to workers. The *maquiladoras* have attracted manufacturing jobs from other parts of North America to Mexico. As of mid-2007, 1.2 million people were employed in the *maquiladoras*, where the take-home pay for entry-level workers, including benefits, was $3 per hour. Since many of these firms come from the United States and sell their products to Mexico's vast domestic market, their operations deepen the impact of U.S. consumer culture on Mexico's urban and rural areas (Cañas et al. 2007).

The *maquiladoras* have contributed to Mexico's economic development, but not without some cost. This development were hastened by passage of the North American Free Trade Agreement (NAFTA), which eliminated most restrictions on trade among Mexico, the United States, and Canada when it took effect in 1994. Conflict theorists note that unregulated growth allows owners of *maquiladoras* to exploit workers with jobs that lack security, possibilities for advancement, and decent wages. Moreover, many of the U.S.-owned factories require female job applicants to take a urine test to screen out those who are pregnant—a violation of Mexican law as well as of NAFTA, and the source of numerous cases of sex discrimination. Social activists also complain that tens of thousands of Mexicans work on *maquiladora* assembly lines for wages that are very low compared to those in the United States (Dillon 1998; J. Dougherty and Holthouse 1999).

Ironically, the *maquiladoras* are now experiencing the same challenge from global trade as U.S. manufacturing plants did. Beginning in 2001, some companies began shifting their operations to China. While Mexican labor costs (wages plus benefits) are just $3 an hour, Chinese labor costs are even lower—72 cents an hour. Of the 700,000 new *maquiladora* jobs created in NAFTA's first seven years, 43 percent were eliminated between 2000 and 2003 (Cañas et al. 2007).

When people in the United States think about the borderlands, they generally think about immigration, a controversial political issue in the United States—especially near the Mexican border. For its part, Mexico is concerned about the priorities and policies of its powerful northern neighbor. From the Mexican

48th among 188 nations in this respect—well ahead of Great Britain, the United States, and France (Bureau of the Census 2007a: Table 1331; Inter-Parliamentary Union 2009).

Feminist sociologists emphasize that even when Mexican women work outside the home, they often are not recognized as active and productive household members, whereas men are typically viewed as heads of the household. As one consequence, women find it difficult to obtain credit and technical assistance in many parts of the country, and to inherit land in rural areas. Within manufacturing and service industries, women generally receive little training and tend to work in the least-automated and least-skilled jobs—in good part because there is little expectation that women will pursue career advancement, organize for better working conditions, or become active in labor unions.

In recent decades, Mexican women have begun to organize to address an array of economic, political, and health issues. Since women continue to serve as the household managers for their families, even when they work outside the home, they are well aware of the consequences of the inadequate public services in lower-income urban neighborhoods. As far back as 1973, women in Monterrey—the nation's third-largest city—began protesting the continuing disruptions of the city's water supply. After individual complaints to city officials and the water authority proved fruitless, social networks of women activists began to emerge. These activists sent delegations to confront politicians, organized protest rallies, and blocked traffic as a means of getting media attention. Though their efforts brought improvements in Monterrey's water service, the issue of reliable and safe water remains a concern in Mexico and many developing countries (Bennett et al. 2005).

The Borderlands

Growing recognition of the borderlands reflects the increasingly close and complex relationship between Mexico and the United

FIGURE **10-7** THE BORDERLANDS

MAPPING LIFE WORLDWIDE

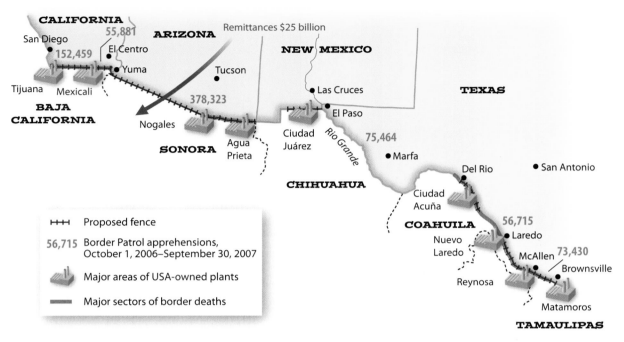

Source: Prepared by the author based on Archibold and Preston 2008; Department of Homeland Security 2008; Llana 2009; and Marosi 2007.
Maquiladoras located just south of the U.S.–Mexican border employ Mexican workers at wages far lower than those earned by U.S. workers. In search of higher wages, undocumented Mexicans often attempt to cross the border illegally, risking their lives in the process. Mexicans who do reach the United States send large amounts of money, called remittances, back to kinfolk in Mexican communities. To counter illegal immigration, the U.S. government has fortified the border, even experimenting with a "virtual fence" of radar towers and ground sensors along a 28-mile stretch of desert in Arizona.

Think about It
Do U.S. consumers benefit from the buildup of factories along the U.S.–Mexican border? How or how not?

point of view, the United States too often regards Mexico simply as a reserve pool of cheap labor, encouraging Mexicans to cross the border when workers are needed but discouraging and cracking down on them when they are not. Some people, then, see immigration more as a labor market issue than a law enforcement issue. Viewed from the perspective of Immanuel Wallerstein's world systems analysis and dependency theory, it is yet another example of a core industrialized nation exploiting a developing nation.

As we saw at the beginning of this case, the risks of immigration are considerable. Following September 11, 2001, when the U.S. government increased surveillance at common entry points along the border, migrants without proper documentation moved to more remote and dangerous locations. In all, about 500 illegal immigrants lose their lives every year while attempting to cross the long border, many of them from dehydration in the intense desert heat (LoMonaco 2006).

The social impact of emigration to the United States is felt throughout Mexico. According to sociological research, the earliest emigrants were typically married men of working age who came from the middle of the stratification system. They

had enough financial resources to afford the costs and risks of emigration, yet were experiencing enough financial strain that entering the United States was attractive to them. Over time, kinship ties to migrants multiplied and emigration became less class-selective, with entire families making the trek to the United States. More recently, the occupational backgrounds of Mexican emigrants have widened further, reflecting not only changes in U.S. immigration policy but the continuing crisis in the Mexican economy (Massey 1998, 2008).

Many Mexicans who have come to the United States send some part of their earnings back across the border to family members still in Mexico. This substantial flow of money, sometimes referred to as **remittances** or *migradollars,* is estimated at a minimum of $25 billion a year and is surpassed only by oil as a source of income. If these funds went solely into the purchase of consumer goods, they would underscore the view of dependency theory, that Mexico's economy is little more than an extension of the economy of the United States. In fact, however, some of these migradollars are used by Mexicans to establish and maintain small business enterprises, such as handicraft workshops and farms. Consequently, the transfer of

Imagine a day when the border between the United States and Mexico is completely open. What would the two countries' economies be like? What would their societies be like?

migradollars does stimulate the local and national economies of Mexico (Llana 2009).

We have seen that inequality is a problem not just in Mexico, but throughout the world. We turn now to an examination of an especially ugly form of social inequality, human rights abuse.

social**policy** and Global Inequality

Universal Human Rights

The Issue

Poised on the third millennium, the world seemed capable of mighty feats, ranging from explorations of distant solar systems to the refinement of tiny genes within human cells. Yet at the same time came constant reminders of how quickly people and their fundamental human rights could be trampled.

Human rights refers to universal moral rights possessed by all people because they are human. The most important elaboration of human rights appears in the Universal Declaration of Human Rights, adopted by the United Nations in 1948. This declaration prohibits slavery, torture, and degrading punishment; grants everyone the right to a nationality and its culture; affirms freedom of religion and the right to vote; proclaims the right to seek asylum in other countries to escape persecution; and prohibits arbitrary interference with one's privacy and the arbitrary taking of a person's property. It also emphasizes that mothers and children are entitled to special care and assistance.

What steps, if any, can the world community take to ensure the protection of these rights? Is it even possible to agree on what those rights are?

The Setting

At first, the United States opposed a binding obligation to the Universal Declaration of Human Rights. The government feared that the declaration would cause international scrutiny of the nation's civil rights controversies (at a time when racial segregation laws were still common). By the early 1960s, however, the United States had begun to use the declaration to promote democracy abroad (Forsythe 1990).

The 1990s brought the term *ethnic cleansing* into the world's vocabulary. In the former Yugoslavia, Serbs initiated a policy intended to "cleanse" Muslims from parts of Bosnia-Herzegovina and ethnic Albanians from the province of Kosovo. Hundreds of thousands of people were killed in fighting there; many others were uprooted from their homes. Moreover, reports surfaced of substantial numbers of rapes of Muslim, Croatian, and Kosovar women by Serbian soldiers. Regrettably, ethnic cleansing has since spread to other parts of the world, including East Timor, Iraq, Kenya, and Sudan.

Governments ratify human rights treaties but often resist efforts to enforce them.

Another human rights concern is the transnational crime of trafficking in humans. Each year an estimated 600,000 to 800,000 men, women, and children are transported across international borders for slavery or sexual exploitation. In 2000, Congress passed the Trafficking Victims Protection Act, which established minimum standards for the elimination of human trafficking. The act requires the State Department to monitor other countries' efforts to vigorously investigate, prosecute, and convict individuals who participate in trafficking—including government officials. Each year the department reports its findings, some of which are shown in Table 10-3 on page 238. Tier 1 and tier 2 countries are thought to be largely in compliance with the act. Tier 2 watch nations are making efforts to comply, though trafficking remains a significant concern. Tier 3 countries are not compliant (Kapstein 2006; Kempadoo and Doezema 1998).

In the wake of the terrorist attacks of September 11, 2001, increased security and surveillance at U.S. airports and border crossings caused some observers to wonder whether human rights were not being jeopardized at home. At the same time, thousands of noncitizens of Arab and south Asian descent were questioned for no other reason than their ethnic and religious

TABLE 10-3 HUMAN TRAFFICKING REPORT

Tier 1 Full Compliance	Tier 2 Significant Effort	Tier 2 Watch Some Effort, but Trafficking Remains a Concern	Tier 3 Noncompliant, No Effort
Australia	Afghanistan	Armenia	Algeria
Canada	Azerbaijan	Bahrain	Burma
Colombia	Brazil	Cambodia	Cuba
Denmark	Greece	China	Iran
France	Israel	Dominican Republic	Kuwait
Germany	Japan	Egypt	Malaysia
Hong Kong	Nicaragua	Honduras	North Korea
Italy	Nigeria	India	Qatar
Morocco	Philippines	Mexico	Saudi Arabia
Norway	Romania	Mozambique	Sudan
Poland	Turkey	Russia	Syria
South Korea	Vietnam	South Africa	Uzbekistan
Spain	Yemen	Ukraine	Venezuela

Note: Table is incomplete; each tier lists only sample nations. Since the Human Trafficking Report is created by the U.S. State Department, the level of compliance by the United States, although not listed, would presumably be "full compliance."
Sources: Ribando 2008:22 for the Department of State.

backgrounds. A few were placed in custody, sometimes without access to legal assistance. As the war on terror moved overseas, human rights concerns escalated. In 2005, the United Nations' secretary-general Kofi Annan criticized the United States and Britain for equating people who were resisting the presence of foreign troops in Afghanistan and Iraq with terrorists. For the foreseeable future, it seems, the United States and other countries will walk a delicate tightrope between human rights and the need for security (Parker 2004; Steele 2005).

Sociological Insights

By its very title, the Universal Declaration of Human Rights emphasizes that such rights should be *universal.* Even so, cultural relativism encourages understanding and respect for the distinctive norms, values, and customs of each culture. In some situations, conflicts arise between human rights standards and local social practices that rest on alternative views of human dignity. For example, is India's caste system an inherent violation of human rights? What about the many cultures of the world that view the subordinate status of women as an essential element in their traditions? Should human rights be interpreted differently in different parts of the world?

In 1993, the United States rejected such a view by insisting that the Universal Declaration of Human Rights set a single standard for acceptable behavior around the world. However, in the late 1990s, certain Asian and African nations were reviving arguments about cultural relativism in an attempt to block sanctions by the United Nations Human Rights Commission. For example, female genital mutilation, a practice that is common in more than 30 countries around the world, has been condemned in Western nations as a human rights abuse. This controversial practice often involves removal of the clitoris, in the belief that its excision will inhibit a young woman's sex drive, making her chaste and thus more desirable to her future husband. Though some countries have passed laws against the practice, they have gone largely unenforced. Immigrants from countries where genital mutilation is common often insist that their daughters undergo the procedure, to protect them from Western cultural norms that allow premarital sex (Religious Tolerance 2008).

In this context, defining human rights becomes a challenge. The feminist perspective places human rights above cultural practices that arise from the political struggle to control women's reproduction and work production. Thus, feminists would reject the extreme cultural relativist position that human rights are whatever a country or its government says they are (Brysk 2005).

It is not often that a nation makes a bold statement on human rights. Policymakers, including those in the United States, more frequently look at human rights issues from an economic perspective. Functionalists would point out how much more quickly we become embroiled in "human rights" concerns when oil is at stake, as in the Middle East, or when military alliances come into play, as in Europe. Governments ratify human rights but resist independent efforts to enforce them within their own borders (Hafner-Burton and Tsutsui 2005).

A recent sociological study compared those nations that do ratify human rights treaties with those that do not. Ironically, the most repressive regimes turned out to be the ones most likely to ratify the agreements. Generally, these countries are the least constrained by watchdog groups that might actually hold them to the agreements. At the same time, participation in the agreements may bring some positive notice, albeit brief, in the court of world opinion. Although research suggests that human rights treaties have not been fully implemented, it also shows a growing global consensus on human rights (Hafner-Burton et al. 2008).

Policy Initiatives

Human rights issues come wrapped up in international diplomacy. For that reason, many national policymakers hesitate to interfere in human rights issues, especially if they conflict with what are regarded as more pressing national concerns. Stepping up to fill the gap are international organizations such as the United Nations and nongovernmental organizations (NGOs) such as Médecins Sans Frontières and Amnesty International. Most initiatives come from these international bodies.

Médecins Sans Frontières (Doctors Without Borders), the world's largest independent emergency medical aid organization, won the 1999 Nobel Peace Prize for its work in countries worldwide. Founded in 1971 and based in Paris, the organization has 27,000 doctors, nurses, laboratory technicians, and others working in nearly 60 countries. "Our intention is to highlight current upheavals, to bear witness to foreign tragedies and reflect on the principles of humanitarian aid," explains Dr. Rony Brauman, the organization's president (Spielmann 1992:12; also see Doctors Without Borders 2008).

In recent years, awareness has been growing of lesbian and gay rights as an aspect of universal human rights. In 1994, Amnesty International (1994:2) published a pioneering report in which it acknowledged that "homosexuals in many parts of the world live in constant fear of government persecution." The report examined abuses in Brazil, Greece, Mexico, Iran, the United States, and other countries, including cases of torture, imprisonment, and extrajudicial execution. Later in 1994, the United States issued an order that would allow lesbians and gay men to seek political asylum in the United States if they could prove they had suffered government persecution in their home countries solely because of their sexual orientation (Johnston 1994).

Ethnic cleansing in the former Yugoslavia, human rights violations in Iraq and Afghanistan, increased surveillance in the name of counterterrorism, violence against women inside and outside the family, government torture of lesbians and gay men—all these are vivid reminders that social inequality today can have life-and-death consequences. Universal human rights remain an ideal, not a reality.

Let's Discuss

1. Why do definitions of human rights vary?
2. Are violations of human rights excusable in time of war? In the aftermath of serious terrorist attacks such as those of September 11, 2001? Why or why not?
3. How well or poorly do you think the United States compares to other countries in terms of respect for human rights, both at home and abroad? Has the nation's record improved or deteriorated in recent years?

getting**involved**

To get involved in the debate over universal human rights, visit this book's Online Learning Center, which offers links to relevant Web sites.

www.mhhe.com/schaefer12e

MASTERING THIS CHAPTER

Summary

Worldwide, stratification can be seen both in the gap between rich and poor nations and in the inequality within countries. This chapter examines the global divide and stratification within the world economic system; the impact of **globalization, modernization,** and **multinational corporations** on developing countries; and the distribution of wealth and income in various nations.

1. Developing nations account for most of the world's population and most of its births, but they also bear the burden of most of its poverty, disease, and childhood deaths.

2. Former colonized nations are kept in a subservient position, subject to foreign domination, through the process of **neocolonialism.**

3. Drawing on the conflict perspective, sociologist Immanuel Wallerstein's **world systems analysis** views the global economic system as one divided between nations that control wealth (core nations) and those from which capital is taken (periphery nations).

4. According to **dependency theory,** even as developing countries make economic advances, they remain weak and subservient to core nations and corporations in an increasingly integrated global economy.

5. **Globalization,** or the worldwide integration of government policies, cultures, social movements, and financial markets through trade and the exchange of ideas, is a controversial trend that critics blame for contributing to the cultural domination of periphery nations by core nations.

6. **Multinational corporations** bring jobs and industry to developing nations, but they also tend to exploit workers in order to maximize profits.

7. Poverty is a worldwide problem that blights the lives of billions of people. In 2000 the United Nations launched the Millennium Project, whose goal is to eliminate extreme poverty worldwide by the year 2015.

8. Many sociologists are quick to note that terms such as **modernization** and even *development* contain an ethnocentric bias.

9. According to **modernization theory,** the development of periphery countries will be assisted by innovations transferred from the industrialized world.

10. Although Mexico is unquestionably a poor country, the gap between its richest and poorest citizens is one of the widest in the world.

11. The subordinate status of Mexico's Indians is but one reflection of the nation's color hierarchy, which links social class to the appearance of racial purity.

12. Growing recognition of the **borderlands** reflects the increasingly close and complex relationship between Mexico and the United States.

13. **Human rights** need to be identified and abuses of those rights corrected in countries throughout the world.

Critical Thinking Questions

1. How have multinational corporations and the trend toward globalization affected you, your family, and your community? List both the pros and the cons. Have the benefits outweighed the drawbacks?

2. Imagine that you have the opportunity to spend a year in Mexico studying inequality in that nation. How would you draw on specific research designs (surveys, observation, experiments, existing sources) to better understand and document stratification in Mexico?

3. How active should the U.S. government be in addressing violations of human rights in other countries? At what point, if any, does concern for human rights turn into ethnocentrism through failure to respect the distinctive norms, values, and customs of another culture?

Key Terms

Borderlands The area of common culture along the border between Mexico and the United States. (page 235)

Colonialism The maintenance of political, social, economic, and cultural domination over a people by a foreign power for an extended period. (223)

Dependency theory An approach that contends that industrialized nations continue to exploit developing countries for their own gain. (223)

Globalization The worldwide integration of government policies, cultures, social movements, and financial markets through trade and the exchange of ideas. (224)

Gross national product (GNP) The value of a nation's goods and services. (227)

Human rights Universal moral rights possessed by all people because they are human. (237)

Modernization The far-reaching process by which periphery nations move from traditional or less developed institutions to those characteristic of more developed societies. (229)

Modernization theory A functionalist approach that proposes that modernization and development will gradually improve the lives of people in developing nations. (229)

Multinational corporation A commercial organization that is headquartered in one country but does business throughout the world. (224)

Neocolonialism Continuing dependence of former colonies on foreign countries. (223)

Remittances The monies that immigrants return to their families of origin. Also called *migradollars*. (236)

World systems analysis A view of the global economic system as one divided between certain industrialized nations that control wealth and developing countries that are controlled and exploited. (223)

Self-Quiz

Read each question carefully and then select the best answer.

1. The maintenance of political, social, economic, and cultural domination over a people by a foreign power for an extended period is referred to as
   a. neocolonialism.
   b. government-imposed stratification.
   c. colonialism.
   d. dependency.

2. In viewing the global economic system as divided between nations that control wealth and those that are controlled and exploited, sociologist Immanuel Wallerstein draws on the
   a. functionalist perspective.
   b. conflict perspective.
   c. interactionist perspective.
   d. dramaturgical approach.

3. Which of the following nations would Immanuel Wallerstein classify as a *core* country within the world economic system?
   a. Germany
   b. South Korea
   c. Ireland
   d. Mexico

4. Which sociological perspective argues that multinational corporations can actually help the developing nations of the world?
   a. the interactionist perspective
   b. the feminist perspective
   c. the functionalist perspective
   d. the conflict perspective

5. Which of the following terms is used by contemporary social scientists to describe the far-reaching process by which peripheral nations move from traditional or less-developed institutions to those characteristic of more developed societies?
   a. dependency
   b. globalization
   c. industrialization
   d. modernization

6. In at least 22 nations around the world, the most affluent 10 percent receives at least what percentage of all income?
   a. 20 percent
   b. 30 percent
   c. 40 percent
   d. 50 percent

7. Karuna Chanana Ahmed, an anthropologist from India who has studied developing nations, calls which group the most exploited of oppressed people?
   a. children
   b. women
   c. the elderly
   d. the poor

8. Which of the following terms is used to refer to Mexico's large, impoverished majority, most of whom have brown skin and a mixed racial lineage due to intermarriage?
   a. *criollo*
   b. *indio*
   c. *mestizo*
   d. *zapatista*

9. In Mexico, women now constitute what percentage of the labor force?
   a. 15 percent
   b. 23 percent
   c. 35 percent
   d. 45 percent

10. Which of the following terms refers to the foreign-owned factories established just across the border in Mexico, where the companies that own them don't have to pay taxes or provide insurance or benefits for their workers?
    a. *maquiladoras*
    b. *hombres*
    c. *mujeres*
    d. *toreadors*

11. Colonial domination established patterns of economic exploitation leading to former colonies remaining dependent on more industrialized nations. Such continuing dependence and foreign domination are referred to as _____.

12. According to Immanuel Wallerstein's analysis, the United States is at the _____ while neighboring Mexico is on the _____ of the world economic system.

13. Wallerstein's world systems analysis is the most widely used version of _____ theory.

14. _____ factories are factories found throughout the developing world that are run by multinational corporations.

15. As _____ industries become a more important part of the international marketplace, many companies have concluded that the low costs of overseas operations more than offset the expense of transmitting information around the world.

16. Viewed from a(n) _____ perspective, the combination of skilled technology and management provided by multinationals and the relatively cheap labor available in developing nations is ideal for a global enterprise.

17. In 2000 the United Nations launched the _____ _____; its objective is to eliminate extreme poverty worldwide by the year 2015.

18. Modernization theory reflects the _____ perspective.

19. At the top of the color hierarchy in Mexico are the_____, the 10 percent of the population who are typically White, well-educated members of the business and intellectual elites, and who have familial roots in Spain.

20. The term _____ refers to the area of a common culture along the border between Mexico and the United States.

THINKING ABOUT MOVIES

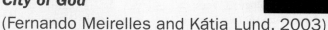

Blood Diamond (Edward Zwick, 2006)

As civil war rages in Sierra Leone, Africa, a fisherman named Solomon Vandy (Djimon Hounsou) is enslaved by a revolutionary group and forced to dig for diamonds. Solomon finds an immense pink diamond that is worth a fortune. He hides this "blood diamond," hoping he can use it to reunite his war-torn family. When a smuggler named Danny Archer (Leonardo DiCaprio) learns about Solomon's diamond, he offers to help him find a buyer.

This fictionalized account of the "conflict diamond trade" illustrates Wallerstein's world systems analysis. *Blood Diamond* shows the unequal distribution of wealth between the industrialized nations that consume diamonds (such as the United States) and the peripheral countries that produce them (such as Sierra Leone). From the film's perspective, multinational corporations use this unequal division of resources to their own advantage, profiting from the inequity.

For Your Consideration

1. What are some of the ways in which this movie illustrates dependency theory?
2. How would you describe the role of diamonds in global stratification, as shown in this film?

City of God (Fernando Meirelles and Kátia Lund, 2003)

In an extremely poor neighborhood west of Rio de Janeiro, Brazil, a young boy named Rocket (Alexandre Rodrigues) survives as best he can. Rocket lives in a *favela,* a shanty town where electricity is limited, shelters are made of recycled materials, and disease runs rampant. These desperate conditions are compounded by gang violence. Rocket's extreme poverty means that he has limited options for upward mobility, but he takes an interest in photography and eventually finds a way out of the *favela* by portraying the violence that surrounds him.

Brazil is a relatively poor country compared to industrialized nations like the United States and Japan. Income inequality is particularly severe there. *City of God,* named after Rocket's *favela,* portrays global inequality by focusing on a community marred by extreme poverty and the violence it engenders.

For Your Consideration

1. How does Rocket cope with his impoverishment? Relate his living conditions to the concept of modernization.
2. In what ways does this movie show the unequal distribution of wealth in South America?

inside

Minority, Racial, and Ethnic
    Groups

Prejudice and Discrimination

Sociological Perspectives
    on Race and Ethnicity

Patterns of Intergroup
    Relations

Race and Ethnicity
    in the United States

Social Policy and Racial and
    Ethnic Inequality:
    Global Immigration

BOXES

Taking Sociology to Work:
    *Prudence Hannis, Liaison
    Officer, National Institute
    of Science Research,
    University of Québec*

Sociology in the Global
    Community: *The
    Aboriginal People
    of Australia*

Research Today: *Social
    Mobility among Latino
    Immigrants*

In Los Angeles, hundreds of
thousands of immigrants march
for immigration reform. Around
the world, racial and ethnic
differences between immigrants
and the dominant groups in
society complicate the extremely
controversial issue of immigration.

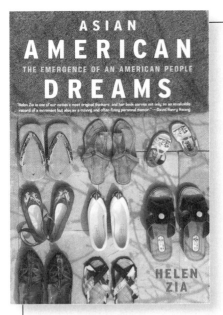

ASIAN AMERICAN DREAMS
THE EMERGENCE OF AN AMERICAN PEOPLE

HELEN ZIA

❝ Ah so. No tickee, no washee. So sorry, so sollee.

Chinkee, Chink. Jap, Nip, zero, kamikaze. Dothead, flat face, flat nose, slant eye, slope. Slit, mamasan, dragon lady. Gook, VC, Flip, Hindoo.

By the time I was ten, I'd heard such words so many times I could feel them coming before they parted lips. I knew they were meant in the unkindest way. Still, we didn't talk about these incidents at home, we just accepted them as part of being in America, something to learn to rise above.

The most common taunting didn't even utilize words but a string of unintelligible gobbledygook that kids—and adults—would spew as they pretended to speak Chinese or some other Asian language. It was a mockery of how they imagined my parents talked to me.

Truth was that Mom and Dad rarely spoke to us in Chinese, except to scold or call us to dinner. Worried that we might develop an accent, my father insisted that we speak English at home. This, he explained, would lessen the hardships we might encounter and make us more acceptable as Americans.

Truth was that Mom and Dad rarely spoke to us in Chinese, except to scold or call us to dinner. Worried that we might develop an accent, my father insisted that we speak English at home.

I'll never know if my father's language decision was right. On the one hand, I, like most Asian Americans, have been complimented countless times on my spoken English by people who assumed I was a foreigner. "My, you speak such good English," they'd cluck. "No kidding, I ought to," I would think to myself, then wonder: should I thank them for assuming that English isn't my native language? Or should I correct them on the proper usage of "well" and "good"?

More often than feeling grateful for my American accent, I've wished that I could jump into a heated exchange of rapid-fire Chinese, volume high and spit flying. But with a vocabulary limited to *"Ni hao?"* (How are you?) and *"Ting bu dong"* (I hear but don't understand), meaningful exchanges are woefully impossible. I find myself smiling and nodding like a dashboard ornament. I'm envious of the many people I know who grew up speaking an Asian language yet converse in English beautifully.

Armed with standard English and my flat New Jersey "a," I still couldn't escape the name-calling. I became all too familiar with other names and faces that supposedly matched mine—Fu Manchu, Suzie Wong, Hop Sing, Madame Butterfly, Charlie Chan, Ming the Merciless—the "Asians" produced for mass consumption. Their faces filled me with shame whenever I saw them on TV or in the movies. They defined my face to the rest of the world: a sinister Fu, Suzie the whore, subservient Hop Sing, pathetic Butterfly, cunning Chan, and warlike Ming. Inscrutable Orientals all, real Americans none. ❞

(Zia 2000:109–110) Additional information about this excerpt can be found on the Online Learning Center at www.mhhe.com/schaefer12e.

Helen Zia, the successful journalist and community activist who wrote this reminiscence from her childhood, is the daughter of Chinese immigrants to the United States. As her story shows, Zia experienced blatant prejudice against Chinese Americans, even though she spoke flawless English. In fact, all new immigrants and their families have faced stereotyping and hostility, whether they were White or non-White, Asian, African, or East European. In this multicultural society, those who are different from the dominant social group have never been welcome.

Today, millions of African Americans, Asian Americans, Hispanic Americans, and many other racial and ethnic minorities continue to experience the often bitter contrast between the "American dream" and the grim realities of poverty, prejudice, and discrimination. Like class, the social definitions of race and ethnicity still affect people's place and status in a stratification system, not only in this country but throughout the world. High incomes, a good command of English, and hard-earned professional credentials do not always override racial and ethnic stereotypes or protect those who fit them from the sting of racism.

What is prejudice, and how is it institutionalized in the form of discrimination? In what ways have race and ethnicity affected the experience of immigrants from other countries? What are the fastest-growing minority groups in the United States today? In this chapter we will focus on the meaning of race and ethnicity. We will begin by identifying the basic characteristics of a minority group and distinguishing between racial and ethnic groups. Then we will examine the dynamics of prejudice and discrimination. After considering four sociological perspectives on race and ethnicity, we'll take a look at common patterns of intergroup relations. The following section will describe the major racial and ethnic groups in the United States. Finally, in the Social Policy section we will explore the issue of global immigration.

Minority, Racial, and Ethnic Groups

Sociologists frequently distinguish between racial and ethnic groups. The term **racial group** describes a group that is set apart from others because of physical differences that have taken on social significance. Whites, African Americans, and Asian Americans are all considered racial groups in the United States. While race does turn on physical differences, it is the culture of a particular society that constructs and attaches social significance to those differences, as we will see later. Unlike racial groups, an **ethnic group** is set apart from others primarily because of its national origin or distinctive cultural patterns. In the United States, Puerto Ricans, Jews, and Polish Americans are all categorized as ethnic groups (Table 11-1).

Minority Groups

A numerical minority is any group that makes up less than half of some larger population. The population of the United States includes thousands of numerical minorities, including television actors, green-eyed people, tax lawyers, and descendants of the Pilgrims who arrived on the *Mayflower*. However, these numerical minorities are not considered to be minorities in the sociological sense; in fact, the number of people in a group does not necessarily determine its status as a social minority (or a dominant group). When sociologists define a minority group, they are concerned primarily with the economic and political power, or powerlessness, of that group. A **minority group** is a subordinate group whose members have significantly less control or power over their own lives than the members of a dominant or majority group have over theirs.

Sociologists have identified five basic properties of a minority group: unequal treatment, physical or cultural traits, ascribed status, solidarity, and in-group marriage (Wagley and Harris 1958):

1. Members of a minority group experience unequal treatment compared to members of a dominant group. For example, the management of an apartment complex may refuse to rent to African Americans, Hispanics, or Jews. Social inequality may be created or maintained by prejudice, discrimination, segregation, or even extermination.

2. Members of a minority group share physical or cultural characteristics that distinguish them from the dominant group. Each society arbitrarily decides which characteristics are most important in defining groups.

3. Membership in a minority (or dominant) group is not voluntary; people are born into the group. Thus, race and ethnicity are considered *ascribed* statuses.

4. Minority group members have a strong sense of group solidarity. William Graham Sumner, writing in 1906, noted that people make distinctions between members of their own group (the *in-group*) and everyone else (the *out-group*). When a group is the object of long-term prejudice and discrimination, the feeling of "us versus them" can and often does become extremely intense.

5. Members of a minority group generally marry others from the same group. A member of a dominant group is often unwilling

Classification	Number in Thousands	Percentage of Total Population
Racial Groups		
Whites (non-Hispanic)	198,553	65.8%
Blacks/African Americans	37,335	12.4
Native Americans, Alaskan Natives	2,365	0.8
Asian Americans	13,668	4.5
Chinese	3,046	1.0
Asian Indians	2,570	0.9
Filipinos	2,412	0.8
Vietnamese	1,508	0.5
Koreans	1,334	0.4
Japanese	803	0.3
Pacific Islanders, Native Hawaiians, and other	1,990	0.7
Ethnic Groups		
White ancestry (single or mixed, non-Hispanic)		
Germans	50,672	16.8
Irish	36,496	12.1
English	28,051	9.3
Italians	17,796	5.9
Scottish and Scotch-Irish	11,462	3.8
Poles	9,140	3.3
French	9,652	3.2
Jews	6,636	2.2
Hispanics (or Latinos)	45,427	15.1
Mexican Americans	29,167	9.7
Puerto Ricans	4,120	1.4
Cubans	1,611	0.5
Salvadorans	1,474	0.5
Dominicans	1,208	0.4
Other Hispanics	7,847	2.6
TOTAL (all groups)	**301,621**	

Note: Percentages do not total 100 and subtotals do not add up to totals in major categories because of overlap between groups (e.g., Polish American Jews or people of mixed ancestry, such as Irish and Italian).
Source: Author estimates based on American Community Survey 2008: Table 50201 and Comparison Profile; Sheskin and Dashefsky 2006.

to marry into a supposedly inferior minority group. In addition, the minority group's sense of solidarity encourages marriage within the group and discourages marriage to outsiders.

Race

The term *racial group* refers to those minorities (and the corresponding dominant groups) set apart from others by obvious physical differences. But what is an "obvious" physical difference? Each society labels those differences that people consider important, while ignoring other characteristics that could serve as a basis for social differentiation.

Social Construction of Race Because race is a social construction, the process of defining races typically benefits those who have more power and privilege than others. In the United States, we see differences in both skin color and hair color. Yet people learn informally that differences in skin color have a dramatic social and political meaning, while differences in hair color do not.

When observing skin color, many people in the United States tend to lump others rather casually into the traditional categories of "Black," "White," and "Asian." More subtle differences in skin color often go unnoticed. In many nations of Central America and South America, in contrast, people recognize color gradients on a continuum from light to dark skin color. Brazil has approximately 40 color groupings, while in other countries people may be described as "Mestizo Hondurans," "Mulatto Colombians," or "African Panamanians." What we see as "obvious" differences, then, are subject to each society's social definitions.

The largest racial minorities in the United States are African Americans (or Blacks), Native Americans (or American Indians), and Asian Americans (Japanese Americans, Chinese Americans, and other Asian peoples). Figure 11-1 provides information about the population of racial and ethnic groups in the United States over the past five centuries. Given current population patterns, it is clear that the nation's diversity will continue to increase. Half of all children now under age 5 belong to racial and ethnic minorities. As those children become students, workers, and parents, the transformation of the U.S. population will continue (Mather 2007).

Racial definitions are crystallized through what Michael Omi and Howard Winant (1994) have called **racial formation,** a sociohistorical process in which racial categories are created, inhibited, transformed, and destroyed. In this process, those who have power define groups of people according to a racist social structure. The creation of a reservation system for Native Americans in the late 1800s is one example of racial formation. Federal officials combined what were distinctive tribes into a single racial group, which we refer to today as Native Americans. The extent and frequency with which peoples are subject to racial formation is such that no one escapes it.

Another example of racial formation from the 1800s was known as the "one-drop rule." If a person had even a single drop of "Black blood," that person was defined and viewed as Black, even if he or she *appeared* to be White. Clearly, race had social significance, enough so that White legislators established official standards about who was "Black" and who was "White."

The one-drop rule was a vivid example of the *social construction of race*—the process by which people come to define a group as a race based in part on physical characteristics, but also on historical, cultural, and economic factors. For example, in the 1800s, immigrant groups such as Italian and Irish Americans were not at first seen as being "White," but as foreigners who were not necessarily trustworthy. The social construction of race is an ongoing process that is subject to debate, especially

FIGURE **11-1** RACIAL AND ETHNIC GROUPS IN THE UNITED STATES, 1500–2100 (PROJECTED)

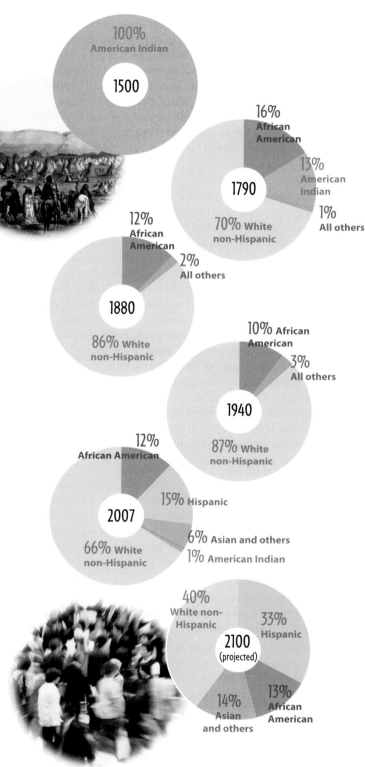

Sources: Author's estimate; American Community Survey 2008; Bureau of the Census 2004a. Data for 2007 and 2100, African Americans and Asian and other are for non-Hispanics.

The racial and ethnic composition of what is today the United States has been undergoing change not just for the past 50 years, but for the past 500. Five centuries ago the land was populated only by indigenous Native Americans.

in a diverse society such as the United States, where each year increasing numbers of children are born to parents of different racial backgrounds.

Recognition of Multiple Identities

In 1900, in an address to the Anti-Slavery Union in London, scholar W. E. B. DuBois predicted that "the color line" would become the foremost problem of the 20th century. DuBois, born a free Black man in 1868, had witnessed prejudice and discrimination throughout the United States. His comment was prophetic. Today, over a century later, race and ethnicity still carry enormous weight in the United States (DuBois [1900] 1969).

The color line has blurred significantly since 1900, however. Interracial marriage is no longer forbidden by law and custom. Thus, Geetha Lakshmi-narayanan, a native of Ann Arbor, Michigan, is both White and Asian Indian. Often mistaken for a Filipina or Latina, she has grown accustomed to the blunt question, "What are you?" (Navarro 2005).

In the late 20th century, with immigration from Latin America rising, the fluid nature of racial formation became evident. Suddenly, people were speaking about the "Latin Americanization" of the United States, or about a biracial, Black/White society being replaced by a triracial one. In a 2008 Bureau of the Census estimate, over 6 million people in the United States (or about 2 percent of the population) reported that they were of two or more races. Half the people classified as multiracial were under age 18, suggesting that this segment of the population will grow in the years to come. People who claimed both White and American Indian ancestry were the largest group of multiracial residents (American Community Survey 2008:Table BO2001; Bonilla-Silva 2004).

This statistical finding of millions of multiracial people obscures how individuals are often asked to handle their identity. For example, the enrollment forms for government programs typically include only a few broad racial-ethnic categories. This approach to racial categorization is part of a long history that dictates single-race identities. Still, many individuals, especially young adults, struggle against social pressure to choose a single identity, and instead openly embrace multiple heritages. Public

figures, rather than hide their mixed ancestry, now flaunt it. Singer Mariah Carey celebrates her Irish American background, and President Barack Obama speaks of being born in Hawai'i to a Kenyan father and a White mother from Kansas. Tiger Woods, the world's best-known professional golfer, considers himself both Asian and African American.

A dominant or majority group has the power not only to define itself legally but to define a society's values. The interactionist William I. Thomas, observing how we assign social meanings, saw that the "definition of the situation" could mold the individual personality. To put it another way, people respond not only to the objective features of a situation or person but also to the *meaning* that situation or person has for them. Thus, we can create false images or stereotypes that become real in their consequences. **Stereotypes** are unreliable generalizations about all members of a group that do not recognize individual differences within the group.

Today, some children of mixed-race families identify themselves as biracial or multiracial, rejecting efforts to place them in a single racial category.

use your sociological *imagination*

Using a TV remote control, how quickly do you think you could find a television show in which all the characters share your own racial or ethnic background? What about a show in which all the characters share a different background from your own—how quickly could you find one?

An ethnic group, unlike a racial group, is set apart from others because of its national origin or distinctive cultural patterns. Among the ethnic groups in the United States are peoples with a Spanish-speaking background, referred to collectively as *Latinos* or *Hispanics,* such as Puerto Ricans, Mexican Americans, Cuban Americans, and other Latin Americans. Other ethnic groups in this country include Jewish, Irish, Italian, and Norwegian Americans. Although these groupings are convenient, they serve to obscure differences *within* ethnic categories (as in the case of Hispanics), as well as to overlook the mixed ancestry of so many people in the United States.

The distinction between racial and ethnic minorities is not always clear-cut. Some members of racial minorities, such as Asian Americans, may have significant cultural differences from other racial groups. At the same time, certain ethnic minorities, such as Latinos, may have obvious physical differences that set them apart from other ethnic groups in the United States.

Despite categorization problems, sociologists continue to feel that the distinction between racial groups and ethnic groups is socially significant. In most societies, including the United States, socially constructed physical differences tend to be more visible than ethnic differences. Partly as a result of this fact, stratification along racial lines is more resistant to change than stratification along ethnic lines. Over time, members of an ethnic minority can sometimes become indistinguishable from the majority—although the process may take generations and may never include all members of the group. In contrast, members of a racial minority find it much more difficult to blend in with the larger society and gain acceptance from the majority.

The inauguration of President Barack Obama in 2009 was clearly historic. To put its significance in perspective, however, Obama's Senate seat was the only one held by a Black man when he left it to become president. More than half of White voters in the 2008 presidential election—57 percent—cast their ballots for candidates other than Obama.

Prejudice and Discrimination

Looking at the United States in the 21st century, some people wonder aloud if race and ethnicity are still relevant to social stratification. After all, African Americans have served as secretary of state, secretary of defense, and chairman of the Joint Chiefs of Staff; the office of attorney general has been held by both an African American and a Hispanic. Most notably, an African American now serves as president. As historic as these leaders' achievements have been, however, in every case their elevation meant that they left behind a virtually all-White government department or assembly.

At the same time, college campuses across the United States have been the scene of bias-related incidents. Student-run newspapers and radio stations have ridiculed racial and ethnic minorities; threatening literature has been stuffed under the doors of minority students; graffiti endorsing the views of White supremacist organizations such as the Ku Klux Klan have been scrawled on university walls. In some cases, there have even been violent clashes between groups of White and Black students (Southern Poverty Law Center 2009). What causes such ugly incidents?

Prejudice

Prejudice is a negative attitude toward an entire category of people, often an ethnic or racial minority. If you resent your roommate because he or she is sloppy, you are not necessarily guilty of prejudice. However, if you immediately stereotype your roommate on the basis of such characteristics as race, ethnicity, or religion, that is a form of prejudice. Prejudice tends to perpetuate false definitions of individuals and groups.

Sometimes prejudice results from **ethnocentrism**—the tendency to assume that one's own culture and way of life represent the norm or are superior to all others. Ethnocentric people judge other cultures by the standards of their own group, which leads quite easily to prejudice against cultures they view as inferior.

One important and widespread ideology that reinforces prejudice is **racism,** the belief that one race is supreme and all others are innately inferior. When racism prevails in a society, members of subordinate groups generally experience prejudice, discrimination, and exploitation. In 1990, as concern mounted about racist attacks in the United States, Congress passed the Hate Crimes Statistics Act. A **hate crime** is a criminal offense committed because of the offender's bias against a race, religion, ethnic group, national origin, or sexual orientation. In 2007 alone, more than 7,600 hate crimes were reported to authorities. As Figure 11-2 shows, more than half those crimes against persons involved racial bias. Most were carried out by one or more individuals.

Color-Blind Racism

Over the past three generations, nationwide surveys have consistently shown growing support among Whites for integration, interracial dating, and the election of minority group members to public office—including the presidency of the United States. How can this trend be explained, given the persistence of residential segregation and the commission of thousands of hate crimes every year? The answer, to some extent, is that prejudice and discriminatory attitudes are no longer expressed as freely as they once were. Often, they are couched in terms of equal opportunity.

FIGURE 11-2 CATEGORIZATION OF REPORTED HATE CRIMES

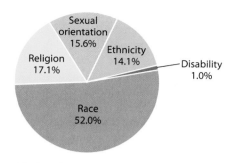

Sexual orientation 15.6%

Religion 17.1%

Ethnicity 14.1%

Disability 1.0%

Race 52.0%

Source: Reported for 2007 in 2008. Department of Justice 2008b.

Color-blind racism is the use of the principle of race neutrality to defend a racially unequal status quo. Proponents of race neutrality claim they believe that everyone should be treated equally. However, the way they apply the principle to government policy is anything but neutral. Proponents of this approach oppose affirmative action (see page 252), public welfare assistance, and to a large extent, government-funded health insurance, all of which they see largely as favors to minority groups. Yet they do not object to practices that privilege Whites, such as college admissions criteria that give preference to the relatives of alumni. Nor do they oppose tax breaks for homeowners, most of whom are White, or government financial aid to college students, who are also disproportionately White. Though race neutrality is not based on theories of racial superiority or inferiority, then, the idea that society should be color-blind only perpetuates racial inequality.

Color-blind racism has also been referred to as "covert racism." Although its proponents rarely speak of racism, other indicators of social status, such as social class or citizenship, tend to become proxies for race. Thus, many White people can convince themselves that they are not racist—nor do they know anyone who is—and yet remain prejudiced against "welfare mothers" and "immigrants." They can conclude, mistakenly, that racial tolerance, or even racial and ethnic equality, has been achieved.

Researchers who have surveyed White attitudes toward African Americans over the past several decades have reached two inescapable conclusions. First, people's attitudes do change. In periods of social upheaval, dramatic attitudinal shifts can occur within a single generation. Second, less racial progress was made in the late 20th and early 21st centuries than in the relatively brief period of the 1950s and 1960s. Today, economically disadvantaged groups such as African Americans and Latinos have become so closely associated with urban decay, homelessness, welfare, and crime that those problems are now viewed as racial issues, even if they are not labeled as such. The tendency to *blame the victims* of these social ills complicates their resolution (see Chapter 9), especially at a time when government's ability to address social problems is limited by antitax initiatives and concern over terrorism. In short, the color line is still in place, even if more and more people refuse to acknowledge its existence (Ansell 2008;

Bonilla-Silva 2006; Coates 2008; M. King 2007:3–4; Quillian 2006; Winant 1994:106–108).

249

Racial and Ethnic Inequality

Discriminatory Behavior

Prejudice often leads to **discrimination,** the denial of opportunities and equal rights to individuals and groups because of prejudice or other arbitrary reasons. Say that a White corporate president with a prejudice against Asian Americans has to fill an executive position. The most qualified candidate for the job is a Vietnamese American. If the president refuses to hire this candidate and instead selects an inferior White candidate, he or she is engaging in an act of racial discrimination.

Prejudiced *attitudes* should not be equated with discriminatory *behavior.* Although the two are generally related, they are not identical; either condition can be present without the other. A prejudiced person does not always act on his or her biases. The White corporate president, for example, might choose—despite his or her stereotypes—to hire the Vietnamese American. That would be prejudice without discrimination. On the other hand, a White corporate president with a completely respectful view of Vietnamese Americans might refuse to hire them for executive posts out of fear that biased clients would take their business elsewhere. In that case, the president's action would constitute discrimination without prejudice.

A field experiment by Devah Pager (2003), a doctoral candidate in sociology at the University of Wisconsin, documented racial discrimination in hiring. Pager sent four polite, well-dressed young men out to look for an entry-level job in Milwaukee, Wisconsin. All were 23-year-old college students, but they presented themselves as high school graduates with similar job histories. Two of the men were Black and two were White. One Black applicant and one White applicant claimed to have served 18 months in jail for a felony conviction—possession of cocaine with intent to distribute.

As one might expect, the four men's experiences with 350 potential employers were vastly different. Predictably, the White applicant with a purported prison record received only half as many callbacks as the other White applicant—17 percent

People who oppose government welfare programs but support other forms of government assistance, such as financial aid to college students, may be exhibiting color-blind racism.

Note: Data released in 2008 for income earned in 2007. Includes only people working full-time, year-round, 25 years old and older. "White" refers to White non-Hispanics.
Sources: DeNavas-Walt et al. 2008; for Native Americans, author's estimate based on Bureau of the Census 2003a.

compared to 34 percent. But as dramatic as the effect of his criminal record was, the effect of his race was more significant. Despite his prison record, he received slightly more callbacks than the Black applicant *with no criminal record* (17 percent compared to 14 percent). Race, it seems, was more of a concern to potential employers than a criminal background.

The implications of this research are not limited to any one city, such as Milwaukee. Similar studies have confirmed discriminatory handling of job applications in Chicago; New York City; Long Island, New York; San Diego; and Washington, D.C. Over time, the cumulative effect of such differential behavior by employers contributes to significant differences in income. Figure 11-3 vividly illustrates the income inequality between White men and almost everyone else (ERASE Racism 2009; Pager 2007a, 2007b; Pager and Shepherd 2008; Pager and Western 2006).

Sometimes racial and ethnic discrimination is overt. Internet forums like Craigslist.org or Roommate.com feature classified ads that state "African Americans and Arabians tend to clash with me" or "Clean, Godly Christian men only." While antidiscrimination laws prevent such notices from being published in the newspapers, existing law has not caught up with online bigotry in hiring and renting (Liptak 2006).

Discrimination persists even for the most educated and qualified minority group members from the best family backgrounds. Despite their talents and experiences, they sometimes encounter attitudinal or organizational bias that prevents them from reaching their full potential. The term **glass ceiling** refers to an invisible barrier that blocks the promotion of a qualified individual in a work environment because of the individual's gender, race, or ethnicity (Schaefer 2010; Yamagata et al. 1997).

In early 1995, the federal Glass Ceiling Commission issued the first comprehensive study of barriers to promotion in the United States. The commission found that glass ceilings continue to block women and minority group men from top management positions in the nation's industries. While White men constitute 45 percent of the paid labor force, they hold down

a much higher proportion of top positions. Even in *Fortune* magazine's 2002 listing of the most diversified corporations, White men held more than 80 percent of both the board of directors seats and the top 50 paid positions in the firms. The existence of this glass ceiling results principally from the fears and prejudices of many middle- and upper-level White male managers, who believe that the inclusion of women and minority group men in management circles will threaten their own prospects for advancement (Bureau of the Census 2008a; Department of Labor 1995a, 1995b; Hickman 2002).

The Privileges of the Dominant

One aspect of discrimination that is often overlooked is the privileges that dominant groups enjoy at the expense of others. For instance, we tend to focus more on the difficulty women have getting ahead at work and getting a hand at home than on the ease with which men manage to make their way in the world and avoid household chores. Similarly, we concentrate more on discrimination against racial and ethnic minorities than on the advantages members of the White majority enjoy. Indeed, most White people rarely think about their "Whiteness," taking their status for granted.

Sociologists and other social scientists are becoming increasingly interested in what it means to be "White," for White privilege is the other side of the proverbial coin of racial discrimination. In this context, **White privilege** refers to rights or immunities granted to people as a particular benefit or favor simply because they are White (Ferber and Kimmel 2008). The feminist scholar Peggy McIntosh (1988) became interested in White privilege after noticing that most men would not acknowledge that there were privileges attached to being male—even if they would agree that being female had its disadvantages. Did White people suffer from a similar blind spot regarding their racial privilege? she wondered. Intrigued, McIntosh began to list all the ways in which she benefited from her Whiteness. She soon realized that the list of unspoken advantages was long and significant.

McIntosh found that as a White person, she rarely needed to step out of her comfort zone, no matter where she went. If she wished to, she could spend most of her time with people of her own race. She could find a good place to live in a pleasant neighborhood, buy the foods she liked to eat from almost any grocery store, and get her hair styled in almost any salon. She could attend a public meeting without feeling that she did not belong, that she was different from everyone else.

McIntosh discovered, too, that her skin color opened doors for her. She could cash checks and use credit cards without suspicion, browse through stores without being shadowed by security guards. She could be seated without difficulty in a restaurant. If she asked to see the manager, she could assume he or she would be of her own race. If she needed help from a doctor or a lawyer, she could get it.

TAKING SOCIOLOGY TO WORK

Prudence Hannis, **Liaison Officer, National Institute of Science Research, University of Québec**

Prudence Hannis is a First Nations (Native American) woman who serves as an official liaison between her people and Canadian researchers. In her position, she interacts with sociologists, anthropologists, political scientists, legal scholars, and researchers in health and medicine at several Canadian universities, all of whom wish to work with First Nations communities. Hannis is enthusiastic about her job, which gives her an opportunity to educate and sensitize would-be researchers who "never set foot in First Nations communities." In 10 years of work on behalf of the native peoples of Canada, Hannis has seen a dramatic change in their representation in Canadian research and policy. "We are everywhere in research efforts and policy consultation, but whether we are listened to is another matter," she notes.

Before taking her current position, Hannis served as a researcher and community activist with Québec Native Women. There she oversaw the women's health portfolio, organized seminars on sexual abuse for local communities, and produced a resource booklet on the subject. "The purpose of my job was to defend First Nations' women's concerns, to be their spokesperson when needed, to analyze critical situations for our sisters, and mostly, to determine ways in which women can empower themselves, their families, and their communities," she says.

Hannis has also worked for the Centre of Excellence on Women's Health, Consortium Université de Montréal, where she focused on First Nations women's health issues. A member of the Abenaki tribe, Hannis received her BA in sociology from the University of Québec at Montréal. She has found her background in the discipline to be invaluable. "Sociology is now, more than it has ever been, a part of my job," she says.

LET'S DISCUSS

1. What may be some of the challenges to improving the health of Native Americans in Canada?
2. In speaking of empowering First Nations women, what sociological perspective do you think Hannis is drawing on?

McIntosh also realized that her Whiteness made the job of parenting easier. She did not need to worry about protecting her children from people who didn't like them. She could be sure that their schoolbooks would show pictures of people who looked like them, and that their history texts would describe White people's achievements. She knew that the television programs they watched would include White characters.

Finally, McIntosh had to admit that others did not constantly evaluate her in racial terms. When she appeared in public, she didn't need to worry that her clothing or behavior might reflect poorly on White people. If she was recognized for an achievement, it was seen as her achievement, not that of an entire race. And no one ever assumed that the personal opinions she voiced should be those of all White people. Because McIntosh blended in with the people around her, she wasn't always onstage.

These are not all the privileges White people take for granted as a result of their membership in the dominant racial group in the United States. As Devah Pager's study showed (see page 249), White job seekers enjoy a tremendous advantage over equally well-qualified—even better-qualified—Blacks. Whiteness *does* carry privileges—to a much greater extent than most White people realize (Fitzgerald 2008; Picca and Feagin 2007).

use your sociological *imagination*

How often do you think people are privileged because of their race or ethnicity? How about yourself—how often are you privileged?

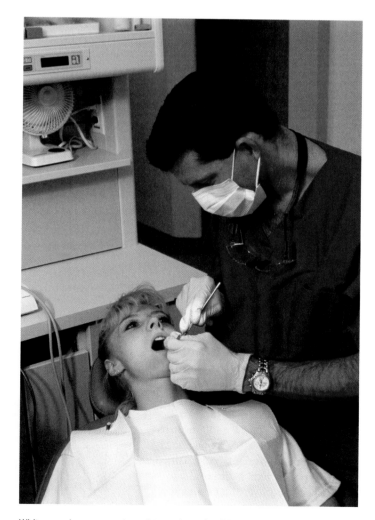

White people are accustomed to seeing other White people in professional positions and jobs with authority and prestige. Whiteness *does* have its privileges.

Discrimination is practiced not only by individuals in one-to-one encounters but also by institutions in their daily operations. Social scientists are particularly concerned with the ways in which structural factors such as employment, housing, health care, and government operations maintain the social significance of race and ethnicity. **Institutional discrimination** refers to the denial of opportunities and equal rights to individuals and groups that results from the normal operations of a society. This kind of discrimination consistently affects certain racial and ethnic groups more than others.

The Commission on Civil Rights (1981:9–10) has identified various forms of institutional discrimination:

- Rules requiring that only English be spoken at a place of work, even when it is not a business necessity to restrict the use of other languages.

- Preferences shown by law and medical schools in the admission of children of wealthy and influential alumni, nearly all of whom are White.

- Restrictive employment-leave policies, coupled with prohibitions on part-time work, that make it difficult for the heads of single-parent families (most of whom are women) to obtain and keep jobs.

Institutional discrimination occurred in the wake of the September 11, 2001, terrorist attacks on the United States. In the heat of demands to prevent terrorist takeovers of commercial airplanes, Congress passed the Aviation and Transportation Security Act, which was intended to strengthen airport screening procedures. The law stipulated that all airport screeners must be U.S. citizens. Nationally, 28 percent of all airport screeners were legal residents but not citizens of the United States; as a group, they were disproportionately Latino, Black, and Asian. Many observers noted that other airport and airline workers, including pilots, cabin attendants, and even armed National Guardsmen stationed at airports, need not be citizens. Efforts are now being made to test the constitutionality of the act. At the least, the debate over its fairness shows that even well-meant legal measures can have disastrous consequences for racial and ethnic minorities (H. Weinstein 2002).

In some cases, even seemingly neutral institutional standards can have discriminatory effects. African American students at a midwestern state university protested a policy under which fraternities and sororities that wished to use campus facilities for a dance were required to pay a $150 security deposit to cover possible damages. African American students complained that the policy had a discriminatory impact on minority student organizations. Campus police countered that the university's policy applied to all student groups interested in using the facilities. However, since the overwhelmingly White fraternities and sororities at the school had their own houses, which they used for dances, the policy indeed affected only African American and other minority organizations.

Attempts have been made to eradicate or compensate for discrimination in the United States. The 1960s saw the passage of many pioneering civil rights laws, including the landmark 1964 Civil Rights Act (which prohibits discrimination in public accommodations and publicly owned facilities on the basis of race, color, creed, national origin, and gender). In two important rulings in 1987, the Supreme Court held that federal prohibitions against racial discrimination protect members of all ethnic minorities—including Hispanics, Jews, and Arab Americans—even though they may be considered White.

For more than 40 years, affirmative action programs have been instituted to overcome past discrimination. **Affirmative action** refers to positive efforts to recruit minority group members or women for jobs, promotions, and educational opportunities. Many people resent these programs, arguing that advancing one group's cause merely shifts the discrimination to another group. By giving priority to African Americans in admissions, for example, schools may overlook more qualified White candidates. In many parts of the country and many sectors of the economy, affirmative action is being rolled back, even though it was never fully implemented. We will discuss affirmative action in more detail in Chapter 18.

Discriminatory practices continue to pervade nearly all areas of life in the United States today. In part, that is because various individuals and groups actually *benefit* from racial and ethnic discrimination in terms of money, status, and influence. Discrimination permits members of the majority to enhance their wealth, power, and prestige at the expense of others. Less qualified people get jobs and promotions simply because they are members of the dominant group. Such individuals and groups will not surrender these advantages easily. We'll turn now to a closer look at this functionalist analysis, as well as the conflict, labeling, and interactionist perspectives on race and ethnicity.

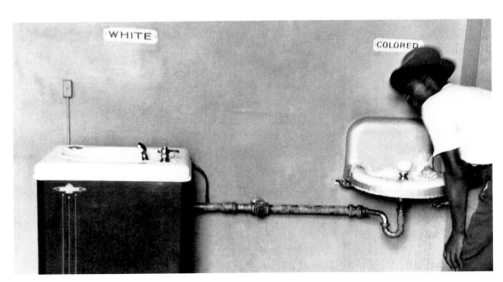

Before passage of the Civil Rights Act (1964), segregation of public accommodations was the norm throughout the South. Whites used the most up-to-date bathrooms, waiting rooms, and even drinking fountains, while Blacks ("Colored") were directed to older facilities in inferior condition. Such separate but unequal arrangements are a blatant example of institutional discrimination.

Sociological Perspectives on Race and Ethnicity

Relations among racial and ethnic groups lend themselves to analysis from four major sociological perspectives. Viewing race from the macro level, functionalists observe that racial prejudice and discrimination serve positive functions for dominant groups. Conflict theorists see the economic structure as a central factor in the exploitation of minorities. With labeling theorists, they note the way in which minorities are singled out for differential treatment by law enforcement officers. On the micro level, interactionist researchers stress the manner in which everyday contact between people from different racial and ethnic backgrounds contributes to tolerance or hostility.

Functionalist Perspective

What possible use could racial bigotry have? Functionalist theorists, while agreeing that racial hostility is hardly to be admired, point out that it serves positive functions for those who practice discrimination.

Anthropologist Manning Nash (1962) has identified three functions of racially prejudiced beliefs for the dominant group:

1. Racist views provide a moral justification for maintaining an unequal society that routinely deprives a minority group of its rights and privileges. Southern Whites justified slavery by believing that Africans were physically and spiritually subhuman and devoid of souls.

2. Racist beliefs discourage the subordinate minority from attempting to question its lowly status, which would be to question the very foundations of society.

3. Racial myths suggest that any major societal change (such as an end to discrimination) would only bring greater poverty to the minority and lower the majority's standard of living. As a result, racial prejudice grows when a society's value system (one underlying a colonial empire or slavery, for example) is threatened.

Although racial prejudice and discrimination may serve the powerful, such unequal treatment can also be dysfunctional for a society, and even for the dominant group. Sociologist Arnold Rose (1951) has outlined four dysfunctions that are associated with racism:

1. A society that practices discrimination fails to use the resources of all individuals. Discrimination limits the search for talent and leadership to the dominant group.

2. Discrimination aggravates social problems such as poverty, delinquency, and crime, and places the financial burden of alleviating those problems on the dominant group.

3. Society must invest a good deal of time and money to defend its barriers to the full participation of all members.

4. Racial prejudice and discrimination often undercut goodwill and friendly diplomatic relations between nations.

Conflict Perspective

Conflict theorists would certainly agree with Arnold Rose that racial prejudice and discrimination have many harmful consequences for society. Sociologists such as Oliver Cox (1948), Robert Blauner (1972), and Herbert M. Hunter (2000) have used the **exploitation theory** (or *Marxist class theory*) to explain the basis of racial subordination in the United States. As we saw in Chapter 9, Karl Marx viewed the exploitation of the lower class as a basic part of the capitalist economic system. From a Marxist point of view, racism keeps minorities in low-paying jobs, thereby supplying the capitalist ruling class with a pool of cheap labor. Moreover, by forcing racial minorities to accept low wages, capitalists can restrict the wages of *all* members of the proletariat. Workers from the dominant group who demand higher wages can always be replaced by minorities who have no choice but to accept low-paying jobs.

The conflict view of race relations seems persuasive in a number of instances. Japanese Americans were the object of little prejudice until they began to enter jobs that brought them into competition with Whites. The movement to keep Chinese immigrants out of the United States became most fervent during the latter half of the 19th century, when Chinese and Whites fought over dwindling work opportunities. Both the enslavement of Blacks and the extermination and removal westward of Native Americans were economically motivated.

However, the exploitation theory is too limited to explain prejudice in its many forms. Not all minority groups have been exploited to the same extent. In addition, many groups (such as the Quakers and the Mormons) have been victimized by prejudice for other than economic reasons. Still, as Gordon Allport (1979:210) concludes, the exploitation theory correctly "points a sure finger at one of the factors involved in prejudice, . . . rationalized self-interest of the upper classes."

Labeling Perspective

One practice that fits both the conflict perspective and labeling theory is racial profiling. **Racial profiling** is any arbitrary action initiated by an authority based on race, ethnicity, or national origin rather than on a person's behavior. Generally, racial profiling occurs when law enforcement officers, including customs officials, airport security, and police, assume that people who fit a certain description are likely to be engaged in illegal activities. Beginning in the 1980s with the emergence of the crack cocaine market, skin color became a key characteristic in racial profiling. This practice is often based on very explicit stereotypes. For example, one federal antidrug initiative encouraged officers to look specifically for people with dreadlocks and for Latino men traveling together.

Today, authorities continue to rely on racial profiling, despite overwhelming evidence that it is misleading. A recent study showed that Blacks are still more likely than Whites to be frisked and handled with force when they are stopped. Yet Whites are more likely than Blacks to possess weapons, illegal drugs, or stolen property (Ridgeway 2007; RAND 2008).

Research on the ineffectiveness of racial profiling, coupled with calls by minority communities to end the stigmatization, has led to growing demands to end the practice. But these efforts came to an abrupt halt after the September 11, 2001, terrorist attacks on the United States, when suspicions arose about Muslim and Arab immigrants. Foreign students from Arab countries were summoned for special questioning by authorities. Legal immigrants who were identified as Arab or Muslim were scrutinized for possible illegal activity and prosecuted for violations that authorities routinely ignored among immigrants of other ethnicities and faiths. National surveys have found little change since 2001 in public support for profiling of Arab Americans at airports. In 2006, 53 percent of Americans favored requiring Arabs, including those who are U.S. citizens, to undergo special, more intensive, security checks than other passengers before boarding planes in or to the United States (Saad 2006; Withrow 2006).

Interactionist Perspective

A Hispanic woman is transferred from a job on an assembly line to a similar position working next to a White man. At first, the White man is patronizing, assuming that she must be incompetent. She is cold and resentful; even when she needs assistance, she refuses to admit it. After a week, the growing tension between the two leads to a bitter quarrel. Yet over time, each slowly comes to appreciate the other's strengths and talents. A year after they begin working together, these two workers become respectful friends. This story is an example of what interactionists call the *contact hypothesis* in action.

The **contact hypothesis** states that in cooperative circumstances, interracial contact between people of equal status will cause them to become less prejudiced and to abandon old stereotypes. People begin to see one another as individuals and discard the broad generalizations characteristic of stereotyping. Note the phrases *equal status* and *cooperative circumstances*. In the story just told, if the two workers had been competing for one vacancy as a supervisor, the racial hostility between them might have worsened (Allport 1979; Fine 2008).

As Latinos and other minorities slowly gain access to better-paying and more responsible jobs, the contact hypothesis may take on even greater significance. The trend in our society is toward increasing contact between individuals from dominant and subordinate groups. That may be one way of eliminating—or at least reducing—racial and ethnic stereotyping and prejudice.

TABLE 11-2 SOCIOLOGICAL PERSPECTIVES ON RACE AND ETHNICITY

summing up

Perspective	Emphasis
Functionalist	The dominant majority benefits from the subordination of racial minorities.
Conflict	Vested interests perpetuate racial inequality through economic exploitation.
Labeling	People are profiled and stereotyped based on their racial and ethnic identity.
Interactionist	Cooperative interracial contacts can reduce hostility.

Another may be the establishment of interracial coalitions, an idea suggested by sociologist William Julius Wilson (1999). To work, such coalitions would obviously need to be built on an equal role for all members.

Table 11-2 summarizes the four major sociological perspectives on race. No matter what the explanation for racial and ethnic distinctions—functionalist, conflict, labeling, or interactionist—these socially constructed inequalities can have powerful consequences in the form of prejudice and discrimination. In the next section, we will see how inequality based on the ascribed characteristics of race and ethnicity can poison people's interpersonal relations, depriving whole groups of opportunities others take for granted.

Patterns of Intergroup Relations

Racial and ethnic groups can relate to one another in a wide variety of ways, ranging from friendships and intermarriages to hostility, from behaviors that require mutual approval to behaviors imposed by the dominant group.

One devastating pattern of intergroup relations is **genocide**—the deliberate, systematic killing of an entire people or nation. This term describes the killing of 1 million Armenians by Turkey beginning in 1915. It is most commonly applied to Nazi Germany's extermination of 6 million European Jews, as well as gays, lesbians, and the Romani people ("Gypsies"), during World War II. The term *genocide* is also appropriate in describing the United States' policies toward Native Americans in the 19th century. In 1800, the Native American (or American Indian) population of the United States was about 600,000; by 1850, it had been reduced to 250,000 through warfare with the U.S. cavalry, disease, and forced relocation to inhospitable environments.

The *expulsion* of a people is another extreme means of acting out racial or ethnic prejudice. In 1979, Vietnam expelled nearly 1 million ethnic

In U.S. retail stores, White customers have different experiences than Black customers. They are less likely than Blacks to have their checks or credit cards refused and less likely to be profiled by security personnel.

Chinese, partly as a result of centuries of hostility between Vietnam and neighboring China. In a more recent example of expulsion (which had aspects of genocide), Serbian forces began a program of "ethnic cleansing" in 1991, in the newly independent states of Bosnia and Herzegovina. Throughout the former nation of Yugoslavia, the Serbs drove more than 1 million Croats and Muslims from their homes. More recently, a genocidal war between the Hutu and Tutsi people in Rwanda left 300,000 school-age children orphaned (Chirot and Edwards 2003; Naimark 2004).

Expulsion and genocide are extreme behaviors. More typical intergroup relations follow four identifiable patterns: (1) amalgamation, (2) assimilation, (3) segregation, and (4) pluralism. Each pattern defines the dominant group's actions and the minority group's responses. Intergroup relations are rarely restricted to only one of the four patterns, although invariably one does tend to dominate. Think of these patterns primarily as ideal types.

Amalgamation

Amalgamation happens when a majority group and a minority group combine to form a new group. Through intermarriage over several generations, various groups in society combine to form a new group. This pattern can be expressed as A + B + C → D, where A, B, and C represent different groups in a society, and D signifies the end result, a unique cultural-racial group unlike any of the initial groups (Newman 1973).

The belief in the United States as a "melting pot" became compelling in the first part of the 20th century, particularly since that image suggested that the nation had an almost divine mission to amalgamate various groups into one people. However, in actuality, many residents were not willing to include Native Americans, Jews, African Americans, Asian Americans, and Irish Roman Catholics in the melting pot. Therefore, this pattern does not adequately describe dominant–subordinate relations in the United States.

Assimilation

In India, many Hindus complain about Indian citizens who copy the traditions and customs of the British. In France, people of Arab and African origin, many of them Muslim, complain they are treated as second-class citizens—a charge that provoked riots in 2005. In Australia, Aborigines who have become part of the dominant society refuse to acknowledge their darker-skinned grandparents on the street. And in the United States, some Italian Americans, Polish Americans, Hispanics, and Jews have changed their ethnic-sounding family names to names that are typically found among White Protestant families.

Assimilation is the process through which a person forsakes his or her own cultural tradition to become part of a different culture. Generally, it is practiced by a minority group member who wants to conform to the standards of the dominant group. Assimilation can be described as a pattern in which A + B + C → A. The majority, A, dominates in such a way that members of minorities B and C imitate it and attempt to become indistinguishable from it (Newman 1973).

Assimilation can strike at the very roots of a person's identity. Alphonso D'Abruzzo, for example, changed his name to Alan Alda. The British actress Joyce Frankenberg changed her name to Jane Seymour. Name changes, switches in religious affiliation, and dropping of native languages can obscure one's roots and heritage. However, assimilation does not necessarily bring

An immigrant from the Philippines studies for his citizenship test. For many immigrants, mastering the information that is part of the naturalization process is one step in the larger cultural process of assimilation.

acceptance to minority group individuals. A Chinese American such as Helen Zia (see the chapter-opening excerpt) may speak English fluently, achieve high educational standards, and become a well-respected professional or businessperson and *still* be seen as different. Other Americans may reject her as a business associate, neighbor, or marriage partner.

use your sociological *imagination*

You have immigrated to another country with a very different culture. What steps might you take to assimilate?

www.mhhe.com/schaefer12e

Segregation

Separate schools, separate seating on buses and in restaurants, separate washrooms, even separate drinking fountains—these were all part of the lives of African Americans in the South when segregation ruled early in the 20th century. **Segregation** refers to the physical separation of two groups of people in terms of residence, workplace, and social events. Generally, a dominant group imposes this pattern on a minority group. Segregation is rarely complete, however. Intergroup contact inevitably occurs, even in the most segregated societies.

From 1948 (when it received its independence) to 1990, the Republic of South Africa severely restricted the movement of Blacks and other non-Whites by means of a wide-ranging system of segregation known as **apartheid.** Apartheid even included the creation of separate homelands where Blacks were expected to live. However, decades of local resistance to apartheid, combined with international pressure, led to marked political changes in the 1990s. In 1994, a prominent Black activist, Nelson Mandela, was elected South Africa's president in the first election in which Blacks (the majority of the nation's population) were allowed to vote. Mandela had spent almost 28 years in South African prisons for his anti-apartheid activities. His election was widely viewed as the final blow to South Africa's oppressive policy of segregation.

Long-entrenched social patterns are difficult to change, however. In the United States today, despite federal laws that forbid housing discrimination, residential segregation is still the norm, as a recent analysis of living patterns in metropolitan areas shows. Across the nation, neighborhoods remain divided along both racial and ethnic lines. Although residential segregation has declined very modestly since 1980, racial isolation remains dramatic. The typical White person lives in a neighborhood that is 80 percent White; the typical Black person resides in an area that is 51 percent Black. The corresponding figures for Latinos and Asian Americans are 46 percent and 18 percent, respectively. Even when we take social class into account, these patterns of minority segregation persist (Lewis Mumford Center 2001; Logan et al. 2004; Wilkes and Iceland 2004).

Whatever the country, residential segregation directly limits people's economic opportunity. Sociologists Douglas Massey and Nancy Denton (1993), in a book aptly titled *American Apartheid*, noted that segregation separates poor people of color from job opportunities and isolates them from successful role models. This pattern repeats itself the world over, from South Central Los Angeles to Oldham, England, and Soweto, South Africa.

Pluralism

In a pluralistic society, a subordinate group does not have to forsake its lifestyle and traditions to avoid prejudice or discrimination. **Pluralism** is based on mutual respect for one another's cultures among the various groups in a society. This pattern allows a minority group to express its own culture and still participate without prejudice in the larger society. Earlier, we described amalgamation as A + B + C → D, and assimilation as A + B + C → A. Using this same approach, we can conceive of pluralism as A + B + C → A + B + C. All the groups coexist in the same society (Newman 1973).

In the United States, pluralism is more of an ideal than a reality. There are distinct instances of pluralism—the ethnic neighborhoods in major cities, such as Koreatown, Little Tokyo, Andersonville (Swedish Americans), and Spanish Harlem—yet there are also limits to cultural freedom. To survive, a society must promote a certain consensus among its members regarding basic ideals, values, and beliefs. Thus, if a Romanian immigrant to the United States wants to move up the occupational ladder, he or she cannot avoid learning the English language.

Switzerland exemplifies the modern pluralistic state. There, the absence of both a national language and a dominant religious faith leads to a tolerance for cultural diversity. In addition, various political devices safeguard the interests of ethnic groups in a way that has no parallel in the United States. In contrast, Great Britain has had difficulty achieving cultural pluralism in a multiracial society. East Indians, Pakistanis, and Blacks from the Caribbean and Africa experience prejudice and discrimination within the dominant White society there. Some British advocate cutting off all Asian and Black immigration, and a few even call for expulsion of those non-Whites currently living in Britain.

Race and Ethnicity in the United States

Few societies have a more diverse population than the United States; the nation is truly a multiracial, multiethnic society. Of course, that has not always been the case. The population of what is now the United States has changed dramatically since the arrival of European settlers in the 1600s, as Figure 11-1 (see page 246) shows. Immigration, colonialism, and in the case of Blacks, slavery determined the racial and ethnic makeup of our present-day society.

Today, the largest racial minorities in the United States are African Americans, Native Americans, and Asian Americans. The largest ethnic groups are Latinos, Jews, and the various White ethnic groups. Figure 11-4 shows where the major racial and ethnic minorities are concentrated.

African Americans

"I am an invisible man," wrote Black author Ralph Ellison in his novel *Invisible Man* (1952:3). "I am a man of substance, of flesh and bone, fiber and liquids—and I might even be said to possess a mind. I am invisible, understand, simply because people refuse to see me."

Over five decades later, many African Americans still feel invisible. Despite their large numbers, they have long been treated as second-class citizens. Currently, by the standards of the federal government, more than 1 out of every 4 African Americans —as opposed to 1 out of every 12 White non-Hispanics—is poor (De Navas-Walt et al. 2008:13).

Contemporary institutional discrimination and individual prejudice against African Americans are rooted in the history of slavery in the United States. Many other subordinate groups had little wealth and income, but as sociologist W. E. B. DuBois (1909) and others have noted, enslaved African Americans were in an even more oppressive situation, because by law, they could not own property and could not pass on the benefits of their labor to their children. Today, increasing numbers of African Americans and sympathetic Whites are calling for *slave reparations* to compensate for the injustices of forced servitude. Reparations could include official expressions of apology from governments such as the United States, ambitious programs to improve

MAPPING LIFE NATIONWIDE

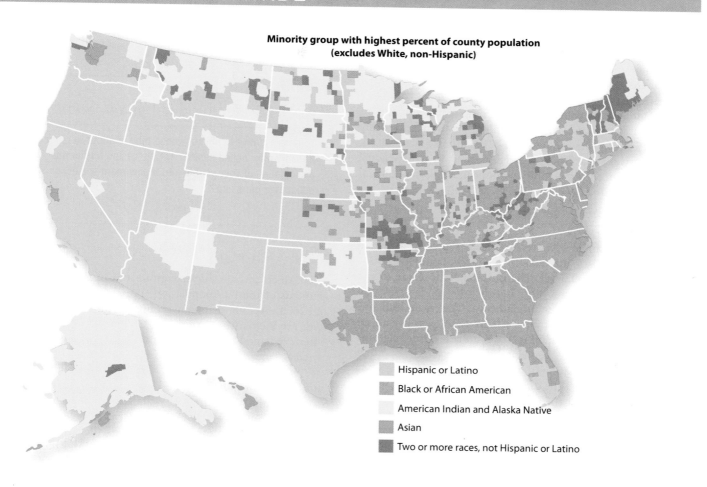

Minority group with highest percent of county population
(excludes White, non-Hispanic)

Hispanic or Latino

Black or African American

American Indian and Alaska Native

Asian

Two or more races, not Hispanic or Latino

Source: C. Brewer and Suchan 2001:20.

Think about It

The United States is a diverse nation. Why, in many parts of the country, can't people see that diversity in their towns?

African Americans' economic status, or even direct payments to descendants of slaves (D. Williams and Collins 2004).

The end of the Civil War did not bring genuine freedom and equality for Blacks. The Southern states passed Jim Crow laws to enforce official segregation, and the Supreme Court upheld them as constitutional in 1896. In addition, Blacks faced the danger of lynching campaigns, often led by the Ku Klux Klan, during the late 1800s and early 1900s. From a conflict perspective, Whites maintained their dominance formally through legalized segregation and informally by means of vigilante terror and violence (Franklin and Moss 2000).

During the 1960s, a vast civil rights movement emerged, with many competing factions and strategies for change. The Southern Christian Leadership Conference (SCLC), founded by Dr. Martin Luther King Jr., used nonviolent civil disobedience to oppose segregation. The National Association for the Advancement of Colored People (NAACP) favored use of the courts to press for equality for African Americans. But many younger

Black leaders, most notably Malcolm X, turned toward an ideology of Black power. Proponents of **Black power** rejected the goal of assimilation into White middle-class society. They defended the beauty and dignity of Black and African cultures and supported the creation of Black-controlled political and economic institutions (Ture and Hamilton 1992).

Despite numerous courageous actions to achieve Black civil rights, Black and White citizens are still separate, still unequal. From birth to death, Blacks suffer in terms of their life chances. Life remains difficult for millions of poor Blacks, who must attempt to survive in ghetto areas shattered by high unemployment and abandoned housing. Today the median household income of Blacks is still 60 percent that of Whites, and the unemployment rate among Blacks is more than twice that of Whites.

Some African Americans—especially middle-class men and women—have made economic gains over the past 50 years. For example, data compiled by the Department of Labor show that the number of African Americans in management increased nationally from 2.4 percent of the total in 1958 to 7.5 percent in 2007. Yet Blacks still represent only 6 percent or less of all physicians, engineers, scientists, lawyers, judges, and marketing managers.

In many respects, the civil rights movement of the 1960s left institutionalized discrimination against African Americans untouched. Consequently, in the 1970s and 1980s, Black leaders worked to mobilize African American political power as a force for social change. Between 1970 and 2007, the number of African American elected officials increased sixfold. Yet today, Blacks remain significantly *underrepresented*, despite the election of President Barack Obama. Their underrepresentation is especially distressing in view of sociologist W. E. B. DuBois's observation over a century ago that Blacks could not expect to achieve equal social and economic opportunity without first gaining political rights (Bureau of the Census 2008a:38, 384–387).

Native Americans

Today, about 2.2 million Native Americans represent a diverse array of cultures distinguishable by language, family organization, religion, and livelihood. The outsiders who came to the United States—European settlers and their descendants—came to know these native peoples' forefathers as "American Indians." By the time the Bureau of Indian Affairs (BIA) was organized as part of the War Department in 1824, Indian–White relations had already included three centuries of hostile actions that had led to the virtual elimination of native peoples (see Figure 11-1, page 245). During the 19th century, many bloody wars wiped out a significant part of the nation's Indian population. By the end of the century, schools for Indians—operated by the BIA or by church missions—prohibited the practice of Native American cultures. Yet at the same time, such schools did little to make the children effective competitors in White society.

Today, life remains difficult for members of the 554 tribal groups in the United States, whether they live in cities or on reservations. For example, one Native American teenager in six has attempted suicide—a rate four times higher than the rate for other teenagers. Traditionally, some Native Americans have chosen to assimilate and abandon all vestiges of their tribal cultures to escape certain forms of prejudice. However, by the 1990s, an increasing number of people in the United States were openly claiming a Native American identity. Since 1960, the federal government's count of Native Americans has tripled. According to the 2000 census, the Native American population increased 26 percent during the 1990s. Demographers believe that more and more Native Americans who previously concealed their identity are no longer pretending to be White (Grieco and Cassidy 2001).

In 2000, on the 175th anniversary of the BIA, director Kevin Guer, a Pawnee, declared that the day was "no occasion for celebration as we express our profound sorrow for what the agency has done in the past." He followed with a formal apology (Stout 2000). The United States is not the only country that has expressed regret over the government's past actions toward indigenous peoples (Box 11-1).

The introduction of gambling on Indian reservations has transformed the lives of some Native Americans. Native Americans got into the gaming industry in 1988, when Congress passed the Indian Gambling Regulatory Act. The law stipulates that states must negotiate agreements with tribes interested in commercial gaming; they cannot prevent tribes from engaging in gambling operations, even if state law prohibits such ventures. The income from these lucrative operations is not evenly distributed, however. About two-thirds of recognized Indian tribes are not involved in gambling ventures. Those tribes that earn substantial revenues from gambling constitute a small fraction of Native Americans (Conner and Taggart 2009).

use your sociological *imagination*

You are a Native American whose tribe is about to open a reservation-based casino. Will the casino further the assimilation of your people into mainstream society or encourage pluralism?

Asian Americans

Asian Americans are a diverse group, one of the fastest-growing segments of the U.S. population (up 69 percent between 1990 and 2000). Among the many groups of Americans of Asian descent are Vietnamese Americans, Chinese Americans, Japanese Americans, and Korean Americans (Figure 11-5).

Asian Americans are also economically diverse. There are rich and poor Japanese Americans, rich and poor Filipino Americans, and so forth. In fact, Southeast Asians living in the United States have the highest rate of welfare dependency of any racial or ethnic group. Though Asian Americans have substantially more schooling than other ethnic groups, their median income is only slightly higher than Whites' income, and their poverty rate is higher. In 2007, for every Asian American family with an annual income of $100,000 or more, there was another earning less than $35,000 a year (DeNavas-Walt et al. 2008:35).

FIGURE **11-5** MAJOR ASIAN AMERICAN GROUPS IN THE UNITED STATES, 2007

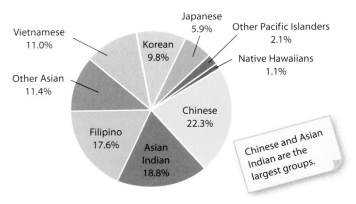

Source: Author's analysis of 2007 data in American Community Survey 2008:Table 50201.

Think about It

Do Asian Americans really have a common identity?

SOCIOLOGY IN THE GLOBAL COMMUNITY

11-1 The Aboriginal People of Australia

The indigenous, or Aboriginal, people of Australia have inhabited their home continent continuously for at least 50,000 years. Today they make up about 2.4 percent of Australia's total population. Although their numbers are small, they are highly visible in Australian society.

The cultural practices of the Aboriginal people are quite diverse, given their many clans, language groups, and communities. Except for occasional connections between kin or trading partners, these groups have little social contact. When Europeans first arrived in Australia, their diversity was even greater: an estimated 600 to 700 different groups of Aboriginals spoke 200 to 250 languages as distinct from each other as French is from German. The existence of many dialects, or variants of languages that were more or less understandable to others, increased the complexity.

Aboriginals' spirituality reflects the diversity not only of their languages and culture, but of the Australian terrain. From the Outback to the tropical rain forests, the Aboriginal peoples see themselves as having arisen from the land itself, and as destined ultimately to return to the land. These beliefs, commonly referred to as Dreaming or Dreamtime, resemble what is known as cosmology or oral folklore in the West.

Like the American Indians, Australia's Aboriginal population declined dramatically following European settlement. New diseases, some of which were not life-threatening to Europeans, had a devastating effect on Aboriginal communities, which lacked immunity to them. Mistreatment under the British colonial regime, dispossession of their land, and the disruption and disintegration of their culture also

overwhelmed the Aboriginal people. Decades of protests and legal efforts regarding their land rights have brought little change.

Historically, the Aboriginal people received little legal recognition from Europeans. Only in 1967 did the government of Australia extend citizenship and voting rights to the Aboriginals, along with access to welfare and unemployment benefits. Yet it would be misleading to view the Aboriginal people as passive victims, either in colonial days or in more recent times. They have worked actively to secure their rights.

As in the United States, Whites' low regard for the Aboriginal people

From 1910 to 1970, thousands of Aboriginal children were forcibly removed from their families so they could be raised by Whites and impressed into the dominant culture.

became the basis for an effort to stamp out their culture. From 1910 to 1970, thousands of Aboriginal children were forcibly removed from their families so they could be raised by Whites and impressed into the dominant culture. Between 10 to 30 percent of all Aboriginal children were affected by this program. Not until 2008 did the Australian government finally apologize to Aboriginals for "the Stolen Generations." The government is now committed to improving

the Aboriginal people's living conditions and their prospects for the future.

LET'S DISCUSS

1. Try to think of a situation in your own culture in which the government might forcibly remove a child from his or her family. Do you know anyone who has had such an experience? If so, what were the repercussions?
2. What kind of reasoning do you think lay behind the Australian government's forced removal of Aboriginal children from their families? In sociological terms, what actually happened?

Sources: W. Anderson 2003; Attwood 2003; Australia 1997, 2008; Schaefer 2008a.

The fact that as a group, Asian Americans work in the same occupations as Whites suggests that they have been successful—and many have. However, there are some differences between the two groups. Asian immigrants, like other minorities and immigrants before them, are found disproportionately in low-paying service occupations. At the same time, better-educated Asian Americans are concentrated near the top in professional and managerial positions, although they rarely reach the pinnacle. Instead, they hit the glass ceiling, or try to "climb a broken ladder," as some put it. In 2002, only 2 percent of the 11,500 people who served on the boards of the nation's 1,000 largest corporations were Asian American (Strauss 2002).

Ironically, Asian Americans are often held up as a **model minority,** or **ideal minority,** supposedly because they have succeeded economically, socially, and educationally despite past prejudice and discrimination, and without resorting to confrontations with Whites. To some Whites, the existence of a model minority seems to reaffirm the notion that anyone can get ahead in the United States through talent and hard work.

The implication is that those minorities that do not succeed are somehow responsible for their failure. Viewed from a conflict perspective, this attitude is yet another instance of *blaming the victims.* Moreover, the stereotype on which it is based is a false one (Bascara 2008; Choi and Lahey 2006).

Vietnamese Americans Each Asian American group has its own history and culture. Vietnamese Americans, for instance, came to the United States primarily during and after the Vietnam War—especially after the U.S. withdrawal from the conflict in 1975. Assisted by local agencies, refugees from the communist government in Vietnam settled throughout the United States, tens of thousands of them in small towns. But over time, Vietnamese Americans have gravitated toward the larger urban areas, establishing Vietnamese restaurants and grocery stores in their ethnic enclaves there.

In 1995, the United States resumed normal diplomatic relations with Vietnam. Gradually, the *Viet Kieu,* or Vietnamese living abroad, began to return to their old country to visit, but usually not to take up permanent residence. Today, more than 30 years after the end of the Vietnam War, sharp differences of opinion remain among Vietnamese Americans, especially the older ones, concerning the war and the present government of Vietnam (Pfeifer 2008).

Chinese Americans Unlike African slaves and Native Americans, the Chinese were initially encouraged to immigrate to the United States. From 1850 to 1880, thousands of Chinese immigrated to this country, lured by job opportunities created by the discovery of gold. However, as employment possibilities decreased and competition for mining jobs grew, the Chinese became the target of a bitter campaign to limit their numbers and restrict their rights. Chinese laborers were exploited, then discarded.

In 1882, Congress enacted the Chinese Exclusion Act, which prevented Chinese immigration and even forbade Chinese in the United States to send for their families. As a result, the Chinese population declined steadily until after World War II. More recently, the descendants of the 19th-century immigrants have been joined by a new influx from Hong Kong and Taiwan. These groups may contrast sharply in their degree of assimilation, desire to live in Chinatowns, and feelings about this country's relations with the People's Republic of China.

Currently, about 3 million Chinese Americans live in the United States. Some Chinese Americans have entered lucrative occupations, yet many immigrants struggle to survive under living and working conditions that belie the model-minority stereotype. New York City's Chinatown district is filled with illegal sweatshops in which recent immigrants—many of them Chinese women—work for minimal wages. Even in legal factories in the garment industry, hours are long and rewards are limited. Half the households in Chinatown earn less than $20,000 per year. Outside of Chinatown, only 23 percent of Asian Americans fall into that low-income category. At the other end of the income distribution, barely 5 percent of Chinatown's residents earn more than $100,000 a year, compared to 25 percent of Asian Americans who live elsewhere in New york City (Logan et al. 2002; Wong 2006).

Japanese Americans Approximately 1.3 million Japanese Americans live in the United States. As a people, they are relatively recent arrivals. In 1880, only 148 Japanese lived in the United States, but by 1920 there were more than 110,000. Japanese immigrants—called the *Issei* (pronounced EE-say), or first generation—were usually males seeking employment opportunities. Many Whites saw them (along with Chinese immigrants) as a "yellow peril" and subjected them to prejudice and discrimination.

In 1941, the attack on Hawai'i's Pearl Harbor by Japan had severe repercussions for Japanese Americans. The federal government decreed that all Japanese Americans on the West Coast must leave their homes and report to "evacuation camps." In effect, Japanese Americans became scapegoats for the anger that other people in the United States felt concerning Japan's role in World War II. By August 1943, in an unprecedented application of guilt by virtue of ancestry, 113,000 Japanese Americans had been forced into hastily built camps. In striking contrast, only a few German Americans and Italian Americans were sent to evacuation camps (Hosokawa 1969).

Despite their tourist appeal, Chinatowns offer their residents limited job opportunities in return for low wages and long hours.

This mass detention was costly for Japanese Americans. The Federal Reserve Board estimates their total income and property losses at nearly half a billion dollars. Moreover, the psychological effect on these citizens—including the humiliation of being labeled "disloyal"—was immeasurable. Eventually, children born in the United States to the *Issei*, called *Nisei* (pronounced NEE-say), were allowed to enlist in the Army and serve in Europe in a segregated combat unit. Others resettled in the East and Midwest to work in factories.

In 1983, a federal commission recommended government payments to all surviving Japanese Americans who had been held in detention camps. The commission reported that the detention was motivated by "race prejudice, war hysteria, and a failure of political leadership." It added that "no documented acts of espionage, sabotage, or fifth-column activity were shown to have been committed" by Japanese Americans. In 1988, President Ronald Reagan signed the Civil Liberties Act, which required the federal government to issue individual apologies for all violations of Japanese Americans' constitutional rights, and established a $1.25 billion trust fund to pay reparations to the approximately 77,500 surviving Japanese Americans who had been interned (Department of Justice 2000).

Korean Americans At nearly 1.3 million, the population of Korean Americans now exceeds that of Japanese Americans. Yet Korean Americans are often overshadowed by other groups from Asia.

Today's Korean American community is the result of three waves of immigration. The initial wave arrived between 1903 and 1910, when Korean laborers migrated to Hawai'i. The second wave followed the end of the Korean War in 1953; most of those immigrants were wives of U.S. servicemen and war orphans. The third wave, continuing to the present, has reflected the admissions priorities set up in the 1965 Immigration Act. These well-educated immigrants arrive in the United States with professional skills. Yet because of language difficulties and discrimination, many must settle at least initially for positions of lower responsibility than those they held in Korea and must suffer through a period of disenchantment. Stress, loneliness, and family strife may accompany the pain of adjustment.

In the early 1990s, the apparent friction between Korean Americans and another subordinate racial group, African Americans, attracted nationwide attention. In New York City, Los Angeles, and Chicago, Korean American merchants confronted Blacks who were allegedly threatening them or robbing their stores. Black neighborhoods responded with hostility to what they perceived as the disrespect and arrogance of Korean American entrepreneurs. In South Central Los Angeles, the only shops in which to buy groceries, liquor, or gasoline were owned by Korean immigrants, who had largely replaced White businesspeople. African Americans were well aware of the dominant role that Korean Americans played in their local retail markets. During the 1992 riots in South Central Los Angeles, small businesses owned by Koreans were a particular target. More than 1,800 Korean businesses were looted or burned during the riots (Kim 1999).

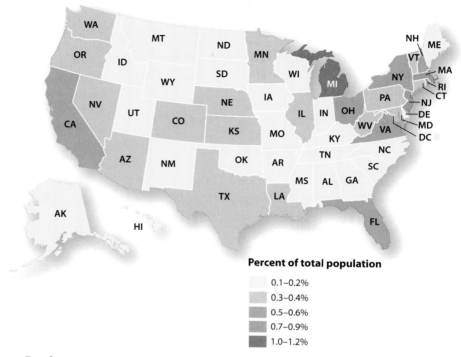

MAPPING LIFE NATIONWIDE

Percent of total population

- 0.1–0.2%
- 0.3–0.4%
- 0.5–0.6%
- 0.7–0.9%
- 1.0–1.2%

Source: Data for 2000 reported in Bureau of the Census 2003b.

Conflict between the two groups was dramatized in Spike Lee's 1989 movie *Do the Right Thing*. The situation stems from Korean Americans' position as the latest immigrant group to cater to the needs of inner-city populations abandoned by those who have moved up the economic ladder. This type of friction is not new; generations of Jewish, Italian, and Arab merchants have encountered similar hostility from what to outsiders seems an unlikely source—another oppressed minority.

Arab Americans

Arab Americans are immigrants and their descendants who hail from the 22 nations of the Arab world. As defined by the League of Arab States, these are the nations of North Africa and what is popularly known as the Middle East, including Lebanon, Syria, Palestine, Morocco, Iraq, Saudi Arabia, and Somalia. Not all residents of those countries are Arab; for example, the Kurds, who live in northern Iraq, are not Arab. And some Arab Americans may have immigrated to the United States from non-Arab countries such as Great Britain or France, where their families have lived for generations.

The Arabic language is the single most unifying force among Arabs, although not all Arabs, and certainly not all Arab Americans, can read and speak Arabic. Moreover, the language has evolved over the centuries so that people in different parts of the Arab world speak different dialects. Still, the fact that the Koran (or Qur'an) was originally written in Arabic gives the language special importance to Muslims, just as the Torah's

composition in Hebrew gives that language special significance to Jews.

Estimates of the size of the Arab American community differ widely. By some estimates, up to 3 million people of Arab ancestry reside in the United States. Among those who identify themselves as Arab Americans, the most common country of origin is Lebanon, followed by Syria, Egypt, and Palestine. In 2000, these four countries of origin accounted for two-thirds of all Arab Americans. As with other racial and ethnic groups, the Arab American population is concentrated in certain areas of the United States (Figure 11-6). Their rising numbers have led to the development of Arab retail centers in several cities, including Dearborn and Detroit, Michigan; Los Angeles; Chicago; New York City; and Washington, D.C. (David 2008).

As a group, Arab Americans are extremely diverse. Many families have lived in the United States for several generations; others are foreign born. Their points of origin range from the metropolis of Cairo, Egypt, to the rural villages of Morocco. Despite the stereotype, most Arab Americans are *not* Muslim, and not all practice religion. Some Arab Americans are Christian. Nor can Arab Americans be characterized as having a specific family type, gender role, or occupational pattern (David 2004).

Despite this great diversity, profiling of potential terrorists at airports has put Arab and Muslim Americans under special surveillance. For years, a number of airlines and law enforcement authorities have used appearance and ethnic-sounding names to identify and take aside Arab Americans and search their belongings. After the terrorist attacks of September 2001, criticism of this practice declined as concern for the public's safety mounted.

Latinos

Together, the various groups included under the general category *Latinos* represent the largest minority in the United States. There are more than 40 million Hispanics in this country, including 26 million Mexican Americans, more than 3 million Puerto Ricans, and smaller numbers of Cuban Americans and people of Central and South American origin (Figure 11-7). The latter group represents the fastest-growing and most diverse segment of the Hispanic community.

According to Census Bureau data, the Latino population now outnumbers the African American population in 6 of the 10 largest cities of the United States: Los Angeles, Houston, Phoenix, San Diego, Dallas, and San Antonio. Hispanics are now the majority of residents in cities such as Miami, Florida; El Paso, Texas; and Santa Ana, California. The rise in the Hispanic population of the United States—fueled by comparatively high birthrates and levels of immigration—has intensified debates over public policy issues such as bilingualism and immigration.

The various Latino groups share a heritage of Spanish language and culture, which can cause serious problems in their assimilation. An intelligent student whose first language is Spanish may be presumed slow or even unruly by English-speaking schoolchildren, and frequently by English-speaking teachers as well. The labeling of Latino children as underachievers, as learning disabled, or as emotionally disturbed can act as a self-fulfilling prophecy for some children. Bilingual education aims at easing the educational difficulties experienced by Hispanic children and others whose first language is not English.

The educational difficulties of Latino students certainly contribute to Hispanics' generally low economic status. In 2007, about 16 percent of all Hispanic households earned less than $15,000, compared to 11 percent of White non-Hispanic households. As of 2007, only 13 percent of Hispanic adults had completed college, compared to 29 percent of White non-Hispanics. In 2007, the poverty rate was 21.5 percent for Hispanics, compared to 8.2 percent for White non-Hispanics. Overall, Latinos are not as affluent as White non-Hispanics, but a middle class is beginning to emerge. Box 11-2 considers Latinos' prospects for social mobility (Bureau of the Census 2008a:145; DeNavas-Walt et al. 2008:13, 33, 36.)

Mexican Americans The largest Latino population is Mexican Americans, who can be further subdivided into those descended from residents of the territories annexed after the Mexican American War of 1848 and those who have immigrated from Mexico to the United States. The opportunity for a Mexican to earn in one hour what it would take an entire day to earn in Mexico has pushed millions of legal and illegal immigrants north.

Aside from the family, the most important social organization in the Mexican American (or Chicano) community is the church, specifically the Roman Catholic church. This strong identification with the Catholic faith has reinforced the already formidable barriers between Mexican Americans and their predominantly White and Protestant neighbors in the Southwest. At the same time, the Catholic Church helps many immigrants to develop a sense of identity and assists their assimilation into the norms and values of the dominant culture of the United States. The complexity of the Mexican American community is underscored by the fact that Protestant churches—especially those that endorse expressive, open worship—have attracted increasing numbers of Mexican Americans.

Puerto Ricans The second-largest segment of Latinos in the United States is Puerto Ricans. Since 1917, residents of Puerto Rico have held the status of American citizens; many have migrated to New York and other eastern cities. Unfortunately, Puerto Ricans have experienced serious poverty both in the United States and on the island. Those who live in the continental United States earn barely half the family income of Whites. As a result, a reverse migration began in the 1970s, when more Puerto Ricans were leaving for the island than were coming to the mainland (Torres 2008).

Politically, Puerto Ricans in the United States have not been as successful as Mexican Americans in organizing for their rights. For many mainland Puerto Ricans—as for many residents of the island—the paramount political issue is the destiny of Puerto Rico itself: Should it continue in its present commonwealth status, petition for admission to the United States as the 51st state, or attempt to become an independent nation? This question has divided Puerto Rico for decades and remains a central issue in Puerto Rican elections. In a 1998 referendum, voters supported a "none of the above" option, effectively favoring continuation of the commonwealth status over statehood or independence.

Cuban Americans Cuban immigration to the United States dates back as far as 1831, but it began in earnest following Fidel Castro's assumption of power in the Cuban revolution (1959). The first wave of 200,000 Cubans included many professionals with relatively high levels of schooling; these men and women were largely welcomed as refugees from communist tyranny. However, more recent waves of immigrants have aroused growing concern, partly because they were less likely to be skilled professionals. Throughout these waves of immigration, Cuban Americans have been encouraged to locate around the United States. Nevertheless, many continue to settle in (or return to) metropolitan Miami, Florida, with its warm climate and proximity to Cuba.

FIGURE **11-7** MAJOR HISPANIC GROUPS IN THE UNITED STATES, 2007

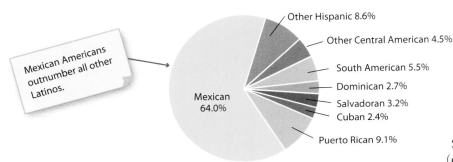

Mexican Americans outnumber all other Latinos.

Other Hispanic 8.6%
Other Central American 4.5%
South American 5.5%
Dominican 2.7%
Salvadoran 3.2%
Cuban 2.4%
Puerto Rican 9.1%
Mexican 64.0%

Source: Author's analysis of 2007 data in American Community Survey 2008:Table 50201.

RESEARCH TODAY

11-2　Social Mobility among Latino Immigrants

The ideal of immigrants coming to the United States to improve their lives and those of their children is well rooted in U.S. culture. Yet the hardships immigrants have experienced are often minimized or overlooked entirely. What is the experience of today's immigrants, most of whom are Latino? Are they getting ahead, and are their children better off as a result?

At best, today's immigrants appear to be achieving a more modest level of upward mobility than past generations. As recently as 1970, the wages of second-generation immigrants exceeded those of nonimmigrants by 9 percent. By 2000, the wage differential had dropped to 5 percent, though the second generation was still earning *more* than comparable nonimmigrants.

This gradual decline in prosperity for immigrants appears to be extending into the 21st century. Today, first-generation immigrants earn 20 percent less income than nonimmigrants, but their children are not likely to make up the difference, much less to surpass the children of native-born parents. Ironically, second-generation Latinos, whose parents typically come from developing nations, fare better compared to their parents than the children of immigrants from industrial nations do. The reason seems to be that the latter group competes with better-skilled, better-educated workers. Some observers have suggested that today's Latino immigrants may follow the pattern of last century's Italian and Polish immigrants, whose relatively limited skills placed them at first in the working class rather than the middle class.

Two of the obstacles to upward mobility among Latinos are a restrictive immigration policy and tightened economic assistance to the poor. Because of heightened border security, today's immigrants are discouraged from traveling back and forth to their home countries, even when job opportunities disappear. Furthermore, under the welfare reform act passed in 1996, even legal immigrants cannot receive food stamps and Supplementary Security Income. Though these policies do not apply to all Latinos, the hardship they cause tends to reinforce negative stereotypes of this ethnic group.

Ironically, second-generation Latinos, whose parents typically come from developing nations, fare better compared to their parents than the children of immigrants from industrial nations do.

Despite this seemingly bleak picture, the first and succeeding generations of Latinos have experienced significant upward mobility, considering their incomes before they entered the country. As time passes, their reference group will shift from those in the home country to their neighbors in the United States, and they may become less satisfied. For now, though, Latinos are optimistic about their quality of life. A 2007 national survey found that about 7 in 10 Hispanics would describe their quality of life as excellent (26 percent) or good (45 percent). A significant 78 percent of respondents say they are very confident or somewhat confident that their children will have better jobs and make more money than they do.

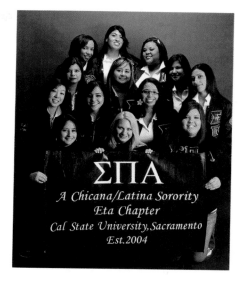

Education is one key to prosperity for the next generation of Latinos. These members of the Latina sorority Sigma Pi Alpha should enjoy significant upward mobility.

LET'S DISCUSS

1. How would you describe your own quality of life? Are you confident that your children will have better jobs and make more money than you?
2. Does the finding that in the past, second-generation immigrants earned more than nonimmigrants surprise you? What might explain their higher incomes?

Sources: Borjas 2006; Economic Mobility Project 2007; Kochhar 2007; Massey 2008; Pew Hispanic Center 2007; Vigdor 2008; Waldinger and Reichl 2006; Waldinger et al. 2007; S. Zimmerman 2008b.

The Cuban experience in the United States has been mixed. Some detractors worry about the vehement anticommunism of Cuban Americans and the apparent growth of an organized crime syndicate that engages in the drug trade and ganglike violence. Recently, Cuban Americans in Miami have expressed concern over what they view as the indifference of the city's Roman Catholic hierarchy. Like other Hispanics, Cuban Americans are underrepresented in leadership positions within the church. Finally—despite many individual success stories—as a group, Cuban Americans in Miami remain behind Anglos (Whites) in income, rate of employment, and proportion of professionals (Masud-Piloto 2008).

Jewish Americans

Jews constitute almost 3 percent of the population of the United States. They play a prominent role in the worldwide Jewish community, because the United States has the world's largest concentration of Jews. Like the Japanese, many Jewish immigrants came to this country and became white-collar professionals in spite of prejudice and discrimination.

Anti-Semitism—that is, anti-Jewish prejudice—has often been vicious in the United States, although rarely so widespread and never so formalized as in Europe. In many cases, Jews have been used as scapegoats for other people's failures. Not surprisingly, Jews have not achieved equality in the United States. Despite high levels of education and professional training, they are still conspicuously absent from the top management of large corporations (except for the few firms founded by Jews). Nonetheless, a national survey in 2009 showed that one out of four people in the United States blame "the Jews" for the financial crisis. In addition, private social clubs and fraternal groups frequently continue to limit membership to Gentiles (non-Jews), a practice upheld by the Supreme Court in the 1964 case *Bell v. Maryland* (Malhotra and Margolit 2009).

The Anti-Defamation League (ADL) of B'nai B'rith funds an annual tally of reported anti-Semitic incidents. Although the number has fluctuated, the 1994 tabulation reached the highest level in the 19 years the ADL has been recording them. In 2007 the total reported incidents of harassment, threats, vandalism, and assaults came to 1,337. Some incidents were inspired and carried out by neo-Nazi skinheads—groups of young people who champion racist and anti-Semitic ideologies. Such threatening behavior only intensifies the fears of many Jewish Americans, who remember the Holocaust—the extermination of 6 million Jews by the Nazi Third Reich during World War II (Anti-Defamation League 2008).

As is true for other minorities discussed in this chapter, Jewish Americans face the choice of maintaining ties to their long religious and cultural heritage or becoming as indistinguishable as possible from Gentiles. Many Jews have tended to assimilate, as is evident from the rise in marriages between Jews and Christians. In marriages that occurred in the 1970s, more than 70 percent of Jews married Jews or people who converted to Judaism. In marriages since 1996, that proportion has dropped to 53 percent. This trend means that today, American Jews are just as likely to marry a Gentile as a Jew. For many, religion is a nonissue—neither parent practices religious rituals. Two-thirds of the children of these Jewish–Gentile marriages are not raised as Jews. Finally, in 2005, two-thirds of Jews felt that the biggest threat to Jewish life was anti-Semitism; only one-third named intermarriage as the major threat (American Jewish Committee 2005; Sanua 2007).

White Ethnics

A significant segment of the population of the United States is made up of White ethnics whose ancestors arrived from Europe within the past century. The nation's White ethnic population includes about 51 million people who claim at least partial German ancestry, 36 million Irish Americans, 18 million Italian Americans, and 9 million Polish Americans, as well as

White Americans often express their ethnicity with special celebrations, such as this Greek Independence Day parade in New York City.

immigrants from other European nations. Some of these people continue to live in close-knit ethnic neighborhoods, while others have largely assimilated and left the "old ways" behind.

Many White ethnics today identify only sporadically with their heritage. **Symbolic ethnicity** refers to an emphasis on concerns such as ethnic food or political issues rather than on deeper ties to one's ethnic heritage. It is reflected in the occasional family trip to an ethnic bakery, the celebration of a ceremonial event such as St. Joseph's Day among Italian Americans, or concern about the future of Northern Ireland among Irish Americans. Except in cases in which new immigration reinforces old traditions, symbolic ethnicity tends to decline with each passing generation (Alba 1990; Winter 2008).

White ethnics and racial minorities have often been antagonistic to one another because of economic competition—an interpretation that agrees with the conflict approach to sociology. As Blacks, Latinos, and Native Americans emerge from the lower class, they must compete with working-class Whites for jobs, housing, and educational opportunities. In times of high unemployment or inflation, any such competition can easily generate intense intergroup conflict.

In many respects, the plight of White ethnics raises the same basic issues as that of other subordinate people in the United States. How ethnic can people be—how much can they deviate from an essentially White, Anglo-Saxon, Protestant norm—before society punishes them for their willingness to be different? Our society does seem to reward people for assimilating, yet as we have seen, assimilation is no easy process. In the years to come, more and more people will face the challenge of fitting in, not only in the United States but around the world, as the flow of immigrants from one country to another continues to increase. In the Social Policy section that follows, we focus on global immigration and its implications for the future.

For practicing Jews, the Hebrew language is an important part of religious instruction. This teacher is showing flashcards of Hebrew alphabetic characters to deaf students.

social**policy** and Racial and Ethnic Inequality

Global Immigration

The Issue

Worldwide, immigration is at an all-time high. Each year, about 191 million people move from one country to another—that is roughly the equivalent of the total populations of Russia and Italy. A million of these immigrants enter the United States legally, to join the 12 percent of the U.S. population who are foreign born.

Globally, these mass migrations have had a tremendous social impact. The constantly increasing numbers of immigrants and the pressure they put on job opportunities and welfare capabilities in the countries they enter raise troubling questions for many of the world's economic powers. Who should be allowed in? At what point should immigration be curtailed (United Nations 2009)?

The Setting

The migration of people is not uniform across time or space. At certain times, war or famine may precipitate large movements of people, either temporarily or permanently. Temporary dislocations occur when people wait until it is safe to return to their home areas. However, more and more migrants who cannot make an adequate living in their home nations are making permanent moves to developed nations. The major migration streams flow into North America, the oil-rich areas of the Middle East, and the industrial economies of western Europe and Asia. Currently, seven of the world's wealthiest nations (including Germany, France, the United Kingdom, and the United States) shelter about one-third of the world's migrant population, but less than one-fifth of the world's total population. As long as disparities in job opportunities exist among countries, there is little reason to expect this international trend to reverse.

One consequence of global immigration is the emergence of **transnationals**—immigrants who sustain multiple social relationships that link their societies of origin with the society of settlement. The Industrial tycoons of the early 20th century, whose power outmatched that of many nation-states, were among the world's first transnationals. But today millions of people, many of very modest means, move back and forth between countries much as commuters do between city and suburbs. More and more of these people have dual citizenship. Rather than being shaped by allegiance to one country, their identity is rooted in their struggle to survive—and in some instances prosper—by transcending international borders (Croucher 2004; Sassen 2005). We will take a closer look at these citizens of the world in the Social Policy section of Chapter 22.

Countries that have long been a destination for immigrants, such as the United States, usually have policies to determine who has preference to enter. Often, clear racial and ethnic biases are built into these policies. In the 1920s, U.S. policy gave preference to people from western Europe, while making it difficult for residents of southern and eastern Europe, Asia, and Africa to enter the country. During the late 1930s and early 1940s, the federal government refused to lift or loosen restrictive immigration quotas in order to allow Jewish refugees to escape the terror of the Nazi regime. In line with this policy, the SS *St. Louis,* with more than 900 Jewish refugees on board, was denied permission to land in the United States in 1939. The ship was forced to sail back to Europe, where it is estimated that at least a few hundred of its passengers later died at the hands of the Nazis (Morse 1967; G. Thomas and Witts 1974).

Since the 1960s, U.S. policy has encouraged the immigration of relatives of U.S. residents as well as of people who have desirable skills. This change has significantly altered the pattern of sending nations. Previously, Europeans dominated, but for the past 40 years, immigrants have come primarily from Latin America and Asia. Thus, an ever-growing proportion of the United States will be Asian or Hispanic (Figure 11-8 on page 266). To a large degree, fear and resentment of growing racial and ethnic diversity is a key factor in opposition to immigration. In many nations, people are concerned that the new arrivals do not reflect their own cultural and racial heritage.

Sociological Insights

Research suggests that immigrants adapt well to life in the United States, becoming an asset to the nation's economy. In some areas, heavy immigration may drain a local community's resources, but in other areas it revitalizes the local economy. Contrary to the notion that Latinos resist learning English, a national survey in 2007 showed that 77 percent of Hispanics believe immigrants should be required to learn English as a condition for remaining in the country (J. Carroll 2007).

Despite people's fears, immigration performs many valuable functions. For the receiving society, it alleviates labor shortages, as it does in health care and technology in the United States. For the sending nation, migration can relieve an economy unable to support large numbers of people. Often overlooked is the large amount of money, called *remittances,* that immigrants send *back* to their home nations. Worldwide, immigrants send more than $300 billion a year back home to their relatives—an amount that surpasses all other forms of foreign aid (International Fund for Agricultural Development 2007).

Immigration can be dysfunctional as well. Although studies generally show that it has a positive impact on the receiving nation's economy, areas that accept high concentrations of immigrants may find it difficult to meet short-term social service needs. And when migrants with skills or educational potential leave developing countries, their departure can be dysfunctional for those nations. No amount of payments sent back home can make up for the loss of valuable human resources from poor nations (Borjas et al. 2006; Kochhar 2006; Sum et al. 2006).

Conflict theorists note how much of the debate over immigration is phrased in economic terms. But the debate intensifies when the arrivals are of a different racial and ethnic background from the host population. For example, Europeans often refer to "foreigners," but the term does not necessarily mean one of foreign birth. In Germany, "foreigners" refers to people of non-German ancestry, even if they were *born* in Germany; it does not refer to people of German ancestry born in another country, who may choose to return to their "mother country." Fear and dislike of "new" ethnic groups divides countries throughout the world.

265

FIGURE 11-8 LEGAL MIGRATION TO THE UNITED STATES, 1820–2010

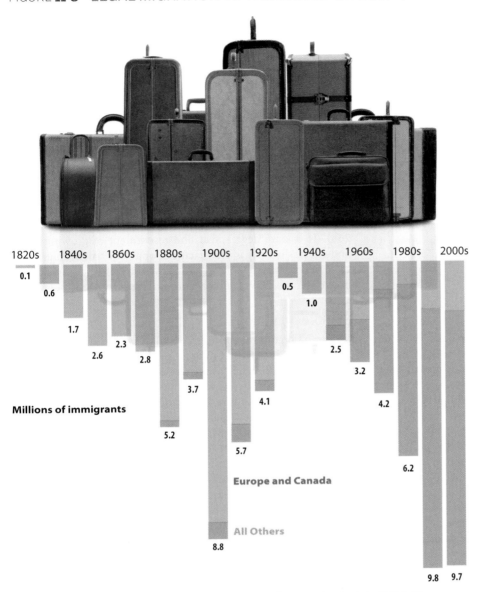

Millions of immigrants

| 1820s | 1840s | 1860s | 1880s | 1900s | 1920s | 1940s | 1960s | 1980s | 2000s |

0.1
0.6
1.7
2.6
2.3
2.8
3.7
5.2
5.7
8.8
4.1
0.5
1.0
2.5
3.2
4.2
6.2
9.8
9.7

Europe and Canada

All Others

Sources: Author's estimates for the period 2000–2010; Office of Immigration Statistics 2008:8–11.

The long border with Mexico provides ample opportunity for illegal immigration into the United States. Throughout the 1980s, the public perception that the United States had lost control of its borders grew. Feeling pressure for immigration control, Congress ended a decade of debate by approving the Immigration Reform and Control Act of 1986. The act marked a historic change in the nation's immigration policy. For the first time, the hiring of illegal aliens was outlawed, and employers caught violating the law became subject to fines and even prison sentences. Just as significant a change was the extension of amnesty and legal status to many illegal immigrants already living in the United States. More than 20 years later, however, the act appears to have had mixed results. Substantial numbers of illegal immigrants continue to enter the country each year, with an estimated 11 million present now at any given time—a marked increase since 2000 (Hoefer et al. 2006).

Recently, immigrants have staged massive marches to pressure Congress to speed the naturalization process and develop ways for illegal immigrants to gain legal residency. Counterdemonstrations by those who are opposed to illegal immigration have called for more resources with which to detect and deport illegal immigrants and to strengthen the U.S.–Mexican border. Despite this widespread public dissatisfaction with the nation's immigration policy, little progress has been made. Congress has had difficulty reaching a bipartisan compromise that pleases both sides—both supporters of strict social control and those who would allow illegal immigrants to remain in the country legally, under some circumstances.

The entire world feels the overwhelming impact of globalization on immigration patterns. The European Union agreement of 1997 gave the governing commission authority to propose a Europe-wide policy on immigration. An EU policy that allows residents of one EU country to live and work in another EU country is expected to complicate efforts by sending nations, such as Turkey, to become members of the EU. Immigrants from Turkey's predominantly Muslim population are not welcome in many EU countries (Denny 2004).

In the wake of the attacks of September 11, 2001, on the World Trade Center and the Pentagon, immigration procedures were complicated by the need to detect potential terrorists. Illegal immigrants especially, but even legal immigrants, have felt increased scrutiny by government officials around the world. For would-be immigrants to many nations, the wait to receive the right to enter a country—even to join relatives—has increased

The feminist perspective pays special attention to the role that women play in global immigration. Immigrant women face all the challenges that immigrant men do, plus some additional ones. Typically, they bear the responsibility for obtaining services for their families, particularly their children. Because the men are likely to be consumed with work, the women are left to navigate through the bureaucratic tangle of schools, city services, and medical facilities, as well as the unfamiliar stores and markets they must visit to feed their families. Women who need special medical services or are victims of domestic violence are often reluctant to seek outside help. Yet they are more likely than the men to serve as the liaison between their households and community and religious associations. Also, because many new immigrants view the United States as a dangerous place to raise a family, women must be especially watchful over their children's lives (Hondagneu-Sotelo 2003).

U.S. employers' demand for low-paid labor fuels illegal immigration.

The intense debate over immigration reflects deep value conflicts in the cultures of many nations. One strand of our culture, for example, has traditionally emphasized egalitarian principles and a desire to help people in time of need. At the same time, hostility to potential immigrants and refugees—whether the Chinese in the 1880s, European Jews in the 1930s and 1940s, or Mexicans, Haitians, and Arabs today—reflects not only racial, ethnic, and religious prejudice, but a desire to maintain the dominant culture of the in-group by keeping out those viewed as outsiders.

Let's Discuss

1. Did you or your parents or grandparents immigrate to the United States from another nation? If so, when and where did your family come from, and why?

2. On balance, do the functions of immigration to the United States outweigh the dysfunctions?

3. Do you live, work, or study with recent immigrants to the United States? If so, are they well accepted in your community, or do they face prejudice and discrimination?

substantially, as immigration officials scrutinize more closely what were once routine applications.

getting**involved**

To get involved in the debate over global immigration, visit this book's Online Learning Center, which offers links to relevant Web sites.

www.mhhe.com/schaefer12e

MASTERING THIS CHAPTER

Summary

The social dimensions of race and ethnicity are important factors in shaping people's lives, both in the United States and in other countries. In this chapter, we examine the meaning of race and ethnicity and study the major **racial** and **ethnic groups** of the United States.

1. A **racial group** is set apart from others by physical differences; an **ethnic group** is set apart primarily by national origin or cultural patterns.

2. When sociologists define a **minority group,** they are concerned primarily with the economic and political power, or powerlessness, of the group.

3. The meaning people attach to the physical differences between races gives social significance to race, producing **stereotypes.**

4. **Prejudice** often but not always leads to **discrimination.** Sometimes, through **color-blind racism,** prejudiced people try to use the principle of racial neutrality to defend a racially unequal status quo.

5. **Institutional discrimination** results from the normal operations of a society.

6. Functionalists point out that discrimination is both functional and dysfunctional for a society. Conflict theorists explain racial subordination through **exploitation theory.** Interactionists pose the **contact hypothesis** as a means of reducing prejudice and discrimination.

7. **Racial profiling** is any arbitrary action initiated by an authority based on race, ethnicity, or national origin rather than on a person's behavior. Based on false stereotypes of certain racial and ethnic groups, the practice is not an effective way to fight crime.

8. Four patterns describe typical intergroup relations in North America and elsewhere: **amalgamation, assimilation, segregation,** and **pluralism.** Pluralism remains more of an ideal than a reality.

9. Contemporary prejudice and discrimination against African Americans are rooted in the history of slavery in the United States.

10. Asian Americans are commonly viewed as a **model** or **ideal minority,** a false stereotype that is not necessarily beneficial to members of that group.

11. The various groups included under the general term *Latinos* represent the largest ethnic minority in the United States.

12. Worldwide, immigration is at an all-time high, fueling controversy not only in the United States but in the European Union. A new kind of immigrant, the **transnational,** moves back and forth across international borders in search of a better job or an education.

Critical Thinking Questions

1. Why is institutional discrimination even more powerful than individual discrimination? How would functionalists, conflict theorists, and interactionists study institutional discrimination?

2. How is color-blind racism expressed in everyday conversation? In news coverage?

3. Examine the relations between dominant and subordinate racial and ethnic groups in your hometown or your college. Can the community in which you grew up or the college you attend be viewed as a genuine example of pluralism?

Key Terms

Affirmative action Positive efforts to recruit minority group members or women for jobs, promotions, and educational opportunities. (page 252)

Amalgamation The process through which a majority group and a minority group combine to form a new group. (255)

Anti-Semitism Anti-Jewish prejudice. (263)

Apartheid A former policy of the South African government, designed to maintain the separation of Blacks and other non-Whites from the dominant Whites. (256)

Assimilation The process through which a person forsakes his or her own cultural tradition to become part of a different culture. (255)

Black power A political philosophy, promoted by many younger Blacks in the 1960s, that supported the creation of Black-controlled political and economic institutions. (257)

Color-blind racism The use of the principle of race neutrality to defend a racially unequal status quo. (249)

Contact hypothesis An interactionist perspective which states that in cooperative circumstances, interracial contact between people of equal status will reduce prejudice. (254)

Discrimination The denial of opportunities and equal rights to individuals and groups because of prejudice or other arbitrary reasons. (249)

Ethnic group A group that is set apart from others primarily because of its national origin or distinctive cultural patterns. (245)

Ethnocentrism The tendency to assume that one's own culture and way of life represent the norm or are superior to all others. (248)

Exploitation theory A Marxist theory that views racial subordination in the United States as a manifestation of the class system inherent in capitalism. (253)

Genocide The deliberate, systematic killing of an entire people or nation. (254)

Glass ceiling An invisible barrier that blocks the promotion of a qualified individual in a work environment because of the individual's gender, race, or ethnicity. (250)

Hate crime A criminal offense committed because of the offender's bias against a race, religion, ethnic group, national origin, or sexual orientation. (248)

Institutional discrimination The denial of opportunities and equal rights to individuals and groups that results from the normal operations of a society. (252)

Minority group A subordinate group whose members have significantly less control or power over their own lives than the members of a dominant or majority group have over theirs. (245)

Model, or ideal, minority A subordinate group whose members supposedly have succeeded economically, socially, and educationally despite past prejudice and discrimination, and without resorting to confrontations with Whites. (259)

Pluralism Mutual respect for one another's cultures among the various groups in a society, which allows minorities to express their own cultures without experiencing prejudice. (256)

Prejudice A negative attitude toward an entire category of people, often an ethnic or racial minority. (248)

Racial formation A sociohistorical process in which racial categories are created, inhibited, transformed, and destroyed. (246)

Racial group A group that is set apart from others because of physical differences that have taken on social significance. (245)

Racial profiling Any arbitrary action initiated by an authority based on race, ethnicity, or national origin rather than on a person's behavior. (253)

Racism The belief that one race is supreme and all others are innately inferior. (248)

Segregation The physical separation of two groups of people in terms of residence, workplace, and social events; often imposed on a minority group by a dominant group. (255)

Stereotype An unreliable generalization about all members of a group that does not recognize individual differences within the group. (247)

Symbolic ethnicity An ethnic identity that emphasizes concerns such as ethnic food or political issues rather than deeper ties to one's ethnic heritage. (264)

Transnational An immigrant who sustains multiple social relationships that link his or her society of origin with the society of settlement. (265)

White privilege Rights or immunities granted to people as a particular benefit or favor simply because they are White. (250)

Self-Quiz

Read each question carefully and then select the best answer.

1. Sociologists have identified five basic properties of a minority group. Which of the following is *not* one of those properties?
   a. unequal treatment
   b. physical traits
   c. ascribed status
   d. cultural bias

2. The largest racial minority group in the United States is
   a. Asian Americans.
   b. African Americans.
   c. Native Americans.
   d. Jewish Americans.

3. Racism is a form of which of the following?
   a. ethnocentrism
   b. discrimination
   c. prejudice
   d. both b and c

4. Suppose that a White employer refuses to hire a Vietnamese American and hires an inferior White applicant. This decision is an act of
   a. prejudice.
   b. ethnocentrism.
   c. discrimination.
   d. stigmatization.

5. Suppose that a workplace requires that only English be spoken, even when it is not a business necessity to restrict the use of other languages. This requirement would be an example of
   a. prejudice.
   b. scapegoating.
   c. a self-fulfilling prophecy.
   d. institutional discrimination.

6. Working together as computer programmers for an electronics firm, a Hispanic woman and a Jewish man overcome their initial prejudices and come to appreciate each other's strengths and talents. This scenario is an example of
   a. the contact hypothesis.
   b. a self-fulfilling prophecy.
   c. amalgamation.
   d. reverse discrimination.

7. Intermarriage over several generations, resulting in various groups combining to form a new group, would be an example of
   a. amalgamation.
   b. assimilation.
   c. segregation.
   d. pluralism.

8. Alphonso D'Abruzzo changed his name to Alan Alda. His action is an example of
   a. amalgamation.
   b. assimilation.

c. segregation.

d. pluralism.

9. In which of the following racial or ethnic groups has one teenager in every six attempted suicide?

   a. African Americans

   b. Asian Americans

   c. Native Americans

   d. Latinos

10. Advocates of *Marxist class theory* argue that the basis for racial subordination in the United States lies within the capitalist economic system. Another representation of this point of view is reflected in which of the following theories?

   a. exploitation

   b. functionalist

   c. interactionist

   d. contact

11. Sociologists consider race and ethnicity to be _____ statuses, since people are born into racial and ethnic groups.

12. The one-drop rule was a vivid example of the social _____ of race—the process by which people come to define a group as a race based in part on physical characteristics, but also on historical, cultural, and economic factors.

13. _____ are unreliable generalizations about all members of a group that do not recognize individual differences within the group.

14. Sociologists use the term _____ to refer to a negative attitude toward an entire category of people, often an ethnic or racial minority.

15. When White Americans can use credit cards without suspicion, and browse through stores without being shadowed by security guards, they are enjoying_____ _____.

16. _____ _____ refers to positive efforts to recruit minority group members or women for jobs, promotions, and educational opportunities.

17. After the Civil War, the Southern states passed "_____ _____" laws to enforce official segregation, and the Supreme Court upheld them as constitutional in 1896.

18. In the 1960s, proponents of _____ _____ rejected the goal of assimilation into White, middle-class society. They defended the beauty and dignity of Black and African cultures and supported the creation of Black-controlled political and economic institutions.

19. Asian Americans are held up as a(n) _____ or _____ minority group, supposedly because despite past suffering from prejudice and discrimination, they have succeeded economically, socially, and educationally without resorting to confrontations with Whites.

20. Together, the various groups included under the general category _____ represent the largest minority group in the United States.

Answers

1 (d); 2 (b); 3 (c); 4 (c); 5 (d); 6 (a); 7 (a); 8 (b OR d); 9 (c); 10 (a); 11 ascribed; 12 construction; 13 Stereotypes; 14 prejudice; 15 White privilege; 16 Affirmative action; 17 Jim Crow; 18 Black power; 19 model; ideal; 20 Latinos OR Hispanics

THINKING ABOUT MOVIES

Crash (Paul Haggis, 2005)

In this movie the lives of many different characters collide, revealing multiple layers of prejudice toward a wide range of races and ethnicities. One story involves Graham Waters (Don Cheadle), an African American police officer who is personally involved with a fellow officer named Ria (Jennifer Esposito). In a tension-filled conversation, Graham refers to Ria as White, then calls her Mexican. Ria reminds him that her father comes from Puerto Rico and her mother from El Salvador. Rather than hear Ria's call for understanding, Graham responds by insulting Latino culture.

From a sociological perspective, *Crash* offers a wealth of examples of prejudice involving many different groups. Over a two-day period in Los Angeles, we watch as Latinos, Persian Americans, African Americans, Whites, and Asian Americans generalize about other people's behavior based on their racial and ethnic identities.

For Your Consideration

1. Identify three characters in *Crash* and explain why their behavior is prejudiced or discriminatory.

2. In *Crash,* pluralism is more of an ideal than a reality in American culture. Do you agree?

The Great Debaters
(Denzel Washington, 2007)

Melvin Tolson (Denzel Washington) coaches the debate team for Wiley College, an all-Black school in Texas. The movie is set in the 1930s, so both Melvin and his students are subject to high levels of prejudice and discrimination. Nevertheless, he inspires the debate team to greatness, winning contest after contest. Because of segregation, all the team's debates are held at Black colleges—that is, until their tremendous success brings invitations from White institutions, leading eventually to a debate at Harvard University.

This drama reminds us of the historic struggle against segregation, as well as the vestiges of racism that linger today. The initial refusal of White schools to debate Wiley's team serves as an example of institutional discrimination. Watch for the scene in which the team first competes against a White school. Forced to hold the debate in a tent because administrators have refused to hold the contest on campus, Wiley's debaters make some eloquent and forceful arguments for the integration of universities.

For Your Consideration

1. What examples of the privileges of the dominant does this movie show?

2. Why is a movie like *The Great Debaters* important today?

inside

Social Construction
of Gender

Sociological Perspectives
on Gender

Women: The Oppressed
Majority

Women in the Workforce
of the United States

Emergence of a Collective
Consciousness

Social Policy and Gender
Stratification: The Battle
over Abortion from
a Global Perspective

BOXES

Sociology on Campus: *The
Debate over Title IX*

Sociology in the Global
Community: *The Head
Scarf and the Veil:
Complex Symbols*

Taking Sociology to Work:
*Abigail E. Drevs, Former
Program and Volunteer
Coordinator, Y-ME Illinois*

Gender stratification exists in all
societies. Around the world, most
occupations are dominated by
either men or women.

Young people sought Elvis's café [in Tehran, Iran] as refuge from the relentless ugliness that pervaded most public gathering places. Even in the rainy winter, people would crowd outside in the drizzle for an hour, smoking soggy cigarettes and waiting for a table. It was the only café in Tehran designed with innovative elegance and attracted young people starved for aesthetic beauty—the artists, writers, and musicians whose sensibilities suffered acutely in a city draped with grim billboards of war martyrs.

Elvis's coffeehouse inspired imitations all over the neighborhood and then the city. In early 2000, when Celine and I first began to haunt the tiny, modern nook, it was one of a kind. By the following summer of 2001, dozens of tastefully decorated cafés dotted the city, but Elvis's remained the original. In the Gandhi shopping complex, where it was located, at least six others sprang up, and the area became center stage in a café scene of shocking permissiveness. By that time, the dress code was so relaxed that everyone buzzed with tales of "You'll never believe what I saw this girl wearing!"; the fashion spring was likened to a silent coup.

Girls dressed in every color imaginable—veils of bright emerald, violet, buttercup—and in short, coat-like tunics called *manteaus* (also known by the Farsi word *roopoosh*) that hugged their curves, Capri pants that exposed long stretches of calf, pedicured toes in delicate sandals. They sat at the tables outside, in mixed groups, alone with boyfriends, laughing and talking into the late evening, past eleven. For a few weeks, Tehran actually had something like nightlife in public, not just sequestered parties inside people's houses. . . .

Often, once we finished discussing work, men, and the new styles of head scarf we coveted, Celine and I would sit and people-watch. The throng of students and young professionals flirted brazenly, and the coquettish slipping of veils produced nothing less than social theater. The Tehran of the revolution was one of the most sexualized milieus I had ever encountered. Even the chat rooms, Celine informed me, were rife with erotic discussion. People really, really wanted to talk about sex.

. . . Made neurotic by the innate oppressiveness of restriction, Iranians were preoccupied with sex in the manner of dieters constantly thinking about food. The subject meant to be *unmentionable*—to which end women were forced to wear veils, sit in the back of the bus, and order hamburgers from the special "women's line" at fast food joints—had somehow become the most mentioned of all. The constant exposure to covered flesh—whether it was covered hideously, artfully, or plainly—brought to mind, well, flesh.

The relaxing of the dress code encouraged this tendency, by breathing sexuality back into public space. Women walked down the street with their elbows, necks, and feet exposed, their figures outlined in form-fitting tunics. After two decades in exile, skin was finally back. And so imaginations flared, everyone eagerly thought about and talked about sex a lot, as though they were afraid if they didn't exploit the new permissiveness in dress and mood, they might wake up to find it had disappeared.

Often, once we finished discussing work, men, and the new styles of head scarf we coveted, Celine and I would sit and people-watch. The throng of students and young professionals flirted brazenly, and the coquettish slipping of veils produced nothing less than social theater.

(Moaveni 2005a:69–70, 71) Additional information about this excerpt can be found on the Online Learning Center at www.mhhe.com/schaefer12e.

Azadeh Moaveni, the author of *Lipstick Jihad*, was born in California after her parents, both Iranian, fled the political turbulence of the Iranian revolution. In 1979, Islamic religious leaders overthrew the U.S.-backed monarchy that had ruled the country for decades. Almost overnight, the country was transformed from a relatively secular, Western-oriented society into a conservative Muslim state. Women who had been accustomed to dressing much as American women did were suddenly expected to cover themselves in dark robes. Young women, who had been required to attend school and serve in the armed forces under the old regime, were now forbidden even to appear in public without a male escort.

Though Moaveni grew up in the United States, she was conversant with her Persian cultural heritage, albeit from a distance. After graduating from college, she lived in Iran for two years, where she covered the country's affairs as a news correspondent. There she found a different society from the one her parents had fled a generation before. The lipstick jihad she refers to in the title of her book is an allusion to the recent relaxation of the strict standards for women's dress and behavior—a change that Iranian women effected by personally defying government sanctions. (*Jihad* is the Arabic term for one's inner struggle against the forces of ungodliness. [Moaveni 2005b]).

In her current role as *Time* magazine's correspondent from Tehran, Moaveni (2007, 2009) continues to observe women's lives inside the Islamic Republic of Iran. She has noted a new trend in the formerly austere capital—an appetite for high-priced designer-label fashion accessories, particularly among the young. Today, *nouveau riche* Iranians are indulging in Western-style conspicuous consumption—something their parents would never have

Azadeh Moaveni, author of *Lipstick Jihad*, was born in California to refugees from the Iranian revolution. In 1998 she moved to Iran and found a very different society from the one her parents had left in 1979.

done. Iranian housewives can be seen driving through the city in BMW SUVs, Burberry scarves showing beneath their full-length black *chadors* (coats).

How do gender roles differ from one culture to another? Are women in the United States still oppressed because of their gender? Have men's and women's positions in society changed? In this chapter we will study these and other questions by looking first at how various cultures, including our own, assign women and men to particular social roles. Then we will consider socio-logical explanations for gender stratification. We will see that around the world, women constitute an oppressed majority of the population. We'll learn that only recently have women begun to develop a collective consciousness of their oppression and the way in which their gender combines with other factors to create social inequality. Finally, we will close the chapter with a Social Policy section on the controversy over a woman's right to abortion.

Social Construction of Gender

How many airline passengers do you think are startled on hearing a female captain's voice from the cockpit? What do we make of a father who announces that he will be late for work because his son has a routine medical checkup? Consciously or unconsciously, we are likely to assume that flying a commercial plane is a *man's* job and that most parental duties are, in fact, a *woman's*. Gender is such a routine part of our everyday activities that we typically take notice only when someone deviates from conventional behavior and expectations.

Although a few people begin life with an unclear sexual identity, the overwhelming majority begin with a definite sex and quickly receive societal messages about how to behave. In fact, virtually all societies have established social distinctions between females and males that do not inevitably result from biological differences between the sexes (such as women's reproductive capabilities).

In studying gender, sociologists are interested in the gender-role socialization that leads females and males to behave differently. In Chapter 4, **gender roles** were defined as expectations regarding the proper behavior, attitudes, and activities of males and females. The application of dominant gender roles leads to many forms of differentiation between women and men. Both sexes are capable of learning to cook and sew, yet most Western societies determine that women should perform those tasks. Both men and women are capable of learning to weld and to fly air-planes, but those functions are generally assigned to men.

Most people do not display strictly "masculine" or "feminine" qualities all the time. Indeed, such standards can be ambiguous. For instance, though men are supposed to be unemotional, they are allowed to become emotional when their favorite athletic team wins or loses a critical game. Yet our society still focuses on "masculine" and "feminine" qualities as if men and women must be evaluated in those terms. Despite recent inroads by women into male-dominated occupations, our construction of gender continues to define significantly different expectations for females and males (J. Howard and Hollander 1997; West and Zimmerman 1987).

Gender roles are evident not only in our work and behavior but in how we react to others. We are constantly "doing gender" without realizing it. If the father mentioned earlier sits in the doc-tor's office with his son in the middle of a workday, he will prob-ably receive approving glances from the receptionist and from other patients. "Isn't he a wonderful father?" runs through their minds. But if the boy's mother leaves *her* job and sits with the son in the doctor's office, she will not receive such silent applause.

We socially construct our behavior so as to create or exag-gerate male/female differences. For example, men and women come in a variety of heights, sizes, and ages. Yet traditional norms regarding marriage and even casual dating tell us that in hetero-sexual couples, the man should be older, taller, and wiser than the woman. As we will see throughout this chapter, such social norms help to reinforce and legitimize patterns of male dominance.

Gender Roles in the United States

Gender-Role Socialization Male babies get blue blankets; females get pink ones. Boys are expected to play with trucks, blocks, and toy soldiers; girls receive dolls and kitchen goods. Boys must be masculine—active, aggressive, tough, daring, and dominant—but girls must be feminine—soft, emotional, sweet, and submissive. These traditional gender-role patterns have been influential in the socialization of children in the United States.

An important element in traditional views of proper "mascu-line" and "feminine" behavior is **homophobia,** fear of and preju-dice against homosexuality. Homophobia contributes significantly

TABLE 12-1 AN EXPERIMENT IN GENDER NORM VIOLATION BY COLLEGE STUDENTS

Norm Violations by Women	Norm Violations by Men
Send men flowers	Wear fingernail polish
Spit in public	Needlepoint in public
Use men's bathroom	Throw Tupperware party
Buy jock strap	Cry in public
Buy/chew tobacco	Have pedicure
Talk knowledgeably about cars	Apply to baby-sit
Open doors for men	Shave body hair

Source: Nielsen et al. 2000:287.

In an experiment testing gender-role stereotypes, sociology students were asked to behave in ways that might be regarded as violations of gender norms, and to keep notes on how others reacted. This is a sample of their choices of behavior over a seven-year period. Do you agree that these actions test the boundaries of conventional gender behavior?

In our society, men and women receive different messages about the ideal body image. For women, the Miss America pageant promotes a very slim, statuesque physique. For men, "action figures" like the G.I. Joe doll promote an exaggerated muscularity typical of professional wrestlers (Angier 1998; Byrd-Bredbenner and Murray 2003).

to rigid gender-role socialization, since many people stereotypically associate male homosexuality with femininity and lesbianism with masculinity. Consequently, men and women who deviate from traditional expectations about gender roles are often presumed to be gay. Despite the advances made by the gay liberation movement, the continuing stigma attached to homosexuality in our culture places pressure on all males (whether gay or not) to exhibit only narrow masculine behavior and on all females (whether lesbian or not) to exhibit only narrow feminine behavior (Seidman 1994; see also Lehne 1995).

It is *adults,* of course, who play a critical role in guiding children into those gender roles deemed appropriate in a society. Parents are normally the first and most crucial agents of socialization. But other adults, older siblings, the mass media, and religious and educational institutions also exert an important influence on gender-role socialization, in the United States and elsewhere.

It is not hard to test how rigid gender-role socialization can be. Just try transgressing some gender norm—say, by smoking a cigar in public if you are female, or by carrying a purse if you are male. That was exactly the assignment given to sociology students at the University of Colorado and Luther College in Iowa. Professors asked students to behave in ways that they thought violated the norms of how a man or woman should act. The students had no trouble coming up with gender-norm transgressions (Table 12-1), and they kept careful notes on others' reactions to their behavior, ranging from amusement to disgust (Nielsen et al. 2000).

Women's Gender Roles How does a girl come to develop a feminine self-image, while a boy develops one that is masculine? In part, they do so by identifying with females and males in their families and neighborhoods and in the media. If a young girl regularly sees female television characters of all ages and body types, she is likely to grow up with a normal body image. And it will not hurt if the women she knows—her mother, sister, parents' friends, and neighbors—are comfortable with their body types, rather than constantly obsessed with their weight. In contrast, if this young girl sees only wafer-thin actresses and models on television, her self-image will be quite different. Even if she grows up to become a well-educated professional, she may secretly regret falling short of the media stereotype—a shapely, sexy young woman in a bathing suit.

Television is far from alone in stereotyping women. Studies of children's books published in the United States in the 1940s, 1950s, and 1960s found that females were significantly underrepresented in central roles and illustrations. Virtually all female characters were portrayed as helpless, passive, incompetent, and in need of a strong male caretaker. Studies of picture books published from the 1970s through the 1990s found some improvement, but males still dominated the central roles. While males were portrayed as a variety of characters, females tended to be shown mostly in traditional roles, such as mother, grandmother,

SOCIOLOGY ON CAMPUS

12-1 The Debate over Title IX

Few federal policies have had such a visible effect on education over the past 30 years as Title IX, which mandates gender equity in education in federally funded schools. Congressional amendments to the Education Act of 1972, together with guidelines for their implementation developed by the Department of Health, Education, and Welfare in 1974–1975, have brought significant changes for both men and women at all levels of schooling. Title IX eliminated sex-segregated classes, prohibited sex discrimination in admissions and financial aid, and mandated that girls receive more opportunities to play sports, in proportion to their enrollment and interest.

Today, Title IX is still one of the more controversial attempts ever made by the federal government to promote equality for all citizens. Its consequences for the funding of college athletics programs are hotly debated, while its real and lasting effects on college admissions and employment are often forgotten. Critics charge that men's teams have suffered from proportional funding of women's teams and athletic scholarships, since schools with tight athletic budgets can expand women's sports only at the expense of men's sports.

To a certain extent, non-revenue-producing men's sports such as wrestling and golf do appear to have suffered as women's teams

Critics charge that men's teams have suffered from proportional funding of women's teams and athletic scholarships.

have been added. But the high expense of some men's sports, particularly football, would be beyond many schools' means even without Title IX expenditures. And the gains for women have more than made up for the losses to men. In 1971, when there were few opportunities for women athletes on college campuses, 300,000 girls participated in high school sports. In 2004, more than three decades after Title IX opened college athletics to women, the figure was 2.6 million.

For minority women, however, the results have been less satisfactory. Most of the women's sports that have benefited from increases in scholarships over the past 20 years, like rowing, lacrosse, and volleyball, traditionally have not attracted minority women. Twenty-five years ago, just 2 percent of female college athletes were African American. Today, the percentage is a disappointing 2.7 percent.

Sociologists note, too, that the social effects of sports on college campuses are not all positive. Michael A. Messner, professor of sociology at the University of Southern California, points to some troubling results of a survey by the Women's Sports Foundation. The study shows that teenage girls who play sports simply for fun have more positive body images than girls who don't play sports. But those who are "highly involved" in sports are more likely than other girls to take steroids and to become binge drinkers and risk takers. "Everyone has tacitly agreed, it seems, to view men's sports as the standard to which women should strive to have equal access," Messner writes. He is skeptical of a system that propels a lucky few college athletes to stardom each year while leaving the majority, many of them African American, without a career or an education. Certainly that was not the kind of equal opportunity legislators envisioned when they wrote Title IX.

LET'S DISCUSS

1. Has Title IX had an effect on you personally? If so, explain. On balance, do you think the increase in women's participation in sports has been good for society as a whole?
2. How might Title IX affect the way students and the public view gender roles?

Sources: V. Gutierrez 2002; H. Mason 2003; Messner 2002; Pennington 2008; L. Smith 2007; Spencer 2008.

---

or volunteer, even if they also held nontraditional roles, such as working professional (Etaugh 2003).

The pervasiveness of these traditional gender roles extends even to education. Box 12-1 considers the impact of the federal mandate called Title IX on gender equity in college athletics.

Traditional gender roles have restricted females more severely than males. This chapter shows how women have been confined to subordinate roles in the political and economic institutions of the United States. Yet it is also true that gender roles have restricted males.

Men's Gender Roles Stay-at-home fathers? Until recent decades such an idea was unthinkable. Yet in a nationwide survey done in 2002, 69 percent of respondents said that if one parent stays home with the children, it makes no difference whether that parent is the mother or the father. Only 30 percent thought that the mother should be the one to stay home. But while people's conceptions of gender roles are obviously changing, the fact is that men who stay home to care for their children are still an unusual phenomenon. For every stay-at-home dad there are 38 stay-at-home moms (Jason Fields 2004:11–12; Robison 2002).

While attitudes toward parenting may be changing, studies show little change in the traditional male gender role. Men's roles are socially constructed in much the same way as women's are. Family, peers, and the media all influence how a boy or man comes to view his appropriate role in society. The male gender role, besides being antifeminine (no "sissy stuff"), includes proving one's masculinity at work and sports—often by using force in dealing with others—as well as initiating and controlling all sexual relations.

Males who do not conform to the socially constructed gender role face constant criticism and even humiliation, both from children when they are boys and from adults as men. It can be agonizing to be treated as a "chicken" or a "sissy" as a youth— particularly if such remarks come from one's father or brothers. And grown men who pursue nontraditional occupations, such as preschool teaching or nursing, must constantly deal with others' misgivings and strange looks. In one study, interviewers found that such men frequently had to alter their behavior

Gender roles serve to discourage men from entering certain low-paying female-dominated occupations, such as child care. Only 5 percent of day care workers are male.

in order to minimize others' negative reactions. One 35-year-old nurse reported that he had to claim he was "a carpenter or something like that" when he "went clubbing," because women weren't interested in getting to know a male nurse. The subjects made similar accommodations in casual exchanges with other men (Cross and Bagilhole 2002:215).

At the same time, boys who successfully adapt to cultural standards of masculinity may grow up to be inexpressive men who cannot share their feelings with others. They remain forceful and tough, but as a result they are also closed and isolated. In fact, a small but growing body of scholarship suggests that for men as well as women, traditional gender roles may be disadvantageous. In many communities across the nation, girls seem to outdo boys in high school, grabbing a disproportionate share of the leadership positions, from valedictorian to class president to yearbook editor—everything, in short, except captain of the boys' athletic teams. Their advantage continues after high school. In the 1980s, girls in the United States became more likely than boys to go to college. By 2006, women accounted for over 57 percent of college students nationwide. And in 2002, for the first time, more women than men in the United States earned doctoral degrees (Bureau of the Census 2008a:174).

Aside from these problems, many men find that traditional masculinity does not serve them well in the job market. The growth of a service economy over the past two generations has created a demand for skills, attitudes, and behaviors that are the antithesis of traditional masculinity. Increasingly, this sector is the place where low-skilled men must look for jobs. As a recent British study showed, many out-of-work men are reluctant to engage in the kind of sensitive, deferential behavior required by service sector jobs (D. Nixon 2009).

In the past 40 years, inspired in good part by the contemporary feminist movement (examined later in the chapter), increasing numbers of men in the United States have criticized the

restrictive aspects of the traditional male gender role. Some men have taken strong public positions in support of women's struggle for full equality and have even organized voluntary associations for the purpose. However, their actions have been countered by other men who feel they are unfairly penalized by laws related to alimony, child support and custody, family violence, and affirmative action (Kimmel 2008; National Organization for Men Against Sexism 2009).

Recent research on gender roles has shown that in fact there is no single, simple characterization of the male gender role. Australian sociologist R. W. Connell (1987, 2002, 2005) has spoken of **multiple masculinities,** meaning that men play a variety of gender roles, including a nurturing-caring role and an effeminate-gay role, in addition to their traditional gender role of dominating women. Nevertheless, society reinforces their traditional, dominating role more than any other role.

One example of multiple masculinities is the difference between the roles of extremely advantaged men with high-status positions and those of working-class men, whose roles are not necessarily devalued, but afford fewer opportunities for advancement. For example, an analysis of the attack on the World Trade Center on September 11, 2001, contrasts the roles of men from different social classes. Consider the relatively modest status of first responders to the disaster compared with the high status of the affluent managerial professionals who worked at the trade center. Many of the first responders lost their lives to rescue the high-status men in upper-echelon positions in finance and investment banking. One can only imagine the firefighters climbing up the stairwells as the financiers made their way down (Langewiesche 2002).

use your sociological *imagination*

You are living in a society in which there are no gender roles. What is your life like?

Cross-Cultural Perspective

To what extent do actual biological differences between the sexes contribute to the cultural differences associated with gender? This question brings us back to the debate over "nature versus nurture." In assessing the alleged and real differences between men and women, it is useful to examine cross-cultural data.

Around the world, anthropologists have documented highly diverse constructions of gender that do not always conform to our own ideals of masculinity and femininity. Beginning with

Gender roles vary considerably from one country to another. After studying the Minangkabau women of West Sumatra, Indonesia, anthropologist Peggy Reeves Sanday concluded that they wield more authority than the supposedly emancipated women of North America and Europe.

the path-breaking work of Margaret Mead ([1935] 2001) and continuing through contemporary fieldwork, these scholars have shown that gender roles can vary greatly from one physical environment, economy, and political system to the next. Peggy Reeves Sanday's (2002, 2008) work in West Sumatra, Indonesia, for example, describes the 4-million-member Minangkabau society as one in which men and women are not competitors, but partners for the common good. This society is based on a nurturing approach to the environment, blended with Islamic religious ethics. Women control the land through inheritance; in the event of a divorce, the ex-husband leaves with only his clothes. The larger community may be governed by men, women, or both men and women working together. Sanday's findings, together with Mead's, confirm the influential role of culture and socialization in gender-role differentiation. There appear to be no innate or biologically determined gender roles for men and women.

In any society, gender stratification requires, not only individual socialization into traditional gender roles within the family, but the promotion and support of those traditional roles by other social institutions, such as religion and education. Moreover, even with all major institutions socializing the young into conventional gender roles, every society has women and men who resist and successfully oppose the stereotypes: strong women who become leaders or professionals, gentle men who care for children, and so forth. It seems clear that differences between

the sexes are not dictated by biology. Indeed, the maintenance of traditional gender roles requires constant social controls—and those controls are not always effective.

We can see the social construction of gender roles in process in societies strained by war and social upheaval. By summer 2004, a year after the war in Iraq began, young girls in Baghdad seldom ventured out to the park or swimming pool. When they did, their parents made sure they were dressed conservatively, in loose clothing and perhaps a head scarf. The overthrow of Saddam Hussein's secular regime had emboldened Islamic fundamentalists, who had begun visiting schools, urging young women to wear long sleeves and cover their heads. Though school officials resisted, many girls dropped out, some out of fear for their safety and others because of financial hardship. In the atmosphere of violence and lawlessness that followed the 2003 occupation, young women wondered what the future would hold for them, and whether they would ever have the opportunity to become educated professionals, as their mothers had (Sengupta 2004).

Sociological Perspectives on Gender

Cross-cultural studies indicate that societies dominated by men are much more common than those in which women play the decisive role. Sociologists have turned to all the major theoretical perspectives to understand how and why these social distinctions are established. Each approach focuses on culture rather than biology as the primary determinant of gender differences. Yet in other respects, advocates of these sociological perspectives disagree widely.

Functionalist View

Functionalists maintain that gender differentiation has contributed to overall social stability. Sociologists Talcott Parsons and Robert Bales (1955) argued that to function most effectively, the family requires adults who specialize in particular roles. They viewed the traditional gender roles as arising out of the need to establish a division of labor between marital partners.

Parsons and Bales contended that women take the expressive, emotionally supportive role and men the instrumental, practical role, with the two complementing each other. **Instrumentality** refers to an emphasis on tasks, a focus on more distant goals, and a concern for the external relationship between one's family and other social institutions. **Expressiveness** denotes concern for the maintenance of harmony and the internal emotional affairs of the family. According to this theory, women's interest in expressive goals frees men for instrumental tasks, and vice versa. Women become anchored in the family as wives, mothers, and household managers; men become anchored in the occupational world outside the home. Of course, Parsons and Bales offered this framework in the 1950s, when many more women were full-time homemakers than is true today. These theorists did not explicitly endorse traditional gender roles, but they implied that dividing tasks between spouses was functional for the family as a unit.

Given the typical socialization of women and men in the United States, the functionalist view is initially persuasive. However, it would lead us to expect girls and women who have no interest in children to become babysitters and mothers. Similarly, males who love spending time with children might be programmed into careers in the business world. Such differentiation might harm the individual who does not fit into prescribed roles, as well as deprive society of the contributions of many talented people who feel confined by gender stereotyping. Moreover, the functionalist approach does not convincingly explain why men should be assigned categorically to the instrumental role, and women to the expressive role.

Conflict Response

Viewed from a conflict perspective, the functionalist approach masks the underlying power relations between men and women. Parsons and Bales never explicitly presented the expressive and instrumental roles as being of unequal value to society, yet their inequality is quite evident. Although social institutions may pay lip service to women's expressive skills, men's instrumental skills are more highly rewarded, whether in terms of money or prestige. Consequently, according to feminists and conflict theorists, any division of labor by gender into instrumental and expressive tasks is far from neutral in its impact on women.

Conflict theorists contend that the relationship between females and males has traditionally been one of unequal power, with men in a dominant position over women. Men may originally have become powerful in preindustrial times because their size, physical strength, and freedom from childbearing duties allowed them to dominate women physically. In contemporary societies, such considerations are not so important, yet cultural beliefs about the sexes are long established, as anthropologist Margaret Mead and feminist sociologist Helen Mayer Hacker (1951, 1974) both stressed. Such beliefs support a social structure that places males in controlling positions.

Conflict theorists, then, see gender differences as a reflection of the subjugation of one group (women) by another group (men). If we use an analogy to Marx's analysis of class conflict, we can say that males are like the bourgeoisie, or capitalists; they control most of the society's wealth, prestige, and power. Females are like the proletariat, or workers; they can acquire valuable resources only by following the dictates of their bosses. Men's work is uniformly valued; women's work (whether unpaid labor in the home or wage labor) is devalued.

Feminist Perspective

A significant component of the conflict approach to gender stratification draws on feminist theory. Although use of the term *feminist theory* is comparatively recent, the critique of women's position in society and culture goes back to some of the earliest works that have influenced sociology. Among the most important are Mary Wollstonecraft's *A Vindication of the Rights of Women* (originally published in 1792), John Stuart Mill's *The Subjection of Women* (originally published in 1869), and Friedrich Engels's *The Origin of the Family, Private Property, and the State* (originally published in 1884).

Engels, a close associate of Karl Marx, argued that women's subjugation coincided with the rise of private property during industrialization. Only when people moved beyond an agrarian economy could males enjoy the luxury of leisure and withhold rewards and privileges from women. Drawing on the work of Marx and Engels, many contemporary feminist theorists view women's subordination as part of the overall exploitation and injustice that they see as inherent in capitalist societies. Some radical feminist theorists, however, view the oppression of women

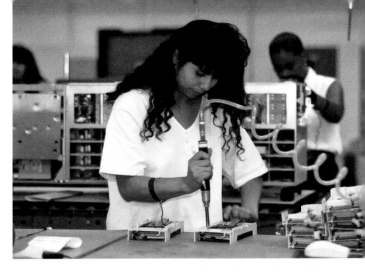

Conflict theorists emphasize that men's work is uniformly valued, while women's work (whether unpaid labor in the home or wage labor) is devalued. This woman is assembling computer parts in a factory in Austin, Texas.

as inevitable in *all* male-dominated societies, whether they are labeled capitalist, socialist, or communist (L. Feuer 1989; Tuchman 1992; R. Tucker 1978: 734–759).

Feminist sociologists would find little to disagree with in the conflict theorists' perspective, but are more likely to embrace a political agenda. Feminists would also argue that until recently, the very discussion of women and society, however well meant, was distorted by the exclusion of women from academic thought, including sociology. We have noted the many accomplishments of Jane Addams and Ida Wells-Barnett, but they generally worked outside the discipline, focusing on what we would now call applied sociology and social work. At the time, their efforts, while valued as humanitarian, were seen as unrelated to the research and conclusions being reached in academic circles, which of course were male academic circles (Andersen 2007; J. Howard 1999).

Contemporary feminists recognize the differential treatment of some women, not only because of their gender, but also because of their race, ethnicity, and socioeconomic status. Simply put, Whites dominate these poor, non-White women because they are non-White; men dominate them because they are women; and the affluent dominate them because they are poor. The African American feminist theorist Patricia Hill Collins (2000) has termed the convergence of social forces that contributes to the subordinate status of these low-status women the **matrix of domination** (Figure 12-1).

Gender, race, and social class are not the only sources of oppression in the United States, though they profoundly affect women and people of color. Other forms of categorization and stigmatization that might be included in the matrix are sexual orientation, religion, disability, and age. If we apply the matrix to the world as a whole, we might add citizenship status or perceived colonial or neocolonial status to the list (Winant 2006).

Though feminists have addressed themselves to the needs of minority women, these women are oppressed much more by their race and ethnicity than by their gender. The question for Latinas (Hispanic women), African American women, Asian American women, and Native American women appears to be whether they should unite with their brothers against racism or challenge them for their sexism. The answer is that our society

FIGURE 12-1 MATRIX OF DOMINATION

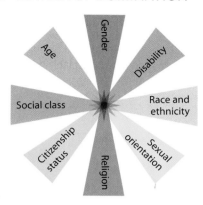

Source: Developed by author.

The matrix of domination illustrates how several social factors, including gender, social class, and race and ethnicity, can converge to create a cumulative impact on a person's social standing.

must eradicate both sexism and racism (Beisel and Kay 2004; Breines 2007; Epstein 1999).

The discussion of gender roles among African Americans has always provoked controversy. Advocates of Black nationalism contend that feminism only distracts women from participating fully in the African American struggle. The existence of feminist groups among Blacks, in their view, simply divides the Black community, thereby serving the dominant White majority. In contrast, Black feminists such as bell hooks (1994) argue that little is to be gained by accepting the gender-role divisions of the dominant society, which place women in a separate, subservient position. Though the media commonly portray Black women in a negative light—as illiterates, welfare queens, or prostitutes—Black feminists emphasize that it is not solely Whites and the White-dominated media who focus on such negative images. Black men (most recently, Black male rap artists) have also portrayed Black women in a negative way (Raybon 1989; Threadcraft 2008).

Historically, Native Americans stand out as an exception to the patriarchal tradition in North America. At the time of the European settlers' arrival, Native American gender roles varied greatly from tribe to tribe. Southern tribes, for reasons unclear to today's scholars, were usually matriarchal and traced their descent through the mother. European missionaries, who sought to make the native peoples more like Europeans, set out to transform this arrangement, which was not entirely universal. Like members of other groups, some Native American women have resisted gender stereotypes (Marubbio 2006).

Latinas are usually considered as part of either the Hispanic or feminist movements, and their distinctive experience ignored. In the past, they have been excluded from decision making in the two social institutions that most affect their daily lives: the family and the church. Particularly in the lower class, the Hispanic family suffers from the pervasive tradition of male domination. And the Catholic Church relegates women to supportive roles, while reserving the leadership positions for men (Browne 2001; De Anda 2004).

Prior to this chapter, much of our discussion has focused on the social effects of race and ethnicity, coupled with poverty, low incomes, and meager wealth. The matrix of domination highlights the confluence of these factors with gender discrimination, which we must include to fully understand the plight of women of color.

Interactionist Approach

While functionalists and conflict theorists who study gender stratification typically focus on macro-level social forces and institutions, interactionist researchers tend to examine gender stratification on the micro level of everyday behavior. The key to this approach is the way gender is socially constructed in everyday interactions. We "do gender" by reinforcing traditionally masculine and feminine actions. For example, a man "does masculinity" by opening a door for his girlfriend; she "does femininity" by consenting to his assistance. Obviously, the social construction of gender goes beyond these relatively trivial rituals. Interactionists recognize, too, that people can challenge traditional gender roles. A female golfer who uses the men's tees and a man who actively arranges a birthday luncheon at work are redoing gender (Deutsch 2007; West and Zimmerman 1987).

One continuing subject of investigation is the role of gender in cross-sex conversations (sometimes referred to as "crosstalk"), specifically the idea that men interrupt women more than women interrupt men. Interestingly, empirical research does not clearly support this assertion. True, people in positions of authority or status—who are much more likely to be male than female—dominate interpersonal conversations. That does not necessarily mean that women per se cannot be heard, however. Future research results may deemphasize the clichéd advice that women must speak up and focus instead on the situational structures that cast men in dominant positions (Cameron 2007; Hyde 2005; Tannen 1990).

Table 12-2 on page 280 summarizes the major sociological perspectives on gender.

Women: The Oppressed Majority

Many people, both male and female, find it difficult to conceive of women as a subordinate and oppressed group. Yet take a look at the political structure of the United States: women remain noticeably underrepresented. As of mid-2009, for example, only 6 of the nation's 50 states had a female governor (Arizona, Connecticut, Hawaii, Michigan, North Carolina, and Washington).

Women have made slow but steady progress in certain political arenas. In 1981, out of 535 members of Congress, there were only 21 women: 19 in the House of Representatives and 2 in the Senate. In contrast, the Congress that held office in mid-2009 had 90 women: 73 in the House and 17 in the Senate. Yet the membership and

Summing up

TABLE 12-2 SOCIOLOGICAL PERSPECTIVES ON GENDER

Theoretical Perspective	Emphasis
Functionalist	Gender differentiation contributes to social stability
Conflict	Gender inequality is rooted in the female–male power relationship
Feminist	Women's subjugation is integral to society and social structure
Interactionist	Gender distinctions and "doing gender" are reflected in people's everyday behavior

leadership of Congress remain overwhelmingly male (Center for American Women and Politics 2009).

In October 1981, Sandra Day O'Connor was sworn in as the nation's first female Supreme Court justice. Still, no woman has ever served as president of the United States, vice president, or chief justice of the Supreme Court.

Sexism and Sex Discrimination

Just as African Americans are victimized by racism, women in our society are victimized by sexism. **Sexism** is the ideology that one sex is superior to the other. The term is generally used to refer to male prejudice and discrimination against women. In Chapter 11, we noted that Blacks can suffer from both individual acts of racism and institutional discrimination. **Institutional discrimination** was defined as the denial of opportunities and equal rights to individuals and groups that results from the normal operations of a society. In the same sense, women suffer from both individual acts of sexism (such as sexist remarks and acts of violence) and institutional sexism.

It is not simply that particular men in the United States are biased in their treatment of women. All the major institutions of our society—including the government, armed forces, large corporations, the media, universities, and the medical establishment—are controlled by men. These institutions, in their normal, day-to-day operations, often discriminate against women and perpetuate sexism. For example, if the central office of a nationwide bank sets a policy that single women are a bad risk for loans—regardless of their incomes and investments—that bank will discriminate against women in state after state. It will do so even at branches where loan officers hold no personal biases toward women, but are merely "following orders."

Our society is run by male-dominated institutions, yet with the power that flows to men come responsibility and stress. Men have higher reported rates of certain types of mental illness than women, and a greater likelihood of death due to heart attack or stroke. The pressure on men to succeed, and then to remain on top in the competitive world of work, can be especially intense. That is not to suggest that gender stratification is as damaging to men as it is to women. But it is clear that the power and privilege men enjoy are no guarantee of personal well-being.

The Status of Women Worldwide

A detailed overview of the status of the world's women, issued by the United Nations in 2001, noted that women and men live in two different worlds. In too many nations women are denied equal pay, sexually harassed at work, or dismissed from their jobs because they are pregnant. These abuses happen even in places where such treatment is prohibited by law. Women who assert their rights are routinely ignored or even punished for their protests. To achieve gender equality, the report concludes, society must hold the powerful accountable to women (United Nations Development Fund for Women 2009).

This critique applies to Western as well as non-Western countries. Although Westerners tend to view some societies—for example, Muslim countries—as being particularly harsh toward women, that perception is actually an overgeneralization. Muslim countries are exceedingly varied and complex and do not often fit the stereotypes created by the Western media. For a detailed discussion of the status of Muslim women today, see Box 12-2.

Regardless of culture, however, women everywhere suffer from second-class status. It is estimated that women grow half the world's food, but they rarely own land. They constitute one-third of the world's paid labor force, but are generally found in the lowest-paying jobs. Single-parent households headed by women, which appear to be on the rise in many nations, are typically found in the poorest sections of the population. The feminization of poverty has become a global phenomenon. As in the United States, women around the world are underrepresented politically.

Despite these challenges, women are not responding passively. They are mobilizing, individually and collectively. Given the significant underrepresentation of women in government offices and national legislatures, however, the task is difficult, as we shall see in Chapter 17.

Not surprisingly, there is a link between the wealth of industrialized nations and the poverty of women in developing countries. Viewed from a conflict perspective or through the lens of Immanuel Wallerstein's world systems analysis, the economies of developing nations are controlled and exploited by industrialized countries and multinational corporations based in those countries. Much of the exploited labor in developing nations, especially in the nonindustrial sector, is performed by women. Women workers typically toil long hours for low pay, but contribute significantly to their families' incomes (Chubb et al. 2008).

In industrial countries, women's unequal status can be seen in the division of housework, as well as in the jobs they hold and the pay they earn. Sociologist Makiko Fuwa (2004) analyzed

SOCIOLOGY IN THE GLOBAL COMMUNITY

12-2   The Head Scarf and the Veil: Complex Symbols

The wearing of a veil or head scarf by women is common to many but not all Middle Eastern societies. However, Muslim women are not alone in their observance of certain standards for dress. All Muslims, men and women alike, are expected to cover themselves and avoid revealing clothes designed to accentuate the body's contours or emphasize its physical beauty. The Koran does permit Muslims to wear revealing garments in private, with their families or with members of the same sex.

The Prophet Muhammad recommended that women cover all of their bodies except for the face, hands, and feet. The Koran adds that a woman's headcovering should fall over the neck and upper chest. A variety of women's outergarments comply with these guidelines for modest attire; collectively, they are referred to as the *hijab*. Face veils are dictated by cultural tradition, however—not by Islam.

In effect, the veil represents a rejection of the beauty myth (see Chapter 8), which is so prevalent in Western societies. By covering themselves almost completely, Muslim women assure themselves and their families that their physical appearance will not play a role in their contacts outside the family. Rather, these women will be known only for their faith, their intellect, and their personalities.

In the 20th century, the veil was politicized by modernization movements that pitted Western cultural values against traditional Islamic values. In Turkey, for instance, in the early 20th century, government officials attempted to subordinate traditional ethnic and religious influences to their nationalistic goals. Though women weren't forbidden to wear the veil, they were not allowed to veil themselves in public places like schools.

Not surprisingly, many Muslims resented these forced social changes.

In the United States today, Muslim women select from an array of traditional garments, including a long, loose tailored coat and a loose black overgarment that is worn with a scarf or perhaps a face veil. However, they are just as apt to wear an overblouse and a long skirt or loose pants, which they can buy at local clothing stores.

> *In effect, the veil represents a rejection of the beauty myth, which is so prevalent in Western societies.*

Researchers have identified three perspectives on the *hijab* among Muslim women in the United States and other non-Islamic countries. Younger, better-educated women who support wearing the *hijab* in public draw on Western ideas of individual rights, arguing in favor of veiling as a form of personal expression. In contrast, older, less-well-educated women who support the *hijab* do so without referring to Western ideology; they cannot see why veiling should be an issue. A third group of women, of all ages and educational backgrounds, opposes the *hijab*.

In some non-Muslim countries, notably France, officials have come under fire for banning the *hijab*, or the head scarf, in public schools (see Chapter 4). The custom generally has not been an issue in the United States, though one 11-year-old had to go to federal court to establish her right to wear a head scarf at school in Muskogee, Oklahoma. Interestingly, the U.S. Department of Justice supported her lawsuit.

The head scarf—an expression of modesty, a woman's right as an individual, or a sign of oppression?

LET'S DISCUSS

1. Consider life in a society in which women wear veils. Can you see any advantages, from the woman's point of view? From the man's?
2. Do you find the Western emphasis on physical beauty oppressive? If so, in what ways?

Sources: Al-Jadda 2006; Haeri 2004; Killian 2003; J. Scott 2007; Selod 2008b.

---

gender inequality in 22 industrial countries using data from the International Social Survey Programme. Fuwa looked first at how couples divided their housework. Then she compared that data to society-wide measures of women's presence in high-status occupations, as well as their wages relative to men's. Figure 12-2 on page 282 shows that while gender differences in empowerment vary widely from one country to the next, equality between the sexes is rare.

Women in the Workforce of the United States

More than 30 years ago, the U.S. Commission on Civil Rights (1976:1) concluded that the passage in the Declaration of Independence proclaiming that "all men are created equal" has been taken too literally for too long—especially with respect to women's opportunities for employment. In this section we will see how gender bias has limited women's opportunities for employment outside the home, at the same time that it forces them to carry a disproportionate burden inside the home.

Labor Force Participation

Women's participation in the paid labor force of the United States increased steadily throughout the 20th century and into the 21st century (Figure 12-3 on page 282). Today, millions of women—married or single, with or without children, pregnant or recently having given birth—are working in the labor force. Overall, 60 percent of adult women in the United States were in the labor force in 2007, compared to 41 percent in 1970. (The data for men are 76 percent in 2007, compared to 76 percent in 1970.) Among married mothers, 62 percent of those with children under age 6

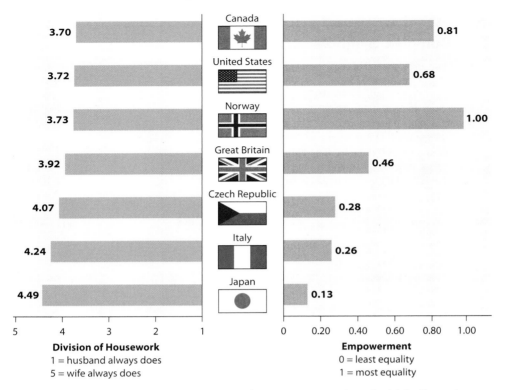

Division of Housework
1 = husband always does
5 = wife always does

Empowerment
0 = least equality
1 = most equality

Notes: Housework includes laundry, grocery shopping, dinner preparation, and care for sick family members. Empowerment includes the proportions of women in parliament, in management, and in professional/technical positions, as well as gender inequality in income.
Source: Adapted from Fuwa 2004:757.

Striking differences exist in women's empowerment—that is, the percentage of women in leadership positions—from one country to the next (right). Yet there is much less difference in the division of housework, even in the same countries (left).

typical of industrial countries. In Great Britain, for example, only 29 percent of computer analysts are women, while 81 percent of cashiers and 90 percent of nurses are women (Cross and Bagilhole 2002).

Women from all groups and men from minority groups sometimes encounter attitudinal or organizational bias that prevents them from reaching their full potential. As we saw in Chapter 11, the term **glass ceiling** refers to an invisible barrier that blocks the promotion of a qualified individual in a work environment because of the individual's gender, race, or ethnicity. A study of the *Fortune* 500 largest corporations in the United States showed that in 2008, barely 15 percent of the seats on their boards of directors were held by women. Furthermore, less than 7 percent of the top earners were female (Catalyst 2009a, 2009b).

This type of inequality is not unique to the United States. Worldwide, women hold less than 1 percent of corporate managerial positions. In recognition of the underrepresentation of women on boards of directors, the Norwegian legislature established minimum quotas for the number of female board members. As the architects of the plan put it, "instead of assuming what people *can't* do at work, provide opportunities for employees to prove what they can do." The goal was not complete equity for women, but 40 percent representation by 2008. The percentage in Norway now stands at 36—much higher than Europe's average of 9 percent. About one in six of Norway's biggest companies have failed to meet the quota, however, and a handful still have no women on their boards (Center for Corporate Diversity 2008; Fouché 2008; Goering 2008).

were in the labor force in 2007, compared to 30 percent in 1970 (Bureau of the Census 2008a:375–376).

Still, women entering the job market find their options restricted in important ways. Particularly damaging is occupational segregation, or confinement to sex-typed "women's jobs." For example, in 2007, women accounted for 99 percent of all dental hygienists and 83 percent of all librarians. Entering such sex-typed occupations places women in "service" roles that parallel the traditional gender-role standard under which housewives "serve" their husbands.

Women are *underrepresented* in occupations historically defined as "men's jobs," which often carry much greater financial rewards and prestige than women's jobs. For example, in 2007, women accounted for approximately 46 percent of the paid labor force of the United States, yet they constituted only 12 percent of civil engineers, 28 percent of dentists and computer systems analysts, and 30 percent of physicians (Table 12-3).

Such occupational segregation is not unique to the United States but

FIGURE **12-3**   TRENDS IN U.S. WOMEN'S PARTICIPATION IN THE PAID LABOR FORCE, 1890–2007

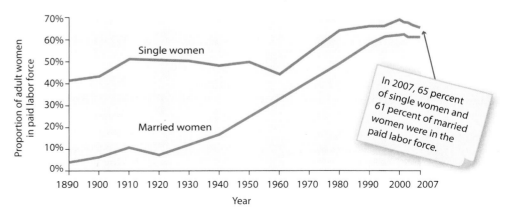

Sources: Bureau of the Census 1975, 2008a:375.

TABLE 12-3 U.S. WOMEN IN SELECTED OCCUPATIONS, 2007: WOMEN AS A PERCENTAGE OF ALL WORKERS IN THE OCCUPATION

Underrepresented		Overrepresented	
Aircraft pilots	2%	High school teachers	57%
Firefighters	5	Cashiers	76
Civil engineers	12	Elementary teachers	81
Police officers	14	File clerks	82
Clergy	15	Social workers	82
Laborers	19	Librarians	83
Chefs and head cooks	21	Tellers	88
Computer systems analysts	28	Word processors and typists	90
Dentists	28	Registered nurses	92
Physicians	30	Receptionists	93
Lawyers	33	Child care workers	95
Mail carriers	37	Dental hygienists	99

Note: Women constitute 46 percent of the entire labor force.
Source: Data for 2007 reported in Bureau of the Census 2008a:384–387.

Compensation

He works. She works. Both are physicians—a high-status occupation with considerable financial rewards. He makes $140,000. She makes $88,000.

These median earnings for physicians in the United States were released by the Census Bureau in 2004. They are typical of the results of the bureau's detailed study of occupations and income. Take air traffic controllers. He makes $67,000; she makes $56,000. Or housekeepers: he makes $19,000; she makes $15,000. What about teachers' assistants? He makes $20,000; she makes $15,000. Statisticians at the bureau looked at the median earnings for no fewer than 821 occupations ranging from dishwasher to chief executive. After adjusting for workers' ages, education, and work experience, they came to an unmistakable conclusion: across the board, there is a substantial gender gap in the median earnings of full-time workers.

Men do not always earn more than women for doing the same work. Researchers at the Census Bureau found 2 occupations out of 821 in which women typically earn about 1 percent more income than men: hazardous materials recovery and telecommunications line installation. These two occupations employed less than 1 out of every 1,000 workers the bureau studied. Forecasting analyses show no convincing evidence that the wage gap is narrowing.

What accounts for these yawning wage gaps between men and women in the same occupation? Scholars at the Census Bureau studied the following characteristics of men and women in the same occupation:

- Age and degree of formal education
- Martial status and the presence of children at home
- Specialization within the occupation (for example, family practice versus surgical practice)
- Years of work experience
- Hours worked per year

Taking all these factors into consideration reduced the pay gap between men and women by only 3 cents. Women still earned 80 cents for every dollar earned by men. In sum, the disparity in pay between men and women cannot be explained by pointing to women's career choices (Government Accountability Office 2003; Weinberg 2004, 2007).

Legally, sex discrimination in wage payments is difficult to prove. Witness the case of former Goodyear worker Lilly Ledbetter, who learned 19 years after she was hired that she was being paid less than men doing the same job. Ledbetter sued and was awarded damages, only to have the Supreme Court overturn the decision on the grounds that she made her claim more than six months after the first discriminatory paycheck was issued. Congress relaxed this restriction in 2009 (Pear 2009).

While women are at a disadvantage in male-dominated occupations, the same is not true for men in female-dominated occupations. Sociologist Michelle Budig (2002) examined a national database containing career information on more than 12,000 men, collected over the course of 15 years. She found that men were uniformly advantaged in female occupations. Though male nurses, grade school teachers, and librarians may experience some scorn in the larger society, they are much more likely than women to be encouraged to become administrators. Observers of the labor force have termed this advantage for men in female-dominated occupations the *glass escalator*—quite a contrast to the glass ceiling (J. Jacobs 2003; C. L. Williams 1992, 1995).

Social Consequences of Women's Employment

Today, many women face the challenge of trying to juggle work and family. Their situation has many social consequences. For one thing, it puts pressure on child care facilities, public financing of day care, and even the fast-food industry, which provides many of the meals women used to prepare themselves. For another, it raises questions about what responsibility male wage earners have in the household.

Who does the housework when women become productive wage earners? Studies indicate that there is a clear gender gap in the performance of housework, although it has been narrowing (see Figure 12-2, page 282). Women do more housework and spend more time on child care than men do, whether on a workday or a nonworkday. Taken together, then, a woman's workday on and off the job is much longer than a man's (Sayer et al. 2004).

Sociologist Arlie Hochschild (1989, 1990, 2005) has used the phrase **second shift** to describe the double burden—work outside the home followed by child care and housework—that many women face and few men share equitably. On the basis of interviews with and observations of 52 couples over an eight-year period, Hochschild reports that the wives (and not their husbands) drive home from the office while planning domestic schedules and play dates for children—and then begin their second shift. Drawing on national studies, she concludes that women spend 15 fewer hours each week in leisure activities than their husbands. In a year, these women work an extra month of 24-hour days because of the second shift; over a dozen years, they work an extra year of 24-hour days. Hochschild found that the married couples she studied were fraying at the edges, and so were their careers and their marriages. With such reports in mind, many feminists have advocated greater governmental and corporate support for child care, more flexible family leave policies, and other reforms designed to ease the burden on the nation's families (Moen and Roehling 2005).

The greater amounts of time women put into caring for their children, and to a lesser degree into housework, take a special toll on women who are pursuing careers. In a survey published in the *Harvard Business Review*, about 40 percent of women indicated that they had voluntarily left work for months or years, compared to only 24 percent of men. As Figure 12-4 shows, women were much more likely than men to take time off for family reasons.

Though women in the United States have a long way to go toward equality in housework, they are doing as well as or better than women in most other countries, including industrial nations. By one measure, 30 percent of the couples in U.S. households share most of the housework, compared to 4 percent in Japan, 25 percent in Great Britain, 27 percent in Sweden, and 32 percent in Canada (C. Geist 2005).

use your sociological *imagination*

In your opinion, how important is it for a couple to share the housework?

Emergence of a Collective Consciousness

Feminism is the belief in social, economic, and political equality for women. The feminist movement of the United States was born in upstate New York, in a town called Seneca Falls, in the summer of 1848. On July 19, the first women's rights convention began, attended by Elizabeth Cady Stanton, Lucretia Mott, and other pioneers in the struggle for women's rights. This first wave of *feminists,* as they are currently known, battled ridicule and scorn as they fought for legal and political equality for women. They were not afraid to risk controversy on behalf of their cause; in 1872, Susan B. Anthony was arrested for attempting to vote in that year's presidential election.

Ultimately, the early feminists won many victories, among them the passage and ratification of the Nineteenth Amendment to the Constitution, which granted women the right to vote in national elections beginning in 1920. But suffrage did not lead to other reforms in women's social and economic position, and in the early and middle 20th century the women's movement became a much less powerful force for social change.

The second wave of feminism in the United States emerged in the 1960s and came into full force in the 1970s. In part, the movement was inspired by three pioneering books arguing for women's rights: Simone de Beauvoir's *The Second Sex,* Betty Friedan's *The Feminine Mystique,* and Kate Millett's *Sexual Politics.* In addition, the general political activism of the 1960s led women—many of whom were working for Black

FIGURE **12-4** WHY LEAVE WORK?

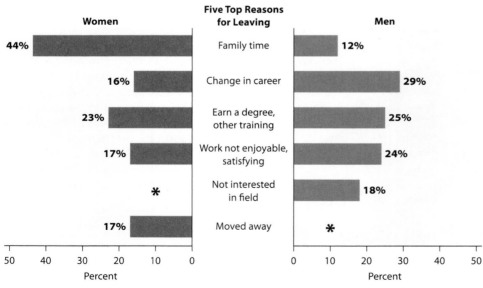

* Not one of top 5 reasons

Note: Based on a representative Harris Interactive survey of "highly qualified" workers, defined as those with a graduate degree, a professional degree, or a high honors undergraduate degree.
Source: Figure adapted from Sylvia Ann Hewlett and Carolyn Burk Luce, 2005. "Off-Ramps and On-Ramps: Keeping Talented Women on the Road to Success," *Harvard Business Review,* March 2005. Copyright © 2005 by the Harvard Business School Publishing Corporation, all rights reserved. Reprinted by permission of *Harvard Business Review.*

TAKING SOCIOLOGY TO WORK

Abigail E. Drevs, **Former Program and Volunteer Coordinator, Y-ME Illinois**

For two and a half years Abigail Drevs served as the program and volunteer coordinator for the Illinois affiliate of Y-ME National Breast Cancer Organization. Y-ME's mission is to provide support and educational outreach through workshops and peer-led support groups, to ensure that no one faces breast cancer alone.

As the coordinator, Drevs was responsible for recruiting, training, and retaining the volunteers who staff the organization's support groups. She also presented workshops about breast cancer and how to detect it early. To make sure that services were available to all and that funding was being managed effectively, she met with community leaders and organizations, corporate partners, and medical institutions. "A typical work week, in one word, was juggling," she says. "In a small nonprofit, few people do the work of many."

Occasionally, Drevs traveled to conferences to network with other organizations dedicated to working with certain populations of breast cancer survivors, including young women. These organizations have banded together to develop a pilot program that will address young women's concerns with intimacy and infertility after breast cancer.

In Chicago, Drevs strove to raise the awareness of breast cancer among African American women from all walks of life. "As a middle-class white woman, the issue of race had been a very academic one in my experience," she says. "I read Studs Terkel and took racial disparities curricula, but never truly understood the issues until I became immersed in the community." Drevs's experience with Y-ME helped her to understand the position of thousands of underinsured African American women in that city: "limited access to health care, distrust of the system, and the importance of their community and social networks."

Asked what insights she has drawn from her training in sociology, Drevs replies, "It reaffirmed my belief that no one perspective is the only perspective. From fundamental social theory to social conflict to developing nations, there are many ways to explain something, and oftentimes, there is something that can be gained from each perspective."

Drevs is currently working for her alma mater, Dartmouth College, as the program manager for young alumni, students, and diversity at the Office of Alumni Relations. Her advice to current students of sociology: "Even if you don't major in this, make sure to take it with you wherever you go. Many of the world's problems can be traced to not communicating properly and not understanding another group's perspective. A good basis in sociology can serve you well, no matter what you do."

LET'S DISCUSS

1. Do some research on breast cancer. Does the survival rate differ among different racial and ethnic groups? What about different social classes? Why are education and early detection important?
2. Relate what you have learned about breast cancer to what you have learned about gender. What social patterns does your research illustrate?

---

civil rights or against the war in Vietnam—to reexamine their own powerlessness. The sexism often found within allegedly progressive and radical political circles convinced many women that they needed to establish their own movement for women's liberation (Breines 2007; Freeman 1973, 1975).

As more and more women became aware of sexist attitudes and practices, including attitudes they themselves had accepted through socialization into traditional gender roles, they began to challenge male dominance. A sense of sisterhood, much like the class consciousness that Marx hoped would emerge in the proletariat, became evident. Individual women identified their interests with those of the collectivity *women*. No longer were women happy in submissive, subordinate roles ("false consciousness" in Marxist terms).

National surveys done today, however, show that while women generally endorse feminist positions, they do not necessarily accept the label *feminist*. Some 57 percent of women considered themselves feminists in 1987; the proportion had dropped to about 25 percent in 2001. Feminism as a unified political cause, requiring one to accept a similar stance on everything from abortion to sexual harassment to pornography to welfare, has fallen out of favor. Both women and men prefer to express their views on these complex issues individually, rather than under a convenient umbrella like feminism. Still, feminism is very much alive in the growing acceptance of women in nontraditional roles, and even the basic acknowledgment that a married mother not

only can work outside the home but perhaps *belongs* in the labor force. A majority of women say that given the choice, they would prefer to work outside the home rather than stay home and take care of a house and family, and about one-quarter of women prefer *Ms.* to *Miss* or *Mrs.* (Feminist Majority Foundation 2007; Robison 2002).

The women's movement has undertaken public protests on a wide range of issues. Feminists have endorsed passage of the equal rights amendment, government subsidies for child care (see Chapter 4), affirmative action for women and minorities (see Chapter 18), federal legislation outlawing sex discrimination in education (see Chapter 16), greater representation of women in government (see Chapter 17), and the right to a legal abortion (discussed in the Social Policy section of this chapter).

---

use your sociological *imagination*

Do you know many people who refer to themselves explicitly as feminists? What about people who make it clear that they are not feminists—how many do you know?

socialpolicy and Gender Stratification

The Battle over Abortion from a Global Perspective

The Issue

Few issues seem to stir as much intense conflict as abortion. A critical victory in the struggle for legalized abortion in the United States came in 1973, when the Supreme Court granted women the right to terminate pregnancies. This ruling, known as *Roe v. Wade,* was based on a woman's right to privacy. The Court's decision was generally applauded by pro-choice groups, which believe women should have the right to make their own decisions about their bodies and should have access to safe and legal abortions. It was bitterly condemned by those opposed to abortion. For these pro-life groups, abortion is a moral and often a religious issue. In their view, human life begins at the moment of conception, so that its termination through abortion is essentially an act of murder.

The Setting

The debate that has followed *Roe v. Wade* revolves around prohibiting abortion altogether or, at the very least, limiting it. In 1979, for example, Missouri required parental consent for minors wishing to obtain an abortion, and the Supreme Court upheld the law. Parental notification and consent have become especially sensitive issues in the debate. Pro-life activists argue that the parents of teenagers should have the right to be notified about—and to permit or prohibit—abortions. In their view, parental authority deserves full support at a time when the traditional nuclear family is embattled. However, pro-choice activists counter that many pregnant teenagers come from troubled families where they have been abused. These young women may have good reason to avoid discussing such explosive issues with their parents.

Changing technology has had its impact on the debate. "Morning-after" pills, which have been available in some nations since 1998, are now prescribed in the United States. These emergency contraception pills can prevent pregnancy after unprotected sex. In 2000, the U.S. government approved RU-486, an abortion-inducing pill that can be used in the first seven weeks of pregnancy. The regime requires doctor visits but no surgical procedures. In addition, doctors, guided by ultrasound, can now end a pregnancy as early as eight days after conception. Pro-life activists are concerned that the use of ultrasound technology will allow people to abort unwanted females in nations where a premium is placed on male offspring.

In the United States, people support a woman's right to a legal abortion, but with reservations. According to a 2009 national survey, 23 percent oppose a woman's right to a legal abortion under *all* circumstances. However, 22 percent feel that abortion should be legal under *all* circumstances. These findings have held for the past 35 years (Saad 2009).

The United States is not alone in debating abortion. Latin American countries typically have the strictest measures against the practice, but changes occasionally occur. In 2006, while protesters took to the streets, the Nicaraguan government joined five other states (Chile, East Timor, El Salvador, Malta, and Vatican City) in outlawing all forms of abortion, including procedures performed to save a pregnant woman's life. And in 2007, Mexico loosened decade-old restrictions to permit legal abortions during the first three months, for any reason (R. Carrol 2006; Ellingwood 2008).

Sociological Insights

Sociologists see gender and social class as the defining issues surrounding abortion. That is, the intense conflict over abortion reflects broader differences over women's position in society. Feminists involved in defending abortion rights typically believe that men and women are essentially similar. They

FIGURE **12-5** RESTRICTIONS ON PUBLIC FUNDING FOR ABORTION

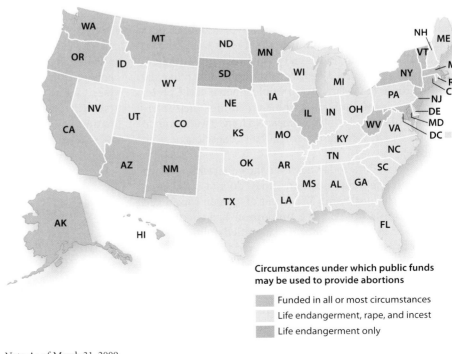

MAPPING LIFE NATIONWIDE

Circumstances under which public funds may be used to provide abortions

- Funded in all or most circumstances
- Life endangerment, rape, and incest
- Life endangerment only

Note: As of March 31, 2009.
Source: NARAL Pro-Choice America 2009.

FIGURE **12-6** THE GLOBAL DIVIDE ON ABORTION

MAPPING LIFE WORLDWIDE

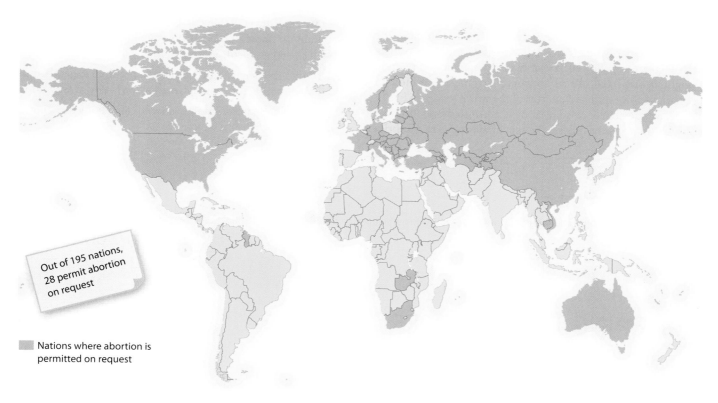

Out of 195 nations, 28 permit abortion on request

■ Nations where abortion is permitted on request

Note: Data current as of November 2007.
Source: Developed by the author based on United Nations Population Division 2007.

support women's full participation in work outside the home and oppose all forms of sex discrimination. Feminists also claim that pregnancy and childbirth have been socially constructed by male-centered health care systems and patriarchal religious traditions. In contrast, most antiabortion activists believe that men and women are fundamentally different. In their view, men are best suited to the public world of work, while women are best suited to the demanding and crucial task of rearing children. These activists are troubled by women's growing participation in work outside the home, which they view as destructive to the family and ultimately to society (Lorber 2005).

In regard to social class, the first major restriction on the legal right to terminate a pregnancy affected poor people. In 1976, Congress passed the Hyde Amendment, which banned the use of Medicaid and other federal funds for abortions. The Supreme Court upheld this legislation in 1980. State laws also restrict the use of public funds for abortions (Figure 12-5).

Another obstacle facing the poor is access to abortion providers. In the face of vocal pro-life sentiment, fewer and fewer hospitals throughout the world are allowing physicians to perform abortions, except in extreme cases. To avoid controversy, many medical schools have ceased to offer training in the procedure. Moreover, some doctors who work in clinics, intimidated by death threats and murders, have stopped performing abortions. For poor people in rural areas, this reduction in service

makes it more difficult to locate and travel to a facility that will accommodate their wishes. Viewed from a conflict perspective, this is one more financial burden that falls especially heavily on low-income women.

Policy Initiatives

In 1973 the Supreme Court supported the general right to terminate a pregnancy by a narrow 5–4 majority. Although pro-life activists continue to hope for an overruling of *Roe v. Wade,* they have focused in the interim on weakening the decision through tactics such as limiting the use of fetal tissue in medical experiments and prohibiting certain late-term abortions, which they term "partial-birth" abortions. The Supreme Court continues to hear cases involving such restrictions. In 2005, speculation arose over a potential narrowing of the applicability of *Roe v. Wade* following the appointment of new justices, who may hold more conservative positions than those they replaced.

What is the policy in other countries? As in the United States, many European nations responded to public opinion and liberalized abortion laws beginning in the 1970s. However, many of those nations limit the procedure to the first 12 weeks of a pregnancy. (The United States, in contrast, allows abortions up to about the 24th week and beyond.) Inspired by the strong antiabortion movement in the United States, antiabortion activists in Europe have become more outspoken, especially in Great Britain, France, Spain, Italy, and Germany.

The policies of the United States are intertwined with those of developing nations. Beginning in the 1980s, members of Congress who opposed abortion successfully blocked foreign aid to countries that might use the funds to encourage abortion. (This practice ended in 2009.) Yet developing nations generally have the most restrictive abortion laws. As Figure 12-6 on page 287 shows, it is primarily in Africa, Latin America, and parts of Asia that women are not allowed to terminate a pregnancy on request. As might be expected, illegal abortions are most common in those nations. An estimated quarter of the world's women live in countries where abortion is illegal or is permitted only if a woman's life is in jeopardy. Indeed, the rate of abortions in countries with legal restrictions on the procedure matches the rate in countries that permit it. Hence, 40 percent of abortions worldwide—about 16 million procedures each year—are performed illegally (P. Baker 2009; Guttmacher Institute 2008).

Let's Discuss

1. How easy do you think it is for a young adult woman to obtain an abortion? What do you think should be the first step she takes in considering one?

2. Do you think teenage girls should be required to get their parents' consent before having an abortion? Why or why not?

3. Under what circumstances should abortions be allowed? Explain your reasoning.

getting**involved**

To get involved in the debate over abortion, visit this book's Online Learning Center, which offers links to relevant Web sites.

www.mhhe.com/schaefer12e

MASTERING THIS CHAPTER

Summary

Gender is an ascribed status that provides a basis for social differentiation. This chapter examines the social construction of gender, theories of stratification by gender, women as an oppressed majority group, women in the workforce of the United States, and the emergence of a collective consciousness.

1. In the United States, the social construction of gender continues to define significantly different expectations for females and males.

2. **Gender roles** show up in our work and behavior and in how we react to others. Throughout history, these roles have restricted women much more than they have men.

3. Though men may exhibit a variety of different gender roles, called **multiple masculinities**, society reinforces their traditional role of dominating women.

4. Anthropological research points to the importance of cultural conditioning in defining the social roles of males and females.

5. Functionalists maintain that sex differentiation contributes to overall social stability, but conflict theorists charge that the relationship between females and males is one of unequal power, with men dominating women. This dominance shows up in people's everyday interactions.

6. Many women experience differential treatment, not only because of their gender, but because of their race, ethnicity, and social class. Patricia Hill Collins has termed this convergence of social forces the **matrix of domination.**

7. As one example of their micro-level approach to the study of gender stratification, interactionists have analyzed men's verbal dominance over women through conversational interruptions.

8. Women around the world suffer from **sexism** and **institutional discrimination.**

9. In the United States today, almost as many women as men participate in the paid labor force, but women are underrepresented in managerial positions and underpaid compared to men with the same jobs.

10. As women have taken on more and more hours of paid employment outside the home, they have been only partially successful in getting their husbands to take on more homemaking duties, including child care.

11. Many women agree with the positions of the feminist movement but reject the label *feminist.*

12. The issue of abortion has bitterly divided the United States (as well as other nations), pitting pro-choice activists against pro-life activists.

Critical Thinking Questions

1. Imagine that you are assigned the opposite gender at birth, but that your race, ethnicity, religion, and social class remain the same. Drawing on the information contained in this chapter, describe how your life as a member of the opposite sex might differ from your life today.

2. In what ways is the social position of White women in the United States similar to that of African American women, Latinas (Hispanic women), and Asian American women? In what ways are women's social positions markedly different, given their racial and ethnic status?

3. Imagine that you have been asked to study political activism among women. How might you employ surveys, observations, experiments, and existing sources to better understand such activism?

Key Terms

Expressiveness Concern for the maintenance of harmony and the internal emotional affairs of the family. (277)

Feminism The belief in social, economic, and political equality for women. (284)

Gender role Expectations regarding the proper behavior, attitudes, and activities of males and females. (273)

Glass ceiling An invisible barrier that blocks the promotion of a qualified individual in a work environment because of the individual's gender, race, or ethnicity. (282)

Homophobia Fear of and prejudice against homosexuality. (273)

Institutional discrimination The denial of opportunities and equal rights to individuals and groups that results from the normal operations of a society. (280)

Instrumentality An emphasis on tasks, a focus on more distant goals, and a concern for the external relationship between one's family and other social institutions. (277)

Matrix of domination The cumulative impact of oppression because of race and ethnicity, gender, and social class, as well as religion, sexual orientation, disability, age, and citizenship status. (278)

Multiple masculinities A variety of male gender roles, including nurturing-caring and effeminate-gay roles, that men may play along with their more pervasive traditional role of dominating women. (276)

Second shift The double burden—work outside the home followed by child care and housework—that many women face and few men share equitably. (284)

Sexism The ideology that one sex is superior to the other. (280)

Self-Quiz

Read each question carefully and then select the best answer.

1. Both males and females are physically capable of learning to cook and sew, yet most Western societies determine that women should perform these tasks. This illustrates the operation of
   a. gender roles.
   b. sociobiology.
   c. homophobia.
   d. comparable worth.

2. An important element in traditional views of proper "masculine" and "feminine" behavior is fear of homosexuality. This fear, along with accompanying prejudice, is referred to as
   a. lesbianism.
   b. femme fatalism.
   c. homophobia.
   d. claustrophobia.

3. The most crucial agents of socialization in teaching gender roles in the United States are
   a. peers.
   b. teachers.
   c. media personalities.
   d. parents.

4. Research by anthropologists Margaret Mead and Peggy Reeves Sanday has shown that
   a. biology is the most important factor in determining the social roles of males and females.
   b. cultural conditioning is the most important factor in determining the social roles of males and females.
   c. biology and cultural conditioning have an equal impact in determining the social roles of males and females.
   d. biology and cultural conditioning have a negligible impact in determining the social roles of males and females.

5. Which sociological perspective acknowledges that it is not possible to change gender roles drastically without dramatic revisions in a culture's social structure?
   a. functionalist perspective
   b. conflict perspective
   c. interactionist perspective
   d. both a and b

6. The term *sexism* is generally used to refer to
   a. female prejudice and discrimination against men.
   b. male prejudice and discrimination against women.
   c. female discrimination against men and male discrimination against women equally.
   d. discrimination between members of the same sex.

7. Which of these statements is true?
   a. More boys than girls take AP exams.
   b. Women in the United States are more likely to attend college than men.
   c. Women in the United States are less likely to obtain doctoral degrees than men.
   d. all of the above

8. Which sociological perspective distinguishes between instrumental and expressive roles?
   a. functionalist perspective
   b. conflict perspective
   c. interactionist perspective
   d. labeling theory

9. Contemporary feminists recognize the differential treatment of some women, not only because of their gender, but also because of their
   a. race.
   b. ethnicity.
   c. socioeconomic status.
   d. all of the above

10. The sense of sisterhood that became evident during the rise of the contemporary feminist movement resembled the Marxist concept of
    a. alienation.
    b. dialectics.
    c. class consciousness.
    d. false consciousness.

11. Talcott Parsons and Robert Bales contend that women take the _____, emotionally supportive role in the family and that men take the _____, practical role, with the two complementing each other.

12. A significant component of the _____ approach to gender stratification draws on feminist theory.

13. It is not simply that particular men in the United States are biased in their treatment of women. All the major institutions of our society—including the government, the armed forces, large corporations, the media, the universities, and the medical establishment—are controlled by men. This situation is symptomatic of institutional _____.

14. Women from all groups and men from minority groups sometimes encounter attitudinal or organizational bias that prevents them from reaching their full potential. This is known as the_____.

15. Sociologist Arlie Hochschild has used the phrase _____ _____ to describe the double burden that many women face and few men share equitably: work outside the home followed by child care and housework.

16. Within the general framework of their theory, _____ sociologists maintain that gender differentiation has contributed to overall social stability.

17. Through the rise of contemporary _____, women are developing a greater sense of group solidarity.

18. _____ contributes significantly to rigid gender-role socialization, since many people stereotypically associate male homosexuality with femininity and lesbianism with masculinity.

19. The term _____ _____ _____ was coined by feminist theorist Patricia Hill Collins to describe the convergence of social forces that contributes to the subordinate status of poor, non-White women.

20. The author of the pioneering argument for women's rights, *The Feminine Mystique*, is_____.

THINKING ABOUT MOVIES

Billy Elliot (Stephen Daldry, 2000)

In this movie, set in a mining town in Northern England, Billy Elliot (Jamie Bell) is a young boy with talent and the inclination to become a professional ballet dancer. His father, Tony (Jamie Draven), a coal miner, at first forbids Billy to take dancing lessons. Tony is socializing Billy to be a man, and he sees ballet as an inappropriate occupation for his son. Gradually, however, he begins to see dance as a way for his son to escape the poverty of his declining industrial town.

Sociologically, if Billy Elliot were to assume a traditional gender role and disavow his love for ballet, his life chances would be minimized. Facing discrimination from many of his peers, Billy fights against traditional gender-role expectations to improve his social status.

For Your Consideration

1. What are the gender norms portrayed in the film? How does Billy support his masculinity and how does he subvert it?

2. What does Tony, the father, do to "properly" socialize Billy as a male?

Boys Don't Cry (Kimberly Peirce, 1999)

In this movie, based on a true story, Brandon Teena (Hillary Swank) is a transgendered person—someone whose identity cuts across the conventional male/female boundary. Brandon was born with the body of a woman but lives as a man. To disguise his female form, he assumes a man's gender role and moves to the small town of Falls City, Nebraska, where no one will know his background. Reveling in his acceptance there, he makes friends and enters a romantic relationship. But when he is thrown in jail on a minor charge, his physical sex is exposed. A tragic confrontation follows, and Brandon feels the wrath of those who do not tolerate his alternative lifestyle.

This movie illustrates the social construction of gender, revealing that a person's identity as a man or a woman is a social role, not a biological fact. Brandon's dress, speech, and behavior—not his body—constitute his male identity. When his physical sex is discovered, he suffers greatly for it, revealing the rigidity of gender-role socialization.

For Your Consideration

1. What does it take for Brandon to play the role of a man, and what does that say about the social construction of gender?

2. Why does Brandon's transformed gender incite such a violent reaction? How might the answer to this question change depending on whether a functionalist or an interactionist answers it?

inside

Aging and Society

Sociological Perspectives
on Aging

Aging Worldwide

Role Transitions throughout
the Life Course

Age Stratification in
the United States

Social Policy and Age
Stratification: The Right
to Die Worldwide

BOXES

Taking Sociology to Work:
*A. David Roberts, Social
Worker*

Sociology in the Global
Community: *Aging,
Japanese Style*

Research Today: *Elderspeak
and Other Signs of Ageism*

These "silver surfers" in
California still enjoy life to the
fullest, just as they did when they
were young. Staying active and
involved has been shown to be
healthy for the older population.

Stratification by Age 13

tuesdays with Morrie

an old man, a young man, and life's greatest lesson

Mitch Albom

> "Later that day, we talked about aging. Or maybe I should say the fear of aging—another of the issues on my what's-bugging-my-generation list. On my ride from the Boston airport, I had counted the billboards that featured young and beautiful people. There was a handsome young man in a cowboy hat, smoking a cigarette, two beautiful young women smiling over a shampoo bottle, a sultry-looking teenager with her jeans unsnapped, and a sexy woman in a black velvet dress, next to a man in a tuxedo, the two of them snuggling a glass of scotch.
>
> Not once did I see anyone who would pass for over thirty-five. I told Morrie I was already feeling over the hill, much as I tried desperately to stay on top of it. I worked out constantly. Watched what I ate. Checked my hairline in the mirror. I had gone from being proud to say my age—because of all I had done so young—to not bringing it up, for fear I was getting too close to forty and, therefore, professional oblivion.
>
> Morrie had aging in better perspective.

All this emphasis on youth—I don't buy it," he said. "Listen, I know what a misery being young can be, so don't tell me it's so great. All these kids who came to me with their struggles, their strife, their feelings of inadequacy, their sense that life was miserable . . .

> "All this emphasis on youth—I don't buy it," he said. "Listen, I know what a misery being young can be, so don't tell me it's so great. All these kids who came to me with their struggles, their strife, their feelings of inadequacy, their sense that life was miserable, so bad they wanted to kill themselves . . .
>
> "And, in addition to all the miseries, the young are not wise. They have very little understanding about life. Who wants to live every day when you don't know what's going on? When people are manipulating you, telling you to buy this perfume and you'll be beautiful, or this pair of jeans and you'll be sexy—and you believe them! It's such nonsense."
>
> Weren't you *ever* afraid to grow old, I asked?
>
> "Mitch, I *embrace* aging."
>
> Embrace it?
>
> "It's very simple. As you grow, you learn more. If you stayed at twenty-two, you'd always be as ignorant as you were at twenty-two. Aging is not just decay, you know. It's growth. It's more than the negative that you're going to die, it's also the positive that you understand you're going to die, and that you live a better life because of it."
>
> Yes, I said, but if aging were so valuable, why do people always say, "Oh, if I were young again." You never hear people say, "I wish I were sixty-five."
>
> He smiled. "You know what that reflects? Unsatisfied lives. Unfulfilled lives. Lives that haven't found meaning. Because if you've found meaning in your life, you don't want to go back. You want to go forward. You want to see more, do more. You can't wait until sixty-five. . . . "

(Albom 1997:117–118) Additional information about this excerpt can be found on the Online Learning Center at www.mhhe.com/schaefer12e.

In *Tuesdays with Morrie*, journalist Mitch Albom (1997) recounted his final class with his favorite college professor, the respected Brandeis University sociologist Morrie Schwartz. Albom, who had graduated years before, contacted Schwartz when he learned the professor was dying of amyotrophic lateral sclerosis (ALS), also known as Lou Gehrig's disease. To his surprise, he found that his series of conversations with Morrie, held always on Tuesday, were more about life than death. From this sage man he learned that age has its benefits and that growing old can also mean growing wise.

Age, like race or gender, is socially constructed. It is an ascribed status that dominates people's perceptions of others, obscuring individual differences. Rather than suggesting that a particular elderly person is no longer competent to drive, for instance, we may condemn the entire age group: "Those old codgers shouldn't be allowed on the road." Unless people can begin to look at the life course as a continuum, rather than as a series of finite stages with predictable consequences, such stereotypical attitudes toward age and aging are not likely to change.

How do people's roles change as they age? What are the social implications of the growing number of elderly in the United States? How does ageism affect an older person's employment opportunities? In this chapter we will look at the process of aging throughout the life course. We will examine aging around the world, focusing primarily on the United States. After exploring various theories of the impact of aging, both on the individual and on society, we will discuss the role transitions typical of the major stages in the life course. In the process we will consider the challenges facing the "sandwich generation," middle-aged people who care for both their children and their aging parents. We will pay particular attention to the effects of prejudice and discrimination on older people, and to the rise of a political consciousness among the elderly. Finally, in the Social Policy section we will discuss the controversial issue of the right to die.

Aging and Society

The Sherpas—a Tibetan-speaking Buddhist people in Nepal—live in a culture that idealizes old age. Almost all elderly members of the Sherpa culture own their homes, and most are in relatively good physical condition. Typically, older Sherpas value their independence and prefer not to live with their children. Among the Fulani of Africa, however, older men and women move to the edge of the family homestead. Since that is where people are buried, the elderly sleep over their own graves, for they are viewed socially as already dead. Like gender stratification, age stratification varies from culture to culture. One society may treat older people with great reverence, while another sees them as unproductive and "difficult" (M. Goldstein and Beall 1981; Stenning 1958; Tonkinson 1978).

It is understandable that all societies have some system of age stratification that associates certain social roles with distinct periods in life. Some of this age differentiation seems inevitable; it would make little sense to send young children off to war, or to expect most older citizens to handle physically demanding tasks, such as loading freight at shipyards. However, as is the case with stratification by gender, in the United States age stratification goes far beyond the physical constraints on human beings at different ages.

"Being old" is a master status that commonly overshadows all others in the United States. Thus, the insights of labeling theory can help us in analyzing the consequences of aging. Once people have been labeled "old," the designation has a major impact on how others perceive them, and even on how they view themselves. Negative stereotypes of the elderly contribute to their position as a minority group subject to discrimination, as we will see later in the chapter.

The model of five basic properties of a minority or subordinate group (introduced in Chapter 11) can be applied to older people in the United States to clarify their subordinate status:

1. Older people experience unequal treatment in employment and may face prejudice and discrimination.

2. Older people share physical characteristics that distinguish them from younger people. In addition, their cultural preferences and leisure-time activities often differ from those of the rest of society.

3. Membership in this disadvantaged group is involuntary.

4. Older people have a strong sense of group solidarity, as is reflected in the growth of senior citizens' centers, retirement communities, and advocacy organizations.

5. Older people generally are married to others of comparable age.

There is one crucial difference between older people and other subordinate groups, such as racial and ethnic minorities or women: *all* of us who live long enough will eventually assume the ascribed status of an older person (Barron 1953; Levin and Levin 1980; Wagley and Harris 1958).

In Korea, certain birthdays are celebrated as milestones, complete with a formal feast. At a 60th birthday celebration, for example, all the younger family members bow before the fortunate elder one by one, in order of their ages, and offer gifts. Later they compete with one another in composing poetry and singing songs to mark the occasion. Unfortunately, not all older people are so lucky; in many other cultures, being old is considered next to being dead.

Sociological Perspectives on Aging

Aging is one important aspect of socialization—the lifelong process through which an individual learns the cultural norms and values of a particular society. There are no clear-cut definitions for different periods of the aging cycle in the United States. *Old age* has typically been regarded as beginning at 65, which corresponds to the retirement age for many workers, but not everyone in the United States accepts that definition. With the increase in life expectancy, writers are beginning to refer to people in their 60s as the "young old," to distinguish them from those in their 80s and beyond (the "old old").

The particular problems of the elderly have become the focus of a specialized field of research and inquiry known as gerontology. **Gerontology** is the scientific study of the sociological and psychological aspects of aging and the problems of the aged. It originated in the 1930s, as an increasing number of social scientists became aware of the plight of the elderly.

Gerontologists rely heavily on sociological principles and theories to explain the impact of aging on the individual and society. They also draw on psychology, anthropology, physical education, counseling, and medicine in their study of the

use your sociological *imagination*

Time has passed, and you are now in your 70s or 80s. How does old age in your generation compare with your parents' or grandparents' experience of old age?

TAKING SOCIOLOGY TO WORK

A. David Roberts, **Social Worker**

Dave Roberts admits to being a "people person," a trait that sociology courses fostered by showing how "everybody has differences; there are little bits of different cultures in all of us." He also had the benefit of "a lot of great teachers" at Florida State University, including Dr. Jill Quadagno in a course on aging. It was this class that sparked his interest in aging issues, which led to a certificate in gerontology in addition to a sociology degree in 1998. He realized that there was a good job market in working with the aging baby boom generation.

Volunteer work with the Meals on Wheels program steered him toward working with the elderly. Today Roberts is a social worker in a nursing home, where he is responsible for patients' care plans. In the course of his work, he meets regularly with patients, family members, and medical residents. Roberts finds that the concept of teamwork he learned in group projects in college has helped him in his job. Also, the projects he had to do in school taught him to work on a schedule. Perhaps most important, sociology has helped him "to grow as a person, to explore different angles, different theories. . . . I'm a better person."

His advice to sociology students: "Just give it a chance; they throw everything into an intro course. Don't get overwhelmed; take it as it comes."

LET'S DISCUSS

1. What other types of employment might be open to a college graduate with a certificate in gerontology?
2. What might be the special rewards of working with elderly people?

---

aging process. Two influential views of aging—disengagement theory and activity theory—can best be understood in terms of the sociological perspectives of functionalism and interactionism, respectively. The conflict perspective also contributes to our sociological understanding of aging.

Functionalist Approach: Disengagement Theory

After studying elderly people in good health and relatively comfortable economic circumstances, Elaine Cumming and William Henry (1961) introduced their **disengagement theory,** which implicitly suggests that society and the aging individual mutually sever many of their relationships. In keeping with the functionalist perspective, disengagement theory emphasizes that passing social roles on from one generation to another ensures social stability.

According to this theory, the approach of death forces people to drop most of their social roles—including those of worker, volunteer, spouse, hobby enthusiast, and even reader. Younger members of society then take on these functions. The aging person, it is held, withdraws into an increasing state of inactivity while preparing for death.

Since it was first outlined five decades ago, disengagement theory has generated considerable controversy. Today, gerontologists and sociologists are more likely to see the elderly in terms of social connectedness, postretirement employment, and volunteerism. For their part, producers and retailers of electronic products are likely to see the older set as e-savvy consumers. Since 2008, they note, growth in computer and digital camera sales has been greatest in that market segment. And retirement homes have had to make room for residents who want to bowl or play tennis on Nintendo's Wii system (Bureau of Labor Statistics 2009; Cornwell et al. 2008; NPD Group 2008).

Interactionist Approach: Activity Theory

How important is it for older people to stay actively involved, whether at a job or in other pursuits? A tragic disaster in Chicago in 1995 showed that it can be a matter of life and death. An intense heat wave lasting more than a week—with a heat index exceeding 115 degrees on two consecutive days—resulted in 733 heat-related deaths. About three-fourths of the deceased were 65 and older. Subsequent analysis showed that older people who lived alone had the highest risk of dying, suggesting that support networks for the elderly literally help to save lives. Older Hispanics and Asian Americans had lower death rates from the heat wave than other racial and ethnic groups. Their stronger social networks probably resulted in more regular contact with family members and friends (Klinenberg 2002; Schaefer 1998).

Often seen as an opposing approach to disengagement theory, **activity theory** suggests that those elderly people who remain active and socially involved will be best adjusted. Proponents of this perspective acknowledge that a person age 70 may not have the ability or desire to perform various social roles that he or she had at age 40. Yet they contend that old people have essentially the same need for social interaction as any other group.

The improved health of older people—sometimes overlooked by social scientists—has strengthened the arguments of activity theorists. Illness and chronic disease are no longer quite the scourge of the elderly that they once were. The recent emphasis on fitness, the availability of better medical care, greater control of infectious diseases, and the reduction of fatal strokes and heart attacks have combined to mitigate the traumas of growing old. Accumulating medical research also points to the importance of remaining socially involved. Among those who decline in their mental capacities later in life, deterioration is most rapid in those who withdraw from social relationships and activities. Fortunately, older people are finding new ways to remain socially engaged, as evidenced by their increasing use of the Internet, especially to keep in touch with family and friends (Zedlewski and Butrica 2007).

Admittedly, many activities open to older adults involve unpaid labor, for which younger adults may receive salaries. Unpaid elderly workers include hospital volunteers (versus aides and orderlies), drivers for charities such as the Red Cross (versus chauffeurs), tutors (as opposed to teachers), and craftspeople

According to the interactionist activity theory, older people who remain active and socially involved will be best adjusted.

for charity bazaars (as opposed to carpenters and dressmakers). However, some companies have recently begun programs to hire retirees for full-time or part-time work.

Though disengagement theory suggested that older people find satisfaction in withdrawal from society, conveniently receding into the background and allowing the next generation to take over, proponents of activity theory view such withdrawal as harmful to both the elderly and society. Activity theorists focus on the potential contributions of older people to the maintenance of society. In their opinion, aging citizens will feel satisfied only when they can be useful and productive in society's terms—primarily by working for wages (Civic Ventures 2009; Dowd 1980; Quadagno 2008).

Labeling Theory

Just who are "the elderly"? Labeling theorists, who study the way reality is constructed through our culture and social interactions, have noted that recently, our society has begun to reconsider what makes a person old.

As early as 1975, social scientists were suggesting that old age should be defined not in terms of how old one is, but of how long one can be expected to live. As life expectancy lengthens, then, the age at which one is labeled old rises. Some have suggested that the threshold of old age should begin in the last 10 or 15 years of a person's expected life. Using that definition, old age would begin at about age 70 or 75, at least for those of us who live in the United States.

Is this new definition of old age likely to be accepted? From the labeling perspective, it all depends on who you are. Understandably, many people would prefer to be considered old later rather than sooner. Those who advocate for the elderly would prefer a broader definition. For example, the AARP (see pages 304–305) offers membership to anyone age 50 or older. They argue that people should begin planning for old age in their 50s, but clearly, encouraging the "young old" to join gives them strength in numbers.

The labeling of old age also differs from one culture to the next, due in part to differences in physical health and life

opportunities. In relatively prosperous cultures like the United States, 70 is the new 60. But in countries whose health and social support systems have been significantly weakened over the past 20 years—Russia, for example—50 is the new 60 (Sanderson and Scherbov 2008).

Conflict Approach

Conflict theorists have criticized both disengagement theorists and activity theorists for failing to consider the impact of social structure on aging patterns. Neither approach, they say, questions why social interaction must change or decrease in old age. In addition, they often ignore the impact of social class on the lives of elderly people.

The privileged upper class generally enjoys better health and vigor and less likelihood of dependency in old age. Affluence cannot forestall aging indefinitely, but it can soften the economic hardships people face in later years. Although pension plans, retirement packages, and insurance benefits may be developed to assist older people, those whose wealth allows them access to investment funds can generate the greatest income for their later years.

In contrast, the working class often faces greater health hazards and a greater risk of disability; aging is particularly difficult for those who suffer job-related injuries or illnesses. Working-class people also depend more heavily on Social Security benefits and private pension programs. During inflationary times, their relatively fixed incomes from these sources barely keep pace with the escalating costs of food, housing, utilities, and other necessities (Atchley and Barusch 2004).

According to the conflict approach, the treatment of older people in the United States reflects the many divisions in our society. The low status of older people is seen in prejudice and discrimination against them, in age segregation, and in unfair job practices—none of which are directly addressed by either disengagement or activity theory.

Conflict theorists have noted, too, that in the developing world, the transition from agricultural economies to industrialization and capitalism has not always been beneficial to the elderly. As a society's production methods change, the traditionally valued role of older people tends to erode. Their wisdom is no longer relevant in the new economy.

In sum, the four perspectives considered here take different views of the elderly. Functionalists portray older people as socially isolated, with reduced social roles; interactionists see them as involved in new networks and changing social roles. Labeling theorists see old age as a life stage that is defined by society. Conflict theorists see it as a time when people are victimized and their social roles devalued. Table 13-1 on page 298 summarizes these perspectives.

use your sociological *imagination*

Have you noticed signs of second-class treatment of older people ? If so, in what ways?

TABLE **13-1** SOCIOLOGICAL PERSPECTIVES
ON AGING

summing up

Sociological Perspective	View of Aging	Social Roles	Portrayal of Elderly
Functionalist	Disengagement	Reduced	Socially isolated
Interactionist	Activity	Changed	Involved in new networks
Labeling	Socially constructed	Changing	Varies by audience
Conflict	Competition	Relatively unchanged	Victimized, organized to confront their victimization

Aging Worldwide

Around the world more than 449 million people were age 65 or over in 2008. Together they constituted about 6.7 percent of the world's population. By 2045, more than twice that proportion, or 15.2 percent of the world's people, will be over 65. In an important sense, this trend toward the aging of the world's population represents a major success story, one that unfolded during the latter years of the 20th century. Through the efforts of national governments and international agencies, many societies have drastically reduced their incidence of disease, and with it their rate of death. As a result, these nations—particularly the industrialized countries of Europe and North America—have a high and steadily rising proportion of older members (Figure 13-1); (Haub 2008; Sanderson and Scherbov 2008).

Overall, Europe's population is older than that of any other continent. Though many European countries have long prided themselves on their generous pension programs, as the proportion of older people continues to rise, government officials have reluctantly begun to reduce pension benefits and raise the age at which workers can receive them. Japan, too, has a relatively old population; the Japanese enjoy a life expectancy of 82 years, compared to 78 in the United States. But though four more years of life may sound like a bonus, it presents a real and growing challenge to Japanese society (Box 13-1).

In most developing countries, people over 60 are likely to be in poorer health than their counterparts in industrialized nations. Yet few of those countries are in a position to offer extensive financial support to the elderly. Ironically, though the modernization of the developing world has brought many social and economic advances, it has undercut the traditionally

high status of the elderly. In many cultures, the earning power of younger adults now exceeds that of their older relatives (Haub 2006; He et al. 2005; Kinsella and Phillips 2005; Vidal 2004).

Role Transitions throughout the Life Course

As noted in Chapter 4 and throughout this textbook, socialization is a lifelong process. We simply do not experience things the same way at different points in the life course. For example, one study found that even falling in love differs according to where we are in the life course. Young unmarried adults tend to treat love as a noncommittal game or an obsession characterized by possessiveness and dependency. People over age 50 are much more likely to see love as involving commitment, and they tend to take a practical approach to finding a partner who meets a set of rational criteria. The life course, then, affects the manner in which we relate to one another (Montgomery and Sorell 1997).

How we move through the life course varies dramatically, depending on our personal preferences and circumstances. Some of us marry early, others late; some have children and some don't. These individual patterns are influenced by social factors such as class, race, and gender. Only in the most general terms, then, can we speak of stages or periods in the life course (M. Shanahan 2000).

One transitional stage, identified by psychologist Daniel Levinson, begins at the time at which an individual gradually enters the adult world, perhaps by moving out of the parental home, beginning a career, or entering a marriage. The second transitional period, the midlife transition, typically begins at about age 40. Men and women often experience a stressful period of self-evaluation, commonly known as the **midlife crisis,** in which they realize that they have not achieved basic goals and

FIGURE **13-1** WORLD'S "OLDEST" COUNTRIES VERSUS THE UNITED STATES, 2006

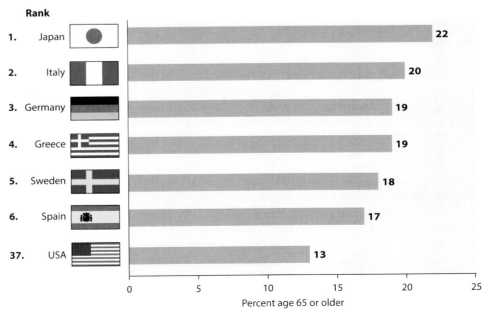

Source: Haub 2008.

SOCIOLOGY IN THE GLOBAL COMMUNITY

13-1 Aging, Japanese Style

An electric water kettle is wired so that people in another location can determine whether it has been used in the previous 24 hours. This arrangement may seem a zany use of modern technology, but it symbolizes a change that is taking place around the globe: the growing needs of an aging population. The Japanese Welfare Network Ikebukuro Honcho installed these wired hotpots so that volunteers can monitor whether the elderly have prepared morning tea. An unused pot initiates contacts to see whether that person needs help. This technological monitoring system indicates not just the tremendous growth in Japan's elderly population, but the increasing numbers of elderly people who live alone.

Indeed, Japan is struggling to confront the challenges posed by the world's most rapidly aging population. For generations, Japanese families have lived with and cared for their aging parents and grandparents. But this tradition of living under the same roof with one's elders is fading as more and more couples and even single adults strike out on their own. Hence the need for the wired hotpots. Compared to the United States and Canada, Japan is less well equipped to deal with this social phenomenon.

Assisted living, in-home services, and nursing homes are all much less common in Japan than they are in North America.

One challenge many aging couples face is the "retired-husband syndrome." In their working days, most older Japanese men labored long hours in workplaces where women traditionally did not hold supervisory positions. When these men retire and begin to stay home full-time, some of them tend to treat their wives as

An unused pot initiates contacts to see if the older person needs help.

subservient laborers. Moreover, many of them were so "married" to their jobs that they failed to develop hobbies or outside interests that might occupy them in retirement. Their wives, who have had free rein around the house all their lives, often find sharing the home with their dictatorial husbands a real challenge. Though Japanese gender roles are changing as record numbers of women enter positions of real responsibility, the senior generation is still hampered by yesterday's stereotypes.

The aging of Japan's workforce has forced government officials to reexamine the nation's policy toward immigrant workers (see Box 10-3, page 231). Although work opportunities dried up during the global economic downturn, the government does not want to lose this small group of immigrants, given Japan's looming labor shortage. So policymakers are devising programs that will allow immigrant workers to stay and will encourage their countrymen to join them when Japan's economy rebounds.

LET'S DISCUSS

1. What do you think caused the change in housing patterns that has resulted in so many elderly Japanese living alone? Could the change in housing patterns be related to the change in life expectancy? How?
2. How might living alone contribute to the retired-husband syndrome noted among aging Japanese couples?

Sources: Crump 2006; Faiola 2005, 2006; Hani 1998; Harden 2009; Haub 2008.

---

ambitions and have little time left to do so. Thus, Levinson (1978, 1996) found that most adults surveyed experienced tumultuous midlife conflicts within the self and with the external world.

Not all the challenges at this time of life come from career or one's partner. In the next section we will examine a special challenge faced by a growing number of middle-aged adults: caring for two generations at once.

The Sandwich Generation

During the late 1990s social scientists focused on the **sandwich generation**—adults who simultaneously try to meet the competing needs of their parents and their children. That is, caregiving goes in two directions: (1) to children, who even as young adults may still require significant direction, and (2) to aging parents, whose health and economic problems may demand intervention by their adult children.

Like the role of caring for children, the role of caring for aging parents falls disproportionately on women. Overall, women provide 60 percent of the care their parents receive, and even more as the demands of the role grow more intense and time consuming. Increasingly, middle-aged women and younger are finding themselves on the "daughter track," as their time and attention are diverted by the needs of their aging mothers and fathers (Gross 2005).

The last major transition identified by Levinson occurs after age 60—sometimes well after that age, given advances in health care, greater longevity, and gradual acceptance within society of older people. Nonetheless, there is a point at which people

transition to a different lifestyle. As we will see, this is a time of dramatic changes in people's everyday lives.

Adjusting to Retirement

Retirement is a rite of passage that marks a critical transition from one phase of a person's life to another. Typically, symbolic events are associated with this rite of passage, such as retirement gifts, a retirement party, and special moments on the last day on the job. The preretirement period itself can be emotionally charged, especially if the retiree is expected to train his or her successor (Atchley 1976).

From 1950 to the mid-1990s, the average age at retirement in the United States declined, but over the past few years it has reversed direction. In 2008, 5 percent of women and 10 percent of men over 75 were still working. A variety of factors explains this reversal: changes in Social Security benefits, an economic shift away from hard manual labor, and workers' concern with maintaining their health insurance and pension benefits. At the same time, longevity has increased, and the quality of people's health has improved (Bureau of Labor Statistics 2009).

Phases of Retirement. Gerontologist Robert Atchley (1976) has identified several phases of the retirement experience:

- *Preretirement,* a period of anticipatory socialization as the person prepares for retirement
- *The near phase,* when the person establishes a specific departure date from his or her job

A sandwich-generation mom cares for her bedridden parent as her older child feeds the younger one. Increasingly, members of the baby boom generation find themselves caring for two generations at once.

- *The honeymoon phase,* an often euphoric period in which the person pursues activities that he or she never had time for before
- *The disenchantment phase,* in which retirees feel a sense of letdown or even depression as they cope with their new lives, which may include illness or poverty
- *The reorientation phase,* which involves the development of a more realistic view of retirement alternatives
- *The stability phase,* a period in which the person has learned to deal with life after retirement in a reasonable and comfortable fashion
- *The termination phase,* which begins when the person can no longer engage in basic, day-to-day activities such as self-care and housework

Retirement is not a single transition, then, but rather a series of adjustments that varies from one person to another. The length and timing of each phase will differ for each individual, depending on such factors as financial status and health. A particular person will not necessarily go through all the phases identified by Atchley (Reitzes and Mutran 2006).

Some factors, such as being forced into retirement or being burdened with financial difficulties, can further complicate the retirement process. People who enter retirement involuntarily or without the necessary means may never experience the honeymoon phase. In the United States, many retirees continue in the paid labor force, often taking part-time jobs to supplement their pensions. Though most younger workers expect to retire before age 65, nearly three-fourths of older workers in the United States (those over age 50) anticipate that they will need to continue working after retirement (Figure 13-2).

Like other aspects of life in the United States, the experience of retirement varies according to gender, race, and ethnicity. White males are most likely to benefit from retirement wages, as well as to have participated in a formal retirement preparation program. As a result, anticipatory socialization for retirement is most systematic for White men. In contrast, members of racial and ethnic minority groups—especially African Americans—are more likely to exit the paid labor force through disability than through retirement. Because of their comparatively lower incomes and smaller savings, men and women from racial and ethnic minority groups work intermittently after retirement more often than older Whites (National Institute on Aging 1999; Quadagno 2008).

Naturally Occurring Retirement Communities (NORCs). With recent improvements in health care, older Americans have gained new choices in where to live. Today, rather than residing in nursing homes or planned retirement communities, many of them congregate in areas that have gradually become informal

"Have you given much thought to what kind of job you want after you retire?"

FIGURE 13-2 EXPECTED RETIREMENT AGE

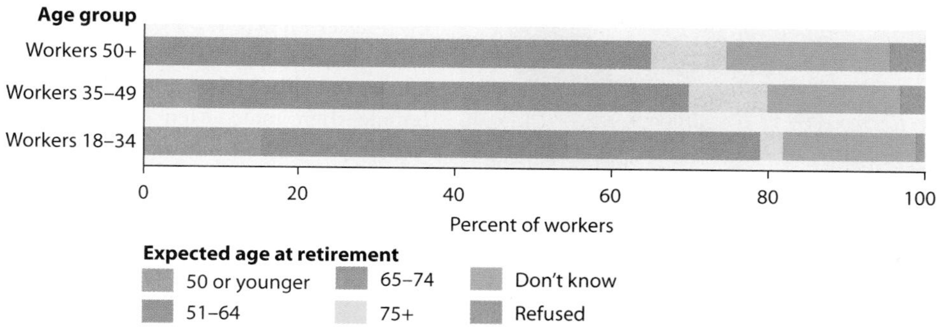

Age group

Workers 50+

Workers 35–49

Workers 18–34

0   20   40   60   80   100

Percent of workers

Expected age at retirement

- 50 or younger
- 51–64
- 65–74
- 75+
- Don't know
- Refused

Note: Survey of 1,053 workers 18 and over conducted in July 2006.
Source: S. K. Brown 2006.

Think about It

At what age do you expect to retire completely, without working for pay at all?

use your sociological *imagination*

How have people close to you, such as relatives, personally handled their retirement from the labor force?

centers for senior citizens. Social scientists have dubbed such areas **naturally occurring retirement communities (NORCs).**

Using observation research, census data, and interviews, sociologists have developed some interesting conclusions about NORCs. These communities can be as small as a single apartment building or as large as a neighborhood in a big city. Often, they emerge as singles and young couples move out and older people move in. Sometimes couples simply remain where they are; as they grow older, the community becomes noticeably grayer. In time, business establishments that cater to the elderly—pharmacies, medical supply outlets, small restaurants—relocate to NORCs, making them even more attractive to older citizens.

Unfortunately, residents of some of these communities are threatened by gentrification, or the takeover of low-income neighborhoods by higher-income residents. In Chicago, a high-rise building known as Ontario Place is converting to a condominium, at prices that current residents cannot afford. About half the building's occupants are Russian immigrants; most of the others are elderly or disabled people living on fixed incomes. These people are distressed not just because they will need to move, but because their community is being destroyed (A. Feuer 2002; Lansprey 1995; J. Perry 2001; Sheehan 2005).

Death and Dying

Among the role transitions that typically (but not always) come later in life is death. Until recently, death was viewed as a taboo topic in the United States. However, psychologist Elisabeth Kübler-Ross (1969), through her pioneering book *On Death and Dying,* greatly encouraged open discussion of the process of dying. Drawing on her work with 200 cancer patients, Kübler-Ross identified five stages of the experience: denial, anger, bargaining, depression, and finally acceptance.

Despite its popular appeal, the five-stage theory of dying has been challenged. Observers often cannot substantiate these stages. Moreover, research suggests that each person declines in his or her own way. Thus, one should not expect—much less counsel—a person to approach death in any particular way (R. Epstein 2005; Fitchett 1980).

Functionalists would see those who are dying as fulfilling distinct social functions. Gerontologist Richard Kalish (1985) lists among the tasks of the dying: completing unfinished business, such as settling insurance and legacy matters; restoring harmony to social relationships and saying farewell to friends and family; dealing with medical needs; and making funeral plans and other arrangements for survivors. In accomplishing these tasks, the dying person actively contributes to meeting society's need for smooth intergenerational transitions, role continuity, compliance with medical procedures, and minimal disruption of the social system, despite the loss of one of its members.

This functionalist analysis brings to mind the cherished yet controversial concept of a "good death." One researcher described a good death among the Kaliai, a people of the South Pacific. In that culture, the dying person calls together all his relatives, settles his debts, disposes of his possessions, and then announces that it is time for him to die (Counts 1977).

The Kaliai concept of a good death has a parallel in Western societies, where people may speak of a "natural death," an "appropriate death," or "death with dignity." The practice of **hospice care,** introduced in London, England, in 1967, is founded on this concept. Hospice workers seek to improve the quality of a dying person's last days by offering comfort and by helping the person to remain at home, or in a homelike setting at a hospital or other special facility, until the end. Currently there are more than 3,200 hospice programs serving over 960,000 people a year through federal programs such as Medicare and Medicaid alone (Hospice Association of America 2008).

Although the Western ideal of the good death makes the experience of dying as positive as possible, some critics fear that acceptance of the concept of a good death may direct both individual efforts and social resources

Coffins in Ghana sometimes reflect the way the dead lived their lives. This Methodist burial service honors a woman who died at age 85, leaving behind 11 children, 82 grandchildren, and 60 great-grandchildren. Her coffin, designed to resemble a mother hen, features 11 chicks nestling beneath the wings (Secretan 1995).

away from attempts to extend life. Still others argue that fatally ill older people should not just passively accept death, but should forgo further treatment in order to reduce public health care expenditures. Such issues are at the heart of current debates over the right to die and physician-assisted suicide.

Today, in many varied ways, people have broken through the historic taboos about death and are attempting to arrange certain aspects of the idealized good death. For example, bereavement practices—once highly structured—are becoming increasingly varied and therapeutic. More and more people are actively addressing the inevitability of death by making wills, leaving "living wills" (health care proxies that explain their feelings about the use of life-support equipment), donating organs, and providing instructions for family members about funerals, cremations, and burials. Given medical and technological advances and a breakthrough in open discussion and negotiation regarding death and dying, it is possible that good deaths may become a social norm in the United States.

Age Stratification in the United States

The "Graying of America"

When Lenore Schaefer, a ballroom dancer, tried to get on the *Tonight Show,* she was told she was "too young": she was in her early 90s. When she turned 101, she made it. But even at that age, Lenore is no longer unusual in our society. Today, people over 100 constitute, proportionately, the country's fastest-growing age group. They are part of the increasing proportion of the population of the United States that is composed of older people (Himes 2001; Rimer 1998).

As Figure 13.3 shows, in the future, an increasing proportion of the U.S. population will be composed of older people. This trend is expected to continue well into the 21st century, as the mortality rate declines and members of the postwar baby boom age. At the same time, the "oldest old"—that is, the segment of

the population representing those who are age 85 or older—will grow at an even faster rate.

Compared with the rest of the population, the elderly are more likely to be female than male. Men tend to have higher death rates than women at every age. By old age, women outnumber men by a ratio of 3 to 2. The gap widens with advancing age, so that among the oldest old, the ratio is 5 to 2.

The elderly are also more likely than others to be White: about 80 percent of the elderly are White and non-Hispanic. Although this segment of the population is becoming more racially and ethnically diverse, the higher death rates of racial and ethnic minorities, together with the continuing immigration of younger Latinos and Asians, is likely to keep it more White than the nation as a whole. Yet the overall pattern of an increasingly diversified population will show up among older Americans. As the projections in Figure 13.4 show, as the 21st century advances, non-Whites and Latinos will make up an increasing proportion of those who are 65 and over.

Finally, the elderly are more likely than the rest of the population to live in certain states. The highest proportions of older people are found in Florida, Pennsylvania, Rhode Island, Iowa, West Virginia, and Arkansas. However, that will soon change. In 2000, Florida was the state most populated by the elderly, with 17.6 percent of the population over age 65. Yet as Figure 13-5 shows, in about another 25 years, more than half the states will have an even greater proportion of elderly people than Florida does now.

The graying of the United States is a phenomenon that can no longer be ignored, either by social scientists or by government

FIGURE **13-3** ACTUAL AND PROJECTED GROWTH OF THE ELDERLY POPULATION OF THE UNITED STATES, 1980–2050

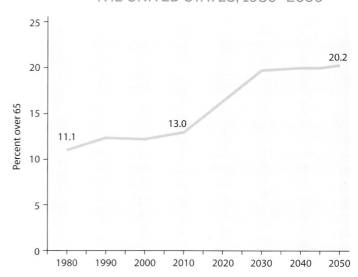

Sources: Bureau of the Census 2008a:10, 2008b; J. Meyer 2001; Sutch and Carter 2006.

policymakers. Advocates for the elderly have spoken out on a wide range of issues. Politicians court the votes of older people, since they are the age group most likely to register and vote. In fact, in the 2008 presidential election, despite the upsurge in the youth vote, people over 60 made up 23 percent of those who voted, compared to 18 percent for those under 30 (Connelly 2008).

Wealth and Income

There is significant variation in wealth and poverty among the nation's older people. Some individuals and couples find themselves poor in part because of fixed pensions and skyrocketing health care costs (see Chapter 19). Nevertheless, as a group, older people in the United States are neither homogeneous nor poor. The typical elderly person enjoys a standard of living that is much higher now than at any point in the nation's past. Class differences among the elderly remain evident, but tend to narrow somewhat: those older people who enjoyed middle-class incomes while younger tend to remain better off after retirement, but less so than before (Denise Smith and Tillipman 2000).

To some extent, older people owe their overall improved standard of living to a greater accumulation of wealth—in the form of home ownership, private pensions, and other financial assets. But much of the improvement is due to more generous Social Security benefits. While modest when compared with other countries' pension programs, Social Security nevertheless provides 39 percent of all income received by older people in the United States. Still, about 10 percent of the nation's elderly population lives below the poverty line. At the extremes of poverty are those groups who were more likely to be poor at earlier points in the life cycle: female-headed households and racial and ethnic minorities (He et al. 2005).

Viewed from a conflict perspective, it is not surprising that older women experience a double burden; the same is true of elderly members of racial and ethnic minorities. For example, in 2005 the proportion of older Latinos with incomes below the poverty level (17.1 percent) was more than twice as large as the proportion of older White non-Hispanics (7.4 percent). Moreover, 23.2 percent of older African Americans fell below the federal government's poverty line (Butrica 2008; DeNavas-Walt et al. 2008:53–57).

Ageism

Physician Robert Butler (1990) became concerned 30 years ago when he learned that a housing development near his home in metropolitan Washington, D.C., barred the elderly. Butler coined the term **ageism** to refer to prejudice and discrimination based on a person's age. For example, we may choose to assume that someone cannot handle a rigorous job because he is "too old," or we may refuse to give someone a job with authority because she is "too young."

Ageism is especially difficult for the old, because at least youthful recipients of prejudice know that in time they will be "old enough." For many, old age symbolizes disease. With ageism all too common in the United States, it is hardly surprising that older people are barely visible on television. In 2002, the Senate Special Committee on Aging convened a panel on the media's portrayal of older people and sharply criticized media and marketing executives for bombarding audiences with negative images of the aged. The social consequences of such images are significant. Research shows that older people who have positive perceptions of aging live an average of 7.5 years

FIGURE **13-4** MINORITY POPULATION AGE 65 AND OLDER, PROJECTED

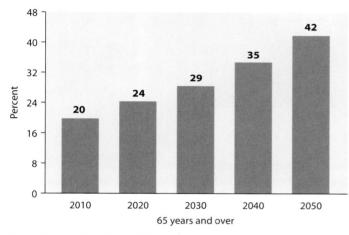

65 years and over

Source: Bureau of the Census 2008b.

FIGURE **13-5** TWENTY-EIGHT FLORIDAS BY 2030

MAPPING LIFE NATIONWIDE

States where at least 20 percent of the population will be over age 65

Source: Bureau of the Census 2005a.

longer than those who have negative perceptions (M. Gardner 2003; Levy et al. 2002; Ramirez 2002).

www.mhhe.com/schaefer12e

---

use your sociological *imagination*

It is September and you are channel-surfing through the new fall TV series. How likely are you to watch a television show that is based on older characters who spend a lot of time together?

Competition in the Labor Force

Participation in paid work is not typical after age 65. In 2008, 36 percent of men ages 65 to 69 and 26 percent of women participated in the paid labor force. That year, because of an economic downturn that threatened pension programs, some older workers postponed their retirement. Their decision further eroded job opportunities for younger workers, already handicapped by the highest unemployment rates in a generation. Unfortunately, some people view older workers as "job stealers"—a biased judgment similar to that directed against illegal immigrants—instead of as experienced contributors to the labor force. Moreover, unemployed workers in their 50s find that potential employers rarely give them serious consideration. These difficulties not only intensify age conflict but lead to age discrimination (Bureau of Labor Statistics 2009; S. Greenhouse 2009a; Luo 2009).

The federal Age Discrimination in Employment Act (ADEA), which went into effect in 1968, was passed to protect workers who are age 40 or older from being fired because of their age and replaced with younger workers, who would presumably receive lower salaries. The Supreme Court strengthened federal protection against age discrimination in 1996, ruling unanimously that such lawsuits can be successful even if an older worker is replaced by someone who is older than 40. Consequently, firing a 65-year-old employee to make way for a 45-year-old can be construed as age discrimination.

The courts have made some significant decisions in favor of older workers. In *Meachan v. Knolls Atomic Power Laboratory* (2008), the Supreme Court ruled 7–1 that, under ADEA, employers must prove that the layoff of an older worker is based, not on age, but on "some reasonable factor." The employer in that case maintained that older workers were less "flexible" or "retrainable," but failed to present any convincing evidence for the layoffs, which affected 31 employees—30 of whom were old enough to be covered by the ADEA (L. Greenhouse 2008).

While firing people simply because they are old violates federal law, courts have upheld the right to lay off older

The AARP is a major voice for the elderly. By featuring actor-comedian Robin Williams (born in 1953) on the cover of its widely distributed magazine, the organization is signaling a desire to represent the younger members of the older generation, as well as to portray the active lives many older people lead.

workers for economic reasons. Critics contend that later, the same firms hire young, cheaper workers to replace experienced older workers. When economic growth began to slow in 2008 and companies cut back on their workforces, complaints of age bias grew sharply as older workers began to suspect they were bearing a disproportionate share of the layoffs (R. Johnson 2008).

Given recent legislative and legal advances, has the climate changed significantly for older workers? Box 13-2 presents several studies that have attempted to assess the extent of ageism, both in everyday life and in hiring.

The Elderly: Emergence of a Collective Consciousness

During the 1960s, students at colleges and universities across the country, advocating "student power," collectively demanded a role in the governance of educational institutions. In the following decade, many older people became aware that *they* were being treated as second-class citizens and turned to collective action. The largest organization representing the nation's elderly is the AARP, founded in 1958 by a retired school principal who was having difficulty getting insurance because of age

RESEARCH TODAY

13-2 Elderspeak and Other Signs of Ageism

"Who did you used to be?" This comment reveals an unflattering assumption about what happens to people when they grow old. Unfortunately, such remarks are far too frequent. In fact, condescending language is so often directed at elderly people that gerontologists have come to call it *elderspeak*.

According to scholars who have done observation research in nursing homes and retirement facilities, staff in these institutions tend to relate to the elderly residents in a manner befitting infants, calling them "dear," "good girl," and "sweetie." Medical professionals may patronize elderly patients, asking "Did you understand what I said?" or cajole them with "You don't want to upset your family, do you?" Pharmacists, without being asked, will sometimes give older customers a special container intended to help them manage their dosing regimens. Although the people who take these actions and make these remarks do not regard them as derogatory, older people find the unintended insults demoralizing.

Many older people experience ageism long before they retire. They may find that past a certain age, they will not be hired or even interviewed for a job. Yet research has shown that older workers can be an asset to employers. According to a 1991 study, older workers can be retrained in new technologies, have lower rates of absenteeism than younger employees, and are often more effective salespeople. This study was done at two corporations based in the United States—the hotel chain Days Inns of America and the holding company Travelers Corporation of Hartford, both of which have long-term experience in hiring people over age 50—as well as at a British retail chain. In response to such findings, some U.S. corporations, including Borders and Home Depot, are actively recruiting retired people.

Yet many older people still have difficulty finding work, often as the result of ageism. Economist Johanna Lahey sent similar resumes for fictitious women of different ages to employers in Boston and St. Petersburg, Florida. The results were striking. In Boston, a younger worker was 42 percent more likely than an older worker to be offered an interview for an entry-level job, such as a clerical position. In St. Petersburg, the difference was 46 percent.

To determine why the older applicants had more difficulty getting an interview, Lahey tried making them look more desirable.

About 30 percent of older workers choose to remain on the job past the usual retirement age. Research shows they can be retrained in new technologies and are more dependable than younger workers.

Many older people experience ageism long before they retire. They may find that past a certain age, they will not be hired or even interviewed for a job.

To prevent a 62-year-old applicant from being seen as inflexible, undependable, out of touch, or an insurance risk, she added one of the following to the person's application:

- Statement of willingness to embrace change
- Attendance award
- Certificate of completion of a recent computer course
- Indication of health insurance coverage

However, these "extras" had no effect on the call-back rate.

This study mirrored the results of one done two decades earlier, which showed that younger applicants are significantly more welcome in the job market than older applicants. Although further research might be done, the pattern seems clear: ageism is entrenched in our society.

LET'S DISCUSS

1. Have you ever worked alongside an older person? If so, did that person's age affect the way he or she did the job? In what ways?
2. Are older people the only ones who experience ageism? What signs of ageism might those who are not old experience?

Sources: Bendick et al. 1993; Freudenheim 2005; Lahey 2006; Leland 2008; Lohr 2008; Telsch 1991; K. Williams et al. 2009.

---

prejudice. Many of the AARP's services involve discounts and insurance for its 37 million members (43 percent of Americans age 50 or older), but the organization is also a powerful lobbying group. Recognizing that many elderly people are still gainfully employed, it has dropped its full name, American Association of *Retired* Persons (Donnelly 2007).

The potential power of the AARP is enormous. It is the third-largest voluntary association in the United States (behind only the Roman Catholic Church and the American Automobile Association), representing one out of every four registered voters in the United States. The AARP has endorsed voter registration campaigns, nursing home reforms, and pension reforms. In acknowledgment of its difficulties recruiting members of racial and ethnic minority groups, the AARP recently began a Minority Affairs Initiative. The spokeswoman for the initiative, Margaret

Dixon, became the AARP's first African American president in 1996 (Birnbaum 2005).

People grow old in many different ways. Not all elderly people face the same challenges or enjoy the same resources. While the AARP lobbies to protect the elderly in general, other groups work in more specific ways. For example, the National Committee to Preserve Social Security and Medicare, founded in 1982, successfully lobbied Congress to keep Medicare benefits for the ailing poor elderly. Other large special interest groups represent retired federal employees, retired teachers, and retired union workers (Quadagno 2008).

Still another manifestation of the new awareness of older people is the formation of organizations for elderly homosexuals. One such group, Senior Action in a Gay Environment (SAGE), was established in New York City in 1977 and now oversees a nationwide network of community groups, as well as affiliates in Canada and Germany. Like more traditional senior citizens' groups, SAGE sponsors workshops, classes, dances, and food deliveries to the homebound. At the same time, the group must deal with special concerns, such as informing gay people of their rights, supporting gay people with Alzheimer's, and advocating for gays who face eviction (Senior Action in a Gay Environment 2009).

The elderly in the United States are better off today both financially and physically than ever before. Many of them have strong financial assets and medical care packages that will meet almost any health need. But as we have seen, a significant segment is impoverished, faced with the prospect of declining health and mounting medical bills. And some older people must now add being aged to a lifetime of disadvantage. Like people in all other stages of the life course, the aged constitute a diverse group in the United States and around the world.

social**policy** and Age Stratification

The Right to Die Worldwide

The Issue

On August 4, 1993, Dr. Jack Kevorkian, a retired pathologist, helped a 30-year-old Michigan man with Lou Gehrig's disease to commit suicide in a van. The patient died after inhaling carbon monoxide through a mask designed by Dr. Kevorkian; in doing so, he became the 17th person to commit suicide with Kevorkian's assistance. Kevorkian was openly challenging a Michigan law (aimed at him) that makes it a felony—punishable by up to four years in jail—to assist in a suicide. Since then Kevorkian has assisted in numerous other suicides, but not until he did it on television in 1998 did the charges brought against him result in his imprisonment for second-degree murder. Kevorkian completed his sentence in 2007.

The issue of physician-assisted suicide is but one aspect of the larger debate in the United States and other countries over the ethics of suicide and euthanasia. The term **euthanasia** has been defined as the "act of bringing about the death of a hopelessly ill and suffering person in a relatively quick and painless way for reasons of mercy" (Council on Ethical and Judicial Affairs, American Medical Association 1992:229). This type of mercy killing reminds us of the ideal of the "good death" discussed earlier in the chapter. The debate over euthanasia and assisted suicide often focuses on cases involving older people, although it can involve younger adults with terminal and degenerative diseases, or even children.

National surveys show that public opinion on this controversial practice is divided. In 2007, 71 percent of respondents said that a physician should be legally permitted to end a patient's life if both the patient and the patient's family make such a request. However, an earlier survey found that only half of respondents could even imagine a situation in which they themselves would request physician-assisted suicide (J. Carroll 2007b; Jost 2005).

The Setting

Many societies are known to have practiced *senilicide*—"killing of the aged"—because of extreme difficulties in providing basic necessities such as food and shelter. In a study of the treatment of elderly people in 41 nonindustrialized societies, Anthony Glascock (1990) found some form of "death-hastening" behavior in 21 of them. Killing of elderly people was evident in 14 of the societies; abandoning them was evident in 8. Typically, death hastening occurs when older people become decrepit and are viewed as already dead. In these nonindustrialized cultures it is open and socially approved. Family members generally make the decisions, often after open consultation with those who are about to die.

Currently, public policy in the United States does not permit *active euthanasia* (such as a deliberate injection of lethal drugs into a terminally ill patient) or physician-assisted suicide. Although suicide itself is no longer a crime, assisting suicide is illegal in at least 29 states. There is greater legal tolerance for *passive euthanasia* (such as disconnecting life-support equipment from a comatose patient).

Sociological Insights

Although formal norms concerning euthanasia may be in flux, informal norms seem to permit mercy killings. According to an estimate by the American Hospital Association, as many as 70 percent of all deaths in the United States are quietly negotiated, with patients, family members, and physicians agreeing not to use life-support technology. In an informal poll of internists, one in five reported that he or she had assisted or helped cause the death of a patient. In a period in which AIDS-related deaths are common,

Dr. Jack Kevorkian with the apparatus that administered a lethal injection to those who wanted assistance in committing suicide.

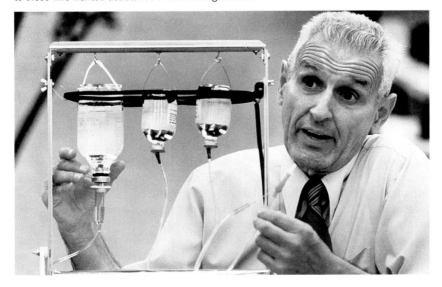

an AIDS underground is known to share information and assistance regarding suicide (N. Gibbs 1993; Martinez 1993).

Conflict theorists ask questions about the values raised by such decisions. By endorsing physician-assisted suicide, are we devaluing the disabled through an acceptance of their premature death? Critics note that we are all only temporarily able-bodied; disease or a speeding automobile can place any one of us among the disabled. By establishing a precedent for ending the lives of selected disabled people, we may unwittingly contribute to negative social views and labeling of all disabled people. Further reflecting the conflict perspective, gerontologist Elizabeth Markson (1992:6) argues that the "powerless, poor or undesirable are at special risk of being 'encouraged' to choose assisted death."

Despite these concerns, research to date shows little bias. In studies of physician-assisted suicide in Oregon and the Netherlands, researchers looked at how implementation of the controversial policy might affect people who were vulnerable because of their disability, age, mental health, or race and ethnicity. People with AIDS proved to be the only vulnerable group with a heightened use of physician-assisted suicide. Overall, those people who died with a doctor's help were more likely to be socially, economically, and educationally privileged than to be particularly vulnerable (Battin et al. 2007).

Policy Initiatives

In the industrialized world, euthanasia is legal and widely accepted in only three countries: the Netherlands, where about 3,800 such procedures are carried out legally each year; Belgium, which records about 350 procedures a year; and Switzerland, which records 200 a year. Unlike the Netherlands and Belgium, Switzerland allows foreigners to be euthanized; about 55 foreign nationals are euthanized there every year. While physician-assisted suicide is accepted by the public in all three countries, the "suicide tourism" that occurs in Switzerland is controversial (*The Economist* 2005a).

In the United States, the only state to allow assisted suicide is Oregon, where the Death with Dignity Act became law in 1997. In 2008, 60 terminally ill Oregonians took their lives with the assistance of a physician; about 30 obtained the necessary authorizations but chose not to end their lives. Similar measures have failed to win support in at least 20 other states, where the issue has encountered sharp opposition. President George W. Bush's administration made an unsuccessful attempt to stop the prescription of lethal drugs to terminally ill patients in Oregon. In 2006 the Supreme Court ruled 6 to 3 that the federal government had overstepped its authority in punishing doctors in Oregon who had helped terminally ill patients to end their lives. Two years later, voters in Washington State passed a law similar to Oregon's, which took effect in 2009. Some local courts and state legislatures are also moving to legalize the practice, despite strong opposition (Fausset 2009; Yardley 2009).

Advances in technology now allow us to prolong life in ways that were unimaginable decades ago. But should people be forced or expected to prolong lives that are unbearably painful, or that are in effect "lifeless"? Unfortunately, medical and technological advances cannot provide answers to these complex ethical, legal, and political questions.

Let's Discuss

1. Why do you think "death-hastening" behavior is common in nonindustrialized countries?

2. In what ways are conflict theory and disengagement theory relevant to the debate over the "right to die"?

3. Do you think someone should be allowed to choose to die? Why or why not?

getting**involved**

To get involved in the debate over the right to die, visit this text's Online Learning Center, which offers links to relevant Web sites.

www.mhhe.com/schaefer12e

MASTERING THIS CHAPTER

Summary

Age, like gender and race, is an ascribed status that forms the basis for social differentiation. This chapter examines sociological perspectives on aging, role transitions in the life course, age stratification in the United States, the growing political activism of the nation's elderly population, and the controversy surrounding the right to die.

1. Like other forms of stratification, age stratification varies from culture to culture.

2. In the United States, being old is a master status that seems to overshadow all others.

3. The particular problems of the aged have become the focus for a specialized area of research and inquiry known as **gerontology.**

4. **Disengagement theory** implicitly suggests that society should help older people to withdraw from their accustomed social roles.

In contrast, **activity theory** suggests that the elderly person who remains active and socially involved will be better adjusted.

5. Labeling theorists note that people of the same age are labeled differently in different societies, based largely on differences in physical health, life opportunities, and life expectancy in those societies.

6. From a conflict perspective, the low status of older people is reflected in prejudice and discrimination against them and in unfair job practices.

7. About 40 percent of those who look after their elderly relatives still have children to care for; these people have been dubbed the **sandwich generation.**

8. As we age, we go through role transitions, including adjustment to retirement and preparation for death.

307

9. An increasing proportion of the population of the United States is composed of older people.

10. **Ageism** reflects a deep uneasiness about growing old on the part of younger people.

11. The AARP is a powerful lobbying group that backs legislation to benefit senior citizens.

12. The "right to die" often entails physician-assisted suicide, a controversial issue worldwide.

Critical Thinking Questions

1. Are there elderly students at your college or university? If so, how are they treated by younger students and by faculty members? Is there a subculture of older students? How do younger students view faculty members in their 50s and 60s?

2. Is age segregation functional or dysfunctional for older people in the United States? Is it functional or dysfunctional for society as a whole? What are the manifest functions, the latent functions, and the dysfunctions of age segregation?

3. If you were hired to run a senior center where you live, how would you use what you have learned in this chapter to better the lives of your community's seniors?

Key Terms

Activity theory An interactionist theory of aging that suggests that those elderly people who remain active and socially involved will be best adjusted. (page 296)

Ageism Prejudice and discrimination based on a person's age. (303)

Disengagement theory A functionalist theory of aging that suggests that society and the aging individual mutually sever many of their relationships. (296)

Euthanasia The act of bringing about the death of a hopelessly ill and suffering person in a relatively quick and painless way for reasons of mercy. (306)

Gerontology The scientific study of the sociological and psychological aspects of aging and the problems of the aged. (295)

Hospice care Treatment of the terminally ill in their own homes, or in special hospital units or other facilities, with the goal of helping them to die easily, without pain. (301)

Midlife crisis A stressful period of self-evaluation that begins at about age 40. (298)

Naturally occurring retirement community (NORC) An area that has gradually become an informal center for senior citizens. (301)

Sandwich generation The generation of adults who simultaneously try to meet the competing needs of their parents and their children. (299)

Self-Quiz

Read each question carefully and then select the best answer.

1. Activity theory is associated with the
   a. functionalist perspective.
   b. conflict perspective.
   c. interactionist perspective.
   d. labeling perspective.

2. What is the one crucial difference between older people and other subordinate groups, such as racial and ethnic minorities or women?
   a. Older people do not experience unequal treatment in employment.
   b. Older people have a strong sense of group solidarity and other groups do not.
   c. All of us who live long enough will eventually assume the ascribed status of being an older person.
   d. Older people are generally married to others of comparable age and other minorities do not marry within their group.

3. Which field of study was originally developed in the 1930s as an increasing number of social scientists became aware of the plight of the elderly?
   a. sociology
   b. gerontology
   c. gerontocracy
   d. senilicide

4. Which sociological perspective is most likely to emphasize the important role of social networks in providing life satisfaction for elderly people?
   a. functionalist perspective
   b. conflict perspective
   c. interactionist perspective
   d. labeling theory

5. Elaine Cumming and William Henry introduced an explanation of the impact of aging known as
   a. disengagement theory.
   b. activity theory.

   c. labeling theory.
   d. the contact hypothesis.

6. According to psychologist Elisabeth Kübler-Ross, the first stage of the experience of dying that a person may undergo is
   a. denial.
   b. anger.
   c. depression.
   d. bargaining.

7. Which of the following statements about the elderly is correct?
   a. Being old is a master status.
   b. Once people are labeled as "old," the designation has a major impact on how others perceive them, and even on how they view themselves.
   c. Negative stereotypes of the elderly contribute to their position as a minority group subject to discrimination.
   d. all of the above

8. The text points out that the model of five basic properties of a minority or subordinate group can be applied to older people in the United States. Which of the following is *not* one of those basic properties?
   a. Older people experience unequal treatment in employment and may face prejudice and discrimination.
   b. Statistically, the elderly represent a majority.
   c. Membership in this group is involuntary.
   d. Older people have a strong sense of group solidarity.

9. Which of the following theories argues that elderly people have essentially the same need for social interaction as any other group and that those who remain active and socially involved will be best adjusted?
   a. conflict theory
   b. functionalist theory

    c. activity theory
    d. disengagement theory

10. According to your text, which of the following statements is true?
    a. Functionalists portray the elderly as being socially isolated, with reduced social roles.

    b. Interactionists see older people as being involved in new networks of people and in changing social roles.
    c. Conflict theorists regard older people as being victimized by social structure, with their social roles relatively unchanged but devalued.
    d. all of the above

11. The elderly are _____ regarded in the traditional Sherpa (Tibet) culture.

12. In keeping with the _____ perspective of sociology, disengagement theory emphasizes that a society's stability is ensured when social roles are passed on from one generation to another.

13. The final phase of retirement, according to Robert Atchley, is the _____, which begins when the person can no longer engage in basic, day-to-day activities such as self-care and housework.

14. _____ theorists argue that both the disengagement and the activity perspectives often ignore the impact of social class in the lives of elderly people.

15. The fastest-growing age group in the United States is people over age _____.

16. _____ is the scientific study of the sociological and psychological aspects of aging and the problems of the aged. It originated in the 1930s as an increasing number of social scientists became aware of the plight of elderly people.

17. Based on a study of elderly people in good health and relatively comfortable economic circumstances, _____ theory suggests that society and the aging individual mutually sever many of their relationships.

18. During the late 1990s, social scientists focused on the _____ _____—adults who simultaneously try to meet the competing needs of their parents and their children.

19. In 2000, _____ was the state most populated by the elderly, with 17.6 percent of the population over age 65.

20. Physician Robert Butler coined the term _____ to refer to prejudice and discrimination based on a person's age.

THINKING ABOUT MOVIES

Quinceañera (Richard Glatzer and Wash Westmoreland, 2006)

Magdalena (Emily Rios) is excited about her *quinceañera,* a 15th-birthday celebration that is for many Latinas a rite of passage into adulthood. While her family fights over the party arrangements, Magdalena becomes pregnant by her boyfriend and must cope with adult issues sooner than expected. Her parents treat her harshly when they hear the news, forcing her to take refuge with her uncle Tomas. There she meets a young cousin who is experimenting with his sexuality. Magdalena begins to rethink her values and her definition of family.

From a sociological point of view, *Quinceañera* shows a young girl going through a difficult stage of the life course. As Magdalena struggles to manage multiple social roles, we see her rebel against her nuclear family, one agent of socialization, and turn instead to her extended family, where she is exposed to different cultural influences from the ones she was raised with.

For Your Consideration

1. What is the social significance of the *quinceañera,* and what is the celebration meant to accomplish for a young girl?

2. How would you describe Magdalena's resocialization after she goes to live with her uncle?

Gran Torino (Clint Eastwood, 2008)

Walt Kowalski (Clint Eastwood), a retired auto worker who sneers at his immigrant neighbors, lives in a changing part of Detroit. Walt severed most of his ties with his family after his wife's death; now he lives out his days drinking beer and biding his time. But when gang violence strikes the neighborhood, bringing Walt together with the extended family of Hmong immigrants next door, he comes out of his shell and befriends the teenage son, Thao Vang Lor (Bee Vang). Under the specter of continued gang violence, Thao and Walt learn from each other.

Gran Torino is valuable for its sociological perspective on aging. Walt's disengagement from society after his wife's death illustrates the functionalist approach to aging. When he reestablishes connections with his Hmong neighbors, we see aging from the interactionist perspective.

For Your Consideration

1. From the perspective of activity theory, how would you evaluate Walt's social needs? How are those needs met by Thao's family?

2. Which sociological approach do you find most useful in understanding Walt's social status, and why?

inside

Global View of the Family

Sociological Perspectives on the Family

Marriage and Family

Divorce

Diverse Lifestyles

Social Policy and the Family: Gay Marriage

BOXES

Sociology in the Global Community: *One Wife, Many Husbands: The Nyinba*

Research Today: *Arranged Marriage, American-Style*

Research Today: *Divorce and Military Deployment*

Marriage is a cultural universal. This couple is about to be married at a Shinto shrine in Tokyo.

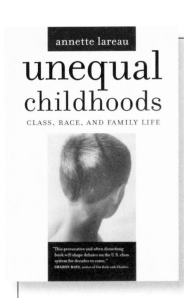

" A Black fourth-grader, Alexander Williams, is riding home from a school open house. His mother is driving their beige, leather-upholstered Lexus. It is 9:00 p.m. on a Wednesday evening. Ms. Williams is tired from work and has a long Thursday ahead of her. She will get up at 4:45 a.m. to go out of town on business and will not return before 9:00 p.m. On Saturday morning, she will chauffeur Alexander to a private piano lesson at 8:15 a.m., which will be followed by a choir rehearsal and then a soccer game. As they ride in the dark, Alexander's mother, in a quiet voice, talks with her son, asking him questions and eliciting his opinions.

Discussions between parents and children are a hallmark of middle-class child rearing. Like many middle-class parents, Ms. Williams and her husband see themselves as "developing" Alexander to cultivate his talents in a concerted fashion. Organized activities, established and controlled by mothers and fathers, dominate the lives of middle-class children. . . . By making certain their children have these and other experiences, middle-class parents engage in a process of *concerted cultivation*. From this, a robust sense of entitlement takes root in the children. . . .

Only twenty minutes away, in blue-collar neighborhoods, and slightly farther away, in public housing projects, childhood looks different.

Like many middle-class parents, Ms. Williams and her husband see themselves as "developing" Alexander to cultivate his talents in a concerted fashion. Organized activities, established and controlled by mothers and fathers, dominate the lives of middle-class children. . . .

Mr. Yanelli, a white working-class father, picks up his son Little Billy, a fourth-grader, from an after-school program. They come home and Mr. Yanelli drinks a beer while Little Billy first watches television, then rides his bike and plays in the street. Other nights, he and his Dad sit on the sidewalk outside their house and play cards. . . . Many nights Little Billy's uncle stops by, sometimes bringing Little Billy's youngest cousin. In the spring, Little Billy plays baseball on a local team. For Little Billy, baseball is his only organized activity outside of school during the entire year. . . .

Farther away, a Black fourth-grade boy, Harold McAllister, plays outside on a summer evening in the public housing project in which he lives. His two male cousins are there that night, as they often are. After an afternoon spent unsuccessfully searching for a ball so they could play basketball, the boys had resorted to watching sports on television. Now they head outdoors for a twilight water balloon fight. Harold tries to get his neighbor, Miss Latifa, wet. People sit in white plastic lawn chairs outside the row of apartments. Music and television sounds waft through the open windows and doors.

The adults in the lives of Billy . . . and Harold want the best for them. Formidable economic constraints make it a major life task for these parents to put food on the table, arrange for housing, negotiate unsafe neighborhoods, take children to the doctor (often waiting for city buses that do not come), clean children's clothes, and get children to bed and have them ready for school the next morning. But unlike middle-class parents, these adults do not consider the concerted development of children, particularly through organized leisure activities, an essential aspect of good parenting. "

(Lareau 2003:1–3) Additional information about this excerpt can be found on the Online Learning Center at www.mhhe.com/schaefer12e.

In this excerpt from *Unequal Childhoods: Class, Race, and Family Life,* Annette Lareau vividly illustrates how different types of stratification—class, race, gender, and age—define family life, molding the social relationships that develop among household members. Lareau, a sociologist who teaches at Temple University, based her book on the observation research she did in schools and homes. She also interviewed families from different social class backgrounds, both White and African American. Among these varied families, she found markedly different approaches to parenting—approaches, Lareau believes, that have much to do with their children's futures.

Just as stratification affects family life, so does the period in which a family lives. The family of today is not what it was a century ago, or even a generation ago. New roles, new gender distinctions, new child-rearing patterns have all combined to create new forms of family life. Today, for example, more and more women are taking the breadwinner's role, whether married or as a single parent. Blended families—the result of divorce and remarriage—are almost the norm. And many people are seeking intimate relationships without being married, whether in gay partnerships or in cohabiting arrangements.

This chapter addresses family and intimate relationships in the United States as well as other parts of the world. As we will see, family patterns differ from one culture to another and even within the same culture. Despite the differences, however, the family is universal—found in every culture. A **family** can be defined as a set of people related by blood, marriage or some other agreed-on relationship, or adoption, who share the primary responsibility for reproduction and caring for members of society.

What are families in different parts of the world like? How do people select their mates? When a marriage fails, how does the divorce affect the children? What are the alternatives to the nuclear family, and how prevalent are they? In this chapter we will look at the family and intimate relationships from the functionalist, conflict, interactionist, and feminist points of view. We'll examine variations in marital patterns and family life, including child rearing, paying particular attention to the increasing numbers of people in dual-income and single-parent families. We'll examine divorce in the United States and consider diverse lifestyles such as cohabitation, lesbian and gay relationships, and marriage without children. In the Social Policy section we will confront the controversial issue of gay marriage.

Global View of the Family

Among Tibetans, a woman may be married simultaneously to more than one man, usually brothers. This system allows sons to share the limited amount of good land. Among the Betsileo of Madagascar, a man has multiple wives, each one living in a different village where he cultivates rice. Wherever he has the best rice field, that wife is considered his first or senior wife. Among the Yanomami of Brazil and Venezuela, it is considered proper to have sexual relations with your opposite-sex cousins if they are the children of your mother's brother or your father's sister. But if your opposite-sex cousins are the children of your mother's sister or your father's brother, the same practice is considered to be incest (Haviland et al. 2008; Kottak 2009).

As these examples illustrate, there are many variations in the family from culture to culture. Yet the family as a social institution exists in all cultures. Moreover, certain general principles concerning its composition, kinship patterns, and authority patterns are universal.

Composition: What Is the Family?

If we were to take our information on what a family is from what we see on television, we might come up with some very strange scenarios. The media do not always present a realistic view of the family. Moreover, many people still think of the family in very narrow terms—as a married couple and their unmarried children living together, like the family in the old *Cosby Show*. However, this is but one type of family, what sociologists refer to as a **nuclear family.** The term *nuclear family* is well chosen, since this type of family serves as the nucleus, or core, on which larger family groups are built.

Most people in the United States see the nuclear family as the preferred family arrangement. Yet by 2000, only about a third of the nation's family households fit this model. The proportion of households in the United States that is composed of married couples with children at home has decreased steadily over the past 40 years and is expected to continue shrinking. At the same time, the number of single-parent households has increased (Figure 14-1).

A family in which relatives—such as grandparents, aunts, or uncles—live in the same home as parents and their children is known as an **extended family.** Although not common, such living arrangements do exist in the United States. The structure of the extended family offers certain advantages over that of the nuclear family. Crises such as death, divorce, and illness put less strain on family members, since more people can provide assistance and emotional support. In addition, the extended family constitutes a larger economic unit than the nuclear family. If the family is engaged in a common enterprise—a farm or a small business—the additional family members may represent the difference between prosperity and failure.

In considering these different family types, we have limited ourselves to the form of marriage that is characteristic of the United States—monogamy. The term **monogamy** describes a form of marriage in which one woman and one man are married only to each other. Some observers, noting the high rate of divorce in the United States, have suggested that "serial monogamy" is a more accurate description of the form marriage takes in this country. In **serial monogamy,** a person may

FIGURE **14-1** U.S. HOUSEHOLDS BY FAMILY TYPE, 1940–2010

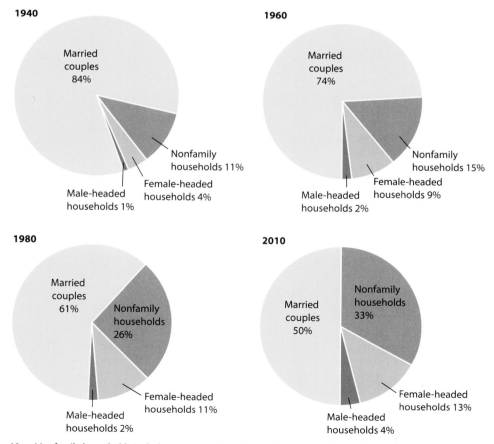

1940
Married couples 84%
Nonfamily households 11%
Female-headed households 4%
Male-headed households 1%

1960
Married couples 74%
Nonfamily households 15%
Female-headed households 9%
Male-headed households 2%

1980
Married couples 61%
Nonfamily households 26%
Female-headed households 11%
Male-headed households 2%

2010
Married couples 50%
Nonfamily households 33%
Female-headed households 13%
Male-headed households 4%

Note: Nonfamily households include women and men living alone or exclusively with people to whom they are not related, as in a college dormitory, homeless shelter, or military base.
Sources: Author's estimate based on Bureau of the Census 1996; Jason Fields 2004; see also McFalls 2003:23.

SOCIOLOGY IN THE GLOBAL COMMUNITY

14-1   One Wife, Many Husbands: The Nyinba

The Nyinba culture of Nepal and Tibet is an agrarian society located in the remote valleys of the Himalaya Mountains, more than 9,000 feet above sea level. Despite the Nyinba's isolation, they have been closely studied. Scholars from around the world have traveled to the Himalayas to observe this people, one of the few remaining cultures on earth to practice polyandry.

Favoritism toward a particular husband is frowned on by the Nyinba. Thus, it is the wife's responsibility to see that each husband shares time with her in a rotational fashion.

In the physically challenging environment of the Himalayas, polyandry seems to work well. Because the land and climate make it difficult to sustain crops, farming is labor-intensive: many Nyinba laborers must work the fields to support a single family. Thus, a typical marriage involving three brothers and one wife provides the necessary adult male laborers, yet minimizes the number of offspring—a necessity in a place where the food supply is limited.

While an outsider might suppose that Nyinba women dominate their families, in fact authority and inheritance rest on the husband or son. The birth of a son is celebrated, while the birth of a daughter, regardless of who might be the father, brings disappointment. Paternity appears to be a nonissue in this culture, since households are shared by brothers from the same family. The literal head of the household is the oldest brother, who typically chooses a wife from outside his extended family.

A Nyinba family threshing buckwheat in the field. At left is the wife; in the center, one of her five husbands (with raised mallet); at right, her mother-in-law.

Favoritism toward a particular husband is frowned on by the Nyinba. Thus, it is the wife's responsibility to see that each husband shares time with her in a rotational fashion. Often, over the morning meal, she will indicate which husband will sleep with her that night. To avoid any confusion, the chosen husband will place his shoes outside her bedroom door.

As in any society (for example, the United States), not all Nyinba households conform to the social norm. If a family has only one son, he must of necessity marry monogamously—an unfortunate outcome in this society. If a wife is unable to have children, a second wife, typically her sister or cousin, may be welcomed into the marriage.

LET'S DISCUSS

1. Why would a monogamous marriage be considered an unfortunate one in the Nyinba culture?
2. What might be some other ways for a society to handle the physical constraints of life in a mountainous terrain?

Sources: N. Levine 1988; Stockard 2002; Zeitzen 2008.

---

have several spouses in his or her lifetime, but only one spouse at a time.

Some cultures allow an individual to have several husbands or wives simultaneously. This form of marriage is known as **polygamy.** In fact, most societies throughout the world, past and present, have preferred polygamy to monogamy. Anthropologist George Murdock (1949, 1957) sampled 565 societies and found that in more than 80 percent, some type of polygamy was the preferred form. While polygamy declined steadily through most of the 20th century, in at least five countries in Africa 20 percent of men still have polygamous marriages (Population Reference Bureau 1996).

There are two basic types of polygamy. According to Murdock, the most common—endorsed by the majority of cultures he sampled—is **polygyny.** Polygyny refers to the marriage of a man to more than one woman at the same time. The wives are often sisters, who are expected to hold similar values and have already had experience sharing a household. In polygynous societies, relatively few men actually have multiple spouses. Most individuals live in monogamous families; having multiple wives is viewed as a mark of status.

The other principal variation of polygamy is **polyandry,** in which a woman may have more than one husband at the same time. Such is the case in the culture of the Nyinba, described in Box 14-1. Polyandry, however, is exceedingly rare today, though it is accepted in some extremely poor societies. Like many other societies, polyandrous cultures devalue the social worth of women (Zeitzen 2008).

Kinship Patterns: To Whom Are We Related?

Many of us can trace our roots by looking at a family tree or by listening to elderly family members talk about their lives—and about the lives of ancestors who died long before we were born. Yet a person's lineage is more than simply a personal history; it also reflects societal patterns that govern descent. In every culture, children encounter relatives to whom they are expected to show an emotional attachment. The state of being related to others is called **kinship.** Kinship is culturally learned, however, and is not totally determined by biological or marital ties. For example, adoption creates a kinship tie that is legally acknowledged and socially accepted.

The family and the kin group are not necessarily one and the same. Whereas the family is a household unit, kin do not always live together or function as a collective body on a daily basis. Kin groups include aunts, uncles, cousins, in-laws, and so forth. In a society such as the United States, the kinship group may come together only rarely, for a wedding or funeral. However, kinship ties frequently create obligations and responsibilities. We may feel compelled to assist our kin, and we may feel free to call on them for many types of aid, including loans and babysitting.

How do we identify kinship groups? The principle of descent assigns people to kinship groups according to their relationship to a mother or father. There are three primary ways of determining descent. The United States follows the system of **bilateral descent,** which means that both sides of a person's family are regarded as equally important. For example, no higher value is given to the brothers of one's father than to the brothers of one's mother.

Most societies—according to George Murdock, 64 percent—give preference to one side of the family or the other in tracing descent. In **patrilineal** (from the Latin *pater,* "father") **descent,** only the father's relatives are significant in terms of property, inheritance, and emotional ties. Conversely, in societies that favor **matrilineal** (from the Latin *mater,* "mother") **descent,** only the mother's relatives are significant.

New forms of reproductive technology will necessitate a new way of looking at kinship. Today, a combination of biological and social processes can "create" a family member, requiring that more distinctions be made about who is related to whom.

Authority Patterns: Who Rules?

Imagine that you have recently married and must begin to make decisions about the future of your new family. You and your spouse face many questions. Where will you live? How will you furnish your home? Who will do the cooking, the shopping, the cleaning? Whose friends will be invited to dinner? Each time a

Though spouses in an egalitarian family may not share all their decisions, they regard themselves as equals. This pattern of authority is becoming more common in the United States.

decision must be made, an issue is raised: Who has the power to make the decision? In simple terms, who rules the family? Conflict theorists examine these questions in the context of traditional gender stratification, under which men have held a dominant position over women.

Societies vary in the way power is distributed within the family. A society that expects males to dominate in all family decision making is termed a **patriarchy.** In patriarchal societies, such as Iran, the eldest male often wields the greatest power, although wives are expected to be treated with respect and kindness. An Iranian woman's status is typically defined by her relationship to a male relative, usually as a wife or daughter. In many patriarchal societies, women find it more difficult to obtain a divorce than a man does. In contrast, in a **matriarchy,** women have greater authority than men. Matriarchies, which are very uncommon, emerged among Native American tribal societies and in nations in which men were absent for long periods because of warfare or food-gathering expeditions (Farr 1999).

In a third type of authority pattern, the **egalitarian family,** spouses are regarded as equals. That does not mean, however, that all decisions are shared in such families. Wives may hold authority in some spheres, husbands in others. Many sociologists believe the egalitarian family has begun to replace the patriarchal family as the social norm in the United States.

use your sociological *imagination*

In your own family, which relatives do you have a significant relationship with? Which do you hardly ever see?

Sociological Perspectives on the Family

Do we really need the family? A century ago, Friedrich Engels ([1884] 1959), a colleague of Karl Marx, described the family as the ultimate source of social inequality because of its role in the transfer of power, property, and privilege. More recently, conflict theorists have argued that the family contributes to societal injustice, denies women opportunities that are extended to men, and limits freedom in sexual expression and mate selection. In contrast, the functionalist view focuses on the ways in which the family gratifies the needs of its members and contributes to social stability. The interactionist view considers the intimate, face-to-face relationships that occur in the family. And the feminist approach examines the role of the wife and mother, especially in the absence of an adult male.

Functionalist View

The family performs six paramount functions, first outlined more than 70 years ago by sociologist William F. Ogburn (Ogburn and Tibbits 1934):

1. **Reproduction.** For a society to maintain itself, it must replace dying members. In this sense, the family contributes to human survival through its function of reproduction.

2. **Protection.** In all cultures, the family assumes the ultimate responsibility for the protection and upbringing of children.

3. **Socialization.** Parents and other kin monitor a child's behavior and transmit the norms, values, and language of their culture to the child.

4. **Regulation of sexual behavior.** Sexual norms are subject to change both over time (for instance, in the customs for dating) and across cultures (compare strict Saudi Arabia to the more permissive Denmark). However, whatever the time period or cultural values of a society, standards of sexual behavior are most clearly defined within the family circle.

5. **Affection and companionship.** Ideally, the family provides members with warm and intimate relationships, helping them to feel satisfied and secure. Of course, a family member may find such rewards outside the family—from peers, in school, at work—and may even perceive the home as an unpleasant or abusive setting. Nevertheless, we expect our relatives to understand us, to care for us, and to be there for us when we need them.

6. **Provision of social status.** We inherit a social position because of the family background and reputation of our parents and siblings. The family presents the newborn child with an ascribed status based on race and ethnicity that helps to determine his or her place within society's stratification system. Moreover, family resources affect children's ability to pursue certain opportunities, such as higher education.

Traditionally, the family has fulfilled a number of other functions, such as providing religious training, education, and recreational outlets. But Ogburn argued that other social institutions have gradually assumed many of those functions. Education once took place at the family fireside; now it is the responsibility of professionals working in schools and colleges. Even the family's traditional recreational function has been transferred to outside groups such as Little Leagues, athletic clubs, and Internet chat rooms.

Conflict View

Conflict theorists view the family not as a contributor to social stability, but as a reflection of the inequality in wealth and power that is found within the larger society. Feminist and conflict theorists note that the family has traditionally legitimized and perpetuated male dominance. Throughout most of human history—and in a wide range of societies—husbands have exercised overwhelming power and authority within the family. Not until the first wave of contemporary feminism in the United States, in the mid-1800s, was there a substantial challenge to the historic status of wives and children as the legal property of husbands.

While the egalitarian family has become a more common pattern in the United States in recent decades—owing in good part to the activism of feminists beginning in the late 1960s and early 1970s—male dominance over the family has hardly disappeared. Sociologists have found that while married men are increasing their involvement in child care, their wives still perform a disproportionate amount of it. Furthermore, for every stay-at-home dad there are 38 stay-at-home moms (Jason Fields 2004:11–12; Garcia-Moreno et al. 2005; Sayer et al. 2004). And unfortunately, many husbands reinforce their power and control over wives and children through acts of domestic violence.

Conflict theorists also view the family as an economic unit that contributes to societal injustice. The family is the basis for transferring power, property, and privilege from one generation to the next. Although the United States is widely viewed as a land of opportunity, social mobility is restricted in important ways. Children inherit the privileged or less-than-privileged social and economic status of their parents (and in some cases, of earlier generations as well). As the chapter-opening excerpt showed, the social class of parents significantly influences children's socialization experiences and the degree of protection they receive. Thus, the socioeconomic status of a child's family will have a marked influence on his or her nutrition, health care, housing, educational opportunities, and in many respects, life chances as an adult. For this reason, conflict theorists argue that the family helps to maintain inequality.

Interactionists are particularly interested in the ways in which mothers and fathers relate to each other and to their children. This mother and her two children are expressing a close and loving relationship, one of the foundations of a strong family.

Interactionist View

Interactionists focus on the micro level of family and other intimate relationships. They are interested in how individuals interact with one another, whether they are cohabiting partners or longtime married couples. For example, in a study of both Black and White two-parent households, researchers found that when fathers are more involved with their children (reading to them, helping them with homework, or restricting their television viewing), the children have fewer behavior problems, get along better with others, and are more responsible (Mosley and Thomson 1995).

Another interactionist study might examine the role of the stepparent. The increased number of single parents who remarry has sparked an interest in those who are helping to raise other people's children. Studies have found that stepmothers are more likely than stepfathers to accept the blame for bad relations with their stepchildren. Interactionists theorize that stepfathers (like most fathers) may simply be unaccustomed to interacting directly with children when the mother isn't there (Bray and Kelly 1999; F. Furstenberg and Cherlin 1991).

Feminist View

Because "women's work" has traditionally focused on family life, feminist sociologists have taken a strong interest in the family as a social institution. As we saw in Chapter 12, research on gender roles in child care and household chores has been extensive. Sociologists have looked particularly closely at how women's work outside the home impacts their child care and housework—duties Arlie Hochschild (1989, 1990, 2005) has referred to as the "second shift." Today, researchers recognize that for many women, the second shift includes the care of aging parents as well.

Feminist theorists have urged social scientists and social agencies to rethink the notion that families in which no adult male is present are automatically a cause for concern, or even dysfunctional. They have also contributed to research on single women, single-parent households, and lesbian couples. In the case of single mothers, researchers have focused on the resiliency of many such households, despite economic stress. According to Velma McBride Murray and her colleagues (2001) at the University of Georgia, such studies show that among African Americans, single mothers draw heavily on kinfolk for material resources, parenting advice, and social support. Considering feminist research on the family as a whole, one researcher concluded that the family is the "source of women's strength" (V. Taylor et al. 2009).

Finally, feminists who take the interactionist perspective stress the need to investigate neglected topics in family studies. For instance, in a growing number of dual-income households, the wife earns a higher income than the husband. In 2005, a study of 58 married couples revealed that 26 percent of the wives earned more than their husbands. In 1981, the proportion was just 16 percent. Yet beyond individual case studies, little research has been done on how these families may differ from those in which the husband is the major breadwinner (Wills and Risman 2006).

Table 14-1 summarizes the four major theoretical perspectives on the family.

Marriage and Family

Currently, over 95 percent of all men and women in the United States marry at least once during their lifetimes. Historically, the most consistent aspect of family life in this country has been the high rate of marriage. In fact, despite the high rate of divorce, there are some indications of a miniboom in marriages of late.

In this part of the chapter, we will examine various aspects of love, marriage, and parenthood in the United States and contrast them with cross-cultural examples. Though we're used to thinking of romance and mate selection as strictly a matter of individual preference, sociological analysis tells us that social

TABLE **14-1** SOCIOLOGICAL PERSPECTIVES ON THE FAMILY

summingup

Theoretical Perspective	Emphasis
Functionalist	The family as a contributor to social stability Roles of family members
Conflict	The family as a perpetuator of inequality Transmission of poverty or wealth across generations
Interactionist	Relationships among family members
Feminist	The family as a perpetuator of gender roles Female-headed households

Chapter 14

institutions and distinctive cultural norms and values also play an important role.

Courtship and Mate Selection

"My rugby mates would roll over in their graves," says Tom Buckley of his online courtship and subsequent marriage to Terri Muir. But Tom and Terri are hardly alone these days in turning to the Internet for matchmaking services. A generation or two ago, most couples met in high school or college, but now that people are marrying later in life, the Internet has become the new meeting place for the romantically inclined. Today, thousands of Web sites offer to help people find mates. A 2005 survey found that 12 percent of couples who visited an online wedding site had met online. Success stories like these notwithstanding, online dating services are only as good as the people who use them. Subscribers' personal profiles—the basis for potential matches—often contain false or misleading information (Kapos 2005; B. Morris 1999:D1).

Internet romance is only the latest courtship practice. In the central Asian nation of Uzbekistan and many other traditional cultures, courtship is defined largely through the interaction of two sets of parents, who arrange marriages for their children. Typically, a young Uzbekistani woman will be socialized to eagerly anticipate her marriage to a man whom she has met only once, when he is presented to her family at the time of the final inspection of her dowry. In the United States, in contrast, courtship is conducted primarily by individuals who have a romantic interest in each other. In our culture, courtship often requires these individuals to rely heavily on intricate games, gestures, and signals. Despite such differences, courtship—whether in the United States, Uzbekistan, or elsewhere—is influenced by the norms and values of the larger society (Carol J. Williams 1995).

One unmistakable trend in mate selection is that the process appears to be taking longer today than in the past. A variety of factors, including concerns about financial security and personal independence, has contributed to this delay in marriage. Most people are now well into their 20s before they marry, both in the United States and in other countries (Figure 14-2).

Aspects of Mate Selection Many societies have explicit or unstated rules that define potential mates as acceptable or unacceptable. These norms can be distinguished in terms of endogamy and exogamy. **Endogamy** (from the Greek *endon,* "within") specifies the groups within which a spouse must be found and prohibits marriage with others. For example, in the United States, many people are expected to marry within their own racial, ethnic, or religious group, and are strongly discouraged or even prohibited from marrying outside the group. Endogamy is intended to reinforce the cohesiveness of the group by suggesting to the young that they should marry someone "of their own kind."

In contrast, **exogamy** (from the Greek *exo,* "outside") requires mate selection outside certain groups, usually one's own family or certain kinfolk. The **incest taboo,** a social norm common to virtually all societies, prohibits sexual relationships between certain culturally specified relatives. For those of us in the United States, this taboo means that we must marry outside the nuclear family. We cannot marry our siblings, and in most states we cannot marry our first cousins.

Endogamous restrictions may be seen as preferences for one group over another. In the United States, such preferences are

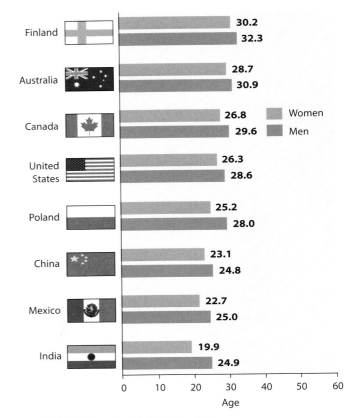

FIGURE **14-2** MEDIAN AGE AT FIRST MARRIAGE IN EIGHT COUNTRIES

Source: United Nations Statistical Division 2009.

Think about It
Why do people marry earlier in India than in Finland?

most obvious in racial barriers. Until the 1960s, some states outlawed interracial marriage. Nevertheless, the number of marriages between African Americans and Whites in the United States has increased more than nine times in recent decades, jumping from 51,000 in 1960 to 464,000 in 2007. Marriage across ethnic lines is even greater among Hispanics: 36 percent of all married Hispanics have a non-Hispanic spouse. But while these examples of racial exogamy are noteworthy, endogamy is still the social norm in the United States (Bureau of the Census 1998, 2008a:52).

Another factor that influences the selection of a marriage partner is **homogamy,** the conscious or unconscious tendency to select a mate with personal characteristics similar to one's own. The "like marries like" rule can be seen in couples with similar personalities and cultural interests. However, mate selection is unpredictable. Though some people may follow the homogamous pattern, others observe the rule that opposites attract: one person is dependent and submissive—almost childishly so—while the other is dominant and controlling.

Recently, the concept of homogamy has been incorporated into the process of seeking a date or marital partner online. The Internet dating site eHarmony, which claims to be the first to use a "scientific approach" to matching people based on a variety of

Although most interracial couples are not as visible as Seal and Heidi Klum, such unions are becoming increasingly common and accepted. They are also blurring the definitions of race. Will the children of these couples be considered Black or White? Why do you think so?

abilities and interests, says that it "facilitates" 46 marriages a day. Sociologist Pepper Schwartz, who works as a consultant for the competing site PerfectMatch.com, has developed a 48-question survey that covers everything from prospective mates' decision-making style to their degree of impulsivity (Gottlieb 2006; Kalmijn 1998).

The Love Relationship   Today's generation of college students seems more likely to hook up or cruise in large packs than to engage in the romantic dating relationships of their parents and grandparents. Still, at some point in their adult lives, the great majority of today's students will meet someone they love and enter into a long-term relationship that focuses on creating a family.

Parents in the United States tend to value love highly as a rationale for marriage, so they encourage their children to develop intimate relationships based on love and affection. Songs, films, books, magazines, television shows, and even cartoons and comic books reinforce the theme of love. At the same time, our society expects parents and peers to help a person confine his or her search for a mate to "socially acceptable" members of the opposite sex.

Though most people in the United States take the importance of falling in love for granted, the coupling of love and marriage

is by no means a cultural universal. Many of the world's cultures give priority in mate selection to factors other than romantic feelings. In societies with *arranged marriages* engineered by parents or religious authorities, economic considerations play a significant role. The newly married couple is expected to develop a feeling of love *after* the legal union is formalized, if at all. Box 14-2 on page 320 describes the marriages that some immigrants to the United States arrange for their children.

Even where arranged marriage is the norm, new media technologies have changed the mating game. Today, when young people exchange phone numbers, a flurry of short text messages is more likely to follow than a series of extended phone conversations. In India, where most young people defer to their parents' wishes when they marry, much of this text messaging is recreational. Still, it can test the limits of traditional dating norms, by reducing the formality of social interactions between men and women (Giridharadus 2008).

In some societies, neither the parents nor the bride has a say in whom she marries. Since at least the 12th century, men in the central Asian nation of Kyrgyzstan have literally kidnapped their future wives from the street in a custom known as *ala kachuu*, which translates roughly as "grab and run." In its most benign form, this custom is a kind of elopement in which the man whisks off his girlfriend. Men do it to avoid the "bride price" that parents often demand in return for their consent. But as of 2005, one-third of the brides in Kyrgyzstan had been abducted against their will. Many of them—perhaps 80 percent—eventually assent to the kidnapping, often at their parents' urging. For these women, romantic love does not precede marriage, though love may well develop over time (Craig Smith 2005).

use your sociological *imagination*

Your parents and/or a matchmaker are going to arrange a marriage for you. What kind of mate will they select? Will your chances of having a successful marriage be better or worse than if you selected your own mate?

www.mhhe.com/schaefer12e

Variations in Family Life and Intimate Relationships

Within the United States, social class, race, and ethnicity create variations in family life. Studying these variations will give us a more sophisticated understanding of contemporary family styles in our country.

Social Class Differences   Various studies have documented the differences in family organization among social classes in the United States. In the upper class, the emphasis is on lineage and maintenance of family position. If you are in the upper class, you are not simply a member of a nuclear family, but rather a member of a larger family tradition (think of the Rockefellers or the Kennedys). As a result, upper-class families are quite concerned about what they see as proper training for children.

RESEARCH TODY

14-2 Arranged Marriage, American-Style

Leona Singh, a 25-year-old Californian, met her future mate, from Iowa, through her father. The two were introduced at a relative's home and later went out alone. Several months later, when they felt "90 percent certain" that their relationship would be a good one, the two Indian Americans married. Years later Leona looked back. "From the beginning, I felt there was a physical chemistry, but it took years to develop a mature bond, and I guess you could call that love" (Bellafante 2005:A15).

For many young people like Leona, the question is not "Does he or she love me?" but "Whom do my parents want me to marry?" In an *arranged marriage*, parents or matchmakers choose a marital partner for a young person based on considerations other than mutual attraction. Typically, couples whose marriages have been arranged don't even know each other. They are assumed to be compatible, however, since they have been carefully chosen to share the same social, economic, and cultural background.

In cultures in which arranged marriage is the norm, young people are socialized to expect and desire such unions.

Historically, arranged marriages have not been unusual; even today they are common in many parts of Asia and Africa. In cultures in which arranged marriage is the norm, young people are socialized to expect and desire such unions. But what happens in cultures that send a very different message to youths? In the United States and Canada, for example, immigrants from countries such as India, Pakistan, and Bangladesh may want to arrange their children's marriages. Their sons and daughters, however, are growing up in a culture in which their schoolmates are obsessed with dating as a prelude to marriage.

Studies of these young people, whose parents still cling to the tradition of arranging their children's marriages, document the challenges

When the children of immigrants to the United States want a husband or wife, they often bow to their parents' wishes and agree to an arranged marriage.

they face. Many of them do still embrace their parents' traditions. As one Princeton student of Indian ancestry put it, "In a lot of ways it's easier. I don't have pressure to look for a boyfriend" (Herschthal 2004). These youths may even accept a partner selected from their parents' country of origin. Nevertheless, though systematic, nationwide studies of this demographic group are lacking, the available research points to a trend away from arranged marriage.

In response to cultural pressure, some Indian immigrant families have replaced formally arranged marriage with *assisted marriage*, in which the parents identify a limited number of potential mates for their children based on caste, family background, and geography. The children can then choose a mate from the candidates approved by their parents. Because of their continued reliance on arranged and now

assisted marriage, Indian immigrants have the highest rate of ethnic endogamy of any major immigrant group in the United States: about 90 percent in 2003.

LET'S DISCUSS

1. Can you, under any circumstances, imagine yourself accepting an arranged marriage? Take a poll of your classmates to see how many agree with you. Can you see an ethnic difference in the responses?
2. For Indian Americans as a group rather than as individuals, what might be some long-term benefits of arranged marriage? Might those benefits give them an advantage over other ethnic groups?

Sources: Bellafante 2005; Davé 2009; Herschthal 2004; Talbani and Hasanali 2000; Zaidi and Shuraydi 2002.

Lower-class families do not often have the luxury of worrying about the "family name"; they must first struggle to pay their bills and survive the crises often associated with a life of poverty. Such families are more likely to have only one parent at home, which creates special challenges in child care and financial management. Children from lower-class families typically assume adult responsibilities—including marriage and parenthood—at an earlier age than children from affluent homes. In part, that is because they may lack the money needed to remain in school.

Social class differences in family life are less striking today than they once were. In the past, family specialists agreed that the contrasts in child-rearing practices were pronounced. Lower-class families were found to be more authoritarian in rearing children and more inclined to use physical punishment. Middle-class families were more permissive and more restrained in punishing their children. And compared to lower-class families, middle-class families tended to schedule more of their children's time, or even to overstructure it. However, these differences may have narrowed as more and more families from all social classes turned to the same books, magazines, and even television talk shows for advice on rearing children (Kronstadt and Favreault 2008; Luster et al. 1989).

Among the poor, women often play a significant role in the economic support of the family. Men may earn low wages, may be unemployed, or may be entirely absent from the family. In 2007, 28 percent of all families headed by women with no husband present fell below the government poverty line. In comparison, the poverty rate for married couples was only 4.9 percent. The disproportionate representation of female-headed households among the poor is a persistent and growing trend, referred to by sociologists as the *feminization of poverty*: see Chapter 9 (DeNavas-Walt et al. 2008:13).

Many racial and ethnic groups appear to have distinctive family characteristics. However, racial and class factors are often closely related. In examining family life among racial and ethnic minorities, keep in mind that certain patterns may result from class as well as cultural factors.

Racial and Ethnic Differences The subordinate status of racial and ethnic minorities in the United States profoundly affects their family lives. For example, the lower incomes of African Americans, Native Americans, most Hispanic groups, and selected Asian American groups make creating and maintaining successful marital unions a difficult task. The economic restructuring of the past 60 years, described by sociologist William Julius Wilson (1996, 2009) and others, has especially affected people living in inner cities and desolate rural areas, such as reservations. Furthermore, the immigration policy of the United States has complicated the successful relocation of intact families from Asia and Latin America.

The African American family suffers from many negative and inaccurate stereotypes. It is true that in a significantly higher proportion of Black than White families, no husband is present in the home (Figure 14-3). Yet Black single mothers often belong to stable, functioning kin networks, which mitigate the pressures of sexism and racism. Members of these networks—predominantly female kin such as mothers, grandmothers, and aunts—ease financial strains by sharing goods and services. In addition to these strong kinship bonds, Black family life has emphasized deep religious commitment and high aspirations for achievement (DuBois [1909] 1970; F. Furstenberg 2007).

Like African Americans, Native Americans draw on family ties to cushion many of the hardships they face. On the Navajo reservation, for example, teenage parenthood is not regarded as the crisis that it is elsewhere in the United States. The Navajo trace their descent matrilineally. Traditionally, couples reside with the wife's family after marriage, allowing the grandparents to help with the child rearing. While the Navajo do not approve of teenage parenthood, the deep emotional commitment of their extended families provides a warm home environment for children, even when no father is present or involved (Dalla and Gamble 2001).

Sociologists also have taken note of differences in family patterns among other racial and ethnic groups. For example, Mexican American men have been described as exhibiting a sense of virility, personal worth, and pride in their maleness that is called **machismo.** Mexican Americans are also described as being more

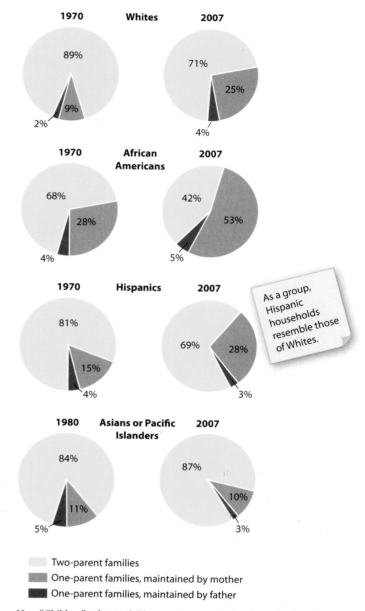

Note: "Children" refers to children under 18. Early data for Asian Americans are for 1980. Hispanics can be of any race. Not included are unrelated people living together with no children present. All data exclude the 4 percent of children in nonparental households.
Sources: Bureau of the Census 2008a:56; Kreider 2008.

familistic than many other subcultures. **Familism** refers to pride in the extended family, expressed through the maintenance of close ties and strong obligations to kinfolk outside the immediate family. Traditionally, Mexican Americans have placed proximity to their extended families above other needs and desires.

Although familism is often seen as a positive cultural attribute, it may also have negative consequences. Sociologists who have studied the relatively low college application rates of Hispanic students have found they have a strong desire to stay at home. Even the children of college-educated parents express this preference, which diminishes the likelihood of their getting a four-year degree and dramatically reduces the possibility

When nine-year-old Blake Brunson shows up for a basketball game, so do his *eight* grandparents—the result of his parents' remarriages. Blended families can be very supportive to children, but what message do they send to them on the permanency of marriage?

that they will apply to a selective college (Desmond and Turley 2009)

These family patterns are changing, however, in response to changes in Latinos' social class standing, educational achievements, and occupations. Like other Americans, career-oriented Latinos in search of a mate but short on spare time are turning to Internet sites. As Latinos and other groups assimilate into the dominant culture of the United States, their family lives take on both the positive and negative characteristics associated with White households (Landale and Oropesa 2007).

Child-Rearing Patterns

The Nayars of southern India acknowledge the biological role of fathers, but the mother's eldest brother is responsible for her children. In contrast, uncles play only a peripheral role in child care in the United States. Caring for children is a universal function of the family, yet the ways in which different societies assign this function to family members can vary significantly. Even within the United States, child-rearing patterns are varied. We'll take a look here at parenthood and grandparenthood, adoption, dual-income families, single-parent families, and stepfamilies.

Parenthood and Grandparenthood The socialization of children is essential to the maintenance of any culture. Consequently, parenthood is one of the most important (and most demanding) social roles in the United States. Sociologist Alice Rossi (1968, 1984) has identified four factors that complicate the transition to parenthood and the role of socialization. First, there is little anticipatory socialization for the social role of caregiver. The normal school curriculum gives scant attention to the subjects most relevant to successful family life, such as child care and home maintenance. Second, only limited learning occurs during the period of pregnancy itself. Third, the transition to parenthood is quite abrupt. Unlike adolescence, it is not prolonged; unlike the transition to work, the duties of caregiving cannot be taken on gradually. Finally, in Rossi's view, our society lacks clear and helpful guidelines for successful parenthood. There is little consensus on how parents can produce happy and well-adjusted offspring—or even on what it means to be well-adjusted. For these reasons, socialization for parenthood involves difficult challenges for most men and women in the United States.

One recent development in family life in the United States has been the extension of parenthood, as adult children continue to live at home or return home after college. In 2008, 56 percent of men and 44 percent of women ages 18 to 24 lived with their parents. Some of these adult children were still pursuing an education, but in many instances, financial difficulties lay at the heart of these living arrangements. While rents and real estate prices have skyrocketed, salaries for younger workers have not kept pace, and many find themselves unable to afford their own homes. Moreover, with many marriages now ending in divorce—most commonly in the first seven years of marriage—divorced sons and daughters often return to live with their parents, sometimes with their own children (Bureau of the Census 2008c:Table A2).

Is this living arrangement a positive development for family members? Social scientists have just begun to examine the

phenomenon, sometimes called the "boomerang generation" or the "full-nest syndrome" in the popular press. One survey in Virginia seemed to show that neither the parents nor their adult children were happy about continuing to live together. The children often felt resentful and isolated, but the parents suffered too: learning to live without children in the home is an essential stage of adult life, and may even be a significant turning point for a marriage (*Berkeley Wellness Letter* 1990; Mogelonsky 1996).

In some homes, the full nest holds grandchildren. In 2004, 6.5 million children, or 9 percent of all children in the United States, lived in a household with a grandparent. In about a third of these homes, no parent was present to assume responsibility for the youngsters. Special difficulties are inherent in such relationships, including legal custodial concerns, financial issues, and emotional problems for adults and youths alike. It is not surprising that support groups such as Grandparents as Parents have emerged to provide assistance (Kreider 2008).

Adoption In a legal sense, **adoption** is a "process that allows for the transfer of the legal rights, responsibilities, and privileges of parenthood" to a new legal parent or parents (E. Cole 1985:638). In many cases, these rights are transferred from a biological parent or parents (often called birth parents) to an adoptive parent or parents. At any given time, about 2 million adults in the United States are raising adopted children (Jo Jones 2009).

Viewed from a functionalist perspective, government has a strong interest in encouraging adoption. Policymakers, in fact, have both a humanitarian and a financial stake in the process. In theory, adoption offers a stable family environment for children who otherwise might not receive satisfactory care. Moreover, government data show that unwed mothers who keep their babies tend to be of lower socioeconomic status and often require public assistance to support their children. The government can lower its social welfare expenses, then, if children are transferred to economically self-sufficient families. From an interactionist perspective, however, adoption may require a child to adjust to a very different family environment and parental approach to child rearing.

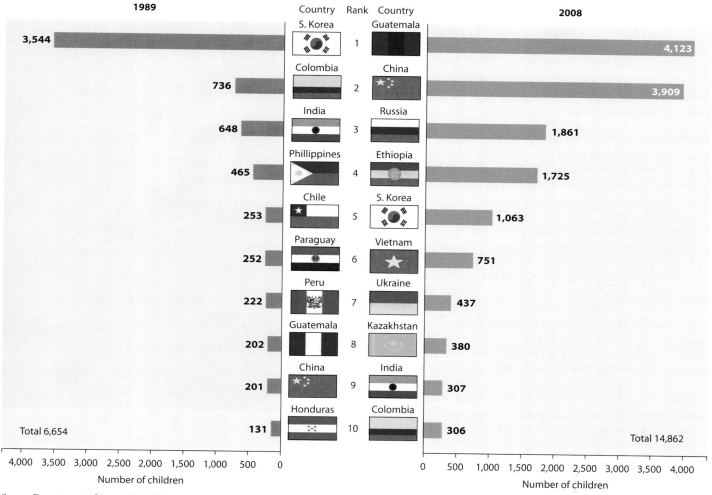

1989		Country	Rank	Country		2008
3,544		S. Korea	1	Guatemala		4,123
736		Colombia	2	China		3,909
648		India	3	Russia		1,861
465		Phillippines	4	Ethiopia		1,725
253		Chile	5	S. Korea		1,063
252		Paraguay	6	Vietnam		751
222		Peru	7	Ukraine		437
202		Guatemala	8	Kazakhstan		380
201		China	9	India		307
131		Honduras	10	Colombia		306

Total 6,654

Total 14,862

4,000 3,500 3,000 2,500 2,000 1,500 1,000 500 0
Number of children

0 500 1,000 1,500 2,000 2,500 3,000 3,500 4,000
Number of children

Source: Department of State 2001, 2009.

Think about It

Why did so many foreign-born adopted children come from these countries in particular? What accounts for the children countries of origin from 1989 to 2008?

About 4 percent of all people in the United States are adopted, about half of whom were adopted by persons not related to them at birth. There are two legal methods of adopting an unrelated person: the adoption may be arranged through a licensed agency, or in some states it may be arranged through a private agreement sanctioned by the courts. Adopted children may come from the United States or from abroad. In 2008 over 17,000 children entered the United States as the adopted children of U.S. citizens. Figure 14-4 shows how the countries of origin have changed over time. International adoptions began to decline in 2004 after a long and steady increase. Recently China, the source for about one-third of overseas adoptions, tightened the

rules for foreign adoptions, effectively reducing their number. Applicants for adoption who are single, obese, or older than 50 are now automatically disqualified.

In some cases the adopters are not married. In 1995, an important court decision in New York held that a couple does not need to be married to adopt a child. Under this ruling, unmarried heterosexual couples, lesbian couples, and gay male couples can all legally adopt children in New York. Writing for the majority, Chief Justice Judith Kaye argued that by expanding the boundaries of who can be legally recognized as parents, the state may be able to assist more children in securing "the best possible home." With this ruling, New York became the third state (after Vermont and Massachusetts) to recognize the right of unmarried couples to adopt children (Dao 1995).

For every child who is adopted, many more remain the wards of state-sponsored child protective services. At any given time, around half a million children in the United States are living in foster care. Every year, about 51,000 of them are adopted; another 130,000 are eligible and waiting to be adopted (Department of Health and Human Services 2009).

Dual-Income Families The idea of a family consisting of a wage-earning husband and a wife who stays at home has largely given way to the dual-income household. Among married people between ages 25 and 34, 96 percent of the men and 69 percent of the women were in the labor force in 2007 (Bureau of the Census 2008a:375).

Why has there been such a rise in the number of dual-income couples? A major factor is economic need, coupled with a desire by both men *and* women to pursue their careers. Evidence of this trend can be found in the rise in the number of married couples living apart for reasons other than marital discord. The 3.6 million couples who now live apart represent 1 out of every 33 marriages. More than half of them live farther than 100 miles apart, and half of those live 1,000 or more miles apart. Of course, couples living apart are nothing new; men have worked at transient jobs for generations as soldiers, truck drivers, or traveling salesmen. Now, however, the woman's job is often the one that creates the separation. The existence of such household arrangements reflects an acceptance of the egalitarian family type (L. Cullen 2007; Holmes 2006).

Single-Parent Families The 2004 *American Idol* winner Fantasia Barrino's song "Baby Mama" offers a tribute to young single mothers—a subject she knows about. Barrino was 17 when she became pregnant with her daughter. Though critics charged that the song sends the wrong message to teenage girls, Barrino says it is about encouraging teens to have sex. Rather, she sees the song as an anthem for young mothers courageously trying to raise their children alone (Cherlin 2006).

In recent decades, the stigma attached to unwed mothers and other single parents has significantly diminished. **Single-parent families,** in which only one parent is present to care for the children, can hardly be viewed as a rarity in the United States. In 2007, a single parent headed about 29 percent of White families with children under 18, 31 percent of Hispanic families with children, and 58 percent of African American families with children (see Figure 14-3 on page 321).

Interestingly, since 1995 the greatest increase in unwed motherhood has occurred among women in their 20s and 30s. This age group still constitutes a smaller proportion of unwed mothers than teens. In 2007, however, 45 percent of births to women in their 20s were to unmarried women (S. Ventura 2009).

The lives of single parents and their children are not inevitably more difficult than life in a traditional nuclear family. It is as inaccurate to assume that a single-parent family is necessarily deprived as it is to assume that a two-parent family is always secure and happy. Nevertheless, life in a single-parent family can be extremely stressful, in both economic and emotional terms. A family headed by a single mother faces especially difficult problems when the mother is a teenager.

Bent Balle, 40, an electronics technician who works in Denmark, talks with his wife Laurel Minikel, who practices obstetrics and gynecology in San Francisco. The number of couples who live apart for long periods increased 31 percent between 2000 and 2005.

Why might low-income teenage women wish to have children and face the obvious financial difficulties of motherhood? Viewed from an interactionist perspective, these women tend to have low self-esteem and limited options; a child may provide a sense of motivation and purpose for a teenager whose economic worth in our society is limited at best. Given the barriers that many young women face because of their gender, race, ethnicity, and class, many teenagers may believe they have little to lose and much to gain by having a child.

According to a widely held stereotype, "unwed mothers" and "babies having babies" in the United States are predominantly African American. However, this view is not entirely accurate. African Americans account for a disproportionate share of births to unmarried women and teenagers, but the majority of all babies born to unmarried teenage mothers are born to White adolescents. Moreover, since 1980, birthrates among Black teenagers have generally declined (J. Martin et al. 2009).

Although 88 percent of single parents in the United States are mothers, the number of households headed by single fathers more than quadrupled from 1987 to 2007. Though single mothers often develop social networks, single fathers are typically more isolated. In addition, they must deal with schools and social service agencies that are more accustomed to women as custodial parents (Bureau of the Census 1994, 2008a).

Stepfamilies Approximately 45 percent of all people in the United States will marry, divorce, and then remarry. The rising rates of divorce and remarriage have led to a noticeable increase in stepfamily relationships.

The exact nature of blended families has social significance for adults and children alike. Certainly resocialization is required when an adult becomes a stepparent or a child becomes a stepchild and stepsibling. Moreover, an important distinction must be made between first-time stepfamilies and households where there have been repeated divorces, breakups, or changes in custodial arrangements.

In evaluating the rise of stepfamilies, some observers have assumed that children would benefit from remarriage because they would be gaining a second custodial parent, and would potentially enjoy greater economic security. However, after reviewing many studies of stepfamilies, sociologist Andrew J. Cherlin (2008a:800) concluded that "the well-being of children in stepfamilies is no better, on average, than the well-being of children in divorced, single-parent households."

Stepparents can play valuable and unique roles in their stepchildren's lives, but their involvement does not guarantee an improvement in family life. In fact, standards may decline. Studies suggest that children raised in families with stepmothers are likely to have less health care, education, and money spent on their food than children raised by biological mothers. The measures are also negative for children raised by stepfathers, but only half as negative as in the case of stepmothers. These results don't mean that stepmothers are "evil"—it may be that the stepmother holds back out of concern for seeming too intrusive, or relies mistakenly on the biological father to carry out parental duties (Schmeeckle 2007; Schmeeckle et al. 2006).

Divorce

In the United States, the pattern of family life includes a commitment both to marriage and to self-expression and personal growth. Needless to say, the tension between those competing commitments can undermine a marriage, working against the establishment of a lasting relationship. This approach to family life is distinctive to the United States. In some nations, such as Italy, the culture strongly supports marriage and discourages divorce. In others, such as Sweden, people treat marriage the same way as cohabitation, and both arrangements are just as lasting (Cherlin 2009).

Statistical Trends in Divorce

Just how common is divorce? Surprisingly, this is not a simple question; divorce statistics are difficult to interpret. The media frequently report that one out of every two marriages ends in divorce, but that figure is misleading. It is based on a comparison of all divorces that occur in a single year (regardless of when the couples were married) with the number of new marriages in the same year.

Most households in the United States do not consist of two parents living with their unmarried children.

In many countries, divorce began to increase in the late 1960s but then leveled off; since the late 1980s, it has declined by 30 percent (for the pattern in the United States, see Figure 14-5). This trend is due partly to the aging of the baby boomer population and the corresponding decline in the proportion of people of marriageable age. But it also indicates an increase in marital stability in recent years (Coontz 2006).

Getting divorced obviously does not sour people on marriage. About 63 percent of all divorced people in the United States have remarried. Women are less likely than men to remarry because many retain custody of their children after a divorce, which complicates a new adult relationship (Bianchi and Spain 1996; Saad 2004).

Some people regard the nation's high rate of remarriage as an endorsement of the institution of marriage, but it does lead to the new challenges of a kin network composed of both current and prior marital relationships. Such networks can be particularly complex if children are involved or if an ex-spouse remarries.

Factors Associated with Divorce

Perhaps the most important factor in the increase in divorce over the past hundred years has been the greater social *acceptance* of divorce. It is no longer considered necessary to endure an

FIGURE **14-5** TRENDS IN MARRIAGE AND DIVORCE IN THE UNITED STATES, 1920–2008

Sources: Bureau of the Census 1975:64; *National Vital Statistics Reports* 2008.

RESEARCH TODAY

14-3   Divorce and Military Deployment

Today, the majority of soldiers in all branches of the military are married. What is the impact of war on them and their spouses? To answer this question, the Defense Department launched a study of military marriages. Researchers analyzed the Pentagon's personnel records on all members of the U.S. military from 1996 through 2005—that is, five years before and five years after the start of recent military operations. The data covered members of the active military, the reserves, and the National Guard. A separate analysis was done on couples married after 2002, because newly married couples are normally at greatest risk for divorce.

After all the data had been analyzed, researchers found that they did not support the commonsense notion that war might strain military marriages to the breaking point. In fact, soldiers who had been deployed overseas were *less* likely to end their marriages than those who had not been deployed. The longer the deployment, the lower the risk of divorce. Other studies of soldiers who served in the Vietnam War and the 1991 Persian Gulf War have come to the same conclusion.

There were some negative findings of the study. Female service members were found to be twice as likely as male service members to end their marriages. Moreover, enlisted service members were more likely than officers to end their marriages. This second disparity may be due to the fact that officers tend to be older than enlisted personnel, and older couples are less likely than younger couples to divorce.

Unfortunately, studies of the impact of overseas deployment on couples' children have not been nearly as reassuring. In 2007, an Army-funded study found that the rate of child neglect among military families was almost four times higher when husbands were deployed than when they were home. Physical abuse of children in those cases was nearly twice as high when husbands were away. Given these findings, one can only hope that support programs for families separated by war will be strengthened.

How can we explain the resiliency of service members' marriages in the face of war? Although wartime separation is undeniably

Welcome home! Military families reunite after a long, anxious separation.

stressful for couples, the researchers speculated that it might also benefit them, perhaps through higher earnings (combat pay) or the potential for career advancement. Moreover, many couples reported finding meaning and fulfillment in the deployment, which they saw as an important

> *Soldiers who had been deployed overseas were less likely to end their marriages than those who had not been deployed. The longer the deployment, the lower the risk of divorce.*

service to the nation. Finally, the spouses who are left behind are not totally isolated. The military provides strong social support, along with health care, child care, and housing subsidies. All these forms of support offer some protection from the impact of stress.

There is a need for further research on this topic. The information that researchers have covers only the short term and pertains only to those soldiers who remained in the military. Could the long-term impact on military couples be more telling? Could the outcome be different for those who leave the military soon after a war? And might soldiers consider marriage more carefully than the average person, knowing that their futures are uncertain? As with even the most detailed research, this study's conclusions raise new questions for scientific investigation.

LET'S DISCUSS

1. Do you know any married couples who have been separated by military deployment overseas? If so, how did they cope? What was the effect on their children?
2. Can you think of some other reasons why military marriages might survive the strain of war as well as they do?

Sources: Gibbs et al. 2007; Karney and Crown 2007; Krauss 1993; T. Perry 2007; Priest 2008; RAND 2007; A. Stone and Bello 2009.

---

unhappy marriage. More important, various religious denominations have relaxed their negative attitudes toward divorce, so that most religious leaders no longer treat it as a sin.

The growing acceptance of divorce is a worldwide phenomenon. A decade ago, Sunoo, South Korea's foremost matchmaking service, had no divorced clients. Few Koreans divorced; those

who did felt social pressure to resign themselves to the single life. But in one recent seven-year period, South Korea's divorce rate doubled. Today, 15 percent of Sunoo's membership are divorced (Onishi 2003).

In the United States, several factors have contributed to the growing social acceptance of divorce:

- Most states have adopted more liberal divorce laws in the past three decades. No-fault divorce laws, which allow a couple to end their marriage without fault on either side (by specifying adultery, for instance), accounted for an initial surge in the divorce rate after they were introduced in the 1970s, but appear to have had little effect beyond that.

- Divorce has become a more practical option in newly formed families, since families tend to have fewer children now than in the past.

- A general increase in family incomes, coupled with the availability of free legal aid to some poor people, has meant that more couples can afford costly divorce proceedings.

- As society provides greater opportunities for women, more and more wives are becoming less dependent on their husbands, both economically and emotionally. They may feel more able to leave a marriage if it seems hopeless.

What about the stress of separation caused by military duty? Forced transfer overseas, the tension of war, new duties at home, and anxiety over a spouse's return might seem a recipe for marital failure. Box 14-3 considers military marriages' vulnerability while the husband or wife is away at war.

Impact of Divorce on Children

Divorce is traumatic for all involved, but it has special meaning for the more than 1 million children whose parents divorce each year. Of course, for some of these children, divorce signals the welcome end to a very dysfunctional relationship. Perhaps that is why a national study that tracked 6,332 children both before and after their parents' divorce found that their behavior did not suffer from the marital breakups. Other studies have shown greater unhappiness among children who live amidst parental conflict than among children whose parents are divorced. Still, it would be simplistic to assume that children are automatically better off following the breakup of their parents' marriage. The interests of the parents do not necessarily serve children well (Zi 2007).

---

use your sociological *imagination*

In a society that maximizes the welfare of all family members, how easy should it be for couples to divorce? How easy should it be to get married?

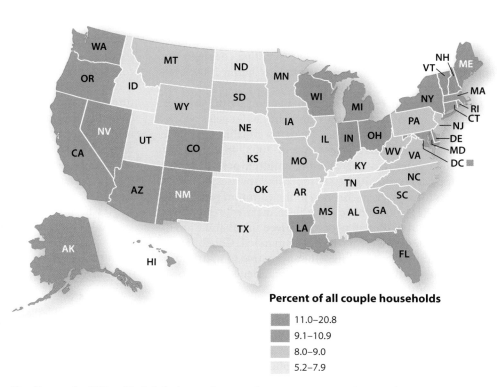

FIGURE **14-6** UNMARRIED-COUPLE HOUSEHOLDS BY STATE 327

MAPPING LIFE NATIONWIDE

Percent of all couple households

- 11.0–20.8
- 9.1–10.9
- 8.0–9.0
- 5.2–7.9

Note: Data are for 2000 and include both opposite-sex and same-sex partners. U.S. average is 9.1 percent.
Source: Simmons and O'Connell 2003:4.

Diverse Lifestyles

Marriage is no longer the presumed route from adolescence to adulthood. In fact, it has lost much of its social significance as a rite of passage. The nation's marriage rate has declined since 1960 because people are postponing marriage until later in life, and because more couples, including same-sex couples, are deciding to form partnerships without marriage.

Cohabitation

In the United States, testing the marital waters by living together before making a commitment is a common practice among marriage-wary 20- and 30-somethings. The tremendous increase in the number of male–female couples who choose to live together without marrying, a practice called **cohabitation,** is one of the most dramatic trends of recent years.

About half of all *currently* married couples in the United States say that they lived together before marriage. This percentage is likely to increase. The number of unmarried-couple households in the United States rose sixfold in the 1960s and increased another 72 percent between 1990 and 2000. Presently over 8 percent of opposite-sex couples are unmarried. Cohabitation is more common among African Americans and American Indians than among other racial and ethnic groups; it is least common among Asian Americans. Figure 14-6 shows regional variations in cohabitation (Peterson 2003; Simmons and O'Connell 2003).

In much of Europe, cohabitation is so common that the general sentiment seems to be "Love, yes; marriage, maybe." In

Iceland, 62 percent of all children are born to single mothers; in France, Great Britain, and Norway, the proportion is about 40 percent. Government policies in these countries make few legal distinctions between married and unmarried couples or households. Perhaps as a result, partnerships between cohabiting adults are not necessarily brief or lacking in commitment. Children born to a cohabiting couple in Sweden, for example, are less likely than children born to a cohabiting couple in the United States to see their parents break up (Cherlin 2009; Lyall 2002; M. Moore 2006).

People commonly associate cohabitation with younger couples. But according to a study done in Los Angeles, working couples are almost twice as likely to cohabit as college students. And census data show that in 2003, 45 percent of unmarried couples had one or more children present in the household. These cohabitants are more like spouses than dating partners. Moreover, in contrast to the common perception that people who cohabit have never been married, researchers report that about half of all people involved in cohabitation in the United States have been previously married. Cohabitation serves as a temporary or permanent alternative to matrimony for many men and women who have experienced their own or their parents' divorces (Jason Fields 2004; Popenoe and Whitehead 1999).

Periodically, legislators attempt to bolster the desirability of a lifelong commitment to marriage. In 2002, President George W. Bush backed funding for an initiative to promote marriage among those who receive public assistance. Under the Healthy Marriage Initiative, the federal government created a resource center that promoted marriage-related programs. Critics charged that the effort was underfunded or an inappropriate mission for the federal government. Still, the Obama administration has indicated a desire to continue the initiative, although the worsening economy may jeopardize its funding (Jayson 2009).

Remaining Single

Looking at TV programs today, you would be justified in thinking that most households are composed of singles. Although that is not the case, it is true that more and more people in the United States are *postponing* entry into a first marriage. Over one out of three households with children in the United States is a single-parent household. Even so, fewer than 4 percent of women and men in the United States are likely to remain single throughout their lives (Bureau of the Census 2008a).

The trend toward maintaining a single lifestyle for a longer period is related to the growing economic independence of young people. This trend is especially significant for women. Freed from financial needs, women don't necessarily need to marry to enjoy a satisfying life. Divorce, late marriage, and longevity also figure into this trend.

There are many reasons why a person may choose not to marry. Some singles do not want to limit their sexual intimacy to one lifetime partner. Some men and women do not want to

become highly dependent on any one person—and do not want anyone depending heavily on them. In a society that values individuality and self-fulfillment, the single lifestyle can offer certain freedoms that married couples may not enjoy. Even divorced parents may not feel the need to remarry. Sociologist Andrew J. Cherlin (2009) contends that a single parent who connects with other adults, such as grandparents, to form a solid, supportive relationship for child rearing should not feel compelled to re-partner.

Nevertheless, remaining single represents a clear departure from societal expectations; indeed, it has been likened to "being single on Noah's Ark." A single adult must confront the inaccurate view that he or she is always lonely, is a workaholic, or is immature. These stereotypes help to support the traditional assumption in the United States and most other societies that to be truly happy and fulfilled, a person must get married and raise a family. To counter these societal expectations, singles have formed numerous support groups (Hertz 2006; Lundquist 2006).

Marriage without Children

There has been a modest increase in childlessness in the United States. According to census data, about 16 to 17 percent of women will now complete their childbearing years without having borne any children, compared to 10 percent in 1980. As many as 20 percent of women in their 30s expect to remain childless (Biddlecom and Martin 2006).

Childlessness within marriage has generally been viewed as a problem that can be solved through such means as adoption and artificial insemination. More and more couples today, however, choose not to have children and regard themselves as child-free rather than childless. They do not believe that having children automatically follows from marriage, nor do they feel that reproduction is the duty of all married couples. Childless couples have formed support groups (with names like No Kidding) and set up Web sites.

Economic considerations have contributed to this shift in attitudes; having children has become quite expensive. According to a government estimate made for 2007, the average middle-class family will spend $204,060 to feed, clothe, and shelter a child from birth to age 18. If the child attends college, that amount could double, depending on the college chosen. Aware of the financial pressures, some couples are having fewer children than they otherwise might, and others are weighing the advantages of a child-free marriage (Lino 2008).

Childless couples are beginning to question current practices in the workplace. While applauding employers' efforts to provide child care and flexible work schedules, some nevertheless express concern about tolerance of employees who leave early to take children to doctors, ballgames, or after-school classes. As more dual-career couples enter the paid labor force and struggle to balance career and familial responsibilities, conflicts with employees who have no children may increase (Biddlecom and Martin 2006).

---

use your sociological *imagination*

What would happen to our society if many more married couples suddenly decided not to have children? How would society change if cohabitation and/or singlehood became the norm?

Lesbian and Gay Relationships

Twenty-one-year-old Parke, a junior in college, grew up in a stable, loving family. A self-described fiscal conservative, he credits his parents with instilling in him a strong work ethic. Sound like an average child of an average family? The only break with traditional expectations in this case is that Parke is the son of a lesbian couple (P. L. Brown 2004).

The lifestyles of lesbians and gay men are varied. Some live in long-term, monogamous relationships; others live alone or with roommates. Some remain in "empty-shell" heterosexual marriages and do not publicly acknowledge their homosexuality. Others live with children from a former marriage or with adopted children. Based on election exit polls, researchers for the National Health and Social Life Survey and the Voter News Service estimate that 2 to 5 percent of the adult population identify themselves as either gay or lesbian. An analysis of the 2000 census shows a minimum of at least 600,000 gay households, and a gay and lesbian adult population approaching 10 million (E. O. Laumann et al. 1994b:293; David M. Smith and Gates 2001).

Gay and lesbian couples face discrimination on both a personal and a legal level. Their inability to marry denies them many rights that married couples take for granted, from the ability to make decisions for an incapacitated partner to the right to receive government benefits to dependents, such as Social Security payments. Though gay couples consider themselves families just like the straight couples who live down the street, they are often treated as if they are not.

Precisely because of such inequities, many gay and lesbian couples are now demanding the right to marry. In the Social Policy section that follows, we will examine the highly controversial issue of gay marriage.

---

social**policy** and the Family

Gay Marriage

The Issue

In the United States, attitudes toward marriage are complex. As always, society and popular culture suggest that a young man or woman should find the perfect mate, settle down and marry, and live happily ever after. But young people are also bombarded by messages implying the frequency of adultery and the acceptability of divorce. In this atmosphere, the idea of same-sex marriage strikes some people as only the latest of many attacks on traditional marriage. To others, it seems an overdue acknowledgment of the formal relationships that faithful, monogamous gay couples have long maintained.

The Setting

What has made gay marriage the focus of national attention? Events in two states brought the issue to the forefront. In 1999, Vermont gave gay couples the legal benefits of marriage through civil union, but stopped short of calling the arrangement a marriage. Then, in 2003, the Massachusetts Supreme Court ruled 4–3 that under the state's constitution, gay couples have the right to marry—a ruling the U.S. Supreme Court has refused to review. Now, with gay married couples in this state passing their 5th anniversaries and approaching their 10th, scholars are beginning to study their experiences compared to those of opposite-sex couples.

Sociological Insights

Functionalists have traditionally seen marriage as a social institution that is closely tied to human reproduction. Same-sex marriage would at first appear not to fit that arrangement. But many same-sex couples are entrusted with the socialization of young children, whether or not their relationship is recognized by the state. Functionalists also wonder whether religious views toward marriage can be ignored. The courts have focused on civil marriage, but religious

Kate Kendell, executive director of the National Center for Lesbian Rights, demonstrates for gay marriage outside the California Supreme Court.

views are hardly irrelevant, even in a country like the United States, which observes a separation between religion and the state. Indeed, religious teachings have led even some staunch supporters of gay rights to oppose same-sex marriage on spiritual grounds.

Conflict theorists have charged that denial of the right to marry reinforces the second-class status of gays and lesbians. Some have compared the ban against gay marriage to past policies that until 1967 banned interracial marriage in 32 states (Liptak 2004).

Interactionists generally avoid the policy question and focus instead on the nature of same-sex households. They ask many of the same questions about gay partner relations and child rearing that they ask about conventional couples. Of course, much less research has been done on same-sex households than on other families, but the studies published to date raise the same issues as those that apply to conventional married couples, plus a few more. For gay couples, the support or opposition of family, co-workers, and friends looms large (Dundas and Kaufman 2000; Dunne 2000).

Recently, national surveys of attitudes toward gay marriage in the United States have shown an almost even split among the public. In 2007, 46 percent of those surveyed felt that marriages between same-sex couples should be considered valid, while 53 percent felt that they should not be recognized. These results reflect a gradual shift in the level of acceptance of gay marriage since 1982, when 34 percent of respondents felt that it should be legal (Gallup 2008b).

Policy Initiatives

The United States is not the first nation to consider this issue. Recognition of same-sex partnerships is common in Europe, including legal recognition of same-sex marriage in Belgium, Netherlands, Norway, Spain, and Sweden. Today, as many as 8 percent of all marriages in the Netherlands are same-sex. The trend is toward recognition in North America as well, since gay couples can marry legally in Canada.

Many nations strongly oppose such measures, however. For example, when Kofi Annan, then secretary general of the United Nations (UN), proposed extending the benefits that married UN employees receive to employees' same-sex partners in 2004, so many countries rose in protest that he reneged. Annan decided that such benefits would extend only to those UN employees whose member nations extend the same benefits to their citizens (Cowell 2005; Farley 2004; Wines 2005).

In the United States, many local jurisdictions have passed legislation allowing for the registration of domestic partnerships, and have extended employee benefits to those relationships. Under such policies, a **domestic partnership** may be defined as two unrelated adults who share a mutually caring relationship, reside together, and agree to be jointly responsible for their dependents, basic living expenses, and other common necessities. Domestic partnership benefits can apply to couples' inheritance, parenting, pensions, taxation, housing, immigration, workplace fringe benefits, and health care. Even though the most passionate support for domestic partnership legislation has come from lesbian and gay activists, the majority of those eligible for such benefits would be cohabiting heterosexual couples.

In the United States, marriage has traditionally been under the jurisdiction of state lawmakers. But recently, pressure has been mounting for national legislation. The Defense of Marriage Act, passed in 1996, provided that no state is obliged to recognize same-sex marriages performed in another state. However, some legal scholars doubt that the law could withstand a constitutional challenge, since it violates a provision in the Constitution that requires states to recognize one another's laws. In 2003, therefore, opponents of gay marriage proposed a constitutional amendment that would limit marriage to heterosexual couples. The measure was introduced in the Senate in 2006, but failed to receive sufficient support to come to a vote.

Within the United States, state courts in California, Iowa, and Massachusetts have ruled that there is no state law that precludes same-sex marriage. In California, 18,000 same-sex couples were married before voters amended the state constitution to prohibit such marriages in the future. However, in 2009, Maine and Vermont extended full legality to same-sex marriages. Although gay unions may be legal within these states, their status out of state is much less clear, as is the future of gay marriage. Gay rights activists claim their movement is gathering momentum, but opponents argue that their high-profile actions have galvanized conservatives who wish to define marriage as the union of one man and one woman.

Let's Discuss

1. If marriage is good for heterosexual couples and their families, why isn't it good for homosexual couples and their families?

2. How can interactionist studies of gay couples and their families inform policymakers who are dealing with the issue of gay marriage? Give a specific example.

3. Who are the stakeholders in the debate over gay marriage, and what do they stand to gain or lose? Whose interest do you think is most important?

getting**involved**

To get involved in the debate over gay marriage, visit this book's Online Learning Center, which offers links to relevant Web sites.

www.mhhe.com/schaefer12e

MASTERING THIS CHAPTER

Summary

The **family**, in its many varying forms, is present in all human cultures. This chapter examines the state of marriage, the family, and other intimate relationships in the United States and considers alternatives to the traditional **nuclear family**.

1. **Families** vary from culture to culture and even within the same culture.

2. The structure of the **extended family** can offer certain advantages over that of the **nuclear family**.

3. Societies determine **kinship** by descent from both parents (**bilateral descent**), from the father only (**patrilineal descent**), or from the mother only (**matrilineal descent**).

4. Sociologists do not agree on whether the **egalitarian family** has replaced the patriarchal family as the social norm in the United States.

5. William F. Ogburn outlined six basic functions of the family: reproduction, protection, socialization, regulation of sexual behavior, companionship, and the provision of social status.

6. Conflict theorists argue that male dominance of the family contributes to societal injustice and denies women opportunities that are extended to men.

7. Interactionists focus on how individuals interact in the family and in other intimate relationships.

8. Feminists stress the need to broaden research on the family. Like conflict theorists, they see the family's role in socializing children as the primary source of sexism.

9. People select mates in a variety of ways. Some marriages are arranged; in other societies people choose their own mates. Some societies require mates to be chosen within a certain group (**endogamy**) or outside certain groups (**exogamy**). And consciously or unconsciously, many people look for a mate with similar personal characteristics (**homogamy**).

10. In the United States, family life varies with social class, race, and ethnicity.

11. Currently, in the majority of all married couples in the United States, both husband and wife work outside the home.

12. **Single-parent families** account for an increasing proportion of U.S. families.

13. Among the factors that contribute to the rising divorce rate in the United States are greater social acceptance of divorce and the liberalization of divorce laws in many states.

14. More and more people are living together without marrying, a practice known as **cohabitation**. People are also staying single longer, and some married couples are deciding not to have children.

15. The gay marriage movement, which would confer equal rights on gay and lesbian couples and their dependents, is strongly opposed by conservative religious and political groups.

Critical Thinking Questions

1. In an increasing proportion of couples in the United States, both partners work outside the home. What are the advantages and disadvantages of the dual-income model for women, for men, for children, and for society as a whole?

2. Choose three television programs that portray the family, either from the current season or from the past. Using your newly acquired understanding of the family in the United States, analyze each program.

3. Given the high rate of divorce in the United States, would it be more appropriate to view divorce as dysfunctional or as a normal part of our marriage system? What would be the implications of viewing divorce as normal rather than dysfunctional?

Key Terms

Adoption In a legal sense, a process that allows for the transfer of the legal rights, responsibilities, and privileges of parenthood to a new legal parent or parents. (page 322)

Bilateral descent A kinship system in which both sides of a person's family are regarded as equally important. (315)

Cohabitation The practice of living together as a male–female couple without marrying. (327)

Domestic partnership Two unrelated adults who share a mutually caring relationship, reside together, and agree to be jointly responsible for their dependents, basic living expenses, and other common necessities. (330)

Egalitarian family An authority pattern in which spouses are regarded as equals. (315)

Endogamy The restriction of mate selection to people within the same group. (318)

Exogamy The requirement that people select a mate outside certain groups. (318)

Extended family A family in which relatives—such as grandparents, aunts, or uncles—live in the same home as parents and their children. (313)

Familism Pride in the extended family, expressed through the maintenance of close ties and strong obligations to kinfolk outside the immediate family. (321)

Family A set of people related by blood, marriage or some other agreed-on relationship, or adoption, who share the primary responsibility for reproduction and caring for members of society. (312)

Homogamy The conscious or unconscious tendency to select a mate with personal characteristics similar to one's own. (318)

Incest taboo The prohibition of sexual relationships between certain culturally specified relatives. (318)

Kinship The state of being related to others. (315)

Machismo A sense of virility, personal worth, and pride in one's maleness. (321)

Matriarchy A society in which women dominate in family decision making. (315)

Matrilineal descent A kinship system in which only the mother's relatives are significant. (315)

Monogamy A form of marriage in which one woman and one man are married only to each other. (313)

Nuclear family A married couple and their unmarried children living together. (313)

Patriarchy A society in which men dominate in family decision making. (315)

Patrilineal descent A kinship system in which only the father's relatives are significant. (315)

Polyandry A form of polygamy in which a woman may have more than one husband at the same time. (314)

Polygamy A form of marriage in which an individual may have several husbands or wives simultaneously. (314)

Polygyny A form of polygamy in which a man may have more than one wife at the same time. (314)

Serial monogamy A form of marriage in which a person may have several spouses in his or her lifetime, but only one spouse at a time. (313)

Single-parent family A family in which only one parent is present to care for the children. (324)

Self-Quiz

Read each question carefully and then select the best answer.

1. Alice, age seven, lives in a private home with her parents, her grandmother, and her aunt. Alice's family is an example of a(n)
  a. nuclear family.
  b. dysfunctional family.
  c. extended family.
  d. polygynous family.

2. In which form of marriage may a person have several spouses in his or her lifetime, but only one spouse at a time?
  a. serial monogamy
  b. monogamy
  c. polygamy
  d. polyandry

3. The marriage of a woman to more than one man at the same time is referred to as
  a. polygyny.
  b. monogamy.
  c. serial monogamy.
  d. polyandry.

4. Which system of descent is followed in the United States?
  a. matrilineal
  b. patrilineal
  c. bilateral
  d. unilateral

5. According to the functionalist perspective, which of the following is *not* one of the paramount functions performed by the family?
  a. mediation
  b. reproduction
  c. regulation of sexual behavior
  d. affection and companionship

6. Which norm requires mate selection outside certain groups, usually one's own family or certain kinfolk?
  a. exogamy
  b. endogamy

  c. matriarchy
  d. patriarchy

7. According to the discussion of social class differences in family life and intimate relationships, which of the following statements is true?
  a. Social class differences in family life are more striking than they once were.
  b. The upper class emphasizes lineage and maintenance of family position.
  c. Among the poor, women usually play an insignificant role in the economic support of the family.
  d. In examining family life among racial and ethnic minorities, most patterns result from cultural, but *not* class, factors.

8. One recent development in family life in the United States has been the extension of parenthood as adult children continue to live at home or return home after college. The reason for this is
  a. the rising divorce rate.
  b. skyrocketing rent and real estate prices.
  c. financial difficulties.
  d. all of the above

9. In the United States, the *majority* of all babies born to unmarried teenage mothers are born to whom?
  a. African American adolescents
  b. White adolescents
  c. Latina adolescents
  d. Asian American adolescents

10. Which of the following factors is associated with the high divorce rate in the United States?
  a. the liberalization of divorce laws
  b. the fact that contemporary families have fewer children than earlier families did
  c. the general increase in family incomes
  d. all of the above

11. The principle of _____ assigns people to kinship groups according to their relationship to an individual's mother or father.

12. _____ emerged among Native American tribal societies, and in nations in which men were absent for long periods because of warfare or food-gathering expeditions.

13. In the view of many sociologists, the _____ family has begun to replace the patriarchal family as the social norm in the United States.

14. As _____ theorists point out, the social class of couples and their children significantly influences the socialization experiences to which the children are exposed, and the protection they receive.

15. _____ focus on the micro level of family and other intimate relationships; for example, they are interested in whether people are cohabiting partners or are longtime married couples.

16. The rule of _____ specifies the groups within which a spouse must be found and prohibits marriage with others.

17. Social class differences in family life are less striking today than they once were; however, in the past, _____-class families were found to be more authoritarian in rearing children and more inclined to use physical punishment.

18. Caring for children is a(n) _____ function of the family, yet the ways in which different societies assign this function to family members can vary significantly.

19. Viewed from the _____ perspective, the government has a strong interest in encouraging adoption.

20. The rising rates of divorce and remarriage have led to a noticeable increase in _____ relationships.

THINKING ABOUT MOVIES

Juno (Jason Reitman, 2007)

High school student Juno MacGuff (Ellen Page) gets pregnant and must decide what to do about the baby. Juno's birth mother has essentially abandoned her; now she lives in a blended family with her father and stepmother. Opting to put her child up for adoption, she responds to a local advertisement by a seemingly loving couple. As she comes to know the prospective adoptive parents, Juno is forced to make difficult decisions about her unborn child's future.

This movie shows adoption from the perspectives of both the birth mother and the adoptive parents. At the same time, it validates alternative families and single mothers. Watch for signs of the social-class differences between Juno and the adoptive couple.

For Your Consideration

1. How do Juno's perspective on the adoptive parents and her hopes for her child's socialization in their family change as she comes to know them?

2. In what ways does Juno's stepfamily affect her socialization and her effort to find a home for her unborn child?

The Host
(Joon-ho Bong, 2007)

On the banks of the River Han in Seoul, South Korea, people are enjoying a leisurely summer's day when a terrifying monster emerges from the deep and goes on a rampage, killing or capturing several victims. Before escaping into the sewers, the monster seizes Park Hyun-seo (Ah-sung Ko), a young girl whose father, Park Gang-Du (Kang-ho Song), works in a snack shop by the river. Gang-Du and his extended family work together to find the monster's lair and rescue Hyun-seo. As they search for her, we learn more about their familial ties, as well as some ways in which children are raised in single-parent families.

Though on the surface *The Host* seems like a conventional creature feature, it is also a delicate portrayal of an extended family that includes two nuclear families whose fathers are the primary caregivers. Pay particular attention to the early scenes that establish the relationships between three generations of the Park family.

For Your Consideration

1. How does the Park family's social network contribute to their child rearing?

2. In what ways does the movie overcome the stigma and stereotypes associated with single-parent families?

inside

Durkheim and the
Sociological Approach
to Religion

World Religions

Sociological Perspectives
on Religion

Components of Religion

Religious Organization

Case Study: Religion in India

Social Policy and Religion:
Religion in the Schools

BOXES

Research Today: *Income and
Education, Religiously
Speaking*

Research Today: *Islam in
the United States*

Research Today: *The Church
of Scientology: Religion
or Quasi-Religion?*

Buddhist monks processing
at Shweyanpyay Monastery,
Myanmar. Around the world,
enormous diversity can be
seen in people's religious
beliefs and practices.

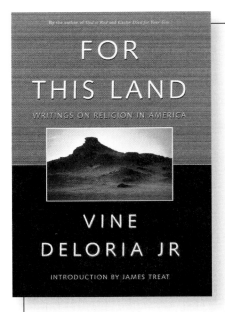

FOR THIS LAND

WRITINGS ON RELIGION IN AMERICA

VINE DELORIA JR

INTRODUCTION BY JAMES TREAT

" Growing up in a small mixed-blood community of seven hundred on the eastern edge of the Pine Ridge Reservation in South Dakota, I uncritically accepted the idea that the old Dakota religion and Christianity were both "true" and in some mysterious way compatible with each other. There were, to be sure, Christian fundamentalists with their intolerance and the old traditional Indians who kept their practices hidden, but the vast majority of the people in the vicinity more or less assumed that a satisfactory blend had been achieved that guaranteed our happiness.

Although my father was an Episcopal priest with a large number of chapels in a loosely organized Episcopal missionary district known (to Episcopalians) as "Corn Creek," he was far from an orthodox follower of the white man's religion. I always had the feeling that within the large context of "religion," which in a border town meant the Christian milieu, there was a special area in his spiritual life in which the old Dakota beliefs and practices reigned supreme. He knew thirty-three songs; some of them social, some ancient, and several spiritual songs used in a variety of ceremonial contexts. Driving to his chapels to hold Christian services he would open the window of the car and beat the side of the door with his hand for the drum beat and sing song after song. . . .

Although my father was an Episcopal priest with a large number of chapels in a loosely organized Episcopal missionary district known (to Episcopalians) as "Corn Creek," he was far from an orthodox follower of the white man's religion.

When I went to college I was exposed to a much larger canvas of human experience upon which various societies had left their religious mark. My first reaction was the belief that most of the religious traditions were simply wrong, that a few of them had come close to describing religious reality, but that it would take some intensive study to determine which religious traditions would best assist human beings in succeeding in the world. It was my good fortune to have as a religion and philosophy professor a Christian mystic who was trying to prove the deepest mysteries of the faith. He also had some intense personal problems which emerged again and again in his beliefs, indicating to me that religion and the specific individual path of life were always intertwined.

Over several years and many profound conversations he was able to demonstrate to me that each religious tradition had developed a unique way to confront some problems and that they had something in common if only the search for truth and the elimination of many false paths. But his solution, after many years, became untenable for me. I saw instead religion simply as a means of organizing a society, articulating some reasonably apparent emotional truths, but ultimately becoming a staid part of social establishments that primarily sought to control human behavior and not fulfill human individual potential. It seemed as if those religions that placed strong emphasis on certain concepts failed precisely in the areas in which they claimed expertise. Thus religions of "love" could point to few examples of their efficacy; religions of "salvation" actually saved very few. The more I learned about world religions, the more respect I had for the old Dakota ways. "

(Deloria 1999:273–275) Additional information about this excerpt can be found on the Online Learning Center at www.mhhe.com/schaefer12e.

In this excerpt from *For This Land*, the late Vine Deloria—a Standing Rock Sioux—revealed his deep personal ties to the religion of his ancestors, undiluted by the overlays of missionary Christian theology. Even though his father was an Episcopal priest, Deloria was keenly aware of how tribal beliefs intruded to color his father's religious sensibility. He was also aware of the fact that Native American rites and customs had been appropriated by a generation of non-Indians seeking a kind of New Age "magic." For Deloria, Indian spiritual beliefs were an integral part of the Native American culture and helped to define that culture. Mixing those beliefs with the beliefs of other religions or systems of thought threatened to undermine the culture's strength.

Religion plays a major role in people's lives, and religious practices of some sort are evident in every society. That makes religion a cultural universal, along with other common practices or beliefs found in every culture, such as dancing, food

preparation, the family, and personal names. At present, an estimated 4 billion people belong to the world's many religious faiths.

When religion's influence on other social institutions in a society diminishes, the process of **secularization** is said to be under way. During this process, religion will survive in the private sphere of individual and family life (as in the case of many Native American families); it may even thrive on a personal level. But at the same time, other social institutions—such as the economy, politics, and education—maintain their own sets of norms, independent of religious guidance. Even so, religion is enormously resilient. Although specific faiths or organizations may change, their transformation does not signal the demise of religious faith. Rather, it contributes to the diversity of religious expression and organization. Figure 15-1 gives an idea of the variety of faiths in the United States alone (Christian Smith 2008; Stark 2004).

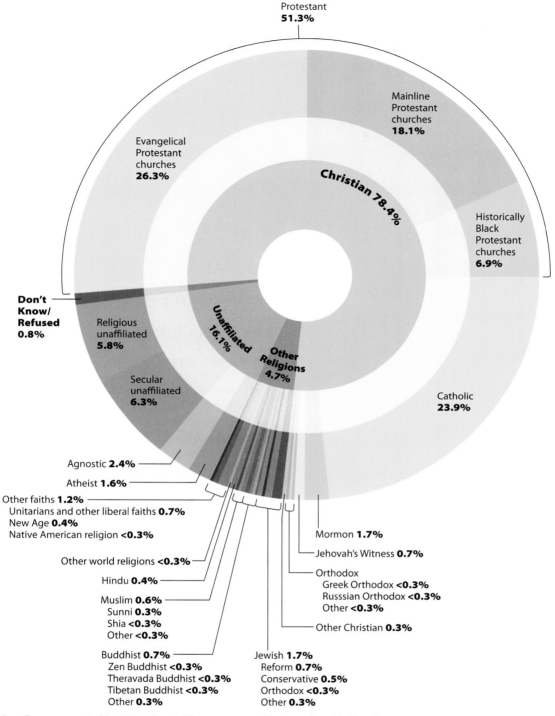

Protestant 51.3%

Mainline Protestant churches 18.1%

Evangelical Protestant churches 26.3%

Christian 78.4%

Historically Black Protestant churches 6.9%

Don't Know/ Refused 0.8%

Religious unaffiliated 5.8%

Unaffiliated 16.1%

Other Religions 4.7%

Catholic 23.9%

Secular unaffiliated 6.3%

Agnostic **2.4%**

Atheist **1.6%**

Other faiths **1.2%**
Unitarians and other liberal faiths **0.7%**
New Age **0.4%**
Native American religion **<0.3%**

Other world religions **<0.3%**

Hindu **0.4%**

Muslim **0.6%**
Sunni **0.3%**
Shia **<0.3%**
Other **<0.3%**

Buddhist **0.7%**
Zen Buddhist **<0.3%**
Theravada Buddhist **<0.3%**
Tibetan Buddhist **<0.3%**
Other **0.3%**

Jewish **1.7%**
Reform **0.7%**
Conservative **0.5%**
Orthodox **<0.3%**
Other **0.3%**

Other Christian **0.3%**

Orthodox
Greek Orthodox **<0.3%**
Russsian Orthodox **<0.3%**
Other **<0.3%**

Mormon **1.7%**

Jehovah's Witness **0.7%**

Note: Due to rounding, figures may not add to 100 and nested figures may not add to the subtotal indicated.
Source: Pew Forum on Religion and Public Life 2008:5.

As bewildering as this representation of religion may seem at first glance, it accurately reflects the diversity of faith in the United States.

Think about It
Where would you place yourself in this diagram? How about your best friends?

What social purposes does religion serve? Does it help to hold society together or foster social change? What happens when religion mixes with politics? This chapter concentrates on the formal systems of religion that characterize modern industrial societies. We will begin with a brief description of the sociological perspectives on religion, followed by an overview of the world's major religions. Next, we will explore religion's role in societal integration, social support, social change, and social control. We'll examine three important components of religious behavior—belief, ritual, and experience—as well as the basic forms of religious organization, including new religious movements. In a special case study, we'll take a fascinating look at religion in India. The chapter will close with a Social Policy section on the controversy over religion in U.S. public schools.

Durkheim and the Sociological Approach to Religion

If a group believes that it is being directed by a "vision from God," sociologists do not attempt to prove or disprove the revelation. Instead, they assess the effects of the religious experience on the group. What sociologists are interested in is the social impact of religion on individuals and institutions.

Émile Durkheim was perhaps the first sociologist to recognize the critical importance of religion in human societies. He saw its appeal for the individual, but more important, he stressed the *social* impact of religion. In Durkheim's view, religion is a collective act that includes many forms of behavior in which people interact with others. As in his work on suicide, Durkheim was not so interested in the personalities of religious believers as he was in understanding religious behavior within a social context.

Durkheim defined **religion** as a "unified system of beliefs and practices relative to sacred things." In his view, religion involves a set of beliefs and practices that are uniquely the property of religion, as opposed to other social institutions and ways of thinking. Durkheim ([1893] 1933; [1912] 2001) argued that religious faiths distinguish between certain transcending events and the everyday world. He referred to those realms as the *sacred* and the *profane*.

The **sacred** encompasses elements beyond everyday life that inspire awe, respect, and even fear. People become part of the sacred realm only by completing some ritual, such as prayer or sacrifice. Because believers have faith in the sacred, they accept what they cannot understand. In contrast, the **profane** includes the ordinary and commonplace. This concept can be confusing, however, because the same object can be either sacred or profane, depending on how it is viewed. A normal dining

room table is profane, but becomes sacred to some Christians if it bears the elements of a communion. A candelabra becomes sacred to Jews if it is a menorah. For Confucians and Taoists, incense sticks are not mere decorative items, but highly valued offerings to the gods in religious ceremonies that mark the new and full moons.

Following the direction established by Durkheim almost a century ago, contemporary sociologists view religion in two different ways. First, they study the norms and values of religious faiths by examining their substantive beliefs. For example, it is possible to compare the degree to which Christian faiths interpret the Bible literally, or Muslim groups follow the Qur'an (or Koran), the sacred book of Islam. At the same time, sociologists examine religion in terms of the social functions it fulfills, such as providing social support or reinforcing social norms. By exploring both the beliefs and the functions of religion, we can better understand its impact on the individual, on groups, and on society as a whole.

World Religions

Worldwide, tremendous diversity exists in religious beliefs and practices (Figure 15-2). Overall, about 85 percent of the world's population adheres to some religion; only about 15 percent is nonreligious. This level of adherence changes over time and also varies by country and age group. In the United States today, those who are nonreligious account for less than 10 to 14 percent of the population; in 1900, they constituted a mere 1.3 percent of all Americans. And in 2008, 21 percent of incoming U.S. college students had no religious preference, compared to 11 percent of their mothers (Hout and Fischer 2002; Pryor et al. 2008; Winseman 2005).

Christianity is the largest single faith in the world; the second largest is Islam (Table 15-1 on page 340). Although global news events often suggest an inherent conflict between Christians and Muslims, the two faiths are similar in many ways. Both are monotheistic (based on a single deity); both include a belief in prophets, an afterlife, and a judgment day. In fact, Islam recognizes Jesus as a prophet, though not the son of God. Both faiths impose a moral code on believers, which varies from fairly rigid proscriptions for fundamentalists to relatively relaxed guidelines for liberals.

The followers of Islam, called *Muslims*, believe that Islam's holy scriptures were received from Allah (God) by the prophet Mohammad nearly 1,400 years ago. They see Mohammad as the last in a long line of prophets, preceded by Adam, Abraham, Moses, and Jesus. Islam is more communal in its expression than Christianity, particularly the more individualistic Protestant denominations. Consequently, in countries that are predominantly Muslim, the separation of religion and the state is not considered necessary or even desirable. In fact, Muslim governments often reinforce Islamic practices through their laws. Muslims do vary sharply in their interpretation of several traditions, some of which—such as the wearing of veils by women—are more cultural than religious in origin.

Like Christianity and Islam, Judaism is monotheistic. Jews believe that God's true nature is revealed in the Torah, which

FIGURE **15-2** RELIGIONS OF THE WORLD

MAPPING LIFE WORLDWIDE

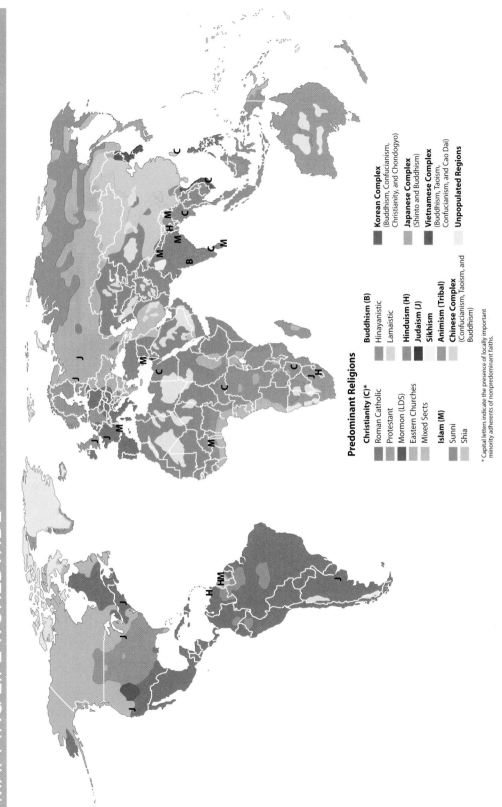

Predominant Religions

Christianity (C)*
Roman Catholic
Protestant
Mormon (LDS)
Eastern Churches
Mixed Sects

Islam (M)
Sunni
Shia

Buddhism (B)
Hinayanistic
Lamaistic

Hinduism (H)

Judaism (J)

Sikhism

Animism (Tribal)

Chinese Complex
(Confucianism, Taoism, and
Buddhism)

Korean Complex
(Buddhism, Confucianism,
Christianity, and Chondogyo)

Japanese Complex
(Shinto and Buddhism)

Vietnamese Complex
(Buddhism, Taoism,
Confucianism, and Cao Dai)

Unpopulated Regions

* Capital letters indicate the presence of locally important
minority adherents of nonpredominant faiths.

Source: J. Allen 2010:31.
Religious adherence is one of the defining social characteristics of a culture.

Christians know as the first five books of the Old Testament. According to these scriptures, God formed a covenant, or pact, with Abraham and Sarah, the ancestors of the tribes of Israel. Even today, Jews believe, this covenant holds them accountable to God's will. If they follow both the letter and spirit of the Torah, a long-awaited Messiah will one day bring paradise to earth. Although Judaism has a relatively small following compared to other major faiths, it forms the historical foundation for both Christianity and Islam. That is why Jews revere many of the same sacred Middle Eastern sites as Christians and Muslims.

Two other major faiths developed in a different part of the world, India. The earliest, Hinduism, originated around 1500 B.C. Hinduism differs from Judaism, Christianity, and Islam in that it embraces a number of gods and minor gods, although most worshippers are devoted primarily to a single deity, such as Shiva or Vishnu. Hinduism is also distinguished by a belief in reincarnation, or the perpetual rebirth of the soul after death. Unlike Judaism, Christianity, and Islam, which are based largely on sacred texts, Hindu beliefs have been preserved mostly through oral tradition.

A second religion, Buddhism, developed in the sixth century B.C. as a reaction against Hinduism. This faith is founded on the teachings of Siddhartha (later called Buddha, or "the enlightened one"). Through meditation, followers of Buddhism strive to overcome selfish cravings for physical or material pleasures, with the goal of reaching a state of enlightenment, or nirvana. Buddhists created the first monastic orders, which are thought to be the models for monastic orders in other religions, including Christianity. Though Buddhism emerged in India, its followers were eventually driven out of that country by the Hindus. It is now found primarily in other parts of Asia. (Contemporary adherents of Buddhism in India are relatively recent converts.)

Although the differences among religions are striking, they are exceeded by variations within faiths. Consider the variations within Christianity, from relatively liberal denominations such as Presbyterians or the United Church of Christ to the more conservative Mormons and Greek Orthodox Catholics. Similar variations exist within Hinduism, Islam, and other world religions (Barrett et al. 2008; Swatos 1998).

use your sociological *imagination*

What evidence do you see of different religions in the area surrounding your college or university? What about on campus?

TABLE **15-1** MAJOR WORLD RELIGIONS   summing**up**

Faith	Current Following, in Millions (and Percentage of World Population)	Primary Location of Followers Today	Founder (and Approximate Birth Date)	Important Texts (and Holy Sites)
Buddhism	386 (5.8%)	Southeast Asia, Mongolia, Tibet	Gautama Siddhartha (563 B.C)	Triptaka (areas in Nepal)
Christianity	2,200 (33.3%)	Europe, North America, South America	Jesus (6 B.C.)	Bible (Jerusalem, Rome)
Hinduism	876 (13.2%)	India, Indian communities overseas	No specific founder (1500 B.C.)	Sruti and Smrti texts (seven sacred cities, including Vavansi)
Islam	1,387 (21.0%)	Middle East, Central Asia, North Africa, Indonesia	Mohammad (A.D. 570)	Qur'an, or Koran (Mecca, Medina, Jerusalem)
Judaism	11 (0.2%)	Israel, United States, France, Russia	Abraham (2000 B.C.)	Torah, Talmud (Jerusalem)

Source: Author based on Barrett et al. 2008; Swatos 1998.

Sociological Perspectives on Religion

Since religion is a cultural universal, it is not surprising that it plays a basic role in human societies. In sociological terms, it performs both manifest and latent functions. Among its *manifest* (open and stated) functions, religion defines the spiritual world and gives meaning to the divine. It provides an explanation for events that seem difficult to understand, such as what lies beyond the grave. The *latent* functions of religion are unintended, covert, or hidden. Even though the manifest function of a church service is to offer a forum for religious worship, it might at the same time fulfill a latent social function as a meeting ground for unmarried members.

Functionalists and conflict theorists both evaluate religion's impact on human societies. We'll consider a functionalist view of religion's role in integrating society, providing social support, and promoting social change, and then look at religion from the conflict perspective, as a means of social control. Note that for the most part, religion's impact is best understood from a macro-level viewpoint that is oriented toward the larger society. Its social support function is an exception: it is best viewed on the micro, or individual, level.

The Integrative Function of Religion

Émile Durkheim viewed religion as an integrative force in human society—a perspective that is reflected in functionalist thought today. Durkheim sought to answer a perplexing question: "How can human societies be held together when they are generally composed of individuals and social groups with diverse interests and aspirations?" In his view, religious bonds often transcend these personal and divisive forces. Durkheim acknowledged that religion is not the only integrative force; nationalism or patriotism may serve the same end.

How does religion provide this "societal glue"? Religion, whether it be Buddhism, Islam, Christianity, or Judaism, gives meaning and purpose to people's lives. It offers certain ultimate values and ends to hold in common. Although they are subjective and not always fully accepted, these values and ends help society to function as an integrated social system. For example, funerals, weddings, bar and bat mitzvahs, and confirmations serve to integrate people into larger communities by providing shared beliefs and values about the ultimate questions of life.

Religion also serves to bind people together in times of crisis and confusion. Immediately after the terrorist attacks of September 11, 2001, on New York City and Washington, D.C., attendance at worship services in the United States increased dramatically. Muslim, Jewish, and Christian clerics made joint appearances to honor the dead and urge citizens not to retaliate against those who looked, dressed, or sounded different from others. A year later, however, attendance levels had returned to normal (D. Moore 2002).

The integrative power of religion can be seen, too, in the role that churches, synagogues, and mosques have traditionally played and continue to play for immigrant groups in the United States. For example, Roman Catholic immigrants may settle near a parish church that offers services in their native language, such as Polish or Spanish. Similarly, Korean immigrants may join a Presbyterian church that has many Korean American members

and follows religious practices like those of churches in Korea. Like other religious organizations, these Roman Catholic and Presbyterian churches help to integrate immigrants into their new homeland.

Religion also strengthens social integration within specific faiths and denominations. In many faiths, members share certain characteristics that help to bind them together, including their race, ethnicity, and social class. Box 15-1 on page 342 examines the income and educational levels characteristic of specific denominations in the United States.

In some instances, religious loyalties are *dysfunctional;* that is, they contribute to tension and even conflict between groups or nations. During the Second World War, the German Nazis attempted to exterminate the Jewish people; approximately 6 million European Jews were killed. In modern times, nations such as Lebanon (Muslims versus Christians), Israel (Jews versus Muslims, as well as Orthodox versus secular Jews), Northern Ireland (Roman Catholics versus Protestants), and India (Hindus versus Muslims, and more recently, Sikhs) have been torn by clashes that are in large part based on religion. (See the case study on page 352 for a more detailed discussion of religious conflict in India.)

Religious conflict (though on a less violent level) has been increasingly evident in the United States as well. Sociologist James Davison Hunter (1991) has referred to the "cultural war" taking place in the United States. In many communities, Christian fundamentalists, conservative Catholics, and Orthodox Jews have joined forces in a battle against liberal denominations for control of the secular culture. The battlefield is an array of familiar social issues, among them multiculturalism, child care (Chapter 4), abortion (Chapter 12), gay marriage (Chapter 14), school prayer, media censorship, and government funding for the arts.

Religion and Social Support

Most of us find it difficult to accept the stressful events of life—the death of a loved one, serious injury, bankruptcy, divorce, and so forth—especially when something "senseless" happens. How can family and friends come to terms with the death of a talented college student, not even 20 years old?

Through its emphasis on the divine and the supernatural, religion allows us to "do something" about the calamities we face. In some faiths, adherents can offer sacrifices or pray to a deity in the belief that such acts will change their earthly condition. On a more basic level, religion encourages us to view our personal misfortunes as relatively unimportant in the broader perspective of human history—or even as part of an undisclosed divine purpose. Friends and relatives of the deceased college student may see his death as being "God's will," or as having some ultimate benefit that we cannot understand now. This perspective may be much more comforting than the terrifying feeling that any of us can die senselessly at any moment—and that there is no divine answer to why one person lives a long and full life, while another dies tragically at a relatively early age.

Faith-based community organizations have taken on more and more responsibilities in the area of social assistance. In fact, President George W. Bush created the Office of Faith-Based and Community Initiatives to give socially active religious groups access to government funding. Renamed the Office of Faith-Based and Neighborhood Partnerships under the Obama

RESEARCH TODAY

Sociologists have found that religions are distinguished not just by doctrinal issues, but by secular criteria as well. Research has consistently shown that denominations and faiths can be arranged in a hierarchy based on their members' social class. The associated differences in financial means have a noticeable impact on the religious bodies, affecting everything from the appearance of their houses of worship to their congregations' ability to undertake social outreach activities.

Data from a national survey conducted in 2007 by the Pew Forum on Religion and Public Life shows that Jews, Presbyterians, and Episcopalians claim a higher proportion of affluent members than other faiths and denominations (see the accompanying figure, top). Their relative affluence can often be seen in the architecture and furnishings of their houses of worship. Members of less affluent groups, such as Muslims and Baptists, may compensate for their lesser means by donating their time and talent to outreach programs. Or they may pledge a higher proportion of their income to the church.

Research has consistently shown that denominations and faiths can be arranged in a hierarchy based on their members' social class.

Of course, all religious groups draw some members from each social stratum. Group differences among the faiths reflect a variety of social factors. For example, some denominations have more followers in urban areas or in the Northeast, where salaries are generally higher. Other faiths, notably Roman Catholicism, have a disproportionate share of immigrants from Latin America and Eastern Europe, where formal schooling is more limited than in the United States. Nonetheless, the existence of wide income differences means that religion can become a mechanism for signaling social mobility. A family that is moving up in wealth and power may seek a faith that is associated with a higher social ranking, moving from, say, the Roman Catholic to the Episcopal church.

Educational differences among faiths and denominations are even more striking. In the United States, Jews are more than three times more likely than Baptists to have a college education or higher (see the accompanying figure, bottom). But a closer look at the data reveals a more complex picture. Those whose faiths are associated with a lower level of formal

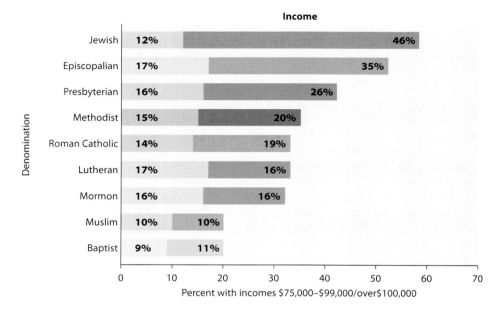

Income

Percent with incomes $75,000–$99,000/over $100,000

Denomination	
Jewish	12% / 46%
Episcopalian	17% / 35%
Presbyterian	16% / 26%
Methodist	15% / 20%
Roman Catholic	14% / 19%
Lutheran	17% / 16%
Mormon	16% / 16%
Muslim	10% / 10%
Baptist	9% / 11%

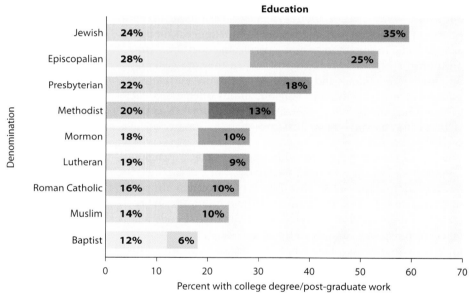

Education

Percent with college degree/post-graduate work

Denomination	
Jewish	24% / 35%
Episcopalian	28% / 25%
Presbyterian	22% / 18%
Methodist	20% / 13%
Mormon	18% / 10%
Lutheran	19% / 9%
Roman Catholic	16% / 10%
Muslim	14% / 10%
Baptist	12% / 6%

schooling—Baptists, Lutherans, and Roman Catholics—also benefit from the strongest church-sponsored educational programs. So while members of these groups may have fewer years of schooling than others, they are much more likely to have been educated in an atmosphere that encourages allegiance to their faith.

LET'S DISCUSS

1. Which faiths and denominations maintain houses of worship in your hometown? Do their facilities differ in terms of their size and construction? If so, do the differences mirror the size of the congregations, or do they represent social class differences as well?

2. Besides religions, what other group affiliations might suggest a person's income or educational level?

Source: Based on interviews with a representative sample of 35,000 adults conducted May–August 2007 and reproduced in the Pew Forum on Religion and Public Life 2008:78–79, 84–85.

Protestant Reformation, emphasized a disciplined work ethic, this-worldly concerns, and a rational orientation to life that have become known as the **Protestant ethic.** One by-product of the Protestant ethic was a drive to accumulate savings that could be used for future investment. This "spirit of capitalism," to use Weber's phrase, contrasted with the moderate work hours, leisurely work habits, and lack of ambition that Weber saw as typical of the times.

Few books on the sociology of religion have aroused as much commentary and criticism as Weber's work. It has been hailed as one of the most important theoretical works in the field and an excellent example of macro-level analysis. Like Durkheim, Weber demonstrated that religion is not solely a matter of intimate personal beliefs. He stressed that the collective nature of religion has consequences for society as a whole.

Weber provided a convincing description of the origins of European capitalism. But this economic system has now been adopted by non-Calvinists in many parts of the world. Studies done in the United States today show little or no difference in achievement orientation between Roman Catholics and Protestants. Apparently, the "spirit of capitalism" has emerged as a generalized cultural trait rather than a specific religious tenet (Greeley 1989).

Conflict theorists caution that Weber's theory—even if it is accepted—should not be regarded as an analysis of mature capitalism, as reflected in the rise of multinational corporations. Marxists would disagree with Weber not on the origins of capitalism, but on its future. Unlike Marx, Weber believed that capitalism could endure indefinitely as an economic system. He added, however, that the decline of religion as an overriding force in society opened the way for workers to express their discontent more vocally (R. Collins 1980).

Liberation Theology Sometimes the clergy can be found in the forefront of social change. Many religious activists, especially in the Roman Catholic Church in Latin America, support **liberation theology**—the use of a church in a political effort to eliminate poverty, discrimination, and other forms of injustice from a secular society. Advocates of this religious movement sometimes sympathize with Marxism. Many believe that radical change, rather than economic development in itself, is the only acceptable solution to the desperation of the masses in impoverished developing countries. Activists associated with liberation theology believe that organized religion has a moral responsibility to take a strong public stand against the oppression of the poor, racial and ethnic minorities, and women (Christian Smith 1991).

The term *liberation theology* dates back to the publication in 1973 of the English translation of *A Theology of Liberation.* The book was written by a Peruvian priest, Gustavo Gutiérrez, who lived in a slum area of Lima during the early 1960s. After years of exposure to the vast poverty around him, Gutiérrez concluded that "in order to serve the poor, one had to move into political action" (R. M. Brown 1980:23; G. Gutiérrez 1990). Eventually, politically committed Latin American theologians came under the influence of social scientists who viewed the domination of capitalism and multinational corporations as central to the hemisphere's problems. One result was a new approach to theology that built on the cultural and religious traditions of Latin America rather than on models developed in Europe and the United States.

Liberation theology may be dysfunctional, however. Some Roman Catholic worshippers have come to believe that by focusing

administration, the agency has acquired three new tasks: encouraging pro-life and pro-choice advocates to cooperate in reducing abortions; dealing with the special problems of children raised in fatherless homes; and fostering interfaith dialogue with religious leaders around the world. There is some evidence of such groups' effectiveness in helping others. Sociologist William Julius Wilson (1999) has singled out faith-based organizations in 40 communities from California to Massachusetts as models of social reform. These organizations identify experienced leaders and assemble them into nonsectarian coalitions that are devoted to community development (White House 2009).

Religion and Social Change

The Weberian Thesis When someone seems driven to work and succeed, we often attribute the Protestant work ethic to that person. The term comes from the writings of Max Weber, who carefully examined the connection between religious allegiance and capitalist development. Weber's findings appeared in his pioneering work *The Protestant Ethic and the Spirit of Capitalism* ([1904] 2009).

Weber noted that in European nations with both Protestant and Catholic citizens, an overwhelming number of business leaders, owners of capital, and skilled workers were Protestant. In his view, this fact was no mere coincidence. Weber pointed out that the followers of John Calvin (1509–1564), a leader of the

344 on political and governmental injustice, the clergy are no longer addressing their personal and spiritual needs. Partly as a result of such disenchantment, some Catholics in Latin America are converting to mainstream Protestant faiths or to Mormonism.

use your sociological *imagination*

The social support that religious groups provide is suddenly withdrawn from your community. How will your life or the lives of others change? What will happen if religious groups stop pushing for social change?

Religion and Social Control: A Conflict View

Liberation theology is a relatively recent phenomenon that marks a break with the traditional role of churches. It was this traditional role that Karl Marx ([1844] 1964) opposed. In his view, religion *impeded* social change by encouraging oppressed people to focus on otherworldly concerns rather than on their immediate poverty or exploitation. Marx described religion as an opiate that was particularly harmful to oppressed peoples. He felt that religion often drugged the masses into submission by offering a consolation for their harsh lives on earth: the hope of salvation in an ideal afterlife. For example, during the period of slavery in the United States, White masters forbade Blacks to practice native African religions, while encouraging them to adopt Christianity, which taught them that obedience would lead to salvation and eternal happiness in the hereafter. Viewed from a conflict perspective, Christianity may have pacified certain slaves and blunted the rage that often fuels rebellion.

Today, however, people around the world see religion more as a source of support through adversity than a source of oppression. In a combination of public opinion polls taken across 143 nations, over 90 percent of those who lived in the poorest countries said religion was an important part of their daily lives. The proportion was smaller but still significant in other countries: 76 percent in middle-income nations and 44 percent in countries with the highest per capita income (Crabtree and Pelham 2009).

Religion does play an important role in propping up the existing social structure. The values of religion, as already noted, tend to reinforce other social institutions and the social order as a whole. From Marx's perspective, however, religion's promotion of social stability only helps to perpetuate patterns of social inequality. According to Marx, the dominant religion reinforces the interests of those in power.

For example, contemporary Christianity reinforces traditional patterns of behavior that call for the subordination of the less powerful. The role of women in the church is an example of this uneven distribution of power. Assumptions about gender roles leave women in a subservient position both within Christian churches and at home. In fact, women find it as difficult to achieve leadership positions in many churches as they do in large corporations. A "stained glass ceiling" tends to stunt clergywomen's career development, even in the most liberal denominations.

Most religions are patriarchal in both their ideology and their leadership. A significant exception to that pattern is the Christian Scientists, founded in the early 20th century by Mary Baker Eddy.

Like Marx, conflict theorists argue that to whatever extent religion actually does influence social behavior, it reinforces existing patterns of dominance and inequality. From a Marxist perspective, religion keeps people from seeing their lives and societal conditions in political terms—for example, by obscuring the overriding significance of conflicting economic interests. Marxists suggest that by inducing a "false consciousness" among the disadvantaged, religion lessens the possibility of collective political action that could end capitalist oppression and transform society.

Feminist Perspective

Drawing on the feminist approach, researchers and theorists have stressed the fundamental role women play in religious socialization. Most people develop their allegiance to a particular faith in their childhood, with their mothers playing a critical role in the process. Significantly, nonworshipping mothers tend to influence their children to be highly skeptical of organized religion.

On the other hand, women generally take a subordinate role in religious governance. Indeed, most faiths have a long tradition of exclusively male spiritual leadership. Furthermore, because most religions are patriarchal, they tend to reinforce men's dominance in secular as well as spiritual matters. Women do play a vital role as volunteers, staff, and religious educators, but even today, religious decision making and leadership typically fall to the men. Exceptions to this rule, such as the Shakers and Christian Scientists, as well as Hinduism with its long goddess heritage, are rare (Schaefer and Zellner 2007).

TABLE **15-2** SOCIOLOGICAL PERSPECTIVES ON RELIGION summing**up** 345

Theoretical Perspective	Emphasis
Functionalist	Religion as a source of social integration and unification
	Religion as a source of social support for individuals
Conflict	Religion as a potential obstacle to structural social change
	Religion as a potential source of structural social change (through liberation theology)
Interactionist	Individual religious expression through belief, ritual, and experience
Feminist	Religion as an instrument of women's subordination, except for their role in religious socialization

In the United States, women are much more likely than men to be affiliated with religion, to pray, to believe in God, to claim that religion is important in their lives, and to attend weekly worship services. Yet organized religion typically does not give them leadership roles. Nationally, women compose 15.1 percent of U.S. clergy, though they account for 34 percent of students enrolled in theological institutions. Women clerics typically have shorter careers than men, often in related fields that do not involve congregational leadership, such as counseling. In faiths that restrict leadership positions to men, women serve unofficially. For example, about 4 percent of Roman Catholic congregations are led by women who hold nonordained pastoral positions—a necessity in a church that faces a shortage of male priests (Association of Theological Schools 2009; Bureau of the Census 2008a:384; Stange 2009).

Table 15-2 summarizes the four major sociological perspectives on religion.

Components of Religion

All religions have certain elements in common, yet those elements are expressed in the distinctive manner of each faith. These patterns of religious behavior, like other patterns of social behavior, are of great interest to sociologists—especially interactionists—since they underscore the relationship between religion and society.

Religious beliefs, religious rituals, and religious experience all help to define what is sacred and to differentiate the sacred from the profane. Let's examine these three components of religion, as seen through the eyes of interactionists.

Belief

Some people believe in life after death, in supreme beings with unlimited powers, or in supernatural forces. **Religious beliefs** are statements to which members of a particular religion adhere. These views can vary dramatically from religion to religion.

In the late 1960s, something rather remarkable took place in the expression of religious beliefs in the United States. Denominations that held to relatively liberal interpretations of religious scripture (such as the Presbyterians, Methodists, and Lutherans) declined in membership, while those that held to more conservative interpretations grew in numbers. Furthermore, in most faiths, those members who held strict views of scripture became more outspoken, questioning those who remained open to a variety of newer interpretations.

The term **fundamentalism** refers to such a rigid adherence to fundamental religious doctrines. Often, fundamentalism is

accompanied by a literal application of scripture or historical beliefs to today's world. The phrase "religious fundamentalism" was first applied to Protestant believers in the United States who took a literal interpretation of the Bible, but fundamentalism is found worldwide among most major religious groups, including Roman Catholicism, Islam, and Judaism. Fundamentalists vary immensely in their behavior. Some stress the need to be strict in their own personal faith but take little interest in broad social issues. Others are watchful of societal actions, such as government policies, that they see as conflicting with fundamentalist doctrine.

The Adam and Eve account of creation found in Genesis, the first book of the Old Testament, is an example of a religious belief. Many people in the United States strongly adhere to this biblical explanation of creation, and even insist that it be taught in public schools. These people, known as *creationists*, are worried by the secularization of society, and oppose teaching that directly or indirectly questions biblical scripture. The Social Policy section at the end of this chapter examines the issue of religion in the schools in depth.

Pilgrims on *hajj* to the Grand Mosque in Mecca, Saudi Arabia. Islam requires all Muslims who are able to undertake this religious ritual.

In general, spirituality is not as strong in industrialized nations as in developing nations. The United States is an exception to the trend toward secularization, in part because the government encourages religious expression (without explicitly supporting it) by allowing religious groups to claim charitable status, and even to receive federal aid for activities such as educational services. And although belief in God is relatively weak in formerly communist states such as Russia, surveys show a growth in spirituality in those countries over the past 10 years (Norris and Inglehart 2004).

Ritual

Religious rituals are practices required or expected of members of a faith. Rituals usually honor the divine power (or powers) worshipped by believers; they also remind adherents of their religious duties and responsibilities. Rituals and beliefs can be interdependent; rituals generally affirm beliefs, as in a public or private statement confessing a sin. Like any social institution, religion develops distinctive norms to structure people's behavior. Moreover, sanctions are attached to religious rituals, whether rewards (bar mitzvah gifts) or penalties (expulsion from a religious institution for violation of norms).

In the United States, rituals may be very simple, such as saying grace at a meal or observing a moment of silence to commemorate someone's death. Yet certain rituals, such as the process of canonizing a saint, are quite elaborate. Most religious rituals in our culture focus on services conducted at houses of worship. Attendance at a service, silent and spoken prayers, communion, and singing of spiritual hymns and chants are common forms of ritual behavior that generally take place in group settings. From an interactionist perspective, these rituals serve as important face-to-face encounters in which people reinforce their religious beliefs and their commitment to their faith.

For Muslims, a very important ritual is the *hajj*, a pilgrimage to the Grand Mosque in Mecca, Saudi Arabia. Every Muslim who is physically and financially able is expected to make this trip at least once. Each year 2 million pilgrims go to Mecca during the one-week period indicated by the Islamic lunar calendar. Muslims from all over the world make the *hajj*, including those in the United States, where many tours are arranged to facilitate the trip.

In recent decades, participation in religious rituals has tended to hold steady or decline in most countries. Figure 15-3 shows the change in religious participation in selected countries from 1981 to 2001.

FIGURE 15-3 RELIGIOUS PARTICIPATION IN SELECTED COUNTRIES, 1981 AND 2001

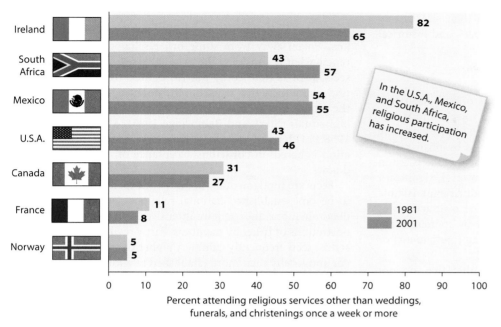

In the U.S.A., Mexico, and South Africa, religious participation has increased.

Percent attending religious services other than weddings, funerals, and christenings once a week or more

Note: World Values survey data for 2001.
Source: Norris and Inglehart 2004:74.

Think about It

Why did religious participation decrease in Ireland but increase in South Africa?

Experience

In the sociological study of religion, the term **religious experience** refers to the feeling or perception of being in direct contact with the ultimate reality, such as a divine being, or of being overcome with religious emotion. A religious experience may be rather slight, such as the feeling of exaltation a person receives from hearing a choir sing Handel's "Hallelujah Chorus." But many religious experiences are more profound, such as a Muslim's experience on a *hajj*. In his autobiography, the late African American activist Malcolm X (1964:338) wrote of his *hajj* and how deeply moved he was by the way that Muslims in Mecca came together across race and color lines. For Malcolm X, the color blindness of the Muslim world "proved to me the power of the One God."

Another profound religious experience, for many Christians, is being "born again"—that is, at a turning point in one's life, making a personal commitment to Jesus. According to a 2008 national survey, 40 percent of people in the United States claim they have had a born-again Christian experience at some time in their lives. An earlier survey found that Southern Baptists (75 percent) were the most likely to report such experiences; in contrast, only 21 percent of Catholics and 24 percent of Episcopalians stated that they had been born again. The collective nature of religion, as emphasized by Durkheim, is evident in these statistics. The beliefs and rituals of a particular faith can create an atmosphere either friendly or indifferent to this type of religious experience. Thus, a Baptist would be encouraged to come forward and share such experiences with others, whereas an Episcopalian who claims to have been born again would receive much less interest (Gallup 2009c; Gallup Opinion Index 1978).

Table 15-3 summarizes the three components of religion.

use your sociological *imagination*

Choose a religious tradition other than your own. How would your religious beliefs, rituals, and experience differ if you had been raised in that tradition?

TABLE 15-3 COMPONENTS OF RELIGION

Element	Definition	Examples
Belief	Statement to which members of a particular religion adhere	Creation account Sacred characters or people
Ritual	Practice required or expected of members of a faith	Worship Prayer Singing or chanting
Experience	Feeling or perception of being in direct contact with the ultimate reality (such as a divine being) or of being overcome with religious emotion	Born-again experience Communion with holy spirit

Religious Organization

The collective nature of religion has led to many forms of religious association. In modern societies, religion has become increasingly formalized. Specific structures such as churches and synagogues have been constructed for religious worship; individuals have been trained for occupational roles within various fields. These developments make it possible to distinguish clearly between the sacred and secular parts of one's life—a distinction that could not be made easily in earlier times, when religion was largely a family activity carried out in the home.

Sociologists find it useful to distinguish between four basic forms of organization: the ecclesia, the denomination, the sect, and the new religious movement, or cult. We can see differences among these four forms of organization in their size, power, degree of commitment expected from members, and historical ties to other faiths.

Ecclesiae

An **ecclesia** (plural, *ecclesiae*) is a religious organization that claims to include most or all members of a society and is recognized as the national or official religion. Since virtually everyone belongs to the faith, membership is by birth rather than conscious decision. Examples of ecclesiae include Islam in Saudi Arabia and Buddhism in Thailand. However, significant differences exist within this category. In Saudi Arabia's Islamic regime, leaders of the ecclesia hold vast power over actions of the state. In contrast, the Lutheran church in contemporary Sweden holds no such power over the Riksdag (parliament) or the prime minister.

Generally, ecclesiae are conservative, in that they do not challenge the leaders of a secular government. In a society with an ecclesia, the political and religious institutions often act in harmony and reinforce each other's power in their relative spheres of influence. In the modern world, ecclesiae are declining in power.

Denominations

A **denomination** is a large, organized religion that is not officially linked to the state or government. Like an ecclesia, it tends to have an explicit set of beliefs, a defined system of authority, and a generally respected position in society. Denominations claim as members large segments of a population. Generally, children accept the denomination of their parents and give little thought to membership in other faiths. Denominations also resemble ecclesiae in that they make few demands on members. However, there is a critical difference between these two forms of religious organization. Although the denomination is considered respectable and is not viewed as a challenge to the secular government, it lacks the official recognition and power held by an ecclesia (Doress and Porter 1977).

The United States is home to a large number of denominations. In good measure, this diversity is a result of our nation's immigrant heritage. Many settlers brought with them the religious commitments native to their homelands. Some Christian denominations in the United States, such as the Roman Catholics, Episcopalians, and Lutherans, are the outgrowth of ecclesiae established in Europe. New Christian denominations also emerged, including the Mormons and Christian Scientists. Within the past generation, immigrants have increased the number of Muslims, Hindus, and Buddhists living in the United States.

Although by far the largest denomination in the United States is Roman Catholicism, at least 24 other Christian faiths have 1 million or more members. Protestants collectively accounted for about 34 percent of the nation's adult population in 2008, compared to 25 percent for Roman Catholics and 2 percent for Jews. There are also 5 million Muslims in the United States, and large numbers of people adhere to Eastern faiths such as Buddhism (3 million) and Hinduism (1 million) (Barrett et al.

2008; Kosmin and Keysar 2009; Lindner 2008). Box 15-2 takes a closer look at Islam in the United States.

Sects

A **sect** can be defined as a relatively small religious group that has broken away from some other religious organization to renew what it considers the original vision of the faith. Many sects, such as that led by Martin Luther during the Reformation, claim to be the "true church," because they seek to cleanse the established faith of what they regard as extraneous beliefs and rituals (Stark and Bainbridge 1985). Max Weber ([1916] 1958:114) termed the sect a "believer's church," because affiliation is based on conscious acceptance of a specific religious dogma.

Sects are fundamentally at odds with society and do not seek to become established national religions. Unlike ecclesiae and denominations, they require intensive commitments and demonstrations of belief by members. Partly owing to their outsider status, sects frequently exhibit a higher degree of religious fervor and loyalty than more established religious groups. Recruitment focuses mainly on adults, and acceptance comes through conversion.

Sects are often short-lived. Those that are able to survive may become less antagonistic to society over time and begin to resemble denominations. In a few instances, sects have been able to endure over several generations while remaining fairly separate from society. Sociologist J. Milton Yinger (1970:226–273) uses the term **established sect** to describe a religious group that is the outgrowth of a sect, yet remains isolated from society. The Hutterites, Jehovah's Witnesses, Seventh-Day Adventists, and Amish are contemporary examples of established sects in the United States.

New Religious Movements or Cults

In 1997, 38 members of the Heaven's Gate cult were found dead in Southern California after a mass suicide timed to occur with the appearance of the Hale-Bopp comet. They believed the comet hid a spaceship on which they could catch a ride once they had broken free of their "bodily containers."

Partly as a result of the notoriety generated by such groups, the popular media have stigmatized the word *cult,* associating it with the occult and the use of intense and forceful conversion techniques. The stereotyping of cults as uniformly bizarre and unethical has led sociologists to abandon the term and refer instead to a *new religious movement (NRM).* While some NRMs exhibit strange behavior, many do not. They attract new members just like any other religion, and often follow teachings similar to those of established Christian denominations, though with less ritual.

Sects are difficult to distinguish from cults. A **new religious movement (NRM)** or **cult** is generally a small, secretive religious group that represents either a new religion or a major innovation of an existing faith. NRMs are similar to sects in that they tend to be small and are often viewed as less respectable than more established faiths. Unlike sects, however, NRMs normally do not result from schisms or breaks with established ecclesiae or denominations. Some cults, such as those focused on UFO sightings, may be totally unrelated to existing faiths. Even when a cult does accept certain fundamental tenets of a dominant faith—such as a belief in Jesus as divine or in Mohammad as a

RESEARCH TODAY

The growing presence of Islam in the United States is promoting better understanding of the significant diversity *within* Islam. Throughout the world, including the United States, Muslims are divided into a variety of sects, such as Sunni and Shia (or Shiite). These divisions sometimes result in antagonism, just as rivalries between Christian denominations can cause friction. Yet the Islamic faith is expressed in many different ways, even among Sunnis or Shia. To speak of Muslims as either Sunni or Shia would be like speaking of Christians as either Roman Catholic or Baptist.

The great majority of Muslims in the United States are Sunni Muslims—literally, those who follow the *Sunnah,* or way of the Prophet. Compared to other Muslims, Sunnis tend to be more moderate in their religious orthodoxy. The Shia, who come primarily from Iraq and Iran, are the second-largest group. Shia Muslims are more attentive to guidance from accepted Islamic scholars than are Sunnis. In sufficient numbers, these two Muslim groups will choose to worship separately, even if they must cross ethnic or linguistic lines to do so. That certainly is the case in U.S. cities with large and varied Muslim communities.

Estimating the number of Muslim Americans in the United States is even more difficult than estimating the number of Arab Americans (see Chapter 11). There are no census data on Muslim Americans, and Islamic institutions such as mosques tend to operate autonomously. Even the most scientific analyses of the topic vary widely in their estimates. Based on the most recent studies, we can say that there are between 3 million and 5.7 million or more Muslims in the United States. About two-thirds of those residents are native-born citizens. In terms of ethnic and racial background, the estimated breakdown of Muslim Americans is as follows:

- 20–42 percent African American
- 24–33 percent South Asian (Afghan, Bangladeshi, Indian, and Pakistani)
- 12–32 percent Arab
- 10–22 percent "other" (Bosnian, Iranian, and Turk, as well as White and Hispanic converts)

All scholars agree that the Muslim population in the United States is growing rapidly, through both immigration and religious conversion.

From these data, we can determine that African Americans who embrace Islam form a significant segment of the Muslim American community. The history of Black American Islam began in the 17th century, when members of some Muslim tribes were forcibly transported to the American colonies. An estimated 10 percent of African slaves were Muslim. Today's Black Islamic community emerged in the 20th century, however, based on the teachings of Elijah Muhammad.

In the United States, Muslim Americans must focus strongly on their faith to survive within the permissive mainstream culture. This Islamic school allows Muslim girls to play basketball without compromising their modesty.

The Nation of Islam, a sect that focuses on the condition of Blacks in the United States as well as on the teachings of the Qur'an, was formed by Muhammad's followers. Today, African American adherents of Islam reflect a variety of orientations, some unique to the United States and others tied to the larger Muslim community.

> *To many Muslim Americans, the popular culture of the United States resembles a pagan cult that celebrates money and sex.*

Though mosques are becoming more common in the United States, these houses of worship attract a different kind of attention than a traditional church with a steeple. To many people in the United States, the mosque represents not religious freedom and diversity, but a "foreign threat." Some communities have attempted to block the construction of Muslim religious centers. In return for a permit, local authorities may require that the buildings be stripped of the usual cultural symbols, perhaps even the traditional dome. On college campuses, administrators have responded more constructively to growing numbers of Muslim students, by hiring part-time imams (prayer leaders) to minister to their needs, dedicating space for daily prayer, and providing for Muslim dietary restrictions.

How does being Muslim in the United States differ from being Muslim in an Islamic country? In the United States, Muslim Americans reflect the diversity of the worldwide Islamic faith, but they practice their faith in a nation where Christianity is the dominant cultural influence. Some Islamic scholars argue that the democracy, religious diversity, and freedom of expression that Muslims experience in the United States have encouraged a stronger, more correct Islamic practice, uninhibited by the government interference that is characteristic of many Islamic states.

Other scholars contend that what makes the Muslim American experience unique is that followers must focus even more strongly on their religion in order to survive in a culture that is so permissive. Indeed, U.S. culture encourages many behaviors that are prohibited by Islamic law or cultural tradition. To many Muslim Americans, the popular culture of the United States resembles a pagan cult that celebrates money and sex. Muslim Americans, then, feel both the freedom to practice their faith as they choose and the pressure to remain Muslim.

LET'S DISCUSS

1. Is there a mosque in your community or a Muslim congregation on your campus? If so, are the members primarily Sunni or Shia? Immigrants or African Americans?
2. Should communities be allowed to block the construction of mosques or dictate their appearance? Would your answer be the same if your community tried to block the construction of a church or temple?

Sources: Belt 2002; Grossman 2008; Leonard 2003; McCloud 1995; Pew Forum on Religion and Public Life 2008; Selod 2008a.

RESEARCH TODAY

15-3 The Church of Scientology: Religion or Quasi-Religion?

From the public statements of entertainers Tom Cruise, Kirstie Alley, and John Travolta to representations on *South Park*, probably no faith has come under as much scrutiny in the past 60 years, or been more misunderstood, than the Church of Scientology. Scientology bears little if any relationship to any other organized religious group, either historically or ideologically. Indeed, its detractors—and there are many, as we will see—question whether it should even be considered a religion.

The Church of Scientology was founded and continues to be based on the voluminous writings of L. Ron Hubbard (1911–1986). Hubbard described a spiritual system that he called Dianetics, in which the individual strives to achieve a heightened, positive state of mind. Essential to Dianetics is a process known as auditing, which is usually the first step in becoming a Scientologist. Auditing is a form of personal counseling in which the auditor, always a church member, measures a person's mental state using an Electropsychometer ("E-Meter"), a device developed by Hubbard.

Scientology bears little if any relationship to any other organized religious group, either historically or ideologically.

Members of the Church of Scientology call it the only major new religion to have emerged in the 20th century. They consider their faith to be similar to the Judeo-Christian and Eastern religions, particularly Buddhism. Skeptics find this claim to be far-fetched. The fact that an organization has declared its doctrine to be a religion does not make it so, they counter. Indeed, some scholars treat the Church of Scientology as a **quasi-religion**, a category that includes organizations that may see themselves as religious but are seen by others as "sort of

religious." Included in this category are Maharishi Mahesh Yogi's Transcendental Meditation (TM), introduced in 1958, and the New Age movements.

Though research on the Church of Scientology is admittedly limited, scholars are moving toward accepting it as a religion. Scientology is a body of belief that offers an explanation for the world, a purpose for humankind, and answers to issues like salvation and the afterlife. Acknowledging this body of belief as a religion, however, would not mean that scholars regard it as an accurate world view, any more than they might consider Episcopalian or Hindu doctrine to be accurate.

Organizationally, many scholars of religion find Scientology's method of financing its operations problematic. Most religious organizations seek voluntary contributions toward their operating expenses, along with payment for specific services, such as child care programs and youth activities. They do not construe these monies as direct payments for instruction in their doctrine. In contrast, the Church of Scientology's doctrine includes the concept of "reciprocity," meaning that members are expected to pay for the spiritual benefits they receive through auditing and training.

LET'S DISCUSS

1. What do you think of the practice of measuring a person's mental state with an

Religion or quasi-religion? Founded in the 20th century, the Church of Scientology (shown here in Los Angeles, California) is a successful and growing organization.

Electropsychometer? If you were considering becoming a Scientologist, what questions would you ask your auditor about this device?

2. Do you agree that Scientology should be considered a religion? Why or why not?

Sources: Bromley and Bracey Jr. 1998; Hubbard 1950; Religious Tolerance 2007; Schaefer and Zellner 2007:280–306.

---

messenger of God—it will offer new revelations or insights to justify its claim to being a more advanced religion (Stark and Bainbridge 1979, 1985).

Like sects, NRMs may be transformed over time into other types of religious organization. An example is the Christian Science Church, which began as a new religious movement under the leadership of Mary Baker Eddy. Today, this church exhibits the characteristics of a denomination. In fact, most major religions, including Christianity, began as cults. NRMs may be in the early stages of developing into a denomination

or new religion, or they may just as easily fade away through the loss of members or weak leadership (Schaefer and Zellner 2007).

Comparing Forms of Religious Organization

How can we determine whether a particular religious group falls into the sociological category of ecclesia, denomination, sect, or NRM? As we have seen, these types of religious organization

Characteristic	Ecclesia	Denomination	Sect	New Religious Movement (or Cult)
Size	Very large	Large	Small	Small
Wealth	Extensive	Extensive	Limited	Variable
Religious services	Formal, little participation	Formal, little participation	Informal, emotional	Variable
Doctrines	Specific, but interpretation may be tolerated	Specific, but interpretation may be tolerated	Specific, purity of doctrine emphasized	Innovative, pathbreaking
Clergy	Well-trained, full-time	Well-trained, full-time	Trained to some degree	Unspecialized
Membership	By virtue of being a member of society	By acceptance of doctrine	By acceptance of doctrine	By an emotional commitment
Relationship to the state	Recognized, closely aligned	Tolerated	Not encouraged	Ignored or challenged

Source: Adapted from Vernon 1962; see also Chalfant et al. 1994.

have somewhat different relationships to society. Ecclesiae are recognized as national churches; denominations, although not officially approved by the state, are generally widely respected. In contrast, sects and NRMs are much more likely to be at odds with the larger culture.

Still, ecclesiae, denominations, and sects are best viewed as types along a continuum rather than as mutually exclusive categories. Table 15-4 summarizes some of the primary characteristics of these ideal types. Since the United States has no ecclesiae, sociologists studying this country's religions have focused on the denomination and the sect. These religious forms have been pictured on either end of a continuum, with denominations accommodating to the secular world and sects protesting against established religions. Although NRMs are included in Table 15-4, they lie outside the continuum, because they generally define themselves in terms of a new view of life rather than in terms of existing religious faiths. In fact, one of the most controversial NRMs, the Church of Scientology, may not fully qualify as a religion (Box 15-3).

Sociologists look at religion from an organizational perspective, which tends to stress the stability of religious adherence, but there are other ways to view religion. From an individual perspective, religion and spirituality are remarkably fluid. People often change their places of worship or move from one denomination to another. In many countries, including the United States, churches, temples, and mosques operate in a highly competitive market (Pew Forum on Religion and Public Life 2008; Wolfe 2008).

One sign of this fluidity is the rapid rise of still another form of religious organization, the electronic church. Facilitated by cable television and satellite transmission, *televangelists* (as they are called) direct their messages to more people—especially in the United States—than are served by all but the largest denominations. While some televangelists are affiliated with religious denominations, most give viewers the impression that they are dissociated from established faiths.

At the close of the 1990s, the electronic church began to take on yet another dimension: the Internet. Today, rather than going to a service in person, many people shop online for a church or faith. Surfers can go to GodTube.com, a video-sharing and social-networking Web site, for spiritually oriented content. Even the Second Life virtual world (described in Chapter 5) has a rich spiritual landscape, with functioning congregations of Buddhist, Jewish, Muslim, and Christian avatars (Kiper 2008; MacDonald 2007; Simon 2007).

use your sociological *imagination*

Suppose the political landscape in the United States has changed. The two mainstream parties, which once appealed to a broad cross section of U.S. voters, have begun to champion specific religious beliefs. As you prepare to cast your vote, what are your concerns, both personal and societal? Assuming that one of the parties supports your religious views, would you vote for its candidates on that basis? What would you do if neither party was sympathetic to your beliefs?

www.mhhe.com/schaefer12e

casestudy Religion in India

From a sociological point of view, the nation of India is large and complex enough that it might be considered a world of its own. Four hundred languages are spoken in India, 16 of which are officially recognized by the government. Besides the two major religions that originated there—Hinduism and Buddhism—several other faiths animate this society. Demographically the nation is huge, with over a billion residents. This teeming country is expected to overtake China as the most populous nation in the world in about three decades (Third World Institute 2007).

The Religious Tapestry in India

Hinduism and Islam, the two most important religions in India, were described on pages 338 and 340. Islam arrived in India in A.D. 1000, with the first of many Muslim invasions. It flowered there during the Mogul empire (1526–1857), the period when the Taj Mahal was built. Today, Muslims account for 13 percent of India's population; Hindus make up 83 percent.

The presence of one dominant faith influences how a society views a variety of issues, even secular ones. For example, India has emerged as a leader in biotechnology, due at least partly to the Hindu faith's tolerance of stem cell research and cloning—techniques that have been questioned in nations where Christianity dominates. Hinduism is open to the latest biomedical techniques, as long as no evil is intended. The only legal prohibition is that fetuses cannot be terminated for the purpose of providing stem cells. Because of its respect for life in all its forms, Hinduism has no major conflict with engineered life-forms of any kind, such as clones (Religion Watch 2006; Sengupta 2006).

Another religion, the Sikh faith, originated in the 15th century with a Hindu named Nanak, the first of a series of gurus (prophets). Sikhism shows the influence of Islam in India, in that it is monotheistic (based on a belief in one god rather than many). It resembles Buddhism in its emphasis on meditation and spiritual transcendence of the everyday world. *Sikhs* (learners) pursue their goal of spiritual enlightenment through meditation with the help of a guru.

Sikh men have a characteristic mode of dress that makes them easy to identify. They do not cut their beards or hair, and they wrap their heads in turbans. (Because of their distinctive dress, the 400,000 Sikhs who live in the United States are often mistaken—and discriminated against—as Muslims.) Sikhs are highly patriotic. Though their 20 million members make up just 2 percent of India's population, they account for 25 percent of India's army. Their presence in the military gives them a much larger voice in the governance of the country than might be expected, given their numbers (Fausset 2003; Watson 2005).

Another faith that has been influential beyond its numbers in India is Jainism (pronounced *Jinism*). This religion was founded six centuries before the birth of Christ—about the same time as Buddhism—by a young Hindu named Mahavira. Offended by the Hindu caste system—the rigid social hierarchy that reduces some people to the status of outcastes based solely on their birth—and by the numerous Hindu deities, Mahavira left his family and his wealth behind to become a beggar monk. His teachings attracted many followers, and the faith grew and flourished until the Muslim invasions of the 12th century.

According to the Jain faith, there is no god; each person is responsible for his or her own spiritual well-being. By following a strict code of conduct, Jains believe they can ultimately free their souls from the endless cycle of death and rebirth and attain *nirvana* (spiritual enlightenment). Jains are required to meditate; forswear lying and stealing; limit their personal wealth; and practice self-denial, chastity, and nonviolence. Because they will not knowingly harm other living beings, including plants and animals, Jains shun meat, fish, or even vegetables whose harvest kills the entire plant, such as carrots and potatoes. They will not work in the military, in farming or fishing, or in the manufacture or sale of alcohol and drugs. Though the Jains are a relatively small group (about 4 million), they exercise considerable influence in India through their business dealings and charitable contributions.

Another group that forms a small segment of the faithful, Christians, also plays a disproportionate role in the country's social safety net. Christian schools, hospitals, and other social service organizations serve non-Christians as well as Christians. Interestingly, hundreds of priests who were trained at churches in India have since immigrated to the United States to ease the shortage of priests there. Together with Jains and Buddhists, Christians make up 4 percent of India's population (Embree 2003; Goodstein 2008).

Adherents of the Hindu religion participate in fire worship at a celebration in Kerala, India. The Hindu faith is enormously influential in India, the country where most Hindus live.

Religion and the State in India

Religion was influential in India's drive to overturn British colonialism. The great Mohandas K. Gandhi (1869–1948) led the long struggle to regain India's sovereignty, which culminated in its independence in 1947. A proponent of nonviolent resistance, Gandhi persuaded Hindus and Muslims, ancient enemies, to join in defying British domination. But his influence as a peacemaker could not override the Muslims' demand for a separate state of their own. Immediately after independence was granted, India was partitioned into two states, Pakistan for the Muslims and India for the Hindus. The new arrangement caused large-scale migrations of Indians, especially Muslims, from one nation to the other, and sparked boundary disputes that continue to this day. In many areas Muslims were forced to abandon places they considered sacred. In the chaotic months that followed, centuries of animosity between the two groups boiled over into riots, ending in Gandhi's assassination in January 1948.

Today, India is a secular state that is dominated by Hindus (see Figure 15-2 on page 339). Though the government is officially tolerant of the Muslim minority, tensions between Hindus and Muslims remain high in some states. Conflict also exists among various Hindu groups, from fundamentalists to more secular and ecumenical adherents (Embree 2003).

Many observers see religion as the moving force in Indian society. As in so many other parts of the world, religion is being redefined in India. To the dismay of Sikh spiritual leaders, increasing numbers of young Sikh men are trimming their long hair and abandoning the traditional turban. To show that the 300-year-old tradition is still cool in the 21st century, Sikh leaders now offer a CD-ROM called "Smart Turban 1.0" (Gentleman 2007b).

socialpolicy and Religion

Religion in the Schools

The Issue

Should public schools be allowed to sponsor organized prayer in the classroom? How about Bible reading, or just a collective moment of silence? Can athletes at public schools offer up a group prayer in a team huddle? Should students be able to initiate voluntary prayers at school events? Each of these situations has been an object of great dissension among those who see a role for prayer in the schools and those who want to maintain strict separation of church and state.

Another controversy concerns the teaching of theories about the origin of humans and the universe. Mainstream scientific thinking holds that humans evolved over billions of years from one-celled organisms, and that the universe came into being 15 billion years ago as a result of a "big bang." These theories are challenged by people who hold to the biblical account of the creation of humans and the universe some 10,000 years ago—a viewpoint known as **creationism.** Creationists, many of whom are Christian fundamentalists, want their belief taught in the schools as the only one—or at the very least, as an alternative to the theory of evolution.

Who has the right to decide these issues, and what is the "right" decision? Religion in the schools is one of the thorniest issues in U.S. public policy today.

The Setting

The issues just described go to the heart of the First Amendment's provisions regarding religious freedom. On the one hand, the government must protect the right to practice one's religion; on the other, it cannot take any measures that would seem to establish one religion over another (separation of church and state).

In the key case of *Engle v. Vitale,* the Supreme Court ruled in 1962 that the use of nondenominational prayer in New York schools was "wholly inconsistent" with the First Amendment's prohibition against government establishment of religion. In finding that organized school prayer violated the Constitution—even when no student was required to participate—the Court argued, in effect, that promoting religious observance was not a legitimate function of government or education. Subsequent Court decisions have allowed *voluntary* school prayer by students, but forbid school officials to *sponsor* any prayer or religious observance at school events. Despite these rulings, many public schools still regularly lead their students in prayer recitations or Bible readings. Other states have enacted "moments of silence" during the public school day, which many see as prayer in disguise (Robelon 2007).

School prayer is not the only issue that pits religion against public schools. Unlike Europeans, many people in the United States seem highly skeptical of evolutionary theory, which is taught as a matter of course in science classes. In 2007 a national survey showed that 43 percent of adults believe that God created humans in their present form. Another 38 percent believe that humans developed their present form with divine guidance. Only 14 percent believe that humans developed without divine guidance. And only 18 percent of respondents believe the central tenet of evolutionary theory, that human beings developed over millions of years from less advanced forms of life (Gallup 2009c).

The controversy over whether the biblical account of creation should be presented in school curricula recalls the famous "monkey trial" of 1925. In that trial, high school biology teacher John T. Scopes was convicted of violating a Tennessee law making it a crime to teach the scientific theory of evolution in public

353

People on both sides of the debate between science and creationism invoke the name of Albert Einstein. Evolutionists emphasize the need for verifiable scientific data, like that which confirmed Einstein's groundbreaking scientific theories. Advocates of intelligent design quote the Nobel Prize–winning physicist's assertion that religion and science should coexist.

schools. Today, creationists have gone beyond espousing fundamentalist religious doctrine; they are attempting to reinforce their position regarding the origins of humanity and the universe with quasi-scientific data.

In 1987, the Supreme Court ruled that states could not compel the teaching of creationism in public schools if the primary purpose was to promote a religious viewpoint. In response, those who believe in the divine origin of life have recently advanced a concept called **intelligent design (ID),** the idea that life is so complex that it could only have been created by intelligent design. Though this concept is not based explicitly on the biblical account of creation, fundamentalists feel comfortable with it. Supporters of intelligent design consider it a more accurate account of the origin of life than Darwinism and hold that, at the very least, ID should be taught as an alternative to the theory of evolution. But in 2005, in *Kitzmiller v. Dove Area School District,* a federal judge ended a Pennsylvania school district's plans to require teachers to present the concept in class. In essence, the judge found ID to be "a religious belief," a subtler but similar approach to creationism in that both find God's fingerprints in nature. The issue continues to be hotly debated and is expected to be the subject of future court cases (Clemmitt 2005; W. Tierney and Holley 2008).

Sociological Insights

Supporters of school prayer and of creationism feel that strict Court rulings have forced too great a separation between what Émile Durkheim called the *sacred* and the *profane*. They insist that the use of nondenominational prayer can in no way lead to the establishment of an ecclesia in the United States. Moreover, they believe that school prayer—and the teaching of creationism—can provide the spiritual guidance and socialization that many children today do not receive from parents or regular church attendance. Many communities also believe that schools should transmit the dominant culture of the United States by encouraging prayer.

Opponents of school prayer and creationism argue that a religious majority in a community might impose viewpoints specific to its faith at the expense of religious minorities. These critics question whether school prayer can remain truly voluntary. Drawing on the interactionist perspective and small-group research, they suggest that children will face enormous social pressure to conform to the beliefs and practices of the majority.

Policy Initiatives

Public school education is fundamentally a local issue, so most initiatives and lobbying have taken place at the local or state level. Federal courts have taken a hard line on religion in the schools. In a decision that the Supreme Court reversed in 2004, a federal appeals court ruled that reciting the phrase "under God" during the Pledge of Allegiance that opens each school day violates the U.S. Constitution (Religion News Service 2003).

Religion–school debates show no sign of ending. The activism of religious fundamentalists in the public school system raises the question: whose ideas and values deserve a hearing in classrooms? Critics see this campaign as one step toward sectarian religious control of public education. They worry that at some point in the future, teachers may not be able to use books or make statements that conflict with fundamentalist interpretations of the Bible. For advocates of a liberal education and of intellectual (and religious) diversity, this is a genuinely frightening prospect (Wilgoren 2005).

Let's Discuss

1. Was there organized prayer in any school you attended? Was creationism part of the curriculum?

2. Do you think that promoting religious observance is a legitimate function of education?

3. How might a conflict theorist view the issue of organized school prayer?

gettinginvolved

To get involved in the debate over religion in the schools, visit this text's Online Learning Center, which offers links to relevant Web sites.

www.mhhe.com/schaefer12e

MASTERING THIS CHAPTER

Summary

Religion is a **cultural universal** found throughout the world in various forms. This chapter examines the major world religions, the functions and dimensions of religion, and the four basic types of religious organization.

1. Émile Durkheim stressed the social impact of religion in attempting to understand individual religious behavior within the context of the larger society.

2. Eighty-five percent of the world's population adheres to some form of **religion.** Tremendous diversity exists in religious beliefs and practices, which may be heavily influenced by culture.

3. Religion helps to integrate a diverse society and provides social support in time of need.

4. Max Weber saw a connection between religious allegiance and capitalistic behavior in a religious orientation he termed the **Protestant ethic.**

5. In **liberation theology,** the teachings of Christianity become the basis for political efforts to alleviate poverty and social injustice.

6. From a Marxist point of view, religion serves to reinforce the social control of those in power. It discourages collective political action, which could end capitalist oppression and transform society.

7. Religious behavior is expressed through **religious beliefs, rituals,** and **experience.**

8. Sociologists have identified four basic types of religious organization: the **ecclesia,** the **denomination,** the **sect,** and the **new religious movement (NRM),** or **cult.**

9. Advances in communications have led to a new type of church organization, the electronic church. Televangelists now preach to more people than belong to many denominations, and every day millions of people use the Internet for religious purposes.

10. India is a secular state that is dominated by a religious majority, the Hindus. The creation of a separate nation, Pakistan, for the Muslim minority following India's independence in 1947 did not end the centuries-old strife between the two groups, which has worsened with their political polarization.

11. Today, the question of how much religion, if any, should be permitted in the U.S. public schools is a matter of intense debate.

Critical Thinking Questions

1. From a conflict point of view, explain how religion could be used to bring about social change. Can you think of an example?

2. What role do new religious movements (or cults) play in the organization of religion? Why are they so often controversial?

3. Do politics and religion mix? Explain your reasoning.

Key Terms

Creationism A literal interpretation of the Bible regarding the creation of humanity and the universe, used to argue that evolution should not be presented as established scientific fact. (page 353)

Denomination A large, organized religion that is not officially linked to the state or government. (348)

Ecclesia A religious organization that claims to include most or all members of a society and is recognized as the national or official religion. (348)

Established sect A religious group that is the outgrowth of a sect, yet remains isolated from society. (348)

Fundamentalism Rigid adherence to fundamental religious doctrines, often accompanied by a literal application of scripture or historical beliefs to today's world. (345)

Intelligent design (ID) The idea that life is so complex, it could only have been created by intelligent design. (354)

Liberation theology Use of a church, primarily Roman Catholicism, in a political effort to eliminate poverty, discrimination, and other forms of injustice from a secular society. (343)

New religious movement (NRM) or **cult** A small, secretive religious group that represents either a new religion or a major innovation of an existing faith. (348)

Profane The ordinary and commonplace elements of life, as distinguished from the sacred. (338)

Protestant ethic Max Weber's term for the disciplined work ethic, this-worldly concerns, and rational orientation to life emphasized by John Calvin and his followers. (343)

Quasi-religion A scholarly category that includes organizations that may see themselves as religious but are seen by others as "sort of religious." (350)

Religion A unified system of beliefs and practices relative to sacred things. (338)

Religious belief A statement to which members of a particular religion adhere. (345)

Religious experience The feeling or perception of being in direct contact with the ultimate reality, such as a divine being, or of being overcome with religious emotion. (347)

Religious ritual A practice required or expected of members of a faith. (346)

Sacred Elements beyond everyday life that inspire awe, respect, and even fear. (338)

Sect A relatively small religious group that has broken away from some other religious organization to renew what it considers the original vision of the faith. (348)

Secularization The process through which religion's influence on other social institutions diminishes. (336)

Self-Quiz

Read each question carefully and then select the best answer.

1. Which of the following sociologists stressed the social impact of religion and was perhaps the first to recognize the critical importance of religion in human societies?
   a. Max Weber
   b. Karl Marx
   c. Émile Durkheim
   d. Talcott Parsons

2. A Roman Catholic parish church offers services in the native language of an immigrant community. This is an example of
   a. the integrative function of religion.
   b. the social support function of religion.
   c. the social control function of religion.
   d. none of the above

3. Sociologist Max Weber pointed out that the followers of John Calvin emphasized a disciplined work ethic, this-worldly concerns, and a rational orientation to life. Collectively, this point of view has been referred to as
   a. capitalism.
   b. the Protestant ethic.
   c. the sacred.
   d. the profane.

4. The use of a church, primarily Roman Catholic, in a political effort to eliminate poverty, discrimination, and other forms of injustice evident in a secular society is referred to as
   a. creationism.
   b. ritualism.
   c. religious experience.
   d. liberation theology.

5. Many people in the United States strongly adhere to the biblical explanation of the beginning of the universe. Adherents of this point of view are known as
   a. liberationists.
   b. creationists.

   c. ritualists.
   d. experimentalists.

6. The Adam and Eve account of creation found in Genesis, the first book of the Old Testament, is an example of a religious
   a. ritual.
   b. experience.
   c. custom.
   d. belief.

7. Which of the following is *not* an example of an ecclesia?
   a. the Lutheran church in Sweden
   b. Islam in Saudi Arabia
   c. Buddhism in Thailand
   d. the Episcopal church in the United States

8. Religion defines the spiritual world and gives meaning to the divine. These are _____ functions of religion.
   a. manifest
   b. latent
   c. positive
   d. negative

9. Which sociological perspective emphasizes the integrative power of religion in human society?
   a. functionalist perspective
   b. conflict perspective
   c. interactionist perspective
   d. all of the above

10. John Calvin, a leader of the Protestant Reformation, emphasized
    a. disciplined work ethic.
    b. this-worldly concerns.
    c. a rational orientation to life.
    d. all of the above

11. The _____ encompasses elements beyond everyday life that inspire awe, respect, and even fear, as compared to the _____, which includes the ordinary and the commonplace.

12. Religion defines the spiritual world and gives meaning to the divine. These are _____ functions of religion.

13. _____ is the largest single faith in the world; the second largest is _____.

14. _____ _____ are statements to which members of a particular religion adhere.

15. A(n) _____ is a religious organization that claims to include most or all members of a society and is recognized as the national or official religion.

16. Because they are _____, most religions tend to reinforce men's dominance in secular as well as spiritual matters.

17. The single largest denomination in the United States is _____ _____.

18. The "big bang" theory is challenged by _____, who hold to the biblical account of creation of humans and the universe.

19. Unlike ecclesiae and denominations, _____ require intensive commitments and demonstrations of belief by members.

20. A possible dysfunction of _____ _____ would be the belief that when Roman Catholics focus on political and governmental injustice, the clergy are no longer addressing people's personal and spiritual needs.

THINKING ABOUT MOVIES

Trembling before G-D
(Sandi Simcha DuBowski, 2001)

Tension between religious belief and sexual orientation is the central theme of *Trembling before G-D*. This documentary tells the stories of several gay and lesbian individuals who are struggling to hold on to their faith. All are Hasidic or Orthodox Jews, a subset of the Jewish denomination that generally adheres to a fundamentalist interpretation of the Bible. Biblical scripture strictly forbids homosexuality, as do Jewish religious institutions.

We can view *Trembling before G-D* as an exploration of the integrative function of religion, in that it explores how people with different social characteristics can share a common religious experience. The film also illustrates the overlap of religion and sociology regarding the expression of sexual orientation within a traditional population.

For Your Consideration

1. How would Émile Durkheim interpret the stories presented in *Trembling before G-D*?

2. In what ways do those who are interviewed in the documentary come to terms with the conflict between their sexual orientation and fundamentalist religious teachings?

Saved! (Brian Dannelly, 2004)

A young woman named Mary (Jena Malone) attends American Eagle Christian High School, where she is a member of a popular clique called the "Christian Jewels." When Mary's boyfriend, Dean (Chad Faust), questions his own sexuality, Mary thinks she can "cure" his condition by having sex with him. Eventually, Dean's parents learn of what they regard as his deviant inclinations and ship him off to a reform school, leaving the pregnant Mary alone and abandoned by many of her friends. Mary questions both her religious beliefs and the educational institution she attends, where she is beginning to feel oppressed. Ultimately, she reaffirms her faith, with help from some fellow outcasts.

This film shows numerous religious rituals. Watch for the scene in which a band concert creates a place for students to exhibit their faith. One way of looking at *Saved!* is as a satire of Christian fundamentalism, with Mary trying to find her own voice amidst the rigid doctrine espoused by school authorities.

For Your Consideration

1. What are some of Mary's religious beliefs? How do they change during the movie?

2. Using a functionalist approach, explain the religious rituals shown in the film.

inside

Sociological Perspectives
    on Education

Schools as Formal
    Organizations

Social Policy and Education:
    No Child Left Behind Act

BOXES

Sociology on Campus: *Google
    University*

Taking Sociology to Work:
    *Ray Zapata, Business
    Owner and Former Regent,
    Texas State University*

Research Today: *Violence
    in the Schools*

Students relax on the lawn
outside the University of Seville
in Spain. From informal learning
in the family to formal study at
an institution of higher learning,
education is a cultural universal.

Education 16

JONATHAN
KOZOL

THE
SHAME
OF THE
NATION

THE RESTORATION OF APARTHEID
SCHOOLING IN AMERICA

66 "Dear Mr. Kozol," said the eight-year-old, "we do not have the things you have. You have Clean things. We do not have. You have a clean bathroom. We do not have that. You have Parks and we do not have Parks. You have all the thing and we do not have all the thing. . . . Can you help us?"

The letter, from a child named Alliyah, came in a fat envelope of 27 letters from a class of third grade children in the Bronx.

. . . I had visited many elementary schools in the South Bronx and in one northern district of the Bronx as well. I had also made a number of visits to a high school where a stream of water flowed down one of the main stairwells on a rainy afternoon and where green fungus molds were growing in the office where the students went for counseling. . . .

In another elementary school, which had been built to hold 1,000 children but was packed to busting with some 1,500 boys and girls, the principal poured out his feelings to me in a room in which a plastic garbage bag had been attached somehow to cover part of the collapsing ceiling. "This," he told me, pointing to the garbage bag, then gesturing around him at the other indications of decay and disrepair

I had also made a number of visits to a high school where a stream of water flowed down one of the main stairwells on a rainy afternoon and where green fungus molds were growing in the office where the students went for counseling.

one sees in ghetto schools much like it elsewhere, "would not happen to white children." . . .

In 1970, when substantial numbers of white children still attended New York City's schools, 400 doctors had been present to address the health needs of the children. By 1993, the number of doctors had been cut to 23, most of them part-time—a cutback that affected most acutely children in the city's poorest neighborhoods where medical provision was perennially substandard and health problems faced by children most extreme. During the 1990s, for example, the rate of pediatric asthma in the South Bronx, already one of the highest in the nation, was exacerbated when the city chose to build a medical waste incinerator in their neighborhood after a plan to build it on the East Side of Manhattan was abandoned in the face of protests from the parents of that area. Hospitalization rates for these asthmatic children in the Bronx were as much as 20 times more frequent than for children in the city's affluent communities. Teachers spoke of children who came into class with chronic wheezing and, at any moment of the day, might undergo more serious attacks, but in the schools I visited there were no doctors to attend to them. . . .

The disrepair and overcrowding of these schools in the South Bronx "wouldn't happen for a moment in a white suburban school district like Scarsdale," says former New York State Commissioner of Education Thomas Sobol, who was once the superintendent of the Scarsdale schools and is now a professor of education at Teachers College in New York. "I'm aware that I could never prove that race is at the heart of this if I were called to testify before a legislative hearing. But I've felt it for so long, and seen it operating for so long, I know it's true. . . ." 99

(Kozol 2005:39, 40–41, 42, 43) Additional information about this excerpt can be found on the Online Learning Center at www.mhhe.com/schaefer12e.

For several decades Jonathan Kozol, the author of this passage from *The Shame of the Nation,* toured public schools throughout the United States. He found that while White students in affluent suburban towns enjoyed state-of-the-art science labs, superb music and art programs, and elaborate athletic facilities, inner-city children were crowded into antiquated, decrepit buildings, deprived of even the most basic requirements—textbooks, classrooms, computers, counselors. An educator himself, Kozol challenged his readers to confront the social implications of this stark contrast in educational resources.

Education, like the family and religion, is a cultural universal. As such it is an important aspect of socialization, the lifelong process of learning the attitudes, values, and behavior considered appropriate to members of a particular culture. As we saw in Chapter 4, socialization can occur in the classroom or at home, through interactions with parents, teachers, friends, and even strangers. Exposure to books, films, television, and other forms of communication also promotes socialization.

When learning is explicit and formalized—when some people consciously teach, while others adopt the role of learner—the process of socialization is called **education.** But students learn far more about their society at school than what is included in the curriculum.

This chapter focuses in particular on the formal systems of education that characterize modern industrial societies. Do public schools offer everyone a way up the socioeconomic ladder, or do they reinforce existing divisions among social classes? What is the "hidden curriculum" in U.S. schools? And what have sociologists learned about the latest trends in education, such as competency testing? We will begin with a discussion of four theoretical perspectives on education: functionalist, conflict, feminist, and interactionist. An examination of schools as formal organizations—as bureaucracies and subcultures of teachers and students—follows. One contemporary educational trend, homeschooling, merits special mention. The chapter closes with a Social Policy section on the controversial No Child Left Behind Act.

Sociological Perspectives on Education

Besides being a major industry in the United States, education is the social institution that formally socializes members of our society. In the past few decades, increasing proportions of people have obtained high school diplomas, college degrees, and advanced professional degrees. For example, the proportion of people age 25 or over with a high school diploma increased from 41 percent in 1960 to more than 84 percent in 2007. The proportion of those with a college degree rose from 8 percent in 1960 to 28 percent in 2007. Figure 16-1 shows the proportion of the college-educated population in selected countries (Crissey 2009).

Throughout the world, education has become a vast and complex social institution that prepares citizens for the roles demanded by other social institutions, such as the family, government, and the economy. The functionalist, conflict, feminist, and interactionist perspectives offer distinctive views of education as a social institution.

Functionalist View

Like other social institutions, education has both manifest (open, stated) and latent (hidden) functions. The most basic *manifest* function of education is the transmission of knowledge. Schools teach students how to read, speak foreign languages, and repair automobiles. Another important manifest function is the bestowal of status. Because many believe this function is performed inequitably, we will consider it later, in the section on the conflict view of education.

In addition to these manifest functions, schools perform a number of *latent* functions: transmitting culture, promoting social and political integration, maintaining social control, and serving as an agent of change.

Transmitting Culture As a social institution, education performs a rather conservative function—transmitting the dominant culture. Schooling exposes each generation of young people to the existing beliefs, norms, and values of their culture. In our society, we learn respect for social control and reverence for established institutions, such as religion, the family, and the presidency. Of course, this statement is true of many other cultures as well. While schoolchildren in the United States are hearing about the accomplishments of George Washington and Abraham Lincoln, British children are hearing about the distinctive contributions of Queen Elizabeth I and Winston Churchill.

In Great Britain, the transmission of the dominant culture through schools goes far beyond learning about monarchs and prime ministers. In 1996, the government's chief curriculum adviser—noting the need to fill a void left by the diminishing authority of the Church of England—proposed that British schools should socialize students into a set of core values. The list included honesty, respect for others, politeness, a sense of fair play, forgiveness, punctuality, nonviolent behavior, patience, faithfulness, and self-discipline (Charter and Sherman 1996).

Sometimes nations reassess the ways in which they transmit culture to students. Recently the Chinese government revised the nation's history curriculum. Students are now taught that the Chinese Communist Party, not the United States, played a central role in defeating Japan in World War II. No mention is made of the estimated 30 million Chinese who died from famine because of party founder Mao Zedong's disastrous Great Leap Forward (1958–1962), a failed effort to transform China's agrarian economy into an industrial powerhouse. In the urban, Western-oriented areas of Shanghai, textbooks acknowledge the technological advances made in Western industrial countries but avoid any criticism of past policies of the Chinese government (French 2004; Kahn 2006).

Culture has been transmitted to students in schools, through books and the spoken word, for centuries. Today, however, the Internet offers a new and potentially revolutionary way of transmitting culture. Box 16-1 on page 362 discusses the educational impact of Google and other search engines.

FIGURE **16-1** HIGHER EDUCATION COMPLETION RATES (BA/BS), SELECTED COUNTRIES

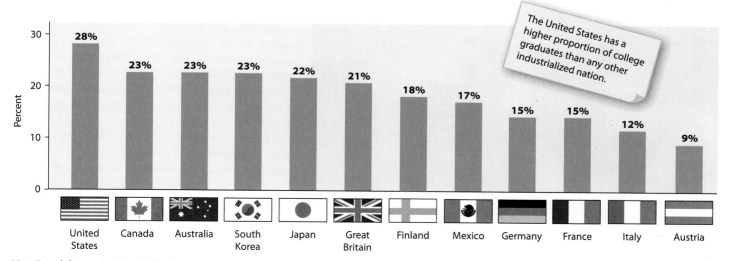

Note: For adults ages 25 to 64 in 2005.
Sources: Bureau of the Census 2008a:823; Crissey 2009:3.

SOCIOLOGY ON CAMPUS

16-1 Google University

From comic books, television, and fast-paced video games to educational films and online college courses, technological innovations in communication have been seen as both a threat to culture and a boon to education. Like these new media, the search engine called Google has been greeted with both praise and scorn. Founded by two students at Stanford University in 1998, Google now handles some 70 percent of all Internet searches in the United States. Its familiar multicolored logo stands for one of the most trusted brands in the world (see Figure 7-1, page 145).

Using Google or some other search engine, a researcher can now retrieve facts, viewpoints, images, and sounds within minutes. Just a few years ago, that task would have taken days. As Nicholas Carr (2008b:56), former editor of the *Harvard Business Review,* notes, "Once I was a scuba diver in the sea of words. Now I zip along the surface like a guy on a Jet Ski." Yet some critics charge that placing more and more of the world's knowledge just a mouse click away has made students lazy. Quick access to information, they point out, does not necessarily encourage concentration, let alone contemplation.

The availability of information online may also be changing the way people read. Educators worry that habitual skimming of the computer screen may carry over to students' print reading. Some have found that younger readers, faced with anything of length online, such as a short PDF file, simply ignore it. In response, researchers have begun to study whether those who read online in preference to books and other printed media still read sentence by sentence, as they were taught to do in school.

> *Like the invention of the printing press, Google's advent is changing not just the university, but the universe of learning.*

Ultimately, education is more than just collecting, organizing, and comprehending information. Accessing information and arguments regarding political and social issues is a form of civic engagement. Thus, the search feature on a Web page becomes a portal to a virtual town square. Perhaps that is why today's students not only are spending more time online than yesterday's students, but are doing more volunteer work.

Well before the advent of the Internet, much less Google, sociologist Daniel Bell (1973) wrote that *intellectual technologies* tend to institutionalize new approaches to the gathering and dissemination of information. Like the invention of the printing press, Google's advent is changing not just the university, but the universe of learning.

LET'S DISCUSS

1. Do you prefer to do your reading online or in a magazine, newspaper, or book? Has the availability of online information changed the way that you read the written word?
2. Have you participated in any social or political causes or volunteered your time while on campus? If so, did you use the Internet to organize or disseminate information about your activities?

Sources: Bauerlein 2008; Brabazon 2007; N. Carr 2008a, 2008b; Vaidhyanathian 2008; Workman 2008.

Though the school that Harry Potter attends in the film *Harry Potter and the Half-Blood Prince* is fictitious, like real schools, it transmits a socially sanctioned culture to students.

Promoting Social and Political Integration Many institutions require students in their first year or two of college to live on campus, to foster a sense of community among diverse groups. Education serves the latent function of promoting social and political integration by transforming a population composed of diverse racial, ethnic, and religious groups into a society whose members share—to some extent—a common identity. Historically, schools in the United States have played an important role in socializing the children of immigrants into the norms, values, and beliefs of the dominant culture. From a functionalist perspective, the common identity and social integration fostered by education contribute to societal stability and consensus (Touraine 1974).

In the past, the integrative function of education was most obvious in its emphasis on promoting a common language. Immigrant children were expected to learn English. In some instances, they were even forbidden to speak their native language on school grounds. More recently, bilingualism has been defended both for its educational value and as a means of encouraging cultural diversity. However, critics argue that bilingualism undermines the social and political integration that education has traditionally promoted.

Maintaining Social Control

In performing the manifest function of transmitting knowledge, schools go far beyond teaching skills like reading, writing, and mathematics. Like other social institutions, such as the family and religion, education prepares young people to lead productive and orderly lives as adults by introducing them to the norms, values, and sanctions of the larger society.

Through the exercise of social control, schools teach students various skills and values essential to their future positions in the labor force. They learn punctuality, discipline, scheduling, and responsible work habits, as well as how to negotiate the complexities of a bureaucratic organization. As a social institution, education reflects the interests of both the family and another social institution, the economy. Students are trained for what is ahead, whether it be the assembly line or a physician's office. In effect, then, schools serve as a transitional agent of social control, bridging the gap between parents and employers in the life cycle of most individuals (Bowles and Gintis 1976; M. Cole 1988).

Schools direct and even restrict students' aspirations in a manner that reflects societal values and prejudices. School administrators may allocate ample funds for athletic programs but give much less support to music, art, and dance. Teachers and guidance counselors may encourage male students to pursue careers in the sciences but steer female students into careers as early childhood teachers. Such socialization into traditional gender roles can be viewed as a form of social control.

Serving as an Agent of Change

So far, we have focused on the conservative functions of education—on its role in transmitting the existing culture, promoting social and political integration, and maintaining social control. Yet education can also stimulate or bring about desired social change. Sex education classes were introduced to public schools in response to the soaring pregnancy rate among teenagers. Affirmative action in admissions—giving priority to females or minorities—has been endorsed as a means of countering racial and sexual discrimination. Project Head Start, an early childhood program that serves more than 908,000 children annually, has sought to compensate for the disadvantages in school readiness experienced by children from low-income families (Bureau of the Census 2008a:360).

Education also promotes social change by serving as a meeting ground where people can share distinctive beliefs and traditions. In 2007–2008, U.S. campuses hosted over 623,000 international students. That number, an all-time high, followed a temporary decline in foreign enrollments after September 11, 2001. Figure 16-2 on page 364 shows the major sending nations of foreign students in the United States (left) and the primary destinations of U.S. students seeking to enrich their college experience abroad (right).

Numerous sociological studies have revealed that additional years of formal schooling are associated with openness to new ideas and more liberal social and political viewpoints. Sociologist Robin Williams points out that better-educated people tend to have greater access to factual information, to hold more diverse opinions, and to possess the ability to make subtle distinctions in analysis. Formal education stresses both the importance of qualifying statements (in place of broad generalizations) and the need at least to question (rather than simply accept) established truths and practices. The scientific method, which relies on *testing* hypotheses, reflects the questioning spirit that characterizes modern education (R. Williams et al. 1964).

Conflict View

The functionalist perspective portrays contemporary education as a basically benign institution. For example, it argues that schools rationally sort and select students for future high-status positions, thereby meeting society's need for talented and expert personnel. In contrast, the conflict perspective views education as an instrument of elite domination. Conflict theorists point out the sharp inequalities that exist in the educational opportunities available to different racial and ethnic groups. In 2004, the nation marked the 50th anniversary of the Supreme Court's landmark decision *Brown v. Board of Education,* which declared unconstitutional the segregation of public schools. Yet today, our schools are still characterized by racial isolation. Nationwide, White students are the most isolated: only 23 percent of their classmates came from minority groups in the 2005–2006 school year. In comparison, Black and Latino students have more

In response to a high pregnancy rate among adolescent girls, many schools now offer sex education courses that promote abstinence. When schools attempt to remedy negative social trends, they are serving as an agent of social change.

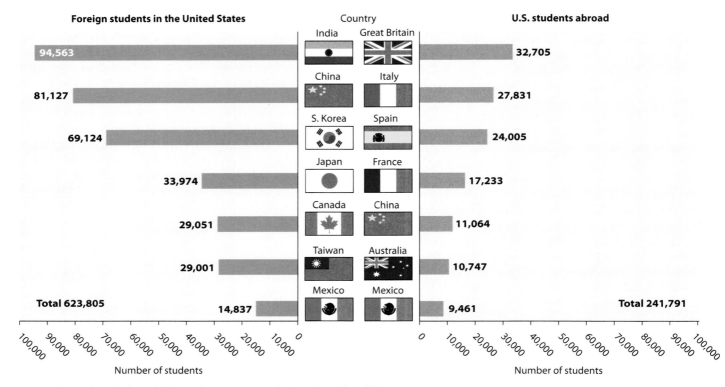

Note: Foreign students in the United States for 2007–2008 and U.S. students abroad for 2006–2007.
Source: Institute of International Education 2008, 2009.

Studies conducted since 1987 suggest that the funding inequities between richer and poorer school districts have widened in recent years.

classmates from different racial and ethnic backgrounds, though they typically do not include Whites (Orfield and Lee 2007).

Conflict theorists also argue that the educational system socializes students into values dictated by the powerful, that schools stifle individualism and creativity in the name of maintaining order, and that the level of change they promote is relatively insignificant. From a conflict perspective, the inhibiting effects of education are particularly apparent in the "hidden curriculum" and the differential way in which status is bestowed.

The Hidden Curriculum   Schools are highly bureaucratic organizations, as we will see later. Many teachers rely on rules and regulations to maintain order. Unfortunately, the need for control and discipline can take precedence over the learning process. Teachers may focus on obedience to the rules as an end in itself, in which case students and teachers alike become victims of what Philip Jackson (1968) has called the *hidden curriculum.*

The term **hidden curriculum** refers to standards of behavior that are deemed proper by society and are taught subtly in schools. According to this curriculum, children must not speak until the teacher calls on them, and must regulate their activities according to the clock or bells. In addition, they are expected to concentrate on their own work rather than to assist other students who learn more slowly. A hidden curriculum is evident in schools around the world. For example, Japanese schools offer guidance sessions that seek to improve the classroom experience and develop healthy living skills. In effect, these sessions instill values and encourage behavior useful in the Japanese business world, such as self-discipline and openness to group problem solving and decision making (Okano and Tsuchiya 1999).

In a classroom that is overly focused on obedience, value is placed on pleasing the teacher and remaining quiet rather than on creative thought and academic learning. Habitual obedience to authority may result in the type of distressing behavior documented by Stanley Milgram in his classic obedience studies.

Credentialism   Fifty years ago, a high school diploma was the minimum requirement for entry into the paid labor force of the United States. Today, a college diploma is virtually the bare minimum. This change reflects the process of **credentialism**—a term used to describe an increase in the lowest level of education needed to enter a field.

In recent decades, the number of occupations that are viewed as professions has risen. Credentialism is one symptom of this trend. Employers and occupational associations typically contend that such changes are a logical response to the increasing complexity of many jobs. However, in many cases, employers raise the degree requirements for a position simply because all applicants have achieved the existing minimum credential (D. Brown 2001; Hurn 1985).

Conflict theorists observe that credentialism may reinforce social inequality. Applicants from poor and minority backgrounds are especially likely to suffer from the escalation of qualifications, since they lack the financial resources needed to obtain degree after degree. In addition, upgrading of credentials serves the self-interest of the two groups most responsible for this trend. Educational institutions profit from prolonging the investment of time and money that people make by staying in school. Moreover, as C. J. Hurn (1985) has suggested, current jobholders have a stake in raising occupational requirements, since credentialism can increase the status of an occupation and lead to demands for higher pay. Max Weber anticipated this possibility as early as 1916, concluding that the "universal clamor for the creation of educational certificates in all fields makes for the formation of a privileged stratum in businesses and in offices" (Gerth and Mills 1958:240–241).

use your sociological *imagination*

How would you react if the job you have or plan to pursue suddenly required a higher-level degree? If suddenly the requirements were lowered?

Bestowal of Status Sociologists have long recognized that schooling is central to social stratification. Both functionalist and conflict theorists agree that education performs the important function of bestowing status. As noted earlier, an increasing proportion of people in the United States are obtaining high school diplomas, college degrees, and advanced professional degrees. From a functionalist perspective, this widening bestowal of status is beneficial not only to particular recipients but to society as a whole. According to Kingsley Davis and Wilbert E. Moore (1945), society must distribute its members among a variety of social positions. Education can contribute to

this process by sorting people into appropriate levels and courses of study that will prepare them for positions in the labor force.

Conflict theorists are far more critical of the *differential* way in which education bestows status. They stress that schools sort pupils according to their social class backgrounds. Although the educational system helps certain poor children to move into middle-class professional positions, it denies most disadvantaged children the same educational opportunities afforded to children of the affluent. In this way, schools tend to preserve social class inequalities in each new generation. Higher education in particular acts more like a sieve that sorts people out of the educated classes than a social ladder that helps all with ambition to rise (Giroux 1988; Pinkerton 2003; M. Stevens et al. 2008).

Even a single school can reinforce class differences by putting students in tracks. The term **tracking** refers to the practice of placing students in specific curriculum groups on the basis of their test scores and other criteria. Tracking begins very early, often in reading groups during first grade. The practice can reinforce the disadvantages that children from less affluent families may face if they haven't been exposed to reading materials, computers, and other forms of educational stimulation during their early childhood years. To ignore this connection between tracking and students' race and social class is to fundamentally misunderstand how schools perpetuate the existing social structure.

Not surprisingly, most recent research on tracking raises questions about its effectiveness, especially for low-ability students. In one study of low-income schools in California, researchers discovered a staggering difference between students who were tracked and those who were not. At one school, all interested students were allowed to enroll in advanced placement (AP) courses, not just those who were selected by the administration. Half the open enrollment students scored high enough to qualify for college credit—a much higher proportion than in selective programs, in which only 17 percent of students qualified for college credit. Tracking programs do not necessarily identify those students with the potential to succeed (B. Ellison 2008; Sacks 2007).

Conflict theorists hold that the educational inequalities produced by tracking are designed to meet the needs of modern capitalist societies. Samuel Bowles and Herbert Gintis (1976) have argued that capitalism requires a skilled, disciplined labor force, and that the educational system of the United States is structured with that objective in mind. Citing numerous studies, they offer support for what they call the **correspondence principle.** According to this approach, schools promote the values

Ray Zapata, **Business Owner and Former Regent, Texas State University**

Ray Zapata, investor, community activist, and restaurant owner, thinks his degree in sociology was the best preparation he could have received for a life spent in business and politics. A graduate of Angelo State University in Texas, Zapata finds that his understanding of society and social diversity has given him perspective on his community and helped him to cooperate with others from different backgrounds. "I think that I can pretty much fit anywhere, whether I'm in New York, London, or South Africa, and I think that's very, very important," he remarks.

Zapata was the second Hispanic to be appointed to the Board of Regents of the Texas State University system. As a regent, he was charged with overseeing both the financial and educational management of the system, which includes working with the state legislature to gain funding for new programs and facilities. During his term he presided over a half-billion-dollar construction program, including a major expansion at his alma mater, Angelo State.

More than the buildings that went up during his term, though, Zapata prides himself on the open admissions policy the Board instituted during his tenure. "If you put education out of reach of the working class or poor people in our society, then I think you lose an opportunity for great minds," he says. One of the most wonderful moments for this regent came when he watched a Hispanic woman who had worked as a janitor at Southwest State University graduate at the top of her class. Zapata wants to see more students like her, including senior citizens, on Texas State campuses. "Education will never hurt you at any age," he says.

LET'S DISCUSS

1. How does an open admissions policy benefit society?
2. In what ways do elderly people benefit from education?

---

expected of individuals in each social class and perpetuate social class divisions from one generation to the next. Thus, working-class children, assumed to be destined for subordinate positions, are likely to be placed in high school vocational and general tracks, which emphasize close supervision and compliance with authority. In contrast, young people from more affluent families are likely to be directed to college preparatory tracks, which stress leadership and decision making—the skills they are expected to need as adults (McLanahan and Percheski 2008).

Feminist View

The educational system of the United States, like many other social institutions, has long been characterized by discriminatory treatment of women. In 1833, Oberlin College became the first institution of higher learning to admit female students—some 200 years after the first men's college was established. But Oberlin believed that women should aspire to become wives and mothers, not lawyers and intellectuals. In addition to attending classes, female students washed men's clothing, cared for their rooms, and served them at meals. In the 1840s, Lucy Stone, then an Oberlin undergraduate and later one of the nation's most outspoken feminist leaders, refused to write a commencement address because it would have been read to the audience by a male student.

In the 20th century, sexism in education showed up in many ways—in textbooks with negative stereotypes of women, counselors' pressure on female students to prepare for "women's work," and unequal funding for women's and men's athletic programs. But perhaps nowhere was educational discrimination more evident than in the employment of teachers. The positions of university professor and college administrator, which hold relatively high status in the United States, were generally filled by men. Public school teachers, who earn much lower salaries, were largely female.

Women have made great strides in one area: the proportion of women who continue their schooling. As recently as 1969, twice as many men as women received college degrees; today, women outnumber men at college commencements. Moreover, women's access to graduate education and to medical, dental, and law schools has increased dramatically in the past few decades as a result of the Education Act of 1972. Box 12-1 on page 275 examines the far-reaching effects of Title IX, the part of the act that concerns discrimination against women in education.

Much has been made of the superior academic achievement of girls and women. Today, researchers are beginning to examine the reasons for their comparatively strong performance in school—or to put it another way, for men's lackluster performance. Some studies suggest that men's aggressiveness, together with the fact that they do better in the workplace than women, even with less schooling, predisposes them to undervalue higher education. While the "absence of men" on many college campuses has captured headlines, it has also created a false crisis in public discourse. Few students realize their potential exclusively through formal education; other factors, such as ambition and personal talent, contribute to their success. And many students, including low-income and immigrant children, face much greater challenges than the so-called gender gap in education (Buchmann et al. 2008; Corbett 2008; Kimmel 2006).

In cultures in which traditional gender roles remain the social norm, women's education suffers appreciably. Since September 11, 2001, the growing awareness of the Taliban's repression of Afghan women has dramatized the gender disparities in education in developing nations. Research has demonstrated that women are critical to economic development and good governance, and that education is instrumental in preparing them for those roles. Educating women, especially young girls, yields high social returns by lowering birthrates and improving agricultural productivity through better management (I. Coleman 2004).

Interactionist View

High school students know who they are—the kids who qualify for a free lunch. So stigmatized are they that in some schools, these students will buy a bit of food in the cash line or simply go without eating to avoid being labeled a "poor kid." School officials in San Francisco are so concerned about their plight that they are moving to cashless cafeterias, in which everyone, rich or poor, uses a debit card (Pogash 2008).

The labeling approach suggests that if we treat people in particular ways, they may fulfill our expectations. Children who are labeled as "troublemakers" may

Although the Chinese government is attempting to address educational inequalities, girls continue to receive less education than boys—especially in rural areas.

come to view themselves as delinquents. Similarly, a dominant group's stereotyping of racial minorities may limit their opportunities to break away from expected roles.

Can the labeling process operate in the classroom? Because of their focus on micro-level classroom dynamics, interactionist researchers have been particularly interested in this question. Howard S. Becker (1952) studied public schools in low-income and more affluent areas of Chicago. He noticed that administrators expected less of students from poor neighborhoods, and wondered if teachers accepted their view. A decade later, in *Pygmalion in the Classroom,* psychologist Robert Rosenthal and school principal Lenore Jacobson (1968, 1992) documented what they referred to as a **teacher-expectancy effect**—the impact that a teacher's expectations about a student's performance may have on the student's actual achievements. This effect is especially evident in the lower grades (through grade three).

In the first experiment, children in a San Francisco elementary school were administered a verbal and reasoning pretest. Rosenthal and Jacobson then *randomly* selected 20 percent of the sample and designated them as "spurters"—children of whom teachers could expect superior performance. On a later verbal and reasoning test, the spurters were found to score significantly higher than before. Moreover, teachers evaluated them as more interesting, more curious, and better adjusted than their classmates. These results were striking. Apparently, teachers' perceptions that the students were exceptional led to noticeable improvements in their performance.

Studies in the United States have revealed that teachers wait longer for an answer from a student they believe to be a high achiever and are more likely to give such children a second chance. In one experiment, teachers' expectations were even shown to have an impact on students' athletic achievements. Teachers obtained better athletic performance—as measured in the number of sit-ups or push-ups performed—from those students of whom they *expected* higher numbers. Despite the controversial nature of these findings, researchers continue to

document the existence of the teacher-expectancy effect. Interactionists emphasize that ability alone may be less predictive of academic success than one might think (Babad and Taylor 1992; Brint 1998; R. Rosenthal and Jacobsen 1992:247–262).

Table 16-1 on page 368 summarizes the four major theoretical perspectives on education.

use your sociological *imagination*

What kinds of labels do school authorities apply to students? What is the outcome of those labels?

Schools as Formal Organizations

Nineteenth-century educators would be amazed at the scale of schools in the United States in the 21st century. For example, California's public school system, the largest in the nation, currently enrolls as many children as there were in secondary schools in the entire country in 1950 (Bureau of the Census 1975:368; 2006a).

In many respects, today's schools, when viewed as an example of a formal organization, are similar to factories, hospitals, and business firms. Like those organizations, schools do not operate autonomously; they are influenced by the market of potential students. This statement is especially true of private schools, but could have broader impact if acceptance of voucher plans and other school choice programs increases. The parallels between schools and other types of formal organizations will become more apparent as we examine the bureaucratic nature of schools, teaching as an occupation, and the student subculture (K. Dougherty and Hammack 1992).

TABLE **16-1** SOCIOLOGICAL PERSPECTIVES ON EDUCATION

summing up

Theoretical Perspective	Emphasis
Functionalist	Transmission of the dominant culture
	Integration of society
	Promotion of social norms, values, and sanctions
	Promotion of desirable social change
Conflict	Domination by the elite through unequal access to schooling
	Hidden curriculum
	Credentialism
	Bestowal of status
Interactionist	Teacher-expectancy effect
Feminist	Treatment of female students
	Role of women's education in economic development

Bureaucratization of Schools

It simply is not possible for a single teacher to transmit culture and skills to children of varying ages who will enter many diverse occupations. The growing number of students being served by school systems and the greater degree of specialization required within a technologically complex society have combined to bureaucratize schools.

Max Weber noted five basic characteristics of bureaucracy, all of which are evident in the vast majority of schools, whether at the elementary, secondary, or even college level:

1. **Division of labor.** Specialized experts teach particular age levels and specific subjects. Public elementary and secondary schools now employ instructors whose sole responsibility is to work with children with learning disabilities or physical impairments.

2. **Hierarchy of authority.** Each employee of a school system is responsible to a higher authority. Teachers must report to principals and assistant principals, and may also be supervised by department heads. Principals are answerable to a superintendent of schools, and the superintendent is hired and fired by a board of education.

3. **Written rules and regulations.** Teachers and administrators must conform to numerous rules and regulations in the performance of their duties. This bureaucratic trait can become dysfunctional; the time invested in completing required forms could instead be spent in preparing lessons or conferring with students.

4. **Impersonality.** As class sizes have swelled at schools and universities, it has become more difficult for teachers to give personal attention to each student. In fact, bureaucratic norms may actually encourage teachers to treat all students in the same way, despite the fact that students have distinctive personalities and learning needs.

5. **Employment based on technical qualifications.** At least in theory, the hiring of instructors is based on professional competence and expertise. Promotions are normally dictated by written personnel policies; people who excel may be granted lifelong job security through tenure.

Functionalists take a generally positive view of the bureaucratization of education. Teachers can master the skills needed to work with a specialized clientele, since they no longer are expected to cover a broad range of instruction. The chain of command within schools is clear. Students are presumably treated in an unbiased fashion because of uniformly applied rules. Finally, security of position protects teachers from unjustified dismissal. In general, then, functionalists stress that the bureaucratization of education increases the likelihood that students, teachers, and administrators will be dealt with fairly—that is, on the basis of rational and equitable criteria.

In contrast, conflict theorists argue that the trend toward more centralized education has harmful consequences for disadvantaged people. The standardization of educational curricula, including textbooks, will generally reflect the values, interests, and lifestyles of the most powerful groups in our society, and may ignore those of racial and ethnic minorities. In addition, the disadvantaged, more so than the affluent, will find it difficult to sort through complex educational bureaucracies and to organize effective lobbying groups. Therefore, in the view of conflict theorists, low-income and minority parents will have even less influence over citywide and statewide educational administrators than they have over local school officials (Bowles and Gintis 1976; Katz 1971).

Sometimes schools can seem overwhelmingly bureaucratic, with the effect of stifling rather than nourishing intellectual curiosity in students. This concern has led many parents and policymakers to push for school choice programs—allowing parents to choose the school that suits their children's needs, and forcing schools to compete for their "customers."

Despite efforts to establish positive relationships among students and between teachers and students, many young people view their schools as impersonal institutions.

16-2 Violence in the Schools

Littleton, Colorado; Red Lake, Minnesota; Jonesboro, Arkansas; West Paducah, Kentucky; Pearl, Mississippi; Edinboro, Pennsylvania; Springfield, Oregon—these are now more than just the names of small towns and medium-size cities. They resonate with the sound of gunshots, of kids killing kids on school grounds. As a result, people no longer perceive schools as safe havens. But how accurate is that impression?

Studies of school violence put the recent spate of school killings in perspective:

- A child has less than a one in a million chance of being killed at school.

- Ninety-nine percent of violent deaths of school-age children in 1992–2004 occurred *outside* school grounds.

- Fewer students are now being found with guns in school.

- With the exception of 1999, school-associated violent deaths declined every year from 1992 through 2006.

- Twenty-three times more children are killed in gun *accidents* than in school killings.

Schools, then, are safer than neighborhoods, but people are still unnerved by the perception of an alarming rise in schoolyard violence generated by heavy media coverage of recent incidents. Some conflict theorists object to the huge outcry about recent violence in schools. After all, they note, violence in and around inner-city schools has a long history. It seems that only when middle-class White children are the victims does school violence become a plank on the national policy agenda. When violence hits the middle class, the problem is viewed not as an extension of delinquency, but as a structural issue in need of legislative remedies, such as gun control (see the Social Policy section in Chapter 8).

A child has less than a one in a million chance of being killed at school.

Feminists observe that virtually all the offenders in these incidents are male, and in some instances, such as the case in Jonesboro, the victims are disproportionately female. The precipitating factor in the violence is often a broken-off dating relationship—yet another example of the violence of men against women (or in this case, boys against girls).

Increasingly, efforts to prevent school violence are focusing on the ways in which the socialization of young people contributes to violence. For example, the American Medical Association has invested in a violence prevention curriculum for elementary school students that teaches social skills related to anger management, impulse control, and empathy.

Some people believe that a key ingredient in the prevention of violence, in or out of school, is greater parental supervision of and responsibility for their children. In her book *A Tribe Apart*, Patricia Hersch documents the lives of eight teens growing up in a Virginia suburb over a three-year period. Her conclusion: children need meaningful adult relationships in their lives. And former Secretary of Education Richard Riley cites studies showing that youths who feel connected to their parents and schools are less likely than others to engage in high-risk behaviors.

LET'S DISCUSS

1. Has a shooting or other violent episode ever occurred at your school? If so, how did students react? Do you feel safer at school than at home, as experts say you are?
2. What steps have administrators at your school taken to prevent violence? Have they been effective, or should other steps be taken?

Sources: American Medical Association 2009; Centers for Disease Control and Prevention 2008b; Department of Education 1999, 2004; Donohue et al. 1998; Hersch 1998; National Center for Education Statistics 2002.

In the United States, another significant countertrend to the bureaucratization of schools is the availability of education over the Internet. Increasingly, colleges and universities are reaching out via the Web, offering entire courses and even majors to students in the comfort of their homes. Online curricula provide flexibility for working students and others who may have difficulty attending conventional classes because of distance or disability. Research on this type of learning is just beginning, so the question of whether teacher–student contact can thrive online remains to be settled. Computer-mediated instruction may also have an impact on instructors' status as employees, which we will discuss next, as well as on alternative forms of education like homeschooling.

use your sociological *imagination*

How would you make your school less bureaucratic? What would it be like?

Teachers: Employees and Instructors

Whether they serve as instructors of preschoolers or of graduate students, teachers are employees of formal organizations with bureaucratic structures. There is an inherent conflict in serving as a professional in a bureaucracy. The organization follows the principles of hierarchy and expects adherence to its rules, but professionalism demands the individual responsibility of the practitioner. This conflict is very real for teachers, who experience all the positive and negative consequences of working in bureaucracies (see Table 6-2, page 127).

A teacher undergoes many perplexing stresses every day. While teachers' academic assignments have become more specialized, the demands on their time remain diverse and contradictory. Conflicts arise from serving as an instructor, a disciplinarian, and an employee of a school district at the same time. In too many schools, discipline means dealing with violence (Box 16-2). Burnout is one result of these stresses: between a quarter and a third of new teachers quit within their first three years, and as many as half leave poor urban schools in their first five years (Wallis 2008).

Given these difficulties, does teaching remain an attractive profession in the United States? In 2008, 4.1 percent of first-year college students indicated that they were interested in becoming elementary school teachers, and 4.2 percent, high school

MAPPING LIFE NATIONWIDE

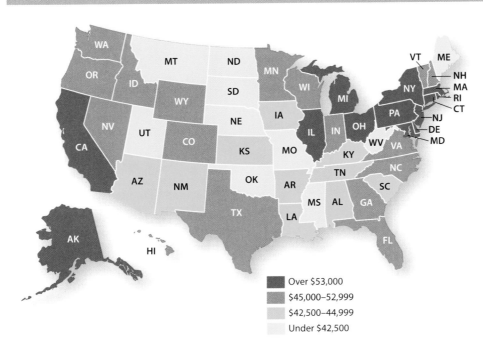

Over $53,000
$45,000–52,999
$42,500–44,999
Under $42,500

Note: Data released in 2008 for 2006–2007.
Source: Di Carlo 2008.

State averages for teacher salaries range from a low of $35,378 in South Dakota to a high of $63,640 in Massachusetts.

teachers. These figures are dramatically lower than the 11 percent of first-year male students and 37 percent of first-year female students who held those occupational aspirations in 1966 (Pryor et al. 2007: 122, 76; 2008:33).

Undoubtedly, economic considerations enter into students' feelings about the attractiveness of teaching. In 2008 the average salary for all public elementary and secondary school teachers in the United States was reported at $51,009, placing teachers somewhere near the average of all the nation's wage earners. In most other industrial countries, teachers' salaries are higher in relation to the general standard of living. Of course, teachers' salaries vary considerably from state to state (Figure 16-3), and even more from one school district to another. Nevertheless, the economic reward for teaching is miniscule compared to some career options: the CEO of a major corporation makes more money in a day than the average teacher makes in a year.

The status of any job reflects several factors, including the level of education required, financial compensation, and the respect given the occupation by society. The teaching profession (see Table 9-2, page 202) is feeling pressure in all three of these areas. First, the level of formal schooling required for teaching remains high, and the public has begun to call for new competency examinations. Second, the statistics just cited demonstrate that teachers' salaries are significantly lower than those of many professionals and skilled workers. Finally, the overall prestige of the teaching profession has declined in the past decade. Many teachers have become disappointed and frustrated and have left the educational world for careers in other professions.

Student Subcultures

An important latent function of education relates directly to student life: schools provide for students' social and recreational needs. Education helps toddlers and young children develop interpersonal skills that are essential during adolescence and adulthood. In their high school and college years, students may meet future husbands and wives and establish lifelong friendships.

When people observe high schools, community colleges, or universities from the outside, students appear to constitute a cohesive, uniform group. However, the student subculture is actually complex and diverse. High school cliques and social groups may crop up according to race, social class, physical attractiveness, placement in courses, athletic ability, and leadership roles in the school and community. In his classic community study of "Elmtown," August B. Hollingshead (1975) found some 259 distinct cliques in a single high school. The cliques, whose average size was five, were centered on the school itself, on recreational activities, and on religious and community groups.

Amid these close-knit and often rigidly segregated cliques, gay and lesbian students are particularly vulnerable. Peer group pressure to conform is intense at this age. Although coming to terms with one's sexuality is difficult for all adolescents, it can be downright dangerous for those whose sexual orientation does not conform to societal expectations.

Teachers and administrators are becoming more sensitized to these issues. Perhaps more important, some schools are creating gay–straight alliances (GSAs), school-sponsored support groups that bring gay teens together with sympathetic straight peers. Begun in Los Angeles in 1984, these programs numbered nearly 3,000 nationwide in 2005; most were founded after the murder of Matthew Shepard, a gay college student, in 1998. In some districts parents have objected to these organizations, but the same court rulings that protect the right of conservative Bible groups to meet on school grounds also protect GSAs. In 2003, the gay–straight movement reached a milestone when the New York City public schools moved an in-school program for gays, bisexuals, and transgender students to a separate school of their own. The Harvey Milk High School was named in memory of San Francisco's first openly gay city supervisor, who was assassinated in 1978 (Gay, Lesbian and Straight Education Network 2009).

We can find a similar diversity of student groups at the college level. Burton Clark and Martin Trow (1966) and more recently, Helen Lefkowitz Horowitz (1987) have identified four distinctive subcultures among college students:

1. The *collegiate* subculture focuses on having fun and socializing. These students define what constitutes a "reasonable"

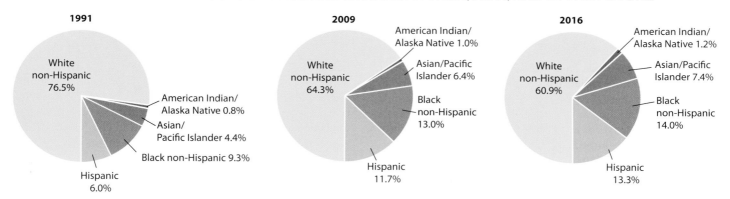

1991
- White non-Hispanic 76.5%
- American Indian/Alaska Native 0.8%
- Asian/Pacific Islander 4.4%
- Black non-Hispanic 9.3%
- Hispanic 6.0%

2009
- White non-Hispanic 64.3%
- American Indian/Alaska Native 1.0%
- Asian/Pacific Islander 6.4%
- Black non-Hispanic 13.0%
- Hispanic 11.7%

2016
- White non-Hispanic 60.9%
- American Indian/Alaska Native 1.2%
- Asian/Pacific Islander 7.4%
- Black non-Hispanic 14.0%
- Hispanic 13.3%

Note: Percentages do not add to 100 due to rounding error.
Source: National Center for Education Statistics 2006.

amount of academic work (and what amount of work is "excessive" and leads to being labeled as a "grind"). Members of the collegiate subculture have little commitment to academic pursuits. Athletes often fit into this subculture.

2. The *academic* subculture identifies with the intellectual concerns of the faculty and values knowledge for its own sake.

3. The *vocational* subculture is interested primarily in career prospects, and views college as a means of obtaining degrees that are essential for advancement.

4. Finally, the *nonconformist* subculture is hostile to the college environment, and seeks ideas that may or may not relate to academic studies. This group may find outlets through campus publications or issue-oriented groups.

Each college student is eventually exposed to these competing subcultures and must determine which (if any) seems most in line with his or her feelings and interests.

The typology used by the researchers reminds us that school is a complex social organization—almost like a community with different neighborhoods. Of course, these four subcultures are not the only ones evident on college campuses in the United States. For example, one might find subcultures of Vietnam veterans or former full-time homemakers at community colleges and four-year commuter institutions. And as more and more students from minority groups decide to continue their formal education beyond high school, subcultures based on race and ethnicity will become more evident. As Figure 16-4 shows, college campuses are increasingly diverse.

Sociologist Joe R. Feagin has studied a distinctive collegiate subculture: Black students at predominantly White universities. These students must function academically and socially within universities where there are few Black faculty members or Black administrators, where harassment of Blacks by campus police is common, and where the curricula place little emphasis on Black contributions. Feagin (1989:11) suggests that "for minority students life at a predominantly White college or university means long-term encounters with pervasive whiteness." In Feagin's view, African American students at such institutions experience both blatant and subtle racial discrimination, which has a cumulative impact that can seriously damage the students' confidence (see also Feagin et al. 1996).

Student subcultures are more diverse today than in the past. Many adults are returning to college to obtain further education, advance their careers, or change their line of work.

use your sociological *imagination*

What distinctive subcultures can you identify at your college?

Homeschooling

When most people think of school, they think of bricks and mortar and the teachers, administrators, and other employees who staff school buildings. But for an increasing number of students in the United States, home is the classroom and the teacher is a parent. About 1.5 million students are now being educated at home. That is about 3 percent of the K–12 school population. For these students, the issues of bureaucratization and social structure are less significant than they are for public school students (National Center for Education Statistics 2009).

In the 1800s, after the establishment of public schools, families that taught their children at home lived in isolated environments or held strict religious views that were at odds with the secular environment of public schools. But today, homeschooling is attracting a broader range of families not necessarily tied to organized religion. Poor academic quality, peer pressure, and school violence are motivating many parents to teach their children at home. In addition, some immigrants choose homeschooling as a way to ease their children's transition to a new society. For example, the growing Arab American population recently joined the movement toward homeschooling (MacFarquhar 2008; National Center for Education Statistics 2008).

While supporters of homeschooling believe children can do just as well or better in homeschools as in public schools, critics counter that because homeschooled children are isolated from the larger community, they lose an important chance to improve their socialization skills. But proponents of homeschooling claim their children benefit from contact with others besides their own age group. They also see homeschools as a good alternative for children who suffer from attention-deficit/hyperactivity disorder (ADHD) and learning disorders (LDs). Such children often do better in smaller classes, which present fewer distractions to disturb their concentration.

Quality control is an issue in homeschooling. While homeschooling is legal in all 50 states, 10 states require no notification that a child will be homeschooled, and another 14 require notification only. Other states may require parents to submit their children's curricula or test scores for professional evaluation. Despite the lack of uniform standards, a research review by the Home School Legal Defense Association (2005) reports that homeschooled students score higher than others on standardized tests, in every subject and every grade.

Who are the people who are running homeschools? In general, they tend to have higher-than-average incomes and educational levels. Most are two-parent families, and their children watch less television than average—both factors that are likely to support superior educational performance. The same students, with the same support from their parents, would probably do just as well in the public schools. As research has repeatedly shown, small classes are better than big classes, and strong parental and community involvement is key (R. Cox 2003:28).

social**policy** and Education

No Child Left Behind Act

The Issue

The consensus was clear: too many public schools in the United States were failing to educate their students—failing to meet even minimum performance standards. In the 2000 presidential election campaign, President George W. Bush had promised to "leave no child behind" if he were elected. The president had advocated an educational reform plan that he had instituted in the Texas public schools while he was governor of that state. In 2001, the U.S. House of Representatives voted 381–41, and the Senate 87–10, to approve the president's No Child Left Behind (NCLB) Act, an initiative designed to improve the performance of public schools in the United States. The NCLB increased federal standards of accountability for states, school districts, and schools, and gave parents more flexibility in choosing which schools their children would attend.

The apparent consensus for educational reform soon disappeared, however. Supporters charged that the act was not being enforced stringently enough; others felt the legislation went too far. What does this state of affairs say about the NCLB in particular, and about the school reform movement in general?

The Setting

The NCLB must be viewed in the context of the United States' unusual educational system. In this country, unlike most others, public schools are locally run and financed, albeit with some federal and state aid. The United States does not have a national education program that follows a common curriculum. Until the 1940s, in fact, the federal government had very little involvement with public education. But in the 1990s, public concern over poor student performance in the United States, compared to that of other countries, led to the establishment of national educational standards.

The NCLB built on those national standards, and for the first time set penalties for failure to meet them. States are now required to conduct annual assessments of all public school students, grades K–12. The resulting performance data must be cross-tabulated by students' race, ethnicity, gender, social class, and disability. Schools whose students do not perform well on the required tests are subject to restructuring, and their students are eligible to transfer to different schools. Theoretically, the testing requirements and the penalties associated with substandard performance should reduce the achievement gap between advantaged and disadvantaged students, allowing the nation to "leave no child behind." The program's ambitious goal is for every student in the nation to be proficient in reading and mathematics by the year 2014.

The NCLB has created a national debate about how best to offer high-quality schooling to all children. Some critics have charged that the program has no substance—that the required testing is just an academic exercise. Others charge that it overemphasizes reading and math at the expense of other subjects, such as art, music, and social studies. Indeed, many principals have reworked their curricula and staff to emphasize the subjects that are tested under the NCLB. Finally, state and local educators have complained bitterly about federal intrusion into local schools. They insist that they need more federal funding if they are to have any hope of complying with the act (Schneider and Keesler 2007).

Sociological Insights

From a functionalist point of view, the development of common curricular objectives promotes social integration. Because the NCLB requires scores to be broken out by gender, race, income, ethnicity, and disability, it prevents schools from disguising low achievement by disadvantaged students. The result should be better educational achievement across the board. Conflict theorists support the need to educate all students, regardless of their socioeconomic status, but they question the wisdom of pursuing that goal through testing programs.

Even before the NCLB, educational testing was a hot issue. From preschool screening through entry-level professional examinations, the practice has always been controversial. Critics have raised serious questions about the reliability and validity of such tests. Recall from Chapter 2 that **validity** refers to the degree to which a measure or scale truly reflects the phenomenon under study. Does an aptitude test really measure the likelihood of future academic success, for instance? **Reliability** refers to the extent to which a measure provides consistent results. If an exam supposedly measures a student's readiness to study high school algebra, it should yield the same result, no matter who administers and scores it.

Reliability and validity are major issues in constructing any test; rarely are these concerns totally resolved. Scholars who design standardized tests are constantly tweaking the questions to improve the tests' reliability and validity. From preschool to graduate and professional programs, the reliability and validity of tests affect everything from the allocation of funds to admissions decisions in highly competitive programs. With high-stakes testing—testing that determines whether a public school closes or remains open, for instance—these issues become even more important.

Policy Initiatives

National policy efforts like the NCLB overlay a patchwork of state and local programs. Educational reformers have yet to come up with a solution that fits all schools in all states. Former Representative Dick Gephardt, a Democrat who voted for the act, has complained that the program does not do what it claimed it would: "We were all fooled into it. It is a fraud." Still, many educators see the NCLB as their best hope so far for improving the nation's schools. According to Peggy Hinckley, an Indiana School superintendent, "We are living in a results-oriented

A statue of President George W. Bush stands outside Hamilton High School in Ohio, where the president signed the No Child Left Behind Act in 2002. Two years later, Hamilton High was labeled a failing school under the act's tough standards.

society. Everybody is looking for results and we will do whatever we can to achieve them" (Dobbs 2004:29; Schrag 2004:40).

In 2007, an independent commission advocated maintaining the 2014 goals, even though by its own estimate, only a small portion of the nation's schools would reach the objectives. By that time, only 13 percent of the nation's eighth graders are expected to reach the mathematics objectives. A maximum of 33 percent of all third graders are expected to meet the reading objectives. Indeed, several states have purposefully been moving very slowly toward meeting the objectives, assuming they would be revised downward. As of 2009, however, there was little indication that Congress planned to move in that direction (Dillon 2008; Tommy Thompson and Barnes 2007:69).

Let's Discuss

1. What are the public schools like in the community where you live? Are some schools in trouble because of high-stakes testing? Does the school system have adequate funding, or are administrators forced to cut corners to stay within budget?

2. What do you think of the practice of restructuring or closing schools whose students do not perform well on national tests? What will be the short-term effect on individual students? The long-term effect on students and schools?

3. Can you think of a better way to improve the nation's public schools?

getting**involved**

To get involved in the debate over the No Child Left Behind program, visit this book's Online Learning Center, which offers links to relevant Web sites.

MASTERING THIS CHAPTER

Summary

Education is a cultural universal found throughout the world, although in varied forms. This chapter examines sociological views of education and analyzes schools as an example of formal organizations.

1. The transmission of knowledge and bestowal of status are manifest functions of education. Among the latent functions are transmitting culture, promoting social and political integration, maintaining social control, and serving as an agent of social change.

2. In the view of conflict theorists, education serves as an instrument of elite domination by creating standards for entry into occupations, bestowing status unequally, and subordinating the role of women.

3. Teacher expectations about a student's performance can sometimes have an impact on the student's actual achievements.

4. Today, most schools in the United States are organized in a bureaucratic fashion. Weber's five basic characteristics of bureaucracy are all evident in schools.

5. Homeschooling has become a viable alternative to traditional public and private schools. An estimated 1.7 million or more American children are now educated at home.

6. The No Child Left Behind Act is a controversial initiative designed to improve the performance of public schools in the United States by increasing federal standards of accountability. Critics charge that the program is underfunded, that it overemphasizes reading and math, and that the tests used to determine whether a school is meeting federal standards are flawed.

Critical Thinking Questions

1. What are the functions and dysfunctions of tracking in schools? Viewed from an interactionist perspective, how would tracking of high school students influence the interactions between students and teachers? In what ways might tracking have positive and negative impacts on the self-concepts of various students?

2. Are the student subcultures identified in this text evident on your campus? What other student subcultures are present? Which subcultures have the highest (and the lowest) social status? How might functionalists, conflict theorists, and interactionists view the existence of student subcultures on a college campus?

Key Terms

Correspondence principle The tendency of schools to promote the values expected of individuals in each social class and to prepare students for the types of jobs typically held by members of their class. (page 365)

Credentialism An increase in the lowest level of education required to enter a field. (364)

Education A formal process of learning in which some people consciously teach while others adopt the social role of learner. (360)

Hidden curriculum Standards of behavior that are deemed proper by society and are taught subtly in schools. (364)

Reliability The extent to which a measure produces consistent results. (373)

Teacher-expectancy effect The impact that a teacher's expectations about a student's performance may have on the student's actual achievements. (367)

Tracking The practice of placing students in specific curriculum groups on the basis of their test scores and other criteria. (365)

Validity The degree to which a measure or scale truly reflects the phenomenon under study. (373)

Self-Quiz

Read each question carefully and then select the best answer.

1. Which sociological perspective emphasizes that the common identity and social integration fostered by education contribute to overall societal stability and consensus?
   a. the functionalist perspective
   b. the conflict perspective
   c. the interactionist perspective
   d. labeling theory

2. Which one of the following was introduced into school systems to promote social change?
   a. sex education classes
   b. affirmative action programs
   c. Project Head Start
   d. all of the above

3. The correspondence principle was developed by
   a. Max Weber.
   b. Karl Marx and Friedrich Engels.
   c. Samuel Bowles and Herbert Gintis.
   d. James Thurber.

4. The student subculture that is hostile to the college environment and seeks out ideas that may or may not relate to studies is called the
   a. collegiate subculture.
   b. academic subculture.

   c. vocational subculture.
   d. nonconformist subculture.

5. Most recent research on ability grouping raises questions about its
   a. effectiveness, especially for lower-achieving students.
   b. failure to improve the prospects of higher-achieving students.
   c. ability to improve the prospects of lower- and higher-achieving students.
   d. both a and b

6. The most basic *manifest* function of education is
   a. transmitting knowledge.
   b. transmitting culture.
   c. maintaining social control.
   d. serving as an agent of change.

7. Fifty years ago, a high school diploma was the minimum requirement for entry into the paid labor force of the United States. Today, a college diploma is virtually the bare minimum. This change reflects the process of
   a. tracking.
   b. credentialism.
   c. the hidden curriculum.
   d. the correspondence principle.

8. Samuel Bowles and Herbert Gintis have argued that capitalism requires a skilled, disciplined labor force and that the educational system of the United States

is structured with that objective in mind. Citing numerous studies, they offer support for what they call
- **a.** tracking.
- **b.** credentialism.
- **c.** the correspondence principle.
- **d.** the teacher-expectancy effect.

9. The teacher-expectancy effect is most closely associated with
- **a.** the functionalist perspective.
- **b.** the conflict perspective.
- **c.** the interactionist perspective.
- **d.** anomie theory.

10. Sociologist Max Weber noted five basic characteristics of bureaucracy, all of which are evident in the vast majority of schools, whether at the elementary, secondary, or even college level. Which of the following is *not* one of them?
- **a.** division of labor
- **b.** written rules and regulations
- **c.** impersonality
- **d.** shared decision making

11. The _____ perspective stresses the importance of education in transmitting culture, maintaining social control, and promoting social change.

12. In the past, the integrative function of education was most obvious through its emphasis on promoting a common _____.

13. The _____ subculture identifies with the intellectual concerns of the faculty and values knowledge for its own sake.

14. _____ and _____ are major issues in constructing any test, but rarely are they totally resolved.

15. Women's education tends to suffer in those cultures with traditional _____ _____.

16. Schools perform a variety of _____ functions, such as transmitting culture, promoting social and political integration, and maintaining social control.

17. Sociologist _____ _____ points out that better-educated people tend to have greater access to information, to hold more diverse opinions, and to possess the ability to make subtle distinctions in analysis.

18. The term _____ _____ refers to standards of behavior that are deemed proper by society and are taught subtly in schools. According to this curriculum, children must not speak until the teacher calls on them and must regulate their activities according to the clock or the bell.

19. _____ is the practice of placing students in specific curriculum groups on the basis of their test scores and other criteria.

20. Of the four distinctive subcultures among college students discussed in the text, the _____ subculture is interested primarily in career prospects, and views college as a means of obtaining degrees that are essential for advancement.

THINKING ABOUT MOVIES

Freedom Writers (Richard LaGravenese, 2007)

Erin Gruwell (Hillary Swank) teaches English at a high school in Long Beach, California. One of her goals is to help students understand racism and learn tolerance for other ethnic and racial groups. To acquaint them with anti-Semitism and the Holocaust, Erin assigns *The Diary of Anne Frank* and asks students to talk with Holocaust survivors. Realizing that gang violence is common in their neighborhoods, she encourages them to express their feelings by telling their own stories through journals. Gradually, the "freedom writers" learn to deal with their anger and share the experience of growing up in an impoverished community.

This film portrays the difficulty of teacher–student relationships through conflict between the students and Erin, who stands in for the larger bureaucracy. *Freedom Writers* also shows conflict between student subcultures and suggests a path toward mutual understanding.

For Your Consideration

1. How does the movie show the hierarchy of authority at the school, and how does that hierarchy affect social relationships?
2. What do you think of the strategies Erin uses to overcome the impersonality of the educational bureaucracy?

Happy-Go-Lucky (Mike Leigh, 2008)

In this film, set in London, Poppy Cross (Sally Hawkins) is a primary school teacher with an infectious effervescence and a gift for seeing the good in people. In the classroom and in everyday life, Poppy does her best to help others. The film shows her efforts to help two men with anger problems, one of whom is her student and the other her driving instructor. Poppy views education as a vehicle for social integration, particularly for those who need a little extra attention.

Happy-Go-Lucky shows how schools can serve as agents for social change. Although Poppy's flighty demeanor tends to undermine discipline in her classroom, her skills help her to identify a student who is showing symptoms of domestic abuse. Watch for the scene in which Poppy joins with a social worker to draw out the student and encourage him to speak about his problems.

For Your Consideration

1. Which sociological approach do you think best describes Poppy's approach to education?
2. What is the relationship between Poppy's educational efforts and the maintenance of social control?

inside

Power and Authority

Types of Government

Political Behavior in the United States

Models of Power Structure in the United States

War and Peace

Political Activism on the Internet

Social Policy and Politics: Campaign Financing

BOXES

Sociology in the Global Community: *Charisma: The Beatles and the Maharishi Mahesh Yogi*

Taking Sociology to Work: *Joshua Johnston, Congressional Aide, Office of Congressman Norm Dicks*

Research Today: *Why Don't More Young People Vote?*

A volunteer speaks with a prospective voter at a mobile voter registration station in Coney Island, New York. Despite efforts to increase political participation by young people, turnout among the young is still low compared to other age groups.

Government 17
and Politics

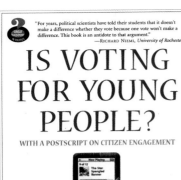

IS VOTING FOR YOUNG PEOPLE?

WITH A POSTSCRIPT ON CITIZEN ENGAGEMENT

MARTIN P. WATTENBERG
AUTHOR OF *Where Have All the Voters Gone?*

"For years, political scientists have told their students that it doesn't make a difference whether they vote because one vote won't make a difference. This book is an antidote to that argument."
—RICHARD NIEMI, *University of Rochester*

❝ "Voting is for Old People," proclaimed a T-shirt printed and distributed in 2004 by Urban Outfitters, a popular American clothing company. At Harvard's Kennedy School of Government, the perceived message of the shirt hit a raw nerve. Its director issued a public statement criticizing the slogan, saying that it could not be further from the truth—that voting is for everyone. In response, Urban Outfitters said they never intended to discourage anyone from voting. Rather, they asserted that their goal was to draw attention to the relative lack of participation of young adults in politics, a problem that many analysts and politicians acknowledge but few seem to be genuinely concerned about. . . .

Over the last three decades, politics and voting have indeed become more and more the province of the elderly, which will be shown to be the case not only in the United States but also *throughout the world's advanced industrialized democracies.* There is in fact a rift between politicians and young adults, although not one of mutual contempt but rather of mutual neglect. Many young people don't vote simply because they don't follow politics. Moreover, because so many young people don't follow politics and don't vote, parties and

All too often, low turnout rates among the young are considered to be a natural part of political life, and hence not worth fretting about.

politicians frequently don't bother with young people, thereby further widening the age bias in electoral participation.

All too often, low turnout rates among the young are considered to be a natural part of political life, and hence not worth fretting about. Scholars often write of a life cycle pattern in which people become more aware of the political world as they age, and hence are more likely to vote. As such, it is often thought that today's young nonvoters will eventually show up at the polls and have their voices heard. If such a life cycle truly exists, it ought to be consistently found in: (1) different eras; and (2) across a wide range of democracies. The data . . . from a number of countries in the 1970s contradict the life cycle hypothesis. . . .

Communications technology is one . . . aspect of political life that has undergone transformation throughout the world's advanced industrialized societies . . . in recent years. . . . Changes in media habits from generation to generation have led to a new situation in which young people are far less likely to be exposed to news about public affairs than their elders. Young adults have not consciously decided to avoid political news in recent years; rather, having been socialized in a markedly different communications environment, they just have not picked up the same media habits that their parents and grandparents did. These media habits, which older people developed long ago in a different world, continue to serve them well in today's political environment—making them substantially more likely to follow politics and become familiar with the issues of the day. And the more one learns about public affairs and follows current events, the more one is likely to realize the stakes involved at the polls. ❞

(Wattenberg 2008:1–2, 3) Additional information about this excerpt can be found on the Online Learning Center at www.mhhe.com/schaefer12e.

In this excerpt from *Is Voting for Young People?* Martin P. Wattenberg, a professor of political science at the University of California at Irvine, confronts the generation gap in politics, not only in the United States but in industrialized countries around the world. Wattenberg thinks that the absence of young people from the voting booth reflects a generational difference in the way that citizens use the mass media. Few young people nowadays read the newspapers, so few know much about politics or think that it has any relevance for them. Most spend their time surfing the Internet, downloading music to their iPods and MP3s, text-messaging and snapping photos using their cell phones. Only in countries where these technological marvels are not available to the average youth is apathy among young people not a noteworthy phenomenon.

Those who vote (or who choose not to) operate within the framework of the existing political system, be it local, state, national, or international. By **political system,** sociologists

mean the social institution that is founded on a recognized set of procedures for implementing and achieving society's goals, such as the allocation of valued resources. Like religion and the family, the political system is a cultural universal: it is found in every society. In the United States, the political system holds the ultimate responsibility for addressing the social policy issues examined in this textbook: child care, the AIDS crisis, welfare reform, and so forth.

Are young people more interested in what's playing on their portable media players than in the political issues confronting their nation? How does government maintain its power, and how do political parties and public interest groups attempt to exert theirs? Does our campaign finance system put some groups at a disadvantage? In this chapter we will analyze the impact of government on people's lives from a sociological point of view. We will begin with a macro-level analysis of the sources of political power and authority, and the four major types of government in which that power and authority is exerted. We will see how politics works, with particular attention to citizens' participation and the changing role of women and minority groups. We'll look at two models of power in the United States, the elite and the pluralist models. Then we'll touch briefly on war, peace, and terrorism, and see how political activists have begun using the Internet to promote their causes. Finally, the Social Policy section will explore the controversy over campaign financing, an issue that vividly illustrates the close relationship between government and the moneyed elite who seek to influence the political process.

Power and Authority

In any society, someone or some group—whether it be a tribal chief, a dictator, or a parliament—makes important decisions about how to use resources and how to allocate goods. One cultural universal, then, is the exercise of power and authority. Inevitably, the struggle for power and authority involves **politics,** which political scientist Harold Lasswell (1936) tersely defined as "who gets what, when, and how." In their study of politics and government, sociologists are concerned with social interactions among individuals and groups and their impact on the larger political and economic order.

Power

Power lies at the heart of a political system. According to Max Weber, **power** is the ability to exercise one's will over others. To put it another way, whoever can overcome the resistance of others and control their behavior is exercising power. Power relations can involve large organizations, small groups, or even people in an intimate association.

Because Weber developed his conceptualization of power in the early 1900s, he focused primarily on the nation-state and its sphere of influence. Today scholars recognize that the trend toward globalization has brought new opportunities, and with them new concentrations of power. Power is now exercised on a global as well as a national stage, as countries and multinational corporations vie to control access to resources and manage the distribution of capital (R. Schaefer 2008b; Sernau 2001).

There are three basic sources of power within any political system: force, influence, and authority. **Force** is the actual or threatened use of coercion to impose one's will on others. When leaders imprison or even execute political dissidents, they are applying force; so, too, are terrorists when they seize or bomb an embassy or assassinate a political leader.

In the 21st century, force has taken on new meaning as nations clamp down on use of the Internet to oppose the central government or assert freedom of expression, human rights, and minority or religious views. When a military coup overthrew the democratically elected government of Thailand in September 2006, for example, citizens lost access to Web sites that criticized the takeover. As of 2008, 16 nations maintained selective to pervasive political controls on Internet content (Figure 17-1 on page 380). Censorship of online content is just as much a use of force as closing down a newspaper or arresting dissidents (Deibert et al. 2008; OpenNet Initiative 2008; Zittrain and Palfrey 2008).

Influence, on the other hand, refers to the exercise of power through a process of persuasion. A citizen may change his or her view of a Supreme Court nominee because of a newspaper editorial, the expert testimony of a law school dean before the Senate Judiciary Committee, or a stirring speech by a political activist at a rally. In each case, sociologists would view such efforts to persuade people as examples of influence. Now let's take a look at the third source of power, *authority.*

Types of Authority

The term **authority** refers to institutionalized power that is recognized by the people over whom it is exercised. Sociologists commonly use the term in connection with those who hold legitimate power through elected or publicly acknowledged positions. A person's authority is often limited. Thus, a referee has the authority to decide whether a penalty should be called during a football game, but has no authority over the price of tickets to the game.

Max Weber ([1913] 1947) developed a classification system for authority that has become one of the most useful and frequently cited contributions of early sociology. He identified three ideal types of authority: traditional, rational-legal, and charismatic. Weber did not insist that only one type applies to a given society or organization. All can be present, but their relative importance will vary. Sociologists have found Weber's typology valuable in understanding different manifestations of legitimate power within a society.

Traditional Authority Until the middle of the last century, Japan was ruled by a revered emperor whose absolute power was passed down from generation to generation. In a political system based on **traditional authority,** legitimate power is conferred by custom and accepted practice. A king or queen is accepted as ruler of a nation simply by virtue of inheriting the crown; a tribal chief rules because that is the accepted practice. The ruler may be loved or hated, competent or destructive; in terms of legitimacy, that does not matter. For the traditional leader, authority rests in custom, not in personal characteristics, technical competence, or even written law. People accept the ruler's authority because that is how things have always been done. Traditional authority is absolute when the ruler has the ability to determine laws and policies.

Rational-Legal Authority The U.S. Constitution gives Congress and our president the authority to make and enforce laws and policies. Power made legitimate by law is known as **rational-legal authority.** Leaders derive their rational-legal authority from the written rules and regulations of political systems, such as a constitution. Generally, in societies based on rational-legal authority, leaders are thought to have specific areas of competence and

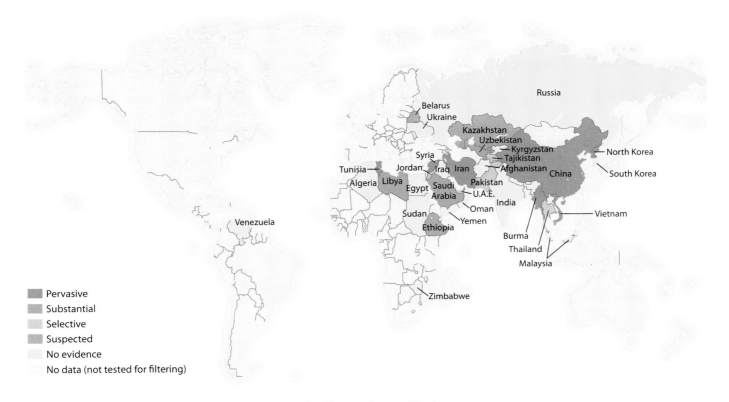

MAPPING LIFE WORLDWIDE

Russia
Belarus
Ukraine
Kazakhstan
Uzbekistan
Kyrgyzstan
Tajikistan
North Korea
Syria
Afghanistan
South Korea
Jordan
Iraq
Iran
China
Tunisia
Pakistan
Algeria
Libya
Egypt
Saudi
Arabia
U.A.E.
India
Vietnam
Oman
Venezuela
Sudan
Yemen
Ethiopia
Burma
Thailand
Malaysia
Zimbabwe

■ Pervasive
■ Substantial
□ Selective
■ Suspected
□ No evidence
□ No data (not tested for filtering)

Note: "No data" (see the gray portions of the map) does not necessarily indicate an absence of filtering.
Sources: OpenNet Initiative 2008; see also Deibert et al. 2008; Faris and Villeneuve 2008.
This map highlights nations that filter or restrict content that expresses views that oppose those of the current government, or are related to human rights, freedom of expression, minority rights, and religious movements.

authority but are not thought to be endowed with divine inspiration, as in certain societies with traditional forms of authority.

Charismatic Authority Joan of Arc was a simple peasant girl in medieval France, yet she was able to rally the French people and lead them into major battles against English invaders. How was this possible? As Weber observed, power can be legitimized by the *charisma* of an individual. The term **charismatic authority** refers to power made legitimate by a leader's exceptional personal or emotional appeal to his or her followers.

Charisma lets a person lead or inspire without relying on set rules or traditions. In fact, charismatic authority is derived more from the beliefs of followers than from the actual qualities of leaders. So long as people perceive a charismatic leader such as Jesus, Joan of Arc, Gandhi, Malcolm X, or Martin Luther King Jr. as having qualities that set him or her apart from ordinary citizens, that leader's authority will remain secure and often unquestioned.

Box 17-1 examines the role of the charismatic spiritual leader Maharishi Mahesh Yogi in the Beatles' ascent to worldwide fame and fortune.

Observing charismatic authority from an interactionist perspective, sociologist Carl Couch (1996) points out that the growth of the electronic media has facilitated the development of charismatic authority. During the 1930s and 1940s, the heads of state of the United States, Great Britain, and Germany all used radio to issue direct appeals to citizens. Now, television and the Internet allow leaders to "visit" people's homes and communicate with them. In both Taiwan and South Korea in 1996, troubled political leaders facing reelection campaigns spoke frequently to national audiences and exaggerated military threats from neighboring China and North Korea, respectively.

As we noted earlier, Weber used traditional, rational-legal, and charismatic authority as ideal types. In reality, particular leaders and political systems combine elements of two or more of these forms. Presidents Franklin D. Roosevelt, John F. Kennedy, and Ronald Reagan wielded power largely through the rational-legal basis of their

SOCIOLOGY IN THE GLOBAL COMMUNITY

17-1 Charisma: The Beatles and the Maharishi Mahesh Yogi

Mention charisma in the same breath with the Beatles, and most people will think of the Fab Four's personal magnetism and its effect on millions of fans worldwide. Yet in reality, the Beatles' compelling mystique owes much to their celebrated Indian spiritual leader, the charismatic Maharishi Mahesh Yogi.

The Beatles first became aware of the Maharishi in 1967, when he visited London on his reported final tour of the West. A popular advocate of transcendental meditation, he maintained that a person could ultimately attain happiness by meditating 20 minutes a day on a *mantra*, a secret Sanskrit word unique to each meditator. Impressed by the man and his message, the Beatles made a highly publicized pilgrimage to the Maharishi's retreat in India in what turned out to be their last trip together outside Britain.

People often change their lifestyles and personal allegiances after experiencing the aura and magnetism of a charismatic authority figure.

With his trademark flowing beard and long hair, Maharishi Mahesh Yogi had long captivated audiences. When the Beatles became his disciples, his fame spread around the world. He used his newly expanded following to launch the Natural Law Party, a worldwide organization dedicated to promoting peace and forward-looking solutions to the world's problems. From a conventional perspective, the NLP has not enjoyed much success. In 2000 its candidate for president of the United States received 83,714 votes out of 105 million.

Though George Harrison remained respectful of the Maharishi, after a few months his band mates disavowed their discipleship.

Maharishi Mahesh Yogi poses in India with the four Beatles and his followers.

Nevertheless, their brief period of study with the Maharishi is credited with unleashing a floodgate of creativity, including the *White Album, Abbey Road,* and Lennon's solo album, *Imagine.* The Maharishi's counsel also helped the four to overcome the deeply felt loss of their manager, Brian Epstein.

Not surprisingly, the Beatles showed the influence of the Maharishi's spirituality in both their music and their dress. People often change their lifestyles and personal allegiances after experiencing the aura and magnetism of a charismatic authority figure. Similarly, in the 2008 presidential campaign, many Americans became politically active or changed their political affiliations in response to the historic campaigns of three charismatic candidates, Hillary Clinton, Barack Obama, and a "true American hero," John McCain.

LET'S DISCUSS

1. Have you ever personally seen or met a charismatic leader? If so, what effect did that person have on you, if any?
2. Are you familiar with the Beatles' music before and after their acquaintance with the Maharishi Mahesh Yogi? If so, can you hear the Maharishi's effect on the Beatles in their music?

Sources: *The Economist* 2008a; Federal Election Commission 2001; J. Gould 2007; Kozinn 2008; Natural Law Party 2008.

---

authority. At the same time, they were unusually charismatic leaders who commanded the personal loyalty of large numbers of citizens.

use your sociological *imagination*

What would our government be like if it were founded on traditional rather than rational-legal authority? What difference would it make to the average citizen?

Types of Government

Each society establishes a political system through which it is governed. In modern industrial nations, these formal systems of government make a significant number of critical political decisions. We will survey five basic types of government here: monarchy, oligarchy, dictatorship, totalitarianism, and democracy.

Monarchy

A **monarchy** is a form of government headed by a single member of a royal family, usually a king, queen, or some other hereditary ruler. In earlier times, many monarchs claimed that God had granted them a divine right to rule. Typically, they governed on the basis of traditional forms of authority, sometimes accompanied by the use of force. By the beginning of the 21st century, however, monarchs held genuine governmental power in only a few nations, such as Monaco. Most monarchs now have little practical power; they serve primarily ceremonial purposes.

Oligarchy

An **oligarchy** is a form of government in which a few individuals rule. A rather old method of governing that flourished in ancient Greece and Egypt, oligarchy now often takes the form of military rule. In developing nations in Africa, Asia, and Latin America, small factions of military officers will forcibly seize power, either from legally elected regimes or from other military cliques.

Strictly speaking, the term *oligarchy* is reserved for governments that are run by a few selected individuals. However, the People's Republic of China can be classified as an oligarchy if we stretch the meaning of the term. In China, power rests in the hands of a large but exclusive ruling *group*, the Communist Party. In a similar vein, drawing on conflict theory, one might argue that many industrialized nations of the West should be considered oligarchies (rather than democracies), since only a powerful few—leaders of big business, government, and the military—actually rule. Later in this chapter, we will examine the "elite model" of the U.S. political system in greater detail.

Dictatorship and Totalitarianism

A **dictatorship** is a government in which one person has nearly total power to make and enforce laws. Dictators rule primarily through the use of coercion, which often includes torture and executions. Typically, they *seize* power rather than being freely elected (as in a democracy) or inheriting power (as in a monarchy). Some dictators are quite charismatic and manage to achieve a certain popularity, though their supporters' enthusiasm is almost certainly tinged with fear. Other dictators are bitterly hated by the people over whom they rule.

Frequently, dictators develop such overwhelming control over people's lives that their governments are called *totalitarian.* (Monarchies and oligarchies may also achieve this type of dominance.) **Totalitarianism** involves virtually complete government control and surveillance over all aspects of a society's social and political life. Germany during Hitler's reign, the Soviet Union in the 1930s, and North Korea today are classified as totalitarian states.

Democracy

In a literal sense, **democracy** means government by the people. The word *democracy* originated in two Greek roots—*demos,* meaning "the populace" or "the common people," and *kratia,* meaning "rule." Of course, in large, populous nations such as the United States, government by the people is impractical at the national level. Americans cannot vote on every important issue that comes before Congress. Consequently, popular rule is generally maintained through **representative democracy,** a form of government in which certain individuals are selected to speak for the people.

The United States is commonly classified as a representative democracy, since the elected members of Congress and state legislatures make our laws. However, critics have questioned how representative our democracy really is. Do Congress and the state legislatures genuinely represent the masses? Are the people of the United States legitimately self-governing, or has our

North Korea has a totalitarian government whose leadership attempts to control all aspects of people's lives. This billboard, a blatant example of government propaganda, portrays the country's ruthless leader as a benevolent father figure.

government become a forum for powerful elites? We will explore these issues in the remainder of the chapter.

Political Behavior in the United States

Citizens of the United States take for granted many aspects of their political system. They are accustomed to living in a nation with a Bill of Rights, two major political parties, voting by secret ballot, an elected president, state and local governments distinct from the national government, and so forth. Yet each society has its own ways of governing itself and making decisions. Just as U.S. residents expect Democratic and Republican candidates to compete for public office, residents of Cuba and the People's Republic of China are accustomed to one-party rule by the Communist Party. In this section, we will examine several aspects of political behavior within the United States.

Participation and Apathy

In theory, a representative democracy will function most effectively and fairly if an informed and active electorate

TAKING SOCIOLOGY TO WORK

Joshua Johnston, **Congressional Aide, Office of Congressman Norm Dicks**

For Joshua Johnston, deciding on a major was easy: everything he was interested in fell into the area of sociology. Johnston, an avid people watcher, appreciates the discipline's focus on everyday social life. "Whether the subject is conspicuous consumption or people standing against the walls in elevators, you can see it all around you," he says.

A graduate of the University of Washington (2003), Johnston is now an aide to a congressional representative from the Seattle area. "I am the person that people work with when they want a meeting with the congressman or they would like him to attend an event," he explains. "A lot of my job is event coordinating and planning." Johnston's week begins with a Monday morning conference at which he schedules upcoming meetings and events. Working with labor unions is another of his responsibilities, one he particularly enjoys: "They are hard-working men and women who are trying to support their families and make an honest living." Once or twice a week, Johnston spends the evening at a community event.

Johnston appreciates the opportunity to work on issues that are important to people in the Pacific Northwest, such as salmon recovery. One of his first assignments as a congressional aide was to organize a hearing on the issue, so that congressional representatives from the area could

hear expert opinions on the topic. He also relishes the chance to meet well-known politicians. When Al Gore visited Seattle to talk about climate change, Johnston worked with Gore's staff to set up the event. He has also met John Edwards and Barack Obama.

Of all the topics Johnston studied in his sociology courses, he finds his knowledge of social networks to be most helpful on the job. "We all have to work with social networks, and we need the tools to be able to work effectively within them," he notes. But he also sees a broader benefit to majoring in sociology: "Sociology has given me the tools that I need to be able to think critically about a subject," he explains. "Above all else, I think this is the one tool that has been the most important to me in my life. Being able to think critically about a subject has given me the chance to analyze why I believe a certain thing, and then have true conviction when people ask me a question about my beliefs."

LET'S DISCUSS

1. How has your study of sociology helped to clarify your thinking on issues that are important to you?
2. Relate what you have learned about networking to the field of politics. In what kind of politics is networking especially useful? How have new technologies that support networking changed politics?

---

communicates its views to government leaders. Unfortunately, that is hardly the case in the United States. Virtually all citizens are familiar with the basics of the political process, and most tend to identify to some extent with a political party. (In 2009, about 35 percent of registered voters in the United States saw themselves as Democrats, 35 percent as independents, and 28 percent as Republicans.) However, only a small minority of citizens, often members of the higher social classes, actually participate in political organizations on a local or national level. Studies reveal that only 8 percent of Americans belong to a political club or organization. Not more than one in five has ever contacted an official of national, state, or local government about a political issue or problem (Gallup 2009e; Orum 2001).

By the 1980s, it had become clear that many people in the United States were beginning to be turned off by political parties, politicians, and big government. The most dramatic indication of this growing alienation came from voting statistics. Today, voters of all ages and races appear to be less enthusiastic than ever about elections, even presidential contests. For example, in the presidential election of 1896, almost 80 percent of eligible voters in the United States went to the polls. Yet by the 2008 election, despite its drama and historic nature, turnout was only 62 percent of all eligible voters—well below the levels of the 1960s. Obviously, even modestly higher voter turnout could dramatically change an election outcome, as the razor-thin margin in the 2000 presidential election demonstrated (McDonald 2008, 2009a).

Although a few nations still command high voter turnout, increasingly, national leaders of other countries also complain of voter apathy. Even so, among the 140 countries that held parliamentary elections between 1945 and 1998, the United States

ranked 114th in voter turnout. No other industrial nation has recorded a lower average turnout (Figure 17-2 on page 384).

Despite poor voter turnout, participation in politics may be increasing, especially on the Internet. In terms of both antigovernment activities and financial contributions to political parties (both of which we will return to later in this chapter), online participation rivals the political rallies and doorbell-ringing efforts of yesteryear. Fifty-five percent of the entire adult population of the United States went online in 2008 to get news and information about the presidential election. One in every five of those online participants went so far as to post their thoughts for others to read (A. Smith 2009).

In the end, political participation makes government accountable to the voters. If participation declines, government operates with less of a sense of accountability to society. This issue is most serious for the least powerful individuals and groups in the United States. Voter turnout has been particularly low among members of racial and ethnic minorities. In postelection surveys, fewer African Americans and Hispanics than Whites report that

---

use your sociological *imagination*

Were you brought up to consider political involvement an important civic duty? If so, do you take that duty seriously by informing yourself about the issues and voting?

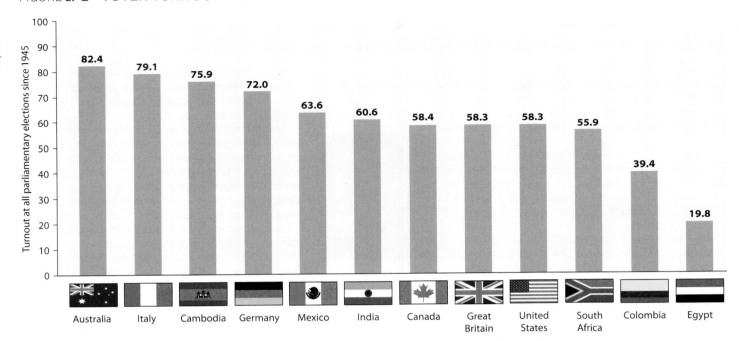

Note: Based on turnout in recent elections for seats in national congress or parliament. Data are for 2008 except for Australia (2007), Cambodia and Mexico (2006), Egypt, Germany, and Great Britain (2005), and India and South Africa (2004).
Source: International Institute for Democracy and Electoral Assistance 2009a.

they actually voted. Many more potential voters fail to register to vote. The poor—whose focus understandably is on survival—are traditionally underrepresented among voters as well. The low turnout found among these groups is explained at least in part by their common feeling of powerlessness. Yet these low statistics encourage political power brokers to continue to ignore the interests of the less affluent and the nation's minorities. The segment of the voting population that has shown the most voter apathy is the young, as discussed in Box 17-2 (Holder 2006; International Institute for Democracy and Electoral Assistance 2009b).

Race and Gender in Politics

Because politics is synonymous with power and authority, we should not be surprised that political strength is lacking in marginalized groups, such as women and racial and ethnic minorities. Nationally, women did not get the vote until 1920. Most Chinese Americans were turned away from the polls until 1926. And African Americans were disenfranchised until 1965, when national voting rights legislation was passed. Predictably, it has taken these groups some time to develop their political power and begin to exercise it effectively.

Progress toward the inclusion of minority groups in government has been slow. As of mid-2009, 17 out of 100 U.S. senators were women. One senator was an African American, 2 were Latinos, and 2 were Asian Americans, leaving 78 White non-Hispanic men. Among the 435 members of the U.S. House of Representatives, 314 were White non-Hispanic men. Seventy were women, 38 were African Americans (including 10

women), 23 were Latinos (including 6 Latinas), 6 were Asian Americans (including 1 woman), and 1 was an Asian Indian. These numbers, although low, represent a high-water mark for most of these groups.

Today, with record-high numbers of Blacks and Latinos holding elective office, many critics still decry what has been termed "fiesta politics." White power brokers tend to visit racial and

Minnesota Democrat Keith Ellison created quite a stir in 2007 when he became the first person to take the Congressional oath of office on a Qur'an instead of a Bible. The newly elected member of the House of Representatives, who is Muslim, thought the Qur'an would make his oath more meaningful than a Bible. Speaker of the House Nancy Pelosi (left) responded by borrowing Thomas Jefferson's two-volume Qur'an for the occasion—a reminder that acknowledging diversity is nothing new in U.S. politics.

RESEARCH TODAY

All through the 1960s, young people in the United States participated actively in a range of political issues, from pushing civil rights to protesting the Vietnam War. They were especially disturbed by the fact that young men were barred from voting but were being drafted to serve in the military and were dying for their country. In response to these concerns, the Twenty-Sixth Amendment to the Constitution was ratified in 1971, lowering the voting age from 21 to 18.

Now, more than 35 years later, we can consider the available research and see what happened. Frankly, what is remarkable is what did *not* happen. First, young voters (those between ages 18 and 21) have not united in any particular political sentiment. We can see in the way the young vote the same divisions of race, ethnicity, and gender that are apparent among older age groups.

Second, while the momentum for lowering the voting age came from college campuses, the majority of young voters are not students at all. Many are already part of the workforce and either live with their parents or have established their own households.

Third, and particularly troubling, is their relatively low turnout. The 2008 presidential election, held against a background of war in Iraq, the historic candidacy of Barack Obama, and a global economic decline, did pique the interest of young voters. In that election, 51.4 percent of voters under age 30 turned out, compared to 49 percent in 2004.

What lies behind this voter apathy among the young? The popular explanation is that people—especially young people—are alienated from the political system, turned off by the shallowness and negativity of candidates and campaigns. True, studies have documented that young voters are susceptible to cynicism and distrust, but those qualities are not necessarily associated with voter apathy. Numerous studies show that the relationship between how people perceive the candidates and issues and their likelihood of voting is a very complex one. Young people do vote as they age.

While the momentum for lowering the voting age came from college campuses, the majority of young voters are not students at all.

Other explanations for the lower turnout among the young seem more plausible. First, the United States is virtually alone in requiring citizens to vote twice, in effect. They must first *register* to vote, often at a time when issues are not on the front burner and candidates haven't even declared. Second, though citizens in the United States tend to be more active in politics at the community level than those in other countries, young people often feel unmoved by local issues such as public school financing.

One way in which youths *are* impacting elections is through their reliance on the Internet for information. Today, every political campaign maintains a presence on the Web, not only through an official Web site but on social networking sites like Facebook and MySpace. During the 2008 presidential election, two-thirds of young adults with online profiles took part in some form of political activity on those sites. Online activity continued through Election Day, when over one out of every four adults turned to the Internet to learn where to vote. Time will tell whether the Internet will ultimately reduce political apathy among younger citizens.

LET'S DISCUSS

1. How often do you vote? If you do not vote, what accounts for your apathy? Are you too busy to register? Are community issues uninteresting to you?

2. Do you think voter apathy is a serious social problem? What might be done to increase voter participation in your age group and community?

Sources: Alwin 2002; Clymer 2000; Higher Education Research Institute 2004; McDonald 2009b; Patterson 2005; A. Smith 2009; Vargas 2007; Wattenberg 2008.

REASONS FOR NOT VOTING, 18- TO 24-YEAR-OLDS

Too busy, conflicting schedule
Don't know or refused
Out of town
Other reason
Not interested
Registration problems
Forgot to vote
Illness or disability
Did not like candidates or campaign issues
Inconvenient polling place
Transportation problems
Bad weather conditions

0   5   10   15   20   25
Percent

Source: Holder 2006:13.

ethnic minority communities only when they need electoral support, making a quick appearance on a national or ethnic holiday to get their pictures taken and then vanishing. When the election is over, they too often forget to consult the residents who supported them about community needs and concerns.

Female politicians may be enjoying more electoral success now than in the past, but there is some evidence that the media cover them differently from male politicians. A content analysis of newspaper coverage of recent gubernatorial races showed that reporters wrote more often about a female candidate's personal life, appearance, or personality than a male candidate's, and less often about her political positions and voting record. Furthermore, when political issues were raised in newspaper articles, reporters were more likely to illustrate them with statements made by male candidates than by female candidates (Devitt 1999; Jost 2008).

Figure 17-3 shows the representation of women in selected national legislatures. While the proportion of women in national legislatures has increased in the United States and many other nations, in all but one country women still do not account for half the members of the national legislature. The African Republic of Rwanda, the exception, ranks the highest, with 56.3 percent of its legislative seats held by women. Overall, the United States ranked 84th among 188 nations in the proportion of women serving as national legislators in 2009.

To remedy this situation, many countries have adopted quotas for female representatives. In some, the government sets aside a certain percentage of seats for women, usually from 14 to 30 percent. In others, political parties have decided that 20 to 40 percent of their candidates should be women. Thirty-two countries now have some kind of female quota system (Rubin and Dagher 2009; Vasagar 2005).

Such quotas may be needed in part because of the disproportionate influence of men in fund-raising. Significantly, in the United States, elite male fund-raisers out-raise women fund-raisers anywhere from 3 to 1 to 10 to 1 (Schauten 2008).

use your sociological *imagination*

Imagine a world in which women, not men, held the majority of elective offices. What kind of world would it be?

Models of Power Structure in the United States

Who really holds power in the United States? Do "we the people" genuinely run the country through our elected representatives? Or is it true that behind the scenes, a small elite controls both the government and the economic system? It is difficult to determine the location of power in a society as complex as the United States. In exploring this critical question, social scientists have developed two basic views of our nation's power structure: the power elite and the pluralist models.

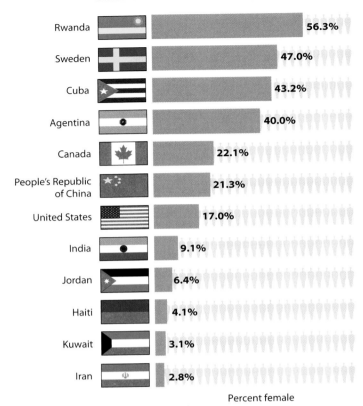

FIGURE 17-3 WOMEN IN NATIONAL LEGISLATURES, SELECTED COUNTRIES, 2008

Rwanda	56.3%
Sweden	47.0%
Cuba	43.2%
Agentina	40.0%
Canada	22.1%
People's Republic of China	21.3%
United States	17.0%
India	9.1%
Jordan	6.4%
Haiti	4.1%
Kuwait	3.1%
Iran	2.8%

Percent female

Notes: Data are for lower legislative houses only, as of February 28, 2009; data on upper houses, such as the U.S. Senate or the U.K. House of Lords, are not included. In 2005, the all-male Kuwaiti Parliament granted women the right to vote and serve in elected offices, which allowed women to run for office in 2007. *Source:* Inter-Parliamentary Union 2009.

Think about It
Why do you think being elected to Congress is so difficult for women?

Power Elite Models

Karl Marx believed that 19th-century representative democracy was essentially a sham. He argued that industrial societies were dominated by relatively small numbers of people who owned factories and controlled natural resources. In Marx's view, government officials and military leaders were essentially servants of this capitalist class and followed their wishes. Therefore, any key decisions made by politicians inevitably reflected the interests of the dominant bourgeoisie. Like others who hold an **elite model** of power relations, Marx believed that society is ruled by a small group of individuals who share a common set of political and economic interests.

Mills's Model Sociologist C. Wright Mills took this model a step further in his pioneering work *The Power Elite* ([1956] 2000b). Mills described a small group of military, industrial, and government leaders who controlled the fate of the United States—the **power elite.** Power rested in the hands of a few, both inside and outside government.

FIGURE **17-4** POWER ELITE MODELS

387

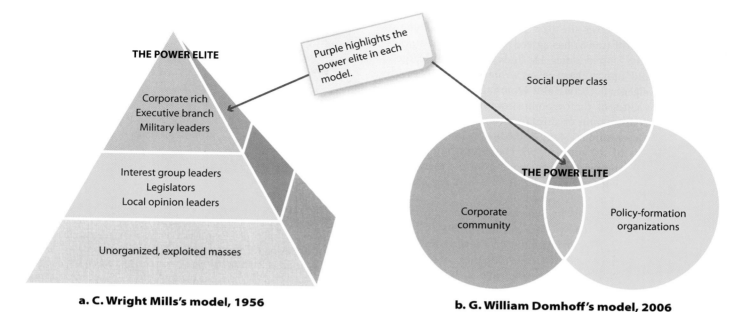

a. C. Wright Mills's model, 1956

b. G. William Domhoff's model, 2006

Source: Left, author based on Mills [1956] 2000b; right, Domhoff 2006:105.

A pyramid illustrates the power structure of the United States in Mills's model (Figure 17-4a). At the top are the corporate rich, leaders of the executive branch of government, and heads of the military (whom Mills called the "warlords"). Directly below are local opinion leaders, members of the legislative branch of government, and leaders of special-interest groups. Mills contended that these individuals and groups would basically follow the wishes of the dominant power elite. At the bottom of the pyramid are the unorganized, exploited masses.

The power elite model is, in many respects, similar to the work of Karl Marx. The most striking difference is that Mills believed that the economically powerful coordinate their maneuvers with the military and political establishments to serve their common interests. He rejected Marx's belief that by itself, the economic structure of capitalism could create a ruling class. Still, the powerless masses at the bottom of Mills's power elite model certainly bring to mind Marx's portrait of the oppressed workers of the world, who have "nothing to lose but their chains."

A fundamental element in Mills's thesis is that the power elite not only includes relatively few members but also operates as a self-conscious, cohesive unit. Although not necessarily diabolical or ruthless, the elite comprises similar types of people who interact regularly with one another and have essentially the same political and economic interests. Mills's power elite is not a conspiracy, but rather a community of interest and sentiment among a small number of influential people (A. Hacker 1964).

Admittedly, Mills failed to clarify when the elite opposes protests and when it toler-

ates them; he also failed to provide detailed case studies that would substantiate the interrelationships among members of the power elite. Nevertheless, his challenging theories forced scholars to look more critically at the democratic political system of the United States.

In commenting on the scandals that have rocked major corporations such as Enron and AIG over the past fifteen years, observers have noted that members of the business elite *are* closely interrelated. In a study of the members of the boards of directors of Fortune 1000 corporations, researchers found that each director can reach *every* other board of directors in just 3.7 steps. That is, by consulting acquaintances of acquaintances, each director can quickly reach someone who sits on each of the other 999 boards. Furthermore, the face-to-face contact directors regularly have in their board meetings makes them a highly cohesive elite. Finally, the corporate elite is not only wealthy, powerful, and cohesive; it is also overwhelmingly White and male (G. Davis 2003, 2004; Kentor and Jang 2004; Mizruchi 1996; R. Schaefer 2008b; Strauss 2002).

One outgrowth of Mills's power elite model is current research on the presence of a *global* power elite—that is, those business, political, and former military leaders who exercise influence across national borders. Because this avenue of scholarship is relatively new, there is some disagreement on the definition of the term. Must the members of the global power elite demonstrate as much consensus as the members of Mills's power elite? Or can the global power elite include such diverse voices as the publisher Rupert Murdoch, the illegal arms dealer Viktor Bout, and former President

Bill Clinton, in his role as head of the Clinton Global Initiative (L. Miller 2008; Rothkopf 2008)?

Domhoff's Model Over the past three decades, sociologist G. William Domhoff (2006) has agreed with Mills that a powerful elite runs the United States. He finds that it is still largely White, male, and upper class, as he wrote in his book with Richard L. Zweigenhaft (2006). But Domhoff stresses the role played both by elites of the corporate community and by the leaders of policy-formation organizations, such as chambers of commerce and labor unions. Many of the people in both groups are also members of the social upper class. And he notes the presence of a small number of women and minority men in key positions—groups that were excluded from Mills's top echelon and are still underrepresented today.

Though the three groups in Domhoff's power elite model overlap, as Figure 17-4b shows, they do not necessarily agree on specific policies. Domhoff notes that in the electoral arena, two different coalitions have exercised influence. A *corporate-conservative coalition* has played a large role in both political parties, generating support for particular candidates through direct-mail appeals. A *liberal-labor coalition* is based in unions, local environmental organizations, a segment of the minority group community, liberal churches, and the university and arts communities (Zweigenhaft and Domhoff 2006).

Pluralist Model

Several social scientists insist that power in the United States is shared more widely than the elite models indicate. In their view, a pluralist model more accurately describes the nation's political system. According to the **pluralist model,** many competing groups within the community have access to government, so that no single group is dominant.

The pluralist model suggests that a variety of groups play a significant role in decision making. Typically, pluralists make use of intensive case studies or community studies based on observation research. One of the most famous—an investigation of decision making in New Haven, Connecticut—was reported by Robert Dahl (1961). Dahl found that although the number of people involved in any important decision was rather small, community power was nonetheless diffuse. Few political actors exercised decision-making power on all issues. One individual or group might be influential in a battle over urban renewal, but have little impact on educational policy.

The pluralist model, however, has not escaped serious questioning. Domhoff (1978, 2006) reexamined Dahl's study of decision making in New Haven and argued that Dahl and other pluralists had failed to trace how local elites who were prominent in decision making belonged to a larger national ruling class. In addition, studies of community power, such as Dahl's work in New Haven, can examine decision making only on issues that become part of the political agenda. They fail to address the potential power of elites to keep certain matters entirely out of the realm of government debate.

Dianne Pinderhughes (1987) has criticized the pluralist model for failing to account for the exclusion of African Americans from the political process. Drawing on her studies of Chicago politics, Pinderhughes points out that the residential and occupational segregation of Blacks and their long political disenfranchisement

Pluralism can be seen in action in the activity of lobbying groups attempting to influence public policy. The highly publicized battle over stem cell research is one example; it has pitted conservative religious groups against health advocacy groups, dividing political leaders in the process. Though legislation to support the controversial research technique had the backing of several prominent Republican lawmakers, including Senator Orrin Hatch (R-Utah), shown here with actor and activist Michael J. Fox, it fell victim to a presidential veto in 2006.

violates the logic of pluralism—which would hold that such a substantial minority should always have been influential in community decision making. This critique applies to many cities across the United States, where other large racial and ethnic minorities, among them Asian Americans, Puerto Ricans, and Mexican Americans, are relatively powerless.

Historically, pluralists have stressed ways in which large numbers of people can participate in or influence governmental decision making. New communications technologies like the Internet are increasing the opportunity to be heard, not just in countries such as the United States but in developing countries the world over. One common point of the elite and pluralist perspectives stands out, however: in the political system of the United States, power is unequally distributed. All citizens may be equal in theory, yet those who are high in the nation's power structure are "more equal." New communications technology may or may not change that distribution of power (McFarland 2007).

Perhaps the ultimate test of power, no matter what a nation's power structure, is the decision to go to war. Because the rank and file of any army is generally drawn from the lower classes—the least powerful groups in society—such a decision has life-and-death consequences for people far removed from the center of power. In the long run, if the general population is not convinced that war is necessary, military action is unlikely to succeed. Thus, war is a risky way in which to address conflict between nations. In the following section we will contrast war and peace as ways of addressing societal conflict, and more recently, the threat of terrorism.

War and Peace

Conflict is a central aspect of social relations. Too often it becomes ongoing and violent, engulfing innocent bystanders as well as intentional participants. Sociologists Theodore Caplow and Louis Hicks (2002:3) have defined **war** as conflict between organizations that possess trained combat forces equipped with deadly weapons. This meaning is broader than the legal definition, which typically requires a formal declaration of hostilities.

FIGURE **17-5** U.S. PUBLIC OPINION ON THE NECESSITY OF WAR, 1971–2007 389

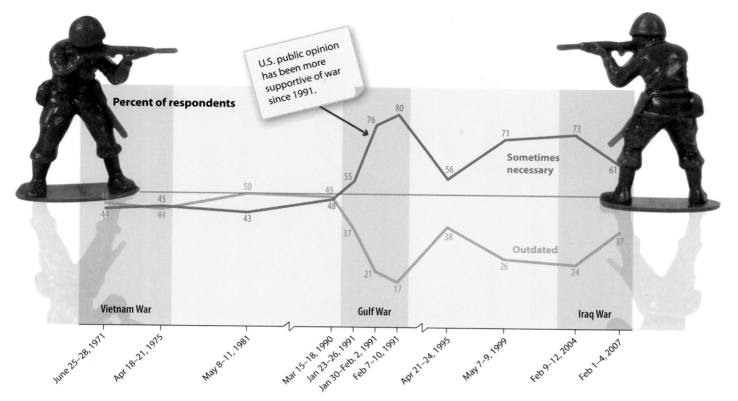

U.S. public opinion has been more supportive of war since 1991.

Note: Respondents replied to the following question: "Some people feel that war is an outmoded way of settling differences between nations. Others feel that wars are sometimes necessary to settle differences. With which point of view do you agree?"
Source: Gallup 2009d.

War

Sociologists approach war in three different ways. Those who take a global view study how and why two or more nations become engaged in military conflict. Those who take a nation-state view stress the interaction of internal political, socioeconomic, and cultural forces. And those who take a micro view focus on the social impact of war on individuals and the groups they belong to (Kiser 1992).

The internal decision-making process that leads to war has been much studied. During the Vietnam War, Presidents Johnson and Nixon both misled Congress, painting a falsely optimistic picture of the likely outcome. Based on their intentional distortions, Congress appropriated the military funds the two administrations requested. But in 1971 the *New York Times* published a set of classified documents now known as "The Pentagon Papers," which revealed the real prospects for the war. Two years later—over Nixon's veto—Congress passed the War Powers Act, which requires the president to notify Congress of the reasons for committing combat troops to a hostile situation (Patterson 2003).

Although the decision to go to war is made by government leaders, public opinion plays a significant role in its execution. By 1971, the number of U.S. soldiers killed in Vietnam had surpassed 50,000, and antiwar sentiment was strong. Surveys done at that time showed the public was split roughly equally on the question of whether war was an appropriate way to settle differences between nations (Figure 17-5). This division in public opinion continued until the United States became involved in the Gulf War following

Iraq's invasion of Kuwait in 1990. Since then, U.S. sentiment has been more supportive of war as a means of resolving disputes.

A major change in the composition of the U.S. military is the growing presence of women. Over 197,000 women, or about 14 percent of active U.S. military forces, are now in uniform, serving not just as support personnel but as an integral part of combat units. The first casualty of the war in Iraq, in fact, was Private First Class Lori Piestewa, a member of the Hopi tribe and a descendant of Mexican settlers in the Southwest (Bureau of the Census 2008a:328).

From a micro point of view, war can bring out the worst as well as the best in people. In 2004, graphic images of the abuse of Iraqi prisoners by U.S. soldiers at Iraq's Abu Ghraib prison shocked the world. For social scientists, the deterioration of the guards' behavior brought to mind Philip Zimbardo's mock prison experiment, done in 1971. Although the results of the experiment, highlighted in Chapter 5, have been applied primarily to civilian correctional facilities, Zimbardo's study was actually funded by the Office of Naval Research. In July 2004, the U.S. military began using a documentary film about the experiment to train military interrogators to avoid mistreatment of prisoners (Zarembo 2004; Zimbardo 2004).

Peace

Sociologists have considered **peace** both as the absence of war and as a proactive effort to develop cooperative relations among nations. While we will focus here on international relations, we should note that in the 1990s, 90 percent of the world's

MAPPING LIFE WORLDWIDE

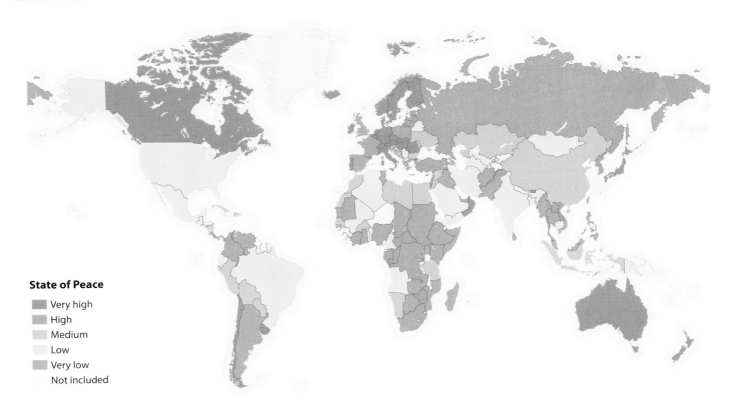

State of Peace

- Very high
- High
- Medium
- Low
- Very low
- Not included

Source: Institute for Economics and Peace 2008.

armed conflicts occurred *within* rather than between states. Often, outside powers became involved in these internal conflicts, either as supporters of particular factions or in an attempt to broker a peace accord. In at least 28 countries where such conflicts occurred—none of which would be considered core nations in world systems analysis—at least 10,000 people died (Kriesberg 1992; Dan Smith 1999).

Another way of picturing the relative peacefulness of nations around the world is the Global Peace Index (Figure 17-6). This index is based on 24 indicators, including organized internal conflict, violent crime, political instability, the potential for terrorist acts, and a nation's level of military expenditures compared to its neighbors'. Currently, Iceland is at the top of the index (very peaceful); Iraq, Somalia, and Sudan are at the bottom. The United States ranks 97 on this list of 121 nations, between Jamaica and Ecuador.

Sociologists and other social scientists who draw on sociological theory and research have tried to identify conditions that deter war. One of their findings is that international trade may act as a deterrent to

A representative of the International Red Crescent Society delivers an aid parcel in the southern Iraqi town of Safwan. The Red Crescent provides emergency aid to victims of war and disaster in Muslim communities. Such nongovernmental organizations (NGOs) help to bind countries together, promoting peaceful relations.

armed conflict. As countries exchange goods, people, and then cultures, they become more integrated and less likely to threaten

FIGURE **17-7** THE GLOBAL REACH OF TERRORISM

391

Government and Politics

MAPPING LIFE WORLDWIDE

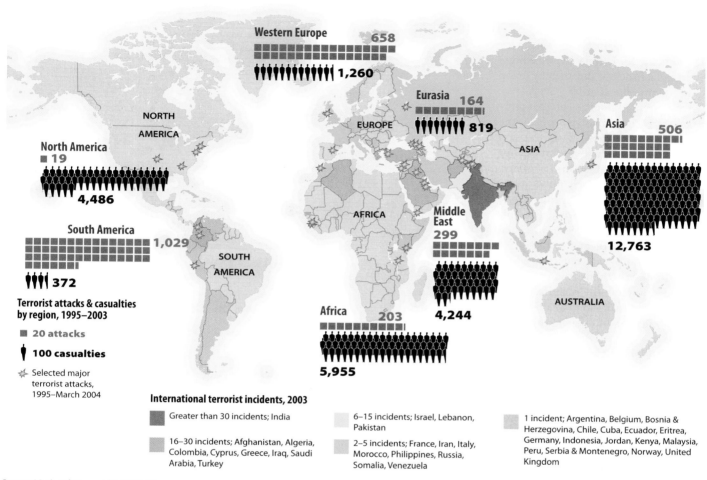

Western Europe 658
1,260

Eurasia 164
819

Asia 506
12,763

NORTH AMERICA

North America 19
4,486

South America 1,029
372

SOUTH AMERICA

Terrorist attacks & casualties by region, 1995–2003

■ **20 attacks**

♦ **100 casualties**

✦ Selected major terrorist attacks, 1995–March 2004

Middle East 299
4,244

Africa 203
5,955

AUSTRALIA

International terrorist incidents, 2003

■ Greater than 30 incidents; India

■ 16–30 incidents; Afghanistan, Algeria, Colombia, Cyprus, Greece, Iraq, Saudi Arabia, Turkey

□ 6–15 incidents; Israel, Lebanon, Pakistan

□ 2–5 incidents; France, Iran, Italy, Morocco, Philippines, Russia, Somalia, Venezuela

□ 1 incident; Argentina, Belgium, Bosnia & Herzegovina, Chile, Cuba, Ecuador, Eritrea, Germany, Indonesia, Jordan, Kenya, Malaysia, Peru, Serbia & Montenegro, Norway, United Kingdom

Source: National Geographic 2005:17.

each other's security. Viewed from this perspective, not just trade but immigration and foreign exchange programs have a beneficial effect on international relations.

Another means of fostering peace is the activity of international charities and activist groups called nongovernmental organizations (NGOs). The Red Cross and Red Crescent, Doctors Without Borders, and Amnesty International donate their services wherever they are needed, without regard to nationality. In the past decade or more, these global organizations have been expanding in number, size, and scope. By sharing news of local conditions and clarifying local issues, they often prevent conflicts from escalating into violence and war. Some NGOs have initiated cease-fires, reached settlements, and even ended warfare between former adversaries.

Finally, many analysts stress that nations cannot maintain their security by threatening violence. Peace, they contend, can best be maintained by developing strong mutual security agreements between potential adversaries (Etzioni 1965; Shostak 2002).

In recent years, the United States has begun to recognize that its security can be threatened not just by nation-states, but by

political groups that operate outside the bounds of legitimate authority. Indeed, terrorism is now considered the foremost threat to U.S. security—one the U.S. military is unaccustomed to fighting.

use your sociological *imagination*

Do you hear much discussion of how to promote worldwide peace, or do the conversations you hear focus more on ending a particular conflict?

www.mhhe.com/schaefer12e

Terrorism

Acts of terror, whether perpetrated by a few or by many people, can be a powerful political force. Formally defined, **terrorism** is the use or threat of violence against random or symbolic targets in pursuit of political aims. For terrorists, the end justifies the means. They believe the status quo is oppressive, and desperate measures are essential to end the suffering of the deprived. Convinced that working through the formal political process will not effect the desired political change, terrorists insist that illegal actions—often directed against innocent people—are needed. Ultimately, they hope to intimidate society and thereby bring about a new political order.

An essential aspect of contemporary terrorism involves use of the media. Terrorists may wish to keep secret their individual identities, but they want their political messages and goals to receive as much publicity as possible. Drawing on Erving Goffman's dramaturgical approach, sociologist Alfred McClung Lee has likened terrorism to the theater, where certain scenes are played out in predictable fashion. Whether through calls to the media, anonymous manifestos, or other means, terrorists typically admit responsibility for and defend their violent acts.

Figure 17-7 on page 391 shows the global reach of terrorism. Since September 11, 2001, governments worldwide have renewed their efforts to fight terrorism. Although the public generally regards increased surveillance and social control as a necessary evil, these measures have nonetheless raised governance issues. For example, some citizens in the United States and elsewhere have questioned whether measures such as the USA Patriot Act of 2001 threaten civil liberties. Citizens also complain about the heightened anxiety created by the vague alerts issued by the federal government from time to time. Worldwide, immigration and the processing of refugees have slowed to a crawl, separating families and preventing employers from filling job openings. As these efforts to combat political violence illustrate, the term *terrorism* is an apt one (R. Howard and Sawyer 2003; Lee 1983; R. Miller 1988).

Like many other aspects of society, terrorism can be viewed from a feminist perspective. That is, terrorism and terrorist movements can be seen symbolically as enactments of masculinity. Thus, organizers and leaders of terrorism are even more likely to be male than members of conventional political organizations. Terrorist acts by women, such as female suicide bombers, are so rare that they attract significant media and societal attention (Ferber and Kimmel 2008).

Political Activism on the Internet

By any measure, the Internet has emerged as a force to be reckoned with in politics. While television and newspapers remain the primary sources of political news, use of the Internet for news gathering more than doubled between the 2002 and 2006 elections. Increasingly, surfing the net is the way people "watch"

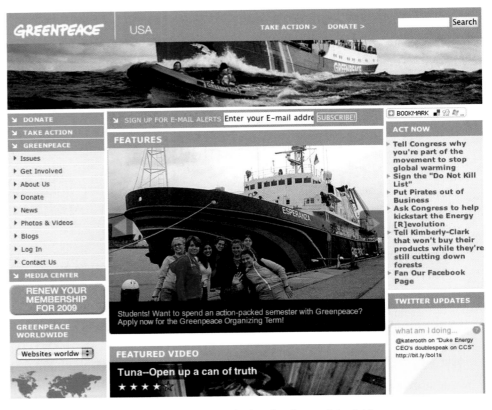

The Web site for Greenpeace, an international organization of environmental activists, encourages interested citizens to get involved in public affairs.

television news shows and "read" the daily paper. The majority of Internet users now look for information about candidates' positions online. During the 2006 election, 41 percent of them went online to check the accuracy of candidates' claims. Many people also visit video-sharing sites like YouTube, which provide up-to-the-minute clips of candidates' appearances that may or may not be flattering.

Not only is the Internet affecting the way people get their news; it is changing the way they think about politics. In one survey, 43 percent of Internet users said the information they received online affected their vote. Modern technology may not eliminate voter apathy, but it is one more way to motivate people to get involved in politics (Rainie and Horrigan 2007).

Is reliance on the Internet a healthy development? A national survey taken in 2007 shows that the general public is divided on this issue. Forty-five percent of respondents said that the "citizen journalism" acquired through Internet Web sites and cell phone cameras is more reliable than traditional journalism. Only 48 percent saw those outlets as less reliable than traditional news organizations (Gallup 2007c).

On the Internet, political activity is not limited to traditional party politics, and certainly not to domestic politics. In far-flung places including China, Mexico, Indonesia, Kosovo, and Malaysia, citizens are making themselves heard through *cyberactivism* or Net Activism—the use of the Internet for political purposes. In China, 10,000 members of the fast-growing Falun Gong religious sect surprised government officials with a mass rally organized on the Web and through YouTube videos. In Kosovo, the staff of Koha Ditore, a dissident newspaper, took to the Web after Serbian soldiers closed their office. And in Mexico, the revolutionary Zapatista movement gained support from an online campaign for self-rule in the state of Chiapas.

As these incidents illustrate, organizers find the Web especially useful in circumventing the restrictive controls of authoritarian regimes. In fact, groups branded as terrorists in a variety of states have used the Web to their advantage. Web sites can be established outside a country's borders, beyond the control of government officials yet still accessible to the country's citizens.

The use of online technology by political activists has not been lost on traditional sources of authority, be they charismatic, legal-rational, or traditional. From Queen Elizabeth II to Prime Minister Manmohan Singh of India, legitimate authority figures have mounted a major effort to create an online presence, sometimes called *e-government*. The competition is on, both online and offline (Lucas 2008).

Also growing in importance are borderless organizations that unite people of like mind—from peace activists to terrorists—around the world. These are very tightly knit communities, notes Professor Juan Enriquez of Harvard University.

Labor groups and environmental organizations such as Greenpeace have become particularly adept at using e-mail to mobilize activists quickly, wherever they are needed. The result: a completely new kind of power structure, compared to the more familiar face-to-face approach of Washington lobbyists. "The new people with power are those with credibility and an e-mail list," says political consultant Jennifer Laszlo. "You have no idea who they are, where they are, what color they are" (Engardio 1999:145).

use your sociological *imagination*

Imagine a future in which everyone in the United States has access to the Internet, and the Internet is the foremost political medium. How would government in that society differ from government today?

social**policy** and Politics

Campaign Financing

The Issue

How much does it cost to become president of the United States? All told, Barack Obama's campaign spent $739 million; John McCain's, $333 million. If we include all presidential and congressional candidates in 2008, win or lose, the price tag was over $5 billion.

Is the enormous cost of modern political campaigns a big issue with voters? The answer is yes and no. Surveys show that 57 percent of voters favor limits on campaign spending. Yet 38 percent feel that a candidate—maybe their candidate?—should be allowed to spend whatever he or she wants (Center for Responsive Politics 2008, 2009; Gallup 2008c).

The Setting

Regulation of campaign contributions has a long history, beginning with efforts to bar the requirement that government employees contribute to their bosses' campaign funds. More recently, the focus on both the state and national levels has been on remedying the shortcomings of the Federal Campaign Act of 1974, which placed restrictions on so-called *hard money*, or donations made to specific candidates for national office. Hard money is now limited to $10,000 per organization or $2,000 per individual donor per election cycle (the primary and election being separate cycles). These limits were intended to keep national candidates or elected officials from being "bought" by the wealthy or by powerful special-interest groups.

However, soon after passage of the act, contributors and potential recipients—that is, politicians—found loopholes in the new law. In 2002, Congress passed the Bipartisan Campaign Reform Act (BCRA) to address some of those shortcomings.

For the first time, limitations were placed on contributions of *soft money*—donations to the major political parties, leadership committees, and political action committees by corporations and special-interest groups. Now, no soft money is permitted in federal elections, and its use in state and local elections is limited.

Under the BCRA, major political parties are still allowed to spend soft money freely on *independent expenditures*, or purchases made on behalf of a political position rather than an individual candidate. This *issue advocacy money*, as it has been called, has become an important way of supporting a particular candidate while escaping contribution limits. To support a pro-environment, or "green," candidate, for example, donors would purchase television ads expressing concern about the environment and pollution.

Soon after the BCRA was passed, political pundits began to speculate on how politicians might still amass huge campaign war chests, regardless of the new restrictions. Some speculated that the law would encourage political parties and political interest groups to rely more on direct mail, phone banks, voter mobilization drives, and other unregulated activities. Few thought that the massive amounts that had once been raised as soft money would disappear from politics. New ways would be found to channel such huge amounts of money in conformity with the BCRA. And predictably, those new innovations in spending would be followed by fresh cries for reform (Campaign Legal Center 2004).

Perhaps the weakest link in campaign finance regulations is the fact that most of them do not apply to candidates who refuse public funding. In the 2004 presidential primary, both George W. Bush and John Kerry declined to accept federal campaign financing. More dramatic was Barack Obama's decision to forgo public funding in the 2008 general election, which allowed him great latitude in receiving private funds. Although Obama argued that his fund-raising was transparent, the sky was, in effect, the limit (Luo 2008).

Sociological Insights

Functionalists would say that political contributions keep the public involved in the democratic process and connected to the candidates. Issue advocacy money also offers voters a way to express their views on issues directly, rather than through the candidates. But conflict theorists would counter that since money brings influence, this use of material wealth allows donors to influence government policymakers in ways that tend to preserve their own wealth. In increasing numbers of cases, candidates like the multimillionaires Ross Perot and Steve Forbes have used their own private fortunes to finance their campaigns—an approach that allows them to sidestep public disclosure requirements.

Interactionists would point out the symbolic significance of the public perception that big money drives elections in the United States. Accurate or not, this impression encourages voter apathy, which is reflected in low turnout at the polls. What good does participating in politics do, voters may wonder, when special interests can spend millions to counteract their efforts?

Policy Initiatives

The rise of online campaign financing may represent a new challenge to efforts to reign in campaign spending. Such reforms attempt to limit how much or how often an individual can contribute to a candidate, party, or political action group. However, violations can be difficult to identify when donations are made by credit card. More and more, donations *are* being made by wire transfer or credit card. Among 2008 voters with online access, 15 percent of Obama backers made online contributions, compared to 6 percent of McCain backers (A. Smith 2009).

On the national level, traditional reform groups—Common Cause, the League of Women Voters, and Ralph Nader's organization Public Citizen—continue to call for tighter limits on contributions by both individuals and organizations. Other interest

"I PREFER NOT TO THINK OF MYSELF AS A FORMER CONGRESSMAN, BUT RATHER AS A FUTURE LOBBYIST."

The high cost of financing political campaigns tends to create a too-cozy relationship between elected officials and lobbyists for special-interest groups.

groups, including the American Civil Liberties Union and the Cato Institute, claim that limiting anyone's involvement in the political process is unfair. The BCRA addresses citizens' complaints that politicians are routinely "bought" by wealthy special interests. Yet it also raises the specter of limits on citizens' freedom to support the candidates of their choice. With voter apathy on the rise, such limits may be too high a price to pay for campaign finance reform.

Let's Discuss

1. Did you vote in the most recent election? Does your vote count, or do special-interest groups wield more power than voters like you?

2. Do you work for or contribute to political candidates? What about groups that promote special issues, like school prayer, gun control, and free trade? Which is more important to you, the candidate or the issue?

3. Would strict across-the-board spending limits on all candidates for public office help to make the political process more democratic? What about limits on political contributions of all kinds?

getting**involved**

To get involved in the debate over campaign financing, visit this book's Online Learning Center, which offers links to relevant Web sites.

www.mhhe.com/schaefer12e

MASTERING THIS CHAPTER

Summary

Every society must have a **political system** in order to allocate valued resources. This chapter examines the sources of **power** and **authority** in such systems; the four major types of government; political behavior, including voter apathy and women's representation in government; two basic models of power structure in the United States; **war** and **peace**; political activism on the Internet; and campaign finance reform.

1. There are three basic sources of **power** within any political system: **force, influence,** and **authority.**

2. Max Weber identified three ideal types of authority: **traditional, rational-legal,** and **charismatic.**

3. There are four basic types of government: **monarchy, oligarchy, dictatorship,** and **democracy.**

4. Political participation makes government accountable to citizens, but voters display a great deal of apathy, both in the United States and in other countries.

5. Women are still underrepresented in politics, but are becoming more successful at winning election to public office.

6. Advocates of the **elite model** of the U.S. power structure see the nation as being ruled by a small group of individuals who share common political and economic interests (a **power elite**). Advocates of a **pluralist model** believe that power is shared more widely among conflicting groups.

7. **War** may be defined as conflict between organizations that possess trained combat forces equipped with deadly weapons—a definition that includes conflict with terrorist organizations.

8. Around the world, the Internet has become a potent political arena, one that dissident groups can use to oppose the power of authoritarian regimes.

9. Despite legislative efforts to reform campaign financing methods, wealthy donors and special-interest groups still wield enormous power in U.S. government through their contributions to candidates, political parties, and issue advocacy.

Critical Thinking Questions

1. In many places in the world, the United States is considered a model political system. Drawing on material presented in earlier chapters of this textbook, discuss the values and beliefs on which this political system is founded. Have those values and beliefs changed over time? Has the system itself changed?

2. Who really holds power in the college or university you attend? Describe the distribution of power at your school, drawing on the elite and pluralist models where relevant.

3. Imagine that you have joined your state representative's legislative staff as a summer intern. She has assigned you to a committee that is working on solutions to the problem of school violence. How could you use what you have learned about sociology to conceptualize the problem? What type of research would you suggest the committee undertake? What legislative solutions might you recommend?

Key Terms

Authority Institutionalized power that is recognized by the people over whom it is exercised. (page 379)

Charismatic authority Power made legitimate by a leader's exceptional personal or emotional appeal to his or her followers. (380)

Democracy In a literal sense, government by the people. (382)

Dictatorship A government in which one person has nearly total power to make and enforce laws. (382)

Elite model A view of society as being ruled by a small group of individuals who share a common set of political and economic interests. (386)

Force The actual or threatened use of coercion to impose one's will on others. (379)

Influence The exercise of power through a process of persuasion. (379)

Monarchy A form of government headed by a single member of a royal family, usually a king, queen, or some other hereditary ruler. (381)

Oligarchy A form of government in which a few individuals rule. (382)

Peace The absence of war, or more broadly, a proactive effort to develop cooperative relations among nations. (389)

Pluralist model A view of society in which many competing groups within the community have access to government, so that no single group is dominant. (388)

Political system The social institution that is founded on a recognized set of procedures for implementing and achieving society's goals. (378)

Politics In Harold Lasswell's words, "who gets what, when, and how." (379)

Power The ability to exercise one's will over others. (379)

Power elite A small group of military, industrial, and government leaders who control the fate of the United States. (386)

Rational-legal authority Power made legitimate by law. (379)

Representative democracy A form of government in which certain individuals are selected to speak for the people. (382)

Terrorism The use or threat of violence against random or symbolic targets in pursuit of political aims. (391)

Totalitarianism Virtually complete government control and surveillance over all aspects of a society's social and political life. (382)

Traditional authority Legitimate power conferred by custom and accepted practice. (379)

War Conflict between organizations that possess trained combat forces equipped with deadly weapons. (388)

Self-Quiz

Read each question carefully and then select the best answer.

1. Which one of the following is a cultural universal?
   a. religion
   b. the political system
   c. family
   d. all of the above

2. A king or queen is accepted as ruler of a nation simply by virtue of inheriting the crown. This is an example of
   a. totalitarianism.
   b. charismatic authority.
   c. traditional authority.
   d. rational-legal authority.

3. Totalitarian states typically control which of the following institutions?
   a. family
   b. economy
   c. politics
   d. all of the above

4. G. William Domhoff's model is an example of
   a. an elite theory of power.
   b. a pluralist theory of power.
   c. a functionalist theory of power.
   d. an interactionist theory of power.

5. In terms of voter turnout, the United States typically ranks
   a. highest among all countries.
   b. highest among industrial nations.
   c. lowest among industrial nations.
   d. lowest among all countries.

6. Political scientist Harold Lasswell defined *politics* as
   a. the struggle for power and authority.
   b. the allocation of valued resources.
   c. who gets what, when, and how.
   d. a cultural universal.

7. What are the three basic sources of power within any political system?
   a. force, influence, and authority
   b. force, influence, and democracy
   c. force, legitimacy, and charisma
   d. influence, charisma, and bureaucracy

8. Which of the following is *not* part of the classification system of authority developed by Max Weber?
   a. traditional authority
   b. pluralist authority
   c. legal-rational authority
   d. charismatic authority

9. According to C. Wright Mills, power rests in the hands of the
   a. people.
   b. representative democracy.
   c. aristocracy.
   d. power elite.

10. The use or threat of violence against random or symbolic targets in pursuit of political aims is referred to as
    a. politics.
    b. power.
    c. authority.
    d. terrorism.

11. _____ is the actual or threatened use of coercion to impose one's will on others.

12. In most of today's_____, kings and queens have little practical power.

13. The elite model of political power implies that the U.S. has a(n) _____ as its form of government.

14. As of mid-2009, only _____ out of 100 United States senators were women.

15. Sexism has been the most serious barrier to women interested in holding public office. To remedy this situation, many countries have adopted _____ for female representatives.

16. _____ is the exercise of power through a process of persuasion.

17. Joan of Arc, Gandhi, Malcolm X, Adolf Hitler, and Martin Luther King Jr., all possessed _____ authority.

18. _____ involves virtually complete government control and surveillance over all aspects of a society's social and political life.

19. The United States is commonly classified as a(n)_____ _____, because the elected members of Congress and state legislatures make our laws.

20. Advocates of the _____ model suggest that competing groups within the community have access to government, so that no single group is dominant.

Answers
1 (d); 2 (c); 3 (d); 4 (a); 5 (c); 6 (c); 7 (a); 8 (b); 9 (d); 10 (d); 11 Force; 12 monarchies; 13 oligarchy; 14 17; 15 quotas; 16 influence; 17 charismatic; 18 Totalitarianism; 19 representative democracy; 20 pluralist

THINKING ABOUT MOVIES

The Last King of Scotland
(Kevin MacDonald, 2006)

Scottish expatriate Nicholas Garrigan (James McAvoy) serves as an aid worker in Uganda. By chance he becomes the personal physician of dictator Idi Amin (Forest Whitaker), known for his legendary brutality. At first, Garrigan is impressed by Amin's charisma and his populist rhetoric about his planned social programs. As he becomes more familiar with Amin, however, he begins to grasp the lengths to which Amin will go to preserve his power.

This movie shows charismatic authority in action. Amin's power is made legitimate by his ability to appeal to his followers' emotions. Moreover, the movie shows the tactics a dictator employs to maintain social control, including coercion and murder.

For Your Consideration

1. How would you define Idi Amin's authority, and how is it related to his style of governing?

2. What does the movie say about the use and abuse of power by prominent politicians?

The Visitor
(Thomas McCarthy, 2008)

When Professor Walter Vale (Richard Jenkins) returns to his Manhattan apartment after a long absence, he is shocked to find two strangers living there. Realizing that the couple, Zainab and Tarek Khalil (Danai Gurira and Haaz Sleiman), have nowhere else to go, he takes pity on them and allows them to stay until they can find another apartment. Walter and Tarek form a friendship based on their mutual love of music, and the three residents begin to feel comfortable with one another.

All goes well until Tarek is stopped by police over a misunderstanding at a subway turnstile. Because he is an illegal alien facing deportation, he is taken into custody. When Walter joins Tarek's family in an attempt to get Tarek released, he confronts the harsh realities of the U.S. justice system.

The Visitor illustrates how governments use their rational-legal authority to exert power over individuals. Watch for the scene in which Walter and Tarek's mother confront the employees at a holding facility for illegal immigrants, and witness the concepts of power, force, and authority in action.

For Your Consideration

1. In what ways does government exercise power in *The Visitor*? What are Tarek's options for resistance?

2. What different forms of governmental authority are shown in the film?

397

inside

Economic Systems

Case Study: Capitalism in China

Work and Alienation

Changing Economies

Social Policy and the Economy: Global Offshoring

BOXES

Sociology in the Global Community: *Working Women in Nepal*

Taking Sociology to Work: *Amy Wang, Product Manager, Norman International Company*

Research Today: *Affirmative Action*

Fresh produce tempts shoppers at an outdoor market in Strasbourg, France. In any society, the exchange of goods and services depends on the interaction of people.

Where Am I Wearing? A Global Tour to the Countries, Factories, and People that Make Our Clothes

❝I was made in America. My *Jingle These* Christmas boxers were made in Bangladesh.

I had an all-American childhood in rural Ohio. My all-American blue jeans were made in Cambodia.

I wore flip-flops every day for a year when I worked as a SCUBA diving instructor in Key West. They were made in China.

One day while staring at a pile of clothes on the floor, I noticed the tag of my favorite T-shirt: "Made in Honduras."

I read the tag. My mind wandered. A quest was born.

Where am I wearing? It seems like a simple question with a simple answer. It's not.

The question inspired the quest that took me around the globe. It cost me a lot of things, not the least of which was my consumer innocence. Before the quest, I could put on a piece of clothing without reading its tag and thinking about Arifa in Bangladesh or Dewan in China, about their children, their hopes and dreams, and the challenges they face.

Where am I wearing? This isn't so much a question related to geography and clothes, but about the people who make our clothes and the texture of their lives. This quest is about the way *we* live and the way *they* live; because when it comes to clothing, others make it, and we have it made. And there's a big, big difference. . . .

Workers flood the narrow alley beside the Delta Apparel Factory in San Pedro Sula, Honduras. They rush to catch one of the many waiting buses at the highway. Merchants hoping to part them from a portion of their daily earnings—$4 to $5—fight for their attention. Vehicles push through the crowd. A minivan knocks over a girl in her midtwenties and then runs over her foot. She curses, is helped to her feet, and limps onto a waiting bus.

The buildings behind the fence are shaded in Bahamian pastels and very well kept. The shrubs have been recently shaped, and the grass trimmed. In the bright Honduran sun, they seem as pleasant as a factory can get.

The lady at Delta Apparel, based in Georgia, giggled at me on the phone when I told her my plans. She was happy to tell me that their Honduran factory was located in the city of Villanueva just south of San Pedro Sula. She even wished me good luck.

Now that I'm in Honduras, the company doesn't think it's very funny.

I stand among the chaos overwhelmed. A thousand sets of eyes stare at me; perhaps they recognize my T-shirt. The irony that this is Tattoo's tropical paradise wore off long ago—somewhere between the confrontation with the big-bellied guards at the factory gate who had guns shoved down their pants like little boys playing cowboy and the conversation with the tight-lipped company representative who failed to reveal much of anything about my T-shirt or the people who assembled it. There was no way I was getting onto the factory floor. All I learned was that eight humans of indiscriminate age and sex stitched my shirt together in less than five minutes—not exactly information that required traveling all the way to Honduras to obtain. ❞

Where am I wearing? This isn't so much a question related to geography and clothes, but about the people who make our clothes and the texture of their lives.

(Timmerman 2009:xiii–xiv, 14) Additional information about this excerpt can be found on the Online Learning Center at www.mhhe.com/schaefer12e.

In his book *Where Am I Wearing? A Global Tour to the Countries, Factories, and People that Make Our Clothes,* journalist Kelsey Timmerman recounts his travels to the countries where his jeans, T-shirts, and flip-flops were made. From Honduras to Bangladesh, from Cambodia to the United States, he tracked down the factories and befriended the seamstresses who labored there. Though owners were reluctant to allow him on the factory floor, they couldn't prevent him from visiting workers' homes and families. Timmerman found that both inside and outside the factory, garment workers lived in what would be considered substandard conditions in the United States. He argues that global apparel companies should take responsibility for conditions at their suppliers' factories, even if those factories are located halfway around the world (Fairtrade Foundation 2009).

While acknowledging Timmerman's point of view, sociologists also try to see foreign workers and factory owners from the perspective of their own cultures—an approach called **cultural relativism** (see Chapter 3). That is, besides comparing factory work in developing countries to similar work in industrial nations, sociologists would compare it to the other jobs available to foreign workers. Sweatshops certainly aren't the sort of places where people in industrial countries would want to work, but from the foreign worker's perspective, they may be preferable to a farm in an isolated rural area or a lower-paying job with a local employer. In sum, foreign workers and producers face a different *economic system* from the one in industrial nations, so their attitudes and the choices they make may differ from our own.

The term **economic system** refers to the social institution through which goods and services are produced, distributed, and consumed. As with social institutions such as the family, religion, and government, the economic system shapes other aspects of the social order and is in turn influenced by them. Throughout this textbook, you have been reminded of the economy's impact on social behavior—for example, on individual and group behavior in factories and offices. You have studied the work of Karl Marx and Friedrich Engels, who emphasized that a society's economic system can promote social inequality. And you have learned that foreign investment in developing countries can intensify inequality among residents.

This chapter will present a sociological analysis of the impact of the economy on people's lives. What makes work satisfying? How has the trend toward deindustrialization changed the work people do? What will the workforce of the 21st century look like? We will begin to answer these questions with a macro-level analysis of two ideal types of economic system—capitalism and socialism—and the real-world institution known as the informal economy. A case study on China, a socialist society that has been moving toward capitalism, follows. Next, we will examine various aspects of work, including worker alienation and worker satisfaction. We will also look at the ways in which the world's economies are changing. Finally, in the Social Policy section we will explore the new trend toward global offshoring, an important issue in today's workplace.

Economic Systems

The sociocultural evolution approach developed by Gerhard Lenski categorizes preindustrial society according to the way in which the economy is organized. The principal types of preindustrial society, as you recall, are hunting-and-gathering societies, horticultural societies, and agrarian societies.

As we noted in Chapter 5, the *Industrial Revolution*—which took place largely in England during the period 1760 to 1830—brought about changes in the social organization of the workplace. People left their homesteads and began working in central locations such as factories. As the Industrial Revolution proceeded, a new form of social structure emerged: the **industrial society,** a society that depends on mechanization to produce its goods and services.

Two basic types of economic system distinguish contemporary industrial societies: capitalism and socialism. As described in the following sections, capitalism and socialism serve as ideal types of economic system. No nation precisely fits either model. Instead, the economy of each individual state represents a mixture of capitalism and socialism, although one type or the other is generally more useful in describing a society's economic structure.

Capitalism

In preindustrial societies, land functioned as the source of virtually all wealth. The Industrial Revolution changed all that. It required that certain individuals and institutions be willing to take substantial risks in order to finance new inventions, machinery, and business enterprises. Eventually, bankers, industrialists, and other holders of large sums of money replaced landowners as the most powerful economic force. These people invested their funds in the hope of realizing even greater profits, and thereby became owners of property and business firms.

The transition to private ownership of business was accompanied by the emergence of the capitalist economic system. **Capitalism** is an economic system in which the means of production are held largely in private hands and the main incentive for economic activity is the accumulation of profits. In practice, capitalist systems vary in the degree to which the government regulates private ownership and economic activity (D. Rosenberg 1991).

Immediately following the Industrial Revolution, the prevailing form of capitalism was what is termed **laissez-faire** ("let them do"). Under the principle of laissez-faire, as expounded and endorsed by British economist Adam Smith (1723–1790), people could compete freely, with minimal government intervention in the economy. Business retained the right to regulate itself and operated essentially without fear of government interference (Smelser 1963).

Two centuries later, capitalism has taken on a somewhat different form. Private ownership and maximization of profits still remain the most significant characteristics of capitalist economic systems. However, in contrast to the era of laissez-faire, capitalism today features government regulation of economic relations. Without restrictions, business firms can mislead consumers, endanger workers' safety, and even defraud the companies' investors—all in the pursuit of greater profits. That is why the government of a capitalist nation often monitors prices, sets safety and environmental standards for industries, protects the rights of consumers, and regulates collective bargaining between labor unions and management. Yet under capitalism as an ideal type, government rarely takes over ownership of an entire industry.

Contemporary capitalism also differs from laissez-faire in another important respect: capitalism tolerates monopolistic practices. A **monopoly** exists when a single business firm controls the market. Domination of an industry allows the firm to effectively control a commodity by dictating pricing, quality standards, and availability. Buyers have little choice but to yield to the firm's decisions; there is no other place to purchase the product or service. Monopolistic practices violate the ideal of free competition cherished by Adam Smith and other supporters of laissez-faire capitalism.

Some capitalistic nations, such as the United States, outlaw monopolies through antitrust legislation. Such laws prevent any business from taking over so much of the competition in an industry that it controls the market. The U.S. federal government allows monopolies to

For more than a century, the board game of Monopoly has entertained millions of people around the world. In the game, players strive to dominate the fictitious economy, gleefully bankrupting other players. Ironically, Monopoly was developed to demonstrate the weaknesses of capitalist economies, such as excessive rents and the tendency for money to accumulate in the hands of a few.

The Federal Reserve's Board of Governors confers with the presidents of regional reserve banks. The 12-member board, which meets behind closed doors, exerts economic power by controlling key interest rates. Because of the Fed's involvement in economic regulation—a function much publicized during the economic downturn that began in 2008—the United States is not considered a laissez-faire economy.

exist only in certain exceptional cases, such as the utility and transportation industries. Even then, regulatory agencies scrutinize these officially approved monopolies to protect the public. The protracted legal battle between the Justice Department and Microsoft, owner of the dominant operating system for personal computers, illustrates the uneasy relationship between government and private monopolies in capitalistic countries.

Conflict theorists point out that although *pure* monopolies are not a basic element of the economy of the United States, competition is still much more restricted than one might expect in what is called a *free enterprise system.* In numerous industries, a few companies largely dominate the field and keep new enterprises from entering the marketplace.

During the severe economic downturn that began in 2008, the United States moved even further away from the laissez-faire ideal. To keep major financial institutions from going under, the federal government invested hundreds of millions of dollars in distressed banking, investment, and insurance companies. Then in 2009, the government bailed out the failing automobile industry, taking a 60 percent interest in General Motors. The Canadian government took another 12 percent.

As we have seen in earlier chapters, globalization and the rise of multinational corporations have spread the capitalistic pursuit of profits around the world. Especially in developing countries, governments are not always prepared to deal with the sudden influx of foreign capital and its effects on their economies. One particularly striking example of how unfettered capitalism can harm developing nations is found in the Democratic Republic of Congo (formerly Zaire). The Congo has significant deposits of the metal columbite-tantalite—coltan, for short—which is used in the production of electronic circuit boards. Until the market for cell phones, pagers, and laptop computers heated up recently, U.S. manufacturers got most of their coltan from Australia. But at the height of consumer demand, they turned to miners in the Congo to increase their supply.

Predictably, the escalating price of the metal—as much as $400 a kilogram at one point, or more than three times the average Congolese worker's yearly wages—attracted undesirable attention. Soon the neighboring countries of Rwanda, Uganda, and Burundi, at war with one another and desperate for resources to finance the conflict, were raiding the Congo's national parks, slashing and burning to expose the coltan underneath the forest floor. Indirectly, the sudden increase in the demand for coltan was financing war and the rape of the environment. U.S. manufacturers have since cut off their sources in the Congo in an effort to avoid abetting the destruction. But their action has only penalized legitimate miners in the impoverished country (Austin 2002; Friends of the Congo 2009).

Socialism

Socialist theory was refined in the writings of Karl Marx and Friedrich Engels. These European radicals were disturbed by the exploitation of the working class that emerged during the Industrial Revolution. In their view, capitalism forced large numbers of people to exchange their labor for low wages. The owners of an industry profit from the labor of workers primarily because they pay workers less than the value of the goods produced.

As an ideal type, a socialist economic system attempts to eliminate such economic exploitation. Under **socialism,** the means of production and distribution in a society are collectively rather than privately owned. The basic objective of the economic system is to meet people's needs rather than to maximize profits. Socialists reject the laissez-faire philosophy that free competition benefits the general public. Instead, they believe that the central government, acting as the representative of the people, should make basic economic decisions. Therefore, government ownership of all major industries—including steel production, automobile manufacturing, and agriculture—is a primary feature of socialism as an ideal type.

In practice, socialist economic systems vary in the extent to which they tolerate private ownership. For example, in Great

A worker mines for coltan with sweat and a stick. The sudden increase in demand for the metal by U.S. computer manufacturers caused incursions into the Congo by neighboring countries hungry for capital to finance a war. Too often, globalization can have unintended consequences for a nation's economy and social welfare.

Britain, a nation with some aspects of both a socialist and a capitalist economy, passenger airline service is concentrated in the government-owned corporation British Airways. Yet private airlines are allowed to compete with it.

Socialist societies differ from capitalist nations in their commitment to social service programs. For example, the U.S. government provides health care and health insurance to the elderly and poor through the Medicare and Medicaid programs. But socialist countries typically offer government-financed medical care to *all* citizens. In theory, the wealth of the people as a collectivity is used to provide health care, housing, education, and other key services to each individual and family.

Marx believed that socialist states would eventually "wither away" and evolve into *communist* societies. As an ideal type, **communism** refers to an economic system under which all property is communally owned and no social distinctions are made on the basis of people's ability to produce. In recent decades, the Soviet Union, the People's Republic of China, Vietnam, Cuba, and nations in Eastern Europe were popularly thought of as examples of communist economic systems. However, this usage represents an incorrect application of a term with sensitive political connotations. All nations known as communist in the 20th century actually fell far short of the ideal type (Walder and Nguyen 2008).

By the early 1990s, Communist parties were no longer ruling the nations of Eastern Europe. As of 2007, however, China, Cuba, Laos, and Vietnam remained socialist societies ruled by Communist parties. Even in those countries, however, capitalism had begun to make inroads. In China, fully 25 percent of the country's production originated in the private business sector. (See the case study Capitalism in China, pages 404–406, for a fuller discussion.)

As we have seen, capitalism and socialism serve as ideal types of economic system. In reality, the economy of each industrial society—including the United States, the European Union, and Japan—includes certain elements of both capitalism and socialism (Table 18-1). Whatever the differences—whether a society more closely fits the ideal type of capitalism or socialism—all industrial societies rely chiefly on mechanization in the production of goods and services.

The Informal Economy

In many countries, one aspect of the economy defies description as either capitalist or socialist. In the **informal economy,** transfers of money, goods, or services take place but are not reported to the government. Examples of the informal economy include trading services with someone—say, a haircut for a computer lesson; selling goods on the street; and engaging in illegal transactions, such as gambling or drug deals. Participants in this type of economy avoid taxes and government regulations.

In developing nations, the informal economy represents a significant and often unmeasured part of total economic activity. Yet because this sector of the economy depends to a large extent on the labor of women, work in the informal economy

is undervalued or even unrecognized the world over. Box 18-1 on page 404 explains how the informal economy operates in Nepal.

Functionalists contend that bureaucratic regulations sometimes contribute to the rise of an informal economy. In the developing world, governments often set up burdensome business regulations that overworked bureaucrats must administer. When requests for licenses and permits pile up, delaying business projects, legitimate entrepreneurs find they need to "go underground" to get anything done. Despite its apparent efficiency, this type of informal economy is dysfunctional for a country's overall political and economic well-being. Since informal firms typically operate in remote locations to avoid detection, they cannot easily expand when they become profitable. And given the limited protection for their property and contractual rights, participants in the informal economy are less likely than others to save and invest their income.

Whatever functions an informal economy may serve, it is in some respects dysfunctional for workers. Working conditions in these illegal businesses are often unsafe or dangerous, and the jobs rarely provide any benefits to those who become ill or cannot continue to work. Perhaps more significant, the longer a worker remains in the informal economy, the less likely that person is to make the transition to the regular economy. No matter how efficient or productive a worker, employers expect to see experience in the formal economy on a job application. Experience as a successful street vendor or self-employed cleaning person does not carry much weight with interviewers (Venkatesh 2006).

use your sociological *imagination*

Some of your relatives are working full-time in the informal economy—for example, babysitting, lawn cutting, house cleaning—and are earning all their income that way. What will be the consequences for them in terms of job security and health care? Will you try to persuade them to seek formal employment, regardless of how much money they are making?

TABLE **18-1** CHARACTERISTICS OF THE THREE MAJOR ECONOMIC SYSTEMS summing**up**

Economic System	Characteristics	Contemporary Examples
Capitalism	Private ownership of the means of production Accumulation of profits the main incentive	Canada Mexico United States
Socialism	Collective ownership of the means of production Meeting people's needs the basic objective	Germany Russia Sweden
Communism	Communal ownership of all property No social distinctions made on basis of people's ability to produce	Cuba North Korea Vietnam

Note: Countries listed in column 3 are typical of one of the three economic systems, but not perfectly so. In practice, the economies of most countries include a mix of elements from the three major systems.

SOCIOLOGY IN THE GLOBAL COMMUNITY

18-1   Working Women In Nepal

Nepal, a small and mountainous Asian country of about 27 million people, has a per capita gross domestic product (GDP) of just $1,040 per year. (The comparable figure in the United States is $45,850.) But gross domestic product seriously understates the true production level in Nepal, for several reasons. Among the most important is that many Nepalese women work in the informal economy, whose activities are not included in the GDP.

Because women's work is undervalued in this traditional society, it is also underreported and underestimated. Official figures state that women account for 27 percent of GDP and form 40 percent of the labor force. But Nepalese women are responsible for 60 percent of additional nonmarket production—that is, work done in the informal economy—and 93 percent of the housework (figure).

> *Because women's work is undervalued in this traditional society, it is also underreported and underestimated.*

Most female workers cultivate corn, rice, and wheat on the family farm, where they spend hours on labor-intensive tasks such as fetching water and feeding livestock. Because much of the food they raise is consumed at home, however, it is considered to be nonmarket production. At home, women concentrate on food processing and preparation, caregiving, and other household tasks, such as clothes making. Childbearing and rearing and elder care are particularly crucial activities. Yet none of these chores are considered part of GDP; instead, they are dismissed as "women's work," both by economists and by the women themselves.

The figures on housework and nonmarket production in Nepal come from an independent economic study. To compile them, researchers had to adapt the conventional accounting

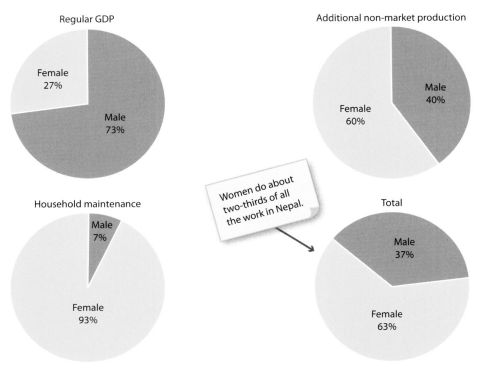

GENDER CONTRIBUTIONS TO GDP AND HOUSEHOLD MAINTENANCE IN NEPAL

Regular GDP
Female 27%
Male 73%

Additional non-market production
Male 40%
Female 60%

Household maintenance
Male 7%
Female 93%

Women do about two-thirds of all the work in Nepal.

Total
Male 37%
Female 63%

Source: Survey by M. Acharya as cited in Mahbub ul Haq Human Development Centre 2000:54.

system by adding a special account dedicated to household maintenance activities. When they did so, women's "invisible work" suddenly became visible and valuable. Not just in Nepal but in every country, economists need to expand their definitions of work and the labor force to account for the tremendous contributions women make to the world economy.

LET'S DISCUSS

1. In your own family, is "women's work" taken for granted? Have you ever tried to figure out what it would cost your family to pay for all the unpaid work women do?
2. Why is recognizing women's work important? How might life for both men and women change if the true economic value of women's work were recognized?

Sources: Acharya 2000; Haub 2008; Mahbub ul Haq Human Development Centre 2000:54–57.

---

casestudy Capitalism in China

Today's China is not the China of past generations; it is expected to become the world's largest economy by 2020. (Figure 18-1 shows the world's largest economies over the past 20 years.) In this country where the Communist Party once dominated people's lives, few now bother to follow party proceedings. Instead, after a decade of rapid economic growth, most Chinese are more interested in acquiring the latest consumer goods. Ironically, it

was party officials' decision to transform China's economy by opening it up to capitalism that reduced the once omnipotent institution's influence (*The Economist* 2006a).

The Road to Capitalism

When the communists assumed leadership of China in 1949, they cast themselves as the champions of workers and peasants and the enemies of those who exploited workers, namely landlords and capitalists. Profit making was outlawed, and those who engaged in it were arrested. By the 1960s, China's economy was dominated by huge state-controlled enterprises, such as factories. Even private farms were transformed into community-owned organizations. Peasants essentially worked for the government, receiving payment in goods based on their contribution to the collective good. In addition, they could receive a small plot of land on which to produce food for their families or for exchange with others. But while the centralization of production for the benefit of all seemed to make sense ideologically, it did not work well economically.

In the 1980s, the government eased restrictions on private enterprise somewhat, permitting small businesses with no more than seven employees. But business owners could not hold policymaking positions in the

On this seemingly endless assembly line in Dehui City, China, factory workers process chicken parts. China's huge economy will soon become the world's largest.

FIGURE 18-1 WORLD'S LARGEST ECONOMIES, 2007

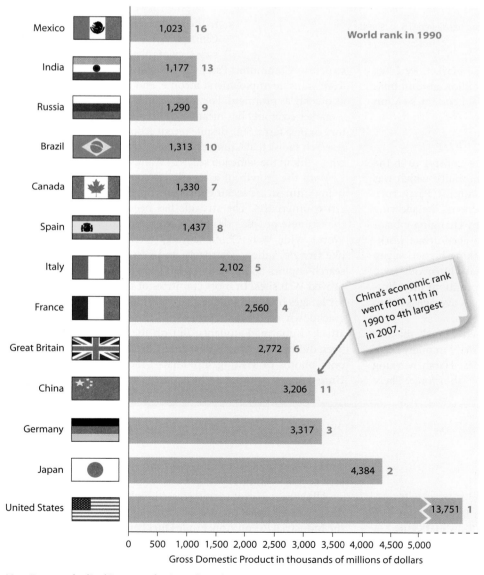

World rank in 1990

Country	GDP	Rank
Mexico	1,023	16
India	1,177	13
Russia	1,290	9
Brazil	1,313	10
Canada	1,330	7
Spain	1,437	8
Italy	2,102	5
France	2,560	4
Great Britain	2,772	6
China	3,206	11
Germany	3,317	3
Japan	4,384	2
United States	13,751	1

China's economic rank went from 11th in 1990 to 4th largest in 2007.

0   500   1,000 1,500 2,000 2,500 3,000 3,500 4,000 4,500 5,000

Gross Domestic Product in thousands of millions of dollars

Note: Data standardized in terms of estimated purchasing power parity to eliminate differences in buying power.
Sources: World Bank, 2007:194–196; 2009:208–210.

party, at any level. Late in the decade, party leaders began to make market-oriented reforms, revising the nation's legal structure to promote private business. For the first time, private entrepreneurs were allowed to compete with some state-controlled businesses. By the mid-1990s, impressed with the results of the experiment, party officials had begun to hand some ailing state-controlled businesses over to private entrepreneurs, in hopes they could be turned around (D. Bell 2008).

The Chinese Economy Today

Today, the entrepreneurs who weathered government harassment during the Communist Party's early years are among the nation's wealthiest capitalists. Some even hold positions on government advisory boards. The growing free-market economy they spawned has brought significant inequality to Chinese workers, however, especially between urban and rural workers. Though the move toward market-driven development has been slowing, questions are still being raised about the accumulation of wealth by a few (Sicular et al. 2006).

Chinese capitalists have had to compete with multinational corporations, which can operate more easily in China now, thanks to government economic reforms. General Motors (GM) first became interested in China in 1992, hoping to use the nation's low-cost labor to manufacture cars for overseas markets. But more and more, foreign-owned

405

For better or worse, the expansion of capitalism in China has linked U.S. businesses to that expanding economy.

enterprises like GM are selling to the Chinese market. By 2006, GM's Chinese operation was producing 6 million automobiles a year, at a profit much higher than in the United States (Kahn 2003; Krebs 2006).

Chinese Workers in the New Economy

For Chinese workers, the loosening of state control over the economy has meant a rise in occupational mobility, which was severely limited in the early days of Communist Party rule. The new markets created by private entrepreneurs are allowing ambitious workers to advance their careers by changing jobs or even cities. On the other hand, many middle-aged urban workers have lost their jobs to rural migrants seeking higher wages. Moreover, the privately owned factories that churn out lawn chairs and power tools for multinational corporations offer limited opportunities and very long hours. Wages average $120 to $200 a month for a six-day workweek.

Serious social problems have accompanied China's massive economic growth. Because safety is not a priority in many businesses, workers suffer from high injury rates. Harsh working conditions contribute to rapid turnover in the labor force. There is no pension system in China, so retirees must struggle to find other ways to support themselves. Pollution is common in urban areas, and environmental problems are extraordinary (Barboza 2008; French 2008).

For the average worker, party membership is less important now than in the past. Instead, managerial skill and experience are much in demand. Hong Kong sociologist Xiaowei Zang (2002) surveyed 900 workers in a key industrial city and found that party members still had an advantage in government and state-owned companies, where they earned higher salaries than other workers. But in private businesses, seniority and either managerial or entrepreneurial experience were what counted. As might be expected, being male and well educated also helped.

Women have been slower to advance in the workplace than men. Traditionally, Chinese women have been relegated to subservient roles in the patriarchal family structure. Communist Party rule has allowed them to make significant gains in employment, income, and education, although not as quickly as promised. For rural women in China, the growth of a market economy has meant a choice between working in a factory or on a farm. Still, despite recent economic changes, emerging research shows that Chinese women receive lower wages than men who work in the same job sectors (Wang and Cai 2006).

With the growth of a middle class and increased education, many Chinese are seeking the same opportunities as their Western counterparts. The struggle has been particularly visible in the Chinese people's desire for open, unrestricted access to the World Wide Web. China requires even U.S.-based companies like Google, Yahoo, Microsoft, and Cisco Systems to alter their search engines and blogging tools so as to block access to unapproved Web sites. In most countries of the world, a Web search for images of Tiananmen Square will call up photos of the 1989 crackdown on student protesters, in which soldiers in tanks attacked unarmed students. But on the other side of what has been dubbed the Great Firewall of China, the same search yields only photos of visiting diplomats—including those from the United States—posing in the square (Deibert et al. 2008).

Work and Alienation

"A moron could learn this job, it's so easy," says one Burger King worker in George Ritzer's study of the fast-food industry (2000:137). Doing repetitive tasks that take minimal skills can be demoralizing, leading to a sense of alienation and isolation in the workplace. Jeremy Rifkin, as we saw in the chapter-opening excerpt, took this concern a step further: as work becomes more and more automated, human skills become obsolete and workers lose their jobs altogether, or are forced into low-skills service jobs (Rifkin 1996).

All the pioneers of sociological thought were concerned about the negative impact on workers of the changes brought about by the Industrial Revolution. Émile Durkheim ([1893] 1933) argued that as labor becomes more and more differentiated, individuals experience *anomie*, or loss of direction. Workers can't feel as much fulfillment from performing one specialized task in a factory as they did when they were totally responsible for creating

TAKING SOCIOLOGY TO WORK

Amy Wang, **Product Manager, Norman International Company**

When Amy Wang entered the University of Texas at Austin in 1999, she didn't know what subject she wanted to major in, but she soon became fascinated by sociology. "Sociology was intriguing in the sense that it combined everything in life," she explains. "I am a people person and I enjoy knowing and learning about all aspects of how people live and interact in society." Wang particularly enjoyed the criminology course she took, as well as another on the sociology of gender, which she found to be eye-opening.

Wang's employer, Norman International Company, is a manufacturer of fine, hand-crafted interior window furnishings. In launching a new product, Wang works closely with a research and development team based in China. Part of her job is to research the domestic market and suggest which options are likely to be popular with U.S. consumers—a task in which she puts her training in doing sociological research to good use. After the R&D team has finalized a new product's specifications, Wang outsources the production of samples to vendors in China. When the product is finally ready for sale, she coordinates the company's U.S.-based operations, including information systems, advertising, and shipping, to ensure a smooth introduction.

Wang, who was born in Taiwan, grew up in a suburb of Dallas, where she became assimilated to mainstream U.S. culture. When she began work with Norman International, the company sent her to southern China for a month and a half to meet the R&D team and work with them closely on a new product. "It was an exciting experience, because it was the first time I had been to China," she remembers. "I was absorbing all of the cultural differences and their way of life. It is very different than the U.S. and I really appreciated my life in the States afterwards."

Wang believes that her background in sociology helps her to adjust to different cultures when she travels on the job. She also thinks that a familiarity with the interactionist perspective fosters teamwork, which is essential to success in business. "Not only do you have to do your job well, but you have to get along with your co-workers so that projects can be finished efficiently," she emphasizes. In a global marketplace, that insight is especially important.

LET'S DISCUSS

1. Given what you have learned about globalization, how likely do you think it is that you will someday be working abroad, on either a temporary or a permanent basis? Do you feel ready for that challenge?
2. What kind of cultural differences might complicate business relations between employees in two different countries—for example, the United States and China?

---

a product. Clearly, the impersonality of bureaucratic organizations can produce a cold and uncaring workplace. But the most penetrating analysis of the dehumanizing aspects of industrialization was offered by Karl Marx.

Marx's View

Marx believed that as the process of industrialization advanced, workers were robbed of any meaningful relationship to their work. The emphasis on the specialization of tasks, he believed, contributed to a growing sense of alienation among industrial workers. The term **alienation** refers to a condition of estrangement or dissociation from the surrounding society. Consider today's telemarketers, who make "cold calls" to sell people products and services. Do they feel a part of the financial institution that employs them? But it wasn't just the monotonous repetition of the same tasks that concerned Marx. In his view, an even deeper cause of alienation was the *powerlessness* of workers in a capitalist economic system. Workers had no control over their occupational tasks, the products of their labor, or the distribution of profits. Moreover, they were constantly producing property that was owned by others (the members of the capitalist class) (Erikson 1986).

The solution to the problem of workers' alienation, according to Marx, was to give workers greater control over the workplace and the products of their labor. Marx didn't focus on the limited reform of factory life; rather, he envisioned a revolutionary overthrow of capitalist oppression. After a transition to collective ownership of the means of production (socialism), the ideal of communism would eventually be achieved. Yet the trend in capitalist societies has been toward concentration of ownership by giant corporations. Through mergers and acquisitions, such corporations become even larger, and individual workers find themselves dwarfed by firms of overwhelming size and power.

When Marx wrote about work and alienation in 1844, the physical conditions of labor were much harsher than they are today. Yet his writings inspired research that persists today, even though the majority of workers now enjoy safer, more comfortable surroundings. Most studies of alienation have focused on how structural changes in the economy serve to increase or decrease worker satisfaction. In fact, the growth of the size of businesses, the emergence of huge franchise chains, and the dominance of multinational corporations have only increased the isolation of laborers. Large business organizations report an escalation in episodes of "desk rage," in which employees or angry ex-employees act out their frustrations, disrupting the workplace and often raising other workers' alienation in the process (Hodson and Sullivan 1995; Hymowitz and Silverman 2001).

Marx focused on alienation among the proletariat, whom he viewed as powerless to effect change in capitalist institutions. **407**

But by the 1980s, the term *burnout* was increasingly being used to describe the stress experienced by a wide range of workers, including professionals, self-employed persons, and even unpaid volunteers. The concept of work-related anxiety now covers alienation even among more affluent workers, who have a greater degree of control over their working conditions. From a conflict perspective, we have masked the fact that alienation falls most heavily on the lower and working classes by making it appear to be endemic, from the boardroom to the shop floor.

Working at the checkout counter may help to pay the bills, but it isn't likely to provide much job satisfaction—especially in a large supermarket where workers enjoy little responsibility or personal recognition.

Worker Satisfaction

In general, people with greater responsibility for a finished product (such as white-collar professionals and managers) experience more satisfaction than those with less responsibility. For women and men working in blue-collar jobs, the repetitive nature of work can be particularly unsatisfying. Repeatedly assembling parts for a cell phone or laptop computer is monotonous work. Not surprisingly, Robert Blauner's (1964) classic research study revealed that printers—who often work in small shops and supervise apprentices—were more satisfied with their work than laborers who performed repetitive tasks on automobile assembly lines.

Factors in Job Satisfaction A number of general factors can reduce the level of dissatisfaction of contemporary industrial workers. Higher wages give workers a sense of accomplishment apart from the task before them. A shorter workweek is supposed to increase the amount of time people can devote to recreation and leisure, reducing some of the discontent of the workplace. But the number of hours Americans work actually *increased* in the 1990s, by the equivalent of about one workweek. Short staffing because of low unemployment rates may have accounted for part of the increase in hours worked; however, many Americans took a second job during this period, just to make ends meet (Gerson and Jacobs 2004).

Numerous studies have shown that positive relationships with co-workers can make a boring job tolerable or even enjoyable. In his often cited "banana time" study, sociologist Donald Roy (1959) examined worker satisfaction in a two-month participant observation of a small group of machine operators. Drawing on the interactionist perspective, Roy carefully recorded the social interactions among members of his work group, including many structured "times" and "themes" designed to break up long days of simple, repetitive work. For example, the workers divided their food breaks into coffee time, peach time, banana time, fish time, Coke time, and lunch time—each of which occurred daily and involved distinctive responsibilities, jokes, and insults. Roy (1959:166) concluded that his observations "seem to support the generally accepted notion that one key source of job satisfaction lies in the informal interaction shared by members of a work group." The patterned conversation and horseplay of these workers reduced the monotony of their workdays.

Sociologist George Ritzer (1977, 2000) has suggested that the relatively positive impression many workers present is misleading. In his view, manual workers are so deeply alienated that they come to expect little from their jobs. Their satisfaction comes from nonwork tasks, and any job-related gratification results from receiving wages. Ritzer's interpretation explains why manual workers—although they say they are satisfied with their occupations—would not choose the same line of work if they could begin their lives over.

Job Satisfaction in Japan One of the major economic developments of the 1980s was the emergence of Japan as an industrial giant. In earlier decades, many people had attributed Japan's economic accomplishments to low wages combined with the production of inexpensive goods. However, in the 1980s Japanese salaries were comparable to those of other industrial nations. A more likely explanation of Japan's remarkable success at that time focused instead on the unusual pride Japanese workers took in their products. In Japanese plants and factories, workers are expected to assume the role of quality-control inspector. Although employees perform specialized production tasks, they can still identify with the finished product.

One of the drawbacks of this manufacturing model is the work schedule, which can be overwhelming. Many Japanese workers suffer from fatigue or even lasting health problems; those who develop a long-term disability can apply for worker compensation. Of the 869 *Karoshi* ("death from overwork") claims submitted to the Japanese government in 2005, 330 were approved (Huff 2007; Wokutch 1992).

For a long time, the collectivist orientation of Japanese culture heavily influenced its economic system. An individual was perceived as an extension of his or her family, business, or community, and as bound together with others in a common purpose. In contrast to U.S. firms, most Japanese companies maintained an ideal of "lifetime employment" for some of their employees. Because they made substantial investments in training, they were reluctant to lay off employees during a business slump. The employer–employee relationship was paramount. Companies even operated reception halls, gymnasiums and swimming pools, mortgage-lending institutions, and cultural programs for the benefit of their workers.

By the close of the 1990s this situation had changed. A severe economic recession had hit Japan, resulting in record unemployment.

While joblessness was still low compared to European countries, almost twice as many people were looking for jobs as there were job openings. Companies facing the impact of a lingering recession and increased competition from abroad set aside the notion of lifetime employment. Interactionists observed that Japanese men—accustomed to job security—were so embarrassed over losing a job that they would keep it secret from their families for days, if not weeks (see Chapter 4). Men in their 50s were looking for work along with recent college graduates. As a result of the restructuring, the bonds between workers and employers are currently weakening. The feelings of worker isolation that Marx and Ritzer wrote about in Europe and North America are becoming increasingly evident in Japan (French 2002).

In 2006 Muhammad Yunus, founder of the Grameen Bank, was awarded the Nobel Peace Prize for his work in championing the concept of microfinancing. The small loans his bank makes to the poor, many of them women, have improved the quality of life of countless families.

---

use your sociological *imagination*

In thinking about the work you will seek after graduation, which is more important to you, job satisfaction or salary?

Changing Economies

As advocates of the power elite model point out, the trend in capitalist societies has been toward concentration of ownership by giant corporations, especially multinational ones. In the following sections, we will examine two outgrowths of this trend in the United States, deindustrialization and the changing face of the workforce, as well as a countertrend: the rise of microfinancing in developing countries. As these trends show, any change in the economy has social and political implications.

Microfinancing

In some respects it offers a small solution to a big problem. **Microfinancing** is lending small sums of money to the poor so they can work their way out of poverty. Borrowers use the money to get small businesses off the ground—to buy the tools, equipment, and bamboo to make stools, yarn to weave into cloth, or cows to produce milk. The products they produce are then sold in the local shops. Typically, microloans are less than $100, often as little as $12. The recipients are people who ordinarily would not be able to qualify for banking services.

Sometimes referred to as "banking the unbanked," microfinancing was the brainchild of Bangladeshi economist Muhammad Yunus. In 1976, in the midst of a devastating famine in Bangladesh, Yunus founded the Grameen (meaning "Village") Bank. The idea came to him when he reached into his pocket to lend $27 to a group of villagers who had asked him for help. Working through local halls or meeting places, the Grameen Bank has now extended credit to nearly 7 million people. The idea has spread, and has even been underwritten by for-profit banks and multinational organizations like the International Monetary Fund. Estimates were that microfinancing would reach over 50 million people by 2007 (Microfinance Information Exchange 2008, 2009).

Microfinancing works well in countries that have experienced economic devastation. At the start of 2002, after decades of conflict and military occupation, Afghanistan did not have a single functioning bank. Five years later, with the help of the World Bank and other donors, Afghans could get microloans and other financial services in 22 of the country's 34 provinces. The new microlenders are the first evidence of a formal financial sector that Afghanistan has seen in years. Their funds have helped to start businesses and allowed farmers to convert from opium growing to other crops.

Because an estimated 90 percent of the recipients of microcredit are women, feminist theorists are especially interested in the growth of microfinancing. Women's economic status has been found to be critical to the well-being of their children, and the key to a healthy household environment. In developing countries, where women often are not treated as well as men, being entrusted with credit is particularly empowering to them. In recognition of these social and economic contributions of microfinancing, the United Nations proclaimed 2005 the International year of Microcredit (Dugger 2006).

Microfinancing is not a sweeping solution to world poverty. The very poorest of the world's people face challenges that prevent them from starting businesses. And the global credit crunch that began in 2008 may dry up many sources for microloans. Yet for millions of people, microfinancing remains an innovative path to prosperity (Beddoes 2008; LeMonde 2009; Selinger 2008).

The Changing Face of the Workforce

The workforce in the United States is constantly changing. During World War II, when men were mobilized to fight abroad, women entered the workforce in large numbers. And with the rise of the civil rights movement in the 1960s, minorities found numerous job opportunities opening to them. Box 18-2 on page 410 takes a closer look at the active recruitment of women and minorities into the workplace, known as *affirmative action.*

Although predictions are not always reliable, sociologists and labor specialists foresee a workforce increasingly composed of women and racial and ethnic minorities. In 1960 there were twice as many men in the labor force as women. From 1984 to 2014, however, 54 percent of new workers are expected to be

RESEARCH TODAY

18-2   Affirmative Action

Jessie Sherrod began picking cotton in the fields of Mississippi when she was eight years old, earning $1.67 for a 12-hour day. Today she is a Harvard-educated pediatrician who specializes in infectious diseases. But the road from the cotton fields to the medical profession was hardly an easy one. "You can't make up for 400 years of slavery and mistreatment and unequal opportunity in 20 years," she says angrily. "We had to ride the school bus for five miles . . . and pass by a white school to get to our black elementary school. Our books were used books. Our instructors were not as good. We didn't have the proper equipment. How do you make up for that?" (Stolberg 1995:A14). Some people think it should be done through affirmative action programs.

Critics warn against hiring and admissions quotas, complaining that they constitute a kind of "reverse discrimination" against White males.

The term *affirmative action* first appeared in an executive order issued by President John F. Kennedy in 1961. That order called for contractors to "take affirmative action to ensure that applicants are employed, and that employees are treated during employment, without regard to their race, creed, color, or national origin." In 1967, the order was amended by President Lyndon Johnson to prohibit discrimination on the basis of sex as well, but affirmative action remained a vague concept. Currently, **affirmative action** refers to positive efforts to recruit minority group members or women for jobs, promotions, and educational opportunities.

Sociologists—especially conflict and feminist theorists—view affirmative action as a legislative attempt to reduce the inequality embedded in the social structure by increasing opportunities for groups who were deprived in the past, such as women and African Americans. Despite the clear disparity in earnings between White males and other groups, however, many people

doubt that everything done in the name of affirmative action is desirable. Critics warn against hiring and admissions quotas, complaining that they constitute a kind of "reverse discrimination" against White males.

Affirmative action became a prominent issue in state and national political campaigns in 1996, when California's voters approved by a 54 to 46 percent margin the California Civil Rights Initiative. Better known as Proposition 209, this measure amends the state constitution to *prohibit* any program that gives preference to women and minorities in college admissions, hiring, promotion, or government contracts. In other words, it aims to abolish affirmative action programs. The courts have since upheld the measure. In 1998, voters in Washington state passed a similar anti–affirmative action measure.

In 2003, focusing specifically on college admissions in a pair of decisions involving policies at the University of Michigan, the Supreme Court ruled that colleges may consider race and ethnicity as one factor in their admissions decisions. However, they cannot assign a specific value to being a minority candidate in such a way that race becomes the overriding factor in a decision. The ruling allowed many colleges and universities to continue their existing affirmative action policies.

Increasingly, critics of affirmative action are calling for color-blind policies that would end affirmative action. Presumably, such policies would allow all applicants to be judged fairly. However, opponents warn against the danger of **color-blind racism**—the use of the principle

The Supreme Court's many decisions on the constitutionality of affirmative action programs have made it difficult for organizations to encourage diversity without transgressing the law.

of race neutrality to defend a racially unequal status quo (see Chapter 11). Will "color-blind" policies put an end to institutional practices that now favor Whites, they ask? According to the latest data, for example, Harvard University admits 40 percent of those applicants who are children of alumni—almost all of whom are White—compared to 11 percent of nonalumni children. Ironically, studies show that children of alumni are far more likely than either minority students or athletes to run into trouble academically.

LET'S DISCUSS

1. Is affirmative action part of the admissions policy at the college or university you attend? If so, do you think the policy has helped to level the playing field? Might it have excluded some qualified White applicants?
2. Take a poll of your classmates. What percentage of the class supports affirmative action in hiring and college admissions? How does that group break down in terms of gender, race, and ethnicity?

Sources: Massey and Mooney 2007; Pincus 2003, 2008; Stolberg 1995; University of Michigan 2003.

---

women. The dynamics for minority-group workers are even more dramatic, as the number of Black, Latino, and Asian American workers continues to increase at a faster rate than the number of White workers (Toossi 2006).

More and more, then, the workforce reflects the diversity of the population, as ethnic minorities enter the labor force and immigrants and their children move from marginal jobs or employment in the informal economy to positions of greater visibility and responsibility. The impact of this changing labor force is not merely statistical. A more diverse workforce means

that relationships between workers are more likely to cross gender, racial, and ethnic lines. Interactionists note that people will soon find themselves supervising and being supervised by people very different from themselves. In response to these changes, 75 percent of businesses had instituted some type of cultural diversity training program as of 2000 (Melia 2000).

Deindustrialization

What happens when a company decides it is more profitable to move its operations out of a long-established community to

Gutted factories like this one in Boston, Massachusetts, contrast with the glamorous corporate campus of Google Corporation in Mountain View, California. Deindustrialization and the rise of high technology have shifted the U.S. labor market, displacing many workers in the process.

another part of the country, or out of the country altogether? People lose jobs; stores lose customers; the local government's tax base declines and it cuts services. This devastating process has occurred again and again in the past decade or so.

The term **deindustrialization** refers to the systematic, widespread withdrawal of investment in basic aspects of productivity, such as factories and plants. Giant corporations that deindustrialize are not necessarily refusing to invest in new economic opportunities. Rather, the targets and locations of investment change, and the need for labor decreases as advances in technology continue to automate production. First, companies may move their plants from the nation's central cities to the suburbs. The next step may be relocation from suburban areas of the Northeast and Midwest to the South, where labor laws place more restrictions on unions. Finally, a corporation may simply relocate *outside* the United States to a country with a lower rate of prevailing wages. General Motors, for example, decided to build a multibillion-dollar plant in China rather than in Kansas City or even in Mexico (Lynn 2003).

Although deindustrialization often involves relocation, in some instances it takes the form of corporate restructuring, as companies seek to reduce costs in the face of growing worldwide competition. When such restructuring occurs, the impact on the bureaucratic hierarchy of formal organizations can be significant. A large corporation may choose to sell off or entirely abandon less productive divisions and to eliminate layers of management viewed as unnecessary. Wages and salaries may be frozen and fringe benefits cut—all in the name of restructuring. Increasing reliance on automation also spells the end of work as we have known it.

The term **downsizing** was introduced in 1987 to refer to reductions taken in a company's workforce as part of deindustrialization. Viewed from a conflict perspective, the unprecedented attention given to downsizing in the mid-1990s reflected the continuing importance of social class in the United States. Conflict theorists note that job loss has long been a feature of deindustrialization among blue-collar workers. But when large numbers of middle-class managers and other white-collar employees with substantial incomes began to be laid off, suddenly the media began expressing great concern over downsizing. The Social

Policy section that follows highlights the latest version of this issue, the outsourcing of service jobs at U.S. companies to workers in foreign countries (Meyerson 2006).

The extended economic downturn that began in 2008 accelerated the processes of deindustrialization and downsizing. As the recession deepened, many plants shut down either temporarily or permanently, releasing more and more workers from their jobs. With those jobs and shuttered plants went any hope of restoring or expanding heavy industry, including automobile manufacturing. The bankruptcy of Chrysler and General Motors hit the midwestern states particularly hard.

The social costs of deindustrialization and downsizing cannot be overemphasized. Plant closings lead to substantial unemployment in a community, which has a devastating impact on both the micro and macro levels. On the micro level, the unemployed person and his or her family must adjust to a loss of spending power. Painting or re-siding the house, buying health insurance or saving for retirement, even thinking about having another child must be put aside. Both marital happiness and family cohesion may suffer as a result. Although many dismissed workers eventually reenter the paid labor force, they must often accept less desirable positions with lower salaries and fewer benefits. Unemployment and underemployment are tied to many of the social problems discussed throughout this textbook, among them the need for child care and the controversy over welfare. In the minds of many displaced workers in the United States, the source of all these ills is the offshoring of U.S. jobs to overseas workers—the subject of the following Social Policy section.

use your sociological *imagination*

Do you see any evidence of deindustrialization or downsizing in your hometown?

Global Offshoring

The Issue

Anney Unnikrishnan's situation is not unusual. In fact, she is one of thousands of Indians who work in global call centers, answering phone calls from all over the world or dialing out to solicit business. The occupation is so common that it has become the subject of a Bollywood musical. In *Hello,* bright young Indians offer technical assistance to clueless American callers, including one who has removed the top from an oven and wants to know why it has stopped working (*The Week* 2008).

Anney received her MBA in India before taking the entrance exams to Purdue University. But after concluding that she couldn't afford Purdue, she realized that because U.S. corporations were setting up shop in India, she didn't need to emigrate to the United States. Anney sums up what she considers her enviable position in this way: "So I still get my rice and sambar (a traditional Indian dish). . . . I don't need to . . . learn to eat coleslaw and cold beef . . . and I still work for a multinational. Why should I go to America?" (Friedman 2005:28).

Offshoring is global: it occurs not just between North America and India, but between North America and Europe (see Box 10-2 on page 229) and between other industrial and developing countries. Online services in the United States enlist Romanians to represent well-to-do video game players. Japan enlists Chinese speakers of Japanese—a legacy of Japan's bitter occupation of China—to create databases or develop floor plans for Japanese construction firms. In Africa, over 54,000 people work in call centers, some specializing in French and others serving the English-speaking market. People all over the world are affected by this issue (Friedman 2005; Lacey 2005).

The Setting

U.S. firms have been *outsourcing* certain types of work for generations. For example, moderate-sized businesses such as furniture stores and commercial laundries have long relied on outside

It may not look like it, but this photograph shows offshoring in action. Ramya Tadikonda, a 26-year-old mother with a college degree, tutors students in the United States from her home in Chennai, India, through U.S.-based TutorVista. For her work, Ramya makes $2 an hour.

TABLE 18-2 OCCUPATIONS MOST VULNERABLE TO OFFSHORING

Rank	Occupation
1	Computer programming
2	Data entry
3	Electrical and electronics drafting
4	Mechanical drafting
5	Computer and information science, research
6	Actuarial science
7	Mathematics
8	Statistics
9	Mathematical science (all other)
10	Film and video editing

Source: Bureau of Labor Statistics data cited in Hira 2008; Moncarz et al. 2008.

trucking firms to make deliveries to their customers. The new trend toward **offshoring** carries this practice one step further, by transferring other types of work to foreign contractors. (Table 18-2 lists the occupations most likely to be offshored.) Now, even large companies are turning to overseas firms, many of them located in developing countries. Offshoring has become the latest tactic in the time-worn business strategy of raising profits by reducing costs.

Offshoring began when U.S. companies started transferring manufacturing jobs to foreign factories, where wage rates were much lower. But the transfer of work from one country to another is no longer limited to manufacturing. Office and professional jobs are being exported, too, thanks to advanced telecommunications and the growth of skilled, English-speaking labor forces in developing nations with relatively low wage scales. The trend includes even those jobs that require considerable training, such as accounting and financial analysis, computer programming, claims adjustment, telemarketing, and hotel and airline reservations. Today, when you call a toll-free number to reach a customer service representative, chances are that the person who answers the phone will not be speaking from the United States.

Sociological Insights

Because offshoring, like outsourcing in general, tends to improve the efficiency of business operations, it can be viewed as functional to society. Offshoring also increases economic interdependence in the production of goods and services, both among enterprises located just across town from one another and among those across the globe.

Conflict theorists charge that this aspect of globalization furthers social inequality. While moving high-tech work to India does help to lower a company's costs, the impact on those technical and service workers who are displaced is clearly devastating. Certainly middle-class workers in industrial countries are alarmed by the trend. Though economists favor some assistance for workers who have been displaced by offshoring, they oppose broad-based efforts to block the practice.

There is a downside to offshoring for foreigners, as well. Although outsourcing is a significant source of employment for India's upper middle class, hundreds of millions of other Indians have seen little to no positive impact from the trend. Most households in India do not possess any form of high technology: only about 1 out of 14 have a telephone, and just 3 out of 1,000 a computer. Instead of improving these people's lives, the new business centers have siphoned water and electricity away from those who are most in need. Even the high-tech workers are experiencing negative consequences. Many suffer from stress disorders such as stomach problems and difficulty sleeping; more than half quit their jobs before the end of a year. On the other hand, the new call centers have brought significant improvements in India's infrastructure, particularly in telecommunications and power generation. The long-term impact of offshoring on India and other developing nations is difficult to predict (Waldman 2004a, 2004b, 2004c).

Policy Initiatives

According to a report published in 2007, 75 percent of the 2,000 largest companies in the world are engaged in offshoring. Alan S. Blinder, former vice chairman of the Federal Reserve, predicts that offshoring will become the "third Industrial Revolution"—a life-altering shift in the way goods and services are produced and consumed. Blinder says we have barely seen the "tip of the offshoring iceberg." While offshoring may not lead to large-scale unemployment, it will likely produce a shift in Western labor markets. Jobs that are easily outsourced, like accounting and computer programming, will migrate to developing countries, leaving those that must be done on site, like nursing and construction, at home (Blinder 2006; Weier 2007).

Despite concerns over the impact of offshoring on the labor force, little legislative action has been taken. Most policymakers, while they bemoan the loss of jobs, see offshoring as part of the "natural" process of globalization, one more manifestation of the gains that come from international trade. In their view, the resulting dislocation of workers at home is just another job change—one that more and more workers will have to adjust to at some point in their lives.

Let's Discuss

1. Do you know anyone whose job has been transferred to a foreign country? If so, was the person able to find a comparable job in the same town, or did he or she have to relocate? How long was the person unemployed?

2. What do you think should be done, if anything, about the growing trend toward offshoring? Do you see it as a serious political issue?

3. How might the number of foreign students who are educated in the United States contribute to the trend toward offshoring? On balance, do you think the gain from training foreign students outweighs the loss from exported jobs?

getting**involved**

To get involved in the debate over global offshoring, visit this book's Online Learning Center, which offers links to relevant Web sites.

www.mhhe.com/schaefer12e

MASTERING THIS CHAPTER

Summary

The **economic system** of a society has an important influence on social behavior and on other social institutions. This chapter examines the major economic systems, the rise of **capitalism** in China, work and **alienation** from work, the changing economy, and the trend toward global **offshoring.**

1. With the Industrial Revolution, a new form of social structure emerged: the **industrial society.**

2. Systems of **capitalism** vary in the degree to which the government regulates private ownership and economic activity, but all emphasize the profit motive.

3. The basic objective of **socialism** is to eliminate economic exploitation and meet people's needs.

4. Marx believed that **communism** would evolve naturally out of socialism.

5. In developing nations, the **informal economy** represents a significant part of total economic activity. Yet because this sector depends largely on women's work, it is undervalued.

6. In the 1980s, the Chinese Communist Party began allowing Chinese entrepreneurs to experiment with capitalist ventures. Today, multinational corporations are capitalizing on China's huge workforce to produce goods and services for sale not just to those in industrial nations, but to the people of China.

7. Industrial jobs can lead to a sense of **alienation** in the workplace. Karl Marx expected that powerless workers would eventually overthrow the capitalist system.

8. **Affirmative action** is intended to remedy the effects of discrimination against minority groups and women in education and the workplace. The concept is controversial, however, because some people see it as reverse discrimination against majority groups.

413

9. The world's economies are changing, both in the United States and abroad. In developing countries, **microfinancing** is improving the lives of millions of poor people. In the United States, workers are coping with **deindustrialization** and employers are training an increasingly diverse workforce.

10. **Offshoring,** or the transfer of work to foreign contractors, has become a global phenomenon involving both developed and developing nations. Today, even professional services can be outsourced to nations like India, which possess a large, well-educated English-speaking population that will work for comparatively low wages.

Critical Thinking Questions

1. The United States has long been put forward as the model of a capitalist society. Drawing on material in earlier chapters of this book, discuss the values and beliefs that have led people in the United States to cherish a laissez-faire, capitalist economy. To what degree have those values and beliefs changed over the past hundred years? What aspects of socialism are now evident in the nation's economy? Have our values and beliefs changed to support certain principles traditionally associated with socialist societies?

2. Describe some of the service workers in the college or university you attend. Do you see any signs of alienation in the workplace?

3. Imagine that you have been assigned to study possible changes in the economy of the city nearest you. How could you use surveys, observation research, experiments, and existing sources to complete the task?

Key Terms

Affirmative action Positive efforts to recruit minority group members or women for jobs, promotions, and educational opportunities. (page 410)

Alienation A condition of estrangement or dissociation from the surrounding society. (407)

Capitalism An economic system in which the means of production are held largely in private hands and the main incentive for economic activity is the accumulation of profits. (401)

Color-blind racism The use of the principle of race neutrality to defend a racially unequal status quo. (410)

Communism As an ideal type, an economic system under which all property is communally owned and no social distinctions are made on the basis of people's ability to produce. (403)

Cultural relativism The viewing of people's behavior from the perspective of their own culture. (400)

Deindustrialization The systematic, widespread withdrawal of investment in basic aspects of productivity, such as factories and plants. (411)

Downsizing Reductions taken in a company's workforce as part of deindustrialization. (411)

Economic system The social institution through which goods and services are produced, distributed, and consumed. (400)

Industrial society A society that depends on mechanization to produce its goods and services. (401)

Informal economy Transfers of money, goods, or services that are not reported to the government. (403)

Laissez-faire A form of capitalism under which people compete freely, with minimal government intervention in the economy. (401)

Microfinancing Lending small sums of money to the poor so they can work their way out of poverty. (409)

Monopoly Control of a market by a single business firm. (401)

Offshoring The transfer of work to foreign contractors. (412)

Socialism An economic system under which the means of production and distribution are collectively owned. (402)

Self-Quiz

Read each question carefully and then select the best answer.

1. Which two basic types of economic system distinguish contemporary industrial societies?
   a. capitalism and communism
   b. capitalism and socialism
   c. socialism and communism
   d. capitalism and dictatorship

2. According to the discussion of capitalism in the text, which of the following statements is true?
   a. The means of production are held largely in private hands.
   b. The main incentive for economic activity is the accumulation of profits.
   c. The degree to which the government regulates private ownership and economic activity will vary.
   d. all of the above

3. Which sociological perspective points out that while *pure* monopolies are not a basic element of the economy of the United States, competition is much more restricted than one might expect in what is called a *free enterprise system*?
   a. the functionalist perspective
   b. the conflict perspective
   c. the interactionist perspective
   d. labeling theory

4. Which of the following is *not* an example of the informal economy?
   a. trading a haircut for a computer lesson
   b. selling illegal drugs on the street
   c. working as a computer programmer for a major corporation
   d. providing child care out of a private home, without reporting the income to the IRS

5. The systematic, widespread withdrawal of investment in basic aspects of productivity such as factories and plants is called
   a. deindustrialization.
   b. downsizing.
   c. postindustrialization.
   d. gentrification.

6. Karl Marx is associated with which of the following concepts?
   a. anomie
   b. assimilation
   c. apartheid
   d. alienation

7. Sociologists and labor specialists foresee a workforce increasingly composed of
   a. women.
   b. racial minorities.
   c. ethnic minorities.
   d. all of the above

8. Currently, _____ _____ refers to positive efforts to recruit minority group members or women for jobs, promotions, and educational opportunities.
   a. equal rights
   b. affirmative action
   c. work programs
   d. equal action

9. The principle of laissez-faire was expounded and endorsed by the British economist
   a. John Maynard Keynes.
   b. Adam Smith.
   c. Paul Samuelson.
   d. Arthur Scargill.

10. Which sociologist, using the interactionist perspective, noted that "one key source of job satisfaction lies in the informal interaction shared by members of a work group"?
   a. Robert Blauner
   b. Donald Roy
   c. George Ritzer
   d. Karl Marx

11. The term _____ _____ refers to the social institution through which goods and services are produced, distributed, and consumed.

12. The principle of_____ _____, as expounded and endorsed by the British economist Adam Smith, was the prevailing form of capitalism immediately following the Industrial Revolution.

13. Under _____, the means of production and distribution in a society are collectively rather than privately owned, and the basic objective of the economic system is to meet people's needs rather than to maximize profits.

14. _____ is an economic system under which all property is communally owned and no social distinctions are made based on people's ability to produce.

15. The term _____ was introduced in 1987 to refer to reductions taken in a company's workforce as part of deindustrialization.

16. A(n) _____ society depends on mechanization to produce its goods and services.

17. _____ theorists point out that while pure monopolies are not a basic element of the economy of the United States, competition is much more restricted than one might expect in what is called a free enterprise system.

18. Émile Durkheim argued that as labor becomes more and more differentiated, individuals experience _____, or loss of direction.

19. Most studies of _____ have focused on factors that serve to increase or decrease worker satisfaction.

20. Some capitalist nations, such as the United States, outlaw _____ through antitrust legislation.

Answers

1 (b); 2 (d); 3 (b); 4 (c); 5 (a); 6 (d); 7 (d); 8 (b); 9 (b); 10 (b); 11 economic system; 12 laissez-faire; 13 socialism; 14 Communism; 15 downsizing; 16 industrial; 17 Conflict; 18 anomie; 19 alienation; 20 monopolies

THINKING ABOUT MOVIES

The Devil Wears Prada
(David Frankel, 2006)

In a coming-of-age tale about a recent college graduate, Andy Sachs (Anne Hathaway) embarks on a career in the fashion industry. Trained as a journalist, Andy settles for an entry-level job as an assistant to the editor of a widely circulated fashion magazine. The editor, Miranda Priestly (Meryl Streep), is known for being impossible to please. Though she makes extreme demands on Andy, she sees herself in the young woman, and sets her on a path to power in the fashion industry.

This movie shows how the fashion industry controls the products that are available for purchase in our consumption-oriented society. To a large extent, powerful people like Miranda dictate what goes in and out of style not just in the United States, but around the world. Watch for the scene in which Andy first meets Miranda. Andy proclaims her disinterest in fashion, but Miranda takes one look at her sweater and proves that everyone who wears clothes is affected by the fashion industry.

For Your Consideration

1. What does the fashion industry do to support a capitalist economy?

2. How does the fashion industry control the consumer purchases of people like you and your friends?

Modern Times
(Charles Chaplin, 1936)

In his classic role as the Tramp, Charlie Chaplin plays an assembly-line worker who cannot keep up with the fast pace of production. A casualty of industrialization, he suffers from the shock of the repetitive physical labor that was typical of the industrial era. The film is an implicit critique of capitalism and its treatment of the workers who labor to accumulate the factory owner's profit.

Modern Times illustrates the modes of production that were common before the deindustrialization of the Western world. Although its title may seem an anachronism, the film remains relevant even in the 21st century. Throughout the world, many people still suffer from the arduous working conditions associated with factory labor.

For Your Consideration

1. How does the Tramp's working experience illustrate Marx's concept of alienation?

2. What aspects of capitalism can be seen in *Modern Times*? Which still hold true today and which seem outdated?

inside

Culture and Health

Sociological Perspectives
on Health and Illness

Social Epidemiology
and Health

Health Care in the
United States

Mental Illness in the
United States

Sociological Perspectives
on the Environment

Environmental Problems

Social Policy and the
Environment:
Environmentalism

BOXES

Taking Sociology to Work:
*Lola Adedokun,
Independent Consultant,
Health Care Research*

Research Today: *The
AIDS Epidemic*

Research Today:
Medical Apartheid

Sociology in the Global
Community:
*The Mysterious Fall
of the Nacirema*

Sierra Club members rally
to protect the environment,
a major influence on our
health and well-being.

THE SCALPEL AND THE SILVER BEAR

The First Navajo Woman Surgeon Combines Western Medicine and Traditional Healing

LORI ARVISO ALVORD, M.D.
AND
ELIZABETH COHEN VAN PELT

❝ I knew that Navajo people mistrusted Western medicine, and that Navajo customs and beliefs, even Navajo ways of interacting with others, often stood in direct opposition to the way I was trained at Stanford to deliver medical care. I wanted to make a difference in the lives of my people, not only by providing surgery to heal them but also by making it easier for them to understand, relate to, and accept Western medicine. By speaking some Navajo with them, by showing respect for their ways, and by being one of them, I could help them. I watched my patients. I listened to them. Slowly I began to develop better ways to heal them, ways that respected their culture and beliefs. I desired to incorporate these traditional beliefs and customs into my practice. . . .

Navajo patients simply didn't respond well to the brusque and distanced style of Western doctors. To them it is not acceptable to walk into a room, quickly open someone's shirt and listen to their heart with a stethoscope, or stick something in their mouth or ear. Nor is it acceptable to ask probing and personal questions. As I adapted my practice to my culture, my patients relaxed in situations that could otherwise have been highly stressful to them. As they became more comfortable and at ease, something even more remarkable—astonishing, even—happened. When patients were trusting and accepting before surgery, their operations seemed to be more successful. If they were anxious, distrustful, and did not understand, or had resisted treatment, they seemed to have more operative or postoperative complications. Could this be happening? The more I watched, the more I saw it was indeed true. Incorporating Navajo philosophies of balance and symmetry, respect and connectedness into my practice, benefited my patients and allowed everything in my two worlds to make sense.

Navajos believe in *hózhǫ́* or *hózhǫ́ni*—"Walking in Beauty"—a worldview in which everything in life is connected and influences everything else. A stone thrown into a pond can influence the life of a deer in the forest, a human voice and a spoken word can influence events around the world, and all things possess spirit and power. So Navajos make every effort to live in harmony and balance with everyone and everything else. Their belief system sees sickness as a result of things falling out of balance, of losing one's way on the path of beauty. In this belief system, religion and medicine are one and the same. . . .

As I have modified my Western techniques with elements of Navajo culture and philosophy, I have seen the wisdom and truth of Navajo medicine too, and how Navajo patients can benefit from it. In this way I am pulling the strands of my life even closer together. The results have been dazzling—*hózhǫ́ni.* It has been beautiful. ❞

> *Navajos believe in hózhǫ́ or hózhǫ́ni—"Walking in Beauty"—a worldview in which everything in life is connected and influences everything else.*

(Alvord and Van Pelt 1999:13–15) Additional information about this excerpt can be found on the Online Learning Center at www.mhhe.com/schaefer12e.

In this excerpt from *The Scalpel and the Silver Bear,* Dr. Lori Arviso Alvord, the first Navajo woman to become a surgeon, describes her effort to bridge the cultural gap between Western medicine and traditional Native American healing. Dropping the impersonal clinical manner she had learned in medical school, Alvord reached out to her Navajo patients, acknowledging their faith in holistic healing practices. Her account communicates the wonder she felt as she watched their health improve. By walking in beauty, Dr. Alvord had become a healer as well as a surgeon.

Dr. Alvord's account illustrates the powerful effect of culture on both health and medicine. Culture affects the way people interact with doctors and healers, the way they relate to their families when they are sick, and even the way they think about health. Are some health problems peculiar to certain cultures? Who defines what illness is? How does health care vary from one social class to another and from one nation to another? In this chapter, we will consider first the relationship between culture and health. Then we present a sociological overview of health, illness, health care, medicine as a social institution, and issues related to mental illness. We begin by examining how functionalists, conflict theorists, interactionists, and labeling theorists look at health-related issues. Then we study the distribution of diseases in a society by social class, race and ethnicity, gender, and age.

We'll look too at the evolution of the U.S. health care system. Sociologists are interested in the roles people play in the health care system and the organizations that deal with issues of health and sickness. Therefore, we will analyze the interactions among physicians, nurses, and patients; alternatives to traditional health care; and the role of government in providing health care services to the needy. The discussion concludes with a sociological analysis of mental illness and its treatment.

Later in the chapter, we examine the environmental problems facing the world in the 21st century, and we draw on the functionalist and conflict perspectives to better understand environmental issues. We'll see that it is important not to oversimplify the relationship between health and the environment. Finally, the Social Policy section explores the recently renewed interest in environmentalism.

Culture and Health

The communities people live in have an impact on their health. In rural areas, for example, residents must travel many miles to see a doctor. The nearest hospital may be hundreds of miles away. On the other hand, people who live in the country escape many of the stresses and strains that plague people who live in cities.

Culture, too, contributes to differences in medical care and even how health is defined. In Japan, for instance, organ transplants are rare. The Japanese do not generally favor harvesting organs from brain-dead donors. Researchers have shown that diseases, too, are rooted in the shared meanings of particular cultures. The term **culture-bound syndrome** refers to a disease or illness that cannot be understood apart from its specific social context (Shepherd 2003; U.S. Surgeon General 1999).

In the United States, a culture-bound syndrome known as anorexia nervosa has received increasing attention over the past few decades. First described in England in the 1860s, this condition is characterized by an intense fear of becoming obese and a distorted image of one's body. Those who suffer from anorexia nervosa (primarily young women in their teenage years or 20s) lose weight drastically through self-induced semistarvation. Anorexia nervosa is best understood in the context of Western culture, which typically views the slim, youthful body as healthy and beautiful, and the fat person as ugly and lacking in self-discipline.

Until recently, U.S. researchers dealt with the concept of culture-bound syndromes only in cross-cultural studies. However, recent increases in immigration, along with efforts by the medical establishment to reach out to immigrant communities, have led to a belated recognition that not everyone views medicine in the same way. Medical practitioners are now being trained to recognize cultural beliefs that are related to medicine. Table 19-1 gives some examples.

Culture can also influence the relative incidence of a disease or disorder. In *The Scalpel and the Silver Bear*, Dr. Lori Arviso Alvord writes of the depression and alcoholism that attend life on the reservation. These diseases, she says, are born from "historical grief": "Navajo children are told of the capture and murder of their forefathers and mothers, and then they too must share in the legacy. . . ." Not just for the Navajo, Alvord writes, but for Black Americans as well, the weight of centuries of suffering, injustice, and loss too often manifests itself in despair and addiction. The rate of alcoholism mortality among Native Americans served by the Indian Health Service is five times that of the general population of the United States (Alvord and Van Pelt 1999:12).

Sociological Perspectives on Health and Illness

How can we define health? Imagine a continuum with health on one end and death on the other. In the preamble to its 1946 constitution, the World Health Organization defined **health** as a "state of complete physical, mental, and social well-being, and not merely the absence of disease and infirmity" (Leavell and Clark 1965:14).

In this definition, the "healthy" end of the continuum represents an ideal rather than a precise condition. Along the continuum, people define themselves as healthy or sick on the basis of criteria established by themselves and relatives, friends, co-workers, and medical practitioners. Because health is relative, then, we can view it in a social context and consider how it varies in different situations or cultures.

Why is it that you may consider yourself sick or well when others do not agree? Who controls definitions of health and illness in our society, and for what ends? What are the consequences of viewing yourself (or of being viewed) as ill or disabled? By drawing on four sociological perspectives—functionalism, conflict theory, interactionism, and labeling theory—we can gain greater insight into the social context that shapes definitions of health and the treatment of illness.

Functionalist Approach

Illness entails breaks in our social interactions, both at work and at home. From a functionalist perspective, being sick must therefore be controlled, so that not too many people are released from their societal responsibilities at any one time. Functionalists contend that an overly broad definition of illness would disrupt the workings of a society.

TABLE 19-1 CULTURAL CHALLENGES TO MEDICINE

Culture	Cultural Challenge	Implications for Medical Decision Making and Treatment
Central Americans	May consider pain a consequence of "earthly misconduct" or imbalance of nature.	May give the impression of acquiescing to a doctor's suggestion (through silence or nodding) because of reluctance to disagree with a person of such authority.
Ethiopians, Eritreans	Traditionally have viewed pregnancy as a dangerous state, blaming sorcery for miscarriages and other bad outcomes.	May have little knowledge or understanding of treatment procedures. A patient who is asked to sign consent forms may become very anxious.
Koreans	May seek care from a *hanui*, a traditional herbal medicine doctor.	Often keep bad medical news from a family member who is ill, believing that such information would wipe out hope.
Muslims	Concerns for personal modesty among women.	Hospital staff should knock and wait for permission to enter to give female patients time to cover themselves.

Sources: Based on Buchanan 2008; S. Levine 2006:31.

Sickness requires that one take on a social role, if only temporarily. The **sick role** refers to societal expectations about the attitudes and behavior of a person viewed as being ill. Sociologist Talcott Parsons (1951, 1975), well known for his contributions to functionalist theory, outlined the behavior required of people who are considered sick. They are exempted from their normal, day-to-day responsibilities and generally do not suffer blame for their condition. Yet they are obligated to try to get well, which includes seeking competent professional care. This obligation arises from the common view that illness is dysfunctional, because it can undermine social stability. Attempting to get well is particularly important in the world's developing countries. Modern automated industrial societies can absorb a greater degree of illness or disability than horticultural or agrarian societies, in which the availability of workers is far more critical (Conrad 2005).

According to Parsons's theory, physicians function as "gatekeepers" for the sick role. They either verify a patient's condition as "illness" or designate the patient as "recovered." The ill person becomes dependent on the physician, because the latter can control valued rewards (not only treatment of illness, but also excused absences from work and school). Parsons suggests that the physician–patient relationship is somewhat like that between parent and child. Like a parent, the physician helps the patient to enter society as a full and functioning adult (Weitz 2007).

The concept of the sick role is not without criticism. First, patients' judgments regarding their own state of health may be related to their gender, age, social class, and ethnic group. For example, younger people may fail to detect warning signs of a dangerous illness, while elderly people may focus too much on the slightest physical malady. Second, the sick role may be more applicable to people who are experiencing short-term illnesses than to those with recurring, long-term illnesses. Finally, even simple factors, such as whether a person is employed, seem to affect one's willingness to assume the sick role—as does the impact of socialization into a particular occupation or activity. For example, beginning in childhood, athletes learn to define certain ailments as "sports injuries" and therefore do not regard themselves

as "sick." Nonetheless, sociologists continue to rely on Parsons's model for functionalist analysis of the relationship between illness and societal expectations of the sick (Curry 1993).

---

use your sociological *imagination*

Describe some situations you have witnessed that illustrate different definitions of the "sick role."

---

www.mhhe.com/schaefer12e

Conflict Approach

Conflict theorists observe that the medical profession has assumed a preeminence that extends well beyond whether to excuse a student from school or an employee from work. Sociologist Eliot Freidson (1970:5) has likened the position of medicine today to that of state religions yesterday—it has an officially approved monopoly of the right to define health and illness and to treat illness. Conflict theorists use the term *medicalization of society* to refer to the growing role of medicine as a major institution of social control (Conrad 2009; McKinlay and McKinlay 1977; Zola 1972, 1983).

The Medicalization of Society Social control involves techniques and strategies for regulating behavior in order to enforce the distinctive norms and values of a culture. Typically, we think of informal social control as occurring within families and peer groups, and formal social control as being carried out by authorized agents such as police officers, judges, school administrators, and employers. Viewed from a conflict perspective, however, medicine is not simply a "healing profession"; it is a regulating mechanism.

How does medicine manifest its social control? First, medicine has greatly expanded its domain of expertise in recent decades. Physicians now examine a wide range of issues, among them sexuality, old age, anxiety, obesity, child development, alcoholism, and drug addiction. We tolerate this expansion of the boundaries of medicine because we hope that these experts can bring new "miracle cures" to complex human problems, as they have to the control of certain infectious diseases.

The social significance of this expanding medicalization is that once a problem is viewed using a *medical model*—once medical experts become influential in proposing and assessing relevant public policies—it becomes more difficult for common people to join the discussion and exert influence on decision making. It also becomes more difficult to view these issues as being shaped by social, cultural, or psychological factors, rather than simply by physical or medical factors (Caplan 1989; Conrad 2009).

Second, medicine serves as an agent of social control by retaining absolute jurisdiction over many health care procedures. It has even attempted to guard its jurisdiction by placing health care professionals such as chiropractors and nurse-midwives outside the realm of acceptable medicine. Despite the fact that

In U.S. society, people who are sick are supposed to stay home and rest until they feel better. Though different societies have different expectations of a person who is seen as being ill, all recognize the significance of the *sick role*.

The growing concern about obesity among the young has focused attention on their eating habits and their need for exercise. Concern about obesity is a sign of the medicalization of society.

FIGURE 19-1 INFANT MORTALITY RATES IN SELECTED COUNTRIES

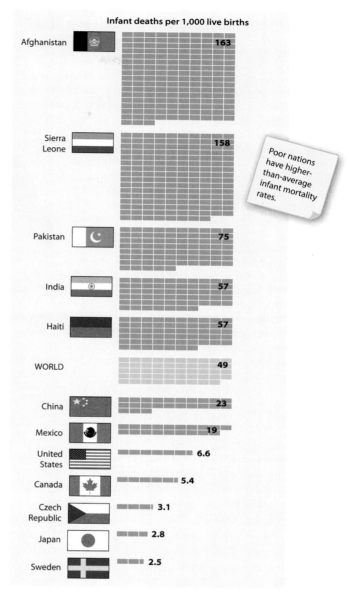

Infant deaths per 1,000 live births

Afghanistan	163
Sierra Leone	158
Pakistan	75
India	57
Haiti	57
WORLD	49
China	23
Mexico	19
United States	6.6
Canada	5.4
Czech Republic	3.1
Japan	2.8
Sweden	2.5

Poor nations have higher-than-average infant mortality rates.

Source: Haub 2008.

midwives first brought professionalism to child delivery, they have been portrayed as having invaded the "legitimate" field of obstetrics, both in the United States and Mexico. Nurse-midwives have sought licensing as a way to achieve professional respectability, but physicians continue to exert power to ensure that midwifery remains a subordinate occupation (Scharnberg 2007).

Inequities in Health Care The medicalization of society is but one concern of conflict theorists as they assess the workings of health care institutions. As we have seen throughout this textbook, in analyzing any issue, conflict theorists seek to determine who benefits, who suffers, and who dominates at the expense of others. Viewed from a conflict perspective, glaring inequities exist in health care delivery in the United States. For example, poor areas tend to be underserved because medical services concentrate where people are wealthy.

Similarly, from a global perspective, obvious inequities exist in health care delivery. Today, the United States has about 27 physicians per 10,000 people, while African nations have fewer than 1 per 10,000. This situation is only worsened by the **brain drain**— the immigration to the United States and other industrialized nations of skilled workers, professionals, and technicians who are desperately needed in their home countries. As part of this

brain drain, physicians, nurses, and other health care professionals have come to the United States from developing countries such as India, Pakistan, and various African states. Conflict theorists view their emigration out of the Third World as yet another way in which the world's core industrialized nations enhance their quality of life at the expense of developing countries. One way the developing countries suffer is in lower life expectancy. In Africa and much of Latin America and Asia, life expectancy is far lower than in industrialized nations (Bureau of the Census 2008a: Table 154; World Bank 2007a:92–94).

Conflict theorists emphasize that inequities in health care have clear life-and-death consequences. From a conflict perspective, the dramatic differences in *infant mortality rates* around the world (Figure 19-1) reflect, at least in part, unequal distribution of health care resources based on the wealth or poverty of various nations. The **infant mortality rate** is the number of

TAKING SOCIOLOGY TO WORK

Lola Adedokun, **Independent Consultant, Health Care Research**

When Lola Adedokun entered Dartmouth College, she was thinking of concentrating in biology and premedical studies. But after taking a sociology course on racial disparities, she realized that sociology was the only subject that offered courses on topics she was passionate about. Eventually, she settled on sociology, along with a special social science major in health policy that she created herself.

Today, Adedokun is a consultant on a number of health-related research projects. One, funded by the National Institutes of Health (NIH), is a follow-up study of an international training program for researchers and clinicians working on HIV/AIDS. Another, funded by the Centers for Disease Control and Prevention (CDC), focuses on the sexual behaviors of heterosexuals at high risk of contracting HIV. "Understanding human behavior and human sexual behavior as well as the cultural and social issues that drive this behavior is essential," she explains. Adedokun is also a graduate research assistant at the National Center for Children in Poverty, where she conducts and analyzes interviews with families, children, and mental health professionals.

Each week is different for this self-employed researcher. Often she works from home, conducting interviews over the phone and analyzing data on her own computer. At other times she works at her clients' offices, using their proprietary software. Adedokun also trains teams of interviewers and serves as a liaison between agencies. "I have a lot of face-to-face contact interviewing clients and researching people from high-risk communities," she says. "The nature of the work is much like the field of sociology—it is

vast and broad, and I'm thinking about it all the time. In that way, my work does not feel like work."

Travel has been one of the high points in Adedokun's career. "The most amazing opportunity I have had in the last few years was traveling to Asia, Africa, and Latin America to conduct interviews with some of the world's leading HIV/AIDS researchers," she says. "I was able to truly get a sense of the challenges and the achievements that these researchers have encountered."

Asked what advice she would give to current students of sociology, Adedokun replies, "One piece of advice is that you would be doing yourself a disservice to distance yourself from this important material. It is the fundamentals of sociology that will be most relevant to any area that you choose to pursue in your future," she continues, "so ask questions, debate, discuss, and argue, as the knowledge that you will pull from that will prove to be the greatest academic lessons you may ever learn."

LET'S DISCUSS

1. What social issue or problem do you feel passionate about, and how can sociology help to address it?
2. Adedokun is a self-starter who created her own major and is now pursuing a career on her own. Have you ever considered creating your own career path, rather than relying on large institutions to map your future? What might be the benefits of such an approach? The drawbacks?

---

deaths of infants under one year old per 1,000 live births in a given year. This measure is an important indicator of a society's level of health care; it reflects prenatal nutrition, delivery procedures, and infant screening measures. Still, despite the wealth of the United States, at least 46 nations have *lower* infant mortality rates, among them Canada, Sweden, and Japan. Conflict theorists point out that unlike the United States, these countries offer some form of government-supported health care for all citizens, which typically leads to greater availability and use of prenatal care.

Interactionist Approach

From an interactionist point of view, patients are not passive; often, they actively seek the services of a health care practitioner. In examining health, illness, and medicine as a social institution, then, interactionists engage in micro-level study of the roles played by health care professionals and patients. Interactionists are particularly interested in how physicians learn to play their occupational role. According to Brenda L. Beagan (2001), the technical language students learn in medical school becomes the basis for the script they follow as novice physicians. The familiar white coat is their costume—one that helps them to appear confident and professional at the same time that it identifies them as doctors to patients and other staff members. Beagan found that many medical students struggle to project the appearance of competence that they think their role demands.

Sometimes patients play an active role in health care by *failing* to follow a physician's advice. For example, some patients stop taking medications long before they should. Some take an incorrect dosage on purpose, and others never even fill their prescriptions. Such noncompliance results in part from the prevalence of self-medication in our society; many people are accustomed to self-diagnosis and self-treatment. On the other hand, patients' active involvement in their health care can sometimes have very *positive* consequences. Some patients read books about preventive health care techniques, attempt to maintain a healthful and nutritious diet, carefully monitor any side effects of medication, and adjust the dosage based on perceived side effects.

Labeling Approach

Labeling theory helps us to understand why certain people are *viewed* as deviants, "bad kids," or criminals, whereas others whose behavior is similar are not. Labeling theorists also suggest that the designation "healthy" or "ill" generally involves social definition by others. Just as police officers, judges, and other regulators of social control have the power to define certain people as

	Functionalist	Conflict	Interactionist	Labeling
Major emphasis	Control of the number of people who are considered sick	Overmedicalization Gross inequities in health care	Doctor–patient relationship Interaction of medical staff	Definition of illness and health
Controlling factors	Physician as gatekeeper	Medical profession Social inequities	Medical profession	Medical profession
Proponents	Talcott Parsons	Paul Starr Thomas Szasz Irving Zola	Doug Maynard	Thomas Szasz

criminals, health care professionals (especially physicians) have the power to define certain people as sick. Moreover, like labels that suggest nonconformity or criminality, labels that are associated with illness commonly reshape how others treat us and how we see ourselves. Our society attaches serious consequences to labels that suggest less-than-perfect physical or mental health (H. Becker 1963; C. Clark 1983; H. Schwartz 1987).

A historical example illustrates perhaps the ultimate extreme in labeling social behavior as a sickness. As enslavement of Africans in the United States came under increasing attack in the 19th century, medical authorities provided new rationalizations for the oppressive practice. Noted physicians published articles stating that the skin color of Africans deviated from "healthy" white skin coloring because Africans suffered from congenital leprosy. Moreover, the continuing efforts of enslaved Africans to escape from their White masters were classified as an example of the "disease" of drapetomania (or "crazy runaways"). The prestigious *New Orleans Medical and Surgical Journal* suggested that the remedy for this "disease" was to treat slaves kindly, as one might treat children. Apparently, these medical authorities would not entertain the view that it was healthy and sane to flee slavery or join in a slave revolt (Szasz 1971).

According to labeling theorists, we can view a variety of life experiences as illnesses or not. Recently, premenstrual syndrome, post-traumatic stress disorders, and hyperactivity have been labeled medically recognized disorders. In addition, the medical community continues to disagree over whether chronic fatigue syndrome constitutes a medical illness.

Probably the most noteworthy medical example of labeling is the case of homosexuality. For years, psychiatrists classified being gay or lesbian not as a lifestyle but as a mental disorder subject to treatment. This official sanction became an early target of the growing gay and lesbian rights movement in the United States. In 1974, members of the American Psychiatric Association voted to drop homosexuality from the standard manual on mental disorders (Conrad 2009).

Table 19-2 summarizes four major sociological perspectives on health and illness. Although they may seem quite different, two common themes unite them. First, any person's health or illness is more than an organic condition, since it is subject to the interpretation of others. The impact of culture, family and friends, and the medical profession means that health and illness are not purely biological occurrences, but sociological occurrences as well. Second, since members of a society (especially industrial societies) share the same health care delivery system,

health is a group and societal concern. Although health may be defined as the complete well-being of an individual, it is also the result of his or her social environment, as the next section will show (Cockerham 2007).

Social Epidemiology and Health

Social epidemiology is the study of the distribution of disease, impairment, and general health status across a population. Initially, epidemiologists concentrated on the scientific study of epidemics, focusing on how they started and spread. Contemporary social epidemiology is much broader in scope, concerned not only with epidemics but also with nonepidemic diseases, injuries, drug addiction and alcoholism, suicide, and mental illness. Recently, epidemiologists took on the new role of tracking bioterrorism. In 2001 they mobilized to trace the anthrax outbreak and prepare for any terrorist use of smallpox or other lethal microbes. Epidemiologists draw on the work of a wide variety of scientists and researchers, among them physicians, sociologists, public health officials, biologists, veterinarians, demographers, anthropologists, psychologists, and meteorologists.

Researchers in social epidemiology commonly use two concepts: *incidence* and *prevalence*. **Incidence** refers to the number of new cases of a specific disorder that occur within a given population during a stated period, usually a year. For example, the incidence of AIDS in the United States in 2005 was 40,608 cases. In contrast, **prevalence** refers to the total number of cases of a specific disorder that exist at a given time. The prevalence of HIV/AIDS in the United States through 2008 was about 1 million cases. Worldwide, the prevalence of HIV/AIDS varies from less than 0.1 percent to 15–28 percent of a country's population (Figure 19-2 on page 424; Centers for Disease Control and Prevention 2007b).

When disease incidence figures are presented as rates, or as the number of reports per 100,000 people, they are called **morbidity rates**. The term **mortality rate** refers to the incidence of *death* in a given population. Sociologists find morbidity rates useful because they reveal that a specific disease occurs more frequently in one segment of a population than another. As we shall see, social class, race, ethnicity, gender, and age can all affect a population's morbidity rates. Box 19-1 on page 425 shows how sociology contributes to our understanding of the AIDS epidemic (Centers for Disease Control and Prevention 2007b).

MAPPING LIFE WORLDWIDE

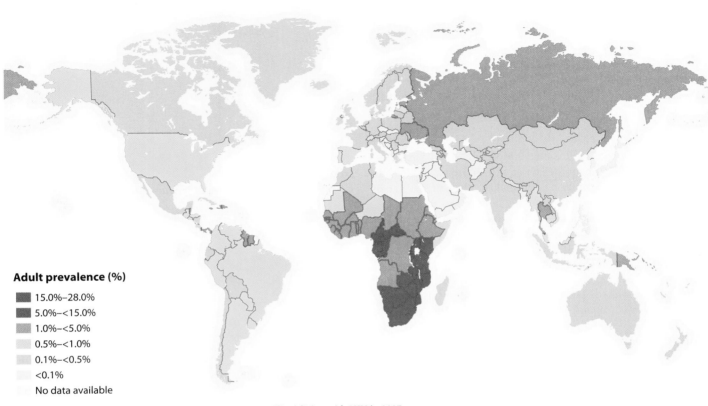

Adult prevalence (%)

- 15.0%–28.0%
- 5.0%–<15.0%
- 1.0%–<5.0%
- 0.5%–<1.0%
- 0.1%–<0.5%
- <0.1%
- No data available

Note: Data for the 33 million people (estimated range, 30–36 million) living with HIV in 2007.
Source: UNAIDS 2008.

Social Class

Social class is clearly associated with differences in morbidity and mortality rates. Studies in the United States and other countries have consistently shown that people in the lower classes have higher rates of mortality and disability than others.

Why is class linked to health? Crowded living conditions, substandard housing, poor diet, and stress all contribute to the ill health of many low-income people in the United States. In certain instances, poor education may lead to a lack of awareness of measures necessary to maintain good health. Financial strains are certainly a major factor in the health problems of less affluent people.

What is particularly troubling about social class differences is that they appear to be cumulative. Little or no health care in childhood or young adulthood is likely to mean more illness later in life. The longer that low income presents a barrier to adequate health care, the more chronic and difficult to treat illness becomes (Syme 2008).

Another reason for the link between social class and health is that the poor—many of whom belong to racial and ethnic minorities—are less able than others to afford quality medical care. As Figure 19-3 shows, the affluent are more likely than others to have health insurance, either because they can afford it or because they have jobs that provide it. This situation has been deteriorating over time, as employer-provided coverage (the most common form of health insurance) declined steadily from

When people who do not have health insurance seek medical care, their condition is often more critical than it would be had they been receiving regular preventive care from a primary care provider. And the care they receive, especially in an emergency room, is much more expensive than the care in a doctor's office.

RESEARCH TODAY

19-1 The AIDS Epidemic

AIDS is the acronym for acquired immune deficiency syndrome. Rather than being a distinct disease, AIDS is actually a predisposition to disease that is caused by a virus, the human immunodeficiency virus (HIV). The virus gradually destroys the body's immune system, leaving the carrier vulnerable to infections that those with healthy immune systems can generally resist, such as pneumonia. Transmission of the virus from one person to another appears to require either intimate sexual contact or an exchange of blood or bodily fluids. Contaminated hypodermic needles or syringes and transfusions of infected blood can transmit the virus. It can also be passed from an infected mother to her child either before or during birth.

The first cases of AIDS in the United States were reported in 1981. Although the numbers of new cases and deaths seem to be declining, still, more than 1 million people in the United States were living with AIDS or HIV by December 2008. Women account for a growing proportion of new cases, especially among racial and ethnic minorities. Worldwide, AIDS is stabilizing, with only gradual increases in reported cases. An estimated 33 million people are now infected. The disease is not evenly distributed, however. Those areas that are least equipped to deal with it—the developing nations of sub-Saharan Africa—face the greatest challenge (see Figure 19-2).

Dramatic crises like the AIDS epidemic are likely to transform a society's social structure.

From a functionalist perspective, if established social institutions cannot meet a crucial need, new social networks are likely to emerge to perform that function. In the case of AIDS, self-help groups have organized, especially in the gay communities of major cities, to care for the sick, educate the healthy, and lobby for more responsive public policies.

Viewed from a conflict perspective, policymakers were slow to respond to the AIDS crisis because those in high-risk groups—gay men and IV drug users—were comparatively powerless.

The label "person with AIDS" or "HIV-positive" often functions as a master status. From the labeling perspective, people who have AIDS or are infected with the virus face a powerful dual stigma. Not only are they associated with a lethal and contagious disease, but they have a disease that disproportionately afflicts already stigmatized groups, such as gay males and intravenous drug users. From the beginning, this link to stigmatized groups delayed recognition of the severity of the AIDS epidemic. Indeed, the media took little interest in the disease until it seemed to be spreading beyond the gay community.

Viewed from a conflict perspective, policymakers were slow to respond to the AIDS crisis because those in high-risk groups—gay men and IV drug users—were comparatively powerless. Furthermore, studies show that African Americans and Latinos are diagnosed later and are slower to receive treatment than other racial and ethnic groups. New programs have been launched to address this disparity in treatment.

On the micro level of social interaction, observers once forecasted that AIDS would lead to a more conservative sexual climate among both homosexuals and heterosexuals, in which people would be much more cautious about becoming involved with new partners. Yet it appears that many sexually active people in the United States have not heeded precautions about "safe sex." Data from studies conducted in the early 1990s indicated a growing complacency about AIDS, even among those who were most vulnerable.

LET'S DISCUSS

1. Do the people you know take few risks sexually because of the danger of becoming infected with the AIDS virus? If not, why not?
2. Aside from the obvious humanitarian reasons, why should the United States help developing countries in the fight against AIDS?

Sources: S. Bernstein 2004; Centers for Disease Control and Prevention 2008b; Glanton 2007; UNAIDS 2008.

FIGURE **19-3** PERCENTAGE OF PEOPLE WITHOUT HEALTH INSURANCE

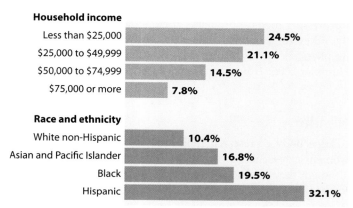

Source: Data for 2007 in DeNavas-Walt et al. 2008:22.

Think about It

Do you know people who don't have health insurance? If so, how has the lack of insurance affected their decisions about medical treatment?

2000 through 2007. In 2008, as a deep recession took hold, more and more people reported going without health care because they could not pay for it. And increasingly, pharmacists reported that people were purchasing only those medications they "needed the most," or were buying in small quantities, such as four pills at a time. Not surprisingly, these problems were most common among those with low incomes and among the growing numbers of unemployed. Yet simultaneously, the general public became less likely to support the federal government's role in ensuring health care for all, as Washington strained to deal with the growing economic challenge (DeNavas-Walt et al. 2008:20–21; Gallup 2009f; Gallup Healthways 2009; Sack 2009).

The most serious consequence of a lack of health insurance is a death that might have been prevented. Uninsured women who develop breast cancer tend to be diagnosed later—when treatment is less effective—than insured women. Uninsured men who develop high blood pressure are more likely than others to forgo screenings and medication, a decision that jeopardizes their health. The best estimates for 2006 place the number of preventable deaths among the uninsured at 22,000 (Dorn 2008).

Another discouraging aspect of the relationship between health and social class is the link between health and economic **425** mobility. Specifically, poor health has clearly been shown to hinder upward mobility. So we have a vicious cycle in which low-income people and the uninsured have the worst health, which in turn may limit their ability to escape poverty or even to obtain health insurance (Kronstadt 2008b).

In the view of Karl Marx and contemporary conflict theorists, capitalist societies such as the United States care more about maximizing profits than they do about the health and safety of industrial workers. As a result, government agencies do not take forceful action to regulate conditions in the workplace, and workers suffer many preventable job-related injuries and illnesses. As we will see later in this chapter, research also shows that the lower classes are more vulnerable to environmental pollution than are the affluent, not only where they work but where they live.

---

use your sociological *imagination*

Does the cost of health care affect the way you receive medical services?

Race and Ethnicity

The health profiles of many racial and ethnic minorities reflect the social inequality evident in the United States. The poor economic and environmental conditions of groups such as African Americans, Hispanics, and Native Americans are manifested in high morbidity and mortality rates for those groups. It is true that some afflictions, such as sickle-cell anemia among Blacks, have a clear genetic basis. But in most instances, environmental factors contribute to the differential rates of disease and death.

In many respects, the mortality rates for African Americans are distressing. Compared with Whites, Blacks have higher death rates from heart disease, pneumonia, diabetes, and cancer. The death rate from stroke is twice as high among African Americans. Such epidemiological findings reflect in part the fact that a high proportion of Blacks are found among the nation's lower classes. According to the National Center for Health Statistics, Whites can expect to live 74.7 years. In contrast, the life expectancy for Blacks is 71.7 years (Arias et al. 2008).

As noted earlier, infant mortality is regarded as a primary indicator of health care. There is a significant gap in the United States between the infant mortality rates of African Americans and Whites. Generally, the rate of infant death is more than twice as high among Blacks. African Americans account for 15 percent of all live births in the nation but 29 percent of infant deaths. Puerto Ricans and Native Americans have infant mortality rates that are lower than African Americans' but higher than Whites' (MacDorman et al. 2005).

The medical establishment is not exempt from racism. Unfortunately, the media often focus on obvious forms of racism, such as hate crimes, while overlooking more insidious forms in social institutions like the medical establishment. Minorities receive inferior medical care even when they are insured. Despite having access to care, Blacks, Latinos, and American Indians are treated unequally as a result of racial prejudice and differences in the quality of various health care plans. Furthermore, national clinical studies have shown that even allowing for differences in income and insurance coverage, racial and ethnic minorities are less likely than other groups to receive both standard health care and life-saving treatment for conditions such as HIV infection (Commonwealth Fund 2008; Long and Msai 2009; Mays et al. 2007; Weden 2007).

The roots of this unequal treatment extend back to slavery. Scholars from a variety of disciplines have investigated the history of African American health care and found some shocking abuses of the Hippocratic oath. Box 19-2 details the deliberate misuse of medicine that lies at the foundation of what some have called *medical apartheid*.

Drawing on the conflict perspective, sociologist Howard Waitzkin (1986) suggests that racial tensions also contribute to the medical problems of Blacks. In his view, the stress that results from racial prejudice and discrimination helps to explain the higher rates of hypertension found among African Americans (and Hispanics) compared to Whites. Hypertension—twice as common in Blacks as in Whites—is believed to be a critical factor in Blacks' high mortality rates from heart disease, kidney disease, and stroke (Morehouse Medical Treatment and Effectiveness Center 1999).

Some Mexican Americans and many other Latinos adhere to cultural beliefs that make them less likely to use the established medical system. They may interpret their illnesses according to traditional Latino folk medicine, or **curanderismo**—a form of holistic health care and healing. *Curanderismo* influences how one approaches health care and even how one defines illness. Most Hispanics probably use folk healers, or *curanderos,* infrequently, but perhaps 20 percent rely on home remedies. Some define such illnesses as *susto* (fright sickness) and *atague* (or fighting attack) according to folk beliefs. Because these complaints often have biological bases, sensitive medical practitioners need to deal with them carefully in order to diagnose and treat illnesses accurately. Moreover, it would be a mistake to blame the poor health care that Latinos receive on cultural differences. Latinos are much more likely to seek treatment for pressing medical problems at clinics and emergency rooms than they are to receive regular preventive care through a family physician (Council on Scientific Affairs 1999; Durden and Hummer 2006; Trotter and Chavira 1997).

Gender

A large body of research indicates that compared with men, women experience a higher prevalence of many illnesses, although they tend to live longer. There are some variations—for example, men are more likely to have parasitic diseases, whereas women are more likely to become diabetic—but as a group, women appear to be in poorer health than men.

The apparent inconsistency between the ill health of women and their greater longevity deserves an explanation, and researchers have advanced a theory. Women's lower rate of cigarette smoking (reducing their risk of heart disease, lung cancer, and emphysema), lower consumption of alcohol (reducing the risk of auto accidents and cirrhosis of the liver), and lower rate of

RESEARCH TODAY

19-2 Medical Apartheid

Numerous studies have shown that even when medical care is accessible to African Americans, many are reluctant to trust the U.S. medical establishment. From seeking medical care to giving blood or signing an organ donation card, African Americans are less likely than others to participate in life-saving medical programs. Unfortunately, there appears to be good reason for their reluctance to take advantage of a world-class medical system: a long and continuing history of mistreatment. Banned from medical schools, denied access to "White blood" as soldiers until after World War II, and prohibited from joining the American Medical Association until the 1960s, Blacks have long suffered from explicit discrimination at the hands of the medical establishment.

Even so, their wary attitude toward medicine has more to do with the way African Americans have been treated as patients. In the notorious Tuskegee syphilis study, begun by the federal government in 1932, doctors knowingly infected Black men from Alabama with syphilis in order to observe the disease's progression. Despite the discovery of antibiotic treatments for the disease in 1945, the men did not receive medical treatment until the press exposed the unethical program in 1972. This deliberate abuse of African Americans' human rights has made contemporary Blacks particularly leery of the medical establishment.

Regrettably, Tuskegee was not an isolated case, nor was it the first or the last. For generations before Tuskegee, medical practitioners' role with respect to people of color was either to verify their worth as slaves, by certifying them as healthy, or to determine whether they were truly sick or feigning illness to avoid slave labor.

Even after Tuskegee was exposed, the abuse continued. In Baltimore in 1991, in a program that was applauded by some observers as a way to "reduce the underclass," researchers implanted the now-defunct birth control device Norplant in African American teenagers. And from 1992 to 1997, in a study meant to determine whether there is a biological or genetic basis for violent behavior, researchers at Columbia University misled the parents of their young subjects, all of whom were Black males, by telling them that the

In the notorious Tuskegee syphilis study, begun by the federal government in 1932, doctors knowingly infected Black men from Alabama with syphilis in order to observe the disease's progression.

children would undergo no more than a series of tests and questions. In fact, the boys were given potentially risky doses of the same drug found in the now-banned Fen-phen weight-loss pill, which causes heart irregularities.

Given these ethical violations, the Black community's suspicious attitude toward the medical community is understandable. Unfortunately, their absence from research trials has also hurt them. Only 1 percent of the nearly 20 million Americans currently enrolled in biomedical studies and clinical trials is Black. Yet research shows that in well-managed clinical trials, African Americans' participation is no different from that of Whites; they are simply less likely than other groups to be included. Thus,

Blacks often miss out on the latest medical breakthroughs. Virtually no Blacks were included in the original studies of the HIV inhibitor AZT, for example. Because the Food and Drug Administration had little evidence of its impact on Black patients when the drug came into widespread use in 1991, the agency erroneously reported that it was ineffective in the treatment of African Americans.

In sum, medical abuse of the African American community is not some distant historical fact. Observers maintain that rather than leaving the issue to journalists and historians, the medical profession should acknowledge the flagrant mistakes of the past, along with the more subtle ones of today. For this community to be healed, the focus must shift from Black Americans' well-publicized concerns about medicine to the demonstrated untrustworthiness of U.S. medical research.

LET'S DISCUSS

1. Do you know anyone who has experienced deliberately inferior or unethical medical treatment? If so, do you think that racism was the reason for the mistreatment? Were any other factors involved?
2. Drawing on what you have learned in this course, what, other than racism, do you think might explain the behavior of the doctors who agreed to participate in experiments that clearly violated their professional oaths?

Sources: Centers for Disease Control and Prevention 2007; Goodwin 2006; Head 2007; Lewis-Elligan 2008; Reverby 2000; Washington 2007; Richard Williams 2007.

---

employment in dangerous occupations explain about one-third of their greater longevity than men. Moreover, some clinical studies suggest that the differences in morbidity may actually be less pronounced than the data show. Researchers argue that women are much more likely than men to seek treatment, to be diagnosed as having a disease, and thus to have their illnesses reflected in the data examined by epidemiologists.

From a conflict perspective, women have been particularly vulnerable to the medicalization of society, with everything from birth to beauty being treated in an increasingly medical context. Such medicalization may contribute to women's higher morbidity rates compared to those of men. Ironically, even though women have been especially affected by medicalization, medical researchers have often excluded them from clinical studies. Female physicians and researchers charge that sexism lies at the heart of such research practices, and insist

there is a desperate need for studies of female subjects (Rieker and Bird 2000).

Age

Health is the overriding concern of the elderly. Most older people in the United States report having at least one chronic illness, but only some of those conditions are potentially life threatening or require medical care. At the same time, health problems can affect the quality of life of older people in important ways. Almost half of older people in the United States are troubled by arthritis, and many have visual or hearing impairments that can interfere with the performance of everyday tasks.

Older people are also especially vulnerable to certain mental health problems. Alzheimer's disease, the leading cause of dementia in the United States, afflicts an estimated 5 million people age 65 or over—that is, 13 percent of that segment of the population.

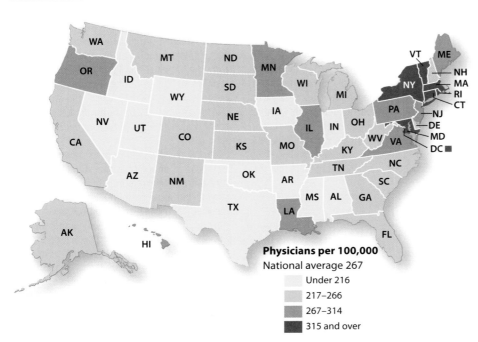

MAPPING LIFE NATIONWIDE

Physicians per 100,000
National average 267

- Under 216
- 217–266
- 267–314
- 315 and over

Source: Data for 2006 in Bureau of the Census 2008a:109.

The rising costs of medical care are especially burdensome in the event of catastrophic illnesses or confinement to a nursing home. Bills of tens of thousands of dollars are not unusual in the treatment of cancer, Alzheimer's disease, and other chronic illnesses requiring custodial care.

The health care system of the United States has moved far beyond the days when general practitioners living in a neighborhood or community typically made house calls and charged modest fees for their services. How did health care become a big business involving nationwide hospital chains and marketing campaigns? How have these changes reshaped the interactions between doctors, nurses, and patients? We will address these questions in the next section of the chapter.

A Historical View

Today, state licensing and medical degrees confer an authority on medical professionals that is maintained from one generation to the next. However, health care in the United States has not always followed this model. The "popular health movement" of the 1830s and 1840s emphasized preventive care and what is termed "self-help." Strong criticism was voiced of "doctoring" as a paid occupation. New medical philosophies or sects established their own medical schools and challenged the authority and methods of more traditional doctors. By the 1840s, most states had repealed medical licensing laws.

In response, through the leadership of the American Medical Association (AMA), founded in 1848, "regular" doctors attacked lay practitioners, sectarian doctors, and female physicians in

While some individuals with Alzheimer's exhibit only mild symptoms, the risk of severe problems resulting from the disease rises substantially with age (Alzheimer's Association 2008:9).

Not surprisingly, older people in the United States (age 75 and older) are five times more likely to use health services than younger people (ages 15–24). The disproportionate use of the U.S. health care system by older people is a critical factor in all discussions about the cost of health care and possible reforms of the health care system (Bureau of the Census 2008a:111).

In sum, to achieve greater access and reduce health disparities, federal health officials must overcome inequities that are rooted not just in age, but in social class, race and ethnicity, and gender. If that were not enough, they must also deal with a geographical disparity in health care resources. Figure 19-4 shows the differences in the presence of physicians from one state to another. Dramatic differences in the availability of physicians, hospitals, and nursing homes also exist between urban and rural areas in the same state.

Health Care in the United States

As the entire nation is well aware, the costs of health care have skyrocketed in the past 35 years. In 1997, total expenditures for health care in the United States crossed the trillion-dollar threshold—more than four times the 1980 figure (Figure 19-5). In 2000, the amount spent on health care equaled that spent on education, defense, prisons, farm subsidies, food stamps, and foreign aid combined. By the year 2017, total expenditures for health care in the United States are expected to exceed $4.2 trillion.

FIGURE 19-5 TOTAL HEALTH CARE EXPENDITURES IN THE UNITED STATES, 1970–2017 (PROJECTED)

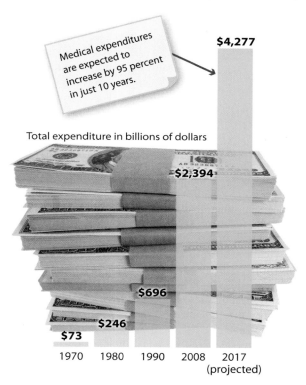

Medical expenditures are expected to increase by 95 percent in just 10 years.

$4,277

Total expenditure in billions of dollars

$2,394

$696

$246

$73

| 1970 | 1980 | 1990 | 2008 | 2017 (projected) |

Sources: Centers for Medicare and Medicaid Services 2008:Table 1 (2008–2017 data); Health Care Financing Administration 2001 (1970–1990 data).

Think about It

What social changes in the United States might account for the rise in health care costs from $73 billion in 1970 to almost 2.4 trillion in 2008?

general. Once they had institutionalized their authority through standardized programs of education and licensing, they conferred it on all who successfully completed their programs. The authority of the physician no longer depended on lay attitudes or on the person occupying the sick role; increasingly, it was built into the structure of the medical profession and the health care system. As the institutionalization of health care proceeded, the medical profession gained control over both the market for its services and the various organizational hierarchies that govern medical practice, financing, and policymaking. By the 1920s, physicians controlled hospital technology, the division of labor of health personnel, and indirectly, other professional practices such as nursing and pharmacy (R. Coser 1984).

Physicians, Nurses, and Patients

Traditionally, physicians have held a position of dominance in their dealings with both patients and nurses. The functionalist and interactionist perspectives offer a framework for understanding the professional socialization of physicians as it relates to patient care. Functionalists suggest that established physicians and medical school professors serve as mentors or role models who transmit knowledge, skills, and values to the passive learner—the medical student. Interactionists emphasize that students are molded by the medical school environment as they interact with their classmates.

Both approaches argue that the typical training of physicians in the United States leads to rather dehumanizing physician–patient encounters. As Dr. Lori Arviso Alvord writes in *The Scalpel and the Silver Bear,* "I had been trained by a group of physicians who placed much more emphasis on their technical abilities and clinical skills than on their abilities to be caring and sensitive" (Alvord and Van Pelt 1999:13). Despite many efforts to formally introduce a humanistic approach to patient care into the medical school curriculum, patient overload and cost-cutting by hospitals have tended to undercut positive relations. Moreover, widespread publicity about malpractice suits and high medical costs has further strained the physician–patient relationship. Interactionists have closely examined compliance and negotiation between physician and patient. They concur with Talcott Parsons's view that the relationship is generally asymmetrical, with doctors holding a position of dominance and controlling rewards.

Just as physicians have maintained dominance in their interactions with patients, they have controlled interactions with nurses. Despite their training and professional status, nurses commonly take orders from physicians. Traditionally, the relationship between doctors and nurses has paralleled the male dominance of the United States: most physicians have been male, while virtually all nurses have been female.

Like other women in subordinate roles, nurses have been expected to perform their duties without challenging the authority of men. Psychiatrist Leonard Stein (1967) refers to this process as the *doctor–nurse game.* According to the rules of this "game," the nurse must never openly disagree with the physician. When she has recommendations concerning a patient's care, she must communicate them indirectly, in a deferential tone. For example,

As if the status differences between nurses and physicians were not clear to all, the cheery uniform of nurses and the formal white doctor's coat reinforce the distinction.

if asked by a hospital's medical resident, "What sleeping medication has been helpful to Mrs. Brown in the past?" (an indirect request for a recommendation), the nurse will respond with a disguised recommendation, such as "Pentobarbital 100 mg was quite effective night before last." Her careful response allows the physician to authoritatively restate the same prescription as if it were *his* idea.

Like nurses, female physicians have traditionally found themselves in a subordinate position because of gender. In fall 2008, 48 percent of all new medical school students in the United States were female, along with 34 percent of all faculty members at medical schools. A study of male and female medical residents suggests that the increasing number of women physicians may alter the traditional doctor–patient relationship. Male residents were found to be more focused on the intellectual challenges of medicine and the prestige associated with certain medical specialties. In contrast, female residents were more likely to express a commitment to caring for patients and devoting time to them. In terms of the functionalist analysis of gender stratification offered by sociologists Talcott Parsons and Robert Bales, male residents took the *instrumental,* achievement-oriented role, while female residents took the *expressive,* interpersonal-oriented role. As women continue to enter and move higher in the hierarchies of the medical profession, sociological studies will surely be done to see whether these apparent gender differences persist (Association of American Medical Colleges 2008, 2009).

Patients have traditionally relied on medical personnel to inform them of health care issues, but increasingly they are turning to the media for health care information. Recognizing this change, pharmaceutical firms are advertising their prescription drugs directly to potential customers through television and magazines. The Internet is another growing source for patient information. Medical professionals are understandably suspicious of these new sources of information. A study published in the *Journal of the American Medical Association* in 2001 found that health information on the Internet is often incomplete and inaccurate, even on the best sites. Nevertheless, there is little doubt that Web research is transforming an increasing proportion of patient–physician encounters, as patients arrive for their doctor's appointments armed with the latest printout from the Internet (Berland 2001; Gerencher 2007).

use your sociological *imagination*

If you were a patient, would you put yourself entirely in the physician's hands? Or would you do some research about your illness on your own? If you were a doctor, would you want your patient checking medical information on the Internet? Explain your positions.

Alternatives to Traditional Health Care

In traditional forms of health care, people rely on physicians and hospitals for the treatment of illness. Yet at least one out of every three adults in the United States attempts to maintain good health or respond to illness through the use of alternative health care techniques. For example, in recent decades interest has been growing in *holistic* (also spelled *wholistic*) medical principles, first developed in China. **Holistic medicine** refers to therapies in which the health care practitioner considers the person's physical, mental, emotional, and spiritual characteristics. The individual is regarded as a totality rather than a collection of interrelated organ systems. Treatment methods include massage, chiropractic medicine, acupuncture (which involves the insertion of fine needles into surface points), respiratory exercises, and the use of herbs as remedies. Nutrition, exercise, and visualization may also be used to treat ailments that are generally treated through medication or hospitalization (Sharma and Bodeker 1998).

The Navajo concept of *hózhǫ́* (walking in beauty) is another example of a holistic approach to health (see the chapter introduction). Practitioners of holistic medicine do not necessarily function totally outside the traditional health care system. Some, like Dr. Lori Arviso Alvord, have medical degrees and rely on X-rays and EKG machines for diagnostic assistance. Others who staff holistic clinics, often referred to as *wellness clinics,* reject the use of medical technology. The recent resurgence of holistic medicine comes amid widespread recognition of the value of nutrition and the dangers of overreliance on prescription drugs (especially those used to reduce stress, such as Valium).

The medical establishment—professional organizations, research hospitals, and medical schools—has generally served as a stern protector of traditionally accepted health care techniques. However, a major breakthrough occurred in 1992 when the federal government's National Institutes of Health—the nation's major funding source for biomedical research—opened an Office of Alternative Medicine, empowered to accept grant requests. NIH-sponsored national surveys conducted in 2002 and 2007 found that one in four adults in the United States had used some form of "complementary and alternative medicine" during the previous month or year. Examples included acupuncture, folk medicine, meditation, yoga, homeopathic treatments, megavitamin therapy, and chiropractic treatment. When prayer was included as an alternative or complementary form of medicine, the proportion of adults who used alternative medicine rose to over 62 percent (Figure 19-6).

On the international level, the World Health Organization (WHO) has begun to monitor the use of alternative medicine around the world. According to WHO, 80 percent of people who live in the poorest countries in the world use some form of alternative medicine, from herbal treatments to the services of a faith healer. In most countries, these treatments are largely unregulated, even though some of them can be fatal. For

FIGURE 19-6 USE OF COMPLEMENTARY AND ALTERNATIVE MEDICINE

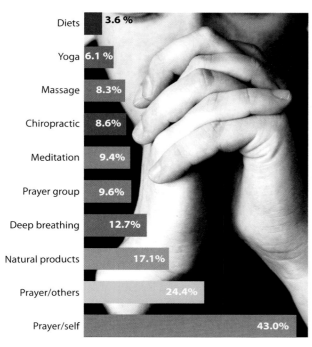

Diets	3.6 %
Yoga	6.1 %
Massage	8.3%
Chiropractic	8.6%
Meditation	9.4%
Prayer group	9.6%
Deep breathing	12.7%
Natural products	17.1%
Prayer/others	24.4%
Prayer/self	43.0%

Note: Data from 2007 survey, except for prayer data from 2002 survey.
Source: Barnes et al. 2004, 2008.

example, Kavakava, an herbal tea used in the Pacific Islands to relieve anxiety, can be toxic to the liver in concentrated form. But other alternative treatments have been found to be effective in the treatment of serious diseases, such as malaria and sickle-cell anemia. WHO's goal is to compile a list of such practices, as well as to encourage the development of universal training programs and ethical standards for practitioners of alternative medicine. To date, the organization has published findings on about 100 of the 5,000 plants believed to be used as herbal remedies (McNeil 2002).

The Role of Government

Not until the 20th century did health care receive federal aid. The first significant involvement was the 1946 Hill-Burton Act, which provided subsidies for building and improving hospitals, especially in rural areas. A far more important change came with the enactment in 1965 of two wide-ranging government assistance programs: Medicare, which is essentially a compulsory health insurance plan for the elderly, and Medicaid, which is a noncontributory federal and state insurance plan for the poor. These programs greatly expanded federal involvement in health care financing for needy men, women, and children.

Given the high rates of illness and disability among elderly people, Medicare has had a huge impact on the health care system. Initially, Medicare simply reimbursed health care providers such as physicians and hospitals for the billed costs of their services. However, in 1983, as the overall costs of Medicare increased dramatically, the federal government introduced a price-control system. Under this system, private hospitals often transfer patients whose treatment may be unprofitable to public facilities. In fact, many private hospitals have begun to conduct "wallet biopsies"—that is, to investigate the financial status of potential patients. Those judged undesirable are then refused admission or dumped. Although a federal law passed in 1987 made it illegal for any hospital receiving Medicare funds to dump patients, the practice continues (E. Gould 2007; Light 2004).

Mental Illness in the United States

The words *mental illness* and *insanity* evoke dramatic and often inaccurate images of emotional problems. Though the media routinely emphasize the most violent behavior of those with emotional disturbances, mental health and mental illness can more appropriately be viewed as a continuum of behavior that we ourselves move along. Using this definition, we can consider a person to have a mental disorder "if he or she is so disturbed that coping with routine, everyday life is difficult or impossible." The term **mental illness** should be reserved for a disorder of the brain that disrupts a person's thinking, feeling, and ability to interact with others (J. Coleman and Cressey 1980:315; National Alliance for the Mentally Ill 2000).

How prevalent is mental illness? According to the World Bank, mental disorders are a significant cause of disability in industrial economies. In the United States, about one out of every four Americans suffers from some form of mental illness. Yet in industrial countries, less than half of all serious cases receive any kind of treatment. In developing nations, the percentage is only one-fifth (World Health Organization 2004; P. Wing et al. 2007).

People in the United States have traditionally maintained a negative and suspicious view of those with mental disorders. Holding the status of "mental patient" or even "former mental patient" can have unfortunate and undeserved consequences. Voting rights are denied in some instances, acceptance for jury duty is problematic, and past emotional problems are an issue in divorce and custody cases. Moreover, content analysis of network television programs and films shows that mentally ill characters are uniformly portrayed in a demeaning and derogatory fashion; many are labeled as "criminally insane," "wackos," or "psychos." From an interactionist perspective, a key social institution is shaping social behavior by manipulating symbols and intensifying people's fears about the mentally ill (Diefenbach and West 2007).

Despite this stigmatization of mental illness, more people are seeking care and professional assistance than in the past. In the military services, the depression and post-traumatic stress that many veterans experience is receiving growing attention. And increasingly, legislators are recognizing the need to provide services for all who suffer from mental illness (Kessler 2006; Tanielian 2009).

Even so, the need for mental health care seems to outstrip the available resources. In 2009, for example, mental health professionals expressed concern for the well-being of children and adults who had been displaced by Hurricane Katrina. In the aftermath of the disaster, residents of New Orleans were displaying unusually high levels of depression, anxiety, suicide, drug and alcohol abuse, and other high-risk behaviors. The crisis called for new intervention strategies, but the city's health care system was already overwhelmed (Abramson et al. 2007; Guarino 2009; Waelde et al. 2009).

Theoretical Models of Mental Disorders

In studying mental illness, we can draw on both a medical model and a more sociological approach derived from labeling theory. Each model rests on distinctive assumptions regarding treatment of people with mental disorders.

According to the *medical model,* mental illness is rooted in biological causes that can be treated through medical intervention. Problems in brain structure or in the biochemical balance in the brain, sometimes due to injury and sometimes due to genetic inheritance, are thought to be at the bottom of these disorders. The U.S. Surgeon General (1999) released an exhaustive report on mental health in which he declared that the accumulated weight of scientific evidence leaves no doubt about the physical origins of mental illness.

Social factors such as war can jeopardize a person's mental health. Many people who once lived in war zones, like these Sundanese fleeing the horrors of genocide in Darfur, later suffer from symptoms of severe mental trauma, including depression, nightmares, and flashbacks to violent events.

That is not to say that social factors do not contribute to mental illness. Just as culture affects the incidence and prevalence of illness in general, its treatment, and the expression of certain culture-bound syndromes, so too it can affect mental illness. In fact, the very definition of mental illness differs from one culture to the next. Mainstream U.S. culture, for instance, considers hallucinations highly abnormal. But many traditional cultures view them as evidence of divine favor, and confer a special status on those who experience them. As we have noted throughout this textbook, a given behavior may be viewed as normal in one society, disapproved of but tolerated in a second, and labeled as sick and heavily sanctioned in a third.

In contrast to the medical model, *labeling theory* suggests that some behaviors that are viewed as mental illnesses may not really be illnesses, since the individual's problems arise from living in society and not from physical maladies. For example, the U.S. Surgeon General's report (1999:5) notes that "bereavement symptoms" of less than two months' duration do not qualify as a mental disorder, but beyond that they may be redefined. Sociologists would see this approach to bereavement as labeling by those with the power to affix labels rather than as an acknowledgment of a biological condition.

Psychiatrist Thomas Szasz (1974), in his book *The Myth of Mental Illness,* which first appeared in 1961, advanced the view that numerous personality disorders are not diseases, but simply patterns of conduct labeled as disorders by significant others. The response to Szasz's challenging thesis was sharp: the commissioner of the New York State Department of Hygiene demanded his dismissal from his university position because Szasz did not "believe" in mental illness. But many sociologists embraced his model as a logical extension of examining individual behavior in a social context.

In sum, the medical model is persuasive because it pinpoints the causes of mental illness and offers treatment for disorders. Yet proponents of the labeling perspective maintain that mental illness is a distinctively social process, whatever other processes are involved. From a sociological perspective, the ideal approach to mental illness integrates the insights of labeling theory with those of the medical approach (Horwitz 2002).

Patterns of Care

For most of human history, those who suffered from mental disorders were deemed the responsibility of their families. Yet mental illness has been a matter of governmental concern much longer than physical illness has. That is because severe emotional disorders threaten stable social relationships and entail prolonged incapacitation. As early as the 1600s, European cities began to confine the insane in public facilities along with the poor and criminals. Prisoners, indignant at being forced to live with "lunatics," resisted this approach. The isolation of the mentally ill from others in the same facility and from the larger society soon made physicians the central and ultimate authority over their welfare.

A major policy development in caring for those with mental disorders came with the passage of the Community Mental Health Centers Act (1963). The CMHC program, as it is known, not only increased the federal government's involvement in the treatment of the mentally ill. It also established community-based mental health centers to treat clients on an *outpatient* basis, thereby allowing them to continue working and living at home. The program showed that outpatient treatment could be more effective than the institutionalized programs of state and county mental hospitals.

Expansion of the federally funded CMHC program decreased inpatient care. By the 1980s, community-based mental health care had replaced hospitalization as the typical form of treatment. Across the United States, deinstitutionalization of the mentally ill reached dramatic proportions. State mental hospitals that had held almost 560,000 long-term patients in 1955 had fewer than 63,000 by 1998. Deinstitutionalization had been conceived as a social reform that would effectively reintegrate the mentally ill into the outside world. However, the authentic humanitarian concern behind deinstitutionalization proved to be a convenient front for politicians whose goal was simply cost cutting (Bureau of the Census 2002:117; Grob 1995).

In a marked shift from public policy over the past three decades, several states have recently made it easier to commit mental patients to hospitals involuntarily. These changes have

At a community mental health center, outpatients create a newsletter for their day program. In the 1980s, community-based mental health care replaced hospitalization as the typical form of treatment for people with serious mental illnesses.

come in part because community groups and individual residents have voiced increasing fear and anger about the growing number of mentally ill homeless people living in their midst, many of them on the streets. All too often, the severely mentally ill end up in jail or prison after committing crimes that lead to their prosecution. Ironically, family members of these mentally ill men and women complain that they cannot get adequate treatment for their loved ones *until* they have committed violent acts. Nevertheless, civil liberties advocates and voluntary associations of mentally ill people worry about the risks of denying people their constitutional rights, and cite horror stories about the abuses people have experienced during institutionalization (Marquis and Morain 1999; Shogren 1994).

Finally, although mental health care is often considered to be qualitatively different from other types of health care, many of the observations that apply to traditional medicine also apply to mental health care. For example, African Americans, Latinos, and American Indians have higher prevalence rates for several mental disorders, but are much less likely than Whites to receive treatment. Documented prejudice by practitioners contributes to the disparity, along with inadequate insurance and geographic isolation. In both rural and inner-city areas, mental health care is difficult to access and often poor in quality, especially for members of minority groups (McGuire and Miranda 2008).

use your sociological *imagination*

How are your views of mental illness different from or similar to your views of physical illness?

Sociological Perspectives on the Environment

We have seen that the environment people live in has a noticeable effect on their health. Those who live in stressful, overcrowded places suffer more from disease than those who do not. Likewise,

people have a noticeable effect on their environment. Around the world, increases in population, together with the economic development that accompanies them, have had serious environmental consequences. We can see signs of despoliation almost everywhere: our air, our water, and our land are being polluted, whether we live in St. Louis, Mexico City, or Lagos, Nigeria.

Though environmental problems may be easy to identify, devising socially and politically acceptable solutions to them is much more difficult. In this section we will see what sociologists have to say about the trade-off between economic growth and development and its effects on the environment. In the section that follows we will look more closely at specific environmental problems.

Human Ecology

Human ecology is an area of study that is concerned with the interrelationships between people and their environment. As the environmentalist Barry Commoner (1971:39) put it, "Everything is connected to everything else." Human ecologists focus on how the physical environment shapes people's lives and on how people influence the surrounding environment.

In an application of the human ecological perspective, sociologists and environmentalists have identified several relationships

In a makeshift recycling center, a Chinese woman uses a hammer to open an old cathode ray tube. She wants the copper that is inside, but in the process she will release several pounds of lead into the soil and groundwater. Scientists have found alarmingly high levels of toxic heavy metals in the rivers that flow by such rural recycling operations.

between the environment and people. Among them are the following:

1. **The environment provides the resources essential for life.** These include air, water, and materials used to create shelter, transportation, and needed products. If human societies exhaust these resources—for example, by polluting the water supply or cutting down rain forests—the consequences could be dire.

2. **The environment serves as a waste repository.** More so than other living species, humans produce a huge quantity and variety of waste products—bottles, boxes, papers, sewage, garbage, and so on. Various types of pollution have become more common because human societies are generating more wastes than the environment can safely absorb.

3. **The environment "houses" our species.** It is our home, our living space, the place where we reside, work, and play. At times we take this truism for granted, but not when day-to-day living conditions become unpleasant and difficult. If our air is "heavy," if our tap water turns brown, if toxic chemicals seep into our neighborhood, we remember why it is vital to live in a healthful environment.

There is no shortage of illustrations of the interconnectedness of people and their environment. For example, scientific research has linked pollutants in the physical environment to people's health and behavior. The increasing prevalence of asthma, lead poisoning, and cancer have all been tied to human alterations to the environment. Similarly, the rise in melanoma (skin cancer) diagnoses has been linked to global warming. And ecological changes in our food and diet have been related to early obesity and diabetes.

With its view that "everything is connected to everything else," human ecology stresses the trade-offs inherent in every decision that alters the environment. In facing the environmental challenges of the 21st century, government policymakers and environmentalists must determine how they can fulfill humans' pressing needs for food, clothing, and shelter while

preserving the environment as a source of resources, a waste repository, and our home.

Conflict View of the Environment

In Chapter 10 we drew on world systems analysis to show how a growing share of the human and natural resources of developing countries is being redistributed to the core industrialized nations. This process only intensifies the destruction of natural resources in poorer regions of the world. From a conflict perspective, less affluent nations are being forced to exploit their mineral deposits, forests, and fisheries in order to meet their debt obligations. The poor turn to the only means of survival available to them: they plow mountain slopes, burn plots in tropical forests, and overgraze grasslands (Livernash and Rodenburg 1998).

Brazil exemplifies this interplay between economic troubles and environmental destruction. Each year more than 5.7 million acres of forest are cleared for crops and livestock. The elimination of the rain forest affects worldwide weather patterns, heightening the gradual warming of the earth. These socioeconomic patterns, with their harmful environmental consequences, are evident not only in Latin America but in many regions of Africa and Asia.

Although deforestation of the rain forest has long been a concern, only in the past few years have policymakers begun to listen to the indigenous peoples who live in these areas. In 2008, native peoples from Brazil, the Congo, and Indonesia convened to make the case that wealthier countries should compensate them for conservation of the tropical rain forests. Preservation of the rain forests may make sense at the global level, but for many local peoples, it limits their efforts to cultivate crops or graze cattle (Barrionuevo 2008).

Conflict theorists are well aware of the environmental implications of land use policies in the Third World, but they contend that focusing on the developing countries is ethnocentric. Who, they ask, is more to blame for environmental deterioration: the poverty-stricken and "food-hungry" populations of the world or the "energy-hungry" industrialized nations? These theorists point out that the industrialized nations of North America and Europe account for only 12 percent of the world's population but are responsible for 60 percent of worldwide consumption. The money their residents spend on ocean cruises each year could provide clean drinking water for everyone on the planet. Ice cream expenditures in Europe alone could be used to immunize every child in the world. Thus, conflict theorists charge, the most serious threat to the environment comes from the global consumer class (Gardner et al. 2004).

Allan Schnaiberg (1994) further refined this analysis by shifting the focus from affluent consumers to the capitalist system as the cause of environmental troubles. In his view, a capitalist system creates a "treadmill of production" because of its inherent need to build ever-expanding profits. This treadmill necessitates the creation of increasing demand for products, the purchase of natural resources at minimal cost, and the manufacturing of products as quickly and cheaply as possible—no matter what the long-term environmental consequences.

Environmental Justice

In autumn 1982, nearly 500 African Americans participated in a six-week protest against a hazardous waste landfill in North Carolina. Their protests and legal actions against the dangerous cancer-causing chemicals continued until 2002, when decontamination of the site finally began. This 20-year battle could be seen as yet another "not in my backyard" (NIMBY) event. But today, the Warren County struggle is viewed as a transformative moment in contemporary environmentalism: the beginning of the *environmental justice* movement (Bullard 1993; McGurty 2000; North Carolina Department of Environment and Natural Resources 2008).

Environmental justice is a legal strategy based on claims that racial minorities are subjected disproportionately to environmental hazards. Some observers have heralded environmental justice as the "new civil rights of the 21st century" (Kokmen 2008:42). Since the start of the environmental justice movement, activists and scholars have discovered other environmental disparities that break along racial and social class lines. In general, poor people and people of color are much more likely than others to be victimized by the everyday consequences of our built environment, including the air pollution from expressways and incinerators.

Sociologists Paul Mohai and Robin Saha (2007) examined over 600 identified hazardous waste treatment, storage, and disposal facilities in the United States. They found that non-Whites and Latinos make up 43 percent of the people who live within one mile of these dangerous sites. There are two possible explanations for this finding. Either racial and ethnic minorities possess less power than others, so that they cannot prevent toxic sites from being located in their backyards. Or they end up living near the sites after they are constructed, because economics and the forces of discrimination push them into the least desirable living areas.

Following reports from the Environmental Protection Agency (EPA) and other organizations documenting the discriminatory location of hazardous waste sites, President Bill Clinton issued an executive order in 1994 that requires all federal agencies to ensure that low-income and minority communities have access to better information about their environment and an opportunity to participate in shaping government policies that affect their health. Initial efforts to implement the policy, along with increased activity by the environmental justice movement, aroused widespread opposition because of the delays it imposes in establishing new industrial sites. Some observers question the wisdom of an order that slows economic development in areas that are in dire need of employment opportunities. Others point out that such businesses employ few unskilled or less skilled workers, and only make the environment less livable (Laszewski 2008; Stretesky 2006; D. Taylor 2000).

Meanwhile, the poor and oppressed continue to bear the brunt of environmental pollution. In the 1990s, the federal government, unable to find a disposal site for spent nuclear fuel, turned to tribal reservations. Agents eventually persuaded a tiny band of Goshute Indians in Skull Valley, Utah, to accept more than 44,000 barrels of the hot, highly radioactive substance, which will remain dangerous for an estimated 10,000 years. The government dropped the plan

From her apartment in Harlem, New York, environmental activist Millicent Redick looks out over a hazy skyline. Redick's home is located near a bus depot, whose fumes have been linked to her children's asthma.

> ## use your sociological *imagination*
>
> Your community has been designated as a site for the burial of toxic waste. How will you react? Will you organize a protest? Or will you make sure the authorities carry out the project safely? How can such sites be chosen fairly?

www.mhhe.com/schaefer12e

only after opposition from surrounding towns and cities, whose residents objected to the movement of the material through their communities. This was not the first time the nation attempted to persuade the impoverished tribe to accept environmentally objectionable installations. The military's nerve gas storage facility resides on or near the reservation, along with the Intermountain Power Project, which generates coal-fired electrical power for consumers in California (Eureka County 2006; Foy 2006).

Sociologists, then, have emphasized both the interconnectedness of humans and the environment and the divisiveness of race and social class in their work on humans and their alteration of the environment. Scientists, too, have taken different approaches, disagreeing sharply on the likely outcomes of environmental change. Of course, when their disagreements threaten to affect government policy and economic regulations, they become highly politicized. For some perspective on this struggle between environmental preservation and economic self-interest, let's revisit the Nacirema, introduced in the opening excerpt for Chapter 3. Box 19-3 on page 436 presents this unusual culture through the eyes of environmentalists.

Environmental Problems

Unfortunately, the environmental problems caused by unbridled development have effects far beyond the places where they are created. Witness Muhammad Ali, a Bangladeshi man who

SOCIOLOGY IN THE GLOBAL COMMUNITY

19-3 The Mysterious Fall of the Nacirema

Chapter 3 opened with anthropologist Horace Miner's description of the strange rituals practiced by the Nacirema (*American* spelled backward). Sixteen years after Miner first described the culture, American Studies scholar Neil B. Thompson wrote a follow-up article, "The Mysterious Fall of the Nacirema," that was in effect the culture's epitaph.

The Nacirema, Thompson wrote, were master engineers who had created extensive networks of "narrow ribbons, called streets," which covered the landscape. From the air, the ribbons around major population centers could be seen to be very elaborate. The purpose of these networks, Thompson speculated, might have been to promote the centralization of government or to separate "persons of lower caste" from others, in neighborhoods referred to as "ottehgs."

A special group of highly privileged priests, called the "ssenisub community," directed such massive projects. The priests lived in gated areas secured by electronic alarm systems. The ssenisub enjoyed complete freedom in creating their vast engineering marvels. "There is no evidence,"

Thompson wrote, "to suggest that any restraints—moral, sociological, or engineering—were placed on their self-determined enterprises."

Looking back over the past 300 "solar cycles" of the culture, Thompson noted that the Nacirema had devoted a great deal of time and attention to changing the color of the air and water. For the first 250 cycles they had little success, "but dur-

> *Looking back over the past 300 "solar cycles" of the culture, Thompson noted that the Nacirema had devoted a great deal of time and attention to changing the color of the air and water.*

ing the short period before the fall of the culture, they mastered their art magnificently," changing the water from bluish-green to reddish-brown and the air from blue to grayish-yellow.

To accomplish this great engineering feat, the Nacirema built huge plants near large cities.

"These plants constantly produced a variety of reagents . . . which were then pumped into the rivers and lakes or released into the atmosphere in the form of hot gases." To solve the problem of what to do with the by-products of these processes, the Nacirema distributed them to people's homes, where they were kept for a short time before being sent to a landfill.

Thompson wrote his article in 1972. To date, archeologists have not been able to explain the demise of this fascinating culture.

LET'S DISCUSS

1. Have you ever visited a foreign culture and been struck by something that seemed odd to you, but perfectly normal to everyone else? If so, did you discuss your reaction with others? Could they see your point of view?
2. If all of us could step back and take an objective look at what we are doing to the environment, would our society change for the better? Why or why not?

Sources: Miner 1956; N. Thompson 1972.

---

has had to flee flood waters five times in the past decade. Scientists believe that global warming is to blame, both for worsening monsoons and for the raging waters of the Jamuna River, swollen by abnormally high glacier melt from the Himalayas. Every time the river floods, Ali tears down his house, made of tin and bamboo, and moves to higher ground. But he is running out of land to move to. "Where we are standing, in five days it will be gone," he says. "Our future thinking is that if this problem is not taken care of, we will be swept away" (Goering 2007).

Increasingly, people are recognizing the need to address such challenges to the environment. Yet in the United States, survey respondents do not see environmental issues as the most pressing of problems, and they often balk at proposed solutions. In 2006, two-thirds of people in the United States were pessimistic about the environment. Yet in 2008, 49 percent of adults said that protection of the environment should be given priority. Forty-two percent said that the government should pursue economic growth even if the environment suffers. On the other hand, 63 percent agreed that the effects of global warming are already manifest, or will occur within five years (Gallup 2008e; Jacobe 2008).

We will discuss the enormous challenge of global warming in this section, along with three broad areas of environmental concern. Two of them, air and water pollution, are thought to be contributors to global warming.

Air Pollution

Worldwide, more than 1 billion people are exposed to potentially health-damaging levels of air pollution. Unfortunately, in cities around the world, residents have come to accept smog and polluted air as normal. Urban air pollution is caused primarily by emissions from automobiles and secondarily by emissions from electric power plants and heavy industries. Smog not only limits visibility; it can lead to health problems as uncomfortable as eye irritation and as deadly as lung cancer. Such problems are especially severe in developing countries. The World Health Organization estimates that up to 700,000 premature deaths *per year* could be prevented if pollutants were brought down to safer levels (Carty 1999; World Resources Institute 1998).

People are capable of changing their behavior, but they are also unwilling to make such changes permanent. During the 1984 Olympics in Los Angeles, residents were asked to carpool and stagger their work hours to relieve traffic congestion and improve the quality of the air athletes would breathe. These changes resulted in a remarkable 12 percent drop in ozone levels. But when the Olympians left, people reverted to their normal behavior and the ozone levels climbed back up. Similarly, in the 2008 Olympics, China took drastic action to ensure that Beijing's high levels of air pollution did not mar the games. Construction work in the city ceased, polluting factories and power plants closed down, and roads were swept and sprayed with water several times a day. But this temporary solution hardly solved China's ongoing problem (*The Economist* 2008b).

On an everyday basis—that is, when cities are not holding down their emissions because of global sports events—air pollution is still a serious issue in the United States. According to a study published in 2009, 6 out of every 10 people in the United States live in communities with dangerously high levels of air

pollution, either short-term or year-round. Solutions range from community efforts to clean up power plants and enforce or strengthen air quality standards to individual actions, like driving less often or using less electricity (American Lung Association 2009; *The Economist* 2008b).

Water Pollution

Throughout the United States, dumping of waste materials by industries and local governments has polluted streams, rivers, and lakes. Consequently, many bodies of water have become unsafe for drinking, fishing, and swimming. Around the world, pollution of the oceans is an issue of growing concern. Such pollution results regularly from waste dumping and is made worse by fuel leaks from shipping and occasional oil spills. When the oil tanker *Exxon Valdez* ran aground in Prince William Sound, Alaska, in 1989, its cargo of 11 million gallons of crude oil spilled into the sound and washed onto the shore, contaminating 1,285 miles of shoreline. All together, about 11,000 people joined in a massive cleanup effort that cost over $2 billion. Globally, oil spills occur regularly. In 2002 the oil tanker *Prestige* spilled twice as much fuel as the *Valdez*, greatly damaging coastal areas in Spain and France (ITOPF 2006).

Less dramatic than large-scale accidents or disasters, but more common in many parts of the world, are problems with the basic water supply. Worldwide, over 1.1 billion people lack safe and adequate drinking water, and 2.6 billion have no acceptable means of sanitation—a problem that further threatens the quality of water supplies. The health costs of unsafe water are enormous (United Nations Development Programme 2006).

Like so many other valuable resources, water is a highly contested commodity in many parts of the world. In the United States, competition over water is intense, especially in booming Las Vegas and the Southwest. In the Middle East, the immense political challenges posed by ethnic and religious conflict are often complicated by battles over water. There, competing nations accuse each other of taking unfair advantage of existing water supplies, and water tanks are a likely target for both military and terrorist forces (Carmichael 2007).

Based primarily on complex computer models, scientists have made hundreds of projections of global warming. The term *global warming* refers to the significant rise in the earth's surface temperatures that occurs when industrial gases like carbon dioxide turn the planet's atmosphere into a virtual greenhouse. Even one additional degree of warmth in the globe's average surface temperature can increase the likelihood of wildfires, shrinkage of rivers and lakes, expansion of deserts, and torrential downpours, including typhoons and hurricanes. As Figure 19-7 on page 438 shows, scientists now track and project carbon dioxide emissions around the world (Lynas 2008).

Although scientific concern over global warming has heated up, climate change remains low on policymakers' list of concerns. The problem seems abstract, and in many countries, officials think that the real impact of any action they may take depends on decisive action by other nations. The Kyoto Protocol (1997) was intended to reduce global emissions of heat-trapped gases, which can contribute to global warming and climate change. To date, 169 countries have signed the accord, but the United States, which produces 24 percent of the world's carbon dioxide, has failed to ratify it. Opponents of the protocol argue that doing so would place the nation at a disadvantage in the global marketplace. But in 2009, shortly after Barack Obama became president, the United States pledged to become involved in negotiating a new, broader agreement. Besides reducing greenhouse emissions, the proposed agreement would give technical assistance to developing countries struggling to cope with climate change (E. Rosenthal 2009; United Nations Framework Convention on Climate Change 2009).

In writing about the global environment, activists often assert, "We're all in this together." Though we are all in this together, the reality is that globally, the most vulnerable countries tend to be the poorest. Developing nations are more likely than others to have economies that are built on limited resources or on a small number of crops vulnerable to drought, flood, and fluctuations in worldwide demand (Revkin 2007).

MAPPING LIFE WORLDWIDE

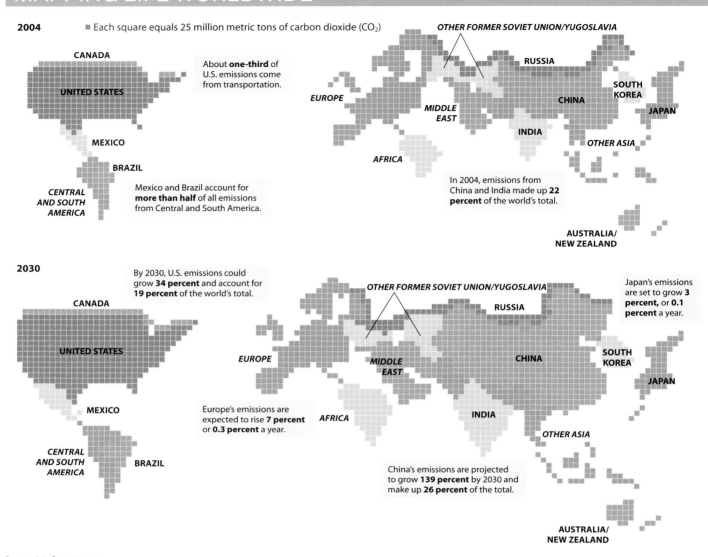

2004 ■ Each square equals 25 million metric tons of carbon dioxide (CO₂)

About **one-third** of U.S. emissions come from transportation.

Mexico and Brazil account for **more than half** of all emissions from Central and South America.

In 2004, emissions from China and India made up **22 percent** of the world's total.

2030

By 2030, U.S. emissions could grow **34 percent** and account for **19 percent** of the world's total.

Japan's emissions are set to grow **3 percent**, or **0.1 percent** a year.

Europe's emissions are expected to rise **7 percent** or **0.3 percent** a year.

China's emissions are projected to grow **139 percent** by 2030 and make up **26 percent** of the total.

Source: Mufson 2007:6.
Throughout the world, carbon dioxide emissions are expected to increase over the coming generation. However, new global agreements may stem the projected increases.

We can view global warming from the point of view of world systems analysis. Historically, core nations have been the major emitters of greenhouse gases. Today, however, manufacturing has moved to semi-periphery and periphery nations, where greenhouse gas emissions are escalating. Ironically, many of the forces that are now calling for a reduction in the human activity that contributes to global warming are located in core nations, which have contributed disproportionately to the problem. We want our hamburgers, but we decry the destruction of the rain forests to create grazing land for cattle. We want inexpensive clothes and toys, but we condemn developing countries for depending on coal-fired power plants, which are expected to increase 46 percent by 2030. The challenge of global warming, then, is closely tied to global inequality (M. Jenkins 2008; J. Roberts et al. 2003).

What are the causes of this global environmental crisis? Some observers, such as Paul Ehrlich and Anne Ehrlich, see the pressure of world population growth as the central factor in environmental deterioration. They argue that population control is essential in preventing widespread starvation and environmental decay. Barry Commoner, a biologist, counters that the primary cause of environmental ills is the increasing use of technological innovations that are destructive to the environment—among them plastics, detergents, synthetic fibers, pesticides, herbicides, and chemical fertilizers. Conflict theorists see the despoliation of the environment through the lens of world systems analysis. And interactionists stress efforts by informed individuals and groups to reduce their carbon footprint—that is, their daily or even lifetime production of greenhouse gases—through careful selection of the goods they

Vacation in an unspoiled paradise! Increasingly, people from developed countries are turning to ecotourism as an environmentally friendly way to see the world. The new trend bridges the interests of environmentalists and businesspeople, especially in developing countries. These birdwatchers are vacationing in Belize.

consume (Carbon Trust 2009; Commoner 1990, 2007; Ehrlich and Ellison 2002).

use your sociological *imagination*

As you think about all the problems facing our society, how often do you consider global warming? How often do your friends give it much thought?

The Impact of Globalization

Globalization can be both good and bad for the environment. On the negative side, it can create a race to the bottom, as polluting companies relocate to countries with less stringent environmental standards. Similarly, globalization allows multinationals to reap the resources of developing countries for short-term profit. From Mexico to China, the industrialization that often accompanies globalization has increased pollution of all types.

Yet globalization can have a positive impact, as well. As barriers to the international movement of goods, services, and people fall, multinational corporations have an incentive to carefully consider the cost of natural resources. Overusing or wasting resources makes little sense, especially when they are in danger of depletion (Kwong 2005).

One reflection of the interplay between globalization and the environment is the emergence of so-called *environmental refugees*. Europe in particular is beginning to see an influx of such immigrants from developing nations. According to a European Union report, global warming can be viewed as a "threat multiplier" that exacerbates prolonged droughts and a shortage of arable land, and along with them, poverty, poor health, and poor living conditions. Viewed through the lens of world systems analysis, periphery countries may become overburdened by environmental problems, precipitating either migrations to industrial nations or conflicts that cause mass displacements of their populations. "Europe must expect substantially increased migratory pressure" from these environmental refugees, the report concludes (Traynor 2008).

Against these potentially negative effects of globalization we must note the potential for new jobs in what are called green industries. Installing solar panels, weatherizing homes, brewing biofuels, building hybrid cars, growing organic foods, manufacturing organic garments, and erecting giant wind turbines are all classified as *green-collar jobs*. However, skeptics question how many such jobs will be created, and to what degree they will offset job losses in pollution-prone industries like oil, gas, and coal mining (S. Greenhouse 2008b; R. Pinderhughes 2008).

Environmentalism

The Issue

On April 22, 1970, in a dramatic manifestation of growing grassroots concern over preservation of the environment, an estimated 25 million people turned out to observe the nation's first Earth Day. Two thousand communities held planned celebrations, and more than 2,000 colleges and 10,000 schools hosted environmental teach-ins. In many parts of the United States, citizens marched on behalf of specific environmental causes. That same year, the activism of these early environmentalists convinced Congress to establish the Environmental Protection Agency. The Clean Air, Clean Water, and Endangered Species acts soon followed (Brulle and Jenkins 2008).

The Setting

Several social trends helped to mobilize the environmental movement. First, the activist subculture of the 1960s and early 1970s encouraged people, especially young people, to engage in direct action regarding social issues. Second, the dissemination of scientific knowledge about serious environmental problems like oil spills and air pollution alarmed many Americans. And third, the growing popularity of outdoor recreation increased the number of people who were concerned about the environment. In this climate of broad-based interest in environmental issues, many organizations that had once focused narrowly on the conservation of natural resources evolved into full-fledged environmental groups (Dunlap and Mertig 1991).

Today, Earth Day has been enshrined on the calendars of city councils, zoos, and museums worldwide. Increasingly, efforts to publicize environmental concerns and create support for action have moved to the Internet. Although times have changed, two beliefs continue to galvanize environmentalists: that the environment is in dire need of protection, and the government must take strong action in response. Although environmentalists recognize that they must "think locally" and monitor their own carbon footprints, they also see preservation of the environment as a global challenge. They note that while significant progress has been made toward environmental protection, government regulation of the environment has been curtailed in some ways (Brulle and Jenkins 2008; Schneider 1995; Sieber et al. 2006).

The general public has a mixed reaction to environmental issues. Many people question the scientific arguments behind the theory of global warming. And although the economic cost of environmental protection has always been an issue, the broad economic downturn that began in 2008 tipped the balance of public opinion in favor of economic growth. In 2009, for the first time since Americans were first asked about the trade-off between the economy and the environment, a majority of people gave economic growth priority over the environment

Americans from around the country joined residents of the nation's capital on the Mall in Washington, D.C., on Earth Day 2009. Since its beginning in 1970, Earth Day has grown into a global celebration, a reminder of the need to preserve our fragile environment.

(Figure 19-8). In times of economic stress, the public puts off or ignores environmental concerns. What is more, today's college students show less interest in the environment than students of past decades. In 2008, less than a third of first-year students wanted to clean up the environment—down from 42.5 percent in 1972 (see Figure 3-4 on page 66).

The contemporary environmental movement has evolved in several directions. At the local level, the number of grassroots organizations that deal with perceived environmental hazards has increased markedly. At the same time, the largest and most powerful environmental organizations have become increasingly bureaucratic. Led by relatively well-paid professional management, they often focus on particular issues, such as air or water pollution, wildlife preservation, or energy conservation. These national organizations work for social change through educational efforts, lobbying, lawsuits, and electoral politics. In contrast, smaller environmental groups distrust virtually all major social institutions, and sometimes resort to sabotage or other illegal tactics. Consequently, the environmental movement is now more fragmented than it was in the 1970s (S. Cable and C. Cable 1995; Dunlap and Mertig 1991; E. Johnson 2008; McCloskey 1991).

Sociological Insights

Even those who support environmentalists' goals are troubled by the fact that nationwide, the most powerful environmental organizations are predominantly White, male-dominated, and affluent. One study notes that while women are overrepresented in the environmental movement (particularly in grassroots environmental groups), men continue to hold most of

FIGURE **19-8** THE ENVIRONMENT VERSUS THE ECONOMY

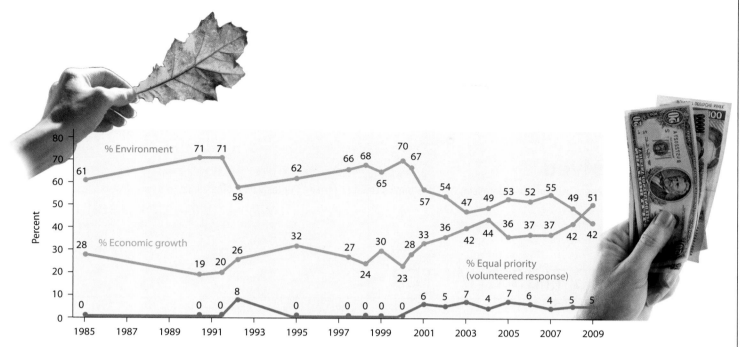

Source: Gallup 2009 cited in Newport 2009.

the high-profile upper-management positions in mainstream national organizations. The perceived middle-class orientation of the movement is especially relevant given the class, racial, and ethnic factors associated with environmental hazards. Sociologist Robert Bullard (1990) has shown that low-income communities and areas with significant minority populations are more likely than affluent White communities to be located near waste sites.

Viewed from a conflict perspective, it is significant that some environmental organizations accept funding from oil companies, chemical giants, and other powerful corporations. Perhaps as a result, the environmental movement has often emphasized limited reform rather than profound structural change. For example, activists may recommend making cars more energy-efficient instead of drastically reducing the number of vehicles on the road (Navarro 2009; Sale 1993).

Like any social movement, the environmental movement has aroused resistance. In this case, the opposition has itself become a social movement. The "wise-use" (or "sustainable-use") movement, founded in 1988, argues that we must balance our need for clean air, unspoiled waters, and pristine wilderness with our need for jobs, energy, and tourism. Wise-use advocates hope to open *all* public lands to mining, grazing, logging, and energy development. They oppose what they view as the special privileges granted by the federal government, through which Native Americans can control or limit development on reservation lands.

Another source of opposition comes from those who promote other issues with remedies that would seem to thwart environmental interests. For example, some question the environmentalists' move to replace fossil fuels such as coal and oil with biofuels such as ethanol. They complain that diverting corn and other crops into fuel production will raise food prices, hampering their efforts to reduce global hunger (Helvarg 1994; Pontin 2009).

Policy Perspectives

The global economic downturn of 2008–2009 has been a mixed blessing for environmentalists. As noted earlier, public opinion in the United States currently favors economic growth over environmental protection. Yet at the same time, the recession has sharply reduced the use of fossil fuels such as coal and oil. Moreover, the federal government's efforts to stimulate economic activity have emphasized the creation of green-collar jobs. By one estimate, every $1 billion invested in well-conceived green programs generates over 30,000 jobs and $450 million in cost savings per year. More specific environmental measures, such as raising federal gas mileage standards for automobiles, face a tough battle in Congress (Houser et al. 2009).

Environmentalism has moved onto a much bigger stage than the one it occupied on the first Earth Day. In 2008, for the first time, the leaders of the G8 economic powers (the United States, Japan, Germany, Great Britain, France, Italy, Canada, and Russia) set an explicit long-term target for eliminating greenhouse gases, which scientists have long warned were warming the planet. "Long-term" may be an understatement: their target date for cutting greenhouse gases in half is 2050. Environmentalists sharply criticized the G8's failure to set specific goals for the nearer term. The challenge is significant, given the fact that G8 emissions *increased* 35 percent over the preceding 15 years (Stolberg 2008).

Conventional wisdom holds that concern for environmental quality is limited to wealthy industrialized nations. However, the results of a 47-nation survey show that around the world, people are increasingly reluctant to ignore environmental issues. Concern has risen sharply in Latin America and Europe, as well as in Japan and India. The survey also noted a general increase in the percentage of people who cite pollution and environmental problems as a top global threat. Around the world, many people blame the United States, and to a lesser extent China, for environmental problems, **441** and look to Washington, D.C., for a solution. Time will tell whether policymakers in the United States or elsewhere will address their concern for the environment (Pew Global Attitudes Project 2007).

Let's Discuss

1. In your community, how would you act locally to preserve the environment? Describe your community's environmental problems and explain how you would seek to solve them.

2. How do you see the trade-off between the economy and the environment? Which is more important? Is it possible to improve both at the same time? Explain.

3. Thinking globally about the environment, list what you consider the most pressing priorities. How important are world hunger and economic justice compared to global warming, clean air and water, and economic development? Are some of your priorities related? In what way?

getting**involved**

To get involved in the debate over environmentalism, visit this book's Online Learning Center, which offers links to relevant Web sites.

www.mhhe.com/schaefer12e

MASTERING THIS CHAPTER

Summary

Both culture and the environment have a significant effect on our health and well-being. The concept of health is shaped by social definitions of behavior. This chapter considers the relationship between culture and health; sociological perspectives on health and the environment; the distribution of disease in a society; the evolution of the U.S. health care system; and the environmental problems facing our planet.

1. The effect of culture on **health** can be seen in the existence of **culture-bound syndromes,** as well as in cultural differences in medical care and the **incidence** and **prevalence** of certain diseases.

2. According to Talcott Parsons's functionalist perspective, physicians function as "gatekeepers" for the **sick role,** either verifying a person's condition as "ill" or designating the person as "recovered."

3. Conflict theorists use the term *medicalization of society* to refer to medicine's growing role as a major institution of social control.

4. Labeling theorists suggest that the designation of a person as "healthy" or "ill" generally involves social definition by others. These definitions affect how others see us and how we view ourselves.

5. Contemporary **social epidemiology** is concerned not only with epidemics but with nonepidemic diseases, injuries, drug addiction and alcoholism, suicide, and mental illness.

6. Studies have consistently shown that people in the lower classes have higher rates of mortality and disability than others.

7. Racial and ethnic minorities have higher rates of morbidity and mortality than Whites. Women tend to be in poorer health than men but live longer. Older people are especially vulnerable to mental health problems, such as Alzheimer's disease.

8. The preeminent role of physicians in the U.S. health care system has given them a position of dominance in their dealings with nurses and patients.

9. Many people use alternative health care techniques, such as **holistic medicine** and self-help groups.

10. Mental disorders may be viewed from two different perspectives, the medical model and the sociological model, which are based on labeling theory. In the United States, society has traditionally taken a negative, suspicious attitude toward people with mental disorders.

11. The human ecological perspective suggests that the natural environment serves three basic functions: it provides essential resources, serves as a waste repository, and houses our species.

12. Conflict theorists charge that the most serious threat to the environment comes from Western industrialized nations.

13. **Environmental justice** addresses the disproportionate subjection of minorities to environmental hazards.

14. Four broad areas of environmental concern include air and water pollution, global warming, and globalization. Though globalization can contribute to environmental woes, it can also have beneficial effects.

15. Environmentalism is a social movement that is dominated by affluent White people from industrialized countries. Increasingly, however, people of all races, ethnicities, social classes, and nationalities are becoming concerned about global warming and the threat it poses to our planet's health.

Critical Thinking Questions

1. Sociologist Talcott Parsons has argued that the doctor–patient relationship is similar to that between parent and child. Does this view seem accurate? Should the doctor–patient relationship be more egalitarian? How might functionalist and conflict theorists differ in their views of the power of physicians in the U.S. health care system?

2. Relate what you have learned about social epidemiology to the question of universal health care coverage. If the United States were to

adopt a system of universal coverage, what might be the effect on the incidence and prevalence of disease among Americans of all classes, races and ethnicities, genders, and ages? What might be the ultimate effect of such changes on health care costs?

3. Imagine that you have been asked to study the issue of air pollution in the largest city in your state. How might you draw on surveys, observation research, experiments, and existing sources to study the issue?

Key Terms

Brain drain The immigration to the United States and other industrialized nations of skilled workers, professionals, and technicians who are desperately needed in their home countries. (page 421)

Culture-bound syndrome A disease or illness that cannot be understood apart from its specific social context. (419)

Curanderismo Latino folk medicine, a form of holistic health care and healing. (426)

Environmental justice A legal strategy based on claims that racial minorities are subjected disproportionately to environmental hazards. (435)

Health As defined by the World Health Organization, a state of complete physical, mental, and social well-being, and not merely the absence of disease and infirmity. (419)

Holistic medicine Therapies in which the health care practitioner considers the person's physical, mental, emotional, and spiritual characteristics. (430)

Human ecology An area of study that is concerned with the interrelationships between people and their environment. (433)

Incidence The number of new cases of a specific disorder that occur within a given population during a stated period. (423)

Infant mortality rate The number of deaths of infants under one year old per 1,000 live births in a given year. (421)

Mental illness A disorder of the brain that disrupts a person's thinking, feeling, and ability to interact with others. (431)

Morbidity rate The incidence of disease in a given population. (423)

Mortality rate The incidence of death in a given population. (423)

Prevalence The total number of cases of a specific disorder that exist at a given time. (423)

Sick role Societal expectations about the attitudes and behavior of a person viewed as being ill. (420)

Social epidemiology The study of the distribution of disease, impairment, and general health status across a population. (423)

Self-Quiz

Read each question carefully and then select the best answer.

1. Which sociologist developed the concept of the sick role?
   a. Émile Durkheim
   b. Talcott Parsons
   c. C. Wright Mills
   d. Erving Goffman

2. Regarding health care inequities, the conflict perspective would note that
   a. physicians serve as "gatekeepers" for the sick role, either verifying a patient's condition as "illness" or designating the patient as "recovered."
   b. patients play an active role in health care by failing to follow a physician's advice.
   c. emigration out of the Third World by physicians is yet another way that the world's core industrialized nations enhance their quality of life at the expense of developing countries.
   d. the designation "healthy" or "ill" generally involves social definition by others.

3. Which one of the following nations has the lowest infant mortality rate?
   a. the United States
   b. Mozambique
   c. Canada
   d. Sweden

4. Compared with Whites, Blacks have higher death rates from
   a. heart disease.
   b. diabetes.
   c. cancer.
   d. all of the above

5. Which theorist notes that capitalist societies, such as the United States, care more about maximizing profits than they do about the health and safety of industrial workers?
   a. Thomas Szasz
   b. Talcott Parsons
   c. Erving Goffman
   d. Karl Marx

6. Which program is essentially a compulsory health insurance plan for the elderly?
   a. Medicare
   b. Medicaid
   c. Blue Cross
   d. Healthpac

7. Which of the following is a criticism of the sick role?
   a. Patients' judgments regarding their own state of health may be related to their gender, age, social class, and ethnic group.
   b. The sick role may be more applicable to people experiencing short-term illnesses than to those with recurring long-term illnesses.
   c. Even such simple factors as whether a person is employed or not seem to affect the person's willingness to assume the sick role.
   d. all of the above

8. Which of the following terms do conflict theorists use in referring to the growing role of medicine as a major institution of social control?
   a. the sick role
   b. the medicalization of society
   c. medical labeling
   d. epidemiology

9. According to sociologists and environmentalists, which one of the following is *not* a basic function that the natural environment serves for humans?
   a. It provides the resources essential for life.
   b. It serves as a waste depository.
   c. It provides a natural setting for social inequalities.
   d. It "houses" our species.

10. Conflict theorists would contend that blaming developing countries for the world's environmental deterioration contains an element of
    a. ethnocentrism.
    b. xenocentrism.
    c. separatism.
    d. goal displacement.

11. _____ affects the way people interact with doctors and healers, the way they relate to their families when they are sick, and even the way they think about health.

12. From a(n) _____ perspective, "being sick" must be controlled so as to ensure that not too many people are released from their societal responsibilities at any one time.

13. The immigration to the United States and other industrialized nations of skilled workers, professionals, and technicians who are desperately needed by their home countries is known as the_____ _____.

14. Traditionally, the relationship between doctors and nurses has paralleled _____ dominance of the larger society.

15. Sociologists find it useful to consider _____ rates because they reveal that a specific disease occurs more frequently among one segment of a population compared with another.

16. The system of reimbursement used by Medicare has contributed to the controversial practice of "_____," under which patients whose treatment may be unprofitable are transferred by private hospitals to public facilities.

17. As defined by the World Health Organization, _____ is a "state of complete physical, mental, and social well-being, and not merely the absence of disease and infirmity."

18. In an application of the _____ _____ perspective, sociologists suggest that the natural environment serves three basic functions for humans and for many animal species.

19. Regarding environmental problems, four broad areas of concern stand out: _____ pollution, _____ pollution, _____ _____, and _____.

20. _____ _____ is a legal strategy based on claims that racial minorities are subjected disproportionately to environmental hazards.

_____

THINKING ABOUT MOVIES

Sicko (Michael Moore, 2007)

Made by the controversial documentary filmmaker Michael Moore, *Sicko* tells the story of the U.S. health care system. From Moore's perspective, the system serves insurance companies and the pharmaceutical industry more than the needs of middle-class Americans. His proposed solution is socialized medicine: a comprehensive, government-sponsored system that cares for all. Through interviews with individuals who have been denied care and comparisons to the socialized health care systems in countries like France and Canada, Moore builds the case for drastic change in our health care system.

This movie shows the enormous control that certain companies and individuals have over people's health in the United States. Though Moore's facts and his means of presentation can be disputed, the larger picture is difficult to ignore: systemic inequalities determine the medical treatment that many groups of Americans receive or fail to receive.

For Your Consideration

1. According to *Sicko,* what is the relationship between social class and medical care in the United States?

2. Who is in a position to define which people receive medical treatment in the United States? From the conflict perspective, what are the implications of your answer?

Into the Wild
(Sean Penn, 2007)

Christopher McCandless (Emile Hirsch), a recent college graduate, rejects the consumerism and industrialism inherent in U.S. society. He gives all his money to charity, renames himself "Alexander Supertramp," and hitchhikes his way to Alaska, where he hopes to live in closer communion with nature. Along the way, Alexander develops relationships with several people who try to convince him that he can't live in isolation from others. Adamant about his need to strike out on his own, however, he pushes on. His stubbornness ends in his tragic death.

From Christopher's (Alexander's) perspective, we see many of the environmental and social ills of modern-day society. Feeling out of place, Christopher tries to revert to a more primitive way of living, but his upbringing leaves him ill equipped for the transition.

For Your Consideration

1. What are some of the different environments shown in the movie, and how do they affect the people who live in them?

2. How does Christopher understand society's effect on the environment, and what is his personal solution to the problem?

glossary

Numbers following the definitions indicate pages where the terms were identified. Consult the index for further page references.

A

Absolute poverty A minimum level of subsistence that no family should be expected to live below. (205)

Achieved status A social position that a person attains largely through his or her own efforts. (100, 193)

Activity theory An interactionist theory of aging that suggests that those elderly people who remain active and socially involved will be best adjusted. (296)

Adoption In a legal sense, a process that allows for the transfer of the legal rights, responsibilities, and privileges of parenthood to a new legal parent or parents. (322)

Affirmative action Positive efforts to recruit minority group members or women for jobs, promotions, and educational opportunities. (252, 410)

Ageism Prejudice and discrimination based on a person's age. (303)

Agrarian society The most technologically advanced form of preindustrial society. Members are engaged primarily in the production of food, but increase their crop yields through technological innovations such as the plow. (110)

Alienation A condition of estrangement or dissociation from the surrounding society. (125, 407)

Amalgamation The process through which a majority group and a minority group combine to form a new group. (255)

Anomie Durkheim's term for the loss of direction felt in a society when social control of individual behavior has become ineffective. (10, 174)

Anomie theory of deviance Robert Merton's theory of deviance as an adaptation of socially prescribed goals or of the means governing their attainment, or both. (174)

Anticipatory socialization Processes of socialization in which a person "rehearses" for future positions, occupations, and social relationships. (90)

Anti-Semitism Anti-Jewish prejudice. (263)

Apartheid A former policy of the South African government, designed to maintain the separation of Blacks and other non-Whites from the dominant Whites. (256)

Applied sociology The use of the discipline of sociology with the specific intent of yielding practical applications for human behavior and organizations. (16)

Argot Specialized language used by members of a group or subculture. (58)

Ascribed status A social position assigned to a person by society without regard for the person's unique talents or characteristics. (100, 193)

Assembling perspective A theory of collective behavior introduced by McPhail and Miller that seeks to examine how and why people move from different points in space to a common location. (477)

Assimilation The process through which a person forsakes his or her own cultural tradition to become part of a different culture. (255)

Authority Institutionalized power that is recognized by the people over whom it is exercised. (379)

Avatar A three-dimensional model, two-dimensional icon, or constructed personality that is assumed by the user of an Internet site. (108)

B

Basic sociology Sociological inquiry conducted with the objective of gaining a more profound knowledge of the fundamental aspects of social phenomena. Also known as *pure sociology*. (18)

Bilateral descent A kinship system in which both sides of a person's family are regarded as equally important. (315)

Bilingualism The use of two or more languages in a particular setting, such as the workplace or schoolroom, treating each language as equally legitimate. (69)

Birthrate The number of live births per 1,000 population in a given year. Also known as the *crude birthrate*. (450)

Black power A political philosophy, promoted by many younger Blacks in the 1960s, that supported the creation of Black-controlled political and economic institutions. (257)

Borderlands The area of common culture along the border between Mexico and the United States. (235)

Bourgeoisie Karl Marx's term for the capitalist class, comprising the owners of the means of production. (197)

Brain drain The immigration to the United States and other industrialized nations of skilled workers, professionals, and technicians who are desperately needed in their home countries. (421)

Bureaucracy A component of formal organization that uses rules and hierarchical ranking to achieve efficiency. (125)

Bureaucratization The process by which a group, organization, or social movement becomes increasingly bureaucratic. (127)

C

Capitalism An economic system in which the means of production are held largely in private hands and the main incentive for economic activity is the accumulation of profits. (197, 401)

Caste A hereditary rank, usually religiously dictated, that tends to be fixed and immobile. (193)

Causal logic The relationship between a condition or variable and a particular consequence, with one event leading to the other. (30)

Census An enumeration, or counting, of a population. (450)

Charismatic authority Max Weber's term for power made legitimate by a leader's exceptional personal or emotional appeal to his or her followers. (380)

Class A group of people who have a similar level of wealth and income. (198)

Class consciousness In Karl Marx's view, a subjective awareness held by members of a class regarding their common vested interests and need for collective political action to bring about social change. (197)

Class system A social ranking based primarily on economic position in which achieved characteristics can influence social mobility. (195)

Classical theory An approach to the study of formal organizations that views workers as being motivated almost entirely by economic rewards. (127)

Clinical sociology The use of the discipline of sociology with the specific intent of altering social relationships or restructuring social institutions. (18)

Closed system A social system in which there is little or no possibility of individual social mobility. (209)

Coalition A temporary or permanent alliance geared toward a common goal. (123)

Code of ethics The standards of acceptable behavior developed by and for members of a profession. (38)

Cognitive theory of development Jean Piaget's theory that children's thought progresses through four stages of development. (83)

Cohabitation The practice of living together as a male–female couple without marrying. (327)

Collective behavior In the view of sociologist Neil Smelser, the relatively spontaneous and unstructured behavior of a group of people who are reacting to a common influence in an ambiguous situation. (474)

Colonialism The maintenance of political, social, economic, and cultural domination over a people by a foreign power for an extended period. (223)

Color-blind racism The use of the principle of race neutrality to defend a racially unequal status quo. (249, 410)

Communism As an ideal type, an economic system under which all property is communally owned and no social distinctions are made on the basis of people's ability to produce. (403)

Community A spatial or political unit of social organization that gives people a sense of belonging, based either on shared residence in a particular place or on a common identity. (448)

Concentric-zone theory A theory of urban growth devised by Ernest Burgess that sees growth in terms of a series of rings radiating from the central business district. (459)

Conflict perspective A sociological approach that assumes that social behavior is best understood in terms of tension between groups over power or the allocation of resources, including housing, money, access to services, and political representation. (14)

Conformity Going along with peers—individuals of our own status who have no special right to direct our behavior. (166)

Contact hypothesis An interactionist perspective which states that in cooperative circumstances, interracial contact between people of equal status will reduce prejudice. (254)

Content analysis The systematic coding and objective recording of data, guided by some rationale. (37)

Control group The subjects in an experiment who are not introduced to the independent variable by the researcher. (36)

Control theory A view of conformity and deviance that suggests that our connection to members of society leads us to systematically conform to society's norms. (170)

Control variable A factor that is held constant to test the relative impact of an independent variable. (33)

Corporate welfare Tax breaks, direct payments, and grants that the government makes to corporations. (213)

Correlation A relationship between two variables in which a change in one coincides with a change in the other. (30)

Correspondence principle A term used by Bowles and Gintis to refer to the tendency of schools to promote the values expected of individuals in each social class and to prepare students for the types of jobs typically held by members of their class. (365)

Counterculture A subculture that deliberately opposes certain aspects of the larger culture. (60)

Craze An exciting mass involvement that lasts for a relatively long period. (480)

Creationism A literal interpretation of the Bible regarding the creation of humanity and the universe, used to argue that evolution should not be presented as established scientific fact. (353)

Credentialism An increase in the lowest level of education required to enter a field. (364)

Crime A violation of criminal law for which some governmental authority applies formal penalties. (179)

Cross-tabulation A table or matrix that shows the relationship between two or more variables. (45)

Crowd A temporary gathering of people in close proximity who share a common focus or interest. (477)

Cultural capital Noneconomic goods, such as family background and education, which are reflected in a knowledge of language and the arts. (13)

Cultural convergence The flow of content across multiple media, and the accompanying migration of media audiences. (141)

Cultural relativism The viewing of people's behavior from the perspective of their own culture. (55, 400)

Cultural transmission A school of criminology that argues that criminal behavior is learned through social interactions. (176)

Cultural universal A common practice or belief found in every culture. (54)

Culture The totality of learned, socially transmitted customs, knowledge, material objects, and behavior. (53)

Culture-bound syndrome A disease or illness that cannot be understood apart from its specific social context. (419)

Culture industry The worldwide media industry that standardizes the goods and services demanded by consumers. (54)

Culture lag A period of maladjustment when the nonmaterial culture is still struggling to adapt to new material conditions. (58, 498)

Culture shock The feeling of surprise and disorientation that people experience when they encounter cultural practices that are different from their own. (60)

Culture war The polarization of society over controversial cultural elements. (66)

Curanderismo Latino folk medicine, a form of holistic health care and healing. (426)

D

Death rate The number of deaths per 1,000 population in a given year. Also known as the *crude death rate*. (450)

Degradation ceremony An aspect of the socialization process within some total institutions, in which people are subjected to humiliating rituals. (91)

Deindustrialization The systematic, widespread withdrawal of investment in basic aspects of productivity, such as factories and plants. (411)

Democracy In a literal sense, government by the people. (382)

Demographic transition A term used to describe the change from high birthrates and death rates to low birthrates and death rates. (452)

Demography The scientific study of population. (452)

Denomination A large, organized religion that is not officially linked to the state or government. (348)

Dependency theory An approach that contends that industrialized nations continue to exploit developing countries for their own gain. (223)

Dependent variable The variable in a causal relationship that is subject to the influence of another variable. (30)

Deviance Behavior that violates the standards of conduct or expectations of a group or society. (170)

Dictatorship A government in which one person has nearly total power to make and enforce laws. (383)

Differential association A theory of deviance proposed by Edwin Sutherland that holds that violation of rules results from exposure to attitudes favorable to criminal acts. (176)

Differential justice Differences in the way social control is exercised over different groups. (178)

Diffusion The process by which a cultural item spreads from group to group or society to society. (57)

Digital divide The relative lack of access to the latest technologies among low-income groups, racial and ethnic minorities, rural residents, and the citizens of developing countries. (147, 208)

Disaster A sudden or disruptive event or set of events that overtaxes a community's resources, so that outside aid is necessary. (478)

Discovery The process of making known or sharing the existence of an aspect of reality. (56)

Discrimination The denial of opportunities and equal rights to individuals and groups because of prejudice or other arbitrary reasons. (249)

Disengagement theory A functionalist theory of aging that suggests that society and the aging individual mutually sever many of their relationships. (296)

Domestic partnership Two unrelated adults who share a mutually caring relationship, reside together, and agree to be jointly responsible for their dependents, basic living expenses, and other common necessities. (330)

Dominant ideology A set of cultural beliefs and practices that helps to maintain powerful social, economic, and political interests. (66, 148, 300)

Double consciousness The division of an individual's identity into two or more social realities. (12)

Downsizing Reductions taken in a company's workforce as part of deindustrialization. (411)

Dramaturgical approach A view of social interaction, popularized by Erving Goffman, in which people are seen as theatrical performers. (15, 82)

Dysfunction An element or process of a society that may disrupt the social system or reduce its stability. (14)

Dyad A two-member group. (124)

Ecclesia A religious organization that claims to include most or all members of a society and is recognized as the national or official religion. (348)

Economic system The social institution through which goods and services are produced, distributed, and consumed. (400)

Education A formal process of learning in which some people consciously teach while others adopt the social role of learner. (360)

Egalitarian family An authority pattern in which spouses are regarded as equals. (315)

Elite model A view of society as being ruled by a small group of individuals who share a common set of political and economic interests. (386)

Emergent-norm perspective A theory of collective behavior proposed by Turner and Killian that holds that a collective definition of appropriate and inappropriate behavior emerges during episodes of collective behavior. (476)

Endogamy The restriction of mate selection to people within the same group. (318)

Environmental justice A legal strategy based on claims that racial minorities are subjected disproportionately to environmental hazards. (435)

Equilibrium model Talcott Parsons's functionalist view that society tends toward a state of stability or balance. (496)

Established sect J. Milton Yinger's term for a religious group that is the outgrowth of a sect, yet remains isolated from society. (348)

Estate system A system of stratification under which peasants were required to work land leased to them by nobles in exchange for military protection and other services. Also known as *feudalism.* (195)

Esteem The reputation that a specific person has earned within an occupation. (201)

Ethnic group A group that is set apart from others primarily because of its national origin or distinctive cultural patterns. (245)

Ethnocentrism The tendency to assume that one's own culture and way of life represent the norm or are superior to all others. (54, 248)

Ethnography The study of an entire social setting through extended systematic observation. (35)

Euthanasia The act of bringing about the death of a hopelessly ill and suffering person in a relatively quick and painless way for reasons of mercy. (306)

Evolutionary theory A theory of social change that holds that society is moving in a definite direction. (495)

Exogamy The requirement that people select a mate outside certain groups. (318)

Experiment An artificially created situation that allows a researcher to manipulate variables. (36)

Experimental group The subjects in an experiment who are exposed to an independent variable introduced by a researcher. (36)

Exploitation theory A Marxist theory that views racial subordination in the United States as a manifestation of the class system inherent in capitalism. (253)

Expressiveness Concern for the maintenance of harmony and the internal emotional affairs of the family. (277)

Extended family A family in which relatives—such as grandparents, aunts, or uncles—live in the same home as parents and their children. (313)

F

Face-work A term used by Erving Goffman to refer to the efforts people make to maintain the proper image and avoid public embarrassment. (82)

Fad A temporary pattern of behavior that involves large numbers of people and is independent of preceding trends. (479)

False consciousness A term used by Karl Marx to describe an attitude held by members of a class that does not accurately reflect their objective position. (198, 484)

Familism Pride in the extended family, expressed through the maintenance of close ties and strong obligations to kinfolk outside the immediate family. (321)

Family A set of people related by blood, marriage or some other agreed-upon relationship, or adoption, who share the primary responsibility for reproduction and caring for members of society. (312)

Fashion A pleasurable mass involvement that has a line of historical continuity. (479)

Feminism The belief in social, economic, and political equality for women. (284)

Feminist view A sociological approach that views inequity in gender as central to all behavior and organization. (14)

Feminization of poverty A trend in which women constitute an increasing proportion of the poor people of the United States. (207)

Fertility The level of reproduction in a society. (449)

Folkway A norm governing everyday behavior whose violation raises comparatively little concern. (63)

Force The actual or threatened use of coercion to impose one's will on others. (379)

Formal norm A norm that has been written down and that specifies strict punishments for violators. (63)

Formal organization A group designed for a special purpose and structured for maximum efficiency. (125)

Formal social control Social control that is carried out by authorized agents, such as police officers, judges, school administrators, and employers. (168)

Functionalist perspective A sociological approach that emphasizes the way in which the parts of a society are structured to maintain its stability. (13)

Fundamentalism Rigid adherence to fundamental religious doctrines, often accompanied by a literal application of scripture or historical beliefs to today's world. (345)

G

Gatekeeping The process by which a relatively small number of people in the media industry control what material eventually reaches the audience. (144)

Gemeinschaft A term used by Ferdinand Tönnies to describe a close-knit community, often found in rural areas, in which strong personal bonds unite members. (109)

Gender role Expectations regarding the proper behavior, attitudes, and activities of males and females. (84, 273)

Generalized other A term used by George Herbert Mead to refer to the attitudes, viewpoints, and expectations of society as a whole that a child takes into account in his or her behavior. (80)

Genocide The deliberate, systematic killing of an entire people or nation. (254)

Gentrification The resettlement of low-income city neighborhoods by prosperous families and business firms. (467)

Gerontology The scientific study of the sociological and psychological aspects of aging and the problems of the aged. (295)

Gesellschaft A term used by Ferdinand Tönnies to describe a community, often urban, that is large and impersonal, with little commitment to the group or consensus on values. (109)

Glass ceiling An invisible barrier that blocks the promotion of a qualified individual in a work environment because of the individual's gender, race, or ethnicity. (250, 282)

Globalization The worldwide integration of government policies, cultures, social movements, and financial markets through trade and the exchange of ideas. (19, 224)

Goal displacement Overzealous conformity to official regulations of a bureaucracy. (126)

Gross national product (GNP) The value of a nation's goods and services. (227)

Group Any number of people with similar norms, values, and expectations who interact with one another on a regular basis. (103, 121)

Groupthink Uncritical acceptance of or conformity to the prevailing viewpoint. (124)

Growth rate The difference between births and deaths, plus the difference between immigrants and emigrants, per 1,000 population. (451)

H

Hate crime A criminal offense committed because of the offender's bias against a race, religion, ethnic group, national origin, or sexual orientation. (248)

Hawthorne effect The unintended influence that observers of experiments can have on their subjects. (37)

Health As defined by the World Health Organization, a state of complete physical, mental, and social well-being, and not merely the absence of disease and infirmity. (419)

Hidden curriculum Standards of behavior that are deemed proper by society and are taught subtly in schools. (364)

Holistic medicine Therapies in which the health care practitioner considers the person's physical, mental, emotional, and spiritual characteristics. (430)

Homogamy The conscious or unconscious tendency to select a mate with personal characteristics similar to one's own. (318)

Homophobia Fear of and prejudice against homosexuality. (273)

Horizontal mobility The movement of an individual from one social position to another of the same rank. (209)

Horticultural society A preindustrial society in which people plant seeds and crops rather than merely subsist on available foods. (110)

Hospice care Treatment of the terminally ill in their own homes, or in special hospital units or other facilities, with the goal of helping them to die easily, without pain. (301)

Human ecology An area of study that is concerned with the interrelationships between people and their environment. (433, 459)

Human relations approach An approach to the study of formal organizations that emphasizes the role of people, communication, and participation in a bureaucracy and tends to focus on the informal structure of the organization. (128)

Human rights Universal moral rights possessed by all people because they are human. (237)

Hunting-and-gathering society A preindustrial society in which people rely on whatever foods and fibers are readily available in order to survive. (109)

Hypothesis A speculative statement about the relationship between two or more variables. (30)

I

Ideal type A construct or model for evaluating specific cases. (10, 125)

Impression management A term used by Erving Goffman to refer to the altering of the presentation of the self in order to create distinctive appearances and satisfy particular audiences. (81)

Incest taboo The prohibition of sexual relationships between certain culturally specified relatives. (318)

Incidence The number of new cases of a specific disorder that occur within a given population during a stated period. (423)

Income Salaries and wages. (193)

Independent variable The variable in a causal relationship that causes or influences a change in a second variable. (30)

Index crimes The eight types of crime reported annually by the FBI in the *Uniform Crime Reports:* murder, rape, robbery, assault, burglary, theft, motor vehicle theft, and arson. (180)

Industrial city A relatively large city characterized by open competition, an open class system, and elaborate specialization in the manufacturing of goods. (457)

Industrial society A society that depends on mechanization to produce its goods and services. (111, 401)

Infant mortality rate The number of deaths of infants under one year old per 1,000 live births in a given year. (421, 450)

Influence The exercise of power through a process of persuasion. (379)

Informal economy Transfers of money, goods, or services that are not reported to the government. (403)

Informal norm A norm that is generally understood but not precisely recorded. (63)

Informal social control Social control that is carried out casually by ordinary people through such means as laughter, smiles, and ridicule. (168)

In-group Any group or category to which people feel they belong. (122)

Innovation The process of introducing a new idea or object to a culture through discovery or invention. (56)

Institutional discrimination The denial of opportunities and equal rights to individuals and groups that results from the normal operations of a society. (252, 280)

Instrumentality An emphasis on tasks, a focus on more distant goals, and a concern for the external relationship between one's family and other social institutions. (277)

Intelligent design (ID) The idea that life is so complex, it could only have been created by intelligent design. (354)

Interactionist perspective A sociological approach that generalizes about everyday forms of social interaction in order to explain society as a whole. (15)

Intergenerational mobility Changes in the social position of children relative to their parents. (209)

Interview A face-to-face or telephone questioning of a respondent to obtain desired information. (34)

Intragenerational mobility Changes in social position within a person's adult life. (209)

Invention The combination of existing cultural items into a form that did not exist before. (56)

Iron law of oligarchy A principle of organizational life developed by Robert Michels, under which even a democratic organization will eventually develop into a bureaucracy ruled by a few individuals. (127)

K

Kinship The state of being related to others. (315)

L

Labeling theory An approach to deviance that attempts to explain why certain people are viewed as deviants while others engaged in the same behavior are not. (177)

Labor union Organized workers who share either the same skill or the same employer. (133)

Laissez-faire A form of capitalism under which people compete freely, with minimal government intervention in the economy. (401)

Language An abstract system of word meanings and symbols for all aspects of culture; includes gestures and other nonverbal communication. (61)

Latent function An unconscious or unintended function that may reflect hidden purposes. (14)

Law Governmental social control. (63, 170)

Liberation theology Use of a church, primarily Roman Catholicism, in a political effort to eliminate poverty, discrimination, and other forms of injustice from a secular society. (343)

Life chances Max Weber's term for the opportunities people have to provide themselves with material goods, positive living conditions, and favorable life experiences. (208)

Life course approach A research orientation in which sociologists and other social scientists look closely at the social factors that influence people throughout their lives, from birth to death. (89)

Life expectancy The median number of years a person can be expected to live under current mortality conditions. (451)

Looking-glass self A concept used by Charles Horton Cooley that emphasizes the self as the product of our social interactions. (79)

Luddites Rebellious craft workers in 19th century England who destroyed new factory machinery as part of their resistance to the Industrial Revolution. (498)

M

Machismo A sense of virility, personal worth, and pride in one's maleness. (321)

Macrosociology Sociological investigation that concentrates on large-scale phenomena or entire civilizations. (12)

Manifest function An open, stated, and conscious function. (14)

Mass media Print and electronic means of communication that carry messages to widespread audiences. (140)

Master status A status that dominates others and thereby determines a person's general position in society. (101)

Material culture The physical or technological aspects of our daily lives. (58)

Matriarchy A society in which women dominate in family decision making. (315)

Matrilineal descent A kinship system in which only the mother's relatives are significant. (315)

Matrix of domination The cumulative impact of oppression because of race and ethnicity, gender, and social class, as well as religion, sexual orientation, disability, age, and citizenship status. (278)

McDonaldization The process by which the principles of the fast-food restaurant are coming to dominate more and more sectors of American society as well as of the rest of the world. (120)

Mean A number calculated by adding a series of values and then dividing by the number of values. (45)

Mechanical solidarity A collective consciousness that emphasizes group solidarity, characteristic of societies with minimal division of labor. (108)

Median The midpoint or number that divides a series of values into two groups of equal numbers of values. (45)

Megalopolis A densely populated area containing two or more cities and their suburbs. (459)

Mental illness A disorder of the brain that disrupts a person's thinking, feeling, and ability to interact with others. (431)

Microfinancing Lending small sums of money to the poor so they can work their way out of poverty. (409)

Microsociology Sociological investigation that stresses the study of small groups, often through experimental means. (13)

Midlife crisis A stressful period of self-evaluation that begins at about age 40. (298)

Migration The relatively permanent movement of people, with the purpose of changing their place of residence. (456)

Minority group A subordinate group whose members have significantly less control or power over their own lives than the members of a dominant or majority group have over theirs. (245)

Mode The single most common value in a series of scores. (45)

Model or ideal minority A subordinate group whose members supposedly have succeeded economically, socially, and educationally despite past prejudice and discrimination, and without resorting to confrontations with Whites. (259)

Modernization The far-reaching process by which periphery nations move from traditional or less developed institutions to those characteristic of more developed societies. (229)

Modernization theory A functionalist approach that proposes that modernization and development will gradually improve the lives of people in developing nations. (229)

Monarchy A form of government headed by a single member of a royal family, usually a king, queen, or some other hereditary ruler. (381)

Monogamy A form of marriage in which one woman and one man are married only to each other. (313)

Monopoly Control of a market by a single business firm. (401)

Morbidity rate The incidence of disease in a given population. (423)

Mores Norms deemed highly necessary to the welfare of a society. (63)

Mortality rate The incidence of death in a given population. (423)

Multinational corporation A commercial organization that is headquartered in one country but does business throughout the world. (224)

Multiple masculinities A variety of male gender roles, including nurturing-caring and effeminate-gay roles, that men may play along with their more pervasive traditional role of dominating women. (276)

Multiple-nuclei theory A theory of urban growth developed by Harris and Ullman that views growth as emerging from many centers of development, each of which reflects a particular urban need or activity. (460)

N

Narcotizing dysfunction The phenomenon in which the media provide such massive amounts of coverage that the audience becomes numb and fails to act on the information, regardless of how compelling the issue. (144)

Natural science The study of the physical features of nature and the ways in which they interact and change. (5)

Naturally occurring retirement community (NORC) An area that has gradually become an informal center for senior citizens. (301)

Neocolonialism Continuing dependence of former colonies on foreign countries. (223)

Net neutrality The principle that the government should remain non-selective or neutral toward online content. (114)

New religious movement(NRM) or cult A small, secretive religious group that represents either a new religion or a major innovation of an existing faith. (348)

New social movement An organized collective activity that addresses values and social identities, as well as improvements in the quality of life. (485)

New urban sociology An approach to urbanization that considers the interplay of local, national, and worldwide forces and their effect on local space, with special emphasis on the impact of global economic activity. (401)

Nonmaterial culture Ways of using material objects, as well as customs, beliefs, philosophies, governments, and patterns of communication. (58)

Nonperiodic assembly A nonrecurring gathering of people that often results form word-of-mouth information. (477)

Nonverbal communication The sending of messages through the use of gestures, facial expressions, and postures. (15)

Norm An established standard of behavior maintained by a society. (63)

Nuclear family A married couple and their unmarried children living together. (313)

O

Obedience Compliance with higher authorities in a hierarchical structure. (166)

Objective method A technique for measuring social class that assigns individuals to classes on the basis of criteria such as occupation, education, income, and place of residence. (201)

Observation A research technique in which an investigator collects information through direct participation and/or by closely watching a group or community. (35)

Offshoring The transfer of work to foreign contractors. (412)

Oligarchy A form of government in which a few individuals rule. (382)

Open system A social system in which the position of each individual is influenced by his or her achieved status. (209)

Operational definition An explanation of an abstract concept that is specific enough to allow a researcher to assess the concept. (30)

Opinion leader Someone who influences the opinions and decisions of others through day-to-day personal contact and communication. (154)

Organic solidarity A collective consciousness that rests on mutual interdependence, characteristic of societies with a complex division of labor. (109)

Organized crime The work of a group that regulates relations between criminal enterprises involved in illegal activities, including prostitution, gambling, and the smuggling and sale of illegal drugs. (181)

Out-group A group or category to which people feel they do not belong. (122)

P

Panic A fearful arousal or collective flight based on a generalized belief that may or may not be accurate. (480)

Patriarchy A society in which men dominate in family decision making. (315)

Patrilineal descent A kinship system in which only the father's relatives are significant. (315)

Peace The absence of war or, more broadly, a proactive effort to develop cooperative relations among nations. (389)

Percentage A portion of 100. (44)

Periodic assembly A recurring, relatively routine gathering of people, such as a college class. (477)

Personality A person's typical patterns of attitudes, needs, characteristics, and behavior. (77)

Peter principle A principle of organizational life, originated by Laurence J. Peter, according to which every employee within a hierarchy tends to rise to his or her level of incompetence. (126)

Pluralism Mutual respect for one another's cultures among the various groups in a society, which allows minorities to express their own cultures without experiencing prejudice. (256)

Pluralist model A view of society in which many competing groups within the community have access to government, so that no single group is dominant. (388)

Political system The social institution that is founded on a recognized set of procedures for implementing and achieving society's goals. (378)

Politics In Harold Lasswell's words, "who gets what, when, and how." (379)

Polyandry A form of polygamy in which a woman may have more than one husband at the same time. (314)

Polygamy A form of marriage in which an individual may have several husbands or wives simultaneously. (314)

Polygyny A form of polygamy in which a man may have more than one wife at the same time. (314)

Population pyramid A special type of bar chart that shows the distribution of a population by gender and age. (453)

Postindustrial city A city in which global finance and the electronic flow of information dominate the economy. (458)

Postindustrial society A society whose economic system is engaged primarily in the processing and control of information. (111)

Postmodern society A technologically sophisticated society that is preoccupied with consumer goods and media images. (111)

Power The ability to exercise one's will over others. (198, 379)

Power elite A term used by C. Wright Mills to refer to a small group of military, industrial, and government leaders who control the fate of the United States. (386)

Precarious work Employment that is poorly paid, and from the worker's perspective, insecure and unprotected. (205)

Preindustrial city A city of only a few thousand people that is characterized by a relatively closed class system and limited mobility. (457)

Prejudice A negative attitude toward an entire category of people, often an ethnic or racial minority. (248)

Prestige The respect and admiration that an occupation holds in a society. (201)

Prevalence The total number of cases of a specific disorder that exist at a given time. (423)

Primary group A small group characterized by intimate, face-to-face association and cooperation. (121)

Profane The ordinary and commonplace elements of life, as distinguished from the sacred. (338)

Professional criminal A person who pursues crime as a day-to-day occupation, developing skilled techniques and enjoying a certain degree of status among other criminals. (180)

Proletariat Karl Marx's term for the working class in a capitalist society. (197)

Protestant ethic Max Weber's term for the disciplined work ethic, this-worldly concerns, and rational orientation to life emphasized by John Calvin and his followers. (343)

Public A dispersed group of people, not necessarily in contact with one another, who share an interest in an issue. (481)

Public opinion Expressions of attitudes on matters of public policy that are communicated to decision makers. (481)

Q

Qualitative research Research that relies on what is seen in field or naturalistic settings more than on statistical data. (34)

Quantitative research Research that collects and reports data primarily in numerical form. (34)

Quasi-religion A scholarly category that includes organizations that may see themselves as religious but are seen by others as "sort of religious." (350)

Questionnaire A printed or written form used to obtain information from a respondent. (34)

R

Racial formation A sociohistorical process in which racial categories are created, inhibited, transformed, and destroyed. (246)

Racial group A group that is set apart from others because of physical differences that have taken on social significance. (245)

Racial profiling Any arbitrary action initiated by an authority based on race, ethnicity, or national origin rather than on a person's behavior. (253)

Racism The belief that one race is supreme and all others are innately inferior. (248)

Random sample A sample for which every member of an entire population has the same chance of being selected. (30)

Rational-legal authority Power made legitimate by law. (379)

Reference group Any group that individuals use as a standard for evaluating themselves and their own behavior. (122)

Relative deprivation The conscious feeling of a negative discrepancy between legitimate expectations and present actualities. (483)

Relative poverty A floating standard of deprivation by which people at the bottom of a society, whatever their lifestyles, are judged to be disadvantaged *in comparison with the nation as a whole.* (206)

Reliability The extent to which a measure produces consistent results. (32, 373)

Religion According to Émile Durkheim, a unified system of beliefs and practices relative to sacred things. (338)

Religious belief A statement to which members of a particular religion adhere. (345)

Religious experience The feeling or perception of being in direct contact with the ultimate reality, such as a divine being, or of being overcome with religious emotion. (347)

Religious ritual A practice required or expected of members of a faith. (346)

Remittances The monies that immigrants return to their families of origin. Also called *migradollars.* (236)

Representative democracy A form of government in which certain individuals are selected to speak for the people. (382)

Research design A detailed plan or method for obtaining data scientifically. (33)

Resocialization The process of discarding former behavior patterns and accepting new ones as part of a transition in one's life. (91)

Resource mobilization The ways in which a social movement utilizes such resources as money, political influence, access to the media, and personnel. (483)

Rite of passage A ritual marking the symbolic transition from one social position to another. (89)

Role conflict The situation that occurs when incompatible expectations arise from two or more social positions held by the same person. (101)

Role exit The process of disengagement from a role that is central to one's self-identity in order to establish a new role and identity. (103)

Role strain The difficulty that arises when the same social position imposes conflicting demands and expectations. (102)

Role taking The process of mentally assuming the perspective of another and responding from that imagined viewpoint. (80)

Rumor A piece of information gathered informally that is used to interpret an ambiguous situation. (480)

S

Sacred Elements beyond everyday life that inspire awe, respect, and even fear. (338)

Sample A selection from a larger population that is statistically representative of that population. (30)

Sanction A penalty or reward for conduct concerning a social norm. (65, 165)

Sandwich generation The generation of adults who simultaneously try to meet the competing needs of their parents and their children. (299)

Sapir-Whorf hypothesis A hypothesis concerning the role of language in shaping our interpretation of reality. It holds that language is culturally determined. (61)

Science The body of knowledge obtained by methods based on systematic observation. (5)

Scientific management approach Another name for the classical theory of formal organizations. (127)

Scientific method A systematic, organized series of steps that ensures maximum objectivity and consistency in researching a problem. (29)

Second shift The double burden—work outside the home followed by child care and housework—that many women face and few men share equitably. (284)

Secondary analysis A variety of research techniques that make use of previously collected and publicly accessible information and data. (37)

Secondary group A formal, impersonal group in which there is little social intimacy or mutual understanding. (121)

Sect A relatively small religious group that has broken away from some other religious organization to renew what it considers the original vision of the faith. (348)

Secularization The process through which religion's influence on other social institutions diminishes. (336)

Segregation The physical separation of two groups of people in terms of residence, workplace, and social events; often imposed on a minority group by a dominant group. (255)

Self According to George Herbert Mead, a distinct identity that sets us apart from others. (79)

Serial monogamy A form of marriage in which a person may have several spouses in his or her lifetime, but only one spouse at a time. (313)

Sexism The ideology that one sex is superior to the other. (280)

Sick role Societal expectations about the attitudes and behavior of a person viewed as being ill. (420)

Significant other A term used by George Herbert Mead to refer to an individual who is most important in the development of the self, such as a parent, friend, or teacher. (81)

Single-parent family A family in which only one parent is present to care for the children. (324)

Slavery A system of enforced servitude in which some people are owned by other people. (193)

Small group A group small enough for all members to interact simultaneously—that is, to talk with one another or at least be well acquainted. (123)

Social capital The collective benefit of social networks, which are built on reciprocal trust. (13)

Social change Significant alteration over time in behavior patterns and culture, including norms and values. (494)

Social constructionist perspective An approach to deviance that emphasizes the role of culture in the creation of the deviant identity. (177)

Social control The techniques and strategies for preventing deviant human behavior in any society. (165)

Social disorganization theory The theory that crime and deviance are caused by the absence or breakdown of communal relationships and social institutions. (176)

Social epidemiology The study of the distribution of disease, impairment, and general health status across a population. (423)

Social inequality A condition in which members of society have differing amounts of wealth, prestige, or power. (19, 192)

Social institution An organized pattern of beliefs and behavior centered on basic social needs. (103)

Social interaction The ways in which people respond to one another. (98)

Social mobility Movement of individuals or groups from one position in a society's stratification system to another. (209)

Social movement An organized collective activity to bring about or resist fundamental change in an existing group or society. (482)

Social network A series of social relationships that links a person directly to others, and through them indirectly to still more people. (106)

Social role A set of expectations for people who occupy a given social position or status. (101)

Social science The study of the social features of humans and the ways in which they interact and change. (6)

Social structure The way in which a society is organized into predictable relationships. (98)

Socialism An economic system under which the means of production and distribution are collectively owned. (402)

Socialization The lifelong process in which people learn the attitudes, values, and behaviors appropriate for members of a particular culture. (76)

Societal-reaction approach Another name for *labeling theory*. (177)

Society A fairly large number of people who live in the same territory, are relatively independent of people outside their area, and participate in a common culture. (53)

Sociobiology The systematic study of how biology affects human social behavior. (55)

Sociocultural evolution Long-term trends in societies resulting from the interplay of continuity, innovation, and selection. (109)

Socioeconomic status (SES) A measure of social class that is based on income, education, and occupation. (202)

Sociological imagination An awareness of the relationship between an individual and the wider society, both today and in the past. (5)

Sociology The scientific study of social behavior and human groups. (5)

Squatter settlement An area occupied by the very poor on the fringe of a city, in which housing is constructed by the settlers themselves from discarded material. (462)

Status A term used by sociologists to refer to any of the full range of socially defined positions within a large group or society. (100)

Status group A term used by Max Weber to refer to people who have the same prestige or lifestyle, independent of their class positions. (198)

Stereotype An unreliable generalization about all members of a group that does not recognize individual differences within the group. (148, 247)

Stigma A label used to devalue members of certain social groups. (172)

Stratification A structured ranking of entire groups of people that perpetuates unequal economic rewards and power in a society. (192)

Subculture A segment of society that shares a distinctive pattern of mores, folkways, and values that differs from the pattern of the larger society. (58)

Suburb According to the Census Bureau, any territory within a metropolitan area that is not included in the central city. (464)

Survey A study, generally in the form of an interview or questionnaire, that provides researchers with information about how people think and act. (33)

Symbol A gesture, object, or word that forms the basis of human communication. (62)

Symbolic ethnicity An ethnic identity that emphasizes concerns such as ethnic food or political issues rather than deeper ties to one's ethnic heritage. (264)

T

Teacher-expectancy effect The impact that a teacher's expectations about a student's performance may have on the student's actual achievements. (367)

Technology Information about how to use the material resources of the environment to satisfy human needs and desires. (57, 109, 498)

Telecommuter An employee who works full-time or part-time at home rather than in an outside office, and who is linked to supervisor and colleagues through phone lines, Wi-Fi, the Internet, and smartphones. (131)

Terrorism The use or threat of violence against random or symbolic targets in pursuit of political aims. (391)

Theory In sociology, a set of statements that seeks to explain problems, actions, or behavior. (8)

Total fertility rate (TFR) The average number of children born alive to any woman, assuming that she conforms to current fertility rates. (450)

Total institution A term coined by Erving Goffman to refer to an institution that regulates all aspects of a person's life under a single authority, such as a prison, the military, a mental hospital, or a convent. (91)

Totalitarianism Virtually complete government control and surveillance over all aspects of a society's social and political life. (382)

Tracking The practice of placing students in specific curriculum groups on the basis of their test scores and other criteria. (365)

Traditional authority Legitimate power conferred by custom and accepted practice. (379)

Trained incapacity The tendency of workers in a bureaucracy to become so specialized that they develop blind spots and fail to notice obvious problems. (126)

Transnational An immigrant who sustains multiple social relationships that link his or her society of origin with the society of settlement. (265, 505)

Transnational crime Crime that occurs across multiple national borders. (182)

Triad A three-member group. (124)

U

Underclass The long-term poor who lack training and skills. (208)

Urban ecology An area of study that focuses on the interrelationships between people and their environment in urban areas. (459)

Urbanism A term used by Louis Wirth to describe distinctive patterns of social behavior evident among city residents. (458)

V

Validity The degree to which a measure or scale truly reflects the phenomenon under study. (32, 373)

Value A collective conception of what is considered good, desirable, and proper—or bad, undesirable, and improper—in a culture. (65)

Value-added model A theory of collective behavior proposed by Neil Smelser to explain how broad social conditions are transformed in a definite pattern into some form of collective behavior. (476)

Value neutrality Max Weber's term for objectivity of sociologists in the interpretation of data. (40)

Variable A measurable trait or characteristic that is subject to change under different conditions. (30)

Verstehen The German word for "understanding" or "insight"; used by Max Weber to stress the need for sociologists to take into account the subjective meanings people attach to their actions. (10)

Vertical mobility The movement of an individual from one social position to another of a different rank. (209)

Vested interests Veblen's term for those people or groups who will suffer in the event of social change, and who have a stake in maintaining the status quo. (497)

Victimization survey A questionnaire or interview given to a sample of the population to determine whether people have been victims of crime. (184)

Victimless crime A term used by sociologists to describe the willing exchange among adults of widely desired, but illegal, goods and services. (180)

Visitability The accessibility of private homes to visitors with disabilities. (488)

Vital statistics Records of births, deaths, marriages, and divorces gathered through a registration system maintained by governmental units. (450)

Voluntary association An organization established on the basis of common interest, whose members volunteer or even pay to participate. (129)

W

War Conflict between organizations that possess trained combat forces equipped with deadly weapons. (388)

Wealth An inclusive term encompassing all a person's material assets, including land, stocks, and other types of property. (193)

White-collar crime Illegal acts committed by affluent, "respectable" individuals in the course of business activities. (182)

White privilege Rights or immunities granted to people as a particular benefit or favor simply because they are White. (250)

World systems analysis Immanuel Wallerstein's view of the global economic system as one divided between certain industrialized nations that control wealth and developing countries that are controlled and exploited. (223, 461)

Z

Zero population growth (ZPG) The state of a population in which the number of births plus immigrants equals the number of deaths plus emigrants. (455)

references

A

Abercrombie, Nicholas, Bryan S. Turner, and Stephen Hill, eds. 1990. *Dominant Ideologies.* Cambridge, MA: Unwin Hyman.

———, Stephen Hill, and Bryan S. Turner. 1980. *The Dominant Ideology Thesis.* London: George Allen and Unwin.

Aberle, David F., A. K. Cohen, A. K. Davis, M. J. Leng, Jr., and F. N. Sutton. 1950. "The Functional Prerequisites of a Society." *Ethics 60* (January):100–111.

Abrahamson, Mark. 1978. *Functionalism.* Englewood Cliffs, NJ: Prentice Hall.

Abramovitz, Janet N. 2001a. "Averting Unnatural Disasters." Pp. 123–142 in *State of the World 2001,* edited by Lester R. Brown, Christopher Flavin, and Hilary French. New York: Norton.

———. 2001b. *Unnatural Disasters.* Washington DC: Worldwatch Institute.

Abramson, David, Irwin Redlener, Tasha Stehling-Ariza, and Elizabeth Fuller. 2007. *The Legacy of Katrina's Children: Estimating the Numbers of At-Risk Children in the Gulf Coast States of Louisiana and Mississippi.* New York: Columbia University Mailman School of Public Health.

Acharya, Meena. 2000. *Labor Market Developments and Poverty: With Focus on Economic Opportunities for Women.* Kathmandu, Nepal: Tanka Prasad Acharya Foundation/FES.

Acosta, R. Vivian, and Linda Jean Carpenter. 2001. "Women in Intercollegiate Sport: A Longitudinal Study: 1977–1998." Pp. 302–308 in *Sport in Contemporary Society: An Anthology,* 6th ed., edited by D. Stanley Eitzen. New York: Worth.

Adams, Tyrene L., and Stephen A. Smith. 2008. *Electronic Tribes: The Virtual Worlds of Geeks, Gamas, Shamans, and Scammers.* Austin: University of Texas Press.

Adamy, Janet. 2008. "Starbucks Plans to License 150 Stores in Europe." *New York Times,* June 12, p. B3.

Addams, Jane. 1910. *Twenty Years at Hull-House.* New York: Macmillan.

———. 1930. *The Second Twenty Years at Hull-House.* New York: Macmillan.

Adler, Freda. 1975. *Sisters in Crime: The Rise of the New Female Criminal.* New York: McGraw-Hill.

———, Gerhard O. W. Mueller, and William S. Laufer. 2007. *Criminology and the Criminal Justice System.* 6th ed. New York: McGraw-Hill.

Adler, Patricia A. 1993. *Wheeling and Dealing: An Ethnography of an Upper-Level Drug Dealing and Smuggling Community.* 2nd ed. New York: Columbia University Press.

———, and Peter Adler. 1991. *Backboards and Blackboards.* New York: Columbia University Press.

———, and ———. 1998. *Peer Power: Preadolescent Culture and Identity.* New Brunswick, NJ: Rutgers University Press.

———, and ———. 2003. "The Promise and Pitfalls of Going into the Field." *Contexts* (Spring):41–47.

———, and ———. 2004. *Paradise Laborers: Hotel Work in the Global Economy.* Ithaca, NY: Cornell University Press.

———, and ———. 2007. "The Demedicalization of Self-Injury: From Psychopathology to Sociological Deviance." *Journal of Contemporary Ethnography* 36 (October):537–570.

———, and ———. 2008a. "Of Rhetoric and Representation: The Four Faces of Ethnography." *Sociological Quarterly* (No. 1).

———, and ———. 2008b. "The Cyber Worlds of Self-Injurers: Deviant Communities, Relationships, and Selves." *Symbolic Interaction* 31 (1):33–56.

———, ———, and John M. Johnson. 1992. "Street Corner Society Revisited." *Journal of Contemporary Ethnography* 21 (April):3–10.

Adler, Roy D. 2008. "Counting on the Middle-Class." *Miller-McCune* (November/December):20–23.

Adorno, Theodor. [1971] 1991. *The Culture Industry.* London: Routledge.

Aguirre, Benigno E., E. L. Quarantelli, and Jorge L. Mendoza. 1988. "The Collective Behavior of Fads: The Characteristics, Effects, and Career of Streaking." *American Sociological Review* 53 (August):569–584.

Alain, Michel. 1985. "An Empirical Validation of Relative Deprivation." *Human Relations* 38 (8):739–749.

Alba, Richard D. 1990. *Ethnic Identity: The Transformation of White America.* New Haven, CT: Yale University Press.

Albas, Daniel, and Cheryl Albas. 1988. "Aces and Bombers: The Post-Exam Impression Management Strategies of Students." *Symbolic Interaction* 11 (Fall):289–302.

Albom, Mitch. 1997. *Tuesdays with Morrie.* New York: Doubleday.

Albrecht, Gary L. 1995. "Review of Disability Laws, Enabling Acts: Disability Rights in Britain and America." *Contemporary Sociology* 24 (5):627–629.

———. 1997. "Disability Is Area Rich with Sociological Opportunity." *Footnotes* 25 (December): 6.

———. 2004. "Disability: Sociological Perspectives." Pp. 3710–3713 in *International Encyclopedia of the Social and Behavioral Sciences,* edited by Neil J. Smelser and Paul B. Baltes. New York: Elsevier.

———, ed. 2005. *Encyclopedia of Disability.* Thousand Oaks, CA: Sage.

Al-Jadda, Souheila. 2006. "A Veil Doesn't Mean 'Oppressed.'" *USA Today,* June 22, p. 13A.

Al-Jadda, Souheila. 2007. "Does Al-Jazeera Belong in the USA?" *USA Today,* December 19, p. 13A.

Al Jazeera. 2009. Home page. Accessed February 5 (http://english.alijeera.net/HomePage).

Allen, Bem P. 1978. *Social Behavior: Fact and Falsehood.* Chicago: Nelson-Hall.

Allen, John L. 2010. *Student Atlas of World Geography.* 6th ed. New York: McGraw-Hill.

Allport, Gordon W. 1979. *The Nature of Prejudice.* 25th anniversary ed. Reading, MA: Addison-Wesley.

Alvord, Lori Arviso, and Elizabeth Cohen Van Pelt. 1999. *The Scalpel and the Silver Bear.* New York: Bantam.

Alwin, Duane F. 2002. "Generations X, Y, and Z: Are They Changing America?" *Contexts* (Fall/Winter):42–51.

Alzheimer's Association. 2008. *2008 Alzheimer's Disease Facts and Figures.* Chicago: Alzheimer's Association.

American Academy of Cosmetic Surgery. 2008. "2007 Procedural Survey Reveals a Two-Year Increase in Age of Patients Seeking Cosmetic Surgery." Press release. Accessed at www.cosmeticsurgery.org/media/pr_031308.pdf.

American Community Survey. 2008. "2007 American Community Survey." Accessed at http://factfinder.census.gov.

American Jewish Committee. 2005. *2005 Annual Survey of American Jewish Opinion.* New York: AJC.

American Lung Association. 2003. "Scene-smoking." Accessed December 19 (www.scenesmoking.org).

———. 2009. *State of the Air 2009.* Washington DC: ALA.

American Medical Association. 2009. "Violence prevention." Accessed April 14 (www.ama-assn.org/ama/pub/physician-resources/public-health/promoting-healthy-lifestyles/violence-prevention.shtml).

American Psychological Association. 2008. "Being Gay Is Just as Healthy as Being Straight." Accessed February 25 (www.apa.org).

American Sociological Association. 1997. *Code of Ethics.* Washington, DC: American Sociological Association. Available at www.asanet. org/members/ecoderev.html.

———. 2005. "Need Today's Data Yesterday." Accessed December 17 (www.asanet.org).

———. 2006. *Careers in Sociology with an Undergraduate Degree in Sociology.* 7th ed. Washington, DC: ASA.

———. 2009a. *2008 Guide to Graduate Departments of Sociology.* Washington, DC: ASA.

———. 2009b. "What Are Sections?" Accessed January 9 (www.asanet.org/cs/root/leftnav/sections/overview).

Amnesty International. 1994. *Breaking the Silence: Human Rights Violations Based on Sexual Orientation.* New York: Amnesty International.

Andersen, Margaret. 2007. *Thinking About Women: Sociological Perspectives on Sex and Gender,* 7th ed. New York: Allyn and Bacon.

Anderson, Elijah. 1990. *Streetwise: Race, Class, and Change in an Urban Community.* Chicago: University of Chicago Press.

Anderson, John Ward, and Molly Moore. 1993. "The Burden of Womanhood." *Washington Post National Weekly Edition* 10 (March 22–28):6–7.

Anderson, Warwick. 2003. *The Cultivation of Whiteness: Science, Health and Racial Destiny in Australia.* New York: Perseus.

Andrejevic, Mark. 2007. *iSpy: Surveillance and Power in the Interactive Era.* Lawrence, KS: University Press of Kansas.

Angier, Natalie. 1998. "Drugs, Sports, Body Image and G.I. Joe." *New York Times,* December 22, pp. D1, D3.

References

Annan, Kofi. 2009. *Africa: Preserving Progress at a Time of Global Crisis.* Geneva: Africa Progress Panel.

Ansell, Amy E. 2008. "Color Blindness." Pp. 320–321, vol. 1, in *Encyclopedia of Race, Ethnicity, and Society,* edited by Richard T. Schaefer. Thousand Oaks, CA: Sage.

Anti-Defamation League. 2008. "Anti-Semitic Incidents Decline for Third Straight Year in U.S., According to Annual ADL Audit." Accessed March 5 (www.adl.org).

Archibold, Randal C. 2006a. "Appeals Court Bars Arrests of Homeless in Los Angeles." *New York Times,* April 15, p. A9.

———. 2006b. "Las Vegas Rule Makes Feeding Homeless Illegal." *New York Times,* July 28, pp. A1, A23.

———, and Julia Preston. 2008. "Homeland Security Stands by Its Fence." *New York Times,* May 21.

Argetsinger, Amy, and Jonathan Krim. 2002. "Stopping the Music." *Washington Post National Weekly Edition* 20 (December 2):20.

Arias, Elizabeth, Lester R. Curtin, Rong Wei, and Robert N. Anderson. 2008. "U.S. Decennial Life Tables for 1999–2001, United States Life Tables." *National Vital Statistics Reports* 57 (August 5).

Armer, J. Michael, and John Katsillis. 1992. "Modernization Theory." Pp. 1299–1304, vol. 4, in *Encyclopedia of Sociology,* edited by Edgar F. Borgatta and Marie L. Borgatta. New York: Macmillan.

Armour, Stephanie. 2008. "New Faces Join Ranks of Nation's Homeless." *USA Today,* June 26, pp. B1–B2.

Asian American Journalists Association. 2007. "Media Advisory: Coverage on Virginia Tech Shooting Incident." Accessed May 16 (www.aaja.org).

Association of American Medical Colleges. 2008. *Facts Applicants, Matriculates and Graduates.* Accessed April 28, 2009 (www.aamc.org/data/facts/2008/2008summary.htm).

———. 2009. Table 9. "Distribution of U.S. Medical School Faculty by Sex and Rank." Accessed April 2 (www.aamc.org/data/facultyroster/usmsf08/08Table9.pdf).

Association of Theological Schools. 2009. "2008–09 Annual Data Tables." Accessed April 9 (www.ats.edu/Pages/default.aspx).

Astin, Alexander, Sarah A. Parrott, William S. Korn, and Linda J. Sax. 1994. *The American Freshman: Thirty Year Trends.* Los Angeles: Higher Education Research Institute.

Atchley, Robert C. 1976. *The Sociology of Retirement.* New York: Wiley.

———, and Amanda S. Barusch. 2004. *Social Forces and Agency: An Introduction to Social Gerontology.* 10th ed. Belmont, CA: Thomson.

Attwood, Bain. 2003. *Rights for Aborigines.* Crows Nest, Australia: Allen and Unwin.

Austin, April. 2002. "Cellphones and Strife in Congo." *Christian Science Monitor,* December 5, p. 11.

Australia. 1997. "Bringing Them Home: Report of the National Inquiry into the Separation of Aboriginal and Torres Strait Islander Children from Their Families." Accessed at www.humanrights.gov.au.

———. 2008. "Apology to Australia's Indigenous Peoples, House of Representatives, Parliament House, Canberra." Accessed February 13 (www.pm.gov.au/media/speech/2008/speech_0073.cfm).

Axtell, Roger E. 1990. *Do's and Taboos around the World.* 2nd ed. New York: Wiley.

Azumi, Koya, and Jerald Hage. 1972. *Organizational Systems.* Lexington, MA: Heath.

B

Babad, Elisha Y., and P. J. Taylor. 1992. "Transparency of Teacher Expectancies Across Language, Cultural Boundaries." *Journal of Educational Research* 86:120–125.

Baby Name Wizard. 2009. "Name Voyager." Accessed January 13 (www.babynamewizard.com).

Bacon Lovers' Talk. 2009. "Bacon Lovers' Talk." Accessed February 4 (www.bacontalk.com/).

Bainbridge, William Sims. 2007. "The Scientific Research Potential of Virtual Worlds." *Science* 317 (July 27):472–476.

Baker, C. Edwin. 2007. *Media Concentration and Democracy: Why Ownership Matters.* New York: Cambridge University Press.

Baker, Peter. 2009. "Obama Reverses Rules on U.S. Abortion Aid." *New York Times,* January 24.

Baker, Therese L. 1999. *Doing Social Research.* 3rd ed. New York: McGraw-Hill.

Barbaro, Michael. 2008. "Wal-Mart Says Most Workers Have Health Plan." *New York Times,* January 22.

Barboza, David. 2006. "Citing Public Sentiment, China Cancels Release of 'Geisha.'" *New York Times,* February 1, p. B6.

———. 2008. "Reform Stalls in Chinese Factories." *New York Times,* January 5, pp. B1, B6.

Barnes, Patricia, Eve Powell-Griner, Ken McFann, and Richard L. Nation. 2004. "Complementary and Alternative Medicine Use Among Adults: United States, 2002." *Advance Data from Vital and Health Statistics,* No. 343. Hyattsville MD: National Center for Health Statistics.

———. Barbara Bloom, and Richard Nahin. 2008. "Complementary and Alternative Medicine Use Among Adults and Children: United States, 2007." *National Health Statistics Reports,* December 10.

Barnow, Burt S. 2008. "The Employment Rate of People with Disabilities." *Monthly Labor Review* (November):44–50.

Barr, Cameron W. 2002. "Top Arab TV Network to Hit US Market." *Christian Science Monitor,* December 26, pp. 1, 7.

Barrett, David B., Todd M. Johnson, and Peter F. Crossing. 2008. "The 2007 Annual Megacensus of Religions." Chicago: Encyclopedia Britannica.

Barrionuevo, Alexei. 2008. "Amazon's 'Forest Peoples' Seek a Role in Striking Global Climate Agreements." *New York Times,* April 6, p. 6.

Barron, Milton L. 1953. "Minority Group Characteristics of the Aged in American Society." *Journal of Gerontology* 8:477–482.

Bartlett, Thomas. 2009a. "How the International Essay Mill Has Changed Cheating." *Chronicle of Higher Education,* March 20, pp. A1, A22–A25.

Barton, Bernadette. 2006. *Stripped: Inside the Lives of Exotic Dancers.* New York: New York University Press.

Bascara, Victor. 2008. "Model Minority." Pp. 910–912, vol. 2, in *Encyclopedia of Race, Ethnicity, and Society,* edited by Richard T. Schaefer. Thousand Oaks, CA: Sage.

Battin, Margaret P., Agnes van der Heide, and Bregje D. Onwuleaka-Philipsen. 2007. "Legal Physician-Assisted Dying in Oregon and the Netherlands: Evidence Concerning the Impact on Patients in 'Vulnerable' Groups." *Journal of Medical Ethics* 33 (October):591–597.

Bauerlein, Monika. 1996. "The Luddites Are Back." *Utne Reader* (March/April):24, 26.

Baum, Katrina. 2006. "Identity Theft, 2004." *Bureau of Justice Statistics Bulletin* (April).

Bauman, Kurt J. 1999. "Extended Measures of Well-Being: Meeting Basic Needs." *Current Population Reports,* ser. P-70, no. 67. Washington, DC: U.S. Government Printing Office.

Baverlein, Mark. 2008. "Online Literacy Is a Lesser Kind." *Chronicle of Higher Education,* September 19, pp. B10–B11.

Bazar, Emily. 2009. "Tent Cities Filling up with Casualties of the Economy. *USA Today,* May 5, pp. 1A–2A.

BBC News. 2005. "Indonesian Village Report: January 12, 2005." Accessed January 19 (www.theworld.org).

Beagan, Brenda L. 2001. " 'Even If I Don't Know What I'm Doing I Can Make It Look Like I Know What I'm Doing': Becoming a Doctor in the 1990s." *Canadian Review of Sociology and Anthropology* 38:275–292.

Bearman, Peter S., James Moody, and Katherine Stovel. 2004. "Chains of Affection: The Structure of Adolescent Romantic and Sexual Networks." *American Journal of Sociology* 110 (July):44–91.

Becker, Anne E. 2007. "Facets of Acculturation and Their Diverse Relations to Body Shape Concerns in Fiji." *International Journal of Eating Disorders* 40 (No. 1).

Becker, Howard S. 1952. "Social Class Variations in the Teacher-Pupil Relationship." *Journal of Educational Sociology* 25 (April):451–465.

———. 1963. *The Outsiders: Studies in the Sociology of Deviance.* New York: Free Press.

———, ed. 1964. *The Other Side: Perspectives on Deviance.* New York: Free Press.

———. 1973. *The Outsiders: Studies in the Sociology of Deviance.* Rev. ed. New York: Free Press.

Beddoes, Zanny Minton. 2008. "Whatever Next." Pp. 143–144, in *The World in 2009.* London: The Economist.

Beisel, Nicola and Tamara Kay. 2004. "Abortion, Race, and Gender in Nineteenth-Century America." *American Sociological Review* 69 (4):498–518.

Beiser, Vince. 2009. "Contrepreneurship." *Miller-McCune* (May–June):40–45.

Bell, Daniel. 1953. "Crime as an American Way of Life." *Antioch Review* 13 (Summer):131–154.

———. 1973. *The Coming of Post-Industrial Society.* New York: Basic Books.

———. 1999. *The Coming of Post-Industrial Society: A Venture in Social Forecasting.* With new foreword. New York: Basic Books.

———. 2009. *China's New Confucianism: Politics and Everyday Life in a Changing Society.* Princeton, NJ: Princeton University Press.

Bell, Wendell. 1981. "Modernization." Pp. 186–187 in *Encyclopedia of Sociology.* Guilford, CT: DPG Publishing.

Bellafante, Ginia. 2005. "Young South Asians in America Embrace 'Assisted' Marriages." *New York Times,* August 23, pp. A1, A15.

Belt, Don. 2002. "The World of Islam." *National Geographic* (January):26–85.

Bendick, Marc, Jr., Charles W. Jackson, and J. Horacio Romero. 1993. *Employment Discrimination against Older Workers: An Experimental Study of Hiring Practices.* Washington, DC: Fair Employment Council of Greater Washington.

Bendix, B. Reinhard. 1968. "Max Weber." Pp. 493–502 in *International Encyclopedia of the Social Sciences,* edited by David L. Sills. New York: Macmillan.

Benford, Robert D. 1992. "Social Movements." Pp. 1880–1887, vol. 4, in *Encyclopedia of Sociology,* edited by Edgar F. Borgatta and Marie Borgatta. New York: Macmillan.

Bennett, Vivienne, S. Dávila-Poblete, and M. N. Rico, eds. 2005. *Opposing Currents: The Politics of Water and Gender in Latin America.* Pittsburg: University of Pittsburg Press.

Bergen, Raquel Kennedy. 2006. *Marital Rape: New Research and Directions.* Harrisburg, PA: VAW Net.

Berger, Peter, and Thomas Luckmann. 1966. *The Social Construction of Reality.* New York: Doubleday.

Berk, Richard A., and Howard E. Aldrich. 1972. "Patterns of Vandalism during Civil Disorders as an Indicator of Selection of Targets." *American Sociological Review* 37 (October):533–547.

Berkeley Wellness Letter. 1990. "The Nest Refilled." 6 (February):1–2.

Berland, Gretchen K. 2001. "Health Information on the Internet: Accessibility, Quality, and Readability in English and Spanish." *Journal of the American Medical Association* 285 (March 23):2612–2621.

Berman, Paul. 2003. *Terror and Liberalism.* New York: Norton.

Bernasek, Anna. 2006. "A Poverty Line That's Out of Date and Out of Favor." *New York Times,* August 14, p. 8.

Bernstein, Elizabeth. 2007. "Colleges Move Boldly on Student Drinking." *Wall Street Journal,* December 6, pp. D1, D2.

Bernstein, Sharon. 2004. "Under the Radar, HIV Worsens." *Los Angeles Times,* October 16, pp. A1, A12.

Bhagat, Chetan. 2007. *One Night at the Call Centre.* London: Black Swan.

Bianchi, Suzanne M., and Daphne Spain. 1996. "Women, Work, and Family in America." *Population Bulletin* 51 (December).

Biddlecom, Ann, and Steven Martin. 2006. "Childless in America." *Contexts* 5 (Fall):54.

Bielby, Denise D., and William T. Bielby. 2002. "Hollywood Dreams, Harsh Realities: Writing for Film and Television." *Contexts* 1 (Fall/Winter):21–25.

———, and C. Lee Harrington. 2008. *Global TV: Exporting Television and Culture in the World Market.* New York: New York University Press.

Billings, Andrew C., J. R. Angelini, and S. T. Eastman. 2008. "Wie Shock: Television Commentary about Playing on the PGA and LPGA Tours." *Howard Journal of Communications* 19 (1):64–84.

Birnbaum, Jeffrey H. 2005. "Listen to the Wallet." *Washington Post National Weekly Edition,* April 4, p. 11.

Black, Donald. 1995. "The Epistemology of Pure Sociology." *Law and Social Inquiry* 20 (Summer):829–870.

Blau, Peter M., and Otis Dudley Duncan. 1967. *The American Occupational Structure.* New York: Wiley.

———, and Marshall W. Meyer. 1987. *Bureaucracy in Modern Society.* 3rd ed. New York: Random House.

Blauner, Robert. 1964. *Alienation and Freedom.* Chicago: University of Chicago Press.

———. 1972. *Racial Oppression in America.* New York: Harper and Row.

Blinder, Alan S. 2006. "Offshoring: The Next Industrial Revolution." *Foreign Affairs* (March/April).

Blumberg, Stephen J., and Julian V. Luke. 2007. "Coverage Bias in Traditional Telephone Surveys of Low-Income and Young Adults." *Public Opinion Quarterly* 71 (5):734–749.

Blumer, Herbert. 1955. "Collective Behavior." Pp. 165–198 in *Principles of Sociology,* 2nd ed., edited by Alfred McClung Lee. New York: Barnes and Noble.

———. 1969. *Symbolic Interactionism: Perspective and Method.* Englewood Cliffs, NJ: Prentice Hall.

Boase, Jeffery, John B. Horrigan, Barry Wellman, and Lee Rainie. 2006. *The Strength of Internet Ties.* Washington, DC: Pew Internet and American Life Project.

Bondy, Christopher. 2008. "Burakumin." Pp. 213–215, vol. 2, in *Encyclopedia of Race, Ethnicity, and Society,* edited by Richard T. Schaefer. Thousand Oaks, CA: Sage.

Bonilla-Silva, Eduardo. 2004. "From Bi-Racial to Tri-Racial: Towards a New System of Racial Stratification in the USA." *Ethics and Racial Studies* 27 (November):931–950.

———. 2006. *Racism Without Racists.* Lanham, MD: Rowman and Littlefield.

Borjas, George S. 2006. "Making It in America: Social Mobility in the Immigrant Population." *Future of Children* 16 (Fall):55–71.

———, Jeffrey Grogger, and Gordon H. Hanson. 2006. "Immigration and African-American Employment Opportunities: The Response of Wages, Employment, and Incarceration to Labor Supply Shocks." Working paper 12518. Cambridge, MA: National Bureau of Economic Research.

Bornschier, Volker, Christopher Chase-Dunn, and Richard Rubinson. 1978. "Cross-National Evidence of the Effects of Foreign Investment and Aid on Economic Growth and Inequality: A Survey of Findings and a Reanalysis." *American Journal of Sociology* 84 (November):651–683.

Bottomore, Tom, and Maximilien Rubel, eds. 1956. *Karl Marx: Selected Writings in Sociology and Social Philosophy.* New York: McGraw-Hill.

Boudreaux, Richard. 2002. "Indian Rights Law Is Upheld in Mexico." *Los Angeles Times,* September 7, p. A3.

Bourdieu, Pierre, and Jean-Claude Passerson. 1990. *Reproduction in Education, Society and Culture,* 2nd ed. London. Sage. Originally published as *La reproduction.*

Boushey, Heather. 2005. *Student Debt: Bigger and Bigger.* Washington, DC: Center for Economic and Policy Research.

Bouvier, Leon F. 1980. "America's Baby Boom Generation: The Fateful Bulge." *Population Bulletin* 35 (April).

Bowles, Samuel, and Herbert Gintis. 1976. *Schooling in Capitalistic America: Educational Reforms and the Contradictions of Economic Life.* New York: Basic Books.

Box Office Mojo. 2009. "Box Office: All Time" and "Box Office: Yearly 2008." Accessed February 5 (www.boxofficemojo.com/).

Brabazon, Tara. 2007. *The University of Google: Education in the (post) Information Age.* Burlington, VT: Ashgate.

Brady Campaign. 2009. "Stop Illegal Gun Trafficking Now." Accessed February 23 (www.bradycampaign.org/action/trafficking/background/).

Brandchannel.com. 2009. "Paul Blart: Mall Cop." Accessed February 4 (www.brandchannel.com/brandcameo_films.asp).

Brannigan, Augustine. 1992. "Postmodernism." Pp. 1522–1525 in *Encyclopedia of Sociology,* vol. 3, edited by Edgar F. Borgatta and Marie L. Borgatta. New York: Macmillan.

Brannon, Rush. 1995. "The Use of the Concept of Disability Culture: A Historian's View." *Disability Studies* 15 (Fall):3–15.

Braverman, Amy. 2002. "Open Door Sexuality." *University of Chicago Magazine* 95 (October): 20–21.

Braxton, Greg. 2007. "Is Prime Time Quietly Becoming Colorblind?" *Chicago Tribune,* March 20, sec. 5, p. 3.

Braxton, Gregory. 2009. "'Reality Television' in More Ways Than One." *Los Angeles Times,* February 17, pp. A1, A15.

Bray, James H., and John Kelly. 1999. *Stepfamilies: Love, Marriage, and Parenting in the First Decade.* New York: Broadway Books.

Breines, Winifred. 2007. "Struggling to Connect: White and Black Feminism in the Movement Years." *Contexts* 6 (Winter):18–24.

Brewer, Cynthia A., and Trudy A. Suchan. 2001. *Mapping Census 2000: The Geography of U.S. Diversity.* Washington, DC: U.S. Government Printing Office.

Brewer, Rose M., and Nancy A. Heitzeg. 2008. "The Racialization of Criminal Punishment." *American Behavioral Scientist* 51 (January):625–644.

Brint, Steven. 1998. *Schools and Societies.* Thousand Oaks, CA: Pine Forge Press.

Bromley, David G., and Mitchell L. Bracey, Jr. 1998. "The Church of Scientology: A Quasi-Religion." Pp. 141–156 in *Sects, Cults, and Spiritual Communities: A Sociological Analysis,* edited by William W. Zellner and Marc Petrowsky. Westport, CT: Praeger.

Brower, Brock. 1988. "The Pernicious Power of the Polls." *Money,* March 17, pp. 144–163.

Brown, David K. 2001. "The Social Sources of Educational Credentialism: Status Cultures, Labor Markets, and Organizations." *Sociology of Education* 74 (Extra issue):19–34.

Brown, Geoff. 2008a. "Cities Under Fire." *Johns Hopkins Public Health* (Fall).

———. 2008b. "Building a Safer Gun." *John Hopkins Public Health* (Fall).

Brown, Michael, and Amy Goldin. 1973. *Collective Behavior: A Review and Reinterpretation of the Literature.* Pacific Palisades, CA: Goodyear.

Brown, Patricia Leigh. 2004. "For Children of Gays, Marriage Brings Joy." *New York Times,* March 19, p. A13.

Brown, Robert McAfee. 1980. *Gustavo Gutierrez.* Atlanta: John Knox.

Brown, Roger W. 1954. "Mass Phenomena." Pp. 833–873, vol. 2, in *Handbook of Social Psychology,* edited by Gardner Lindzey. Reading, MA: Addison-Wesley.

Brown, S. Kathi. 2006. *Attitudes Toward Work and Job Security.* Washington, DC: AARP.

Browne, Irene, ed. 2001. *Latinas and African American Women at Work: Race, Gender, and Economic Inequlity.* New York: Russell Sage Foundation.

Brubaker, Bill. 2008. "Social Insecurity: Many People's Numbers Are Readily Available Online to Identity Thieves." *Washington Post National Weekly Edition,* (January 14), p. 34.

Brulle, Robert, and J. Craig Jenkins. 2008. "Fixing the Bungled U.S. Environmental Movement." *Contexts* 7 (Spring):14–18.

Brysk, Alison. 2005. *Human Rights and Private Wrongs: Constructing Global Civil Society.* New York: Routledge.

Buchanan, Joy. 2008. "Medicine Meets a Culture Gap." *USA Today,* February 14, p. 9D.

Buchholz, Barbara Ballinger. 2003. "Expanded Access." *Chicago Tribune,* January 26, sec. 16, pp. 1R, 5R.

Buchmann, Claudia, Thomas A. DiPrete, and Anne McDaniel. 2008. "Gender Inequalities in Education." *Annual Review of Sociology* 34:319–337.

Buckingham, David. 2007. "Selling Childhood? Children and Consumer Culture." *Journal of Children and Media* 1 (1):15–24.

Budig, Michelle J. 2002. "Male Advantage and the Gender Composition of Jobs: Who Rides the Glass Escalator?" *Social Problems* 49 (2):258–277.

Bullard, Robert D. 1993. *Dumping in Dixie: Race, Class, and Environmental Quality.* 2nd ed. Boulder, CO: Westview Press.

———, and Beverly Wright. 2009. *Race, Place, and Environmental Justice After Hurricane Katrina.* Boulder CO: Westview Press.

Bulle, Wolfgang F. 1987. *Crossing Cultures? Southeast Asian Mainland.* Atlanta: Centers for Disease Control.

Burawoy, Michael. 2005. "For Public Sociology." *American Sociological Review* 70 (February):4–28.

Bureau of Economic Analysis. 2009. National Income and Product Accounts Table: Table 2.1. Personal Income and Its Disposition. Accessed June 7 (www.bea.gov/national/nipaweb/ TableView.asp?SelectedTable=58&Freq=Qtr& FirstYear=2007&last year=2009).

Bureau of Justice Statistics. 2008. "Background Checks for Firearm Transfers, 2007." Accessed February 22, 2009 (www.ojp.usdoj.gov/bjs/pub/ html/bcft/2007/bcft07st.htm).

Bureau of Labor Statistics. 2006. "Number of Jobs Held, Labor Market Activity, and Earnings Growth Among the Youngest Baby Boomers: Results from a Longitudinal Survey." *News,* August 25, 2006. Washington, DC: BLS.

———. 2009a. "Union Members in 2008." Accessed January 30 (www.bls.gov/opub/ted/2009/jan/ wk4/arto5.htm).

———. 2009b. "Characteristics of Minimum Wage Workers: 2007." Accessed January 29 (www.bls .gov/cps/minwage2007.htm).

———. 2009c. "Household Data: Table 3." *Employment Status of Civilian Noninstitutional Population by Age, Sex, and Race.* Accessed March 15 (www.bls.gov/cps/cpsaat3.pdf).

Bureau of the Census. 1975. *Historical Statistics of the United States, Colonial Times to 1970.* Washington, DC: U.S. Government Printing Office.

———. 1994. *Statistical Abstract of the United States, 1994.* Washington, DC: U.S. Government Printing Office.

———. 1996. "Percent Distribution of Projected Households by Type: 1995 to 2010." Released May 1996. Accessed March 1, 2006 (www.census.gov).

———. 1998. "Race of Wife by Race of Husband." Internet release of June 10.

———. 2002. *Statistical Abstract of the United States, 2002.* Washington, DC: U.S. Government Printing Office.

———. 2003a. *Characteristics of American Indians and Alaska Natives. By Tribe and Language: 2000.* Washington, DC: U.S. Government Printing Office.

———. 2003b. TM-PCT023 *Percent of Persons of Arab Ancestry 2000.* Accessed March 4, 2004 (http://factfinder.census.gov).

———. 2004a. *Statistical Abstract of the United States, 2004–2005.* Washington, DC: U.S. Government Printing Office.

———. 2005a. *Florida, California and Texas Future Population Growth,* Census Bureau Reports, CB05-52. Washington, DC: U.S. Government Printing Office.

———. 2005f. "American Fact Finder: Places with United States." Accessed December 12 (http://factfinder.census.gov).

———. 2006a. *Statistical Abstract of the United States 2007.* Washington, DC: U.S. Government Printing Office.

———. 2006b. "American Community Survey 2006: Table R1601.Percent of People 5 Years and Over Who Speak a Language Other Than English at Home." Accessed October 14, 2007 (http://factfinder.census.gov).

———. 2007a. *Statistical Abstract, 2008.* Washington, DC: U.S. Government Printing Office.

———. 2007b. "America's Families and Living Arrangements: 2006." Current Population Survey accessible at www.census.gov.

———. 2008a. *Statistical Abstract, 2008.* Washington, DC: U.S. Government Printing Office.

———. 2008b. "Total Midyear Population for the World:1900–2050." (Data updated 3/27/2008.) Accessed April 9 (www.census.gov).

———. 2008c. "America's Families and Living Arrangements 2008." Accessed at www.census.gov/ population/www/socdemo/hh-fam/cps2008.html.

———. 2008d. "An Older and More Diverse Nation by Midcentury." Accessed August 14 (www.census.gov/Press-Release/www/releases/ archives/population/012496.html).

———2009a. *Statistical Abstract of the United States 2010.* Washington, DC: U.S. Government Printing Office.

———. 2009b. Population Analysis. Accessed at www.census.gov.

———. 2009c. Table A-3. "Immigration, Outmigration, and Net Migration for Metropolitan Areas: 1985–2008." Accessed May 2 (www.census.gov/population/socdemo/ migration/tab-a-3.pdf).

———. 2009d. "International Data Base." Accessed May 2 (www.census.gov/ipc/www/idbnew.html).

Burgdorf, Robert L., Jr. 2005. "Americans with Disabilities Act of 1990 (United States)." Pp. 93–101 in *Encyclopedia of Disability,* edited by Gary Albrecht. Thousand Oaks, CA: Sage.

Burger, Jerry M. 2009. "Replicating Milgram: Would People Still Obey Today?" *American Psychologist* 64 (January):1–11.

Burger King. 2009. "Whopper Sacrifice." Accessed February 4 (www.whoppersacrifice.com/).

Burgess, Ernest W. 1925. "The Growth of the City." Pp. 47–62 in *The City,* edited by Robert E. Park, Ernest W. Burgess, and Roderick D. McKenzie. Chicago: University of Chicago Press.

Burkeman, Oliver. 2007. "Virtual World Wakes Up to Violent Protest." *Manchester Guardian,* February 16, p. 6.

Butler, Daniel Allen. 1998. *"Unsinkable": The Full Story.* Mechanicsburg, PA: Stackpole Books.

Butler, Robert N. 1990. "A Disease Called Ageism." *Journal of American Geriatrics Society* 38 (February):178–180.

Butrica, Barbara A. 2008. *Do Assets Change the Racial Profile of Poverty among Older Adults?* Washington, DC: Urban Institute.

Byrd-Bredbenner, Carol, and Jessica Murray. 2003. "Comparison of the Anthropometric Measurements of Idealized Female Body Images in Media Directed to Men, Women, and Mixed Gender Audiences." *Topics in Clinical Nutrition* 18 (2):117–129.

Bystydzienski, Jill M., and Joti Sekhon. 1999. *Democratization and Women's Grassroots Movements.* Bloomington: Indiana University Press.

C

Cable, Sherry, and Charles Cable. 1995. *Environmental Problems/Grassroots Solutions: The Politics of Grassroots Environmental Conflict.* New York: St. Martin's Press.

Calhoun, Craig. 1998. "Community without Propinquity Revisited." *Sociological Inquiry* 68 (Summer):373–397.

———. 2003. "Belonging in the Cosmopolitan Imaginary." *Ethnicities* 3 (December):531–553.

Call, V. R., and Teachman, J. D. 1991. "Military Service and Stability in the Family Life Course." *Military Psychology* 3:233–250.

Cameron, Deborah. 2007. *The Myth of Mars and Venus.* Oxford: Oxford University Press.

Campaign Legal Center. 2004. "National Party Finances." *Weekly Reports,* November 19.

Campbell, Mary, Robert Haveman, Gary Sandefur, and Barbara Wolte. 2005. "Economic Inequality and Educational Attainment Across a Generation." *Focus* 23 (Spring):11–15.

Cañas, Jesus, Roberto Coronado, and Robert W. Gilman. 2007. "Southwest Economy." (March/ April). Accessed April 18 (http://dallasfed.org/ research/swe/2007/swe0702b.cfm).

Cantril, Hadley. 1940. *The Invasion from Mars: A Study in the Psychology of Panic.* Princeton, NJ: Princeton University Press.

Caplan, Ronald L. 1989. "The Commodification of American Health Care." *Social Science and Medicine* 28 (11):1139–1148.

Caplow, Theodore, and Louis Hicks. 2002. *Systems of War and Peace.* 2nd ed. Lanham, MD: University Press of America.

Carbon Trust. 2009. "About the Carbon Trust." Accessed April 28 (www.carbontrust.co.uk/default.ct).

Carmichael, Mary. 2007. "Troubled Waters." *Newsweek* 149 (June 4):52–56.

Carr, Nicholas. 2008a. *The Big Switch: Rewiring the World: From Edison to Google.* New York: Norton.

———. 2008b. "Is Google Making Us Stoopid?" *Atlantic* (July/August):56–58, 60, 62–63.

Carroll, Joseph. 2005. "Who Supports Marijuana Legalization?" November 1. Accessed January 19, 2007 (www.galluppoll.com).

———. 2006. "Public Continues to Support Right-to-Die for Terminally Ill Patients." Accessed June 26, 2007 (www.gallup.com).

———. 2007a. "Hispanics Support Requiring English Proficiency for Immigrants." Accessed July 24 (www.galluppoll.com).

———. 2007b. "Public Divide Over Moral Acceptability of Doctor-Assisted Suicide." Accessed June 18, 2009. (www.galluppoll.com).

Carroll, Rory. 2006. "Nicaragua Votes to Outlaw Abortion." *The Guardian (Manchester)*, October 27.

Carter, Bill. 2008. "TV Casting May Feel an Obama Effect." *New York Times*, November 29, pp. C1, C11.

Carty, Win. 1999. "Greater Dependence on Cars Leads to More Pollution in World's Cities." *Population Today* 27 (December):1–2

Castañeda, Jorge G. 1995. "Ferocious Differences." *Atlantic Monthly* 276 (July):68–69, 71–76.

Castells, Manuel. 1983. *The City and the Grass Roots*. Berkeley: University of California Press.

———. 1997. *The Power of Identity*. Vol. 1 of *The Information Age: Economy, Society and Culture*. London: Blackwell.

———. 1998. *End of Millennium*. Vol. 3 of *The Information Age: Economy, Society and Culture*. London: Blackwell.

———. 2000. *The Information Age: Economy, Society and Culture* (3 vols.). 2nd ed. Oxford and Malden, MA: Blackwell.

———. 2001. *The Internet Galaxy: Reflections on the Internet, Business, and Society*. New York: Oxford University Press.

Catalyst. 2009a. *2008 Catalyst Census of Women Corporate Officers and Top Earners of the Fortune 500*. New York: Catalyst.

———. 2009b. *Women in U.S. Management*. New York: Catalyst.

Cauchon, Dennis 2009. "Benefit Spending Soars to New High." *USA Today*, June 4, p. A1.

CBS News. 1979. Transcript of *Sixty Minutes* segment, "I Was Only Following Orders." March 31, pp. 2–8.

Center for Academic Integrity. 2006. *CAI Research*. Accessed January 10 (www.academicintegrity.org).

Center for American Women and Politics. 2009. *Fact Sheet: Women in the U.S. Congress 2009 and Statewide Elective Women 2009*. Rutgers, NJ: CAWP.

Center for Corporate Diversity. 2008. "Nordic 500, 2006–2008." Accessed March 17 (www .managementwomen.no).

Centers for Disease Control and Prevention. 2007. "U.S. Public Health Service Syphilis Study at Tuskegee." Accessed April 25 (www.cdc.gov).

———. 2008a. *HIV and AIDS in the United States: A Picture of Today's Epidemic*. Atlanta GA: CDC.

———. 2008b. "School-Associated Student Homicides—United States, 1992–2006." *MMWR Weekly* 57 (January 18):33–36.

Center for Responsible Politics. 2008. "U.S. Election Will Cost $5.3 Billion, Center for Responsive Politics Predicts." Accessed April 16 (www. opensecrets.org/news/2008/10/us-election-will-cost-53-billi.html).

———. 2009. "Banking on Becoming President." Accessed April 16 (www.opensecrets.org/pres08/index.php).

Centers for Medicare and Medicaid Services. 2008. "NHE Projections 2007–2017." Accessed March 23 (www.cms.hhs.gov).

Cerulo, Karen A., Janet M. Ruane, and Mary Chagko. 1992. "Technological Ties That Bind: Media Generated Primary Groups." *Communication Research* 19:109–129.

Chalfant, H. Paul, Robert E. Beckley, and C. Eddie Palmer. 1994. *Religion in Contemporary Society*. 3rd ed. Itasca, IL: F. E. Peacock.

Chambliss, William. 1973. "The Saints and the Roughnecks." *Society* 11 (November/December): 24–31.

Chan, Sewell. 2009. "City Unveils Facebook Page to Encourage Condom Use." *New York Times*, February 12, p. A32.

Charter, David, and Jill Sherman. 1996. "Schools Must Teach New Code of Values." *London Times*, January 15, p. 1.

Chase-Dunn, Christopher, and Peter Grimes. 1995. "World-Systems Analysis." Pp. 387–417 in *Annual Review of Sociology*, 1995, edited by John Hagan. Palo Alto, CA: Annual Reviews.

———, Yukio Kawano, and Benjamin D. Brewer. 2000. "Trade Globalization Since 1795: Waves of Integration in the World System." *American Sociological Review* 65 (February):77–95.

Chen, Shaohua, and Martin Ravallion. 2008. *The Developing World Is Poorer Than We Thought, But No Less Successful in the Fight against Poverty*. Geneva: Development Research Group, The World Bank.

Cheng, Shu-Ju Ada. 2003. "Rethinking the Globalization of Domestic Service." *Gender and Society* 17 (2):166–186.

Cherlin, Andrew J. 2003. "Should the Government Promote Marriage?" *Contexts* 2 (Fall):22–29.

———. 2006. On Single Mothers "Doing" Family. *Journal of Marriage and Family* 68 (November):800–803.

———. 2008a. *Public and Private Families: An Introduction*. 5th ed. New York: McGraw-Hill.

———. 2008b. "Can the Left Learn the Lessons of Welfare Reform?" *Contemporary Sociology* 37 (March):101–104.

———. 2009. *The Marriage-go-round: The State of Marriage and the Family in America Today*. New York: Knopf.

Chesney-Lind, Meda. 1989. "Girls' Crime and Woman's Place: Toward a Feminist Model of Female Delinquency." *Crime and Delinquency* 35:5–29.

Chicago Tribune. 1997. "In London, Prince Meets a Pauper, an Ex-Classmate." December 5, p. 19.

Children Now. 2004. *Fall Colors: 2003–04 Prime Time Diversity Report*. Oakland, CA: Children Now.

Chin, Kolin. 1996. *Chinatown Gangs: Extortion, Enterprise, and Ethnicity*. New York: Oxford University Press.

Chirot, Daniel, and Jennifer Edwards. 2003. "Making Sense of the Senseless: Understanding Genocide." *Contexts* 2 (Spring):12–19.

Choi, Yoonsun, and Benjamin B. Lahey. 2006. "Testing the Model Minority Stereotype: Youth Behaviors Across Racial and Ethnic Groups." *Social Science Review* (September):419–452.

Christakis, Nicholas A., and James H. Fowler. 2008. "The Collective Dynamics of Smoking in a Large Social Network." *New England Journal of Medicine* 358 (May 22):2249–2258.

Chronic Poverty Research Centre. 2008. *The Chronic Poverty Report 2008–09: Escaping Poverty Traps*. Geneva: Chronic Poverty Research Centre.

Chu, Henry. 2005. "Tractors Crush Heart of a Nation." *Los Angeles Times*, July 10, p. A9.

———. 2007. "English Divides India's Call-Centre Hub." *Guardian* 176 (February 16):3.

Chubb, Catherine, Simone Melis, Louisa Potter, and Raymond Storry. 2008. *The Global Gender Pay Gap*. London: Incomes Data Services.

Citizens Commission on Homelessness. 2004. *Home Again*. Portland, OR: Bureau of Housing and Community Development.

Civil Ventures. 2009. Home page. Accessed March 18 (www.civicventures.org).

Clark, Burton, and Martin Trow. 1966. "The Organizational Context." Pp. 17–70 in *The Study of College Peer Groups*, edited by Theodore M. Newcomb and Everett K. Wilson. Chicago: Aldine.

Clark, Candace. 1983. "Sickness and Social Control." Pp. 346–365 in *Social Interaction: Readings in Sociology*, 2nd ed., edited by Howard Robboy and Candace Clark. New York: St. Martin's Press.

Clarke Adele E., Janet K. Shim, Laura Maro, Jennifer Ruth Fusket, and Jennifer R. Fishman. 2003. "Bio Medicalization: Technoscientific Transformations of Health, Illness, and U.S. Biomedicine." *American Sociological Review* 68 (April):161–194.

Clarke, Lee. 2002. "Panic: Myth or Reality?" *Contexts* 1 (Fall):21–26.

Clawson, Dan, and Naomi Gerstel. 2002. "Caring for Our Young: Child Care in Europe and the United States." *Contexts* 1 (Fall/Winter):23–35.

Clemmitt, Marcia. 2005. "Intelligent Design." *CQ Researcher* 15 (July 29):637–660.

———. 2006. "Cyber Sociology." *CQ Researcher* 16 (July 28), pp. 625–648.

Clifford, Stephanie. 2008. "Billboards That Look Back." *New York Times*, May 31.

———. 2009. "Teaching Teenagers About Harassment." *New York Times*, January 27, p. B1.

Clinard, Marshall B., and Robert F. Miller. 1998. *Sociology of Deviant Behavior*. 10th ed. Fort Worth: Harcourt Brace.

Clymer, Adam. 2000. "College Students Not Drawn to Voting or Politics, Poll Shows." *New York Times*, January 2, p. A14.

Coates, Rodney. 2008. "Covert Racism in the USA and Globally." *Sociology Compass* 2:208–231.

Cockerham, William C. 2007. *Medical Sociology*. 10th ed. Upper Saddle River, NJ: Prentice Hall.

Cole, Elizabeth S. 1985. "Adoption, History, Policy, and Program." Pp. 638–666 in *A Handbook of Child Welfare*, edited by John Laird and Ann Hartman. New York: Free Press.

Cole, Mike. 1988. *Bowles and Gintis Revisited: Correspondence and Contradiction in Educational Theory*. Philadelphia: Falmer.

Coleman, Isobel. 2004. "The Payoff from Women's Rights." *Foreign Affairs* 83 (May/June):80–95.

Coleman, James William. 2006. *The Criminal Elite: Understanding White-Collar Crime*. 6th ed. New York: Worth.

522

———, and Donald R. Cressey. 1980. *Social Problems.* New York: Harper and Row.

Collier, Paul. 2007. *The Bottom Billion.* Oxford: Oxford University Press.

Collins, Patricia Hill. 2000. *Black Feminist Thought: Knowledge, Consciousness, and the Politics of Empowerment.* Revised 10th Anniv. 2nd ed. New York: Routledge.

Collins, Randall. 1975. *Conflict Sociology: Toward an Explanatory Sociology.* New York: Academic Press.

———. 1980. "Weber's Last Theory of Capitalism: A Systematization." *American Sociological Review* 45 (December):925–942.

———. 1986. *Weberian Sociological Theory.* New York: Cambridge University Press.

———. 1995. "Prediction in Macrosociology: The Case of the Soviet Collapse." *American Journal of Sociology* 100 (May):1552–1593.

Collura, Heather. 2007. "Roommate Concerns Fed by Facebook." *USA Today,* August 8, p. 6D.

Colucci, Jim. 2008. "All the World's a Screen." *Watch!* (June):50–53.

Columbia Accident Investigation Board. 2003. "*Columbia* Accident Investigation Board Report: Volume I." Washington, DC: CAIB, NASA.

Commission on Civil Rights. 1976. *A Guide to Federal Laws and Regulations Prohibiting Sex Discrimination.* Washington, DC: U.S. Government Printing Office.

———. 1981. *Affirmative Action in the 1980s: Dismantling the Process of Discrimination.* Washington, DC: U.S. Government Printing Office.

Commoner, Barry. 1971. *The Closing Circle.* New York: Knopf.

———. 1990. *Making Peace with the Planet.* New York: Pantheon.

———. 2007. "At 90, an Environmentalist from the 70's Still Has Hope." *New York Times,* June 19, p. D2.

Commonwealth Fund. 2008. *Why Not the Best?* New York: Commonwealth Fund.

Comstock, P., and M. B. Fox. 1994. "Employer Tactics and Labor Law Reform." Pp. 90–109 in *Restoring the Promise of American Labor Law,* edited by S. Friedman, R. W. Hurd, R. A. Oswald, and R. L. Seeber. Ithaca, NY: ILR Press.

Connell, R. W. 1987. *Gendered Power: Society, the Person, and Sexual Politics.* Stanford, CA: Stanford University Press.

———. 2002. *Gender.* Cambridge, UK: Polity Press.

———. 2005. *Masculinities.* 2nd ed. Berkeley: University of California Press.

Connelly, Marjorie. 2008. "Dissecting the Changing Electorate." *New York Times,* November 8, sec. WK.

Conner, Thaddeus, and William A. Taggart. 2009. "The Impact of Gaming on the Indian Nations in New Mexico." *Social Science Quarterly* 90 (March):52–70.

Conrad, Peter, ed. 2005. *The Sociology of Health and Illness: Cultural Perspectives.* 7th ed. New York: Worth.

———. 2009. *The Medicalization of Society: On the Transformation of Human Conditions into Treatable Disorders.* 11th ed. Baltimore, MD: John Hopkins University.

Cooley, Charles. H. 1902. *Human Nature and the Social Order.* New York: Scribner.

Coontz, Stephanie. 2006. "A Pop Quiz on Marriage." *New York Times,* February 19, p. 12.

Cooper, Jeremy. 2005. "Disability Law: Europe." Pp. 444–449 in *Encyclopedia of Disability,* edited by Gary Albrecht. Thousand Oaks, CA: Sage.

Cooper, K., S. Day, A. Green, and H. Ward. 2007. "Maids, Migrants and Occupational Health in the London Sex Industry. *Anthropology and Medicine* 14 (April):41–53.

Corbett, Christianne, Catherine Hill, and Andresse St. Rose. 2008. *Where the Girls Are: The Facts About Gender Equity in Education.* Washington, DC: American Association of University Women.

Cornwell, Benjamin, Edward O. Laumann, and L. Phip Schumm. 2008. "The Social Connectedness of Older Adults: A National Profile." *American Sociological Review* 73 (April):185–203.

Coser, Lewis A. 1977. *Masters of Sociological Thought: Ideas in Historical and Social Context.* 2nd ed. New York: Harcourt, Brace and Jovanovich.

Coser, Rose Laub. 1984. "American Medicine's Ambiguous Progress." *Contemporary Sociology* 13 (January):9–13.

Côté, James E. 2000. *Arrested Adulthood: The Changing Nature of Identity and Maturity in the Late World.* New York: New York University.

Couch, Carl J. 1968. "Collective Behavior: An Examination of Some Stereotypes." *Social Problems* 15:310–322.

———. 1996. *Information Technologies and Social Orders.* Edited with an introduction by David R. Maines and Shing-Ling Chien. New York: Aldine de Gruyter.

Council on Ethical and Judicial Affairs, American Medical Association. 1992. "Decisions Near the End of Life." *Journal of the American Medical Association* 267 (April 22–29):2229–2333.

Council on Scientific Affairs. 1999. "Hispanic Health in the United States." *Journal of the American Medical Association* 265 (January 9):248–252.

Counts, D. A. 1977. "The Good Death in Kaliai: Preparation for Death in Western New Britain." *Omega* 7:367–372.

Cowell, Alan. 2005. "Gay Britons Signing Up as Unions Become Legal." *New York Times,* December 5.

Cox, Oliver C. 1948. *Caste, Class, and Race: A Study in Social Dynamics.* Detroit: Wayne State University Press.

Cox, Rachel S. 2003. "Home Schooling Debate." *CQ Researcher* 13 (January 17):25–48.

Crabtree, Steve, and Brett Pelham. 2009. "Religion Provides Emotional Boost to World's Poor." Accessed April 9 (www.gallup.com/poll/116449/Religion-Provides-Emotional-Boost-World-Poor.aspx).

Crissey, Sarah R. 2009. "Educational Attainment in the United States: 2007." *Current Population Reports,* ser. P20-S60. Washington, DC: U.S. Government Printing Office.

Cross, Simon, and Barbara Bagilhole. 2002. "Girls' Jobs for the Boys? Men, Masculinity and Non-Traditional Occupations." *Gender, Work, and Organization* 9 (April):204–226.

Croteau, David, and William Hoynes. 2003. *Media/Society: Industries, Images, and Audiences.* 3rd ed. Thousand Oaks, CA: Pine Forge Press.

———. 2006. *The Business of the Media: Corporate Media and the Public Interest.* 2nd ed. Thousand Oaks, CA: Pine Forge Press.

Croucher, Sheila L. 2004. *Globalization and Belonging: The Politics of Identity in a Changing World.* Lanham, MD: Rowman and Littlefield.

Crouse, Kelly. 1999. "Sociology of the *Titanic.*" *Teaching Sociology Listserv.* May 24.

Crowe, Jerry, and Valli Herman. 2005. "NBA Lists Fashion Do's and Don'ts." *Los Angeles Times,* October 19, pp. A1, A23.

Crump, Andy. 2006. "Suicide in Japan." *Lancet* 367 (April 8): 1143.

Cuff, E. C., W. W. Sharrock, and D. W. Francis, eds. 1990. *Perspectives in Sociology.* 3rd ed. Boston: Unwin Hyman.

Cullen, Francis T., Jr., and John B. Cullen. 1978. *Toward a Paradigm of Labeling Theory,* ser. 58. Lincoln: University of Nebraska Studies.

Cullen, Lisa Takevchi. 2007. "Till Work Do Us Part." *Time,* October 8, pp. 63–64.

Cumming, Elaine, and William E. Henry. 1961. *Growing Old: The Process of Disengagement.* New York: Basic Books.

Currie, Elliot. 1985. *Confronting Crime: An American Challenge.* New York: Pantheon.

Currie, Elliot. 1998. *Crime and Punishment in America.* New York: Metropolis Books.

Curry, Timothy Jon. 1993. "A Little Pain Never Hurt Anyone: Athletic Career Socialization and the Normalization of Sports Injury." *Symbolic Interaction* 26 (Fall):273–290.

Curtis, J., Douglas Baer, and E. Grabb. 2001. "Nations of Joiners: Explaining Voluntary Association Memberships in Democratic Societies." *American Sociological Review* 66(6):783–805.

Curtiss, Susan. 1977. *Genie: A Psycholinguistic Study of a Modern Day "Wild Child."* New York: Academic Press.

———. 1985. "The Development of Human Cerebral Lateralization." Pp. 97–116 in *The Dual Brain,* edited by D. Frank Benson and Eran Zaidel. New York: Guilford.

Cushing-Daniels, Brenda, and Sheila R. Zedlewski. 2008. "Tax and Spending Policy and Economic Mobility." Washington, DC: Economic Mobility Project. Also accessible at www.economic-mobility.org/reports_and_research/literature_reviews?id=0004.

D

Dahl, Robert A. 1961. *Who Governs?* New Haven, CT: Yale University Press.

Dahrendorf, Ralf. 1958. "Toward a Theory of Social Conflict." *Journal of Conflict Resolution* 2 (June):170–183.

———. 1959. *Class and Class Conflict in Industrial Sociology.* Stanford, CA: Stanford University Press.

Daley, Suzanne. 1999. "Doctors' Group of Volunteers Awarded Nobel." *New York Times,* October 16, pp. A1, A6.

Daley-Harris, Sam, ed. 2002. *Pathways out of Poverty: Innovations in Microfinance for the Poorest Families.* Bloomfield, CT: Komarian Press.

Dalla, Rochelle L., and Wendy C. Gamble. 2001. "Teenage Mothering and the Navajo Reservation: An Examination of Intergovernmental Perceptions and Beliefs." *American Indian Culture and Research Journal* 25 (1):1–19.

Daniels, Arlene Kaplan. 1987. "Invisible Work." *Social Problems* 34 (December):403–415.

————. 1988. *Invisible Careers.* Chicago: University of Chicago Press.

Daniszewski, John. 2003. "Al-Jazeera TV Draws Flak Outside—and Inside—the Arab World." *Los Angeles Times,* January 5, pp. A1, A5.

Dao, James. 1995. "New York's Highest Court Rules Unmarried Couples Can Adopt." *New York Times,* November 3, pp. A1, B2.

Darlin, Damon. 2006. "It's O.K to Fall Behind the Technology Curve." *New York Times,* December 30, p. B6.

Darwin, Charles. 1859. *On the Origin of Species.* London: John Murray.

Dash, Erich. 2006. "Executive Pay: A Special Project." *New York Times,* April 9, sec. 3, pp. 1, 5.

Davé, Shiipa. 2009. "No Life Without Wife: Interracial Pairings." Transnationalism, and Arranged Marriage in South Asian America." Paper presented at the annual meeting of the American Studies Association.

David, Gary. 2004. "Scholarship on Arab Americans Distorted Past 9/11." *Al Jadid* (Winter/Spring):26–27.

————. 2008. "Arab Americans." Pp. 84–87, vol. 1, in *Encyclopedia of Race, Ethnicity, and Society,* edited by Richard T. Schaefer. Thousand Oaks, CA: Sage.

Davies, Christie. 1989. "Goffman's Concept of the Total Institution: Criticisms and Revisions." *Human Studies* 12 (June):77–95.

Davis, Darren W., and Brian D. Silver. 2003. "Stereotype Threat and Race of Interviewer Knowledge." *American Journal of Political Science* 47 (January):33–45.

Davis, Donald B., and Karen A. Polonko. 2001. *Telework America 2001 Summary.* Accessed March 3, 2003 (www.workingfromanywhere.org/telework/twa2001.htm).

Davis, Gerald. 2003. *America's Corporate Banks Are Separated by Just Four Handshakes.* Accessed March 7 (www.bus.umich.edu/research/davis.html).

————. 2004. "American Cronyism: How Executive Networks Inflated the Corporate Bubble." *Contexts* (Summer):34–40.

Davis, James A., Tom W. Smith, and Peter V. Marsden. 2007. *General Social Surveys, 1972–2006: Cumulative Codebook.* Chicago: National Opinion Research Center.

————. 2009. *General Social Surveys, 1972–2008: Cumulative Codebook.* Chicago: National Opinion Research Center.

Davis, Kingsley. 1940. "Extreme Social Isolation of a Child." *American Journal of Sociology* 45 (January):554–565.

————. 1947. "A Final Note on a Case of Extreme Isolation." *American Journal of Sociology* 52 (March):432–437.

————, and Wilbert E. Moore. 1945. "Some Principles of Stratification." *American Sociological Review* 10 (April):242–249.

————. [1949] 1995. *Human Society.* Reprint. New York: Macmillan.

Davis, Mike. 2005. *Planet of Slums.* London: Verso.

Davis, Nanette J. 1975. *Sociological Constructions of Deviance: Perspectives and Issues in the Field.* Dubuque, IA: Wm. C. Brown.

De Anda, Roberto M. 2004. *Chicanas and Chicanos in Contemporary Society.* 2nd ed. Lanham, MD: Rowman and Littlefield.

Death Penalty Information Center. 2009. "Executions in the United States, 1608–1976, 1976 to Present, By State." Accessed February 22 (www.deathpenaltyinfo.org/executions-united-states-1608-1976-state).

Deegan, Mary Jo, ed. 1991. *Women in Sociology: A Bio-Biographical Sourcebook.* Westport, CT: Greenwood.

————. 2003. "Textbooks, the History of Sociology, and the Sociological Stock of Knowledge." *Sociological Theory* 21 (November):298–305.

Deflem, Mathieu. 2005. "'Wild Beasts Without Nationality': The Uncertain Origins of Interpol, 1898–1910." Pp. 275–285 in *Handbook of Transnational Crime and Justice,* edited by Philip Rerchel. Thousand Oaks, CA: Sage.

Deibert, Ronald J., John Palfrey, Rafal Rohozinski, and Jonathan Zittrain. 2008. *Access Denied: The Practice and Policy of Global Internet Filtering.* Cambridge, MA: MIT Press.

Delaney, Kevin J. 2005. "Big Mother Is Watching." *Wall Street Journal,* November 26, pp. A1, A6.

Della Porta, Donatella, and Sidney Tarrow, eds. 2005. *Transnational Protest and Global Activism.* Lanham, MD: Rowman and Littlefield.

Deloria, Vine, Jr. 1999. *For This Land: Writings on Religion in America.* New York: Routledge.

DeNavas-Walt, Carmen, Bernadette D. Proctor, and Jessica C. Smith. 2008. "Income, Poverty, and Health Insurance Coverage in the United States: 2007." Pp. 60–235 in *Current Population Survey.* Washington DC: U.S. Government Printing Office.

Denny, Charlotte. 2004. "Migration Myths Hold No Fears." *Guardian Weekly,* February 26, p. 12.

Denzin, Norman K. 2004. "Postmodernism." Pp. 581–583 in *Encyclopedia of Social Theory,* edited by George Ritzer. Thousand Oaks, CA: Sage.

DeParle, Jason. 2007. "Migrant Money Flow: A \$300 Billion Current." *New York Times,* November 18, Work section p. 3.

————. 2009. "The 'W' Word, Re-Engaged." *New York Times,* February 8, Week in Review, p. 1.

Department of Agriculture. 2004. *2002 Census of Agriculture: Preliminary Report AC-02-A-PR.* Washington, DC: U.S. Government Printing Office.

Department of Education. 1999. *Report on State Implementation of the Gun-Free Schools Act. School Year 1997–98.* Rockville, MD: Westat.

————. 2004. *Crime and Safety in America's Public Schools.* Washington, DC: U.S. Government Printing Office.

Department of Education. 2006. *Integrated Postsecondary Education Data Systems, Completions, 1995–2004.* Washington, DC: NCES.

Department of Energy. 2004. *Permanent Markers Implementation Plan.* Carlsbad, NM: Carlsbad Field Office, Department of Energy.

Department of Health and Human Sciences. 2009. "Trends in Foster Care and Adoption—FY 2002–FY 2007." Accessed April 6 (www.acf.hhs.gov/programs/cb/stats_research/afcars/secllgbll).

Department of Homeland Security. 2008. "Immigration Enforcement Actions: 2007." In *Annual Report December 2008.* Washington, DC: Department of Homeland Security.

Department of Justice. 2000. *The Civil Liberties Act of 1988: Redress for Japanese Americans.* Accessed June 29 (www.usdoj.gov/crt/ora/main.html).

————. 2008a. *Crime in the United States, 2007.* Washington, DC: U.S. Government Printing Office.

————. 2008b. "Hate Crime Statistics, 2007." Accessible at www.Fbi.gov/ucr/ucr.htm.

Department of Labor. 1995a. *Good for Business: Making Full Use of the Nation's Capital.* Washington, DC: U.S. Government Printing Office.

————. 1995b. *A Solid Investment: Making Full Use of the Nation's Human Capital.* Washington, DC: U.S. Government Printing Office.

Department of State. 2001. "Immigrant Visas Issued to Orphans Coming to the U.S." Accessed August 1 (http://travel.state.gov/orphan_numbers.html).

————. 2009. "Total Adoptions to the United States." Accessed April 5 (http://adoption.state.gov/news/total_chart.html?css=print).

Desai, Manisha. 1996. "If Peasants Build Their Own Dams, What Would the State Have Left to Do?" Pp. 209–224, Vol. 19, in *Research in Social Movements, Conflicts and Change,* edited by Michael Dobkowski and Isidor Wallimann. Greenwich, CT: JAI Press.

Desmond, Matthew and Ruth N. López Turley. 2009. The Role of Familism in Explaining the Hispanic-White College Application Gap. *Social Problems* 56 (2):311–334.

Deutsch, Francine M. 2007. "Undoing Gender." *Gender and Society* 21 (February):106–127.

Devitt, James. 1999. *Framing Gender on the Campaign Trail: Women's Executive Leadership and the Press.* New York: Women's Leadership Conference.

Di Carlo, Matthew, and Nate Johnson, with Pat Cochran. 2008. *Survey and Analysis of Teacher Salary Trends 2007.* Washington, DC: American Federation of Teachers.

Diamond, Jared. 2003. "Globalization, Then." *Los Angeles Times,* September 14, pp. M1, M3.

Diamond, Shari Seidman, and Mary R. Rose. 2005. "Real Juries." Pp. 255–284 in *Annual Review of Law and Social Science 2005.* Palo Alto, CA: Annual Reviews.

Diefenbach, Donald L., and Mark D. West. 2007. "Television and Attitudes Toward Mental Health Issues: Cultivation Analysis and the Third Person Effect." *Journal of Community Psychology* 35 (2):181–195.

Diehl, William C., and Esther Prins. 2008. "Unintentional Outcomes in Second Life: Intercultural Literacy and Cultural Identity in a Virtual World." *Language and Intercultural Communication* 8(2):101–116.

DiFonzo, Nicholas, and Prashant Bordia. *Rumor Psychology: Social and Organizational Approaches.* Washington, DC: American Psychological Association.

Dillon, Sam. 1998. "Sex Bias at Border Plants in Mexico Reported by U.S." *New York Times,* January 13, p. A6.

————. 2004. "Education Can Be Long, Hard Haul for Nation's Rural Kids." *Chicago Tribune,* May 28, p. 13.

Dillon, Sam. 2008. "Under 'No Child' Law, Even Solid Schools Falter." *New York Times,* October 15, pp. A1, A14.

DiMaggio, Paul, Eszter Hargittai, W. Russell Neuman, and John P. Robinson. 2001. "Social Implications of the Internet." Pp. 307–336 in *Annual Review of Sociology, 2001,* edited by Karen S. Cook and John Hogan. Palo Alto, CA: Annual Reviews.

Directors Guild of America. 2002. *Diversity Hiring Special Report.* Los Angeles: DGA.

Disaster Research Center. 2009. "About the DRC." Accessed May 5 (www.udel.edu/DRC/aboutus/about.html).

Dobbs, Michael. 2004. "'No Child' Law Leaves a Good Deal Behind." *Washington Post National Weekly Edition,* May 9, p. 29.

Doctors Without Borders. 2008. *Speaking Out.* New York: Doctors Without Borders.

Dodds, Klaus. 2000. *Geopolitics in a Changing World.* Harlow, England: Pearson Education.

Domhoff, G. William. 1978. *Who Really Rules? New Haven and Community Power Reexamined.* New Brunswick, NJ: Transaction.

———. 2006. *Who Rules America?* 5th ed. New York: McGraw-Hill.

Dominick, Joseph R. 2009. *The Dynamics of Mass Communication: Media in the Digital Age.* 10th ed. New York: McGraw-Hill.

Donadio, Rachel. 2009. "Facebook 'Fans' of the Mafia May Be More, Authorities Say." *New York Times,* January 20, pp. A1, A8.

Donnelly, Sally B. 2007. "Growing Younger." *Time* (January bonus section):A13–A14.

Donohue, Elizabeth, Vincent Schiraldi, and Jason Ziedenberg. 1998. *School House Hype: School Shootings and Real Risks Kids Face in America.* New York: Justice Policy Institute.

Doress, Irwin, and Jack Nusan Porter. 1977. *Kids in Cults: Why They Join. Why They Stay, Why They Leave.* Brookline, MA: Reconciliation Associates.

Dorn, Stan. 2008. *Uninsured and Dying Because of It.* Washington, DC: Urban Institute.

Dorning, Mike. 2009. "Muslim World Outreach." *Chicago Tribune,* January 25, p. 6.

Dotson, Floyd. 1991. "Community." P. 55 in *Encyclopedic Dictionary of Sociology.* 4th ed. Guilford, CT: Dushkin.

Dougherty, John, and David Holthouse. 1999. "Bordering on Exploitation." Accessed March 5 (www.phoenixnewtime.com/issies/1998-07-09/feature.html).

Dougherty, Kevin, and Floyd M. Hammack. 1992. "Education Organization." Pp. 535–541 in *Encyclopedia of Sociology,* vol. 2, edited by Edgar F. Borgatta and Marie L. Borgatta. New York: Macmillan.

Dreifus, Claudia. 2003. "A Conversation with Lee Clarke." *New York Times,* May 20, Science Times section, p. 2.

———. 2004. "A Sociologist with an Advanced Degree in Calamity." *New York Times,* September 7, p. D2.

———. 2005. "A Sociologist Confronts 'the Messy Stuff' of Race, Genes and Disease." *New York Times,* October 18.

DuBois, W. E. B. [1899] 1916. *The Philadelphia Negro: A Social Study.* Philadelphia: University of Pennsylvania Press.

———. [1900] 1969. "To the Nations of the World." Pp. 19–23 in *An ABC of Color,* edited by W. E. B. DuBois. New York: International Publishers.

———. [1903] 1961. *The Souls of Black Folks: Essays and Sketches.* New York: Fawcett.

———. [1903] 2003. *The Negro Church.* Walnut Creek, CA: Alta Mira Press.

———. [1909] 1970. *The Negro American Family.* Atlanta University. Reprinted 1970. Cambridge, MA: M.I.T. Press.

———. [1940] 1968. *Dusk of Dawn.* New York: Harcourt, Brace. Reprint, New York: Schocken Books.

Dugger, Celia. 2006. "Peace Prize to Pioneer of Loans for Those Too Poor to Borrow." *New York Times,* October 14, pp. A1, A6.

Dukes, Richard L., Tara M. Bisel, Karoline N. Burega, Eligio A. Lobato, and Matthew D. Owens. 2003. "Expression of Love, Sex, and Hurt in Popular Songs: A Content Analysis of All-Time Greatest Hits." *Social Science Journal:* 40 (4) 643–650.

Dundas, Susan, and Miriam Kaufman. 2000. "The Toronto Lesbian Family Study." *Journal of Homosexuality* 40 (20):65–79.

Duneier, Mitchell. 1994a. "On the Job, but Behind the Scenes." *Chicago Tribune,* December 26, pp. 1, 24.

———. 1994b. "Battling for Control." *Chicago Tribune,* December 28, pp. 1, 8.

———. 1999. *Sidewalk.* New York: Farrar, Straus and Giroux.

Dunlap, Riley E., and Angela G. Mertig. 1991. "The Evolution of the U.S. Environmental Movement from 1970 to 1990: An Overview." *Society of National Resources* 4 (July–September):209–218.

Dunne, Gillian A. 2000. "Opting into Motherhood: Lesbians Blurring the Boundaries and Transforming the Meaning of Parenthood and Kinship." *Gender and Society* 14 (February):11–35.

Durden, T. Elizabeth, and Robert A. Hummer. 2006. "Access to Healthcare Among Working-Aged Hispanic Adults in the United States." *Social Science Quarterly* 87 (December):1319–1343.

Durkheim, Émile. [1893] 1933. *Division of Labor in Society.* Translated by George Simpson. Reprint. New York: Free Press.

———. [1895] 1964. *The Rules of Sociological Method.* Translated by Sarah A. Solovay and John H. Mueller. Reprint. New York: Free Press.

———. [1897] 1951. *Suicide.* Translated by John A. Spaulding and George Simpson. Reprint. New York: Free Press.

———. [1912] 2001. *The Elementary Forms of Religious Life.* A new translation by Carol Cosman. New York: Oxford University Press.

Durrenberger, E. Paul. 2007. "The Anthropology of Organized Labor in the United States." *Annual Review of Anthropology* 36:73–88.

Duster, Troy. 2002. "Sociological Stranger in the Land of the Human Genome Project." *Contexts* 1 (Fall):69–70.

Dykman, Jason. 2006. "America by the Numbers." Time 168 (October):41–54.

F

Eaton, Leslie. 2007. "Urban to Care, Storm Evacuees Give Farm a Try." *New York Times,* April 28, pp. A1, A9.

Ebaugh, Helen Rose Fuchs. 1988. *Becoming an Ex: The Process of Role Exit.* Chicago: University of Chicago Press.

Eckenwiler, Mark. 1995. "In the Eyes of the Law." *Internet World* (August):74, 76–77.

Eckstein, Megan. 2009. "Focusing on Education, White House Touts Perkins Loan for Middle Class." *Chronicle of Higher Education,* March 20, p. A21.

Economic Mobility Project. 2007. *Economic Mobility of Immigrants in the United States.* Washington, DC: Pew Charitable Trust.

———. 2009. *Findings from a National Survey and Focus Groups on Economic Mobility.* Washington, DC: Pew Charitable Trusts.

The Economist. 2003b. "The One Where Pooh Goes to Sweden." (April 5):59.

———. 2004. "Battle on the Home Front." (February 21):8–10.

———. 2005a. "The Policeman's Dilemma." 377 (October 15):58–59.

———. 2005b. "We Are Tous Québécois." (January 8):39.

———. 2005c. "Behind the Digital Divide." (March 2):22–25.

———. 2005f. "The Hidden Wealth of the Poor." (November 5):1–14.

———. 2006a. "The World's Largest Economies." (April 1):84.

———. 2006b. "The New Organization." (January 21):3–18.

———. 2006c. "Splitting the Digital Difference." (September 23), 3–4.

———. 2007a. "Giving to Charity: Bring Back the Victorians." 382 (February 17):56–57.

———. 2007b. "Africa and the Internet: The Digital Gap." (October 12):64.

———. 2007c. "Going Hybrid: A Special Report on Business in Japan." (December 21):3–18.

———. 2008a. "Maharishi Mahesh Yogi." (February 16):95.

———. 2008b. "A Ravenous Dragon: A Special Report on China's Quest for Resources." (March 15):1–22.

———. 2008c. "Has 'a dollar a day' had its day?" (May 24):100.

———. 2008d. "Following the Crowd." (September 6):10–11.

———. 2009. "Burgeoning Bourgeoisie." (February 14):1–22.

Ehrenreich, Barbara. 2001. *Nickel and Dimed: On (Not) Getting By in America.* New York: Metropolitan.

Ehrlich, Paul R. 1968. *The Population Bomb.* New York: Ballantine.

———, and Anne H. Ehrlich. 1990. *The Population Explosion.* New York: Simon and Schuster.

———, and Katherine Ellison. 2002. "A Looming Threat We Won't Face." *Los Angeles Times,* January 20, p. M6.

Eitzen, D. Stanley. 2009. *Fair and Foul: Beyond the Myths and Paradoxes of Sport.* 4th ed. Lanham, MD: Rowman and Littlefield.

Ellingwood, Ken. 2008. "Mexico Court Backs Abortion Rights." *Los Angeles Times,* August 29, p. A3.

Ellison, Brandy. 2008. "Tracking." Pp. 301–304, vol. 2, in *Encyclopedia of Race, Ethnicity, and Society,* edited by Richard T. Schaefer. Thousand Oaks, CA: Sage.

Ellison, Jesse. 2008. "A New Grip on Life." *Newsweek* 152 (December 15):64.

Ellison, Nicole, Charles Stein Field, and Cliff Lampe. 2007. "The Benefits of Facebook 'friends': Exploring the Relationship between College Students' Use of Online Social Networks and Social Capital." *Journal of Computer-Mediated Communication* 12 (4):1143–1168.

Ellison, Ralph. 1952. *Invisible Man.* New York: Random House.

Ely, Robin J. 1995. "The Power of Demography: Women's Social Construction of Gender Identity at Work." *Academy of Management Journal* 38 (3):589–634.

Embree, Ainslie. 2003. "Religion." Pp. 101–220 in *Understanding Contemporary India,* edited by Sumit Ganguly and Neil DeVotta. Boulder, CO: Lynne Rienner.

Emery, David. 1997. "The Kidney Snatchers." Accessed December 21, 1999 (http://urbanlegends.about.com/culture/urbanlegends/library/blkid.htm).

Engardio, Pete. 1999. "Activists Without Borders." *BusinessWeek,* October 4, pp. 144–145, 148, 150.

Engels, Friedrich [1884] 1959. "The Origin of the Family, Private Property, and the State." Pp. 392–394, excerpted in *Marx and Engels: Basic Writings on Politics and Philosophy,* edited by Lewis Feuer. Garden City, NY: Anchor Books.

Entine, Jon, and Martha Nichols. 1996. "Blowing the Whistle on Meaningless 'Good Intentions.'" *Chicago Tribune,* June 20, sec. 1, p. 21.

Epstein, Cynthia Fuchs. 1999. "The Major Myth of the Women's Movement." *Dissent* (Fall):83–111.

Epstein, Robert. 2005. "Psychology's Top 10 Misguided Ideas." *Psychology Today* 38 (January/February):55–58, 60.

Erikson, Kai. 1966. *Wayward Puritans: A Study in the Sociology of Deviance.* New York: Wiley.

———. 1986. "On Work and Alienation." *American Sociological Review* 51 (February):1–8.

Escárcega, Sylvia. 2008. "Mexico." Pp. 898–902, vol. 2, in *Encyclopedia of Race, Ethnicity, and Society,* edited by Richard T. Schaefer. Thousand Oaks, CA: Sage.

ESPN. 2009. "PGA and LPGA Money Leaders—2008." Accessed January 8 (http://sports.espn.go.com/golf/moneyleaders).

Etaugh, Claire. 2003. "Witches, Mothers and Others: Females in Children's Books." *Hilltopics* (Winter):10–13.

Etzioni, Amitai. 1964. *Modern Organization.* Englewood Cliffs, NJ: Prentice Hall.

———. 1965. *Political Unification.* New York: Holt, Rinehart, and Winston.

Eureka County. 2006. "EPA Hears Testimony on Proposed Radiation Rule." *Nuclear Waste Office Newsletter* (Eureka County Yucca Mountain Information Office) 11 (Winter).

European Union. 2009. "Treaty of Lisbon: Taking Europe into the 21st Century." Accessed May 5 (http://europa.eu/lisbon_treaty/index_en.htm).

Evergeti, Venetia, and Elisabetta Zontini. 2006. "Introduction: Some Critical Reflections on Social Capital, Migration and Transnational Families." *Ethnic and Racial Studies* 29 (November):1025–1039.

F

Facebook. 2009. Statistics. Accessed January 21 (www.facebook.com/press/info.php?statistics).

Fackler, Martin. 2007. "Career Women in Japan Find a Blocked Path." *New York Times,* August 6.

Faiola, Anthony. 2005. "Their Husbands Made Them Sick." *Washington Post National Weekly Edition* 23 (October 24):18.

———. 2006. "Japan's Vulnerable Elderly." *Washington Post National Weekly Edition* 23 (February 27):18.

Fairtrade Foundation. 2009. "Retail Products." Accessed April 30 (www.fairtrade.org.uk/products/retail_products/default.aspx).

Faith, Nazila. 2005. "Iranian Cleric Turns Blogger in Campaign for Reform." *New York Times,* January 16, p. 4.

Fallows, Deborah. 2006. *Pew Internet Project Data.* Washington, DC: Pew Internet and American Life Project.

Faris, Robert, and Nart Villeneuve. 2008. "Measuring Global Internet Filtering." Pp. 5–56 in *Access Denied: The Practice and Policy of Global Internet Filtering,* edited by Ronald Deibert, John Palfrey, Rafal Rohozinski, and Jonathan Zittrain. Cambridge, MA: MIT Press.

Farley, Maggie. 2004. "U.N. Gay Policy Is Assailed." *Los Angeles Times,* April 9, p. A3.

Farley, Melissa, and Victor Malarek. 2008. "The Myth of the Victimless Crime." *New York Times,* March 12, p. A27.

Farr, Grant M. 1999. *Modern Iran.* New York: McGraw-Hill.

Fausset, Richard. 2003. "Sikhs Mark New Year, Fight Post-September 11 Bias." *Los Angeles Times,* April 14, pp. B1, B7.

———. 2009. "Assisted-Suicide Debate Heats Up." *Los Angeles Times,* February 27, pp. A1, A20.

Favreault, Melissa. 2008. "Discrimination and Economic Mobility." Washington, DC: Economic Mobility Project. Also. accessible at www.economicmobility.org/reports_and_research/literature_reviews?id=0004.

Feagin, Joe R. 1983. *The Urban Real Estate Game: Playing Monopoly with Real Money.* Englewood Cliffs, NJ: Prentice Hall.

———. 1989. *Minority Group Issues in Higher Education: Learning from Qualitative Research.* Norman, OK: Center for Research on Minority Education, University of Oklahoma.

———. 2001. "Social Justice and Sociology: Agenda for the Twenty-First Century." *American Sociological Review* 66 (February):1–20.

———, Harnán Vera, and Nikitah Imani. 1996. *The Agony of Education: Black Students at White Colleges and Universities.* New York: Routledge.

Featherman, David L., and Robert M. Hauser. 1978. *Opportunity and Change.* New York: Aeodus.

Federal Election Commission. 2001. "2000 Official Presidential General Election Results." Accessed March 16, 2008 (www.fec.gov/pubrec/2000presgeresults.htm).

Fellmann, Jerome D., Arthur Getis, and Judith Getis. 2007. *Human Geography.* 9th ed. New York: McGraw-Hill.

Felson, David, and Akis Kalaitzidis. 2005. "A Historical Overview of Transnational Crime." Pp. 3–19 in *Handbook of Transnational Crime and Justice,* edited by Philip Reichel. Thousand Oaks, CA: Sage.

Feminist Majority Foundation. 2007. "Feminists Are the Majority." Accessed February 25 (www.feminist.org).

Ferber, Abby L., and Michael S. Kimmel. 2008. "The Gendered Face of Terrorism." *Sociology Compass* 2:870–887.

Ferree, Myra Marx. 2005. "It's Time to Mainstream Research on Gender." *Chronicle of Higher Education* 51 (August 21):B10.

———, and David A. Merrill. 2000. "Hot Movements, Cold Cognition: Thinking about Social Movements in Gendered Frames." *Contemporary Society* 29 (May):454–462.

Feuer, Alan. 2002. "High-Rise Colony of Workers Evolves for Their Retirement." *New York Times,* August 5, pp. A1, A15.

Feuer, Lewis S. 1989. *Marx and Engels: Basic Writings on Politics and Philosophy.* New York: Anchor Books.

Fiala, Robert. 1992. "Postindustrial Society." Pp. 1512–1522 in *Encyclopedia of Sociology,* vol. 3, edited by Edgar F. Borgatta and Marie L. Borgatta. New York: Macmillan.

Field, John. 2008. *Social Capital.* 2nd ed. London: Routledge.

Fields, Jason. 2004. "America's Families and Living Arrangements: 2003." *Current Population Reports,* ser. P-20, no. 553. Washington, DC: U.S. Government Printing Office.

Fields, Jessica. 2005. "'Children Having Children': Race, Innocence, and Sexuality Education." *Social Problems* 52 (4):549–571.

Fiji TV. 2009. Home page. Accessed January 18 (www.fijitv.com.fj).

Finch, Emily, and Vanessa E. Munro. 2005. "Juror Stereotypes and Blame Attribution in Rape Cases Involving Intoxicants." *British Journal of Criminology* 45 (June):25–38.

———. 2007. "The Demon Drink and the Demonized Woman: Socio-Sexual Stereotypes and Responsibility Attribution in Rape Trials Involving Intoxicants." 16 (4):591–614.

———. 2008. "Lifting the Veil: The Use of Focus Groups and Trial Simulations in Legal Research." *Journal of Law and Society* 35:30–51.

Fine, Gary C. 1987. *With the Boys: Little League Baseball and Preadolescent Culture.* Chicago: University of Chicago Press.

———. 2008. " Robbers Cave." Pp. 1163–1164, vol. 3, in *Encyclopedia of Race, Ethnicity, and Society,* edited by Richard T. Schaefer. Thousand Oaks, CA: Sage.

Finkel, Steven E., and James B. Rule. 1987. "Relative Deprivation and Related Psychological Theories of Civil Violence: A Critical Review." *Research in Social Movements* 9:47–69.

Fiss, Peer C., and Paul M. Hirsch. 2005. "The Discourse of Globalization: Framing of an Emerging Concept." *American Sociological Review* (February):29–52.

Fitchett, George. 1980. "It's Time to Bury the Stage Theory of Death and Dying." *Oncology Nurse Exchange II* (Fall).

Fitzgerald, Kathleen J. 2008. "White Privilege." Pp. 1403–1405, vol. 3, in *Encyclopedia of Race, Ethnicity, and Society,* edited by Richard T. Schaefer. Thousand Oaks, CA: Sage.

———, and Diane M. Rodgers. 2000. "Radical Social Movement Organization: A Theoretical Model." *The Sociological Quarterly* 41 (4):573–592.

Flacks, Richard. 1971. *Youth and Social Change.* Chicago: Markham.

Fletcher, Connie. 1995. "On the Line: Women Cops Speak Out." *Chicago Tribune Magazine,* February 19, pp. 14–19.

Flora, Cornelia Butler, and Jan L. Flora, with Susan Fey. 2004. *Rural Communities: Legacy and Change.* 2nd ed. Boulder, CO: Westview Press.

Florio, Gwen. 2006. "Vacant Seat Tough to Fill If 'Districts' Empty, Too." *USA Today,* January 24, p. 3A.

Flynn, Laurie J. 2008. "MySpace Mind-Set Finally Shows Up at the Office." *New York Times,* April 9, p. H7.

References

Fonseca, Felicia. 2008. "Dine College on Quest to Rename Navajo Cancer Terms." *News from Indian Country* 22 (January 7):11.

Forsythe, David P. 1990. "Human Rights in U.S. Foreign Policy: Retrospect and Prospect." *Political Science Quarterly* 105 (3):435–454.

Fortune. 2007. "Global 500," (July 14).

———. "Global 500". Accessed October 1 (http://money.cnn.com/magazines/fortune/global500/2008/).

Fouché, Gladys. 2008. "Norway's Gender Deadline Passes." *The Guardian Weekly,* April 1, p.15.

Foy, Paul. 2006. "Interior Rejects Goshute Nuclear Waste Stockpile." *Indian Country Today* 20 (September 18):1.

Frank, Robert. 2007. *Richistan.* New York: Crown Books.

———. 2009a. "A Recession Rolls-Royce? Bad Idea." Accessed March 16 (http://blogs.wsj.com/wealth/2009/03/05/a-recession-rolls-royce-bad-idea/tab/print/).

———. 2009b. "Can a 15,000-Square-Foot Mansion Be 'Green'?" Accessed March 16 (http://blogs/wsj.com/weatlh/2009/03/02/can-a-15000-square-foot-mansion-be-green/).

Franke, Richard Herbert, and James D. Kaul. 1978. "The Hawthorne Experiments: First Statistical Interpretation." *American Sociological Review* 43 (October):623–643.

Franklin, John Hope, and Alfred A. Moss. 2000. *From Slavery to Freedom: A History of African Americans.* 8th ed. Upper Saddle River, NJ: Prentice Hall.

FreeBabarAhmad. 2009. "Home page." Accessed May 5 (www.freebabarahmad.com).

Freeman, Jo. 1973. "The Origins of the Women's Liberation Movement." *American Journal of Sociology* 78 (January):792–811.

———. 1975. *The Politics of Women's Liberation.* New York: McKay.

Freidson, Eliot. 1970. *Profession of Medicine.* New York: Dodd, Mead.

French, Howard W. 2000. "The Pretenders." *New York Times Magazine,* December 3, pp. 86–88.

———. 2002. "Teaching Japan's Salarymen to Be Their Own Men." *New York Times,* November 27, p. A4.

———. 2004. "China's Textbooks Twist and Omit History." *New York Times,* December 6, p. A10.

———. 2008. "Lines of Grinding Poverty, Untouched by China's Boom." *New York Times,* January 13, p. 4.

Freudenburg, William R. 2005. "Seeing Science, Courting Conclusions: Reexamining the Intersection of Science, Corporate Cash, and the Law." *Sociological Forum* 20 (March):3–33.

Freudenheim, Milt. 2005. "Help Wanted: Oldest Workers Please Apply." *New York Times,* March 23, pp. A1, C3.

Fridlund, Alan. J., Paul Erkman, and Harriet Oster. 1987. "Facial Expressions of Emotion; Review of Literature 1970–1983." Pp. 143–224 in *Nonverbal Behavior and Communication,* 2nd ed., edited by Aron W. Seigman and Stanley Feldstein. Hillsdale, NJ: Erlbaum.

Friedan, Betty. 1963. *The Feminine Mystique.* New York: Dell.

Friedman, Thomas L. 2005. *The World Is Flat: A Brief History of the Twenty-first Century.* New York: Farrar, Straus and Giroux.

Friend, David. 2007. *Watching the World Change: The Stories Behind the Images of 911.* New York: Picador.

Friends of the Congo. 2009. "Coltan: What You Should Know." Accessed April 20 (www.friendsofthecongo.org/new/coltan.php).

Fry, Richard. 2009. *The Rapid Growth and Changing Complexion of Suburban Public Schools.* Washington, DC: Pew Hispanic Center.

Fudge, Judy, and Rosemary Owens, eds. 2006. *Precarious Work, Women, and the New Economy: The Challenge to Legal Norms.* Oxford, UK: Hart.

Furstenberg, Frank F. 2007. "The Making of the Black Family: Race and Class in Qualitative Studies in the Twentieth Century." *Annual Review of Sociology* 33:429–348.

Furstenberg, Frank, and Andrew Cherlin. 1991. *Divided Families: What Happens to Children When Parents Part.* Cambridge, MA: Harvard University Press.

Furstenberg, Sheela Kennedy, Jr., Vonnie C. McCloyd, Rubén G. Rumbaut, and Richard A. Setterstein, Jr. 2004. "Growing Up Is Harder to Do." *Contexts* 3:33–41.

Fuwa, Makiko. 2004. "Macro-Level Gender Inequality and the Division of Household Labor in 22 Countries." *American Sociological Review* 69 (December):751–767.

G

Gailey, Robert. 2007. "As History Repeats Itself, Unexpected Developments Move Us Forward." *Journal of Rehabilitation Research and Development* 44 (4):vii–xiv.

Galbraith, John Kenneth. 1977. *The Age of Uncertainty.* Boston: Houghton Mifflin.

Gale Cengage Learning. 2009. "Associations Unlimited." Accessed January 27 (www.gale.cengage.com).

Gallup. 2007c. "Media Use and Evaluation." Accessed April 19 (www.gallup.com).

———. 2008a. "Environment." Accessed March 18 (www.gallup.com).

———. 2008b. "Homosexual Relations." Accessed March 6 (www.gallup.com).

———. 2008c. "Campaign Financing Appears to Be Non-Issue for Voters." Accessed April 16, 2009 (www.gallup.com/poll/111652/Campaign-Financing-Appears-Nonissue-Voters.aspx).

———. 2008e. "Religion." Accessed March 14 (www.gallup.com).

———. 2009a. "Gallup's Pulse of Democracy: Gun Laws." Accessed February 23 (www.gallup.com/).

———. 2009c. "Religion." Accessed April 9 (www.gallup.com).

———. 2009d. "Military and National Defense." Accessed April 17 (www.gallup.com/poll/1666/military-national-defense-aspx).

———. 2009e. "Party Affiliation." Accessed April 17 (www.gallup.com/poll/15370/Party-Affiliation.aspx).

———. 2009f. "Healthcare System." Accessed April 27 (www.gallup.com/poll/4708/Healthcare-System.aspx?version=print).

Gallup Healthways. 2009. "Gallup Healthways Well-Being Index Findings: Snapshot Findings." Accessed April 28 (www.well-beingindex.com/SnapshotFindings.asp).

Gallup Opinion Index. 1978. "Religion in America, 1977–1978." 145 (January).

Gamson, Joshua. 1989. "Silence, Death, and the Invisible Enemy: AIDS Activism and Social Movement 'Newness.' " *Social Problems* 36 (October):351–367.

———, and Pearl Latteier. 2004. "Do Media Monsters Devour Diversity?" *Contexts* (Summer):26–32.

Gans, Herbert J. 1991. *People, Plans, and Policies: Essays on Poverty, Racism, and Other National Urban Problems.* New York: Columbia University Press and Russell Sage Foundation.

———. 1995. *The War against the Poor: The Underclass and Antipoverty Policy.* New York: Basic Books.

Garcia-Moreno, Claudia, Henrica A. F. M. Jansen, Mary Ellsberg, Lori Heise, and Charlotte Watts. 2005. *WHO Multi-country Study on Women's Health and Domestic Violence Against Women.* Geneva, Switzerland: WHO.

Gardner, Gary, Erik Assadourian, and Radhika Sarin. 2004. "The State of Consumption Today." Pp. 3–21 in *State of the World 2004,* edited by Brian Halweil and Lisa Mastny. New York: Norton.

Gardner, Marilyn. 2003. "This View of Seniors Just Doesn't 'Ad' Up." *Christian Science Monitor,* January 15, p. 15.

Garfinkel, Harold. 1956. "Conditions of Successful Degradation Ceremonies." *American Journal of Sociology* 61 (March):420–424.

Garner, Roberta. 1996. *Contemporary Movements and Ideologies.* New York: McGraw-Hill.

———. 1999. "Virtual Social Movements." Presented at Zaldfest: A conference in honor of Mayer Zald. September 17, Ann Arbor, MI.

Garreau, Joel. 1991. *Edge City: Life on the New Frontier.* New York: Doubleday.

Gaudin, Sharon. 2009. "Facebook Has Whopper of a Problem with Burger King Campaign." *Computerworld,* January 15.

Gay, Lesbian and Straight Education Network. 2009. "About GLSEN." Accessed April 14 (www.glsen.org).

Gecas, Viktor. 2004. "Socialization, Sociology of." Pp. 14525–14530 in *International Encyclopedia of the Social and Behavioral Sciences,* edited by Neil J. Smelser and Paul B. Baltes. Cambridge, MA: Elsevier.

Geist, Claudia. 2005. "The Welfare State and the Home: Regime Differences in the Domestic Division of Labour." *European Sociological Review 2005* 21 (1):23–4.

Gentile, Carmen. 2009. "Student Fights Record of 'Cyberbullying.'" *New York Times,* February 8, p. 20.

Gentleman, Amelia. 2006. "Bollywood Captivated by the Call Centre Culture." *Guardian Weekly,* June 2, p. 17.

———. 2007a. "Police Ignore Serial Killings in Delhi Slum, Exposing Unequal Justice for India's Poor." *New York Times,* January 7, p. 8.

———. 2007b. "Young Sikh Men Get Haircuts, Annoying Their Elders." *New York Times,* March 29, p. A3.

Gerencher, Kristen. 2007. "New Online Consumer Health Site Aims Big." Accessed May 20 (www.marketwatch.com).

Gerson, Kathleen, and Jerry A. Jacobs. 2004. "The Work-Home Crunch." *Contexts* 3 (Fall):29–37.

Gerth, H. H., and C. Wright Mills. 1958. *From Max Weber: Essays in Sociology.* New York: Galaxy.

Gertner, Jon. 2005. "Our Ratings, Ourselves." *New York Times Magazine,* April 10, pp. 34–41, 56, 58, 64–65.

Gibbs, Deborah A., Sandra L. Mortin, Lawrence L. Kupper, and Ruby E. Johnson. 2007. "Child Maltreatment in Enlisted Soldiers' Families During Combat-Related Deployments." *Journal of the American Medical Association* 298 (5):528–535.

Gibbs, Nancy. 1993. "Rx for Death." *Time,* May 31, pp. 34–39.

Giddens, Anthony. 1991. *Modernity and Self-Identity: Self and Society in the Late Modern Age.* Cambridge, UK: Polity.

Giddings, Paul J. 2008. *Ida: A Sword Among Lions.* New York: Amistad.

Gilley, Brian Joseph. 2006. *Becoming Two-Spirit: Gay Identity and Social Acceptance in Indian Country.* Lincoln, NE: University of Nebraska Press.

Giordano, Peggy C. 2003. "Relationships in Adolescence." Pp. 257–281 in *Annual Review of Sociology, 2003,* edited by Karen S. Cook and John Hagan. Palo Alto, CA: Annual Reviews.

———, Stephen A. Cernkovich, and Alfred DeMaris. 1993. "The Family and Peer Relations of Black Adolescents." *Journal of Marriage and Family* 55 (May): 277–287.

Giridharadas, Anand. 2008. "Flirting by Text Message, Indians Test Social Limits." *New York Times,* March 21, p. A8.

Giroux, Henry A. 1988. *Schooling and the Struggle for Public Life: Critical Pedagogy in the Modern Age.* Minneapolis: University of Minnesota Press.

Gitlin, Todd. 2002. *Media Unlimited: How the Torrent of Images and Sounds Overwhelms Our Lives.* New York: Henry Holt.

Glanton, Dahleen. 2007. "Law AIDS Awareness Adds to Crisis." *Chicago Tribune,* February 7, p. 3.

Glascock, Anthony P. 1990. "By Any Other Name, It Is Still Killing: A Comparison of the Treatment of the Elderly in American and Other Societies." Pp. 44–56 in *The Cultural Context of Aging: Worldwide Perspective,* edited by Jay Sokolovsky. New York: Bergen and Garvey.

Glenn, David. 2004. "A Dangerous Surplus of Sons?" *Chronicle of Higher Education* 50 (April 30):A14–A16, A18.

Glenn, David. 2007. "Anthropologists in a War Zone: Scholars Debate Their Role." *Chronicle of Higher Education* 54 (September 30):A1, A10–A12.

Global Alliance for Workers and Communities. 2003. *About Us.* Accessed April 28 (www.theglobalalliance.org).

Global Digital Solidarity Fund. 2008. Accessed January 11 (www.dsffsn.org/cms/component/ option,com_magazine/func,show_magazine/ id,11/ltemid,194/lang,fr/).

Goering, Laurie. 2007. "The First Refugees of Global Warming." *Chicago Tribune,* May 2, pp. 1, 25.

———. 2008. "Women Urge Larger Role in Easing World's Ills." *Chicago Tribune,* March 11, p. 11.

Goffman, Erving. 1959. *The Presentation of Self in Everyday Life.* New York: Doubleday.

———. 1961. *Asylums: Essays on the Social Situation of Mental Patients and Other Inmates.* Garden City, NY: Doubleday.

———. 1963. *Stigma: Notes on Management of Spoiled Identity.* Englewood Cliffs, NJ: Prentice Hall.

———. 1979. *Gender Advertisements.* Cambridge, MA: Harvard University Press.

Goldstein, Amy. 2009. From Middle Class to Welfare. *Washington Post National Weekly Edition* 26 (January 4):33.

Goldstein, Greg. 1998. "World Health Organization and Housing." Pp. 636–637 in *The Encyclopedia of Housing,* edited by Willem van Vliet. Thousand Oaks, CA: Sage.

Goldstein, Melvyn C., and Cynthia M. Beall. 1981. "Modernization and Aging in the Third and Fourth World: Views from the Rural Hinterland in Nepal." *Human Organization* 40 (Spring):48–55.

Gonzalez, David. 2003. "Latin Sweatshops Pressed by U.S. Campus Power." *New York Times,* April 4, p. A3.

Gooding, Caroline. 1994. *Disability Laws, Enabling Acts: Disability Rights in Britain and America.* Boulder, CO: Westview Press.

Goodstein, Laurie. 2008. "India, Exporter of Priests, May Keep Them Home." *New York Times,* December 30, p. A1.

Goodwin, Michele. 2006. *Black Markets: The Supply and Demand of Body Parts.* New York: Cambridge University Press.

Gordon, Rachel. 2009. "BART Signs 20-Year Deal for Wi-Fi." *San Francisco Chronicle,* January 31.

Gordon, Raymond G., Jr., ed. 2005. *Ethnologue: Languages of the World.* 15th ed. Dallas, TX: SIL International.

Gottdiener, Mark, and Joe R. Feagin. 1988. "The Paradigm Shift in Urban Sociology." *Urban Affairs Quarterly* 24 (December):163–187.

———, and Ray Hutchison. 2006. *The New Urban Sociology.* 3rd ed. Boulder, CO: Westview Press.

Gottfredson, Michael, and Travis Hirschi. 1990. *A General Theory of Crime.* Palo Alto, CA: Stanford University Press.

Gottlieb, Lori. 2006. "How Do I Love Thee?" *Atlantic Monthly* (March):58, 60, 62–68, 70.

———. 2007. "The Health-Finance Debate Reaches a Fever Pitch." *Chronicle of Higher Education,* April 13, pp. B14, B15.

Gould, Jonathan. 2007. *Can't Buy Me Love: The Beatles, Britain, and America.* New York: Harmony Books.

Gould, Larry A. 2002. "Indigenous People Policing Indigenous People: The Potential Psychological and Cultural Costs." *Social Science Journal* 39:171–188.

Gouldner, Alvin. 1960. "The Norm of Reciprocity." *American Sociological Review* 25 (April):161–177.

———. 1970. *The Coming Crisis of Western Sociology.* New York: Basic Books.

Government Accountability Office. 2003. "Women's Earnings: Work Patterns Partially Explain Difference Between Men's and Women's Earnings." Washington, DC: U.S. Government. Printing Office.

Gramsci, Antonio. 1929. *Selections from the Prison Notebooks.* Antonio Gramsci. Edited and translated by Quintin Hoare and Geoffrey Nowell Smith. London: Lawrence and Wishort.

———. 2008b. "Wealth and Economic Mobility." Washington, DC: Economic Mobility Project. Also accessible at www. economicmobility.org/reports_and_research/ literature_reviews?id=0004.

Greeley, Andrew M. 1989. "Protestant and Catholic: Is the Analogical Imagination Extinct?" *American Sociological Review* 54 (August):485–502.

Greenblatt, Alan. 2005. "Upward Mobility." *CQ Researcher* 15 (April 29).

Greenhouse, Linda. 2008. "D.C. Ban Rejected. Landmark Decision on Covert Meaning of 2nd Amendment." *New York Times,* June 27, pp. A1, A12.

Greenhouse, Steven. 2007. "Low Pay and Broken Promises Greet Guest Workers in U.S." *New York Times,* February 28, pp. A1, A14.

———. 2008a. "Unions Look for New Life in the World of Obama." *New York Times,* December 29, p. B6.

———. 2008b. "Millions of Jobs of a Different Collar." *New York Times,* March 26.

———. 2009a. "A Face-Off for Jobs." *New York Times,* March 13, pp. 1, 5.

———. 2009b. "In America, Labor Has an Unusually Long Fuse." *New York Times,* April 5, Week in Review News, p. 3.

Greenwald, John. 1990. "Bitter Cup of Protest." *Time,* May 28.

Gregory, Katherine. 2007. "Drawing a Virtual Gun." Pp. 98–111 in *Open Fire: Understanding Global Gun Cultures,* edited by Charles Fruehling Springwood. New York: Berg.

Grieco, Elizabeth M., and Rachel C. Cassidy. 2001. "Overview of Race and Hispanic Origin." *Current Population Reports Series* CENBR/01–1. Washington, DC: U.S. Government Printing Office.

Grier, Peter. 2005. "Rich-Poor Gap Gaining Attention." *Christian Science Monitor,* June 14.

Griswold, Wendy. 2004. *Cultures and Societies in a Changing World.* 2nd ed. Thousand Oaks, CA: Pine Forge Press.

Grob, Gerald N. 1995. "The Paradox of Deinstitutionalization." *Society* 32 (July/August):51–59.

Groening, Chad. 2007. "Media Coverage of Virginia Tech Massacre Shows Anti-Gun Bias, Says Watchdog." Accessed May 16 (www .onenewsnow.com).

Gross, Jane. 2005. "Forget the Career. My Parents Need Me at Home." *New York Times,* November 24, pp. A1, A20.

Grossman, Cathy Lynn. 2008. "Muslim Census a Difficult Count." *USA Today,* August 6, p. 5D.

Groza, Victor, Daniela F. Ileana, and Ivor Irwin. 1999. *A Peacock or a Crow: Stories, Interviews, and Commentaries on Romanian Adoptions.* Euclid, OH: Williams Custom Publishing.

Guarino, Mark. 2009. "New Orleans' 'Katrina Generation' Struggles with Drugs and Depression." *Christian Science Monitor,* May 13.

Guo, Guang, Michael E. Roettger, and Tianji Cai. 2008. "The Integration of Genetic Propensities into Social-Control Models of Delinquency and Violence among Male Youths." *American Sociological Review* 73 (August):543–568.

Guterman, Lila. 2000. "Why the 25-Year-Old Battle over Sociology Is More Than Just 'An Academic Sideshow.'" *Chronicle of Higher Education,* July 7, pp. A17–A18.

Gutierrez, Valerie. 2002. "Minority Women Get Left Behind by Title IX." *Los Angeles Times,* June 23, pp. D1, D12.

Gutiérrez, Gustavo. 1990. "Theology and the Social Sciences." Pp. 214–225 in *Liberation Theology at the Crossroads: Democracy or Revolution?* edited by Paul E. Sigmund. New York: Oxford University Press.

Guttmacher Institute. 2008. *Facts on Induced Abortion Worldwide.* New York: Guttmacher.

Ha, Anthony. 2008. "Meraki Brings Free WiFi to 100,000 San Franciscans." Accessed February 4 (http://venturebeat.com/2008/07/03/meraki-brings-free-wifi-to-100000-san-franciscans/).

Hacker, Andrew. 1964. "Power to Do What?" Pp. 134–146 in *The New Sociology,* edited by Irving Louis Horowitz. New York: Oxford University Press.

Hacker, Helen Mayer. 1951. "Women as a Minority Group." *Social Forces* 30 (October):60–69.

———. 1974. "Women as a Minority Group, Twenty Years Later." Pp. 124–134 in *Who Discriminates against Women?* edited by Florence Denmark. Beverly Hills, CA: Sage.

Haeri, Shaykh Fadhilalla. 2004. *The Thoughtful Guide to Islam.* Alresford, UK: O Books.

Hafner-Burton, Emilie M., and Kiyoteru Tsutsui. 2005. "Human Rights in a Globalizing World: The Paradox of Empty Promises." *American Journal of Sociology* 110 (March):1373–1411.

———, Kiyoteru Tsutsui, and John W. Meyer. 2008. "International Human Rights Law and the Politics of Legitimation." *International Society* 23 (1):115–141.

Haines, David W., Makito Minami, and Shinji Yamashita. 2007. "Transnational Migration in East Asia: Japan in Comparative Focus." *International Migration Review* 4 (Winter):963–967.

Hall, Mimi. 2005. "Senators 'to Demand Answers' on Slow Action." *USA Today,* September 6, p. 4A.

Hallinan, Maureen T. 1997. "The Sociological Study of Social Change." *American Sociological Review* 62 (February):1–11.

Hamilton, Anita. 2007. "Is Facebook Overrated?" *Time* 170 (December 3):46–48.

Hamm, Steve. 2007. "Children of the Web." *Business Week,* July 2, pp. 50–56, 58.

Hani, Yoko. 1998. "Hot Pots Wired to Help the Elderly." *Japan Times Weekly International Edition,* April 13, p. 16.

Hank, Karsten. 2001. "Changes in Child Care Could Reduce Job Options for Eastern German Mothers." *Population Today* 29 (April):3, 6.

Hanson, Ralph E. 2005. *Mass Communication: Living in a Media World.* New York: McGraw-Hill.

Harden, Blaine. 2009. "Revising History: Japan Helps Immigrants Find Work, Realizing That Its Aging Population Can't Support Itself." *Washington Post National Weekly Edition* (February):20.

Harlow, Harry F. 1971. *Learning to Love.* New York: Ballantine.

Harrington, Michael. 1962. *The Other America: Poverty in the United States.* Baltimore: Penguin.

———. 1980. "The New Class and the Left." Pp. 123–138 in *The New Class,* edited by B. Bruce Briggs. Brunswick, NJ: Transaction.

Harris Interactive. 2008. "Cell Phone Usage Continues to Increase." Accessed January 13 (www.harrisinteractive.com).

Harris, Chauncy D., and Edward Ullman. 1945. "The Nature of Cities." *Annals of the American Academy of Political and Social Science* 242 (November):7–17.

Haskins, Ron. 2006. "Welfare Reform, 10 Years Later." *Poverty Research Insights* (Fall).

Haub, Carl. 2006. *2006 World Population Data Sheet.* Washington, DC: Population Reference Bureau.

———. 2008. *2008 World Population Data Sheet.* Washington, DC: Population Reference Bureau.

Havilard, William A., Harald E. L. Prins, Dana Walrath, and Bunny McBride. 2008. *Cultural Anthropology—The Human Challenge.* 12th ed. Belmont, CA: Wadsworth.

Hayden, H. Thomas. 2004. "What Happened at Abu Ghraib." Accessed August 7 (www.military.com).

He, Wan, Manisha Sengupta, Victoria A. Velkoff, and Kimberly A. DeBarros. 2005. "65+ in the United States: 2005." *Current Population Reports,* ser. P-23, no. 209. Washington, DC: U.S. Government Printing Office.

Head, John F. 2007. "Why, Even Today, Many Blacks Are Wary about American Medicine." *Crisis* (January):48–49.

Health and Human Services. 2009. "TANF Families as of April 18, 2008." Accessed March 15, 2009 (www.acf.hhs.gov/programs.ofa.caseload/2007/tanf_family.htm).

Health Care Financing Administration. 2001. *National Health Care Expenditures Projections.* Accessed August 10 (www.hcfa.gov/stats/NHE-proj/).

Hebel, Sara. 2006. "In Rural America, Few People Harvest 4-Year Degrees." *Chronicle of Higher Education* 53 (November 3):A21–A24.

Heckert, Druann, and Amy Best. 1997. "Ugly Duckling to Swan: Labeling Theory and the Stigmatization of Red Hair." *Symbolic Interaction* 20 (4):365–384.

Hedley, R. Alan. 1992. "Industrialization in Less Developed Countries." Pp. 914–920 vol. 2, in *Encyclopedia of Sociology,* edited by Edgar F. Borgatta and Marie L. Borgatta. New York: Macmillan.

Heilman, Madeline E. 2001. "Description and Prescription: How Gender Stereotypes Prevent Women's Ascent up the Organizational Ladder." *Journal of Social Issues* 57 (4):657–674.

Hellmich, Nanci. 2001. "TV's Reality: No Vast American Waistlines." *USA Today,* October 8, p. 7D.

Helvarg, David. 1994. *The War Against Greens: The "Wise Use" Movement, the New Right and Anti-Environmental Violence.* San Francisco: Sierra Club Books.

Hendershott, Ann. 2002. *The Politics of Deviance.* San Francisco: Encounter Books.

Henly, Julia R. 1999. "Challenges to Finding and Keeping Jobs in the Low-Skilled Labor Market." *Poverty Research News* 3 (1):3–5.

Hersch, Patricia. 1998. *A Tribe Apart: A Journey into the Heart of the American Adolescence.* New York: Fawcett Books.

Herschthal, Eric. 2004. "Indian Students Discuss Pros, Cons of Arranged Marriages." *Daily Princetonian,* October 20.

Hertz, Rosanna. 2006. *Single by Chance, Mothers by Choice.* New York: Oxford University Press.

Hewlett, Sylvia Ann, and Carolyn Buck Luce. 2005. "Off-Ramps and On-Ramps: Keeping Talented Women on the Road to Success." *Harvard Business Review* (March):43–53.

Hickman, Jonathan. 2002. "America's 50 Best Corporations for Minorities." *Fortune* 146 (July 8):110–120.

Higher Education Research Institute. 2004. *Trends in Political Attitudes and Voting Behavior Among College Freshmen and Early Career College Graduates: What Issues Could Drive This Election?* Los Angeles: HERI, University of California, Los Angeles.

Hill, Michael R., and Susan Hoecker-Drysdale, eds. 2001. *Harriet Martineau: Theoretical and Methodological Perspectives.* New York: Routledge.

Hillery, George A. 1955. "Definitions of Community: Areas of Agreement." *Rural Sociology* (2):111–123.

Hira, Ron. 2008. "An Overview of the Offshoring of U.S. Jobs." Pp. 14–15 in Marlene A. Lee and Mark Mather. "U.S. Labor Force Trends." *Population Bulletin* 63 (June).

Hirsch, Paul M., and Michaela De Soucey. 2006. "Organizational Restructuring and Its Consequences: Rhetorical and Structural." Pp. 171–189 in *Annual Review of Sociology 2006,* edited by Karen S. Cook and Douglas S. Massey. Palo Alto, CA: Annual Reviews.

Hirschi, Travis. 1969. *Causes of Delinquency.* Berkeley: University of California Press.

Hirst, Paul, and Grahame Thompson. 1996. *Globalization in Question: The International Economy and the Possibilities of Governance.* Cambridge, UK: Polity Press.

Hitlin, Steven, and Jane Allyn Piliavin. 2004. "Values: Reviving a Dormant Concept." Pp. 359–393 in *Annual Review of Sociology, 2004,* edited by Karen S. Cook and John Hagan. Palo Alto, CA: Annual Reviews.

Hochschild, Arlie Russell. 1990. "The Second Shift: Employed Women Are Putting in Another Day of Work at Home." *Utne Reader* 38 (March/April): 66–73.

———. 2005. *The Commercialization of Intimate Life: Notes from Home and Work.* Berkeley: University of California Press.

———, with Anne Machung. 1989. *The Second Shift: Working Parents and the Revolution at Home.* New York: Viking Penguin.

Hodson, Randy, and Teresa A. Sullivan. 1995. *The Social Organization of Work.* 2nd ed. Belmont, CA: Wadsworth.

Hoefer, Michael, Nancy Rytina, and Christopher Campbell. 2006. Estimates of the Unauthorized Immigrant Population Residing in the United States: January 2005. Rev. Number 2006. Washington, DC: Policy Directorate Office of Immigration Statistics.

Hoepker, Thomas. 2006. "I Took That 9/11 Photo." Posted at *Slate,* September 14, 2006. Accessed January 2, 2008 (www.slate.com/toolbar.aspx?action=print&id=2149675).

Hoffman, Adonis. 1997. "Through an Accurate Prism." *Los Angeles Times,* August 8, p. M1.

Hoffman, Lois Wladis. 1985. "The Changing Genetics/Socialization Balance." *Journal of Social Issues* 41 (Spring):127–148.

Holden, Constance. 1980. "Identical Twins Reared Apart." *Science* 207 (March 21):1323–1328.

———. 1987. "The Genetics of Personality." *Science* 257 (August 7):598–601.

Holder, Kelly. 2006. "Voting and Registration in the Election of November 2004." *Current Population Reports,* ser. P-20, no. 556. Washington, DC: U.S. Government Printing Office.

Hollingshead, August B. 1975. *Elmtown's Youth and Elmtown Revisited.* New York: Wiley.

Holmes, Mary. 2006. "Love Lives at a Distance: Distance Relationships over the Lifecourse." *Sociological Research Online* 11 (3).

Homans, George C. 1979. "Nature versus Nurture: A False Dichotomy." *Contemporary Sociology* 8 (May):345–348.

Home School Legal Defense Association. 2005. "State Laws" and "Academic Statistics on Homeschooling." Accessed May 12 (www.hslda.org).

Hondagneu-Sotelo, Pierrette, ed. 2003. *Gender and U.S. Immigration: Contemporary Trends.* Berkeley: University of California Press.

hooks, bell. 1994. *Feminist Theory: From Margin to Center.* 2nd ed. Boston: South End Press.

Horgan, John. 1993. "Eugenics Revisited." *Scientific American* 268 (June):122–128, 130–133.

Horkheimer, Max, and Theodore Adorno. [1944] 2002. *Dialectic of Enlightenment.* Palo Alto, CA: Stanford University Press.

Horowitz, Helen Lefkowitz. 1987. *Campus Life.* Chicago: University of Chicago Press.

Horrigan, John B. 2007. *A Typology of Information and Communication Technology Users.* Washington, DC: Pew Internet and American Life Project.

Horwitz, Allan V. 2002. *Creating Mental Illness.* Chicago: University of Chicago Press.

Hosokawa, William K. 1969. *Nisei: The Quiet Americans.* New York: Morrow.

Hospice Association of America. 2008. *Hospice Facts and Statistics.* Washington, DC: Hospice Association of America.

Houseman, John. 1972. *Run Through.* New York: Simon and Schuster.

Houser, Trevor, Shashank Mohamad, and Robert Heilmayer. 2009. *A Green Global Recovery? Assessing U.S. Economic Stimulus and the Prospects for International Coordination.* Washington, DC: World Resources Institute of Peterson Institute for International Economics.

Housing and Urban Development. 2008. *The Annual Homeless Assessment Report to Congress.* Washington, DC: U.S. Government Printing Office.

Hout, Michael, and Claude S. Fischer. 2002. "Why More Americans Have No Religious Preference: Politics and Generations." *American Sociological Review* 67 (April):165–190.

Howard, Judith A. 1999. "Border Crossings between Women's Studies and Sociology." *Contemporary Sociology* 28 (September):525–528.

———, and Jocelyn Hollander. 1997. *Gendered Situations, Gendered Selves.* Thousand Oaks, CA: Sage.

Howard, Michael C. 1989. *Contemporary Cultural Anthropology.* 3rd ed. Glenview, IL: Scott, Foresman.

Howard, Russell D., and Reid L. Sawyer. 2003. *Terrorism and Counterterrorism: Understanding the New Security Environment.* Guilford, CT: McGraw-Hill/Dushkin.

Huang, Gary. 1988. "Daily Addressing Ritual: A Cross-Cultural Study." Presented at the annual meeting of the American Sociological Association, Atlanta.

Hubbard, L. Ron. 1950. *Dianetics.* Hollywood, CA: Bridge.

Huber, Bettina J. 1985. *Employment Patterns in Sociology: Recent Trends and Future Prospects.* Washington, DC: American Sociological Association.

Huff, Charlotte. 2007. "Survival of the Fittest." *American Way,* May 1, pp. 30–35.

Huffstutter, P. J. 2003. "See No Evil." *Los Angeles Times,* January 12, pp. 12–15, 43–45.

Hughes, Everett. 1945. "Dilemmas and Contradictions of Status." *American Journal of Sociology* 50 (March):353–359.

Hughlett, Mike. 2008. "Sitting Pretty." *Chicago Tribune,* September 14, sec. 5, pp. 1, 7.

Human Genome Project. 2009. "Human Genome Project Information." Accessed May 5 (www.ornl.gov).

Hundley, Tom, and Margaret Ramirez. 2008. "Young Muslims Put Faith in Facebook." *Chicago Tribune,* February 10, p. 12.

Hunt, Darnell. 1997. *Screening the Los Angeles "Riots": Race, Seeing, and Resistance.* New York: Cambridge University Press.

Hunter, Herbert M., ed. 2000. *The Sociology of Oliver C. Cox: New Perspectives: Research in Race and Ethnic Relations,* vol. 2. Stamford, CT: JAI Press.

Hunter, James Davison. 1991. *Culture Wars: The Struggle to Define America.* New York: Basic Books.

Huntington, Samuel P. 1993. "The Clash of Civilizations?" *Foreign Affairs* 72 (Summer): 22–49.

Hurn, Christopher J. 1985. *The Limits and Possibilities of Schooling,* 2nd ed. Boston: Allyn and Bacon.

Hyde, Janet Shibley. 2005. "The Gender Similarities Hypothesis." *American Psychologist* 60 (6):581–592.

Hymowitz, Carol, and Rachel Emma Silverman. 2001. "Can Work Place Stress Get Worse?" *Wall Street Monitor,* January 16, pp. B1, B4.

Ibata-Arens, Kathryn. 2008. "Comparing National Innovation Systems in Japan and the United States: Push, Pull, Drag and Jump Factors in the Development of New Technology." *Asia Pacific Business Review* 14 (July):315–338.

Igo, Sarah E. 2007. *The Average American: Surveys, Citizens, and the Making of a Mass Public.* Cambridge, MA: Harvard University Press.

Immervoll, Herwig, and David Barber. 2005. *Can Parents Afford to Work? Childcare Costs, Tax-Benefit Policies and Work Incentives.* Paris: Organisation for Economic Co-operational and Development.

Inglehart, Ronald, and Wayne E. Baker. 2000. "Modernization, Cultural Change, and the Persistence of Traditional Values." *American Sociological Review* 65 (February):19–51.

Institute for Economics and Peace. 2008. "Global Peace Index." Accessed June 11 (www.visionofhumanity.org/gpi/results/world-map.php).

Institute of International Education. 2008. "U.S. Study Abroad Up 8%, Continuing Decade-Long Growth." Accessed at http://opendoors.iienetwork.org/?p=131592.

———. 2009. "Open Doors 20/08 'Fast Facts.'" Accessed at www.ies.org.

Instituto del Tercer Mundo. 2005. *The World Guide 2005/2006.* Oxford: New Internationalist Publications.

Interbrand. 2008. *Best Global Brands 2008.* New York: Interbrand.

Interface Group Report (Virginia Tech). 2007. *Presidential Internal Review.* Blacksburg, VA: Virginia Polytechnic Institute and State University.

International Centre for Prison Studies. 2009. "Prison Brief—Highest to Lowest Rates."

Accessed February 21 (www.kcl.ac.uk/depsta/law/research/icps/worldbrief/wpb_stats.php?area=all&category=wb_poprate).

International Crime Victim Survey. 2004. *Nationwide Surveys in the Industrialized Countries.* Accessed February 20 (www.ruljis.leidenuniv.nl/group/jfcr/www/icvs).

International Fund for Agricultural Observation. 2007. *Sending Money Home: Worldwide Remittance Flows to Developing and Transition Countries.* Rome: LIFAD.

International Gay and Lesbian Human Rights Commission. 2009. Home page. Accessed February 21. (www.iglhrc.org).

International Institute for Democracy and Electoral Assistance. 2009a. "Voter Turnout." Accessed April 15 (www.idea.int/vt/index.cfm).

———. 2009b. "Turnout in the World—Country by Country Performance (1945–1998)." Accessed April 15 (www.idea.int/vt/survey/voter_turnout_pop2-2.vtm).

International Monetary Fund. 2000. *World Economic Outlook: Asset Prices and the Business Cycle.* Washington, DC: International Monetary Fund.

International Trade Union Confederation. 2009. "Davos: World Unions Call for Action Against Corporate Grand Theft." Accessed January 31 (www.ituc-csi.org/spip.php?article2736).

Internet Crime Complaint Center. 2008. *2007 Internet Crime Report.* Washington, DC: National White Collar Crime Center, Bureau of Justice Assistance, and Federal Bureau of Investigation.

Internet World Stats. 2009. "Usage and Population Statistics" and "Internet World Users by Language." Accessed May 5 (www.internetworldstats.com).

Inter-Parliamentary Union. 2009. *Women in National Parliaments.* February 28. Accessed March 16 (www.ipu.org).

Isaacs, Julia B. 2007a. *Economic Mobility of Families Across Generations.* Washington, DC: Economic Mobility Project, Pew Charitable Trusts.

———. 2007b. *Economic Mobility of Men and Women.* Washington, DC: Economic Mobility Project.

———, Isabel V. Sawhill, and Ron Haskins. 2008. *Getting Ahead or Losing Ground: Economic Mobility in America.* Washington, DC: Pew Charitable Trust.

ITOPF. 2006. "Statistics: International Tanker Owners Pollution Federation Limited." Accessed May 2 (www.itopf.com/stats.html).

Jackson, Elton F., Charles R. Tittle, and Mary Jean Burke. 1986. "Offense-Specific Models of the Differential Association Process." *Social Problems* 33 (April):335–356.

Jackson, Philip W. 1968. *Life in Classrooms.* New York: Holt.

Jacobe, Dennis. 2008. "Half of Public Favors the Environment Over Growth." Accessed April 9 (www.gallup.com).

Jacobs, Andrew. 2008. "One-Child Policy Lifted for Parents of China Quake Victims." *New York Times,* May 27, p. A8.

———. 2009. "Chinese Learn Limits of Online Freedom as the Filter Tightens." *New York Times,* February 5, p. A8.

References

Jacobs, Jerry. 2003. "Detours on the Road to Equality: Women, Work and Higher Education." *Contexts* (Winter):32–41.

Jain, Saranga, and Kathleen Kurz. 2007. *New Insights on Preventing Child Marriage: A Global Analysis of Factors and Programs.* Washington, DC: International Center for Research on Women.

James, Meg. 2007. "Latinos Join TV Ratings Picture." *Chicago Tribune,* September 3, sec. 3, pp. 1, 4.

Janis, Irving. 1967. *Victims of Groupthink.* Boston: Houghton Mifflin.

Jargowsky, Paul A., and Rebecca Yang. 2006. "The 'Underclass' Revisited: A Social Problem in Decline." *Journal of Urban Affairs* 28 (1):55–70.

Jasper, James M. 1997. *The Art of Moral Protest: Culture, Biography, and Creativity in Social Movements.* Chicago: University of Chicago Press.

Jayson, Sharon. 2009. "Holding Up the Value of Marriage." *USA Today,* February 18, pp. D1, D2.

Jecker, Nancy. 2000. "Review of Medical Apartheid." *New England Journal of Medicine* (November 23).

Jencks, Christopher, Joe Swingle, and Scott Winship. 2006. "Welfare Redux." *American Prospect* (March):36–40.

Jenkins, Henry. 2006. *Convergence Culture: Where Old and New Media Collide.* New York: New York University Press.

Jenkins, J. Craig, and William Form. 2005. "Social Movements and Social Change." Pp. 1446–1528 in *The Handbook of Political Sociology,* edited by Thomas Janoski, Robert Alford, Alexander Hicks, and Mildred Schwartz. New York: Cambridge University Press.

Jenkins, Matt. 2008. "A Really Inconvenient Truth." *Miller-McCure* 1 (March–April):38–41.

Jenkins, Richard. 1991. "Disability and Social Stratification." *British Journal of Sociology* 42 (December):557–580.

Jenness, Valerie, David A. Smith, and Judith Stepan-Norris. 2008. "Editors' Note: Lessons or Welfare Reform?" *Contemporary Sociology* 37 (March):vii–viii.

Jensen, Gary F. 2005. *Social Organization Theory.* In *Encyclopedia of Criminology,* edited by Richard A. Wright and J. Mitchell Miller. Chicago. Fitzrog Dearborn.

Jervis, Rick. 2008. "New Orleans Homicides up 30% over 2006 Level." *USA Today,* January 3, p. 3A.

Jesella, Kara. 2008. "Blogging's Glass Ceiling." *New York Times,* July 27, Style section, pp. 1, 2.

Johnson, Anne M., Jane Wadsworth, Kaye Wellings, and Julie Field. 1994. *Sexual Attitudes and Lifestyles.* Oxford: Blackwell Scientific.

Johnson, Benton. 1975. *Functionalism in Modern Sociology: Understanding Talcott Parsons.* Morristown, NJ: General Learning.

Johnson, Erik W. 2008. Social Movement Size, Organizational Diversity and the Making of Federal Law. *Social Forces* (March):967–993.

Johnson, Kenneth M. 1999. "The Rural Rebound." *Reports on America* 1 (September).

———. 2006. *Demographic Trends in Rural and Small Town America.* Durham: Casey Institute, University of New Hampshire.

Johnson, Richard A. 1985. *American Fads.* New York: Beech Tree.

Johnson, Richard W. 2008. *How Is the Recession Affecting Older Workers?* Washington, DC: Urban Institute. Accessed March 15 (www.Retirement-Policy.org).

Johnston, David Cay. 1994. "Ruling Backs Homosexuals on Asylum." *New York Times,* June 12, pp. D1, D6.

Jones, Del, and Barbara Hansen. 2009. "CEO Pay Packages Sink with Economy." *USA Today,* May 4, pp. B1–B2.

Jones, Jeffrey M., and Joseph Carroll. 2007. "Americans and the Super Bowl Phenomenon." Accessed February 2, 2008 (www.gallup.com).

Jones, Jo. 2009. "Who Adopts? Characteristics of Women and Men Who Have Adopted Children." *NCHS Data Brief* (12).

Jordan, Miriam. 2009. "As U.S. Job Opportunities Fade, More Mexicans Look Homeward." *Wall Street Journal,* February 13, p. A14.

Joseph, Jay. 2004. *The Gene Illusion: Genetic Research in Psychiatry and Psychology under the Microscope.* New York: Algora Books.

Jost Kenneth. 2005. "Right to Die." *CQ Researcher,* May 13.

———. 2008. "Women in Politics." *CQ Researcher* 18 (March 21).

Juhasz, Anne McCreary. 1989. "Black Adolescents' Significant Others." *Social Behavior and Personality* 17 (2):211–214.

Kahn, Joseph. 2003. "Made in China, Bought in China." *New York Times,* January 5, sec. 3, pp. 1, 10.

———. 2006. "Where's Mao? Chinese Revise History Books." *New York Times,* September 1, pp. A1, A6.

Kaiser Family Foundation. 2005. *Sex on TV4.* Santa Barbara, CA: Kaiser Family Foundation.

———. 2007. "Parents Say They're Getting Control of Their Children's Exposure to Sex and Violence in the Media—Even Online." Accessed January 2, 2008 (www.kff.org/entmedia/entmedia061907nr.cfm).

Kalish, Richard A. 1985. *Death, Grief, and Caring Relationships.* 2nd ed. Monterey, CA: Brooks/Cole.

Kalita, S. Mitra. 2006. "On the Other End of the Line." *Washington Post National Week Edition,* January 9, pp. 20–21.

Kalleberg, Arne L. 2009. "Precarious Work, Insecure Workers: Employment Relations in Transition." *American Sociological Review* 74 (February):1–22.

Kalmijn, Matthijs. 1998. "Intermarriage and Homogeny: Causes, Patterns, Trends." *Annual Review of Sociology* 24:395–421.

Kambayashi, Takehiko. 2008. "Japanese Men Shout the Oft-unsaid 'I love you." *Christian Science Monitor,* February 13.

Kamenetz, Anya. 2006. *Generation Debt.* New York: Riverhead.

Kandel, William. 2005. "Rural Hispanics at a Glance." *Economic Information Bulletin* (December).

Kapos, Shia. 2005. "Bloom Falls Off the Rose for Internet Matchups." *Chicago Tribune,* February 14, sec. 4, pp. 1, 7.

Kapstein, Ethan B. 2006. "The New Global Slave Trade." *Foreign Affairs* 85 (November/December): 103–115.

Karney, Benjamin R., and John S. Crown. 2007. "Families Under Stress: An Assessment of Data, Theory, and Research on Marriage and Divorce in the Military." Santa Monica, CA: RAND.

Katel, Peter. 2005. "Ending Poverty." *CQ Researcher* 15 (September 9):733–760.

Katovich, Michael A. 1987. Correspondence. June 1.

Katz, Michael. 1971. *Class, Bureaucracy, and the Schools: The Illusion of Educational Change in America.* New York: Praeger.

Kaufman, Sarah. 2006. "The Criminalization of New Orleanians in Katrina's Wake." Accessed April 4 (www.ssrc.org).

Kavada, Anastasia. 2005. "Exploring the Role of the Interest in the 'Movement for Alternative Globalization': The Case of the Paris 2003 European Social Forum." *Westminster Papers in Communication and Culture* 2 (1):72–95.

Keeter, Scott, and Courtney Kennedy. 2006. "The Cell Phone Challenge to Survey Research." Washington, DC: Pew Research Center.

———, Michael Dimock, and Leah Christian. 2008. "Cell Phones and the 2008 Vote: An Update." Accessed October 2 (http://pewresearch.org/pubs/964/cell-phones-and-the-2008-vote-an-update).

Kempadoo, Kamala, and Jo Doezema, eds. 1998. *Global Sex Workers: Rights, Resistance, and Redefinition.* New York: Routledge.

Kent, Mary M., and Carl Haub. 2005. "Global Demographic Divide." *Population Bulletin* 60 (December).

Kentor, Jeffrey, and Yong Suk Jang. 2004. "Yes, There Is a (Growing) Transnational Business Community." *International Sociology* 19 (September):355–368.

———. 2009. *Social Stratification and Inequality: Class Conflict in Historical, Comparative, and Global Perspective.* 7th ed. New York: McGraw-Hill.

Kerbo, Harold R. 2006. *World Poverty: The Roots of Global Inequality and the World System.* New York: McGraw-Hill.

Kessler, Ronald C., Emil F. Coccaro, Maurizio Fava, Savina Jaeger, Robert Jin, and Ellen Walters. 2006. "The Prevalence and Correlates of DSM-IV Intermittent Explosive Disorder in the National Comorbidity Survey Replication." *Archives of General Psychiatry* 63 (June):669–678.

Kilborn, Peter T. 2001. "Rural Towns Turn to Prisons to Reignite Their Economies." *New York Times,* August 1, pp. A1, A11.

Killian, Caitlin. 2003. "The Other Side of the Veil: North Africa Women in France Respond to the Headscarf Affair." *Gender and Society* (August 17):576–590.

Kim, Kwang Chung. 1999. *Koreans in the Hood: Conflict with African Americans.* Baltimore: Johns Hopkins University Press.

Kimmel, Michael S. 2006. "A War Against Boys?" *Dissent* (Fall):65–70.

———. 2008. *The Gendered Society,* 3rd ed. New York: State University of New York at Stony Brook.

King, Leslie. 1998. "France Needs Children: Pronatalism, Nationalism, and Women's Equity." *Sociological Quarterly* 39 (Winter):33–52.

King, Meredith L. 2007. *Immigrants in the U.S. Health Care System.* Washington, DC: Center for American Progress.

King, Sharon A. 1999. "Mania for 'Pocket Monsters' Yields Billions for Nintendo." *New York Times,* April 26, pp. A1, A18.

Kingsbury, Alex. 2008. "Q and A: Sudhir Venkatesh." *U.S. News and World Report,* January 21, p. 14.

Kinsella, Kevin, and David R. Phillips. 2005. "Global Aging: The Challenge of Success." *Population Bulletin* 60 (March).

Kinsey, Alfred C., Wardell B. Pomeroy, and Paul H. Gebhard. 1953. *Sexual Behavior in the Human Female.* Philadelphia: Saunders.

———, Wardell B. Pomeroy, and Clyde E. Martin. 1948. *Sexual Behavior in the Human Male.* Philadelphia: Saunders.

Kiper, Dmitry. 2008. "GodTube.com Puts Christian Worship Online." *Christian Science Monitor,* February 6.

Kirsten, Adèle. 2008. *A Nation Without Guns? The Story of Gun Free South Africa.* Scottsville, South Africa: University of Kwa Zulu-Natal Press.

Kiser, Edgar. 1992. "War." Pp. 2243–2247 in *Encyclopedia of Sociology,* edited by Edgar F. Borgatta and Marie L. Borgatta. New York: Macmillan.

Kitchener, Richard F. 1991. "Jean Piaget: The Unknown Sociologist." *British Journal of Sociology* 42 (September):421–442.

Klein, Naomi. 1999. *No Logo: Money, Marketing, and the Growing Anti-Corporate Movement.* New York: Picador (St. Martin's Press).

Kleiner, Art. 2003. "Are You In with the In Crowd?" *Harvard Business Review* 81 (July):86–92.

Kleinknecht, William. 1996. *The New Ethnic Mobs: The Changing Face of Organized Crime in America.* New York: Free Press.

Kleniewski, Nancy. 2002. *Cities, Change, and Conflict: A Political Economy of Urban Life.* 2nd ed. Belmont, CA: Wadsworth.

Klinenberg, Eric. 2002. *Heat Wave: A Social Autopsy of Disaster in Chicago.* Chicago: University of Chicago Press.

——— 2007. *Fighting for Air: The Battle to Control America's Media.* New York: Metropolitan Books.

Klinger, Jeffrey. 2007. "What Now?" *Time* 169 (April 6):30–109.

Kochhar, Rakesh. 2006. "Growth in the Foreign-Born Workforce and Employment of the Nature Born." Washington, DC: Pew Hispanic Center.

———. 2007. "1995–2005: Foreign Born Latinos Make Progress on Wages." Washington, DC: Pew Hispanic Center.

———. 2008. *Latino Workers in the Ongoing Recession: 2007–2008.* Washington, DC: Pew Hispanic Center.

Kohut, Andrew. 2008. "The Internet Gains on Politics." Accessed January 11 (www.pewinternet.org/PPF/r/234/report_display.asp).

——— et al. 2005. *American Character Gets Mixed Reviews: 16-Nation Pew Global Attitudes Survey.* Washington, DC: Pew Global Project Attitudes.

———, et al. 2007. *Global Unease with Major World Powers: Rising Environmental Concern in 47-Nation Survey.* Washington, DC: Pew Global Project Attitudes.

Kokmen, Leyla. 2008. "Environmental Justice for All." *Utne Reader* (March–April):42–46.

Kolata, Gina. 2008. "Study Finds Strong Social Factor in Quitting Smoking." *New York Times,* May 22, pp. A18, A24.

Koolhaas, Rem, et al. 2001. *Mutations.* Barcelona, Spain: Actar.

Kornblum, Janet. 2007. "Meet the 'Tech-No's': People Who Reject Plugging into the Highly Wired World." *USA Today,* January 11, pp. A1, A2.

Kosmin, Barry A., and Ariela Keysar. 2009. *American Religious Identification Survey.* Hartford, CT: Trinity College.

Kottak, Conrad. 2009. *Anthropology: The Explanation of Human Diversity.* 13th ed. New York: McGraw-Hill.

Kozinn, Allan. 2008. "Meditation on the Man Who Saved the Beatles." *New York Times,* February 7.

Kozol, Jonathan. 2005. *The Shame of the Nation: The Restoration of Apartheid Schooling.* New York: Crown Books.

Kraft Foods. 2009. "Hoaxes and Rumors." Accessed February 4 (http://brands.kraftfoods.com/oscarmayer/hoaxes_rumors).

Krauss, C. 1993. "Marine Leader Contritely Admits He Erred on 'Singles Only' Order." *New York Times,* August 12, p. A1.

Krebs, Michelle. 2006. "Chinese Lessons: What GM Has Learned in China." Inside Line.

Kreider, Rose M. 2008. "Living Arrangements of Children: 2004." *Current Population Reports,* ser. no. 114. Washington, DC: U.S. Government. Printing Office.

———. 2005. "Number, Timing, and Duration of Marriages and Divorces: 2001." *Current Population Reports,* pp. 70–97. Washington, DC: U.S. Government Printing Office.

Kriesberg, Louis. 1992. "Peace." Pp. 1432–1436 in *Encyclopedia of Sociology,* edited by Edgar F. Borgatta and Marie L. Borgatta. New York: Macmillan.

Kristof, Nicholas D. 1998. "As Asian Economies Shrink, Women Are Squeezed Out." *New York Times,* June 11, pp. A1, A12.

———. 2006. "Race Against Death." *New York Times,* June 4, sec. WK, p. 15.

Kroll, Luisa, Matthew Miller, and Tatiana Serafin. 2009. "The World's Billionaires." *Forbes* 183 (March 30):75–144. Accessed March 17 (www.forbes.com/2009/03/11/worlds-richest-people-billionaires-2009_land.html).

Kronstadt, Jessica. 2008a. "Genetics and Economic Mobility." Washington, DC: Economic Mobility Project. Also accessible at www.economicmobility.org/reports_and_research/literature_reviews?id=0004.

———. 2008b. "Health and Economic Mobility." Washington, DC: Economic Mobility Project. Also accessible at www.economicmobility.org/reports_and_research/literature_reviews?id=0004.

———, and Melissa Favreault. 2008. "Families and Economic Mobility." Washington, DC: Economic Mobility Project. Also accessible at www.economicmobility.org/reports_and_research/literature_reviews?id=0004.

Kübler-Ross, Elisabeth. 1969. *On Death and Dying.* New York: Macmillan.

Kwong, Jo. 2005. "Globalization's Effects on the Environment." *Society* 42 (January/February): 21–28.

Lacey, Marc. 2005. "Accents of Africa: A New Outsourcing Frontier." *New York Times,* February 2, pp. C1, C6.

Ladner, Joyce. 1973. *The Death of White Sociology.* New York: Random House.

Lague, David. 2006. "Official Union Set Up in China at Wal-Mart." *New York Times,* July 31, pp. C1, C8.

Lahey, Joanna. 2006. *Age, Women, and Hiring: An Experimental Study.* Boston: Center for Retirement Research, Boston College. Accessed at http://escholarship.bc.edu/retirement_papers/134.

Landale, Nancy S., and R. S. Oropesa. 2007. "Hispanic Families: Stability and Change." *Annual Review of Sociology* 33:381–405.

———, and Michael Barbaro. 2006. "No, Not Always." *New York Times,* August 2, pp. C1, C4.

Landler, Mark, and David E. Sanger. 2009. "World Leaders Pledge $1.1 Trillion to Tackle Crisis." *New York Times,* April 3, pp. A1, A11.

Landtman, Gunnar. [1938] 1968. *The Origin of Inequality of the Social Class.* New York: Greenwood (original edition 1938, Chicago: University of Chicago Press).

Landy, Heather. 2008. "Behind the Big Paydays." *Washington Post National Weekly Edition* 26 (November 24):7.

Lang, Robert E., and Jennifer B. LeFurgy. 2007. *Boomburbs: The Rise of America's Accidental Crisis.* Washington, DC: Brookings Institution.

Langewiesche, William. 2002. *American Ground: Unbuilding the World Trade Center.* New York: North Point Press.

Lanier, Charles S., William Bowers, and James R. Acker. 2009. *The Future of America's Death Penalty: An Agenda for the Next Generation of Capital Punishment Research.* Durham, NC: Carolina Academic Press.

Lansprey, Susan. 1995. "AAAs and 'Naturally Occurring Retirement Communities' (NORCs)." Accessed August 4, 2003 (www.aoa.gov/housing/norcs.html).

Lareau, Annette. 2003. *Unequal Childhoods: Class, Race, and Family Life.* Berkeley: University of California Press.

Laska, Shirley. 2005. "The Role of Social Science Research in Disaster Preparedness and Response." Testimony before U.S. House of Representatives, Science Committee, Subcommittee on Research.

Lasswell, Harold D. 1936. *Politics: Who Gets What, When, How.* New York: McGraw-Hill.

Laszewski, Chuck. 2008. "The Sociologists' Take on the Environment." *Contexts 7* (Spring):20–24.

Lauer, Robert H. 1982. *Perspectives on Social Change.* 3rd ed. Boston: Allyn and Bacon.

Laumann, Anne E., and Amy J. Derick. 2006. "Tattoos and Body Piercings in the United States: A National Data Set." *Journal of the American Academy of Dermatology* 55 (September):413–421.

Laumann, Edward O., John H. Gagnon, and Robert T. Michael. 1994a. "A Political History of the National Sex Survey of Adults." *Family Planning Perspectives* 26 (February):34–38.

———, John H. Gagnon, Robert T. Michael, and Stuart Michaels. 1994b. *The Social Organization of Sexuality: Sexual Practices in the United States.* Chicago: University of Chicago Press.

Lavrakas, Paul J., Charles D. Shuttles, Charlotte Steel, and Howard Fienberg. 2007. "The State of Surveying Cell Phone Numbers in the United States: 2007 and Beyond." *Public Opinion Quarterly* 71 (5):840–854.

Lawler, Edward J., Shane R. Thye, and Jeongkou Youn. 2008. "Social Exchange and Micro Social Order." *American Sociological Review* 73 (August):519–542.

Lawson, Sandra. 2008. *Girls Count.* New York: Goldman Sachs.

Lazarsfeld, Paul, Bernard Beretson, and H. Gaudet. 1948. *The People's Choice.* New York: Columbia University Press.

———, and Robert K. Merton. 1948. "Mass Communication, Popular Taste, and Organized Social Action." Pp. 95–118 in *The Communication of Ideas,* edited by Lymon Bryson. New York: Harper and Brothers.

Le Monde, François Galichet. 2009. "Class Struggle Is Not Over." *The Guardian,* June 2, p. 20.

Lear, Norman, and Robert W. McChesney. 2006. "Does Big Media Need to Get Bigger?" *Los Angeles Times,* August 5, p. B17.

Leavell, Hugh R., and E. Gurney Clark. 1965. *Preventive Medicine for the Doctor in His Community: An Epidemiologic Approach.* 3rd ed. New York: McGraw-Hill.

Lee, Alfred McClung. 1983. *Terrorism in Northern Ireland.* Bayside, NY: General Hall.

Lehne, Gregory K. 1995. "Homophobia among Men: Supporting and Defining the Male Role." Pp. 325–336 in *Men's Lives,* edited by Michael S. Kimmel and Michael S. Messner. Boston: Allyn and Bacon.

Leland, John. 2008. "In 'Sweetie' and 'Dear,' a Hurt Beyond Insult for the Elderly." *New York Times,* October 7, pp. A1, A22.

Lengermann, Patricia Madoo, and Jill Niebrugge-Brantley. 1998. *The Women Founders: Sociology and Social Theory, 1830–1930.* Boston: McGraw-Hill.

———, Mary Madden, and Paul Hitlin. 2005. *Teens and Technology.* Washington, DC: Pew Internet and American Life Project.

———. 2007. *Social Networking Websites and Teens: An Overview.* Washington, DC: Pew Internet and American Life Project.

Lenhart, Amanda. 2009. "Pew Internet Project Data Memo: Adults and Social Network Websites." Accessed at www.pewinternet.org/PPF/r/272/report_display.asp.

Lenski, Gerhard. 1966. *Power and Privilege: A Theory of Social Stratification.* New York: McGraw-Hill.

Leonard, Koren Isakser. 2003. *Muslims in the United States: The State of Research.* New York: Russell Sage Foundation.

Leonhardt, David. 2004. "As Wealthy Fill Top Colleges Concerns Grow Over Fairness." *New York Times,* April 22, pp. A1, A12.

———. 2007. "Middle-Class Squeeze Comes with Nuances." *New York Times,* April 25, pp. C1, C12.

Lerach, William S. 2007. "Guilty: Why Is Wall Street So Bullish on Bad CEOs?" *Washington Post National Weekly Edition,* November 19, p. 29.

Levin, Jack, and William C. Levin. 1980. *Ageism.* Belmont, CA: Wadsworth.

Levine, Nancy. 1988. *The Dynamics of Polyandry: Kinship, Domesticity, and Population on the Tibetan Border.* Chicago: University of Chicago Press.

Levine, Susa. 2006. "Culturally Sensitive Medicine." *Washington Post National Weekly Edition* 23 (March 26):31.

Levinson, Daniel J. 1978. *The Seasons of a Man's Life.* With Charlotte N. Darrow et al. New York: Knopf.

———. 1996. *The Seasons of a Woman's Life.* With Judy D. Levinson. New York: Knopf.

Levitt, Peggy, and B. Nadya. Jaworsky. 2007. "Transnational Migration Studies: Past Developments and Future Trends." *Annual Review of Sociology* 33:129–156.

Levitt, Steven D., and Stephen J. Dubner. 2006. *Freakonomics: A Rogue Economist Explores the Hidden Side of Everything.* Revised and Expanded Edition. New York: Morrow.

Levy, Becca R., Martin D. Slade, Suzanne R. Kunkel, and Stanislav V. Kasl. 2002. "Longevity Increased by Positive Self-Perceptions of Aging." *Journal of Personality and Social Psychology* 83 (2):261–270.

Lewis Mumford Center. 2001. *Ethnic Diversity Grows, Neighborhood Integration Is at a Standstill.* Albany, NY: Lewis Mumford Center.

Lewis-Elligan, Tracy. 2008. "Medical Experimentation." Pp. 883–885, vol. 2, in *Encyclopedia of Race, Ethnicity, and Society,* edited by Richard T. Schaefer. Thousand Oaks, CA: Sage.

Lichtblau, Eric. 2009. Telecom Companies Win Dismissal of Wiretap Suits. *New York Times,* June 4, p. A14.

Lieberman, David. 2007. "View of Media Ownership Limits Changes." *USA Today,* January 29, pp. B1–B2.

Lieberson, Stanley. 2000. *A Matter of Taste: How Names, Fashions, and Culture Change.* New Haven, CT: Yale University Press.

Light, Donald W. 2004. "Dreams of Success: A New History of the American Health Care System." *Journal of Health and Social Behavior* 45 (Extra issue):1–24.

Light, Paul C. 2005. "Katrina's Lesson in Readiness." *Washington Post,* September 1.

Lim, Louisa. 2007. "Digital Culture: China's 'Gold Farmers' Play a Grim Game." May 14, 2007 broadcast on NPR. Accessed at www.npr.org.

Lindner, Eileen, ed. 2008. *Yearbook of American and Canadian Churches, 2008.* Nashville: Abingdon Press.

Linn, Susan, and Alvin F. Poussaint. 1999. "Watching Television: What Are Children Learning About Race and Ethnicity?" *Child Care Information Exchange* 128 (July):50–52.

Lino, Mark. 2008. *Expenditures on Children by Families, 2007.* Washington, DC: U.S. Department of Agriculture, Center for Nutrition Policy and Promotion.

Lio, Shoon, Scott Melzer, and Ellen Reese. 2008. "Constructing Threat and Appropriating 'Civil Rights': Rhetorical Strategies of Gun Rights and English Only Leaders." *Symbolic Interaction* 31 (1):5–31.

Lipka, Sara. 2009. "Do Crime Statistics Keep Students Safe?" *The Chronicle of Higher Education* 55 (January 30):A15–A17.

Lipson, Karen. 1994. " 'Nell' Not Alone in the Wilds." *Los Angeles Times,* December 19, pp. F1, F6.

Liptak, Adam. 2004. "Bans on Interracial Unions Offer Perspective on Gay Ones." *New York Times,* March 17, p. A16.

———. 2006. "The Ads Discriminate, but Does the Web?" *New York Times,* March 5, p. 16.

———. 2008. "From One Footnote, a Debate Over the Tangles of Law, Science and Money." *New York Times,* November 25, p. A13.

Liska, Allen E., and Steven F. Messner. 1999. *Perspectives on Crime and Deviance.* 3rd ed. Upper Saddle River, NJ: Prentice Hall.

Little, Kenneth. 1988. "The Role of Voluntary Associations in West African Urbanization." Pp. 211–230 in *Anthropology for the Nineties: Introductory Readings,* edited by Johnnetta B. Cole. New York: Free Press.

Livernash, Robert, and Eric Rodenburg. 1998. "Population Change, Resources, and the Environment." *Population Bulletin* 53 (March).

Livingstone, Sonia. 2004. "The Challenge of Changing Audiences." *European Journal of Communication* 19 (March):75–86.

Llana, Sara Miller. 2009. "Mexican Workers Send Less Cash Home from the U.S." *Christian Science Monitor,* January 28.

Loeb, Susanna, Bruce Fuller, Sharon Lynn Kagan, and Bidemi Carrol. 2004. "Child Care in Poor Communities: Early Learning Effects of Type, Quality, and Stability." *Child Development* 75 (January/February):47–65.

Lofland, John. 1981. "Collective Behavior: The Elementary Forms." Pp. 441–446 in *Social Psychology: Sociological Perspectives,* edited by Morris Rosenberg and Ralph Turner. New York: Basic Books.

———. 1985. *Protests: Studies of Collective Behavior and Social Movements.* Rutgers, NJ: Transaction.

Lofland, Lyn H. 1975. "The 'Thereness' of Women: A Selective Review of Urban Sociology." Pp. 144–170 in *Another Voice,* edited by M. Millman and R. M. Kanter. New York: Anchor/Doubleday.

Logan, John R., Brian J. Stults, and Reynolds Farley. 2004. "Segregation of Minorities in the Metropolis: Two Decades of Change." *Demography* 41 (February):1–22.

Lohr, Steve. 2008. "For a Good Retirement, Find Work. Good Luck." *New York Times,* June 22, p. 3.

LoMonaco, Claudine. 2006. "U.S.-Mexico Border: The Season of Death Dispatches June 27, 2006." Accessed February 19, 2007 (www.pbs.org).

Long, Sharon K., and Paul B. Mass. 2009. *Access to and Affordability of Carte in Massachusetts as of Fall 2008: Geographic and Racial/Ethnic Differences.* Washington, DC: Urban Institute.

Lorber, Judith. 2005. *Breaking the Bowls: Degendering and Feminist Change.* New York: Norton.

Lucas, Edward. 2008. "The Electronic Bureaucrat." *The Economist* 186 (February 16, special report).

Ludwig, Jens, and Isabell Sawhill. 2007. *Success by Ten: Interviewing Early, Often, and Efficiently in the Education of Young Children.* Washington, DC: Brookings Institution.

Lukacs, Georg. 1923. *History and Class Consciousness.* London: Merlin.

Lumpe, Lora. 2003. "Taking Aim at the Global Gun Trade." *Amnesty Now* (Winter):10–13.

Lundquist, Jennifer Hickes. 2006. "Choosing Single Motherhood." *Contexts* 5 (Fall):64–67.

Luo, Michael. 2008. "What Happens to Public Financing, When Obama Thrived Without It?" *New York Times,* November 3, p. A17.

———. 2009. "Longer Periods of Unemployment for Workers 45 and Older." *New York Times,* April 13, p. A11.

Luster, Tom, Kelly Rhoades, and Bruce Haas. 1989. "The Relation between Parental Values and Parenting Behavior: A Test of the Kohn Hypothesis." *Journal of Marriage and the Family* 51 (February):139–147.

Luttinger, Nina, and Gregory Dicum. 2006. *The Coffee Book: Anatomy of an Industry from Crop to the Last Drop.* Revised and Updated. New York: New Press.

Lyall, Sarah. 2002. "For Europeans, Love, Yes; Marriage, Maybe." *New York Times,* March 24, pp. 1–8.

Lykes, M. Brinton, Ali Banuazizi, Ramsay Liem, and Michael Morris, eds. 1996. *Myths about the Powerless: Contesting Social Inequalities.* Philadelphia: Temple University Press.

Lynas, Mark. 2008. *Six Degrees: Our Future on a Hotter Planet.* Washington, DC: National Geographic.

Lynn, Barry C. 2003. "Trading with a Low-Wage Tiger." *The American Prospect* 14 (February):10–12.

M

MacDonald, G. Jeffrey. 2007. "Go in Search of a Church by Way of the Web." *USA Today,* October 17, p. 8D.

MacDorman, Marian, et al. 2005. "Explaining the 2001–2002 Infant Mortality Increase: Data from the Linked Death/Infant Death Data Set." *National Vital Statistics Reports* 53 (January 24).

MacFarquhar, Neil. 2008. "Resolute or Fearful, Many Muslims Turn to Home Schooling." *New York Times,* March 26, p. A1.

Mack, Mick G. 2003. "Does Exercise Status Influence the Impressions Formed by College Students?" *College Student Journal* 3.7 (December).

Mack, Raymond W., and Calvin P. Bradford. 1979. *Transforming America: Patterns of Social Change.* 2nd ed. New York: Random House.

MacLeod, Scott, and Vivienne Walt. 2005. "Live from Qatar." *Time,* bonus section, June, pp. A6–A8.

Magga, Ole Henrik. 2006. "Diversity in Sami Terminology for Reindeer, Snow, and Ice." *International Social Science Journal* 58 (March):25–34.

Magnier, Mark. 2004. "China Clamps Down on Web News Discussion." *Los Angeles Times,* February 26, p. A4.

Mahbub ul Haq Human Development Centre. 2000. *Human Development in South Asia 2000.* Oxford, England: Oxford University Press for Mahbub ul Haq Human Development Centre.

Malcolm X, with Alex Haley. 1964. *The Autobiography of Malcolm X.* New York: Grove.

Malcolm, Andrew H. 1974. "The 'Shortage' of Bathroom Tissue: A Classic Study in Rumor." *New York Times,* February 3, p. 29.

Malhotra, Neil, and Yotam Margalit. 2009. "State of the Nation: Anti-Semitism and the Economic Crisis." *Boston Review* (May/June). Accessible at http://bostonreview.net/BR34.3/malhotra_margalit.php.

Malthus, Thomas Robert, Julian Huxley, and Frederick Osborn. [1824] 1960. *Three Essays on Population.* Reprint. New York: New American Library.

Mangum, Garth L., Stephen L. Magnum, and Andrew M. Sum. 2003. *The Persistence of Poverty in the United States.* Baltimore: Johns Hopkins University Press.

Marijuana Policy Project. 2008. "State-By-State Medical Marijuana Laws." Accessed February 21, 2009 (www.mpp.org/assets/pdfs/download-materials/SBSR_NOV2008.pdf).

Mark, Gloria, Victor M. Gonzalez, and Justin Harris. 2005. "No Task Left Behind? Examining the Nature of Fragmented Work." Paper presented at CHI 2005, Portland, Oregon.

Markoff, John. 2006. "For $150, Third-World Laptop Stirs a Big Debate." *New York Times,* November 30, pp. A1, C6.

———. 2007. "At Davos, the Squabble Resumes on How to Wire the Third World." *New York Times,* January 29, pp. C1, C2.

———. 2008. "Intel Quits Efforts to Get Computers to Children." *New York Times,* January 5.

Markson, Elizabeth W. 1992. "Moral Dilemmas." *Society* 29 (July/August):4–6.

Marosi, Richard. 2007. "The Nation: A Once-Porous Border Is a Turning-Back Point." *Los Angeles Times,* March 21, pp. A1, A20.

Marquis, Julie, and Dan Morain. 1999. "A Tortuous Path for the Mentally Ill." *Los Angeles Times,* November 21, pp. A1, A22, A23.

Marr, Phebe. 2003. "Civics 101, Taught by Saddam Hussein: First, Join the Paramilitary." *New York Times,* April 20.

Martin, Dominique, Jean-Luc Metzger, and Philippe Pierre. 2006. "The Sociology of Globalization: Theoretical and Methodological Reflections." *International Sociology* 21 (July):499–521.

Martin, Joyce A., Brady E. Hamilton, Paul D. Sutton, Stephanie J. Ventura, Fay Menacker, Sharon Kirmeyer, and T. J. Mathews. 2009. "Births: Final Data for 2006." *National Vital Statistics Reports* 57 (January 7).

Martin, Marvin. 1996. "Sociology Adapting to Changes." *Chicago Tribune,* July 21, sec. 18, p. 20.

Martin, Susan E. 1994. "Outsider Within the Station House: The Impact of Race and Gender on Black Women Politics." *Social Problems* 41 (August):383–400.

Martineau, Harriet. [1837] 1962. *Society in America.* Edited, abridged, with an introductory essay by Seymour Martin Lipset. Reprint. Garden City, NY: Doubleday.

———. [1838] 1989. *How to Observe Morals and Manners.* Philadelphia: Leal and Blanchard. Sesquentennial edition, edited by M. R. Hill, Transaction Books.

Martinez, Elizabeth. 1993. "Going Gentle into That Good Night: Is a Rightful Death a Feminist Issue?" *Ms.* 4 (July/August):65–69.

Marubbio, M. Elise. 2006. *Killing the Indian Maiden: Images of Native American Women in Film.* Lexington, KY: University Press of Kentucky.

Marx, Karl, and Friedrich Engels. [1847] 1955. *Selected Work in Two Volumes.* Reprint. Moscow: Foreign Languages Publishing House.

Marx, Karl. [1844] 1964. "Contribution to the Critique of Hegel's Philosophy of Right." In *On Religion,* Karl Marx and Friedrich Engels. New York: Schocker Books.

Maryanski, Alexandra R. 2004. "Evaluation Theory." Pp. 257–263 in *Encyclopedia of Social Theory,* edited by George Ritzer. Thousand Oaks, CA: Sage.

Mason, Heather. 2003. "What Do Americans See in Title IX's Future?" *Gallup Poll Tuesday Briefing.* Accessed January 28, 2003 (www.gallup.com).

Mason, J. W. 1998. "The Buses Don't Stop Here Anymore." *American Prospect* 37 (March):56–62.

Mason, Matt. 2008. *The Pirate's Dilemma: How Youth Culture Is Reinventing Capitalism.* New York: Free Press.

Massey, Douglas S. 1998. "March of Folly: U.S. Immigration Policy After NAFTA." *The American Prospect* (March/April):22–23.

———, and Nancy A. Denton. 1993. *American Apartheid: Segregation and the Making of the Underclass.* Cambridge, MA: Harvard University Press.

———, and Margarita Mooney. 2007. "The Effects of America's Three Affirmative Action Programs on Academic Performance." *Social Problems* 54 (1):99–117.

———. 2007. *Categorically Unequal: The American Stratification System.* New York: Russell Sage Foundation.

———. 2008. "A Mexican Apartheid." Pp. 55–57, vol. 2, in *Encyclopedia of Race, Ethnicity, and Society,* edited by Richard T. Schaefer. Thousand Oaks CA: Sage.

Masuda, Takahiko, Phoebe C. Ellsworth, Batja Mesquita, Janxin Leu, Shigehito Tanida, and Ellen Van de Veerdonk. 2008. "Attitudes and Social Cognition: Placing the Face in Context: Cultural Differences in the Perception of Facial Emotion." *Journal of Personality and Social Psychology* 94 (3):365–381.

Masud-Piloto, Felix. 2008. "Cuban Americans." Pp. 357–359, vol. 1, in *Encyclopedia of Race, Ethnicity, and Society,* edited by Richard T. Schaefer. Thousand Oaks, CA: Sage.

Masur, Louis P. 2007. "How the Truth Gets Framed by the Camera." *Chronicle of Higher Education* November 23: pp. B6–B8.

Mather, Mark. 2007. "The New Generation Gap." Washington, DC: Population Reference Bureau. Accessible at www.prb.org.

Matthews, Sarah H. 2007. "A Window on the 'New' Sociology of Childhood." *Sociology Compass* 1 (1):322–334.

Mays, Vickie M., Susan D. Cochran, and Namdi W. Barnes. 2007. "Race, Race-Based Discrimination, and Health Outcomes Among African Americans." *Annual Review of Psychology* 58:201–225.

Mazumder, Bhashkar. 2008. *Upward Intergenerational Economic Mobility in the United States.* Washington, DC: Economic Mobility Project.

McCabe, Donald L., Tony Fenghaliod, and Hanin Abdellah. 2008. "Academic Dishonesty in the Middle East: Individual and Contextual Factors." *Research in Higher Education* 49 (August):451–467.

McCloskey, Michael. 1991. "Twenty Years of Change in the Environmental Movement: An Insider's View." *Society and Natural Resources* 4 (July–September): 273–284.

McCloud, Aminah Beverly. 1995. *African American Islam.* New York: Routledge.

McDonald, Michael P. 2008. "The Return of the Voter: Voter Turnout in the 2008 Presidential Election." *The Forum* 6(4): Article 4.

———. 2009a. "Voter Turnout." Accessed April 8 (http://elections.gmu.edu/voter_turnout.htm).

———. 2009b. "2008 Current Population Survey Voting and Registration Supplement." Accessed April 16 (http://elections.gmu.edu/CPS_2008.html).

McFalls, Joseph A., Jr. 2003. "Population: A Lively Introduction." *Population Bulletin* 58 (December).

———. 2007. *Population: A Lively Introduction.* 5th ed. Washington, DC: Population Reference Bureau.

McFarland, Andrew S. 2007. "Neopluralism." *Annual Review of Political Science* 10:45–66.

McFarland, Daniel A., and Reuben J. Thomas. 2006. "Bowling Young: How Youth Voluntary Associations Influence Adult Political Participation." *American Sociological Review* 71 (June):401–425.

534

References

McGue, Matt, and Thomas J. Bouchard, Jr. 1998. "Genetic and Environmental Influence on Human Behavioral Differences." Pp. 1–24 in *Annual Review of Neurosciences.* Palo Alto, CA: Annual Reviews.

McGuire, Thomas G., and Jeanne Miranda. 2008. "New Evidence Regarding Racial and Ethnic Disparities in Mental Health: Policy Implications." *Health Affairs* 27 (2):393–403.

McGurty, Eileen Maura. 2000. "Warren County, NC, and the Emergence of the Environmental Justice Movement: Unlikely Coalitions and Shared Meanings in Local Collective Action." *Society and Natural Resources* 13:373–387.

McIntosh, Peggy. 1988. "White Privilege and Male Privilege: A Personal Account of Coming to See Correspondence Through Work and Women's Studies." Working Paper No. 189, Wellesley College Center for Research on Women, Wellesley, MA.

McKinlay, John B., and Sonja M. McKinlay. 1977. "The Questionable Contribution of Medical Measures to the Decline of Mortality in the United States in the Twentieth Century." *Milbank Memorial Fund Quarterly* 55 (Summer):405–428.

McLanahan, Sara, and Christine Percheski. 2008. "Family Structure and the Reproduction of Inequalities." *Annual Review of Sociology* 38:257–276.

McLuhan, Marshall. 1964. *Understanding Media: The Extensions of Man.* New York: New American Library.

———, and Quentin Fiore. 1967. *The Medium Is the Message: An Inventory of Effects.* New York: Bantam Books.

McNeil, Donald G., Jr. 2002. "W.H.O. Moves to Make AIDS Drugs More Accessible to Poor Worldwide." *New York Times,* August 23, p. D7.

———. 2004. "Plan to Battle AIDS Worldwide Is Falling Short." *New York Times,* March 28, pp. 1, 14.

McPhail, Clark. 1991. *The Myth of the Madding Crowd.* New York: De Gruyter.

———. 1994. "The Dark Side of Purpose in Riots: Individual and Collective Violence." *Sociological Quarterly* 35 (January):i–xx.

———. 2006. "The Crowd and Collective Behavior: Bringing Symbolic Interaction Back In." *Symbolic Interaction* 29 (Issue 4):433–464.

———, and David Miller. 1973. "The Assembling Process: A Theoretical Empirical Examination." *American Sociological Review* 38 (December): 721–735.

———. 2008. "Crowd." *Contexts* (Spring):78–79.

Mead, George H. 1934. In *Mind, Self and Society,* edited by Charles W. Morris. Chicago: University of Chicago Press.

———. 1964a. In *On Social Psychology,* edited by Anselm Strauss. Chicago: University of Chicago Press.

———. 1964b. "The Genesis of the Self and Social Control." Pp. 267–293 in *Selected Writings: George Herbert Mead,* edited by Andrew J. Reck. Indianapolis: Bobbs-Merrill.

Mead, Margaret. [1935] 2001. *Sex and Temperament in Three Primitive Societies.* New York: Perennial, HarperCollins.

Mehl, Matthias R., Simine Vazire, Nairán Ramírez-Esparza, Richard B. Slatcher, and James W. Pennebacker. 2007. "Are Women Really More Talkative Than Men?" *Science* 317 (July 6):82.

Melia, Marilyn Kennedy. 2000. "Changing Times." *Chicago Tribune,* January 2, sec. 17, pp. 12–15.

Mendez, Jennifer Bickman. 1998. "Of Mops and Maids: Contradictions and Continuities in Bureaucratized Domestic Work." *Social Problems* 45 (February):114–135.

Merton, Robert. 1948. "The Bearing of Empirical Research upon the Development of Social Theory." *American Sociological Review* 13 (October):505–515.

———. 1968. *Social Theory and Social Structure.* New York Free Press.

———, and Alice S. Kitt. 1950. "Contributions to the Theory of Reference Group Behavior." Pp. 40–105 in *Continuities in Social Research: Studies in the Scope and Methods of the American Soldier,* edited by Robert K. Merton and Paul L. Lazarsfeld. New York: Free Press.

Messner, Michael A. 2002. "Gender Equity in College Sports: 6 Views." *Chronicle of Higher Education.* 49 (December 6):B9–B10.

———, Margaret Carlisle Duncan, and Nicole Williams. 2006. "This Revolution Is Not Being Televised." *Contexts* 5 (Summer):34–38.

Meston, Cindy M., and David M. Buss. 2007. "Why Humanoids Have Sex." *Archives of Sexual Behavior* 36 (August).

Meyer, Julie. 2001. *Age: 2000.* Census 2000 Brief. Washington, DC: U.S. Government Printing Office.

Meyer, Karen. 2007. "Match the Disability." April 31. Unpublished paper. Chicago: DePaul University.

———. 2008. "Americans with Disabilities Act." In *Encyclopedia of Race, Ethnicity, and Society,* edited by Richard T. Schaefer. Thousand Oaks, CA: Sage.

Meyerson, Harold. 2006. "How Capitalism Works Now." *Prospect Magazine* 17 (November):54–55.

Michals, Jennifer M. 2003. "The Price We Pay to Get Richer: A Look at Student Indebtedness." Unpublished M.A. paper, DePaul University, Chicago, IL.

Michels, Robert. 1915. *Political Parties.* Glencoe, IL: Free Press (reprinted 1949).

Microfinance Information Exchange. 2008. *The MicroBanking Bulletin* 17 (Autumn).

———. 2009. "Growth of Numbers of Borrowers and Savers." Accessed April 20 (www.themix.org/node/936).

Milgram, Stanley. 1963. "Behavioral Study of Obedience." *Journal of Abnormal and Social Psychology* 67 (October):371–378.

———. 1975. *Obedience to Authority: An Experimental View.* New York: Harper and Row.

Miller, Dan E. 2006. "Rumor: An Examination of Some Stereotypes." *Symbolic Interaction* 28 (4):505–519.

Miller, David L. 2000. *Introduction to Collective Behavior and Collective Action.* 2nd ed. Prospect Heights, IL: Waveland Press.

———. and JoAnne DeRoven Darlington. 2002. *Fearing for the Safety of Others: Disasters and the Small World Problem.* Paper presented at Midwest Sociological Society, Milwaukee, WI.

Miller, Jacqueline W., Timothy S. Naimi, Robert D. Brewer, and Sherry Everett Jones. 2007. "Binge Drinking and Associated Health Risk Behaviors Among High School Students." *Pediatrics* 119 (January): 76–85.

Miller, Laura. 2008. "The Rise of the Superclass." Accessed in *Salon* May 2 (www.salon.com/books/review/2008/03/14/superclass/print.html).

Miller, Reuben. 1988. "The Literature of Terrorism." *Terrorism* 11 (1):63–87.

Mills, C. Wright. [1959] 2000a. *The Sociological Imagination.* 40th Anniversary Edition: New Afterword by Todd Gitlin. New York: Oxford University Press.

———. [1956] 2000b. *The Power Elite.* A New Edition. Afterword by Alan Wolfe. New York: Oxford University Press.

Miner, Horace. 1956. "Body Ritual among the Nacirema." *American Anthropologist* 58 (June): 503–507.

Minnesota Center for Twin and Family Research. 2009. "Research at the MCTFR." Accessed January 20 (http://mctfr.psych.umn.edu/research/).

Mizruchi, Mark S. 1996. "What Do Interlocks Do? An Analysis, Critique, and Assessment of Research on Interlocking Directorates." Pp. 271–298 in *Annual Review of Sociology,* 1996, edited by John Hagan and Karen Cook. Palo Alto, CA: Annual Reviews.

Moaveni, Azadeh. 2005a. *Lipstick Jihad. A Memoir of Growing Up Iranian in America and American in Iran.* New York: Public Affairs.

———. 2005b. "Fast Times in Tehran." *Time,* June 12; pp. 38–42.

———. 2007. "The Unbearable Chic-ness of Jihad." *Time,* April 10.

———. 2009. *Honeymoon in Tehran: Two Years of Love and Danger in Iran.* New York: Random House.

Moeller, Susan D. 1999. *Compassion Fatigue.* London: Routledge.

Moen, Phyllis, and Patricia Roehling. 2005. *The Career Mystique: Cracks in the American Dream.* Lanham, MD: Rowman and Littlefield.

Mogelonsky, Marcia. 1996. "The Rocky Road to Adulthood." *American Demographics* 18 (May):26–29, 32–35, 56.

Mohai, Paul, and Robin Saha. 2007. "Racial Inequality in the Distribution of Hazardous Waste.: A National-Level Reassessment." *Social Problems* 54 (3):343–370.

Mokhtarian, Patricia L., Ilan Salomon, and Sangho Choo. 2005. "Measuring the Measurable: Why Can't We Agree on the Number of Telecommuters in the U.S." *Quality and Quantity* 35:423–452.

Mollen, Milton. 1992. *"A Failure of Responsibility": Report to Mayor David N. Dinkins on the December 28, 1991, Tragedy at City College of New York.* New York: Office of the Deputy Mayor for Public Safety.

Monaghan, Peter. 1993. "Sociologist Jailed Because He 'Wouldn't Snitch' Ponders the Way Research Ought to Be Done." *Chronicle of Higher Education* 40 (September 1):A8, A9.

Monahan, Mary T. 2007. *2007 Identity Fraud Survey Report: Identity Fraud Is Dropping, Continued Vigilance Necessary.* Pleasanton, CA: Javelin Strategy and Research.

Moncarz, Roger J., Michael G. Wolf, and Benjamin Wright. 2008. "Service-Providing Occupations, Offshoring, and the Labor Market." *Monthly Labor Review* (December): 71–86.

Money. 1987. "A Short History of Shortages." 16 (Fall, special issue):42.

Montgomery, Marilyn J., and Gwendolyn T. Sorell. 1997. "Differences in Love Attitudes Across Family Life Stages." *Family Relations* 46:55–61.

Moore, David W. 2002. "Americans' View of Influence of Religion Settling Back to Pre-September 11 Levels." *Gallup Poll Tuesday Briefing;* December 31.

Moore, Molly. 2006. "Romance, but not Marriage." *Washington Post National Weekly Edition,* November 27; p. 18.

Moore, Solomon. 2007. "States Export Their Inmates As Prisons Fill." *New York Times,* July 31, pp. A1, A14.

Moore, Wilbert E. 1967. *Order and Change: Essays in Comparative Sociology.* New York: Wiley.

———. 1968. "Occupational Socialization." Pp. 861–883 in *Handbook of Socialization Theory and Research,* edited by David A. Goslin. Chicago: Rand McNally.

Morehouse Medical Treatment and Effectiveness Center. 1999. *A Synthesis of the Literature: Racial and Ethnic Differences in Acccess to Medical Care.* Menlo Park, CA: Kaiser Family Foundation.

Morris, Aldon. 2000. "Reflections on Social Movement Theory: Criticisms and Proposals." *Contemporary Sociology* 29 (May):445–454.

Morris, Bonnie Rothman. 1999. "You've Got Romance! Seeking Love on Line." *New York Times,* August 26, p. D1.

Morrison, Denton E. 1971. "Some Notes toward Theory on Relative Deprivation, Social Movements, and Social Change." *American Behavioral Scientist* 14 (May/June):675–690.

Morse, Arthur D. 1967. *While Six Million Died: A Chronicle of American Apathy.* New York: Ace.

Morselli, Carlo, Pierre Tremblay, and Bill McCarthy. 2006. "Mentors and Criminal Achievement." *Criminology* 44 (1):17–43.

Mosley, J., and E. Thomson. 1995. Pp. 148–165 in *Fatherhood: Contemporary Theory, Research and Social Policy,* edited by W. Marsiglo. Thousand Oaks, CA: Sage.

Moss, Michael, and Ford Fessenden. 2002. "New Tools for Domestic Spying, and Qualms." *New York Times,* December 10, pp. A1, A18.

Mueller, G. O. 2001. "Transnational Crime: Definitions and Concepts." Pp. 13–21 in *Combating Transnational Crime: Concepts, Activities, and Responses,* edited by P. Williams and D. Vlassis. London: Franklin Cass.

Mufson, Steven. 2007. "Turning Down the Heat." *Washington Post National Weekly Edition* 24 (July):6–8.

Mumbere, Virginie. 2008. "With Microloans, Flour Milling and Literacy Teaching, Widows Are Given the Chance to Start a New Life." *The Guardian Weekly* (May 30):25.

Muñoz, José A. 2008. "Protest and Human Rights Networks: The Case of the Zapatista Movement." *Sociology Compass* (April): 1045–1058.

Murdock, George P. 1945. "The Common Denominator of Cultures." Pp. 123–142 in *The Science of Man in the World Crisis,* edited by Ralph Linton. New York: Columbia University Press.

———. 1949. *Social Structure.* New York: Macmillan.

———. 1957. "World Ethnographic Sample." *American Anthropologist* 59 (August):664–687.

Murphy, Caryle. 1993. "Putting Aside the Veil." *Washington Post National Weekly Edition* 10 (April 12–18):10–11.

Murphy, Dean E. 1997. "A Victim of Sweden's Pursuit of Perfection." *Los Angeles Times,* September 2, pp. A1, A8.

Murray, Velma McBride, Amanda Willert, and Diane P. Stephens. 2001. "The Half-Full Glass: Resilient African American Single Mothers and Their Children." *Family Focus* (June):F4–F5.

NAACP. 2008. *Out of Focus—Out of Sync Take 4.* Baltimore MD: NAACP.

NACCRRA. 2007. "Child Care in America." Accessed January 31 (www.naccrra.org).

———. 2008. "Child Care in America: 2008 State Fact Sheets." Accessed January 20, 2009 (www.naccrra.org).

Naimark, Norman M. 2004. "Ethnic Cleansing, History of." Pp. 4799–4802 in *International Encyclopedia of Social and Behavioral Sciences,* edited by N. J. Smelser and P. B. Baltes. New York: Elsevier.

Nakao, Keiko, and Judith Treas. 1994. "Updating Occupational Prestige and Socioeconomic Scores: How the New Measures Measure Up." *Sociological Methodology* 24:1–72.

NARAL Pro-Choice America. 2009. "Who Decides? Restrictions on Low-Income Women's Access to Abortion." Accessed March 31 (www.prochoiceamerica.org).

Nash, Manning. 1962. "Race and the Ideology of Race." *Current Anthropology* 3 (June):285–288.

National Advisory Commission on Criminal Justice. 1976. *Organized Crime.* Washington, DC: U.S. Government Printing Office.

National Alliance for the Mentally Ill. 2000. "What Is Mental Illness?" Accessed January 18 (www.nami.org/disorder/whatis.html).

National Alliance to End Homelessness. 2009. *Homeless Counts.* Washington, DC: National Alliance to End Homelessness.

National Center for Education Statistics. 2002. *Indicators of School Crime and Safety.* Washington, DC: U.S. Government Printing Office.

National Center for Education Statistics. 2006. "Projections of Education Statistics to 2016." Table 22. Accessed April 14, 2009 (http://nces.ed.gov/programs/projections/projections2016/tables/table_22.asp?referrer=list).

———. 2009. *Homeschooled Students.* Accessed May 31 (http://nces.ed.gov/programs/coe/2009/section1/indicator06.asp).

National Center on Addiction and Substance Abuse at Columbia University. 2007. *Wasting the Best and the Brightest: Substance Abuse at America's Colleges and Universities.* New York: NCASA at Columbia University.

National Council on Disability. 2004. *Righting the ADA.* Washington, DC: NCD.

National Geographic. 2005. *Atlas of the World.* 8th ed. Washington, DC: *National Geographic.*

National Institute of Justice. 2005. *Sexual Assault on Campus: What Colleges and Universities Are Doing About It.* Washington, DC: National Institute of Justice.

National Institute on Aging. 1999. *Early Retirement in the United States.* Washington, DC: U.S. Government Printing Office.

National Institute on Alcohol Abuse and Alcoholism. 2009. "College Drinking—Changing the Culture." Accessed February 21 (www.collegedrinkingprevention.gov/StatsSummaries/snapshot.aspx).

National Law Center on Homelessness and Poverty. 2006. *A Dream Denied: The Criminalization of Homelessness in U.S. Cities.* Washington, DC: National Law Center on Homelessness and Poverty.

———. 2009. "Maryland 1st to Protect Homeless from Hate Crimes." Accessed May 8 (www.nlchp.org/news.cfm?id=98).

National Organization for Men Against Sexism. 2009. Home page. Accessed March 31 (www.nomas.org).

National Right to Work Legal Defense Foundation. 2009. *Right to Work States.* Accessed January 27 (www.nrtw.org/rtws.htm).

National Vital Statistics Reports. 2008. "Births, Marriages, Divorces, and Deaths: Provisional Data for June 2008." *National Vital Statistics Reports* 57 (April 3).

Natural Law Party. 2008. "Natural Law Party: A Reason to Vote." Accessed March 16 (www.natural-law.org).

Navarro, Mireya. 2002. "Trying to Get Beyond the Role of the Maid." *New York Times,* May 16, pp. E1, E4.

———. 2005. "When You Contain Multitudes." *New York Times,* April 24, pp. 1, 2.

———. 2009. "In Environmental Push, Looking to Add Diversity." *New York Times,* March 10, p. A13.

Neckerman, Kathryn M., and Florencia Torche. 2007. "Inequality: Causes and Consequences." *Annual Review of Sociology* 33:335–357.

Nelson, Emily. 2004. "Goodbye, 'Friends'; Hello, New Reality." *Wall Street Journal,* February 9, pp. B6, B10.

Nemoto, Kumiko. 2008. "Japan." Pp. 778–781, vol. 2, in *Encyclopedia of Race Ethnicity, and Society,* edited by Richard T. Schaefer. Thousands Oaks, CA: Sage.

Neuman, Lawrence W. 2009. *Understanding Research.* Boston: Allyn and Bacon.

Neuwirth, Robert. 2004. *Shadow Cities: A Billion Squatters, a New Urban World.* New York: Routledge.

Newman, William M. 1973. *American Pluralism: A Study of Minority Groups and Social Theory.* New York: Harper and Row.

Newport, Frank. 2009. "Americans: Economy Takes Precedence Over Environment." Accessed April 27 (www.gallup.com/poll/116962/Americans-Economy-Takes-Precedence-Environment.aspx).

Newsday. 1997. "Japan Sterilized 16,000 Women." September 18, p. A19.

NewsHour. 2007. "New National Approach Focuses on Chronically Homeless." Accessed April 28 (www.pbs.org).

New York Times. 2007. "University Officials Accused of Hiding Campus Homicide." June 24, p. 19.

New York Times. 2008. "Law and Order." January 6, pp. 10–11.

NICHD. 2007. "Children Who Complete Intensive Early Childhood Program Show Gains in Adulthood: Greater College Attendance, Lower Crime and Depression." Accessed January 7, 2008 (www.nichd.nih.gov/news.releases/early_interventions_082107.cfm).

References

Nielsen Media Research. 2009. "Nielsen Reports Growth of 4.4% in Asian and 4.3% in Hispanic U.S. Households for 2008–2009 Television Season." Accessed February 5 (www.nielsenmedia.com).

Nielsen, Joyce McCarl, Glenda Walden, and Charlotte A. Kunkel. 2000. "Gendered Heteronormativity: Empirical Illustrations in Everyday Life." *Sociological Quarterly* 41 (2): 283–296.

Niezen, Ronald. 2005. "Digital Identity: The Construction of Virtual Selfhood in the Indigenous Peoples' Movement." *Comparative Studies in Society and History* 47 (3):532–551.

Nislow, Jennifer. 2003. "The Wrong Time to Find Out That Emerging Alert System Doesn't Work." *Law Enforcement News* 29 (March).

Nixon, Darren. 2009. "'I Can't Put a Smiley Face On': Working-Class Masculinity, Emotional Labor and Service Work in the 'New Economy.'" *Gender, Work and Organization* 16 (3):300–322.

Nixon, Howard L., II. 1979. *The Small Group.* Englewood Cliffs, NJ: Prentice Hall.

Nolan, Patrick, and Gerhard Lenski. 2009. *Human Societies: An Introduction to Macrosociology.* 11th ed. Boulder, CO: Paradigm.

Noonan, Rita K. 1995. "Women Against the State: Political Opportunities and Collective Action Frames in Chile's Transition to Democracy." *Sociological Forum* 10:81–111.

Norris, Poppa, and Ronald Inglehart. 2004. *Sacred and Secular: Religion and Politics Worldwide.* Cambridge: Cambridge University Press.

North Carolina Department of Environmental and Natural Resources. 2008. "Warren County PCB Landfill Fact Sheet." Accessed April 9 (www.wastenotnc.org/WarrenCo_Fact_Sheet.htm).

NPD Group. 2008. "Wired Baby Boomers Going Digital, Visiting Social Networks and Watching Videos on the Web." Accessed March 18 (www.npd.com/press/releases/press_080909.html).

Nussbaum, Bruce. 2006. "Can Wal-Mart Make It in India?" November 28. Accessed January 23, 2007 (www.businessweek.com).

O

Oberschall, Anthony. 1973. *Social Conflict and Social Movements.* Englewood Cliffs, NJ: Prentice Hall.

O'Connor, Anne-Marie. 2004. "Time of Blogs and Bombs." *Los Angeles Times,* December 27, pp. E1, E14–E15.

O'Donnell, Mike. 1992. *A New Introduction to Sociology.* Walton-on-Thames, United Kingdom: Thomas Nelson and Sons.

Office of Immigration Statistics. 2008. "2007 Yearbook of Immigration Statistics." Washington, DC: U.S. Department of Homeland Security.

Office of Justice Programs. 1999. "Transnational Organized Crime." *NCJRS Catalog* 49 (November/December):21.

Ogburn, William F. 1922. *Social Change with Respect to Culture and Original Nature.* New York: Huebsch (reprinted 1966, New York: Dell).

———, and Clark Tibbits. 1934. "The Family and Its Functions." Pp. 661–708 in *Recent Social Trends in the United States,* edited by Research Committee on Social Trends. New York: McGraw-Hill.

O'Hare, William P., and Brenda Curry-White. 1992. "Is There a Rural Underclass?" *Population Today* 20 (March):6–8.

O'Hare, William, and Mark Mather. 2008. *Child Poverty Is Highest in Rural Counties in U.S.* Washington DC.: Population Reference Bureau.

O'Harrow, Jr., Robert. 2005. "Mining Personal Data." *Washington Post National Weekly Edition,* February 6, pp. 8–10.

Okano, Kaori, and Motonori Tsuchiya. 1999. *Education in Contemporary Japan: Inequality and Diversity.* Cambridge: Cambridge University Press.

Oliver, Melvin L., and Thomas M. Shapiro. 2006. *Black Wealth/White Wealth: New Perspectives on Racial Inequality.* 2nd ed. New York: Routledge.

———. 2008. "Sub-Prime as a Black Catastrophe." *American Prospect* (October):A9–A11.

Omi, Michael, and Howard Winant. 1994. *Racial Formation in the United States,* 2nd ed. New York: Routledge.

One Laptop per Child. 2009. "One Laptop per Child." Accessed May 5 (www.laptop.org).

Onishi, Norimitso. 2003. "Divorce in South Korea: Striking a New Attitude." *New York Times,* September 21, p. 19.

———. 2009. "Japan's Outcasts Still Wait for Society's Embrace." *New York Times,* January 16, pp. A1, A6.

OpenNet Initiative. 2008. Home page. Accessed January 12 (http://opennet.net).

Orfield, Gary, and Chungmei Lee. 2007. *Historic Reversals, Accelerating Resegregation, and the Need for New Integration Strategies.* Los Angeles: Civil Rights Project, UCLA.

Organisation for Economic Co-Operation and Development. 2007. "Poverty at a Glance. Table EQ7.1." Accessed March 6, 2009 (www.oecd.org/dataoecd/26/40/38785295.htm).

———. 2008. "Growing Unequal? Income Distribution and Poverty in OECD Countries." Geneva: OECD.

———. 2009. "Geographical Distribution of Financial Flows to Developing Countries 2003–2007." Geneva: OECD. Accessed March 16 (www.oecd.org/document/57/0,3343,en_2649_34485_1897081_1_1_1_1,00.html).

Ormond, James. 2005. "The McDonaldization of Football." Accessed January 23, 2006 (http://courses.essex.ac.uk/sc/sc111).

Orum, Anthony M. 1989. *Introduction to Political Sociology: The Social Anatomy of the Body Politic.* 3rd ed. Englewood Cliffs, NJ: Prentice Hall.

———. 2001. *Introduction to Political Sociology.* 4th ed. Upper Saddle River, NJ: Prentice Hall.

Osberg, Lars, and Timothy Smeeding. 2006. "'Fair' Inequality? Attitudes Toward Pay Differentials: The United States in Comparative Perspective." *American Sociological Review* 71 (June): 450–473.

Ouchi, William. 1981. *Theory Z: How American Businesses Can Meet the Japanese Challenge.* Reading, MA: Addison-Wesley.

Outside the Classroom. 2009. "College Students Spend More Time Drinking Than Studying." Accessed March 11 (www.outsidetheclassroom.com).

P

Pace, David. 2006. "FEC Won't Regulate Internet Politics." *Associated Press,* May 27.

Page, Charles H. 1946. "Bureaucracy's Other Face." *Social Forces* 25 (October):89–94.

Pager, Devah. 2003. "The Mark of a Criminal Record." *American Journal of Sociology* 108 (March):937–975.

———. 2007a. *Marked: Race, Crime, and Funding Work in an Era of Mass Incarceration.* Chicago: University of Chicago Press.

———. 2007b. "The Use of Field Experiments for Studies of Employment Discrimination: Contributions, Critiques, and Directions for the Future." *Annals* 609 (January):104–133.

———, and Hana Shepherd. 2008. "The Sociology of Discrimination: Racial Discrimination in Employment, Housing, Credit, and Consumer Markets." *Annual Review of Sociology* 34:181–209.

———, and Bruce Western. 2006. *Race at Work: Realities of Race and Criminal Record in the NYC Job Market.* Report prepared for the 50th Anniversary of the New York City Museum on Human Rights. Accessible at www.princeton.edu/~pager/race_at_work.pdf.

Parish, William, Edward Lavmann, and Sanyu Mojola. 2007. "Sexual Behavior in China: Trends and Comparisons." *Population of Development Review* 33 (December):729–756.

Park, Robert E. 1916. "The City: Suggestions for the Investigation of Human Behavior in the Urban Environment." *American Journal of Sociology* 20 (March):577–612.

———. 1922. *The Immigrant Press and Its Control.* New York: Harper.

———. 1936. "Succession, an Ecological Concept." *American Sociological Review* 1 (April):171–179.

Parker, Alison. 2004. "Inalienable Rights: Can Human-Rights Law Help to End U.S. Mistreatment of Noncitizens?" *American Prospect* (October):A11–A13.

Parsons, Talcott. 1951. *The Social System.* New York: Free Press.

———. 1966. *Societies: Evolutionary and Comparative Perspectives.* Englewood Cliffs, NJ: Prentice Hall.

———. 1975. "The Sick Role and the Role of the Physician Reconsidered." *Milbank Medical Fund Quarterly Health and Society* 53 (Summer):257–278.

———, and Robert Bales. 1955. *Family: Socialization and Interaction Process.* Glencoe, IL: Free Press.

Passero, Kathy. 2002. "Global Travel Expert Roger Axtell Explains Why." *Biography* (July):70–73, 97–98.

Patterson, Thomas E. 2003. *We the People.* 5th ed. New York: McGraw-Hill.

———. 2005. "Young Voters and the 2004 Election." Cambridge, MA: Vanishing Voter Project, Harvard University.

Pattillo-McCoy, Mary. 1999. *Black Picket Fences: Privilege and Peril among the Black Middle Class.* Chicago: University of Chicago Press.

Patton, Carl V., ed. 1988. *Spontaneous Shelter: International Perspectives and Prospects.* Philadelphia: Temple University Press.

Pear, Robert. 1997. "Now, the Archenemies Need Each Other." *New York Times,* June 22, sec. 4, pp. 1, 4.

———. 2009. "Congress Relaxes Rules on Suits Over Pay Inequity." *New York Times,* January 28, p. A14.

Pendergrast, Mark. 1999. *Uncommon Grounds: The History of Coffee and How It Transformed Our World.* New York: Basic Books.

Peng, Liang. 2008. "Venture Capital in Japan and Enlightenment to China." *China Business Review* 7 (January):10–20.

Pennington, Bill. 2008. "College Athletic Scholarships: Expectations Lose Out to Reality." *New York Times,* March 10, pp. A1, A15.

Perry, Joellen. 2001. "For Most, There's No Place Like Home." *U.S. News and World Report* 130 (June 4):66.

Perry, Tony. 2007. "Study: Deployment Does Not Increase Divorce." *Los Angeles Times,* April 16.

Peter, Laurence J., and Raymond Hull. 1969. *The Peter Principle.* New York: Morrow.

Petersen, John L. 2009. "How 'Wild Cards' May Reshape Our Future." *The Futurist* (May–June):19–20.

Petersen, William. 1979. *Malthus.* Cambridge, MA: Harvard University Press.

Peterson, Karen S. 2003. "Unmarried with Children: For Better or Worse." *USA Today,* August 18, pp. 1A, 8A.

Petrášová, Alexandra. 2006. *Social Protection in the European Union.* Brussels: European Union.

Pew Forum on Religion and Public Life. 2008. *U.S. Religious Landscape Survey.* Washington, DC: Author.

Pew Global Altitudes Project. 2007. *Global Unease with Major World Powers.* Washington DC: Pew Global.

Pew Hispanic Center. 2007. "2007 National Survey of Latinos: As Illegal Immigration Issue Heats Up, Hispanics Feel a Chill." Washington, DC: Author.

Pew Internet Project. 2008. "Demographics of Internet Users." Accessed April 18 (www.pewinternet. org/trends/User_Demo_2.15.08.htm).

———. 2009. "Demographics of Internet Users." Accessed February 4 (www.pewinternet.org/ trends/User_Demo_Jan_2009.htm).

Pew Research Center. 2009. "Americans Now Divided Over Both Issues: Public Takes Conservative Turn on Gun Control, Abortion." News release. Washington, DC: Pew Research Center.

Pfeifer, Mark. 2008. "Vietnamese Americans" Pp. 1365–1368, vol. 3, in *Encyclopedia of Race, Ethnicity, and Society,* edited by Richard T. Schaefer. Thousand Oaks, CA: Sage.

Phillips, E. Barbara. 1996. *City Lights: Urban–Suburban Life in the Global Society.* New York: Oxford University Press.

Phillips, Susan A. 1999. *Wallbangin': Graffiti and Gangs in L.A.* Chicago: University of Chicago Press.

Phillips, Tom. 2005. "Farewell to the Favelas?" *Guardian Weekly* 173 (November 17):29.

Piaget, Jean. 1954. *Construction of Reality in the Child.* Translated by Margaret Cook. New York: Basic Books.

Picca, Leslie Houts, and Joe R. Feagin. 2007. *Two-Faced Racism: Whites in Backstage and Frontstage.* New York: Routledge.

Pierre, Robert E. 2002. "When Welfare Reform Stops Working." *Washington Post National Weekly Edition,* January 13, pp. 29–30.

Piller, Charles. 2006. "An Alert Unlike Any Other." *Los Angeles Times,* May 3, pp. A1, A8.

Pincus, Fred L. 2003. *Reverse Discrimination: Dismantling the Myth.* Boulder, CO: Lynne Rienner.

———. 2008. "Reverse Discrimination." Pp. 1159–1161, vol. 3, in *Encyclopedia of Race, Ethnicity, and Society,* edited by Richard T. Schaefer. Thousand Oaks, CA: Sage.

Pinderhughes, Dianne. 1987. *Race and Ethnicity in Chicago Politics: A Reexamination of Pluralist Theory.* Urbana: University of Illinois Press.

Pinderhughes, Raquel. 2008. "Green Collar Jobs." Accessed June 29 (www.urbanhabitat.org/ node/528).

Pinkerton, James P. 2003. "Education: A Grand Compromise." *Atlantic Monthly* 291 (January/ February):115–116.

Piven, Frances Fox, and Richard A. Cloward. 1996. "Welfare Reform and the New Class War." Pp. 72–86 in *Myths about the Powerless: Contesting Social Inequalities,* edited by M. Brinton Lykes, Ali Banuazizi, Ramsay Liem, and Michael Morris. Philadelphia: Temple University Press.

Plomin, Robert. 1989. "Determinants of Behavior." *American Psychologist* 44 (February):105–111.

Plüss, Caroline. 2005. "Constructing Globalized Ethnicity." *International Sociology* 20 (June):201–224.

Pogash, Carol. 2008. "Poor Students in High School Suffer Stigma from Lunch Aid." *New York Times,* March 1, pp. A1, A14.

Polletta, Francesca, and James M. Jasper. 2001. "Collective Identity and Social Movements." Pp. 283–305 in *Annual Review of Sociology, 2001,* edited by Karen S. Cook and Leslie Hogan. Palo Alto, CA: Annual Reviews.

Poniewozik, James. 2001. "What's Wrong with This Picture?" *Time* 157 (May 28):80–81.

Pontin, Jason. 2007. "First, Cure Malaria. Next, Global Warming." *New York Times,* June 3, p.3.

Popenoe, David, and Barbara Dafoe Whitehead. 1999. *Should We Live Together? What Young Adults Need to Know About Cohabitation Before Marriage.* Rutgers, NJ: The National Marriage Project.

Population Reference Bureau. 1996. "Speaking Graphically." *Population Today* 24 (June/July):b.

Portes, Alejandro, Cristina Escobar, and Renelinda Arana. 2008. "Bridging the Gap: Transnational and Ethnic Organizations in the Political Incorporation of Immigrants in the United States." *Ethnic and Racial Studies* 31 (September 6): 1056–1090.

Prah, Pamela M. 2005. "Labor Unions' Future." *CQ Researcher* 15 (September 2):709–731.

Prehn, John W. 1991. "Migration." Pp. 190–191 in *Encyclopedia of Sociology,* 4th ed. Guilford, CT: Dushkin.

Priest, Dana. 2008. "Soldiers on the Edge." *Washington Post National Weekly* Edition 25 (February 4):8–9.

Pryor, John H., Sylvia Hurtado, Linda DéAngelo, Jessica Sharkness, Laura C. Romero, William S. Korn, and Serge Tran. 2008. *The American Freshman: National Norms Fall 2008.* Los Angeles: Higher Education Research Institute, UCLA.

Pryor, John H., Sylvia Hurtado, Victor B. Saenz, José Luis Santos, and William S. Korn. 2007. *The American Freshman: Forty Year Trends.* Los Angeles: Higher Education Research Institute, UCLA.

Puentes, Robert, and David Warrenn. 2006. *One-Fifth of America: A Comprehensive Guide to American's First Suburbs.* Washington, DC: Brookings Institution.

Quadagno, Jill. 2008. *Aging and the Life Course: An Introduction to Social Gerontology.* 4th ed. New York: McGraw-Hill.

Quarantelli, Enrico L. 1957. "The Behavior of Panic Participants." *Sociology and Social Research* 41 (January):187–194.

———, and Russell R. Dynes. 1970. "Property Norms and Looting: Their Patterns in Continuity Crises." *Phylon* (Summer):168–182.

———, and James R. Hundley, Jr. 1975. "A Test of Some Propositions about Crowd Formation and Behavior." Pp. 538–554 in *Readings in Collective Behavior,* edited by Robert R. Evans. Chicago: Rand McNally.

Quillian, Lincoln. 2006. "New Approaches to Understanding Racial Prejudice and Discrimination." *Annual Review of Sociology* 32:299–328.

Quinney, Richard. 1970. *The Social Reality of Crime.* Boston: Little, Brown.

———. 1974. *Criminal Justice in America.* Boston: Little, Brown.

———. 1979. *Criminology.* 2nd ed. Boston: Little, Brown.

———. 1980. *Class, State and Crime.* 2nd ed. New York: Longman.

Rainie, Lee. 2005. *Sports Fantasy Leagues Online.* Washington, DC: Pew Internet and American Life Project.

———, and John Horrigan. 2007. *Election 2006 Online.* Washington, DC: Pew Research Center.

Rajan, Gita, and Shailja Sharma. 2006. *New Cosmopolitanisms: South Asians in the US.* Stanford, CA: Stanford University Press.

Ramet, Sabrina. 1991. *Social Currents in Eastern Europe: The Source and Meaning of the Great Transformation.* Durham, NC: Duke University Press.

Ramirez, Eddy. 2002. "Ageism in the Media Is Seen as Harmful to Health of the Elderly." *Los Angeles Times,* September 5, p. A20.

RAND. 2007. "RAND Study Finds Divorce Among Soldiers Has Not Spiked Higher Despite Stress Created by Battlefield Deployments." News release. April. 12 (www.rand.org).

———. 2008. *Do NYPD's Pedestrian Stop Data Indicate Racial Bias?* Santa Monica CA: RAND.

Rand, Michael R. 2008. "Criminal Victimization, 2007." *Bureau of Justice Statistics Bulletin* (December).

Rawlinson, Linnie, and Nick Hunt. 2009. "Jackson Dies, Almost Takes Internet with Him." Accessed July 1 (www.cnn.com/2009/TECH/06/26/ michael.jackson.internet/).

Ray, Raka. 1999. *Fields of Protest: Women's Movement in India.* Minneapolis: University of Minnesota Press.

Raybon, Patricia. 1989. "A Case for 'Severe Bias.'" *Newsweek* 114 (October 2):11.

Read, Brock. 2006. "Can Technology Save the Developing World?" *Chronicle of Higher Education* 52 (July 21):A27–A29.

Reed, Mark. 2008. *American Indian Network Diversity Report Card for 2008.* Shadow Hills, CA: American Indians in Film and TV.

Reed, Matt. 2007. "Tattoos: Official Blots on Reputations?" *USA Today,* July 23, p. 3A.

Reinharz, Shulamit. 1992. *Feminist Methods in Social Research.* New York: Oxford University Press.

Reitzes, Donald C., and Elizabeth J. Mutran. 2006. "Lingering Identities in Retirement." *Sociological Quarterly* 47: 333–359.

Religion News Service. 2003. "New U.S. Guidelines on Prayer in Schools Get Mixed Reaction." *Los Angeles Times,* February 15, p. B24.

Religion Watch. 2006. "Hinduism Shaping India's Pragmatic Use of Biotechnology." April.

Religious Tolerance. 2007. "Prejudice of Americans towards Various Religions." Accessed January 7, 2007 (www.religioustolerance.org/amer_intol .htm).

———. 2008. "Female Genital Mutilation (FGM): Informational Materials." Accessed March 1 (www.religioustolerance.org).

Renard, J. B. 2003. "Rumors and Urban Legends." *International Encyclopedia of the Social and Behavioral Sciences.* Amsterdam: Elsevier.

Rennison, Callie. 2002. *Criminal Victimization 2001. Changes 2000–01 with Trends 1993–2001.* Washington, DC: U.S. Government Printing Office.

RepRap. 2008. "What Is RepRap." Accessed March 11 (http://reprap.org/bin/view/main/webhome).

Reschovsky, Clara. 2004. *Journey to Work: 2000.* Census 2000 Brief C2KBR-23. Washington, DC: U.S. Government Printing Office.

Reuters. 2009. "Terrorism Suspect Wins Police Brutality Claim." Accessed May 18 (http://uk.reuters.com).

Reverby, Susan M., ed. 2000. *Tuskegee's Truths: Rethinking the Tuskegee Syphilis Study.* Chapel Hill, NC: University of North Carolina Press.

Revkin, Andrew C. 2007. "Wealth and Poverty, Drought and Flood: Report from Four Fronts in the War on Warming." *New York Times,* April 3, pp. D4–D5.

Rheingold, Howard. 2003. *Smart Mobs: The Next Social Revolution.* Cambridge, MA: Perseus.

Ribando, Clare M. 2008. *CRS Report for Congress: Trafficking in Persons.* Washington, DC: Congressional Research Service.

Rideout, Victoria, Donald F. Roberts, and Ulla G. Foehr. 2005. *Executive Summary: Generation M: Media in the Lives of 8–18-year-olds.* Menlo Park, CA: Kaiser Family Foundation.

Ridgeway, Greg. 2007. "Analysis of Racial Disparities in the New York Police Department's Stop, Question, and Frisk Practices." Santa Monica, CA: RAND.

Riding, Alan. 1998. "Why 'Titanic' Conquered the World." *New York Times,* April 26, sec. 2, pp. 1, 28, 29.

———. 2005. "Unesco Adopts New Plan Against Cultural Invasion." *New York Times,* October 21, p. B3.

Rieker, Patricia R., and Chloe E. Bird. 2000. "Sociological Explanations of Gender Differences in Mental and Physical Health." Pp. 98–113 in *Handbook of Medical Sociology,* edited by Chloe Bird, Peter Conrad, and Allan Fremont. New York: Prentice Hall.

Rifkin, Jeremy. 1995. *The End of Work; The Decline of the Global Labor Force and the Dawn of the Post-Market Era.* New York: Tarcher/ Putnam.

———. 1996. "Civil Society in the Information Age." *The Nation* 262 (February 26):11–12, 14–16.

Riley, Matilda White, Robert L. Kahn, and Anne Foner. 1994a. *Age and Structural Lag.* New York: Wiley InterScience.

———, Robert L. Kahn, and Anne Foner, in association with Karin A. Mock. 1994b. "Introduction: The Mismatch between People and Structures." Pp. 1–36 in *Age and Structural Lag,* edited by Matilda White Riley, Robert L. Kahn, and Anne Foner. New York: Wiley InterScience.

Riley, Nancy E. 2004. "China's Population: New Trends and Challenges." *Population Bulletin* 59 (June).

Rimer, Sara. 1998. "As Centenarians Thrive, 'Old' Is Redefined." *New York Times,* June 22, pp. A1, A14.

Ritzer, George. 1977. *Working: Conflict and Change.* 2nd ed. Englewood Cliffs, NJ: Prentice Hall.

———. 2000. *The McDonaldization of Society.* New Century Edition. Thousand Oaks, CA: Pine Forge Press.

———. 2002. *McDonaldization: The Reader.* Thousand Oaks, CA: Pine Forge Press.

———. 2004. *The Globalization of Nothing.* Thousand Oaks, CA: Pine Forge Press.

———. 2008. *The McDonaldization of Society 5.* Thousand Oaks, CA: Sage.

Robelon, Erik W. 2007. "'Moment-of-Silence' Generates Loud Debate in Illinois." *Education Week,* (October 24).

Roberts, J. Timmons, Peter E. Grines, and Jodie L. Mańale. 2003. "Social Roots of Global Environmental Change: A World-Systems Analysis of Carbon Dioxide Emissions." *Journal of World-Systems Research* 9 (Summer):277–315.

Robertson, Roland. 1988. "The Sociological Significance of Culture: Some General Considerations." *Theory, Culture, and Society* 5 (February):3–23.

Robison, Jennifer. 2002. "Feminism—What's in a Name?" Accessed February 25, 2007 (www.galluppoll.com).

Rose, Arnold. 1951. *The Roots of Prejudice.* Paris: UNESCO.

Rose, Peter I., Myron Glazer, and Penina Migdal Glazer. 1979. "In Controlled Environments: Four Cases of Intense Resocialization." Pp. 320–338 in *Socialization and the Life Cycle,* edited by Peter I. Rose. New York: St. Martin's Press.

Rosenberg, Douglas H. 1991. "Capitalism." Pp. 33–34 in *Encyclopedic Dictionary of Sociology,* 4th ed., edited by Dushkin Publishing Group. Guilford, CT: Dushkin.

Rosenberg, Howard. 2003. "Snippets of the 'Unique' Al Jazeera." *Los Angeles Times,* April 4, pp. E1, E37.

Rosenthal, Elisabeth. 2009. "Obama's Backing Increases Hopes for Climate Pact." *New York Times,* December 1, pp. 1, 10.

Rosenthal, Robert, and Lenore Jacobson. 1968. *Pygmalion in the Classroom.* New York: Holt.

———. 1992. *Pygmalion in the Classroom: Teacher Expectations and Pupils' Intellectual Development.* Newly expanded edition. Bancy Felin, UK: Crown House.

Rosnow, Ralph L., and Gary L. Fine. 1976. *Rumor and Gossip: The Social Psychology of Hearsay.* New York: Elsevier.

Ross, John. 1996. "To Die in the Street: Mexico City's Homeless Population Booms as Economic Crisis Shakes Social Protections." *SSSP Newsletter* 27 (Summer):14–15.

Rossi, Alice S. 1968. "Transition to Parenthood." *Journal of Marriage and the Family* 30 (February): 26–39.

———. 1984. "Gender and Parenthood." *American Sociological Review* 49 (February):1–19.

Rossi, Peter H. 1987. "No Good Applied Social Research Goes Unpunished." *Society* 25 (November/December):73–79.

Rossides, Daniel W. 1997. *Social Stratification: The Interplay of Class, Race, and Gender.* 2nd ed. Upper Saddle River, NJ: Prentice Hall.

Roszak, Theodore. 1969. *The Making of a Counter-culture.* Garden City, NY: Doubleday.

Rothkopf, David. 2008. *Superclass: The Global Power Elite and the World They Are Making.* New York: Farrar, Straus, and Giroux.

Roy, Donald F.1959."'Banana Time': Job Satisfaction and Informal Interaction." *Human Organization* 18 (Winter):158–168.

Rubin, Alissa J. 2003. "Pat-Down on the Way to Prayer." *Los Angeles Times,* November 25, pp. A1, A5.

———, and Sam Dagher. 2009. "Election Quotas for Iraqi Women Are Weakened, Provoking Anger as Vote Nears." *New York Times,* January 14, p. A13.

Ruebain, David. 2005. "Disability Discrimination Act of 1995 (United Kingdom)." Pp. 420–422 in *Encyclopedia of Disability,* edited by Gary Albrecht. Thousand Oaks, CA: Sage.

Rumbaut, Rubén G. 2008. "Immigration's Complexities, Assimilation's Discontents."*Contexts* 7 (1):72.

Rumbaut, Rubén, Douglas S. Massey, and Frank D. Bean. 2006. "Linguistic Life Expectancies: Immigrant Language Retention in Southern California."*Population and Development Review* 32 (3):447–460.

Ryan, William. 1976. *Blaming the Victim.* Rev. ed. New York: Random House.

Rymer, Russ. 1993. *Genie: An Abused Child's Flight from Science.* New York: HarperCollins.

S

Saad, Lydia. 2004. "Divorce Doesn't Last." *Gallup Poll Tuesday Briefing,* March 30 (www.gallup. com).

———. 2006. "'Grin and Bear It' Is Motto for Most Air Travelers." Accessed January 28, 2008 (www.gallup.com/poll).

———. 2008. "Economic Anxiety Surges in Past Year." Accessed May 3 (http://www.gallup.com/ poll/105802/Economic-Anxiety-Surges-Past-Year.aspx).

———. 2009. "More Americans 'Pro-Life' Than 'Pro-Choice' for First Time." Accessed May 15 (www.gallup.com/poll/118399/More-Americans-Pro-Life-Than-Pro-Choice-First-Time.aspx).

Sabbathday Lake. 2008. Interview by author with Sabbathday Lake Shaker Village. January 8.

Sabol, William J., and Heather Couture. 2008. "Prison Inmates at Midyear 2007." *Bureau of Justice Statistics Bulletin* (June).

Sachs, Jeffrey D. 2005. *The End of Poverty: Economic Possibilities for Our Time.* New York: Penguin.

Sack, Kevin. 2009. Slump Pushing Cost of Drugs Out of Reach. *New York Times,* June 4, pp. A1, A3.

Sacks, Peter. 2007. *Tearing Down the Gates: Confronting the Class Divide in American Education.* Berkeley: University of California Press.

Sadeghi, Akbar. 2008. "The Births and Deaths of Business Establishments in the United States." *Monthly Labor Review* (December):3–18.

Saez, Emmanuel. 2008. "Striking It Richer: The Evolution of Top Incomes in the United States." *Pathways* (Winter): 6–8.

Sagarin, Edward, and Jose Sanchez. 1988. "Ideology and Deviance: The Case of the Debate over the Biological Factor." *Deviant Behavior* 9 (1):87–99.

Said, Edward W. 2001. "The Clash of Ignorance." *The Nation,* October 22.

Sale, Kirkpatrick. 1996. *Rebels against the Future: The Luddites and Their War on the Industrial Revolution* (with a new preface by the author). Reading, MA: Addison-Wesley.

Salem, Richard, and Stanislaus Grabarek. 1986. "Sociology B.A.s in a Corporate Setting: How Can They Get There and of What Value Are They?" *Teaching Sociology* 14 (October):273–275.

Sampson, Robert J., and W. Byron Graves. 1989. "Community Structure and Crime: Testing Social-Disorganization Theory." *American Journal of Sociology* 94 (January): 774–802.

Samuelson, Paul A., and William D. Nordhaus. 2010. *Economics.* 19th ed. New York: McGraw-Hill.

Sanday, Peggy Reeves. 2002. *Women at the Center: Life in a Modern Matriarchy.* Ithaca, NY: Cornell University Press.

———. 2008. Home page. Accessed March 15 (www.sas.upenn.edu/ psanday/).

Sandefur, Rebecca L. 2008. "Access to Civil Justice and Race, Class, and Gender Inequality." *Annual Review of Sociology* 34:339–358.

Sanders, Edmund. 2004. "Coming of Age in Iraq." *Los Angeles Times,* August 14, pp. A1, A5.

Sanderson, Warren, and Sergei Scherbov. 2008. "Rethinking Age and Aging." *Population Bulletin* 63 (December).

Sanua, Marianne R. 2007. "AJC and Intermarriage: The Complexities of Jewish Continuity, 1960–2006." Pp. 3–32 in *American Jewish Yearbook 2007,* edited by David Singer and Lawrence Grossman. New York: American Jewish Committee.

Sapir, Edward. 1929. "The State of Linguistics as a Science." *Language* 5 (4):207–214.

Saporito, Bill. 2007. "Restoring Wal-Mart." *Time* 170 (November 12):46–48, 50, 52.

Sassen, Saskia. 2005. "New Global Classes: Implications for Politics." Pp. 143–170 in *The New Egalitarianism,* edited by Anthony Giddens and Patrick Diamond. Cambridge: Polity.

Sawhill, Isabel, and John E. Morton. 2007. *Economic Mobility: Is the American Dream Alive and Well?* Washington, DC: Economic Mobility Project, Pew Charitable Trusts.

Sayer, Liana C., Suzanne M. Bianchi, and John P. Robinson. 2004. "Are Parents Investing Less in Children? Trends in Mothers' and Fathers' Time with Children." *American Journal of Sociology* 110 (July):1–43.

Scarce, Rik. 1994. "(No) Trial (But) Tribulations: When Courts and Ethnography Conflict." *Journal of Contemporary Ethnography* 23 (July):123–149.

———. 1995. "Scholarly Ethics and Courtroom Antics: Where Researchers Stand in the Eyes of the Law." *American Sociologist* 26 (Spring):87–112.

———. 2005. "A Law to Protect Scholars." *Chronicle of Higher Education,* August 12, p. 324.

Schachter, Jason. 2001. "Geographical Mobility: Population Characteristics." *Current Population Reports,* ser. P-20, no. 538. Washington, DC: U.S. Government Printing Office.

Schaefer, Peter. 2008. *Digital Divide.* Pp. 388–389, vol. 1, in *Encyclopedia of Race, Ethnicity, and Society in the United States.* Thousand Oaks, CA: Sage.

Schaefer, Richard T. 1998. "Differential Racial Mortality and the 1995 Chicago Heat Wave." Presentation at the annual meeting of the American Sociological Association, August, San Francisco.

———, and William W. Zellner. 2007. *Extraordinary Groups.* 8th ed. New York: Worth.

———. 2008a. "Australia, Indigenous People." Pp. 115–119, vol. 1, in *Encyclopedia of Race, Ethnicity, and Society,* edited by Richard T. Schaefer. Thousand Oaks CA: Sage.

———. 2008b. "'Power' and 'Power Elite.'" In *Encyclopedia of Social Problems,* edited by Vincent Parrillo. Thousand Oaks, CA: Sage.

———. 2010. *Race and Ethnicity in the United States.* 12th ed. Upper Saddle River, NJ: Prentice Hall.

Scharnberg, Kirsten. 2002. "Tattoo Unites WTC's Laborers." *Chicago Tribune,* July 22, pp. 1, 18.

———. 2007. "Black Market for Midwives Defies Bans."*Chicago Tribune,* November 25, pp. 1, 10.

Scherer, Ron. 2009. "Job Migration to Suburbs: An Unstoppable Flow?" *New York Times,* April 6.

Schlesinger, Traci. 2009. "The Failure of Race-Neutral Policies: How Mandatory Terms and Sentencing Enhancements Increased Racial Disparities in Prison Admission Rates." *Crime & Delinquency.* Forthcoming. Published online 2008 (http://cad.sagepub.com/pap.dtl).

Schmeeckle, Maria. 2007. "Gender Dynamics in Stepfamilies: Adult Stepchildren's Views." *Journal of Marriage and Family* 69 (February):174–189.

———, Roseann Giarrusso, Du Feng, and Vern L. Bengtson. 2006. "What Makes Someone Family? Adult Children's Perceptions of Current and Former Stepparents." *Journal of Marriage and Family* 68 (August):595–610.

Schnaiberg, Allan. 1994. *Environment and Society: The Enduring Conflict.* New York: St. Martin's Press.

Schneider, Barbara L., and Venessa A. Keesler. 2007. "School Reform 2007: Transforming Education into a Scientific Enterprise." *Annual Review of Sociology* 33:197–217.

Schneider, Keith. 1995. "As Earth Day Turns 25, Life Gets Complicated." *New York Times,* April 16, p. E6.

Schouten, Fredreka. 2008. "In Fundraising Ranks, a Gender Gap Is Showing." *USA Today,* July 31, p. 5A.

Schrag, Peter. 2004. "Bush's Education Fraud." *American Prospect* 15 (February):38–41.

Schulman, Gary I. 1974. "Race, Sex, and Violence: A Laboratory Test of the Sexual Threat of the Black Male Hypothesis." *American Journal of Sociology* 79 (March):1260–1272.

Schumpeter, Joseph A. 1975 [1942]. *Capitalism, Socialism, and Democracy.* New York: Harper.

Schur, Edwin M. 1965. *Crimes without Victims: Deviant Behavior and Public Policy.* Englewood Cliffs, NJ: Prentice Hall.

———. 1968. *Law and Society: A Sociological View.* New York: Random House.

———. 1985. "'Crimes without Victims': A 20 Year Reassessment." Paper presented at the annual meeting of the Society for the Study of Social Problems.

Schwartz, Howard D., ed. 1987. *Dominant Issues in Medical Sociology.* 2nd ed. New York: Random House.

Schwartz, John. 2004. "Leisure Pursuits of Today's Young Man." *New York Times,* March 29.

———. 2005. "NASA Shuts Down Shuttle Program, over Foam Debris." *New York Times,* July 28, pp. A1, A19.

Schwartz, Shalom H., and Anat Bardi. 2001. "Value Hierarchies Across Cultures: Taking a Similarities Perspective." *Journal of Cross-Cultural Perspective* 32 (May):268–290.

Scotch, Richard. 1989. "Politics and Policy in the History of the Disability Rights Movement." *The Milbank Quarterly* 67 (Suppl. 2):380–400.

———. 2001. *From Good Will to Civil Rights: Transforming Federal Disability Policy.* 2nd ed. Philadelphia: Temple University Press.

Scott, Alan. 1990. *Ideology and the New Social Movements.* London: Unwin Hyman.

Scott, Gregory. 2001. "Broken Windows behind Bars: Eradicating Prison Gangs through Ecological Hardening and Symbolic Cleansing." *Corrections Management Quarterly* 5 (Winter):23–36.

———. 2005. "Public Symposium: HIV/AIDS, Injection Drug Use and Men Who Have Sex with Men." Pp. 38–39 in *Scholarship with a Mission,* edited by Susanna Pagliaro. Chicago: DePaul University.

Scott, Joan Wallach. 2007. "Veiled Politics." *Chronicle of Higher Education* 54 (November 23):B10-B11.

Scott, W. Richard. 2003. *Organizations: Rational, Natural, and Open Systems.* 5th ed. Upper Saddle River, NJ: Prentice Hall.

———. 2004. "Reflections on a Half-Century of Organizational Sociology." Pp. 1–21 in *Annual Review of Sociology 2004,* edited by Karen S. Cook and John Hagan. Palo Alto, CA: Annual Reviews.

Second Life. 2009. "Economic Statistics." Accessed January 26 (http://secondlife.com/whatis/ economy_stats.php).

Secretan, Thierry. 1995. *Going into Darkness: Fantastic Coffins from Africa.* London: Thames and Hudson.

Security on Campus. 2008. "Complying with the Jeanne Clery Act." Accessed January 13 (www. securityoncampus.org/crimestats/index.html).

Segerstråle, Ullica. 2000. *Defense of the Truth: The Battle for Science in the Sociobiology Debate and Beyond.* New York: Oxford University Press.

Seidman, Steven. 1994. "Heterosexism in America: Prejudice against Gay Men and Lesbians." Pp. 578–593 in *Introduction to Social Problems,* edited by Craig Calhoun and George Ritzer. New York: McGraw-Hill.

Selinger, Evan. 2008. "Does Microsoft 'Empower'? Reflections on the Grameen Bank Debate." *Human Studies* 31:27–41.

Sellers, Frances Stead. 2004. "Voter Globalization." *Washington Post National Weekly Edition,* November 29, p. 22.

Selod, Saher Farooq. 2008a. "Muslim Americans." Pp. 920–923, vol. 2, in *Encyclopedia of Race, Ethnicity, and Society,* edited by RichardT. Schaefer. Thousand Oaks, CA: Sage.

———. 2008b. "Veil." Pp. 1359–1360, vol. 3, in *Encyclopedia of Race, Ethnicity, and Society,* edited by Richard T. Schaefer. Thousand Oaks, CA: Sage.

Semuels, Alana. 2007. "Second Life Proves Hard Sell."*Chicago Tribune,* July 23, p. 5.

———. 2009. "You in Back, Yes You, the Half-lynx." *Los Angeles Times,* May 10, pp. A1, A23.

Sengupta, Somini. 2004. "For Iraqi Girls, Changing Land Narrows Lines." *New York Times,* June 27, pp. A1, A11.

———. 2006. "Report Shows Muslims Near Bottom of Social Ladder." *New York Times,* November 29, p. A4.

———. 2009. "An Empire for Poor Working Women, Guided by a Gandhian Approach." *New York Times,* March 7, p. A6.

Senior Action in a Gay Environment. 2009. Home page. Accessed March 18 (www.sageusa.org).

Sernau, Scott. 2001. *Worlds Apart: Social Inequalities in a New Century.* Thousand Oaks, CA: Pine Forge Press.

Shanahan, Michael J. 2000. "Pathways to Adulthood in Changing Socities: Variability and Mechanisms in Life Cause Perspective." Pp. 667–692 in *Annual Review of Sociology 2000,* edited by Karen S. Cook. Palo Alto, CA: Annual Reviews.

Shapiro, Joseph P. 1993. *No Pity: People with Disabilities Forging a New Civil Rights Movement.* New York: Times Books.

Shapiro, Julianne. 2009. "Students, Faculty React to Cal Poly Drinking Death." *Spartan Daily,* February 4.

Shapiro, Thomas M. 2004. *The Hidden Cost of Being African American: How Wealth Perpetuates Inequality.* New York: Oxford University Press.

Sharma, Hari M., and Gerard C. Bodeker. 1998. "Alternative Medicine." Pp. 228–229 in *Britannica Book of the Year 1998.* Chicago: Encyclopaedia Britannica.

Sharp, Ansel M., Charles A. Register, and Paul W. Grimes. 2008. *Economics of Social Issues.* 18th ed. New York: McGraw-Hill.

Sharp, Jeff S., and Jill K. Clark. 2008. "Between the Country and the Concrete: Rediscovering the Rural-Urban Fringe." *City and Community* 7 (March):61–77.

Shaw, Claude, and Henry D. McKay. 1942. *Juvenile Delinquency and Urban Areas.* Chicago: University of Chicago Press.

Sheehan, Charles. 2005. "Poor Seniors Take On Plans of Condo Giant." *Chicago Tribune,* March 22, pp.1,9.

Shepherd, Jean. 2003. *Japan Performs First Transplants from Brain-Dead Donor.* Accessed June 14 (www.pntb.org/ff-rndwrld.html).

Sheridan, Mary Beth. 2009. "A Dire Situation." *Washington Post National Weekly Edition* 26 (April 27):19.

Sheskin, Ira M., and Arnold Dashefsky. 2006. "Jewish Population of the United States, 2006." In *American Jewish Year Book 2006,* edited by David Singer and Lawrence Grossman. New York: American Jewish Committee.

Shibutani, Tamotshu. 1966. *Improvised News: A Sociological Study of Rumor.* Indianapolis: Bobbs-Merrill.

Shin, Hyon B., and Rosalind Bruno. 2003. "Language Use and English-Speaking Ability: 2000." *Census 2000 Brief,* C2KBR-29. Washington, DC: U.S. Government Printing Office.

Shipler, David K. 2005. *The Working Poor: Invisible in America.* New York: Knopf.

Shogren, Elizabeth. 1994. "Treatment against Their Will." *Los Angeles Times,* August 18, pp. A1, A14–A15.

Shorrocks, Anthony, James Davies, Susanna Sandström, and Edward Wolff. 2006. *The World Distribution of Household Wealth.* Helsinki, Finland: United Nations University and World Institute for Development Economics Research.

Shortliffe, E. H., and V. L. Patel. 2004. "Internet: Psychological Perspectives." Pp. 7852–7855 in *International Encyclopedia of the Social and Behavioral Sciences,* edited by Neil J. Smelser and Paul B. Baltes. New York: Elsevier.

Shostak, Arthur B. 2002. "Clinical Sociology and the Art of Peace Promotion: Earning a World Without War." Pp. 325–345 in *Using Sociology: An Introduction from the Applied and Clinical Perspectives,* edited by Roger A. Straus. Lanham, MD: Rowman and Littlefield.

Shupe, Anson D., Jr., and David G. Bromley. 1980. *The New Vigilantes: Deprogrammers, Anti-Cultists, and the New Religions.* Beverly Hills: Sage.

Sicular, Terry, Ximing Yue, Bjorn Gustafsson, and Shi Li. 2006. *The Urban-Rural Income Gap and Inequality in China.* Research Paper No. 2006/135, United Nations University—World Institute for Development Economic Research.

Sieber, Renée E., Daniel Spitzberg, Hannah Muffatt, Kristen Brewer, Blanka Füleki, and Naomi Arbit. 2006. *Influencing Climate Change Policy: Environmental Non-Governmental Organizations (ENGOs) Using Virtual and Physical Activism.* Montreal: McGill University.

Silver, Ira. 1996. "Role Transitions, Objects, and Identity." *Symbolic Interaction* 10 (1):1–20.

Simmel, Georg. [1917] 1950. *Sociology of Georg Simmel.* Translated by K. Wolff. Glencoe, IL: Free Press (originally written in 1902–1917).

Simmons, Tavia, and Martin O'Connell. 2003. "Married-Couple and Unmarried-Partner Households: 2000." *Census 2000 Special Reports,* CENBR-5. Washington, DC: U.S. Government Printing Office.

Simon, Stephanie. 2007. "It's Easter; Shall We Gather at the Desktops?" *Los Angeles Times,* April 8, p. A13.

Simons, Marlise. 1997. "Child Care Sacred as France Cuts Back the Welfare State." *New York Times,* December 31, pp. A1, A6.

Sipser, Walter. 2006. "It's Me in that 9/11 Photo." Posted at *Slate,* September 13, 2006. Accessed January 2, 2008 (www.slate.com/toolbar. aspx?action=print&id=2149578).

Sisson, Carmen K. 2007. "The Virtual War Family." *Christian Science Monitor,* May 29.

Sjoberg, Gideon. 1960. *The Preindustrial City: Past and Present.* Glencoe, IL: Free Press.

Skinner, E. Benjamin. 2008. "People for Sale." *Foreign Policy* (March–April).

Slack, Jennifer Daryl, and J. Macgregor Wise. 2007. *Culture + Technology.* New York: Peter Lang.

Slackman, Michael. 2008. "9/11 Rumors That Harden into Conventional Wisdom." *New York Times,* September 9, p. A16.

Slavin, Barbara. 2007. "Child Marriage Rife in Nations Getting U.S. Aid." *USA Today,* July 17, p. 6A.

Slavin, Robert E., and A. Cheung. 2003. *Effective Reading Programs for English Language Learners: A Best-Evidence Synthesis.* Baltimore, MD: Johns Hopkins University, Center for Research on the Education of Students Placed at Risk.

Slug-Lines.com. 2008. "A Unique Commuter Solution." Accessed January 9 (www.slug-lines.com).

Smart, Barry. 1990. "Modernity, Postmodernity, and the Present." Pp. 14–30 in *Theories of Modernity and Postmodernity,* edited by Bryan S. Turner. Newbury Park, CA: Sage.

Smeeding, Timothy M. 2008. "Poorer by Comparison: "Poverty, Work, and Public Policy in Comparative Perspective." *Pathways* (Winter):3–5.

Smelser, Neil. 1962. *Theory of Collective Behavior.* New York: Free Press.

———. 1963. *The Sociology of Economic Life.* Englewood Cliffs, NJ: Prentice Hall.

———. 1981. *Sociology.* Englewood Cliffs, NJ: Prentice Hall.

Smith, Aaron. 2009. *The Internet's Role in Campaign 2000.* Washington, DC: Pew Internet and American Life Project.

Smith, Christian. 1991. *The Emergence of Liberation Theology: Radical Religion and Social Movement Theory.* Chicago: University of Chicago Press.

———. 2007. "Getting a Life: The Challenge of Emerging Adulthood." *Books and Culture: A Christian Review* (November–December).

———. 2008. "Future Directions of the Sociology of Religion." *Social Forces* 86 (June):1564–1589.

Smith, Craig S. 2005. "Abduction, Often Violent, a Kyrgyz Wedding Rite." *New York Times,* April 30, pp. A1, A7.

———. 2006. "Romania's Orphans Face Widespread Abuse, Group Says." *New York Times,* May 10, p. A3.

Smith, Dan. 1999. *The State of the World Atlas.* 6th ed. London: Penguin.

Smith, David A. 1995. "The New Urban Sociology Meets the Old: Rereading Some Classical Human Ecology." *Urban Affairs Review* 20 (January): 432–457.

———, and Michael Timberlake. 1993. "World Cities: A Political Economy/Global Network Approach." Pp. 181–207 in *Urban Sociology in Transition,* edited by Ray Hutchison. Greenwich, CT: JAI Press.

Smith, David M., and Gary J. Gates. 2001. *Gay and Lesbian Families in the United States: Same-Sex Unmarried Partner Households.* Washington, DC: Human Rights Campaign.

Smith, Denise, and Hava Tillipman. 2000. "The Older Population in the United States." *Current Population Reports,* ser. P-20, no. 532. Washington, DC: U.S. Government Printing Office.

Smith, Kirsten P., and Nicholas A. Christakis. 2008. "Social Networks and Health." *Annual Review of Sociology* 34:405–429.

Smith, Lauren. 2007. "Black Female Participation Languishes Outside Basketball and Track." *Chronicle of Higher Education* 53 (June 29): A34.

Smith, Michael Peter. 1988. *City, State, and Market.* New York: Basil Blackwell.

Smith, Peter. 2008. "Going Global: The Transnational Politics of the Debt Movement." *Globalizations* 5 (March):13–33.

Smith, Tom. 2003. *Coming of Age in 21st Century America: Public Attitudes Toward the Importance and Timing of Transition to Adulthood.* Chicago: National Opinion Research Center.

Snow, David A., Louis A. Zurcher, Jr., and Robert Peters. 1981. "Victory Celebrations as Theater: A Dramaturgical Approach to Crowd Behavior." *Symbolic Interaction* 4:21–42.

Snyder, Thomas D. 1996. *Digest of Education Statistics 1996.* Washington, DC: U.S. Government Printing Office.

Somavia, Juan. 2008. "The ILO at 90 Working for Social Justice." *World of Work* 64 (December):4–5.

Sorokin, Pitirim A. [1927] 1959. *Social and Cultural Mobility.* New York: Free Press.

Southern Poverty Law Center. 2009. "10 Ways to Fight Hate on Campus." Accessed March 20 (www.tolerance.org/campus).

Spalter-Roth, Roberta, and Nicole Van Vooren. 2008a. "What Are They Doing with a Bachelor's Degree in Sociology?" Washington, DC: American Sociological Association. Accessible at http://asanet.org/galleries/research/ ASAresearchbrief_corrections.pdf.

———. 2008b. "Skills, Reasons and Jobs. What Happened to the Class of 2005." Washington, DC: American Sociological Association. Accessible at http://asanet.org.

Speak, Suzanne, and Graham Tipple. 2006. "Perceptions, Persecution and Pity: The Limitations of Interventions for Homelessness in Developing Countries." *International Journal of Urban and Regional Research* 30 (March): 172–188.

Spencer, Nancy. 2008. "Title IX." Pp. 1308–1310, vol. 3, in *Encyclopedia of Race, Ethnicity, and Society,* edited by Richard T. Schaefer. Thousand Oaks, CA: Sage.

Spielmann, Peter James. 1992. "11 Population Groups on 'Endangered' List." *Chicago Sun-Times,* November 23, p. 12.

Spitzer, Steven. 1975. "Toward a Marxian Theory of Deviance." *Social Problems* 22 (June):641–651.

Sprague, Joey. 2005. *Feminist Methodologies for Critical Research: Bridging Differences.* Lanham, MD: AltaMira Press.

Springwood, Charles Fruehling, ed. 2007. *Open Fire: Understanding Global Gun Culture.* New York: Berg.

Squires, Gregory D., ed. 2002. *Urban Sprawl: Causes, Consequences and Policy Responses.* Washington, DC: Urban Institute.

Stahler-Sholk, Richard. 2008. "Zapatista Rebellion." Pp. 1423–1424, vol. 3, in *Encyclopedia of Race, Ethnicity, and Society,* edited by Richard T. Schaefer. Thousand Oaks, CA: Sage.

Standing, Guy. 2004. *Economic Security for a Better World.* Geneva: International Labour Organization.

Stange, Mary Zeiss. 2009. "Do Women Have a Prayer?" *USA Today,* March 23, p. 11A.

Stanley, Alessandra. 2007. "Deadly Rampage and No Loss for Words." *New York Times,* April 17.

Stark, Rodney, and William Sims Bainbridge. 1979. "Of Churches, Sects, and Cults: Preliminary Concepts for a Theory of Religious Movements." *Journal for the Scientific Study of Religion* 18 (June):117–131.

———, and William Sims Bainbridge. 1985. *The Future of Religion.* Berkeley: University of California Press.

Stark, Rodney. 2004. *Exploring the Religious Life.* Baltimore: Johns Hopkins University Press.

Starr, Paul. 1982. *The Social Transformation of American Medicine.* New York: Basic Books.

Steele, Jonathan. 2005. "Annan Attacks Britain and U.S. over Erosion of Human Rights." *Guardian Weekly,* March 16, p. 1.

Stein, Leonard I. 1967. "The Doctor-Nurse Game." *Archives of General Psychology* Volume 16: 699–703.

Stein, Rob. 2008. "Circles of Acquaintances." *Washington Post National Weekly Edition,* June 2, p. 37.

Steinberg, Jacques. 2009. "Goal Is College. Hurdle Is Aid." *New York Times,* May 1, pp. A1–A15.

Stenning, Derrick J. 1958. "Household Viability among the Pastoral Fulani." Pp. 92–119 in *The Developmental Cycle in Domestic Groups,* edited by John R. Goody. Cambridge, England: Cambridge University Press.

Stevens, Mitchell L., Elizabeth A. Armstrong, and Richard Arum. 2008. "Sieve, Incubator, Temple, Hub: Empirical and Theoretical Advances in the Sociology of Higher Education." *Annual Review of Sociology* 38:127–151.

Stockard, Janice E. 2002. *Marriage in Culture.* Belmont, CA: Thomson Wadsworth.

Stolberg, Sheryl Gay. 2008. "Richest Nations Pledge to Halve Greenhouse Gas." *New York Times,* July 9, pp. A1, A13.

Stolberg, Sheryl. 1995. "Affirmative Action Gains Often Come at a High Cost." *Los Angeles Times,* March 29, pp. A1, A13–A16.

Stone, Andrea, and Marisol Bello. 2009. "Mom's Plight Shows Army Strain." *USA Today,* March 4, p. 3A.

Stone, Brad. 2007. "Using Web Cams but Few Inhibitions, the Young Turn to Risky Social Sites." *New York Times,* January 2, pp. C1, C2.

Stoner, Madeleine R. 2008. "Homelessness." pp. 641–644, vol. 2, in *Encyclopedia of Race, Ethnicity, and Society,* edited by Richard T. Schaefer. Thousand Oaks, CA: Sage.

Stout, David. 2000. "At Indian Bureau, a Milestone and an Apology." *New York Times,* September 9: p. A7.

Strassman, W. Paul. 1998. "Third World Housing." Pp. 589–592 in *The Encyclopedia of Housing,* edited by Willem van Vliet. Thousand Oaks, CA: Sage.

Strauss, Gary. 2002. "'Good Old Boys' Network Still Rules Corporate Boards." *USA Today,* November 1, pp. B1, B2.

Street, Marc D. 1997. "Groupthink: An Examination of Theoretical Issues, Implications, and Future Research Systems." *Small Group Research* 28 (February):72–93.

Stretesky, Paul B. 2006. "Corporate Self-Policing and the Environment." *Criminology* 44 (3):671.

Subramaniam, Mangala. 2006. *The Power of Women's Organization: Gender, Caste, and Class in India.* Lanham, MD: Lexington Books.

Suitor, J. Jill, Staci A. Minyard, and Rebecca S. Carter. 2001. "'Did You See What I Saw?' Gender Differences in Perceptions of Avenues to Prestige Among Adolescents." *Sociological Inquiry* 71 (Fall):437–454.

Sullivan, Harry Stack. [1953] 1968. *The Interpersonal Theory of Psychiatry.* Edited by Helen Swick Perry and Mary Ladd Gawel. New York: Norton.

Sullivan, Kevin. 2006. "Bridging the Digital Divide." *Washington Post National Weekly Edition* 25 (July 17):11–12.

Sum, Andrew, Paul Harrington, and Ishwar Khatiwada. 2006. *The Impact of New Immigrants on Young Native-Born Workers, 2000–2005.* Washington, DC: Center for Immigration Studies.

Sumner, William G. 1906. *Folkways.* New York: Ginn.

Sunstein, Cass. 2002. *Republic.com.* Rutgers, NJ: Princeton University Press.

Surk, Barbara. 2007. "MTV Flag Planted on Arab Airwaves." *Chicago Tribune,* November 19, p. 16.

Sutch, Richard, and Susan B. Carter. 2006. *Historical Statutes of US: Earliest Time to the Present.* Cambridge, England: Cambridge University Press.

Sutcliffe, Bob. 2002. *100 Ways of Seeing an Unequal World.* London: Zed Books.

Sutherland, Edwin H. 1937. *The Professional Thief.* Chicago: University of Chicago Press.

———. 1940. "White-Collar Criminality." *American Sociological Review* 5 (February):1–11.

———. 1949. *White Collar Crime.* New York: Dryden.

———. 1983. *White Collar Crime: The Uncut Version.* New Haven, CT: Yale University Press.

———, Donald R. Cressey, and David F. Luckenbill. 1992. *Principles of Criminology.* 11th ed. New York: Rowman and Littlefield.

Suzuki, Atsuko, ed. 2007. *Gender and Career in Japan.* Translated by Leonie R. Stickland. Melbourne: Trans Pacific Review.

Swatos, William H., Jr., ed. 1998. *Encyclopedia of Religion and Society.* Lanham, MD: Alta Mira.

Sweet, Kimberly. 2001. "Sex Sells a Second Time." *Chicago Journal* 93 (April):12–13.

Swidler, Ann. 1986. "Culture in Action: Symbols and Strategies." *American Sociological Review* 51 (April): 273–286.

Syme, S. Leonard. 2008. "Reducing Racial and Social-Class Inequalities in Health: The Need for a New Approach." *Health Affairs* 27 (March–April):456–459.

Szasz, Thomas S. 1971. "The Same Slave: An Historical Note on the Use of Medical Diagnosis as Justificatory Rhetoric." *American Journal of Psychotherapy* 25 (April):228–239.

———. 1974. *The Myth of Mental Illness.* Rev. ed. New York: Harper and Row.

Tach, Laura, and Sarah Halpern-Meekin. 2009. "How Does Premarital Cohabitation Affect Trajectories of Marital Quality?" *Journal of Marriage and Family* 71(2):298–317.

Taub, Richard P. 1988. *Community Capitalism: Banking Strategies and Economic Development.* Cambridge, MA: Maynard Business School Press.

———. 2004. *Doing Development in Arkansas.* Fayetteville: University of Arkansas Press.

Talbani, Aziz, and Parveen Hasanali. 2000. "Adolescent Females between Tradition and Modernity: Gender Role Socialization in South Asian Immigrant Culture." *Journal of Adolescence* 23:615–627.

Talbot, David. 2008. "The Fleecing of the Avatars." *Technology Review* (January/February).

Tanielian, Terri. 2009. "Assessing Combat Exposure and Post-Traumatic Stress Disorder in Troops and Estimating the Costs to Society." Testimony presented before the House Veterans' Affairs Committee, Subcommittee on Disability Assistance and Memorial Affairs, March 24.

Tannen, Deborah. 1990. *You Just Don't Understand: Women and Men in Conversation.* New York: Ballantine.

Tarrow, Sidney. 2005. *The New Transnational Activism.* Boulder, CO: Rowman and Littlefield.

Taylor, Dorceta E. 2000. "The Rise of the Environmental Justice Paradigm."*American Behavioral Scientist* 43 (January): 508–580.

Taylor, Verta, Leila J. Rupp, and Nancy Whittier. 2009. *Feminist Frontiers.* 8th ed. New York: McGraw-Hill.

Taylor, Verta. 1999. "Gender and Social Movements: Gender Processes in Women's Self-Help Movements." *Gender and Society* 13:8–33.

———. 2004. "Social Movements and Gender." Pp. 14348–14352 in *International Encyclopedia of the Social and Behavioral Sciences,* edited by Neil J. Smelser and Paul B. Baltes. New York: Elsevier.

Tedeschi, Bob. 2006. "Those Born to Shop Can Now Use Cellphones." *New York Times,* January 2.

Telsch, Kathleen. 1991. "New Study of Older Workers Finds They Can Become Good Investments." *New York Times,* May 21, p. A16.

Tessler, Joelie. 2006. "Privacy Erosion: A 'Net' Loss." *CQ Weekly,* February 20, p. 480.

Third World Institute. 2007. *The World Guide,* 11th ed. Oxford. New Internationalist Publications.

This Week. 2008. "Delhi: Film Shows Stupid Americans." October 31, p. 11.

Thomas, Gordon, and Max Morgan Witts. 1974. *Voyage of the Damned.* Greenwich, CT: Fawcett Crest.

Thomas, Pradip N., and Zaharom Nain. 2004. *Who Owns the Media: Global Trends and Local Resistance.* London: WACC/Zed Books.

Thomas, R. Murray. 2003. "New Frontiers in Cheating." In *Encyclopedia Britannica 2003 Book of the Year.* Chicago: Encyclopedia Britannica.

Thomas, William I. 1923. *The Unadjusted Girl.* Boston: Little, Brown.

Thomasrobb.com. 2007. "WhitePride TV." Accessed May 7 (http://thomasrobb.com).

Thompson, Clive. 2005. "Meet the Life Hackers." *New York Times Magazine,* October 16, pp. 40–45.

Thompson, Ginger. 2001. "Why Peace Eludes Mexico's Indians." *New York Times,* March 11, sec. WK, p. 16.

Thompson, Neil B. 1972. "The Mysterious Fall of the Nacirema." *Natural History* (December).

Thompson, Tommy G., and Roy E. Barnes. 2007. *Beyond NCLB: Fulfilling the Promise to Our Nation's Children.* Washington, DC: Aspen Institute.

Thompson, Tony. 2005. "Romanians Are Being Paid to Play Computer Games for Westerners." *Guardian Weekly,* March 25, p. 17.

Threadcraft, Shatema. 2008. "Welfare Queen." In *Encyclopedia of Race, Ethnicity and Society,* edited by Richard T. Schaefer. Thousand Oaks, CA: Sage.

Thurow, Lester. 1984. "The Disappearance of the Middle Class." *New York Times,* February 5, sec. 5, p. 2.

Tibbles, Kevin. 2007. "Web Sites Encourage Eating Disorders." *Today,* February 18. Accessed May 7 (www.msabc.msn.com).

Tierney, John. 1990. "Betting the Planet." *New York Times Magazine,* December 2, pp. 52–53, 71, 74, 76, 78, 80–81.

———. 2003. "Iraqi Family Ties Complicate American Efforts for Change." *New York Times,* September 28, pp. A1, A22.

Tierney, Kathleen J. 2007. "From the Margins to the Mainstream? Disaster Research at the Crossroads." *Annual Review of Sociology* 33:503–525.

Tierney, Kathleen. 1980. "Emergent Norm Theory as 'Theory': An Analysis and Critique of Turner's Formulation." Pp. 42–53 in *Collective Behavior: A Source Book,* edited by Meredith David Pugh. St. Paul, MN: West.

Tierney, William G., and Karri A. Holley. 2008. "Intelligent Design and the Attack on Scientific Inquiry." *Cultural Studies Critical Methodologies* 8 (February): 39–49.

Tilly, Charles. 1993. *Popular Contention in Great Britain 1758–1834.* Cambridge, MA: Harvard University Press.

———. 2004. *Social Movements, 1768–2004.* Boulder, CO: Paradigm.

———. 2007. "Trust Networks in Transnational Migration." *Sociological Forum* 22 (March):3–24.

Timmerman, Kelsey. 2009. *Where Am I Wearing?* Hoboken NJ: Wiley.

Tolbert, Kathryn. 2000. "In Japan, Traveling Alone Begins at Age 6." *Washington Post National Weekly Edition* 17 (May 15):17.

Tonkinson, Robert. 1978. *The Mardudjara Aborigines.* New York: Holt.

Tönnies, Ferdinand. [1887] 1988. *Community and Society.* Rutgers, NJ: Transaction.

Toossi, Mitra. 2006. "A New Look at Long-Term Labor Force Projects to 2050." *Monthly Labor Review* (November):19–39.

Toro, Paul A. 2007. "Toward an International Understanding of Homelessness." *Journal of Social Issues* 63 (3):461–481.

Torres, Lourdes. 2008. "Puerto Rican Americans" and "Puerto Rico." Pp. 1082–1089, vol. 3, in *Encyclopedia of Race, Ethnicity, and Society,* edited by Richard T. Schaefer. Thousand Oaks, CA: Sage.

Touraine, Alain. 1974. *The Academic System in American Society.* New York: McGraw-Hill.

Transactional Records Access Clearinghouse. 2008. "TRAC Monthly Bulletins by Topic, September 2008." Accessed February 21, 2009 (www.trac.syr.edu/tracreports/bulletins/monthly_list.shtml).

Traynor, Ian. 2008. "Europe Expects a Flood of Climate Refugees."*The Guardian Weekly,* March 14, p. 1–2.

Trotter III, Robert T., and Juan Antonio Chavira. 1997. *Curanderismo: Mexican American Folk Healing.* Athens, GA: University of Georgia Press.

Trumbull, Mark. 2006. "America's Younger Workers Losing Ground on Income." *Christian Science Monitor,* February 27.

Tuchman, Gaye. 1992. "Feminist Theory." Pp. 695–704 in *Encyclopedia of Sociology,* vol. 2, edited by Edgar F. Borgatta and Marie L. Borgatta. New York: Macmillan.

Tucker, Robert C. (ed.) 1978. The Marx-Engels Reader. 2nd ed. New York: Norton.

Tumin, Melvin M. 1953. "Some Principles of Stratification: A Critical Analysis." *American Sociological Review* 18 (August):387–394.

———. 1985. *Social Stratification.* 2nd ed. Englewood Cliffs, NJ: Prentice Hall.

Ture, Kwame, and Charles Hamilton. 1992. *Black Power: The Politics of Liberation.* Rev. ed. New York: Vintage Books.

Turek, Melanie. 2006. "The Number of Telecommuters Is on the Rise." November 27. Accessed February 10, 2007 (www.collaborationloop.com).

Turkle, Sherry. 2004. "How Computers Change the Way We Think." *Chronicle of Higher Education* 50 (January 30):B26–B28.

Turner, Bryan S., ed. 1990. *Theories of Modernity and Postmodernity.* Newbury Park, CA: Sage.

Turner, Margery Austin, Marla McDaniel, and Daniel Kuehn. 2007. *Racial Disparities and the New Federalism.* Washington, DC: Urban Institute.

Turner, Ralph, and Lewis M. Killian. 1987. *Collective Behavior.* 3rd ed. Englewood Cliffs, NJ: Prentice Hall.

Turner, S. Derek, and Mark Cooper. 2006. *Out of the Picture: Minority and Female TV Station Ownership in the United States.* Washington, DC: Free Press.

Twenge, Jean M. 2009. "Change Over Time in Obedience: The Jury's Still Out, But It Might Be Decreasing." *American Psychologist* 64 (1):28–31.

U

UNAIDS. 2008. "A Global View of HIV Infection." Accessed April 28, 2009 (http://data.unaids.org/pub/GlobalReport/2008/GR08_2007_HIVPrevWallMap_Gr08_en.jpg).

UN-Habitat. 2009. "Urban Indicators." Accessed May 3 (www.unhabitat.org/stats/Default.aspx).

UNICEF. 2002. *Young People and HIV/AIDS: Opportunity in Crisis.* New York: UNICEF.

United Nations Development Fund for Women. 2009. *Who Answers to Women?* New York: UNIFEM.

United Nations Development Programme. 1995. *Human Development Report 1995.* New York: Oxford University Press.

———. 2000. *Poverty Report 2000: Overcoming Human Poverty.* Washington, DC: UNDP.

———. 2006. *Human Development Report 2006. Beyond Scarcity: Power, Poverty and the Global Water Crisis.* New York: UNDP.

United Nations Framework Convention on Climate Change. 2009. "Countdown to Copenhagen." Accessed April 28 (http://unfccc.int/2860.php).

United Nations Office on Drugs and Crime. 2005. "The United Nations Convention Against Transnational Organized Crime and Its Protocols." Accessed March 18 (www.unodc.org).

United Nations Population Division. 2007. *World Abortion Policies 2007.* New York: UNDP.

United Nations Statistical Division. 2008. "Singulate Mean Age at Marriage." Accessed March 1, 2009 (http://data.un.org/search.aspx?q=marriage).

United Nations. 2005a. *The Millennium Development Goals Report.* Washington, DC: United Nations.

———. 2005b. *In Larger Freedom: Towards Development, Security and Human Rights for All.* New York: United Nations.

United Nations. 2009. *International Migration Report 2006: A Global Assessment.* New York: United Nations, Economic and Social Affairs.

University of Michigan. 2003. *Information on Admissions Lawsuits.* Accessed August 8 (www.umich.edu/urel/admissions).

Urban Dictionary. 2009. "Urban Amish." Accessed March 16 (www.urbandictionary.com/define.php?term=urgan%20amish).

Urbina, Ian. 2002. "Al Jazeera: Hits, Misses and Ricochets." *Asia Times,* December 25.

U.S. Committee for Refugees and Immigrants. 2008. *World Refugee Swing 2008.* Washington, DC: US Committee for Refugees and Immigrants.

U.S. Conference of Mayors. 2004. *Hunger and Homeless Survey.* Washington, DC: United States Conference of Mayors and SODEXHO USA.

U.S. English. 2009. "Making English the Official Language." Accessed January 18 (www.us-english.org/inc/).

U.S. Surgeon General. 1999. *Surgeon General's Report on Mental Health.* Washington, DC: U.S. Government Printing Office.

U.S. Trade Representative. 2007. "Trade Promotion Authority Delivers Jobs, Growth, Prosperity, and Security at Home." January 31 Fact Sheet. Accessed February 19 (www.ustr.gov).

V

Vaidhyanathan, Siva. 2008. "Generational Myth: Not All Young People Are Tech-Savvy." *Chronicle of Higher Education,* September 19, pp. B7–B9.

van den Berghe, Pierre. 1978. *Race and Racism: A Comparative Perspective.* 2nd ed. New York: Wiley.

Van Gennep, Arnold. 1960 [1909]. *The Rites of Passage.* Translated by Monika B. Vizedom and Gabrielle L. Caffee. Chicago: University of Chicago Press.

van Vucht Tijssen, Lieteke. 1990. "Women between Modernity and Postmodernity." Pp. 147–163 in *Theories of Modernity and Post-modernity,* edited by Bryan S. Turner. London: Sage.

Vargas, Jose Antonio. 2007. "YouTube Gets Serious with Links to Candidates." *Washington Post,* March 2, p. C1.

Vasagar, Jeeran. 2005. "'At Last Rwanda Is Known for Something Positive." *Guardian Weekly,* July 22, p. 18.

Vaughan, Diane. 1996. *The Challenger Launch Decision: Risky Technology, Culture, and Deviance at NASA.* Chicago: University of Chicago Press.

———. 1999. "The Dark Side of Organizations: Mistake, Misconduct, and Disaster." Pp. 271–305 in *Annual Review of Sociology,* edited by Karen J. Cook and John Hagan. Palo Alto, CA: Annual Reviews.

Vaughan, R. M. 2007. "Cairo's Man Show." *Utne Reader* (March–April): 94–95.

Venkatesh, Sudhir Alladi. 2000. *American Project: The Rise and Fall of a Modern Ghetto.* Cambridge, MA: Harvard University Press.

———. 2008b. "Glimpses." *University of Chicago Magazine* (March–April): 44–45.

Veblen, Thorstein. [1899] 1964. *Theory of the Leisure Class.* New York: Macmillan. New York: Penguin.

———. 1919. *The Vested Interests and the State of the Industrial Arts.* New York: Huebsch.

Venkatesh, Sudhir Alladi. 2006. *Off the Books: The Underground Economy of the Urban Poor.* Cambridge, MA: Harvard University Press.

———. 2008a. *Gang Leader for a Day: A Rogue Sociologist Takes to the Streets.* New York: Penguin Press.

Ventura, Stephanie M. 2009. "Changing Patterns of Nonmarital Childbearing in the United States." *NCHS Data Brief* (No. 18, May).

Vernon, Glenn. 1962. *Sociology and Religion.* New York: McGraw-Hill.

Vidal, John. 2004. "One in Three People Will Be Elderly by 2050." *Guardian Weekly,* April 1, p. 5.

Vigdor, Jacob L. 2008. "Measuring Immigrant Assimilation in the United States." *Manhattan Institute.* Accessed at www.manhattan-institute.org/.

Villarreal, Andrés. 2004. "The Social Ecology of Rural Violence: Land Scarcity, the Organization of Agricultural Production, and the Presence of the State." *American Journal of Sociology* 110 (September):313–348.

Viramontes, Helena Maria. 2007. "Loyalty Spoken Here." *Los Angeles Times,* September 23, p. R7.

Visitability. 2009. "Visitability: Becoming a National Trend." Accessed May 5 (www.visitability.org).

Visser, Jelle. 2006. "Union Membership Statistics in 24 Countries." *Monthly Labor Review* (January):38–49.

W

Wachtendorf, Tricia. 2002. "A Changing Risk Environment: Lessons Learned from the 9/11 World Trade Center Disaster." Presentation at the Sociological Perspectives on Disasters, Mt. Macedon, Australia, July.

Waelde, L. C. 2008. "A Pilot Study of Mediation for Mental Health Workers Following Hurricane Katrina." *Journal of Traumatic Stress* 21 (5):497–500.

Wages for Housework Campaign. 1999. *Wages for Housework Campaign.* Circular. Los Angeles.

Wagley, Charles, and Marvin Harris. 1958. *Minorities in the New World: Six Case Studies.* New York: Columbia University Press.

Waite, Linda. 2000. "The Family as a Social Organization: Key Ideas for the Twentieth Century." *Contemporary Sociology* 29 (May):463–469.

Waitzkin, Howard. 1986. *The Second Sickness: Contradictions of Capitalist Health Care.* Chicago: University of Chicago Press.

Wal-Mart. 2007. "The 'Ten-Foot Attitude." Accessed January 23 (www.wal-martchina.com).

Walder, Andrew G., and Giang Hoang Nguyen. 2008. "Ownership, Organization, and Income Inequality: Market Transition in Rural Vietnam." *American Sociological Review* 73 (April):251–269.

Waldinger, Roger, and David Fitzgerald. 2004. "Transnationalism in Question." *American Journal of Sociology* 109 (March):1177–1195.

———, Nelson Lim, and David Cort. 2007. "Bad Jobs, Good Jobs, No Jobs? The Employment Experience of the Mexican American Second Generation." *Journal of Ethnic and Migration Studies* 33 (January):1–35.

———, and Renee Reichl. 2006. "Second-Generation Mexicans: Getting Ahead or Falling Behind?" Washington, DC: Migration Policy Institute. Accessed May 23 (www.migrationinformation.org).

Waldman, Amy. 2004a. "India Takes Economic Spotlight, and Critics Are Unkind." *New York Times,* March 7, p. 3.

———. 2004b. "Low-Tech or High, Jobs Are Scarce in India's Boon." *New York Times,* May 6, p. A3.

———. 2004c. "What India's Upset Vote Reveals: The High Tech Is Skin Deep." *New York Times,* May 15, p. A5.

Walker, Marcus, and Roger Thurow. 2009. U.S., Europe Are Ocean Apart on Human Toll of Joblessness. *Wall Street Journal,* May 7, pp. A1, A14.

Wall Street Journal. 2006. "The Web's Worst New Idea." *Wall Street Journal,* May 18.

Wallace, Ruth A., and Alison Wolf. 1980. *Contemporary Sociological Theory.* Englewood Cliffs, NJ: Prentice Hall.

Wallerstein, Immanuel. 1974. *The Modern World System.* New York: Academic Press.

———. 1979a. *Capitalist World Economy.* Cambridge, England: Cambridge University Press.

———. 1979b. *The End of the World as We Know It: Social Science for the Twenty-First Century.* Minneapolis: University of Minnesota Press.

———. 2000. *The Essential Wallerstein.* New York: The New Press.

Wallis, Claudia. 2008. "How to Make Great Teachers." *Time* 171 (February 25):28–34.

Wang, Meiyan, and Fand Cai. 2006. *Gender Wage Differentials in China's Urban Labor Market.* Research Paper No. 2006/141. United Nations University World Institute for Development Economics Research.

Washington, Harriet. 2007. *Medical Apartheid: The Dark History of Medical Experimentation on Black Americans from Colonial Times to Present.* New York: Doubleday.

Watson, Paul. 2005. "Defying Tradition." *Los Angeles Times,* April 24, p. 56.

Wattenberg, Martin P. 2008. *Is Voting for Young People?* New York: Pearson Longman.

Weber, Max. [1913–1922] 1947. *The Theory of Social and Economic Organization.* Translated by A. Henderson and T. Parsons. New York: Free Press.

———. [1904] 1949. *Methodology of the Social Sciences.* Translated by Edward A. Shils and Henry A. Finch. Glencoe, IL: Free Press.

———. [1916] 1958. *The Religion of India: The Sociology of Hinduism and Buddhism.* New York: Free Press.

———. [1904] 2009. *The Protestant Ethic and the Spirit of Capitalism,* 4th ed. Translated by Stephen Kalberg. New York: Oxford University Press.

Wechsler, Henry, J. E. Lee, M. Kuo, M. Seibring, T. F. Nelson, and H. Lee. 2002. "Trends in College Binge Drinking During a Period of Increased Prevention Efforts: Findings from Four Harvard School of Public Health College Alcohol Surveys: 1993–2001." *Journal of American College Health* 50 (5):203–217.

———, Mark Seibring, I-Chao Liu, and Marilyn Ahl. 2004. "Colleges Respond to Student Binge Drinking: Reducing Student Demand or Limiting Access." *Journal of American College Health* 52 (4):159–168.

Weden, Margaret M. 2007. *Twentieth Century U.S. Racial Inequalities in Mortality.* Santa Monica, CA: RAND.

Weeks, John R. 2008. *Population: An Introduction to Concepts and Issues.* 10th ed. Belmont, CA: Wadsworth.

Weier, Mary Hayes. 2007. "The Second Decade of Offshore Outsourcing: Where We're Headed." *InformationWeek* (November 3). Accessed June 6, 2008 (www.information-week.com).

Weil, Nancy. 1998. "Internet Tax Freedom Act Heads to full House." June 19. Accessed January 30, 2007 (www.cnn.com).

Weinberg, Daniel H. 2004. *Evidence from Census 2000 About Earnings by Detailed Occupation for Men and Women.* CENSR-15. Washington, DC: U.S. Government Printing Office.

———, 2007. "Earnings by Gender: Evidence from Census 2000." *Monthly Labor Review* (July/August):26–34.

Weinstein, Henry. 2002. "Airport Screener Curb Is Regretful." *Los Angeles Times,* November 16, pp. B1, B14.

References

Weinstein, Michael A., and Deena Weinstein. 2002. "Hail to the Shrub." *American Behavioral Scientist* 46 (December):566–580.

Weisbrot, Mark, Dean Baker, and David Rusnick. 2005. *The Scorecard on Development: 25 Years of Diminished Progress.* Washington, DC: Center for Economic and Policy Research.

Weitz, Rose. 2007. *The Sociology of Health, Illness, and Heath Care,* 4th ed. Belmont, CA: Thomson.

Wells-Barnett, Ida B. 1970. *Crusade for Justice: The Autobiography of Ida B. Wells.* Edited by Alfreda M. Duster. Chicago: University of Chicago Press.

Wentling, Tre, Elroi Windsor, Kristin Schilt, and Betsy Lucal. 2008. "Teaching Transgender." *Teaching Sociology* 36 (January):49–57.

Wentz, Laurel, and Claire Atkinson. 2005. " 'Apprentice' Translators Hope for Hits All Over Globe." *Advertising Age,* February 14, pp. 3, 73.

West, Candace. 1987. "Doing Gender." *Gender and Society* 1 (June):125–151.

West, Heather, and William J. Sabol. 2009. "Prisons in 2007." *Bureau of Justice Statistics Bulletin* (December 2008, revised 2/12/09).

Westergaard-Nielsen, Niels. 2008. *Low-Wage Work in Denmark.* New York: Russell Sage Foundation.

White House. 2009. "Obama Announces White House Office of Faith-based and Neighborhood Partnerships." *Briefing Room* (February 5). Accessed at www.whitehouse.gov.

White, David Manning. 1950. " 'The Gatekeeper': A Case Study in the Selection of News." *Journalism Quarterly* 27 (Fall):383–390.

Whitlock, Craig. 2005. "The Internet as Bully Pulpit." *Washington Post National Weekly Edition* 22 (August 22):9.

———. 2008. "Stumbling in the Midwest." *Washington Post National Weekly Edition,* July 7, p. 10.

Whyte, William Foote. 1981. *Street Corner Society: Social Structure of an Italian Slum.* 3rd ed. Chicago: University of Chicago Press.

Whyte, William H., Jr. 1952. "Groupthink." *Fortune* (March):114–117, 142, 146.

Wickman, Peter M. 1991. "Deviance." Pp. 85–87 in *Encyclopedic Dictionary of Sociology,* 4th ed., edited by Dushkin Publishing Group. Guilford, CT: Dushkin.

Wilford, John Noble. 1997. "New Clues Show Where People Made the Great Leap to Agriculture." *New York Times,* November 18, pp. B9, B12.

Wilgoren, Jodi. 2005. "In Kansas, Darwinism Goes on Trial Once More." *New York Times,* May 6, p. A14.

Wilkes, Rima, and John Iceland. 2004. "Hypersegregation in the Twenty-First Century." *Demography* 41 (February):23–36.

Wilkinson, Alec. 2007. "No Obstacles." *New Yorker* (April 16):106–108, 110, 112–114, 116.

Williams, Carol J. 1995. "Taking an Eager Step Back." *Los Angeles Times,* June 3, pp. A1, A14.

Williams, Christine L. 1992. "The Glass Escalator: Hidden Advantages for Men in the 'Female' Professions." *Social Problems* 39 (3):253–267.

———. 1995. *Still a Man's World: Men Who Do Women's Work.* Berkeley: University of California Press.

Williams, David R., and Chiquita Collins. 2004. "Reparations." *American Behavioral Scientist* 47 (March):977–1000.

Williams, Kristine N., Ruth Herman, Byron Gajewski, and Kristel Wilson. 2009. "Elderspeak Communication: Impact on Dementia Care." *American Journal of Alzheimer's Disease and Other Dementias* 24 (March):11–20.

Williams, Richard Allen. 2007. "Cultural Diversity, Health Care Disparities, and Cultural Competency in American Medicine." *Journal of American Academy of Orthopedic Surgery* 15 (Suppl. 1):552–558.

Williams, Robin M., Jr. 1970. *American Society.* 3rd ed. New York: Knopf.

———, with John P. Dean and Edward A. Suchman. 1964. *Strangers Next Door: Ethnic Relations in American Communities.* Englewood Cliffs, NJ: Prentice Hall.

Williams, Wendy M. 1998. "Do Parents Matter? Scholars Need to Explain What Research Really Shows." *Chronicle of Higher Education* 45 (December 11):B6–B7.

Wills, Jeremiah B., and Barbara J. Risman. 2006. "The Visibility of Feminist Thought in Family Studies." *Journal of Marriage and Family* 68 (August):690–700.

Wilson, Edward O. 1975. *Sociobiology: The New Synthesis.* Cambridge, MA: Harvard University Press.

———. 1978. *On Human Nature.* Cambridge, MA: Harvard University Press.

———. 2000. *Sociobiology: The New Synthesis.* Cambridge, MA: Belknap Press, Harvard University Press.

Wilson, John. 1973. *Introduction to Social Movements.* New York: Basic Books.

Wilson, William Julius. 1980. *The Declining Significance of Race: Blacks and Changing American Institutions.* 2nd ed. Chicago: University of Chicago Press.

———. 2009. *More Than Just Race: Being Black and Poor in the Inner City.* New York: Norton.

———. 1987. *The Truly Disadvantaged: The Inner City, the Underclass and Public Policy.* Chicago: University of Chicago Press.

———. 1996. *When Work Disappears: The World of the New Urban Poor.* New York: Knopf.

———. 1999. *The Bridge over the Racial Divide: Rising Inequality and Coalition Politics.* Berkeley: University of California Press.

———, J. M. Quane, and B. H. Rankin. 2004. "Underclass." In *International Encyclopedia of Social and Behavioral Sciences.* New York: Elsevier.

———, and Richard P. Taub in collaboration with Reuben A. Buford May and Mary Pattillo. 2006. "Groveland: A Stable African American Community." Pp. 128–160 in *There Goes the Neighborhood* by William Julius Wilson and Richard P. Taub. New York: Alfred A. Knopf.

Winant, Howard B. 1994. *Racial Conditions: Politics, Theory, Comparisons.* Minneapolis: University of Minnesota Press.

———. 2006. "Race and Racism: Towards a Global Future." *Ethnic and Racial Studies* 29 (September): 98–1003.

Wines, Michael. 2005. "Same-Sex Unions to Become Legal in South Africa." *USA Today,* December 2, p. A6.

Wing, Philip S., et al. 2007 "Use of Mental Heath Services for Anxiety, Mood, and Substance Disorders in 17 Countries in the WHO World Mental Health Surveys." *Lancet,* September 8, pp. 841–850.

Winickoff, Jonathan P., Joan Friebely, Susanne E. Tanski, Cheryl Sherrod, George E. Matt, Mebourne F. Hovell, and Robert C. McMillen. 2009. "Beliefs About the Health Effects of 'Thirdhand' Smoke and Home Smoking Bans." *Pediatrics* 123 (January):74–79.

Winkler, Adam. 2009. "Heller's Catch-22." *UCLA Law Review* 56 (June).

Winseck, Dwayne. 2008. "The State of Media Ownership and Media Markets: Competition or Concentration and Why Should We Care?" *Sociology Compass* 2 (1):34–47.

Winseman, Albert L. 2005. "Religion in America: Who Has None?" December 6, 2005. Accessed March 4, 2007 (www.gallup.com).

Winslow, Robert W., and Sheldon X. Zhang. 2008a. *Criminology: A Global Perspective.* New York: Pearson Prentice Hall.

———. 2008b. "Crime and Society: A Comparative Tour of the World." Accessed January 28 (www.rohan.sdsu.edu/faculty/rwinslow).

Winter, J. Allen. 2008. "Symbolic Ethnicity." Pp. 1288–1290, vol. 3, in *Encyclopedia of Race, Ethnicity, and Society,* edited by Richard T. Schaefer. Thousand Oaks, CA: Sage.

Wirth, Louis. 1928. *The Ghetto.* Chicago: University of Chicago Press.

———. 1931. "Clinical Sociology." *American Journal of Sociology* 37 (July):49–60.

———. 1938. "Urbanism as a Way of Life." *American Journal of Sociology* 44 (July):1–24.

Withrow, Brian L. 2006. *Racial Profiling: From Rhetoric to Reason.* Upper Saddle River, NJ: Prentice Hall.

Witte, Griff. 2005. "The Vanishing Middle Class." *Washington Post National Weekly Edition,* September 27, pp. 6–9.

Wokutch, Richard E. 1992. *Worker Protection, Japanese Style: Occupational Safety and Health in the Auto Industry.* Ithaca, NY: Cornell University, ILR Press.

Wolf, Naomi. 1992. *The Beauty Myth: How Images of Beauty Are Used Against Women.* New York: Anchor Books.

Wolf, Richard. 2006. "How Welfare Reform Changed America." *USA Today,* July 18, pp. 1A, 6A.

Wolfe, Alan. 2008. "Pew in the Pews." *Chronicle of Higher Education,* March 21, pp. B5–B6.

Wolfe, Richard. 2008. "New Week, Bush's Agenda Is Africa." *USA Today,* February 15, p. 6A.

Wolff, Edward N. 2002. *Top Heavy.* Updated ed. New York: New Press.

Wolraich, M., et al. 1998. "Guidance for Effective Discipline." *Pediatrics* 101 (April):723–728.

Wong, Morrison G. 2006. "Chinese Americans." Pp. 110–145 in *Asian Americans: Contemporary Trends and Issues,* 2nd ed., edited by Pyong Gap Min. Thousand Oaks, CA: Sage.

Wood, Julia T. 1994. *Gendered Lives: Communication, Gender and Culture.* Belmont, CA: Wadsworth.

Word, David L., Charles D. Coleman, Robert Nunziator, and Robert Kominski. 2007. "Demographic Aspects of Surnames from Census 2000." Accessed January 2, 2008 (www.census.gov/genealogy/www/surnames.pdf).

Working Women's Forum. 2007. Home page. Accessed May 7 (www.workingwomensforum.org).

Workman, Thomas A. 2008. "The Real Impact of Virtual Worlds." *Chronicle of Higher Education,* September 19, pp. B12–B13.

World Bank. 2001. *World Development Report 2002. Building Instructions for Markets.* New York: Oxford University Press.

———. 2003. *World Development Report 2003: Sustainable Development in a Dynamic World.* Washington, DC: World Bank.

———. 2006a. *World Development Indicators 2006.* New York: World Bank.

———. 2006b. *Global Economic Prospects 2006.* Washington, DC: World Bank.

———. 2007. *World Development Indicators 2007.* New York: World Bank.

———. 2009. *World Development Indicators 2009.* Washington, DC: World Bank.

World Development Forum. 1990. "The Danger of Television." 8 (July 15):4.

World Economic Forum. 2008. *The Global Information Technology Report 2007–2008.* Davos, Switzerland: World Economic Forum.

World Health Organization. 2000. *The World Health Report 2000. Health Systems: Improving Performance.* Geneva, Switzerland: WHO.

———. 2004. "Prevalence, Severity, and Unmet Need for Treatment of Mental Disorders in the World Health Organization World Mental Health Surveys." *Journal of the American Medical Association* (June 2):2581–2590.

———. 2006. "Pesticides Are a Leading Suicide Method." Accessed December 4 (www.who.org).

———. 2009. "Biotechnology (GM Foods)." Accessed May 11 (www.who.int/foodsafety/biotech/en/).

World Resources Institute. 1998. *1998–1999 World Resources: A Guide to the Global Environment.* New York: Oxford University Press.

Worth, Robert F. 2008. "As Taboos Ease, Saudi Girl Group Dares to Rock." *New York Times,* November 24, pp. A1, A9.

Wortham, Robert A. 2008. "DuBois, William Edward Burghardt." Pp. 423–427, vol. 1, in *Encyclopedia of Race, Ethnicity, and Society,* edited by Richard T. Schaefer. Thousand Oaks CA: Sage.

Wray, Matt; Matthew Miller, Jill Gurvey, Joanna Carroll, and Ichiro Kawachi. 2008. "Leaving Las Vegas: Exposure to Las Vegas and Risk of Suicide." *Social Science and Medicine* 67:1882–1888.

———. 2008. "China Says One-Child Policy Will Stay for at Least Another Decade." *New York Times,* March 11, p. A10.

Wright, Charles R. 1986. *Mass Communication: A Sociological Perspective.* 3rd ed. New York: Random House.

Wright, Eric R., William P. Gronfein, and Timothy J. Owens. 2000. "Deinstitutionalization, Social Rejection, and the Self-Esteem of Former Mental Patients." *Journal of Health and Social Behavior* (March).

Wright, Erik Olin, David Hachen, Cynthia Costello, and Joy Sprague. 1982. "The American Class Structure." *American Sociological Review* 47 (December):709–726.

Yamagata, Hisashi, Kuang S. Yeh, Shelby Stewman, and Hiroko Dodge. 1997. "Sex Segregation and Glass Ceilings: A Comparative Statistics Model of Women's Career Opportunities in the Federal Government over a Quarter Century." *American Journal of Sociology* 103 (November):566–632.

Yap, Kioe Sheng. 1998. "Squatter Settlements." Pp. 554–556 in *The Encyclopedia of Housing,* edited by Willem van Vliet. Thousand Oaks, CA: Sage.

Yardley, Jim. 2005. "Fearing Future, China Starts to Give Girls Their Due." *New York Times,* January 31, p. A3.

———. 2008. "China Says One-Child Policy Will Stay for at Least Another Decade." *New York Times* (March 11), p. A10.

Yardley, William. 2009. "A 2nd State Lets Doctors Lend Help in Suicide." *New York Times,* March 5, p. A15.

Yinger, J. Milton. 1970. *The Scientific Study of Religion.* New York: Macmillan.

Young, Kevin, ed. 2004. *Sporting Bodies, Damaged Selves.* New York: Elsevier.

Zaidi, Arishia U., and Muhammad Shuraydi. 2002. "Perceptions of Arranged Marriages by Young Pakistani Muslim Women Living in a Western Society." *Journal of Comparative Family Studies* 33 (Autumn):495–515.

Zang, Xiaowei. 2002. "Labor Market Segmentation and Income Inequality in Urban China."*Sociological Quarterly* 43 (1):27–44.

Zarembo, Alan. 2004. "A Theater of Inquiry and Evil." *Los Angeles Times,* July 15, pp. A1, A24, A25.

Zedlewski, Sheila R., and Barbara A. Butrica. 2007. *Perspectives on Productive Aging.* Washington, DC: Urban Institute.

Zeitzen, Miriam Koktvedgaard. 2008. *Polygamy: A Cross-Cultural Analysis.* Oxford, England: Berg.

Zellner, William M. 1995. *Counter Cultures: A Sociological Analysis.* New York: St. Martin's Press.

Zernike, Kate. 2002. "With Student Cheating on the Rise, More Colleges Are Turning to Honor Codes." *New York Times,* November 2, p. A10.

Zi, Jui-Chung Allen. 2007. *The Kids Are OK: Divorce and Children's Behavior Problems.* Santa Monica: RAND.

Zia, Helen. 2000. *Asian American Dreams: The Emergence of an American People.* New York: Farrar, Straus, and Giroux.

Zimbardo, Philip G., 2004. "Power Turns Good Soldiers into 'Bad Apples.'" *Boston Globe,* May 9. Also available at www.prisonexp.org.

———. 2007a. "Revisiting the Stanford Prison Experiment: A Lesson in the Power of the Situation." *Chronicle of Higher Education* 53 (March 20):B6, B7.

———. 2007b. *The Lucifer Effect: Understanding How Good People Turn Evil.* New York: Random House.

———, Ann L. Weber, and Robert Johnson. 2003. *Psychology: Core Concepts.* 4th ed. Boston: Allyn and Bacon.

Zimmerman, Ann, and Emily Nelson. 2006. "With Profits Elusive, Wal-Mart to Exit Germany." *Wall Street Journal,* July 29, pp. A1, A6.

Zimmerman, Seth. 2008a. "Globalization and Economic Mobility." Washington, DC: Economic Mobility Project. Also. accessible at www.economicmobility.org/reports_and_research/literature_reviews?id=0004.

———. 2008b. "Immigration and Economic Mobility." Washington, DC: Economic Mobility Project. Also accessible at www.economicmobility.org/reports_and_research/literature_reviews?id=0004.

———. 2008c. *Labor Market Institutions and Economic Mobility.* Washington DC: Pew Charitable Trust.

Zipp, Yvonne. 2009. Courts Divided on Police Use of GPS Tracking. *Christian Science Monitor,* May 15.

Zirin, Dave. 2008. "Calling Sports Sociology off the Bench." Contexts (Summer):28–31.

Zittrain, Jonathan, and John Palfrey. 2008. "Reluctant Gatekeepers: Corporate Ethics on a Filtered Internet." Pp. 103–122 in *Access Denied,* edited by Ronald Deibert, John Palfrey, Rafal Rohozinski, and Jonathan Zittrain. Cambridge, MA: The MIT Press.

Zola, Irving K. 1972. "Medicine as an Institution of Social Control." *Sociological Review* 20 (November):487–504.

———. 1983. *Socio-Medical Inquiries.* Philadelphia: Temple University Press.

Zweigenhaft, Richard L., and G. William Domhoff. 2006. *Diversity in the Power Elite: How It Happened, Why It Matters.* 2nd ed. New York: Rowman and Littlefield

Zywica, Jolene, and James Danowski. 2008. "The Faces of Facebookers: Investigating Social Enhancement and Social Compensation Hypotheses; Predicting Facebook and Offline Popularity from Sociability and Self-Esteem, and Mapping the Meanings of Popularity with Semantic Networks." *Journal of Computer-Mediated Communication* 14:1–34.

acknowledgments

Chapter 1

page 4: Excerpt from Barbara Ehrenreich. 2001. "Evaluation," pp. 6, 197–198 from *Nickel and Dimed: On (Not) Getting By in America*. Copyright © 2001 by Barbara Ehrenreich. Reprinted by arrangement with Henry Holt and Company, LLC, and by permission of International Creative Management, Inc.

page 19: Cartoon by Jim Morin, copyright 2007, the Miami Herald. Used by permission of Cartoonists & Writers Syndicate.

Chapter 2

page 28: Excerpt from Patricia A. Adler and Peter Adler. 2007. "The Demedicalization of Self-Injury: From Psychopathology to Sociological Deviance," *Journal of Contemporary Ethnography* 36, Issue 5, (October 2007):537–570. Copyright 2007. Reprinted by permission of Sage Publications Inc.

page 33: Figure 2-4 Author's analysis of *General Social Survey 2006* in J. A. Davis et al. 2007. Used by permission of National Opinion Research Center.

page 38: Figure from Laura Wattenberg. 2009. *The Baby Name Wizard*.

page 43: Figure 2-5 From Henry J. Kaiser Family Foundation. November 2005. Sex on TV 4, Executive Summary; a Biennial Report of the Kaiser Family Foundation (#7399). This information was reprinted with permission from the Henry J. Kaiser Family Foundation. The Kaiser Family Foundation is a non-profit, private operating foundation, based in Menlo Park, CA, dedicated to producing and communicating the best possible information, research, and analysis on health issues.

page 45: Figures 2-7, 2-8 from The Gallup Poll, "Who Supports Marijuana Legalization," by Joseph Carroll. Copyright © 2005 The Gallup Organization, Princeton, NJ. All rights reserved. Reprinted with permission.

Chapter 3

page 52: Excerpt from Horace Miner. 1956. "Body Ritual among the Nacirema," *American Anthropologist*, vol. 58(3), 1956: pp. 503–504. © 1956 American Anthropological Association.

page 54: Figure 3-1 From Jerome Fellmann et al. 2007. *Human Geography,* ninth edition. © 2007 by The McGraw-Hill Companies. Reproduced by permission.

page 60: Cartoon by Sidney Harris. © ScienceCartoonsPlus.com.

page 66: Figure 3-4 as reported in Astin et al. 1994; Pryor et al. 2007, 2008. From UCLA Higher Education Research Institute. *The American Freshman: National Norms for Fall* 2007, 2008. © 2008 The Regents of the University of California. All rights reserved.

page 70: Figure 3-6 From Rubén Rumbaut, Douglas S Massey, and Frank D. Bean. 2006. "Linguistic Life Expectancies: Immigrant Language Retention in Southern CA," *Population and Development Review* 32, No. 3 (Sept. 2006). Reprinted by permission of Blackwell Publishing Ltd.

Chapter 4

page 76: Excerpt from Mary Pattillo-McCoy. 1999. *Black Picket Fences: Privilege and Peril among the Black Middle Class,* pp. 100–102. Copyright 1999. Reprinted by permission of University of Chicago Press.

page 78: Figure 4-1 From Susan Curtiss. 1977. *Genie: a Psycholinguistic Study of a Modern-Day "Wild Child,"* p. 275. Copyright Academic Press 1977. Reprinted with permission of Elsevier.

page 82: Quotation from Daniel Albas and Cheryl Albas. 1988. "Aces and Bombers: The Post-Exam Impression Management Strategies of Students." *Symbolic Interaction.* University of California Press–Journals. Reproduced by permission of the authors.

page 86: Table 4-3 Adapted from Jill Suitor, Staci A. Minyard, and Rebecca S. Carter. 2001. "Did You See What I Saw? Gender Difference in Perceptions of Avenues to Prestige Among Adolescents," *Sociological Inquiry* 71 (Fall 2001):445, Table 2. University of Texas Press. Reprinted by permission of Blackwell Publishing Ltd.

page 89: Figure B Adapted from Frederic Stutzman, "An Evaluation of Identity-Sharing Behavior in Social Network Communities," *International Digital Media and Art Journal* 3 (No. 1), 2007. Used with permission of IDMAA/Frederic Stutzman.

page 90: Table 4-4 From Tom Smith. 2003. "Coming of Age in 21st Century America: Public Attitudes Toward the Importance and Timing of Transition to Adulthood." Based on the 2002 General Social Survey of 1,398 people. Used by permission of National Opinion Research Center.

page 93: Figure 4-3 Adapted from Herwig Immervoll and David Barber, "Can Parents Afford to Work? Childcare Costs, Tax-Benefit Policies and Work Incentives," Figure 2.3 Overall childcare costs including benefits and tax concessions: two-earner couple, two children, pp. 21–22; and Figure 2.4 Overall childcare costs including benefits and tax concessions: lone parents, two children, p. 25. OECD Social, Employment and Migration Working Papers No. 31, OECD 2005.

Chapter 5

page 98: Excerpt from Philip G. Zimbardo. 2007. *The Lucifer Effect: Understanding How Good People Turn Evil*. Copyright © 2007 by Philip G. Zimbardo, Inc. Used by permission of Random House, Inc.; and published by Rider, used by permission of the Random House Group Ltd.

page 107: Figure From The Washington Post, May 26 © 2008 The Washington Post. All rights reserved. Used by permission and protected by the Copyright Laws of the United States. The printing, copying, redistribution, or retransmission of the Material without express written permission is prohibited.

page 108: Screenshot from Second Life. Second Life® is a trademark of Linden Research, Inc. Certain materials have been reproduced with the permission of Linden Research, Inc.

page 109: Cartoon © The New Yorker Collection 1986 Dean Vietor from cartoonbank.com. All rights reserved.

page 113: Cartoon by Sidney Harris. © ScienceCartoonsPlus.com.

Chapter 6

page 120: Excerpt from George Ritzer. 2008. *The McDonaldization of Society 5*. 2008:1–2, 3, 4, 11. Copyright © 2008 by Sage Publications Inc. Books. Reproduced with permission of Pine Forge Press, a Division of Sage Publications, Inc. via Copyright Clearance Center.

page 122: Cartoon © The New Yorker Collection 1979 Robert Weber from cartoonbank.com. All rights reserved.

page 130: Figure 6-1 from James Allan Davis and Tom W. Smith. 2007. *General Social Surveys 2007*. Published by the Roper Center, Storrs, CT. Reprinted by permission of National Opinion Research Center.

Chapter 7

page 140: Excerpt from Mark Andrejevic. 2007. *iSpy: Surveillance and Power in the Interactive Era*. Used with permission of the University Press of Kansas.

page 142: Logo used by permission of New York City Department of Health and Mental Hygiene.

page 142: Table 7-1 Adapted from the Pew Internet & American Life Project, John B. Horrigan, *A Typology of Information and Communication Technology Users*, May 7, 2007, pp. 5–11, www.pewinternet.org/Reports/2007/A-Typology-of-Information-and-Communication-Technology-Users.aspx. Reprinted with permission.

page 146: Figure 7-2 Adapted from OpenNet Initiative 2008. Copyright © The OpenNet Initiative 2008. All rights reserved.

page 148: Cartoon by David Simonds, The Economist Newspaper.

page 151: Figure 7-3 Adapted from Michael A. Messner, Margaret Carlisle Duncan, and Nicole William. 2006. "The Revolution Is Not Being Televised," *Contexts*, (Summer 2006), p. 35. American Sociological Association. Copyright 2006 by University of California Press–Journals. Used by permission of University of California Press–Journals via the Copyright Clearance Center.

page 153: Figure 7-5 Adapted from the Pew Internet & American Life Project. Based on a November 2008 national survey released January 6, 2009. Data taken from "Demographics of Internet Users," updated 1/6/09, accessible at www.pewinternet.org/trends/User_Demo_Jan_2009.htm. Reprinted with permission.

page 158: Cartoon by Daryl Cagle. © 2004 Daryl Cagle and PoliticalCartoons.com

Chapter 8

page 164: Excerpt from Sudhir Venkatesh. 2008. *Gang Leader for a Day.* Copyright 2008 by Sudhir Venkatesh. Used by permission of The Penguin Press, a division of Penguin Group (USA) Inc. and by Penguin Books Ltd.

page 169: Figure from Henry Wechsler et al. 2002. "Trends in College Binge Drinking During a Period of Increased Prevention Efforts," *Journal of American College Health*, 2002:208. Reprinted with permission of the Helen Dwight Reid Educational Foundation. Published by Heldref Publications, 1319 18th St. NW, Washington, DC 20036-1802. Copyright © 2002.

page 171: Figure 8-2 Used by permission of the Marijuana Policy Project.

page 174: Table 8-1 From Robert K. Merton. 1968. *Social Theory and Social Structure*, Revised and Enlarged Edition. Adapted by permission of The Free Press, a Division of Simon & Schuster, Inc. Copyright © 1967, 1968 by Robert K. Merton. Copyright renewed 1985 by Robert K. Merton. All rights reserved.

page 182: Cartoon by Harley Schwadron. Reprinted with permission.

page 186: Cartoon by Jonathan Shapiro. 2004. © Copyright Zapiro. Used by permission.

Chapter 9

page 192: Excerpt from Robert Frank. 2007. *Richistan: A Journey Through the American Wealth Boom and the Lives of the New Rich*, copyright © 2007 by Robert L. Frank. Used by permission of Crown Publishers, a division of Random House, Inc.

page 202: Figure 9-3 From "America by the Numbers," Project directed by Jackson Dykman, *TIME*, 10/30/06, pp. 48–49. © 2006 Time Inc. All rights reserved.

page 202: Table 9-2 from James. A. Davis and Tom W. Smith. 2007. *General Social Surveys, 1972–2006* Used by permission of the National Opinion Research Center.

page 204: Figure 9-4 Data on wealth from Edward N. Wolff. 2002. "Recent Trends in the Distribution of Household Wealth Ownership." In *Back to Shared Prosperity: The Growing Inequality of Wealth and Income in America*, ed. Ray Marshall. New York: M. E. Sharpe. Reprinted by permission of the author.

page 210: Cartoon by Matt Davies. © Tribune Media Services, Inc. All Rights Reserved. Reprinted with permission.

page 211: Figure 9-7 From Bhashkar Mazumder. 2008. *Upward Intergenerational Economic Mobility in the United States*. Washington DC: Economic Mobility Project, An initiative of the Pew Charitable Trusts. Used by permission of Dr. Bhashkar Mazumder.

Chapter 10

page 220: Excerpt from Paul Collier. 2007. *The Bottom Billion: Why the Poorest Countries Are Failing and What Can Be Done About It*. © 2007 Paul Collier. Used with permission of Oxford University Press, UK.

page 221: Figure 10-1 Adapted from Bob Sutcliffe. 2002. *100 Ways of Seeing an Unequal World*, Fig 1, p. 18. London: Zed Books. Reprinted by permission.

page 222: Figure 10-2 Adapted in part from John R. Weeks. 2008. *Population* 10E. © 2008 Wadsworth, a part of Cengage Learning Inc. Reproduced by permission of www.cengage.com/permissions. And adapted in part from Carl Haub. 2008. *World Population Data Sheet 2008*. Used by permission of Population Reference Bureau.

page 225: Table 10-1 Adapted in part from *Fortune*. 2008. FORTUNE Global 500, http://money.cnn.com/magazines/fortune/global500/2008/full_list/index.html. © 2008 Time Inc. All rights reserved. And adapted in part from World Bank. 2009. W*orld Development Indicators 2009*. Copyright 2009 by World Bank. Used by permission of the International Bank for Reconstruction and Development/World Bank via the Copyright Clearance Center.

page 226: Figure 10-4 From Chronic Poverty Research Centre. 2005. Administered by Institute for Development Policy and Management, School of Environment and Development, University of Manchester, UK. Used by permission.

page 229: Table from Soumitra Dutta and Irene Mia, *The Global Information Technology Report* 2008–2009. Reproduced with permission of Palgrave Macmillan.

page 232: Figure 10-6 World Bank. 2007. W*orld Development Indicators 2007*. Copyright 2007 by World Bank. Used by permission of the International Bank for Reconstruction and Development/World Bank via Copyright Clearance Center.

page 237: Cartoon by Horsey, Seattle Post-Intelligencer.

Chapter 11

page 244: Excerpt from Helen Zia. 2000. *Asian American Dreams: The Emergence of an American People*. Copyright © 2000 Helen Zia. Published by Farrar, Straus & Giroux, LLC. Reprinted by permission.

page 248: Cartoon by Nick Anderson. Used with permission of Nick Anderson and the Washington Post Writers Group in conjunction with the Cartoonist Group. All rights reserved.

page 267: Cartoon by Ed Stein, edsteinink.com.

Chapter 12

page 272: Excerpt from Azadeh Moaveni. 2005. *Lipstick Jihad: A Memoir of Growing up Iranian in America and American in Iran*. Copyright © 2005 by Azadeh Moaveni. Reprinted by permission of PublicAffairs, a member of the Perseus Books Group.

page 274: Table 12-1 From Joyce McCarl Nielsen, et al. 2000. "Gendered Heteronormativity: Empirical Illustrations in Everyday Life," *Sociological Quarterly* 41 (No. 2):287. © 2000 by Blackwell Publishing, reprinted by permission.

page 282: Figure 12-2 Adapted from Makiko Fuwa. 2004. "Macro-level Gender Inequality and the Division of Household Labor in 22 Countries," *American Sociological Review* 69: December 2004, Table 2, page 757. Used by permission of the American Sociological Association and the author.

page 286: Figure 12-5 From NARAL Pro-Choice America Foundation 2009. Used by permission of NARAL, Washington, DC.

Chapter 13

page 294: Excerpt from Mitch Albom. *Tuesdays with Morrie*. 1997. Copyright © 1997 by Mitch Albom. Used by permission of Doubleday, a division of Random House, Inc., and by permission of the Little, Brown Books Group Ltd.

page 300: © The New Yorker Collection 2006 Barbara Smaller from cartoonbank.com. All rights reserved.

page 301: Figure 13-2 © AARP. 2006. *Attitudes Toward Work and Job Security*, (Washington, DC: AARP, 2006).

Chapter 14

page 312: Excerpt from Annette Lareau. 2003. *Unequal Childhoods: Class, Race, and Family Life*. Copyright 2003 by University of California Press–Books. Reproduced with permission of the University of California Press–Books via Copyright Clearance Center.

page 313: Figure 14-1 In part from Joseph A. McFalls, Jr. 2003. "Population: A Lively Introduction," fourth edition, *Population Bulletin* 58 (December):23. Used by permission of the Population Reference Bureau.

page 325: Cartoon by Signe Wilkinson. Used by permission of Cartoonists & Writers Syndicate.

Chapter 15

page 336: Excerpt from Vine Deloria, Jr. 1999. *For This Land: Writings on Religion in America*. Copyright © 1999 by Taylor & Francis Group LLC–Books. Reproduced by permission of Routledge Publishing Inc. a division of Taylor & Francis Group LLC via Copyright Clearance Center.

page 337: Figure 15-1 Data from the Pew Research Center, U.S. Religious Landscape Survey, Feb. 2008.

page 339: Figure 15-2 From John L. Allen. 2010. *Student Atlas of World Geography*, sixth edition. Copyright © 2010 by The McGraw-Hill Companies. Reproduced by permission of McGraw-Hill Contemporary Learning Series, 501 Bell Street, Dubuque, IA 52001.

page 347: Figure 15-3 Adapted from Pippa Norris and Ronald Inglehart. 2004. *Sacred and Secular: Religion and Politics Worldwide*: Table 3.6, p.74. Cambridge University Press © 2004. Reprinted with permission of Cambridge University Press.

page 354: Cartoon by Sandy Huffaker. © 2005 Sandy Huffaker and PoliticalCartoons.com.

Chapter 16

page 360: Excerpt from Jonathan Kozol. 2005. *The Shame of the Nation*. Copyright © 2005 by Jonathan Kozol. Reprinted by permission of Crown Publishers, a division of Random House, Inc.

page 362: Google logo © Google Inc., 2009. Reprinted with permission.

page 364: Cartoon by Kirk Anderson. Used by permission of Kirk Anderson, www.kirktoons.com.

page 378: Excerpt from Martin P. Wattenberg. 2008. *Is Voting for Young People?* pp. 1–2, 3. Copyright © 2008 by Pearson Education, Inc. Reprinted by permission. Users may not reproduce copies without permission of Pearson Education.

page 380: Figure 17-1 Adapted from OpenNet Initiative 2008. Copyright © The OpenNet Initiative 2008. All rights reserved.

page 387: Figure 17-4 (right) From G. William Domhoff. 2006. *Who Rules America,* fifth edition. © 2006 by The McGraw-Hill Companies. Reproduced by permission.

page 389: Figure 17-5 Military and National Defense from The Gallup Poll. Copyright © 2009 The Gallup Organization, Princeton, NJ. All rights reserved. Reprinted with permission.

page 390: Figure 17-6 2008 Global Peace Index, Institute for Economics and Peace.

page 391: Figure 17-7 Adapted from *National Geographic Atlas of the World,* eighth edition. National Geographic Society, 2005. NG Maps/National Geographic Image Collection.

page 392: Screenshot © Greenpeace.

page 394: Cartoon by Drew Sheneman. © Tribune Media Services, Inc. All rights reserved. Reprinted with permission.

Chapter 18

page 400: Excerpt from Kelsey Timmerman. 2009. *Where Am I Wearing? A Global Tour to the Countries, Factories, and People that Make Our Clothes.* © 2009. Reproduced with permission of John Wiley & Sons, Inc.

page 404:-Figure from M. Acharya. 2000. In Mahbub ul Haq Human Development Centre, *Human Development in South Asia 2000: The Gender Question,* p. 54. Oxford University Press, Karachi. Reprinted by permission.

page 406: Cartoon by Mike Thompson, Detroit Free Press.

page 410: Cartoon by Mike Keefe. © 2003 Mike Keefe, The Denver Post, and PoliticalCartoons.com.

page 410: Quotation from Sheryl Stolberg. 1995. "Affirmative Action Gains Often Come at a High Cost," *Los Angeles Times,* March 29, 1995:A14. Copyright 1995 Los Angeles Times. Reprinted by permission.

Chapter 19

page 418: Excerpt from Lori Arviso Alvord M.D. & Elizabeth Cohen Van Pelt. 1999. *The Scalpel and the Silver Bear,* copyright © 1999 by Lori Arviso Alvord & Elizabeth Cohen Van Pelt. Used by permission of Bantam Books, a division of Random House, Inc. and the author.

page 421: Figure 19-1 From Carl Haub and Mary Mederios Kent. 2008. *World Population Data Sheet 2008.* Used by permission of Population Reference Bureau.

page 424: Figure 19-2 From UNAIDS. 2008. Adapted from A global view of HIV infection. 2008 Report on the global AIDS epidemic, July 2008, UNAIDS. Courtesy UNAIDS, Geneva, Switzerland.

page 428: Cartoon by Sidney Harris. © ScienceCartoonsPlus.com.

page 436: Quotation from Neil B. Thompson. 1972. Reprinted from *Natural History,* December 1972; copyright © Natural History Magazine, Inc. 1972.

page 437: Cartoon by Mike Luckovich. Reprinted by permission of Mike Luckovich and Creators Syndicate, Inc.

page 438: Figure 19-7 From the Washington Post © 2007 The Washington Post. All rights reserved. Used by permission and protected by the Copyright Laws of the U.S. The printing, copying, redistribution, or retransmission of the Material without express written permission is prohibited.

page 440: Figure 19-8 Frank Newport 2009, Americans: Economy Takes Precedence Over Environment, from The Gallup Poll. Copyright © 2009 The Gallup Organization, Princeton, NJ. All rights reserved. Reprinted with permission.

Chapter 20

page 448: Excerpt from Mitchell Duneier. 1999. *Sidewalk,* pp. 17–18. Copyright © 1999 by Mitchell Duneier. Reprinted by permission of Farrar, Straus & Giroux, LLC, and the author.

page 451: Figure 20-1 From Carl Haub and Mary Mederios Kent. 2008. *World Population Data Sheet 2008.* Used by permission of Population Reference Bureau.

page 453: Cartoon by Signe Wilkinson. Used by permission of Cartoonists & Writers Syndicate.

page 458: Table 20-2 Based on Gideon Sjoberg. 1960. *The Preindustrial City: Past and Present*: 323–328. Adapted with permission of The Free Press, a Division of Simon & Schuster Adult Publishing Group. Copyright © 1960 by The Free Press. Copyright © renewed 1968 by Gideon Sjoberg. All rights reserved. And based on E. Barbara Phillips. 1996. *City Lights: Urban-Suburban Life in the Global Society,* second edition. Copyright © 1981 by E. Barbara Phillips and Richard T. LeGates, 1996 by E. Barbara Phillips. Oxford University Press. Used by permission.

page 459: Figure 20-4 Adapted from *National Geographic Atlas of the World,* eighth edition. National Geographic Society, 2005. NG Maps/National Geographic Image Collection. Used by permission.

page 460: Figure 20-5 Adapted from Chauncy Harris and Edward Ullmann. 1945. "The Nature of Cities," *Annals of the American Academy of Political and Social Science,* 242 (November):13. Reprinted by permission of American Academy of Political and Social Science, Philadelphia.

page 466: Figure 20-6 Homelessness Research Institute at the National Alliance to End Homelessness, 2009. Used with permission.

Chapter 21

page 474: Excerpt from Howard Rheingold. 2003. *Smart Mobs, The Next Social Revolution: Transforming Cultures and Communities in the Age of Instant Access.* Copyright © 2003 Howard Rheingold. Reprinted by permission of Basic Books, a member of Perseus Books LLC.

page 474: Cartoon by Baloo, from The Wall Street Journal, permission Cartoon Features Syndicate.

page 484: Illustration reprinted by permission of the publisher from John B. Christiansen and Sharon N. Barnartt, *Deaf President Now! The 1988 Revolution at Gallaudet University* (Washington DC: Gallaudet University Press, 1995) p. 22. Copyright 1995 by Gallaudet University.

page 488: Table 21-3 Adapted from Karen Meyer, "Match the Disability." April 30, 2007. Chicago: DePaul University. Reproduced with permission.

Chapter 22

page 494: Excerpt from Matt Mason. 2008. *The Pirates Dilemma: How Youth Culture is Reinventing Capitalism.* Reprinted and edited with permission of The Free Press, a Division of Simon & Schuster, Inc. Copyright © 2008 by Matt Mason. All rights reserved.

page 505: Figure 22-1 Adapted from *National Geographic Atlas of the World,* eighth edition. National Geographic Society, 2005. NG Maps / National Geographic Image Collection.

The World as a Village

Data in this presentation are based on author's estimates from the following sources: *The World Almanac and Book of Facts 2008.* New York: Reader's Digest Book, NJ: World Almanac Books, pp. 728–729; World Bank. 2009. *World Development Indicators 2009.* Washington, DC: World Bank, pp. 24, 30, 69, 94, 100, 104, 184, 308, 312; Carl V. Haub. 2008. *World Population Data Sheet 2008.* Washington, DC: Population Reference Bureau. "The State of the Village Report," Donella Meadows Archive Sustainability Institute, accessed February 27, 2008 at www.sustainer.org; "World Religions," *2007 Encyclopedia Britannica Book of the Year.* Chicago: Encyclopedia Britannica; and Mac/PC System Shootouts. 2008. "iPod Sales." Accessed May 12, 2009 at http://www.systemsshootouts.org/?q=node/209. The concept of considering the entire world as a community of 1,000 people has often been done in a variety of depictions quite dissimilar to this representation. The inspiration for this presentation first appeared, to the author's knowledge, in Donella H. Meadows, 1994. "If the World Were a Village of 1,000 People," in Doug Aberley (ed.), *Futures by Design: The Practice of Ecological Planning.* Gabuola Island, British Columbia: New Society Publishers, pp. 27–31. Donella (Dana) Meadows was a biophysicist who passed away in 2001.

photo credits

Ribound/Magnum Photos; p. 368: © Dennis MacDonald/Alamy; p. 371: © Andrew Holbrooke/Image Works; p. 373: © Chicago Tribune photo by Candice C. Cruisic. All rights reserved. Used with permission. **Chapter 17:** Opener: © Andy Kropa/Redux Pictures; p. 378: Photo by Editorial Image, LLC; p. 379: © C Squared Studios/Getty Images; p. 380: © Frank Micelotta/Getty Images; p. 381: © Hulton Archive/Getty Images; p. 382: © Joren Gerhard; p. 383: Courtesy Joshua Johnston; p. 384: © Win McNamee/Getty Images; p. 385: © Ryan McVay/Getty Images; p. 387: © Photodisc Collection/Getty Images; p. 388: © AP Images/Haraz Ghanbari; p. 389: © iStockphoto.com/Valerie Loiseleux; p. 390: © Reuters/Yannis Behrakis/Landov.
Chapter 18: Opener: © Rene Mattes/Hemis/Corbis; p. 400: © Masterfile RF; p. 401: © Mark Steinmetz/Amanita Pictures; p. 402(top): © Board of Governors of the Federal Reserve System; p. 402(bottom): © Ramadhan Khamis/Panapress; p. 405: © Edward Burtynsky; p. 407(top): Courtesy of Amy Wang; p. 407(bottom): © Royalty-Free/Corbis; p. 408: © Chuck Keeler/Stone/Getty Images; p. 409: © Jesus Castillo/ITSPress/Atlaspress; p. 411(left): © Age Fotostock/Superstock; p. 411(right): © Erin Lubin/Bloomberg News/Landov; p. 412: © Namas Bhojini/Redux Pictures. **Chapter 19:** Opener: © Barry Lewis/Alamy; p. 420: © Jupiterimages/BananaStock/Alamy; p. 421: © Bob Daemmrich/Image Works; p 422(top): Courtesy of Lola Adedokun; p. 422(bottom): © Photodisc Collection/Getty Images; p. 424: © Ryan McVay/Photodisc/Getty Images; p. 429 (top): © Comstock Images/Alamy; p. 430: © Anthony Saint James/Getty Images; p. 431: © iStockphoto.com/Duncan Walker; p. 432: © Mustafa Ozer/AFP/Getty Images; p. 433(top): © Rhonda Sidney/Stock Boston; p. 433(bottom): © Basel Action Network; p. 434: © Royalty-Free/Corbis; p. 435: © Jennifer S. Altman; p. 437: © Steve Allen/Brand X Pictures; p. 439(top): © Macduff Everton/Corbis; p. 439(bottom): © The McGraw-Hill Companies, Inc./John

Flournoy, photographer; p. 440: © Nancy Ostertag/Getty Images; p. 441 (left): Dynamicgraphics/Jupiterimages; p. 441 (right): © Image Source/Alamy: p. 499: © Creatas/Superstock. **Chapter 20:** Opener: © Thomas Cockrem/Alamy; p. 448(bottom): © Ovie Carter; p. 449: © Gianni Muratore/Alamy; p. 450: © Royalty-Free/CORBIS; p. 453: © Josef Polleross/Image Works; p. 455: © Goh Chai Hin/AFP/Getty Images; p. 456(top): © AP Images; p. 456(bottom): © C Squared Studios/Getty Images; p. 458: © Mark Henley/Panos Pictures; p. 461: © Sarah Leen/National Geographic/Getty Images; p. 463: © AP Images/Max Nash; p. 465: © Steve Warmowski/Image Works; p. 467: © Steffan Hacker/Habitat for Humanity.
Chapter 21: Opener: © Mark Henley/Panos Pictures; p. 475(top): © AP Images/Kaspar Wenstrup, Nordphoto; p. 475(bottom): © Amos Morgan/Getty Images; p. 477: © Chung Sung-Jun/Getty Images; p. 478, p. 479: © AP Images; p. 480: © Scott Barbour/Reportage/Getty Images; p. 481: © Raoul Minsart/Superstock; p. 482(left): © AP Images/George Nikitin; p. 482(right): © AP Images/Jeff Chiu; p. 483: © AP Images/Ed Andrieski; p. 484: © Joshua Roberts/Getty Images; p. 486: © Dr. Parvinder Sethi; p. 487: © Photodisc Collection/Getty Images; p. 488: © AP Images/Jason R. Davis. **Chapter 22:** Opener: © Pavel Filatov/Alamy; p. 494: Jacket design of THE PIRATES DILEMMA: *How Youth Culture is Reinventing Capitalism* by Matt Mason, published by The Free Press. Copyright © 2008 by Simon & Schuster, Inc. Reproduced with permission of the publisher. All rights reserved.; p. 496: © 2002 Joseph Rodriguez/Stockphoto.com; p. 497: © Jim West/jimwestphoto.com; p. 498: © ScotStock/Alamy; p. 499(left): © Peter Menzel/Menzel Photography; p. 499(right): © Melanie Stetson Freeman/The Christian Science Monitor/Getty Images; p. 501: Courtesy of One Laptop Per Child; p. 502: © Photodisc/Alamy; p. 503: Courtesy, Troy Duster; p. 504: © Pedro Armestre/epa/Corbis.

name index

Page numbers in *italics* indicate photos or cartoons. Page numbers followed by a *f* indicate figures; page numbers followed by a *t* indicate tables.

A

Abercrombie, Nicholas, 200
Aberle, David F., 103
Abraham, 338, 340
Abrahamson, Mark, 173
Abramovitz, Janet M., 478
Abramson, David, 431
Acharya, Menna, 404
Adams, Evan, 73
Adams, Tyrene, 142
Adamy, Janet, 20
Addams, Jane, 12, *12*, 16, 41, 278
Adedokun, Lola, 422
Adler, Freda, 179, 180
Adler, Patricia A., 28, 29, 35
Adler, Peter, 28, 29, 35, 36
Adler, Roy D., 232
Adorno, Theodor, 54
Aguilera, Christina, 53
Aguirre, Benigno E., 479
Ahmed, Karuna Chanana, 232
Alain, Michel, 483
Alba, Richard D., 264
Albas, Cheryl, 82
Albas, Daniel, 82
Albom, Mitch, 294
Albrecht, Gary L., 102, 489
Alda, Alan, 255
Aldrich, Howard, 477
Ali, Muhammad, 100, 143*t*
Allen, Bem P., 167
Allen, John L., 339
Alley, Kirstie, 350
Allport, Gordon, 253, 254
Alvord, Lori Arviso, 418, 419, 429, 430
Alwin, Duane F., 385
Ameche, Don, 117
Andersen, Margaret, 278
Anderson, Elijah, 16
Anderson, John Ward, 232
Anderson, Warwick, 259
Andrejevic, Mark, 140
Angier, Natalie, 274
Aniston, Jennifer, 143*t*
Annan, Kofi, 228, 330
Ansell, Amy E., 249
Anthony, Susan B., 284
Apatow, Judd, 189
Arail, Robert, 199
Archibold, Randal C., 236, 467
Argetsinger, Amy, 67
Arias, Elizabeth, 426
Arishi, Takako, 231
Armer, J. Michael, 230
Aronofsky, Darren, 95
Astin, Alexander, 66
Atchley, Robert, 297, 299, 300
Atkinson, Claire, 148

Attwood, Bain, 259
Austin, April, 402
Avramovitz, Rakefet, 85, *85*
Axtell, Roger E., 80
Azumi, Koya, 125

B

Babad, Elisha Y., 367
Bagilhole, Barbara, 276, 282
Baichwal, Jennifer, 509
Bainbridge, William Sims, 108, 348, 350
Baker, C. Edwin, 158
Baker, Dean, 213
Baker, Peter, 288
Baker, Theresa, 42
Baker, Wayne E., 230
Bales, Robert, 277
Balle, Bent, 324
Banks, Enos, 207
Barbaro, Michael, 68
Barber, David, 92, 93
Barboza, David, 148, 406
Bardi, Anat, 66
Barnes, Roy E., 373
Barnow, Burt S., 102
Barr, Cameron W., 156
Barrett, David R., 340
Barrino, Fantasia, 324
Barrionuevo, Alexei, 434
Barron, Milton L., 295
Bartlett, Thomas, 67
Barton, Bernadette, 178
Barusch, Amanda, 297
Bascara, Victor, 259
Battin, Margaret P., 307
Bauerlein, Monika, 362, 498
Baum, Katrina, 182
Bauman, Kurt J., 205
Bazar, Emily, 205
Beach, Adam, 73
Beagan, Brenda L., 422
Beall, Cynthia M., 295
Bearman, Peter S., 106
Becker, Anne E., 52
Becker, Howard S., 177, 180, 367, 423
Beddoes, Zanny Milton, 409
Beisel, Nicola, 279
Bell, Daniel, 111, 181, 362, 405, 498
Bell, Wendell, 229
Bellafante, Ginia, 320
Bellamy, Ralph, 117
Bello, Marisol, 326
Belt, Don, 349
Bendick, Marc, Jr., 305
Bendix, B. Reinhard, 40
Benford, Robert D., 482
Bennett, Vivienne, 235
Bergen, Raquel Kennedy, 179
Berger, Peter, 99, 106
Berk, Richard, 477
Berland, Gretchen K., 430
Berman, Paul, 66
Bernasek, Anna, 206

Bernstein, E., 169
Bernstein, Sharon, 425
Berry, Halle, 143*t*
Best, Amy, 172
Bhagat, Chetan, 60
Bianchi, Suzanne M., 325
Biddlecom, Ann, 328
Bielby, Denise D., 149
Bielby, William T., 148, 149, 150, 158
Black, Donald, 63, 170
Blau, Peter M., 210
Blauner, Robert, 253, 408
Blinder, Alan S., 413
Blonsky, Nikki, 137
Blumberg, Stephen J., 35
Blumer, Herbert, 99, 481, 482
Boase, Jeffrey, 151
Bogart, Humphrey, 143
Bondy, Christopher, 231
Bong, Joon-ho, 333
Bonilla-Silva, Eduardo, 247, 249
Bono, 143*t*
Bordia, Prashant, 481
Borjas, George S., 263, 265
Bornschier, Volker, 230
Bottomore, Tom, 496
Bouchard, Thomas J., 79
Boudreaux, Richard, 234
Bourdieu, Pierre, 13, 60
Boushey, Heather, 210
Bout, Victor, 387
Bouvier, Leon F., 455
Bowles, Samuel, 85, 363, 365, 368
Brabazon, Tara, 362
Bracey, Mitchell L., Jr., 350
Bradford, Calvin, 103
Brady, Jim, 185
Brannigan, Augustine, 111
Brannon, Rush, 487
Brauman, Rony, 239
Braverman, Amy, 44
Braxton, Greg, 149
Bray, James H., 317
Breines, Winnifred, 279, 285
Brewer, Cynthia A., 257
Brewer, Rose M, 178
Brockovich, Erin, 49
Bromley, David, 36, 350
Brower, Brock, 481
Brown, David K., 365
Brown, Geoff, 187
Brown, Michael, 476
Brown, Patricia Leigh, 329
Brown, Robert McAfee, 342
Brown, Roger W., 480
Browne, Irene, 279
Brubaker, Bill, 182
Brulle, Robert, 440
Bruno, Rosalind, 69
Brunson, Blake, 322
Brysk, Alison, 238
Buchholz, Barbara Ballinger, 489
Buchmann, Claudia, 366
Buckley, Terri, 318

Buckley, Tom, 318
Buddha, 340
Budig, Michelle, 283
Bullard, Robert D., 208, 435, 441
Bulle, Wolfgang F., 64
Burawoy, Michael, 16
Burgdorf, Robert L., Jr., 488
Burger, Jerry, 168
Burkeman, Oliver, 108
Burkeman, Oliver, 108
Burtynsky, Edward, 509
Bush, George H. W., 143*t*
Bush, George W., 328, 341, 373*f*, 393
Buss, David M., 34, 36
Butler, Robert, 303
Butrica, Barbara A., 296, 303
Byrd-Bredbenner, Carol, 274
Bystydreinski, Jill Mind, 486

C

Cable, Charles, 441
Cable, Sherry, 441
Cai, Fand, 406
Calhoun, Craig, 485, 486, 506
Calvin, John, 342
Cameron, Deborah, 279
Cameron, James, 217
Campbell, Mary, 210
Cañas, Jesus, 235
Cantril, Hadley, 480
Caplan, Ronald, L., 420
Caplow, Theodore, 388
Car, Nicholas, 362
Carey, Mariah, 247
Carmichael, Mary, 436
Carrol, Rory, 286
Carroll, Diahann, 143*t*
Carroll, Joseph, 45, 71, 265, 306
Carson, Johnny, 480
Carter, Bill, 149
Carter, Susan B., 183, 302, 495
Carty, Win, 436
Cassidy, Rachel C., 258
Castañeda, Jorge, 234
Castells, Manuel, 108, 131, 156, 229, 462, 486
Castro, Fidel, 262, 483
Cauchon, Dennis, 213
Cerulo, Karen A., 151
Chalfant, H. Paul, 351
Chambliss, William, 177
Chan, Sewell, 142
Chang, Yung, 509
Charles, Prince of Wales, 466
Chase-Dunn, Christopher, 223, 227
Chavira, Juan Antonio, 426
Cheadle, Don, 161, 269
Cheng, Mitchell J., 227
Cheng, Shu-Ju Ada, 42
Cherlin, Andrew J., 21, 213, 214, 317, 324, 325, 328
Chesney-Lind, Meda, 179, 180
Cheung, A., 69
Chin, Ko-lin, 181
Chirot, Daniel, 255

Choi, Yoonsun, 259
Christ, Jesus, 143t, 338, 340
Christakis, Nicholas A., 107
Chu, Henry, 59, 60
Chubb, Catherine, 280
Churchill, Winston, 361
Clark, Burton, 370
Clark, Candace, 423
Clark, E. Gurney, 419
Clark, Jill K., 464
Clarke, Adele, 502
Clarke, Lee, 480
Clawson, Daniel, 92
Clay, Cassius, 100
Clemmitt, Marcia, 114, 354
Clifford, Stephanie, 142, 151
Clinard, Marshall B., 175
Clinton, Bill, 143t
Clooney, George, 145
Cloward, Richard A., 213
Clymer, Adam, 385
Coates, Rodney, 249
Cockerham, William C., 423
Cole, Elizabeth, 322
Cole, Mike, 363
Coleman, Isobel, 367
Coleman, James William, 182, 431
Collier, Paul, 220
Collins, Chiquita, 257
Collins, Patricia Hill, 278
Collins, Randall, 200, 342, 498
Collura, Heather, 106
Colucci, Jim, 148
Commoner, Barry, 433, 438, 439
Comstock, P., 134
Comte, Auguste, 9, 495
Condon, Bill, 49
Connell, R. W., 276
Connelly, Marjorie, 303
Conner, Thaddieus, 258
Conrad, Peter, 420, 423
Cooley, Charles Horton, 12, 79–80, 83, 120, 182
Coontz, Stephanie, 325
Cooper, Jeremy, 489
Cooper, K., 42
Cooper, Mark, 158
Corbette, Christianne, 366
Cornwell, Benjamin, 296
Cosby, Bill, 143t
Coser, Lewis A., 200
Coser, Rose Laub, 10, 429
Côté, James E., 90
Couch, Carl, 380, 478
Counts, D. A., 301
Couture, Heather, 168
Cox, Oliver, 253
Cox, Rachel S., 372
Crabtree, Steve, 344
Creamer, Paula, 17
Cressey, Donald R., 361, 431
Cross, Simon, 276, 282
Croteau, David, 154, 156, 158
Croucher, Sheila A., 265
Crowe, Jerry, 15
Crowe, Russell, 189
Crown, John S., 8, 326
Cruise, Tom, 143t, 350
Crump, Andy, 299
Cuff, E. C., 200
Cullen, Frances T., Jr., 177
Cullen, John B., 177

Cullen, Lisa Tekevchi, 324
Cumming, Elaine, 296
Currie, Elliot, 185
Curry, Timothy John, 420
Curry-White, Brenda, 208
Curtis, James, 130
Curtiss, Susan, 77, 78
Cushing-Daniels, Brenda, 92, 204

D

Dagher, Sam, 386
Dahl, Robert, 388
Dahrendorf, Ralf, 14, 200, 496, 497
Daldry, Stephen, 291
Daley-Harris, Sam, 486
Dalla, Rochelle L., 321
Damon, Britt, 36
Damon, Matt, 95
Daniels, Arlene Kaplan, 130
Daniszewski, John, 156
Dannelly, Brian, 357
Danowski, James, 89
Dao, James, 324
Darlin, Damon, 499
Darlington, JoAnne DeRoven, 142
Darwin, Charles, 10, 55, 495
Dashefsky, Arnold, 245
Davé, Shiipa, 320
David, Gary, 261
Davies, Christie, 91
Davies, James, 33
Davis, Darren W., 34
Davis, Donald B., 131
Davis, Gerald, 387
Davis, James A., 130, 202
Davis, Kingsley, 77, 199, 200, 365
Davis, Mike, 467
Davis, Nanette J., 173, 177
De Anda, Roberto M., 279
de Beauvoir, Simone, 284
De Soucey, Michaela, 131, 131
de Tocqueville, Alexis, 129
Deegan, Mary Jo, 9, 12
Deflem, Mathieu, 183
Deibert, Ronald J., 146, 379, 380
Delaney, Kevin J., 147
Della Porta, Donatella, 483, 485
Deloria, Vine, 336
DeNavas-Walt, Carmen, 45, 195, 196, 204, 205, 206, 207, 250, 256, 258, 262, 303, 321, 425
Denny, Charlotte, 266
Denton, Nancy, 463
Denzin, Norman K., 112
DeParle, Jason, 213, 505
Derick, Amy J., 172
Desai, Manisha, 486
Desegrais, Helene, 212
Desmond, Matthew, 322
Deutsch, Francine M., 279
Devitt, James, 386
Di Carlo, Matthew, 370
Diamond, Jared, 506
Diamond, Shari Seidman, 124
Diaz, Cameron, 142
DiCaprio, Leonardo, 95, 217, 241
Dicum, Gregory, 20
Diefenbach, Donald L., 431
DiFonzo, Nicholas, 481
Dillon, Sam, 235, 373, 465

DiMaggio, Paul, 131, 132
Dixon, Margaret, 306
Dobbs, Michael, 373
Dodds, Klaus, 57
Doezema, Jo, 237
Domhoff, G. William, 387, 387f, 388
Dominick, Joseph R., 150
Donadio, Rachel, 89
Donnelly, Sally B., 305
Donohue, Elisabeth, 369
Doress, Irwin, 348
Dorn, Stan, 426
Dorning, Mike, 156
Dougherty, John, 235
Dougherty, Kevin, 367
Dowd, James J., 297
Draven, Jamie, 291
Dreifus, Claudia, 479, 503
Drevs, Abigail, 285
DuBois, W. E. B., 11, 11–12, 16, 19, 41, 247, 256, 258, 321
Dubner, Stephen J., 38, 175
DuBowski, Sandi Simcha, 357
Dugger, Celia, 409
Dukes, Richard L., 37
Duncan, Otis Dudley, 210
Dundas, Susan, 330
Duneier, Mitchell, 105, 448
Dunlap, Riley E., 440, 441
Dunne, Gillian, 330
Durden, T. Elizabeth, 426
Durkheim, Émile, 8, 10, 11, 40, 107, 108, 112, 165, 173, 174, 180, 205, 338, 341, 406, 495
Durrenberger, E. Paul, 133
Duster, Troy, 503
Dykman, Jason, 203, 204
Dylan, Bob, 143t
Dynes, Russell R., 478

E

Eastwood, Clint, 309
Eaton, Leslie, 465
Ebaugh, Helen Rose Fuchs, 103
Eberbach, Dave, 41
Eckenwiler, Mark, 502
Eckhart, Aaron, 161
Eddy, Mary Baker, 344, 350
Edwards, Jennifer, 255
Ehrenreich, Barbara, 4, 5, 19, 35, 206
Ehrlich, Anne, 438, 439
Ehrlich, Paul, 438, 439, 450
Einstein, Albert, 106, 354f
Eisenhower, Dwight D., 143t
Elizabeth I, 361
Elizabeth II, 393
Ellingwood, Ken, 286
Ellison, Jesse, 503
Ellison, Keith, 384
Ellison, Nicole, 89
Ellison, Ralph, 256
Embree, Ainslie, 352, 353
Emery, David, 481
Engels, Friedrich, 10, 11, 19, 125, 135, 278, 316, 402, 483
Enriquez, Juan, 393
Entine, Jon, 225
Epstein, Cynthia Fuchs, 279
Erikson, Kai, 173, 407
Escárcega, Sylvia, 234

Esposito, Jennifer, 269
Etaugh, Claire, 275
Etzioni, Amitai, 125, 390
Evergeti, Venetia, 506
Eyre, Chris, 73

F

Fackler, Martin, 231
Faiola, Anthony, 299
Faith, Nazila, 107
Fallows, Deborah, 151
Faris, Robert, 146, 380
Farley, Melissa, 180
Farley, Reynolds, 330
Farr, Grant M., 315
Fatina, Helac, 452
Fausset, Richard, 307, 352
Favreault, Melissa, 211, 321
Feagin, Joe R., 19, 251, 371, 461
Featherman, David L., 210
Fellmann, Jerome D., 54
Felson, David, 183
Ferber, Amy L., 250, 390
Ferree, Myra Marx, 15, 484, 485
Feuer, Alan, 301
Fiala, Robert, 498
Field, John, 13
Fields, Jason, 275, 313, 316, 328
Fields, Jessica, 18
Finch, Emily, 124
Fine, Gary Alan, 254
Fiore, Quentin, 154
Fischer, Claude S., 338
Fiss, Peer C., 19
Fitchett, George, 301
Fitzgerald, David, 505
Fitzgerald, Kathleen J., 251, 484
Flacks, Richard, 60
Fletcher, Connie, 102
Flora, Cornelia Butter, 465
Flora, Jan L., 465
Flynn, Laurie J., 106
Fonseca, Felicia, 61
Forbes, Steve, 394
Ford, Gerald, 143t
Form, William, 484
Forsythe, David P., 237
Foster, Jodie, 77
Fouché, Gladys, 282
Fowler, James H., 107
Fox, M. B., 134
Fox, Michael J., 388f
Foy, Paul, 435
Frank, Robert, 134, 192, 220
Franke, Richard Herbert, 37
Franklin, John Hope, 257
Freeman, Jo, 285
Freidson, Eliot, 420
French, Howard W., 82, 361, 406, 409
Freud, Sigmund, 82–83
Freudenheim, Milt, 305
Frey, William H., 464, 465
Fridlund, Alan J., 62
Friedan, Betty, 284, 455
Friedman, Thomas L., 412
Friend, David, 104
Fudge, Judy, 205
Furstenberg, Frank, 317, 321
Furstenberg, Sheela Kennedy, Jr., 90
Fuwa, Makiko, 280, 282

G

Gailey, Robert, 503
Galbraith, Kenneth, 192
Gamble, Wendy C., 321
Gamson, Joshua, 158, 484
Gandhi, Mohandas K., 353, 380
Gans, Herbert J., 463
Garcia-Moreno, Claudia, 316
Gardner, Gary, 434
Gardner, Marilyn, 304
Garfinkel, Harold, 91
Garner, Roberta, 485
Garreau, Joel, 460
Gaudin, Sharon, 152
Gecas, Viktor, 91
Gentile, Carmen, 142
Gentleman, Amelia, 60, 179, 353
Gephardt, Dick, 373
Gere, Richard, *64*
Gerson, Kathleen, 408
Gerstel, Naomi, 92
Gerth, H. H., 10
Gertner, Jon, 147
Gibbs, Nancy, 307, 326
Giddens, Anthony, 14, 57
Gilley, Brian Joseph, 178
Gintis, Herbert, 85, 365, 368
Giordano, Peggy C., 81, 86
Giridharadas, Anand, 319
Giroux, Henry A., 365
Gitlin, Todd, 155
Glanton, Dahleen, 425
Glascock, Anthony, 306
Glenn, David, 36
Goering, Laurie, 282, 435
Goffman, Erving, 15, 37, 81–82, *83*, 91, 102, 172, 177, 182, 390
Goldin, Amy, 476
Goldstein, Amy, 214
Goldstein, Greg, 467
Goldstein, Melvyn C., 295
Gonzalez, David, 225
Gooding, Caroline, 489
Goodstein, Laurie, 352
Goodwin, Michele, 427
Gorbachev, Mikhail, 499
Gordon, Rachel, 61, 140
Gottdiener, Mark, 461
Gottfredson, Michael, 170
Gottlieb, Lori, 319
Gould, Elise, 431
Gould, Larry, 102, 381
Gouldner, Alvin, 40, 496
Grabarek, Stanislaus, 21
Gramsci, Antonio, 66
Graves, Byron, 176
Grawe, Nathan, 204
Greeley, Andrew M., 342
Greenblatt, Alan, 197
Greenhouse, Linda, 304
Greenhouse, Steven, 134, 193, 304, 439
Greenwald, John, 20
Gregory, Katherine, 186
Grieco, Elizabeth M., 258
Grier, Peter, 204
Grimes, Peter, 223, 227
Griswold, Wendy, 58
Grob, Gerald N., 432
Groening, Chad, 147

Gross, Jane, 299
Grossman, Ler, 349
Groza, Victor, 78
Guarino, Mark, 431
Guo, Guang, 55
Guterman, Lila, 56
Gutiérrez, Gustavo, 342
Gutiérrez, Valerie, 275
Guttmacher Institute, 288

H

Ha, Anthony, 140
Hacker, Andrew, 387
Hacker, Helen Mayer, 278
Haeri, Shaykh Fadhilalla, 281
Hafner-Burton, Emilie M., 238
Hage, Jerald, 125
Haggis, Paul, 269
Haines, David W., 231
Hall, Mimi, 479
Hallinan, Maureen, 498, 499
Hamilton, Charles, 108, 257
Hamm, Steve, 129
Hammack, Floyd M., 367
Hani, Yoko, 299
Hank, Karsten, 93
Hannis, Prudence, 251
Hansen, Barbara, 198
Hanson, Ralph E., 144
ul Haq, Mahbub, 404
Harden, Blaine, 231, 299
Harlow, Harry, 78
Harold, Clive, 466
Harrington, Michael, 111, 148, 150, 158, 207
Harris, Chauncy D., 460
Harris, Marvin, 245, 295
Harrison, George, 143*t*
Hart, Johnny, 174
Hasanali, Parveen, 320
Haskins, Ron, 214
Hatch, Orrin, 388*f*
Haub, Carl, 207, 228, 234, 298, 299, 404, 451, 453, 454
Hauser, Robert M., 210
Havel, Vaclav, 483
Haviland, William A., 61, 313
Hawkins, Sally, 375
Hayden, H. Thomas, 167
He, Wan, 298, 303
Hebel, Sara, 465
Heckert, Druann, 172
Hedley, R. Alan, 230
Heilman, Madeline E., 212
Heitzeg, Nancy A., 178
Hellmich, Nanci, 148
Helvarg, David, 441
Hendershott, Ann, 178
Hendrix, Jimi, 143*t*
Henly, Julia R., 106
Henry, William, 296
Hepburn, Katharine, 143
Herman, Valli, 15
Hersch, Patricia, 369
Herschtal, Eric, 320
Hertz, Rosanna, 328
Hewlett, Sylvia Ann, 284
Hickman, Jonathan, 250
Hicks, Louis, 388
Hill, Michael R., 9

Hilton, Perez, 142
Himes, Christine L., 302
Hinckley, John, 185
Hinckley, Peggy, 373
Hira, Ron, 412
Hirsch, Paul M., 19, 131
Hirschi, Travis, 170
Hirst, Paul, 57
Hitlin, Steven, 66
Hochschild, Arlie, 284, 317
Hodson, Randy, 407
Hoecker-Drysdale, Susan, 9
Hoepker, Thomas, 104
Hoffman, Adonis, 149
Hoffman, Lois Wladis, 55, 56
Holden, Constance, 79
Holder, Kelly, 384
Hollander, Jocelyn A., 273
Holley, Karri A., 354
Hollingshead, August B., 370
Holmes, Mary, 324
Holthouse, David, 235
Homans, George C., 77
Hondagneu-Sotelo, Pierette, 266
hooks, bell, 15
Horgan, John, 79
Horkheimer, Max, 54
Horne, Lena, 143*t*
Horowitz, Helen Lefkowitz, 370
Horrigan, John B., 142, 390
Horwitz, Allan V., 432
Hosokawa, William K., 260
Hounsou, Dijmon, 241
Houseman, John, 480
Houser, Trevor, 441
Houston, Whitney, 143*t*
Hout, Michael, 338
Howard, Judith, 273, 278
Howard, Michael C., 80
Howard, Russell D., 390
Hoynes, William, 154, 156, 158
Huang, Gary, 100
Hubbard, L. Ron, 350
Huber, Bettina J., 22
Huff, Charlotte, 131, 408
Huffstutter, P. J., 151
Hughlett, Mike, 57
Hull, Raymond, 126
Hummer, Robert A., 426
Hundley, James R., 89, 476
Hunt, Courtney, 137
Hunt, Darnell, 154
Hunt, Nick, 142
Hunter, Herbert M., 253
Hunter, James Davison, 66, 341
Huntington, Samuel P., 66
Hurn, Christopher J., 365
Hussein, Saddam, 85, 86, 277, 478
Hutchison, Ray, 461
Hyde, Janet Shibley, 279
Hymowitz, Carol, 407

I

Ibata-Arens, Kathryn, 132
Iceland, John, 256
Igo, Sarah E., 31, 43
Immervoll, Herwig, 92, 93
Inglehart, Ronald, 230, 346, 347
Isaacs, Julia B., 209, 210, 211, 212
ITOPF, 436

J

Jackson, Elton F., 176
Jackson, Janet, 143*t*
Jackson, Michael, 142, 143*t*
Jackson, Philip, 364
Jacobe, Dennis, 435
Jacobs, Andrews, 145, 455
Jacobs, Jerry A., 283, 408
Jacobson, Lenore, 367
Jagger, Mick, 143*t*
Jain, Saranga, 55, 56
James, LeBron, 149
Janis, Irving, 125
Jargowski, Paul A., 208
Jasper, James M., 485, 497
Jaworsky, Nadya, 505, 506
Jayson, Sharon, 328
Jencks, Christopher, 213
Jenkins, Henry, 141
Jenkins, J. Craig, 440, 484
Jenkins, Matt, 438
Jenkins, Richard, 196
Jenness, Valerie, 213
Jensen, Gary F., 176
Jervis, Rick, 7
Jesella, Kara, 151
Jobs, Steve, 132
Johnson, Anne M., 44
Johnson, Benton, 496
Johnson, Judy, 466
Johnson, Kenneth M, 457, 465
Johnson, Lyndon B., 143*t*
Johnson, Richard A., 479
Johnson, Richard W., 304
Johnston, David Cay, 239
Johnston, Joshua, 383
Jones, Del, 198
Jones, Jeffrey M., 144
Jones, Jo, 322
Jordan, Miriam, 234
Joseph, Jay, 79
Jost, Kenneth, 386
Juárez, Benito, 234
Juhasz, Anne McCreary, 81
Jung, Andrea, 212

K

Kabama, Mbwebwe, 207
Kahn, Joseph, 361
Kalaitzidis, Akis, 183
Kalish, Richard, 301
Kalita, S. Mitra, 60
Kalleberg, Arne, 205
Kalmijn, Matthijs, 319
Kambayashi, Takehiko, 99
Kamenetz, Anya, 210
Kandel, William, 465
Kapos, Shia, 318
Kapstein, Ethan B., 237
Karney, Benjamin R., 8, 326
Karzai, Hamid, 145
Katel, Peter, 228
Katovich, Michael A., 167
Katsillis, John, 230
Katz, Bari, 233
Katz, Michael, 368
Kaufman, Miriam, 330
Kaufman, Sarah, 7

Name Index

Kaul, James D., 37
Kavada, Anastasia, 485
Kay, Tamara, 279
Kaye, Judith, 323
Keesler, Venessa A., 372, 431
Keeter, Scott, 35
Kelly, John, 317
Kempadoo, Kamala, 237
Kennedy, Courtney, 35
Kennedy, John F., 185, 198, 380
Kennedy, John F., Jr., 143t
Kennedy, Robert, 185
Kent, Mary M., 453
Kentor, Jeffrey, 387
Kerbo, Harold R., 200, 227, 230
Kerry, John, 393
Kevorkian, Jack, 306, 307
Keysar, Ariela, 348
Kidman, Nicole, 143t
Kilborn, Peter T., 465
Killian, Caitlin, 281, 481
Killian, Lewis, 476
Kim, Kwang Chung, 261
Kimmel, Michael, 250, 276, 366, 390
King, Leslie, 93
King, Meredith L., 249
King, Martin Luther, Jr., 185, 257, 380, 484
King, Rodney, 476
King, Sharon A., 480
Kingsbury, Alex, 175
Kinsella, Kevin, 298
Kinsey, Alfred C., 43, 49
Kiper, Dmitry, 351
Kirsten, Adèle, 187
Kiser, Edgar, 389
Kitchener, Richard F., 83
Klein, Naomi, 155
Kleiner, Art, 129
Kleinknecht, William, 181
Kleniewski, Nancy, 464
Klinenberg, Eric, 157, 296
Klum, Heidi, 319
Knowles, Beyoncé, 37
Kochhar, Rakesh, 211, 263, 265
Kohut, Andrew, 66, 142
Kolata, Gina, 107
Koolhaas, Rem, 458
Kornblum, Janet, 499
Kosmin, Barry A., 348
Kottak, Conrad, 313
Kozinn, Alan, 381
Kozol, Jonathan, 360
Krauss, C., 326
Kreider, Rose M., 321, 322, 495
Kriesberg, Louis, 390
Krim, Jonathan, 67
Kristof, Nicholas D., 232
Kroc, Ray, 120
Kroll, Luisa, 234
Kronstadt, Jessica, 79, 321, 426
Kübler-Ross, Elisabeth, 301
Kurz, Karin, 55, 56
Kwong, Jo, 439

Lacey, Marc, 412
Ladner, Joyce, 41
LaGravenese, Richard, 375
Lague, David, 135

Lahey, Benjamin B., 259, 305
Lakshmi-Narayanan, Geetha, 247
Landale, Nancy, 322
Landler, Mark, 68, 228
Landtman, Gunnar, 199
Landy, Heather, 198, 231
Lane, George, 488
Lang, Robert E., 460
Langewiesche, William, 276
Lanier, Charles S., 165
Lansprey, Susan, 301
Lareau, Annette, 312
Laska, Shirley, 7
Lasswell, Harold, 379
Laszewski, Chuck, 435
Laszlo, Jennifer, 393
Latteier, Pearl, 158
Laumann, Edward, 44, 172, 329
Lawler, Edward J., 124
Lawson, Sandra, 232
Lazarsfeld, Paul, 141, 144, 154
Le Monde, François Galichet, 409
Lear, Norman, 158
Leavell, Hugh R., 419
Ledbetter, Lilly, 283
Lee, Alfred McClung, 390
Lee, Ang, 56
Lee, Chungmei, 364
Lee, Spike, 25, 261
LeFurgy, Jennifer B., 460
Leigh, Mike, 375
Leland, John, 305
Lemmons, Kasi, 161
Lengermann, Patricia Madoo, 12
Lennon, John, 143t, 185
Lenski, Gerhard, 57, 107, 109, 110, 111, 112, 201
Leo, Melissa, 137
Leonhardt, David, 197, 210, 349
Lerach, William S., 198
Levin, Jack, 295
Levin, William C., 295
Levine, Nancy, 314
Levinson, Daniel, 299
Levitt, Peggy, 175, 505, 506
Levitt, Steven D., 38
Levy, Becca R., 304
Lewis-Elligan, Tracy, 427
Lichtblau, Eric, 502
Lieberman, David, 158
Lieberson, Stanley, 38
Light, Donald W., 431
Light, Paul C., 479
Lim, Louisa, 229
Linn, Susan, 84
Lino, Mark, 328
Lio, Shoon, 186
Lipson, Karen, 77
Liptak, Adam, 250, 330
Liska, Allen E., 177
Little, Kenneth, 130
Livernash, Robert, 434
Livingston, Sonia, 154
Llana, Sarah Miller, 236
Loeb, Susanna, 92
Lofland, John, 42, 479, 480
Logan, John R., 256, 260
Lohr, Steve, 305
LoMonaco, Claudine, 236

Long, Sharon K., 426
Lopez, Jennifer, 209
Lorber, Judith, 287
Lowe, Rob, 161
Lucas, Samuel R., 393
Luce, Carolyn Burk, 284
Luckmann, Thomas, 99, 106
Ludwig, Jens, 92
Lukacs, George, 66
Luke, Julian V., 35
Lumpe, Lora, 181, 187
Lund, Kátia, 241
Lundquist, Jennifer Hickes, 328
Luo, Michael, 304, 394
Luster, Tom, 321
Luther, Martin, 348
Luttinger, Nina, 20
Lynas, Mark, 437
Lynn, Barry C., 411

M

MacDorman, Marian, 426
MacFarquhar, Neil, 372
Mack, Raymond, 103
MacLeod, Scott, 156
Madonna, 143t
Magga, Ole Henrik, 61
Maggi, Blairo, 59
Maharishi Mahesh Yogi, 380, 381f
Mahavira, 352
Malarek, Victor, 180
Malcolm, Andrew H., 480
Malcolm X, 101, 257, 347, 380
Malhotra, Neil, 263
Malone, Jean, 357
Malthus, Thomas, 449–450
Mandela, Nelson, 256
Mangum, Garth L., 208
Margalit, Yotam, 263
Mark, Gloria, 132
Markoff, John, 501
Markson, Elizabeth, 307
Marosi, Richard, 236
Marquis, Julie, 433
Marr, Phebe, 86
Marshall, Jim, 205
Martin, Dominique, 57
Martin, Joyce A., 324
Martin, Marvin, 18
Martin, Susan E., 102
Martin, Steve, 328
Martineau, Harriet, 9, 9
Martinez, Elizabeth, 307
Marubbio, M. Elise, 279
Marx, Karl, 10–11, 11, 14, 19, 66, 111, 125, 135, 197, 200, 205, 223, 278, 316, 344, 386, 387, 402, 407, 426, 450, 483, 484, 496
Maryanski, Alexandra R., 495
Mason, Heather, 275
Mason, J. W., 464
Mason, Matt, 494
Mass, Paul B., 426
Massey, Douglas S., 192, 197, 236, 263, 410, 463
Masuda, Takahiko, 15
Masud-Piloto, Felix, 263
Masur, Louis P., 104
Mather, Mark, 246, 465
Matthews, Sarah H., 84

Mazumuder, Bhashkar, 211
McCabe, Donald, 67
McCain, John, 393, 394
McCartney, Paul, 143t
McChesney, Robert W., 158
McCloskey, Michael, 441
McDonald, Kim A., 383, 385
McFalls, Joseph A., Jr., 313, 456
McFarland, Daniel A., 130, 388
McGue, Matt, 79
McGuire, Thomas G., 433
McGurty, Eileen, 435
McIntosh, Peggy, 250, 251
McKay, Henry, 176, 180
McKinlay, John B., 420
McKinlay, Sonja M., 420
McLanahan, Sara, 366
McLuhan, Marshall, 154, 157
McNeil, Donald G., Jr, 221, 431
McPhail, Clark, 476, 477, 478
Mead, George Herbert, 15, 16, 79, 80–81, 83
Mead, Margaret, 277, 278
Mehl, Matthias R., 8
Meirelles, Fernando, 241
Melia, Marilyn Kennedy, 410
Mendez, Jennifer Bickman, 127
Merrill, David A., 484, 485
Mertig, Angela G., 440, 441
Merton, Robert, 12–13, 14, 33, 122, 123, 126, 141, 144, 165, 174, 175, 180
Messner, Michael A., 151, 177, 275
Meston, Cindy M., 34, 36
Meyer, Julie, 302
Meyer, John W., 489
Meyerson, Harold, 411
Michals, Jennifer M., 210
Michels, Robert, 127, 131, 134, 484
Milgram, Stanley, 166, 167, 364
Milk, Harvey, 370
Mill, John Stuart, 278
Miller, Dan E., 481
Miller, David, 142, 477
Miller, Jacqueline W., 169
Miller, Reuben, 392
Miller, Robert F., 175
Millett, Kate, 284
Mills, C. Wright, 5, 10, 144, 386–387
Miner, Horace, 52, 436
Miranda, Jeanne, 433
Mizruchi, Mark S., 387
Moaveni, Azadeh, 272, 273
Moeller, Susan D., 144
Moen, Phyllis, 284
Mogelonsky, Marcia, 322
Mohai, Paul, 435
Mohammad, 338, 340, 348
Mokhtarian, Patricia L., 131
Monaghan, Peter, 39
Monahan, Mary T., 182
Moncarz, Roger J., 412
Montgomery, Marilyn J., 298
Moody, James, 106
Mooney, Margarita, 410
Moore, David W., 341
Moore, Molly, 328
Moore, Michael, 185
Moore, Solomon, 168
Moore, Wilbert E., 87, 199, 200, 365
Morain, Dan, 433
Morris, Aldon, 484

Morris, Bonnie Rothman, 318
Morris, Neisha, 76
Morrison, Denton E., 483
Morse, Arthur D., 265
Morselli, Carlo, 176
Morton, John E., 209, 211
Moses, 338
Mosley, J., 317
Moss, Alfred A., 257
Mott, Lucretia, 284
Muccino, Gabriele, 217
Mueller, G. O., 183
Mufson, Steven, 438
Mumbere, Virginie, 229
Muñoz, José A., 234
Munro, Vanessa, 124
Murdock, George, 54, 314
Murdock, Rupert, 157, 387
Murphy, Dean E., 102
Murphy, Eddie, 117
Murray, Carol, 274
Murray, Jessica, 274
Murray, Velma McBride, 317
Mutran, Elizabeth J., 300

N

NACCRRA, 92, 93
Nader, Ralph, 394
Nain, Zaharom, 157
Nair, Mira, 73
Nakao, Keiko, 201, 202
Nanak, 352
Nash, Manning, 253
Navarro, Mirey, 247, 441
Navarro, Vicente, 149
Neckerman, Kathryn M., 204
Neeson, Liam, 49
Negroponte, Nicholas, 501
Nelson, Emily, 68, 141
Nemoto, Kumiko, 231
Neuman, W. Lawrence, 30
Neuwirth, Robert, 462
Newman, William M., 255
Nguyen, Giang Hoang, 403
NICHD 2007, 92
Nichols, Martha, 225
Niebrugge-Brantley, Jill, 12
Nielsen, Joyce McCarl, 274
Niezen, Ronald, 486
Nislow, Jennifer, 157
Nixon, David, 276
Nixon, Howard L., II, 124
Nixon, Richard M., 143t
Nolan, Patrick, 57, 109, 110, 201
Noonan, Rita K., 484
Nordhaus, William D., 202
Norris, Poppa, 346, 347
NPD Group, 296
Nussbaum, B., 68

O

Obama, Barack, 35, 99, 104, 105, 149,
154f, 156, 247, 248f, 258, 381, 385,
393, 394
Obama, Michelle, 149, 154f
O'Connell, Martin, 327
O'Connor, Anne–Marie, 107
O'Connor, Sandra Day, 280

O'Donnell, Mike, 201
Ogburn, William F., 58, 316, 497, 498, 503
O'Hare, William P., 208, 465
O'Harrow, Robert Jr., 502
Okano, Kaori, 364
Oliver, Melvin L., 204, 211
Omi, Michael, 246
Onassis, Jackie, 143t
Onishi, Norimitso, 231, 326
Orfield, Gary, 364
Ormond, James, 128
Oropesa, R. S., 322
Orum, Anthony M., 383, 483
Osberg, Lars, 204
Ouchi, William, 131

P

Page, Charles, 128
Page, Ellen, 333
Pager, Devah, 249, 250, 251
Palfrey, John, 379
Parish, William, 44
Park, Robert, 141, 459
Parker, Alison, 238
Parsons, Talcott, 13, 277, 420, 496
Passero, Kathy, 62
Passerson, Jean-Claude, 13
Patterson, Thomas E., 389
Pattillo-McCoy, Mary, 76, 84
Patton, Carl V., 462
Pear, Robert, 123
Peirce, Kimberly, 291
Pelham, Brett, 344
Pelosi, Nancy, 384
Pendergrast, Mark, 20
Peng, Liang, 132
Penn, Kal, 73
Pennington, Bill, 275
Percheski, Christine, 366
Perot, Ross, 394
Perry, Juellen, 301
Perry, Tony, 326
Peter, Lawrence J., 126, 127
Petersen, John L., 503
Peterson, Karen S., 327
Petrasova, Alexandra, 214
Phillips, David R., 298
Phillips, E. Barbara, 458
Phillips, Tom, 462
Piaget, Jean, 83, 83
Picasso, Pablo, 56
Picca, Leslie Houts, 261
Pierre, Robert E., 212
Piestewa, Lori, 389
Piliavin, Jane Allyn, 66
Piller, Charles, 62
Pincus, Fred L., 410
Pinderhughes, Dianne, 388
Pinderhughes, Raquel, 439
Pinkerton, James P., 365
Pitt, Brad, 143t
Piven, Frances Fox, 213
Plüss, Caroline, 506
Pogash, Carol, 367
Poitier, Sidney, 143t
Polletta, Francesca, 485
Polonko, Karen A., 131
Poniewozik, James, 149
Pontin, Jason, 441

Popenoe, David, 328
Porter, Jack Nusan, 348
Portes, Alejandro, 506
Poussaint, Alvin F., 84
Prah, Pamela M., 133
Preston, Julia, 236
Priest, Dana, 326
Prins, Harald E. L., 106
Pryor, John H., 66, 338, 370
Puentes, Robert, 464

Q

Quadagno, Jill, 297, 300, 306
Quarantelli, Enrico L., 476, 478, 480
Quillian, Lincoln, 249
Quinney, Richard, 178, 180

R

Rainie, Lee, 151, 390
Rajan, Gita, 506
Ramet, Sabrina, 482
Ramirez, Eddy, 89, 304
RAND, 253, 326
Rand, Michael R. 185
Ravallion, Martin, 227
Rawlinson, Linnie, 142
Raybon, Patricia, 279
Read, Brock, 501
Reagan, Ronald, 133, 143t, 185, 380
Redick, Millicent, 436
Reed, Mark, 149, 172
Reichl, Renee, 263
Reinharz, Shulamit, 41, 42
Reitman, Jason, 161, 333
Reitzes, Donald C., 300
Rembrandt, 53
Rennison, Callie, 185
Reschovsky, Clara, 464
Reverby, Susan M., 427
Revkin, Andrew C., 436
Rheingold, Howard, 474
Richards, Keith, 143t
Rideout, Victoria, 86
Ridgeway, Greg, 253
Riding, Alan, 150
Rifkin, Jeremy, 406, 498
Riggen, Patricia, 25
Riley, Matilda White, 498
Riley, Nancy, 455
Rimer, Sara, 302
Rios, Emily, 309
Risman, Barbara J., 317
Ritzer, George, 20, 57, 120, 128, 405, 408, 502
Robelon, Erik W., 353
Robert, Julia, 49
Roberts, A. David, 296
Roberts, Ed, 487
Roberts, J. Timmons, 438
Roberts, Julia, 143t
Robertson, Roland, 200
Robison, Jennifer, 275, 285
Rodenburg, Eric, 434
Rodgers, Diane M., 484
Rodrigues, Alexandre, 241
Roehling, Patricia, 284
Rogen, Seth, 189
Roosevelt, Franklin D., 380
Rose, Arnold, 253

Rose, Mary, 124
Rose, Peter I., 91
Rosenberg, Douglas H., 401
Rosenberg, Howard, 156
Rosenthal, Elisabeth, 436
Rosenthal, Robert, 367
Ross, John, 467
Rossi, Alice, 322
Rossi, Peter, 41
Rossides, Daniel, 195
Roszak, Theodore, 60
Rourke, Mickey, 95
Roy, Donald, 408
Rubel, Maximilien, 496
Rubin, Alyssa J., 64
Ruebain, David, 489
Rule, James, 483
Rumbaut, Ruben G., 70, 503
Ryan, William, 208
Rymer, Russ, 77

S

Saad, Lydia, 254, 286, 325, 467
Sabol, William J., 168
Sachs, Jeffrey D., 221, 227
Sack, Kevin, 425
Sadeghi, Akbar, 132
Saez, Emmanuel, 204
Sagarin, Edward, 173
Saha, Robin, 435
Said, Edward W., 66
Sale, Kirkpatrick, 441, 498
Salem, Richard, 21
Sampson, Robert J., 176
Samuelson, Paul, 202
Sanchez, Jose, 173
Sanday, Peggy Reeves, 277
Sandefur, Gary, 178
Sanders, Edmund, 86
Sanderson, Warren, 297, 298
Sanger, Margaret, 228
Sanua, Marianne R., 264
Sapir, Edward, 61
Saporito, Bill, 68
Sassen, Saskia, 265
Sawhill, Isabel V., 92, 209, 211
Sawyer, Reid L., 390
Sayer, Liana C., 284, 316
Scarce, Rik, 39
Schachter, Jason, 457
Schaefer, Lenore, 302
Schaefer, Peter, 148
Schaefer, Richard T., 70, 102, 103, 148, 250,
259, 296, 344, 350, 379, 387, 456
Scharnberg, Kirsten, 15, 421
Scherbov, Sergei, 297, 298
Scherer, Ron, 464
Schlesinger, Traci, 178
Schmeeckle, Maria, 325
Schnaiberg, Allan, 434
Schneider, Barbara L., 372
Schneider, Keith, 440
Schulman, Gary, 167
Schumpeter, Joseph, 132
Schur, Edwin M., 170, 180
Schwartz, Howard D., 423
Schwartz, John, 129
Schwartz, Morrie, 294
Schwartz, Pepper, 319

Schwartz, Shalom, 66, 158
Scopes, John T., 353
Scorsese, Martin, 95
Scotch, Richard, 488
Scott, Alan, 485
Scott, Gregory, 14
Scott, Joan Wallach, 281
Scott, Ridley, 189
Scott, W. Richard, 129, 131
Seal, 319
Segerstråle, Ullica, 56
Seidman, Steven, 274
Sekhon, Joti, 486
Selinger, Evan, 409
Sellers, Frances Stead, 506
Selod, Saher Farooq, 281, 349
Semuels, Alana, 108
Sengupta, Manisha, 486
Sengupta, Somini, 277
Sernau, Scott, 57, 211, 379
Seymour, Jane, 255
Shanahan, Suzanne, 298
Shankman, Adam, 137
Shapiro, Joseph, 102
Shapiro, Julianne, 169
Shapiro, Thomas M., 204, 211
Sharma, Shailja, 506
Sharp, Jeff S., 464
Shaw, Clifford, 176, 180
Sheehan, Charles, 301
Shepard, Matthew, 370
Shepherd, Jean, 250, 419
Sheskin, Ira M., 245
Shethy, Shilpa, *64*
Shibutani, Tamotsu, 481
Shin, Hyon B., 69
Shipler, David K., 197
Shortliffe, E. H., 113
Shostak, Arthur B., 390
Shupe, Anson, 36
Shurayi, Muhammad, 320
Sicular, Terry, 405
Siddhartha, 340
Sieber, Renée E., 440
Silver, Brian D., 34
Silver, Ira, 103
Silverman, Rachel Emma, 407
Simmel, Georg, 124
Simmons, Tavia, 327
Simon, Stephanie, 351
Simons, Marlise, 212
Simpson, Jessica, 154
Singh, Leona, 320
Singh, Manmohan, 393
Sipser, Walter, 104
Sisson, Carmen K., 107
Skinner, E. Benjamin, 193
Slack, Jennifer Daryl, 498
Slackman, Michael, 481
Slavin, Barbara, 55
Slavin, Robert E., 69
Slug-lines.com, 15
Smart, Barry, 112
Smeeding, Timothy M., 204, 206
Smelser, Neil, 401, 474, 476
Smith, Aaron, 383, 394
Smith, Adam, 401
Smith, Christian, 90, 336, 342
Smith, Craig, 78, 319
Smith, David A., 458, 461

Smith, Dan, 390
Smith, David M., 329
Smith, Denise, 303
Smith, Kirsten P., 107
Smith, Lauren, 275
Smith, Peter, 194
Smith, Stephen A., 142
Smith, Tom, 90
Smith, Will, 217
Snow, David A., 477
Snyder, Thomas D., 498
Soderbergh, Steven, 49
Somavia, Juan, 205
Song, Kang-ho, 333
Sorokin, Pitirim, 209
Sorrell, Gwendolyn T., 298
Spain, Daphne, 325
Spalter-Roth, Roberta, 22
Speak, Suzanne, 468
Spears, Britney, 57, 143*t*
Spencer, Herbert, 10
Spencer, Nancy, 275
Spielmann, Peter James, 239
Spitzer, Steven, 178
Sprague, Joey, 42
Springsteen, Bruce, 143*t*
Springwood, Charles Fruehling, 187
Stahler-Sholk, Richard, 234
Standing, Guy, 506
Stanley, Alessandra, 147
Stanton, Elizabeth Cady, 284
Stark, Rodney, 336, 348, 350
Starkey, Carson, 169
Starr, Paul, 497
Steele, Jonathan, 238
Stein, Leonard, 107, 429
Stein, Rob, 107
Stenning, Derrick J., 295
Stevens Mitchell L., 365
Stewart, Martha, 182
Stockard, Janice E., 314
Stohr, Oskar, 78, 79, *79*
Stolberg, Sheryl, 410, 441
Stone, Andrea, 326
Stone, Brad, 113
Stoner, Madeleine R., 467
Stout, David, 258
Stovel, Katherine, 106
Strassman, W. Paul, 468
Strauss, Gary, 259, 387
Street, Marc D., 125
Stretesky, Paul B., 435
Stutzman, Frederic, 89
Su, Jessica Houston, 195
Subramaniam, Mangala, 486
Suchan, Trudy A., 257
Suitor, J. Jill, 86
Sullivan, Harry Stack, 81
Sullivan, Kevin, 87
Sullivan, Theresa A., 407
Sum, Andrew M., 265
Sumner, William Graham, 54, 122
Sunstein, Cass, 152
Surk, Barbara, 150
Sutch, Richard, 183, 302, 495
Sutcliffe, Bob, 221
Sutherland, Edwin H., 176, 180, 181, 182
Suzuki, Atsuko, 231
Swank, Hilary, 178, 291, 375
Swatos, William H., Jr., 340

Sweet, Kimberly, 44
Swidler, Ann, 53
Syme, S. Leonard, 424
Szasz, Thomas, 423, 432

T

Tadikonda, Ramya, 412*f*
Taggart, William A., 258
Talbani, Aziz, 320
Talbot, David, 108
Tanielian, Terri, 431
Tannen, Deborah, 279
Tarrow, Sidney, 483, 485
Taub, Richard, 18
Taylor, Dorceta E., 435
Taylor, Elizabeth, 143*t*
Taylor, P. J., 367
Taylor, Verta, 317, 485
Teachman, J. D., 8
Tedeschi, Bob, 57
Teena, Brandon, 178
Telsch, Kathleen, 305
Tessler, Joelie, 114
Thomas, Gordon, 265
Thomas, Pradip N., 157, 158
Thomas, R. Murray, 67
Thomas, Reuben J., 130
Thomas, William I., 99, 247
Thompson, Clive, 132
Thompson, Ginger, 234
Thompson, Grahame, 57
Thompson, Neil B., 436
Thompson, Tommy G., 373
Thompson, Tony, 229
Thomson, E., 317
Threadcraft, Shatema, 279
Thurow, Lester C., 197, 214
Tibbits, Clark, 316
Tibbles, Kevin, 487
Tierney, John, 55
Tierney, Kathleen J., 476, 478
Tierney, William G., 354
Tillipman, Hava, 303
Tilly, Charles, 485, 505, 506
Timberlake, Michael, 458
Timmerman, Kelsey, 400
Tipple, Graham, 468
Tolbert, Kathryn, 84
Tolstoy, Leo, 56
Tomei, Marisa, 95
Tonkinson, Robert, 295
Tönnies, Ferdinand, 107, 109, 110, 112, 462
Toossi, Mitra, 410
Torche, Florencia, 204
Toro, Paul A., 468
Torres, Lourdes, 262
Touraine, Alain, 362
Travolta, John, 350
Traynor, Ian, 439
Treas, Judith, 201, 202
Trotter, Robert T., III, 426
Trow, Martin, 370
Trudeau, Garry, *34*
Trumbull, Mark, 210
Tschuchiya, Motonori, 364
Tsutsui, Kiyoteru, 238
Tuchman, Gaye, 278
Tucker, Robert C., 125
Tumin, Melvin M., 200

Ture, Kwame, 257
Turek, Melanie, 131
Turley , Ruth N. López, 322
Turner, Bryan S., 112
Turner, Margery Austin, 213
Turner, Ralph, 476, 481
Twenge, Jean M., 168

U

Ullmann, Edward, 460
Unnikrashnan, Anney, 412
Upham, Misty, 137
Urbina, Ian, 156

V

Vaidhyanathan, Siva, 362, 502
Van Cleve, Nicole Martorano, 146
van den Berghe, Pierre, 55
Van Gennep, Arnold, 89
Van Pelt, Elizabeth Cohen, 419, 429
Van Vooren, Nicole, 22
Van Vucht Tijssen, Lieteke, 112
Vang, Bee, 309
Vargas, Jose Antonio, 385
Vasagar, Jeeran, 386
Vaughan, Diane, 62, 129
Veblen, Thorstein, 199, 497
Venkatesh, Sudhir Alladi, 123, 164, 175, 403
Ventura, Stephanie J., 324
Vernon, Glenn, 351
Vezzani, Stephanie, 184
Vigdor, Jacob L., 263
Villarreal, Andrés, 179
Villeneuve, Nart, 146, 380
Viramontes, Helena Maria, 71
Visser, Jelle, 133

W

Wachtendorf, Tricia, 479
Waelde, L. C., 431
Wagley, Charles, 245, 295
Waite, Linda, 151
Waitzkin, Howard, 426
Walder, Andrew G., 403
Waldinger, Roger, 263, 505
Waldman, Amy, 413
Walesa, Lech, 483
Walker, Marcus, 214
Wallace, Ruth A., 496
Wallerstein, Immanuel, 223, 224, 227, 280, 461, 501
Wallis, Claudia, 369
Wang, Amy, 407
Wang, Meiyan, 406
Warren, David, 464
Washington, Denzel, 143*t*, 189, 269
Wattenberg, Martin P., 378, 385
Weber, Max, 10, *11*, 29, 40, 125, 126, 127, 131, 198, 205, 342, 348, 365, 368, 379, 484
Wechsler, Henry, 169
Weden, Margaret, 426
Weier, Mary Hayes, 413
Weil, Nancy, 114
Weinberg, Daniel H., 283
Weinstein, Henry, 252
Weinstein, Michael A., 152
Weisbrot, Mark, 228

Weitz, Rose, 420
Wells, H. G., 480
Wells-Barnett, Ida, 12, 14, *15*, 19, 278
Wentling, Tre, 178
Wentz, Laurel, 148
West, Candace, 273, 279
West, Heather, 168
West, Mark D., 431
Westergaard-Nielsen, Niels, 205
Western, Bruce, 250
Westmoreland, Wash, 309
White, David Manning, 143
Whitehead, Barbara Dafoe, 328
Whitlock, Craig, 156, 487
Whorf, Benjamin Lee, 61
Whyte, William F., 35, 36
Whyte, William H., Jr., 124
Wickman, Peter M., 170
Wilford, John Noble, 110
Wilgoren, Jodi, 354
Wilkes, Rima, 256
Wilkinson, Alec, 59
Williams, Carol J., 318
Williams, Christine L., 283
Williams, David R., 257
Williams, Kristine N., 305

Williams, Michelle, 117
Williams, Richard, 427
Williams, Robin (comedian), 304
Williams, Robin (sociologist), 65, 363
Williams, Wendy M., 84
Wills, Jeremiah B., 317
Wilson, Edward O., 55, 56
Wilson, John, 483
Wilson, William Julius, 76, 123, 207, 211, 254, 321, 342, 464
Wilson-Dorsett, Kelsie, 451
Winant, Howard, 246, 249, 278
Wines, Michael, 330
Wing, Philip S., 431
Winickoff, Jonathan P., 177
Winkler, Adam, 186
Winseck, Dwayne, 158
Winseman, Albert L., 338
Winslet, Kate, 217
Winslow, Robert W., 185
Winter, J. Allen, 264
Wirth, Louis, 18, 458
Wise, J. Macgregor, 498
Witte, Griff, 197
Witts, Max Morgan, 265
Wokutch, Richard F., 408

Wolf, Alison, 496
Wolf, Naomi, 171
Wolf, Richard, 214
Wolff, Edward, 204
Wollstonecraft, Mary, 278
Wolraich, M., 168
Wong, Morrisson G., 260
Wood, Julia T., 151
Woods, Tiger, 247
Word, David L., 38
Workman, Thomas A., 362
Worth, Robert F., 151
Wray, Matt, 9
Wright, Charles R., 141
Wright, Eric R., 177
Wright, Erik Olin, 200, 208

Y

Yamagata, Hisashi, 250
Yang, Rebecca, 208, 387
Yap, Kioe Sheng, 462
Yardley, Jim, 307, 455
Yeltsin, Boris, 483
Yufe, Jack, 78, 79, *79*
Yunus, Muhammad, 409, 409*f*

Z

Zaidi, Arishia U., 320
Zang, Xiaowei, 406
Zapata, Ray, 366
Zarembo, Alan, 389
Zedlewski, Sheila R., 92, 204, 296
Zedong, Mao, 361
Zeitzen, Miriam Koktvedgaard, 314
Zellner, William W., 60, 344, 350
Zernike, Kate, 67
Zhang, Sheldon X., 185
Zhang, Ziyi, 150
Zi, Jui-Chung Allen, 327
Zia, Helen, 244, 255
Zimbardo, Philip, 98, 99, 100, 101, 167, 176, 389
Zimmerman, Ann, 68
Zimmerman, Don H., 273, 279
Zimmerman, Seth, 133, 204, 263
Zittrain, Jonathan, 379
Zola, Irving K., 420
Zontini, Elisabetta, 506
Zweigenhaft, Richard L., 388
Zwick, Edward, 241
Zywica, Jolene, 89

subject index

Page numbers in *italics* indicate photos or cartoons. Page numbers followed by an *f* indicate figures; page numbers followed by a *t* indicate tables.

A

AARP (Association for the Advancement of Retired Persons), 130*f*, 297, 304–305, 308
Aboriginal people, 104, 255, 259
abortion, 286–288, 286*f*, 287*f*
absolute poverty, 205, 206, 215
Abu Ghraib prison, 98–99, 167, 389, 390
abuse, of Internet, 113, 115, 142
academic subculture, 370–371
Academic Universe News, 46
acceptance of norms, 64
Accra, Ghana, 446, 447
ace-ace encounters, 82
ace-bombers encounters, 82
achieved statuses, 100–101, 100*f*, 114, 115, 193, 214, 215
action stage (role exit), 103
activism, on Internet, 392–393
activity theory, 296–297, 307, 308
acupuncture, 430
ADA (Americans with Disabilities Act), 131, 488–489, 490
adaptation theory, of deviance, 12, 174–175, 174*t*, 187, 188
ADHD (attention-deficit/hyperactivity disorder), 372
Adidas, 145*f*
ADL (Anti-Defamation League), 264
Adlers, Hawai'i and, 29
adoptions, 77–78, 322–324, 323*f*, 331
adulthood, 90, 90*t*
advertisements
    commercials and, 39, 86, 143, 146, 148
    mass media and, 143–144, 155
    women and, 37
affection, 64, 316
affirmative action, 252, 267, 268, 409, 410, 410*f*, 413, 414
Afghanistan
    electronically controlled prosthetic devices and, 503
    human rights violations in, 239
    Human Terrain System and, 36, 36, 40
    human trafficking and, 238*t*
    infant mortality rates in, 421*f*
    military marriages and, 8
    Oscar Mayer and, 480
    as periphery nation, 223, 223*f*
    population structure of, 454*f*
    poverty and, 226*f*
    refugees from, 456*f*
Africa. *See also* South Africa
    CO₂ emissions in, 438*f*
    digital divide and, 147–148
    global economy and, 461
    globalization and, 224
    HIV/AIDS cases in, 453*f*
    periphery nations of, 223, 223*f*

prostitution and, 279
    sub-Saharan, 228, 425, 503
    West, child marriage and, 55, 56*f*
Africa Progress Panel, 228
African Americans, 256–258. *See also* civil rights movement; Obama, Barack
    affirmative action and, 252, 267, 268, 409, 410, 413, 414
    Black power and, 257, 267, 268
    class system and, 211
    differential justice and, 178
    double consciousness and, 12, 23
    gangs and, 84
    The Great Debaters and, 269
    in Groveland, 76
    health insurance and, 425*f*
    income and, 250*f*
    Korean Americans, racial friction and, 261
    lynch mobs and, 14, 257, 474
    medical apartheid and, 427
    The Negro Church and, 11
    The Philadelphia Negro and, 11
    poverty and, 207*t*
    as racial group, 245*t*
    racial profiling of, 253
    segregation and, 255–256, 267, 268
    slavery and, 193, 214, 215, 423
    television and, 149
    in U.S., 246*f*, 256–258, 257*f*
"African Panamanians," 246
age
    ageism and, 303–304, 308
    matrix of domination and, 278, 279*f*, 288, 289
age stratification, 292–302
    social policy and, 306–307
    in U.S., 302–306
aging. *See also* elderly
    in Japan, 299
    labeling theory and, 297
    society and, 295
    sociological perspectives on, 295–298, 298*t*
    stratification and, 292–302
    Tuesdays with Morrie and, 294
    worldwide, 298, 298*f*
agrarian societies, 110, 111*t*, 115
Agriculture, Department of, 465
AIDS. *See* HIV/AIDS
air pollution, 436–437
ala kachuu, 319
Alabama
    baby names study and, 38
    Katrina disaster area and, 6–7, 19, 208, 209*f*, 479
    School for the Deaf, 62*f*
    Tuskegee syphilis experiment and, 427
Alaska
    female governor in, 279
    Valdez disaster and, 40, 40
Alaskan Natives
    as racial group, 245*t*
    in U.S., 257*f*
Albania, 237

alcohol abuse
    binge drinking and, 164, 169
    drinking rape victim and, 124
    drunk driving and, 180
    MADD and, 180
    recovering alcoholic and, 103, 172
    SADD and, 180, 189
    teenage, 64
Algeria
    French colonialism and, 223
    human trafficking and, 238*t*
alienation
    defined, 413, 414
    division of labor and, 125–126, 127*t*, 135
    Marx's view on, 407–408
    work and, 125, 135, 406–409, 413, 414
Allianz, 145*f*
AltaVista, 145
alternative medicine, 430–431, 431*f*
Alzheimer's Association, 428
Alzheimer's disease, 306, 427, 428, 442
AMA. *See* American Medical Association
amalgamation, 255, 267, 268
Amazon River, 59
Amazon.com, 57, 501
Amendments
    Eighteenth Amendment, 170
    First Amendment, 172*f*, 353
    Fourth Amendment, 113, 114, 502
    Hyde Amendment, 287
    Nineteenth Amendment, 284
    Second Amendment, 186
    Twenty-Sixth Amendment, 385
America
    graying of, 302–303
    Nacirema people, 52, 436
America Online (AOL), 113, 157
American Academy of Cosmetic Surgery, 172
American Academy of Pediatrics, 168
American Apartheid (Massey & Denton), 256, 463
American Association of Aardvark Aficionados, 129
American Community Survey, 31, 69*f*
American Cultures Center, 503
American dream, 244
American Express, 145*f*
American Hospital Association, 306
American Indians. *See* Native Americans
American Jewish Congress, 129
American Lung Association, 37, 437
American Medical Association (AMA), 306, 369, 427, 428, 430, 497
American Psychiatric Association (APA), 177, 423
American Psychological Association, 177
American Sign Language, 62*f*
American Sociological Association (ASA), 22
    citations/references format and, 46–47
    Code of Ethics, 38–39
    sections of, 6, 6*t*
    Web site, 47
American Sociological Society, 12

Americans with Disabilities Act (ADA), 131, 488–489, 490
Amish people, 4, 83, 348, 498
Amnesty International, 239, 391
Amsterdam, Schiphol airport in, 170*f*
analysis/collection of data (scientific method step), 30–33
ancestral land, Philippines and, 232–233
Andersonville, 256
Angola, 222*f*
animism, 339*f*
anomie, 23, 174, 188
anomie theory of deviance, 174–175, 187, 188
anonymity
    dalit and, 14, 194
    information sources and, 39, 42
    social networking Web sites and, 113, 172
    terrorism and, 392
anorexia nervosa, 172, 419, 487
anthrax, 423
anticipatory socialization, 90–91, 94
Anti-Defamation League (ADL), 264
anti-Semitism, 263–264
Anti-Slavery Union, 247
AOL (America Online), 113, 157
APA. *See* American Psychiatric Association
Apache woman, mudding ceremony and, 90
apartheid, 256, 267, 268, 427, 463
apathy, 382–384
Apple Computer, 132, 212*f*
applied sociology, 16, 18, 23
approaches. *See* sociological perspectives
Arab Americans, 261–262. *See also* Islam; Muslim Americans
    Muslims and, 261
    racial profiling of, 177, 253, 254
    stereotyping of, 170
Al-Arabiya, 156
Argentina
    Buenos Aires, 496*f*
    women legislators in, 386*f*
argot, 58, 59, 71, 72
Arizona
    borderlands and, 233, 235–237, 236*f*, 239, 240, 266
    female governor in, 279
    Mexican immigrant deaths and, 233
Arkansas
    elderly in, 302
    Jonesboro, killing spree in, 369
    neighborhood economic development and, 18
    Wal-Mart and, 68
Armenia
    genocide, Turkey and, 254
    human trafficking and, 238*t*
arms transfers, 187
arranged marriages, 320
"artificial mothers," 78
Arunta people, 10
ASA. *See* American Sociological Association
www.asanet.org, 47
ascribed statuses, 100–101, 114, 193, 214, 215. *See also* aging; gender; race

Asia. *See also* South Asia; Southeast Asia
coffee drinkers in, 56, 57
global economy and, 461
periphery nations of, 223, 223*f*
Asian American Dreams (Zia), 244
Asian American Journalists Association, 147
Asian Americans, 258–261. *See also specific*
Asian American subgroups
health insurance and, 425*f*
income and, 250*f*
poverty and, 207*t*
as racial group, 245*t*
television and, 149
in U.S., 246*f*, 257*f*
Asian Indians
as racial group, 245*t*
in U.S., 258*f*
assemblies, periodic/nonperiodic, 477, 490
assembling perspective, 477, 489, 490
assimilation, 255, 267, 268
assisted marriages, 320
assisted suicide, 306–307, 308
association, differential, 176, 187, 188
Association for Applied Clinical Sociology, 18
Association for the Advancement of Retired
Persons. *See* AARP
Association of American Medical
Colleges, 430
associations. *See also* organizations
voluntary, 129–130, 135, 136
assumptions, culture and, 53–54
asylum seekers. *See* refugees
Atlantic Monthly, 46
attention-deficit/hyperactivity disorder
(ADHD), 372
Audi, 145*f*
audience, mass media and, 152–154
Australia
Aboriginal people of, 104, 255, 259
Arunta people in, 10
child care costs in, 93*f*
CO_2 emissions in, 438*f*
crime and, 187
foreign students and, 364*f*
higher education completion rates
in, 361*f*
human trafficking and, 238*t*
marriage ages in, 318*f*
Perth, 92*f*
poverty rate in, 206*f*
thumbs-up sign in, 62
union membership in, 133*f*
Austria
higher education completion rates
in, 361*f*
McDonald's and, 57
authority
charismatic, 380–381, 395
defined, 379, 395
hierarchy, bureaucracy and, 126, 127*t*
patterns, in families, 315
power and, 379
rational-legal, 379–380, 395
traditional, 379, 395
types of, 379–381
avatars, 106, 108, 113, 115, 351
average. *See* mean
Aviation and Transportation Security
Act, 252
Avon Corporation, 212*f*
AXA, 145*f*

Azerbaijan
filtering information and, 146*f*
human trafficking and, 238*t*

B

Baath Socialist Party, 86
baby boom, 454–455
baby names study, 38, 38*f*
www.babynamewizard.com, 38
babysitting. *See* child care
bad blood, 173
Baghdad, Iraq War and, 86, 277
Bahamas, 451
Bahrain
human trafficking and, 238*t*
Al Jazeera and, 156
bailout legislation, 133, 213, 402. *See also*
recession
Baja California, 236*f*
Bali cockfights, 15
Bally's Fitness, 120
Bangalore, India, 84*f*
Bangladesh
child marriage in, 56*f*
Grameen Bank and, 409
income distribution in, 232*f*
NRI and, 229, 229*t*
poverty and, 226*f*
Toyota Motor *v.*, 225*t*
bankruptcy, 183*t*, 402, 411
Baptists, 45, 342, 347
baseball, 17, 171, 176, 312, 477
basic sociology, 18, 23
basketball, 15, 41, 76, 103, 312, 322, 349,
475–476
BBC News, 20, 155
BCRA (Bipartisan Campaign Reform Act),
393, 394
Beardstown, Illinois, 465*f*
Beatles, Maharishi and, 381
beauty
hózhóni, 418
myth, 171, 281
Beijing, Olympics and, 436
Belarus, 146*f*, 380*f*
Belgium
euthanasia and, 307
GNI for, 222*f*
same-sex marriages and, 330
Wal-Mart *v.*, 225*t*
beliefs, religious, 345, 347*t*, 355
believer's church, 348
Belize, 439*f*
Bell v. Maryland, 263
Beloved Wives Day, 99
Benin, 56, 222
bento box, 56
Berkeley Center for Independent
Living, 487
Berkeley Wellness Letter, 322
Berlitz Method, 61*f*
BET (Black Entertainment Television), 149
Betsileo people, 313
Bhutan, television and, 157, 157*f*
biases, research and, 41
bilateral descent, 315
bilingualism
education and, 67, 69–71, 69*f*
Israeli child care center and, 91
Billboard magazine, 37

bin Laden, Osama, 126, 156
binge drinking, 164, 169. *See also* alcohol
abuse
biology
biological/genetic factors *v.* social
interactions, 55–56, 72
sociobiology and, 55–56, 71, 72, 173
biotechnology, 502–504
bioterrorism, 423
Bipartisan Campaign Reform Act (BCRA),
393, 394
birthrate, 450, 468, 469
bisexuals, 178
Black Americans. *See* African Americans
Black Entertainment Television
(BET), 149
Black Picket Fences (Pattillo-McCoy), 76
Black power, 257, 267, 268
Blackberry, 145*f*
"blame the victims," 176, 208, 249
BMW, 145*f*
B'nai B'rith, 264
body painting. *See* tattooing
"Body Ritual among the Nacirema" (Miner),
52, 436
Bolivia
life expectancy in, 451*f*
NRI and, 229
as periphery nation, 223, 223*f*
Bombay. *See* Mumbai
bomber-bomber encounters, 82
boomerang generation, 322
borderlands, 233, 235–237, 236f, 239,
240, 266
borderless world, 57. *See also* global
community
borders, businesses without, 57
Borders, Doctors Without, 239, 391
Borders bookstore, 305
born-again experience, 347
Boroco people, 59
Bosnia-Herzegovina
6 billionth person and, 452
ethnic cleansing in, 237, 255
Muslim Americans and, 349
terrorism and, 391*f*
Boston. *See also* Massachusetts
ageism and, 305
Boston Pops orchestra, 125, 136
The Departed and, 95
gutted factory in, 411*f*
New Hampshire community and, 112
Street Corner Society, and, 35–36, 48
Boston Pops orchestra, 125
Boston University, 169
Botswana, 102, 451*f*
The Bottom Billion (Collier), 220
boundary-maintenance function, of
deviance, 173
bourgeoisie, 197, 214, 215
BP (British Petroleum), 145*f*, 225*t*
Brady Handgun Violence Prevention Act,
185–186
brain drain, 421, 442
brand casting, 143, 144*f*, 145*f*, 161
Brazil
CO_2 emissions in, 438*f*
cultural survival in, 59
economy of, 405*f*
human trafficking and, 238*t*
income distribution in, 232*f*

poverty and, 226*f*
Wal-Mart and, 68
Yanomami people of, 313
breast cancer, 235
bribery/corruption, 183*t*
Britain. *See* Great Britain
British Elastic Rope Sports Association, 130
British Petroleum (BP), 145*f*, 225*t*
Brooklyn, 25, 104*f*
Brown University, women's rugby team of,
118, 119
Brown v. Board of Education, 363
Buddhism, 64, 338, 339*f*, 340, 340*t*
buddy lists, 113
Buenos Aires, 496*f*
Bulgaria, 222*f*
bulimia, 487
bullfighting, 55
bungee-jumping, 130
Burakumin, 231
Burberry, 273
Bureau of Indian Affairs, 258
Bureau of Justice Statistics, 184, 186
Bureau of Labor Statistics, 87, 134, 203, 296,
299, 304, 412
bureaucracies, 125–129, 135. *See also*
McDonald's
bureaucratization
defined, 127, 135
of schools, 368–369
as way of life, 128
Burger King, 152, 406
Burkina Faso, 56, 222
Burma
human trafficking and, 238*t*
Shweyanppay Monastery in, *334, 335*
Burundi
Congo's national parks and, 402
NRI and, 229, 229*t*
business world
"businesses without borders," 57
net neutrality and, 114
sociology and, 22

C

Cabbage Patch Day, 99
cage fight, 173*f*
Calcutta, 73
California. *See also* Los Angeles; San
Francisco
bilingualism and, 70, 70*f*, 71
borderlands and, 233, 235–237, 236*f*,
239, 240, 266
faith-based organizations and, 343
Filipino Americans in, 70*f*
Genie (isolation case) in, 77–78, 78*f*
Google Corporation in, *411*
houseworkers, tasks of, 127
Santa Ana, Hispanics in, 262
"silver surfers" in, *292, 293*
call center subculture, India and,
59–60, 59*f*
Cambodia
GNI for, 222*f*
human trafficking and, 238*t*
NRI and, 229
symbols and, 175
campaign financing, 393–394
Campaign Legal Center, 393
campus crime, 181

Canada
brands in, 145f
child care costs in, 93f
CO₂ emissions in, 438f
as core nation, 223, 223f
economy of, 405f
foreign aid per capita in, 227f
foreign students and, 364f
G8 conference and, 228, 441, *472, 473*
gender inequality in, 282f
higher education completion
rates in, 361f
human trafficking and, 238t
income distribution in, 232f
infant mortality rates in, 421f
life expectancy in, 451f
marriage ages in, 318f
media penetration in, 155f
NRI and, 229
nuclear power generation and, 58f
poverty rate in, 206f
Quebec, bilingualism and, 70
religious participation in, 347f
sexual behavior research, 44f
Toronto, protesters/police in, *162, 163*
union membership in, 133f
women legislators in, 386f
cancer, 61, 235, 285, 301
Canon, 145f
capital
cultural, 13, 23, 60–61
social, 11, 23
capitalism
characteristics of, 401–402, 403t.
See also globalization
in China, 404–406
defined, 197, 214, 215, 401, 413, 414
The Pirates Dilemma and, 494
car thefts, 184t, 185
carbon dioxide (CO₂) emissions, 438f
careers. *See also* jobs; occupations; workplace
occupational prestige, 201–202, 202t
reasons for leaving, 284f
in sociology, 21–22, 22f
Caribbean, 20, 192, 221, 256, 503, 505
Cartier, 145f
Casa del Mar Hotel, 234f
casinos, Native American, 258
caste system, 193–195, 209, 214, 215
Catalyst, 282
Catholics, 45, 255, 341, 342, 343, 344, 347,
348, 356
Cato Institute, 394
Cats on Stamps Study Group, 129–130
causal logic, 30, 32f, 47
CBS News, 167, 480
CBS Records, 157
ceiling, glass, 249, 267, 268, 282, 289
celibacy, 103. *See also* Shakers
cell phones. *See* mobile phones
censorship, in global community, 501–502
census, 450, 468, 469
Census Bureau, 22, 46
Center for Academic Integrity, 67
Center for American Women and Politics, 280
Centers for Disease Control and Prevention,
369, 422, 423, 425, 427
...al Americans
...emissions in, 438f
...ine challenges and, 419t
..., 462–463

Central Europe, 214
centralization/concentration, of mass media,
157–158, 159
Chad
boiling water in, 499f
development agency and, 220
GNI for, 222f
marriage rates in, 56f
NRI and, 229, 229t
as periphery nation, 222f, 223, 223f
Challenger space shuttle, 129
chances, life, 208–209, 214, 215
Chanel, 145f
change. *See* social change
charismatic authority, 380–381, 395
Charisse, 76
charms, 52
chat rooms, Internet, 42, 58, 86, 142, 172,
272, 316
chatting, women and, 8, 113
cheating, 65–66, 67
chess clubs, 121
Chevron, Peru *v.*, 222t
Chiapas, 235f
Chicago. *See also* Illinois
Casablanca in, *138, 139*
gang study in, 123, 164
Groveland in, 76
homelessness in, 41
Hull House in, 12
law firm, word processors at, 105
McDonald's corporation in, 57
neighborhood economic development
and, 18
Chicago Coalition for the Homeless, 41
Chicago Tribune, 466
Chihuahua, 236f
child care (throughout world), 91–93, 93f
Child Care Law Center, 85
child marriage, 55, 56f
childbirth, 228, 287
childless couples, 463
child-rearing patterns, 322–325
children. *See also* socialization
child pornography and, 178
divorce's impact on, 327
female infanticide and, 232
imitation and, 80, 81
isolation of, 77–78, 78f
marriage without, 328
Romanian orphanages and, 77–78
socialization of, 322–325
Chile
abortion and, 286
foreign-born adoptions and, 323f
GNI for, 222f
terrorism and, 391f
China
capitalism in, 404–406
CO₂ emissions in, 438f
dog meat in, 60
economy of, 405f
elderly and, 100
entrepreneurship and, 405, 406, 413
foreign students and, 364f
foreign-born adoptions and, 323f
Google and, 145, 147, 406
Great Firewall of, 406
Great Leap Forward and, 361
HIV/AIDS prevention and, 44
human trafficking and, 238t

infant mortality rates in, 421f
lead-based paint/toys and, 224f
life expectancy in, 451f
marriage ages in, 318f
media penetration in, 155f
Microsoft and, 406
population policy in, 455
poverty and, 226f
as semiperiphery nation, 223, 223f
Shanghai, 361, 455
social support and, 455
Starbucks in, 72
Tiananmen Square and, 406
Tibet and, 70
Up the Yangtze and, 509
/Vietnam, expulsion and, 254–255
Wal-Mart and, 68, 135
women legislators in, 386f
Chinatown district, 260
Chinese Americans, 260
as racial group, 245t
refugees and, 267
in U.S., 258f
Chinese Communist Party, 413
Chinese Exclusion Act, 260
Chinese Ministry of Health, 44
"Christian Jewels," 357
Christian Scientists, 344, 348
Christianity, 66, 338, 339f, 340, 340t
Chronic Poverty Research Centre, 226
Church of England, 361
Church of Scientology, 350, 355
CIA/FBI division of labor, 126
cigarette smoking. *See* smoking
Cisco systems, 145f
citations/references (research reports),
46–47
cities, 457–458, 468, 469. *See also*
urbanization
central, 462–463
industrial, 457, 458t, 468, 469
issues in, 463–464, 468
postindustrial, 458, 458t, 468, 469
preindustrial, 457, 458t, 468, 469
suburbs and, 464, 468, 469
types of people in, 463
urban dwellers and, 463
Citigroup, 145f
Citizens Commission on Homelessness, 468
City College tragedy, basketball and, 475–476
Civic Ventures, 297
civil disobedience, 257
Civil Liberties Act, 260
Civil Rights Act, 252, 488, 489
civil rights movement, 100, 161, 211, 257,
258, 409, 488
Civil War, 193, 195, 257, 269
"clash of civilizations," 66
class consciousness, 197, 214, 215
classes (social classes/class system),
195–197, 214, 215. *See also* statuses
bourgeoisie, 197, 214, 215
family life and, 319–321
financial aid and, 210
lower, 196, 199
Marx and, 197–198, 200
measuring, 201–202
middle, 196–197
multidimensional model of, 202
proletariat, 197, 214, 215
social epidemiology and, 424–426

stratification by, 201–202
underclass, 207–208, 214, 215
upper, 196
in U.S., 195–197
Weber and, 198
working, 197
classical theory of formal organizations, 127,
135, 136
cleansing, ethnic, 237, 255
Clear Channel Communications, 157
Clery Act, 181
clinical sociology, 18, 23
cliques, 122, 357, 370, 382
clogs, 112
cloning, 352, 498, 502, 503
closed system, 209, 214, 215
CMHC (Community Mental Health
Centers Act), 432
CNN network, 148, 156, 157, 158, 481
CO₂ (carbon dioxide) emissions, 438f
Coahuila, 236f
coal miners, 198f
coalitions, 123, 135, 136
Coca-Cola, 145f, 155, 230
cocaine, 175, 249, 253
cockfights, Bali, 5
code of ethics, 38, 47
Code of Ethics (ASA), 38–39
Coeur d'Alene Indians, 73
coffee
Asian coffee drinkers and, 56, 57
Elvis's café and, 272
globalization and, 20
Guatemala and, 225
Starbucks and, 20, 56, 72, 128, 225
coffins, in Ghana, 302f
cognitive theory of development, 83,
83t, 94
cohabitation, 46, 327–328
Cold War era, 61, 220
collapse
of Hussein regime, 85–86, 277, 478
of Soviet Union, 498, 499
of World Trade Center (case study),
478–479
collection/analysis of data (scientific
method step), 30–33
collective behavior, 474–490, 482t
collective consciousness
elderly and, 304–306
feminism and, 284–285
mechanical solidarity and, 107–109, 115
collective decision making, 131
colleges. *See also* education; students; *specific*
colleges; specific schools
binge drinking, 164, 169
cheating at, 65–66, 67
crime at, 181
educational level/income relationship
(study), 30, 31, 31f, 32, *32*, 32f,
33, 33f
financial aid and, 85, 209, 210, 249, 275
first-year students, values of, 65, 66f
fraternities, 10, 121, 169, 252
gender norm violations (experiment),
274t
Google and, 362
higher education completion rates
(in industrial nations), 361f
impression management in, 82
race/ethnicity percentages in, 371f

sociology careers and, 21–22, 22*f*
sororities, 42, 101, 121, 169, 252, 263
student subcultures in, 370–371
students, environmental issues and, 65, 66*f*
virtual campus tours, 91
collegiate subculture, 370–371
Colombia
foreign-born adoptions and, 323*f*
human trafficking and, 238*t*
wealth and, 230
colonialism, 223–224, 239, 240
color
"color line" and, 247
color-blind racism, 248–249, 267, 268, 410, 414
Mexico and, 234
Colorado
Columbine High School killings in, 122, 147, 185, 369
University of Colorado in, 274
coltan, 402, 402*f*
Columbia Pictures, 157
Columbia Records, 157
Columbia space shuttle, 129
Columbia University, 12, 164
Columbine High School killings, 122, 147, 185, 369
commercials, 39, 86, 143, 146, 148. *See also* advertisements
Commission on Civil Rights, 252, 281
Common Cause, 394
common sense, sociology *v.*, 7–8, 23
Commonwealth Fund, 426
Communicare, 92*f*
communication. *See also* e-mail; language; nonverbal communication; social networking Web sites
electronic, 132
globalization of social movements and, 485–486
Internet and, 113, 156
nonverbal, 15, 23, 62
communications technology. *See also* Internet; mass media; mobile phones; social networking Web sites; television
digital divide and, 113, 147–148, 159, 208–209, 214, 215
distribution of power and, 388
globalization and, 19, 57, 87, 224
user categories for, 142*t*
voting and, 378
communism, 403, 403*t*, 413, 414
Communist League, 11
The Communist Manifesto (Marx), 11, 19, 125
communities, 448–449. *See also* cities; global community
changing, 457–458
defined, 448–449, 468, 469
neighborhood economic development and, 18
types of, 462–464
Community Mental Health Centers Act (CMHC), 432
companionship, families and, 316
compensation, women and, 283
complementary/alternative medicine, 430–431, 431*f*
compulsive gambler, 9, 170, 172, 180
computer crime, 182, 183*t*

computer technology, 501. *See also* Internet; technology
computerized library systems, 46
crime and, 182
NRI and, 229, 229*t*
OLPC campaign and, 501
research and, 42–43
workplace and, 131
XO computers and, 501
concentration/centralization, of mass media, 157–158, 159
concentric-zone theory, 459, 460*f*, 468, 469
concierge doctors, 192
conclusions (scientific method step), 33
concrete operational stage, 83
Coney Island, mobile voter registration station at, 376, 377
confidentiality, 39–40
conflict perspective, 14–15, 16, 23. *See also* feminist perspective; sociological perspectives
conformity, 187
deviance *v.*, 164
Milgram experiments and, 166–168
obedience and, 166–168, 187
Confucianism, 338, 339
congestion zones, 463*f*
Congo. *See* Democratic Republic of the Congo
Congress, rational-legal authority and, 379
connected but hassled (communications technology), 142*t*
Connecticut
female governor in, 279
Milgram experiments and, 166–168
connectors (communications technology), 142*t*
ConocoPhillips, Finland *v.*, 225*t*
consciousness. *See also* collective consciousness; self
class consciousness, 197, 214, 215
double consciousness, 12, 23
false consciousness, 198, 214, 215, 285, 484, 490
conspicuous consumption, 199, 201, 216, 272, 383
conspicuous leisure, 199, 201
Constitution (United States). *See also* Amendments
census and, 450
Defense of Marriage Act and, 330
gun ownership and, 186
rational-legal authority and, 379
school prayer and, 353
voting and, 385
constructing reality, dominant ideology and, 148
consumption, conspicuous, 199, 201, 216, 272, 383
contact hypothesis, 254, 267, 268
content analysis, 37, 47
Contexts journal, 233
control. *See* social control
control group, 36, 47
control theory, 170, 188. *See also* social control
control variables, 33, 47
convenience samples, 32
convergence, cultural, 141, 159
copyright infringement, 67, 173
core culture, 67

core nations, 223, 223*f*
Cornell University, 86
corporate crime, 182
corporate executives, salaries and, 198
Corporate Policy Institute, 149
corporate welfare, 213, 215
corporations
Fortune 500, 18, 282, 387
multinational, 224–227, 239, 240
correlation, 30, 47
correspondence principle, 365–366, 374
corruption/bribery, 183*t*
cosmetic surgery, 172
cosmopolites, 463
Costa Rica, 222*f*
Costco stores, 465
Council on Scientific Affairs, 426
countercultures, 60, 60, 71, 72. *See also* terrorism
countries. *See* nations; *specific countries*
Court. *See* Supreme Court
courtship, 318–319
cows, India and, 13, 13, 14, 55
crack cocaine, 175, 249, 253
crazes, 480, 482*t*, 490
"crazy runaways," 423
creationism, 345, 353, 354, 355
credentialism, 364–365, 374
crime(s), 179–185. *See also* crime rates; deviance; gangs
campus, 181
college, 181
computer, 182, 183*t*
corporate, 182
defined, 179, 187, 188
hate, 248, 249*f*, 267, 268
human trafficking, 238*t*
index, 180, 188
innovation and, 12, 174, 175
intellectual property, 183*t*
international, 185
national crime rates, 184*t*
networking of, 183*t*
organized, 181, 187, 188
professional, 180–181, 187, 188
in rural Mexico, 179
sociological perspectives on, 173–179, 180*t*
statistics, limitations of, 183–185
technology and, 182
transnational, 181, 182–183, 183*t*, 187, 188
types of, 180–183
victimless, 178, 180, 187, 188
white-collar, 179, 182, 183, 189
women and, 179
crime rates, 184*t*, 185
crime waves, 173
criollos, 234
crisis, midlife, 298, 307, 308
Croatia, 222, 237
cross-cultural integration, 111*t*
cross-cultural perspective, on gender, 276–277
cross-tabulation, 45, 47
crowds, 477–478, 482*t*, 489, 490
Cuba
human trafficking and, 238*t*
women legislators in, 386*f*
Cuban Americans, 262–263
as ethnic group, 245*t*
in Miami, 89, 262

quinceañera ceremony of, 89, 309
refugees and, 262
in U.S., 262*f*
cults, 348, 350, 351*t*, 355
cultural capital, 13, 23, 60–61
cultural convergence, 141, 159
cultural relativism, 55, 71, 72, 400, 414
cultural transmission, 175–176, 187, 188, 361
cultural universals, 54, 71, 72. *See also* education; families; funerals; marriage; medicine; political systems; religions; sports
education as, 358, 360, 365, 374
funerals as, 54
marriage as, 54, 310, 319
medicine as, 54
political systems as, 378, 379
religion as, 336, 341, 355
sports as, 54, 71
cultural values. *See* values
cultural variation, 58–60
countercultures and, 60, 60, 71, 72
subcultures and, 58–60, 71, 72
Wal-Mart and, 68, 68*t*
culture(s), 52–73. *See also* subcultures
assumptions and, 53–54
core, 67
countercultures and, 60, 60, 71, 72
defined, 53–54
development of (global), 56–58
dominant ideology and, 66–67
health and, 419
language and, 60–62
material, 58, 72
nonmaterial, 58, 72
nonverbal communication and, 62
society and, 53–54, 66–67, 68*t*
sociobiology and, 55–56, 71, 72, 173
Wal-Mart and, 68, 68*t*
culture industry, 54, 71, 72
culture lag, 58, 72, 498, 507
culture shock, 60, 71, 72, 195
culture war, 66
culture-bound syndrome, 419, 442
curanderismo, 426, 442
cures, miracle, 420
curriculum, hidden, 364, 374
CW, 149
cyberactivism, 392
cyberbullying, 142
cyberspace, 108. *See also* Internet; virtual worlds
Czech Republic
gender inequality in, 282*f*
infant mortality rates in, 421*f*
Czechoslovakia, twins study and, 77–78

D

dalits, 14, 194, 486
dance, 53, 53
Danone, 145*f*
Darfur, genocide and, 432
Darwin's evolution theory, 10, 24, 55, 494, 495
Das Kapital (Marx), 11, 496
data collection/analysis (scientific method step), 30–33
data warehouse, United Way, 41
date rape, 177, 181
dating services, Internet, 112, 152, 318
Days Inns of America, 305

deafness, 9, 62*f*, 77, 108, 264*f*, 477, 484*f*, 489*t*

death and dying, 301–302. *See also* aging
"right to die" and, 306–307, 308

death penalty, 165, 166*f*

Death Penalty Information Center, 166

death rate, 450, 468, 469

The Death of White Sociology (Ladner), 41

decision making. *See* collective decision making; group decision making

Defense, Department of, 326, 501

Defense of Marriage Act, 330

defining problems (scientific method step), 29–30

deforestation
hamburgers and, 438
in Mato Grosso, 59

degradation ceremony, 91, 94

deindustrialization, 410–411, 414

deinstitutionalization, of mentally ill, 208, 432

Delaware
baby names study and, 38
female governor in, 279

Dell Corporation, 147

democracy, 382, 395

Democratic Party, 130

Democratic Republic of the Congo
Kinshasa, 87
Kota people in, 89
mobile phones and, 87
national parks of, 402
poverty and, 226*f*

Democratic voters, 48, 213, 383

demographic transition, 452–453, 452*f*, 468, 469

demography, 449–451, 468, 469

Denmark
child care in, 92
human trafficking and, 238*t*
Millenium Project and, 227
NRI and, 229, 229*t*
poverty rate in, 206*f*

denominations, 348, 351*t*, 355

Department of Agriculture, 465

Department of Defense, 326, 501

Department of Education, 21, 369

Department of Homeland Security, 134, 236, 479

Department of Justice, 181, 183, 184, 185, 249, 260, 281, 402

Department of Labor, 250, 257

Department of Transportation, 488

departure stage (role exit), 103

dependency theory, 223, 230*t*, 239, 240

dependent variables, 30, 32*f*, 47

depression. *See also* recession
economic, anomie and, 174
Great Depression, 104
jurors and, 124
stage, in dying process, 301

deprivation, relative, 483, 485*t*, 490

deprived people, 463

descent, 315, 332

detachment, sociology and, 28, 36. *See also* Hawthorne effect

detention camps, 260

developing conclusions (scientific method step), 33

developing nations. *See also* industrial nations; nations

digital divide and, 113, 147–148, 159, 208–209, 214, 215

gender differences/social mobility and, 232–233

industrial nations *v.*, 221*f*

social mobility in, 231–232

development
of culture, 56–57
of sociological imagination, 18–20
of sociology, 9–13, 23

development biz, 220

development buzz, 220

deviance, 170–179
anomie theory of, 174–175, 187, 188
boundary-maintenance function of, 173
conformity *v.*, 164
cultural transmission and, 175–176, 187, 188
defined, 164, 170, 187, 188
Durkheim's theory of, 173–174
labeling theory and, 177–178, 187, 188
Merton's theory of, 12, 174–175, 174*t*, 187, 188
routine activities theory of, 175
smoking and, 172, 177
sociological perspectives on, 173–179, 180*t*
stigma and, 172
women and, 179

Devoted Husband Organization, 117

Dickinson College, 85

dictatorship, 382, 395

differential association, 176, 187, 188

differential justice, 178, 187, 188

diffusion, 54, 56, 57, 58, 71, 72, 225, 229

digital divide, 113, 147–148, 159, 208–209, 214, 215

digital enclosure, 140

digital television, 158

disabilities
ADA and, 131, 488–489, 490
deafness and, 9, 62*f*, 77, 108, 264*f*, 477, 484*f*, 489*t*
famous people and, 489*t*
as master status, 102
matrix of domination and, 278, 279*f*, 288, 289

disability rights, 487–489

disasters
behavior, 478–479
defined, 478, 482*t*, 490
mass media and, 144
research on, 478–479

disconnect, global, 229*t*

discovery, 56, 71, 72

Discovery space shuttle, 129

discrimination, 249–252
affirmative action and, 252, 267, 268, 409, 410*f*, 413, 414
ageism as, 303–304, 308
defined, 249, 267, 268
glass ceiling and, 249, 267, 268
institutional, 252, 267, 268, 280, 288, 289
prejudice *v.*, 249

diseases. *See also* cancer; illness
Alzheimer's disease, 306, 427, 428, 442
culture-bound syndrome and, 419, 442
sexually transmitted diseases, 43
social epidemiology and, 423–428, 442

disenchantment phase (retirement), 300

disengagement theory, 296, 307, 308

disinformation, e-mail and, 480–481

Disney company, 145*f*, 157

Disneyland, 146

Disneyland Paris, *112*

disobedience, civil, 257

distribution of power, communications technology and, 388

District of Columbia. *See* Washington D.C.

District of Columbia v. Heller, 186

diverse lifestyles, 327–330

divide. *See* digital divide; global divide

division of labor, 125–126, 127*t*, 135

The Division of Labor in Society (Durkheim), 11, 107

divorce, 325–327, 325*f*

D.I.Y. (Do-IT-Yourself) activity, 494

doctors. *See* physicians

Doctors Without Borders (Médecins Sans Frontières), 239, 391

dog meat, China and, 60

Do-IT-Yourself (D.I.Y.) activity, 494

domestic partnerships, 330, 331, 486

Domhoff's power elite model, 387*f*, 388, 395

dominant groups, privileges of, 250–251

dominant ideology
culture and, 66–67
defined, 66, 71, 72, 148, 200, 214, 215
mass media and, 148, 150, 159
stratification and, 200

domination, matrix of, 278, 279*f*, 288, 289

Dominican Republic
child marriage and, 56*f*
GNI and, 222*f*
human trafficking and, 238*t*
as periphery nation, 223, 223*f*
transnationals and, 505

Dominicans
as ethnic group, 245*t*
in U.S., 262*f*

donations
gene, 503
hard money as, 393, 394
organ, 302, 427
service, NGOs and, 391
XO computers and, 501

double consciousness, 12, 23

doubt (role exit stage), 103

downloading, illegal, 67, 173

downsizing, 411, 414

draft resistance, 60

drag racing, 176*f*

drain, brain, 421, 442

dramaturgical approach, 15–16, 23, 82, 83*t*, 94

drapetomania, 423

dream, American, 244

dress codes, 15

"drink till you drop" alcoholic consumption, 164, 169

drinking rape victim, 124

Driving While Black (DWB) violations, 177

drug dealing, 175

drunk driving, 180. *See also* alcohol abuse

dual-income families, 324, 331

Dubai
Al-Arabiya and, 156
MTV Arabia and, 150*f*

Durkheim, Émile
deviance and, 173–174
The Division of Labor in Society by, 11, 107

mechanical/organic solidarity and, 107–109, 115

religion and, 338, 341

suicide theory of, 8, 10

DWB (Driving While Black) violations, 177

dyads, 124, 135, 136

dying. *See* death and dying

dysfunctions
in bureaucracy, 126
defined, 14, 23
Internet, 89, 113, 115, 142
of mass media, 141, 144, 159

E

East Timor, 222, 237, 286

Eastern Europe
end of communism in, 198, 403
global divide and, 221*f*
global immigration and, 265, 342
orphanages in, 77–78

Eastern Michigan University, killing at, 181

eating disorders, 52, 88, 172, 419, 487

Ebay, 57, 145

Ebony magazine, 143*t*

ecclesiae, 348, 351*t*, 355

ecology. *See also* new urban sociology
human, 433–434, 442, 459, 468, 469
urban, 459, 462*t*, 468, 469

economic depression, 174. *See also* recession

Economic Security Index, 506

economic systems, 401–406. *See also* capitalism; global economy; globalization
changes in, 409–411
communism, 403, 413, 414
defined, 400, 413, 414
informal, 403, 413, 414
largest, by country, 405*f*
Mexico and, 234
social order and, 400
socialism, 402–403, 403*t*, 413, 414

The Economist, 70, 132, 148, 207, 229, 232, 234, 307, 381, 404, 436, 437, 478, 501

Economy and Society (Weber), 11

Ecuador, 222*f*, 390, 391*f*

EDSA (Epifanio de los Santas Avenue), 474

education, 358–375. *See also* colleges; schools
bilingualism and, 67, 69–71, 69*f*
cognitive theory of development and, 83, 83*t*, 94
cultural transmission and, 361
as cultural universal, 358, 360, 365, 374
defined, 360, 374
educational level/income relationship (study), 30, 31, 31*f*, 32, 32*f*, 33, 33*f*
Google and, 362
Head Start programs, 92, 363, 374
hidden curriculum and, 364, 374
income/education/religion (study), 342, 342*f*
Internet usage and, 153*f*
social change and, 363
social control and, 363
social mobility and, 211
social/political integration and, 362–363, 368, 373, 374
sociological perspectives on, 361–367, 368*t*
status and, 365–367

Education, Department of, 21, 369

egalitarian families, 307, 315

egocasting, 152

Egypt
holding hands in, 62
human trafficking and, 238t
as periphery nation, 223, 223f

eHarmony.com, 112

Eighteenth Amendment, 170

Einstein, Albert, 106, 354f

El Salvador
abortion and, 286
child marriages and, 56f
coffee and, 20
GNI for, 222f
people in U.S., 70f, 245f, 262f

elderly. *See also* aging; death and dying;
retirement
AARP and, 130f, 297, 304–305, 308
China and, 100
collective consciousness and,
304–306
in Florida, 303, 303f
gerontology and, 295–296, 307, 308
Gray Panthers and, 100
growth of, in U.S., 302f, 303f
income and, 303
in industrial nations, 298, 298t
labor force and, 304
medical epidemiology and, 427–428
"silver surfers" and, *292, 293*
stereotypes and, 90
wealth and, 303

elderspeak, 305

electric torch, 61

electronic communication, 132. *See also*
e-mail

electronically controlled prosthetic
devices, 503

electronics factory, in Malaysia, 232f

Elementary and Secondary Education Act
(ESEA), 70

Elementary Forms of Religious Life
(Durkheim), 11

Elvis's café, 272

e-mail, 132. *See also* Internet
Baghdad youth and, 86
chat rooms and, 42, 58, 86, 142, 172,
272, 316
disinformation and, 480–481
identity information and, 89f
instant messaging and, 88, 108, 113,
154, 168
military and, 107
Patriot Act and, 502
as research source, 39
September 11th attacks and, 142
smart mob behavior and, 474
smiley face on, 62
surveys and, 32
text messaging and, 87, 106, 113, 152,
319, 378, 474, 477, 485
warehouses, 114

embedded journalists, 141

emergent-norm perspective, 475–476,
489, 490

emerging adulthood, 90

emperor rule, Japan and, 379

employment. *See also* careers; workplace
based on technical qualifications
(bureaucracy), 126, 127t

/instruction, teaching profession and,
369–370
as milestone, 90t
women's, social consequences of,
283–284

endangered species, 183, 440, 485

endogamy, 318, 331

England. *See also* Great Britain; Industrial
Revolution; London; United Kingdom
anorexia nervosa and, 419
car thefts in, 185
Church of England, 361
electric torch and, 61
hospice care and, 301
incarceration rates in, 165
Industrial Revolution and, 111, 133,
401, 498
Luddites in, 498, 507
suicide reports from, 8

Engle v. Vitale, 353

English language. *See also* languages
bilingualism and, 67, 69–71, 69f
immigrants and, 70–71
Internet and, 58
Kannada v., 60
as official language in U.S., 70
pluralism and, 256
war terms and, 61

Enron scandal, 387

entertainment, pirated, 67, 172–173

entrepreneurship
China and, 405, 406, 413
drug dealing and, 175
informal economy and, 403
Internet and, 158
Japan and, 57, 132
organized crime and, 189
women and, 212

environment (social environment), 77–78
heredity and, 77, 78–79, 265
isolation and, 77–78, 78f
"nature v. nurture" interaction, 77, 265

environmental crime, 183t

environmental justice, 18, 435, 442

environmental problems, 435–442. *See also*
ecology
college students' values and, 65, 66f
globalization and, 439
hazardous waste sites, 18, 63, 435, 497
Sierra Club and, *416, 417*
social policy and, 440–442
sociological perspectives on, 433–435

environmental refugees, 439

environmental sociology, 18

epidemiology, social, 423–428, 442

Epifanio de los Santas Avenue
(EDSA), 474

equilibrium model, 496, 507

Eritreans, 221, 419t

ESEA (Elementary and Secondary
Education Act), 70

Essays on the Principle of Population
(Malthus), 449

established sects, 348, 351t, 355

estate system, 195, 214, 215

esteem
defined, 201, 215
prestige v., 201
self-esteem, 77, 172, 324

eternal happiness, 344

ethics

Protestant ethic, 11, 343, 355
research ethics, 37–39

Ethiopia
child marriage in, 56f
coffee and, 20
foreign-born adoptions and, 323f
medicine challenges and, 419t
NRI and, 229, 229t
poverty and, 226f

ethnic cleansing, 237, 255

ethnic groups. *See also specific ethnic groups*
defined, 245, 267, 268
racial groups v., 245, 248
in U.S., 245t, 246f, 256–264, 257f

ethnic succession, 181

ethnic villagers, 463

ethnicity
family life and, 321–322
Internet usage and, 153f
/race percentages, in colleges, 371f
race v., 248
/race/gender, income and, 250f
social mobility and, 211
sociological perspectives on, 253–254,
254t
symbolic, 264, 267, 268

ethnics, White. *See* White people

ethnocentrism, 54–55, 71, 72, 248, 267, 268

Ethnograph, 42

ethnography, 35, 47

EU (European Union), 266

Europe. *See also* Central Europe; Eastern
Europe; Western Europe
CO_2 emissions in, 438f
global divide and, 221
SS *St. Louis* and, 265
White ethnics from, 264

European Union (EU), 266

euthanasia, 306–307, 308

evacuation camps, 260

evolution
Darwin's theory of, 10, 24, 55, 494, 495
evolutionary theory (sociology), 495,
507
sociocultural, 109–111, 111t, 115

ex-convict, 172

executions, by state, 165, 166f

existing sources/secondary analysis, 37, 39, 48

exiting, of roles, 102–103

ex-mental patient, 172

exogamy, 318, 331

experiences, religious, 347, 347t, 355

experimental groups, 36, 47

experiments (research design), 36–37, 47.
See also specific experiments

exploitation theory (Marxist class theory),
197–198, 253, 267, 268

Explorers (Miami Police Department), *96, 97*

explosion, population, 453–454

expressiveness, 277, 289

expulsion, 254, 255, 256, 346, 471. *See also*
genocide

extended families, 313, 331, 333

extinction, societies and, 104

Exxon Mobil, 40, *40*, 225t

false consciousness, 198, 214, 215, 285,
484, 490

Falun Gong, 392

families, 310–327
affection and, 316
authority patterns in, 315
child-rearing patterns, 322–325
class differences in, 319–321
companionship and, 316
composition of, 313–314
definitions of, 312–314
dual-income, 324, 331
egalitarian, 315, 331
ethnic differences in, 321–322
extended, 313, 331, 333
functions of, 331
global perspective on, 313–315
marriage and, 317–325
nuclear, 313, 332
race differences in, 321–322
reproduction and, 312, 316, 331
single-parent, 91–93, 324, 331, 332
social support and, 317
socialization and, *74, 75*, 83–84
sociological perspectives on, 316–317,
317t
stepfamilies, 325
types, U.S. households and, 313f
variance in, 319–322

familism, 321, 331

Family Educational Rights and Privacy Act
(FERPA), 88

famous people, disabilities and, 489t

fashions, 479–480, 482t, 489, 490

FBI (Federal Bureau of Investigation), 126,
169–170, 180, 188

FCC (Federal Communications Commission)
ruling, 158

Federal Bureau of Investigation. *See* FBI

Federal Bureau of Narcotics, 179f

Federal Communications Commission (FCC)
ruling, 158

Federal Election Commission, 114

Federal Emergency Management Agency
(FEMA), 479

Federal Reserve Board, 192, 204, 260,
402, 413

females. *See* women

FEMA (Federal Emergency Management
Agency), 479

The Feminine Mystique (Friedan), 284

feminism, 284–285
defined, 284, 289
The Feminine Mystique and, 284
feminist label and, 285
feminist theory and, 278
The Second Sex and, 284
Sexual Politics and, 284

Feminist Majority Foundation, 285

feminist perspective, 14–15, 23. *See also*
conflict perspective; sociological
perspectives
gender stratification and, 278–280
movement origins, 14
research and, 41–42

feminization of poverty, 207, 214, 215, 321

FERPA (Family Educational Rights and
Privacy Act), 88

Ferrari, 145f

fertility, 449, 468, 469. *See also* reproduction

fertility patterns, in U.S., 454–456

feudalism, 195, 214, 215
fiesta politics, 384
Fiji islandlers, television and, 52
file sharing, 113, 173
Filipino Americans
    in California, 70*f*
    as racial group, 245*t*
    in U.S., 245*t*, 258*f*
Filipinos, EDSA and, 474
films. *See* movies
filtering/monitoring. *See* monitoring/
    filtering
financial aid, 85, 209, 210, 249, 275
financial independence, as milestone, 90*t*
financial/economic crisis. *See* recession
financing, campaign, 393–394
Finland
    brands in, 145*f*
    ConocoPhillips *v.*, 225*t*
    higher education completion rates
        in, 361*f*
    marriage ages in, 318*f*
    NRI and, 229, 229*t*
    prison cell in, 165*f*
First Amendment, 172*f*, 353
Flickr, 142, 152
Florida. *See also* Miami
    elderly in, 303, 303*f*
    Katrina disaster area and, 6–7, 19, 208,
        209*f*, 479
folkways, 63–64, 71, 72
football, 5, 41, 62, 64, 80, 275, 379, 475, 477
For This Land (Deloria), 336
force, 379, 395. *See also* power
foreign aid per capita, in nations, 227*f*
foreign students, by country, 364*f*
formal norms, 63, 71, 72
formal operational stage, 83
formal organizations, 125, 135, 136. *See also*
    organizations
formal social control, 168, 187, 188
former Soviet Union. *See* Soviet Union
former Yugoslavia, 237, 255, 438*f*
Fortune 500 corporation, 18, 282, 387
Fortune magazine, 225, 250
forums, Internet, 142, 250
Fourth Amendment, 113, 114, 502
Fox Entertainment Group, 134, 149,
    156, 157
France
    arms transfers and, 187
    brands in, 145*f*
    child care and, 93
    as core nation, 223, 223*f*
    economy of, 405*f*
    foreign students and, 364*f*
    G8 conference and, 228, 441, *472, 473*
    higher education completion rates
        in, 361*f*
    human trafficking and, 238*t*
    media penetration in, 155*f*
    nuclear power generation and, 58*f*
    poverty rate in, 206*f*
    religious participation in, 347*f*
    riots in, 255
    Strasbourg, open market in, *398, 399*
    union membership in, 133*f*
frankenfood, 504
fraternities, 10, 121, 169, 252
Freakonomics (Venkatesh & Levitt), 175
free expression issues, Internet and, 487

Freudian theory, of psychoanalysis,
    82–83, 83*t*
friending, 88
friendship networks, 12, 13, 17, 87,
    88–89, 151, 152, 153*t*. *See also* social
    networking Web sites
Friendster, 88, 113
Fulani people, 295
full-nest syndrome, 322
functionalist perspective, 13–14, 16, 23. *See*
    also sociological perspectives
fundamentalism, 345, 355
funding, research, 40
funerals, 54, 141, 202*t*, 315, 341
future
    sociology and, 20
    technology and, 499

G

G8 conference, 228, 441, *472, 473*
Gaia Online, 113
Gale Cengage Learning, 130
Gallaudet University, 477, 484
Gallup poll, 34
Gambia, 222*f*
gambling, 9, 170, 172, 180
game stage (Mead's stages of self), 80, 81*t*
Gang Leader for a Day (Venkatesh), 164
gangs
    African Americans and, 84
    American Gangster and, 189
    Chicago study of, 123, 164
    City of God and, 241
    crack cocaine and, 175
    Freedom Writers and, 375
    graffiti writing by, 175
    Gran Torino and, 309
    as groups, 12, 121
    Mall Cop and, 144*f*
    prison, 14
    in Russia, 185
    Street Corner Society and, 35–36, 48
Gap corporation, 120, 225
gatekeeping, 144–145, 159
Gay, Lesbian and Straight Education
    Network, 370
gays. *See* homosexuals
gay-straight alliances (GSAs), 370
Gaza Strip, 54*f*
GE, 145*f*
Gemeinschaft, 109, 110*t*, 112, 115, 116,
    130, 131
gender
    cross-cultural perspective on, 276–277
    defined, 273, 288
    family life and, 84
    inequality, in industrial nations, 282*f*
    inequality, Japan and, 231, 282*f*
    languages and, 61
    matrix of domination and, 278, 279*f*,
        288, 289
    occupational prestige and, 201–202,
        202*t*
    politics and, 384, 386
    prestige and, 201–202
    /race/ethnicity, income and, 250*f*
    social construction of, 273–277
    social epidemiology and, 426–427
    /social mobility, nations and, 232–233
    social mobility and, 211–212

social movements and, 484–485
socialization and, 84
sociological perspectives on,
    277–279, 280*t*
sociology degrees by, 21*f*
stratification, 270–291
survey taking and, 34
gender norm violations (experiment), 274*t*
gender roles, 84, 93, 94, 273–276
    defined, 84, 94, 273, 288, 289
    men's, 275–276
    socialization and, 273–274
    women's, 274–275
gender stratification, 270–291
gene donations, 503
gene pool, biotechnology and, 502–504
General Motors (GM), 225*t*, 402, 405, 411
General Social Survey (GSS), 32, 33,
    43, 90*t*
generalized others, 80, 83*t*, 93, 94
Generation Debt, 210
"Generation Txt," 474
Generation Y, 210
genetic manipulation, 502
genetically modified food, 504
genetic/biological factors, social
    interactions *v.*, 55–56, 72
Geneva, G8 conference and, *472, 473*
Genie (girl isolation case), 77–78, 78*f*
genital mutilation, of women, 238
genocide, 254–255, 267, 268
    "clash of civilizations" and, 66
    Darfur and, 432
    defined, 254, 268
    ethnic cleansing and, 237, 255
    expulsion and, 254, 255, 256, 346, 471
    Holocaust and, 167, 254, 264, 341
    Native Americans and, 253, 254
    Rwanda and, 255
Genome Project, Human, 502, 503, 504
gentrification, 467, 468, 469
Georgia (country), 222*f*, 400
Georgia (state)
    high school popularity study and,
        86, 86*t*
    visitability and, 488
Georgio Armani, 145*f*
Germans Americans
    as ethnic group, 245*t*
    evacuation camps and, 260
Germany. *See also Gemeinschaft*;
    Gesellschaft; Nazis
    arms transfers and, 187
    brands in, 145*f*
    child care costs in, 93*f*
    as core nation, 223, 223*f*
    economy of, 405*f*
    elderly percentage in, 298, 298*t*
    foreign aid per capita in, 227*f*
    G8 conference and, 228, 441, *472, 473*
    higher education completion rates
        in, 361*f*
    human trafficking and, 238*t*
    poverty rate in, 206*f*
    totalitarian state and, 382
    union membership in, 133*f*
    U.S. favorability rating and, 66
    Wal-Mart and, 68
gerontology, 295–296, 307, 308
Gesellschaft, 109, 110*t*, 112, 115, 116,
    130, 131

Ghana
    Accra, people in, *446, 447*
    coffins in, 302*f*
    GNI for, 222*f*
G.I. Joe doll, *274*
Gillette, 145f
Ginko Financial, 108
Girl Scouts of America, 129
glass ceiling, 250, 267, 268, 282, 289
Glass Ceiling Commission, 250
Global Alliance for Workers and
    Communities, 225
global community, 57. *See also* globalization;
    Internet
    call center subculture and, 59–60, 59*f*
    censorship in, 501–502
    culture war in, 66
    global disconnect and, 229*t*
    as global village, 57, 154, 155, 157, 157*f*,
        485, 501–502
    globalization and, 57
    immigration and, 265–267
    mass media and, 154–157
    Millennium Project, 227, 228, 239, 241
    news outlets and, 156
    offshoring and, 412–413, 414
    privacy in, 501–502
    recession in, 223, 228. *See also* recession
    religions of, 338–340, 339*f*, 340*t*
    sex worker trafficking and, 42, *42*
    social change in, 493–509, 498–499
    sociology in, 228
    terrorism and, 391*f*
    urbanization in, 459*f*
    world systems analysis and, 223, 223*f*,
        239, 240
global divide, 221–222, 222*f*, 239
    abortion and, 287*f*
    defined, 221
    GNI, by country, 222*f*
    inequalities, by country, 221*f*
global economy
    Africa and, 461
    Asia and, 461
    core nations and, 223, 223*f*
    defined, 229
    dependency theory and, 223, 239, 240
    global disconnect and, 229
    IMF and, 223, 224, 409
    Latin America and, 461
    new urban sociology and, 461, 462*t*,
        468, 469
    rural areas and, 465
    social change and, 22
    unions and, 133
    upward social mobility and, 231–232
    World Bank and, 224
    world systems analysis and, 223, 223*f*,
        239, 240, 461, 468, 469
global inequality, 218–241
    global divide and, 221–222, 222*f*, 239, 287*f*
    sociological perspectives on, 230*t*
Global Peace Index, 390, 390*f*
global perspective
    abortion and, 286–288
    families and, 313–315
    social structures and, 107–112
global profile, of Internet, 500
global torrent, 155
global village, 57, 154, 155, 157, 157*f*, 485,
    501–502. *See also* global community

global warming, 437–439
globalization. *See also* global community;
    global economy; global perspective
    Africa and, 224
    benefits of, 57
    coffee trade and, 20
    communications technology and, 19,
        57, 87, 224
    criticism of, 57
    culture and, 56–58
    defined, 19, 23, 224, 239, 240
    environmental problems from, 439
    global community and, 57
    immigration patterns and, 266
    integration and, 19, 23, 224, 239, 240
    Internet and, 224
    labor unions and, 133
    Latin America and, 224
    mass media and, 84*f*, 224
    McDonaldization and, 57, 120, 126,
        128, 136
    Mongolia and, *492, 493*
    multinational corporations and,
        224–227, 239, 240
    postmodern societies and, 111–112,
        111*t*, 112*f*, 115
    social movements and, 485–486
    social policy and, 504–506
    Starbucks and, 20, 56, 72, 128, 225
    toys/lead-based paint and, 224*f*
    transnationals and, 265, 267, 268,
        504–506
    Western media and, 84*f*
GM. *See* General Motors
GNI (gross national income), by nation, 222*f*
GNP (gross national product), 227, 240
goal displacement, 126, 135, 136
golf, 17, 68, 153, 247, 275, 279, 460
good death, 301
Goodyear worker, female, 283
Google
    as brand, 145*f*, 362
    China and, 145, 147, 406
    Earth map, 141
    education through, 362
    Google Corporation, *411*
    Michael Jackson's death and, 142
    news information and, 158
    plagiarism and, 65
    San Francisco and, 140
    University, 362
    users' Web-browsing activities and, 147
    "Vice President and Chief Internet
        Evangelist" at, 114
    YouTube, 112, 113, 142, 158, 392
Goshute Indians, 435
Goths, 28
government, 381–382. *See also* economic
        systems
    health care and, 431
    homosexual torture by, 239
    religion and, 87, 89
    socialization and, 87, 89, 93
    sociology and, 20, 43
    types of, 381–382
governors, female, 279
graffiti, gangs and, 175
Grameen Bank, 409
grandparenthood, 322
graphs, reading of, 45

Gray Panthers, 100
graying of America, 302–303. *See also* aging
Great Britain. *See also* England; United
        Kingdom
    arms transfers and, 187
    binge drinking in, 169
    brands in, 145*f*
    economy of, 405*f*
    foreign aid per capita in, 227*f*
    foreign students and, 364*f*
    G8 conference and, 228, 441, *472, 473*
    gender inequality in, 282*f*
    higher education completion rates
        in, 361*f*
    income distribution in, 232*f*
    Labour Party and, 134
    life expectancy in, 451*f*
    Muslims, Internet and, 88
    poverty rate in, 206*f*
    sex survey funding and, 44
    survey/researcher in, *26*
    visitability and, 488
Great Clips, 120
Great Depression, 104. *See also* recession
Great Firewall of China, 406
Great Leap Forward, 361
Greater Syria (*Al Sham*), 54*f*
Greece
    elderly percentage in, 298, 298*t*
    human trafficking and, 238*t*
Greek Independence Day parade, 264*f*
Greenpeace, 392, 485, 504
Grinnell College, 41
gross national income (GNI), by
        nation, 222*f*
gross national product (GNP), 227, 240
Ground Zero, 15
group decision making, 124–125, 131
groups, 103, 114, 115, 121–125. *See also*
        ethnic groups; gangs; minority groups;
        racial groups; social networking Web
        sites; social networks
    coalitions, 123, 135, 136
    Cooley and, 12
    defined, 103, 115, 121, 136
    dominant, privileges of, 250–251
    dyads as, 124, 135, 136
    experimental, 36, 47
    in-groups, 121–122, 135, 136
    Marx and, 11
    out-groups, 121–122, 135, 136
    peer, 86, 93
    primary, 121, 136
    reference, 122–123, 135, 136
    secondary, 104*f*, 121, 121*f*, 123, 125, 135,
        136, 137, 153
    self-injury, 28, 88
    sizes of, 123–124
    small, 123, 135, 136
    as social structures, 103
    status, 198, 214, 215
    subordinate, 99, 100, 148, 245, 248, 254,
        256, 268, 295, 308
    triads as, 124, 135, 136
groupthink, 124–125, 135, 136
Groveland (Chicago community), 76
GSS (General Social Survey), 32, 33, 43, 90*t*
Guatemala
    child marriages in, 56*f*
    foreign-born adoptions and, 323*f*
    GNI for, 222*f*

immigrants in U.S., 70*f*
    San Antonio Palopo, *74, 75*
    Starbucks and, 225
Gucci, 145*f*
Guinea
    child marriages and, 56*f*
    GNI for, 222*f*
guinea pig effect, 37
Guinea-Bissau, 222*f*
Gulf Coast, Katrina and, 6–7, 19, 208, 209*f*, 479
gun control, 185–187
Gypsies, 254

H

Habitat for Humanity, 467
Haiti
    infant mortality rates in, 421*f*
    life expectancy in, 451*f*
    as periphery nation, 223, 223*f*
    women legislators in, 386*f*
hajj, 346, 347
Hallmark cards, 145
hamburgers, 128, 272, 438. *See also*
        McDonald's
hand signals, 62
handgun control, 185–187
Handgun Control (organization), 186
happiness, eternal, 344
hard money, 393, 394
Harley-Davidson, 155
Harris poll, 34
Harvard Business Review, 284, 362
Harvard School of Public Health, 169
Harvard University, 12, 13, 40, 169, 195, 198,
        269, 378, 393, 410
Harvard University's John F. Kennedy School
        of Government, 195, 378
Harvey Milk High School, 370, 491
hate crimes, 248, 249*f*, 267, 268
Hate Crimes Statistics Act, 248
Hawai'i
    Adlers and, 29
    female governor in, 279
    Korean Americans and, 260
    Pearl Harbor attack in, 260
Hawai'ians, Native
    as race category, 245*f*
    in U.S., 245*f*, 258*f*
Hawthorne effect, 37, 47
hazardous waste sites, 18, 63, 435, 497
HBO network, 157
head scarf/veil, Middle East and, 281
Head Start programs, 92, 363, 374
health
    culture and, 419
    defined, 442
    labeling theory and, 422–423, 423*t*
    social epidemiology and, 423–428, 442
    sociological perspectives on,
        419–423, 423*t*
health care
    alternatives to, 430–431, 431*f*
    concierge doctors and, 192
    government and, 431
    inequities in, 421–422
    medical sociology and, 6*t*, 18, 21
    as social institution, 103, 114
    in U.S., 428–431
Health Care Financing Administration, 429
health insurance, 424–425, 425*f*

Heaven's Gate cult, 348
Hebrew language, 264*f*
Hennessy, 145*f*
herbalists, 52
heredity, 78–79
    "nature *v.* nurture" interaction, 77, 265
    social environment and, 77, 78–79, 265
    socialization and, 77, 78–79, 93, 265
    twins and, *78*, 78–79, *79*
Hermes, 145*f*
heroin, 189
Herzegovina. *See* Bosnia-Herzegovina
Hewlett-Packard, 132, 145*f*
Hibiya Library, 82
hidden curriculum, 364, 374
hierarchy
    of authority, 126, 127*t*
    minimal, 131
high schools. *See also* education
    Columbine killings, 122, 147, 185, 369
    educational level/income relationship
        (study), 30, 31, 31*f*, 32, *32*, 32*f*,
        33, 33*f*
    in-groups/out-groups at, 122
    popularity study, 86, 86*t*
    romantic relationships (study), 106
    Roughnecks/Saints and, 177
Higher Education Research Institute, 66, 385
hijab, 281
hijacking, of airplanes, 183*t*
Hinduism, 338, 339*f*, 340, 340*t*, 352–353
hippies, 60
Hispanics (Latinos), 262–263. *See also*
        specific Hispanic subgroups
    assimilation and, 255
    class system and, 211
    differential justice and, 187
    as ethnic group, 245*t*
    health insurance and, 425*f*
    income and, 250*f*
    poverty and, 207*t*
    social mobility and, 263
    subgroups, 262*f*
    television and, 149
    in U.S., 246*f*, 257*f*, 262*f*
Hitler Youth movement, 79
HIV/AIDS
    Africa and, 453*f*
    Ashe and, 101
    awareness event, India and, *64*
    child marriage and, 55
    China and, 44
    mass media and, 141
    research and, 425
    sexual behavior studies and, 43, 44
    worldwide, 424*f*
H&M, 145*f*
holding hands, 62
holistic medicine, 442
Holocaust, 167, 254, 264, 341
Home Depot, 305, 465
Home School Legal Defense
        Association, 372
Homeland Security, Department of, 134,
        236, 479
homelessness, 466–468
    in Chicago (study), 41
    Dark Days and, 471
    in New York City, *190, 191*
    social policy and, 466–468
    stigma and, 172

homeschooling, 371–372, 374
homogamy, 318, 331
homophobia, 273–274, 288, 289
homosexuals
    lesbian/gay relationships, 329–330
    military and, 177
    Milk and, 370, 491
    same-sex marriage and, 64, 329–330
    sociopathic personality disorder and, 177
    stigma of, 178
    torture/abuse of, 239
Honda, 145f
Honduras
    BP v., 225t
    foreign-born adoptions and, 323f
    human trafficking and, 238t
honeymoon phase (retirement), 300
Hong Kong
    GNI for, 222f
    homelessness and, 468
    human trafficking and, 238t
    immigrants from, 260
    sex selection clinics and, 57
Hopi woman, Iraq War and, 389
horizontal mobility, 209, 214, 215
horticultural societies, 110–111, 111t, 115
Hospice Association of America, 301
hospice care, 301–302, 308
households
    by family type (U.S.), 313f
    unmarried-couple, by state, 327f
houseworkers' tasks (study), 127
Housing and Urban Development, 467
hózhóni, 418
H&R Block, 120
HSBC, 145f
Hull House, 12
human ecology, 433–434, 442, 459, 468, 469
Human Genome Project, 502, 503, 504
human relations approach, to formal
        organizations, 128, 135, 136
human rights, 237–239. See also rights
Human Rights, Universal Declaration of,
        197, 237, 238
human sexuality. See sexual behavior
Human Terrain System, 36, 36, 40
human trafficking, 183t, 238t
Hummer, 426
Hungary
    child care costs in, 93f
    GNI for, 222f
    Total corporation v., 225t
    venture capital investment and, 132
hunting-and-gathering societies, 109–110,
        111t, 115
Al Hurra, 156
Hurricane Katrina disaster, 6–7, 19, 208,
        209f, 479
Hussein regime collapse, 85–86, 277, 478
Hutu people, 255
Hyde Amendment, 287
hypotheses, 30, 33, 47. See also scientific
        method; theories; specific hypotheses
Hyundai, 145f

IBM, 145f, 230
Iceland
    Global Peace Index and, 390, 390f
    NRI and, 229, 229t

sexual behavior research, 44f
    single mothers and, 328
ICTs (information and communications
        technologies), 141, 142t. See also
        communications technology
ID (intelligent design), 354, 355
Idaho, Coeur d'Alene Indians in, 73
ideal minority group, 259, 267, 268
ideal type, 10, 23, 125, 135, 136
identical twins, 78, 78–79, 79
identity. See also me; roles; self
    multiple identities, 247
    self-identity, 80
    student, Internet and, 89f
identity theft, 182, 184
ideology. See dominant ideology
Ikea, 145f
illegal downloading, 67, 173
illegal drugs, 17, 171, 183t. See also heroin;
        marijuana
illegal money transfers, 183t
illegal sales of firearms and
        ammunition, 183t
Illinois. See also Chicago
    Beardstown, 465f
    Y-Me National Breast Cancer
        Organization in, 285
illness. See also diseases; mental illness
    culture-bound syndrome and,
        419, 442
    labeling theory and, 422–423, 423t
    social epidemiology and, 423–428, 442
    sociological perspectives on,
        419–423, 423t
imagination. See sociological imagination
IMAX, 157
IMF (International Monetary Fund), 223,
        224, 409
imitation. See also conformity;
        McDonaldization
    assimilation and, 255, 267, 268
    children and, 80, 81
    of Elvis's café, 272
    of McDonald's, 120
    of Napster, 173
    of U.S. media, 148
immigration. See also migration
    bilingualism and, 67, 69–71, 69f
    borderlands and, 233, 235–237, 236f,
        239, 240, 266
    English language and, 70–71
    global, social policy and, 265–267
    globalization and, 266
    Hispanic, social mobility and, 263
    protesters, in L.A., 242, 243
    transnationals and, 265, 267, 268,
        504–506
    to U.S., 266f
Immigration Reform and Control Act of
        1986, 266
impersonality (bureaucracy), 126, 127t
impression management, 81–82, 81f, 83t, 93,
        94, 113, 113f
imprisonment. See prison
incarceration rates, international, 185
incest taboo, 318, 331
incidence, 423, 442
income. See also wealth
    defined, 193, 214, 215
    distribution, in nations, 232f
    distribution, in U.S., 203f

educational level/income relationship
        (study), 30, 31, 31f, 32, 32, 32f,
        33, 33f
    education/income/religion (study),
        342, 342f
    elderly and, 303
    GNI, by nation, 222f
    health insurance and, 424–425, 425f
    income/poverty levels, by state, 194f
    intergenerational mobility and, 211f
    Internet usage and, 153f
    /labor migration, 505f
    median household, 45
    by race/ethnicity/gender, 250f
    stratification, 202–204
    wealth v., 193, 202–204
independent variables, 30, 32f, 47
index crimes, 180, 188
India
    AIDS awareness event in, 64
    Bangalore, 84f
    call center subculture and, 59–60, 59f
    caste system and, 193–195, 209,
        214, 215
    child marriage in, 56f
    CO₂ emissions in, 438f
    cow sacredness in, 13, 13, 14, 55
    economy of, 405f
    foreign students and, 364f
    foreign-born adoptions and, 323f
    Hinduism and, 338, 339f, 340, 340t,
        352–353
    human trafficking and, 238t
    infant mortality rates in, 421f
    Internet plagiarism and, 67
    Islam and, 352–353
    life expectancy in, 451f
    marriage ages in, 318
    McDonald's in, 57
    media penetration in, 155f
    Nayars of, 322
    New Delhi slums, killings in, 178–179
    new social movements in, women
        and, 486
    poverty and, 226f
    public displays of affection and, 64
    religion (case study), 352–353
    religious clashes and, 341
    as semiperiphery nation, 223, 223f
    sexual behavior research, 44f
    Simla, 59f
    Slumdog Millionaire and, 471
    Wal-Mart and, 68
    women legislators in, 386f
Indian Gambling Regulatory Act, 258
Indian Health Service, 419
Indian Ocean tsunami, 20, 84
Indiana school superintendent, 373
Indians. See Native Americans
indifferents (communications
        technology), 142t
individualism, 132, 164, 198, 364
Indonesia
    cockfights in, 5
    GNI for, 222f
    Indian Ocean tsunami and, 20, 84
    Islam and, 340t
    Minangkabau society in, 277
    Net activism and, 392
    Nike and, 295
    slaves, in New York, 193

terrorism and, 391f
    West Sumatra, 277
industrial cities, 457, 458t, 468, 469
industrial nations. See also developing
        nations; nations
    core, 223, 223f
    deindustrialization and, 410–411, 414
    developing nations v., 221f
    economies of, by country, 405f
    elderly percentages in, 298, 298t
    gender differences/social mobility
        and, 232–233
    gender inequality in, 282f
    higher education completion rates
        in, 361f
    life expectancy in, 451f
    social mobility in, 230–231
Industrial Revolution, 111, 133, 401, 413,
        457–458t, 498
industrial societies, 111, 111t, 115, 413, 414
inequality. See global inequality; social
        inequality
inexperienced experimenters
        (communications technology), 142t
infant mortality rates, 421–422, 421f, 442,
        450, 468, 469
infiltration of legal businesses, 183t
influence, 379, 395. See also power
informal economies, 403, 413, 414
informal norms, 63, 71, 72
informal social control, 168, 187, 188
information and communications
        technologies (ICTs), 141, 142t. See also
        communications technology
information finding (research reports), 46
information gathering, Internet and, 114
ING Group, 145f, 225t
in-groups, 121–122, 135, 136
innovation, 56, 71, 72, 131, 132. See also
        discovery; invention
    crime and, 12, 174, 175
    forms of, 56, 71
    media, 86
    Merton's theory of deviance and, 12,
        174, 174t, 175
    technology and, 58
instant messaging, 88, 108, 113, 154, 168
institutional discrimination, 252, 267, 268,
        280, 288, 289
institutions. See social institutions
instrumentality, 277, 288, 289
insurance fraud, 183t
integration. See also globalization
    cross-cultural, 111t
    globalization and, 19, 23, 224, 239, 240
    racial, 248, 269
    religion and, 338, 341, 345
    social/political, education and, 362–363,
        368, 373, 374
    transnationals and, 506
Intel, 145f
intellectual property crime, 183t
intelligent design (ID), 354, 355
interactionism, 15
interactionist perspective, 15–16, 23. See also
        sociological perspectives
interactions. See social interactions
intercourse. See sexual behavior
intercultural relations, languages and, 61
intergenerational mobility, 209, 211f, 214,
        215, 231

intergenerational sex, 178
intergroup relations, patterns of, 254–256
Intermountain Power Project, 435
internal migration, 456–457
International Committee of the
     Red Cross, 187
international crime rates, 185
International Gay and Lesbian Human
     Rights Commission, 177
international incarceration rates, 185
International Labor Organization, 506
international migration, 456
International Monetary Fund (IMF), 223,
     224, 409
International Red Crescent Society, 390, 391
International Social Survey Programme, 281
International Women Count Network, 201
internationalization. *See* globalization
Internet. *See also* e-mail; Google; social
     networking Web sites; virtual worlds
   abuse of, 113, 115, 142
   avatars, 106, 108, 113, 115, 351
   chat rooms, 42, 58, 86, 142, 172, 272, 316
   communication and, 113, 156
   dating services, 112, 152, 318
   digital divide and, 113, 147–148, 159,
        208–209, 214, 215
   disinformation and, 480–481
   dysfunctionality of, 89, 113, 115, 142
   e-mail warehouses, 114
   English language and, 58
   entrepreneurship and, 158
   forums, 142, 250
   free expression issues and, 487
   global profile of, 500
   globalization and, 224
   hosts, 501
   illegal downloading and, 67, 173
   information gathering and, 114
   Iraq War and, 487
   Ku Klux Klan and, 487
   languages on, 500f
   Mafia and, 88
   mass media and, 155–156, 159
   misuse of, 113, 115, 142
   monitoring/filtering of, 113, 126f
   Nazis and, 88
   Net activism and, 392
   neutrality, 114, 115
   news and, 157–158
   NRI and, 229, 229t
   off the Net category and, 142t
   penetration, by world region, 500f
   plagiarism on, 67
   political activism on, 142, 392–393
   predators, 113, 115, 142
   profiles, 88, 88f, 89, 106, 113, 114, 318, 385
   regulation of, 112–114, 145
   research and, 42–43, 46
   romance on, 112, 152, 318
   self-injury groups and, 28, 88
   September 11th attacks and, 142
   sexual predators and, 113, 115, 142
   social interactions and, 112–114
   social movements and, 487
   socialization and, 86–87, 88–89, 88f, 93
   surveys, 42–43
   "That's not cool" campaign and, 142
   usage in U.S., 153f
   users, by world region, 500f
   women and, 113

Internet Tax Freedom Act, 114
internment camps, 260
Inter-Parliamentary Union, 231, 235, 386
Interpol, 183
interpersonal violence, 181
interracial marriage, 247
interviews, 34, 47
intimate relationships, 319–322. *See also*
     families
intragenerational mobility, 209, 214, 215
Inuit tribes, 58
invention, 56, 71, 72
Invisible Man (Ellison), 256
Iowa
   arranged marriage and, 320
   elderly in, 302
   Grinnell College in, 41
   Luther College in, 274
   same-sex marriage and, 330
   United Way data warehouse in, 41
Iran
   election protest and media, 142
   Elvis's café in, 272
   filtering information and, 146f, 380f
   homosexual abuse in, 239
   human trafficking and, 238t
   Iraq and, 85
   Lipstick Jihad and, 272–273
   as patriarchal society, 315
   refugees from, 273
   Revolution, 273, 498
   Shia of, 349
   Spiderman ride in, *50*
   Tehran, 272
   terrorism and, 391f
   women in, 272–273
   women legislators in, 386f
Iraq
   Abu Ghraib prison in, 98–99, 167,
        389, 390
   ethnic cleansing and, 237
   family loyalties in, 55
   filtering information and, 146f, 380f
   Global Peace Index and, 390, 390f
   human rights violations in, 239
   Human Terrain System and, 36, *36*, 40
   Hussein regime collapse and, 85–86,
        277, 478
   Iran and, 85
   Kurds in, 261
   Kuwait invasion and, 389
   military marriages and, 8
   nepotism and, 55
   poverty and, 226f
   Red Crescent and, 390
   schools in, 85–86
   Shia of, 349
   terrorism and, 238t, 391f
Iraq War
   Baghdad and, 86, 277
   electronically controlled prosthetic
        devices and, 503
   embedded journalists and, 141
   foreign opinion of U.S. and, 66
   Hopi woman and, 389
   Internet and, 487
   maldistribution of food supplies and, 450
   Oscar Mayer and, 480
   searching/touching of Muslims and,
        63f, 64
   South Korean protesters and, 477f

Ireland. *See also* Northern Ireland
   child care costs in, 93f
   foreign aid per capita in, 227f
   ING Group *v.*, 225f
   poverty rate in, 206f
   religious participation in, 347f
   as semiperiphery nation, 223, 223f
   step dancers, 53, *53*
   union membership in, 133f
iris checks, 170f
Irish Americans
   as ethnic group, 245t
   ethnic succession and, 181
   Northern Ireland and, 264
Irish-Scotch, 245t
iron law of oligarchy, 127, 135, 136
Is Voting for Young People? (Wattenberg), 378
Isabelle (girl isolation case), 77–78
Islam, 338, 339f, 340, 340t. *See also* Middle
     East; Muslims; September 11th attacks
   India and, 352–353
   Koran and, 156, 261, 281, 338, 340
   in U.S., 349
isolation, 77–78, 78f
Israel
   child care center, bilingualism and, 91
   human trafficking and, 238t
   kibbutz, 79
   religious clashes and, 341
   as semiperiphery nation, 223, 223f
   terrorism and, 60
Issei, 260
Italian Americans
   assimilation and, 255
   Do the Right Thing and, 25, 261
   as ethnic group, 245t
   ethnic succession and, 181
   evacuation camps and, 260
   numbers, in U.S., 264
   St. Joseph's Day and, 264
Italy
   brands in, 145f
   economy of, 405f
   elderly percentage in, 298, 298t
   foreign students and, 364f
   G8 conference and, 228, 441, *472, 473*
   gender inequality in, 282f
   higher education completion rates in,
        361f
   human trafficking and, 238t
   Internet, Mafia and, 88
   population structure of, 454f
   poverty rate in, 206f
   sexual behavior research and, 44f
iTunes, 142

J

Jack/Oskar (identical twins), 78–79
Jamaica
   Global Peace Index and, 390, 390f
   income distribution in, 232f
   reggae music from, 111
   sexual behavior research and, 44f
James Bond movies, 57
Japan. *See also* Tokyo
   aging in, 299
   brands in, 145f
   child care costs in, 93f
   CO_2 emissions in, 438f
   as core nation, 223, 223f

disabled women and, 102
economy of, 405f
elderly percentage in, 298, 298t
emperor rule and, 379
entrepreneurship and, 57, 132
face-work in, 82
foreign aid per capita in, 227f
foreign students and, 364f
G8 conference and, 228, 441, *472, 473*
gender inequality in, 231, 282f
higher education completion rates in,
     361f
human trafficking and, 238t
income distribution in, 232f
infant mortality rates in, 421f
innovation and, 132
job satisfaction in, 408–409
life expectancy in, 451f
marriage and, 99
McDonald's and, 57
stratification in, 231
sushi from, 56, 111
union membership in, 133f
Japanese Americans, 260
   evacuation camps and, 260
   as racial group, 245t
   in U.S., 258f
Al Jazeera, 156
Jewish Americans, 263–264
   anti-Semitism and, 263–264
   as ethnic group, 245t
   ethnic succession and, 181
Jews
   anti-Semitism and, 263–264
   Holocaust and, 167, 254, 264, 341
   Judaism and, 338, 339f, 340, 340t
   refugees and, 265, 267
Jiffy Lube, 120
jihad, 272
Jim Crow laws, 257
Joan of Arc, 380, 396
Joblessness and Urban Poverty Research
     Program, 190, 195
jobs. *See also* labor force; occupations;
     workforce; workplace
   /careers in sociology, 21–22, 22f
   job satisfaction, 408–409
   networking and, 106
   precarious work, 205, 214, 215
   reasons for leaving, 284f
Jocks, 122
John F. Kennedy School of Government,
     195, 378
John *v.* Juan (study), 38, 38f
Johns Hopkins University, 69
Jonesboro killing spree, 369
Jordan
   GNI for, 222f
   Al Jazeera and, 156
   terrorism and, 391f
   women legislators in, 386f
Journal of the American Medical
     Association, 430
Juan *v.* John (study), 38, 38f
Judaism, 338, 339f, 340, 340t
jury deliberations, 124
justice
   differential, 178, 187, 188
   environmental, 18, 435, 442
Justice Department, 181, 183, 184, 185, 249,
     260, 281, 402

K

Kaiser Family Foundation, 43
Kannada (language), 60
Kansas
    female governor in, 279
    Obama's mother and, 247
Kansas City, GM and, 411
Katrina disaster, 6–7, 19, 208, 209f, 479
kavakava, 431
Kazakhstan
    filtering information and, 380f
    foreign-born adoptions and, 323f
    GNI for, 222f
Kenya
    ethnic cleansing and, 237
    GNI for, 222f
    Obama's father and, 247
    terrorism and, 391f
    women and, 232
Kevorkian, Jack, 306
kibbutz, 79
killing. *See also* abortion; genocide;
        suicides; war
    Columbine High School attack, 122, 147,
        185, 369
    Eastern Michigan University death, 181
    euthanasia and, 306–307, 308
    executions, by state, 165, 166f
    female infanticide and, 232
    Holocaust and, 167, 254, 264, 341
    Jonesboro killing spree, 369
    Kevorkian and, 306
    in New Delhi slums, 178–179
    rewarding of, war and, 64
    Virginia Tech killing spree, 7, 147, 147f,
        168, 181
King Kong vaults, 59
Kinsey Report, 43, 49
Kinshasa, 87
kinship, 315, 331
kinship patterns, 315
*Kitzmiller v. Dover Area School
        District*, 354
Kiwai Papuans, 199
Kiwanis Club, 129
Klu Klux Klan, 66, 248, 257
Kmart, 185
Koran, 156, 261, 281, 338, 340
Korea, 133. *See also* North Korea; South
        Korea
Korean Americans, 260–261
    /African Americans, racial friction
        and, 261
    Hawai'i and, 260
    Presbyterian church and, 341
    as racial group, 245t
    in U.S., 258f
Koreatown, 256
Kosovo, 237, 392
Kota people, 89
Ku Klux Klan, 66, 248, 257, 487
Kuala Lumpur, electronics factory
        in, 232f
Kurds, 261
Kuwait
    human trafficking and, 238t
    Iraqi invasion of, 389
    women legislators in, 386f
Kyoto Protocol, 437

L

labeling theory, 177–178, 187, 188
    aging and, 297
    defined, 177, 188
    deviance and, 177–178, 187, 188
    health/illness and, 422–423, 423t
    racial profiling and, 177, 253–254,
        267, 268
    sexual deviance and, 177–178
    social constructionist perspective and,
        177, 187, 188
Labor Department, 250, 257
labor force. *See also* workforce
    alienation and, 406–409, 413, 414
    division of labor (bureaucracy),
        125–126, 127t, 135
    elderly and, 304
    low-wage workers, 4, 5, 35
    women in, 281–283, 282f
labor unions, 133–135, 133f, 134f
labor/income migration, 505f
Labour Party, 134
lackluster veterans (communications
        technology), 142t
lag, culture, 498, 507
Lagos, 433
laissez-faire, 414
language(s), 60–62. *See also* communication;
        English language; nonverbal
        communication; *specific languages*
    bilingualism and, 69–71, 69f
    culture and, 60–62
    defined, 61, 72
    gender-related, 61
    intercultural relations and, 61
    on Internet, 500f
    number of, 61
    race stereotypes and, 62
    reality described through, 61
    reality shaped through, 61, 62
    role of, 60–62
    seldom-used, 61f
    symbols and, 15, 61, 62, 63f, 71, 72, 80
language translators, after September 11th
        attacks, 61
Laos
    communism in, 403
    development agency and, 220
    GNI for, 222f
    life expectancy in, 451f
Las Vegas
    population growth in, 460, 461f
    suicides and, 8, 9
    water and, 437
latent functions, 14, 23
Latin America
    global economy and, 461
    globalization and, 224
    as peripheral nation, 501
    periphery nations of, 223, 223f, 501
    Wal-Mart and, 68
Latinos. *See* Hispanics
Latvia
    Exxon Mobil *v.*, 225t
    GNI for, 222f
law(s). *See also* Constitution; norms;
        regulations; social policy; Supreme
        Court
    defined, 63, 71, 72, 170, 187, 188

"right to work," 134f
    society and, 170
lawyers, women, 125
"lazy" secretaries, 105
lead-based paint, toys and, 224f
leadership, 484
League of Women Voters, 129
learning, through Google, 362
Lebanon
    Arab Americans and, 261
    religious clashes and, 341
    terrorism and, 391f
    /U.S. cheating (cross-cultural
        study), 67
legalization, of marijuana, 44, 45, 45f,
        170, 171f
legislatures, women in, 386f
leisure, conspicuous, 199, 201
Lenski, Gerhard
    sociocultural evolution approach of,
        109–111, 111t, 115
    stratification and, 200–201
Leo Burnett USA, 145
lesbians. *See* homosexuals
Lewis Mumford Center, 256
Lexus, 145f
liberation theology, 343, 355
Liberia, 56f, 222f
library catalog, 46
life chances, 208–209, 214, 215
life course
    defined, 94
    rites of passage and, 89–90, 93, 94
    role transitions during, 298–302
    socialization and, 76, 89–91, 94
life event milestones, 90t
life expectancy, 451, 451f, 468, 469
life goals, college students', 65, 66f
lifestyles, diverse, 327–330
light but satisfied (communications
        technology), 142t
Lions Club, 130
Lipstick Jihad (Moaveni), 272–273
literature review (scientific method step), 30
Lithuania, 222f
Little Billy, 312
Little League baseball, 176
Little Tokyo, 256
Littleton, Columbine killings and, 122, 147,
        185, 369
Live 8 gobal benefit concerts, 228
living wills, 302
logic, causal, 30, 32f, 47
"Lollipop," 155
London
    Anti-Slavery Union in, 247
    bungee-jumping in, 130
    Communist League in, 11
    Happy-Go-Lucky and, 375
    hospice care and, 301
    Maharishi in, 381
lood doo na'dziihii (cancer), 61
looking-glass self, 79–80, 83t, 93, 94, 95
L'Oréal, 145f
Los Angeles
    immigration protesters in, *242, 243*
    race riots, 154, 261, 476, 477
    society and, 53
Los Angeles Times, 142
Louis Vuitton, 145f
Louisiana

    Katrina disaster area and, 6–7, 19, 208,
        209f, 479
    University of, high school popularity
        study and, 86, 86t
love relationship, 319–320. *See also*
        romance
lower class, 92, 196, 199, 200
low-wage workers, 4, 5, 35
The Lucifer Effect (Zimbardo), 98
Luddites, 498, 507
Luther College, 274
Luxembourg, 227
lynch mobs, 14, 257, 474

M

machismo, 321, 331
macrosociology, 12, 23
Madagascar, 56f, 222f, 313
MADD (Mothers Against Drunk
        Driving), 180
Mafia, Internet and, 88
magical packets, 52
Maharaja Mac, 57
Maharishi Mahesh Yogi, 381
Mahbub al Haq Human Development
        Centre, 404
mail-back questionnaires, 32
Maine, 4, 104, 459
majority, oppressed, 279–281
males. *See* men
Malawi, 56f, 222f
Malay, 70
Malaysia
    electronics factory in, 232f
    human trafficking and, 238t
    Royal Dutch/Shell *v.*, 225t
male dominance, 14, 64, 112, 113, 273, 278,
        279, 280, 283, 285, 316, 331
male-dominated occupations, 283t
"mall intercepts," 32
Malta, 286
Malthus's thesis, 449–450, 468
Mandarin, 70
manifest functions, 14, 23
Manila, 474
map, pan-Arabism and, 54f
maquiladoras, 235, 236
marijuana, 44, 45, 45f, 170, 171f, 179f
Marijuana Policy Project, 171
marketing, social network Web sites
        and, 152f
Marlboro, 145f
marriage
    arranged, 320
    assisted, 320
    child marriage, 55, 56f
    cohabitation *v.*, 327–328
    as cultural universal, 54, 310, 319
    divorce and, 325–327
    family and, 317–325
    interracial, 247
    Japan and, 99
    as milestone, 90t
    military, 8
    monogamy, 313, 332
    polyandry, 314, 332
    polygamy, 314, 332
    polygyny, 314, 332
    reproduction and, 328, 329
    same-sex, 64, 329–330

serial monogamy, 313–314, 332
at Shinto Shrine, *310, 311*
socialization for, 84
trends, in U.S., 325*f*
without children, 328
Marxist view. *See also* conflict perspective;
sociological perspectives
alienation and, 407–408
class theory (exploitation theory),
197–198, 200, 253, 267, 268
defined, 14
Malthus's thesis and, 450
religion and, 344
social change and, 496
Marx, Karl, 10–11, *11*, 14, 19, 66, 111, 125,
135, 197, 200, 205, 223, 278, 316, 344,
386, 387, 402, 407, 426, 450, 483,
484, 496
Mary Crane Nursery, *12*
Maryland
Bell v. Maryland in, 263
homeless people and, 467
medical marijuana patients and, 171*f*
masculinities, multiple, 276, 288, 289
Mason Club, 130
mass media, 138–161. *See also* globalization;
Internet; movies; television
advertising and, 143–144, 155
audience and, 152–154
concentration/centralization of,
157–158, 159
defined, 140, 159
disasters and, 144
dominant ideology and, 148, 150, 159
dysfunctions of, 141, 144
gatekeeping and, 144–145, 159
global reach of, 154–157
global village and, 154, 155
globalization and, 84*f*, 224
HIV/AIDS and, 141
innovations, 86
Internet and, 155–156, 159
monitoring, 145, 147
narcotizing dysfunction of, 141,
144, 159
norms and, 142
opinion leaders and, 154, 159
penetration, in selected countries, 155*f*
radio and, 86, 86*f*
sexual behavior and, 142
socialization and, 86–87, 141–142
sociological perspectives on, 141–154,
153*t*, 159
status and, 142–143, 143*t*
stereotypes and, 148, 150
technology and, 86–87
U.S., imitation of, 148
women and, 150–151
Massachusetts. *See also* Boston
adoption/unmarried couples and, 324
faith-based organizations and, 343
gay marriage ruling and, 329, 330
gutted factory in, 411*f*
State Police, 95
teacher salaries and, 370*f*
Massachusetts Institute of Technology,
501, 508
Massachusetts Supreme Court, 329
master status, 101, 102, 114, 115
matchmaker services, 319
mate selection, 318–319

material culture, 58, 72
material resources, technology and, 72, 109,
115, 498, 507
Mato Grosso, deforestation in, 59
matriarchy, 315
matrilineal descent, 315, 332
matrix of domination, 278, 279*f*, 288, 289
Mauritania, 54, 56*f*, 222*f*
McCafe, 57
McDonaldization, 57, 120, 126, 128, 136. *See*
also globalization
McDonaldization of Society (Ritzer), 120, 128
McDonald's, 57, 58*f*, 125, 127, 128, 145*f*
McKinney Homeless Assistance Act, 467
me, achieved statuses and, 100*f*
Meachan v. Knolls Atomic Power
Laboratory, 304
Mead's theory of self, 79, 80–81, 81*t*, 93
mean (average), 45, 47
Mecca, 346
mechanical solidarity, 107–109, 115. *See also*
collective consciousness
Médecins Sans Frontières (Doctors Without
Borders), 239, 391
media. *See* mass media
media monitoring, 145, 147
median, 45, 47
median household income, 45
Medicaid, 206, 214, 287, 301, 403, 429, 431
medical apartheid, 427
medical marijuana, 170, 171*f*
medical model, 420
medical sociology, 6*t*, 18, 21
Medicare, 206, 214, 287, 301, 403, 429, 431
medicine. *See also* diseases; health; health
care; illness
alternative, 430–431, 431*f*
cultural challenges to, 419*t*
as cultural universal, 54
curanderismo and, 426, 442
Doctors Without Borders and, 239, 391
holistic, 442
medicalization of society and, 420–421
medicine men, 52
physicians/nurses/patients and,
429–430
The Scalpel and the Silver Bear and, 418,
419*t*, 429
megalopolis, 459, 468, 469
melting pot, 255
men. *See also* gender; male dominance
gender roles of, 84, 275–276
mental illness and, 280
mental illness, 431–433, 442
deinstitutionalization and, 208, 432
homosexuality and, 177
men/women and, 280
The Myth of Mental Illness and, 432
stigma and, 7, 147
welfare and, 214
Mercedes-Benz, 145*f*
Merton's theory of deviance, 12, 174–175,
174*t*, 187, 188
mestizos, 234
Methodists, 302, 342, 345
Mexican Americans, 262
as ethnic group, 245*t*
familism and, 321, 331
family and, 321
machismo and, 321, 331
in U.S., 262, 262*f*

Mexico
CO_2 emissions in, 438*f*
color hierarchy and, 234
economy of, 234, 405*f*
foreign students and, 364*f*
higher education completion rates
in, 361*f*
human trafficking and, 238*t*
immigrant deaths in Arizona and, 233
income distribution in, 232*f*
infant mortality rates in, 421*f*
life expectancy in, 451*f*
maquiladoras and, 235, 236
marriage ages in, 318*f*
media penetration in, 155*f*
migradollars and, 236, 237, 240
Monterrey, 235
municipal dump in, *218, 219*
poverty and, *218, 219*
race relations in, 234
religious participation in, 347*f*
rural, crime in, 179
San Jose del Cabo, 234*f*
as semiperiphery nation, 223, 223*f*
sexual behavior research, 44*f*
Sonora, 233, 236*f*
stratification in, 233–237
/U.S., borderlands and, 233, 235–237,
236*f*, 239, 240, 266
Wal-Mart and, 68
women's status in, 234–235
Zapatistas and, 235, 392, 485
Miami
bilingualism and, 70
Cuban Americans in, 89, 262
Hispanics in, 262
Police Department Explorers, *96, 97*
Michigan
Eastern Michigan University and, 181
female governor in, 279
international migration amounts
and, 456
Kevorkian and, 306
University of Michigan and, 410
microfinancing, 409, 414
microsociology, 12, 23
Microsoft, 145*f*, 402, 406
middle class, 196–197
Middle East
CO_2 emissions in, 438*f*
global migration and, 265
head scarf/veil and, 281
Al Hurra and, 156
Islam and, 340
Al Jazeera and, 156
nations of, 261
oil and, 238
television characters and, 149
terrorism and, 391*f*
U.S. troops in, 107
midlife crisis, 298, 307, 308
midwifery, 421, 497
migradollars, 236, 237, 240
migrant workers, 504, 506
migration. *See also* immigration
defined, 456, 468, 469
internal, 456–457
international, 456
labor/income, 505*f*
population and, 456–457
reverse, 262

Mikes of America, 130
milestones, 90*t*, 352, 498, 502, 503
Milgram experiments, 166–168
military. *See also* war
deployment, divorce and, 326
e-mail and, 107
homosexuals and, 177
marriages and, 8
social support and, 326
U.S. troops in Middle East, 107
Milk, Harvey, 370, 491
Millennium Project, 227, 228, 239, 241
Mills's power elite model, 386–387, 387*f*, 395
Minangkabau society, 277
minimal hierarchies, 131
Minnesota Center for Twin and Family
Research, 79
minority groups, 245, 267, 268
affirmative action and, 252, 267, 268,
409, 410, 413, 414
ideal, 259, 267, 268
model, 259, 267, 268
Minot, train derailment in, 157
miracle cures, 420
Mississippi
affirmative action and, 410
baby names study and, 38
Katrina disaster area and, 6–7, 19, 208,
209*f*, 479
rural nature of, 459
school violence and, 369
misuse, of Internet, 113, 115, 142
mob behavior, smart, 474
mobile centrics (communications
technology), 142*t*
mobile phones
developing nations and, 87
mobile centrics and, 142*t*
Obama and, 35
surveys/polling issues and, 35
mobility. *See* social mobility
mock prison experiment, 98–99, 101, 176
mode, 45, 47
model minority group, 259, 267, 268
modern societies, 10, 107, 108, 157, 229, 347.
See also postmodern societies
modernization, 229, 240
modernization theory, 229–230, 230*t*,
239, 240
modified/new words, in language, 484
Moët & Chandon, 145*f*
Moldova, 146*f*
Monaco, 382
monarchy, 381–382, 395
money laundering, 183*t*
Money magazine, 480
Mongolia
Buddhism and, 340*t*
globalization and, *492, 493*
GNI for, 222*f*
monitoring/filtering
Internet and, 113, 146*f*
media monitoring, 145, 147
political content, 380*f*
social content, 146*f*
monkeys, 78, 353
monogamy, 313, 332
monopolies, 401–402, 414
Monopoly (game), *401*
Monterrey, Mexico, 235
moral development, Piaget and, 83

morbidity rates, 423, 442

Morehouse Medical Treatment and
    Effectiveness, 426

mores, 63, 71, 72

Mormons, 253, 337, 339, 340, 342, 344, 348

Morocco
    human trafficking and, 238t
    ING Group v., 225t
    U.S. favorability rating and, 66

mortality rates, 423, 442

mothers
    artificial, 78
    MADD, 180
    Obama's, 247
    single, Iceland and, 328

Mothers Against Drunk Driving
    (MADD), 180

motion pictures. *See* movies

Mountain View, Google Corporation at, *411*

movements. *See* social movements

movies. *See also* mass media; television
    American Gangster, 189
    Billy Elliot, 291
    Blood Diamond, 241
    Bowling for Columbine, 185
    Boys Don't Cry, 178f, 291
    Casablanca, *138, 139*
    City of God, 241
    Crash, 269
    Dark Days, 471
    The Departed, 95
    The Devil Wears Prada, 415
    Do the Right Thing, 25, 261
    Erin Brockovich, 49
    Frozen River, 137
    Gran Torino, 309
    The Great Debaters, 269
    Hairspray, 137
    Happy-Go-Lucky, 375
    *Harry Potter and the Half-Blood
        Prince*, 362f
    The Host, 333
    Into the Wild, 445
    James Bond, 57
    Juno, 333
    Kinsey, 49
    Knocked Up, 189
    The Last King of Scotland, 397
    Maid in Manhattan, 209
    Mall Cop, 144f
    Manufactured Landscapes, 509
    Matrix Reloaded, 157
    Memoirs of a Geisha, 148, 150f
    Milk, 491
    Modern Times, 415
    The Namesake, 73
    Norma Rae, 491
    product placement and, 143, 144f
    Pursuit of Happyness, 217
    Quinceañera, 309
    Saved!, 357
    Sicko, 445
    Slumdog Millionaire, 471
    Smoke Signals, 73
    smoking in, 37
    socialization and, 86
    Talk to Me, 161
    Thank You for Smoking, 161
    Titanic, 148, 217
    Trading Places, 117
    Trembling Before G-D, 357

Under the Same Moon, 25

Up the Yangtze, 509

The Visitor, 397

Wendy and Lucy, 117

The Wrestler, 95

Mozambique, human trafficking and, 238t

Ms. magazine, 46

MTV Arabia, 150f

mudding ceremony, *90*

multidimensional model of class, 202

multinational corporations, 224–227, 225t,
    239, 240. *See also* globalization

multiple identities, 247

multiple masculinities, 276, 288, 289

multiple measures, for social class, 202

multiple-nuclei theory, 460, 460f, 468, 469

multitasking, 132

Mumbai (formerly Bombay), 471, 486

municipal dump, Mexico and, *218, 219*

murder. *See* killing

Muslim Americans. *See also* Arab Americans
    Islam and, 349
    racial profiling of, 177, 253, 254
    Razanne doll and, 85
    stereotyping of, 170

Muslims, 349
    Arab Americans and, 261
    Great Britain, Internet and, 88
    Hindu/Muslim riots and, 353
    Islam and, 338, 339f, 340, 340t
    medicine challenges and, 419t
    Obama and, 156
    touching/searching, Iraq War and, 63f

Myanmar, Shweyanpyay Monastery at,
    334, 335

MySpace, 28, 88, 106, 108, 112, 113, 114, 141,
    142, 157, 385

The Myth of Mental Illness (Szasz), 432

N

NAACP (National Association for the
    Advancement of Colored People),
    11, 12

NACCRRA, 92

Nacirema people, 52, 436

NAFTA (North American Free Trade
    Agreement), 235

NameVoyager, 38

Namibia, 222f, 230

Napster, 173

narcotizing dysfunction, of mass media, 141,
    144, 159

NASA (National Aeronautics and Space
    Administration), 129

Nation of Islam, 349

National Advisory Commission on Criminal
    Justice, 181

National Aeronautics and Space
    Administration (NASA), 129

National Alliance for the Mentally Ill, 431

National Alliance to End Homelessness,
    466, 467

National Association for the Advancement of
    Colored People (NAACP), 11, 12

National Basketball Association (NBA), 15

National Center for Community and Justice,
    218, 233

National Center for Education Statistics, 369,
    371, 372

National Center for Health Statistics, 426

National Committee to Preserve Social
    Security and Medicare, 305

National Conference for Community and
    Justice, 233

National Council on Disability, 488

national crime rates, 184t

National Crime Victimization Survey, 184, 185

National Geographic, 391, 459, 505

National Guard, 252, 326, 479

National Health and Social Life Survey
    (NHSLS), 44, 44f

National Institute of Child Health and
    Human Development, 44

National Institute on Aging, 300

National Institutes of Health (NIH), 422, 430

National Law Center on Homelessness and
    Poverty, 467

National Opinion Research Center
    (NORC), 32

National Organization for Men Against
    Sexism (NOMAS), 276

National Reconnaissance Office, 126

National Review, 46

National Rifle Association (NRA), 186

National Science Foundation, 40

National Security Agency, 126

National White Collar Crime Center, 182

nations. *See also* developing nations;
        industrial nations; *specific nations*
    core, 223, 223f
    developing, mobile phones and, 87
    foreign aid per capita in, 227f
    gross national income, by nation, 222f
    human trafficking and, 238t
    income distribution in, 232f
    life expectancy in, 451f
    multinational corporations v., 225t
    NRI and, 229, 229t
    periphery, 223, 223f
    semiperiphery, 223, 223f
    stratification within, 230–237
    women in national legislatures, by
        country, 386f
    world poverty and, 226f

Native Alaskans. *See* Alaskan Natives

Native Americans, 258–259. *See also*
        specific tribes
    casinos, 258
    genocide and, 253, 254
    income and, 250f
    powwow, 122f
    as racial group, 245t
    reservation system and, 246
    seldom-used languages and, 61f
    two spirit and, 178
    in U.S., 246f, 257f

Native Hawai'ians. *See also* Hawai'i
    as race category, 245f
    in U.S., 245f, 258f

natural science, 5, 23

natural selection, 55

naturally occurring retirement communities
    (NORCs), 300–301, 308

nature v. nurture, 77, 276. *See also*
    environment; heredity

Navajo
    cancer and, 61
    family and, 321
    Navajo Nation Police Department, 102
    The Scalpel and the Silver Bear and, 418,
        419, 429

Naval Academy (U.S.), 67

Naval Academy seniors, hats and, 89

Nayar people, 322

Nazis
    Hitler Youth movement and, 79
    Holocaust and, 167, 254, 264, 341
    Internet and, 88
    neo-Nazi skinheads, 264
    SS *St. Louis* and, 265
    virtual world and, 108

NBA (National Basketball Association), 15

near phase (retirement), 299

Negroes. *See* African Americans

The Negro Church (duBois), 11

neighborhood economic development, 18

neocolonialism, 223, 239, 240

neo-Luddites, 498, 508

neo-Nazi skinheads, 264

Nepal
    NRI and, 229, 229t
    Nyinba culture of, 314
    poverty and, 226f
    Sherpas and, 295
    women workers in, 404

nepotism, Iraq and, 55

Nescafé, 145f

Net activism, 392

Net neutrality, 114, 115

Netherlands
    Amsterdam, Schiphol airport and, 170f
    arms transfers and, 187
    brands in, 145f
    Millenium Project and, 227
    NRI and, 229, 229t
    physician-assisted suicide and, 307
    same-sex marriages and, 330

Network Center, 105

Networked Readiness Index (NRI),
    229, 229t

networking. *See also* Internet; social
        networking Web sites; social networks
        of criminal organizations, 183t
    social networks and, 106

neutrality
    Internet, 114, 115
    value, 40–41, 43, 48

Nevada, 457. *See also* Las Vegas

New Delhi slums, killings in, 178–179

New Guinea, 61, 199, 222f

New Hampshire
    community, Boston and, 112
    handicap access ramp (for mountain
        shelter) in, 102
    high school popularity study and, 86

New Haven, Milgram experiments and,
    166–168

new identity (role exit stage), 103

New Jersey, 244, 480

New Mexico
    borderlands and, 233, 235–237, 236f,
        239, 240, 266
    death penalty and, 166
    Waste Isolation Pilot Plant, 62, 63f

New Orleans, Katrina and, 6–7, 19, 208,
    209f, 479

*New Orleans Medical and Surgical J
    ournal*, 423

new religious movements (NRMs), 348,
    350, 351t, 355

new social movements, 485, 485t, 486, 490

new urban sociology, 461, 462t, 468, 469

New York (state)
adoption/unmarried couples and, 324
Indonesian slaves in, 193
Oneida Nation of, 61f
Urban Justice Center, 233
New York City. See also September 11th attacks
Brooklyn, 25, 104f
Coney Island, mobile voter registration
station in, 376, 377
homeless man in, 190, 191
New York Corset Club, 130
New York Times, 181, 389
New York University, 233, 503
New Zealand
car thefts in, 185
child care costs in, 93f
CO$_2$ emissions in, 438f
crime and, 187
GNI for, 222f
new/modified words, in language, 484
news. See also mass media
comprehension, television viewing and, 30
Google and, 158
Internet and, 157–158
media concentration and, 157–158
world, 156
News Corporation, Rupert Murdoch's, 157
NGOs (nongovernmental organizations),
238, 390, 391
NHSLS (National Health and Social Life
Survey), 44, 44f
Nicaragua
abortion and, 286
child marriages and, 56f
GNI for, 222f
human trafficking and, 238t
NRI and, 229
Nickel and Dimed (Ehrenreich), 4
Niger
child marriages and, 56f
GNI for, 222f
TFR and, 450
Nigeria
British Petroleum v., 225t
GNI for, 222f
human trafficking and, 238t
Internet plagiarism and, 67
poverty and, 226f
wealth and, 230
nightclub fire, in West Warwick, 476
NIH (National Institutes of Health), 422, 430
nihilists, 28
Nike Corporation, 155
9/11 attacks. See September 11th attacks
Nineteenth Amendment, 284
Nintendo, 145f
Nisei, 260
Nissan, 231
Nivea, 145f
No Child Left Behind Act, 372–373, 374
No Kidding, 328
Nobel Peace Prize, 202, 239, 354, 409
Nokia, 145f
NOMAS (National Organization for Men
Against Sexism), 276
nonconformist subculture, 370–371
nondeviant conformity (Merton's theory of
deviance), 174, 174t
nongovernmental organizations (NGOs),
238, 390, 391
nonmaterial culture, 58, 72

nonperiodic assemblies, 477, 490
nonscientific polls, 32
nonverbal communication
American Sign Language as, 62f
cultures and, 62
defined, 15, 23
symbols and, 15, 61, 62, 63f, 71, 72
NORC (National Opinion Research
Center), 32
NORCs (naturally occurring retirement
communities), 300–301, 308
Nordhaus, 202
Norman International Company, 407
norms, 63–64, 68t, 71, 72. See also laws
acceptance of, 64
mass media and, 142
sanctions v., 64–65, 65t, 71, 72
types of, 63–64
North American Free Trade Agreement
(NAFTA), 235
North Carolina, 279, 435
North Korea
human trafficking and, 238t
medicine challenges and, 419t
poverty and, 226f
as totalitarian state, 382
Northern Ireland
Irish Americans and, 264
religious clashes and, 341
terrorism and, 60
Northwestern University, 146
Norway
foreign aid per capita in, 227f
gender inequality in, 282f
human trafficking and, 238t
Millenium Project and, 227
NRI and, 229, 229t
religious participation in, 347f
same-sex marriages and, 330
Sami people of, 61
Norwegian Americans, 248
NRA (National Rifle Association), 186
NRI (Networked Readiness Index), 229, 229t
NRMs (new religious movements), 348, 350,
351t, 355
nuclear families, 313, 332
nuclear power generation, 58f
nuclear waste, WIPP and, 62, 63f
Nuestro Himno (Star-Spangled Banner), 71
nurses/patients/physicians, 429–430
nurture v. nature, 77, 276. See also
environment; heredity
NVivo 7, 42
Nyinba people, 314

O

Obama, Barack
Abu Ghraib scandal and, 99
campaign costs and, 393
charisma of, 381
father of, 247
fundraising and, 394
inauguration of, 104, 105, 248f
mobile phone users and, 35
mother of, 247
multiple identities and, 247
Muslim world and, 156
television casting and, 149
underrepresentation of Black Americans
and, 258

Us Weekly and, 154f
young voters and, 385
Obama, Michelle, 149, 154f
obedience
conformity and, 166–168, 187
defined, 166, 187, 188
Milgram experiments and, 166–168
obesity, 35, 107, 148, 172, 420, 421f, 434
objective method, of measuring social class,
201, 214, 215
observation, 34–36, 48. See also ethnography
occupational mobility, 210
occupational prestige, 201–202, 202t
occupations
female-dominated, 283t
male-dominated, 283t
prestige rankings of, 201–202, 202t
women in, 283t
OCED (Organization for Economic
Co-operation and Development), 93,
226, 231
off the Net (communications technology), 142t
offshoring, 412–413, 414
Ohio, Isabelle case in, 77–78
Old West, 61
older population. See aging; elderly
oligarchies, 127, 135, 136, 382, 395
Olin Center for Law, Economics, and
Business, 40
OLPC (One Laptop per Child) campaign, 501
Oman
filtering information and, 146f, 380f
GNI for, 222f
omnivores (communications technology), 142t
On Death and Dying (Kübler-Ross), 301
On the Origin of Species (Darwin), 10
One Laptop per Child (OLPC)
campaign, 501
One Night @ the Call Centre, 60
one-drop rule, 246, 269
online. See Internet
online socializing. See social networking
Web sites
open system, 209, 214, 215
operational definitions, 30, 47, 48
opinion, public, 481, 482t, 490
opinion leaders, mass media and, 154, 159
oppressed majority (women), 279–281
order. See social order
Oregon
physician-assisted suicide and, 307
Wendy and Lucy and, 117
organic solidarity, 107–109, 115
organism, society as, 13, 24
Organization for Economic Co-operation and
Development (OECD), 93, 226, 231
organizational culture, bureaucracy and,
127–129
organizational restructuring, 131
organizations, 125–135
classical theory of, 127, 135, 136
formal, 125, 135, 136
human relations approach to, 128,
135, 136
NGOs, 238, 390, 391
religious forms of, 347–351, 351t
schools as, 367–372
scientific management approach to, 127,
135, 136
voluntary, 129–130, 135, 136

organized crime, 181, 187, 188
The Origin of the Family, Private Property,
and the State (Engels), 278
orphanages, in Eastern Europe, 77–78
Oscar Mayer, 480
Oskar/Jack (identical twins), 78–79
others
generalized, 80, 83t, 93, 94
significant, 81, 93, 94
The Other America (Harrington), 111
out-groups, 121–122, 135, 136

P

Pacific Gas & Electric, 49
Pacific Islanders
health insurance and, 425f
poverty and, 207t
as racial group, 245t
in U.S., 258f
Pakistan
infant mortality rates in, 421f
poverty and, 226f
as semiperiphery nation, 223, 223f
Palestinian territories
educational curriculum, pan-Arabism
in, 54f
Israeli child care center and, 91
terrorism and, 60
Panama
"African Panamanians" and, 246
GNI for, 222f
as semiperiphery nation, 223, 223f
pan-Arabism, Palestinian educational
curriculum and, 54f
Panasonic, 145f
Pan-Cordillera Women's Network for Peace
and Development, 233
panics, 480, 482t, 490
paradigms, 120, 140
Paraguay, foreign-born adoptions and, 323f
parenthood, 84, 90t
Paris
child care and, 212
Disneyland, 112
Marx in, 10
McDonaldization and, 120
Médecins Sans Frontières in, 239, 391
parkour, 58–59
Parson's equilibrium model, 496, 507
participant observation, 35, 36
participation, political, 382–384
partnerships, domestic, 330, 331, 486
passage, rites of, 89–90, 93, 94, 299. See also
life course
patents, 39, 132, 495
patients/physicians/nurses, 429–430
patriarchy, 315, 332
patrilineal descent, 315, 332
Patriot Act, 66, 169–170
PDAs (personal digital assistants), 154
peace, 389–391, 395. See also war
Peace Corps, 60, 130
Peace Index, Global, 390, 390f
Pearl Harbor attack, 260
pedophilia, 178
peer groups, 86, 93
Pennsylvania
elderly in, 302
Kitzmiller v. Dover Area School District
and, 354

school violence and, 369
State University, 106
Pentagon, 126, 266, 326, 389, 481. *See also* September 11th attacks
'Pentagon Papers,' 389
People magazine, 143*t*, 157
People's Republic of China. *See* China
percentage, 44–45, 48
PerfectMatch.com, 144, 319
periodic assemblies, 477, 490
periodical indexes, computerized, 46
periphery nations, 223, 223*f*
personal digital assistants (PDAs), 154
Personal Responsibility and Work Opportunity Reconciliation Act, 213
personality, 77, 94
perspectives. *See* global perspective; sociological perspectives
Perth, Australia, 92*f*
Peru
  Chevron *v.*, 225*t*
  filtering information and, 146*f*
  foreign-born adoptions and, 323*f*
  GNI for, 222*f*
  preindustrial societies and, 110
  symbols and, 80
  terrorism and, 391*f*
  A Theology of Liberation and, 343
Peter principle, 126
Pew Internet Project, 148, 151, 153, 209
Pew Research Center, 141, 186
The Philadelphia Negro (duBois), 11
Philippines
  ancestral land protection and, 232–233
  foreign-born adoptions and, 323*f*
  human trafficking and, 238*t*
  Internet plagiarism and, 67
  as periphery nation, 223, 223*f*
Philips, 145*f*
physicians
  assisted suicide and, 306–307, 308
  concierge doctors, 192
  Doctors Without Borders and, 239, 391
  /nurses/patients, 429–430
Piaget, developmental stages of, 83, 83*t*, 94
Piczo, 113
piracy, sea, 183*t*
pirated entertainment, 67, 172–173
The Pirates Dilemma (Mason), 494
Pizza Hut, *121*
placebo effect, 37
plagiarism, 46, 65–66, 67
play stage (Mead's stages of self), 80, 81*t*
pluralism, 256, 267, 268
pluralist model, 388, 395
Poland
  GNI for, 222*f*
  human trafficking and, 238*t*
  marriage ages in, 318*f*
  social movements and, 483
  Warsaw, 453*f*
Polaroid, 145
police/protesters, in Toronto, *162, 163*
policy. *See* social policy
Polish Americans
  assimilation and, 255
  as ethnic group, 245*t*
  in U.S., 245*f*, 264
political activism, on Internet, 142, 392–393
political behavior, in U.S., 382–386

political participation, 382–384
political systems
  as cultural universal, 378, 379
  defined, 381, 395
  types of, 381–382
political/social integration, education and, 362–363
politics. *See also* authority; power
  defined, 395
  fiesta, 384
  gender in, 384, 386
  race in, 384, 386
  television and, 148
polling, 32, 34, 35, 481
pollution, 436–437
polyandry, 314, 332
polygamy, 314, 332
polygyny, 314, 332
poor. *See also* homelessness; poverty
  The Bottom Billion and, 220
  categorization of, 206, 207*t*
  deprived people and, 463
  global divide and, 221–222, 222*f*
  underclass and, 207–208, 214, 215
popularity study, high school, 86, 86*t*
population
  demography and, 449–451, 468, 469
  explosion, 453–454
  growth, stable, 455–456
  growth, unchecked, 460, 461
  Malthus's thesis and, 449–450, 468
  migration and, 456–457
  policy, China and, 455
  pyramid, 453, 454*f*
  world, 451–454, 452*t*
  ZPG and, 455–456, 468, 469
The Population Bomb (Ehrlich), 450
pornography, 151, 178, 180
Porsche, 145*f*
Portugal
  foreign aid per capita in, 227*f*
  GM *v.*, 225*t*
  GNI for, 222*f*
Postal Service (U.S.), 125
postindustrial cities, 458, 458*t*, 468, 469
postindustrial societies, 111, 111*t*, 115
postmodern societies, 111–112, 111*t*, 112*f*, 115. *See also* globalization
poverty, 204–209, 207*t*. *See also* poor
  absolute, 205, 206, 215
  explanations for, 208
  feminization of, 207, 214, 215, 321
  Hurricane Katrina disaster and, 6–7, 19, 208, 209*f*, 479
  income/poverty levels, by state, 194*f*
  Mexico and, *218, 219*
  Millennium Project and, 227, 228, 239, 241
  rates, in countries, 206*f*
  relative, 206, 214, 215
  researching, 205–206
  worldwide, 226*f*
poverty line, 206
power. *See also* authority
  authority and, 379
  Black, 257, 267, 268
  communications technology and, 388
  definitions of, 66, 198, 214, 215, 379, 395
  force as, 379, 395
  influence as, 379, 395
  war and, 388

power elite, 386–387, 387*f*, 395
power elite models, 386–388, 387*f*, 395
power structure models (in U.S.), 386–388
The Power Elite (Mills), 386
powwow, 122*f*
Prada, 145*f*
precarious work, 205, 214, 215
predators, online, 113, 115, 142
preindustrial cities, 457, 458*t*, 468, 469
preindustrial societies, 109–110, 111*t*, 115
prejudice, 248–249, 267, 268. *See also* discrimination
preoperational stage, 83
preparatory stage (Mead's stages of self), 80, 81*t*
preretirement phase, 299
Presbyterians, 340, 341, 342, 345
preschoolers, child care and, 91, 92
presentation of the self, 81–82, 81*f*, 93, 94
presidency. *See* Obama, Barack
prestige, 201–202, 202*t*, 215
prestige symbol, stigma symbol *v.*, 172
prevalence, 423, 442
primary groups, 121, 136
primates, isolation of, 78
Princess Diana, 143, 485
Princess Victoria (Sweden), 143
printing, 3-D, 494
prison
  Abu Ghraib, 98–99, 167, 389, 390
  in Finland, 165*f*
  gangs, 14
  international incarceration rates, 185
  overflow in, 168
  resocialization and, 91*f*
  social control and, 168
  television in, 165*f*
  Zimbardo's mock prison experiment, 98–99, 101, 176
privacy
  censorship and, 501–502
  Fourth Amendment and, 113, 114, 502
  in global community, 501–502
privileges
  of dominant groups, 250–251
  White privilege, 250–251, 267, 268
problem defining (scientific method step), 29–30
product placement, 143, 144*f*
productivity enhancers (communications technology), 142*t*
profane, 338, 355
professional crime, 180–181, 187, 188
profiles
  global, of Internet, 500
  online, 88, 88*f*, 89, 106, 113, 114, 318, 385
profiling, racial, 177, 253–254, 267, 268
project teams, 131
proletariat, 197, 214, 215
prosthetic devices, electronically controlled, 503
prostitution, 15
  African American women and, 279
  Gang Leader for a Day and, 164
  global trafficking of sex workers and, 42, *42*
  organized crime and, 181
  prestige ranking for, 202*t*
  as victimless crime, 180, 187

Protestant ethic, 11, 343, 355
Protestant Ethic and the Spirit of Capitalism (Weber), 11, 343
Protestant Reformation, 343, 348, 356
Protestants, 341, 343, 348
protesters, *162, 163, 472, 473*
psychoanalysis, 82–83, 83*t*
psychological approaches to self, 82–83
Public Citizen, 394
public displays of affection, India and, *64*
public opinion, 481, 482*t*, 490
public policy. *See* social policy
public sociology, 6, 16, 233
publics, 481, 482*t*, 490
Puerto Ricans
  as ethnic group, 245*t*
  reverse migration of, 262
  in U.S., 245, 262, 262*f*, 463
Puerto Rico
  GNI for, 222*f*
  U.S. and, 245, 262, 463
Purdue University, 412
Puritans, 173
Pygmalion in the Classroom, 367
pyramid, population, 453, 454*f*

Q

Al Qaeda terrorist network, 126, 156
Qatar
  human trafficking and, 238*t*
  Al Jazeera and, 156
qualitative research, 34–35, 48. *See also* observation
quantitative research, 34, 48. *See also* polling; surveys
quasi-religions, 350, 355
Quebec, bilingualism and, 70
Québécois, 70
questionnaires, 32, 34, 48
quinceañera ceremony, 89, 309

R

race, 245–247
  /ethnicity percentages, in colleges, 371*f*
  ethnicity *v.*, 248
  /ethnicity/gender, income and, 250*f*
  family life and, 84, 321–322
  Internet usage and, 153*f*
  language/stereotypes and, 62
  matrix of domination and, 278, 279*f*, 288, 289
  Mexico and, 234
  politics and, 384, 386
  social construction of, 246–247
  social epidemiology and, 426
  social mobility and, 211
  socialization and, 84
  sociological perspectives on, 253–254, 254*t*
  stereotypes and, 62, 247
  survey taking and, 34
race riots, Los Angeles, 154, 261, 476, 477
racial formation, 246, 267, 268
racial groups. *See also* specific racial groups
  defined, 245, 267, 268
  ethnic groups *v.*, 245, 248
  in U.S., 245*t*, 246*f*, 256–264, 257*f*, 258*f*
racial profiling, 177, 253–254, 267, 268

racism
color-blind, 248–249, 267, 268, 410, 414
defined, 248, 267, 268
radio, media and, 86, 86f
random samples, 30–31, 48
rape
date rape, 177, 181
drinking rape victim, 124
national crime rate, 184t
of wives, by husbands, 178, 179
rational-legal authority, 379–380, 395
Razanne doll, 85
reality. See also languages
constructing, dominant ideology
and, 148
describing languages and, 61
shaping languages and, 61, 62
social interaction and, 99–100
reality television, 43, 149
rebellion (Merton's theory of deviance),
174t, 175
recession. See also global community;
globalization
bailout legislation and, 133, 213, 402
global, 223, 228
Japan and, 82, 408–409
Millennium Project and, 227, 228,
239, 241
Obama inauguration and, 104
September 11th attacks and, 19
suicide and, 8
U.S. and, 133–134, 411
recording industry, 144
recovering alcoholic, 103, 172
Red Crescent Society, 390, 391
Red Cross, 187
Reebok Corporation, 108, 225
Reese's Pieces candy, 143
reference groups, 122–123, 135, 136
references/citations (research reports),
46–47
Reformation, 343, 348, 356
refugees (asylum seekers)
Afghan, 456f
Chinese, 267
Cuban, 262
environmental, 439
increases in, 456
Iranian, 273
Jewish, 265, 267
processing of, 392
Vietnamese, 259
reggae music, 111
regulations
Internet and, 112–114, 145
/rules, bureaucracy and, 126, 127t
relationships. See also families; groups;
marriage
diverse lifestyles and, 327–330
intergroup, 254–256
lesbian/gay, 329–330
love, 319
relative deprivation approach, 483, 485t, 490
relative poverty, 206, 214, 215
relativism, cultural, 55, 71, 72, 400, 414
reliability, 32, 47, 48, 373, 374
religion(s), 334–357. See also Buddhism;
Christianity; Hinduism; Islam;
Judaism; specific religions
beliefs, 345, 347t, 355
components of, 345–347, 347t

as cultural universal, 336, 341, 355
defining, 338, 355
Durkheim and, 338, 341
education/income/religion (study),
342, 342f
experiences in, 347, 347t, 355
forms of organization in, 347–351, 351t
government and, 87, 89
in India (case study), 352–353
integration and, 341
Marx on, 344
matrix of domination and, 278, 279f,
288, 289
quasi, 350, 355
rituals, 346, 347t, 355
social change and, 343–344
as social institution, 103
social order and, 344
social support and, 341–343, 345t, 355
socialization and, 87, 93
sociological perspectives on, 338,
341–345, 345t
of U.S., 337f
Weberian thesis and, 343, 355
world, 338–340, 339f, 340t
Religion News Service, 354
religious beliefs, 345, 347t, 355
religious experiences, 347, 347t, 355
religious movements, new, 348, 350,
351t, 355
religious organization, forms of,
347–351, 351t
religious rituals, 346, 347t, 355
religious services, 347, 351
Religious Tolerance, 238, 350
remittances, 236, 239, 240, 265
reorientation phase (retirement), 300
reports. See research reports
representative democracy, 382, 395
reproduction
family and, 312, 316, 331
fertility and, 449, 468, 469
marriage and, 328, 329
Republic of Rwanda. See Rwanda
Republic of South Africa. See South Africa
Republican voters, 213, 382, 383, 388
research. See also research designs; specific
research studies
biases and, 41
on disasters, 478–479
ethics of, 37–39
feminist perspective and, 41–42
funding, 40
HIV/AIDS and, 425
Internet and, 42–43, 46
poverty and, 205–206
process of, 29–49
qualitative, 34–35, 48
quantitative, 34, 48
reports, preparation of, 46–47
sociology and, 19
technology and, 42–43
research designs, 33–37, 47, 48. See also
specific research designs
existing sources/secondary analysis,
37, 39, 48
experiments, 36–37, 47
observation, 35–36
summary chart of, 39t
surveys, 33–35
research reports (preparation of), 46–47

reservation system, Native Americans
and, 246
resistance to social change, 497–498
resistance to technology, 498
resocialization, 91, 91f, 94, 95
resource mobilization approach, 483–484,
485t, 490
resources
environmental, 228
material, technology and, 72, 109, 115,
498, 507
social, 217, 301
restructuring, organizational, 131
retirement, 299–301, 301f, 308
retreatist (Merton's theory of deviance),
174, 174t
Reuters, 155
reverse migration, 262
review of literature (scientific method
step), 30
rewards
for killing in warfare, 64
sanctions and, 65
rhesus monkeys, isolation of, 78
Rhode Island
elderly in, 302
nightclub fire and, 475
Richistan (Frank), 192
rights
Civil Rights Act, 252, 488, 489
civil rights movement, 100, 161, 211,
257, 258, 409, 488
disability rights, 487–489
human, 237–239
"right to die," 306–307
"right to work" laws, by state, 134f
Rio de Janeiro, 241
riots
as collective behavior, 475, 476, 477, 478
Do the Right Thing and, 25, 261
in France (2005), 255
Hindu/Muslim, 353
L.A. race riots, 154, 261, 476, 477
potential, Toronto police and, 162, 163
rites of passage, 89–90, 93, 94, 299. See also
life course
ritualist (Merton's theory of deviance), 174,
174t
rituals, religious, 346, 347t, 355
Riyadh, McDonald's in, 58f
Roe v. Wade, 286, 287
roles. See also gender roles
sick, 442
social, 101–103, 114, 115
role conflict, 101–102, 115
role exit, 102–103, 115
role strain, 102, 115
role taking, 80, 94
role transitions, during life course, 298–302
Rolex, 145f
Rolling Stone magazine, 143t
Rolls-Royce, 192
Roman Catholics. See Catholics
romance. See also love relationship
arranged marriages and, 320
individual preference and, 317
Internet dating services and, 112, 152,
318
romantic relationships (high school
study), 106
workplace, 68

Romani people, 264
Romania
human trafficking and, 238t
orphanages in, 77–78
Roughnecks, Saints and, 177
routine activities theory of deviance, 175
Royal Dutch/Shell, Malay v., 225t
RU-486 (abortion pill), 286
rugby team, at Brown University, 118, 119
rules/regulations, bureaucracy and,
126, 127t
rumors, 480–481, 482t, 490
Rupert Murdoch's News Corporation, 157
rural areas, 464–466
Russia. See also Soviet Union
arms transfers and, 187
binge drinking in, 169
CO_2 emissions in, 438f
economy of, 405f
G8 conference and, 228, 441, 472, 473
human trafficking and, 238t
media penetration in, 155f
social support and, 297
Rutgers University, 67
Rwanda
Congo's national parks and, 402
genocide and, 255
GNI for, 222f
women legislators in, 386f

S

sabotage
detention camps and, 260
environmental groups and, 440
industrial, 201
origin of term, 498
sacred
cows, in India, 13, 13, 14, 55
defined, 338, 355
SADD (Students Against Drunk Driving),
180, 189
Safwan, 390
Saints, Roughnecks and, 177
salaries
corporate executives and, 198
teachers and, 370f
Salt Lake City, 184
Salvadorans, in U.S., 70f, 245f, 262f. See also
El Salvador
same-sex marriage, 64, 329–330
Sami people, 61
samples, 30–32, 47, 48. See also specific
sampling techniques
convenience, 32
random, 30–31, 48
snowball, 32
Samsung, 145f
San Antonio Palopo, Guatemala, 74, 75
San Francisco
Child Care Law Center in, 85
Google's plans for, 140
Wi-Fi accessibility and, 140
San Jose del Cabo, 234f
sanctions, 64–65, 65t, 71, 72, 165. See also
norms
sandwich generation, 299, 307, 308
Santa Ana, Hispanics in, 262
SAP, 145f
Sapir-Whorf hypothesis, 61–62, 72. See also
languages

Saudi Arabia
  ecclesiae in, 348
  holding hands in, 62
  human trafficking and, 238t
  Mecca, 346
  Riyadh, McDonald's and, 58f
The Scalpel and the Silver Bear (Alvord), 418, 419, 429
Scarce court case, 39
scarf/veil, Middle East and, 281
scheduled castes, 194
Schiphol airport, 170f
schools. *See also* colleges; high schools
  bureaucratization of, 368–369
  completion, milestone and, 90t
  as formal organizations, 367–372
  homeschooling, 371–372, 374
  Iraqi, socialization and, 85–86
  political integration and, 362–363
  religion in, 353–354
  socialization and, 85–86, 93
  violence in, 369
sciences. *See also* sociology
  defined, 5, 23
  natural, 5, 23
  social, 5–7, 23
  systematic study and, 5, 9, 24, 55, 72
scientific management approach (formal organizations), 127, 135, 136
scientific method, 29–33, 48
  defined, 29, 47, 48
  educational level/income and, 30, 31, 31f, 32, 32, 32f, 33, 33f
  steps in, 29
  summary of, 29f, 33
Scientology, 350, 355
SCLC (Southern Christian Leadership Conference), 257
Scopes Monkey Trial, 353
Scotch-Irish, 245t
screen names, 113
screen time, 140
sea piracy, 183t
search for alternatives (role exit stage), 103
Seattle, 225, 383
SEC (Securities and Exchange Commission), 125
Second Amendment, 186
Second Life virtual world, 106, 108, 351
second shift, 284, 289
secondary analysis/existing sources, 37, 39, 48
secondary groups, 104f, 121, 121f, 123, 125, 135, 136, 137, 153
The Second Sex (de Beauvoir), 284
Secret Service (U.S.), 184
secretaries, "lazy," 105
sects, 348, 351t, 355
secularization, 336, 355
Securities and Exchange Commission (SEC), 125
segregation, 255–256, 267, 268
seldom-used languages, 61f
self
  defined, 79, 94
  looking-glass, 79–80, 83t, 93, 94, 95
  Mead and, 79, 80–81, 81t, 93
  presentation of, 81–82, 81f, 93, 94
  psychological approaches to, 82–83
  self-identity, 80
  socialization and, 79–83

sociological perspectives on, 79–82
  stages of, 80, 81t
self-esteem, 77, 172, 324
self-injury groups, 28, 88
semiperiphery nations, 223, 223f
Senator Hatch, 388f
sensorimotor stage, 83
Seoul, South Korea, 333, 447
September 11th attacks
  bin Laden and, 126, 156
  CIA/FBI division of labor and, 126
  Department of Homeland Security and, 134
  economic decline and, 19
  global culture war and, 66
  identity theft and, 182, 184
  Internet and, 142
  Al Jazeera and, 156
  language translators and, 61
  media outlets and, 142
  Patriot Act and, 66, 169–170
  Pentagon and, 126, 266, 326, 389, 481
  racial profiling and, 177, 253
  social control and, 168–169
  strangers in group and, 104, 104
  surveillance after, 66, 169–170, 239
  tattoos and, 5, 15
  terrorist groups and, 60
  wiretaps and, 147
Serbia
  ethnic cleansing and, 237
  GNI for, 222f
  terrorism and, 391f
serial monogamy, 313–314, 332
SES (socioeconomic status), 202, 215, 216
settlement houses, 12
Seventh-Day Adventists, 348
sex. *See* gender; sexual behavior
sex selection clinics, 57
sex trade. *See* human trafficking
sex workers, global trafficking of, 42, 42. *See also* prostitution
sexism, 280, 288, 289
sexual behavior
  intergenerational sex, 178
  mass media and, 142
sexual behavior research
  HIV/AIDs and, 43, 44
  Kinsey Report, 43, 49
  reasons for sex (study), 34, 36t
  social policy and, 43–44
sexual content, in television, 43, 43f
sexual deviance, 177–178
sexual intercourse. *See* sexual behavior research
sexual orientation. *See also* homosexuals
  hate crimes and, 249f
  matrix of domination and, 278, 279f, 288, 289
Sexual Politics (Millett), 284
sexual predators, online, 113, 115, 142
sexual reproduction. *See* reproduction
sexually explicit words, in songs, 37
sexually transmitted diseases, 43
Shakers, 103–104, 116, 344
Al Sham (Greater Syria), 54f
Shame of the Nation (Kozol), 360
Shanghai, 361, 455
shared values, throughout world, 66
Shell Oil, 145f
Sherpa culture, 295

Shia, 349
shift, second, 284, 289
Shinto Shrine, in Tokyo, 310, 311
shock, culture, 60, 71, 72, 195
Shoshit, Shetkari, Kashtakari, Kamgar, Mukti, Sangharsh (SSKKMS), 486, 491
shrine rooms, 52
Shweyanpyay Monastery, 334, 335
sick role, 442
Sidewalk (Duneier), 448
Siemens, 145f
Sierra Club, 416, 417
Sierra Leone, 241
  Blood Diamond and, 241
  GNI for, 222f
  infant mortality rates in, 421f
Sign Language (American Sign Language), 62f
significant others, 81, 93, 94
Sikhism, 339, 352
Silent Warriors, 62f
Silicon Valley, 192
"silver surfers," 292, 293
Simla, India, 59f
simulated prison experiment, 98–99, 101, 176
Singapore
  bilingualism and, 70
  congestion zones and, 463f
  filtering information and, 146f
  GNI for, 222f
  homelessness and, 468
  NRI and, 229, 229t
single lifestyle, 328
single mothers, Iceland and, 328
single-parent families, 324, 331
  child care and, 91–93
  defined, 332
  in U.S., 321f
Sioux Falls, cage fight in, 173f
Sioux Indians, 336
six billionth person, in world, 452
skinheads, 264
Skull Valley, Utah, 435
skyjacking, 183t
slang words, 53, 72, 498
slapping, 168
slavery, 193, 214, 215, 423
  Anti-Slavery Union, 247
  as closed system, 209
  drapetomania and, 423
  as transnational crime, 183
Slovak Republic, venture capital investment and, 132
Slovenia, 222f
slugging, 15
slumdog, 471
small groups, 123, 135, 136
smart mob behavior, 474
Smart Mobs (Rheingold), 474
smartphones, 131
smiley face, 62
Smirnoff, 145f
smoking. *See also* cancer
  dangers of, 177, 178
  deviance and, 172, 177
  in films, 37
  social networks and, 107
  survey (cartoon), 34f
  thirdhand smoke and, 177
  tobacco-related medical cost reimbursements and, 123

snowball samples, 32
Soboa ceremony, 89
soccer, 41, 155, 312, 475, 476
social capital, 13, 23
social change
  communities and, 457–458
  defined, 494–495, 507
  education and, 363
  global, 498–499
  in global community, 493–509
  global economy and, 22
  Marxist view on, 496
  religion and, 343–344
  resistance to, 497–498
  sociological perspectives on, 495–497, 497t
  theories of, 495–497
  U.S. and, 495t
social classes. *See* classes
social club, 122
social compensation hypothesis, 88
social construction
  of gender, 273–277
  of race, 246–247
social constructionist perspective, 177, 187, 188. *See also* labeling theory
social control, 165–170
  control theory and, 170, 188
  defined, 165
  education and, 363
  formal, 168, 187, 188
  gun control and, 185–187
  informal, 168, 187, 188
  Milgram experiments and, 166–168
  prison and, 168
  September 11th attacks and, 168–169
social disorganization theory, 176, 187, 188
social enhancement hypothesis, 88
social epidemiology, 423–428, 442
social inequality, 4. *See also* classes; digital divide; global divide; global inequality; statuses; stratification
  defined, 19, 23, 192, 214, 215
  global, 218–241
social institutions
  defined, 103, 115
  sociological perspectives on, 103–106, 106t, 114
  survival, functional prerequisites for, 103–104
  total, 91, 94
social interactions
  defined, 98, 114, 115
  genetic/biological factors v., 55–56, 72
  Internet and, 112–114
  reality and, 99–100
  social structures v., 98–99
social mobility, 209–211, 214, 215. *See also* stratification
  in developing nations, 231–232
  education and, 211
  ethnicity and, 211
  gender and, 211–212
  /gender differences, nations and, 232–233
  Hispanic immigrants and, 263
  horizontal, 209, 214, 215
  in industrial nations, 230–231
  intergenerational, 209, 211f, 214, 215, 231
  intragenerational, 209, 214, 215

occupational, 210
race and, 211
types of, 209–210
in U.S., 210–212
vertical, 209, 214, 215
social movements, 482–489
defined, 482t, 489, 490
gender and, 484–485
globalization of, 485–486
Internet and, 487
new, 485, 485t, 486, 490
NRMs, 348, 350, 351t, 355
social networking Web sites, 7. *See also* social
networks; virtual worlds
anonymity and, 113, 172
avatars and, 106, 108, 113, 115, 351
chat rooms and, 42, 58, 86, 142, 172,
272, 316
Facebook, 87, 88, 113, 141, 142, 152, 385
friendship networks and, 87, 88–89,
151, 152
Friendster, 88, 113
Gaia Online, 113
impression management and, 113, 113f
marketing through, 152f
MySpace, 28, 88, 106, 108, 112, 113, 114,
141, 142, 157, 385
online profiles and, 88, 88f, 89, 106, 113,
114, 318, 385
Piczo, 113
screen names and, 113
Second Life virtual world, 106, 108, 351
sexual predators and, 113, 115, 142
Twitter, 88, 142
Xanga, 113
YouTube and, 112, 113, 142, 158, 392
social networks. *See also* social networking
Web sites
defined, 106
friendship, 87, 88–89
smoking and, 107
social capital and, 13, 23
as social structures, 106
social norms. *See* norms
social order
economic systems and, 400
rebel and, 175
religion and, 344
sociological perspectives on, 16t
social policy, 20
abortion issue and, 286–288
age stratification and, 306–307
bilingualism and, 69–71, 69f
campaign financing and, 393–394
defined, 20
disability rights and, 487–489
environmental problems and, 440–442
global immigration and, 265–267
global offshoring and, 412–413, 414
globalization and, 504–506
gun control and, 185–187
homelessness and, 466–468
human rights and, 237–239
Internet regulation and, 112–114
labor unions and, 133–135, 133f, 134f
mass media centralization/
concentration and, 157–158
No Child Left Behind Act and,
372–373, 374
religion in schools and, 353–354
"right to die" and, 306–307

same-sex marriage and, 329–330
sexual behavior research v., 43–44
socialization and, 91–93
transnationals and, 504–506
welfare and, 212–214
social reality. *See* reality
social roles, 101–103, 114, 115. *See also* roles
social sciences, sociology and, 5–7, 23
Social Security Administration, 38
social statuses. *See* statuses
social stigma. *See* stigma
social stratification. *See* stratification
social structures. *See also* groups; social
institutions; social networks; social
roles; statuses; virtual worlds
defined, 98, 114
elements of, 100–107, 114
global perspective on, 107–112
social interactions v., 98–99
social support
China and, 455
families and, 317
military and, 326
mobility in developing nations and, 232
religion and, 341–343, 345t, 355
Russia and, 297
socialism, 402–403, 403t, 413, 414
socialization, 74–95
agents of, 83–89
anticipatory, 90–91, 94
of children, 322–325
defined, 76, 93, 94
environment/heredity and, 77, 78–79,
265
family and, 74, 75, 83–84
gender-role, 273–274
gender's impact on, 84
government and, 87, 89, 93
heredity/environmental factors and, 77,
78–79, 93, 265
Internet and, 86–87, 88–89, 88f, 93
Isabelle and, 77–78
isolation and, 77–78, 78f
life course and, 76, 89–91, 94
for marriage, 84
mass media and, 86–87, 141–142
movies and, 86
for parenthood, 84
peer groups and, 86, 93
race's impact on, 84
religion and, 87, 93
resocialization and, 91, 91f, 94, 95
role of, 77–79
school and, 93
self and, 79–83
social policy and, 91–93
workplace and, 87, 87f, 93
socializing online. *See* social networking
Web sites
social/political integration, education and,
362–363
societal-reaction approach, 177, 188. *See also*
labeling theory
societies. *See also* social structures
aging and, 295
agrarian, 110, 111t, 115
complexity of, 107
culture and, 53–54, 66–67, 68t
defined, 53
extinction of, 104
horticultural, 110–111, 111t, 115

hunting-and-gathering, 109–110,
111t, 115
industrial, 111, 111t, 115, 413, 414
law and, 170
matriarchal, 315
medicalization of, 420–421
modern, 10, 107, 108, 157, 229, 347
as organisms, 13, 24
patriarchal, 315, 332
postindustrial, 111, 111t, 115
postmodern, 111–112, 111t, 112f, 115
preindustrial, 109–110, 111t, 115
technology and, 109
traditional, 20, 456
Society for the Psychological Study of Social
Issues, 55
Society for the Study of Social Problems, 12
Society in America (Martineau), 9
sociobiology, 55–56, 71, 72, 173
sociocultural evolution, 109–111, 111t, 115
socioeconomic status (SES), 202, 215, 216
Sociological Abstracts online, 46
sociological imagination
defined, 5, 22, 23
developing, 18–20
Mills and, 5
sociological perspectives. *See also* conflict
perspective; feminist perspective;
functionalist perspective; global
perspective; interactionist perspective;
labeling theory; Marxist view; social
constructionist perspective
on aging, 295–298, 298t
on cultural variation, 68t
on culture/society, 68t
on deviance and crime, 173–179, 180t
on education, 361–367, 368t
on environmental problems, 433–435
on family, 316–317, 317t
on gender, 277–279, 280t
on global inequality, 230t
on health, 419–423, 423t
on illness, 419–423, 423t
on mass media, 141–154, 153t, 159
on multinational corporations,
224–227, 239, 240
on norms, 68t
on race/ethnicity, 253–254, 254t
on religion, 338, 341–345, 345t
on self, 79–82
on social change, 495–497, 497t
on social institutions, 103–106,
106t, 114
on social order, 16t
on sports, 17
on stratification, 197–199, 201t
on urbanization, 459–461, 462t,
468, 469
on values, 68t
on Wal-Mart and culture, 68t
sociology. *See also* American Sociological
Association; global community;
globalization
applied, 16, 18, 23
basic, 18, 23
breadth of topics in, 4, 6, 29
business world and, 22
careers in, 21–22, 22f
clinical, 18, 23
common sense and, 7–8, 23
defined, 5, 22, 23

degrees, by gender, 21f
detachment and, 28, 36
development of, 9–13, 23
environmental, 18
evolutionary theory in, 495, 507
future and, 20
in global community, 228
government issues and, 20
macrosociology and, 12, 23
medical, 6t, 18, 21
microsociology and, 12, 23
new urban sociology and, 461, 462t,
468, 469
public, 6, 16, 233
research and, 19
social sciences and, 5–7, 23
systematic study and, 5, 9, 24, 55, 72
term, coining of, 9
theories in, 8–9
sociopathic personality disorder,
homosexuality as, 177
solidarity, mechanical/organic, 107–109, 115.
See also collective consciousness
Somalia, 54f, 220
Arab Americans and, 261
Global Peace Index and, 390, 390f
GNI for, 222f
population growth in, 453f
songs, sexually explicit words in, 37
Sonora, 233, 236f
Sonoran Desert, 233
Sony, 145f
sororities, 42, 101, 121, 169, 252, 263
Souls of Black Folk (duBois), 11
sources, for sociological research, 37, 39, 48
South Africa. *See also* Africa
apartheid and, 256, 267, 268
binge drinking in, 169
gun control and, 187
human trafficking and, 238t
life expectancy in, 451f
religious participation in, 347f
Soweto, 256
wealth and, 230
South America
Christianity and, 340t
CO_2 emissions in, 438f
global divide and, 221
Hispanics, in U.S., 262f
knowledge of, 150
on map, 54f
preindustrial societies and, 110f
skin color gradients and, 246
terrorism and, 391f
unequal distribution of wealth in, 241
South Americans, in U.S., 262f
South Asia
child marriage in, 55, 56f
tsunami in, 20, 84
South Dakota
cage fight in, 173f
Minot, train derailment in, 157
South Korea
brands in, 145f
CO_2 emissions in, 438f
foreign students and, 364f
foreign-born adoptions and, 323f
higher education completion rates
in, 361f
human trafficking and, 238t
medicine challenges and, 419t

protesters, Iraq War and, 477*f*
as semiperiphery nation, 223, 223*f*
Seoul, 333, 447
socializing at mall in, 105*f*
union membership in, 133*f*
Wal-Mart and, 68
Southeast Asia
Buddhism and, 64, 340
farmers in, 58
heroin and, 189
people, in U.S., 258
Southern Christian Leadership Conference
(SCLC), 257
Southwest State University, 366
Soviet Union (now Russia)
CO_2 emissions and, 438*f*
collapse of, 498, 499
communism and, 403
Economic Security Index and, 506
as totalitarian state, 382
/U.S., special language schools
and, 61
Soweto, South Africa, 256
space shuttles, 129
Spain
brands in, 145*f*
economy of, 405*f*
elderly percentage in, 298, 298*t*
foreign students and, 364*f*
human trafficking and, 238*t*
same-sex marriages and, 330
sexual behavior research, 44*f*
Spanish Harlem, 256
spanking, 168
species, endangered, 183, 440, 485
Spiderman ride, in Iran, *50*
spoiled identity, 172
sports
Ali and, 100
baseball, 17, 171, 176, 312, 477
basketball, 15, 41, 76, 103, 312, 322, 349,
475–476
as cultural universal, 54, 71
football, 5, 41, 62, 64, 80, 275, 379,
475, 477
golf, 17, 68, 153, 247, 275, 279, 460
men/women, network coverage and,
151*f*
parkour, 58–59
soccer, 41, 155, 312, 475, 476
sociological perspectives on, 17
tennis, 41, 101, 296, 476
Title IX and, 275
Springfield, Al Hurra in, 156
squatter settlements, 461, 462
SS *St. Louis*, 265
SSKKMS (*Shoshit, Shetkari, Kashtakari,
Kamgar, Mukti, Sangharsh*), 486, 491
St. Joseph's Day, 264
stability phase (retirement), 300
stable population growth, 455–456
Standing Rock Sioux, 336
Stanford University, 98
Starbucks, 20, 56, 72, 128, 225
Star-Spangled Banner (*Nuestro Himno*), 71
states. *See* government; United States;
specific states
statistics
crime, limitations of, 183–185
usage of, 44–45
vital, 450, 468, 469

status groups, 198, 214, 215
statuses, 100–101
achieved, 100–101, 100*f*, 114, 115, 193,
214, 215
ascribed, 100–101, 114, 193, 214, 215
defined, 100, 115
education and, 365–367
mass media and, 142–143, 143*t*
master, 101, 102, 114, 115
as social structures, 100–101
step dancers, 53, *53*
stepfamilies, 325
stereotypes
Arab Americans and, 170
contact hypothesis and, 254, 267, 268
defined, 148, 159, 247, 267, 268
elderly and, 90
mass media and, 148, 150
Muslims and, 170
race and, 247
women and, 274–275
stigma
defined, 172, 187, 188
deviance and, 172
of homosexuality, 178
mental illness and, 7, 147
prestige symbol *v.*, 172
stories (individual/group), 57, 85
strain, structural, 476, 489
strangers
groups and, 121
Muslims searched by, 63*f*
September 11th attacks and, 104, *104*
Strasbourg, open market in, *398*, *399*
stratification. *See also* classes; poverty;
social mobility
by age, 292–302
caste system and, 193–195, 209,
214, 215
closed system, 209, 214, 215
defined, 192–193, 214, 215
estate system, 195, 214, 215
by gender, 270–291
income/wealth and, 202–204
in Japan, 231
in Mexico, 233–237
within nations, 230–237
open system, 209, 214, 215
by social class, 201–202
sociological perspectives on,
197–199, 201*t*
systems of, 193–197
*Unequal Childhoods: Class, Race, and
Family Life* and, 312
universality of, 199–201
Weber's view of, 198
in world system, 223–230
Street Corner Society (Whyte), 35–36, 48
street gangs. *See* gangs
structural strain, 476, 489
structures. *See* social structures
students. *See also* colleges; education; high
schools
cheating, 65–66, 67
foreign, by country, 364*f*
identity information, Internet and, 89*f*
impression management and, 82
subcultures, 370–371
values, environment and, 65, 66*f*
Students Against Drunk Driving (SADD),
180, 189

subcultures, 58–60, 71, 72
call center, 59–60, 59*f*
college student, 370–371
The Subjection of Women (Mill), 278
subordinate groups, 99, 100, 148, 245, 248,
254, 256, 268, 295, 308
sub-Saharan Africa, 228, 425, 503
suburbs, 464, 468, 469
Sudan
Darfur region of, 432
ethnic cleansing and, 237
human trafficking and, 238*t*
poverty and, 226*f*
Sudetenland, twins study and, 78–79
Suicide: A Study in Sociology (Durkheim), 11
suicides
assisted, 306–307, 308
Durkheim's theory of, 8, 10
Las Vegas and, 8, 9
Sunnis, 349
Sunoo, 326
support systems. *See* social support
supporting hypotheses, 33. *See also*
hypotheses
Supreme Court (United States)
affirmative action and, 410, 410*f*
age discrimination protection and, 304
assisted suicide and, 307
Bell v. Maryland and, 263
Brown v. Board of Education and, 363
creationism and, 354
District of Columbia v. Heller and, 186
Engle v. Vitale and, 353
Exxon oil tanker *Valdez* and, 40
female Goodyear worker and, 283
gay marriage and, 329
Jim Crow laws and, 257
*Meachan v. Knolls Atomic Power
Laboratory* and, 304
medical marijuana and, 170
racial discrimination prohibitions
and, 252
Roe v. Wade and, 286, 287
Scarce case and, 39
Tennessee v. Lane and Jones and, 488
women in, 280
Surgeon General, 419, 432
surveillance, after September 11th attacks,
66, 169–170, 239
surveys, 26, 33–35, 48, 481. *See also* polling;
specific surveys
forms of, 34
gender/race impact on, 34
Internet, 42–43
/polling issues, mobile phones and, 35
as quantitative research, 34
survival of the fittest, 10, 24
sushi, 56, 111
Swaziland, 222*f*
sweat shops, 230, 260, 485
Sweden
brands in, 145*f*
child care in, 92
clogs from, 112
elderly percentage in, 298, 298*t*
foreign aid per capita in, 227*f*
income distribution in, 232*f*
infant mortality rates in, 421*f*
Millenium Project and, 227
NRI and, 229
Princess Victoria of, 143

same-sex marriages and, 330
Sami people of, 61
union membership in, 133*f*
welfare and, 213*f*, 214
women legislators in, 386*f*
Swedish Americans, Andersonville and, 256
Switzerland
brands in, 145*f*
Exxon Mobil *v.*, 225*t*
G8 conference and, *472*, *473*
NRI and, 229, 229*t*
pluralism and, 256
symbolic ethnicity, 264, 267, 268
symbolic interactionism, 15
symbols. *See also* nonverbal communication
language and, 15, 61, 62, 63*f*, 71, 72, 80
variance of, 80
x/y, variables and, 30, 32
syphilis experiment, Tuskegee, 427
Syria
human trafficking and, 238*t*, 238*t*
Al Sham, 54*f*
systematic study, sociology and, 5, 9,
24, 55, 72

T

tabulation, cross-, 45, 47
Taco Bell, 108
Tagged, 113
Taiwan
foreign students and, 364*f*
GNI for, 222*f*
immigrants and, 260
talkativeness study, 8
Tamago Burger, 57
Tamaulipas, 236*f*
Tamil, 70
Tanzania
child marriages and, 56*f*
GNI for, 222*f*
poverty and, 226*f*
women and, 232
tattooing, 15, 99, 172*f*
teaching profession
employees *v.* instructors in, 369–370
salaries, by state, 370*f*
teacher-expectancy effect, 367, 374
technical qualifications, employment based
on, 126, 127*t*
technology. *See also* communications
technology; computer technology;
Internet
bio-, 502–504
crime and, 182
definitions, 72, 109, 115, 498, 507
deviance and, 172–173
digital divide and, 113, 147–148, 159,
208–209, 214, 215
future and, 499
innovations and, 58
Lenski and, 109
mass media and, 86–87
material culture and, 58, 72
material resources and, 72, 109, 115,
498, 507
research and, 42–43
resistance to, 498
societies and, 109
virtual worlds and, 91
teenage alcoholism, 64

Tehran, 272
Telecommunications Act of 1996, 158
telecommuting, 131, 135, 136
telemarketers, 407, 412
Telemundo (Spanish TV station), 149
telephones. *See* mobile phones
televangelists, 351, 355
television (TV). *See also* mass media;
 movies
 African Americans and, 149
 American Idol, 148
 American Inventor, 132
 The Apprentice, 148
 Asian Americans and, 149
 The Bachelor, 149
 Bhutan and, 157, 157f
 Big Brother, 148
 Black Entertainment Television, 149
 casting, Obama and, 149
 commercials and, 143
 The Cosby Show, 149
 CSI, 124, 142, 148, 149
 Dexter, 149
 Dharma and Greg, 149
 digital, 158
 Fiji islanders and, 52
 Friends, 148
 Gilmore Girls, 52
 Girlfriends, 149f
 Grey's Anatomy, 149
 Hispanics and, 149
 Lost, 52
 Medium, 148
 MTV Arabia, 150f
 news comprehension and, 30
 Oprah Winfrey Show, 157f
 political process and, 148
 prison and, 165f
 reality television, 43, 149
 Saturday Night Live, 149
 sexual content in, 43, 43f
 Survivor, 123, 123f, 148
 Telemundo and, 149
 Ugly Betty, 149
 Univision (Spanish TV station), 149
 Who Wants to be a Millionaire, 148
 Will and Grace, 149
Temple University, 12
temporary workers, 133, 197, 205
Tennessee
 19th Amendment and, 284
 Scopes Monkey Trial in, 353
 Tennessee v. Lane and Jones, 488
tennis, 41, 101, 296, 476
termination phase (retirement), 300
terrorism, 391–392. *See also* September
 11th attacks
 Abu Ghraib prison and, 98–99, 167,
 389, 390
 anonymous manifestos and, 392
 bin Laden and, 126, 156
 bio-, 423
 global reach of, 391f
 in-group/out-group interplay
 and, 122
 Internet and, 487
 Iraq and, 238, 391f
 Israel and, 60
 Palestinian territories and, 60
 Al Qaeda and, 126, 156
 as transnational crime, 183t

Texas
 baby names study and, 38
 borderlands and, 233, 235–237, 236f,
 239, 240, 266
 coalitions in, 123
 visitability and, 488
Texas State University, 366
Tex-Mex border, 70
text messaging, 87, 106, 113, 152, 319, 378,
 474, 477, 485
TFR (total fertility rate), 450, 468, 469
Thailand
 ecclesiae in, 348
 filtering information and, 146f, 380f
 GNI for, 222f
 TFR and, 453
"That's not cool" campaign, 142
theft
 car, 184t, 185
 identity, 182, 184
theology, liberation, 343, 355
A Theology of Liberation (Gutiérrez), 343
theoretical perspectives. *See* sociological
 perspectives
theories, 8–9. *See also* scientific method;
 specific theories
 defined, 8, 23
 sociological, 8–9
third Industrial Revolution, 413
Third World countries, 467. *See also*
 developing nations
thirdhand smoke, 177
Thomasrobb.com, 487
Thomson Reuters, 145f
3-D printing, 494
thumbs-up sign, in Australia, 62
Tiananmen Square, 406
Tibet
 China and, 70
 Nyinba culture of, 314
 polyandry in, 314
tic tac, 59
Time magazine, 46, 143t, 145, 157
Timor-Leste, 222, 229, 237, 286
Titanic (ocean liner), 208
Title IX, 275
TMZ, 142
tobacco-related medical cost
 reimbursements, 123
Togo, 56f
Tokyo
 Cabbage Patch Day, 99
 Hibiya Library in, 82
 Shinto Shrine in, 310, 311
Tonight Show, 302, 480
Tonnies's *Gemeinschaft/Gesellschaft*, 109,
 110t, 112, 115, 116, 130, 131
Torah, 261, 338, 340
Toronto, protesters/police in, 162, 163
torture. *See also* Abu Ghraib prison
 dictatorships and, 382
 Holocaust and, 167, 254, 264, 341
 of homosexuals, by governments, 239
 Universal Declaration of Human Rights
 and, 197, 237, 238
Total Corporation, 225t
total fertility rate (TFR), 450, 468, 469
total institutions, 91, 94
totalitarianism, 382, 395
touching/searching Muslims, Iraq War
 and, 63f

Toyota Motor, 145f, 225t
 toys, lead-based paint and, 224f
Toys "R" Us, 120
tracking, 365, 374
traditional authority, 379, 395
traditional societies, 20, 456
trafficking, of sex workers, 42, 42. *See also*
 prostitution
Trafficking Victims Protection Act, 237
trained incapacity, 126, 135, 136
Transactional Records Access
 Clearinghouse, 182
transgendered individuals, 7, 178, 291, 370
transition. *See also* life course
 to adulthood, 90, 90t
 demographic, 452–453, 452f, 468, 469
transmission, cultural. *See* cultural
 transmission
transnational crime, 181, 182–183, 183t,
 187, 188
transnationals, 265, 267, 268, 504–506
Transportation, Department of, 488
transsexuals, 103, 103f, 178
transvestites, 178
trapped people, 463
Travelers Corporation of Hartford, 305
Trenchcoat Mafia, 122
triads, 124, 135, 136
A Tribe Apart (Hersch), 369
trichotillomania, 28
Trinidad, twins study and, 78–79
Triptaka, 340t
"trophy photos," 98
tsunamis (2004), 20, 84
Tuesdays with Morrie (Albom), 294
Tunisia, 54f
 colonialism and, 223
 filtering information and, 146f, 380f
 GNI for, 222f
Turkey
 EU and, 266
 genocide and, 254
 human trafficking and, 238t
Turkmenistan, 222f
Tuskegee syphilis experiment, 427
Tutsi people, 255
TV. *See* television
Twenty-Sixth Amendment, 385
twins, 78, 78–79, 79
Twitter, 88, 142
two spirit, 178

U

UAE (United Arab Emirates), 222f
UBS, 145f
Uganda
 child marriages and, 56f
 Congo's national parks and, 402
 GNI for, 222f
 The Last King of Scotland and, 397
 poverty and, 226f
Ukraine
 foreign-born adoptions and, 323f
 human trafficking and, 238t, 238t
 Internet plagiarism and, 67
UNAIDS, 424, 425
underclass, 207–208, 214, 215
*Unequal Childhoods: Class, Race, and Family
 Life* (Lareau), 312
unequal societies. *See* social inequality

UNESCO (United Nations Educational,
 Scientific, and Cultural
 Organization), 150
UNICEF, 44f
Uniform Crime Reports, 183
unions, 133–135, 133f, 134f
United Arab Emirates (UAE), 222f
United Farm Workers, 130
United Kingdom. *See also* England; Great
 Britain
 as core nation, 223, 223f
 filtering information and, 146f
 GNI for, 222f
 immigration and, 265
 terrorism and, 391f
United Nations Development Programme,
 202, 233, 280, 437
United Nations Educational, Scientific, and
 Cultural Organization (UNESCO), 150
United Nations General Assembly, 150
United Nations Millennium Project, 227, 228,
 239, 241
United Nations Office on Drugs and
 Crime, 183
United States (U.S.). *See also* Constitution;
 Iraq War; military; Supreme Court;
 war; *specific states*
 abortion funding, by state, 286f
 age stratification in, 302–306
 arms transfers and, 187
 arranged marriages and, 320
 bilingualism, by state, 69f
 brands in, 145f
 child care costs in, 93f
 class system in, 195–197
 CO_2 emissions in, 438f
 as core nation, 223, 223f
 divorce trends, 325f
 economy of, 405f
 educational level/income by state
 (study), 30, 31, 31f, 32, 32, 32f,
 33, 33f
 elderly, by percentages, 298, 298t
 elderly, by state, 303f
 elderly population growth in, 302f, 303f
 ethnic groups in, 245t, 246f, 256–264,
 257f, 258f
 executions, by state, 165, 166f
 female governors in, 279
 fertility patterns in, 454–456
 Filipino Americans in, 245t, 258f
 foreign aid per capita in, 227f
 G8 conference and, 228, 441, 472, 473
 gender inequality in, 282f
 health care in, 428–431
 higher education completion rates
 in, 361f
 households, by family type, 313f
 immigrants in, 266f
 income distribution in, 203f, 232f
 income/poverty levels, by state, 194f
 infant mortality rates in, 421f
 Internet usage and, 153f
 Islam in, 349
 /Lebanon cheating (cross cultural
 study), 67
 life expectancy in, 451f
 marriage ages in, 318f
 marriage trends, 325f
 media penetration in, 155f
 medical marijuana, by state, 171f

mental illness in, 431–433, 442
/Mexico, borderlands and, 233, 235–237, 236f, 236f, 239, 240, 266
national crime rates, 184t
NRI and, 229, 229t
nuclear power generation and, 58f
political behavior in, 382–386
poor (categories) in, 206, 207t
population structure of, 454f
poverty rate in, 206f
poverty/income levels, by state, 194f
power structure models in, 386–388
Puerto Rico and, 262, 463
racial groups in, 245t, 246f, 256–264, 257f, 258f
religions of, 337f
religious participation in, 347f
"right to work" laws, by state, 134f
Salvadorans in, 70f, 245f, 262f
single-parent families in, 321f
social change in, 495t
social mobility in, 210–212
/Soviet Union, special language schools and, 61
teacher salaries, by state, 370f
union membership in, 133f, 134f
unmarried-couple households, by state, 327f
wealth distribution in, 204f
/Western Europe, crime rates in, 185, 187
White House and online media, 142
United States Army Human Terrain System, 36, 36, 40
United States Committee for Refugees and Immigrants, 456
United States Conference of Mayors, 467
United States Constitution. See Constitution
United States Naval Academy, 67, 89
United Way, 41
Universal Declaration of Human Rights, 197, 237, 238
universal human rights, 237–239
universality, of stratification, 199–201
universals, cultural. See cultural universals
universities. See specific universities
University of Akron, 184
University of Chicago, 176
University of Colorado, 274
University of Georgia, 317
University of Louisiana, high school popularity study and, 86, 86t
University of Michigan, 410
University of Quebec, 251
University of Seville, 358, 359
Univision (Spanish TV station), 149
unmarried couples, 324, 327f
untouchables, 14, 194, 486
upper class, 196
urban dwellers, 463
urban ecology, 459, 462t, 468, 469
Urban Justice Center, 233
urban sociology, new, 461, 462t, 468, 469
urbanism, 458, 468, 469
urbanization
  global, 459f
  sociological perspectives on, 459–461, 462t, 468, 469
  urban growth models, 459–461, 460f
US magazine, 154f

USA Patriot Act, 66, 169–170
Utah
  Goshute Indians in, 435
  Salt Lake City, 184
  Senator Hatch and, 388f
Uzbekistan
  arranged marriages and, 318
  human trafficking and, 238t, 238t

V

Valdez disaster, 40, 40
validity, 32, 47, 48, 373, 374
value neutrality, 40–41, 43, 48
value-added model, 476, 489, 490
values (cultural values), 65–66, 68t, 71, 72
  of first-year college students, 65, 66f
  list of, 65
  shared, throughout world, 66
  variance in, 67
variables
  control, 33, 47
  defined, 30, 48
  dependent, 30, 32f, 47
  independent, 30, 32f, 47
  x/y symbols and, 30, 32
variation, cultural, 58–60
varnas, 194
veil/head scarf, Middle East and, 281
Venezuela
  human trafficking and, 238t
  Yanomami people of, 313
venture capital investment, 132
Vermont
  adoption/unmarried couples and, 324
  rural nature of, 459
verstehen, 10, 23
vertical mobility, 209, 214, 215
vested interests, 497, 507
VH-1 (music channel), 153
Viacom, 157
"Vice President and Chief Internet Evangelist," 114
victimization surveys, 184, 185, 188
victimless crimes, 178, 180, 187, 188
Victoria, Princess of Sweden, 143
Viet Kieu, 259
Vietnam
  expulsion of Chinese from, 254–255
  foreign-born adoptions and, 323f
  human trafficking and, 238t
  media penetration in, 155f
  military marriages and, 8
  as periphery nation, 223, 223f
  refugees from, 259
Vietnam War, 14, 166
  Ali and, 100
  countercultures and, 60
Vietnamese Americans, 258f, 259–260
  as racial group, 245t
views. See sociological perspectives
village, global. See global community; global village
A Vindication of the Rights of Women (Wollstonecraft), 278
violence. See also killing
  gun control and, 185–187
  interpersonal, 181
  in schools, 369

Virginia. See also West Virginia
  Springfield, Al Hurra and, 156
  Virginia Tech killing spree, 7, 147, 147f, 168, 181
virtual worlds, 106–107, 114–115
  college campus tours and, 91
  Second Life, 106, 108, 351
  as social structures, 99, 106–107, 108
visitability, 488, 490
vital statistics, 450, 468, 469
vocational subculture, 371
Volkswagen, 145f
voluntary associations, 129–130, 135, 136
voting
  apathy and, 382–384
  communications technology and, 378
  Democrats and, 48, 213, 383
  Is Voting for Young People? and, 378
  reasons for not voting, 385
  Republicans and, 213, 382, 383, 388
  Twenty-Sixth Amendment and, 385
  young people and, 385

W

"Wall Street greed," 182
Wall Street Journal, 123, 192
Wallerstein's world systems analysis, 223, 223f, 239, 240, 461, 468, 469
Wal-Mart
  Arkansas and, 68
  Belgium v., 225t
  China and, 68, 135
  cultural variation and, 68, 68t
war, 388–389. See also genocide; Iraq War; refugees
  Civil War, 193, 195, 257, 269
  Cold War era, 61, 220
  definition of, 388–389, 395
  global culture war, 66
  Holocaust and, 167, 254, 264, 341
  peace and, 389–391, 395
  power and, 388
  rewards for killing and, 64
  term, language and, 61
  Vietnam, 14, 60, 100, 166
  World War I, 127, 223
  World War II, 55, 127, 130, 167, 206, 223, 254, 260, 264, 341, 361, 409
warming, global, 437–439
Warsaw, 453f
Washington
  affirmative action and, 410f
  euthanasia and, 307
  female governor in, 279
  Seattle, 225, 383
Washington D.C. See also September 11th attacks
  District of Columbia v. Heller and, 186
  medical marijuana and, 171f
Waste Isolation Pilot Plant (WIPP), 62, 63f
waste sites, hazardous, 18, 63, 435, 497
water pollution, 437
wealth. See also income
  defined, 193, 214, 215
  distribution, in U.S., 204f
  elderly and, 303
  income v., 193, 202–204
  stratification and, 202–204

web-browsing activities, Google and, 147
Weber, Max
  religion and, 343, 355
  stratification and, 198
Web sites. See Internet; social networking Web sites
welfare, 212–215, 213f
West (Old West), 61
West Africa, child marriage and, 55, 56f. See also Ghana; Sierra Leone
West Sumatra, 277
West Virginia, 302, 459, 465
West Warwick, nightclub fire and, 476
Western Electric Company, 37
Western Europe
  child care in, 92
  global divide and, 221f
  global immigration and, 265
  terrorism and, 391f
  /U.S., crime rates in, 185, 187
Western media. See mass media
Where Am I Wearing? (Timmerman), 400
White people (non-Hispanic), 264
  as ethnic group, 245t
  from Europe, 264
  health insurance and, 425f
  income and, 250f
  multiple identities and, 247
  poverty and, 207t
  privilege, 250–251, 267, 268
  as racial group, 245t
  in U.S., 246f
white-collar crimes, 179, 182, 183, 189
WHO (World Health Organization), 430, 431
Whorf-Sapir hypothesis. See Sapir-Whorf hypothesis
Wi-Fi accessibility, San Francisco, 140
William Shatner Fellowship, 130
WIPP (Waste Isolation Pilot Plant), 62, 63f
wiretaps, 147
Wisconsin, monkey isolation study in, 78
women. See also feminism; feminist perspective; gender
  in advertisements (study), 37
  affirmative action and, 252, 267, 268, 409, 410, 410f, 413, 414
  African American, prostitution and, 279
  beauty myth and, 171, 281
  chatting and, 8, 113
  compensation and, 283
  cosmetic surgery and, 172
  crime and, 179
  deviance and, 179
  disabled, Japan and, 102
  employment, social consequences of, 283–284
  entrepreneurship and, 212
  female infanticide and, 232
  female-dominated occupations, 283t
  gender roles of, 84, 274–275
  genital mutilation of, 238
  Goodyear worker, 283
  as governors, 279
  Hopi, Iraq War and, 389
  inequality of, in industrial nations, 282f
  institutional discrimination of, 280, 288, 289
  Internet and, 113
  in Iran, 272–273
  Kenya and, 232

in labor force, 281–283, 282f
as lawyers, 125
in legislatures (national), 386f
mass media and, 150–151
matrix of domination and, 278, 279f, 288, 289
mental illness and, 280
Mexico and, 234–235
new social movements in India and, 486
in occupations, 283t
as oppressed majority, 279–281
pornography and, 151, 178, 180
second shift of, 284, 289
status of, in Mexico, 234–235
status of, worldwide, 280–281, 282f
stereotyping of, 274–275
in Supreme Court, 280
Tanzania and, 232
"women's line" for hamburgers, 272
workers, in Nepal, 404
in workforce, 281–284
Women's Sports Foundation, 275
word processors, at Chicago law firm, 105
words. See also languages
new/modified, 484
sexually explicit, in songs, 37
slang, 53, 72, 498
work teams, 131
worker satisfaction, 408–409
workforce. See also labor force
affirmative action and, 252, 267, 268, 409, 410f, 413, 414
alienation and, 125, 135, 406–409, 413, 414
changing face of, 409–411

temporary workers, 133, 197, 205
women in, 281–284
working class, 197
workplace
changing, 131–132
romance in, 68
socialization and, 87, 87f, 93
world. See also global community; globalization; Internet; virtual worlds
abortion throughout, 287f
aging throughout, 298, 298f
borderless, 57
brands in, 143, 145f
carbon dioxide emissions throughout, 438f
child care throughout, 91–93
HIV/AIDS throughout, 424f
Internet penetration/usage in, 500f
map, pan-Arabism and, 54f
news outlets, 156
population patterns, 451–454, 452t
poverty and, 226f
religions of, 338–340, 339f, 340t
"right to die" throughout, 306–307
shared values throughout, 66
six billionth person in, 452
women's status throughout, 280–281, 282f
World Bank, 144, 185, 213, 220, 224, 225, 227, 228, 230, 232, 234, 405, 409, 421, 431. See also global economy
World Economic Forum's Networked Readiness Index (NRI), 229, 229t
world economy. See global economy

World Health Organization (WHO), 430, 431
world system
stratification in, 223–230
world systems analysis, 223, 223f, 230t, 239, 240, 461, 468, 469
World Trade Center. See also September 11th attacks
attacks on, 104, 126
collapse (case study), 478–479
multiple masculinities and, 276
parts of, eBay and, 145
tattoos and, 15
World Trade Organization, 474, 483
World War I, 127, 223
World War II, 55, 127, 130, 167, 206, 223, 254, 260, 264, 341, 361, 409

X

x symbol, 30, 32. See also independent variables
Xanga, 113
XO computers, 501

Y

Y Generation, 210
y symbol, 30, 32. See also dependent variables
Yahoo, 113
Yanomami people, 313
Yemen
filtering information and, 146f, 380f
GNI for, 222f
human trafficking and, 238t

YMCA (Young Men's Christian Association), 130
Y-Me National Breast Cancer Organization, 285
Young Men's Christian Association (YMCA), 130
young voters, 385
youthhood, 90
YouTube, 112, 113, 142, 158, 392
Yugoslavia, former, 237, 255, 438f

Z

Zaire. See Democratic Republic of the Congo
Zambia
child marriages and, 56f
GNI for, 222f
poverty and, 227
Zania Turner (avatar), 108
Zapatista National Liberation Army, 235
Zapatistas, 235, 392, 485
Zara, 145f
zebu, 13, 13
zero population growth (ZPG), 455–456, 468, 469
Zimbabwe
filtering information and, 380f
GNI for, 222f
NRI and, 229, 229t
poverty and, 226f
Zimbardo's mock prison experiment, 98–99, 101, 176
ZPG (zero population growth), 455–456, 468, 469

Applications of *Sociology's* Major Theoretical Approaches

Sociology provides comprehensive coverage of the major sociological perspectives. This summary table includes a sample of the topics in the text that have been explored using the major approaches. The numbers in parentheses indicate the pertinent chapters.

FUNCTIONALIST PERSPECTIVE

Defined and explained (1)
Adoption (14)
AIDS epidemic (19)
Anomie theory of deviance (8)
Bilingualism (3)
Bureaucratization of schools (16)
Campaign financing (17)
Cow worship in India (1)
Culture (3, 16)
Davis and Moore's view of stratification (9)
Disengagement theory of aging (13)
Dominant ideology (3)
Durkheim's view of deviance (8)
Dysfunctions of racism (11)
Ethnocentrism (3)
Family (14)
Formal organizations (6)
Functions of dying (13)
Functions of racism (11)
Gans's functions of poverty (9)
Gay marriage (14)
Gender stratification (12)
Global immigration (11)
Health and illness (19)
Human ecology (19, 20)
Human rights (10)
In-groups and out-groups (6)
Integrative function of religion (15)
Media and social norms (7)
Media and socialization (7)
Media and status conferral (7)
Media concentration (7)
Media promotion of consumption (7)
Modernization theory (10)
Multinational corporations (10)
Narcotizing effect of the media (7)
No Child Left Behind Act (16)
Offshoring (18)
Racial prejudice and discrimination (11)
Regulating the Internet (5)
Rumors (21)
Social change (16, 22)
Social control (8, 16)
Social institutions (5)
Socialization in schools (4, 16)
Sports (1)
Subcultures (3)
Transnationals (22)
Urban ecology (20)

CONFLICT PERSPECTIVE

Defined and explained (1)
Abortion (12)
Access to health care (19)
Access to technology (22)
Affirmative action (18)
Age stratification (13)
AIDS epidemic (19)
Bilingualism (3)
Bureaucratization of schools (16)
Campaign financing (17)
Capitalism (15, 18)
Corporate welfare (9)
Correspondence principle (16)
Credentialism (16)
Culture (3)
Day care funding (4)
Deviance (8)
Disability as a master status (5)
Disability rights (21)
Dominant ideology (3, 7, 9)
Downsizing (18)
Elite model of the U.S. power structure (17)
Environmental issues (19)
Environmentalism (19)
Exploitation theory of discrimination (11)
Family (14)
Gay marriage (14)
Gender equity in education (16)
Gender stratification (12)
Global immigration (11)
Gun control (8)
Hidden curriculum (16)
Iron Law of Oligarchy (6)
Labor unions (6)
Marx's view of stratification (9)
Matrix of domination (12)
Media concentration (7)
Media gatekeeping (7)
Media stereotypes (7)
Medicalization of society (19)
Model minority (11)
Multinational corporations (10)
New urban sociology (20)
No Child Left Behind Act (16)
Offshoring (18)
Poverty (9)
Privacy and technology (22)
Racism and health (19)
Regulating the Internet (5)
Religion and social control (15)
Right to die (13)
School violence (16)
Social change (22)
Social control (8)
Social institutions (5)
Socialization in schools (4)
Sports (1)
Subcultures (3)
Tracking (16)
Transnationals (22)
Victimless crimes (8)
White-collar crime (8)
World systems analysis (10, 20, 22)

INTERACTIONIST PERSPECTIVE

Defined and explained (1)
Activity theory of aging (13)
Adolescent sexual networks (5)
Adoption (14)
Affirmative action (18)
AIDS epidemic (19)
Campaign financing (17)
Charismatic authority (17)
Conspicuous consumption (9)
Contact hypothesis (11)
Culture (3)
Differential association (8)
Disability rights (21)
Dramaturgical approach (4, 17)
Electronic communication (7)
Family (14)
Gay marriage (14)
Gender stratification (12)
Gun control (8)
Health and illness (19)
Human relations approach (6)
Media concentration (7)
Obedience (8)
Presentation of the self (4)
Regulating the Internet (5)
Routine activities theory (8)
Small groups (6)
Social institutions (5)
Sports (1)
Tattoo symbols of 9/11 (1)
Teacher-expectancy effect (16)
Teenage pregnancy (14)
Transnationals (22)
Unions (6)

FEMINIST PERSPECTIVE

Defined and explained (1)
Day care funding (4)
Deviance (8)
Dominant ideology (3)
Ethnographic research (2)
Family (14)
Gender gap in education (16)
Gender stratification (12)
Language (3)
Media stereotypes (7)
Pornography (7)
Rape (8)
Regulating the Internet (5)
Religion and social control (15)
School violence (16)
Sports (1)
Victimless crimes (8)

LABELING THEORY

Defined and explained (8)
AIDS epidemic (19)
Disabilities and labeling (5)
Disability rights (21)
Health and illness (19)
Mental illness (19)
Societal reaction approach (8)
Teacher-expectancy effect (16)
Victimless crimes (8)